TEACHER'S MANUAL

Food for Today

Sixth Edition

HELEN KOWTALUK

Alice Orphanos Kopan, M.Ed., M.A., CFCS

GLENCOE
McGraw-Hill

New York, New York   Columbus, Ohio   Mission Hills, California   Peoria, Illinois

Edited by Jody James, Editorial Consultant

Glencoe/McGraw-Hill

*A Division of The **McGraw·Hill** Companies*

Send all inquiries to:
Glencoe/McGraw-Hill
3008 W. Willow Knolls Drive
Peoria, Illinois 61614-1083

ISBN 0-02-642980-2 (Student Text)
ISBN 0-02-642983-7 (Teacher's Wraparound Edition)

Printed in the United States of America

2 3 4 5 6 7 8 9 10 VHJ 01 00 99 98 97

CONTRIBUTORS

Linda R. Glosson, Ph.D., CFCS
Home Economics Teacher
Wylie High School
Wylie, Texas

Nanci Burkhart
Home Economics Teacher
Hueneme High School
Oxnard, California

Anna Sue Couch, Ed.D.
Professor of Home Economics Education
Texas Tech University
Lubbock, Texas

Brenda Barrington Mendiola, M.S., CFCS
Home Economics Teacher
Irion County Schools
Mertzon, Texas

Connie R. Sasse
Former Editor, Tips and Topics
Texas Tech University
Lubbock, Texas

Lynn Steil
Life Management Teacher
Central Middle School
Dowagiac, Michigan

CONTENTS OF TEACHER'S MANUAL

Photo Credits: Ann Garvin, Peerless Photography, Brent Phelps

Teaching with *Food for Today*

Welcome to the Sixth Edition of *Food for Today*. The newest edition of a widely popular text, it is the most up-to-date, complete foods and nutrition program now available. *Food for Today* provides what teachers across the country are looking for:

- Up-to-date information on the Dietary Guidelines, Food Guide Pyramid, food labels, new products, and more.
- Emphasis on critical thinking, decision-making, and resource management.
- Information on current topics: cultural diversity, food technology, nutrition for athletes, eating disorders, the safety of our food supply, and more.
- Short reading segments and a flexible organization.
- A variety of special features to enhance teaching and learning.
- A colorful, appealing design.

In addition, the Sixth Edition of *Food for Today* includes a unique package of program components. They are:

- **Student Text.** The core of the program is this 720-page handbook for learning about foods and nutrition.
- **Teacher's Wraparound Edition (TWE).** This component provides complete lesson plans, teaching suggestions, cross-references, supplemental information, and more—conveniently "wrapped" around every page of the student text.
- **Student Workbook.** The study guides and activity sheets in this softbound book are designed to maximize learning.
- **Teacher's Classroom Resources (TCR).** This file box of supplemental booklets provides a wealth of time-saving reproducible masters and other teaching helps.
- **Color Transparencies.** Ready-to-use color transparencies can enliven your presentations and enhance learning.
- **Testmaker Software.** With this software and a personal computer, you have the capability to quickly and easily create your own personalized tests.

On the following pages, you will find more information about each of these components as well as suggestions for using them effectively. We hope that both you and your students enjoy discovering what *Food for Today* has to offer.

We welcome comments from teachers and students on this and other Glencoe Family and Consumer Sciences publications. Address your letters to:

Director of Family and Consumer Sciences
Glencoe/McGraw-Hill
3008 W. Willow Knolls Drive
Peoria, Illinois 61614

FOOD FOR TODAY—MEETING THE NEEDS
OF TODAY'S FOODS AND NUTRITION TEACHERS

Topic/Need	Student Text	Teacher's Wraparound Edition (TWE)	Teacher's Classroom Resources (TCR)
Science and Technology	• "Science Connection" features • "Technology Tidbit" features • Section 1.4, "Food, Science, and Technology"	• "Science Connection" teaching suggestions • "Food and Nutrition Science" teaching suggestions	• Food Science Resources booklet
Multicultural Awareness/ Global Issues	• "World of Variety" features • Section 1.3, "Food and Culture" • Section 13.3, "The Global Food Supply" • Chapter 22, "Foods of the World" • Chapter 23, "Foods of the U.S. and Canada"	• "World of Variety" teaching suggestions	• Multicultural Resources booklet
Environmental Awareness	• "Earth Watch" features • Section 7.5, "Conserving Natural Resources"	• "Earth Watch" teaching suggestions	
Academic Skills	• Chapter Review, "Linking Your Studies"	• "Key Skill" identification (Student Experiences)	
Higher-Level Thinking Skills	• Section Review, "Discuss Your Ideas" • Chapter Review, "Thinking Critically" • Section 3.3, "Separating Fact from Fiction"	• "Thinking Skills" boxes • "Key Skill" identification (Student Experiences)	• Enrichment Activities booklet
Management Skills, Decision Making, Problem Solving	• Chapter Review, "Making Decisions and Solving Problems" • Section 1.5, "Managing Resources and Making Decisions"	• "Key Skill" identification (Student Experiences)	

Hands-on Application	• Recipes • Section Review, "Apply Your Learning" • Chapter Review, "Learning by Doing"	• "Lab Experience" suggestions • "Using the Recipe" suggestions	• Foods Lab Resources booklet
Cooperative Learning	• Section 8.5, "TIme Management and Teamwork"	• "Cooperative Learning Suggestions" (chapter opening pages) • "Cooperative Learning Techniques" (Teacher's Manual, page T-14)	• Foods Lab Resources booklet
Students with Special Needs		• "Special Needs Strategies" suggestions • "Reteaching" suggestions (end of each section) • "Enrichment" suggestions (end of each section)	• Reteaching Activities booklet • Enrichment Activities booklet

STUDENT TEXT

The *Food for Today* Student Text combines a strong nutrition emphasis with thorough coverage of consumer and food preparation skills.

Flexible Organization

Food for Today uses a unit-chapter-section organization. The purpose is twofold: flexibility for the teacher and short reading segments for the student.

Sections

The shortest segments are the sections. There are 90 sections; most are 4 to 8 pages long. Each section is a self-contained lesson on a specific topic. Each has its own objectives, vocabulary list, and section review, as well as a quiz provided in the Teacher's Classroom Resources box. Choose just the sections you want to teach depending on the focus of your course and the time available. With this built-in flexibility, *Food for Today* can suit a wide variety of courses—beginning or advanced, comprehensive or specialized. (See the Suggested Course Outlines on pages T-24 through T-29.)

Chapters

Chapters are groups of related sections. There are two to five sections per chapter. After you have taught any or all of the sections in a chapter, you may wish to use the chapter review (provided in the text) and the chapter test (provided in the Teacher's Classroom Resources box).

Units

Units are groups of related chapters. The text consists of five units, each focusing on a broad area of food and nutrition studies. Unit tests are provided in the Teacher's Classroom Resources.

Content and Writing Style

The *Food for Today* text has been carefully planned to include the information that is most important to teachers and students. The body of each section is clearly organized into major topics and subtopics through the use of distinctive color headings.

The text is carefully written at a comfortable reading level for high school students. Topics are clearly explained, often with concrete examples. Special care has been taken to ensure that key ideas are easy to find and understand.

Vocabulary terms, in addition to being listed at the beginning of the section, are highlighted and defined in context. Pronunciation guides are included where they may be needed.

Visual Elements

The text pages are designed to be colorful and appealing to students, with hundreds of color photographs and drawings. The illustrations serve an educational purpose by enriching and supporting the text material. They provide examples, clearly show techniques, and help students relate the text concepts to real life. Captions are not only informative, but in many cases ask questions to help students review facts, apply concepts, and develop higher-level thinking skills.

Special Features Within Sections

A number of elements have been included in the text sections to enhance teaching and learning.

Objectives

Each section begins with clearly stated objectives that establish specific learner outcomes. They can help students identify goals before reading the section. They can also help you plan your course and document student learning.

List of Terms

The heading "Look for These Terms" alerts students to key terms introduced in the section. The terms are listed in order of use. They are highlighted and defined with the section and also appear in the Glossary.

Boxed Features

Each section of the text includes one or more brief, interesting features highlighting a topic related to the text discussion. There are seven types of these features, each with a distinctive color logo.

- **Science Connection** features show how food and nutrition topics relate to concepts in biology, chemistry, and physics.

- **Technology Tidbit** features give information about technology in the food industry and in the home, including food- and nutrition-related uses for home computers.

- **World of Variety** features help promote multicultural awareness by providing information about foods and customs from around the world.

- **Earth Watch** features help promote an attitude of caring for the environment with tips for practical ways to conserve natural resources.

- **Healthy Attitudes** features provide nutrition and fitness tips to help students adopt a healthy lifestyle.

- **Tips for Success** features highlight key pointers related to specific topics.

- **Safety Check** features give precautions to help prevent accidents and foodborne illness.

Recipes

The *Food for Today* text includes 29 recipes carefully selected for use in the foods lab. (For additional recipes, see the Foods Lab Resources booklet in the Teacher's Classroom Resources box.) The recipes have been chosen with several criteria in mind. These include nutrition, low cost, reasonable preparation time, appropriate skill level, appeal to teens, ethnic variety, and correlation to text content. The recipes call upon students to use a variety of techniques and equipment, including the microwave oven.

Each recipe is introduced with two questions under the heading "Thinking About the Recipe." These questions help students relate the text content to the recipe. They enable you to use the recipes as a teaching tool even before students prepare the food in the lab. (Answers are provided in the Teacher's Wraparound Edition.)

The recipes follow a standard format for ease of use. Ingredients are listed with both metric and customary amounts. Clear, step-by-step directions are given. Nutrition information is provided at the end of each recipe.

Section Review

Each section concludes with a brief review of five to seven items. (Answers are provided in the Teacher's Wraparound Edition.) The section reviews include three types of items:

- **Recall the Facts**—items to check basic content knowledge.
- **Discuss Your Ideas**—items to encourage thought and discussion.
- **Apply Your Learning**—one or two brief activities, most of which can be done in class with little or no advance preparation.

Career Profiles

Following the final section in each chapter, a special "Career Profile" page introduces students to a worker in a particular job. (These are fictitious profiles that represent the background and experiences typical of workers in the stated job.) Together, the career profiles acquaint students with a wide range of employment opportunities related to foods and nutrition.

Each career profile concludes with two questions to help students think about what they have read. Students are encouraged to find some aspect of each job that appeals to them. Thus, the career profiles help students not only expand their awareness of careers, but also consider their own interests and aptitudes.

Chapter Reviews

At the end of each chapter, a two-page chapter review is provided. (Answers are found in the Teacher's Wraparound Edition.)

For convenience, a section number is given for all items in the chapter review. This enables you to choose the appropriate items in case you did not teach every section in the chapter. It also serves as a study aid for students as they complete the review.

The chapter review includes:

- **Summary**—A recap of the main ideas in each section of the chapter. (Note: If you do not have time to teach all the sections in a chapter, you may wish to use the summary as a way of briefly discussing the sections that were skipped.)
- **Reviewing Facts**—Questions to check students' recall of basic knowledge.

- **Learning by Doing**—Suggestions for hands-on activities, such as foods labs, food science labs, computer labs, demonstrations, and taste tests.
- **Thinking Critically**—Questions that help students practice specific critical thinking skills within the context of the subject matter. Examples of the skills reinforced include identifying cause and effect, recognizing bias, comparing and contrasting, and recognizing fallacies in logic.
- **Making Decisions and Solving Problems**—Realistic scenarios that present students with content-related dilemmas and ask, "What would you do?"
- **Linking Your Studies**—Activities that relate the chapter content to other subject areas. Emphasis is given to applied academics: math, science, writing, literature, social studies, and reading/study skills. In addition, subject areas such as health and fine arts are included when appropriate.

Other Learning Aids

Several learning aids are found in the back of the student text.

Glossary

The Glossary begins on page 690 of the student text. It includes all of the vocabulary listed under "Look for These Terms" (at the beginning of each text section). Pronunciation guides are given when needed, and all terms are clearly defined. The glossary also identifies the section in which each term was introduced. Students can use the glossary to quickly review their understanding of important terms.

Appendix

The Appendix, "Nutritive Value of Foods," begins on page 698 of the student text. This detailed chart provides information about the calorie and nutrient content of commonly eaten foods, including fat, cholesterol, and sodium content.

Index

The student text also includes a detailed alphabetical index for easy reference to text topics. It begins on page 708.

TEACHER'S WRAPAROUND EDITION

The Teacher's Wraparound Edition (TWE) provides maximum teaching support in a convenient, easy-to-use format. Each page of the Teacher's Wraparound Edition consists of a slightly reduced replica of the student text page surrounded by lesson plans and other teaching materials. The quantity and variety of teaching suggestions ensures that you have many options from which to choose in planning your lessons.

Unit Opening Pages

At the beginning of each unit, you will find several helpful items:

- A unit overview to help you quickly identify the focus of each chapter in the unit.
- A list of Teacher's Classroom Resources materials that correlate with the unit as a whole.
- Suggestions for introducing the unit with motivators, activities that help spark student interest.
- Suggestions for completing the unit with review and evaluation.

Chapter Opening Pages

At the beginning of each chapter, the Teacher's Wraparound Edition provides:

- A list of Teacher's Classroom Resources materials that correlate with the chapter as a whole.
- Suggestions for introducing the chapter with a motivating activity.
- Cooperative learning suggestions. These activities can help you use specific cooperative learning techniques in your classroom. For information on the techniques referred to in these activities, see "Cooperative Learning Techniques" on page T-14.

Lesson Plans Within Sections

The Teacher's Wraparound Edition provides a ready-made lesson plan for each section of the text, with suggestions for introducing, completing, and teaching the unit.

Introducing the Section

On the first page of each section, the Teacher's Wraparound Edition provides suggestions for motivating students, introducing the section objectives, introducing the vocabulary terms, and initiating guided reading activities. Also found on this page is a list of Teacher's Classroom Resources materials correlated to the section.

Teaching the Section

Within each section, the basic lesson plan continues. The section is broken down into specific topics, as identified by headings at the top of the Teacher's Wraparound Edition page. For example:

Teaching . . .

• Convenience Food Choices

(text pages 395-396)

This is followed by two types of basic lesson plan material:

- **Comprehension Check** provides questions to help you make sure students have a grasp of the main ideas covered in the text. Answers follow in parentheses.
- **Student Experiences** are activities to help students apply their knowledge and extend their learning. They also help reinforce key skills, ranging from basic academic skills to higher-level thinking skills to life management skills. The key skill is identified in parentheses following each activity.

Completing the Section

On the last page of each section, the Teacher's Wraparound Edition material helps you bring the lesson to a close with:

- Suggestions for review activities.
- Options for evaluation.
- Reteaching suggestions. These are suitable for students who need additional practice to master the lesson.
- An enrichment activity suitable for students who would benefit from independent study or more challenging content.
- A suggestion for bringing the lesson to a close.
- Answers to the Section Review found in the student text.

Special Features Within Sections

In addition to the basic lesson plan, the Teacher's Wraparound Edition provides other types of teaching helps within the sections.

- *Food and Nutrition Science* boxes provide options for bringing additional science content into the course. Some suggest simple experiments, while others provide information beyond the text.

- *Thinking Skills* boxes can be used to help students build their creativity, critical thinking skills, reasoning skills, and problem-solving abilities.

- *Special Needs Strategies* help you effectively teach students who have special needs, ranging from those with physical or learning disabilities to the gifted and talented.

- *Lab Experience* boxes provide suggestions for hands-on learning.

- *Text feature tie-ins* provide discussion suggestions or additional information relating to the text features (Science Connection, Technology Tidbit, World of Variety, Earth Watch, Healthy Attitudes, Tips for Success, Safety Check).

- *Using the Photo* boxes provide suggestions for using text illustrations as a springboard for discussion.

- *"More About"* boxes provide extra information related to the topics covered in the text. You may wish to share this information with students to spark interest and generate discussion, draw upon the information when answering student questions, or use the information to enhance your own understanding of the subject.

- *"See Also"* boxes refer you to related topics in other sections of the text.

Recipe Pages

The Teacher's Wraparound Edition provides information to help you use the recipes found in the student text. The key skill reinforced by each recipe is identified near the top of the page. The "Using the Recipe" box helps you guide students through the steps that lead to success in the kitchen or foods lab: reading the recipe beforehand, noting pre-preparation tasks, reviewing safety and sanitation procedures, making a work plan, checking equipment and ingredients, and evaluating results. It also refers you to coordinated materials in the Foods Lab Resources booklet (part of the Teacher's Classroom Resources). Answers to "Thinking About the Recipe" questions are provided in the bottom margin.

Career Feature Pages

The Teacher's Wraparound Edition also provides support material for the Career Profile at the end of each chapter. Suggestions are given for discussing the features in class. "Student Opportunities" provides practical suggestions for part-time and volunteer work so that students can follow up on their career interests. "Occupational Outlook" identifies ways that people in the featured job may advance in their career. At the bottom of the page, "For More Information" lists addresses of organizations that students may wish to contact to find out more about related careers.

Chapter Review Pages

On the chapter review pages, the Teacher's Wraparound Edition provides suggestions for completing the chapter with review and evaluation. It also provides answers to the chapter review questions.

STUDENT WORKBOOK

The *Food for Today* Student Workbook provides a study guide for each section of the text. These study guides are useful as guided reading activities and to help students review material in preparation for quizzes and tests.

The Student Workbook also provides a variety of well-planned, ready-to-use activity sheets, one for each section of the text. They provide opportunities for independent practice and can help students master concepts, extend their learning, apply basic academic skills, and strengthen thinking skills.

Each sheet is perforated so that they can easily be detached and turned in for checking. Answers are provided in the Teacher's Annotated Edition of the workbook, which is part of the Teacher's Classroom Resources.

Please note that the *Food for Today* Student Workbook is designed as a consumable workbook for use by one student. Reproduction of activity sheets for classroom use is a violation of copyright.

TEACHER'S CLASSROOM RESOURCES

A unique feature of the *Food for Today* program is the Teacher's Classroom Resources (TCR), a file box filled with a multitude of supplemental resources and teaching materials to meet your needs and a variety of student ability levels. Each type of material is bound in its own booklet.

Reproducible Lesson Plans

This booklet provides reproducible, checklist-style lesson plans for each section of *Food for Today*. Each lesson plan is a listing of all the resource materials in the *Food for Today* program that correlate with the section. You can simply check off items used to teach the section, then hand in or file the lesson plan for documentation of your goals and plans.

Student Workbook
(Teacher's Annotated Edition)

This annotated edition of the *Student Workbook* provides answers for all study guides and activities, printed right on the activity page.

Extending the Text

This booklet provides reproducible handout masters for each section of the text. They give students extra information, extending text concepts for in-depth learning. They can be read and discussed by the whole class or given to selected students. The reading level is similar to that of the textbook.

Reteaching Activities

This booklet provides a reteaching activity for each section of the text. These activities offer extra guidance for those students who may need a little more help grasping important concepts. They focus on the main ideas of the section, have a simplified reading level, and often take a visual approach. Answers are provided in the back of the booklet.

Enrichment Activities

This booklet provides an enrichment activity for each chapter of the text. These activities are designed to challenge the more academically able student. For example, they often consist of supplemental readings (at a higher reading level than the text) followed by critical thinking questions. Answers are provided in the back of the booklet.

Section Quizzes

This booklet provides a reproducible one-page quiz for each section of the text. Each quiz includes one or two types of objective items, such as multiple choice, matching, true-false, or completion. The booklet also includes a complete answer key.

Chapter and Unit Tests

This booklet provides a reproducible test for each chapter and unit of *Food for Today*. Two to three types of objective items are included in each test. In addition, two essay questions are included at the end of each test for optional use. Simply delete the essay questions if you do not wish to use them. A complete answer key is included.

Foods Lab Resources

This booklet provides a variety of materials to help you plan and carry out effective foods lab activities. It includes:

- Over 50 tested recipes chosen with foods lab requirements in mind. The recipes are printed on reproducible sheets so that students do not have to take their textbooks into the foods lab.

- An activity sheet for each recipe. These provide questions to help students think about the recipe, prepare for the lab, and evaluate the results.
- An answer key for the recipe worksheets.
- Reproducible handouts such as a work plan form, "Standards Scorecards" for product evaluation, and "Problem Solver" checklists.

Food Science Resources

This booklet provides reproducible experiment sheets to help your students explore food science concepts. Teacher guidelines are provided for each experiment. A planning chart correlates the experiments to the textbook.

The experiments use food and equipment normally found in a high school foods lab. No hazardous chemicals or expensive special equipment is needed.

Multicultural Resources

This booklet provides a variety of materials related to foods from around the world. The materials range from international recipes to maps to handouts that provide information about a variety of cultures. You may wish to use these materials in conjunction with Chapter 22, "Foods of the World," or to supplement the study of food throughout your course. Suggestions are given for projects that could be undertaken cooperatively with other departments, such as social studies and foreign languages.

Additional international recipes and related handouts may be found in Glencoe's *Foods Around the World* booklet, a special bonus provided in the Teacher's Classroom Resources box.

Performance Assessment

Foods, nutrition, and food science classes have long been a place where student performance is assessed in a variety of ways. In addition to grading written tests, teachers must evaluate hands-on foods lab activities and many other types of projects, such as skits, pamphlets, visual displays, and research papers. The *Food for Today* Performance Assessment booklet provides easy-to-use rubrics to help you systematically evaluate student work. Each rubric consists of suggested criteria for evaluation presented in an easy-to-use chart format. The rubrics can be used with many of the activities found throughout the *Food for Today* program.

School to Work

This booklet provides activities and information to help students make a successful transition to the working world. Topics range from finding jobs to building positive relationships at work.

ABCNews InterActive™ Videodiscs Bar Code Correlation

ABCNews InterActive™ videodisc series *Understanding Ourselves* is a multimedia program combining videodiscs, text, and software. Titles in the series include *Food and Nutrition; Tobacco; Alcohol; Drugs and Substance Abuse; Health: AIDS;* and *Teenage Sexuality*. In the Bar Code Correlation booklet, the *Understanding Ourselves* series has been correlated to *Food for Today*. The booklet identifies videodisc segments that can be used to reinforce, apply, or extend the lesson when teaching specific sections of *Food for Today*. The bar codes provided, when used with a bar code scanner, allow quick and easy access to the specified videodisc segments.

Color Transparencies

The Teacher's Classroom Resources box includes a set of over 50 ready-to-use transparencies in full color. You will find them a valuable tool for introducing topics, reinforcing concepts, sparking discussion, and developing thinking skills. Each transparency is accompanied by a sheet of teaching suggestions. They can help you introduce the transparencies, lead discussion, and initiate related activities.

TESTMAKER SOFTWARE

This computer software can help you create personalized quizzes and tests with ease. For example, if you did not choose to teach all the sections in a chapter, you can use the *Testmaker Software* to prepare a chapter test covering only the sections you taught. Hundreds of objective test items are stored on the computer disk. You may choose the test items you want to use, ask the computer to select items randomly, or add questions of your own. You can arrange items in any order and scramble them to create multiple versions of the same test. Answer keys can be printed out to accompany each test. The software can also be used to create homework assignments and study sheets.

Cooperative Learning Techniques

From the workplace to the classroom, emphasis is increasingly being placed on teamwork. In the workplace, employers are increasing productivity and improving quality through the use of quality circles. Quality circles consist of small groups of employees who meet regularly to discuss the way they do their jobs and to recommend changes. In the classroom, teachers are moving from use of lectures to impart information to increased involvement of students through the use of learning teams. Like quality circles, this new approach, called cooperative learning, emphasizes student involvement and cooperation in the learning process.

In cooperative learning students work together in small groups, draw on each other's strengths, and assist each other in completing a task. This method encourages students to develop supportive relationships, good communication skills, and higher-level thinking competencies. Cooperative learning benefits students by fostering cooperation, encouraging positive group relationships, developing students' self-esteem, and improving academic achievement.

In cooperative learning, heterogeneous groups of students work together to reach an instructional goal. Each student is responsible for his or her own learning *and* helping others learn. As in any successful team effort, the strengths of each person are utilized in a way that ensures success for both individuals and the group. Cooperative learning helps students build good communication and social skills. It encourages peer regulation, feedback, support, and encouragement.

ELEMENTS OF COOPERATIVE LEARNING

Cooperative learning activities include five basic elements: 1) positive goal interdependence, 2) face-to-face interaction, 3) individual accountability, 4) social skills, and 5) group processing. Each element contributes to the success of the group.

- *Positive interdependence* occurs when students feel that they need to do their own part for the benefit of the entire group. Positive interdependence is achieved through common goals; division of labor; dividing materials, resources, or information among group members; assigning students different roles; and by giving group rewards. For a learning situation to be cooperative, students must feel a sense of interdependence with other members of their learning group.

- *Face-to-face interaction* requires students to explain how they obtained an answer or how a problem might be solved, to help each other understand a task, check each other's understanding of the material, or summarize what was learned. These interactions facilitate the positive interdependence that enhances educational outcomes.

- *Individual accountability* is achieved by giving both individual and group grades for mastery of learning material. This encourages group members to offer support and assist each other in attaining the required mastery level. This helps to maximize the achievement of each individual student.

- *Social skills* for effective group functioning must be taught to students before involving them in cooperative learning. Students must learn how to follow as well as to lead. For cooperative learning to be effective, students must learn how to ensure that everyone participates, how to listen carefully and critically, the importance of taking turns, how to help students who have difficulty understanding, how to explain one's reasoning, and the importance of respecting each other's viewpoints. They must learn to encourage each other to complete the assigned task, how to ask for assistance when they need it, and how to use appropriate strategies to resolve any conflicts which arise. Developing these skills requires practice. This makes it necessary to set up situations in which these skills can be used and reinforced until they are learned.

- *Group processing skills* must also be taught to students. This involves teaching students to evaluate the group's effectiveness. Students should first reflect on how well the group is working, then determine ways their effectiveness might be improved. Techniques include observations by group members, the teacher, or an individual assigned the role of observer. The observer provided feedback regarding the strengths and weaknesses of the group. Based on the feedback, the group identifies ways to improve the group's functioning.

IMPLEMENTING COOPERATIVE LEARNING

For cooperative learning to be successful, the teacher must plan activities carefully, monitor groups throughout the process, and then evaluate the results. Each of these steps is necessary to ensure the success of the cooperative learning experience.

Planning for cooperative learning involves identifying appropriate tasks or projects, determining how to structure learning groups, and providing clear instructions. Just assigning students to work in groups does not meet the intent of cooperative learning. To fit the cooperative learning model, the task must be structured so that students are interdependent. Cooperative learning activities should be based on clearly specified academic objectives and collaborative skills objectives. The task must be clearly explained and explicit directions describing the procedures to be followed must be given. The teacher may need to define terms, develop concepts, and relate them to previous learning before initiating the cooperative learning process. This will facilitate the groups' efforts when they begin their work.

Decisions must also be made regarding grouping of students. Groups will vary in size depending on the task to be accomplished and the experience of the students. Groups are usually made up of two to six students. Groups should be heterogeneous, varying in academic ability, gender, and racial mix. Desks or tables should be arranged so that students in a group sit together facing each other.

In monitoring the groups, the teacher's role is to make sure everyone is participating. One way to do this is to assign each member of the group a role such as leader, recorder, encourager, and summarizer. The teacher should move from group to group to be sure each group is on task and to answer questions. As groups become more experienced in cooperative learning, the need for teacher monitoring will decrease.

While monitoring groups, the teacher should be alert to problems. Typical problems include the student who tries to do all of the work, the student who dominates the group, and the student who refuses to participate. Assigning each group member a role reduces the potential for such problems to occur. Evaluating how well each student performs the assigned role also helps to minimize problems. Another technique is to structure the task so that each person has an important part of the information that is not available to other group members. This requires each group member to participate and to share information in order to complete the task.

At the end of the cooperative learning activity, time should be provided for the group to analyze how well the task was done and how effectively the group functioned. This can be done through class discussion or by using evaluation forms. Students should evaluate both their own participation and the group's functioning.

COOPERATIVE LEARNING APPROACHES

A variety of approaches to cooperative learning have been developed. All are variations on the basic elements of cooperative learning. The approach selected for a particular activity depends on the task to be accomplished. Several examples of cooperative learning approaches are given below.

Think/Pair/Share

A simple way to increase student participation in a teacher-led discussion begins with a question asked by the teacher, followed by 3 to 10 seconds of silence or "wait time." After giving students time to think about the question, the teacher instructs students to pair with another student and share their thinking. This requires students to articulate their ideas, to give examples, and to clarify when needed. While one student shares, the other student must listen and formulate questions designed to clarify points that are unclear. The activity can be extended by having students combine their ideas into one idea.

Observer Feedback

This approach is similar to the one described above with the addition of an observer. The third group member observes the interaction and provides feedback. The observer may be required to record observable data without becoming involved in the interaction. The observer's role is to give objective and accurate feedback.

Tell/Retell: 2-4-8

This activity begins with students sharing in pairs. Each pair then joins another pair of students. Each partner of the original pair must retell the other's contribution. Each foursome then joins another foursome to form a group of eight and each person must tell a point that he or she has not told or retold before. To summarize, the group tries to recall all eight interactions. This activity requires active listening and is a good way for students to quickly gather and share a lot of ideas.

People Search

The people search requires participants to move about the room and talk with each other while gathering answers to questions. Students are given a list of statements beginning with, "Find someone who...." Participants create informal clusters of two or more students as they try to find answers and gather signatures of the persons who answer the questions. This activity may be used as an ice-breaker, as a pre-learning strategy, or as a review. It encourages students to meet new people and to enter into new groups.

Wraparound

This forced response strategy, sometimes called a wraparound, whip, snake, round robin, or response-in-turn, requires each student to contribute to the discussion. The activity may begin with an individual written response such as an individual journal entry to give students a moment to formulate a response and to refine their thoughts. After completing the written response, students stand to share their responses in the wraparound. As responses are given, the concept or idea takes on new dimensions through students' unique connections. (Note: Responses are not really forced, because students are give the option of saying, "I pass," if they do not want to respond.) This approach is useful for gathering a quick response from each student. It is a good way to establish the expectation for each student to participate.

Human Graph

This approach requires students to physically indicate their agreement or disagreement, preference, or intensity of feelings. The teacher begins with a statement and asks students to literally take a stand on an imaginary or tape-drawn graph. The teacher then asks students to share their reasoning. Students are allowed to rethink, modify, or change their opinion as other students share their reasoning. This technique provides a quick, highly visible reading of group opinions on an issue, idea, or concept. Following the activity, students may be asked to write about the topic.

Groups of Four

This approach involves having four randomly selected students work together on a task. For example, students might review their homework assignment, discuss any differences, decide on the correct answers, and turn in one homework assignment. This encourages discussion and justification of answers. The teacher provides assistance as needed and leads a follow-up discussion. This activity emphasizes communication and social skills.

Jigsaw

In the jigsaw activity, each group member is assigned a part of the task. Each student works independently to research the assigned topic. Each group member then teaches his or her piece of the puzzle to others in the group. Each person is also responsible for mastering the information other group members present in order to master all parts of the puzzle. This activity helps to build individual responsibility within the group. A variation of this technique requires members from all groups who are assigned the same "puzzle" to work together to develop their expertise. Then these "experts" return to their groups to teach.

Co-Op Co-Op

The group chooses a main topic, then divides it into mini-topics. Each student selects a mini-topic, researches it, and shares the information with the group. After discussion, the group compiles the information into a group presentation which it gives to the entire class. Students may be evaluated on individual papers as well as the group presentation. This activity requires students to interact with each other and encourages team-building.

Group Investigation/Small Group Teaching

The teacher assigns an area of study, and student groups of two to six select a related topic of interest. Through cooperative planning, the teacher and students decide how to investigate the topic and group tasks are assigned. The teacher sets up work stations around the room where the research is conducted. Each member carries out an individual investigation, then the group summarizes the findings and prepares an interesting presentation to share with the entire class. By listening to all of the reports, students gain a broad perspective on the topic. In addition, they are expected to learn all of the material. Evaluation is based on observations of how well students use investigative skills. Both individual and group efforts may be evaluated. This approach emphasizes interdependence among groups.

References

Bauwens, J., and Hourcade, J. J. *Cooperative Teaching: Rebuilding the Schoolhouse for All Students.* Austin, TX: PRO-ED, 1994.

Bellanca, J. and Fogarty, R. *Blueprints for Thinking in the Cooperative Classroom*. Palatine, IL: Skylight Publishing, 1990.

Carroll, J. A., and Seaton, M. *Cooperative Learning Throughout the Year.* Carthage, IL: Good Apple, 1992.

Fogarty, R. and Bellanca, J. *Patterns for Thinking—Patterns for Transfer*. Palatine, IL: Skylight Publishing, 1987.

Hilke, E.V. *Cooperative Learning.* Bloomington, IN: Phi Delta Kappa Educational Foundation, 1990.

Holt, L. *Cooperative Learning in Action.* Columbus, OH: National Middle Schools, 1993.

Johnson, D.W., and Johnson, R. *Learning Together and Alone: Cooperative, Competitive, and Individualistic Learning*. 2d ed. Englewood Cliffs, NJ: Prentice-Hall, 1987.

Johnson, D.W., Johnson, R., and Holubec, E. *Cooperation in the Classroom* (revised edition). Edina, MN: Interaction Book Company, 1988.

Johnson, D. W., Johnson, R., and Holubec, E. Johnson. *Cooperative Learning in the Classroom.* Alexandria, VA: Association for Supervision and Curriculum Development, 1994.

Johnson, D. W., Johnson, R., and Holubec, E. Johnson. *The New Circles of Learning: Cooperation in the Classroom and School.* Alexandria, VA: Association for Supervision and Curriculum Development, 1994.

McMullen, M. *Cooperative Learning: ESL Techniques.* White Plains, NY: Longman, 1993.

Putnam, J. W., ed. *Cooperative Learning and Strategies for Inclusion: Celebrating Diversity in the Classroom.* Baltimore: P. H. Brookes, 1993.

Rybak, S. *Cooperative Learning Throughout the Curriculum.* Carthage, IL: Good Apple, 1992.

Scholastic Books staff. *Cooperative Learning: Getting Started.* New York: Scholastic, 1993.

Scope and Sequence

The following chart shows how major themes are woven throughout the *Food for Today* text. You will find it useful for planning your course, sequencing courses, emphasizing particular course themes, and correlating *Food for Today* to your curriculum.

Unit One: Food, Nutrition, and You	
Nutrition and Health	Section 1.1: Food and Health Chapter 2: The Nutrients You Need Chapter 3: Guidelines for Good Nutrition Chapter 4: Planning Daily Food Choices Chapter 5: Food and Fitness Chapter 6: Special Topics in Nutrition
Consumer Information	Section 1.2: Influences on Food Choices Section 1.5: Managing Resources and Making Decisions Section 2.1: The Role of Nutrients Section 3.3: Separating Fact From Fiction Section 4.3: Eating Out Nutritiously
Management	Section 1.5: Managing Resources and Making Decisions Section 4.2: Improving Your Eating Habits Section 5.2: Weight Management Section 6.2: Managing Health Conditions
Safety and Sanitation	Section 5.2: Weight Management
Food and Nutrition Science	Section 1.4: Food, Science, and Technology Section 2.2: Carbohydrates, Fiber, and Proteins Section 2.3: Fats Section 2.4: Vitamins, Minerals, and Water Section 2.5: How Your Body Uses Food Section 5.4: Nutrition for Sports and Fitness
Food Preparation	
Social and Cultural Aspects	Section 1.2: Influences on Food Choices Section 1.3: Food and Culture Section 4.4: Vegetarian Food Choices Section 6.1: Food and the Life Cycle
Trends and Technology	Section 1.2: Influences on Food Choices Section 1.4: Food, Science, and Technology

Unit Two: Workspace, Tools, and Techniques

Nutrition and Health	Section 8.3: Changing a Recipe
Consumer Information	Section 7.4: Storing Food Section 7.5: Conserving Natural Resources Section 9.1: Equipment for Cooking
Management	Section 7.5: Conserving Natural Resources Section 8.5: Time Management and Teamwork
Safety and Sanitation	Section 7.2: Safety in the Kitchen Section 7.3: Sanitation
Food and Nutrition Science	Section 7.3: Sanitation Section 8.3: Changing a Recipe Section 9.2: Heat and Cooking
Food Preparation	Section 8.1: Recipe Basics Section 8.2: Measuring Ingredients Section 8.3: Changing a Recipe Section 8.4: Preparation Tasks Section 8.5: Time Management and Teamwork Section 9.1: Equipment for Cooking Section 9.2: Heat and Cooking Section 9.3: Microwave Cooking Techniques Section 9.4: Conventional Cooking Techniques
Social and Cultural Aspects	Section 10.1: Serving Family Meals Section 10.2: Mealtime Etiquette
Trends and Technology	Section 7.5: Conserving Natural Resources Section 8.3: Changing A Recipe Section 9.1: Equipment for Cooking

Unit Three: Consumer Decisions

Nutrition and Health	Section 11.1: Basic Meal Planning Section 11.2: Challenges in Meal Planning Section 12.2: Food Labels Section 13.2: A Safe Food Supply Section 13.3: The Global Food Supply
Consumer Information	Chapter 11: Planning Meals Chapter 12: Shopping for Food Chapter 13: The Food Supply Chapter 14: Buying for the Kitchen
Management	Section 11.1: Basic Meal Planning Section 11.2: Challenges in Meal Planning Section 11.3: Food Costs and Budgeting Section 12.1: Before You Shop Section 14.2: Choosing Kitchen Equipment
Safety and Sanitation	Section 12.3: In the Supermarket Section 13.2: A Safe Food Supply Section 14.2: Choosing Kitchen Equipment
Food and Nutrition Science	Section 13.2: A Safe Food Supply
Food Preparation	
Social and Cultural Aspects	Section 11.2: Challenges in Meal Planning Section 13.3: The Global Food Supply
Trends and Technology	Section 11.2: Challenges in Meal Planning Section 13.2: A Safe Food Supply Section 14.2: Choosing Kitchen Equipment Section 14.3: Designing a Kitchen

Unit Four: Foods for Meals and Snacks	
Nutrition and Health	Section 15.1: Choosing Convenience Foods Section 16.1: Choosing Fruits and Vegetables Section 17.1: Choosing Grains and Grain Products Section 17.3: Legumes, Nuts, and Seeds Section 18.1: Choosing Dairy Products Section 18.3: Egg Basics Section 19.1: Looking at Meat, Poultry, Fish, and Shellfish Section 20.1: Sandwiches, Snacks, and Packed Lunches Section 20.2: Salads and Dressings Section 20.3: Soups and Sauces Section 20.4: Casseroles and Other Combinations Section 21.1: Ingredients and Techniques for Baking Section 21.2: Quick Breads Section 21.3: Yeast Breads and Rolls Section 21.4: Cakes, Cookies, and Pies
Consumer Information	Section 15.1: Choosing Convenience Foods Section 16.1: Choosing Fruits and Vegetables Section 17.1: Choosing Grains and Grain Products Section 17.3: Legumes, Nuts, and Seeds Section 18.1: Choosing Dairy Products Section 18.3: Egg Basics Section 19.1: Looking at Meat, Poultry, Fish, and Shellfish Section 19.2: Meat Selection and Storage Section 19.3: Poultry Selection and Storage Section 19.4: Fish and Shellfish Selection and Storage
Management	Section 15.2: Cooking with Convenience Section 21.3: Yeast Breads and Rolls
Safety and Sanitation	Section 15.1: Choosing Convenience Foods Section 16.1: Choosing Fruits and Vegetables Section 17.1: Choosing Grains and Grain Products Section 17.3: Legumes, Nuts, and Seeds Section 18.1: Choosing Dairy Products Section 18.3: Egg Basics Section 19.1: Looking at Meat, Poultry, Fish, and Shellfish Section 19.2: Meat Selection and Storage Section 19.3: Poultry Selection and Storage Section 19.4: Fish and Shellfish Selection and Storage Section 20.1: Sandwiches, Snacks, and Packed Lunches

Unit Four (continued)

Food and Nutrition Science	Section 16.2: Preparing Raw Fruits and Vegetables Section 17.1: Choosing Grains and Grain Products Section 18.1: Choosing Dairy Foods Section 18.3: Egg Basics Section 19.1: Looking at Meat, Poultry, Fish, and Shellfish Section 20.2: Salads and Salad Dressings Section 21.1: Ingredients and Techniques for Baking
Food Preparation	Section 15.2: Cooking with Convenience Section 16.2: Preparing Raw Fruits and Vegetables Section 16.3: Cooking Fruits and Vegetables Section 17.2: Preparing Grains and Grain Products Section 17.3: Legumes, Nuts, and Seeds Section 18.2: Preparing Dairy Foods Section 18.3: Egg Basics Section 18.4: Using Eggs in Recipes Section 19.5: Preparing Meat, Poultry, Fish, and Shellfish Chapter 20: Food Combinations Chapter 21: Baking
Social and Cultural Aspects	Section 16.1: Choosing Fruits and Vegetables Section 17.1: Choosing Grains and Grain Products
Trends and Technology	Section 15.1: Choosing Convenience Foods Section 15.2: Cooking with Convenience Section 21.3: Yeast Breads and Rolls

Unit Five: Expanding Your Horizons

Nutrition and Health	Section 24.2: Beverages Section 25.1: Career Opportunities
Consumer Information	Section 24.2: Beverages
Management	Section 24.3: Entertaining Section 25.2: The Successful Worker
Safety and Sanitation	Section 24.4: Outdoor Meals Section 24.5: Preserving Food at Home
Food and Nutrition Science	Section 24.5: Preserving Food at Home Section 25.1: Career Opportunities
Food Preparation	Section 24.1: Creative Techniques Section 24.2: Beverages Section 24.4: Outdoor Meals Section 24.5: Preserving Food at Home
Social and Cultural Aspects	Section 22.1: Latin America Section 22.2: Africa and the Middle East Section 22.3: Europe Section 22.4: Asia and the Pacific Section 23.1: Regional Food of the East, Midwest, and South Section 23.2: Regional Foods of the West and Canada
Trends and Technology	Section 25.1: Career Opportunities

Suggested Course Outlines

The chart on pages T-25 through T-29 shows how *Food for Today* can be adapted for use in a variety of courses. Suggested course outlines are given for eight different types of courses:

- 36-week course covering all sections of the text.
- 18-week course covering all sections of the text.
- 18-week Beginning Foods and Nutrition course.
- 18-week Advanced Foods and Nutrition course.
- 18-week course with Food Science emphasis.
- 18-week course with Sports Nutrition emphasis.

- 6-week section of a Comprehensive Family and Consumer Sciences course.
- 3-week section of a Health course.

To use the chart, find the heading for the desired type of course. Read down the column to see the suggested number of days to spend on each section of the *Food for Today* text. An asterisk (*) indicates that the section can be skipped or summarized. These outlines can easily be adapted to meet your particular needs.

SUGGESTED COURSE OUTLINES

	Foods and Nutrition 36 Weeks	Foods and Nutrition 18 Weeks	Beginning Foods and Nutrition 18 Weeks	Advanced Foods and Nutrition 18 Weeks	Food Science emphasis 18 Weeks	Sports Nutrition 18 Weeks	Section of Comprehensive 6 Weeks	Section of Health 3 Weeks
Chapter 1. Exploring Food Choices								
1.1 Food and Health	1	1	1	*	*	2	*	*
1.2 Influences on Food Choices	1	1	1	2	*	2	*	1
1.3 Food and Culture	1	1	1	*	*	*	*	1
1.4 Food, Science, and Technology	2	1	*	2	3	*	*	*
1.5 Managing Resources and Making Decisions	2	1	1	*	1	*	*	*
Chapter 2. The Nutrients You Need								
2.1 The Role of Nutrients	2	1	*	2	2	2	1	*
2.2 Carbohydrates, Fiber, and Proteins	2	1	*	2	2	2	1	*
2.3 Fats	2	1	*	2	2	2	1	*
2.4 Vitamins, Minerals, and Water	2	1	*	2	2	2	1	*
2.5 How Your Body Uses Food	2	1	*	2	2	2	1	*
Chapter 3. Guidelines for Good Nutrition								
3.1 Dietary Guidelines	2	1	2	1	1	2	1	1
3.2 The Food Guide Pyramid	2	1	2	1	2	2	1	1
3.3 Separating Fact from Fiction	2	1	1	2	2	2	*	*
Chapter 4. Planning Daily Food Choices								
4.1 Daily Meals and Snacks	2	1	2	*	*	2	*	*
4.2 Improving Your Eating Habits	2	1	2	*	*	2	1	*
4.3 Eating Out Nutritiously	2	1	2	*	*	1	*	*
4.4 Vegetarian Food Choices	2	1	*	1	*	1	*	*
Chapter 5. Food and Fitness								
5.1 A Healthy Weight	2	1	2	*	*	2	*	1
5.2 Weight Management	2	1	2	*	*	2	1	1
5.3 Exercise Basics	2	1	2	*	*	2	*	1
5.4 Nutrition for Sports and Fitness	2	1	*	3	*	2	*	1

	Foods and Nutrition 36 Weeks	Foods and Nutrition 18 Weeks	Beginning Foods and Nutrition 18 Weeks	Advanced Foods and Nutrition 18 Weeks	Food Science emphasis 18 Weeks	Sports Nutrition 18 Weeks	Section of Comprehensive 6 Weeks	Section of Health 3 Weeks
Chapter 6. Special Topics in Nutrition								
6.1 Food and the Life Cycle	2	1	2	*	2	2	*	1
6.2 Managing Health Conditions	2	1	1	3	2	2	*	1
6.3 Eating Disorders	2	1	1	3	2	2	*	1
Chapter 7. Kitchen Principles								
7.1 Introduction to the Kitchen	1	1	*	*	1	1	*	*
7.2 Safety in the Kitchen	2	1	2	*	2	1	1	*
7.3 Sanitation	2	1	2	*	2	1	1	*
7.4 Storing Food	2	1	2	*	1	1	*	*
7.5 Conserving Natural Resources	2	1	*	2	2	*	*	1
Chapter 8. Recipe Skills								
8.1 Recipe Basics	1	1	1	*	2	1	1	*
8.2 Measuring Ingredients	2	1	2	*	2	1	1	*
8.3 Changing a Recipe	2	1	*	3	2	1	*	*
8.4 Preparation Tasks	2	1	1	*	2	1	1	*
8.5 Time Management and Teamwork	2	1	1	*	2	1	1	*
Chapter 9. Cooking Methods								
9.1 Equipment for Cooking	2	1	1	*	1	1	*	*
9.2 Heat and Cooking	1	1	2	*	2	1	*	*
9.3 Microwave Cooking Techniques	2	2	2	*	2	1	*	*
9.4 Conventional Cooking Techniques	2	1	2	*	2	1	*	*
Chapter 10. Mealtime Customs								
10.1 Serving Family Meals	2	1	1	*	*	*	1	*
10.2 Mealtime Etiquette	2	1	1	*	*	*	1	*
Chapter 11. Planning Meals								
11.1 Basic Meal Planning	2	1	2	*	1	2	1	*
11.2 Challenges in Meal Planning	2	1	*	3	*	2	*	*
11.3 Food Costs and Budgeting	2	1	*	3	*	*	1	*

	Foods and Nutrition 36 Weeks	Foods and Nutrition 18 Weeks	Beginning Foods and Nutrition 18 Weeks	Advanced Foods and Nutrition 18 Weeks	Food Science emphasis 18 Weeks	Sports Nutrition 18 Weeks	Section of Comprehensive 6 Weeks	Section of Health 3 Weeks
Chapter 12. Shopping for Food								
12.1 Before You Shop	2	1	1	*	*	*	1	*
12.2 Food Labels	2	1	1	*	*	1	1	*
12.3 In the Supermarket	2	1	2	*	*	*	1	*
Chapter 13. The Food Supply								
13.1 Where Does Food Come From?	2	1	*	2	2	*	*	1
13.2 A Safe Food Supply	2	1	*	2	2	*	*	1
13.3 The Global Food Supply	2	1	*	2	1	*	*	1
Chapter 14. Buying for the Kitchen								
14.1 Consumer Skills	2	1	1	*	*	*	*	*
14.2 Choosing Kitchen Equipment	2	1	1	*	*	*	*	*
14.3 Designing a Kitchen	2	1	*	3	*	*	*	*
Chapter 15. Convenience Foods								
15.1 Choosing Convenience Foods	2	1	1	*	*	1	*	*
15.2 Cooking with Convenience	2	2	2	*	1	2	*	*
Chapter 16. Fruits and Vegetables								
16.1 Choosing Fruits and Vegetables	2	2	1	*	*	1	1	*
16.2 Preparing Raw Fruits and Vegetables	2	2	2	*	2	1	*	*
16.3 Cooking Fruits and Vegetables	3	2	3	*	2	2	1	*
Chapter 17. Grains, Legumes, Nuts, and Seeds								
17.1 Choosing Grains and Grain Products	2	1	1	*	1	1	1	*
17.2 Preparing Grains and Grain Products	2	1	3	*	2	2	1	*
17.3 Legumes, Nuts, and Seeds	3	2	2	*	1	1	*	*
Chapter 18. Dairy Foods and Eggs								
18.1 Choosing Dairy Foods	2	1	1	*	1	1	1	*
18.2 Preparing Dairy Foods	3	2	3	*	2	2	1	*
18.3 Egg Basics	2	1	1	*	1	1	*	*
18.4 Using Eggs in Recipes	3	2	3	*	2	1	*	*

	Foods and Nutrition 36 Weeks	Foods and Nutrition 18 Weeks	Beginning Foods and Nutrition 18 Weeks	Advanced Foods and Nutrition 18 Weeks	Food Science emphasis 18 Weeks	Sports Nutrition 18 Weeks	Section of Comprehensive 6 Weeks	Section of Health 3 Weeks
Chapter 19. Meat, Poultry, and Fish								
19.1 Looking at Meat, Poultry, Fish, and Shellfish	2	1	2	*	1	1	1	*
19.2 Meat Selection and Storage	2	1	1	*	1	1	*	*
19.3 Poultry Selection and Storage	2	1	1	*	1	1	*	*
19.4 Fish and Shellfish Selection and Storage	2	1	2	*	1	1	*	*
19.5 Preparing Meat, Poultry, Fish, and Shellfish	3	2	3	*	2	2	1	*
Chapter 20. Food Combinations								
20.1 Sandwiches, Snacks, and Packed Lunches	2	1	*	2	*	2	*	*
20.2 Salads and Dressings	2	1	*	2	2	2	*	*
20.3 Soups and Sauces	2	*	*	2	2	2	*	*
20.4 Casseroles and Other Combinations	2	*	*	2	*	2	*	*
Chapter 21. Baking								
21.1 Ingredients and Techniques for Baking	2	2	1	*	1	*	*	*
21.2 Quick Breads	2	2	2	1	2	*	*	*
21.3 Yeast Breads and Rolls	2	*	*	3	2	*	*	*
21.4 Cakes, Cookies, and Pies	3	*	*	3	*	*	*	*
Chapter 22. Foods of the World								
22.1 Latin America	2	1	*	3	*	*	*	*
22.2 Africa and the Middle East	2	1	*	3	*	*	*	*
22.3 Europe	2	1	*	3	*	*	*	*
22.4 Asia and the Pacific	2	1	*	3	*	*	*	*
Chapter 23. Foods of the U.S. and Canada								
23.1 Regional Foods of the East, Midwest, and South	2	1	2	*	*	*	*	*
23.2 Regional Foods of the West and Canada	3	1	2	*	*	*	*	*

	Foods and Nutrition 36 Weeks	Foods and Nutrition 18 Weeks	Beginning Foods and Nutrition 18 Weeks	Advanced Foods and Nutrition 18 Weeks	Food Science emphasis 18 Weeks	Sports Nutrition 18 Weeks	Section of Comprehensive 6 Weeks	Section of Health 3 Weeks
Chapter 24. Special Ways with Food								
24.1 Creative Techniques	2	*	*	2	*	*	*	*
24.2 Beverages	1	*	*	2	*	*	*	*
24.3 Entertaining	2	*	*	2	*	*	*	*
24.4 Outdoor Meals	2	*	*	2	*	*	*	*
24.5 Preserving Food at Home	2	*	*	3	*	*	*	*
Chapter 25. Careers in Food and Nutrition								
25.1 Career Opportunities	2	*	*	2	1	1	*	*
25.2 The Successful Worker	2	*	*	2	1	1	*	*

Selected References

(Also see the Cooperative Learning references listed on page T-17)

GENERAL REFERENCE

ABCNews InterActive™ Videodiscs, *Alcohol, Drugs and Substance Abuse, Food and Nutrition, Teenage Sexuality, Tobacco, Violence Prevention.* Columbus, OH: Glencoe, 1997.

Frank, Robyn C., and Holly Berry Irving, eds. *Directory of Food and Nutrition Information for Professionals and Consumers.* 2nd ed. Phoenix, Arizona: Oryx, 1992.

Kowtaluk, Helen. *Discovering Food and Nutrition,* 5th ed. Columbus, OH: Glencoe, 1997.

NUTRITION

Books

Gershoff, Stanley. *Tufts University Guide to Total Nutrition.* New York: Harper and Row, 1993.

Haskew, Paul, and Cynthia Adams. *Eating Disorders: Managing Problems with Food.* Columbus, OH: Glencoe, 1989.

Jacobson, Michael F., and Sarah Pritschner. *Fast Food Guide.* New York: Workman Publishing, 1991.

Lyman, Bernard. *Psychology of Food: More Than a Matter of Taste.* New York: Van Nostrand Reinhold, 1988.

Periodicals

Environmental Nutrition

Journal of Nutrition Education

Tufts University Diet and Nutrition Letter

University of California at Berkeley Wellness Letter

Vegetarian Times

Videos

The following videos are available from Glencoe:

Anorexia: Thin Obsession.

Bulimia: The Vicious Cycle.

Controlling Weight Sensibly.

Eating Disorders: Anorexia Nervosa and Bulimia.

Eating Healthy: What's A Serving?

Low-Fat Cooking.

The Exercise and Nutrition Connection.

The New Nutrition Pyramid.

Nutrients and You.

Read the Food Label.

Sensible Weight Control.

Tip-Top Tots: The Nutrition Pyramid for Preschoolers.

Vegetarianism.

You Are What You Eat.

FOODS AND FOOD PREPARATION

Books

Robertson, Laurel, Carol Flinders, and Brian Ruppenthal. *The New Laurel's Kitchen.* Berkeley, CA: Ten Speed Press, 1986.

Vegetarian Times, ed. *Vegetarian Times Cookbook.* New York: Macmillan, 1984.

Better Homes and Gardens Complete Guide to Food and Cooking. Des Moines, IA: Meredith Books, 1991.

Fresh Produce A to Z. Menlo Park, CA: Sunset Books, 1987.

Good Housekeeping Illustrated Microwave Cookbook. New York: Hearst Books, 1989.

Greene, Bert. *The Grains Cookbook.* New York: Workman Publishers, 1989.

Herbst, Sharon Tyler. *Food Lover's Companion: Comprehensive Definitions of Over 3000 Food, Wine, and Culinary Terms.* Hauppauge, NY: Barron, 1990.

Pickarski, Ron. *Friendly Foods.* Berkeley, CA: Ten Speed Press, 1991.

Videos

The following videos are available from Glencoe:

Cooking with Convenience Foods.

Food and Kitchen Safety.

Food Processing, Safety, and Preparation.

Food Safety.

Herbs and Spices.

Measure Up.

Quickbreads.

Safety in the Kitchen.

Timing & Organization in Food Preparation.

FOOD SCIENCE

Books

Edwards, Gabrielle I. *Biology the Easy Way.* Hauppage, NY: Barron, 1990.

McGee, Harold. *The Curious Cook.* San Francisco: North Point Press, 1990.

—. *On Food and Cooking.* New York: Macmillan, 1988.

Mehas, Kay Yockey, and Sharon Lesley Rodgers. *Food Science: The Biochemistry of Food and Nutrition.* 3rd ed. Columbus, OH: Glencoe, 1997.

Video

The following video is available from Glencoe:

An Introduction to Food Science.

PSYCHOLOGICAL AND SOCIAL ASPECTS

Books

Fox, C. Lynn. *Unlocking Doors to Self-Esteem: Supportive Counseling for Professionals and Families.* Rolling Hills Estates, CA: Jalmar Press, 1990.

Post, Elizabeth L. *Emily Post's Etiquette.* New York: Harper Collins Publishers, Inc., 1992.

Periodical

Self-Esteem Today. (National Council for Self-Esteem, P.O. Box 277877, Sacramento, CA 95827-7877)

Videos

The following videos are available from Glencoe:

Good Manners.

Setting the Table.

HISTORICAL AND CULTURAL ASPECTS

Books

Mothershead, Alice B. *Dining Customs Around the World.* Garrett Park, MD: Garrett Park Press, 1982.

Tannahill, Reay. *Food in History.* New York: Crown Publishers, 1984.

Weatherford, Jack M. *Indian Givers: How the Indians of the Americas Transformed the World.* New York: Crown Publishers, 1988.

Videos

The following videos are available from Glencoe:

Overview of Cuisine.

Foods from Other Lands.

CONSUMER AND RESOURCE MANAGEMENT

Books

Designing and Remodeling Kitchens. San Francisco: Ortho Books, 1990.

Ideas for Great Kitchens. Menlo Park, CA: Sunset Books, 1991.

Jacobson, Michael F. *Safe Food.* Berkeley, CA: Berkeley Publishers, 1993.

—. *Safe Food: Eating Wisely in a Risky World.* Los Angeles: Living Planet Press, 1991.

Sass, Lorna J. *Recipes from an Ecological Kitchen.* New York: William Morrow, 1992.

Teitel, Martin. *Rain Forest in Your Kitchen: The Hidden Connection Between Extinction and Your Supermarket.* Washington, DC: Island Press, 1992.

Periodicals

Consumer Reports

Nutrition Action (Center for Science in the Public Interest, 1501 16th Street NW, Washington, DC 20036-1499)

Videos

The following videos are available from Glencoe:

Budget and Credit Live Videos—Budgeting.

Buying Nutritious Food.

Ecology in the Kitchen.

Supermarket Shopping: A Guide to Grocery Store Services.

CAREERS

Books

Kimbrell, Grady, and Ben S. Vinyard. *Entering the World of Work.* Columbus, OH: Glencoe, 1989.

U.S. Department of Labor. *Dictionary of Occupational Titles.* Annual.

Videos

The following video is available from Glencoe:

Careers in Food and Nutrition.

Home Economics Careers. Teaching Aids, Inc., P.O. Box 1798, Costa Mesa, CA 92628-0798.

SOFTWARE SOURCES

Cotton Computer Service
Route 1, Box 34
Bristow, OK 74010

DDA Software
P.O. Box 26
Hamburg, NJ 07419

MCE, Inc.
157 S. Kalamazoo Mall, Suite 250
Kalamazoo, MI 49007

Nutrition Counseling Education Services
P.O. Box 3018
Olathe, KS 66062-8018

Teaching Aids, Inc.
P.O. Box 1798
Costa Mesa, CA 92628-0798

Food for Today

Sixth Edition

Food for Today

Sixth Edition

HELEN KOWTALUK

Alice Orphanos Kopan, M.Ed., M.A., CFCS

GLENCOE
McGraw-Hill

New York, New York   Columbus, Ohio   Mission Hills, California   Peoria, Illinois

Glencoe/McGraw-Hill

A Division of The **McGraw·Hill** *Companies*

Send all inquiries to:
Glencoe/McGraw-Hill
3008 W. Willow Knolls Drive
Peoria, Illinois 61614

ISBN 0-02-642980-2 (Student Text)
ISBN 0-02-642983-7 (Teacher's Wraparound Edition)

Printed in the United States of America

3 4 5 6 7 8 9 10   QPH   02 01 00 99 98 97

Nutrition Consultant

Elizabeth Shipley Moses, M.S., R.D.

Contributors

Gwen Bagaas
Jamestown, New York

Gayle Gardner Erskine, M.S., CFCS
Home Economics Department Chair
Cherry Creek Schools
Aurora, Colorado

Brenda Barrington Mendiola, M.S.
Home Economics Teacher
Irion County Schools
Mertzon, Texas

Elise Zwicky
Pekin, Illinois

Reviewers

Pamela M. Baggett, CFCS
Family and Consumer Sciences Teacher
Middleburg High School
Middleburg, Florida

Ann Branch, M.Ed.
Personal and Family Life Science Instructor
Jefferson Senior High School
Alexandria, Minnesota

Patricia Brodeen, M.S.
Home Economics Teacher
Roosevelt High School
San Antonio, Texas

Jeannine C. Campbell, M.S., CFCS
Family and Consumer Sciences Teacher
F.J. Reitz High School
Evansville, Indiana

Judith Egolf, M.A., CFCS
Family and Consumer Sciences Teacher
Warsaw Community High School
Warsaw, Indiana

Ann Larkin, P.H.E.C.
Family Studies Teacher
Clarke Road Secondary School
London, Ontario

Mary Helen Mays, Ph.D., R.D.
Former Coordinator,
Coordinated Program in Dietetics
University of Texas Pan American
Edinburg, Texas

Vicki McClung
Family and Consumer Sciences Teacher
Trumann High School
Trumann, Arkansas

Paula McKee
Family and Consumer Sciences Teacher
Middleburg High School
Middleburg, Florida

Brenda Barrington Mendiola, M.S.
Home Economics Teacher
Irion County Schools
Mertzon, Texas

Wanda Menghini, M.S.
Home Economics Teacher
Olathe South High School
Olathe, Kansas

JoAnne S. Rowe, M.S.
Research Associate and Instructor of
Family and Consumer Sciences
Indiana State University
Terre Haute, Indiana

CONTENTS

Unit One
Food, Nutrition, and You

Unit Two
Workspace, Tools, and Techniques

Unit Three
Consumer Decisions

Chapter 12. Shopping for Food ··············326

Chapter 13. The Food Supply ··················348

Chapter 14. Buying for the Kitchen ········370

Unit Four
Foods for Meals and Snacks

Chapter 20. Food Combinations ·········522

Chapter 21. Baking ·······························550

Unit Five
Expanding Your Horizons

Chapter 25. Careers in Food and Nutrition ·····················674

SPECIAL TEXT FEATURES

Career Profiles

Earth Watch

Healthy Attitudes

These features highlight suggestions for adopting a healthful lifestyle. They are found throughout the text.

Recipes

Safety Check

Safety, sanitation, and health precautions are highlighted in these features throughout the text.

Science Connection

Technology Tidbit

Tips for Success

Look to these features for helpful suggestions on a variety of topics.

World of Variety

Planning the Unit

Unit Overview

Chapter 1: Exploring Food Choices—Gives an overview of the impacts of food on daily life and the influence of culture and technology on available food choices.

Chapter 2: The Nutrients You Need—Discusses the role of nutrients in health and wellness; explains the different types of nutrients (carbohydrates, fiber, proteins, fats, vitamins, minerals, and water) and how the human body uses food.

Chapter 3: Guidelines for Good Nutrition—Presents dietary guidelines and explains how to differentiate between fact and fiction in food-related discussions.

Chapter 4: Planning Daily Food Choices—Discusses eating habits and nutritious ways to eat at restaurants; also includes food choices for vegetarian diets.

Chapter 5: Food and Fitness—Discusses fitness topics such as weight management and nutrition for sports.

Chapter 6: Special Topics in Nutrition—Explains the role of food in the life cycle and discusses management of health conditions and eating disorders.

Teacher's Classroom Resources—Unit One

Refer to these resources in the TCR package:

Chapter and Unit Tests

Testmaker Software

18

UNIT ONE
Food, Nutrition, and You

19

Introducing the Unit

Motivator

- Before class begins, set up two large tables. On one, place an apple, some grains of corn, a bonnet, a garden trowel, and a cast-iron pot (or other symbols of pioneer cooking methods). On the other table, arrange a basket of tropical fruits, a packaged dinner, canned goods, packages of snacks, a sugary cereal, and a can of diet soda. Ask half the students to be seated at the pioneer table, and half at the other table. Ask the "pioneers" to discuss how they would provide food for their families, both in summer and in winter. How would they keep food from spoiling? Ask the "modern" table to discuss and list how they choose what to eat. How do they pick safe and nutritious food faced with so many choices? Compare the pioneer food system with the risks and responsibilities of choosing nutritious foods today.

Completing the Unit

Review

- Remind students of the scenario they acted out at the beginning of this unit. Assign groups of two or three students to create another scenario in which the same fictional teen finds a way to eat nutritiously without altering his or her schedule or sacrificing daily activities.

Evaluation

- Have students take the test for Unit 1. (Refer to the *Chapter and Unit Tests* booklet or construct your own test using the *Testmaker Software*.)

Planning the Chapter

Chapter Overview

Section 1.1: Food and Health

Section 1.2: Influences on Food Choices

Section 1.3: Food and Culture

Section 1.4: Food, Science, and Technology

Section 1.5: Managing Resources and Making Decisions

Introducing the Chapter

Motivators

- Bring samples of two or three unfamiliar foods to class and ask volunteers to taste them. Have students explain why they like or dislike the foods. Emphasize that people's food choices differ for many reasons.

- In groups have students discuss these questions and summarize their answers on charts. How does food meet your physical and psychological needs? What influences your food choices? How are they affected by cultural background? By science and technology? How do your management and decision-making skills influence your food choices? Post and refer to groups' charts as you study the chapter.

Teacher's Classroom Resources—Chapter One

Refer to these resources in the TCR package:

Enrichment Activities

Food Science Resources

Chapter and Unit Tests

Testmaker Software

CHAPTER 1
Exploring Food Choices

20

Cooperative Learning Suggestions

Have students work in groups to collect articles on new scientific discoveries and technological advances that are likely to affect food choices in the future. Using the articles, have students use the Roundtable approach to write and present a skit describing family food choices in the year 2020. Students should decide together on the theme of the skit, vote on the approach they should take, and then pair up to write the script. The skit might present changes in food production and processing, a futuristic view of food buying, a vision of a 21st century kitchen, or a look at family meals in the future. Have groups explain how their reading contributed to their views.

SECTION 1.1
Food and Health

OBJECTIVES
After studying this section, you should be able to:
- Describe the importance of nutrition and wellness.
- Explain how food helps meet physical and psychological needs.

LOOK FOR THESE TERMS
nutrients
nutrition
wellness
psychological
self-esteem

Troy was headed out the door of the school when he saw a group of his friends. "Hey, how about stopping for something to eat? I'm starving."

Justin shook his head. "I can't. I promised Dad I'd pick up a few things at the supermarket."

Isabel said, "Sorry. It's my turn to get dinner ready."

"I'd like to, but I've got a pep club meeting," said Brian. "We're going to plan our next spaghetti supper."

"I'll go with you, Troy," said Jamal. "We can talk about the weekend while we eat."

On this particular afternoon, the activities of Troy and his friends all revolve around food. Why does food play such an important role in people's lives? As you will see, food helps people meet a variety of needs.

Physical Needs

Food is necessary for survival. When your body needs food, it lets you know—you feel hungry. You begin to think about getting something to eat.

However, food does more than fill the stomach to stop hunger pangs. Food supplies the human body with chemicals called **nutrients.** The human body is a living organism that needs nutrients to carry on its functions.

Nutrition is the study of nutrients and how they are used by the body. The term "nutrition" can also refer to the effect of your food choices on your health. If your food choices provide all the nutrients you need in the right amounts, you are practicing good nutrition.

Good nutrition has many benefits. It can help you feel your best and look your best. It helps you grow and become strong. It helps you stay energetic and healthy, both now and in later life. As part of your study of food, you will learn more about good nutrition and how to make wise food choices.

Teacher's Classroom Resources—Section 1.1

Refer to these resources in the TCR package:

Reproducible Lesson Plans
Student Workbook
Extending the Text

Reteaching Activities
Section Quizzes
Testmaker Software
Color Transparencies

Introducing the Section

Motivators
- Compare taking care of the human body with maintaining an automobile. Discuss what is required to keep each running properly. Emphasize that you are responsible for the health of your body just as you are for the maintenance of your car, if you own one. Ask students what happens if you fail to maintain your car properly. Ask them what happens if you fail to maintain your body properly.
- Ask students to share sayings they have heard or read about the relationship between food and wellness. Example: An apple a day keeps the doctor away. Discuss the accuracy of the statements and their basis in fact, if any.

Objectives
- Have students read the section objectives. Discuss the purpose of studying this section.

Vocabulary
- Pronounce the terms listed under "Look for These Terms." Have students find the terms and their definitions in the section.

Guided Reading
- Have students look at the headings within Section 1.1 to preview the concepts that will be discussed.
- Have students read the section and complete the appropriate part of the Chapter 1 Study Guide in the *Student Workbook*.

Comprehension Check

1. Ask students to identify some of the reasons people eat. *(for nutrition, because they're hungry, for enjoyment)*

2. Ask students to explain the meaning of "nutrients." *(They are the chemicals found in food that the body needs to function properly.)*

3. Discuss the concept of "wellness" and have students list several ways of practicing wellness.

Student Experiences

1. **Defining Terms:** Ask students to define the word "nutrition." *(The study of nutrients and their use by the body.)* Discuss what is meant by "good nutrition." Identify the benefits of good nutrition. *(Key skill: language arts)*

2. **Analyzing Written Materials:** Provide students with articles emphasizing wellness. Ask students to read the articles, then write a paragraph describing what wellness means to them. How does their definition compare with the articles'? *(Key skills: reading, writing)*

Healthy Attitudes

Discuss specific ways students can implement the wellness pointers listed in the feature. For example, how might they ensure that they get plenty of rest? What is included in "routine medical care"? How might they go about learning stress management?

Getting the most out of life depends on feeling your best. Do your daily routines and decisions promote wellness?

Wellness

Good nutrition is an important part of wellness. **Wellness** is a philosophy that encourages people to take responsibility for their own health. That means it's up to you to take the necessary steps to have and enjoy good health throughout your life.

Of course, practicing wellness doesn't guarantee that you will never have a health problem. However, wellness will help you attain the highest level of health that you possibly can.

Wellness involves taking care of yourself in many ways for good physical, mental, and emotional health. By developing good health habits now, you have a better chance of staying healthy throughout your life. Making wise food choices is an important part of anyone's wellness program.

Healthy Attitudes

In addition to making nutritious food choices, you can practice wellness by:

- Exercising regularly.
- Getting plenty of rest and sleep.
- Practicing good hygiene.
- Getting regular checkups and routine medical care when needed.
- Following safety practices.
- Avoiding health risks such as tobacco, alcohol, and other drugs.
- Learning to manage stress.

More About Basic Human Needs

One of several theories developed regarding basic human needs is that of psychologist Abraham Maslow. His theory states that people have several levels of needs. The higher levels build on the lower ones.

According to Maslow, the basic physical needs for food, air, water, and shelter must be met first. Next comes the need for security and safety, followed by the need for love and belonging. The fourth level is the need for self-esteem, self-worth, and confidence. Self-actualization, the highest need, is the level of self-fulfillment and creative growth.

Psychological Needs

Psychological (sie kuh LAHJ-ih-kuhl) means having to do with the mind and emotions. Psychological health is part of wellness and is just as important as physical health. Though you may not realize it, food also helps you meet psychological needs. These include the need for security, a sense of belonging, enjoyment, and self-esteem.

Security

Security is a feeling of being free from harm, fear, and want. One type of security comes from knowing you have the basic necessities of life. Thus, having a good supply of food helps you feel secure.

Security can also be related to emotional needs and desires. In times of stress, people may turn to certain foods that they believe will make them feel better. For example, they may crave favorite foods from childhood because they associate them with feelings of being cared for or rewarded. Later in this chapter you will learn more about how emotions influence food choices.

A Sense of Belonging

People need to feel that they are accepted by others and belong to a group, whether it's a family or friends. Food can help create a bond between people, giving them a sense of belonging.

Food is associated with hospitality. At parties, weddings, family reunions—even when people just "stop by"—guests are usually offered something to eat or drink. This helps people feel welcome and at ease.

Foods that give a sense of security are sometimes called "comfort foods." Many people turn to chicken soup when they don't feel well. Scientists have found that it also offers some physical relief—it can help clear a stuffy head.

Teaching . . .

• Psychological Needs: Security and Belonging

(text pages 23-24)

Comprehension Check

1. Ask students to explain how food contributes to feelings of safety and security. *(Emphasize that while most people in this country have enough food to feel secure, this is not true of all.)*

2. Discuss the role of food in helping to create a sense of belonging to a family or social group.

Student Experiences

1. **Class Discussion:** Ask students to give examples of ways people's emotions affect what, when, and how much they eat. (For example, you may lose your appetite when you are excited.) *(Key skill: critical thinking)*

2. **Poster Project:** Have students prepare posters that illustrate how food appeals to the senses. *(Key skill: creativity)*

3. **Research:** To demonstrate the prevalence of food in our lives and our culture, ask students to count how many nursery rhymes or tall tales (from a collection) mention food. *(Key skill: research)*

See Also . . .

• Section 2.1: "The Role of Nutrients," text page 53.

• Section 6.1: "Food and the Life Cycle," text page 163.

- **Psychological Needs: Enjoyment and Self-Esteem**

(text pages 24-25)

Comprehension Check

1. Ask students to list ways food can help strengthen family relationships.

2. Ask students to give examples of ways food helps to fulfill the emotional needs for enjoyment, self-esteem, and adventure.

3. Ask students to define self-esteem. *(Recognizing your own strengths and weaknesses and understanding that you're just as good as everybody else.)*

Student Experiences

1. **Group Project:** Identify and define the psychological needs people have. Have students work in groups to identify ways food meets the needs for security, a sense of belonging, enjoyment, or self-esteem. Have groups write their lists in chart form to share with the class. Add additional points generated by the class. *(Key skill: critical thinking)*

2. **Community Project:** Invite a representative from a local food bank or other community service agency to talk about the effect of providing food for others on a person's self-esteem. As a class, participate in a food drive or other effort to provide food for needy people in the community. *(Key skill: community service)*

There are real advantages to involving the whole family in food preparation. The work is shared, but so is the fun. It also provides opportunities for passing on family traditions.

Food can also help strengthen family relationships. For instance, Isabel often helps out with meal preparation. She is proud to be making a contribution to her family. She also enjoys the companionship of sharing meal-time with her mother and two younger sisters. It gives them a chance to talk and laugh together.

Food can also help you feel a part of a larger group—all the people with whom you share customs and traditions. Section 1.3 will look at the relationship between food and culture.

Enjoyment

What are your favorite foods? Imagine their appearance, taste, texture, and aroma. It's easy to see that food satisfies the senses. In addition, trying new foods may appeal to your sense of adventure.

Preparing food can bring pleasure as well. Many people enjoy the chance to be creative and the challenge of learning new skills. Turning an assortment of ingredients into a delicious dish for yourself and others to enjoy can bring a great sense of satisfaction.

24   Chapter 1: Exploring Food Choices

More About Food Choices

The ability to make proper choices is an effective tool for living. In making choices, including food choices, watch out for these roadblocks:

- *Old Habits.* Be willing to change old ways of thinking and doing.

- *Misunderstandings.* Check your understanding of the situation. Everyone perceives differently.
- *Fear.* Try to overcome your fears.
- *Emotions.* Don't let your emotions interfere with your ability to think clearly.

Self-Esteem

Brian has been volunteering to help with the pep club's fundraising dinners for the past two years. Half of the money raised goes toward club activities and the rest to a local charity. Brian is glad he got involved. He's made some new friends and is learning to overcome his shyness. The fact that he has a valuable skill to contribute helps him feel good about himself.

Brian may not realize it, but he is developing a strong sense of self-esteem. **Self-esteem** is a healthy recognition of your strengths and weaknesses and the ability to accept yourself as you are. It doesn't mean you're better than anyone else, but you're just as good. Developing your skills, including skills in food and nutrition, can help strengthen your self-esteem. People with good self-esteem not only have confidence in themselves, but respect and support others.

As you can see, food helps people meet a variety of physical and psychological needs. These basic needs are shared by everyone. However, experience tells you that people's food choices differ dramatically. Why do people eat the foods they do? How can the same food be liked by one person and disliked by another? The next section will help you think about the answers to those questions.

Learning new skills boosts your self-esteem. You will feel more confident.

Section 1.1 Review

RECALL THE FACTS

1. What is nutrition? Why is good nutrition important?

2. What are four psychological needs that food can help meet?

3. What psychological need is being met when family members share a meal together?

DISCUSS YOUR IDEAS

4. How might a natural disaster threaten food supplies? How would this affect people's sense of security? How might they react?

5. Do physical and psychological needs for food ever conflict? Explain.

APPLY YOUR LEARNING

6. List foods you might serve at a gathering of family or friends. Identify how these foods could help meet physical and psychological needs.

Section 1.1: Food and Health   **25**

1.1

Completing the Section

Review

- Ask students to summarize the main ideas in this section.

- Have students complete the Section Review. (Answers appear below.)

Evaluation

- Have students write a short essay describing the needs that food helps satisfy.

- Have students take the quiz for Section 1.1. (Refer to the *Section Quizzes* booklet or construct your own quiz using the *Testmaker Software*.)

Reteaching

- Have students prepare a short skit or poster that demonstrates the ways food affects people physically and psychologically.

- Refer to the *Reteaching Activities* booklet for the Section 1.1 activity sheet.

Enrichment

- Have students select a critical community project that seems to need publicity or another form of help and plan a way to provide that help. Have students carry out their plans.

Closure

- Lead a class discussion on the differences between physical and psychological needs and how food helps people meet both kinds of needs.

Answers to Section Review

1. The study of nutrients and how they are used by the body; it affects physical and psychological health.
2. Security, sense of belonging, enjoyment, and self-esteem.

3. Answers will vary. All of the four needs from #2 are acceptable.
4. By damaging crops, destroying means of food transportation, etc.

5. Yes; overeating because of boredom or anxiety can reduce a person's physical fitness.
6. Answers will vary.

S E C T I O N 1 . 2

Influences on Food Choices

OBJECTIVES
After studying this section, you should be able to:
- Identify social influences on food choices.
- Describe how food choices are influenced by available resources and technology.
- Identify personal influences on food choices.

LOOK FOR THESE TERMS
culture
media
resources
lifestyle

Introducing the Section

Motivators

- Ask students to describe one of their family's favorite foods and explain why it is special. For example, it may be an old family recipe or a food that's part of a cultural tradition.

- In advance, prepare six lists of resources needed to get food. Include specific amounts of money, time, knowledge, abilities, equipment, and a place to buy food on each list, but make each list deficient in one or more resources. Divide the class into six groups. Have the groups decide how to overcome the deficiencies and provide food for a family.

Objectives

- Have students read the section objectives. Discuss the purpose of studying this section.

Vocabulary

- Pronounce the terms listed under "Look for These Terms." Have students find the terms and their definitions in the section.

Guided Reading

- Have students look at the headings within Section 1.2 to preview the concepts that will be discussed.

- Have students read the section and complete the appropriate part of the Chapter 1 Study Guide in the *Student Workbook.*

You probably have some very definite ideas about what foods you like and dislike. Where do these preferences come from? You may not be aware of it, but when you make food choices, many influences are at work.

Social Influences

Although you are an individual, you are also a member of various social groups. Many of your preferences begin with the influence of culture, family, friends, and the media.

Culture

Culture refers to the shared customs, traditions, and beliefs of a large group of people, such as a nation, race, or religious group. The distinctive customs help the members of the group develop a common sense of identity.

Food customs are one aspect of culture. Members of different cultures often enjoy distinctive foods. They may also have their own traditional ways of preparing, serving, and eating meals. You will learn about the food customs of many different cultures as you read this book.

Cultural differences are not as pronounced today as they have been in the past. Modern communication and transportation have allowed food customs to be shared and blended much more rapidly than before. Today people can choose from a wonderful wealth of food traditions from around the world. At the same time, they can uphold and celebrate the unique food customs of their own culture to express pride in their heritage.

Cultural influences can change throughout life. For example, Jin Soon was born in Korea but now lives in the United States. Her favorite foods include both traditional Korean dishes, such as *kimchi,* and typical American foods, such as hamburgers.

Teacher's Classroom Resources—Section 1.2

Refer to these resources in the TCR package:
Reproducible Lesson Plans
Student Workbook
Extending the Text

Reteaching Activities
Section Quizzes
Testmaker Software
Color Transparencies

Food customs are part of any culture's traditions. These women in Bali are bringing offerings of food to a local temple.

Kimchi is a spicy-hot Korean relish. It is made from cabbage mixed with ingredients such as onions, hot peppers, and spices. Traditionally, the mixture is put into sealed pots or jars and buried in the ground. Commercially made kimchi can be purchased in Korean markets.

Family

Your family probably has had the greatest influence on your food choices. When you were very young, family members made most of your food choices for you. As you grew, you learned food habits by following your family's example. You saw them enjoying certain foods at certain times of day, for instance.

A family's food customs often reflect cultural background. For instance, the Masinelli family always has two main dishes at Thanksgiving—turkey and lasagne.

In addition, many families have developed their own unique food traditions. In one family, pancakes are a traditional Saturday night meal. Another family wouldn't think of serving pork chops without applesauce. Birthdays might call for a cake served on a special plate.

People tend to feel comfortable with foods that are familiar. If certain foods were never served in your home, you may think you dislike them. However, part of the adventure of eating is trying new foods and finding some that you enjoy.

Section 1.2: Influences on Food Choices   27

Comprehension Check

1. Discuss the resources available to help you meet your food needs. *(money, time, knowledge and skills, ability, equipment, energy, place to buy food)*

2. Ask students to give examples of how technology has changed the food supply in the United States and other highly developed countries. *(Technology makes a wide variety of high-quality food available. In earlier times, people relied on foods that were grown locally and many foods were available only in season.)*

3. Discuss the concept of substituting resources. Emphasize that when some resources are in short supply, wise use of other resources may suffice. Ask students to give examples of various situations in which this happens. *(For example, if you don't have the money to buy a birthday gift, you could use time and skills to make one.)*

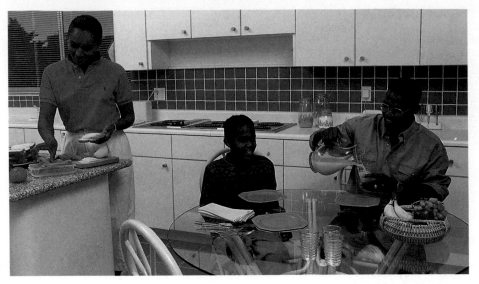

Nutrition experts know that families shape the food habits of young children. That influence often lasts a lifetime. How have your food choices been influenced by your family?

Friends

Food is usually an important part of friendships. You and your friends might get together for pizza, eat at the same table in the school cafeteria, or share a bag of pretzels from a vending machine. It should come as no surprise, then, that you and your friends influence each other's food choices.

As part of the group, you help make the decision as to where and what to eat. Sometimes you may not agree with your friends, but you go along with them anyway. If your friends are from different cultural backgrounds, you might learn to enjoy the foods they commonly eat. What kind of foods do you eat because your friends choose them?

The Media

Newspapers, magazines, television, and radio bring information to large audiences. Together these channels of communication are referred to as **media.** Today, they are major influences in making food choices.

Nutrition has become a popular topic for newspapers, magazines, and television shows. The media also report on new products and new trends in foods. You might make food choices just to try the new foods or be part of the trend.

Think about how often food is mentioned in the media.

28   Chapter 1: Exploring Food Choices

Food and Nutrition Science

Food Processing: The science of food processing allows highly developed countries such as the U.S. to create high-tech methods of preserving food. This increases the variety and amount of food available. Examples of high-tech preservation techniques include freeze-drying, irradiation, and controlled-atmosphere packaging.

Advertising is an especially powerful influence on food choices. Does watching a television commercial for hot, juicy hamburgers or chewy chocolate candy make you hungry? Have you ever chosen a particular cereal or snack food just because the ad made it sound so good?

If you are to make wise food choices, be aware of how the media influences you. Think critically about what you see and hear. You'll learn how in Section 3.3.

Available Resources

Your choice of foods depends a great deal on the resources that are available to you. **Resources** are objects and qualities that can help you reach a goal. For example, this textbook is a resource that helps you learn about food and nutrition.

Many resources are involved in getting the food you need. Money is an obvious one. Time, knowledge, abilities, equipment, and a place to buy food are equally important.

One reason people make different food choices is that their resources differ. No one has an endless supply of all resources, but everyone has some. You can often substitute a resource you have for another that is in short supply. For instance, if you have time and skills, you can save money by cooking at home instead of eating out.

Technology and the Food Supply

One of the resources that influences your food choices is the basic food supply. In other words, the choices you make depend on what you have to choose from. Technology influences the food supply and therefore your choices.

Imagine that you have stepped back in time two or three hundred years. How would your food choices change? In this world of the past, almost everything you eat must be grown by your family or your neighbors. In warm weather, foods are plentiful but spoilage is a problem. In cold weather, the challenge is to make food last until the next harvest.

Preserving food at home once was the only way to insure sufficient food year-round. Today, technology has made food readily available any time of the year. People who preserve food at home usually do so by choice, rather than necessity.

Section 1.2: Influences on Food Choices   29

Student Experiences

1. **Out-of-Class Project:** Have students interview their parents to discuss how time and other resources influence food choice and food preparation at home. *(Key skill: management skills)*

2. **Research:** Have students research ways technology has influenced our food supply or new ways technology is likely to influence our food choices in the future. Have students report their findings to the class. *(Key skill: research)*

Technology Tidbit

Encourage students to discuss other types of food preparation tasks that could be accomplished by robots. Then have students do research to find out whether their ideas have been put in practice by food manufacturers and to discover other uses for robots in the industry.

Thinking Skills

Problem Solving: Ask students to make a list of resources they use every day that are dependent on modern technology (food processing techniques, transportation, etc.) and the needs they meet with those resources. Then ask students to think about people who lived two hundred years ago. How might those people have met the same needs? What could they have used instead of the modern technology we use today?

Comprehension Check

1. Discuss the different types of lifestyles people have and how those lifestyles can affect the foods they choose to eat.

2. Ask students to explain why it is important to recognize the effect of moods on food choices. *(Some food choices determined by moods may be unwise; by recognizing the influence of moods, you may be able to curb unhealthy impulses.)*

Student Experiences

1. **Videotape Viewing:** Give each student a food advertisement from a magazine or newspaper or show videotapes of television food commercials. Ask students to evaluate the ads to determine the methods advertisers use to persuade people to buy their products. Does it appeal to their emotions? their values? priorities? (Key skill: analysis)

2. **Future Forecast:** Have students write a short paper on what their lifestyles might be like in five years and how their food habits might change as a result. (Key skills: writing, creativity)

Technology Tidbit

Did you know that some of the foods you buy may have been prepared with the help of robots? For instance, at some large commercial bakeries, robots take baked loaves out of the pans. This technology helps food companies provide high-quality products.

Today, modern technology has greatly increased the options that are available to you. Jet planes and trucks bring food from around the world to the local supermarket. You can take a frozen, already-prepared main dish out of the freezer and pop it in the microwave. In just minutes it will be hot and ready to eat.

New technology will continue to add to people's food choices. Can you imagine what foods might be available two hundred years in the future?

Personal Influences

Your lifestyle, values, priorities, and emotions also influence your choice of foods. They are part of the reason that your food choices are uniquely your own.

Your Lifestyle

Lifestyle refers to a person's typical way of life. Your lifestyle includes how you spend your time and what is important to you. Lifestyle has a strong influence on what and where you eat, how and where you shop, and how you prepare food.

Today, your lifestyle might include school, a part-time job, family activities, and hobbies. Your busy lifestyle can affect your food choices. For instance, you may buy a snack from a vending machine just because the food is available, easy to carry, and easy to eat quickly.

Values and Priorities

Not everyone spends time or money in the same way. People make different choices based on their own values and priorities.

Food choices, too, depend on your values and priorities. Some people enjoy the time they spend preparing meals. Others would rather spend the time on another activity, such as a hobby or community service. Some people may choose to eat out, even though it costs more than preparing food at home.

It's not always easy to juggle your priorities. Time, money, health, enjoyment—all are important to most people. As you continue your study of food, you will learn ways to meet the challenge of a busy lifestyle.

What are the most powerful influences on your food choices?

Thinking Skills

Creativity: Because lifestyle is often a function of the culture in which we live, people from other cultures may approach food choices in an entirely different manner than we do. Present this scenario to students: Three students from other countries are visiting your school. You have been asked to help them learn about traditional food customs in the United States. The students are from India, Mexico, and Japan. How would you approach this task?

Most celebrations call for special foods. They make such occasions more enjoyable and memorable.

Your Emotions

Emotions and moods can also influence food choices. Some people believe certain kinds of food make them feel better if they are sad or depressed. They may choose different foods if they are happy or celebrating an event.

Food often carries strong associations, which may be pleasant or unpleasant. For instance, Jarod can still remember being forced to eat spinach as a child. He does not like spinach to this day. On the other hand, Tonya loves spinach. It reminds her of meals at her grandmother's house and feelings of comfort and security.

As you can see, even a decision such as what to have for lunch, though it may seem simple, is influenced by many factors. Your background, your lifestyle today, and the world around you all play a part in your food choices.

Advor

Section 1.2 Review

RECALL THE FACTS

1. What is culture? How does it relate to food choices?

2. What is a resource? Name five resources that are involved in obtaining food.

3. What is lifestyle? How does it influence a person's choice of foods?

DISCUSS YOUR IDEAS

4. How has your family influenced your food choices? What are some of your family's food traditions?

5. Imagine that you are an inventor in the 22nd century. Describe a new food product or kitchen appliance that you would like to invent. How would it affect people's food choices?

APPLY YOUR LEARNING

6. Find three food advertisements in magazines. Do they make you want to buy the product? Why or why not?

Section 1.2: Influences on Food Choices   **31**

Completing the Section

Review
- Ask students to summarize the main ideas in this section.
- Have students complete the Section Review. (Answers appear below.)

Evaluation
- Have students prepare a presentation for other classes to demonstrate the effects of social influences and resources on food choices.
- Have students take the quiz for Section 1.2. (Refer to the *Section Quizzes* booklet or construct your own quiz using the *Testmaker Software*.)

Reteaching
- Have students collect or draw pictures that represent the six types of resources that influence food choices. Combine into a display and discuss.
- Refer to the *Reteaching Activities booklet* for the Section 1.2 activity sheet.

Enrichment
- Have students investigate the reasons for food shortages around the world and explore what is being done about them.

Closure
- Lead a discussion on the influences that affect food choices.

Answers to Section Review

1. The shared customs, traditions, or beliefs of a group of people; culture helps form food preferences.
2. An object or quality that helps you reach a goal. *Any five:* money, time, knowledge, abilities, equipment, food stores.
3. A person's typical way of life; by determining the types of foods a person chooses.
4. Answers will vary.
5. Answers will vary. Encourage students to be creative.
6. Answers will vary. Remind students to support their answers.

Section 1.3
Food and Culture

Food and Culture

Introducing the Section

Motivators

- Ask students why many people eat each of the following foods: turkey at Thanksgiving, cake on birthdays, hot dogs on July 4, popcorn at the movies. Discuss the part culture plays in each of these food choices.

- Provide students with magazines and ask them to find pictures of foods associated with different cultural groups or regions around the world. Have students use the pictures to create posters, identifying the foods pictured and the culture or region with which they are associated. Have students present their posters to the class.

Objectives

- Have students read the section objectives. Discuss the purpose of studying this section.

Vocabulary

- Pronounce the terms listed under "Look for These Terms." Have students find the terms and their definitions in the section.

Guided Reading

- Have students look at the headings within Section 1.3 to preview the concepts that will be discussed.

- Have students read the section and complete the appropriate part of the Chapter 1 Study Guide in the *Student Workbook*.

OBJECTIVES

After studying this section, you should be able to:

- Describe the characteristics of a multicultural society.
- Give examples of cultural food customs.
- Explain how food customs have evolved through history.

LOOK FOR THESE TERMS

ethnic group
multicultural
cultural diversity

Eric, Cyrise, Joel, and Amber decided to have lunch in the food court at the mall. Each went to a different food stall. Eric returned with wonton soup and chicken fried rice. Cyrise chose a burrito, while Joel decided on pizza. Amber had a shish kebab and pita bread.

The foods they chose were all made from basic ingredients, such as grains, vegetables, and meat or poultry. However, each dish was distinctly different. Each represented the food customs of a specific culture.

Understanding Culture

As you learned in Section 1.2, "culture" refers to the shared customs, traditions, and beliefs of a group of people. But what makes up a "group of people"?

One example of a cultural group might be the people who live in a particular part of the world. The various nations around the globe have developed many unique customs, including those related to food.

Corn has special significance in some Native American cultures. It is used for ceremonies, as well as for food.

Teacher's Classroom Resources—Section 1.3

Refer to these resources in the TCR package:

Reproducible Lesson Plans
Student Workbook
Extending the Text
Reteaching Activities

Section Quizzes
Testmaker Software
Multicultural Resources
Color Transparencies

A cultural group may also be defined by a common heritage, or past. For instance, Native Americans are descendants of the original dwellers in America. Some people now living in the United States were born in other countries. Most Americans can trace their ancestry back to other parts of the world. A cultural group based on common heritage is often called an **ethnic group.**

Religion is another basis for defining cultural groups. Members of a particular faith usually have a common set of beliefs and follow specific practices.

As you can see, a person may belong to more than one cultural group. In addition, many different cultural groups may exist side by side. The term **multicultural** describes a society that includes many cultures.

The United States has always been a multicultural society. Today it has become even more so, and the trend will almost certainly continue in the future. Many people see this **cultural diversity,** or variety of cultures, as a great strength. In a multicultural society, people are free to share and enjoy the customs of many cultures. At the same time, it's important to respect other people's beliefs and practices, even though they may differ from your own.

Understanding Cultural Food Customs

Food is essential in the everyday life of individuals and families. In addition, food can play an important role in celebrations and ceremonies. It's no wonder that food customs are often a focal point in cultural traditions.

Food-related celebrations are common in this country. One town's annual pumpkin festival offers everything from pumpkin ice cream to pumpkin chili.

Teaching . . .

- **Understanding Culture**
  (text pages 32-33)

Comprehension Check

1. Discuss different types of cultural groups, such as ethnic groups and religious groups, and the effects their heritage has on their food choices.

2. Ask students to explain why the United States is necessarily a multicultural nation. *(Most of its population has its origins in the diverse groups of immigrants who settled here.)*

3. Differentiate between ethnic foods *(brought to the United States from another culture)* and regional foods *(developed in a particular region of the United States).* Ask students to create a class list of ethnic foods and a list of regional foods.

Student Experiences

1. **Guest Speaker:** Invite representatives of several different religious and ethnic backgrounds to discuss food customs, etiquette, and foods for special occasions. *(Key skill: multicultural awareness)*

2. **Visual Display:** Have students develop a visual display (of their choice) illustrating the cultural diversity of the United States. *(Key skill: social studies)*

3. **Research:** Provide a list of ethnic foods. Ask students to research at least one food and report on its origin and any customs that may be associated with it. *(Key skills: research, writing)*

Thinking Skills

Critical Thinking: Have students discuss the advantages of cultural diversity in a society. Are there any potential problems to be guarded against?

Teaching . . .

* **Examples of Food Customs**

(text pages 34-35)

Comprehension Check

1. Ask students to identify differences in mealtime etiquette in different parts of the world. Are there differences among the regions of the United States?

2. Discuss dietary laws and religions and how they may affect people's food choices.

3. Discuss why many holiday customs are related very closely to food customs.

4. Ask students to list special occasions associated with holidays for various cultures and religions. What foods are associated with each holiday?

WORLD of variety

Have student volunteers research food and mealtime customs of their own cultural background or of a culture that interests them. Have them share their findings with the rest of the class.

Examples of Food Customs

Food customs usually involve certain kinds of foods, but that's just the beginning. They also include the way food is prepared, how it is served, and how it is eaten.

Unique Foods

In the example you read at the beginning of this section, the foods chosen by Eric, Cyrise, Joel, and Amber each trace their roots back to a different part of the world. For instance, Eric's wonton soup originated in China. Wontons are dumplings filled with minced vegetables and meat. Amber's shish kebab, made with chunks of meat threaded on a skewer, originated in the Middle East. So did pita bread, a distinctive flat bread that forms a pocket. You can find many other examples of foods from around the world in Chapter 22.

Within a nation, there may also be distinct regional food traditions. In the United States, well-known regional foods include cornbread and grits from the South, chili and barbecue from Texas, sourdough bread from San Francisco, and clam chowder from New England. Although these foods are now available all over the United States, each was developed in a particular section of the country. You can read more about regional foods in Chapter 23.

Dietary Laws

Religious beliefs often include dietary laws, or rules about what foods may be eaten. For example, Jews who follow a kosher diet do not eat meat and dairy products in the same meal. Hindus do not eat beef because they consider cattle to be sacred animals. Muslims eat no pork.

Etiquette

Social customs for serving and eating food also vary, depending on the culture. For instance, not all cultures use forks, knives, and spoons for eating. In China and Japan, chopsticks are the traditional eating utensils. In some countries, such as India, Pakistan, Algeria, and Morocco, it is considered proper to eat many foods using the fingers. In Mexico, food may be scooped up with a tortilla.

Food customs affect not only what is eaten, but how foods are served. How does this scene from a restaurant in China differ from what you might see in an American restaurant?

More About Ethnic Foods and Customs

People in different parts of the world have developed diets of striking diversity. Consider the following foods:

* *Raw fish* is eaten in many parts of the world.

* *Horsemeat* is a delicacy in parts of Europe, Japan, and China.

* *Seaweed* is a staple food in many coastal areas.

* *Bird's nest soup*, popular in China, is

WORLD of variety

If you were a guest at a meal in Laos, a country in Southeast Asia, you would sit on a mat on the floor. The host would bring in the food, crouching to keep his head below the level of yours as a sign of respect. The food would be in small pieces and served in one dish from which everyone would eat. You would eat with a fork in your left hand and a spoon in your right. However, to eat rice you would use your fingers, then wipe them on a napkin.

Special Occasions

Many food customs relate to holidays, festivals, and religious observances. To celebrate Chinese New Year, Judy Chen helps her mother make New Year's dumplings. The small, smooth, round dumplings are made of rice powder and water and filled with a sweet soybean paste. Their shape symbolizes good fortune. For Easter, Poles and Ukrainians color eggs in complex designs. In Italy, a popular Easter food is a ring-shaped coffee cake with colored eggs tucked into the top.

Holiday food customs do not always involve special foods. On Yom Kippur, the Jewish faith observes the Day of Atonement by fasting. Catholics refrain from eating meat on certain church holy days. During Ramadan, a month-long religious observance, Muslims do not eat or drink during the daylight hours. Instead, they eat anytime after sunset and before sunrise.

Easter is celebrated in some countries as both a signal of spring and a religious feast. These intricately decorated eggs from the Ukraine are a symbol of both.

Section 1.3: Food and Culture **35**

made from the nests of swifts. These birds use their gluelike saliva to form cup-shaped nests. Western versions of bird's nest soup use a gel, rather than dried saliva, as the thickener.

Comprehension Check

1. Discuss the effects of geography on food customs.

2. Ask students to explain why different customs arise in different countries and regions. *(because of different circumstances; the availability of different kinds of foods; different ideas and interests)*

3. Ask students to explain the effects of travel on changing food customs and preferences.

4. Ask students to explain what is meant by the phrase "the world is growing smaller."

5. Discuss the influence of television and newspapers on the types of ethnic and regional foods people are willing to try or prepare.

Sometimes food itself is the theme for a festival. Harvest festivals have been common since ancient times. In the United States, Thanksgiving is the official harvest festival. Many communities also have their own festivals to celebrate the harvest of locally grown foods.

How Food Customs Evolve

As you can see, there are as many different ways of preparing, serving, and eating food as there are cultural groups. None of these food customs can be considered "better" than any other. Different customs arise naturally because of different circumstances.

For instance, you may be used to eating leftovers for lunch or dinner. In Japan, this would be considered unusual, even strange. This cultural difference can be understood if you realize that most Japanese do not have large refrigerators for food storage. Food is purchased fresh daily to be eaten that day. Dining on leftovers would be viewed as eating "old" food.

Food Customs Through History

A journey through history can help you understand many other food customs. In the distant past, geography greatly influenced the development of food customs. Differences in climate and soil affected the foods that could be grown in an area. Without modern transportation, food choices were limited. How the foods were cooked often depended on the types and amount of fuel available. For example, in many Asian countries, cooking fuel was scarce. To conserve it, food was cut into small pieces that would cook quickly.

In many cultures, economic conditions created two types of food customs. One was for the rich, who could afford the finest foods prepared by talented chefs in the most elegant manner. The rest of the people were poor and ate only a few basic foods. A typical daily meal might be soup, made with whatever food was available, and coarse, dark bread made from ground whole grain.

Stir-frying small pieces of food probably developed as a way to save scarce fuel. The ingredients used depended on available foods.

However they originated, food customs were passed down from one generation to the next. Still, changes occurred along the way. Explorers took some of their own foods with them on their journeys and brought strange foods from distant lands when they returned. Invading armies often brought new food customs with them.

European explorers who reached the Western Hemisphere found an abundance of foods eaten by the Native Americans. The explorers brought back samples and seeds of foods that were not found in Europe, such as

More About the Origin of Food

- *Sandwich.* In the eighteenth century, the Earl of Sandwich was so fond of playing cards that he would not leave the card table to eat. He asked his servant to bring him slices of roast beef between pieces of bread. The food took his name.

- *Ice Cream Sundae.* At one time, laws prohibited the sale of carbonated drinks, including sodas, on Sunday. A clever clerk omitted the carbonated beverage, placed the ice cream in a dish, and poured sauce over it. This new dessert could be served legally on Sunday.

dry beans, corn, tomatoes, potatoes, sweet potatoes, and cassava, a type of root. Over the centuries, some of these foods became popular in the Eastern Hemisphere.

As food customs traveled around the world, they were often changed and adapted. Perhaps the original ingredients were not as commonly available in the new locale, or people adapted dishes to suit their own tastes. Sometimes an entirely new dish resulted. For example, chop suey is not authentic Chinese food, but an American dish based on the Chinese style of cooking.

A World of Food Choices

Today, the world is becoming "smaller." People and foods can be flown thousands of miles in a few hours. Satellite links allow almost instant communication with any part of the globe.

As a result, food customs travel the world faster than ever. Foods grown halfway around the world are sold in your local supermarket. Television programs can show you the sights of another country or tell you how to prepare dishes from remote parts of the world.

Of course, as discussed earlier, you don't have to turn to another part of the globe to find examples of different cultures. You can find many examples right here. Whenever people gather to share food and fun, they also share each other's food traditions.

It's not surprising, therefore, that ethnic and international foods are now an everyday part of American life. Supermarkets routinely stock a wide variety of ethnic foods, and many restaurants include an assortment on their menus. You probably enjoy many such foods, from tacos to pizza, without thinking of them as being different. They have become as familiar to Americans as steak and potatoes.

This is one of the benefits of living in a multicultural society. Consider the mingling of international flavors in this meal, which Katie's family ate recently. They had chicken curry over rice (India), garlic French bread (France), steamed snow peas and water chestnuts (China), and a dessert of fresh papayas and bananas (Caribbean).

Global flavors are also being combined in recipes. Rachel makes pizza with chili-seasoned ground meat and tops it with grated cheese and salsa (SAL-suh), a spicy, Mexican fresh tomato sauce. At the same time, American fast foods such as fried chicken, french fries, and hamburgers are known around the globe. Fast food places have become popular in major cities around the world, such as Moscow and Tokyo.

Such global diversity enriches everyone's lives. No matter where people go, they can find foods they enjoy and experience the adventure of new flavors.

Mangoes were once available only in tropical climates. Today, they can often be found at the neighborhood supermarket. How often do you try new foods?

Student Experiences

1. **Guest Speaker**: Invite a representative of the local historical society to discuss food customs in your area 100, 200, and possibly even 1,000 years ago. *(Key skill: history)*

2. **Television Viewing**: Have students watch a cooking show on television and identify the cultural origins of the foods demonstrated. What special equipment and techniques were used to prepare the food? *(Key skill: analysis)*

3. **Analyzing Restaurant Menus**: Provide students with local restaurant menus and have students identify examples of regional, ethnic, and international food choices on the menus. Discuss the wide variety of foods available in the United States. *(Key skill: multicultural awareness)*

4. **Supermarket Survey**: Have students survey a supermarket or specialty foods store to identify examples of ethnic and international foods. Ask students to report their findings to the class. *(Key skill: multicultural awareness)*

5. **Small Group Project**: Divide the class into small groups. Have each group design a timeline that traces the use of a certain type of food (such as wheat, rice, or corn) throughout known history. The timeline should show new technologies that influenced changes in the ways the foods are used. *(Key skills: research, social studies)*

Food and Nutrition Science

Food Preservation: Sometimes political or economic conditions may necessitate the a change in food customs or preparation techniques. For example, when the United States entered World War I, a method was needed to preserve food for armies at the front. For the first time, the United States began dehydrating foods on a large scale. This provided a lightweight, compact, long-lasting food source for the armed forces.

Today, dehydration is a major method of food preservation. Techniques have been improved, so the taste and texture of the foods are retained better than before.

Completing the Section

Review

- Ask students to summarize the main ideas in this section.
- Have students complete the Section Review. (Answers appear below.)

Evaluation

- Have students write a short essay describing the concepts presented in this section.
- Have students take the quiz for Section 1.3. (Refer to the *Section Quizzes* booklet or construct your own quiz using the *Testmaker Software*.)

Reteaching

- Ask students to give examples of food customs in their families. Discuss how these customs influence their food choices.
- Refer to the *Reteaching Activities* booklet for the Section 1.3 activity sheet.

Enrichment

- Have students do research to find out how early people may have been able to decide on which foods were edible and which were not.

Closure

- Refer to the posters students made for the first motivator in this section. Discuss the similarities among the basic foods used in different cultures.

This fast food restaurant in Tokyo shows that food customs are being shared around the world.

Section 1.3 Review

RECALL THE FACTS

1. What does "multicultural" mean? What are some advantages of living in a multicultural society?

2. Name four categories of cultural food customs. Give an example of each.

3. What often happens when food customs are introduced into new areas? Why?

DISCUSS YOUR IDEAS

4. Do you think it is important for members of a particular culture to retain some distinct food customs? Why or why not?

5. Do you think differences in food customs will continue to exist in the future? Why or why not?

APPLY YOUR LEARNING

6. List some of your own or your family's favorite foods. Indicate the cultures that are represented.

Answers to Section Review

1. It describes a society that includes many cultures; provides inhabitants with a variety of foods and customs from which to choose.
2. Examples: unique foods (wonton soup); dietary laws (not eating beef); etiquette (eating utensils); special occasions (Easter).
3. They are changed; original ingredients not available; changed to suite different tastes.
4. Answers will vary.
5. Answers will vary.
6. Answers will vary.

Food, Science, and Technology

OBJECTIVES

After studying this section, you should be able to:

- Explain how science is related to nutrition and food preparation.
- Discuss the impact of food-related technology in the food industry and in the home.

LOOK FOR THESE TERMS

science
food science
ergonomics
technology

Stacey wandered down the supermarket aisles, trying to decide on food for her party Saturday night. Finally, she chose a few old favorites but also several new items that looked good. They included fat-free cookies, mini-pizzas made for the microwave, and red, tomato-flavored chips.

It never occurred to Stacey that science and technology were responsible for the wide variety of foods that made her choices so difficult. Science and technology have had a great effect on food, from the kind of food available to how it is prepared.

Scientific Aspects of Food

Science involves research to develop knowledge of a particular part of nature. The study of food and nutrition is related to a number of basic sciences, such as chemistry, biology, and physics. Here's a brief look at some of the ways in which science is directly related to food.

Food technologists help develop new foods and improve existing ones. They rely on knowledge of food, nutrition, science, and technology.

Section 1.4
Food, Science, and Technology

Introducing the Section

Motivators

- Ask students to recall from science classes examples of ways science relates to food (such as the effect of heat of food, the relationships between nutrition and health, or how bacteria cause spoilage). Define food science and explain the relationship between science, nutrition, and food preparation.

- Ask students to compare foods available and meal preparation in the 19th century and today. How has technology influenced how foods are produced, processed, packaged, and shipped?

Objectives

- Have students read the section objectives. Discuss the purpose of studying this section.

Vocabulary

- Pronounce the terms listed under "Look for These Terms." Have students find the terms and their definitions in the section.

Guided Reading

- Have students look at the headings within Section 1.4 to preview the concepts that will be discussed.

- Have students read the section and complete the appropriate part of the Chapter 1 Study Guide in the *Student Workbook*.

Teacher's Classroom Resources—Section 1.4

Refer to these resources in the TCR package:

Reproducible Lesson Plans
Student Workbook
Extending the Text

Reteaching Activities
Section Quizzes
Testmaker Software
Color Transparencies

Teaching . . .

• **Scientific Aspects
of Food**

(text pages 39-41)

Comprehension Check

1. Discuss the ways in which science is related to food *(nutrition, food preparation, ergonomics).*

2. Ask students to define the term *ergonomics. (the study of making tools and equipment comfortable and easy to use)* What are some examples of ergonomics?

3. Ask students to describe two roles scientists play in the science of nutrition. *(discovering nutrients and determining relationships between nutrition and health)*

4. Ask students to describe examples of technologies that aid home food preparation.

Lab Experience

Test a proven theory such as "boiling eggs too long causes a sulfur ring to form around the egg yolk." Have students determine how long an egg needs to cook to be hardcooked. How much time elapses before a sulfur ring forms?

See Also . . .

• Section 2.1: "The Role of Nutrients," text page 53.

• Section 2.5: "How Your Body Uses Food," text page 79.

Nutrition

The science of nutrition is a continuing process. So far, about 40 nutrients have been identified. No one knows how many other nutrients still remain to be discovered. Once nutrients are discovered, scientists continue to research the role they play.

In recent years, scientists have made amazing discoveries about the relationships between nutrition and health. For instance, research shows that beta carotene (BAY-tuh CARE-oh-teen), a form of vitamin A found in fruits and vegetables, may be helpful in preventing certain kinds of cancer.

The Science of Food Preparation

Moira's friend Keisha is a whiz in the kitchen. Inspired by Keisha's example, Moira tried making biscuits and gravy. She followed Keisha's recipes exactly—well, almost exactly—but the biscuits were flat and hard and the gravy was greasy and lumpy. "I guess I just don't have Keisha's magic touch," Moira decided.

What makes the difference between light, flaky biscuits and hard ones, or between smooth and lumpy gravy? The answer isn't found in magic, but in science.

Food preparation is governed by natural laws. When certain foods are heated, chilled, mixed together, or manipulated in other ways, they undergo chemical and physical changes. In fact, you can compare a recipe to a chemistry experiment. If you change the conditions of an experiment, the results are likely to change. In the same way, even a small change in a recipe can cause the final product to turn out differently.

Courses that help you learn about food from a scientific angle are often called **food science** courses. Knowledge of food science can help you understand why certain instructions in a recipe are important. If something doesn't turn out right, food science can help you understand why. Then you'll be able to keep the problem from happening again.

Fresh pineapple contains an enzyme that prevents gelatin from becoming firm. However, the enzyme is destroyed by heat in the canning process. Knowing about science can help you in food preparation.

This book will introduce you to some of the scientific principles of food preparation. For example, you'll learn:

- ❖ Why fresh pineapple makes a gelatin salad turn out more like fruit soup.
- ❖ Why fried chicken is so brown, crispy, and flavorful, and how you can get similar results using other cooking methods.
- ❖ Why an angel food cake recipe has so many egg whites.
- ❖ Why some fruits turn brown when you cut them and how you can prevent it.

Ergonomics

Have you ever felt stiff or sore after sitting in a chair that just didn't seem to fit you? If so, you've experienced the need for ergonomics. **Ergonomics** (urr-guh-NAHM-iks) is the study of how to make tools and equipment easier and more comfortable to use.

Ergonomics plays a key role in the design of kitchens, appliances, and food preparation equipment. For instance, cookware and kitchen tools are ergonomically designed to make food preparation easier and faster.

How might the design of this rubber-handled peeler make it easier and more comfortable to use?

"Work simplification" is an important part of ergonomics. It means looking for the fastest, easiest method for getting a job done. Using work simplification in the kitchen or foods lab can save time and energy, as you will discover.

Technology and Food

Technology is the practical application of scientific knowledge. Through technology, new or improved products and processes are developed. Examples can be found in the food industry and in the home.

The Food Industry

Technology plays a major role in how foods are produced, processed, packaged, and shipped. For instance:

- ❖ Food processors are using computers and robots to help control the quality of their products.
- ❖ New forms of packaging have been developed to keep food safe longer. In some cases, special packaging methods allow foods that traditionally required refrigeration to be stored at room temperature.
- ❖ Food scientists continue to develop new fat and sugar substitutes and new ways to use them in foods.
- ❖ Scientists are learning how to "design" plants with certain traits, using a technique called *genetic engineering*. They have developed tomatoes that stay firm longer after ripening. This allows ripe tomatoes to be shipped long distances without rotting or being damaged. Genetic engineering has also produced disease-resistant squash and pest-resistant potatoes.

Student Experiences

1. **Textbook Review**: Provide students with a variety of science textbooks. Have them find examples of ways science is directly related to food. On the chalkboard, list the related sciences and the examples identified. *(Key skill: science)*

2. **Reading Scientific Reports**: Provide students with scientific reports describing nutrition research. Discuss the new relationships between nutrition and health reported by the articles. *(Key skill: reading)*

3. **Redesigning a Kitchen**: Have students work in groups to apply the principles of ergonomics to the redesign of a kitchen, kitchen appliances, food preparation equipment and tools, or food preparation tasks. Have groups plan and present the results of their efforts to the class in an interesting manner. *(Key skills: critical thinking, creativity)*

4. **Research**: Have students select a nutrient and write a paper explaining its function. What happens if you do not get enough of the nutrient? Students should include recommendations on ways to get appropriate amounts of the nutrient. Sources of information should be cited. *(Key skills: research, writing)*

Food and Nutrition Science

Cancer and Diet: Food scientists are searching for dietary links to cancer and heart disease, two leading causes of death for Americans. One recent study suggests that eating cruciferous vegetables, such as cabbage and broccoli, helps prevent cancer. Another study reports that blood cholesterol levels may be lowered by eating foods high in fiber, such as oats, fruits, and vegetables. Ask students to review current popular literature to find other dietary claims for preventing cancer and heart disease. Are the claims well substantiated?

Teaching . . .

• **Technology and Food**

(text pages 41-44)

Comprehension Check

1. Ask students to describe the benefits of using genetic engineering to develop food products. Are there any disadvantages to using genetic engineering?

2. Discuss the development of the microwave oven and the circumstances that led to its extreme popularity.

3. Discuss ways in which personal computers can be used in food preparation in the home. Ask students to name other ways computers may be used in the future to aid food preparation.

Science Connection

Genes are present in the chromosomes of all plants and animals. Usually, many genes are present on each chromosome. Scientists often use a technique known as "gene splicing" (substituting one gene or set of genes for another) to achieve the desired characteristics. Genetic engineering holds promise for helping improve the quality and quantity of available food.

■ ■ ■

Tomatoes are often shipped green so they won't spoil before they reach the stores. Through genetic engineering, new varieties are being developed that can be left on the vine until they are ripe.

Science Connection

Biology:

Genes and genetic engineering

A *gene* is a tiny chemical unit in a living organism, such as a tomato. Genes allow traits to be passed on from parent to offspring. Each gene carries information about a specific trait. Genetic engineering involves making changes in the gene structure to produce desired characteristics.

■ ■ ■

In later chapters, you will learn more about the food industry and the products that have been developed as a result of technology.

Technology in the Home

Many examples of technology can be found right in the home. These examples show that new technology can have far-reaching effects on people's lives.

The Microwave Oven

The microwave oven was not an instant success. The first models, sold in the 1950s, were about the size of a large refrigerator and cost about $2,500. Many people questioned their safety. The one advantage of the microwave oven was its cooking speed.

As their lives became more fast-paced, people wanted quicker ways to cook. Scientists improved the microwave oven, making it safer. New technology made the ovens smaller and more automatic. The fast-cooking microwave oven gained popularity and became more affordable.

Thinking Skills

Critical Thinking: Ask students to identify what kinds of changes it might be possible to make in organisms through genetic engineering. How might such changes affect foods. What might be potential drawbacks of this technique?

Today, microwave ovens can be found in about 90 percent of U.S. homes and in many workplaces. Hundreds of new food and cookware products have been developed for the microwave. Some people predict that microwave ovens will someday be found in cars.

Other Kitchen Appliances

Like microwave ovens, other appliances—such as ranges, refrigerators, dishwashers, and small appliances—have changed over the years. Designers and manufacturers continually search for ways to make appliances that perform better, are more reliable, require less energy, and are easier to use. Many of today's appliances contain a "brain" in the form of computer chips. Some even alert the user when repair is needed.

New technology does have its drawbacks. Appliances with advanced features are more costly than basic models, making them out of reach for many consumers. In some cases, the advanced features may add to the difficulty and cost of repairs. Learning to use new features and controls can be time-consuming. Still, technology has made many modern conveniences possible. Most people feel that the benefits of technology outweigh the drawbacks.

✓ **SAFETY CHECK**

Learning to use new technology can be exciting, but don't forget about safety. Always read the instructions before using an appliance or other device for the first time.

Microwave ovens are smaller, less expensive, and give better results than when they were first introduced. Many appliances are now available with special features, such as Braille touchpad controls, that make them adaptable for people with physical limitations.

Section 1.4: Food, Science, and Technology **43**

Student Experiences

1. **Guest Speaker**: Invite a buyer or other representative from a supermarket to address the class on the difficulties of maintaining produce quality during shipping and display in the supermarket. How might improved "keeping qualities" impact stores and consumers? *(Key skill: consumer awareness)*

2. **Panel Discussion**: Invite several senior citizens to discuss with the class ways technology has changed the home kitchen in their lifetime. *(Key skill: history)*

3. **Price Comparisons**: Have students use catalogs to compare the prices and features of a basic model and a "high-tech" model of a common kitchen appliance such as a refrigerator or range. Have students draw conclusions based on their findings. *(Key skill: math)*

Safety Check

Kitchen appliances are now so common that many people forget the most elementary safety precautions. Before you operate any electric appliance (mixer, can opener, etc.), be sure that the area around the appliance is not wet and that you are not standing on a wet spot on the floor.

See Also . . .

- Section 13.1: "Where Does Food Come From?" text page 349.
- Section 13.2: "A Safe Food Supply," text page 354.

Review

- Ask students to summarize the main ideas in this section.
- Have students complete the Section Review. (Answers appear below.)

Evaluation

- Have students describe what they have learned in this section in a short written essay.
- Have students take the quiz for Section 1.4. (Refer to the *Section Quizzes* booklet or construct your own quiz using the *Testmaker Software*.)

Reteaching

- Write advice-column questions that can be answered with the information in this section. Have groups of students compose response letters.
- Refer to the *Reteaching Activities* booklet for the Section 1.4 activity sheet.

Enrichment

- Have students write to a manufacturer of a kitchen appliance for more information about its use and safety. Read any responses in class.

Closure

- Ask students to summarize what they have learned by creating short skits presenting food preparation technology yesterday and today.

Personal Computers

A relatively new technology that is finding a place in many people's lives is the personal computer. One of the ways computers are proving helpful is in the area of planning meals. For instance, some people use a computer to store recipes and plan menus. With the right software, they can evaluate whether they are getting a nutritious diet. A computer can also help keep track of food spending and supplies. As home computers become more common, the uses are sure to expand.

A personal computer can help you manage food selection and preparation. A computer program was used to calculate the nutritional content of the recipes in this book.

Food for Tomorrow

What you have read is just a sample of the ways in which science and technology relate to food. You'll find additional information in the "Science Connection" and "Technology Tidbits" features throughout this book.

New discoveries are made every day. Stay informed about the latest developments in science and technology. They have a great influence on what your life will be like in the future.

■ Section 1.4 Review ■

RECALL THE FACTS

1. What is the difference between science and technology?
2. How is a recipe like a chemistry experiment?
3. What is meant when a kitchen tool claims to be ergonomically designed?
4. Give an example of recent technological advances in the food industry.

DISCUSS YOUR IDEAS

5. How do you think the drawbacks of technology compare to the benefits?
6. What are the advantages and disadvantages of using a personal computer to help with meal planning?

APPLY YOUR LEARNING

7. Using a catalogue, compare the price and features of a basic model and a "high-tech" model of a common kitchen appliance, such as a toaster. Draw conclusions.

■ Answers to Section Review ■

1. Science involves research to develop knowledge; technology is the application of that knowledge to practical uses.
2. When you change the conditions or ingredients, the results change also.
3. It is easy and comfortable to use.
4. Answers will vary. Examples include genetic engineering and microwave ovens.
5. Answers will vary.
6. Answers will vary.
7. Answers will vary.

Managing Resources and Making Decisions

OBJECTIVES

After studying this section, you should be able to:

- Give examples of how management techniques relate to the study of food and nutrition.
- List the steps in the decision-making process.

LOOK FOR THESE TERMS

management

In her foods class, Lawanda is learning to make healthful food choices. Even though she keeps busy with school, a job, and after-school activities, she makes time to eat three nutritious meals a day. As part of her studies in foods, she has learned decision-making and management techniques which help her to live more successfully.

What Is Management?

Management refers to specific techniques that help you use resources wisely. As you learned in Section 1.2, resources are objects and qualities that can help you reach your goals. They include time, money, equipment, food, knowledge, and abilities, such as your ability to think and imagine.

With good management you can use whatever resources you have most effectively.

Teacher's Classroom Resources—Section 1.5

Refer to these resources in the TCR package:

Reproducible Lesson Plans
Student Workbook
Extending the Text

Reteaching Activities
Section Quizzes
Testmaker Software
Color Transparencies

Section 1.5
Managing Resources and Making Decisions

Introducing the Section

Motivators

- Ask students to identify the resources involved in providing family meals. List the resources on the chalkboard. Ask students to identify tasks involved in management. List the tasks on the chalkboard. How is managing family meals similar to managing a business?

- Divide the class into groups. Ask students to pretend they are in charge of family meals for the next week. Have them list the decisions that must be made in planning and preparing family meals. In what order do these decisions occur? Compare the lists compiled by different groups.

Objectives

- Have students read the section objectives. Discuss the purpose of studying this section.

Vocabulary

- Pronounce the terms listed under "Look for These Terms." Have students find the terms and their definitions in the section.

Guided Reading

- Have students look at the headings within Section 1.5 to preview the concepts that will be discussed.

- Have students read the section and complete the appropriate part of the Chapter 1 Study Guide in the *Student Workbook*.

1.5

Teaching . . .

- ### What Is Management?

  (text pages 45-46)

Comprehension Check

1. Ask students to discuss the various resources that need to be managed to prepare foods wisely and efficiently. *(time, energy, food, equipment, knowledge, abilities)*

2. Ask students why keeping records is considered a form of management. *(It provides a written record you can use to plan and evaluate.)*

3. Ask student volunteers to describe one or more decisions they have had to make today.

Student Experiences

1. **Case Study**: Have students work in pairs or small groups to apply management skills to a situation which requires decisions about food (for example, deciding what to serve at a party). *(Key skill: management skills)*

2. **Making a Time Schedule**: Have students work in groups to plan a time schedule for preparing a simple meal. Provide recipes for the meal and give the serving time. Have students compare the groups' schedules and identify possible improvements. *(Key skills: management skills, math)*

Earth Watch

Ask students to suggest ways in which they can help conserve natural resources during their everyday activities. Would these suggestions greatly alter their current lifestyle? Why or why not?

Scientists are concerned that destruction of the tropical rainforests could change the global climate. What might be the effects on food production?

As you study food and nutrition, you will find many ways in which management techniques can be useful. For instance:

- ❖ **Managing time and energy** can help you accomplish what you really need and want to do without wearing yourself out. You'll find that time management is an essential part of working in the school foods lab.

- ❖ **Managing your money** can help you meet financial goals and get the most value for your dollar. Unit Three of this book looks at the consumer decisions involved in buying food and kitchen equipment.

- ❖ **Record-keeping** can help you to make plans and evaluate how well you use your resources. For instance, later you will learn how keeping a record of the food you eat for a few days can help you make better food choices.

- ❖ **Organizing** means arranging items in an orderly and logical way. A good way to organize a kitchen is to put items near where they are used. You might organize

Earth Watch

Conserving natural resources, such as fuel, water, and clean air, is part of responsible management. Make protecting the environment a priority in your life. You'll find tips to help you in later chapters.

---

a shopping list by grouping similar items together. Being well-organized saves time and effort in the long run.

Another very important management technique is knowing how to make decisions.

Making Decisions

Throughout this course, and in your daily life, you will be making many decisions related to food and nutrition. For example, what foods will you choose from the lunch menu? Which recipe will you try? Which package of meat will you purchase? What equipment will you use to prepare the recipe?

People often make decisions without thinking them through. They may "flip a coin," picking an option at random. Sometimes they put off making a decision until they no longer have any choices. However, important decisions deserve more careful thought.

See Also . . .

- Section 7.5: "Conserving Natural Resources," text page 213.
- Section 8.5: "Time Management and Teamwork," text page 246.
- Chapter 11: "Planning Meals," text page 304.
- Chapter 12: "Shopping for Food," text page 326.
- Chapter 14: "Buying for the Kitchen," text page 370.

Steps in Making Decisions

Here is a simple seven-step process that can help you make better decisions:

1. *Identify the decision to be made and your goals.* In other words, what do you want the end result to be? For instance, "I need to choose what food to bring to the potluck dinner. It should be easy to fix, easy to keep hot or cold, and something most people will like."

2. *List your resources.* What do you have available that could help you in this situation? A resource for finding recipes might be a cookbook. A resource for keeping food hot at the potluck might be an electric slow cooker.

3. *Identify your options.* Be creative and open to new ideas. As you think of solutions that might work, make a list.

4. *Consider each option.* Imagine the results of each possible choice. If you need to, gather more information. Now list the advantages and disadvantages of each option. How well would it meet the goals you originally set?

5. *Choose the best option.* Often there is no perfect solution. Weigh and compare, then choose the one that seems best. What if none of the choices is acceptable? Try going back to step 3—perhaps there's a solution you've overlooked.

6. *Carry out your decision.* Make a plan based on your choice. For instance, if you decide to take baked beans to the potluck, plan when and how you will make them. Then put your plan in action.

7. *Evaluate the results.* How did your decision turn out? If it worked well, take pride in what you accomplished. However, don't be discouraged if things didn't work quite the way you planned. Accept the fact that you did your best, then try to learn from the experience. As you continue to make decisions and carry them out, the process will become easier.

With practice, the decision-making process will become automatic. You will be more satisfied with the choices you make.

Teaching . . .

• Making Decisions

(text pages 46-47)

Comprehension Check

1. Have students list the steps in the decision-making process. Ask students if these steps could be followed successfully in any other order. Why or why not?

2. Discuss the importance of developing a habit of making wise decisions about the foods you eat.

Student Experiences

1. **Journal**: Have students keep a journal to identify all the decisions they make about food in a day. Have students share examples with the class. *(Key skill: writing)*

2. **Brainstorming**: Ask students to give examples of ways management skills can be used in other situations which require decisions about food. *(Examples include selecting food when you are eating out, making decisions about shopping for food, etc.) (Key skill: critical thinking)*

3. **Decision-Making**: Provide a problem related to food preparation. Have students work in small groups and use the seven decision-making steps to solve the problem. Discuss and compare the different solutions the groups propose. *(Key skill: problem solving)*

More About Making Decisions

Ask students to discuss this scenario: You are returning home from an after-school job. It's 6:30 and your appetite is raging when you catch sight of the familiar sign of a fast-food restaurant. Checking your money, you find you have just enough for a hamburger, fries, and a shake. So you quickly squelch your hunger pangs with a meal high in calories and saturated fat and low in fiber. How might your decision be altered by using management skills? What factors, other than your hunger and ready cash, might you consider in choosing whether to eat at the fast-food restaurant?

1.5

Completing the Section

Review

- Ask students to summarize the main ideas in this section.
- Have students complete the Section Review. (Answers appear below.)

Evaluation

- Ask students to prepare a bulletin board display that explains the seven steps of making decisions.
- Have students take the quiz for Section 1.5. (Refer to the *Section Quizzes* booklet or use the *Testmaker Software*.)

Reteaching

- Select a simple food preparation problem. Set up a station in the classroom for each step of the decision-making process. Each should show how the step can be applied to the problem. Have students visit each station and write a report on their observations.
- Refer to the *Reteaching Activities* booklet for the Section 1.5 activity sheet.

Enrichment

- Have experienced students work in small groups to prepare a meal, using the decision-making steps.

Closure

- Refer students back to the motivators for this section. How have their ideas changed? Ask students to suggest changes to the list.

Decision-Making and Food Choices

A lifetime of good or poor health depends, in part, on the many small decisions you make each day. Often poor food choices are made as a matter of habit, but remember that good choices can also become a habit.

As you continue in this book, you will learn more about the nutrients in foods and how to eat nutritiously at home and away. That knowledge, along with the decision-making process, will help you evaluate and improve your day-to-day food choices.

The food industry offers diverse career opportunities. The need for food workers is expected to increase steadily.

48   Chapter 1: Exploring Food Choices

Career Decisions

One of the most important decisions you will ever make is choosing how you would like to earn your living. When making career decisions, identifying the options is especially important. Too often, people decide on a line of work without really knowing much about it. They are unaware of many other possible careers, any one of which might prove even more satisfying to them.

You might be surprised at the wide range of careers related to food and nutrition. This book can help you learn about the possibilities. At the end of each chapter, you'll find a "Career Profile" describing a particular worker and his or her job. The last chapter of this book provides more information to help you think about and prepare for a career.

■ Section 1.5 Review ■

RECALL THE FACTS

1. What is management?
2. Name three management techniques. Tell how each relates to food and nutrition.
3. What are the seven steps in the decision-making process?

DISCUSS YOUR IDEAS

4. Why is the seventh step in the decision-making process important?
5. Why do you think some people dislike making decisions? What advice would you give them?

APPLY YOUR LEARNING

6. Imagine that your class has been asked to cook a meal for a local senior citizen's group. Identify at least three decisions that would have to be made. Choose one and explain how you would use the decision-making process in this situation.

■ Answers to Section Review ■

1. Specific techniques that help you use your resources wisely.
2. *Any three:* Managing time and energy (food preparation); managing money (get the most value for each food dollar); record-keeping (plan and evaluate food choices); organizing (saves time and effort).
3. 1) Identify decision and goals; 2) list resources; 3) identify options; 4) consider options; 5) choose best option; 6) carry out decision; 7) evaluate results.
4. The first decision may not work; you may need to try a different option.
5. Answers will vary.
6. Answers will vary.

Career PROFILE

Rita Johnson
Caterer

CURRENT POSITION

"I own a small deli/catering service specializing in parties and receptions."

WHY I CHOSE THIS CAREER

"I've enjoyed cooking since I was 11 years old. I'm the type of person who takes cookbooks to the beach instead of paperbacks."

SKILLS

"Of course it's necessary to be a good cook in this business. It also helps to be well-organized and personable."

EDUCATION

"I've taken community college courses in culinary arts, as well as in business management and advertising."

TYPICAL DAY ON THE JOB

"My days vary, depending on the kind of jobs I have lined up. Some days are spent meeting with potential clients, while other days are spent in the kitchen. Because most clients have slightly different needs, no two days are exactly alike!"

FAVORITE PART OF THE JOB

"The flexibility of owning my own business is a real plus. Also, I get a lot of satisfaction from hearing my clients say what a great time their guests had, and would I be available to cater their sister's wedding reception in April?"

- What might be the benefits and drawbacks of owning your own business?
- What aspects of Rita's job do you think you might enjoy? Why?

49

Thinking About . . . Catering

- Have students think of other questions they would like to ask Rita Johnson about the catering occupation. (Examples: "How many hours a week do you usually work?" "What resources did you need to get started in this business?")
- Ask student volunteers to tell what they think would be the most exciting part of the catering business.
- Have students brainstorm decisions that might have to be made in the catering business and use the decision-making steps to develop logical answers.

Student Opportunities

Students who are interested in a career as a caterer should consider vocational food service/culinary arts programs. They can gain experience working in a restaurant, cafeteria, or catering business.

Occupational Outlook

In a catering career, you can begin as a caterer's assistant, earn your credentials as a caterer, then either join a large catering firm or start your own catering business. As a caterer, you have the opportunity to take part in a business as big or as small as you want it to be.

For More Information

For more information about careers in the deli/catering business, encourage interested students to contact:
- American Culinary Federation, P.O. Box 3466, St. Augustine, FL 32084
- Small Business Administration (SBA), 1441 L Street NW, Washington, D.C. 20416
- Small Business Institute, P.O. Box 30149, Baltimore, MD 21270

Completing the Chapter

Review

- Have students complete the Chapter Review. (Answers appear below.)

Evaluation

- Divide the class into two teams (A and B). Each team should brainstorm questions about Chapter 1. Then allow a representative of Team A to ask Team B one question. Then Team B asks Team A a question. Anyone in the responding team may answer. At the end of the questioning period, the team with the most correct answers wins.

- Have students take the test for Chapter 1. (Refer to the *Chapter and Unit Tests* booklet or construct your own test using the *Testmaker Software*.)

■ ANSWERS ■

REVIEWING FACTS

1. *Nutrients:* chemicals the body needs to carry on its functions; *nutrition:* the study of nutrients and how the body uses them; *wellness:* philosophy encouraging people to take responsibility for their health.

2. Answers will vary. Example: guests being offered something to eat or drink when they enter your home is intended to make the guests "feel at home."

3. Answers will vary. Possible answers: newspapers, magazines, television, and radio; they expose you to advertisements encouraging you to buy certain types or brands of food.

4. Answers will vary. Example: A busy person who has a very tight schedule might choose to eat prepackaged, frozen meals.

SUMMARY

SECTION 1.1

Food and Health: Good nutrition is an important part of physical health. Food can also contribute to psychological health by providing security, a sense of belonging, and enjoyment. Developing skills in food and nutrition can help build self-esteem.

SECTION 1.2

Influences on Food Choices: Social influences on food choices include culture, family, friends, and the media. Food choices also depend on available resources. Technology has increased the options available. Personal influences also affect your choice of foods.

SECTION 1.3

Food and Culture: Today's world is becoming an ever more multicultural and global society. Different cultures have distinct food customs. Many food customs originated in the distant past, although they have changed and mingled along the way.

SECTION 1.4

Food, Science, and Technology: The study of food has many scientific aspects. Nutrition is a science in itself, while chemistry and ergonomics play a role in food preparation. New technology is changing the way food is produced and processed, as well as the way people plan and prepare meals.

SECTION 1.5

Managing Resources and Making Decisions: Management techniques help you use resources wisely and are useful in studying food. The decision-making process can help in situations ranging from choosing food to choosing a career.

50

REVIEWING FACTS

1. Define: nutrients, nutrition, wellness. (1.1)

2. Give an example of how food can help provide a sense of belonging. (1.1)

3. Name four forms of media. How does the media influence food choices? (1.2)

4. Give an example of how two people might make different food choices because of differences in lifestyle. (1.2)

5. What is meant by "cultural diversity"? How does it relate to food customs? (1.3)

6. How did geography affect the development of food customs in the past? Why does it have less influence today? (1.3)

7. What do natural laws of science have to do with food preparation? (1.4)

8. Discuss the changes that have resulted from the invention of the microwave oven. (1.4)

9. What is the first step in making a decision? (1.5)

10. What should you do if a decision doesn't turn out as well as you expected? (1.5)

---

5. A variety of cultures coexisting in the same society; exposes people to food customs from other cultures.

6. In the past, people had to eat foods grown or raised locally; now they can choose from foods grown all over the world.

7. They govern physical and chemical changes that occur when foods are heated, chilled, etc.

8. Cooking has become faster, and many new products have been developed especially for the microwave.

9. Identify the decision to be made and your goals.

10. After evaluating it, return to the other options you defined, add to the list if necessary, and try again.

LEARNING BY DOING

1. **Taste-test lab:** Wearing a blindfold, taste food samples prepared by your teacher. Describe the aroma, texture, and flavor. Try to identify the food. Discuss how the senses contribute to the enjoyment of food. What role do they play in making food choices? (1.1, 1.2)

2. **Food science lab:** Cut an apple or banana into slices. Coat half the slices with lemon juice. Let all the slices stand at room temperature for thirty minutes. Observe the appearance of the slices. How does this experiment reinforce the idea that food preparation is governed by scientific principles? (1.4)

3. **Foods lab:** Prepare popcorn in the microwave oven, on the range, and in a popcorn popper. Compare the methods for time, cost, and taste. What are the advantages and disadvantages of each method? Which would you be more likely to choose in the future? (1.4, 1.5)

THINKING CRITICALLY

1. **Identifying evidence:** How might a person determine whether food is successfully meeting physical and psychological needs? (1.1)

2. **Recognizing values:** Some people, if asked to bake a cake, would choose to bake it from scratch. Others would use a cake mix. What values and priorities are reflected by each approach? (1.2, 1.5)

3. **Comparing and contrasting:** Working with a partner, compare and contrast the eating habits of each of your families. Discuss the reasons for similarities and differences. (1.2, 1.3)

4. **Identifying cause and effect:** In what ways has the microwave oven changed daily life? (1.4)

MAKING DECISIONS AND SOLVING PROBLEMS

What Would You Do?

1. You're working in the foods lab, rolling and shaping dough for yeast rolls. You notice that one of your lab partners seems to be having trouble. Most of her rolls are lopsided or falling apart. "I don't know why I even try," you hear her mutter. "I'm no good at anything." (1.1)

2. A new student at your school has invited you home for dinner. When you sit down to eat, you learn that your friend's grandmother has prepared a meal of authentic foods from her native country. You don't recognize any of the foods on your plate. (1.2, 1.3)

3. You are helping your family shop for a new microwave oven. There is a basic model in your price range that looks easy to use. However, you think your family would like some of the special features found in higher-priced models. (1.4, 1.5)

LINKING YOUR STUDIES

1. **Writing:** Describe your favorite food in a paragraph. Focus on details of taste, texture, appearance, and aroma. (1.1)

2. **Social studies:** Choose five foods that originated in five different cultures. Prepare a display that tells what part of the world each food came from and how it came to this country. (1.2, 1.3)

3. **Business:** Explain how the management skills described in the chapter would apply to someone who is a business owner or employee. What other management skills are used in business? How might they apply to food and nutrition? (1.5)

51

THINKING CRITICALLY

1. Possible answer: by using decision-making steps to see if needs are being met, and if not, what changes are needed.

2. Possible answers: time, equipment, ability, experience, priorities.

3. Be sure students discuss both similarities and differences.

4. Help students understand the meaning of the word hypothesis if necessary, and explain how a hypothesis can become the basis for a new experiment.

5. Possible answer: less time spent in kitchen when your schedule is busy.

MAKING DECISIONS AND SOLVING PROBLEMS

Answers to "Making Decisions and Solving Problems" questions will vary. Encourage students to give reasons for their answers.

LINKING YOUR STUDIES

1. Encourage students to use the terms listed on the handout "Vocabulary for Sensory Evaluation." (See *Food Science Resources* booklet.)

2. Have students to be creative in preparing their displays. Have each student present and explain his or her display to the class.

3. Answers will vary. However, students should understand that management skills are necessary in any business endeavor, and are even important in organizing pleasure activities.

LEARNING BY DOING

1. Before beginning the lab, distribute the handout "Vocabulary for Sensory Evaluation." (See *Food Science Resources* booklet.) Encourage students to use the terms listed on the handout

2. Reinforces the idea that mixing foods may cause a chemical or physical effect.

Untreated fruit turned brown by reacting with air. The lemon juice reacted with fruit to keep fruit from reacting with air.

3. Encourage students to consider equipment needed, ease of popping the popcorn, and relative cleanup times needed.

Planning the Chapter

Chapter Overview

Section 2.1: The Role of Nutrients

Section 2.2: Carbohydrates, Fiber, and Proteins

Section 2.3: Fats

Section 2.4: Vitamins, Minerals, and Water

Section 2.5: How Your Body Uses Food

Introducing the Chapter

Motivators

- Create a bulletin board entitled, "You Can't Be the Picture of Health . . . If You Don't Have All the Pieces!" Label large jigsaw puzzle pieces *Carbohydrates, Fiber, Proteins, Fats, Vitamins, Minerals,* and *Water.* Discuss what happens if a piece is missing.

- Ask students for their reactions to the saying, "You are what you eat." In what sense is the statement true? In what ways is it false?

Teacher's Classroom Resources—Chapter 2

Refer to these resources in the TCR package:

Enrichment Activities

Chapter and Unit Tests

Testmaker Software

C H A P T E R 2

The Nutrients You Need

52

Cooperative Learning Suggestions

Divide the class into six groups. Assign each group one of the major types of nutrients for the following Co-op Co-op activity. Have each group develop a game or activity that summarizes the important facts about the nutrient type. Each member of the group should ask questions about the nutrient to make sure no important points are missed. Then, as a chapter review, have each group present their game or activity to the entire class. Have the class try the game and make suggestions.

The Role of Nutrients

OBJECTIVES

After studying this section, you should be able to:
- Name the six major types of nutrients.
- Explain the purpose of RDAs.
- Give guidelines regarding calorie needs and calorie sources.
- Evaluate the use of supplements to meet daily nutritional needs.

LOOK FOR THESE TERMS

carbohydrates
fats
proteins
vitamins
minerals
dietary fiber
nutrient deficiency
malnutrition
RDA
calorie

As you learned in Chapter 1, food provides essential chemicals called nutrients. Nutrients play a vital role in your ability to enjoy life and reach your potential. They work in three basic ways:
- They give you energy.
- They are needed for growth, maintenance, and repair of the body.
- They keep the different systems in your body working smoothly.

Nutrient Teamwork

As you may recall, more than 40 nutrients have been identified so far. Each has a specific job to do to keep the body healthy. You can't substitute one for another, and one nutrient alone can't keep your body healthy. All the nutrients work together to contribute to good health.

You might compare good nutrition to a football team. One player carries the football for a touchdown, but it takes the whole team to make sure that player gets to the goal. The coach decides who will play on the team.

Nutrients work together as a team, each one playing its role. Some are major players, and some are minor, but all are essential to good health. Think of yourself as the coach of the team. Your role is to choose the foods that will provide all the nutrients you need.

Good nutrition is essential for good health.

Section 2.1: The Role of Nutrients   **53**

Introducing the Section

Motivators
- On the chalkboard, use X's and O's to represent the offensive and defensive lineups of two football teams. Discuss the positions of different players. What might happen if a position were left vacant? Then add the names of nutrients to one of the teams in your diagram. Identify these as the "players" in the wellness game. Explain that nutrients act as a team in your body.
- Ask students to share information they have about calories and nutrient supplements. Where do calories come from? Why do people take nutrient supplements? In what forms are they available? Are they necessary?

Objectives
- Have students read the section objectives. Discuss the purpose of studying the section.

Vocabulary
- Pronounce the terms listed under "Look for These Terms." Have students find the terms and their definitions in the section.

Guided Reading
- Have students look at the headings within Section 2.1 to preview the concepts that will be discussed.
- Have students read the section and complete the appropriate part of the Chapter 2 Study Guide in the *Student Workbook*.

Teaching . . .

• Nutrient Teamwork

(text pages 53-55)

Comprehension Check

1. Ask students to list the three basic ways in which nutrients work. *(They give you energy; are needed for body growth, maintenance, and repair; keep body systems working smoothly.)*

2. Ask students to explain the importance of getting the correct amounts of all nutrients, rather than concentrating on just one or two. *(All nutrients work together as a team.)*

3. Ask students to identify the six major types of nutrients and explain their general roles. *(Summarized in left column.)*

4. Ask students to explain what nutrient deficiency is. Discuss the possible effects of nutrient deficiency. *(A severe shortage of a nutrient, which can cause illness or weaken bones and other body systems.)*

5. Discuss the causes of malnutrition. *(People cannot afford food; people make poor food choices.)*

A team relies on each member's contributions. The food you eat must include all vital nutrients in order for your body to function smoothly.

What Nutrients Do You Need?

The nutrients are divided into six major types.

❖ The body's main source of energy is **carbohydrates** (kar-bo-HY-drates).

❖ **Fats** are a concentrated source of energy. They are needed, in moderate amounts, to perform important functions in the body.

❖ The main job of **proteins** is to help build and repair the body. They also provide energy.

❖ **Vitamins** are chemicals needed in small amounts to help the body function properly. They also help other nutrients do their jobs.

❖ Like vitamins, **minerals** help the body work properly. Many also become part of body tissues, such as bone.

❖ Water is considered a nutrient because it is essential to life.

You will learn more about these nutrients in the next two sections of this chapter. You'll also learn about **dietary fiber,** a mixture of plant materials that are not broken down in the digestive system. Like the nutrients, fiber is important for good health.

Effects of Poor Nutrition

When people make poor food choices or do not have enough to eat, they may not get the right balance of nutrients. Poor health can result.

A **nutrient deficiency,** or severe shortage of a nutrient, can cause illness. For instance, a lack of vitamin D can keep children's bones from growing properly. Their bones become weak and they develop bowed legs. In adults, a lack of vitamin D weakens bones so they break more easily. It may also cause muscle spasms.

54   Chapter 2: The Nutrients You Need

Special Needs Strategies

Behaviorally Disabled: Have students pretend they are detectives. As each nutrient is studied, their job is to make a list of important clues that help to solve the mystery of good health. As you give each "clue," hold up a magnifying glass as a cue to take notes. Provide students with a "detective's diary" in which to record their clues. Decorate the pages with appropriate motifs.

Children are at particular risk from malnutrition. Lack of adequate, nutritious food during childhood can have lifelong effects. What programs are available in your area to fight malnutrition?

1. **Nutrient Mapping:** Have students create a cognitive map of types of nutrients. Have them 1) write the word "nutrients" in a circle in the center of a sheet of paper; 2) draw satellites around the center circle and label them with the names of the six major types of nutrients; 3) draw lines from each nutrient on which they list the functions of that nutrient. *(Key skill: language arts)*

2. **Reading About Diets:** Set up a display of magazines and books featuring diets. Include some that recommend a single food or food group. Ask students to select one and explain whether it supports the rule that nutrients work together as a team. *(Key skill: reading)*

3. **Analyzing Photos:** Provide students with magazines that include pictures of people who are malnourished. Ask students to identify physical characteristics resulting from malnutrition. On a map, locate the countries mentioned in the stories. (Note: Include stories about people in the United States who are malnourished, including those who are overweight.) *(Key skills: social studies, analysis)*

Malnutrition refers to serious health problems caused by poor nutrition over a long period of time. Generally, malnutrition occurs when people do not have enough to eat. Bad weather, poor transportation, political problems, or other factors can cause food shortages.

Many people around the world simply cannot afford to buy the food needed for good health. In the United States, it's estimated that 20 percent of children live in poverty.

Poor nutrition can also occur among people who have an abundant food supply and can afford to buy whatever they want. Their problem stems from poor food choices. They choose foods that do not supply enough of the nutrients needed for good health. They may also eat too much or get too much of some nutrients, such as fat.

The food choices you make today will have long-term effects on your health. Poor food choices increase the risk of diseases that can shorten life or reduce the quality of life. By making good choices, you can increase your chances of staying healthy, strong, and active throughout life.

How Much Do You Need?

Scientists have established how much of certain nutrients people need. They have developed **RDA** values, which stands for *Recommended Dietary Allowances.* The RDAs are divided into 18 groups based on age and gender (male or female). They include recommended amounts for protein, 11 vitamins,

Section 2.1: The Role of Nutrients   55

More About Malnutrition

In 1988, some 600 million people, nearly one-ninth of the world's population, suffered from malnutrition. Although population growth has slowed in the industrialized nations, it has accelerated in developing countries, where human demands often overtax life support systems. Tropical forests are rapidly dwindling and soils are eroding at unprecedented rates. With the demise of these natural resources, food and fuel quickly diminish and malnutrition follows.

Teaching . . .

• How Much Do You Need?

(text pages 55-56)

Comprehension Check

1. Ask students to explain why, of the more than 40 nutrients known, only 19 are included in the RDA values. *(Not enough is known about the others.)* Discuss why researchers must determine critical facts such as the amount of the nutrient used by the body, how it is used, and what the effects of an "overdose" of the nutrient are before scientists can recommend amounts.

2. Ask students to explain why scientists use the metric system rather than the customary system to measure amounts of nutrients. *(It includes very small units of measure.)* Can students think of other situations in which the metric system would be more convenient to use?

Student Experiences

1. **Product Comparison:** Obtain a variety of breakfast cereal nutrition charts showing percentages of the daily RDAs (daily values) for a variety of nutrients. Have students (or groups of students) make graphs showing the RDA levels for key nutrients. Compare the graphs for various cereals. Discuss the pros and cons of cereals that provide "total daily nutrition." *(Key skills: math, critical thinking)*

2. **Research:** Have students research Recommended Daily Allowances/Reference Daily Intakes guidelines. How have these guidelines changed through the years? Why have they changed? *(Key skill: research)*

and 7 minerals. Researchers have enough information about these nutrients to be able to recommend specific amounts. Not enough is known about other nutrients, so they are not included. The RDAs are updated periodically as new information is available.

The RDAs are used by professionals such as nutritionists and dietitians. They are an important tool in shaping U.S. nutrition policy and for developing educational programs. They are also used by industry when adding nutrients to foods and developing new products.

The Food and Drug Administration has used the RDAs as the basis for another set of guidelines. These are known by their new name, *Reference Daily Intakes (RDIs),* or by their original name, *U.S. Recommended Daily Allowances (U.S. RDAs).* They are used in nutrition labeling.

How Nutrients Are Measured

Most nutrients are needed in relatively small amounts. It's easier to measure them using the metric system, the system of measurement used by scientists. The metric system includes small units of measure, such as the milligram (mg).

The amount of iron you need each day is small—less than the weight of a single raisin. A cup of raisins contains 3 milligrams of iron.

56   Chapter 2: The Nutrients You Need

For example, teenage females need 15 milligrams (mg) of iron each day. That's equivalent to about 0.0005 ounce.

Energy from Nutrients

As you have learned, some nutrients—carbohydrates, fats, and proteins—supply your body with energy. This energy is measured in units called *kilocalories* (KILL-oh-KAL-uh-rees). For consumer use, kilocalorie has been shortened to **calorie,** the term that will be used throughout this book. (In the metric system, energy is measured in kilojoules [kJ].)

Your Energy Needs

Your body needs energy to carry on basic processes, such as pumping blood, and to fuel activities, such as walking. Therefore, you need a certain number of calories each day. The number depends on your age, weight, level of activity, and whether you are male or female.

Science Connection

Nutrition Science:
Measuring Kilocalories

One kilocalorie is the amount of energy needed to raise the temperature of 1 kilogram (a little more than 4 cups) of water 1 degree Celsius. An instrument called a *calorimeter* is used to calculate the energy content of foods. A measured amount of food is placed in the calorimeter chamber and burned. Scientists calculate how much heat was given off in the process. The results tell them how many kilocalories the food contains.

■ ■ ■

More About Nutrient Guidelines

The newest guidelines based on RDAs are called Daily Values and include both Reference Daily Intakes (RDIs) and Daily Reference Values (DRVs). Under the new guidelines, RDI values include those for vitamins, minerals, and proteins. Values for these nutrients are currently the same as the older U.S. RDAs. DRV values are new values for fat, carbohydrate (including fiber), protein, cholesterol, sodium, and potassium. The new nutrition labels do not distinguish between RDIs and DRVs; all the values are grouped under the term "Daily Values."

Vigorous exercise, such as running or swimming, uses large amounts of energy. That is why athletes usually need more calories per day than nonathletes.

If the number of calories used by the body balances the number of calories from food, your body weight will stay about the same. However, if the calories do not balance, over time you will gain or lose weight. In Chapter 5, you will learn more about weight management.

Recommended Sources of Calories

Scientists have calculated the number of calories provided by each of the three energy-producing nutrients in their pure form. (See the chart below.) Notice that fat is a concentrated source of energy. It has more than twice the number of calories per gram as carbohydrate and protein.

Health experts recommend that you get 30 percent or less of the calories you take in from fat, 55 percent or more from carbohydrates, and 12 to 15 percent from protein. This ratio provides the healthiest balance of the three nutrients.

For instance, Julie, who needs about 2200 calories a day, should get no more than about 660 of those calories from fat (2200 x 0.3 = 660). How many grams of fat will supply 660 calories? There are 9 calories in one gram of fat, so divide 660 by 9. The answer is about 73 grams. For comparison, a double cheeseburger and fries from a fast-food restaurant provide about 47 grams of fat.

The U.S. Department of Agriculture, as part of its nutrition guidelines, offers the following suggestions for calorie intake:

❖ 1600 calories is about right for many sedentary (inactive) women and some older adults.
❖ 2200 calories is about right for most children, teenage girls, active women, and many sedentary men. Women who are pregnant or breastfeeding may need more.
❖ 2800 calories is about right for teenage boys, many active men, and some very active women.

Nutrient	Calories	kJ
1 gram carbohydrate	4	17
1 gram protein	4	17
1 gram fat	9	37

Teaching . . .

• Energy from Nutrients

(text pages 56-58)

Comprehension Check

1. Have students discuss the relationship between caloric intake, exercise, and weight gain or loss.
2. Ask students to list the recommended daily percentages of the different sources of energy (carbohydrates, protein, fats). *(Carbohydrates: 55% or more; protein: 12%-15%; fat: 30% or less)*

Student Experiences

1. **Demonstration:** Show the difference between calories and kilocalories (1000 calories = 1 kilocalorie) and ask students to do some simple equations using this conversion factor. *(Key skill: math)*
2. **Diet Analysis:** Have students analyze the calories supplied by the daily diet of a hypothetical classmate. What percentage of the daily calorie intake comes from carbohydrates? Should any changes be made? *(Key skills: math, critical thinking)*
3. **Computer Analysis:** Have students use computer software to analyze their diets. Check the percentages of calories from carbohydrates, proteins, and fats. What adjustments, if any, are needed for a balanced diet? *(Key skill: computer literacy)*

See Also . . .

• Section 2.2: "Carbohydrates, Fiber, and Proteins," text page 60.
• Section 3.1: "Dietary Guidelines," text page 89.
• Section 5.2: "Weight Management," text page 143.

• Who Needs Supplements?

(text pages 58-59)

Comprehension Check

1. Ask students to define the term *supplements*. What are some common reasons for taking nutrient supplements? *(medication, pregnant/nursing women, convalescents, elderly, people on special diets)*

2. Ask students to discuss the use of nutrient supplements by people other than those listed above. Are the supplements necessary? Do they accomplish any good? Can they be harmful? If so, in what ways?

3. Ask students to list guidelines for taking nutrient supplements. *(See page 59, left column.)*

Student Experiences

1. **Out-of-Class Project:** Ask students to visit a grocery store, pharmacy, or health food store to observe the types of nutrient supplements available. Have them read the labels of several products and record any claims made on the label. Have students prepare a written report of their findings. *(Key skill: writing)*

2. **Developing Nutrient Guidelines:** Provide students with copies of articles about nutrient supplements. Have students read and summarize the articles for the class. Using the information obtained from the articles, have students develop guidelines for choosing and using nutrient supplements. *(Key skill: reading)*

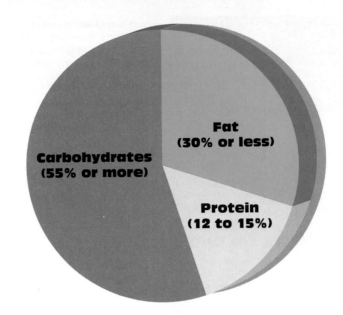

It's not just the number of calories you take in that's important. The sources of those calories also affect nutrition and health. As the chart above shows, health experts recommend that more than half your calories come from carbohydrates, 30 percent or less from fat, and only 12 to 15 percent from protein.

Who Needs Supplements?

Supplements are nutrients people take in addition to the food they eat. Supplements are generally available as pills, capsules, liquids, or powder.

Supplements may be useful for people who are taking certain kinds of medication, pregnant and nursing women, those recovering from illness, the elderly, and people on special diets. In such cases, the people may not be getting enough nutrients from the food they eat.

Most people, however, do not need supplements. They can get all the nutrients they need by eating a variety of nutritious foods. People who rely on supplements to make up for poor food choices may be short-changing themselves.

Technology Tidbit

Computer software is available that can check for a balanced diet. After a list of daily food choices is entered, the computer calculates the percentage of calories from carbohydrates, proteins, and fats. It displays the results in comparison to the recommended goal.

58   Chapter 2: The Nutrients You Need

Thinking Skills

Critical Thinking: Have students debate the topic, "Nutrient supplements are needed to keep people healthy."

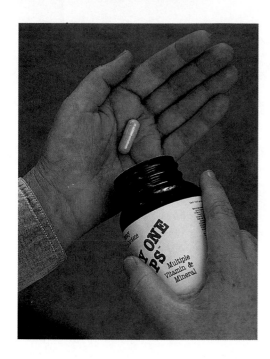

Nutritional supplements are not a substitute for eating nutritious food. Never take large amounts of any supplement without checking with a physician.

Some people believe in "megavitamin therapy," which means taking extra-large amounts of supplements to prevent or cure diseases. This should be done only on the advice of a physician. Excess amounts of many nutrients can accumulate in the body and cause harm. For instance, taking large amounts of vitamin A can lead to liver damage.

Some nutrients are not stored by the body. The excess amounts simply pass out of the body unused. Thus, taking unneeded supplements is a waste of money.

Try to get all your nutrients from food. If you do decide to take supplements:

❖ Avoid mega-doses and single nutrients (unless prescribed by a health professional).

❖ Read the list of ingredients to make sure of what you're getting. Avoid unrecognized nutrients.

❖ If you're taking supplements "just to be safe," consider taking them every other day instead of daily.

✓ SAFETY CHECK

Children often confuse vitimin and mineral pills with candy. They can be harmed by large doses of supplements. If there are children in the home, make sure nutrient supplements are stored in child-resistant packages out of the reach of children.

■ Section 2.1 Review ■

RECALL THE FACTS

1. What are the six major types of nutrients? What are the main functions of each?

2. What purpose does the RDA serve?

3. Which nutrients supply your body with energy? How is food energy measured?

DISCUSS YOUR IDEAS

4. Why do you think nutrient supplements are so popular? Do you think people who use supplements would change their minds if they better understood the drawbacks?

APPLY YOUR LEARNING

5. Jonathan is 15 years old. Approximately how many calories does he need to take in each day? How many of those calories should come from fat? How many grams of fat would supply that many calories?

Section 2.1: The Role of Nutrients   **59**

Completing the Section

Review

- Ask students to summarize the main ideas in this section.
- Have students complete the Section Review. (Answers appear below.)

Evaluation

- Ask students to write a brief summary of the nutrition topics discussed in this section.
- Have students take the quiz for Section 2.1. (Refer to the *Section Quizzes* booklet or use the *Testmaker Software*.)

Reteaching

- Have students read about the importance of nutrients in a selected reference. Then ask them to list four important points made about nutrition. Analyze how these points compare with points made in this chapter.
- Refer to the *Reteaching Activities* booklet for the Section 2.1 activity sheet.

Enrichment

- Have students research a low carbohydrate diet. What problems have been associated with the diet?

Closure

- Hold a class discussion on the nutrients people need and the use of supplements to meet their nutrient needs.

■ Answers to Section Review ■

1. Carbohydrates (energy), fats (energy), proteins (build/repair body), vitamins (body functions), minerals (body functions) and water (essential to life).

2. Used by professionals to help form nutritional policies; used by industry to add nutrients to products and to develop new products.

3. Carbohydrates and fat; calories.
4. Answers will vary.
5. 2800 calories; 840 or less from fat; 93 grams.

Motivators

- Bring to class news or magazine articles about the importance of carbohydrates, dietary fiber, and protein in the diet. Discuss reasons these nutrients are newsworthy.

- Ask students to identify foods that have been the mainstay of the human diet throughout history. Point out that grains, fruits, vegetables, meat, fish, poultry, eggs, legumes, and nuts are important sources of carbohydrates, fiber, and protein. Explain that these nutrients are essential for energy and good health.

Objectives

- Have students read the section objectives. Discuss the purpose of studying the section.

Vocabulary

- Pronounce the terms listed under "Look for These Terms." Have students find the terms and their definitions in the section.

Guided Reading

- Have students look at the headings within Section 2.2 to preview the concepts that will be discussed.

- Have students read the section and complete the appropriate part of the Chapter 2 Study Guide in the *Student Workbook*.

SECTION 2.2

Carbohydrates, Fiber, and Proteins

OBJECTIVES

After studying this section, you should be able to:

- Name sources of simple and complex carbohydrates.
- Tell why soluble and insoluble fiber are needed.
- Distinguish between complete and incomplete proteins.

LOOK FOR THESE TERMS

refined sugars
insoluble fiber
soluble fiber
amino acids
complete proteins
incomplete proteins

As you read in section 2.1, for good health you need six basic nutrients, plus fiber. Read on to learn more about these, beginning with carbohydrates, fiber, and proteins.

Carbohydrates

The body's main source of energy is carbohydrates. You may know them as starches and sugars. They are found mainly in foods from plant sources, such as fruits, vegetables, grain products, and dry beans and peas. For good health, eat a variety of these foods every day. Generally, they are the least expensive form of energy you can buy.

If you don't eat enough carbohydrates, your body will use the other energy-producing nutrients for energy. When it does, however, it keeps those nutrients from doing their specialized jobs.

Carbohydrates include starches, natural sugars, and refined sugars.

Science Connection

Chemistry:
Simple and Complex Carbohydrates

Carbohydrates get their name from their chemical structure. They are composed of the elements carbon, oxygen, and hydrogen. Simple carbohydrates (sugars) are made up of single or short chemical units. Complex carbohydrates (starches) are made up of long chemical units.

■ ■ ■

Teacher's Classroom Resources—Section 2.2

Refer to these resources in the TCR package:

Reproducible Lesson Plans
Student Workbook
Extending the Text

Reteaching Activities
Section Quizzes
Testmaker Software
Color Transparencies

Grain products, dry beans and peas, and fruits and vegetables are important sources of carbohydrates. The starches and sugars they contain provide energy for the body.

Starches

Starches are also known as *complex carbohydrates*. They are found in dry beans, peas, and lentils; vegetables, such as potatoes and corn; and grain products, such as rice, pasta, and breads. These foods are also good sources of proteins, vitamins, minerals, and dietary fiber.

Natural Sugars

Sugars, also called *simple carbohydrates*, are a natural part of many foods. There are several types of natural sugars. *Fructose* (FROOK-tohs) is found in fruits, *maltose* (MALL-tohs) in grain products, and *lactose* (LACK-tohs) in milk. These foods also provide other nutrients, such as proteins, vitamins, and minerals.

Refined Sugars

Refined sugars are sugars that are removed from plants and used as sweeteners. *Sucrose* (SUE-krohs), or table sugar, comes from plants such as sugar cane or sugar beets. It is used as a sweetener in many foods, such as desserts and candy. Other refined sugars include corn syrup, honey, maple syrup, molasses, and brown sugar.

Studies show that refined sugar does not directly pose any health risk. It can, however, lead to tooth decay. Eating large amounts of sweetened foods can lead to excess weight, which can contribute to health problems.

Refined sugar does not supply nutrients other than simple carbohydrates. To meet your energy needs, rely on the starches and natural sugars found in vegetables, dry beans and peas, fruits, and grain products.

Section 2.2: Carbohydrates, Fiber, and Proteins **61**

More About Carbohydrates

Point out that carbohydrates meet many human needs in addition to nutrition:
- We use cellulose, one of the most common carbohydrates, to make clothing (of cotton, rayon, and linen).

- We use cellulose, in the form of wood, to build homes.

Thus, carbohydrates meet the most basic human needs: food, clothing, and shelter. Ask students to think of other needs that can be met using carbohydrates.

Teaching . . .

• Carbohydrates

(text pages 60-61)

Comprehension Check

1. Ask students to name sources of carbohydrates in the diet.
2. Discuss the difference between natural and refined sugars. Which are more beneficial to the body? Why? *(Natural sugars provide nutrients, but refined sugars do not.)*

Student Experiences

1. **Food Comparison:** Have students compare the calories and nutritional content of natural, refined, and processed carbohydrate foods. Have students arrange the foods in order from high calorie to low calorie. Have students note the nutritional content of foods at each end of the range. *(Key skill: consumer awareness)*
2. **Poster Project:** Have students work in groups to make posters illustrating the chemical makeup of sugars, starches, and fiber. Use the posters to explain the differences in simple and complex carbohydrates. *(Key skill: science)*

Science Connection

Point out that complex carbohydrates are formed of repeated units of simple carbohydrates or "simple sugars." The body breaks these down into simple carbohydrates for use as energy. How might this affect the relative ease with which the body can use simple and complex carbohydrates?

Teaching . . .

• Dietary Fiber

(text page 62)

Comprehension Check

1. Ask students to list sources of dietary fiber. *(fruits, vegetables, grains, dry beans and peas)*

2. Ask students to describe the types of fiber the body needs and the function of each. *(Insoluble fiber will not dissolve in water; it helps food move through the large intestine and may lower the risk of colon cancer; soluble fiber dissolves in water; it appears to lower blood cholesterol levels.)*

Student Experiences

1. **Creating a Chart:** Have students create charts listing foods that are high in soluble and insoluble fiber. Discuss the importance of getting plenty of fiber in your diet. *(Key skill: charting)*

2. **Research:** Provide articles from magazines and books that discuss the intake and use of dietary fiber. Ask students to read an article and make a list of its most important points. *(Key skills: research, reading)*

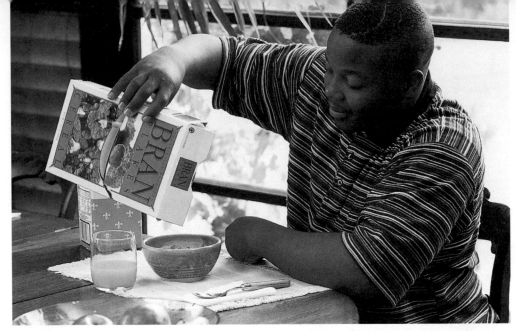

Wheat bran is high in insoluble fiber, which helps move food through the body.

Dietary Fiber

As you learned in section 2.1, dietary fiber consists of plant materials that are not digested. Fiber is found only in foods from plant sources, such as fruits, vegetables, grain products, and dry beans and peas. Foods from animal sources do not contain fiber.

There are two kinds of fiber. Most plant foods contain different amounts of both.

Insoluble fiber will not dissolve in water. It absorbs water and contributes bulk. It helps food move through the large intestine at a normal rate. It promotes regular bowel movements and helps prevent constipation. This type of fiber appears to lower the risk of colon cancer. It is found mainly in fruit and vegetable skins and in whole wheat or wheat bran products.

Soluble fiber dissolves in water. It does not contribute bulk. Studies show it appears to lower blood cholesterol levels. (You will learn about cholesterol in Section 2.3.) Soluble fiber is found in fruits; vegetables; dry beans, peas, and lentils; and oat products.

The National Cancer Institute recommends 20 to 35 grams of dietary fiber a day. To make sure you get enough fiber, eat a wide variety of plant foods such as fruits, vegetables, and whole grain products every day. Increase the fiber gradually and be sure to drink enough liquids. Otherwise, you might develop digestive problems, such as abdominal cramps.

More About Fiber

Many types of fiber are complex carbohydrates. However, these carbohydrates differ from others in that they cannot be broken down into simple sugars. Therefore, the body cannot use them for energy.

Proteins

Proteins are used mainly to help the body grow and to repair worn-out or damaged parts. About one-fifth of your body's total weight is protein. Your hair, eyes, skin, muscles, and bones are made of protein. The proteins you eat help maintain them in good condition.

Proteins also regulate important body processes. For instance, they play a major role in fighting disease because parts of the immune system are proteins.

Proteins can do their job only if the body has enough carbohydrates and fats for energy. If not, the body uses proteins for energy instead of for building and repairing.

Proteins are found in all foods from animal sources, such as meat, poultry, fish, eggs, and dairy products. They are also found in foods from plant sources, especially dry beans and peas, peanuts, vegetables, and grain products. Most Americans eat more protein than they need. Excess amounts are stored by the body as fat.

Many foods are good sources of protein. Those from animal sources (left) are called complete proteins because they contain all the essential amino acids the body needs. Protein can also be obtained by eating a variety of foods from plant sources (below).

Section 2.2: Carbohydrates, Fiber, and Proteins **63**

Complete and Incomplete Proteins

Protein is made up of chemical compounds called **amino acids** (uh-MEE-no). There are about 22 different amino acids. They can be combined into millions of different kinds of protein.

The body can manufacture most of the amino acids it needs to build protein. However, nine amino acids cannot be made in the body and therefore must come from the food you eat. These nine amino acids are called *essential amino acids*.

Complete proteins supply all of the essential amino acids. Foods from animal sources, such as meat, poultry, fish, eggs, and dairy products, provide complete protein.

Incomplete proteins are lacking one or more essential amino acids. Foods from plant sources supply incomplete proteins. However, it is possible to obtain all of the essential amino acids by eating a variety of foods from plant sources.

Many dishes from around the world make use of plant proteins. For instance, meals in India often include *dal,* lentils cooked and seasoned in a variety of ways. Lentils, a close relative of dry beans and peas, are an excellent source of plant protein.

For example, dry beans and peas are high in proteins, but they lack certain essential amino acids. Grain products, nuts, and seeds also lack some essential amino acids. However, they provide the ones that dry beans and peas lack. If dry beans or peas and any grain products, nuts, or seeds are eaten during the same day, they provide all the essential amino acids needed for good health. Each supplies what is missing from the other.

Most Americans get the largest amount of their protein from animal sources. Health experts recommend that people get more of their protein from plant sources. Why? Plant sources have less fat, and low-fat food choices are recommended. You will learn more about fat in the next section.

Section 2.2 Review

RECALL THE FACTS

1. List three foods that supply natural sugars and six foods that supply complex carbohydrates.

2. Why is it important to obtain both soluble and insoluble fiber?

3. What is the difference between complete and incomplete proteins?

DISCUSS YOUR IDEAS

4. In general, Americans eat more refined sugar than is needed for good health. What are some possible reasons?

APPLY YOUR LEARNING

5. Think back to the last meal you ate. Which foods supplied carbohydrates? Fiber? Proteins? What types of carbohydrates, fiber, and proteins were they?

Fats

OBJECTIVES

After studying this section, you should be able to:
- Describe the functions and sources of fats.
- Identify three basic types of fatty acids.
- Discuss the effects of cholesterol and the different fatty acids on health.

LOOK FOR THESE TERMS

cholesterol
saturated
polyunsaturated
monounsaturated
hydrogenation

Fats are in the news a great deal these days. You may have heard or read about cutting down on fats. That's sound advice, as you will see. However, even health experts do not recommend that you avoid fats altogether. This section will help you understand fat's role as a nutrient.

Functions and Sources of Fats

Fat is an essential nutrient that has several important functions.
❖ You need some fat in your diet for healthy skin and normal growth. Specifically, your body needs certain substances called *essential fatty acids,* which are found mainly in vegetable oils.
❖ Fat in the body carries vitamins A, D, E, and K to wherever they are needed.

In addition, the body stores fat to provide a reserve supply of energy. This stored fat also acts as a cushion to protect vital organs such as the heart and liver.

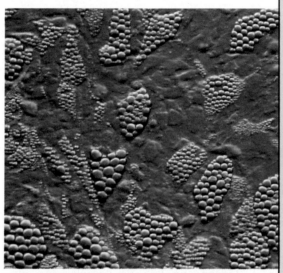

Fat not needed immediately is stored in body tissues for later use. These are fat cells in bone marrow.

Section 2.3: Fats **65**

Teacher's Classroom Resources—Section 2.3

Refer to these resources in the TCR package:

Reproducible Lesson Plans

Student Workbook

Extending the Text

Reteaching Activities

Section Quizzes

Testmaker Software

Color Transparencies

Section 2.3
Fats

Introducing the Section

Motivators
- Ask students to identify sources of fat in the diet. Which of these sources are visible? Which are invisible? Was it harder to give examples of visible or invisible fats? What does this tell you about judging the amount of fat in food? *(Appearance alone cannot be used to judge the amount of fat in a food.)*
- Discuss reasons people are concerned about the amount of cholesterol they consume. What are some reasons for teens to be concerned?

Objectives
- Have students read the section objectives. Discuss the purpose of studying the section.

Vocabulary
- Pronounce the terms listed under "Look for These Terms." Have students find the terms and their definitions in the section.

Guided Reading
- Have students look at the headings within Section 2.3 to preview the concepts that will be discussed.
- Have students read the section and complete the appropriate part of the Chapter 2 Study Guide in the *Student Workbook.*

Teaching . . .

• Functions and Sources of Fats

(text pages 65-66)

Comprehension Check

1. Ask students which substances in fats the human body needs. *(essential fatty acids)*

2. Ask students to list the vitamins that depend on fats for transportation within the body. *(vitamins A, D, E, and K)*

3. Discuss the biggest problem most people have with eating fats. *(They eat too much.)* How can this problem be avoided?

4. Discuss the jobs fat performs, in addition to its major roles of supplying fatty acids and transporting certain vitamins. *(It provides a reserve supply of energy, cushions vital organs, and add flavor to foods.)*

Student Experiences

1. **Poster Project:** Have students work in groups to prepare posters showing or describing the functions of fats in the human body. Display the posters around the school. *(Key skill: creativity)*

2. **Label Analysis:** Provide students with labels from a variety of processed foods. Have students determine the percentage of calories provided by fat for each food. *(Multiply the number of grams of fat by 9 to find the number of calories, then divide by 100.)* Which foods are higher in fat than students anticipated? *(Key skill: analysis)*

Oil, butter, and margarine are obvious sources of fat. However, many other foods also contain high amounts of fat.

Fats also add flavor to food. Because they move through the digestive system slowly, they have satiety (suh-TIE-uh-tee) value. In other words, your hunger remains satisfied for a longer time if you eat foods that include some fat.

The problem with fat is that most people eat too much. Eating too much fat increases the risk of illnesses such as heart disease and cancer. It can also create a health risk by causing the person to become overweight. (Remember, fats have twice as many calories as carbohydrates or proteins.)

Foods high in fat include butter, margarine, oils, cream, sour cream, salad dressings, fried foods, some baked goods, and chocolate. Large amounts are also found in some cuts of meat, nuts and seeds, peanut butter, egg yolk, whole milk, and some cheeses.

Fats cannot be eliminated from the diet completely. However, it is important to moderate, or limit, their use. To cut down on fat, eat more complex carbohydrates and choose low-fat foods. You will learn more about making food choices in Chapters 3 and 4.

Health experts also advise people to pay attention to the types of fats that are eaten. As you will soon discover, some fats create more of a health risk than others.

Cholesterol, Fats, and Health

"My dad is watching his cholesterol." "Brand X oil is high in polyunsaturates." Statements like these can be heard frequently. What does it all mean?

Cholesterol in the Bloodstream

Cholesterol (kuh-LESS-tehr-all) is a fat-like substance present in all body cells. It is needed for many essential body processes. Your body manufactures cholesterol in the liver.

A certain amount of cholesterol circulates in the blood. It does not float through the

More About Essential Fatty Acids

The two essential fatty acids are linoleic acid and linolenic acid. They are called "essential" fatty acids because the body cannot manufacture them, and they are needed to produce various hormones.

bloodstream on its own, but in chemical "packages" called lipoproteins (LIH-po-PRO-teens). There are two major kinds of lipoproteins: LDL and HDL.

❖ **LDL** stands for low-density lipoprotein. The LDL "package" takes cholesterol from the liver to wherever it is needed in the body. However, if too much LDL cholesterol is circulating, excess amounts of cholesterol can build up in artery walls. This increases the risk of heart disease or stroke. Thus, LDL cholesterol has come to be called "bad" cholesterol.

❖ **HDL** stands for high-density lipoprotein. Studies suggest that HDL picks up excess cholesterol and takes it back to the liver, keeping it from causing harm. For this reason, cholesterol in the HDL "package" has come to be known as "good" cholesterol.

Medical tests can determine the amounts of total cholesterol, LDL cholesterol, and HDL cholesterol in the bloodstream. The risk of heart disease is believed to increase if LDL and total cholesterol levels are too high and if the HDL level is too low.

Making wise food choices can help reduce the amount of harmful cholesterol in the bloodstream. As you will see, both cholesterol and fat in foods may affect blood cholesterol levels.

Cholesterol in Foods

In addition to being manufactured in the body, cholesterol is found in some foods. Cutting down on high-cholesterol foods may help reduce the level of harmful cholesterol in the bloodstream.

High levels of cholesterol in the bloodstream can increase the risk of heart disease or stroke. Foods from animal sources contain cholesterol. Limiting how often they are eaten can help reduce cholesterol levels in the blood.

Teaching . . .

- • **Cholesterol in the Bloodstream**
- • **Cholesterol in Foods**

(text pages 66-68)

Comprehension Check

1. Discuss what cholesterol is, its functions, and how it is transported. *(A fatlike substance needed for body processes; transported in the blood in lipoproteins.)*

2. Ask students to explain what LDLs and HDLs are and the differences between them. *(LDL's transport cholesterol to the liver but also allow build-up on artery walls. HDL's seem to help prevent clogged arteries.)*

Student Experiences

1. **Reading Articles:** Provide students with a collection of articles concerning cholesterol, fats, and health. Have each student read one article and summarize it for the class. *(Key skill: reading)*

2. **Cholesterol Analysis:** Provide students with pictures of foods that contain cholesterol. Have students find the cholesterol per serving of each food, then list the foods from least to most cholesterol. What conclusions can they draw? *(Key skill: critical thinking)*

Lab Activity

Have students create their own combinations of reduced-fat potato toppers. Provide toppers such as low-fat plain yogurt, low-fat cottage cheese, green onions, mushrooms, chopped green pepper and tomatoes, shredded carrots, Mexican salsa, sprouts, sunflower seeds, etc. Discuss what makes some combinations more appealing than others.

Thinking Skills

Problem Solving: Ask students to discuss items they could order at a fast-food restaurant to cut down on their intake of fats. If nutrition analysis of menu items are available, ask students to plan a meal that is low in fat and calories. Discuss the ease or difficulty of this activity.

2.3

- **Saturated and Unsaturated Fats**

(text pages 68-69)

Comprehension Check

1. Discuss the difference between saturated and unsaturated fats.

2. Discuss the process of hydrogenation. What does hydrogenation do to liquid fatty acids? *(solidifies them)* Why might such a procedure be performed? *(additional uses in cooking; stick margarine as a butter substitute)*

Student Experiences

1. **Classification:** Display samples of various types of fats. Have students categorize the fats as saturated or unsaturated. *(Key skill: classification)*

2. **Small Group Discussion:** Have students discuss ways to cut down on the amount of total fat, saturated fat, and cholesterol in one's diet. *(Key skill: health)*

Healthy Attitudes

Have students brainstorm other ways in which people can lower their blood cholesterol levels. Make a composite list and post it on the wall of the classroom.

You might also ask a health professional to speak on ways to lower blood cholesterol levels.

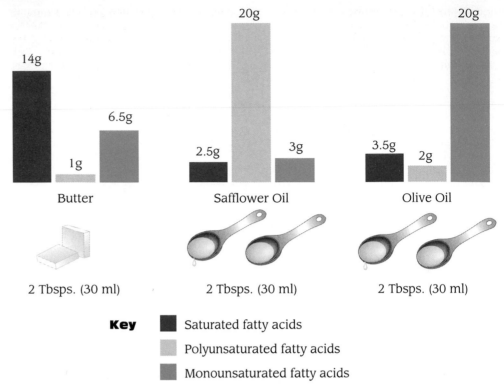

Butter   Safflower Oil   Olive Oil

2 Tbsps. (30 ml)   2 Tbsps. (30 ml)   2 Tbsps. (30 ml)

Key
- ■ Saturated fatty acids
- ■ Polyunsaturated fatty acids
- ■ Monounsaturated fatty acids

Butter, safflower oil, and olive oil each contain all three types of fatty acids. Which is highest in polyunsaturated fatty acids? In saturated fatty acids? Which has the highest amount of monounsaturated fatty acids?

Cholesterol is found only in foods from animal sources. Meat, poultry, and fish all have about the same amount of cholesterol. Foods especially high in cholesterol include liver, egg yolks, and a few types of shellfish.

Saturated and Unsaturated Fats

For most people, the amount and types of fats eaten have an even greater effect on blood cholesterol levels.

The different fats found in food, such as butter, chicken fat, or corn oil, are made up of different combinations of *fatty acids.* There are three basic kinds of fatty acids. Each has a different effect on cholesterol levels. All fats include all three kinds of fatty acids, but in varying amounts.

Saturated (SAT-chur-ay-ted) fatty acids appear to raise the level of LDL ("bad") cholesterol in the bloodstream. Foods relatively high in saturated fatty acids include meat, poultry skin, whole-milk dairy products, and the tropical oils—coconut oil, palm oil, and palm kernel oil.

Polyunsaturated (PAH-lee-uhn-SAT-chur-ay-ted) fatty acids seem to help lower both HDL and LDL cholesterol levels. Many vegetable oils, such as corn oil, soybean oil, and safflower oil, are high in polyunsaturated fatty acids.

Food and Nutrition Science

Chemical Structure of Fats: Fats are sometimes called *triglycerides.* This refers to their structure: three fatty acids attached to a glycerol molecule.

Fatty acids are made up of the elements carbon, oxygen, and hydrogen. These elements are arranged differently in the various kinds of fatty acids. Unsaturated fatty acids have some hydrogen missing from their chemical structure. Depending on the number of hydrogen atoms that are missing, they are either monounsaturated or polyunsaturated. Saturated fatty acids contain as much hydrogen as is possible.

Monounsaturated (MAH-no-uhn-SAT-chur-ay-ted) fatty acids appear to lower only LDL ("bad") cholesterol levels. Foods relatively high in monounsaturated fatty acids include olives, olive oil, avocados, peanuts, peanut oil, and canola oil.

In general, a fat that is solid at room temperature, such as butter or lard, has mainly saturated fatty acids. Fats that are liquid at room temperature, such as vegetable and fish oils, have mainly unsaturated fatty acids.

Vegetable oils can be made solid through a process called **hydrogenation** (hi-DRAH-juh-NAY-shun). Shortening and margarine are examples of hydrogenated fats. The hydrogenation process makes the fat more saturated.

Many people are switching from saturated fats to unsaturated ones in an effort toward better health. They should remember, however, that it's also important to limit the total amount of all fat eaten.

Healthy Attitudes

Besides eating less fat and cholesterol, here are some other health habits that can help lower blood cholesterol levels:

- Eat plenty of soluble fiber (the kind found in dry beans and oats).
- Exercise regularly.
- Maintain a healthy weight.
- Don't smoke.

Section 2.3 Review

RECALL THE FACTS

1. Name two functions of fat.
2. List six foods high in fat.
3. What is cholesterol? Why is LDL cholesterol called "bad" cholesterol?
4. Name three types of fatty acids. Which is considered least healthy? Why? Where is it mainly found?

DISCUSS YOUR IDEAS

5. Suppose you are shopping for peanut butter. One brand has "No Cholesterol" in large letters on the label. The kind you usually buy does not. Would you switch brands? Why or why not?

APPLY YOUR LEARNING

6. Design a magazine ad encouraging people to cut down on fat and cholesterol.

Section 2.4
Vitamins, Minerals, and Water

Introducing the Section

Motivators

- Ask students to name the nutrients that provide energy. List these nutrients (carbohydrates, fats, and proteins) on the chalkboard. Ask students to name other nutrients that are important in the body. List vitamins, minerals, and water on the chalkboard. Point out that while these nutrients do not provide energy, they are equally important for good health.

- Point out that many people think that they can take a vitamin pill and then eat anything they want, without needing to worry about nutrients. They say they are using vitamin pills as "nutritional insurance." Discuss the misinformation behind this thinking.

Objectives

- Have students read the section objectives. Discuss the purpose of studying the section.

Vocabulary

- Pronounce the terms listed under "Look for These Terms." Have students find the terms and their definitions in the section.

Guided Reading

- Have students look at the headings within Section 2.4 to preview the concepts that will be discussed.

- Have students read the section and complete the appropriate part of the Chapter 2 Study Guide in the *Student Workbook.*

SECTION 2.4

Vitamins, Minerals, and Water

OBJECTIVES

After studying this section, you should be able to:
- Identify the types of vitamins and minerals, their functions, and their food sources.
- Explain the importance of water in the diet.

LOOK FOR THESE TERMS

water-soluble vitamins
fat-soluble vitamins
provitamin
macrominerals
electrolytes
trace minerals
osteoporosis

As you have learned, carbohydrates, fats, and proteins are the only nutrients that directly provide energy. However, they are not the only nutrients you need. Vitamins, minerals, and water are just as important.

Vitamins

Although vitamins are needed in very small amounts, they are essential for good health. They help keep your body's tissues healthy and its many systems working properly. They help carbohydrates, fats, and proteins do their work.

Scientists are still learning about the functions of vitamins. Recent studies suggest that some vitamins may protect against illnesses such as heart disease and cancer. More research is needed before scientists can say for certain.

Vitamin C, shown here under a microscope, plays a key role in keeping the body healthy and repairing wounds. Good food sources include citrus fruits, potatoes, and tomatoes.

Teacher's Classroom Resources—Section 2.4

Refer to these resources in the TCR package:

Reproducible Lesson Plans
Student Workbook
Extending the Text

Reteaching Activities
Section Quizzes
Testmaker Software
Color Transparencies

Science Connection

Chemistry:
Chemical Names of Vitamins

When vitamins were first discovered, they were given letter names: vitamin A, vitamin B, and so on. Later, scientists were able to analyze the chemical makeup of the vitamins. For example, vitamin C is ascorbic acid. Today, many vitamins are still commonly referred to by their letter names. Others are known by their chemical names, such as riboflavin and niacin.

■ ■ ■

Types of Vitamins

So far, scientists have identified about 13 different vitamins. **Water-soluble vitamins** dissolve in water. They include vitamin C and eight B vitamins. **Fat-soluble vitamins** dissolve in fat. They include vitamins A, D, E, and K. The charts on pages 72 and 73 list the functions and food sources of these nutrients.

If you eat more fat-soluble vitamins than you need, they are stored in the body's fat and in the liver. The body can draw on these stores if needed. In contrast, water-soluble vitamins remain in the body for only a short time. Therefore, you need them on a daily basis.

A **provitamin** is a substance that your body can convert into a vitamin. An example is *beta carotene* (BAY-tuh CARE-oh-teen). It is used by the body to make vitamin A. Foods high in beta carotene may also help lower the risk of certain types of cancer.

Meeting Your Vitamin Needs

Remember, it's best to obtain vitamins and other nutrients from foods rather than from supplements (unless supplements are advised by a physician). Some vitamins can be found in a wide range of foods. Others are limited to just a few.

Here are some hints for getting the vitamins you need. For more information, refer to the vitamin charts.

❖ Eat plenty of dark green vegetables (such as broccoli and spinach) and deep yellow-orange fruits and vegetables (such as carrots, sweet potatoes, and cantaloupe). These foods are good sources of beta carotene, so they can help meet your need for vitamin A.
❖ Vitamin D is available in fortified milk. It is also made by the body through the action of sunlight on the skin, but this is an unreliable source. If you don't drink fortified milk, be sure to get enough vitamin D from other sources.
❖ Vitamin C occurs only in fruits and vegetables. Be sure to eat some every day.

Foods high in vitamins usually contain substantial amounts of other nutrients as well.

Thinking Skills

Reasoning: Explain that although vitamin D is not commonly found in foods, exposure of skin to sunlight produces vitamin D. Ask students: In what areas of the United States is a deficiency of vitamin D most likely? *(Areas with little sunshine.)*

Teaching . . .

• Vitamins

(text pages 70-71)

Comprehension Check

1. Discuss why vitamins are necessary. With what functions do they help?
2. Ask students to list the fat-soluble vitamins *(A, D, E, K)* and the water-soluble vitamins *(C and B vitamins)*. What is the most important difference between the two kinds of vitamins? *(Fat-soluble are stored; water-soluble are not.)*
3. Which vitamin is found only in fruits and vegetables? *(vitamin C)* What is a good way to get enough vitamin D? *(sunlight or fortified milk)* What foods should you eat to get enough vitamin A? *(dark green and deep yellow-orange vegetables and fruits)*

Student Experiences

1. **Dietary Analysis:** Have students use a computer program to determine whether their food intake for three days is deficient in any vitamins. *(Key skill: computer literacy)*
2. **Favorite Food Sources:** Have students list their favorite food sources of each vitamin and identify vitamins for which they have few favorite food sources. How can they avoid a deficiency of these vitamins? *(Key skill: health)*

Science Connection

Have students find the chemical names of vitamins. Discuss the information, if any, that the chemical name provides. For example, ascorbic acid (vitamin C) is acidic.

■ ■ ■

Teaching . . .

• **Vitamins (Charts)**

(text pages 72-73)

Comprehension Check

1. Ask students to list vitamins that affect the nervous system. What foods supply these vitamins? *(Thiamin, niacin, B₆, B₁₂, pantothenic acid; see chart for food sources.)*

2. Ask students to list the functions performed by vitamin A. If a person had no access to dairy products or liver, how might he or she get enough vitamin A? *(By eating dark green leafy vegetables and deep yellow fruits and vegetables, which contain beta carotene. The body can convert beta carotene into vitamin A.)*

3. Some nutrient advertisements claim that vitamin C can cure a common cold. On what fact might this claim be based? *(Vitamin C helps the body resist infections.)* Why should people not depend on vitamin C to cure a cold? *(The claim has not been proven; megadoses of nutrients can have harmful effects; the "cold" might be something more serious that needs medical treatment, such as bronchitis.)*

Water-Soluble Vitamins	
Vitamin/Functions	Food Sources
Thiamin ❖ Helps turn carbohydrates into energy ❖ Needed for muscle coordination and a healthy nervous system	❖ Enriched and whole grain breads and cereals ❖ Dry beans and peas ❖ Lean pork
Riboflavin ❖ Helps the body release energy from carbohydrates, fats, and proteins	❖ Enriched and whole grain breads and cereals ❖ Milk products ❖ Some vegetables ❖ Dry beans and peas ❖ Meat, poultry, fish
Niacin ❖ Helps the body release energy from carbohydrates, fats, and proteins ❖ Needed for a healthy nervous system and mucous membranes	❖ Meat, poultry, fish ❖ Liver and kidneys ❖ Enriched and whole grain breads and cereals ❖ Dry beans and peas, peanuts
Vitamin B6 ❖ Helps the body use carbohydrates, fats, and proteins ❖ Needed for a healthy nervous system and mucous membranes ❖ Helps protect against infection	❖ Poultry, fish, meat ❖ Dry beans and peas ❖ Whole wheat products ❖ Some fruits and vegetables ❖ Liver
Vitamin B12 ❖ Helps the body use carbohydrates, fats, and proteins ❖ Helps build red blood cells and form genetic material ❖ Needed for a healthy nervous system	❖ Found only in animal foods, such as meat, poultry, fish, shellfish, eggs, and dairy products
Folate *(Folacin, Folic acid)* ❖ Helps build red blood cells and form genetic material	❖ Fruits ❖ Enriched and whole wheat breads ❖ Dark green, leafy vegetables ❖ Dry beans and peas ❖ Liver
Pantothenic acid ❖ Helps the body release energy from carbohydrates, fats, and proteins ❖ Helps the body produce cholesterol ❖ Needed for healthy nerves	❖ Meat ❖ Dairy products ❖ Eggs ❖ Dry beans and peas ❖ Whole grain breads and cereals ❖ Dark green, leafy vegetables
Biotin ❖ Helps the body make fatty acids and use carbohydrates	❖ Dark green, leafy vegetables ❖ Nuts ❖ Liver, kidney ❖ Egg yolk

72   Chapter 2: The Nutrients You Need

More About Vitamin A

For centuries, "dry eye" was a common affliction of malnourished children. The eyes dried and became inflamed, resulting in blindness. In the early 1900s, Dr. Mori, a Japanese physician, cured the disease with cod-liver oil and chicken livers. However, the crucial ingredient remained unidentified.

During World War I, Dr. E. V. McCollum experimented with various diets and discovered that butter cleared up the condition. About the same time, Denmark began exporting all its butter. Danish children drank only skim milk and began to suffer from the eye disease. Danish physician C. E.

Water-Soluble Vitamins (continued)	
Vitamin/Functions	Food Sources
Vitamin C (Ascorbic acid) ❖ Helps maintain healthy capillaries, bones, skin, and teeth ❖ Helps the body heal wounds and resist infections ❖ Aids in absorption of iron ❖ Helps form collagen, which gives structure to bones, cartilage, muscle, and blood vessels ❖ Protects other nutrients from damage by oxygen	❖ Fruits and vegetables, such as citrus fruits, cantaloupes, kiwis, mangos, papayas, cabbage, kale, plantains, potatoes, tomatoes

Fat-Soluble Vitamins	
Vitamin/Functions	Food Sources
Vitamin A ❖ Helps ward off infections ❖ Helps form and maintain healthy skin, hair, mucous membranes, bones, and teeth ❖ Essential for reproduction ❖ Needed for normal vision, especially in dim light	❖ Dairy products ❖ Liver ❖ Egg yolk ❖ Food high in beta carotene (see below)
Vitamin D ❖ Helps the body use calcium and phosphorus ❖ Helps body build strong bones and teeth	❖ Fortified milk ❖ Egg yolk ❖ Fatty fish, such as salmon and mackerel ❖ Liver
Vitamin E ❖ Protects other nutrients from damage by oxygen ❖ Helps form red blood cells and muscles	❖ Vegetable oils ❖ Whole grain breads and cereals; wheat germ ❖ Dark green, leafy vegetables ❖ Dry beans and peas, peanuts ❖ Nuts and seeds
Vitamin K ❖ Necessary for normal blood clotting	❖ Dark green, leafy vegetables ❖ Cauliflower, cabbage, turnips ❖ Egg yolks ❖ Liver
Provitamin/Functions	Food Sources
Beta Carotene ❖ Used by the body to make vitamin A ❖ Protects other nutrients from damage by oxygen	❖ Dark green, leafy vegetables, such as broccoli ❖ Deep yellow-orange vegetables, such as sweet potatoes ❖ Deep yellow-orange fruits, such as mangoes

Section 2.4: Vitamins, Minerals, and Water **73**

Student Experiences

1. **Collages:** Have students work in groups to create collages depicting good food sources of each vitamin. Have groups present their collages to the class. Display the collages in the classroom for future reference. *(Key skill: health)*

2. **Label Reading:** Have students study food labels to determine the percentage of Daily Values or U.S. RDAs for each vitamin provided. Discuss how to use this information in making food choices. *(Key skill: reading)*

3. **Illustrations:** Provide students with line drawings of the human digestive system. Have students use colored pencils to represent fat- and water-soluble vitamins. Use a blue pencil to show that extra amounts of water-soluble vitamins are eliminated in urine. Use a red pencil to show that extra amounts of fat-soluble vitamins are stored in the body's fat and in the liver. Discuss how these facts can help you know how often each type of vitamin must be included in the diet and the effects of consuming too much. *(Key skill: science)*

Bloch read of Dr. McCollum's experiments and cured the disease by feeding the children butter or whole milk.

Meanwhile, fishermen in Newfoundland and Labrador were suffering from night blindness. Some discovered that they could cure the disease by drinking fish-liver oil.

The substance in butterfat was identified as vitamin A, the first individual vitamin to be discovered. Cod-liver oil was found to be the richest available source of vitamin A.

Comprehension Check

1. Ask students to list the three macrominerals and give examples of food sources for each. *(Calcium, phosphorus, magnesium. Examples will vary.)*

2. Discuss osteoporosis and its causes. What can people do to build strong bones and help prevent the development of osteoporosis? *(healthy eating; calcium-rich foods; exercise; avoiding smoking, alcohol, and excess caffeine)*

3. Discuss the function of iron in the body. What are some dietary sources of iron? *(lean red meat, dry beans and peas, dried fruits, dark green leafy vegetables)*

Minerals

Minerals are essential for good health. Most minerals become a part of the body, such as teeth and bones. Others are used to make substances that the body needs.

Types of Minerals

Minerals can be divided into three groups:

❖ **Macrominerals** (MACK-ro-MIHN-uh-ruhls) are needed in relatively large amounts. They include calcium, phosphorus, and magnesium.

❖ **Electrolytes** (ee-LECK-troh-lites) are minerals that work together to help maintain the body's fluid balance. They are potassium, sodium, and chloride.

❖ **Trace minerals** are needed in small amounts, but are just as important as other nutrients. They include iron, copper, zinc, iodine, and selenium, as well as many others. Scientists continue to research trace minerals and their functions.

The charts on pages 76-77 show the functions and food sources of minerals.

Through good nutrition and sufficient exercise now, you can help reduce the risk of osteoporosis later in life. Calcium is a key mineral in building bone mass.

Meeting Your Mineral Needs

Even though some minerals are needed in very tiny amounts, getting the right amount is important to health. For example, getting too much or too little iodine can cause thyroid problems. The thyroid gland, located in the neck, produces substances needed for growth and development. Getting too much sodium, or too little potassium, may be linked to high blood pressure.

Getting the right balance of minerals is not difficult. The key is to eat a wide variety of healthful foods. However, you may need to pay special attention to whether you are getting enough calcium and iron.

Calcium and Strong Bones

As you can see by the chart, calcium has several important functions. One of these is to maintain bone strength. Lack of calcium throughout life is one of the factors that can lead to **osteoporosis** (AH-stee-oh-puh-RO-sis). This is a condition in which the bones gradually lose their minerals, becoming weak and fragile. As a result, posture may become stooped and bones can break easily.

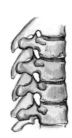

Loss in Height

Normal   **Osteoporosis**

Thinking Skills

Creativity: Ask students to suggest ten ways for people who do not drink milk to increase their calcium consumption. Would their suggestion differ for people of different age groups?

Although it can affect either gender, osteoporosis is most common in women. It's estimated that about 25 percent of women over 65 have osteoporosis.

If you want to reduce your risk of osteoporosis, it's essential that you start now. Bone mass is built up during childhood, the teen years, and young adulthood. The more you do to build strong bones now, the less likely you will be to develop osteoporosis when you are older.

To build strong bones:
* Eat plenty of calcium-rich foods. These include dairy products, dry beans and peas, and dark green, leafy vegetables.
* Follow other basic guidelines for healthy eating. Remember, nutrients work in teams. Many nutrients, such as vitamin D, work together with calcium.
* Exercise regularly. Weight-bearing exercise, such as walking or jogging, helps build and maintain strong bones.

* Avoid smoking, alcohol, and excess caffeine (found in coffee and soft drinks). All may contribute to osteoporosis.

Iron and Red Blood Cells

Iron is essential in making hemoglobin. *Hemoglobin* (HEE-muh-glow-bin) is a substance in red blood cells that carries oxygen to all the cells in the body. If you don't get enough iron, the blood may not be able to carry enough oxygen to the cells. This condition is called iron-deficiency anemia (uh-NEE-me-uh). People with anemia are often tired, weak, short of breath, and pale.

Some sources of iron are lean red meat, dry beans and peas, dried fruits, grain products, and dark green, leafy vegetables. (Other sources are listed in the chart on page 76). Eating foods rich in vitamin C at the same time as iron-rich foods helps the body absorb more of the iron from plant foods. Iron utensils used to cook food are also a good source of iron.

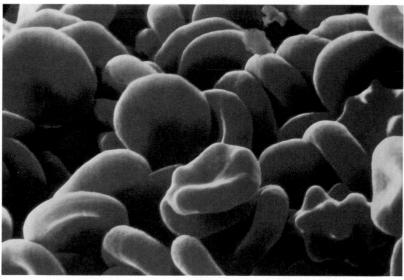

The hemoglobin in blood carries oxygen to the body's cells. Iron from food is needed for the formation of hemoglobin.

Student Experiences
1. **Reading:** Provide students with articles about osteoporosis and its prevention. Have students read the articles and then summarize them for the class. *(Key skill: reading)*
2. **Dietary Analysis:** Have students list what they ate yesterday. Ask students to circle foods that are good sources of iron. Ask students to place a star next to foods that are rich in vitamin C that were consumed at the same time as iron-rich foods. Point out the nutrient teamwork between vitamin C and iron. *(Key skill: analysis)*
3. **Menu Planning:** Have students plan a day's menu that incorporates foods that are high in iron. *(Key skill: creativity)*
4. **Dietary Analysis:** Have students use a computer nutrition program to determine whether their diets are deficient in any minerals. *(Key skill: computer literacy)*

More About Sodium and Potassium

* *Sodium.* Most processed foods contain sodium. When reading food labels, look for the key words "salt" and "sodium" or the chemical symbol "Na" (for sodium). Sodium (or Na) may also appear as part of other ingredient names (such as monosodium glutamate).

* *Potassium.* Fruits and vegetables are the best sources of this vital mineral. Winter squash, black-eyed peas, dried lima beans, and baked potato contain generous amounts. Dried apricots, banana, cantaloupe, oranges, asparagus, and brussels sprouts are also good sources of potassium.

Teaching . . .

• Minerals (Charts)

(text pages 76-77)

Comprehension Check

1. Ask students to list minerals that help the heart work properly. *(copper, selenium, calcium, potassium)* These are critical minerals; yet with the exception of calcium and potassium, they are rarely mentioned in articles about health and nutrition. Ask students why this might be so. *(They are needed only in very small amounts. Anyone who eats a balanced diet is sure to get enough of them.)*

2. Ask students to name minerals that are supplied by dry beans and peas. *(iron, copper, zinc, calcium, phosphorus, magnesium, potassium)* Aside from the protein they contain, why are these good food choices? *(They supply a wide variety of minerals.)*

Student Experiences

1. **Nutrients in Food Charts:** Have students refer to the chart on page 77 to identify good sources of calcium. Have students make a list of calcium-rich foods they consume regularly. *(Key skill: health)*

2. **Research:** Ask students to research the problems caused by deficiency or overconsumption of one of these minerals: calcium, phosphorus, magnesium, chlorine, potassium, sodium, iron, iodine, or zinc. Have the students write a short report on their findings. *(Key skills: research, writing)*

Trace Minerals	
Mineral/Functions	**Food Sources**
Iron ❖Helps carry oxygen in the blood ❖ Helps the cells use oxygen	❖ Meat, fish, shellfish ❖ Egg yolk ❖ Dark green, leafy vegetables ❖ Dry beans and peas ❖ Enriched or whole grain products ❖ Dried fruits
Iodine ❖ Responsible for the body's use of energy	❖ Saltwater fish ❖ Iodized salt ❖ Dairy products ❖ Bakery products
Copper ❖ Helps iron make red blood cells ❖ Helps keep bones, blood vessels, and nerves healthy ❖ Helps the heart work properly	❖ Whole grain products ❖ Shellfish ❖ Organ meats ❖ Dry beans and peas ❖ Nuts and seeds ❖ Potatoes and sweet potatoes
Zinc ❖ Helps the body make proteins, heal wounds, and form blood ❖ Helps in growth and maintenance of all tissues ❖ Helps the body use carbohydrates, fats, and proteins ❖ Affects the senses of taste and smell ❖ Helps the body use vitamin A	❖ Meat, liver, poultry, fish, shellfish ❖ Dairy products ❖ Dry beans and peas, peanuts ❖ Whole grain breads and cereals ❖ Eggs
Selenium ❖ Helps the heart work properly ❖ Protects cells from damage by oxygen	❖ Whole-grain breads and cereals ❖ Vegetables (amount varies with content in soil) ❖ Meat, organ meats, fish, shellfish
Fluoride ❖ Helps strengthen teeth and prevent cavities	❖ In many communities, small amounts are added to the water supply to help improve dental health

More About Electrolytes

When you perspire, you lose sodium, chloride, and other electrolytes, as well as a significant amount of water. Loss of water and electrolytes can results in muscle cramps and dehydration (severe water loss). Several electrolyte replacement products are now on the market to help people who need to replace water and minerals quickly.

The human body can only sweat about 1 liter per hour, and it can keep up that rate for no more than a few hours. If water and essential minerals are not replaced, more serious problems such as heat exhaustion or even heat stroke may occur.

Macrominerals	
Mineral/Functions	**Food Sources**
Calcium ❖ Maintains bone strength; helps prevent osteoporosis ❖ Helps regulate body processes such as blood clotting and nerve activity ❖ Needed for muscle contraction, including the heart	❖ Dairy products ❖ Canned fish eaten with the bones ❖ Dry beans, peas, and lentils ❖ Dark green, leafy vegetables such as broccoli, spinach, and turnip greens ❖ Grain products
Phosphorus ❖ Works with calcium to build strong bones and teeth ❖ Helps release energy from carbohydrates, fats, and proteins ❖ Helps build body cells and tissues	❖ Meat, poultry, fish ❖ Dry beans and peas ❖ Dairy products ❖ Grain products
Magnesium ❖ Helps build bones and make proteins ❖ Helps nerves and muscles work normally ❖ Helps regulate body temperature	❖ Whole grain products ❖ Dark green, leafy vegetables ❖ Dry beans and peas ❖ Nuts and seeds

Electrolytes	
Mineral/Functions	**Food Sources**
Sodium ❖ Helps maintain the fluid balance in the body ❖ Helps with muscle and nerve action	❖ Salt ❖ Many foods
Chloride ❖ Helps maintain the fluid balance in the body	❖ Salt
Potassium ❖ Helps maintain the fluid balance in the body ❖ Helps maintain the heartbeat ❖ Helps with muscle and nerve action	❖ Fruits such as bananas and oranges ❖ Vegetables ❖ Meat, poultry, fish ❖ Dry beans and peas ❖ Dairy products

Section 2.4: Vitamins, Minerals, and Water **77**

Teaching . . .

• Water

(text page 78)

Comprehension Check

1. Discuss the many roles water plays in the body. *(functions in chemical reactions, maintains body temperature)*

2. Discuss why people can live for much longer without food than without water. Why is water so critical?

3. Ask students to explain how much water the body uses each day and list foods and liquids that can help supply the body with water.

Student Experiences

1. **Demonstration:** Weigh a raw potato. Then puree the potato in a food processor. Drain and measure the liquid from the pureed potato. What percentage by weight is the water content? Have students suggest other foods to test for water content. Have students check their results against published references. What might account for any differences? *(Key skill: science)*

2. **Calculating Water Loss:** Have students calculate the amount of water the body uses in one week, one month, and one year, based on an average water loss figure of 2.5 quarts (2.3 liters) per day. *(Key skill: math)*

3. **Research:** Have students find out the water content of several fruits and vegetables and list their findings in a chart. *(Key skills: research, writing)*

Completing the Section

Review

- Ask students to summarize the main ideas in this section.
- Have students complete the Section Review. (Answers appear below.)

Evaluation

- Have students describe what they have learned in this section in a short written essay.
- Have students take the quiz for Section 2.4. (Refer to the *Section Quizzes* booklet or use the *Testmaker Software*.)

Reteaching

- Have students develop a quiz game to review important facts about vitamins, minerals, and water.
- Refer to the *Reteaching Activities* booklet for the Section 2.4 activity sheet.

Enrichment

- Have students research ways the vitamin loss during food preparation and cooking can be minimized. They should present their findings in a poster.

Closure

- Lead a discussion on the importance of eating a variety of healthful foods every day to provide the body with the vitamins and minerals it needs.

Water

Your body needs a regular supply of water to carry on its many life-supporting activities. You may be able to live for weeks without food, but you can live only a few days without water.

About 50 to 60 percent of the body is water. Even your bones contain water. Your blood is 80 percent water.

Water plays a role in the many chemical reactions that constantly go on in the body. It also helps keep your body temperature normal. Think of what happens when you get too warm. You begin to perspire. As the perspiration evaporates into the air, it cools your body.

On the average, the body uses about 2 to 3 quarts (2 to 3 liters) of water a day. To help replace it, be sure to drink about 6 to 8 cups (1.5 to 2 liters) of liquid daily. In hot weather, when you perspire heavily, you might need even more.

Liquids that can help supply your body with water include plain water, fruit juices, milk, and soups. The foods you eat also help meet your need for water. Most foods contain water, with fruits and vegetables having the largest amounts. Watermelon and lettuce, for instance, are about 90 percent water.

Even "solid" foods such as bread and meat contain water. However, you also need to drink plenty of liquids daily.

Healthy Attitudes

Don't wait until you are thirsty to drink water. By the time you feel thirsty, your body may have already lost a quart (liter) of water or more.

Section 2.4 Review

RECALL THE FACTS

1. Which vitamins are fat-soluble? Water-soluble? Why is this distinction important?

2. Why do you need calcium? Iron? What foods provide these nutrients?

3. How much liquid do you need to drink each day to replenish your body's water supply?

DISCUSS YOUR IDEAS

4. Why are trace minerals just as important as other minerals, even though they are needed in such small amounts?

APPLY YOUR LEARNING

5. List ten of your favorite foods. Using the charts in this section, identify the vitamins and minerals they provide.

Answers to Section Review

1. A, E, D, and K. C and the B vitamins; because fat-soluble vitamins can be stored by the body, but water-soluble vitamins can't.
2. Calcium: To build strong bones, help regulate body functions, and aid in muscle contraction; dairy products, dry beans and peas, dark green vegetables. Iron: To help carry and use oxygen; see food sources on page 76.
3. Six to eight cups (1.5 to 2 liters).
4. Answers will vary. Students should realize all nutrients are vital.
5. Answers will vary.

SECTION 2.5

How Your Body Uses Food

OBJECTIVES

After studying this section, you should be able to:

- Outline the process of digestion.
- Explain how nutrients are absorbed, transported, and stored.
- Tell how the body uses food to produce energy.

LOOK FOR THESE TERMS

digestion
esophagus
peristalsis
glucose
glycogen
oxidation
basal metabolism

While you are reading this, your body is busily working. You are inhaling oxygen from the air and exhaling waste products. Your heart is recirculating blood with every beat. In the time it has taken you to read this paragraph, about 100 million of your body cells died and new ones took their place. If you had a meal or snack in the last several hours, your digestive system is breaking down the food into nutrients.

Digestion

The process of breaking down food into usable nutrients is known as **digestion.** It takes place in the digestive system, a long tube that extends from the mouth through the entire body. Here is what happens to food on its journey through the digestive system.

The Mouth

The digestive process starts before you even begin to eat the food. Just smelling and seeing food, or even thinking about it, can start saliva flowing in your mouth. Saliva is the first of many digestive juices that act on food to break it down chemically.

Science Connection

Chemistry:
Enzymes in Digestion

Enzymes are an important part of the digestive process. An *enzyme* helps cause a chemical reaction, but does not actually enter into the reaction. At different stages of the digestive process, specific enzymes go to work to help break down food.

Saliva contains an enzyme called *ptyalin* (TIE-uh-luhn). As food is chewed, ptyalin begins to digest starch, turning it into sugar.

Section 2.5
How Your Body Uses Food

Introducing the Section

Motivator

- Using a wall chart of the digestive system, ask students to list the parts of the body involved in digestion. *(The list should include the mouth, esophagus, stomach, small intestine, and large intestine.)*

Objectives

- Have students read the section objectives. Discuss the purpose of studying the section.

Vocabulary

- Pronounce the terms listed under "Look for These Terms." Have students find the terms and their definitions in the section.

Guided Reading

- Have students look at the headings within Section 2.5 to preview the concepts that will be discussed.
- Have students read the section and complete the appropriate part of the Chapter 2 Study Guide in the Student Workbook.

Teacher's Classroom Resources—Section 2.5

Refer to these resources in the TCR package:
Reproducible Lesson Plans
Student Workbook
Extending the Text
Reteaching Activities
Section Quizzes
Testmaker Software
Food Science Resources
Color Transparencies

Teaching . . .

• Digestion

(text pages 79-81)

Comprehension Check

1. Ask students to describe the two ways in which the mouth participates in the digestive process. *(By producing saliva, a digestive juice, and by grinding the food between the teeth.)*

2. Discuss the importance of chewing food well. What consequences might occur if you do not chew food adequately?

3. Ask students to explain what peristalsis is and its purpose in digestion. *(Peristalsis is the muscular action in the esophagus that moves food into the stomach.)*

4. Discuss the ways in which the stomach breaks food down. *(using gastric juices, peristalsis)*

5. Ask students to compare and contrast the amount of time needed to digest different types of food.

Science Connection

(page 79) Ask a science teacher to demonstrate the effect of ptyalin on a potato or other starchy food.

Digestion begins in the mouth as food is chewed and mixed with saliva.

Food is also broken down physically as your teeth grind it into tiny pieces. Chewing food well is important. It mixes the food with saliva and makes it easier to swallow and digest. Solid food should be chewed until it is the consistency of applesauce.

The Esophagus

Once the food is swallowed, it passes into the **esophagus** (ih-SOFF-uh-gus), a long tube connecting the mouth to the stomach. The muscles of the esophagus contract and relax, creating wavelike movements that force the food into the stomach. This muscular action is called **peristalsis** (PAIR-uh-STALL-suhs).

The Stomach

The stomach is the widest part of the digestive system, a pouch located on the left side of the body inside the rib cage. On the average, it can hold about 2½ pints (1.2 liters) of food.

The walls of the stomach manufacture gastric juices—a combination of acid and enzymes that helps in the chemical breakdown of the food. In addition, the stomach breaks food down physically through peristalsis. The food is churned until it turns into a thick liquid called chyme (KIME).

Different kinds of food take different amounts of time to break down and leave the stomach. Carbohydrates take the shortest amount of time, usually one to two hours. Proteins take longer, about three to five hours. Fats take the longest time to digest, about five to seven hours. That's why a food with fat will keep you from feeling hungry for a longer time.

The Small Intestine

From the stomach, chyme is released into the small intestine a little at a time. The small intestine is a long, winding tube between the stomach and the large intestine. Here, the chyme is acted on by three types of digestive juices:

❖ Bile, a substance that helps your body digest and absorb fats. It is produced in the liver and stored in the gall bladder until needed.

❖ Pancreatic (pan-kree-AT-tick) juice, which contains enzymes that help break down carbohydrates, proteins, and fats. It is produced by the pancreas (PAN-kree-us), a gland connected to the small intestine.

❖ Intestinal juice, produced in the small intestine. This digestive fluid works with the others to break down food.

When fully broken down, carbohydrates are turned into a simple sugar called **glucose.** Glucose, or blood sugar, is the body's basic fuel supply. Fats are changed into fatty acids. Proteins are broken down into amino acids. Vitamins, minerals, and water do not need to be broken down. They can be used by the body in the same form in which they appear in food.

Thinking Skills

Reasoning: Ask students how knowing the length of time carbohydrates, proteins, and fats stay in the stomach could aid an athlete in deciding what and when to eat before a competitive event.

Food and Nutrition Science

Effects of Acids Experiment: See the *Food Science Resources* booklet for the "Effect of Acid on Protein" teaching guidelines and student experiment worksheet. The experiment tests the effects of acids on the physical appearance of proteins.

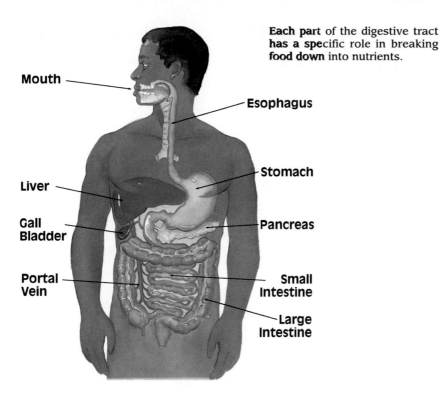

Each part of the digestive tract has a specific role in breaking food down into nutrients.

- Mouth
- Esophagus
- Stomach
- Liver
- Gall Bladder
- Pancreas
- Portal Vein
- Small Intestine
- Large Intestine

Student Experiences

1. **Discussion:** Have students discuss the role the teeth play in digestion. Why is it important for food to be broken into small pieces before it is swallowed? *(Key skill: critical thinking)*

2. **Class Discussion:** Have students discuss what would happen if gravity rather than peristaltic waves directed food from the mouth to the stomach. *(Food might go down too fast. It would stop moving if you were not vertical. It would come back up if you bent over. Astronauts would not be able to digest food in zero gravity.) (Key skill: science)*

3. **Creativity:** Have students write a travel diary of a hamburger's trip through the digestive system. *(Key skills: writing, science)*

Lab Experience

Have students hold small pieces of plain soda cracker on their tongues for 5 minutes. Ask what change in taste occurs. Explain that their saliva is breaking down the starch in the cracker into simple sugars.

Healthy Attitudes

At one time or another, most people have digestive problems. Possible causes include food choices, smoking, and alcohol. Emotions such as worry, fear, anger, and depression can also cause digestive problems.

Here are some guidelines that can help lead to good digestion:

- Eat regular meals every day.
- Chew food thoroughly before swallowing it.
- Relax while you eat.

Negative emotions are one possible cause of digestive problems.

Healthy Attitudes

Have students brainstorm ideas for other guidelines that can lead to good digestion. Then discuss the items on the brainstormed list. Also ask students to identify ways to keep the atmosphere at family meals positive.

Section 2.5: How Your Body Uses Food   81

Food and Nutrition Science

Sphincter muscles: A small, muscular valve, called a *sphincter* (sfink-turr), is located where the esophagus meets the stomach. It works like a one-way gate, letting the food into the stomach but keeping it from being forced back into the esophagus. Another sphincter is located between the stomach and the small intestine.

- **Using the Nutrients**
- **Energy from Nutrients**

(text pages 82-84)

Comprehension Check

1. Ask students to explain the difference between digestion and absorption. *(Digestion breaks foods down into their nutrient components; absorption is the process in which the body takes in the nutrients for future use.)*

2. Discuss the many jobs the liver does. *(turns amino acids into proteins, converts extra glucose into glycogen for storage, stores iron and fat-soluble vitamins)*

3. Ask students to explain what oxidation is and how it is used to supply the body with energy. *(In the body, glucose is combined with oxygen to produce heat and power for the cells.)*

4. Ask students to describe the two basic purposes for which the body uses energy. *(physical activities and automatic processes)*

Using the Nutrients

Once food has been broken down into nutrients, digestion is complete. However, the body still has work to do. It must absorb the nutrients and take them to where they can be used or stored.

Absorption

After digestion, the nutrients are absorbed into the bloodstream. Most absorption takes place in the small intestine. The lining of the small intestine is arranged in folds. It is lined with billions of tiny finger-like projections, called villi (VILL-eye), like velvet cloth or shag carpet. The villi increase the surface area of the intestine so that more nutrients can be absorbed.

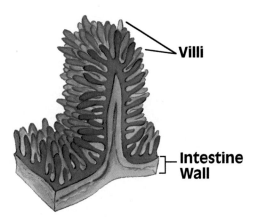

Villi

Intestine Wall

This is a cross-section of the lining of the small intestine. The many small projections, called villi, create a large surface area for absorbing nutrients.

After absorption, some waste material, including fiber, is left in the small intestine. This waste material is moved into the large intestine, also called the colon. The colon removes water, potassium, and sodium from the waste. The remainder is stored as a semi-solid in the rectum (REK-tum), or lower part of the intestine, then eliminated.

Processing and Storing Nutrients

After the nutrients are absorbed by the villi of the small intestine, they are carried through a blood vessel, called the portal vein, to the liver.

One of the liver's many jobs is to turn nutrients into different kinds needed by the body. For instance, it takes amino acids the nturns them into different kinds of proteins. Then the proteins are carried by the blood to wherever they are needed.

Some nutrients, if not needed immediately, can be stored for future use.

❖ The liver converts extra glucose into **glycogen** (GLIE-kuh-juhn), a storage form of glucose. Glycogen is stored in the liver and the muscles.

❖ If there is more excess glucose than can be stored as glycogen, the rest is converted to body fat. Fats are deposited throughout the body as an energy reserve. Excess fatty acids and amino acids are also converted to body fat.

❖ Minerals are stored in various ways. For instance, iron is stored in the liver and in bone marrow.

❖ Fat-soluble vitamins are stored mainly in the liver and in body fat.

Some nutrients, including most water-soluble vitamins, are not stored for long periods. If not needed, they are removed from the body with wastes.

82   Chapter 2: The Nutrients You Need

More About Feeding the Cells

Water and nutrients move into cells through a process called *osmosis*. The cell membrane allows only water and nutrients to pass from the blood into the cell. Waste products pass from the cell into the blood.

To balance fluids and control the flow into and out of cells, the body uses the electrolytes sodium and chloride. An electrolyte is an electrically charged particle called an *ion,* which has either a positive or negative charge. Sodium provides most of the positive ions in the blood. Potassium provides most

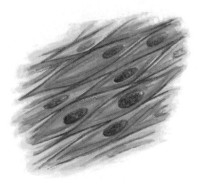

Muscle Cells

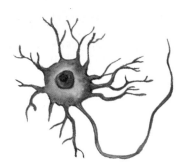

Nerve Cell

Cells differ in appearance. The shape of each type is related to its specialized function.

Red Blood Cells

Feeding the Cells

Nutrients and oxygen are carried throughout the body by the circulatory system. The smallest blood vessels, the capillaries, bring nutrients and oxygen to individual cells. They also remove waste products from the cells.

When they reach the cells, the nutrients are used for their specialized purposes. As you recall, one of these is to provide energy. This is done by combining glucose with water through a process called oxidation.

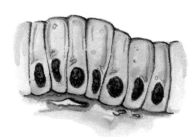

Skin Cells

Student Experiences

1. **Class Discussion:** Discuss why the body stores fat. How is the ability both helpful and harmful? *(The fat cells are the body's main energy reserve. They provide a buffer zone to ward off starvation in times of famine. Since many people no longer experience famine, they seldom dip into their fat reserves. Fat cells accumulate and obesity may result.) (Key skill: critical thinking)*

2. **Creating Models:** Have students create models to illustrate the absorption of nutrients. Have students explain their models to the class. Use the models to create a display on how the body uses food. Place the display in the school library or donate it to a nearby elementary school. *(Key skills: science, creativity)*

3. **Calculation:** Have students find their weight in kilograms (pounds ÷ 2.2 = weight in kilograms). Have them determine their basal energy need (weight in kilograms x 22 [women] or 24 [men] = basal calories needed). Then estimate the percent of basal calories required for their usual activity level (very sedentary, 20%; sedentary, 30%; moderately active, 40%; very active, 50%). Total the calories needed for basal metabolism and activities, then add 10% for specific dynamic effect (SDE: energy expended to digest and absorb nutrients from food) to find total daily energy needs. *(Key skill: math)*

of the positive ions in the cells. When ions are more concentrated in the cells, water and nutrients flow into the cell. When ions are more concentrated in the blood, water and waste products flow out of the cell.

Food and Nutrition Science

Osmosis Experiment: See the *Food Science Resources* booklet for the "Recrisping Celery" teaching guide and student experiment worksheet. The experiment demonstrates the effect of osmosis by placing limp celery stalks in water.

Review

- Ask students to summarize the main ideas in this section.
- Have students complete the Section Review. (Answers appear below.)

Evaluation

- Ask students to prepare a puppet show that explains the processes of food digestion and absorption.
- Have students take the quiz for Section 2.5. (Refer to the *Section Quizzes* booklet or use the *Testmaker Software*.)

Reteaching

- Have students develop a lesson teaching grade school students about digestion. They may use skits, games, or videotapes.
- Refer to the *Reteaching Activities* booklet for the Section 2.5 activity sheet.

Enrichment

- Have interested students research the different enzymes and digestive aids produced by the body and present a five-minute report to the class.

Closure

- Lead a class discussion on digestion and the importance of eating the right balance of foods to aid the digestive process.

Energy from Nutrients

Oxidation is a process in which fuel is combined with oxygen to produce energy. One example of oxidation is a log burning in a fireplace. The fuel in this case is wood. To keep burning, it must have oxygen from the air. Energy is produced in the form of light and heat.

In your body, the fuel is glucose. When glucose reaches the cells, it is combined with oxygen. The result is energy in the form of heat and power for the cells.

As explained in section 2.1, energy supplied by food is measured in calories (actually, kilocalories). The number of calories you need to take in each day depends on how much energy you use.

Your body uses energy for two basic purposes:

❖ **Physical activities,** such as work and exercise. The more active you are, the more energy you use. For instance, you would use more energy walking up a flight of stairs than riding in an elevator.

❖ **Automatic processes** such as breathing, digesting food, and creating new cells. Even when you are resting or sleeping, your body is using energy. This energy is called **basal metabolism** (BAY-suhl muh-TAB-oh-lih-zum).

Generally, about two-thirds of the calories you use are for basal metabolism. However, this varies from person to person. It depends on factors such as age, body size, and body composition (the amount of muscle or fat). The amount of energy used for basal metabolism is sometimes called the basal metabolic rate, or BMR.

As you can see, the human body is an amazing organism. Without your even thinking about it, the body carries on thousands of complex processes every moment. By now you should have a better understanding of how the food you eat provides nutrients and energy to every one of your cells, keeping you alive and healthy.

The energy you need can come only from the nutrients in food. Without good nutrition, you can't do your best.

84   Chapter 2: The Nutrients You Need

Section 2.5 Review

RECALL THE FACTS

1. Summarize the steps in the digestive process.

2. How do nutrients get from the digestive system to the bloodstream?

3. Name two ways in which excess glucose can be stored.

4. What two substances combine to produce energy in the cells? What is this process called?

DISCUSS YOUR IDEAS

5. How might emotions such as worry or fear lead to digestive problems?

APPLY YOUR LEARNING

6. Sketch a design for a poster or bulletin board showing how food is broken down into nutrients and how nutrients travel through the body.

■ Answers to Section Review ■

1. Digestion begins in the mouth (chewing/saliva); food travels through esophagus to stomach (gastric juices/peristalsis); digestive juices in small intestine finish breaking down nutrients.

2. They are absorbed by the villi in the small intestine.

3. As glycogen in the liver and muscles; as body fat.

4. Glucose and oxygen; oxidation.

5. Answers will vary. Students may cite examples such as overeating, losing one's appetite, etc. Point out that emotions and stress can cause the digestive process to slow down or speed up.

6. Students may use a variety of approaches (example: a "road map" with signs to indicate the path taken by food and nutrients).

Career PROFILE

Lisa Yang
Food Scientist

CURRENT POSITION

"I'm a scientist specializing in food research for the U.S. Department of Agriculture."

RESPONSIBILITIES

"My job involves finding ways to increase the nutrition of various foods, such as soybeans and grains."

SKILLS

"Patience is a must in this field, as research can be very time-consuming and sometimes frustrating! You also need a strong background in science."

EDUCATION

"I hold a bachelor's degree in chemistry, and master's and doctoral degrees in food engineering."

WORK ENVIRONMENT

"I spend most of my time running experiments in the lab. Although several scientists may work on the same project, much of my day is spent working on my own. I also spend quite a bit of time documenting my findings."

FAVORITE PART OF THE JOB

"I've always had an inquisitive mind and a love of science, which are perfect for this line of work. I like knowing that my research leads to better tasting and more nutritious foods."

- Does Lisa seem well suited to this job? Why or why not?
- What aspects of Lisa's job do you think you might enjoy? Why?

85

Thinking About . . . Food Science

- Have students think of other questions they would like to ask Lisa Yang about being a food scientist. (Examples: Do you specialize in any particular type of food or food problem? How many hours a week do you work?)
- Ask students to brainstorm a list of the ways food scientists can help people (provide better nutrition, produce better seeds, prevent illness, etc.).

Student Opportunities

Students planning a career in food science or nutrition research should enroll in science and biology classes. For work experience, they should check with local food laboratories for volunteer and employment opportunities. They may also become lab assistants to science teachers in their school.

Occupational Outlook

Most food scientists begin by working in a university, private industry, or nonprofit research foundation. Advancement depends on their education, experience, and quality of their job performance. Food scientists with experience and good job performance may become supervisors of major research programs or may specialize in a certain area of food science.

For More Information

For more information about a career in food or agricultural science, encourage interested students to contact:
- American Society of Agronomy, 677 S. Segoe Rd., Madison, WI 53711
- Office of Higher Education Programs, U.S. Dept. of Agriculture, Administration Bldg., 14th St. and Independence Ave. SW, Washington, D.C. 20250

Review

- Have students complete the Chapter Review. (Answers appear below.)

Evaluation

- Have the students take the test for Chapter 2. (Refer to the *Chapter and Unit Tests* booklet or construct your own test using the *Testmaker Software*.)

CHAPTER 2 REVIEW

■ ANSWERS ■

REVIEWING FACTS

1. Recommended Dietary Allowances; recommended amounts of protein, 11 vitamins, and 7 minerals.

2. Carbohydrates: 55%; protein: 12 to 15%; fat: 30% or less.

3. Starches; in dry beans, peas, and lentils, vegetables such as potatoes and corn, and grain products such as rice, pasta, and breads.

4. Amino acids; because they lack one or more essential amino acids.

5. LDLs (low-density lipoproteins) takes cholesterol from the liver to wherever it is needed in the body; however, excess LDL cholesterol can build up in the arteries. HDLs (high-density lipoproteins) pick up excess cholesterol and take it back to the liver.

6. Corn oil: polyunsaturated; olive oil: monounsaturated; coconut: saturated.

7. It uses beta carotene to produce vitamin A; in dark green and deep yellow-orange fruits and vegetables.

8. Potassium, sodium, and chloride; they work together to help maintain the body's fluid balance.

SUMMARY

SECTION 2.1

The Role of Nutrients: The six major types of nutrients work as a team. Lack of nutrients, or too much of certain nutrients, can result in poor health. Recommended amounts have been established for some nutrients. The energy supplied by carbohydrates, proteins, and fats is measured in calories. Most people do not need nutrient supplements.

SECTION 2.2

Carbohydrates, Fiber, and Proteins: Carbohydrates include starches and sugars. Refined sugars, which are added to many foods, are limited in nutrients. Both soluble and insoluble fiber are important for good health. Complete protein can be obtained by eating animal foods or a wide variety of plant foods.

SECTION 2.3

Fats: Fats perform several important jobs. However, eating too much fat is linked with several health problems. The three types of fatty acids—saturated, polyunsaturated, and monounsaturated—appear to have different effects on blood cholesterol levels. Experts recommend that people limit their intake of total fat, saturated fat, and cholesterol.

SECTION 2.4

Vitamins, Minerals, and Water: Each vitamin and mineral has specific functions and food sources. The body can store fat-soluble vitamins for long periods, but not most water-soluble ones. Some minerals are needed in relatively large amounts and others in very small amounts, but all are important. Every day you must replace the water lost by the body.

SECTION 2.5

How Your Body Uses Food: Digestion is the process of breaking down food into usable nutrients. As food travels through the digestive system, it is broken down by a combination of physical and chemical action. Then the nutrients are absorbed and put to use. Some nutrients can be stored if not needed right away. The bloodstream carries nutrients to all the cells in the body. Glucose and oxygen combine to produce energy for physical activities and basal metabolism.

REVIEWING FACTS

1. What does RDA stand for? What is included in the RDA chart? (2.1)

2. What percentage of daily calories should come from carbohydrates? From proteins? From fats? (2.1)

3. What are complex carbohydrates? In what foods can they be found? (2.2)

4. What are proteins made of? Why are plant proteins considered incomplete? (2.2)

5. What is the difference between HDL and LDL cholesterol? (2.3)

6. Which type of fatty acid is corn oil highest in? Olive oil? Coconut oil? (2.3)

7. How does your body use beta carotene? In what foods is it found? (2.4)

8. Which minerals are electrolytes? What do electrolytes do? (2.4)

9. Name four digestive juices. In what part of the digestive system does each do its work? (2.5)

10. What is basal metabolism? (2.5)

86

9. *Any four:* saliva (mouth); gastric juices (stomach); bile, pancreatic, and intestinal juices (large intestine).

10. The energy a person's body uses when he or she is resting or sleeping.

LEARNING BY DOING

1. **Taste test:** Taste samples of ripe fresh fruits provided by your teacher. Which do you think are highest in natural sugar? (2.2)

2. **Food science lab:** Rub a sample of butter or margarine on a piece of white paper. Label the spot left by the butter. Do the same with samples of ten different foods, such as cheese, a potato, an apple, and a cookie. Let the paper dry for 15 minutes. Which foods left a translucent spot that did not disappear? How does this compare to the spot left by the butter? What do you conclude? (2.3)

3. **Computer lab:** If nutrition software is available, use it to analyze a sample daily menu. How would you rate the menu's balance of carbohydrate, protein, and fat? How would you rate it on vitamins and minerals? After changing some of the foods in the menu, analyze it again. How do the results differ? Why? (2.1, 2.2, 2.3, 2.4)

THINKING CRITICALLY

1. **Recognizing fallacies:** An advertisement claims that a special nutrient supplement will "meet all your daily nutrient needs." What is wrong with this claim? (2.1)

2. **Identifying evidence:** A frozen dinner boasts "only 300 calories per serving." The nutrition information shows that the dinner contains 20 grams of fat. What do you conclude? (2.1, 2.3)

3. **Predicting consequences:** Janine is about your age. She doesn't like milk, and seldom eats vegetables except for corn and potatoes. Unless she changes her eating habits, what health problem is she at risk for? How can she reduce her risk? (2.4)

MAKING DECISIONS AND SOLVING PROBLEMS

What Would You Do?

1. One of your friends often skips meals and fills up on soft drinks, candy, and chips. She says that what she eats doesn't matter because she takes vitamin supplements every day. She encourages you to do the same. (2.1)

2. Your uncle tells you he has decided to increase the fiber in his diet. Since he hasn't eaten much fiber before, he plans to make up for it by eating twice the recommended amount for several days. He asks your opinion. (2.2)

3. The cafeteria supervisor at your school is considering whether to add a salad bar featuring vegetables, fruits, and pasta. Next week, students will be asked to vote on the idea. How will you vote? Why? (2.2, 2.4)

LINKING YOUR STUDIES

1. **Math:** Collect and bring to class three food labels that include nutrition information. Multiply the number of grams of fat by 9 to find the number of calories from fat. Divide by the number of calories per serving, then multiply by 100. The result is the percentage of calories from fat. Compare results with classmates. (2.1, 2.3)

2. **Social Studies/Health:** In regions of the world where food is scarce, certain nutrient deficiencies are common. Using library resources, find information about three specific deficiency diseases. What are the symptoms? How can each be prevented? Treated? (2.1, 2.2, 2.4)

3. **Reading and Study Skills:** Create a game to help you review the digestive process. Be prepared to explain your game to classmates. (2.5)

87

LEARNING BY DOING

1. Encourage students to give reasons for their answers.

2. Answers will depend on the foods used. Students should conclude that those foods that left translucent spots contain fat.

3. Answers will vary. Encourage students to experiment with different food substitutions.

THINKING CRITICALLY

1. Answers will vary. Stress that supplements cannot entirely take the place of good eating habits.

2. Since 180 of the calories in the product come from fat, this frozen dinner is not a diet food, in spite of the low calorie count.

3. Osteoporosis; by including more dairy products in her daily diet and by eating a healthier balance of foods.

MAKING DECISIONS AND SOLVING PROBLEMS

Answers to "Making Decisions and Solving Problems" questions will vary. Encourage students to give reasons for their answers.

LINKING YOUR STUDIES

1. You may wish to have students create a class chart of their findings.

2. To ensure variety, you may wish to assign various deficiency diseases to students.

3. Provide time for students to try their games. Encourage them to take turns trying each other's ideas.

Planning the Chapter

Chapter Overview

Section 3.1: Dietary Guidelines

Section 3.2: The Food Guide Pyramid

Section 3.3: Separating Fact from Fiction

Introducing the Chapter

Motivators

- Have students conduct a brainstorming session to identify their own guidelines for good nutrition. How many servings of different foods do students believe teenagers need?

- Ask students to bring to class articles which give guidelines for good nutrition. Use the articles to create a poster illustrating the types of nutrition information available. Discuss the sources of these guidelines and their reliability.

Teacher's Classroom Resources—Chapter 3

Refer to these resources in the TCR package:

Enrichment Activities

Chapter and Unit Tests

Testmaker Software

CHAPTER 3

Guidelines for Good Nutrition

88

Cooperative Learning Suggestions

Use the Co-op Co-op technique to have students create exhibits illustrating each of the Dietary Guidelines. Group 1: Illustrate nutritious meals that include a variety of foods. Group 2: Show nutritious food choices that would help a person gain or lose weight. Group 3: Show foods that are high and low in fat, saturated fat, and cholesterol. Group 4: Exhibit unfamiliar fruits, vegetables, and grain products. Group 5: Show the amount of sugar in common foods. Group 6: Show processed foods that are high in salt. Have each group present its completed exhibit to the rest of the class and hold a panel discussion on the concepts illustrated.

Dietary Guidelines

OBJECTIVES

After studying this section, you should be able to:

- List six Dietary Guidelines for Americans.
- Tell how each Guideline contributes to good health.
- Describe ways of reducing fats and sodium in your diet.

LOOK FOR THESE TERMS

Dietary Guidelines for Americans

moderation

New discoveries about nutrition and health are constantly being made. To help you take advantage of the latest nutrition knowledge, health experts have developed dietary guidelines—suggestions for making healthful food choices. Following these guidelines can increase your chances of living a long and healthy life.

Dietary Guidelines for Americans

The **Dietary Guidelines for Americans** were developed by the U.S. Department of Agriculture (USDA) and the U.S. Department of Health and Human Services. They include the six guidelines shown in the box on this page.

The Dietary Guidelines for Americans

❖ Eat a variety of foods.

❖ Balance the food you eat with physical activity–maintain or improve your weight.

❖ Choose a diet with plenty of grain products, vegetables, and fruits.

❖ Choose a diet low in fat, saturated fat, and cholesterol.

❖ Choose a diet moderate in sugars.

❖ Choose a diet moderate in salt and sodium.

Teacher's Classroom Resources—Section 3.1

Refer to these resources in the TCR package:

Reproducible Lesson Plans

Student Workbook

Extending the Text

Reteaching Activities

Section Quizzes

Testmaker Software

Food Science Resources

Color Transparencies

Introducing the Section

Motivators

- Create a bulletin board entitled, "You Can Solve the Dietary Puzzle . . . By Following These Guidelines." Label large jigsaw puzzle pieces with the six Dietary Guidelines for Americans. Discuss how each piece of the puzzle increases your chances of living a long and healthy life.

- Ask students to define moderation. Ask them to identify situations in which *moderation* is a good idea. Ask how they think the concept of moderation relates to food choices.

Objectives

- Have students read the section objectives. Discuss the purpose of studying the section.

Vocabulary

- Pronounce the terms listed under "Look for These Terms." Have students find the terms and their definitions in the section.

Guided Reading

- Have students look at the headings within Section 3.1 to preview the concepts that will be discussed.

- Have students read the section and complete the appropriate part of the Chapter 3 Study Guide in the *Student Workbook*.

3.1

Teaching . . .

- **Eat a Variety of Foods**
- **Maintain Healthy Weight**

(text pages 89-90)

Comprehension Check

1. Discuss the relationship between moderation and eating a variety of foods. What is the advantage of eating many different foods in moderation? *(It helps your body get all the nutrients it needs.)*

2. Discuss the health problems associated with improper weight. *(Emphasize that being too thin can be just as harmful as being overweight.)*

Student Experiences

1. **Class Discussion:** We live in a nation of plenty, yet some Americans are malnourished. Discuss why. Relate the discussion to being overweight or underweight. *(Key skill: critical thinking)*

2. **Teenage Diet Analysis:** Have students work in groups to analyze teenagers' diets, based on their own experience. Then have them develop their own list of dietary guidelines for teens. Have each group present its guidelines to the class. Compare the guidelines developed by the groups with the Dietary Guidelines for Americans. *(Key skill: health)*

3. **Research:** Have students research the history of the Dietary Guidelines for Americans. Why were the Dietary Guidelines developed? Who developed them? How can the Dietary Guidelines help Americans improve their diets? *(Key skill: research)*

Eat a Variety of Foods

As you have learned, scientists have identified about 40 different nutrients needed for good health. Many more probably occur in foods but haven't yet been identified. Eating a variety of foods is a good way to get all the nutrients your body needs.

No single food can supply all nutrients in the amounts you need. For instance, sweet potatoes are packed with vitamins A and C, copper, and fiber, but have little calcium or phosphorus. Skim milk is a good source of calcium and phosphorus, but has no fiber and little vitamin C. As you can see, for good health you need to eat a variety of foods.

Moderation, or avoiding extremes, goes hand-in-hand with variety. People often eat a few favorite foods regularly, sometimes in large amounts, and ignore others. Instead, eat moderately sized servings of many different kinds of foods. That way, you'll be getting a wider variety of nutrients for good health.

There are no "bad" or "good" foods. Any food that supplies nutrients can be part of nutritious daily choices. The key is to balance your food choices so that, overall, they lead to good health. Variety and moderation can help you do just that.

Balance the Food You Eat with Physical Activity—Maintain or Improve Your Weight

Achieving and maintaining an appropriate weight is important to your health. That's because your chances of developing a health problem are greater if you are overweight or underweight.

Excess weight is a common problem in the United States. Generally, a few extra pounds are not harmful. Being truly overweight, however, is a health risk. It may contribute to high blood pressure, heart disease, stroke, diabetes, and certain kinds of cancer.

Being too thin can also be a problem. It may mean that you are not eating enough to meet your body's energy and nutrient needs. Some health problems are associated with being underweight.

Maintaining a healthy weight is a balancing act. As you know, food provides energy, and physical activity uses up energy. The key is to balance the energy supplied by the food you eat with the energy your body uses. Chapter 5 will help you learn more about weight management.

Eating a variety of foods in moderation will help insure you get the nutrients you need.

Thinking Skills

Reasoning: Ask students to hypothesize about why researchers have not yet been able to define a healthy weight for individuals. *(Factors such as genetics and bone structure can have an effect on the amount of weight that is considered healthy for a person. Also, the relationship of weight to health risks is still being studied.)*

When planning meals, remember that you need more servings of grain products, vegetables, and fruits than you do of other foods.

Choose a Diet with Plenty of Grain Products, Vegetables, and Fruits

Most of the calories supplied by the food you eat should come from grain products, vegetables, and fruits. They are considered the foundation of a healthful diet for several reasons.

❖ Grain products, vegetables, and fruits are key sources of the carbohydrates your body needs for energy. As you read in Chapter 2, carbohydrates should supply at least 55 percent of your calories.

❖ Dietary fiber is found only in foods from plant sources. Because these foods contain different types of fiber, choose a variety of grain products, vegetables, and fruits to make sure you get the fiber your body needs.

❖ Grain products, vegetables, and fruits are excellent sources of many vitamins and minerals essential to health. Take another look at the vitamin and mineral charts in Section 2.4. Notice how many of the nutrients listed there are supplied by grain products, vegetables, and fruits. Some, such as vitamin C and beta carotene, are found in fruits and vegetables but no other types of foods.

❖ Most grain products, vegetables, and fruits are low in fat. Eating more of these foods can help you cut down on the amount of fat in your diet—as long as you don't add high-fat toppings such as butter, sour cream, or rich sauces.

Get in the habit of eating more grain products, vegetables, and fruits. Think of them as central to your food choices rather than as extras to have "on the side." With so many flavorful choices available, you'll find it an enjoyable habit as well as a healthful one.

Section 3.1: Dietary Guidelines **91**

Thinking Skills

Problem Solving: Discuss why some Americans have better access to fresh fruits and vegetables than others. Who would have the most difficulty obtaining them? What alternatives can students suggest?

Teaching . . .

• **Choose Grain Products, Vegetables, and Fruits**

(text page 91)

Comprehension Check

1. Discuss the reasons why grain products, vegetables, and fruits make a good foundation for daily food•choices. *(They are key sources of carbohydrates, fiber, vitamins, and minerals, and they're low in fat, unless high-fat toppings are added.)*

2. Ask students to give examples of breakfast, lunch, or dinner menus that illustrate this Dietary Guideline. *(Students should suggest menus in which grain products, vegetables, and fruits are present in larger quantities than other foods.)*

Student Experiences

1. Research: Have students report on what the American Cancer Society advises about eating grain products, vegetables, and fruits as a way to reduce the risk of cancer. Are there certain foods that are highly recommended? If so, which ones and why? *(Key skill: reading)*

2. Call an Expert: Have students call the Consumer Nutrition Hotline at 800-366-1655 (weekdays) for information about the Dietary Guidelines or to hear a variety of recorded messages about nutrition. Students may also speak to a registered dietitian or order fact sheets.

Teaching . . .

• Diet Low in Fat

(text pages 92-93)

Comprehension Check

1. Ask students to list the daily percentages of total fat *(30% or less)* and saturated fat *(10% or less)* recommended by the Dietary Guidelines for Americans. Then ask students to comment on reasons why the Dietary Guidelines suggest that people limit their fat intake.

2. Ask students to give examples of ways to lower the amount of cholesterol they consume each day.

3. Foods that are high in fat (or sugar) usually have a lower nutrient density. That is, the nutrients the body receives per calorie decreases. Ask students to explain why this is so.

Suggestions for Lowering Fat		
High-Fat Food	Low-Fat Alternative	Fat Savings
Whole milk (1 cup/250 mL)	Skim milk	8 grams less fat
Fried chicken (3 oz./84 g)	Baked chicken without skin	8 grams less fat
Regular salad dressing (1 Tbsp./15 mL)	Flavored vinegar, lemon juice, or fat-free dressing	9 grams less fat
Potato chips (1 oz./28 g)	Plain popcorn, air popped (1 cup/250 mL)	10 grams less fat
Premium ice cream (1 cup/250 mL)	Low-fat frozen yogurt	20 grams less fat
Cheddar cheese (1 oz./28 g)	Part-skim mozzarella	4 grams less fat
Sour cream on a baked potato (2 Tbsp./30 mL)	Plain nonfat yogurt	6 grams less fat

By becoming more aware of foods high in invisible fats, you can make better food choices.

92   Chapter 3: Guidelines for Good Nutrition

Choose a Diet Low in Fat, Saturated Fat, and Cholesterol

There are several reasons why the Dietary Guidelines encourage people to eat less fat and cholesterol. A high-fat diet is linked with certain kinds of cancer. Fat—especially saturated fat—and cholesterol are linked with increased risk of heart disease. Choosing foods high in fat can lead to overweight.

Health experts have suggested the following goals for fat in making daily food choices:

❖ **Total fat:** 30 percent or less of the calories you eat. (Section 2.1 shows how to calculate the amount of fat that is equal to 30 percent of the day's total calories.)

❖ **Saturated fat:** 10 percent or less of your calories. Remember, the highest proportion of saturated fatty acids are found in animal fats (in meat, poultry, fish, eggs, and dairy products) and in the tropical oils (coconut, palm, and palm kernel oil).

❖ **Cholesterol:** Limit the amount of cholesterol eaten. Only foods from animal sources contain cholesterol.

Visible and Invisible Fats

Studies show that on the average, Americans get 37 percent of calories from fat. Many people are unaware of how much fat is in the food they eat.

Some fat is called *visible fat* because it is easily seen. For example, you can see the butter on a baked potato or the layer of fat around a pork chop. People are usually aware of these sources of fats in their diet.

Much of the fat people eat, however, is *invisible fat*. It is a part of the chemical composition of the food and cannot be seen. Foods such as whole milk, cheese, egg yolks, nuts, and avocado are loaded with invisible fat. So are fried foods and baked goods.

Lowering Fat

Eating low-fat foods can help reduce your risk of health problems. It also allows you to eat more food without increasing your total calories. Remember, a gram of fat has 9 calories, while a gram of protein or carbohydrate has only 4 calories.

It's not difficult to substitute low-fat food choices for high-fat ones. The chart on page 92 gives some examples. As you study this book, you will learn more about choosing low-fat foods and cooking methods.

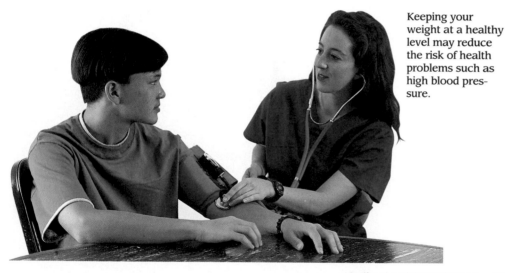

Keeping your weight at a healthy level may reduce the risk of health problems such as high blood pressure.

Student Experiences

1. **Poster Project:** Have students create posters to try to convince people to follow the six Dietary Guidelines. Tell students to be creative and make the posters appealing as well as convincing. Display the posters around the school. *(Key skill: creativity)*

2. **Research:** Have students find and summarize an article on current research theories related to fat, saturated fat, and cholesterol. Ask students to report their findings to the class. Why are health experts concerned about high-fat diets? *(Key skill: reading)*

3. **Substitutions:** Have students identify low-fat substitutions for common high-fat foods other than those listed on page 92. Discuss the effects of cooking method on the amount of fat in foods. *(Key skill: critical thinking)*

Food and Nutrition Science

Invisible Fat Experiment: See the *Food Science Resources* booklet for the "Separating Fat From Cream" teaching guidelines and student experiment worksheet. The experiment demonstrates turning invisible fat into visible fat using agitation.

3.1

- **Diet Moderate in Sugars**
  - **Diet Moderate in Salt/Sodium**
  - **Other Guidelines**

(text pages 94-95)

Comprehension Check

1. Ask students why it is sometimes difficult to know when sugar has been added to a food. *(because of the many ways it may be listed on labels)*

2. Discuss various ways to reduce salt intake.

3. Discuss the possible reasons why more than one set of dietary guidelines exists in the United States. *(Each group has a somewhat different focus.)*

Student Experiences

1. **Display:** Have students research and create a display that uses sugar cubes to represent the amount of sugar in various foods. *(Key skill: science)*

2. **Recipe Search:** Have students find reduced-sodium recipes. What seasonings flavor these foods? *(Key skill: reading)*

3. **Menu Creation:** Have students create a restaurant menu that would allow customers to follow the Dietary Guidelines. *(Key skill: problem solving)*

WORLD of Variety

Ask interested students to research the dietary guidelines produced by countries other than the United States and Japan. Have them share their findings with the class.

Choose a Diet Moderate in Sugars

Natural sugar is a source of energy in many foods, such as fruits and grain products. These foods also provide other nutrients.

The refined sugars that are added to many foods also provide energy. However, they are limited in nutrients. Most healthy people should use only moderate amounts of these sugars. Very active people with high energy needs may be able to use more, as long as their food choices are nutritious ones. People with low energy needs should use refined sugars in very small amounts.

You probably expect to find sugar in foods such as candy, desserts, and baked goods. Other foods, such as cold cuts, ketchup, and peanut butter, may also contain refined sugar as a flavoring. Because there are many different kinds of sugars, you may not be aware that the product you are buying is sweetened. Here are some of the different sugars that may appear on food labels:

- sucrose
- raw sugar
- dextrose
- maltose
- honey
- corn sweetener
- high-fructose corn syrup
- fruit juice concentrate
- brown sugar
- glucose
- fructose
- lactose
- syrup
- molasses

Unsalted, air-popped popcorn is a healthful alternative to snack foods high in fat, sugar, and sodium.

Choose a Diet Moderate in Salt and Sodium

Table salt contains sodium and chloride, both of which are essential nutrients. Most people, however, eat more salt and sodium than they need for good health. Salt is added to most foods and beverages during processing. Many foods also contain natural amounts of sodium.

Excess sodium in food choices has been associated with high blood pressure. People can lower their risk of getting high blood pressure by eating less salt and sodium. Here are some hints for cutting down on salt and sodium:

- Add little, if any, salt to food when cooking and at the table.
- Choose salted snacks, such as chips, crackers, pretzels, and nuts, only occasionally.
- Go easy on processed foods. They generally have more sodium than fresh ones.
- Check labels for the amount of sodium in foods. Choose those lower in sodium most of the time.

Food and Nutrition Science

Cereal Experiment: Conduct a blind taste text of six to eight breakfast cereals with varying sugar contents. Ask students to rank them according to sugar content. Have students compare their perception of sweetness to the information on the box labels. How well do they correspond? Ask students to write a summary of their experiment and discuss their conclusions based on their findings.

Other Nutrition Guidelines

The U.S. government is not alone in issuing recommendations for healthful eating. For example, the National Cancer Institute and the American Cancer Society have issued dietary guidelines that focus on reducing cancer risk. These guidelines give much the same message as the Dietary Guidelines for Americans. They include recommendations to avoid obesity, eat less fat, and eat more fruits, vegetables, and whole grains. In addition, they recommend that people eat fewer smoked, salt-cured, and nitrate-cured foods, such as bacon and some cold cuts.

Dietary guidelines give you goals to help you improve your health. In the next section, you will learn about the Food Guide Pyramid, a tool that can help you meet your goal of good nutrition.

In Japan, the Ministry of Health and Welfare has issued "Dietary Guidelines for Health Promotion." The guidelines recommend that people eat a variety of foods, at least 30 or more different kinds daily. They also emphasize weight management and cutting down on total fat, saturated fats, and salt. One guideline states, "Make all activities pertaining to food and eating pleasurable ones." It encourages Japanese families to sit down to meals together and to enjoy traditional home-cooked dishes.

Making healthier choices doesn't mean giving up all the foods you enjoy. Frozen yogurt, for example, is as satisfying as ice cream—with significantly less fat.

Section 3.1 Review

RECALL THE FACTS

1. What are the six Dietary Guidelines for Americans discussed in this section?

2. Why must you eat a variety of foods for good health?

3. What is meant by "invisible fat"? Name three foods in which it is found.

4. List five examples of different sugars that may appear on food labels.

DISCUSS YOUR IDEAS

5. Which Dietary Guideline do you think is hardest for most people to follow? Why?

6. Discuss the fifth dietary guideline issued by the Japanese government: "Make all activities pertaining to food and eating pleasurable ones." Why do you think this was included?

APPLY YOUR LEARNING

7. Choose one Dietary Guideline and list five to ten suggestions for helping people to follow it.

Section 3.1: Dietary Guidelines   95

Introducing the Section

Motivator

- Referring to the Food Guide Pyramid, ask students to name foods that are high in calories and foods that are low in calories in each groups. Which of the high-calorie foods named are high in sugar? in fat? Explain that low- or moderate-calorie foods provide more important nutrients for the number of calories than their high-calorie counterparts. This means they are more nutrient-dense.

Objectives

- Have students read the section objectives. Discuss the purpose of studying the section.

Vocabulary

- Pronounce the terms listed under "Look for These Terms." Have students find the terms and their definitions in the section.

Guided Reading

- Have students look at the headings within Section 3.2 to preview the concepts that will be discussed.

- Have students read the section and complete the appropriate part of the Chapter 3 Study Guide in the *Student Workbook.*

SECTION 3.2

The Food Guide Pyramid

OBJECTIVES

After studying this section, you should be able to:

- Describe the food groups in the Food Guide Pyramid.
- Give guidelines for using the Food Guide Pyramid to plan daily food choices.

LOOK FOR THESE TERMS

Food Guide Pyramid
nutrient-dense

You probably grew up learning about the "four food groups." Did you know that there are now five food groups?

Over the years, different food group systems have served as tools for planning nutritious meals. Foods are placed in groups based on the major nutrients they contain. Choosing foods from each group gives you a variety of flavorful, nutritious foods every day.

As nutrition knowledge changes, food group systems have also changed. In 1992, the U.S. Department of Agriculture unveiled a food group system called the **Food Guide Pyramid.**

Understanding the Pyramid

The Food Guide Pyramid is designed to help you follow the Dietary Guidelines for Americans. It guides you toward eating a variety of foods in moderate amounts, including plenty of grains, vegetables, and fruits.

The Food Guide Pyramid includes five food groups:

- ❖ Bread, Cereal, Rice, and Pasta Group.
- ❖ Vegetable Group.
- ❖ Fruit Group.
- ❖ Milk, Yogurt, and Cheese Group.
- ❖ Meat, Poultry, Fish, Dry Beans, Eggs, and Nuts Group.

A pyramid shape was chosen to illustrate how each food group fits into a healthful eating plan. Look at the illustration of the Pyramid on page 97. As you can see, foods are arranged in the Pyramid according to the recommended number of servings. For instance, the Bread, Cereal, Rice, and Pasta

---

Teacher's Classroom Resources—Section 3.2

Refer to these resources in the TCR package:

Reproducible Lesson Plans	*Reteaching Activities*
Student Workbook	*Section Quizzes*
Extending the Text	*Testmaker Software*
	Color Transparencies

Food Guide Pyramid
A Guide to Daily Food Choices

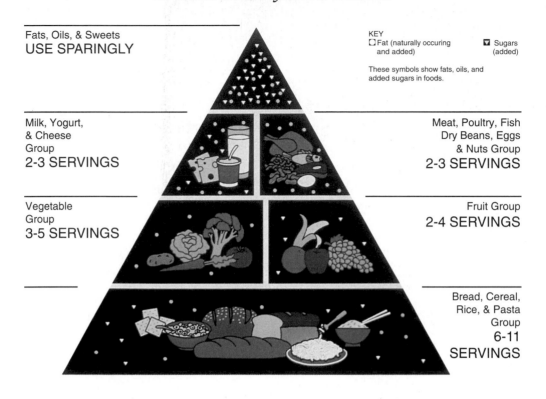

Fats, Oils, & Sweets
USE SPARINGLY

KEY
□ Fat (naturally occuring and added)   ▼ Sugars (added)

These symbols show fats, oils, and added sugars in foods.

Milk, Yogurt, & Cheese Group
2-3 SERVINGS

Meat, Poultry, Fish Dry Beans, Eggs & Nuts Group
2-3 SERVINGS

Vegetable Group
3-5 SERVINGS

Fruit Group
2-4 SERVINGS

Bread, Cereal, Rice, & Pasta Group
6-11 SERVINGS

Keeping the Food Guide Pyramid in mind can help you balance your daily food intake. Which three food groups have the highest number of recommended daily servings?

Group is located at the base of the Pyramid—the largest section—because you need more servings from this group than any of the others.

In addition to the five food groups, the Pyramid includes a section labeled "Fats, Oils, and Sweets." Foods in this category include salad dressings and oils, cream, butter, margarine, refined sugars, soft drinks, candies, and sweet desserts. These foods provide calories from fat and sugar, but little or no vitamins and minerals. Fats and sweets are placed at the small tip of the Pyramid to show that they should be used sparingly.

Section 3.2: The Food Guide Pyramid   97

Teaching . . .

• Understanding the Pyramid

(text pages 96-98)

Comprehension Check

1. Ask students to explain why the "four food groups" used previously has been changed to the "Food Guide Pyramid."

2. Ask students to list the five food groups contained in the Food Guide Pyramid. *(See illustration.)*

3. Ask students to describe how fats and sugars are represented on the Pyramid diagram and discuss why this is necessary. *(Fats are indicated by small circles and sugars by small triangles.)*

Student Experiences

1. **Food Guide History:** Have students trace the history of food guides in the United States. What changes have been made in the food guides as nutritionists learned more about the role of food in good health? *(Key skill: social studies)*

2. **Class Discussion:** Have students study the Food Guide Pyramid. Discuss how the Pyramid graphically depicts the importance of each food group and reminds people to beware of foods that are high in fat and added sugar within each group. *(Key skill: understanding graphics)*

Special Needs Strategies

Learning Disabled: Provide students with pictures of a variety of foods pasted on half-sheets of construction paper. Create a poster-size food pyramid. Have students practice placing the pictures on the correct section of the food pyramid by food group. Using the same pictures, have students practice separating foods that are high in fats, sugars, and calories from those that are nutrient-dense. Also, use the pictures to help students plan meals that meet the Dietary Guidelines for Americans.

Comprehension Check

1. Discuss why it is important to select nutrient-dense foods from the Food Guide Pyramid.

2. Ask students to list foods contained in the Bread, Cereal, Rice, and Pasta Group.

3. Ask students to describe the benefits the body receives from foods in the Vegetable Group. *(vitamins, minerals, fiber, complex carbohydrates)*

4. Discuss the recommended number of servings for the Bread, Cereal, Rice, and Pasta Group *(6 to 11)* and the Vegetable Group *(3 to 5)*. Why does the recommended number of servings vary? *(depends on individual needs)*

5. Ask students to discuss the meaning of "one serving" as it applies to fruits, vegetables, and meats.

6. Ask students to explain why certain groups of people may need more than the standard two servings of milk products each day. *(Discuss teens, young adults, and pregnant or breastfeeding women.)*

On the Pyramid diagram, fats are represented by small circles, and added sugars by small triangles. Notice that these symbols appear not only at the tip of the Pyramid, but also within the food groups. This is to remind you that fats and added sugars can be found in some of the foods within each group.

Using the Pyramid

Now that you are familiar with the basics of the Pyramid, here are some guidelines for putting it to use.

Choosing Nutrient-Dense Foods

Within each food group, there is a wide assortment of foods. They differ in nutrients and calories. Spinach, for example, has more vitamins and minerals than iceberg lettuce. French fries have more fat and calories than a plain baked potato. Peaches canned in syrup have more sugar and calories than fresh peaches.

A food that is low or moderate in calories, yet rich in important nutrients, is said to be **nutrient-dense.** Generally, nutrient-dense foods are low in fats and added sugars. Instead, they supply other nutrients such as complex carbohydrates (starches), fiber, proteins, vitamins, and minerals.

When selecting foods from the food groups, choose nutrient-dense ones. That way, you can get the important nutrients you need without getting more calories, fat, and sugar than you need. Later in this section, and throughout the book, you will find hints for choosing foods from the Pyramid. You may also want to use the chart at the back of this book, "Nutritive Value in Foods," to compare the calories and nutrients in different foods.

The Food Groups

All five food groups are important to health. Each provides some, but not all, of the nutrients you need. One group cannot replace another. You need a variety of food from the food groups each day.

Bread, Cereal, Rice, and Pasta Group

This group includes all kinds of grain products. They supply complex carbohydrates, fiber, vitamins, and minerals.

You need six to eleven servings from this group every day. Some examples of a serving are:

* 1 slice bread.
* 1 ounce (28 g) ready-to-eat cereal.
* 1/2 cup (125 mL) cooked cereal, rice, or pasta.

To get the fiber you need, choose as many whole grain foods as you can, such as whole wheat bread and whole grain cereals. This group includes many low-fat choices, but also some higher-fat ones, such as croissants and other baked goods.

Vegetable Group

Vegetables provide beta carotene, which your body uses to make vitamin A. They also supply vitamin C, folate (a B vitamin), and minerals such as magnesium and iron. They provide fiber and complex carbohydrates and are low in fat.

More About Food Group Systems

Different countries have developed their own food group systems. For instance, a German health newsletter outlines seven food groups. Five of them are similar to the food groups in the Pyramid, except that potatoes are placed in the same group with grain products. There is also a fat group and a "miscellaneous" group.

You should have three to five servings of vegetables daily. Each of the following counts as one serving:

- ❖ 1 cup (250 mL) raw leafy vegetables.
- ❖ 1/2 cup (125 mL) other vegetables, cooked or chopped raw.
- ❖ 3/4 cup (175 mL) vegetable juice.

Different types of vegetables provide different nutrients. For variety, include dark green, leafy vegetables, such as kale; deep yellow-orange vegetables, such as sweet potatoes; starchy vegetables, including corn, peas, and potatoes; dry beans and peas; and others.

Fruit Group

Fruits provide important amounts of beta carotene, vitamin C, and potassium. Edible skins are good sources of fiber. Like vegetables, most fruits are low in fat and sodium.

You need two to four servings of fruit every day. One serving equals:

- ❖ 1 medium fruit such as an apple, banana, or orange.
- ❖ 1/2 cup (125 mL) chopped, cooked, or canned fruit.
- ❖ 3/4 cup (175 mL) fruit juice.

Be sure to have fruits rich in vitamin C regularly, such as citrus fruits, melons, and berries. Eat whole fresh fruits often for the fiber they provide. When choosing canned or frozen fruits, look for products without added sugar. Count only 100 percent fruit juices as a serving of fruit.

Milk, Yogurt, and Cheese Group

Foods in the milk group are high in protein, vitamins, and minerals. They are also one of the best sources of calcium.

Most adults need two servings of milk products daily. Three servings are recommended for pregnant or breastfeeding women, teens, and young adults up to age 24. One serving equals:

- ❖ 1 cup (250 mL) milk or yogurt.
- ❖ 1½ ounces (42 g) natural cheese.
- ❖ 2 ounces (56 g) process cheese.

Low-fat choices from this group include skim milk, nonfat yogurt, and nonfat dry milk. Go easy on high-fat cheese and ice cream. Remember, too, that some milk products, such as flavored yogurt, contain added sugar.

Meat, Poultry, Fish, Dry Beans, Eggs, and Nuts Group

This group is an important source of protein, vitamins, and minerals. Two to three daily servings are recommended.

- ❖ 2 to 3 ounces (56 to 85 g) of cooked lean meat, poultry, or fish equals one serving. This is about the size of an average hamburger or the amount of meat in half a medium chicken breast.
- ❖ Each of the following portions is the equivalent of 1 ounce (28 g) of meat: 1/2 cup (125 mL) cooked dry beans; one egg; or 2 tablespoons (30 mL) peanut butter.

The total of your daily servings should be the equivalent of 5 to 7 ounces (140 to 196 g) of cooked lean meat, poultry, or fish. For instance, you might eat one egg for breakfast, a cup of cooked dry beans in bean soup for lunch, and a lean hamburger for dinner. These foods would give you the equivalent of 6 ounces (168 g) of meat.

To limit the fat in your diet, select lean meats, fish, and poultry without skin. Have dry beans and peas often—they are high in fiber and low in fat. Go easy on eggs, nuts, and seeds. Eggs are high in cholesterol; nuts and seeds are high in fat.

Student Experiences

1. **Class Survey:** Have each student write down the number of servings of vegetables eaten the previous day. Calculate the class average. How does this average compare to the servings suggested in the Pyramid? *(Key skill: math)*

2. **Menu Evaluation:** Distribute copies of the school cafeteria's weekly menu to students. Have them label each food according to the food group(s) represented: G = grain products (bread, cereal, rice, pasta); V = vegetables; F = fruits; D = dairy foods; and M = meat, poultry, fish, dry beans, eggs, and nuts. Are the meals nutritionally balanced? *(Key skill: analysis)*

3. **Food Comparisons:** Have students develop charts comparing the nutrient density of different foods. Have students present their charts as reminders of the importance of choosing nutrient-dense foods. *(Key skill: analysis)*

Lab Experience

Have students prepare recipes that use a mixture of nutritious ingredients. Recipes might include stir-fried dishes, quick breads, and mixed fruit dishes.

Thinking Skills

Reasoning: Ask students what might happen to a person who regularly eats foods high in calories and low in nutrient density. *(The person could become both overweight and malnourished.)*

3.2

Teaching . . .

• The Food Guide Pyramid

(text pages 100-101)

Comprehension Check

1. Discuss the nutrients provided by foods in the Fruit Group. *(beta carotene, vitamin C, potassium)* What is the advantage of eating the skins of some fruits? *(good sources of fiber)*

2. Ask students to list low-fat foods in the Milk, Yogurt, and Cheese Group. *(skim milk, nonfat dry milk, nonfat yogurt)*

3. Ask students to explain the advantage of including dry beans and peas in their protein intake on a regular basis. *(They are low in fat but high in fiber.)*

Student Opportunities

1. **Food Record:** Have students keep a record of the foods they eat for two days. Have them determine how many servings of each of the food groups they have eaten. Ask students to count the number of different foods they ate each day. Did their diets include a variety of foods as well as foods in each food group? Ask them to make suggestions for improving their food intake. *(Key skill: math)*

2. **Food Display:** Ask students to bring empty bread, cereal, rice, and pasta containers from home. Ask them to define terms such as *fortified* and *enriched* found on the labels. Have them recommend a serving size for each item. *(Key skill: reading)*

▲ **Milk, Yogurt, and Cheese Group**
Foods in the milk group are high in protein, vitamins, and minerals and are one of the best sources of calcium. (top left)

▲ **Meat, Poultry, Fish, Dry Beans, Eggs, and Nuts Group**
This group is an important source of protein, vitamins, and minerals. (bottom left)

▲ **Vegetable Group**
Vegetables provide beta carotene, vitamin C, folate and minerals such as magnesium and iron. They provide fiber and complex carbohydrates and are low in fat. (bottom right)

100   Chapter 3: Guidelines for Good Nutrition

Food and Nutrition Science

Alternative Nutrient Sources: Ask students which other food groups include nutrients provided by the Meat, Poultry, Fish, Dry Beans, Eggs, and Nuts Group. *(The Milk, Yogurt, and Cheese Group provides protein; the Fruit Group and Vegetable Group provide iron and B vitamins; the Bread, Cereal, Rice, and Pasta Group provides iron and B vitamins.)* Ask students to discuss the advantages of knowing this. *(It can help them make substitutions when necessary without compromising nutrient intake.)*

▲ Fruit Group
Fruits provide important amounts of beta carotene, vitamin C, potassium, and fiber. (right)

▲ Bread, Cereal, Rice, and Pasta Group
This group includes all kinds of grain products. They supply complex carbohydrates, fiber, vitamins, and minerals. (bottom right)

▲ Fats, Oils, and Sweets
Use these foods sparingly. They provide calories from fat and sugar, but little or no vitamins and minerals. (bottom left)

Section 3.2: The Food Guide Pyramid   101

Teaching . . .

• How Many Servings for You?
(text page 102)

Comprehension Check

1. Discuss the range of servings recommended in the Food Guide Pyramid for each food group. What groups of people should eat servings near the top of the serving range? Near the bottom of the serving range? Why?

2. Ask students to explain why it is important for people to know how much of a food, such as spaghetti, is present on a plate of food. *(The serving size might not correspond to the serving size referred to in the Pyramid.)*

Student Experiences

1. **Class Discussion:** Discuss the importance of understanding that many foods (such as tacos) contain servings from more than one food group. Have students create a list of these foods and discuss how many servings from each group are present in each food. *(Key skill: analysis)*

2. **Research:** Divide the class into groups. Provide each group with a meal plan for a meal from another country. Ask students to find out what food groups make up each food, and how many servings of each food group are included in the meal. *(Key skills: research, multicultural awareness)*

See Also . . .
- Section 5.2: "Weight Management," page 143.
- Section 4.2: "Improving Your Eating Habits," page 118.

Completing the Section

Review

- Ask students to summarize the main ideas in this section.
- Have students complete the Section Review. (Answers appear below.)

Evaluation

- Have students write an essay about the topics covered in this section.
- Have students take the quiz for Section 3.2. (Refer to the *Section Quizzes* booklet or use the *Testmaker Software*.)

Reteaching

- Distribute menus for meals in which one of the food groups is missing. Ask students how they would change each menu to make it nutritionally balanced.
- Refer to the *Reteaching Activities* booklet for the Section 3.2 activity sheet.

Enrichment

- Have students design a poster, handout, or other educational aid showing how the Food Guide Pyramid applies to senior citizens. Have them present their project to a local senior citizens' center.

Closure

- Lead a discussion about the Food Guide Pyramid and the choices that people can make within its guidelines to eat nutritiously.

How Many Servings for You?

As you have seen, the Food Guide Pyramid does not give an exact number of servings for each group. Instead, it gives a range, such as three to five servings of vegetables. This is because people have different needs for calories and nutrients, depending on their age, gender, body size, and activity level.

In general, most teenage boys need the highest number of servings from each food group. For most teenage girls, the middle number of servings (such as nine servings from the bread group) is about right. However, all teens need three servings from the milk group.

You may be used to eating amounts of food that are larger or smaller than what the Food Guide Pyramid considers a serving. For example, if you eat 1 cup (250 mL) of cooked spaghetti, remember to count that as two servings from the bread group, not one.

Some foods include ingredients from more than one food group. If you're eating tacos, you would have servings from the bread group (taco shell), meat group (meat or bean filling), milk group (cheese), and vegetable group (lettuce and tomatoes). Depending on the amounts of the different fillings, you might have full or half servings from the different groups.

The Food Guide Pyramid makes it easy to plan for good nutrition. It is a valuable tool for getting all the nutrients you need in their proper balance.

Healthy Attitudes

The Food Guide Pyramid differs in several ways from the four food groups that were used earlier:

- Fruits and vegetables are placed in separate groups rather than combined.
- The number of recommended servings for fruits, vegetables, and grain products has been increased.
- The Pyramid places more emphasis on making low-fat choices.

All of these changes reinforce the Dietary Guidelines for Americans.

■ Section 3.2 Review ■

RECALL THE FACTS

1. List the five food groups in the Food Guide Pyramid. Give the range of recommended daily servings for each.
2. What does "nutrient-dense" mean? How does it relate to choosing foods from the Pyramid?
3. For each food group, give two examples of serving sizes.

DISCUSS YOUR IDEAS

4. Do you feel the pyramid design is an effective way to get the desired nutrition message across? Why or why not?

APPLY YOUR LEARNING

5. Name two combination foods (other than tacos). List the food groups that are represented by the food's ingredients.
6. Make up a one-day menu that provides the recommended servings from the Food Guide Pyramid for a female teen.

■ Answers to Section Review ■

1. See the Pyramid diagram on page 97.
2. Nutrient-dense means that a food is low or moderate in calories, yet rich in important nutrients.

Choose nutrient-dense foods from the Pyramid.
3. Examples will vary but should be found on pages 98-99 of the text.

4. Answers will vary. Ask students to support their answers.
5. Answers will vary.
6. Answers will vary.

Separating Fact from Fiction

OBJECTIVES

After studying this section, you should be able to:

- Explain how to evaluate advertisements, news reports, and other information related to foods and nutrition.
- Name reliable sources of nutrition information.

LOOK FOR THESE TERMS

critical thinking
quacks
study
myths

"Fish oil prevents heart attacks," exclaimed newspaper headlines in the mid 1980s. Studies of populations that eat large amounts of oily fish, such as natives of the North Arctic, Japan, and Greenland, showed low blood cholesterol levels and few heart attacks. Omega-3 (oh-MAY-guh-3) fatty acids were identified as the "magic" ingredient in the fat.

Almost immediately, omega-3 fatty acids were available in capsules and advertised as a cure for high blood cholesterol levels. Later studies were conflicting. Some verified the original report, but others raised many questions. In 1990, the Food and Drug Administration (FDA) banned the capsule manufacturers from making any health claims for omega-3 fatty acids. According to FDA, there was not enough scientific evidence to support the health claims on fish oils.

This is but one example of confusing nutrition claims. How can you, as a consumer, determine the facts behind the claims? Start by thinking carefully about what you see and hear.

When it was reported that the oil in fish might reduce cholesterol, consumption of fish and fish oil increased sharply. For centuries, native peoples of the Arctic have relied on fish, like these dried salmon, as a main source of food. However, no one factor is responsible for their health.

Section 3.3
Separating Fact from Fiction

Introducing the Section

Motivator

- Bring to class articles and advertisements that represent misleading nutrition claims. Ask students to look for clues in the articles that would help them separate fact from fiction.

Objectives

- Have students read the section objectives. Discuss the purpose of studying the section.

Vocabulary

- Pronounce the terms listed under "Look for These Terms." Have students find the terms and their definitions in the section.

Guided Reading

- Have students look at the headings within Section 3.3 to preview the concepts that will be discussed.
- Have students read the section and complete the appropriate part of the Chapter 3 Study Guide in the *Student Workbook.*

Teacher's Classroom Resources—Section 3.3

Refer to these resources in the TCR package:

Reproducible Lesson Plans
Student Workbook
Extending the Text

Reteaching Activities
Section Quizzes
Testmaker Software
Color Transparencies

Comprehension Check

1. Ask students to list techniques advertisers use to convince people to buy their products. *(Answers may include limited information, positive images, appeals to basic needs, and use of celebrities.)*

2. Discuss questions people can ask themselves when they're evaluating an advertising or promotional campaign.

3. Ask students to define the terms quack and fraud. *(Quacks make misleading or incorrect claims but may actually believe the claims they make; frauds do so for the single purpose of making money.)*

4. Ask students to list key signs they should look for when they are trying to determine whether a claim is true or false.

The Need to Think Critically

Critical thinking means judging an idea on its soundness and truthfulness. It involves asking questions about a claim and the people who make it to decide whether you will accept it as true.

In a society where you have many choices, critical thinking is a valuable skill. It can help you recognize the ways in which advertisements, news reports, and nutrition fads may be misleading.

Evaluating Advertising

Many products related to health and nutrition are advertised on television and radio, in newspapers and magazines, and in other ways. Advertising can be informative and entertaining. Without it, many of the products you enjoy today would not be available.

At times, however, advertisements can be misleading. They can lead people to buy products without thinking about cost or nutrition.

How Advertisers Persuade You

Here are a few of the techniques advertisers use to convince you to buy their products:

❖ *Limited information.* Often, advertisements give you only the facts that will encourage you to buy. They may not tell the whole story.

❖ *Positive images.* An advertisement may use images of things that people feel positively about, such as friendship or good looks. The advertiser hopes you will associate these images and feelings with the product.

❖ *Appeal to basic needs.* Advertisers may focus on ways the product meets a need for security or self-esteem. They try to convince you that the product will make you look or feel better.

❖ *Celebrities.* Some advertisements show popular performers or athletes promoting the product. They don't tell you whether the person actually uses the product in real life.

Advertising can be a valuable source of information about products, but it can be misleading. Children tend to believe everything they see or hear. Thinking critically requires experience and practice.

More About Advertising Techniques

Other advertising techniques include:

• *Repetition.* The same message is repeated many times in different media. This helps imprint the advertiser's name and message in the consumer's mind. Think of one of your favorite foods that is advertised regularly. Do you remember the advertising message?

• *Urgency.* Most advertisements try to motivate consumers to take action right away. For instance, the ad might say, "Buy now," "Limited time offer" or "Limited supply."

Besides advertising, companies use other techniques to promote their products. A soft drink company may lend its name to a sports event or arrange to have its product shown in a movie. Coupons and eye-catching store displays encourage consumers to buy. Even product packages are a form of advertising.

The problem with these techniques is that they often don't give you the facts you need to make an informed choice. Instead, they appeal to your emotions. When evaluating advertising, ask yourself: What facts am I given? What needs or wants does the ad appeal to? What do I know about the people promoting the product?

Remember that the purpose of advertising is to get people to buy a product. Your goal is to get good nutrition at a fair price. Be sure your buying decisions are based on your own priorities, not the advertiser's.

Quacks and Frauds

Quacks are people who promote a particular food, diet, or supplement as a health aid without sound scientific evidence. Some quacks are deliberate frauds—their only goal is to make money in whatever way they can, even if the product hurts someone's health. Others are firm believers in the products they sell.

Understanding how quacks work can help you evaluate information. Here are some signs to look for. An advertisement or other product claim may not be truthful if it:

❖ *Guarantees fast results.* If the claim sounds too good to be true, it usually is.
❖ *Claims to be based on a "scientific breakthrough."* Legitimate scientific research takes time. The "miracle" discovery promoted in the ad may be complete fiction, or it may be based on early, incomplete studies.

Student Experiences

1. **Class Discussion:** Have students name ways, other than advertising, in which companies promote their products. Discuss the following points about these techniques: Do they give you the facts you need to make an informed choice? Do they appeal to your emotions? *(Key skill: critical thinking)*

2. **Evaluating Advertising:** Have students collect advertisements for products related to health and nutrition. Ask students to evaluate the techniques the advertisers used to encourage people to buy the products. What facts are given? What needs or wants does the ad appeal to? What information is given about the people promoting the product? *(Key skill: critical thinking)*

3. **Reading Nutrition Claims:** Provide students with copies of articles and advertisements that make confusing nutrition claims. Ask students how they would decide whether to believe the claims. Have students identify claims that may not be truthful. *(Key skill: reading)*

No product can guarantee good health or weight loss. Make your choices based on facts, not false promises.

Teaching . . .

- **Nutrition in the News**
  - **Myths and Fads**
  - **Getting Facts**

(text pages 106-108)

Comprehension Check

1. Discuss the relevance of news items about research in nutrition. Why should they be read with caution?

2. Discuss ways students can protect themselves against false, unproven, or premature claims made about nutrition.

3. Ask students to define the terms *fad* and *myth*. How do fads and myths contribute to popular beliefs that lead to poor nutrition?

4. Discuss sources of more information about nutrition topics. Where might you look to find the truth behind a current fad or myth?

5. Discuss why it is important to distinguish between fact and fiction in nutrition.

❖ **Uses scare tactics.** For instance, it may play on people's fear of aging or becoming ill. Some ads suggest that common symptoms, such as headaches and fatigue, are signs of an illness that can only be cured by the advertised product. Yet there are many possible causes for such symptoms.

❖ **Relies on personal testimonials.** An advertisement may say that Ms. L.J., of Pine Grove, Oregon, used the product with fantastic results. But who is Ms. L.J.? You can't even be sure she really exists.

❖ **Encourages megadoses of vitamins and minerals.** As you have learned, excess amounts of vitamins and minerals can be a threat to good health.

Realistic expectations about nutrition are your best defense against false claims like these. Quacks are successful because many people are looking for shortcuts to good health. Remember, good health is attained by practicing wellness every day, not by "miracle" products.

Nutrition in the News

Reports of the latest health and nutrition studies appear in the media almost daily. A study is a scientific experiment conducted on a specific group of either people or animals.

There are several reasons why you should be cautious when reading about the latest research results.

❖ Many studies are poorly designed or show vague results.

❖ The people who performed or reported on the study may have been biased (swayed toward a particular conclusion). For example, research performed by a dental resource center reportedly showed that chocolate could fight dental plaque (PLACK), a cause of tooth decay. Investigation revealed that the center received most of its funds from a candy company.

❖ Even a well-designed, unbiased study usually is not the final authority. The results must be verified by other researchers.

Nutrition research can help health professionals learn more about how the body uses food. However, research must be carefully planned and carried out to provide valid information. Think critically about research results reported in the press.

❖ Most studies focus on just a small segment of the population. Some are done on animals. The results may not apply to people in general.

❖ Media reports are often too brief to provide complete information.

❖ News reporters may not have the scientific background needed to correctly interpret the details.

Stay informed about the latest research, but use critical thinking. When you read or hear about an interesting study, don't jump to conclusions. Look for the facts in the report. Get information from other sources. Be patient and wait for further studies instead of allowing yourself to be influenced by just one report.

Food and Nutrition Science

Assessing the Reliability of Information: It's important to know how to read claims about new findings in research. Approach new findings scientifically by considering the following questions when you read articles about research findings:

- Who did the study and where? Who paid for it?
- Who were the subjects of the study? How many subjects were used?
- How was the study designed and carried out?

Food Myths and Fads

Advertiscments and news reports are not the only sources of information that call for critical thinking. People often spread stories about the latest food fad they've heard. They pass along myths, or unsound beliefs, about nutrition. Many books and magazine articles written by so-called "experts" give poor advice about nutrition and health.

Before you follow anyone's advice, ask yourself whether the source is a reliable one. Authors of books and magazine articles should be well-qualified, with an educational background in the particular subject from an accredited university or college.

Many people believe brown eggs are better than white. In fact, they are nutritionally the same. It's true that butter has more cholesterol and saturated fat than margarine, but they have the same amount of total fat and calories. Are muffins a good choice for breakfast? It depends. Many are high in sugar and fat. Check out the facts.

Healthy Attitudes

Here are just a few examples of nutrition myths and the facts behind them.

- **Myth: Eating grapefruit will help you burn fat and lose weight.** Fact: Grapefruit is low in fat and calories, but it has no special fat-burning qualities.
- **Myth: People who are under stress need extra vitamins.** Fact: Eating a balanced variety of nutritious foods, like other wellness habits, can help you handle stress. However, there is little evidence that everyday stress robs the body of vitamins.
- **Myth: If a food is cholesterol-free, it must be fat-free.** Fact: Cholesterol and fat are not the same thing. For instance, cholesterol-free crackers may contain coconut oil, which is high in saturated fatty acids. Remember, eating too much fat—especially saturated fat—may increase the risk of heart disease.

- Who is reporting on the study? What are his or her qualifications?
- Have other studies been done on the subject? How many? What did they show?

Student Experiences

1. **Guest Speaker:** Invite a nutritionist to describe how health and nutrition research is conducted and reported. Ask the speaker to identify potential problems in conducting and reporting the results that create a need for caution when reading reports of research. Ask the speaker how consumers can read reports of health and nutrition research objectively. What are some signs of potential bias? Have student summarize what they learned in a short report. *(Key skill: writing)*

2. **Class Discussion:** Have students identify the perspective of each reliable source of nutrition listed in the text. Why might these sources be more reliable than other sources of nutrition information? *(Key skill: reading)*

3. **Clues About Authors:** Provide students with a variety of nutrition books and articles. Have students work in groups to locate and evaluate information about the background and perspective of the author(s). Ask each group to identify sources of information they would consider reliable and those they would not. Have a spokesperson for each group share the group's conclusions with the class. *(Key skills: reading, critical thinking)*

Healthy Attitudes

Have students share other examples of widely-held nutrition beliefs. Do they think they are facts or myths? Why?

Where to Get the Facts

If you are suspicious about any nutrition information you have received or want more facts, here are some sources to contact:

- ❖ A local nutritionist or dietitian.
- ❖ Your local health department.
- ❖ Your foods and nutrition teacher.
- ❖ A professional organization, such as the American Dietetics Association.
- ❖ The nutrition department at a nearby university or college.

Remember that your health is your responsibility. Separating nutrition fact from fiction is an important part of exercising that responsibility.

A university health center might be one source of accurate nutrition information. What are some others?

Section 3.3 Review

RECALL THE FACTS

1. What is critical thinking?
2. What are two signs that an advertisement may be promoting a "quack" product?
3. Why doesn't any one scientific study provide enough evidence to draw a conclusion?
4. List three reliable sources of information about nutrition.

DISCUSS YOUR IDEAS

5. Why do you think some people continue to believe false claims and myths when there is no evidence for them?

APPLY YOUR LEARNING

6. Bring to class ads that you think are false or misleading. Identify the misleading statements or techniques.

Career PROFILE

Larry Burke
Dietitian

CURRENT POSITION

"I'm an administrative dietitian working for a large public school district."

RESPONSIBILITIES

"I supervise large-scale meal planning and preparation for the entire school district. It's also my responsibility to enforce safety standards and maintain a budget."

SKILLS

"To succeed in this field, you must be able to work well with all types of people. Organizational skills are important, and of course, you need knowledge of nutrition and food service."

EDUCATION

"I have a four-year college degree with a major in food service management. I'm also a registered dietitian and have a master's degree in business administration."

WORK ENVIRONMENT

"I work about 40 hours a week. More than half of that time is spent at my desk, often in front of a computer. I also spend some time supervising the kitchen staff and food servers."

FAVORITE PART OF THE JOB

"I'm very people-oriented. I enjoy the challenge of giving school kids meals that are both good-tasting and healthy."

- Why is it important for Larry to be able to work well with many different people?
- What aspects of Larry's job do you think you might enjoy? Why?

Thinking About . . . Dietetic Careers

- Have students think of other questions they would like to ask Larry Burke about being a dietitian. (Examples: What does it take to become a registered dietitian? For what kinds of tasks do you use a computer?)
- Ask students to give reasons why a dietitian might be needed in a public school district. Interested students might find out how these issues are handled in your school system.

Student Opportunities

Students planning a career as a dietitian may want to volunteer in the kitchens of hospitals, nursing homes, or senior citizen organizations.

Occupational Outlook

Dietitians with experience who wish to advance can accept a position in a related career as assistant or chief director of a dietary department or as the manager of a restaurant.

109

For More Information

For more information about dietetic careers, have students contact:
- The American Dietetic Association, 208 S. LaSalle St., Chicago, IL 60604-1003
- The U.S. Office of Personnel Management, Washington, D.C. 20415.

Review

- Have students complete the Chapter Review. (Answers appear below.)

Evaluation

- Divide the class into three groups. Assign each group one section of Chapter 3. Ask each group to write questions about its section. Then have groups take turns asking their questions to the other two groups.

- Have students take the test for Chapter 3. (Refer to the *Chapter and Unit Tests* booklet or construct your own test using the *Testmaker Software*.)

■ ANSWERS ■

REVIEWING THE FACTS

1. Total fat: 30 percent; saturated fat: 10 percent.

2. They provide starches and fiber, proteins, vitamins, and minerals, yet many of them are low in fat.

3. High blood pressure. *Any three:* add little or no salt to food when cooking and at the table; choose salted snacks only occasionally; go easy on processed foods; check labels for the amount of sodium in foods and choose those that are lower in sodium.

4. Foods at the bottom of the Pyramid are those that have a higher number of recommended servings; number of recommended servings decreases toward the top of the Pyramid.

5. *Bread, Cereal, Rice, and Pasta Group:* complex carbohydrates, fiber, vitamins, and minerals; *Vegetable Group:* complex carbohydrates,

SUMMARY

SECTION 3.1

Dietary Guidelines: The Dietary Guidelines for Americans give advice for healthful eating. Included are recommendations to eat a variety of foods; balance the food you eat with physical activity—maintain or improve your weight; choose a diet with plenty of grain products, vegetables, and fruits; choose a diet low in fat, saturated fat, and cholesterol; choose a diet moderate in sugars; and choose a diet moderate in salt and sodium. Various groups have issued other dietary guidelines.

SECTION 3.2

The Food Guide Pyramid: The Food Guide Pyramid is a tool to help you plan daily food choices. It shows the approximate number of servings you need each day from each of five food groups. Fats, oils, and sweets are placed at the small tip of the Pyramid and should be used sparingly. Choosing nutrient-dense foods from the food groups will help you get the nutrients you need without too many calories.

SECTION 3.3

Separating Fact from Fiction: Critical thinking can help you identify information that may be misleading. Advertisers use a variety of techniques to convince you to buy their products. Quacks promote products as health aids without sound scientific evidence. Avoid jumping to conclusions when reading news of a scientific study. Be wary of food myths and fads, and know where to get accurate information about nutrition.

REVIEWING FACTS

1. What are the recommended limits for fat and saturated fat in the diet? (3.1)

2. What are the benefits of choosing a diet with plenty of grain products, vegetables, and fruits? (3.1)

3. What problems are associated with excess sodium? Give three hints for cutting down on salt and sodium. (3.1)

4. Explain how the position of food groups in the Food Guide Pyramid diagram relates to the recommended number of servings for each. (3.2)

5. Briefly describe the main nutrients provided by each food group. (3.2)

6. Why does the Food Guide Pyramid give the recommended number of servings for each food group as a range instead of an exact number? (3.2)

7. Name three techniques used by advertisers to convince you to buy their products. (3.3)

8. What is meant by the term "nutrition myth"? Give an example. (3.3)

9. How can you tell whether the author of a book on nutrition is a reliable source of information on the subject? (3.3)

LEARNING BY DOING

1. ***Taste test:*** Heat three samples of a canned vegetable, such as green beans: one canned with salt and two canned without salt. Season one of the no-salt samples with a salt alternative, such as herbs or lemon juice. Compare the taste of the vegetables. Which do you prefer? Why? (3.1)

fiber, beta carotene, vitamin C, folate, and minerals such as magnesium and iron; *Fruit Group:* beta carotene, vitamin C, and potassium; *Milk, Yogurt, and Cheese Group:* protein, vitamins, and minerals, especially calcium; *Meat, Poultry, Fish, Dry Beans, Eggs, and Nuts Group:* protein, vitamins, and minerals.

2. **Foods lab:** Compare the amount of fat in different types of ground beef. Weigh out 1/4 pound (112 g) of regular ground beef and the same amount of ground round. Form each portion into a patty. Cook each patty in a separate skillet over medium-low heat until done (about five minutes on each side). After cooking, weigh each patty again. Pour the grease from each pan into a separate measuring cup. Which patty contained more fat? How might you use this information? (3.1, 3.2)

THINKING CRITICALLY

1. **Determining accuracy:** Suppose a friend tells you that honey and molasses are better for you than white or brown sugar. How can you decide whether this is true? (3.1, 3.3)

2. **Predicting consequences:** What may be the consequences of eating too many foods low in nutrient density? (3.2)

3. **Recognizing bias:** Suppose a study on whether vitamin C is effective against colds is being paid for by a company that makes vitamin C tablets. Why does this suggest a possible bias? (3.3)

MAKING DECISIONS AND SOLVING PROBLEMS

What Would You Do?

1. Your sister has learned that carrots are very nutritious. Therefore, she has stopped eating most other vegetables and eats large amounts of carrots at almost every meal. (3.1, 3.2)

2. One of your friends is planning to go on a grapefruit-only diet for a few weeks. She asks you to go on the diet with her. (3.3)

LINKING YOUR STUDIES

1. **Fine arts:** Prepare a song, skit, puppet show, or poster that could be used to teach children about the Food Guide Pyramid. (3.2)

2. **Reading and study skills:** Find a newspaper or magazine article about a nutrition-related study. Identify the following information in the article: What was the purpose of the study? Who did the study and where? Who paid for it? What type of people or animals did the researchers study? How was the study carried out? (3.3)

3. **Writing:** Think of a nutrition claim you have recently seen or heard about. Write a letter to a dietitian asking for information and advice on the subject. (3.3)

LEARNING BY DOING

1. Answers will vary.

2. The regular ground beef contains more fat. To cut down on the amount of fat you consume by buying ground round.

THINKING CRITICALLY

1. Students should list sources they could refer to, such as those listed on page 108.

2. Becoming both overweight and malnourished.

3. Students should realize that the company wants the study to show that vitamin C *is* effective against colds.

MAKING DECISIONS AND SOLVING PROBLEMS

Answers to "Making Decisions and Solving Problems" questions will vary. Encourage students to give reasons for their answers.

LINKING YOUR STUDIES

Answers to "Linking Your Studies" questions will vary. Encourage students to be creative and to explore alternatives where applicable.

111

6. The actual number of servings required for individuals differ according to age and lifestyle.

7. *Any three:* limited information, positive images, appeal to basic needs, and celebrities.

8. An unsound belief about nutrition, such as "eating grapefruit will help you burn fat and lose weight."

9. By finding out more about the author and his or her qualifications; by contacting one or more of the authorities listed in Section 3.3.

Planning the Chapter

Chapter Overview

Section 4.1: Daily Meals and Snacks

Section 4.2: Improving Your Eating Habits

Section 4.3: Eating Out Nutritiously

Section 4.4: Vegetarian Food Choices

Introducing the Chapter

Motivators

- Ask several students to interview the person in a family who plans most meals. Students should ask the person to describe the family's typical eating patterns. How often does the family eat out? Does the family include anyone who is a vegetarian? If so, which type? Have students share the results of their interviews with the class.

- Invite a nutritionist to discuss the importance of planning daily food choices. How can different meal patterns be adapted to meet nutritional needs? What role should snacks play in a person's diet? How can a person make nutritious food choices when eating out? Have students develop a list of additional questions to ask.

CHAPTER 4

Planning Daily Food Choices

112

Cooperative Learning Suggestions

Have students use the Think-Pair-Share method to plan a day's meals following different meal patterns. Have each pair of students take turns suggesting ideas for organizing the meals. They should include snacks in their plans for meeting daily food needs. Provide students with restaurant menus. Have them replace one of their meals with foods selected from the restaurant menu. Finally, have students adapt their menus to fit one of the three types of vegetarian diets. Ask several pairs of students to share their ideas with the class.

Daily Meals and Snacks

OBJECTIVES

After studying this section, you should be able to:

- Identify different eating patterns.
- Discuss how nutritional needs can be met through meals and snacks.

LOOK FOR THESE TERMS

eating patterns
snacks
"grazing"

Barry greeted his friend at the door. "Hi, Manuel. I'm glad you stopped by. We were just sitting down to dinner—would you like to join us?"

"I'm sorry, I didn't know you hadn't eaten yet," said Manuel. "I've already had supper."

"Well, then, how about a snack?" Barry grinned. "Come on in!"

Has something similar ever happened to you? Because of differences in schedules, family background, and habits, people follow different patterns when it comes to meals and snacks.

Eating Patterns

The term **eating patterns** refers to when, what, and how much people eat. Today, many different eating patterns are becoming common. Some people eat three traditional

Your daily schedule is one of the factors that influence your eating pattern. What are some others?

Section 4.1: Daily Meals and Snacks 113

Teacher's Classroom Resources—Section 4.1

Refer to these resources in the TCR package:

Reproducible Lesson Plans
Student Workbook
Extending the Text

Reteaching Activities
Section Quizzes
Testmaker Software
Color Transparencies

Section 4.1
Daily Meals and Snacks

Introducing the Section

Motivators

- Ask students to list the times they usually eat during the day and the term they use to describe each. How many students follow a traditional meal pattern of breakfast, midday meal, and evening meal? How many students usually eat their largest meal in the evening? How many students usually skip breakfast? At what times do they eat snacks?

- If any students have ever lived in another country or have relatives who have done so, ask them to describe the meal patterns of that country. How similar are the meal patterns of the country described to meal patterns in the United States? What may account for the differences?

Objectives

- Have students read the section objectives. Discuss the purpose of studying the section.

Vocabulary

- Pronounce the terms listed under "Look for These Terms." Have students find the terms and their definitions in the section.

Guided Reading

- Have students look at the headings within Section 4.1 to preview the concepts that will be discussed.

- Have students read the section and complete the appropriate part of the Chapter 4 Study Guide in the Student Workbook.

Teaching . . .

- **Eating Patterns**
- **Traditional Meals**

(text pages 113-115)

Comprehension Check

1. Ask students to describe factors that have an effect on the eating pattern a person develops. *(lifestyle, schedule, time available, etc.)*

2. Ask students to list and describe the traditional meals. *(breakfast, midday, and evening)*

3. Discuss the type of breakfast that is most beneficial to students before their school day begins.

4. Discuss the reasons why many people tend to skip breakfast. How can this problem be overcome?

5. Discuss the pros and cons of having the biggest meal of the day at midday and in the evening.

meals a day, while others prefer to eat many small meals. People often eat snacks between meals. Some use different eating patterns from day to day, depending on their schedules.

No matter what your eating pattern is, the goal is to make nutritious food choices throughout the entire day. It's also important to eat regularly. If you try to go too long without food, your body won't have the fuel it needs. Studies show that people who skip meals make up for it by overeating later. Usually, meal skippers eat more in a day than they would if they chose to eat at regular intervals.

Traditional Meals

The traditional meals include breakfast, the midday meal, and the evening meal.

Breakfast

Studies continue to prove that breakfast is the most important meal of the day. You haven't eaten since the evening before, which means your body hasn't had a supply of energy foods for many hours. Breakfast gives you energy and helps you feel alert during the morning hours.

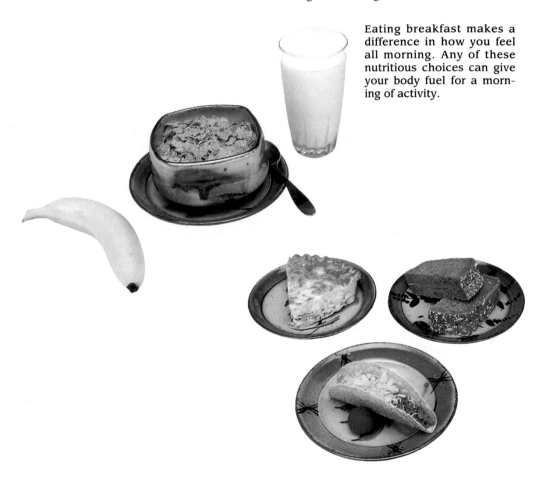

Eating breakfast makes a difference in how you feel all morning. Any of these nutritious choices can give your body fuel for a morning of activity.

Special Needs Strategies

Learning Disabled: Have students practice planning daily meals and snacks using cards that picture a variety of foods. After students make food choices for a day, check their work and make suggestions for improving eating habits, if needed.

Healthy Attitudes

Are you a breakfast skipper? If time is your problem, begin by getting up a few minutes earlier. Make a meal out of "quick" foods, such as:

- Low-fat flavored or plain yogurt, whole grain muffin or bagel, and a banana.
- Peanut butter and jelly sandwich and low-fat milk.
- A breakfast drink made by blending low-fat milk or yogurt, juice, and fruit.

If you skip breakfast, it's harder to concentrate on your schoolwork. Recent studies show that students who eat breakfast get to school on time and score better grades than those who don't eat breakfast.

Not all breakfasts are equal. A breakfast of starch, protein, and fruit, such as whole grain cereal or muffin, milk, and banana, gives you more lasting energy than a doughnut and a soft drink. You may feel fine after eating the doughnut and soft drink, but you will probably experience a mid-morning letdown.

Some people skip breakfast because they are bored with standard breakfast fare. However, any food can be breakfast food, so long as it is nutritious. Try having pizza, tacos, soup with crackers, or refried beans on toast for breakfast. Round out the menu with a serving of fruit and low-fat milk.

Midday and Evening Meals

The midday meal gives you energy and nutrients to carry out the rest of the day's activities. The evening meal is a good time to think about the food you've eaten for the day. It's your chance to fill in any food group servings that are lacking.

"Dinner" traditionally means the largest meal of the day. It may be eaten at midday or in the evening, depending on your personal preference and your schedule.

Some people prefer to eat dinner at midday and a lighter meal, sometimes called supper, in the evening. The larger midday meal provides fuel for the day's activities. Some people find they sleep better if the evening meal is light.

On the other hand, sometimes people prefer to have a light meal, or lunch, at midday. This pattern is often chosen by those who work or go to school. They may prefer to have the largest meal in the evening when all or most family members can eat together. On weekends or special occasions, they may follow a different pattern.

No matter when it is eaten, a dinner usually includes a main dish along with a grain product, vegetables, and a beverage. Sometimes people add dessert. A typical dinner might be stir-fried chicken, broccoli, and water chestnuts over rice; a tossed salad; low-fat milk; a whole wheat roll; and fruit for dessert.

For a lighter lunch or supper, popular choices include sandwiches, soups, main-dish salads, and similar foods. Accompaniments could include fresh fruits and vegetables, whole grain bread, and low-fat milk or yogurt.

In Mexico, the main meal is eaten at midday. A light meal or snack, called *merienda,* may be eaten in the early evening, followed by supper in the late evening.

1. **Quick List:** Give students two minutes to list all the low-nutrient foods they can think of that are commonly eaten for breakfast. Combine students' lists to make one list titled "Eat Breakfast but Skip These Foods." *(Key skill: brainstorming)*

2. **Group Project:** Have students work in groups to plan nutritious and appealing breakfast menus. Have students, as a class, select and later prepare the most nutritious and appealing menu. *(Key skill: health)*

3. **Meal Planning:** Have students plan a week's evening meals that are nutritious and easy to prepare. *(Key skill: health)*

4. **Research:** Have students research meal patterns in another culture. Ask students to report their findings to the class. *(Key skill: social studies)*

Ask students to brainstorm reasons why the meal pattern in Mexico may have evolved. Then have them use references to check their ideas. What types of work do the people do? What foods are available to the majority of the people on a regular basis?

More About Daily Meals

In the past, meals were a family affair. Family members were expected to be prompt for meals, to eat together, and to eat whatever had been prepared.

Mealtime gave family members a chance to socialize and communicate with each other. This helped maintain family stability.

In today's fast-paced society, the ritual of the family meal has become rare. It has been replaced by a new ritual—quickly prepared, simple meals eaten when there's time. As a result, the families often miss out on the important social benefits of meal sharing.

Comprehension Check

1. Discuss the value of eating snacks between regular meals. Are snacks necessarily bad for you? Why or why not?

2. Discuss guidelines people should follow when they eat snacks. *(Don't eat them too close to a regular meal; eat nutritious foods for snacks; keep away from typical "snack foods" that may be high in fat, sugar, and calories.)*

3. Discuss the concept of "grazing." How do people's lifestyles contribute to the need to graze?

Student Experiences

1. **Packaged Food Analysis:** Ask students to bring an empty package from a snack food item. Have them use the nutrition information on the packages to determine the nutrients supplied by the foods. Rank the items from most to least nutritious. *(Key skill: math)*

2. **Recipe Selection:** Have students select nutritious snack recipes they would choose for a party. Evaluate the recipes for appeal and taste. *(Key skill: analysis)*

See Also . . .
- Section 15.1: "Choosing Convenience Foods," text page 395.
- Section 20.1: "Sandwiches, Snacks, and Packed Lunches," text page 523.

Snacks

Snacks are small amounts of food eaten between meals. Snacking is not necessarily a bad habit. Well-chosen snacks can help you meet your energy and nutrient needs throughout the day.

However, many so-called "snack foods" are high in fat, sugar, and calories. These include candy, chips, granola, cookies, and other sweets.

For a nutritious snack, you can choose almost any nutrient-dense food from the five food groups. Try leftovers from the refrigerator, fresh fruits or vegetables, low-fat dairy products, or whole grain breads and cereals.

Also consider the timing of your snacks. If you snack too close to mealtime, you may not be able to eat the nutritious foods included in the meal.

Remember that snacks are as much a part of your eating pattern as breakfast, lunch, or dinner. Choose them wisely.

"Grazing"

Some people prefer to eat five or more small meals throughout the day instead of three larger ones. This eating pattern is sometimes called **"grazing."**

When you choose snacks, consider nutrient density. Snacks like these can satisfy your hunger and provide important nutrients.

Why might a person prefer smaller meals more often instead of three larger meals?

If grazing is your eating pattern, think about your food choices toward the end of the day. Are you lacking any servings from the food groups? If so, eat those foods so you'll be sure to meet the daily recommendations. On the other hand, check to be sure you are not eating too much. The day's total servings and calories should be the right amount for you, just as if you were eating three traditional meals.

As you have learned, eating patterns vary from person to person and day to day. In the end, *when* you eat is less important than *what* you eat. The eating pattern that helps you get the nutrients you need and the right number of calories is the one that's best for you. Identifying your eating pattern can help you plan for good nutrition.

■ Section 4.1 Review ■

RECALL THE FACTS

1. Give three examples of different eating patterns.

2. Why is breakfast considered the most important meal of the day?

3. How can you choose snacks that help meet your nutrient needs?

DISCUSS YOUR IDEAS

4. What eating pattern do you usually follow? How does it reflect your lifestyle?

5. What are some advantages of grazing? What are the disadvantages?

APPLY YOUR LEARNING

6. Make a list of 15 nutritious snack foods that require little preparation. Put a check mark by those you have tried before. Put a star by those you plan to try.

Section 4.1: Daily Meals and Snacks **117**

Section 4.2
Improving Your Eating Habits

Introducing the Section

Motivator

- Ask students to make a list of their good and bad eating habits. Ask students to identify things they would need to know about their current eating habits before they can decide how to improve bad eating habits.

Objectives

- Have students read the section objectives. Discuss the purpose of studying this section.

Vocabulary

- Pronounce the terms listed under "Look for These Terms." Have students find the terms and their definitions in the section.

Guided Reading

- Have students look at the headings within Section 4.2 to preview the concepts that will be discussed.
- Have students read the section and complete the appropriate part of the Chapter 4 Study Guide in the *Student Workbook*.

SECTION 4.2

Improving Your Eating Habits

OBJECTIVES

After studying this section, you should be able to:

- Describe how to keep a food record.
- Suggest practical ways to succeed in changing eating habits for the better.

LOOK FOR THIS TERM

food record

If you are like most people, some of your eating habits are healthful ones. Others, however, could be improved. The first step in improving your eating habits is to recognize the kinds of food choices you make now. Then you can keep your good habits and work on improving the poor ones.

What Are Your Current Habits?

People sometimes aren't aware of how often and what they eat. They may make sound food choices at certain times or in some situations, but not others.

You can become more aware of your habits by keeping a **food record.** This is simply a list of all the food you eat for a specific period of time. Start by carrying a small notebook or scratch pad with you. Each time you eat, no matter how small the amount, make a note in your record. Write down:

❖ The time you ate.
❖ The food eaten and the amount. You don't have to measure the exact amount—just make a reasonable estimate.

❖ A brief description of the eating situation. This might include where you were, what you were doing, your mood, and any other information that could help you understand your food habits.

Keep your food record for three consecutive days, including at least one weekend day. During this time, make your usual food choices. This is not a test you have to pass. It's just a way of letting you know the kind of food choices you are making now.

Reviewing Your Food Record

At the end of the three-day period, take a look at your food choices. For each day, count the number of servings you had from each group in the Food Guide Pyramid (page 97). Compare your totals with the recommended number of servings. Did you eat at least the minimum amount of servings? If not, which foods were you lacking? Were your food choices high or low in fats and added sugars? Remember, fats, oils, and sweets should be eaten sparingly.

Teacher's Classroom Resources—Section 4.2

Refer to these resources in the TCR package:

Reproducible Lesson Plans

Student Workbook

Extending the Text

Reteaching Activities

Section Quizzes

Testmaker Software

Color Transparencies

```
                        Food Record
      Thursday, Feb. 10
          Time              Food and Amount            Situation
       6:30 A.M.       1 small glass orange juice    home—breakfast—
                         1 cup cornflakes              in a hurry
                         1 glass skim milk
        10 A.M.        1 small bag potato chips     school—between classes
         Noon              cheeseburger               school lunch
                      tossed salad with dressing
                           soft drink
                            brownie
       3:30 P.M.       1 large bag french fries        mall—shopping
                         1 diet soda                with Kara and Jason
```

How Can You Improve Your Habits?

Perhaps your food record shows that you are already following the Food Guide Pyramid and the Dietary Guidelines. If so, keep up your good habits.

Most people, however, find that their food choices leave room for improvement. For instance, Roberto discovered that he was not eating enough vegetables. He also saw that high-fat and sugary foods were often among his food choices.

Once you have identified poor eating habits, think about why they occur. Look at your food record again. Did you tend to make poor food choices in certain situations, such as while watching TV or when you were unhappy? Roberto's food record showed that he often snacked on cookies or french fries when he was at the mall with friends.

Roberto's food record made it easier for him to identify ways he could improve his eating habits. Consider keeping track of your own food intake for several days.

TIPS for Success

Developing New Eating Habits
❖ Begin to make changes in your food habits gradually. Work on them one by one.
❖ Allow plenty of time for each new way of eating to become a habit.
❖ If you find yourself slipping back into old ways of eating, don't give up. Review your plan and make sure it's realistic, then try again. If you continue to make the effort, eventually you will succeed.

Section 4.2: Improving Your Eating Habits   **119**

Comprehension Check

1. Ask students to discuss ways to become more aware of their eating habits.
2. Discuss how a food record can be used to help you improve your eating habits.

Student Experiences

1. **Food Journal:** Have students keep a record of the foods they eat for three days. Have them follow the guidelines given in the text. *(Key skill: science)*

2. **Food Review:** Have students study their food records and analyze their current eating habits. Have students count the number of servings from each group in the Food Guide Pyramid. Have them compare their totals with the recommended number of servings. Which foods were lacking? Which foods were high or low in fats and added sugars? *(Key skill: analysis)*

3. **Diet Report:** Have students write an essay describing what they learned about their eating habits in the previous two experiences. Read two or three of the essays anonymously to the class. Compare the essays with typical teenagers' eating habits. *(Key skill: writing)*

Food and Nutrition Science

Modifying Eating Habits: Have students use scientific journals and other references to research ways to change habits successfully. Have students report their findings to the class. Relate the suggestions to changing eating habits. As a class, develop guidelines for positive change.

Have students design an experiment to test the guidelines they have developed. Remind students that they must have both a control group and an experimental group.

Have interested students try the experiment. Ask them to report the results to the class.

Completing the Section

Review

- Ask students to summarize the main ideas in this section.
- Have students complete the Section Review. (Answers appear below.)

Evaluation

- Present a case study of a person who displays poor eating habits and ask students to suggest specific improvements.
- Have students take the quiz for Section 4.2. (Refer to the *Section Quizzes* booklet or use the *Testmaker Software*.)

Reteaching

- Place the title "Habits—Good or Bad?" on a bulletin board. Label one side of the display "Good" and the other "Bad." Have students find and display pictures showing good and bad habits on the appropriate sides of the bulletin board.
- Refer to the *Reteaching Activities* booklet for the Section 4.2 activity sheet.

Enrichment

- Have interested students find out if there are any organizations in your area that can help people change habits. What resources are available?

Closure

- Lead a discussion on the importance of habits in our daily lives and how habits in general influence our eating habits.

In shopping malls, tempting foods seem to be everywhere. Look for nutritious choices.

Next, think about how to solve the problem. Some people just tell themselves, "I'll eat better from now on." That promise is hard to keep because it isn't specific. Instead, decide on specific changes you can make. (You may want to review the decision-making steps explained in Section 1.5.)

The next time he went to the supermarket, Roberto noticed how many different kinds of fresh vegetables there were. He decided to try at least one new vegetable a week. After he had done this for several weeks, he began to work on choosing healthier snacks at the mall.

Remember, eating is an enjoyable part of life. Don't take the pleasure out of it. You can make changes in your food habits and have fun doing it.

Every once in a while, keep another food record for several days. Use the same method to analyze your food choices. Compare it to your previous food record. You can see if you are making the necessary changes that will help you feel and look better. Keeping a food record and analyzing your food choices can help you stay on the track toward good health.

120   Chapter 4: Planning Daily Food Choices

Section 4.2 Review

RECALL THE FACTS

1. What is a food record? What is its purpose?
2. When keeping a food record, what information do you need to write down?
3. Give two tips for successfully changing one's eating habits.

DISCUSS YOUR IDEAS

4. How could you give encouragement to a friend who is working on new eating habits?

APPLY YOUR LEARNING

5. The text describes two specific steps Roberto decided to take to improve his eating habits. List at least five other steps that could help him reach his goals.

Answers to Section Review

1. A record of the foods you eat during a specific period; it allows you to analyze your eating habits.
2. Time, food eaten and amount, description of eating situation.
3. See "Tips for Success" on page 119.
4. By not offering foods the person is trying not to eat or suggesting a snack that is not nutritious, etc.
5. Answers will vary.

Eating Out Nutritiously

OBJECTIVES

After studying this section, you should be able to:

- Give guidelines for making nutritious food choices when eating away from home.
- Explain how eating out fits into overall food choices.

LOOK FOR THESE TERMS

entree

a la carte

Eating out is growing in popularity. Recent studies have shown that Americans eat more than one-fifth of their meals away from home.

Most people enjoy eating out. When it comes to nutrition, however, eating out can be a challenge. Take care to make healthful food choices when eating at restaurants, at school, and on the go.

Restaurant Meals

There are many types of restaurants. Each has advantages and disadvantages when it comes to nutrition.

❖ **Full-service restaurants** offer table service, which means you sit at a table and a server takes your order. Nutrition varies depending on the menu. Some restaurants offer a wide variety of choices.

At full-service restaurants, you usually have many food options. That makes it easier to make healthful choices.

Section 4.3: Eating Out Nutritiously   121

Teaching . . .

• Restaurant Meals

(text pages 121-125)

Comprehension Check

1. Ask students to list the three major types of restaurants *(full-service; cafeterias, buffets, and smorgasbords; fast-food)* and describe the advantages and disadvantages of each *(from a nutritional point of view).*

2. Discuss factors that enter into the choice of a restaurant. *(prices, time available, nutrition)*

3. Discuss the clues that people can look for on restaurant menus to avoid foods that are high in fat content. *(See "Menu Clues," right column.)*

4. Ask students to discuss and make a list of ways to control portion size at restaurants. *(Ask for smaller portions; choose appetizers and side dishes; take home leftovers.)*

5. Ask students to list healthful side dishes that are often available in restaurants.

6. Discuss ways to avoid toppings and "extras" served in restaurants that add fat, sodium, and sugar to otherwise healthful meals.

7. Discuss reasons why fast-food restaurants are now making an effort to offer nutritious foods. Ask students to list fast-food items that are nutritious choices. *(See chart page 124.)*

8. Discuss items to avoid on salad bars and buffets.

Others specialize in certain types of food, such as fish or steaks, or in certain cuisines, such as Italian or Chinese food. Since food is usually cooked to order, there's a good chance you can ask to have some items prepared the way you want—with less fat or salt, for example.

❖ **Cafeterias, restaurant buffets, and smorgasbords** (SHMORE-guhs-boards) are self-serve restaurants. A wide variety of food is displayed on counters, from which you make your selection. This can give you greater control over the kinds and amounts of food you eat. Buffet-type restaurants, however, generally allow you to return as many times as you want for second helpings. They often advertise "all you can eat" for a specific price. Such offers can tempt you to overeat and choose high-fat and sugary foods.

❖ **Fast-food restaurants** are changing to meet customers' requests for more nutritious food. Traditionally, fast food restaurants have offered a limited selection of foods, many of them high in fat, sugar, and sodium. Today, however, many fast-food restaurants are adding more healthful choices to the menu. You can now find broiled and roasted foods, salads, skim milk, and fruit juice. You may or may not have some choice in the way foods are prepared.

Many factors enter into your choice of restaurant, such as the price of a meal and how quickly you want to be served. Nutrition should also be a consideration. Try to select a restaurant that you know offers healthful choices.

Choosing from the Menu

As with at-home meals, wise choices can help you get the most nutrition when you're eating out. The guidelines that follow can help you.

Menu Clues

Pay attention to the way foods are described on the menu. For example, food described as "broiled," "baked," or "steamed" is probably relatively low in fat. On the other hand, the following terms are a clue that the food may be high in fat:

❖ fried	❖ sautéed
❖ breaded	❖ creamed
❖ in its own gravy	❖ au gratin
❖ in a cheese sauce	❖ scalloped
❖ rich	❖ batter-dipped

If you're in doubt, ask the server how foods are prepared. You might also ask whether your food can be prepared or served differently. Perhaps fish could be broiled instead of breaded and fried, for instance.

Many fast-food restaurants now have information available on the nutritional content of the foods on their menu.

122   Chapter 4: Planning Daily Food Choices

Food and Nutrition Science

Menu Development: Many of the larger fast-food restaurant chains employ nutrition experts as well as food scientists to help develop good-tasting foods that are nutritious and can be served in a fast-food environment. Ask the manager of a local fast-food restaurant how you can find out about the role food science plays in that restaurant chain. Share this information with the class.

Portion Size

Many restaurants give large portions—more than you may want or need to eat. How can you avoid this problem?

❖ If there is a choice of sizes on the menu, choose the smaller one. Even if there is no size choice, some restaurants will serve a smaller portion on request.

❖ Portions for the **entree** (AHN-tray), or main course, are often large. Try making a meal of appetizer or side dish selections, such as soup and a leafy green salad.

❖ If you are served a portion that is too large, don't force yourself to eat it all. Ask for a bag to take the leftover food home. Use it for a meal or snack.

Smart Side Dishes

In a full-service restaurant, the price of an item may include certain accompaniments. For instance, a sandwich may come with french fries and cole slaw. To avoid high-fat side dishes, ask if you can order items **a la carte** (ah-lah-CART), or individually. That way you can choose which side dishes you want.

The menu may offer a variety of accompaniments to the meal. Look for healthful choices such as whole grain breads, vegetables (not fried), and fruits. If you can, combine several of these foods with a moderate-sized serving from the meat group. Add skim or low-fat milk for a beverage, and you've put together a meal based on the Dietary Guidelines.

Topping It Off

In many cases, restaurant foods would be light and healthful if it weren't for toppings and other extras. Examples include rich sauce or gravy on an entree, butter or sour cream on a potato, dressing on a salad, and mayonnaise on a sandwich. There are a number of ways to get around the problem.

When the portion you receive is more than you need, don't hesitate to ask for a container to take the extra food home. The food won't be wasted and you won't overeat.

Student Experiences

1. **Selecting Foods:** Distribute restaurant menus to students. Have them practice selecting foods low in fat, sodium, and sugar. Ask them to point out foods high in fat, sodium, and sugar. *(Key skill: health)*

2. **Making Comparisons:** Have students compare full-meal and a la carte choices on restaurant menus. Ask students which is the most and least expensive. Have students decide which option makes it easier to avoid high-fat and high-sodium side dishes and accompaniments. *(Key skills: math, analysis)*

3. **Research:** Assign students to visit restaurants that have a salad bar. Ask students to make a list of the foods on the salad bar. Have students analyze the choices for added fat. Have students plan a nutritious, low-fat salad using foods available on the salad bar. *(Key skill: health)*

4. **Skits:** Ask students to identify possible choices when restaurant portions are more than you may want or need to eat or when toppings and other extras add unwanted fat, sodium, or extra calories. Have students work in pairs to write and present skits demonstrating acceptable ways to handle these situations. *(Key skill: communication)*

Thinking Skills

Creativity: Ask students to think of or create good-tasting toppings for a salad that are low in fats, sodium, and sugar, but highly nutritious. Have students share their ideas. If possible, allow students to try their ideas.

- **Eating at School**
- **Eating on the Go**
- **How Eating Out Fits In**

(text pages 125-126)

Comprehension Check

1. Ask students to list the advantages and disadvantages of bringing a lunch from home as opposed to eating the food provided in the school's cafeteria.

2. Discuss healthful choices people can make at a vending machine.

Healthy Attitudes

Lead a discussion on other substitutions people can make to cut down on fat in restaurant meals. Students can calculate approximate calorie and fat reduction for the substitutions.

See Also . . .

- Chapter 11: "Planning Meals," text page 304.
- Section 20.1: "Sandwiches, Snacks, and Packed Lunches," text page 523.

Salad dressing isn't the only way to enhance the flavor of a tossed salad.

You can:

- ❖ Ask for the food to be served without the topping.
- ❖ Use a substitute. For example, you could ask for a low-fat salad dressing or use lemon juice, vinegar, pepper, or herbs instead.
- ❖ Ask that rich sauces and salad dressings be served on the side (that is, in a separate container). Then you can add just a small amount.

Perhaps you're concerned about getting too much sodium. Often restaurant foods are

Healthy Attitudes

If you're hungry enough for a giant burger with all the fixings, consider having two small plain burgers instead. The extra bun gives you more carbohydrates without added fat.

seasoned with salt or with a flavor enhancer called *monosodium glutamate* (MSG for short). Both contain sodium. You may want to ask whether your food can be prepared without added salt or MSG.

Fast Food Suggestions

Many fast-food restaurants now supply nutrition information to customers. Ask for a brochure or look for a sign that lists the nutrient content of items on the menu.

The box below gives suggestions for items that, in general, may be nutritious choices. However, the nutrient content of similar items can vary quite a bit from one restaurant to another. Check the nutrition information to be sure. Also remember to watch out for those extra toppings that can add fat, sugar, and sodium.

Fast Food Suggestions

Main Dishes
- ❖ Small burger with lettuce and tomato
- ❖ Roast beef sandwich
- ❖ Grilled or roast chicken sandwich
- ❖ Chicken white meat (eat without skin)
- ❖ Salad made with lean meat or poultry

Side Dishes
- ❖ Tossed salad
- ❖ Plain baked potato
- ❖ Mashed potatoes
- ❖ Plain pasta
- ❖ Corn on the cob
- ❖ Baked beans

Beverages
- ❖ Low-fat milk
- ❖ Fruit juice
- ❖ Water

Breakfast Items
- ❖ Whole grain cereal with low-fat milk
- ❖ Bran muffin

Choosing from a Salad Bar or Buffet

Many restaurants have a salad bar. You can choose from a variety of ingredients and toppings to build your own salad. The salad bar may also include ready-made salads and perhaps other foods such as fruit, cottage cheese, or hot soup.

A salad bar is a good way to include fruits and vegetables in your restaurant meal. However, if you don't choose carefully you could also be adding more fat than you realize. Prepared salads that have a creamy or oily dressing, such as potato salad, macaroni salad, or marinated vegetables, can be very high in fat. So can salad dressings and cheeses. Take smaller amounts of these items, but help yourself to plenty of leafy greens, carrots, broccoli, melon, and other nutritious selections.

Buffets are similar to salad bars, but include a wider variety of items. As with salad bars, you can build a healthful or less healthful meal. It's all in what you choose and what toppings you add. Look for nutri-tious, low-fat foods such as fruits, vegetables, whole-grain breads, low-fat dairy products, and lean meat, poultry, and fish.

Eating at School

Most schools have a cafeteria that serves lunch, and often breakfast as well. Usually the cafeteria offers a complete meal that was planned with good nutrition in mind. In some schools, you may also be able to choose from items served a la carte. Be sure to follow the Dietary Guidelines when you choose.

Bringing food from home is also an option. You'll learn how to pack a nutritious lunch or snack in Section 20.1.

Eating on the Go

These days, busy schedules often keep people from sitting down to regular meals. While they are out, they buy ready-to-eat foods from vending machines, convenience

Look for salad bars that include plenty of choices low in both calories and fat. What healthful salad foods are your favorites?

Student Experiences

1. **Class Discussion:** Ask students why it is important to consider the calories and nutrients provided by the entire day's food intake. Why is this especially important with today's busy lifestyles? If food choices are limited when you eat out, how might you compensate during the rest of the day? *(Key skill: management skills)*

2. **Choosing Nutrition:** Have students work in groups to make a list of convenience foods available from each of these sources: vending machines, convenience stores, mall shops, and drive-through windows. Ask students to identify the healthful food choices available from each source. Using the foods available, have each group plan a healthful menu to share with the class. *(Key skill: health)*

Thinking Skills

Creativity: Have students create a different meal for eating "on the go" for five school days. The meals must be nutritious and follow the Dietary Guidelines, but they must also be appealing and portable. Tell students to be creative but realistic in designing their menus. Have students share their ideas with the class.

Completing the Section

Review

- Ask students to summarize the main ideas in this section.
- Have students complete the Section Review. (Answers appear below.)

Evaluation

- Have students use actual menus to select nutritious meals that are low in fat, salt, and sugar.
- Have students take the quiz for Section 4.3. (Refer to the *Section Quizzes* booklet or use the *Testmaker Software.*)

Reteaching

- Have students list their ten favorite restaurant dishes. Help students determine whether the dishes are nutritious and whether they are high or low in fats, salt, and sugar.
- Refer to the *Reteaching Activities* booklet for the Section 4.3 activity sheet.

Enrichment

- Have students contact restaurant chains for any available nutrition information on the foods they serve. Students can make a reference booklet.

Closure

- Lead a class discussion on problems associated with eating out nutritiously and how those problems can be solved.

Fruit juice makes a refreshing snack any time of the day.

stores, mall shops, or drive-through windows. They may eat while working, walking, or driving.

If you find yourself in such a situation, you can still make healthful food choices. For instance, if you're limited to a vending machine, choose fresh fruit, fruit juice, yogurt, or pretzels. Better still, if you know you're not going to have much time to eat, pack nutritious foods to take with you.

How Eating Out Fits In

Keep in mind that variety is one of the keys to good nutrition. When eating out, your choices are likely to be limited. You may be short on some of the foods needed for good health, such as fruits and vegetables. If so, make an extra effort to include many different types of those foods in other meals.

Whether you eat out twice a month or twice a day, the food choices you make at that time are important ones. Remember that the food you eat away from home counts as part of your overall eating plan. Make your choices as nutritious as you can.

In Japan, it's considered bad manners to eat while walking. Snack foods bought from street vendors must be eaten at the food stand.

■ Section 4.3 Review ■

RECALL THE FACTS

1. When it comes to nutrition, what is one advantage of an all-you-can eat buffet? What is a disadvantage?
2. Give three suggestions for making healthful choices from a restaurant menu.
3. Name two vending machine foods that would be relatively nutritious choices.
4. Why is it important to balance restaurant food choices with other food choices?

DISCUSS YOUR IDEAS

5. Why do you think eating out has become so popular?
6. What do you consider when deciding when and where to eat out?

APPLY YOUR LEARNING

7. Create a lunch menu for a fast-food restaurant that emphasizes foods low in fat, sugar, and sodium. Give names to the food items. What would you call your restaurant? Why?

■ Answers to Section Review ■

1. You can choose nutritious items to create a healthful meal. You may be tempted to choose high-fat, high-sugar items.
2. *Any three:* Pay attention to menu clues; choose a smaller portion size; choose side dishes carefully; choose to have toppings put on the side or left off entirely.
3. Answers will vary. Examples: fresh fruit and yogurt.
4. To be sure you get the right amounts of each type of nutrient each day.
5. Answers will vary. Encourage students to give reasons for their answers.
6. Answers will vary.
7. Answers will vary.

Vegetarian Food Choices

OBJECTIVES

After studying this section, you should be able to:

- Identify foods eaten by different types of vegetarians.
- Discuss reasons why people choose to become vegetarians.
- Plan nutritious vegetarian meals.

LOOK FOR THESE TERMS

vegetarians
vegans
lacto-vegetarians
ovo-vegetarians
lacto-ovo vegetarians

Inez and her friends were standing in the lunch line, trying to decide what to eat. After Jennie had made her choices, Inez looked at her tray and said, "What? No hamburger today?"

"No," said Jennie, "I'm thinking of becoming a vegetarian, so I thought I'd stop eating meat for a while and see how it feels."

Vegetarians are people who do not eat meat, poultry, or fish. In addition, some do not eat dairy foods or eggs.

A vegetarian diet can supply complete nutrition. However, as with any way of eating, the food choices require some thought and planning. Before Jennie changes her way of eating, she would be wise to learn more about making vegetarian food choices.

Facts About Vegetarians

Some people are confused about what foods vegetarians eat. In fact, there are several kinds of vegetarians, depending on what foods they include in their diet.

Wise food choices are the key to any eating plan, including vegetarian ones.

Introducing the Section

Motivators

- Ask students if they know anyone who is a vegetarian. Discuss reasons why a person might want to become a vegetarian. Ask students to identify foods usually included in a vegetarian diet.

- Have students taste samples of tofu prepared in different ways. Discuss the role tofu plays in many vegetarian diets. Identify other foods that help meet the vegetarian's protein needs.

Objectives

- Have students read the section objectives. Discuss the purpose of studying the section.

Vocabulary

- Pronounce the terms listed under "Look for These Terms." Have students find the terms and their definitions in the section.

Guided Reading

- Have students look at the headings within Section 4.4 to preview the concepts that will be discussed.

- Have students read the section and complete the appropriate part of the Chapter 4 Study Guide in the *Student Workbook*.

Teacher's Classroom Resources—Section 4.4

Refer to these resources in the TCR package:

Reproducible Lesson Plans
Student Workbook
Extending the Text

Reteaching Activities
Section Quizzes
Testmaker Software
Color Transparencies

Teaching . . .

• Facts About Vegetarians

(text pages 127-128)

Comprehension Check

1. Ask students to list the four basic types of vegetarians *(vegans, lacto-vegetarians, ovo-vegetarians, lacto-ovo vegetarians)* and describe the differences among them.

2. Discuss reasons why people decide to become vegetarians. Ask students if they can add any reasons to those listed in the book.

Student Experiences

1. Guest Panel: Invite a guest panel of people who represent different types of vegetarians to discuss the similarities and differences in what they eat. Why did each person choose to become a vegetarian? What changes has each made to ensure a healthful diet? Which type of vegetarian has the most difficulty in getting all of the needed nutrients? *(Key skill: comparing and contrasting)*

2. Bulletin Board: Divide the class into four groups. Make each group responsible for creating a bulletin board targeted at one of the four types of vegetarian. The displays should show how a person could maintain a healthful diet within that form of vegetarianism. *(Key skills: creativity, health)*

Some people become vegetarians because they feel that raising animals for food is an inefficient use of resources.

❖ **Vegans** (VEE-guns or VEE-juns) are also known as pure vegetarians. They eat only foods from plant sources, such as grain products, dry beans and peas, fruits, vegetables, nuts, and seeds.

❖ **Lacto-vegetarians** eat dairy products in addition to foods from plant sources.

❖ **Ovo-vegetarians** eat eggs in addition to foods from plant sources.

❖ **Lacto-ovo vegetarians** eat foods from plant sources, dairy products, and eggs.

People choose to become vegetarians for many reasons. Close to 50 percent do so because they feel it is healthier. Of course, it's not necessary to become a vegetarian in order to practice healthful eating habits. Still, studies show that well-chosen vegetarian diets are healthier than the average American diet. For instance, most Americans eat too much protein and fat, whereas vegetarian diets can provide enough protein and be relatively low in fat.

Some people are vegetarians for religious reasons. Seventh Day Adventists, for instance, encourage their members not to eat meat. Many Hindus and Buddhists are vegetarians.

Some people become vegetarians because they are concerned about the world food supply. Animals can eat about 5 pounds (2 kg) or more of grain to produce 1 pound (500 g) of meat. Many vegetarians believe that eating meat contributes to the problem of world hunger. They think it would be better to use the grain to feed people around the world.

Others are vegetarians because they do not believe in killing animals. Still others are vegetarians for economic reasons. Vegetarian meals are usually less expensive than meat-based ones.

Good Nutrition for Vegetarians

If they make wise food choices, vegetarians can usually get all the nutrients they need. As with any other eating patterns, the key to good vegetarian nutrition is variety. Although vegetarians choose to avoid some foods, they still have plenty of others from which to select.

128   Chapter 4: Planning Daily Food Choices

Thinking Skills

Critical Thinking: Ask students to think about the effects that becoming a vegetarian would have, not only on their food choices, but also on their lifestyles and habits. What changes would they have to make?

Grain products, dry beans and peas, nuts and seeds, and vegetables are all sources of protien.

Specific Nutrients

It's helpful to take a look at how some specific nutrients are supplied in vegetarian food choices. Of particular interest are protein, fat, iron, calcium, and vitamins B_{12} and D.

Protein

Obtaining enough protein on a vegetarian diet is not difficult, even for vegans. As you may recall, proteins are made up of amino acids. Proteins from plant sources are called incomplete proteins, since they do not provide all of the essential amino acids. However, eating a wide variety of foods from plants can provide complete protein.

✓ SAFETY CHECK

Some extreme vegan diets are too limited. For instance, "macrobiotic" diets recommend cutting out most foods until you are eating only brown rice. Such limited diets can lead to serious health problems.

Section 4.4: Vegetarian Food Choices   **129**

More About Vegetarians

The emphasis on low-fat, low-cholesterol, and high-fiber diets has led many people to become "semi-vegetarians." These people eat mostly cereals, vegetables, fruit, and dairy products. Occasionally, they may eat a little meat, chicken, or fish.

Teaching . . .

- **Good Nutrition for Vegetarians**

(text pages 128-130)

Comprehension Check

1. People usually think of vegetarian diets as diets that are low in fats. Discuss why this might not be true. *(All the types of vegetarians except vegans eat some form of dairy products or eggs, many of which are high in fat. Also, nuts and seeds are high in fat.)*

2. Ask students to explain why vegetarians may run the risk of not getting sufficient iron in their diets, even though many fruits, vegetables, and grains are rich in iron. *(The iron from these sources cannot be easily absorbed by the body.)*

3. Discuss why vegans may need to take vitamin and mineral supplements.

Student Experiences

1. **Recipes:** Provide students with vegetarian cookbooks. Have students identify recipes that appeal to them. *(Key skill: reading)*

2. **Diet Analysis:** Have students analyze typical vegetarian menus. Have students determine which provide protein, fat, iron, calcium, and vitamins B_{12} and D. *(Key skill: analysis)*

Safety Check

Relate this Safety Check to the information in "Separating Fact from Fiction" on text pages 103-108. Ask students to discuss ways to avoid some of the unhealthy versions of vegetarianism or any other type of diet.

Comprehension Check

1. Discuss ways to adapt the Food Guide Pyramid for a vegetarian diet.

2. Ask students to describe several places to find vegetarian recipes. *(in vegetarian cookbooks, in cookbooks from Asia and Central and South America, by revising favorite recipes from nonvegetarian cookbooks)*

3. Have students explain why it is important for vegetarians—especially vegans—to eat plenty of dark green leafy vegetables such as kale and spinach. *(These plants are good alternate sources of calcium for vegetarians who don't eat dairy products.)*

Dry beans or peas, together with any grain products, nuts, or seeds eaten during the same day, can provide all the essential amino acids. In addition, vegetarians who eat dairy products or eggs can get complete protein from those sources.

Fat

You have learned in previous chapters that health experts recommend choosing foods low in fat. A well-chosen vegetarian meal pattern can be low in fat because it emphasizes grain products, fruits, and vegetables. However, vegetarians who rely heavily on whole milk, cheese, or eggs may be eating too much fat, especially saturated fat. Nuts and seeds are also high in fat.

When Angelo became a vegetarian, he enjoyed a wide variety of recipes using dairy foods and eggs. When his weight began to go up, Angelo realized that he was eating more fat than before, so he made some basic changes. He switched to low-fat dairy products and cut back on eggs. He discovered delicious recipes for cooked dry beans and peas and added a variety of whole grain products to his meals. He also ate more fruits and vegetables. Before long, Angelo's weight returned to normal.

Iron

Many fruits, vegetables, and grain products are good sources of iron, especially dry beans and peas and dried fruits. However, vegetarians run the risk of an iron shortage because the iron in foods from plant sources is not easily absorbed.

Vitamin C helps the body absorb iron from plant sources. It's best to eat foods rich in vitamin C at the same time as foods high in iron. If vegetarians eat a wide variety of foods, including rich sources of vitamin C, they will probably meet their iron needs. Another way to get iron is by using cast iron cookware.

Calcium

Getting enough calcium is of particular concern for vegans and others who do not drink milk. As you have learned, a good supply of calcium is essential for healthy bones and teeth.

Dry beans are used in many vegetarian dishes because they supply protein and other nutrients. Dozens of different varieties of beans are available.

Thinking Skills

Reasoning: Some people claim that increasing emphasis on health and fitness may encourage more people to become vegetarians. Ask students whether they think the number of vegetarians will increase, decrease, or remain about the same over the next ten years. Ask them to give reasons for their ideas.

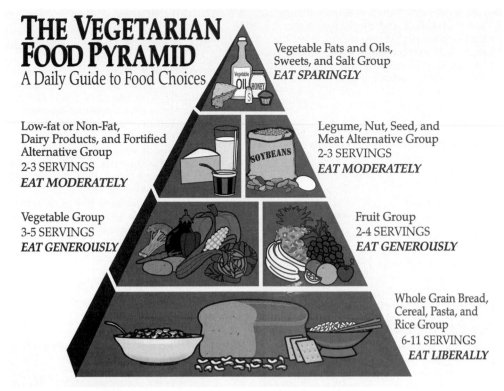

THE VEGETARIAN FOOD PYRAMID
A Daily Guide to Food Choices

Vegetable Fats and Oils, Sweets, and Salt Group
EAT SPARINGLY

Low-fat or Non-Fat, Dairy Products, and Fortified Alternative Group
2-3 SERVINGS
EAT MODERATELY

Legume, Nut, Seed, and Meat Alternative Group
2-3 SERVINGS
EAT MODERATELY

Vegetable Group
3-5 SERVINGS
EAT GENEROUSLY

Fruit Group
2-4 SERVINGS
EAT GENEROUSLY

Whole Grain Bread, Cereal, Pasta, and Rice Group
6-11 SERVINGS
EAT LIBERALLY

How does the Vegetarian Food Pyramid compare to the Food Guide Pyramid? ©The Health Connection, 1994.

Calcium needs can probably be met by eating good plant sources of the nutrient. These include dry beans and green leafy vegetables, such as spinach, kale, and mustard greens.

Even so, it may be difficult for vegans to get enough calcium. They may be advised to drink fortified soy milk. Some health professionals recommend vegans use calcium supplements.

Vitamins B$_{12}$ and D

Another concern regarding vegan diets is vitamins B$_{12}$ and D. Since vitamin B$_{12}$ is not found in foods from plant sources, the Dietary Guidelines recommend that vegans take supplements. Vegans may also need supplements of vitamin D, which is found mainly in fortified milk.

Planning Vegetarian Meals

Planning vegetarian meals can be easy. Just follow the basic guidelines for meal planning you have already studied, but modify them.

The Vegetarian Food Pyramid shown above is based on the Food Guide Pyramid. (You may want to review the serving sizes given in Section 3.2.) Here are some additional suggestions for vegetarian meal planning:

❖ Look for food products made from soybeans and wheat that can be substituted for foods from animal sources. The box on page 132 lists some that can be found in supermarkets or health food stores.

Section 4.4: Vegetarian Food Choices   131

Student Experiences

1. **Tasting:** Provide students with samples of vegetarian dishes made with soy milk, tofu, seitan, and vegetable protein. Ask students to evaluate the taste and appearance of the dishes. *(Key skill: evaluation)*

2. **Menu Planning:** Have students plan and write out a well-balanced vegetarian diet for a day. *(Key skills: health, writing)*

3. **Problem Solving:** Have students work in groups to solve the following problems that can occur in a vegetarian diet. How can a vegetarian reduce fat consumption? How can a vegetarian avoid an iron shortage? How can vegans avoid deficiencies of vitamins B$_{12}$ and D?

**• Eating Out
Vegetarian Style**

(text pages 133-134)

Comprehension Check

1. Ask students to list foods that are readily available in restaurants that are suitable for a vegetarian diet. *(some types of omelets and pizzas, baked potatoes with cheese topping, etc.)*

2. Discuss guidelines for vegetarians to follow when selecting a restaurant. *(Choose a self-serve restaurant; ask server about items on menu that might be suitable; choose ethnic restaurants such as Chinese, East Indian, Mexican, or Mideastern; talk to manager.)*

❖ Get acquainted with the many varieties of grain products and dry beans and peas that are available. (See Chapter 17 for more information about these foods.) For instance, you might want to try grains such as millet, bulgur, and barley.

❖ Each day, make sure you have several good sources of vitamin C, such as citrus fruits, strawberries, and melons.

❖ Use dark green leafy vegetables, such as kale and mustard greens, liberally.

Products to Try

❖ **Soy milk,** a beverage made from soybeans, can be used as a milk substitute. Look for products that are fortified.

❖ **Tofu** (TOE-foo) is also known as soybean curd. High in protein, it has a bland flavor that blends well with other foods. Choose from firm or soft tofu to use in recipes. You can also buy tofu hot dogs, patties, and ready-to-eat frozen foods.

❖ **Seitan** (say-tan) is also known as wheat meat. Although it resembles cooked meat, it's made from wheat dough cooked in a flavored liquid. Seitan can be substituted for meat in many recipes and is also available as ready-to-eat foods.

❖ **Vegetable protein foods** are made of soy protein. You can buy them in granular form to mix in recipes. They are also commercially made into ready-to-eat meat and poultry substitutes, such as breakfast links.

Even people who are not vegetarians may want to collect vegetarian recipes to enjoy from time to time.

Vegetarian Recipes

Many vegetarian recipe books are available. They range from basic information on getting started with vegetarian foods to gourmet and ethnic recipes. Since vegetarian recipes are sometimes high in fat, choose them carefully. You can also adapt favorite non-vegetarian recipes, substituting ingredients such as seitan or bulgur for meat.

Many ethnic cuisines, such as Asian and Central and South American, are based on vegetarian foods. They can provide you with a wealth of menu ideas and recipes as well as introduce you to new foods.

Vegetarian meals can be just as appealing as any others. One of the most famous American chefs is Brother Ron Pickarski, a Franciscan friar and certified executive chef. He heads the American natural foods team, which has won two silver medals at the International Culinary Olympics using only vegan foods.

Food and Nutrition Science

Analyzing Vegetarian Diets: Have students volunteer to follow a vegetarian diet for a week. Students should keep a scientific log of what they eat each day and how they liked it. At the end of the week, they should analyze the nutritional value of the foods they ate. Have students create a written report of their experiment. The report should include their log, their nutritional analysis, and a statement of how they felt after eliminating meat from their diet.

Eating Out Vegetarian Style

Because of demand from their customers, many restaurants are offering at least one vegetarian meal on their menu. Except for vegans, most vegetarians should have no problems making food choices when eating out. They can usually find meatless meals made with milk, eggs, or cheese. Some food choices might include baked potatoes with cheese toppings, pizza, meatless lasagna, bean soup, and omelets.

Since vegans eat no animal products, their choices are more limited. Many restaurants offer salad bars or a selection of salads on the menu, but for those who eat out frequently, this can be tiresome.

Here are some suggestions for vegans when eating out:

❖ Choose self-serve restaurants, such as cafeterias or buffets, whenever possible. They usually have an assortment of hot vegetables and breads, along with fresh fruits and salads. If hot soup is offered, find out if it has meat or is made from a meat stock.

❖ Read the menu descriptions carefully. Sometimes the ingredients for each selection are listed. If not, and an item sounds as though it might be suitable, ask the server what it contains.

❖ Tell the server that you are a vegetarian and ask whether the chef would be willing to make up a plate of cooked vegetables.

❖ Ethnic restaurants, such as Chinese, East Indian, Mexican, and Mideastern, usually offer some vegan meals.

❖ If a restaurant does not offer any vegan meals except salads, talk to the manager. Restaurants are always looking for ways to attract new customers and may be receptive to your ideas.

Today, vegetarians are finding more restaurant choices that suit their way of eating.

Student Experiences

1. **Analyzing Menus:** Provide students with restaurant menus. Have students select menu items for a meal to be eaten by a vegetarian. *(Key skill: reading)*

2. **Choosing Vegetarian Meals:** Take a field trip to a suitable restaurant and have students choose nutritious vegetarian meals. Ask students to write a summary of what they chose, whether they liked it, and why. *(Key skill: writing)*

Lab Experience

Provide a recipe for pizza crust (or provide frozen crusts from a supermarket) and a variety of toppings that would be suitable for lacto-vegetarians. Have students create and critique vegetarian pizzas.

Thinking Skills

Problem Solving: Present this situation to students: You are a vegan attending a dinner meeting with a large group of people at a local restaurant. This is an important meeting for you, since you will be asked to make a presentation. When you get to the restaurant, you discover that none of the foods on the menu are appropriate for a vegan. What do you do?

4.4

Completing the Section

Review

- Ask students to summarize the main ideas in this section.
- Have students complete the Section Review. (Answers appear below.)

Evaluation

- Have students write a short essay on the various types of vegetarians.
- Have students take the quiz for Section 4.4. (Refer to the *Section Quizzes* booklet or use the *Testmaker Software*.)

Reteaching

- Display photographs of various foods and have students practice choosing foods that would be acceptable to different types of vegetarians.
- Refer to the *Reteaching Activities* booklet for the Section 4.4 activity sheet.

Enrichment

- Have interested students research vegetarianism in other countries. What types of recipes do they use? Do they follow the same guidelines as vegetarians in the United States? What differences are there?

Closure

- Lead a class discussion on vegetarianism and its effects on food choices, habits, and lifestyle.

Vegetarian meals aren't just for vegetarians. This spicy bean pizza, for example, would please almost anyone, as would the zucchini-rice soup shown at right.

■ Section 4.4 Review ■

RECALL THE FACTS

1. How are a vegan and a lacto-ovo vegetarian similar? How are they different?

2. List four reasons people give for becoming vegetarians.

3. How can vegetarians be sure to get enough protein? Iron?

4. Give three guidelines for planning vegetarian meals.

DISCUSS YOUR IDEAS

5. Do you think restaurants should offer more choices for vegetarian customers? If they did, would non-vegetarian customers also benefit? Why or why not?

APPLY YOUR LEARNING

6. Plan one day's meals and snacks for a vegetarian. Be prepared to explain the type of vegetarian the menu is for and why you chose those foods.

■ Answers to Section Review ■

1. Neither eats meat; lacto-ovo vegetarian eats eggs and dairy products in addition to vegetables.
2. *Any four:* They think it's healthier; religious reasons; concern about world food supply; do not believe in killing animals.
3. Eat dry beans or peas as well as grain products, nuts, or seeds each day; consume vitamin C along with vegetable sources of iron.
4. *Any three:* Modify the foods listed in the Food Guide Pyramid; use products made from soybeans and wheat instead of meats; use grain products and dry beans and peas; include several good sources of vitamin C; use dark green leafy vegetables.
5. Answers will vary.
6. Answers will vary.

Career PROFILE

Sue Anderson
Cooperative Extension Specialist

CURRENT POSITION

"I'm one of two educators working for the Cooperative Extension Service in a small rural county."

RESPONSIBILITIES

"My job is multi-faceted, but one of my main duties is to educate the public about foods and nutrition. I do this through phone calls that come in to my office, through video programs that I plan and prepare, and through articles that I write for the media."

SKILLS

"Because the majority of my time is spent talking to people, communication skills are very important for this job. Flexibility and creativity are also valued skills."

EDUCATION

"I have a four-year college degree in home economics with a minor in communications."

WORK ENVIRONMENT

"Every day is different. Some days are spent in the office writing press releases or answering telephone calls from the public. Other days are spent out in the community, delivering programs and speeches to groups of people. My hours can vary greatly, including evening and weekend work."

FAVORITE PART OF THE JOB

"Most enjoyable for me is being able to provide people with the kind of information they need in their everyday lives, whether it be food preparation or managing a household budget. I also like the variety that goes with this job."

- Do you think you'd like a job in which every day is different? Why or why not?
- What are the advantages of having hours that vary? What are the disadvantages?

135

For More Information

For more information about careers in family and consumer sciences, contact:
- American Dietetic Association, 216 W. Jackson Blvd., Suite 800, Chicago, IL 60606-6995

- American Association of Family and Consumer Sciences, 1555 King St., Alexandria, VA 22314
- Future Homemakers of America, 1910 Association Dr., Reston, VA 22091

Completing the Chapter

Review

- Have students complete the Chapter Review (Answers appear below.)

Evaluation

- Ask students to plan three nutritious meals for an active teenager: one that can be prepared at home; one that could be chosen from a menu at a restaurant; and one for a person on a vegan diet.

- Have students take the test for Chapter 4. (Refer to the *Chapter and Unit Tests* booklet or construct your own test using the *Testmaker software*.)

■ ANSWERS ■

REVIEWING THE FACTS

1. Find out if it provides the nutrients you need and the right number of calories.

2. Lack of energy during the morning as a result of not eating since the night before; it's harder to concentrate on your schoolwork.

3. Eating five or more small meals at convenient times during the day instead of three large ones.

4. Each time you eat, make a note in a log of the time you ate, the food you ate and the amount of food, and give a brief description of the eating situation.

5. Because a vague promise to yourself such as "I'll eat better from now on" is hard to keep.

6. *Any three:* Fried, breaded, in its own gravy, in a cheese sauce, rich, sautéed, creamed, au gratin, scalloped, batter-dipped.

SUMMARY

SECTION 4.1

Daily Meals and Snacks: People follow many different eating patterns, from three traditional meals a day to "grazing." No matter what eating pattern you follow, be sure your daily food choices provide the right amount of calories and nutrients. It's also important to eat regularly, start the day with a nutritious breakfast, and choose snacks wisely

SECTION 4.2

Improving Your Eating Habits: Keeping a food record is a good way to identify your current eating habits. Then you can evaluate your habits and decide whether you want to change them. Work at improving your eating habits gradually and set specific, realistic goals.

SECTION 4.3

Eating Out Nutritiously: Different types of restaurants have pros and cons when it comes to nutrition. Learn to identify the healthful choices on a restaurant menu, a salad bar, or a buffet. Wise food choices are also important when eating at school or eating on the go.

SECTION 4.4

Vegetarian Food Choices: Some vegetarians eat only foods from plants, while others also eat dairy products or eggs. People become vegetarians for many reasons. The vegetarian way of eating can be healthful as long as wise food choices are made. To plan vegetarian meals, modify the basic guidelines for good nutrition.

REVIEWING FACTS

1. Identify two ways to judge whether an eating pattern is nutritionally sound. (4.1)

2. Name two negative consequences of skipping breakfast. (4.1)

3. What is meant by "grazing"? (4.1)

4. Briefly describe how to keep a food record. (4.2)

5. When planning to improve your food habits, why is it important to decide on specific changes? (4.2)

6. Name three clues that a food on a restaurant menu may be high in fat. (4.3)

7. What does ordering "a la carte" mean? How can it help you choose healthier foods when eating out? (4.3)

8. Name four types of vegetarians and the foods eaten by each. (4.4)

9. Why do some vegetarians need to be careful about eating too much fat? (4.4)

10. Why is calcium a concern for some vegetarians? Name two foods that can help meet their calcium needs. (4.4)

LEARNING BY DOING

1. ***Foods lab:*** Using recipe books or magazines, find three ideas for quick and easy foods that would make a nutritious breakfast. Prepare the foods in class. (4.1)

2. ***Computer lab:*** Using a word processing program or other software, produce a form that could be used when keeping a food record. Include spaces for recording the food eaten, amount, time of day, and situation. (4.2)

3. ***Taste test:*** Taste samples of vegetarian dishes provided by your teacher. Judge them on taste and appearance. (4.4)

7. Choosing items individually from the menu; it can help you avoid any rich foods that may ordinarily be served with the entree at a restaurant.

8. Vegans eat only foods from plant sources; lacto-vegetarians eat foods from plant sources and dairy products; ovo-vegetarians eat foods from plant sources and eggs; lacto-ovo-vegetarians eat foods from plant sources, eggs, and dairy products.

THINKING CRITICALLY

1. **Analyzing a statement:** Your friend tells you that snacking is bad for you. Do you agree or disagree? Why? (4.1)

2. **Analyzing behavior:** Alyssa was reviewing her food record. She noticed that when she ate alone or with her family, she usually made healthful food choices. However, her choices were less wise when she ate out with friends. Why might this be so? (4.2)

3. **Predicting consequences:** How might consumer complaints or suggestions affect menu items offered by a restaurant? What might happen if restaurant owners ignore consumer complaints and suggestions? (4.3, 4.4)

4. **Recognizing stereotypes:** Suppose you and a friend are eating out. You hear a person at the next table asking if there are any vegetarian dishes on the menu. Your friend says, "How dumb. People who don't eat meat are weird. I'll bet he's a real weakling." Is this a reasonable judgment? What can you say to help your friend better understand vegetarians and their way of eating? (4.4)

MAKING DECISIONS AND SOLVING PROBLEMS

What Would You Do?

1. Your dad routinely fixes breakfast for the family. Most mornings he prepares eggs, bacon or sausage, buttered biscuits, and whole milk. You appreciate his willingness to see that you have a hot breakfast each morning. However, you are concerned about the fat and cholesterol in the foods he prepares. (4.1)

2. Analyzing your food record, you find that you are most likely to make poor food choices late in the day, a few hours after the evening meal. You also find you eat very few fruits. (4.2)

3. You would like to eat in your school cafeteria each day. However, you have noticed that many of the foods served seem high in fat. (4.3)

4. One of your cousins is coming to stay with you for a week while his parents are out of town. He has just reminded you that he is a lacto-vegetarian. Your family routinely serves meat at every meal. (4.4)

LINKING YOUR STUDIES

1. **Social studies:** Using library resources, research the eating patterns in two other cultures. Present your findings to the class. Discuss why eating patterns vary from one culture to another. (4.1)

2. **Math:** Use a calorie-counting guide and a one-day food record. Determine approximately how many calories were in each meal and snack. Express the calories for each meal or snack as a percentage of the total calories for the day. (4.1, 4.2)

3. **Math:** At a popular fast-food restaurant chain, a cheeseburger has 305 calories, 9 grams of fat, 50 milligrams of cholesterol, and 725 milligrams of sodium. A small order of fries has 220 calories, 12 grams of fat, no cholesterol, and 110 milligrams of sodium. What is the total amount of calories, fat, cholesterol, and sodium for this meal? If one gram of fat has 9 calories, how many calories does the fat in this meal provide? (4.3)

4. **Writing:** Write a dialogue in which a vegetarian explains his or her food choices to a non-vegetarian. (4.4)

137

LEARNING BY DOING

1. Answers will vary.

2. Food logs will vary. You may need to instruct some students in the use of a simple software program.

THINKING CRITICALLY

1. Answers will vary. Students should realize that it's not the snack that is troublesome, but the type of food eaten. Healthful snacks such as fresh fruit can be beneficial.

2. Answers will vary. Remind students that friends are among the social influences that help determine our eating habits.

3. Answers will vary. Remind students that most restaurants try to improve based on patron suggestions. If a restaurant ignored consumer complaints and suggestions, it might lose business or even go out of business.

4. Answers will vary. Students should realize that a well-balanced vegetarian meal is just as nutritious as any other well-balanced meal. Help students realize that judging a person by the type of food he or she eats can lead to faulty conclusions.

MAKING DECISIONS AND SOLVING PROBLEMS

Answers to "Making Decisions and Solving Problems" questions will vary. Encourage students to give reasons for their answers.

LINKING YOUR STUDIES

Answers to Linking Your Studies questions will vary. Encourage students to be creative and to explore alternatives where applicable.

9. Some ovo- and lacto-vegetarians may tend to depend on foods such as eggs or dairy products that are high in fats to supply protein needs; nuts and seeds also contain a large amount of fat.

10. Vegetarians who do not drink milk may have trouble getting enough calcium. They can eat dry beans and green leafy vegetables or drink fortified soy milk.

Planning the Chapter

Chapter Overview

Section 5.1: A Healthy Weight

Section 5.2: Weight Management

Section 5.3: Exercise Basics

Section 5.4: Nutrition for Sports and Fitness

Introducing the Chapter

Motivators

- Invite a coach or fitness expert to class to discuss food and fitness. Ask the speaker to discuss the roles of food and exercise in weight management. Also ask the person to identify special considerations for athletes. Have students develop a list of questions they would like to ask the guest speaker.

- Take a field trip to a weight control and fitness center. Ask the trainer to discuss the roles of food and exercise in weight management and fitness. Find out what services the center offers clients in weight control and what types of exercises are recommended for overall fitness.

Teacher's Classroom Resources—Chapter 5

Refer to these resources in the TCR package:

Enrichment Activities

Chapter and Unit Tests

Testmaker Software

CHAPTER 5
Food and Fitness

138

Cooperative Learning Suggestions

Ask students to form groups of four to conduct interviews about improving their physical fitness. Each group consists of two pairs of students, who interview each other. One student interviews the other about his or her perceived fitness needs; then each pair reverses roles so that everyone gets interviewed. Then have students share what they learned from their partner with the rest of the group. Together, the group should set goals and work together to reach them.

- Provide students time to weigh and discuss their progress each week.
- Encourage students to meet outside of school for exercise activities.

SECTION 5.1

A Healthy Weight

OBJECTIVES

After studying this section, you should be able to:

- Explain why there is no one ideal body shape.
- Describe methods used to determine whether a person's weight is at a healthy level.

LOOK FOR THIS TERM

waist-to-hip ratio

Section 5.1
A Healthy Weight

Introducing the Section

Motivators

- Ask students to describe their ideas of the "ideal" body. Ask students what has influenced their concept of an "ideal" body. Discuss reasons why a person's "ideal" body may not be realistic.

- Ask students how they would decide whether they are underweight, overweight, or the right weight for their bodies. On the chalkboard, list the sources of information they name. Discuss advantages and disadvantages of using each source.

Objectives

- Have students read the section objectives. Discuss the purpose of studying the section.

Vocabulary

- Pronounce the terms listed under "Look for These Terms." Have students find the terms and their definitions in the section.

Guided Reading

- Have students look at the headings within Section 5.1 to preview the concepts that will be discussed.

- Have students read the section and complete the appropriate part of the Chapter 5 Study Guide in the *Student Workbook*.

Margo was confused. According to the weight charts, she was at least five pounds too heavy for her height. Yet she knew that she ate sensibly and exercised regularly. She also knew that she wasn't as slender as some of her friends. Maybe the weight charts were right.

The Myth of the "Ideal" Body

Like Margo, many people are concerned or dissatisfied with their weight. One reason is a lack of realistic goals.

About half the people trying to lose weight today are not really overweight. Instead, they are trying to reduce to a body size or weight that's impossible for them to reach. Movies and television shows, along with advertisers, set up a slim body as the ideal for everyone.

Inherited characteristics play a major role in determining body shape. DNA molecules, like this one, are located in the nucleus of each cell. They carry the genetic code of characteristics unique to you.

Teacher's Classroom Resources—Section 5.1

Refer to these resources in the TCR package:

Reproducible Lesson Plans
Student Workbook
Extending the Text

Reteaching Activities
Section Quizzes
Testmaker Software
Color Transparencies

Teaching . . .

- **The Myth of the "Ideal" Body**

(text pages 139-140)

Comprehension Check

1. Ask students to explain why it is usually impossible to obtain the "ideal" body as presented in movies and advertisements.

2. Ask students to describe the role genes play in determining the ideal body weight for each individual. *(Through genes, people inherit physical traits such as shoulder width and leg length. These traits affect the weight requirements for individuals.)*

Student Experiences

1. **Class Discussion:** Discuss sources of "ideal" body myths. Ask students to name some famous people who serve as "ideal" body role models. Identify the inherited characteristics of these people. Are any excessively thin? How do these role models influence their admirers? *(Key skill: analysis)*

2. **Reading:** Provide students with an article that describes ways a movie star or model camouflages his or her less desirable traits. How do these efforts contribute to the myth of perfection? *(Key skill: reading)*

In reality, the human body comes in many different shapes and sizes. These differences have nothing to do with being "too fat" or "too thin." They are simply part of each person's inherited traits.

Through the genes, children inherit characteristics from their parents, grandparents, and other ancestors. Some people have inherited wider shoulders or hips than others. Legs may be short, long, or in-between. When you look around, you see many different combinations, from tall, thin bodies to short, stocky ones. How do you judge body shapes? Does shape make one person more worthy than another one?

Most people are much more critical of their own body shape than other people's bodies. In their minds, they have an image of an "ideal" body and try desperately to reach that ideal. In most cases, it's a losing battle. The slim model or movie star inherited that shape, just as you did yours. Unless their genetic makeup allows it, most people cannot possibly change their body shape to match the ideal image.

Successful weight management starts with accepting the body you were born with. Then you can take steps to achieve a healthy weight within your body limits. You may never look like a model or star athlete. However, it's far more important to be fit and healthy, whatever your shape and size.

What Is a Healthy Weight?

Health professionals urge people to maintain a healthy weight. That means a weight that will help you stay healthy throughout your life, within the framework of your own inherited shape.

Health professionals use a variety of methods to evaluate whether a person is overweight or underweight. These include weight charts, body fat tests, and waist-to-hip ratio.

Weight Charts

A weight chart, such as the one below, gives recommendations for healthy weights for adults.

Weight charts are not available for children and teens. That's because they are growing rapidly and at different rates.

Suggested Weights for Adults	
Height[1]	Weight in pounds[2]
5'0"	97-128
5'1"	101-132
5'2"	104-137
5'3"	107-141
5'4"	111-146
5'5"	114-150
5'6"	118-155
5'7"	121-160
5'8"	125-164
5'9"	129-169
5'10"	132-174
5'11"	136-179
6'0"	140-184
6'1"	144-189
6'2"	148-195
6'3"	152-200
6'4"	156-205
6'5"	160-211
6'6"	164-216

[1] Without shoes.
[2] Without clothes. The higher weights in the ranges apply to people who have more muscle and bone, such as many men.

Source: Dietary Guidelines for Americans, 1995.

Thinking Skills

Reasoning: Ask students why men of a certain height and frame size weigh more than women of the same height and frame size. *(Men's small frames are larger than women's small frames. Men tend to have more muscle tissue, which is dense, than women. Women have more fat tissue, which is less dense.)*

Body-Fat Tests

Instead of weight, some health professionals prefer to check the amount of body fat in relation to muscle. In many cases, this gives a truer picture than a number on a scale does.

When Margo saw that she weighed more than the charts recommended, she became concerned. However, body-fat tests showed that the extra pounds were from muscle, not fat. Margo actually had less body fat than average. Her physician reassured her that she did not need to lose weight.

Healthy Attitudes

What if you eat sensibly and exercise regularly, but still feel you're overweight? Ask a physician for advice. It may simply be that you're gaining weight faster than you're growing in height. Later on, your height may catch up.

Waist-to-Hip Ratio

Health professionals also look at how fat is distributed in the body. Researchers have divided people into two groups, according to where fat is located. Adults with a pear-like shape carry most of the fat on the thighs and hips. Those with an apple-like shape carry most of it over the abdomen. Research shows that "apples" may have a greater risk of health problems than the "pears." "Apples," however, seem to be able to lose excess weight more easily than "pears."

Adults can check their body shape very easily. They should stand relaxed and measure their waist without pulling in their stomach. Then they should measure their hips where they are the largest. Divide the waist measurement by the hip measurement. This will give the **waist-to-hip ratio.**

Adult women should have a ratio no higher than 0.80, while men should have no more than 0.95. Ratios above these limits may increase the risk of health problems, even if the scale shows that weight is at a healthy level.

Successful athletes pay careful attention to the ratio of fat to muscle. They understand the vital role nutrition plays in a training program.

Section 5.1: A Healthy Weight   **141**

Teaching . . .

• **What Is a Healthy Weight?**

(text pages 140-142)

Comprehension Check

1. Discuss the importance of maintaining a weight that is healthy for your personal size and shape.

2. Discuss why weight charts do not usually include figures for children and teens. *(They are growing rapidly and at different rates.)*

3. Ask students to explain why some health professionals use body-fat tests instead of relying strictly on weight to determine whether a person is overweight. *(Extra muscle may add weight but not be a health risk.)*

Student Experiences

1. **Body Shapers:** Have students locate articles showing how to select clothing that looks good on different body types. How can dressing properly contribute to self-esteem? *(Key skill: reading)*

2. **Body-Fat Tests:** Provide students with information about body-fat tests, including the pinch test and the body immersion test. Ask them to explain how these tests determine the amount of body fat in relation to muscle. *(Key skill: reading)*

3. **Body Measurements:** Have students work singly or in pairs to take their waist and hip measurements. Have students divide their waist measurements by their hip measurements to find their waist-to-hip ratio. Have students compare their ratios to those listed in the text. *(Key skill: math)*

Food and Nutrition Science

Energy Balance: Emphasize to students that 1 pound (0.45 kg) of body fat contains 3500 calories. This fact is the basis for scientific understanding of weight gain and loss. The energy balance between food eaten and energy expended in metabolism and activities results in weight gain, loss, or maintenance.

Completing the Section

Review

- Ask students to summarize the main ideas in this section.
- Have students complete the Section Review. (Answers appear below.)

Evaluation

- Have students write a short essay describing what they learned in this section.
- Have students take the quiz for Section 5.1. (Refer to the *Section Quizzes* booklet or use the *Testmaker Software*.)

Reteaching

- Give students magazine ads that include people. Ask them what these ads suggest about the body shapes most valued in our society. In what ways might the ads give a false impression?
- Refer to the *Reteaching Activities* booklet for the Section 5.1 activity sheet.

Enrichment

- Have students develop a plan for creating average height-weight charts for students in the school.

Closure

- Lead a class discussion on the "ideal" weight. Discuss why "ideal" differs with each individual.

The Right Weight for You

As you can see, there's more to evaluating a person's weight than meets the eye. If you're wondering about your weight, don't compare yourself to your friends or to a picture in a magazine. Instead, talk to a health professional. He or she can use reliable methods to judge whether your weight is right for you.

No matter what your shape or size, a sound weight management program can benefit you. In the next section, you'll learn some basic guidelines to help you maintain a healthy weight throughout your life.

Be realistic about what is a healthy weight for you. Unrealistic expectations can keep you from feeling good about yourself.

Section 5.1 Review

RECALL THE FACTS

1. Why do people have different body shapes and sizes?
2. Name three methods that health professionals may use to evaluate a person's weight.
3. How is waist-to-hip ratio calculated? Why is it significant?

DISCUSS YOUR IDEAS

4. What "ideal" body shape is shown in the media? Why do you think these physical traits are valued?
5. Why do you think that images of the "ideal" body have such a powerful effect on people?

APPLY YOUR LEARNING

6. In magazines, find pictures showing the "ideal" body shape. Compare and contrast this with more typical body shapes.

Answers to Section Review

1. They inherit different body structures from relatives.
2. Weight charts, body-fat tests, and waist-to-hip ratio.
3. By measuring the waist and the hips and dividing waist measurement by hip measurement. Ratios above 0.80 (for women) or 0.95 (for men) can increase the risk of health problems.
4. Answers will vary.
5. Answers will vary. Students should understand that there is a psychological factor involved. People enjoy being "one of the crowd."
6. Answers will vary.

SECTION 5.2

Weight Management

OBJECTIVES

After studying this section, you should be able to:

- Recognize questionable weight-loss methods.
- Describe techniques for successful weight loss.
- Give guidelines for gaining and maintaining weight.

LOOK FOR THESE TERMS

fad diets
"yo-yo" dieting
behavior modification

A weight management program can help you achieve a healthy weight and maintain it throughout your life. Beginning weight management now can lead to a lifetime of better health. Whether you need to lose weight, gain weight, or keep your weight about where it is now, you'll find tips in this section to help you.

Losing Excess Weight

As you have learned, excess weight can be a health risk. Studies show that overweight is a risk factor in heart disease, diabetes, cancer, and high blood pressure. For many people, losing weight is a positive step toward better health.

By eating right and staying active, you can maintain a healthy weight.

Teacher's Classroom Resources—Section 5.2

Refer to these resources in the TCR package:

Reproducible Lesson Plans

Student Workbook

Extending the Text

Reteaching Activities

Section Quizzes

Testmaker Software

Color Transparencies

**Section 5.2
Weight
Management**

Introducing the Section

Motivators

- Ask students to describe weight-loss methods with which they are familiar. Who recommends each method? How successful are these weight-loss methods in the short term? in the long term? Why do most weight-loss methods have more short-term than long-term success?

- Show before-and-after pictures of someone who has gained weight after being anorexic and someone who has lost weight after being obese. Have students discuss factors they think contributed to the underweight/overweight conditions and how the weight gain or loss might have been accomplished.

Objectives

- Have students read the section objectives. Discuss the purpose of studying the section.

Vocabulary

- Pronounce the terms listed under "Look for These Terms." Have students find the terms and their definitions in the section.

Guided Reading

- Have students look at the headings within Section 5.2 to preview the concepts that will be discussed.

- Have students read the section and complete the appropriate part of the Chapter 5 Study Guide in the *Student Workbook*.

Teaching . . .

• Evaluating Weight-Loss Methods

(text pages 143-145)

Comprehension Check

1. Discuss the relationship between weight and major health problems such as heart disease, diabetes, high blood pressure, and cancer. *(Excess weight increases the risk of these problems.)*

2. Ask students to list three popular methods of losing weight. *(wight-loss diets, weight-control centers, weight-control products)*

3. Discuss the types of diets that you should avoid and the reasons why they are dangerous.

4. Ask students to describe the disadvantages associated with some weight-loss methods.

Using the Photo

(Clogged artery, page 145) If possible, collect additional photos from the science department or from a local heart clinic that show atherosclerosis in various stages, from beginning to advanced. Show the photos in sequence to help students. Then discuss the various ways atherosclerosis can be treated. Emphasize that prevention—choosing low-fat, low-cholesterol foods—is by far the best "cure."

✓ SAFETY CHECK

A woman should never go on a weight-loss diet during pregnancy. Weight gain is very important for expectant mothers. Their own health, and that of the baby, depends on getting enough nutritious food. You can read more about this subject in Section 6.1.

Evaluating Weight-Loss Methods

These days, with so much attention focused on health and appearance, weight loss is big business. Everywhere you turn you can find books, articles, and advertisements that claim to provide the answers to weight loss.

Popular types of weight-loss methods include:

❖ **Weight-loss diets**—eating plans that restrict calorie intake.
❖ **Weight-control centers**—organizations that provide a diet and psychological support.
❖ **Weight-control products**—anything from pills to candies, crackers, milkshakes, and even prepared meals, all sold with the promise of helping people lose weight.

Some of the weight-loss methods that are promoted are based on sound nutrition principles. Many, however, are not. **Fad diets** are current, popular weight-loss methods that ignore good nutrition. Some, as you will see, can even be dangerous to health.

Dangers to Avoid

Many weight-loss plans rely on unsafe methods. Avoid the following:
❖ Very low-calorie diets (800 calories or less per day). These may not provide enough energy or enough of the nutrients needed for good health.
❖ Diets based on a single food, such as grapefruit. As you know, your body needs a variety of foods every day.
❖ Fasting—going without food. This can be extremely damaging to your health.
❖ Diet pills. Some contain drugs that could create serious health problems.
❖ Plans that promise quick weight loss (over 2 pounds, or 1 kg, per week).

Even a weight-loss plan that would be acceptable for an adult may pose a problem for teens. At this point in your life, you are probably still growing. If you follow a weight-loss plan now, you might not get enough nutrients to grow into a healthy adult. If you are overweight now, see a health professional before you begin a weight-loss plan.

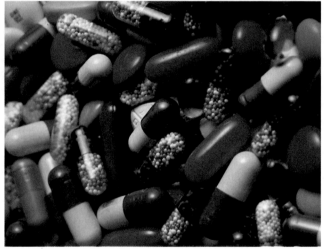

There are no magic ways to lose weight. The advertisements for diet pills, for example, don't tell you they can cause serious health problems.

Special Needs Strategies

Behaviorally Disabled: Have the school nurse weigh students and tell them privately if they are underweight or overweight. Have the nurse suggest ways to reach or maintain their ideal weight. Have students write a brief report summarizing what they learned.

Physically Disabled: Ask a physical education instructor to teach students basic exercises to help them improve their physical fitness. Have students keep a fitness record for a month of the exercises they do. Ask students whether they can tell any difference in how they feel.

SAFETY CHECK

People who lose weight too quickly may develop the following symptoms due to lack of nutrients:

❖ Constant fatigue.
❖ Large, dark circles under the eyes.
❖ Sagging, flaking, or dry skin.
❖ Brittle or soft fingernails.
❖ Dull or thinning hair.

Disadvantages to Consider

Not all weight-loss methods are dangerous to health. However, many have other disadvantages.

Some methods are simply frauds. For instance, some products that claim to suppress appetite may use ingredients that actually have no effect.

Cost is another consideration. Weight control centers and special diet products can be expensive. Think carefully about what you are getting for your money.

Some weight-loss plans offer very limited food choices. Favorite foods are denied and the diet becomes monotonous. As a result, people find it difficult to stay on the plan long enough to get the results they want.

Of those who do manage to lose weight by dieting, at least 95 percent gain it back. The most likely reason is that weight-loss diets are seen as a temporary way of eating. Instead of learning to make healthful food choices, dieters often rely on printed menus or prepackaged meals. As soon as they have lost the weight, they tend to go back to their old eating habits.

Many dieters get caught up in the cycle of **"yo-yo" dieting.** They lose weight when dieting and gain weight when the diet stops. Then they go back on a diet and repeat the same cycle.

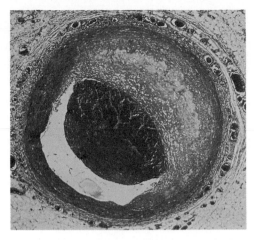

People who are overweight are more likely to suffer from heart disease. Many heart attacks are brought on by atherosclerosis. Fatty deposits—linked to a high-fat diet—build up in the blood vessels. When a vessel becomes completely blocked, the heart is deprived of oxygen. This causes a heart attack.

Research shows the yo-yo dieting is a risk factor in diseases such as high blood pressure and heart disease. What's more, with each diet, more weight is gained back than was lost. The weight becomes harder and harder to lose. Thus, people who practice yo-yo dieting often end up weighing more than when they started the process. They also have a greater risk of health problems.

Successful Weight Loss

If so many weight-loss methods don't work, what does work? The most successful way to manage weight is by making gradual, permanent changes in eating and exercise habits. This is known as **behavior modification.** It is the key to keeping your weight at a healthy level throughout your life.

Section 5.2: Weight Management   145

Teaching . . .

• Successful Weight Loss

(text pages 145-148)

Comprehension Check

1. Discuss the principle of behavior modification and its implications for losing weight.

2. Ask students to explain why it is important for people to set specific, but reasonable, goals when they attempt to lose weight.

3. Discuss why it is important to aim for a weight loss of only 1/2 to 2 pounds per week.

4. Ask students to list reasons why it is important to exercise during a weight-loss attempt. *(Exercise burns calories both during the activity and for some time afterward; it helps ensure that the weight you lose comes from body fat, not muscle.)*

Safety Check

Ask students to think of specific reasons why it is important to see a health professional before beginning a weight-loss program. *(The most important reason is underlying illness or medical conditions that may make such a program dangerous to the person's health. For example, people with heart conditions or diabetes could experience serious harm if they follow a diet that would be harmless for most other people.)*

✔ **SAFETY CHECK**

It's wise to have a medical check-up before beginning any weight loss program. A health professional can help you judge whether you truly have a weight problem that needs attention. You may have to consider other health factors besides excess weight. In addition, a health professional can give you expert advice that will help you succeed.

Set Reasonable Goals

Setting specific goals for weight loss can help motivate you and give you a way to see your progress. However, make sure your goals are reasonable.

First, be realistic about the size and shape of your body. Don't try to reach a weight or clothing size that's not right for you.

If you have a large amount of weight to lose, divide the task into a series of smaller goals. For instance, Deanna needed to lose 40 pounds (18 kg), but her first goal was to lose just 10 pounds (4.5 kg). The smaller goal was easier to reach and gave her the encouragement she needed to stick with her program.

Give yourself plenty of time to reach your goal. Remember, it's taken you a lifetime to develop your eating and exercise habits. You cannot expect to change them in a matter of a few days or weeks.

Aim for a weight loss of no more than 1/2 to 2 pounds (0.25 to 1 kg) a week. The more slowly you lose weight, the better your body can adjust to it. Your weight loss has a greater chance of being permanent.

Get More Exercise

Lack of exercise is one of the basic causes of overweight. Just increasing your physical activity, even without cutting down on food, can often result in a leaner body.

Remember, the balance between energy in food and the energy you use for activities affects your weight. If you use up about the same number of calories as you get from food, your weight should stay at about the same level. If the food you eat provides more calories than you need for your activities, your body stores the extra as fat. Therefore, you gain weight. If you use up more calories in activities than you take in from food, you should lose weight.

In theory, you could change your energy balance just by eating less. In reality, however, it's better to increase your activity level as well. Why? Studies show that exercise not only burns calories during the activity, but also increases metabolism for some time

Exercise is a key element in successful weight loss. Besides using up calories, moderate exercise often seems to reduce appetite.

More About Exercise and Weight Loss

Many Americans lead a sedentary lifestyle—they get only a limited amount of physical activity. People who sit at school all day, for instance, and spend evenings watching television get little physical activi-

ty. Excess weight in teens is often caused by lack of exercise.

Studies show a direct relationship between weight and the number of hours spent watching television. The more hours

Calories Burned in Activities

The more strenuous an activity, the more calories you burn. The following chart shows the approximate number of calories used during one minute of activity. These figures are for someone who weighs 140 pounds (63 kg). Someone who weighs more would burn slightly more calories. Someone who weighs less would burn slightly fewer.

Sitting or standing quietly ....1 to 2 calories per minute
Light activity: cleaning house, playing baseball ....4 calories per minute
Moderate activity: brisk walking, gardening, ...6 calories per minute
cycling, dancing, playing basketball
Strenuous activity: jogging, playing football, ...9 to 10 calories per minute
swimming
Very strenuous activity: running fast,................................12 calories per minute
racquetball, skiing

1. Demonstration: Ask for three student volunteers. Have one student measure the pulse and another check the respiration of the third. *(NOTE: Do not use a student with health problems for this demonstration. Stop immediately if the exercise becomes too strenuous.)* Then have the third student run in place for 2 minutes. Repeat pulse and respiration measurements and record. Let the student rest until his or her pulse and respiration return to normal. Then have the student put on a 25-pound backpack and run in place for another 2 minutes. Record pulse and respiration rates again. Discuss the effects of exercise and extra weight on pulse and respiration rates. Draw conclusions regarding the effects of excess body weight. *(Key skill: health)*

2. Media Survey: Have students survey electronic or printed media for advertisements for "miracle diets." Ask students to discuss the advertising techniques used to sell the diets to the public. *(Key skill: reading)*

3. Developing Guidelines: Have students develop a brochure describing guidelines for successful weight loss. Arrange to place copies of the brochure in local businesses such as laundromats and beauty shops. *(Key skill: writing)*

afterward. In other words, it increases the amount of energy used for basic body processes. Regular exercise also helps ensure that the weight you lose comes from body fat, not muscle.

Whatever your level of physical activity when you start a weight-loss plan, try to increase it. Without the added physical activity, you probably will not lose much weight. Section 5.3 discusses different types of exercise and gives guidelines for planning an exercise program.

Change Your Eating Habits

Establishing new, more healthful eating habits will also help you reach and maintain a healthy weight. Be sure to follow a sensible eating plan that you enjoy and that allows you to eat a reasonable number of calories a day. You can get a reliable plan from a physician, nutritionist, or dietitian.

One of the keys to successful weight loss is to eat less fat. Remember, fat supplies more than twice as many calories as carbohydrates or proteins. Therefore, foods high in fat will make you gain weight much faster than other foods. In addition, studies suggest that fats in food are turned into body fat more easily than excess carbohydrates and proteins.

235 Calories
52% fat

Avoiding high-fat foods can help you lose weight faster. A baked or broiled skinless chicken breast would be a better choice than fried chicken.

Section 5.2: Weight Management   147

people watch television, the more overweight they are. Exercising while watching television is one possible solution. Regular use of an exercise bicycle or a rowing machine might help keep weight down.

Teaching . . .

- **Gaining Needed Weight**
  - **Maintaining a Healthy Weight**

(text pages 148-149)

Comprehension Check

1. Ask students to list some reasons people may need to gain weight and to discuss some things people can do to gain the weight they need.

2. Discuss why it is important to maintain a healthy weight throughout your life.

3. Discuss ways to help maintain a healthy weight if your weight begins to change.

Student Experiences

1. **Group Discussion:** Have students discuss possible reasons for being underweight. Identify problems associated with being underweight. Have students suggest ways to add calories to commonly eaten foods to promote weight gain. *(Key skill: critical thinking)*

2. **Menu Planning:** Haves students develop a list of calorie-rich, nutritious foods that could be added to a diet if the goal is to gain 1 pound (0.45 kg) a week. *(Key skills: writing, brainstorming)*

3. **Menu Planning:** Have students plan a week's menus to meet their personal goals to gain, lose, or maintain weight. *(Key skill: math)*

TIPS for Success

Losing Weight

❖ Weigh yourself no more than once a week. That way the weight loss will be more noticeable. You won't be discouraged by the natural ups and downs in weight that occur from day to day.

❖ Don't give up if you don't show a weight loss for the first three or four weeks. It takes time for your body to adjust.

❖ After you have lost a little weight, you may suddenly stop losing. This is common and is called a "plateau." To continue losing weight, you may have to eat less fat and fewer calories or just increase your daily activity slightly.

❖ Eat slowly. Take time to relax and enjoy the taste of the food. Wait awhile to let your body tell you if it is full before deciding to take a second helping.

❖ If you eat a high-fat, high-calorie favorite, don't feel guilty or give up. Just enjoy the food, then go back to your plan.

❖ About once a month, keep a food record (as explained in Section 4.2). See whether your eating habits are changing as planned.

❖ If possible, find others who are trying to lose weight by changing their eating habits. Give each other moral support.

❖ Reward yourself when you reach a goal. Don't celebrate by going back to old eating habits. Instead, go to a concert or buy a special poster you've wanted.

As you learn to make more sensible food choices, become aware of nutrient-dense foods. They give you the most nutrients for the least number of calories. Select foods carefully from the five food groups. Be sure to choose lean meats and low-fat dairy products. Eat plenty of grain products and fresh fruits and vegetables. By eating less fat and sugar, you may find that you can eat more food instead of less and still lose weight.

If you've read Section 4.2, then you have already found good advice for improving your eating habits. Remember, most people make both sound and poor food choices. The focus is to keep the sensible choices and improve the poor ones. At the same time, the food choices must be enjoyable ones.

Gaining Needed Weight

Although many people are concerned with weight loss, some need to gain weight. For instance, male teens, who have very high energy needs, may find it a challenge to get enough calories each day. Teens who are going through a growth spurt may appear thin until weight catches up with height.

If you're concerned about being too thin, discuss the matter with a physician. There may be a medical reason for inability to put on weight.

Here are some hints to help you gain weight without adding fat to your food choices:

❖ Have larger portions of nutritious foods from the five food groups.
❖ Eat regular meals.
❖ Enjoy healthful snacks between meals.
❖ Avoid high-sugar and high-fat snacks such as candy, chips, and french fries. Instead, rely on snacks with more nutrients, such as yogurt and fresh or dried fruit.

More About Maintaining Weight

To avoid regaining lost weight:

- Motivation is the key to keeping weight off. Learn to enjoy your new body image. Take pride in staying at your best weight.
- Don't emphasize food in your life. Treat food as an essential for health, not a

pleasure or reward. Reward yourself in other ways.
- If you feel old cravings for food returning, take control immediately. Try to find out why you're returning to your old habits.

Whatever your weight goals, make your food choices nutritious ones.

Maintaining a Healthy Weight

Todd has finally filled out. Now he wants to hold his weight steady at this level. His father, who has successfully lost 20 pounds, also wants to keep the healthy weight he has reached. Todd's mother has always been at a healthy weight. However, she is concerned about staying that way as she gets older.

Once a healthy weight has been reached, the next goal is to maintain it. If you continue to follow good eating and exercise habits, you should have no problem maintaining a healthy weight. Still, if your weight starts to change, here are some suggestions:

❖ Keep track of the food you eat for a few days and analyze the results. You may be slipping into poor eating patterns.

❖ If you find your weight going up, be sure you're getting plenty of exercise.

❖ If you find you're eating too much or too little because of stress, look for healthy ways to cope with your problems.

■ Section 5.2 Review ■

RECALL THE FACTS

1. What are the health risks associated with overweight?

2. Name three signs that a weight-loss plan is unsafe.

3. What is behavior modification? How does it relate to weight loss?

4. Give two tips for gaining weight and two tips for maintaining weight.

DISCUSS YOUR IDEAS

5. Why are fad diets popular? What could be done to educate people about the problems associated with them?

APPLY YOUR LEARNING

6. In newspapers and magazines, find ads for weight-loss methods. Evaluate them based on the information you have read in this section.

Section 5.2: Weight Management   149

Completing the Section

Review

- Ask students to summarize the main ideas in this section.

- Have students complete the Section Review. (Answers appear below.)

Evaluation

- Have students prepare a written evaluation of their weight needs and a discussion of how to maintain a healthy weight.

- Have students take the quiz for Section 5.2. (Refer to the *Section Quizzes* booklet or use the *Testmaker Software*.)

Reteaching

- Have students compile a list of high-calorie foods and drinks that total about 3500 calories. Emphasize that this is the amount of calories—and food—a person would have to cut out each week to lose 1 pound (0.45kg).

- Refer to the *Reteaching Activities* booklet for the Section 5.2 activity sheet.

Enrichment

- Have students research companies that make health facilities available on premises for their employees. What are the benefits for employers? for employees? Do students think this trend will continue?

Closure

- Discuss the importance of achieving and maintaining a weight right for you.

■ Answers to Section Review ■

1. Heart disease, diabetes, cancer, and high blood pressure.
2. *Any three:* Very low-calorie diets; diets based on a single food; fasting; diet pills; quick weight loss.
3. Gradual, permanent changes in eating and exercise habits; it helps people lose weight safely and permanently.
4. Gaining *(any two):* have larger portions of nutritious foods; eat regular meals; enjoy healthful snacks; avoid high-sugar and high-fat snacks. Maintaining *(any two):* keep track of the food you eat and analyze the results; be sure to get plenty of exercise; look for healthy ways to cope with stress.
5. Because they promise "miraculous" results; answers will vary.
6. Answers will vary.

Motivators

- Ask students to identify the types of exercise they get regularly. How much time per week is spent in each activity? Do students believe they get enough exercise?

- Ask students why people need to exercise. List responses on the chalkboard. Compare students' responses with the benefits of exercise listed on pages 150-151.

- On the chalkboard, list three basic kinds of exercise. *(stretching, aerobic, strengthening)* Ask students to demonstrate examples of exercises that fit in each category.

Objectives

- Have students read the section objectives. Discuss the purpose of studying this section.

Vocabulary

- Pronounce the terms listed under "Look for These Terms." Have students find the terms and their definitions in the section.

Guided Reading

- Have students look at the headings within Section 5.3 to preview the concepts that will be discussed.

- Have students read the section and complete the appropriate part of the Chapter 5 Study Guide in the *Student Workbook.*

SECTION 5.3

Exercise Basics

OBJECTIVES

After studying this section, you should be able to:
- Explain the benefits of exercise.
- Describe the basic types of exercise.
- Make a plan for an exercise program.

LOOK FOR THIS TERM
aerobic

Almost everywhere you look, you can see people enjoying physical activity—walking in the park, shooting baskets in a school yard, digging in the garden. These people have discovered the physical and emotional benefits provided by regular, enjoyable exercise.

Benefits of Exercise

Exercise does have many benefits:

❖ It helps keep the body mobile. If muscles are not used regularly, they tend to stiffen and movement eventually becomes painful and difficult. Regular exercise can keep the muscles strong and flexible throughout life.

❖ It helps improve psychological health. Regular exercise helps people feel better by reducing stress and anxiety. Studies show that regular exercisers have a brighter outlook on life.

Exercise includes more than running or lifting weights. Hobbies like gardening can reduce stress and increase physical activity.

150   Chapter 5: Food and Fitness

Teacher's Classroom Resources—Section 5.3

Refer to these resources in the TCR package:

Reproducible Lesson Plans

Student Workbook

Extending the Text

Reteaching Activities

Section Quizzes

Testmaker Software

Color Transparencies

- It helps improve physical health. Exercise speeds up the metabolism and increases the flow of energy in the body. It can help people lose and keep off excess weight. Exercise reduces the risk of osteoporosis, the condition marked by weak and brittle bones. It can also lower blood pressure and blood cholesterol levels and reduce the risk of heart disease.
- Just as important, exercise can be fun. Many people of all ages enjoy sports and other physical activities.

Types of Exercise

The many forms of exercise can be divided into three basic kinds. A well-rounded exercise program includes all three.

- Stretching exercises gently stretch the muscles. Performing these exercises correctly will keep the body flexible and can help prevent injury.
- **Aerobic** (uh-ROW-bick) exercises give your heart and lungs a workout. Aerobic means "using oxygen." During the exercise, your body needs more oxygen, so you breathe more deeply. Your heart pumps faster and harder to send blood through your body. As a result, the heart and lungs are exercised. This helps lower the risk of heart disease. Aerobic exercises include walking, jogging, climbing stairs, bicycling, aerobic dance, and swimming.
- Strengthening exercises build strong muscles in the arms, legs, and torso. Having strong muscles aids in everyday activities and helps prevent injury. Strengthening exercises include push-ups and sit-ups. Another way to strengthen muscles is by lifting weights. People generally start with light weights and gradually increase to heavier ones. However, weightlifting exercises are not recommended until the body has reached full adult development. Seek advice from a health professional before starting to lift weights.

Aerobic exercise raises your heart rate. Experts recommend regular aerobic exercise—at least three times per week for 20 to 30 minutes at a time.

✓ **SAFETY CHECK**

Exercise can improve health, but it can also result in injury if you're not careful. Use the proper equipment and follow the correct techniques for each activity. Learn how to warm up and cool down properly. If you feel pain while exercising, stop at once. Following these guidelines will help keep your workouts safe and enjoyable.

Section 5.3: Exercise Basics   **151**

Teaching . . .

- **Benefits of Exercise**
- **Types of Exercise**

(text pages 150-151)

Comprehension Check

1. Discuss the benefits of exercising regularly. Can students think of any other benefits that are not listed in the textbook?
2. Ask students to describe the effects of the three major types of exercises. Why does a well-rounded exercise program include all three?

Student Experiences

1. **Historical Comparison:** Read a passage from *Little House in the Big Woods* by Laura Ingalls Wilder (Chapter 11, "Harvest"). Point out that the need to "get exercise" is a modern phenomenon. Exercise was a basic part of the lives of our agrarian ancestors. *(Key skill: history)*
2. **Class Discussion:** Identify the benefits of exercise. How would being bedridden affect a person's muscles? *(Key skill: health)*
3. **Demonstration:** Invite a physical education teacher to demonstrate exercises that improve flexibility, condition muscles, and strengthen the heart and lungs. Discuss how a person can judge the potential value of specific exercises. What health and safety considerations should one take in selecting an exercise program? *(Key skill: physical fitness)*

Teaching . . .

• **Getting the Exercise Habit**

(text pages 152-153)

Comprehension Check

1. Discuss various exercise options that are available to teenagers. What are the advantages and disadvantages of each exercise option? *(Consider budget, time, location, etc.)*

2. Ask students to list activities that they enjoy doing that include exercise.

Student Experiences

1. **Debate:** Have students debate whether physical education classes in high school should be mandatory or voluntary. *(Key skill: public speaking)*

2. **Cost Comparisons:** Have students compute the costs associated with various types of exercise. Include expenses such as equipment, use of facilities, clothing, and transportation. Which activities are least expensive? Which are most expensive? *(Key skill: math)*

Healthy Attitudes

Ask students to think of other ideas for exercise that they can get every day as they follow their normal pattern of activity. Then have them calculate the approximate number of extra calories they could burn by making these changes.

Getting the Exercise Habit

If you do not exercise regularly, think about starting now. Begin with a medical checkup. Then experiment with different kinds of exercise and choose several that interest you. That way, you won't be bored and will be more likely to exercise regularly. If possible, get other members of the family involved or exercise with friends.

There are exercise options to suit every taste and budget. Depending on the activity, you can exercise outdoors, at school or a fitness center, or at home. You might enjoy playing sports or using fitness equipment such as a stationary bicycle or treadmill. Exercise classes and videotapes offer still more options. Many activities, such as walking or jumping rope, require little more than a comfortable pair of shoes.

Technology Tidbit

You may have seen or used exercise equipment that has computer readouts. For instance, some stationary bicycles have a display that keeps track of your pulse rate, the time and "distance" you have pedaled, and the number of calories you have burned.

If you exercise at home, try listening to music or watching your favorite program. You'll find the time goes faster and you will enjoy it more.

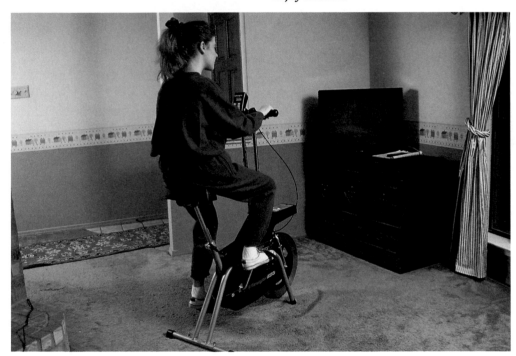

More About the Benefits of Exercise

How does exercise help prevent osteoporosis? Bone is living, growing matter. Weight-bearing exercise, such as walking, basketball, and racquet sports, puts stress on bones. This increases the flow of blood and bone-building nutrients to the bone, which reduces bone loss and stimulates new bone growth.

You don't have to exercise strenuously. Research is beginning to show that even moderate exercise has health benefits. Begin your program by exercising five or ten minutes a day, every other day. Gradually increase the time to about 30 minutes. Exercise at least three times a week, although every day is preferable.

Many people don't exercise because they think they don't have time. When you make out your schedule, allow time for exercise. Don't think of it as one more chore to cram into an already busy day, but as your fun time, a time to enjoy yourself.

The benefits of exercise are well worth the time spent. Like good nutrition, regular exercise is a habit that gives a lifetime of physical and emotional rewards.

Try out a variety of activities to find the ones you enjoy most. Many people prefer activities that let them spend time with friends while they exercise.

Healthy Attitudes

You can easily work exercise into everyday activities. You might try:
- Walking to school or work.
- Taking the stairs instead of the elevator.
- Getting up to change the channel instead of using the remote control.
- Playing upbeat music while doing household chores.
- Planning social activities around physical ones. For example, turn a birthday party into a roller skating party.

■ Section 5.3 Review ■

RECALL THE FACTS

1. Name three benefits of exercise.
2. What are the basic types of exercise? Why is each important?
3. What are the steps for beginning a new exercise program?

DISCUSS YOUR IDEAS

4. Why do you think people are advised to get a medical checkup before beginning a new exercise program?
5. What is your favorite form of exercise? Which of the three basic types of exercise does it involve?

APPLY YOUR LEARNING

6. Make a chart which outlines an exercise plan for the next week. Include at least three exercise sessions and at least two different types of activities. Be prepared to explain the benefits of your plan.

Section 5.3: Exercise Basics   **153**

5.3

Completing the Section

Review
- Ask students to summarize the main ideas in this section.
- Have students complete the Section Review. (Answers appear below.)

Evaluation
- Have students write a brief essay describing what they learned in this section.
- Have students take the quiz for Section 5.3. (Refer to the *Section Quizzes* booklet or use the *Testmaker Software*.)

Reteaching
- Provide pictures of people exercising. Have students classify the exercises as stretching, aerobic, or strengthening exercises.
- Refer to the *Reteaching Activities* booklet for the Section 5.3 activity sheet.

Enrichment
- Have students calculate how many extra calories they would need to eat in a week to maintain their weight, if they started swimming one hour a day. *(2450).* Have students calculate their weekly weight loss if they ate as they do now, but swam one hour a day *(0.3 kg [0.7 lb.] a week).*

Closure
- Lead a discussion on the different types of exercise and how to determine the right exercise program for you.

■ Answers to Section Review ■

1. *Any three:* Improved mobility; psychological health; physical health; fun.
2. Stretching exercises help keep the body flexible and prevent injury; aerobic exercises give heart and lungs a workout; strengthening exercises build muscles.
3. Begin with a medical checkup; choose several exercises that interest you; begin exercising 5 minutes per day every other day; increase to 30 minutes per day. Exercise at least three times a week.
4. Students should realize that they could harm themselves if they undertake an exercise program with any underlying medical problems.
5. Answers will vary.
6. Answers will vary.

Section 5.4
Nutrition for Sports and Fitness

Motivators

- Bring to class sports magazines that include articles on how an athlete's nutrient needs can be met. Do the articles perpetuate any common myths? Discuss the accuracy of the information provided in these articles.

- Ask students to write a paragraph describing how the nutrient needs of athletes are similar to and different from those of the average person. Ask several students to read their paragraphs to the class. Point out that the primary differences in an athlete's nutrient needs are the increased needs for energy and for water.

Objectives

- Have students read the section objectives. Discuss the purpose of studying this section.

Vocabulary

- Pronounce the terms listed under "Look for These Terms." Have students find the terms and their definitions in the section.

Guided Reading

- Have students look at the headings within Section 5.4 to preview the concepts that will be discussed.

- Have students read the section and complete the appropriate part of the Chapter 5 Study Guide in the *Student Workbook*.

S E C T I O N   5 . 4

Nutrition for Sports and Fitness

OBJECTIVES

After studying this section, you should be able to:

- Explain how an athlete's nutrient needs can be met.
- Give suggestions for pre-game meals.
- Point out the dangers of using steroids to build muscles.

LOOK FOR THESE TERMS

dehydration
anabolic steroids

When you think of "athlete," what comes to mind? Perhaps it's a superstar whose career depends on building the physical strength, skill, and stamina needed for success. However, an athlete may also be a high school swimmer or a 50-year-old who enjoys her morning run. Regardless of how seriously they are involved, all athletes' performance can benefit from good nutrition.

Eating right can't improve an athlete's skills—only practice can do that. An athlete's daily food choices, however, can make a difference between a good performance and a poor one.

Nutrient Needs of Athletes

Generally, an athlete's nutrition needs can be met by following the Food Guide Pyramid's recommendations. However, the athlete does have two nutritional needs that far exceed those of the average person: the need for energy and for water.

Successful athletes know that performing their best requires good nutrition.

Teacher's Classroom Resources—Section 5.4

Refer to these resources in the TCR package:

Reproducible Lesson Plans

Student Workbook

Extending the Text

Reteaching Activities

Section Quizzes

Testmaker Software

Color Transparencies

Energy Needs

As you have learned, during digestion carbohydrates are broken down into the simple sugar glucose, which is used for energy. Extra carbohydrates are turned into a storage form of glucose known as glycogen (GLIE-kuh-juhn). Glycogen is stored in the liver and muscles.

During vigorous and extended periods of exercise, the body uses glycogen for fuel. When the glycogen is used up, the athlete runs out of energy. Therefore, it's essential for athletes to eat plenty of carbohydrates to build up their glycogen stores.

During training and competition, athletes may need two or three times as much energy as the average person. To supply this additional energy, complex carbohydrates are the best choice. These include foods such as dry beans and peas, breads, cereal, pasta, rice, and potatoes. About 60 percent of an athlete's calories should come from carbohydrates, about 25 percent from fat, and about 15 percent from protein.

Healthy Attitudes

"Carbohydrate loading" refers to techniques designed to increase the amount of glycogen stored in the muscles. There are many myths about carbohydrate loading. Here are the facts:

- For the average athlete, carbohydrate loading is not necessary. It can, however, be helpful when training for a long, intense event, such as a marathon.
- The proper way to practice carbohydrate loading is simple. Just continue to eat healthfully with an emphasis on complex carbohydrates. A few days before the event, cut back on exercise. This gives the muscles a chance to rest and store glycogen.

Pasta and other complex carbohydrates are an excellent source of the extra energy athletes need.

- ### Energy Needs of Athletes

(text pages 154-155)

Comprehension Check

1. Discuss why athletes need more energy than other people.
2. Discuss why increasing carbohydrate intake is the best way of increasing an athlete's energy. *(Carbohydrates are broken down into glucose, which provides energy for the body.)*

Student Experiences

1. **Guest Speaker:** Invite a registered dietitian to class to speak to students about nutrition for athletes and how athletes should eat during training. *(Key skill: health)*
2. **Applying Science:** Have students study science books or interview a science teacher to learn why athletes need to consume more water. What is dehydration, and why is it dangerous? What causes heat stroke and heat exhaustion? *(Key skill: science)*

See Also . . .
- Section 2.5: "How Your Body Uses Food," page 79.

Comprehension Check

1. Ask students to explain why dehydration can have serious health consequences. *(can cause confusion, weakness, overheating, heat exhaustion, heat stroke)*

2. Ask students how athletes can avoid dehydration. *(Drink plenty of water before, during, and after the athletic activity.)*

3. Ask students to explain why most athletes do not need extra protein. *(A normal diet provides more than enough; extra won't build muscles)*

4. Discuss the use of vitamin and mineral supplements by athletes. Is this practice necessary? Why or why not?

Student Experiences

1. **Menu Planning:** Provide students with a standard 1800-2000 calorie day's menu. Have students adapt the menu to be suitable for a student athlete. *(Key skill: math)*

2. **Library Research:** Have students research common myths about the nutritional needs of athletes. *(Key skills: research, reading)*

Safety Check

Emphasize that heat exhaustion and heat stroke can happen to anyone, not just athletes. These serious conditions can occur any time someone gets overheated and does not take steps to prevent the body from becoming hotter.

Liquid Needs

Athletes lose a great deal of water through perspiration—as much as 3 to 5 quarts (3 to 5 L) during a strenuous workout. If the water is not replaced right away, **dehydration** (dee-high-DRAY-shun), or lack of adequate fluids in the body, can result. This can lead to serious health problems.

An athlete who is dehydrated may become weak and confused. The body can become overheated, especially when exercising in hot weather. Heat exhaustion or heat stroke can result. These are serious conditions requiring first aid.

To prevent dehydration, athletes should drink water before, during, and after an event. They should drink water even if they do not feel thirsty. Thirst is a sign that dehydration has already begun.

One good way to gauge the amount of water to drink is to weigh in before and after the event. Loss of water usually shows up as a loss in body weight. For each pound (500 g) lost during exercise, athletes should drink 2 cups (500 mL) of fluid.

In addition to water, juices and fruit drinks can be used. However, because they are high in sugar, the body absorbs them more slowly. To cut down on sugar, dilute juices and fruit drinks by one-half with water.

Be sure to drink additional water whenever you exercise vigorously. Even if you don't feel thirsty, you need to replace water lost through perspiration.

✓ SAFETY CHECK

Heat stroke is a medical emergency. Signs of heat stroke include very high body temperature; hot, red, dry skin; and rapid pulse. The person may become unconscious. Immediate medical attention is needed.

Heat exhaustion usually results in pale, clammy skin. The person may sweat heavily; feel tired, dizzy, and nauseated; and have a headache. A person with heat exhaustion should lie down (in a cool place, if possible) and sip water.

Sports drinks are also available. They are valuable mainly to athletes involved in exercise lasting more than two hours.

Common Myths

Some athletes believe they need extra protein to build muscles. It's true that dietary protein is needed to build body protein. Remember, however, that most Americans eat far more protein than they need. An athlete's protein requirements can be met easily through normal eating. Excess protein does nothing to build up muscles—only physical training can do that.

Thinking Skills

Critical Thinking: Ask students to explain how myths about athletic nutritional needs get started and why people tend to believe them. Compare myths about athletic nutritional needs to other common myths about food and nutrition. Ask students to discuss similarities and differences.

Likewise, athletes who eat nutritious meals do not need vitamin or mineral supplements. These supplements do not supply anything of special value to an athlete.

Athletes generally do not need salt tablets. It's true that salt and potassium are lost through perspiration. However, these minerals can be easily replaced in well-chosen daily meals.

Timing of Meals

If you eat just before an athletic event, the digestive process competes with your muscles for energy. Instead, eat three to four hours prior to the event to allow for proper digestion.

Follow these suggestions to get the most from your pre-event meal:

❖ Choose a meal that is low in fat and protein and high in complex carbohydrates. As you may recall, fat and protein take the longest to digest.
❖ Eat foods you enjoy and have eaten before. A pre-game meal is no time to experiment with a new food.
❖ Choose foods that you know you can digest easily.

❖ Have a reasonably sized meal, not too large, so the stomach is relatively empty by event time.
❖ Drink large amounts of fluids with the meal.
❖ Avoid sugary foods, such as candy, within an hour before the event. These will give you quick bursts of energy that don't last. This can lead to feelings of fatigue or shakiness during the event.

After an athletic event or a hard workout, you need to refuel your body. In addition to replacing the water you have lost, be sure to eat nutritious food within one to four hours after the event.

Anabolic Steroids

All athletes want to perform well in sports and to have well-developed muscles. Many, however, are in a hurry to build up their muscles. Instead of depending on training alone, they use drugs called **anabolic steroids** (AN-uh-boll-ick STEER-oyds).

Steroid drugs were developed years ago for medical purposes and can be obtained only by prescription. Today, they are rarely prescribed by physicians.

To perform your best, eat a pre-game meal three to four hours before the event starts.

Section 5.4: Nutrition for Sports and Fitness   **157**

5.4

Teaching . . .

• Timing of Meals
• Anabolic Steroids

(text pages 157-158)

Comprehension Check

1. Discuss guidelines athletes should follow when eating before an athletic event.

2. Ask students to explain why pre-event meals should be high in complex carbohydrates and low in fat and protein. *(Fat and protein take longer to digest.)*

3. Ask students to explain what anabolic steroids are and why some teenage athletes are tempted to take them.

4. Discuss the physical and psychological side effects of anabolic steroids.

Student Experiences

1. **Guest Speaker:** Invite a high school coach to discuss the timing of meals before and after athletic events. *(Key skill: health)*

2. **Anabolic Steroids:** Have students write a poem, a song, or a news article describing the dangers of using anabolic steroids. Have volunteers read their pieces aloud. *(Key skill: writing)*

More About Food for Athletes

• Some athletes believe that products such as bee pollen and ginseng root will give them added power. Medical research shows these substances have no power to enhance athletic performance. But bee pollen can cause an allergic reaction, and too much ginseng root can be toxic.

• Athletes use far more energy than the average person, so they need larger amounts of some nutrients involved in producing energy. But since athletes usually have larger appetites, they normally eat enough food to provide the additional nutrients.

5.4

Review

- Ask students to summarize the main ideas in this section.
- Have students complete the Section Review. (Answers appear below.)

Evaluation

- Have students write a short essay describing the concepts presented in this section.
- Have students take the quiz for Section 5.4. (Refer to the *Section Quizzes* booklet or use the *Testmaker Software*.)

Reteaching

- Have students list the hazards of steroid use. Then have them explain the safe way to build muscles.
- Refer to the *Reteaching Activities* booklet for the Section 5.4 activity sheet.

Enrichment

- Have students research other drugs, vitamin supplements, etc., that are sometimes used by athletes. What are the side effects of these items? What dangers are associated with their use?

Closure

- Lead a class discussion on the nutritional needs of athletes and how they differ from those of other people.

Canadian sprinter Ben Johnson was stripped of his Olympic medal, and eventually of the right to compete, for illegal use of steroids. Steroids can cause serious permanent damage to the body.

Besides their medical effect, steroids can increase strength when they are combined with muscle-building exercises. As a result, illegal steroid use is increasing among teenage athletes, who manage to get the drug without a prescription.

Many athletes do not realize that steroids have dangerous side effects which create serious health risks. Steroids interfere with fertility, a person's ability to have children. In teens they can impair bone growth, even though muscles get large. Taken over a period of time, steroids damage the liver, heart, and stomach and cause high blood pressure. Other physical side effects of steroid use include trembling, breath odor, and acne.

Steroids also have psychological side effects. Users become aggressive, irritable, and hyperactive. Some experience hallucinations. Studies suggest that some steroid users suffer from even more serious psychological problems.

Remember that there are no "quick fixes" to improving athletic performance. Careful training and sound nutrition, practiced every day, are the surest ways to long-lasting top athletic performance.

158 Chapter 5: Food and Fitness

■ Section 5.4 Review ■

RECALL THE FACTS

1. How do the nutritional needs of athletes differ from those of nonathletes?
2. Do athletes need more protein than other people? Why or why not?
3. Give three suggestions for planning meals before an athletic event.
4. What are five major negative side effects of steroids?

DISCUSS YOUR IDEAS

5. How could you convince a friend or teammate to avoid using anabolic steroids?

APPLY YOUR LEARNING

6. Use the Food Guide Pyramid and recipe books to plan three meals for an athlete who is in training for a sport of your choice.

■ Answers to Section Review ■

1. Athletes need more energy and more water.
2. No; most people already eat much more protein than they actually need.
3. *Any three:* Eat foods low in fat and protein but high in complex carbohydrates; eat foods you enjoy and have eaten before; choose foods that you know you can digest easily; have a reasonable-sized meal (not too large); avoid sugary foods.
4. *Any five:* Infertility; impair bone growth; damage liver, heart, and stomach; cause high blood pressure; aggressiveness; irritability; hyperactivity; hallucinations.
5. Answers will vary.
6. Answers will vary.

Career PROFILE

Mel Logsdon
Health Club Trainer

CURRENT POSITION

"I work as a personal trainer at a medium-sized health club."

RESPONSIBILITIES

"I teach several exercise classes each day. I also work with individual members, designing fitness programs that suit their needs and goals."

SKILLS

"In addition to knowledge of exercise and weight management, the ability to relate to and work with people is a must."

EDUCATION

"I've taken college courses in nutrition, and I'm also a certified fitness instructor."

FUTURE PLANS

"I'm working toward a degree in sports sciences. A degree is not necessarily required for this job, but I may pursue a job as an athletic trainer in the future."

BIGGEST CHALLENGE

"Believe me, this job requires a lot of energy! That's why it's so important that I pay attention to my own nutrition and health."

FAVORITE PART OF THE JOB

"I like being able to see that I can help make a difference in people's lives when they start shaping up."

> • How might good nutrition help Mel, or anyone, perform better on the job?
> • What aspects of Mel's job do you think you might enjoy? Why?

159

CAREER PROFILE: HEALTH CLUB TRAINER

Thinking About . . . Health Club Trainers

- Have students think of other questions they would like to ask Mel Logsdon about being a health club trainer. (Examples: How many hours do you work each week? Is it possible to schedule your hours so that you can also attend school? What equipment do you use or encourage others to use on a regular basis?)

- Ask students to list the advantages and disadvantages of going to a health club as opposed to exercising on your own. (Advantages: you have the help and experience of a trained professional; you have the use of the equipment at the club; disadvantages: health clubs are usually fairly expensive; you might not exercise as often if you have to go to the club to do it.)

Student Opportunities

Students thinking about a career in the health club industry should join a health club and/or apply for a job at one. Students may also volunteer to work in the training room of nonprofit organizations, such as the YMCA.

Occupational Outlook

Advancement depends on the individual interests of the trainer. Some people advance from working with amateurs to working with professionals in various sports fields. Others may open their own sports clubs and go into management or public relations.

For More Information

For additional information about health club careers, contact:
- The American Aerobic Association (AAA), P.O. Box 633, Richboro, PA 18954
- The American Alliance for Health, Physical Education, Recreation, and Dance, 1900 Association Dr., Reston, VA 22091
- The National Health Council, 622 Third Ave., New York, NY 10017-6765

Review

- Have students complete the Chapter Review (Answers appear below.)

Evaluation

- Provide students with descriptions of two or three hypothetical people who have different weight management needs. Have students describe the steps that each hypothetical person should take.

- Have students take the test for Chapter 5. (Refer to the *Chapter and Unit Tests* booklet or construct your own test using the *Testmaker Software*.)

■ ANSWERS ■

REVIEWING THE FACTS

1. Because children and teens grow and develop at different rates. What is right for one may be entirely wrong for another.

2. "Apple"-shaped figures seem to run more risk of some health problems than "pear"-shaped figures.

3. Repeatedly losing and gaining weight; it can be a risk factor in medical conditions such as high blood pressure and heart disease; also, the weight becomes harder and harder to lose in each cycle, so people often gain more weight than they lose.

4. *Any three:* Be realistic about your body size and shape; divide large weight-loss tasks into several smaller, more obtainable goals; give yourself plenty of time to reach your goal; aim for weight loss of no more than 1/2 to 2 pounds per week.

CHAPTER 5 REVIEW

SUMMARY

SECTION 5.1

A Healthy Weight: Instead of trying to achieve the "ideal body," it's best to accept your inherited body shape and focus on being fit and healthy. Health professionals use several methods to evaluate whether an individual is at a healthy weight. These include weight charts, body-fat tests, and waist-to-hip ratio.

SECTION 5.2

Weight Management: A weight management program can help you achieve and maintain a healthy weight. Many popular weight-loss methods are ineffective, and some are dangerous to health. The best way to lose weight is through gradual, permanent changes in eating and exercise habits. Those who need to gain weight or maintain their present weight can also benefit from a weight-management program.

SECTION 5.3

Exercise Basics: Regular exercise has many physical and psychological benefits. Each of the three basic types of exercise—stretching, aerobic, and strengthening—is important to good health. An exercise program that includes a variety of enjoyable physical activities is more likely to be successful.

SECTION 5.4

Nutrition for Sports and Fitness: Athletes should emphasize complex carbohydrates and drink plenty of fluids.They generally do not need extra protein, nutrient supplements, or salt tablets. Pre-event meals should be planned carefully to avoid digestive problems. Using anabolic steroids to build muscles is not only illegal, but has dangerous side effects.

160

REVIEWING FACTS

1. Why are children and teens excluded from most weight charts? (5.1)

2. In terms of health, what is the difference between having an "apple"-shaped figure and a "pear"-shaped figure? (5.1)

3. What is yo-yo dieting? What are the possible consequences of it? (5.2)

4. List three guidelines for setting a reasonable weight-loss goal. (5.2)

5. Give two suggestions for gaining weight healthfully. (5.2)

6. Name three specific physical benefits of exercise. (5.3)

7. What is meant by aerobic exercise? Give two examples. (5.3)

8. About what percentage of an athlete's calories should come from complex carbohydrates? (5.4)

9. What can happen if an athlete doesn't replace water lost through perspiration? (5.4)

10. About how long before an athletic event should the pre-event meal be eaten? Why? (5.4)

LEARNING BY DOING

1. *Foods lab:* Make a list of simple snacks that would be suitable for a person who is changing eating habits to lose weight. The snacks should be easy to prepare, low in fat and calories, and nutritious. Work in groups to prepare the snacks. (5.2)

2. *Demonstration:* Working in groups, prepare a demonstration of safe exercises for stretching or strengthening muscles. Use books, tapes, magazines, or other references to learn the proper form for each exercise. Demonstrate the exercises to other class members. (5.3)

5. *Any two:* Eat larger quantities of nutritious food; eat regular meals; eat healthful snacks between meals; avoid snacks high in sugar and fat.

6. *Any three:* It helps keep the body mobile; it helps improve psychological health; it helps improve physical health; it can be fun.

3. **Foods lab:** Plan and prepare a pre-event meal for a group of athletes in your school. Prepare a handout giving facts about nutrition and athletic performance to give each participant. Interview members of the team after their performance to find out how they felt during the event. (5.4)

THINKING CRITICALLY

1. **Determining credibility:** Suppose you are interested in losing weight. Several of your friends are following the plan described in a best-selling diet book. Before you decide whether to join them, what information would you want to know about the author? About the diet plan? How will you find the information? How will it influence your decision? (5.2)

2. **Recognizing bias:** Why do you think some children receive more encouragement to participate in exercise and sports than others? How do you think children are affected by such encouragement (or lack of it)? (5.3)

3. **Recognizing fallacies:** A basketball coach recommends a special "power supplement," claiming it will improve performance. After using the supplement for a week, several members of the team say that it helped them shoot more accurately. Do you think they are right? Why or why not? (5.4)

MAKING DECISIONS AND SOLVING PROBLEMS

What Would You Do?

1. Your friend is seriously overweight. It doesn't seem to bother him, but you are concerned about his health. On the other hand, you're also worried about hurting his feelings. (5.1, 5.2)

2. You strain your leg muscle while jogging one day. The doctor tells you to try to stay off your feet for a few weeks. However, you want to continue with some type of exercise during that time. (5.3)

3. A friend of yours is a star player on the football team and counting on a football scholarship to get into college. He tells you that he has begun taking steroids to improve his performance. He asks you not to tell anyone else. (5.4)

LINKING YOUR STUDIES

1. **Math:** Find the waist-to-hip ratio for each of the following adults. (Round off to two decimal places.) Which of the ratios indicate a health risk? (5.1)

   A. Female, waist 27 in., hips 36 in.

   B. Female, waist 33 in., hips 40 in.

   C. Female, waist 35 in., hips 45 in.

   D. Male, waist 36 in., hips 35 in.

   E. Male, waist 34 in., hips 36 in.

2. **Writing:** Write an article for a newspaper or newsletter on one of the following subjects: safe weight loss, planning an exercise program, or nutrition for athletes. (5.2, 5.3, 5.4)

3. **Health:** Conduct library research to find out more about the dangers of anabolic steroids. (5.4)

161

LEARNING BY DOING

1. Snacks will vary.
2. Exercises will vary.
3. Meals will vary.

THINKING CRITICALLY

1. Answers will vary. Students should realize that not all people who write books about weight management are qualified to do so. They should look into the author's educational background and try to find out what health professionals think about the book.
2. Answers will vary.
3. Answers will vary. Students should realize that medical studies have proven that supplements have no effect on athletic ability.

MAKING DECISIONS AND SOLVING PROBLEMS

Answers to "Making Decisions and Solving Problems" questions will vary. Encourage students to give reasons for their answers.

LINKING YOUR STUDIES

1. A: 0.75; B: 0.83 (health risk); C: 0.78; D: 1.03 (health risk); E: 0.94.
2. Articles will vary.
3. Answers will vary.

---

7. Exercise during which your body requires more oxygen. Examples will vary.

8. 60 percent.

9. Dehydration can occur.

10. Three to four hours; to allow for proper digestion.

Planning the Chapter

Chapter Overview

Section 6.1: Food and the Life Cycle

Section 6.2: Managing Health Conditions

Section 6.3: Eating Disorders

Introducing the Chapter

Motivator

- Invite a panel of health experts to discuss current topics relating to nutrition and health. The panel might include a physician, a nurse, a dietitian, a child development expert, and a counselor. Before inviting the panel, have students identify topics in which they are interested and questions they would like the experts to answer. Provide the panel with a copy of the students' questions in advance. Allow time for additional student questions following the presentation.

Teacher's Classroom Resources—Chapter 6

Refer to these resources in the TCR package:

Enrichment Activities

Chapter and Unit Tests

Testmaker Software

Special Topics in Nutrition

162

Cooperative Learning Suggestions

- Initiate a Think-Pair-Share activity. Ask students to select a topic related to the chapter. Then pair up students according to their interests. Have each pair interview a health expert or affected individual, research additional information, and then discuss their ideas and work together to organize the material.
- Using the information collected, have each pair develop a pamphlet and plan a booth for a community fair to be held in conjunction with a school or community event.

Food and the Life Cycle

OBJECTIVES

After studying this section, you should be able to:

- Identify the varying nutritional needs for each stage of the life cycle.
- Explain how to encourage healthful eating habits for people in every stage of the life cycle.

LOOK FOR THESE TERMS

life cycle
fetus
obstetrician
colostrum
pediatrician

A person's movement from one stage of development to the next is called the **life cycle.** The stages of the life cycle include prenatal development, infancy, childhood, adolescence, and adulthood. At each stage, people experience changes in growth and nutrition needs.

To stay healthy throughout your life, you must be aware of the stage of the life cycle you're experiencing. That way, you can make any necessary changes in your wellness program to help you live a long and active life.

Prenatal Development

During the nine months of a normal pregnancy, a single cell grows and develops into a baby able to survive in the outside world. Proper development depends on the right nutrients. However, the unborn baby—called a **fetus** (FEE-tus)—cannot control its own nutrition. That is the most important responsibility of a pregnant woman.

While eating right is essential throughout life, nutritional needs vary at different stages of the life cycle.

Introducing the Section

Motivators

- Have students work in groups to find magazine pictures of people representing different life cycle stages. Also, have students find magazine pictures of foods associated with each life cycle stage. Use the pictures to create a bulletin board.

- List the stages of the life cycle across the top of the chalkboard. Discuss characteristics of each stage. Ask students to identify foods associated with each stage of the life cycle. Write the foods named under the appropriate life cycle stage.

Objectives

- Have students read the section objectives. Discuss the purpose of studying the section.

Vocabulary

- Pronounce the terms listed under "Look for These Terms." Have students find the terms and their definitions in the section.

Guided Reading

- Have students look at the headings within Section 6.1 to preview the concepts that will be discussed.

- Have students read the section and complete the appropriate part of the Chapter 6 Study Guide in the *Student Workbook.*

Teacher's Classroom Resources—Section 6.1

Refer to these resources in the TCR package:

Reproducible Lesson Plans	*Reteaching Activities*
Student Workbook	*Section Quizzes*
Extending the Text	*Testmaker Software*
	Color Transparencies

Teaching . . .

• **Prenatal Development**

(text pages 163-165)

Comprehension Check

1. Ask students to describe the responsibilities of a pregnant woman regarding the nutrients provided to the fetus.

2. Ask students to explain why it is important for expectant mothers to make healthy food choices *(to avoid risking both her health and that of the unborn baby).*

3. Discuss why pregnant teens are at special risk. *(They need additional nutrients for themselves and the fetus; also, since most teens are not fully developed, they are more likely to have difficult pregnancies.)*

4. Discuss general health guidelines for pregnant women.

5. Ask students to explain why women should not go on weight-loss diets during pregnancy.

6. Discuss common problems associated with the use of tobacco and pregnancy. Why should pregnant women avoid these products?

Nutrition During Pregnancy

Concern about good nutrition should begin before pregnancy. A healthy woman who has good eating habits before her pregnancy begins is more likely to have a safe pregnancy and healthy baby. A woman usually does not learn of her pregnancy until a month or more after she has become pregnant. Meanwhile, the food she has been eating has been the only nourishment for the unborn baby. If the expectant mother has been making poor food choices, she runs the risk of health problems for herself and the baby.

Poor nutrition during pregnancy can lead to babies with low birth weight (under 5½ pounds or 2.5 kg). Such babies often have serious physical problems and may have learning problems as well.

Teen Pregnancy

Pregnant teens are at special risk, because they need added nutrients for themselves and the fetus. Poor eating habits can increase the risk of having a baby with health problems. Because most teens are not fully developed, they are also more likely to have difficult pregnancies.

Guidelines for Pregnant Women

As soon as a woman suspects she is pregnant, she should see a health professional, such as a physician or nurse practitioner. Some women see an **obstetrician** (ahb-stuh-TRISH-un), a physician who specializes in pregnancy.

An expectant mother should follow her health professional's recommendations for the kind and amount of food to be eaten.

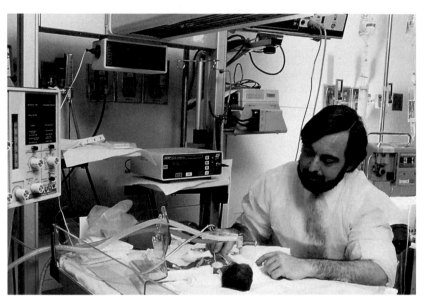

Low birth weight significantly increases the risk a baby will die or have long-term health or learning problems.

Special Needs Strategies

Multicultural and/or Bilingual: Have students collect pictures of foods associated with different stages of the life cycle. Have them use the pictures to create a picture book that includes simple sentences describing eating guidelines for each stage.

During pregnancy, six to eight glasses of liquid are needed daily.

These recommendations may include:

- ❖ Choose low-fat, nutrient-dense foods from the Food Guide Pyramid. (See pages 97-102.)
- ❖ Increase calories slightly to supply enough energy for both mother and fetus.
- ❖ Choose at least four daily servings of high-protein foods, such as fish, poultry, meat, eggs, and dry beans.
- ❖ Have at least three servings of milk or low-fat cheese or yogurt a day (at least four for pregnant teens).
- ❖ Eat foods rich in iron, such as meat, poultry, fish, dry beans, and leafy green vegetables, to help build red blood cells. Foods that contain vitamin C, such as fruits and vegetables, help the body use iron from plant sources more efficiently.
- ❖ Eat foods rich in folate, such as whole-grain breads and cereals, fruits, and dark green vegetables.
- ❖ Drink at least six to eight glasses of liquid daily, including water, juices, and milk.

Women should not go on a weight-loss diet during pregnancy. Dieting deprives the fetus of much-needed nutrients and can seriously affect the baby's health. A weight gain of about 25 to 35 pounds (11 to 16 kg) is nor-

mal. Most of the added weight comes from the fetus, its surrounding fluids, and body changes in the mother. Little of it is fat. Those who have made nutritious food choices should return to their prepregnancy weight within a few months after childbirth.

Pregnant women should avoid using any drugs, medicines, or nutrient supplements unless directed by a physician. Smoking and drinking alcoholic beverages can be especially dangerous to the physical and mental development of the fetus. Smoking often results in low birth weight. Drinking alcoholic beverages may result in severe mental and physical problems known as "fetal alcohol syndrome." The baby is abnormally small at birth with a small brain. Such babies never catch up to normal growth, either physically or mentally. Many have heart defects.

Infancy

The first years of life are a time of exceptional growth and development. Good nutrition plays a key role. The harmful effects of poor nutrition during infancy can last a lifetime.

Feeding Newborns

There are two choices for feeding newborn infants—breast-feeding or bottle-feeding infant formula. Both provide all the nutrients the baby needs for the first four to six months.

Breast milk has the right amount and kind of fat for a baby. The protein is more easily digested and absorbed than the protein in cow's milk.

During about the first three days after the birth, the mother's breasts give **colostrum** (kuh-LAW-strum), a thick, yellowish fluid. It is easily digested, highly nutritious, and contains antibodies that protect the baby from infection. Later, the colostrum changes to true breast milk.

A woman who is breast-feeding should eat the same kinds of foods recommended

Student Experiences

1. **Guest Speaker:** Invite an obstetrician or dietician to speak on the dietary advice given to pregnant women. Ask the speaker to explain why dieting by the pregnant mother can be dangerous for the fetus. Also ask the speaker to discuss the dangers of using any drugs, medicines, or nutrient supplements unless directed by a physician. What effect may smoking have on the fetus? What is fetal alcohol syndrome, and what causes it? *(Key skill: health)*

2. **Guest Speaker:** Invite a neonatal nurse to discuss the causes and effects of low birth weight. What type of immediate care is needed and what are the costs? What are possible long-term effects? Have students write a short summary of what they learn. *(Key skill: writing)*

3. **Posters:** Have students make posters that show factors under the control of the mother that can affect the fetus. *(Key skill: science)*

4. **Menu Planning:** Have students prepare a table that lists the amounts of calories and nutrients needed by pregnant women and at least two specific foods rich in each nutrient. *(Key skill: math)*

Thinking Skills

Reasoning: In a traditional meal pattern, most members of the family eat the same foods each day. Ask students whether this is a good idea. Why or why not? *(Link to life cycle.)*

Comprehension Check

1. Ask students why good nutrition is so important for infants. *(The harmful effects of poor nutrition during infancy can last a lifetime.)*

2. Ask students to list beverages that should not be given to babies *(sugar water, soft drinks, diet beverages, coffee, or tea).*

3. Ask students to explain why it is unnecessary to add salt, sugar, fat, or spices to a baby's food. *(Babies' taste buds are more sensitive than an adult's.)*

Student Experiences

1. **Guest Panel:** Invite the mothers of a newborn and infants under a year of age to demonstrate proper feeding and burping techniques for newborns and infants. *(Key skill: life management)*

2. **Store Survey:** Have students observe the baby food section of a supermarket. What types of food products are available? How much do they cost? Does unit cost vary among brands? How do these products differ from "adult" foods? *(Key skill: consumer awareness)*

Lab Experience

Have students prepare a homemade fruit or vegetable baby food. Taste-test and compare the homemade product with the commercial product made of the same food. How does taste compare? How does cost per serving compare? What conclusions can they draw?

What would be the advantages and disadvantages of bottle-feeding?

during pregnancy and drink plenty of liquids. The right food choices will insure that she produces enough milk to keep the baby well fed and healthy. She should not diet while she is breast-feeding.

Bottle-feeding infant formula can also provide good nutrition. Infant formula is usually made of a nonfat cow's milk base. Vegetable oils and carbohydrates are added to make it more similar to breast milk. Other types of formula are also available. For infants allergic to cow's milk, formulas with a soybean base are often used.

Do not give a baby sugar water, soft drinks, diet beverages, coffee, or tea. Also, do not give a baby honey during the first year of life. The honey may contain microorganisms that are harmful to the baby.

Adding Solid Foods

After the first four to six months, the baby will be ready for solid food. The **pediatrician,** a physician who cares for infants and children, can make recommendations.

A baby's first "solid" foods are actually strained foods that are easy to swallow and

digest. They should be introduced one at a time. That way the cause of any food allergies can be identified. The first solid food is usually iron-fortified rice cereal, followed by strained vegetables and fruits. Other foods can be added later.

During the last half of the first year, infants' eating skills improve. They can be given foods that need some chewing. They begin to learn to pick up solid food with their fingers. Good "finger foods" include pieces of fruit, cooked vegetables, cheese, and crackers. They also begin to learn to use a spoon for self-feeding.

Do not add salt, sugar, fat, or spices to the baby's food. Babies do not need them because their taste buds are more sensitive than an adult's. Added salt, sugar, or fat may also start babies on poor eating habits.

Certain foods should not be fed to infants and small children because they can cause choking. These include nuts, seeds, raw carrots, hot dogs, candy, grapes, popcorn, and peanut butter.

By the end of the first year, a baby usually can eat the same foods as the rest of the

TIPS for Success

Feeding Solid Food to Infants

❖ Offer new foods at the beginning of the meal, when the baby is the most hungry.

❖ Keep mealtime quiet, relaxed, and enjoyable for you and the baby.

❖ When the baby is ready for table foods, cut them into very small pieces for easier handling and safe eating.

❖ Have patience. Until the baby learns to chew and swallow properly, much of the food will end up on the baby and the surroundings. Do not become angry or scold—the baby is doing the best he or she can.

More About Feeding Infants

• Besides being healthy for the baby, breast feeding has several advantages. It costs less than formula and doesn't require sterile bottles, mixing, or heating.

• If the baby refuses certain foods, continue to offer them. Eventually, the baby will accept them.

• Homemade formulas may not contain all the nutrients the baby needs. There is also a risk of bacterial contamination if homemade formula is not handled properly.

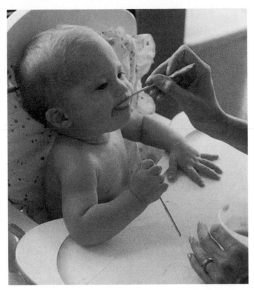

Introducing solid foods one at a time makes it easier to pinpoint any food allergies. Which solid food is usually introduced first?

family, but in smaller amounts. Parents and caregivers should not try to limit the amount of fat that children under age two eat. Babies and toddlers have high energy requirements. They need more fat in their diet than older children and adults do.

Childhood

Young children are active and growing. It is essential that they receive a wide selection of nutritious foods from the five food groups in the Food Guide Pyramid. However, children have small stomachs that cannot hold very much food at one time.

When serving food at meals, keep portions small. Many experts recommend beginning

with 1 tablespoon (15 mL) of a food for each year of the child's life. If the child is still hungry, he or she can be given more. The amount of food needed varies from child to child and week to week. During periods of very rapid growth, called growth spurts, children may eat more than usual. At other times, they may want less food.

Young children need 2 cups (500 mL) of milk each day. It can be served in three or four smaller portions.

Children also need between-meal snacks to help supply them with enough energy and nutrients. Good snacks include juice, yogurt, milk, pieces of fruit or vegetables, cooked meat or poultry, unsweetened cereal, and whole-grain crackers. Avoid foods that are high in fat, sugar, or salt.

Promoting Good Eating Habits

Most children go through phases of strong food likes and dislikes. Usually this is no cause for concern. Eventually they will try new foods.

Young children need nutritious food served attractively. Simply varying the colors and shapes of foods makes meals more inviting.

Section 6.1: Food and the Life Cycle   **167**

Thinking Skills

Problem Solving: How parents manage meal and snack times for infants and children affects the type of eating habits children develop. Have students identify and discuss the types of mealtime behavior that will encourage good eating habits or poor eating habits.

Teaching . . .

• Childhood
(text pages 167-168)

Comprehension Check

1. Discuss why it is important to feed small children nutritious between-meal snacks. *(Their stomachs are too small to hold much at a time, so they get hungry before it's time for another meal.)*

2. Ask students to list tips for promoting good eating habits in small children.

Student Experiences

1. **Childhood Memories:** Ask students to recall pleasant and unpleasant childhood memories that involved food. Based on the discussion, have students develop a list of guidelines for making mealtime pleasant for young children. *(Key skill: writing)*

2. **Class Discussion:** Have students identify ways people use food to show love, give rewards, or impose punishment. Discuss alternative ways to accomplish these goals without using food. *(Key skill: critical thinking)*

3. **Demonstration:** Have students work in groups to plan and demonstrate fun foods for young children. Include finger foods and foods that would have special appeal for young children. *(Key skill: creativity)*

4. **Television Food Ads:** Have students observe Saturday morning children's television. Ask students to write a report listing the foods that were advertised, the techniques advertisers used, and how successful students thought the ads would be. *(Key skills: writing, critical thinking)*

Teaching . . .

- **Adolescence**
- **Adulthood**

(text pages 168-169)

Comprehension Check

1. Ask students to explain why teens need more of almost all nutrients. *(They are growing rapidly and undergoing dramatic physical and psychological changes.)*

2. Ask students to explain why older adults often don't drink as much water as they should. How much do they need? Ask students to think of ways an older adult can be sure of getting enough water each day.

Student Experiences

1. **Class Discussion:** Discuss what happens when adults continue to eat as much food as when they were younger. Why is regular exercise important for adults? What factors in modern lifestyles make it difficult for adults to make good food choices and get enough exercise? *(Key skill: health)*

2. **Field Trip:** Have students take a field trip to a feeding program or center for the elderly. Ask the program director to identify the special challenges some elderly people face in meeting their nutritional needs. How do fixed incomes, health problems, and living alone contribute to the nutritional problems of the elderly? Have interested students find out how they can help in the feeding program or center. *(Key skill: community service)*

Here are some tips to encourage children to develop good eating habits:

- ❖ Teach children how to prepare several simple, nutritious foods by themselves.
- ❖ Let children help prepare a simple part of a meal.
- ❖ Serve colorful foods with different textures and flavors. If foods are attractive, children will be more likely to eat them.
- ❖ Eat meals with children. Model good eating habits and acceptable mealtime behavior. Mealtime companionship may encourage children to try new foods.
- ❖ Avoid using food to reward or punish children. This gives them the wrong impression about the purpose of food and can lead to poor eating habits.
- ❖ Do not force children to eat more than they want or insist that they clean their plates. Doing so only creates negative feelings and makes mealtime unpleasant.
- ❖ Let children decide what foods they want to eat for some meals, when possible.

Adolescence

As adolescents move from childhood to adulthood, dramatic physical and psychological changes occur. The growth rate is rapid and varies widely. As a result, teens have an increased need for almost all nutrients.

Many teens choose foods that often do not provide enough calcium, zinc, iron, or vitamins A and C. Be sure to eat at least the minimum number of servings suggested in the Food Guide Pyramid for adolescents. Teens who are growing or have a high activity level may need the maximum number of servings.

As a teen, you are assuming more responsibility for your life, including food choices. Developing good food and fitness habits at this stage gives you a foundation for a healthy adult life. How sensible are your food choices?

Adulthood

Adults, in general, have lower calorie needs than teens. They are no longer growing and may be less active than they were as teens. If adults continue to eat as much food as when they were younger, they may put on weight.

Although adults may need fewer calories, they still need their full share of nutrients. They should choose a variety of low-fat, low-calorie foods from the Food Guide Pyramid. Continuing to get regular exercise throughout adulthood is important as well.

Most adults have many demands on their time—work, family, community activities, and perhaps additional schooling. They may feel too busy to give time and thought to their eating and exercise habits. However, even under such hectic conditions, adults can still make good food choices. By doing so, they can help insure good health in the future.

During adulthood, many people become less active. What effects might this have on their nutrition and health?

Thinking Skills

Critical Thinking: Financial management is very important for older adults on a fixed income. In times of financial crisis, they may purchase other goods and services instead of food. Have students develop a list of budget-stretching tips that might help an older adult maintain good eating habits during these times.

Many adults don't realize that they have slipped into poor eating and exercise habits until they develop a health problem. Developing healthy habits in your teen years may help eliminate future health problems. It will also be easier to continue these habits throughout life.

Older Adults

As people age, they continue to need the same nutrients. However, the amounts needed may change. Older adults may also need fewer calories. If they're physically active, they can eat as much as younger adults.

With maturity, the body's thirst signal often declines and people don't drink as much water as needed. Older people, like all adults, need to drink six to eight cups (1.5 to 2 liters) of liquid daily.

Special Problems of the Elderly

Some elderly people face special challenges in meeting their nutritional needs. Many live on fixed incomes that are too low to provide enough nutritious food. Those

With proper nutrition, exercise, and good health, many older adults remain very active.

who live alone may not feel like preparing a meal just for one. Some elderly persons have health problems that create nutrition risks.

Many communities have social service programs to help elderly people in these situations. Senior and community centers often offer meals at reduced rates for the elderly. They provide nutritious meals and an opportunity for socializing.

Living alone or on a limited income can make meal planning challenging for people of any age, not just the elderly. Chapter 11 provides helpful suggestions. In addition, people of any age may have to cope with medical problems or physical impairments. You will learn more about these in the next section.

■ Section 6.1 Review ■

RECALL THE FACTS

1. Why are good nutrition habits important for a woman even before she knows she is pregnant?

2. What is colostrum?

3. Identify three good "finger foods" for infants and three good snack foods for young children.

4. How can adults get their full share of nutrients without getting too many calories?

DISCUSS YOUR IDEAS

5. Why do you suppose the text recommends getting children involved in meal preparation? How might this promote good eating habits?

APPLY YOUR LEARNING

6. Think of a simple food that children can prepare for themselves. Write down directions for preparing the food as you would explain it to a child.

Section 6.1: Food and the Life Cycle   **169**

6.1

Completing the Section

Review
- Ask students to summarize the main ideas in this section.
- Have students complete the Section Review. (Answers appear below.)

Evaluation
- Have students create simple, nutritious menus suitable for a small child, a teenager, an adult, and an older adult.
- Have students take the quiz for Section 6.1. (Refer to the *Section Quizzes* booklet or use the *Testmaker Software*.)

Reteaching
- Have students create a time line that represents a typical lifetime for a female. List nutritional needs at the appropriate points. Discuss how the time line would be different for a male.
- Refer to the *Reteaching Activities* booklet for the Section 6.1 activity sheet.

Enrichment
- Have students interview a person who lives alone, asking about eating patterns and habits.

Closure
- Discuss nutritional and caloric requirements at different times in life.

■ Answers to Section Review ■

1. A woman usually does not know she's pregnant for about a month.
2. Fluid the mother's breast releases for about 3 days after the baby is born; it contains antibodies and is highly nutritious.
3. Infants *(any three):* Pieces of fruit, cooked vegetables, cheese, and crackers; children *(any three):* juice, yogurt, milk, pieces of fruit or vegetables, cooked meat or poultry, unsweetened cereal, and whole-grain crackers.
4. By choosing nutrient-dense foods that are low in fat, salt, and sugar.
5. Students should realize that helping prepare meals may increase the child's interest in the food.
6. Answers will vary.

Introducing the Section

Motivators

- Ask students to describe dietary changes someone they know has been required to make as the result of a health condition. List the health conditions and the dietary changes on the chalkboard.

- Have students bring to class newspaper or magazine articles that discuss the special nutrition needs related to various health conditions. Have students categorize the articles by health condition and place them in folders for reference as they study this section.

Objectives

- Have students read the section objectives. Discuss the purpose of studying the section.

Vocabulary

- Pronounce the terms listed under "Look for These Terms." Have students find the terms and their definitions in the section.

Guided Reading

- Have students look at the headings within Section 6.2 to preview the concepts that will be discussed.

- Have students read the section and complete the appropriate part of the Chapter 6 Study Guide in the *Student Workbook.*

SECTION 6.2

Managing Health Conditions

OBJECTIVES

After studying this section, you should be able to:

- Explain the relationship between stress and nutrition.
- Identify the role of nutrition in recovery from illness or injury.
- Give examples of how those with medical conditions or physical impairments can meet their nutritional needs.

LOOK FOR THESE TERMS

stress
convalescence
diabetes
food allergy

As you have learned, good nutrition is essential for anyone's health. However, certain situations result in special nutrition needs or challenges.

Nutrition and Stress

Have you ever lost sleep the night before a big exam or had butterflies in your stomach when meeting someone new? If so, you were experiencing stress. **Stress** is physical or mental tension triggered by an event or situation in your life.

Not everyone finds the same situations stressful. Some people experience "test anxiety," while others don't. A person who works in an office will experience different kinds of job stress than a police officer. Even positive events, such as going on a date or receiving an award, can be stressful.

No two people react in quite the same way to a situation. How does your response to an upcoming test compare with your friends'?

170   Chapter 6: Special Topics in Nutrition

Teacher's Classroom Resources—Section 6.2

Refer to these resources in the TCR package:

Reproducible Lesson Plans
Student Workbook
Extending the Text

Reteaching Activities
Section Quizzes
Testmaker Software
Color Transparencies

Taking time to relax can help you manage the stress in your life.

Teaching . . .

- **Nutrition and Stress**

(text pages 170-172)

Comprehension Check

1. Discuss the various relationships between stress and nutrition. Why are over- and undereating poor ways to deal with stress?

2. Ask students to explain how good nutrition can help a person deal with stress.

3. Ask students to list ways to manage stress without making poor food choices.

Student Experiences

1. **Guest Speaker:** Ask a physical education teacher or fitness instructor to explain how exercise can help alleviate stress. What types of exercises are effective in relieving stress? *(Key skill: health)*

2. **Demonstrations:** Have students demonstrate various relaxation techniques to the class. How can learning to relax reduce stress and aid in digestion? *(Key skill: health)*

3. **Skits:** Have students create skits to demonstrate positive and negative ways to deal with stress. Then hold a class discussion on each method. Is it constructive or destructive? How could students reduce stress more effectively? *(Key skills: creativity, life management)*

Stressful situations are part of life and can't be avoided. The key is in learning how to react to these situations positively. Your reaction makes a big difference in whether stress becomes a problem for you. For healthy ways to cope with stressful situations, see the "Tips for Success" on this page.

When stress is not handled effectively, the body and mind may react in various ways. For some people, stress often brings feelings of worry, fear, or anger. A person may become depressed and lack energy. Stress may also cause physical symptoms, such as a headache, stiff neck, or sore back. Stress even plays a role in serious illnesses such as high blood pressure and heart disease.

Stress and nutrition are related in a number of ways. For example, negative emotions can cause some people to experience digestive problems such as heartburn, diarrhea, or constipation. Others react to stress by changing their eating habits. They may overeat or choose too many foods high in fat, sugar, or salt. On the other hand, stress causes some people to lose their appetite.

TIPS for Success

Managing Stress

❖ Take care of your health. You'll be better able to handle challenges if you eat right, get enough rest, and exercise regularly.

❖ Learn to manage your time. Allow time each day to relax and enjoy yourself.

❖ Take positive action to solve a problem if you can. If the problem is beyond your control, learn to accept it for the time being. Perhaps later you may be able to change it.

❖ Develop your sense of humor. Laughter can relieve tension and help you think more clearly.

❖ Try physical activity when you feel upset. Run, walk, ride a bike, or clean out a closet.

❖ Share your feelings and problems with someone you trust.

TIPS for Success

Ask student volunteers to give examples of times when one of these tips has worked for them. Then ask students to identify other ways to manage stress constructively.

Thinking Skills

Critical Thinking: Obtain a list of stress indicators or a self-test designed to measure the stress level in an adult's life. Ask students to redesign the test to make it applicable to the typical stresses in a teen's life. Ask for permission to conduct the test using another class. What do the results tell about the stress level among that group of teens? Have students write up the results. How valid are they?

Teaching . . .

- **Illness and Convalescence**
- **Special Diets**
- **Physical Impairments**

(text pages 172-174)

Comprehension Check

1. Ask students to explain the importance of good nutrition when a person is ill. *(With good nutrition, the body can better fight the illness.)*

2. Discuss the importance of good nutrition during convalescence. *(Help the healing process.)*

3. Ask students to list some guidelines for serving food to a person who is ill or recovering from an illness.

4. Discuss the types of special diets needed for people with high blood pressure, kidney disease, diabetes, or allergies.

5. Ask students to explain why it is important to read the labels on foods in the supermarket when shopping for someone on a special diet. *(Forbidden foods are not always apparent. Salt, in particular, is a "hidden" ingredient in many packaged items.)*

6. Discuss the effects physical impairments can have on the way people meet their nutritional needs.

7. Ask students to list ideas for foods that would be appropriate for someone who has dental problems and cannot eat hard breads, rolls, uncooked vegetables, and some meats.

Making poor food choices is not a positive way to deal with stress. It does nothing to help you cope with what is causing your stress. Poor eating habits can make you feel worse in the long run—often leading to poor nutrition, an unhealthy weight, and perhaps serious health problems.

In contrast, good nutrition can help reduce stress. Eating right is one way to help prevent stress-related illnesses or manage their symptoms. By reacting to stressful situations in a positive way, people can take control of their lives and reduce the risk of illness.

Illness and Convalescence

Any illness puts an additional strain on the body. Whether fighting off a sore throat or the measles, a healthy, well-nourished body is better equipped to handle the problem. Even though a person who is ill may lose interest in eating, the body needs the nutrients found in good food.

Convalescence is the period of recovery after a serious illness or injury. While the patient is recovering, nutritious food and extra rest aid the healing process.

During illness or convalescence, a physician or a dietitian may give special directions about the patient's diet. For example, the patient may be restricted to liquids or soft foods for a time.

If you are helping to care for someone who is ill or recovering from an illness, here are some guidelines:

- ❖ Ask the physician or pharmacist whether the patient's medication affects the appetite or the way the body uses nutrients.
- ❖ Encourage the patient to get enough rest so healing can take place.
- ❖ Be sure the patient gets enough liquids. The physician may specify how much is needed.
- ❖ Serve nutritious food attractively. A meal that includes foods of various colors, shapes, textures, and temperatures is more appealing.

Hospitals know that good nutrition is essential to the healing process. Dietitians make sure that patients receive a diet that meets their particular needs.

- ❖ Use disposable paper or plastic plates and cups if the patient has an illness that can spread to others.

Special Diets for Medical Conditions

Some people, because of long-term medical conditions, must be especially aware of their food choices. Their physician may prescribe a special diet to keep the medical condition under control. Some common examples of such special diets are:

- ❖ *Low-cholesterol, low-fat diets.* People with heart problems or high blood cholesterol may need to follow a special diet to reduce the amount of cholesterol in the blood. Their choices include low-fat, low-cholesterol foods. For instance, someone who has always enjoyed fried food must learn to adjust to foods that are baked or broiled instead.

Thinking Skills

Problem Solving: Have students plan three days of menus for a child who is allergic to milk. How can students see that the child gets enough calcium and other nutrients normally found in the Milk, Yogurt, and Cheese Group?

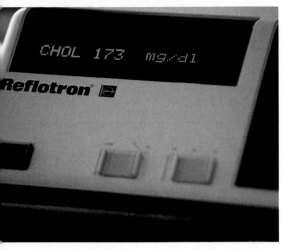

Low-cholesterol, low-fat diets can help lower cholesterol levels in the blood. This can reduce the risk of heart problems. Even children and teens can have elevated cholesterol levels.

Science Connection

Biochemistry:
Insulin and Diabetes

Insulin is a hormone—a chemical substance—produced in the pancreas. It enables glucose, or blood sugar, to enter cells throughout the body for energy use. Diabetes occurs when the pancreas doesn't produce enough insulin or the insulin doesn't work properly. Glucose builds up in the bloodstream, stressing the body and resulting in weakness, fatigue, drowsiness, and thirst.

■ ■ ■

❖ *Low-sodium diets.* With certain medical conditions, such as kidney disease, too much sodium in the diet can cause serious problems. In such cases, people must not add salt when preparing and eating food. They must also limit foods high in sodium, such as processed foods.

❖ *Diabetic diets.* **Diabetes** is a condition in which the body cannot control blood sugar properly, resulting in high blood sugar levels. Diabetes may cause serious damage to the kidneys, the eyes, and other parts of the body. Eating the right balance of food plays a role in controlling the blood sugar level. Like most people, those with diabetes need to eat foods high in complex carbohydrates and fiber and low in fats, cholesterol, sodium, and sugar. Eating all foods in moderation also helps control weight, which is very important for diabetics. Diets for people with diabetes are individually prescribed for each patient and must be closely followed.

❖ *Food allergy diets.* Some people have an unpleasant reaction after eating even a small amount of a certain food. This condition is called a **food allergy.** Symptoms may include itching, rash, hives, abdominal pain, nausea, or difficulty in breathing. Some of the more common allergy-causing foods are cow's milk, eggs, fish, shellfish, nuts, and peanuts. Special tests are used to determine which foods are responsible for the allergy.

It takes time for people who have been put on a special diet to adjust to a new way of eating. If you know of anyone in this situation, offer your support and encouragement. Try to help them look upon the special diet as an opportunity to try new foods.

When shopping for foods to fit a special diet, read labels carefully. Check for fats, sodium, or other ingredients that must be limited. You may be able to find substitute products, such as no-cholesterol egg substitutes.

Section 6.2: Managing Health Conditions   **173**

Student Experiences
1. **Analyzing Diets:** Provide students with copies of diets recommended during illness and convalescence. Discuss situations in which each diet might be prescribed. *(Key skill: analysis)*
2. **Interview:** Have students interview someone on a restricted diet. What foods are restricted or must be included? Does the diet cause problems when the person eats at a restaurant? *(Key skill: health)*
3. **Analyzing Diets:** Have students work in groups to study special diets for people with heart problems or high cholesterol, kidney disease, diabetes, or food allergies. How does each diet differ from that of a person on a regular diet? Have students report their findings to the class.*(Key skills: analysis, public speaking)*

Science Connection

Ask students to find out how insulin is cultured. What new methods are now available? What are the advantages and disadvantages of each method?

■ ■ ■

See Also . . .
• "Kitchen Safety for the Elderly or Handicapped," page 193.
• "Designing Barrier-Free Kitchens," page 388.

More About Illness and Sanitation

When caring for patients at home, follow these hints to keep the illness from spreading to other family members:
• Wash your hands carefully with soap and warm water before and after every contact with the patient.

• Wash patient's dishes and utensils separately from those used by others.
• To dispose of paper or plastic eating utensils and leftover food, put them in a paper bag in the sickroom. Then dispose of the bag immediately.

Review

- Ask students to summarize the main ideas in this section.
- Have students complete the Section Review. (Answers appear below.)

Evaluation

- Have students write a short essay describing adaptations a person with a long-term medical condition or a physical impairment might require.
- Have students take the quiz for Section 6.2. (Refer to the *Section Quizzes* booklet or use the *Testmaker Software*.)

Reteaching

- Have students work in pairs to list stressful situations for teens and ways teens can combat stress.
- Refer to the *Reteaching Activities* booklet for the Section 6.2 activity sheet.

Enrichment

- Have students research ideas and devices people have developed to make it easier to meet their nutritional needs.

Closure

- Name physical illnesses or impairments that may require special diets or using adaptive devices to meet nutritional requirements. Ask students to give specific examples of each.

You might be surprised at the variety of flavorful foods that can be prepared within the limitations of special diets. For instance, you could learn to use different herbs and spices and to make low-fat or low-sodium sauces and gravies. Many hospitals and clinics offer classes on cooking for special diets. Cookbooks focusing on special diets are also available.

Physical Impairments

Sometimes a physical impairment requires that a person make adaptations in order to meet his or her nutritional needs. This can be true of some elderly people or some people with physical handicaps. However, it can also be true in a number of other situations. Generally the person's nutrition needs are no different from those of anyone else who is

A physical impairment sometimes makes it difficult to prepare food in a standard kitchen. Adapting the kitchen for easier use encourages independence and good nutrition.

similar in age, gender, and activity level. However, physical limitations may affect how those needs are met.

For instance, some people have dental problems. Hard breads and rolls, raw fruits and vegetables, and certain meats may be difficult for them to eat. Try substituting softer foods that are also nutritious, such as:

- ❖ High-fiber cereal softened with milk.
- ❖ Ground meat, ground poultry, or fish.
- ❖ Soft, enriched breads and rolls.
- ❖ Canned, unsweetened fruits.

Other examples of physical impairments might include limited mobility, limited use of the hands, or vision problems. Physical limitations such as these might make it difficult to use standard kitchen equipment. In this case, the solution is to adapt the kitchen and its equipment. In Chapters 7 and 14 you will read about adaptations to help those with physical impairments be self-sufficient.

■ Section 6.2 Review ■

RECALL THE FACTS

1. What is stress? Give three examples of how a negative reaction to stress can affect nutrition.

2. What is convalescence? How does nutrition play a part in it?

3. Give three suggestions for planning and preparing meals to fit a medically prescribed special diet.

4. In general, how do physical impairments relate to nutrition needs?

DISCUSS YOUR IDEAS

5. Discuss ways that good nutrition might help you handle stress more effectively.

APPLY YOUR LEARNING

6. Imagine that you are caring for someone who is convalescing from surgery. Identify at least six ways that you could make meals more enjoyable for this person.

■ Answers to Section Review ■

1. Physical or mental tension triggered by an event or situation in your life; examples will vary.
2. The recovery period after an illness or injury; nutritional foods aid the recovery process.
3. *Any three:* Ask the physician or pharmacist whether the patient's medication affects appetite or the way the body uses nutrients; encourage patient to get enough rest; be sure patient gets enough liquids; serve nutritious foods attractively; use disposable paper or plastic plates and cups if the illness is contagious.
4. They can make it more difficult to meet nutritional needs; special adaptations may be necessary.
5. Answers will vary.
6. Answers will vary.

Eating Disorders

OBJECTIVES

After studying this section, you should be able to:

- Identify the characteristics of anorexia nervosa and bulimia nervosa.
- Describe the effects of eating disorders on health.
- Explain what can be done to help someone with an eating disorder.

LOOK FOR THESE TERMS

eating disorder
anorexia nervosa
bulimia nervosa

When Charlene began to lose excess weight, her friends supported her efforts. As the weeks passed, Charlene reached a weight considered healthy for her age and height. However, she continued her diet.

Months later, Charlene had lost so much weight that she almost looked like a skeleton. She was lightheaded, had stopped menstruating, and felt tired all the time. Concerned, her family scheduled a medical checkup. After a thorough evaluation, Dr. Cho diagnosed Charlene's problem as an eating disorder.

What Are Eating Disorders?

The term **eating disorder** describes extreme, unhealthy behavior relating to food, eating, and weight. The causes of eating disorders are not clearly understood, although research continues.

People with eating disorders are unable to view their weight and eating habits realistically. Without treatment, eating disorders can cause serious health problems or even death.

Section 6.3: Eating Disorders   **175**

Teaching . . .

• What Are Eating Disorders?

(text pages 175-176)

Comprehension Check

1. Discuss the problems associated with eating disorders. What do researchers know about eating disorders? What don't they know?

2. Discuss the differences between anorexia nervosa and bulimia nervosa.

Student Experiences

1. **Reading about Eating Disorders:** Ask students to find and read newspaper, magazine, or journal articles about the eating disorders anorexia nervosa and bulimia nervosa. What methods do people who have these disorders use to lose weight? Why is it difficult to determine the causes of eating disorders? *(Key skill: reading)*

2. **Survey:** Have the class develop a body image survey and administer it to the students in the school. Include questions about ideal body shape, size, and weight. Ask questions about weight loss methods students are using, including extremely low-calorie diets, laxatives, diet aids, forced vomiting, strenuous exercise for long periods. Tally the results and draw conclusions. *(Key skills: math, drawing conclusions)*

Eating disorders generally occur among teens and young adults, especially females. It's estimated that from 1 to 10 percent of all teens suffer from an eating disorder.

The term "eating disorder" usually refers to two specific problems called *anorexia nervosa* and *bulimia nervosa*. Both are related to an overwhelming desire to gain control in life through controlling weight.

Anorexia Nervosa

Anorexia nervosa (an-uh-RECK-see-yuh ner-VOH-suh) involves an irresistible urge to lose weight through self-starvation. It is often described as "dieting out of control." No matter how thin anorexics become, they "feel fat." They see themselves as being overweight and show an obsessive fear of gaining weight.

Anorexics will do anything to lose as much weight as possible. They refuse to eat or eat very little. They may use laxatives and diet aids or force themselves to vomit after a meal. In spite of feeling tired, some exercise strenuously every day for long periods of time. Still, most deny that they have any problem and believe that their behavior is normal.

Bulimia Nervosa

Bulimia nervosa (byou-LIM-ee-yuh ner-VOH-suh) involves episodes of binge eating, or rapidly consuming very large amounts of food. The binge is followed by purging—using self-induced vomiting, laxatives, or vigorous exercise to prevent weight gain. Unlike anorexics, most bulimics are usually within 10 to 15 pounds (5 to 8 kg) of a healthy weight.

Bulimics use secret eating binges in an attempt to cope with problems such as anger, loneliness, boredom, and frustration. Usually they binge on high-fat, high-calorie foods which they might normally consider "forbidden," such as pastries, candy, chips, and ice cream. The foods are eaten in a short time, usually within two hours. It's not unusual for bulimics to eat 3,000 to 5,000 calories at a time. During a day of repeated bingeing, some can eat as many as 20,000 calories. They stop eating only when their stomach hurts, they fall asleep, they run out of food, or someone interrupts them.

After bingeing, bulimics feel guilty and depressed. Because they don't want to gain weight, they follow the binge with purging. A typical bulimic has two or more eating binges a week. The binge-purge cycle becomes a way of life.

People with bulimia nervosa have frequent episodes of bingeing on foods high in calories and fat.

Food and Nutrition Science

Anorexia and Brain Damage: Permanent brain damage can result from anorexia nervosa. This occurs because the brain needs a steady supply of glucose. When it doesn't get enough glucose from dietary or stored carbohydrate, protein is metabolized. However, anorexics may have little excess protein to break down into glucose. This lack of glucose can cause brain damage.

Effects of Eating Disorders

Eating disorders can create serious health problems. Anorexia can result in lowered heart rate and body temperature, constipation, and lowered blood pressure and breathing rate. Female anorexics stop menstruating. About 10 percent of anorexics die of starvation.

Bulimics lose fluid and potassium, which may result in fatigue, heart problems, and kidney damage. The vomiting damages their esophagus, teeth, and gums. Their salivary glands, located on each side of the neck, enlarge. Many bulimics have a sore throat almost all the time.

What steps might you take if a friend shows several signs that might indicate an eating disorder?

What Can Be Done?

It's important to realize that anorexics and bulimics have an illness. Most can't stop their self-destructive behavior on their own. Often it's up to others to recognize the problem and encourage the person to get help.

Recognizing Eating Disorders

Anorexics often exhibit warning signs. In addition to losing large amounts of weight, eating little, and exercising for hours, they may:

❖ Show sensitivity to cold temperatures.
❖ Seem preoccupied with food and calories.
❖ Develop food-related rituals, such as always cutting food into very tiny pieces.
❖ Prepare elaborate meals, but not eat them. Some actually become gourmet cooks.
❖ Begin to avoid their friends and spend more time by themselves.

Section 6.3: Eating Disorders   **177**

6.3

Teaching . . .

• **Effects of Eating Disorders**
• **What Can Be Done?**

(text pages 177-178)

Comprehension Check

1. Discuss the health problems that can result from anorexia nervosa and bulimia nervosa.

2. Ask students to list the signs of anorexia nervosa and bulimia nervosa. Why is it more difficult to detect bulimics than anorexics?

3. Ask students to describe the professional help needed to cure eating disorders. What might be the advantage of staying in a hospital for a time? *(It's more difficult to hide the problem; foods and exercise can be regulated.)*

Student Experiences

1. **Reading:** Have students read articles about the effects of eating disorders on teenagers and young adults. Have students list the effects identified in the article. Have students pool their information to create a class list. *(Key skills: reading, writing)*

2. **Guest Speaker:** Invite a health care professional or counselor to discuss symptoms of eating disorders, sources of help, and treatment procedures. *(Key skill: health)*

More About Anorexia Nervosa

Anorexics may be described as having low self-esteem. They often feel that others are controlling their lives. Anorexics attempt to gain control in their lives by constantly losing weight.

6.3

Completing the Section

Review

- Ask students to summarize the main ideas in this section.
- Have students complete the Section Review. (Answers appear below.)

Evaluation

- Have students write a short essay describing the topics they studied in this section.
- Have students take the quiz for Section 6.3. (Refer to the *Section Quizzes* booklet or use the *Testmaker Software*.)

Reteaching

- Have students use a two-column table to list the causes of eating disorders, along with their effects.
- Refer to the *Reteaching Activities* booklet for the Section 6.3 activity sheet.

Enrichment

- Have students report on the latest research into the causes of eating disorders and on current treatment methods.

Closure

- Lead a class discussion on eating disorders, their symptoms, and their treatment.

Bulimics are aware that they have no control over their unusual eating habits. They are embarrassed by their lack of self-control. As a result, they are very secretive and can hide their unusual eating habits quite successfully. For this reason, and because they generally maintain their weight, bulimics are much harder to recognize than anorexics. Warning signs include:

❖ Preoccupation with food and eating.
❖ Physical changes, such as swollen glands or tooth problems.

Professional help is needed to recover from an eating disorder. Some residential treatment centers are devoted solely to eating disorders.

Getting Help

Eating disorders stem from complex problems that require professional help. Treatment usually includes nutritional and psychological counseling as well as medical help. Often the person must be hospitalized in an eating disorder clinic.

People with eating disorders can recover, but the process is very slow. It usually takes at least one or two years of treatment for full recovery to occur. As with any other illness, support from family and friends is an important part of the recovery process.

Section 6.3 Review

RECALL THE FACTS

1. List four characteristics of anorexia nervosa.
2. Describe two key ways in which bulimia differs from anorexia.
3. Name three health problems that may occur as a result of eating disorders.
4. What help is available to persons who suffer from eating disorders?

DISCUSS YOUR IDEAS

5. In recent years, a number of celebrities have admitted having eating disorders. Do you think such publicity has a positive or negative effect? Explain.

APPLY YOUR LEARNING

6. Imagine that Charlene—the girl described at the beginning of the section—is a friend of yours. You have just learned about her eating disorder. Write a journal entry describing the signs that led you to suspect there was a problem. Close by explaining how you plan to give support to Charlene.

Answers to Section Review

1. *Any four:* sensitivity to cold temperatures; preoccupied with food and calories; develop food-related rituals; prepare elaborate meals, but not eat them; avoid their friends.
2. Bulimics are aware that they have no control over their unusual eating habits, and they generally maintain their weight at close to normal.
3. *Any three:* Lowered heart rate and body temperature; constipation; lowered blood pressure and breathing rate; lack of menstruation in females; some die of starvation.
4. Nutritional and psychological counseling and medical help.
5. Answers will vary.
6. Answers will vary.

Career PROFILE

Carmen Ragusa
Hospital Volunteer

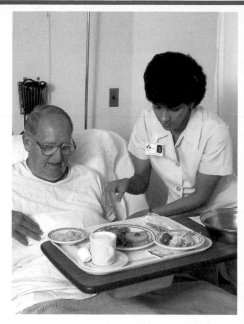

CURRENT POSITION

"I volunteer three evenings a week at a community hospital."

RESPONSIBILITIES

"Basically, I go wherever I'm needed. I make sure patients have fresh water, I help serve their meal trays, and I try to make them comfortable in any way I can—sometimes just by talking with them or buying them magazines at the gift shop."

WHY I CHOSE THIS JOB

"I was interested in working at a hospital, but I wasn't sure if I was suited for it. Volunteering has given me a chance to explore my options."

SKILLS

"In this job, you have to be willing to do anything and be cheerful while you're doing it, even if you aren't feeling particularly cheerful at the moment."

FAVORITE PART OF THE JOB

"I really like it when I can take a tray to a person who's feeling down and leave him in a better mood by showing him genuine concern and compassion. Not everyone is receptive, though, so I do take my cues from the patient."

FUTURE PLANS

"I'm still exploring my options, but I'm leaning toward a career as a clinical dietitian. I think I would enjoy teaching people good nutrition practices."

- What are the advantages of volunteering?
- What aspects of Carmen's job do you think you might enjoy? Why?

179

CAREER PROFILE: HOSPITAL VOLUNTEERS

Thinking About . . . Hospital Volunteers

- Have students think of other questions they would like to ask Carmen Ragusa about being a volunteer at the hospital. (Examples: How many hours a week do you volunteer? How does your volunteer work fit in with your school work?)
- Ask students to brainstorm a list of nonmedical things a hospital volunteer could do to make patients more comfortable while they're in the hospital.

Student Opportunities

Students interested in hospital work can volunteer at hospitals or nursing homes. No specific training is needed. If you have an area of special interest, such as nutrition or obstetrics, you can sometimes be placed on a ward where you can observe people working in these areas.

Occupational Outlook

Although being a hospital volunteer is not a paying job, it can be very rewarding. It can also be good preparation for any career within the nutrition, medical, and nursing fields. The contacts you make while you volunteer can be valuable in these fields, too. However, to advance into these related fields, you will need specialized training.

For More Information

For more information about hospital careers, contact:
- The National Health Council, 622 Third Ave., New York, NY 10017-6765
- American Hospital Association, 840 North Lake Shore Dr., Chicago, IL 60611
- American Health Care Association, 1200 15th St. NW, Washington, D.C. 20005

Review

- Have students complete the Chapter Review. (Answers appear below.)

Evaluation

- Have students write an outline of the topics discussed in Chapter 6. They may use the headings and subheads from the chapter, but they should include important points within the sections to fill out the outline.

- Have students take the test for Chapter 6. (Refer to the *Chapter and Unit Tests* booklet or construct your own test using the *Testmaker Software*.)

■ ANSWERS ■

REVIEWING THE FACTS

1. Because their bodies are still developing, growing, and changing.

2. *Any five:* nuts, seeds, raw carrots, hot dogs, candy, grapes, popcorn, and peanut butter.

3. They keep eating the same amounts of the same foods but their caloric requirements go down.

4. Extremely low budget and a reluctance to make a meal just for one.

5. *Any four:* Take care of your health; learn to manage your time so that you have time for enjoyment; take positive action to solve a problem if you can or accept it if you can't; develop your sense of humor; physical activity; share your feelings and problems with someone you trust.

6. A condition in which the body cannot control blood sugar properly; they must be high in complex carbohydrates and fiber and low in fats, cholesterol, sodium, and sugar.

CHAPTER 6 REVIEW

SUMMARY

SECTION 6.1

Food and the Life Cycle: At each stage of the life cycle, people experience changes in nutritional needs. Good nutrition during pregnancy is essential for the health of the baby. Infants and children need the right kinds of food for health and growth. Children should also be encouraged to develop good eating habits. Through adolescence and adulthood, changing energy needs are a consideration. Some elderly people face special challenges to nutrition.

SECTION 6.2

Managing Health Conditions: Good nutrition is essential in preventing and managing stress-related illnesses. Along with rest, nutritious food helps the body heal itself during illness and convalescence. Some people have long-term medical conditions requiring special diets. Physical impairments sometimes require that a person make adaptations in order to meet nutritional needs.

SECTION 6.3

Eating Disorders: Anorexia nervosa involves losing weight through self-starvation. Bulimia nervosa involves bingeing and purging. Both eating disorders can cause serious damage to health. Warning signs may indicate a problem. People with eating disorders need professional help.

REVIEWING FACTS

1. Why is nutrition of particular concern for pregnant teens? (6.1)

2. Name five foods that should not be given to infants or small children because they may cause choking. (6.1)

3. Why do people often tend to put on weight as they move from the teen years to adulthood? (6.1)

4. Name two factors that may keep some elderly people from eating nutritious meals. (6.1)

5. List four positive ways to cope with stress. (6.2)

6. What is diabetes? Give two characteristics of a diet to control diabetes. (6.2)

7. List three nutritious, easy-to-chew foods appropriate for a person with dental problems. (6.2)

8. In which groups of people do eating disorders occur most often? (6.3)

9. Describe the binge-purge cycle characteristic of bulimia. (6.3)

10. Why is it usually more difficult to recognize bulimia than anorexia? (6.3)

LEARNING BY DOING

1. *Foods lab:* List ideas for making nutritious foods that would appeal to young children. Consider using unusual colors, animal shapes, funny faces, etc. Prepare samples of the foods. Serve them to classmates or to a group of young children, if possible. (6.1)

2. *Foods lab:* Find and prepare a simple recipe designed for a special diet, such as diabetic, low-salt, or wheat-free. Rate the food for appearance, texture, and flavor. (6.2)

7. *Any three:* High-fiber cereal softened with milk; ground meat, ground poultry, or fish; soft, enriched breads and rolls; canned, unsweetened fruits.

8. Teens and young adults, especially females.

9. A person overeats (binges) and then "purges" by inducing vomiting, taking laxatives, or getting extreme amounts of exercise. Then the person feels guilty about it and resolves not to do it again. However, the cycle repeats.

3. **Foods lab:** Prepare a simple meal, such as soup and a sandwich. Place it on a tray as if you were serving it to someone who was in bed recovering from an illness. Show how you would make the meal attractive as well as easy to eat. (6.2)

THINKING CRITICALLY

1. **Analyzing cause and effect:** The text states that using food to reward or punish children can lead to poor eating habits. Give some examples to show how this might happen. (6.1)

2. **Determining accuracy:** Some people believe that certain foods can help cure certain illnesses—for example, that chicken soup helps cure a cold. Do you think there is any truth to these beliefs? Why or why not? How might a scientist try to test such theories? (6.2)

3. **Predicting consequences:** How might family members be affected if a member of the family is suffering from an eating disorder? (6.3)

MAKING DECISIONS AND SOLVING PROBLEMS

What Would You Do?

1. Next week, you will start babysitting your neighbor's five-year-old after school each day. The parents want you to give the child a nutritious snack. You've been told the child is a very picky eater. (6.1)

2. Your elderly neighbor has poor vision and no longer drives a car. He does his grocery shopping only when someone is available to drive him to the supermarket. You are worried that he isn't getting regular, nutritious meals. (6.1, 6.2)

3. Each morning, your sister prepares an elaborate sack lunch. You've often seen her throw the lunch in the trash as soon as she arrives at school. She often cooks dinner for the family but seldom eats any of it, claiming she is still full from lunch. She is getting thinner and thinner. (6.3)

LINKING YOUR STUDIES

1. **Writing:** Work in groups to write, illustrate, and produce a pamphlet discussing the importance of good nutrition during pregnancy. Distribute the pamphlet in your school or community. (6.1)

2. **Science:** Using library sources, research the connection between nutrition and the healing process. Possible topics include: What effect does nutrition have on the immune system? What nutrients are important for bone and muscle repair and rebuilding? Do some diets seem to help with chronic or terminal illnesses? Report your findings to the class. (6.2)

3. **Literature:** Find a book written by or about someone with an eating disorder. (You may want to ask your teacher or a librarian for suggestions.) After reading the book, write a brief report discussing how the person's story affected you. (6.3)

181

LEARNING BY DOING

1. Foods will vary.

2. Recipes and foods will vary. Remind students to be objective in their evaluation of the foods.

3. Answers will vary.

THINKING CRITICALLY

1. Examples will vary.

2. Answers will vary. A scientist might begin testing such a theory by finding several people who have the same illness at the same stage, along with several healthy people. To half of the ill people and half of the well people, the scientist would feed chicken soup. The other half of both groups would not get chicken soup. He would then record the results and note any improvement due to chicken soup.

3. Answers will vary. Family members should be supportive of the person with the eating disorder.

MAKING DECISIONS AND SOLVING PROBLEMS

Answers to "Making Decisions and Solving Problems" questions will vary. Encourage students to give reasons for their answers.

LINKING YOUR STUDIES

1. Pamphlets will vary. Check the content of the pamphlets before allowing students to distribute them.

2. Answers will vary.

3. Answers will vary. *Starving for Attention* by Cherry Boone O'Neill is one such book.

10. Bulimics realize that they have a problem and become very skilled at hiding the symptoms.

COMPLETING THE UNIT

Refer to page 19 for suggestions for completing the unit.

Planning the Unit

Unit Overview

Chapter 7: Kitchen Principles— Gives an overview of the proper layout of a kitchen and discusses safety, sanitation, and conservation techniques for the kitchen.

Chapter 8: Recipe Skills— Discusses basic skills associated with reading, interpreting, and collecting recipes; measuring units and tools; how to change a recipe; preparation tasks; and time management.

Chapter 9: Cooking Methods— Gives an overview of cooking appliances and tools, discusses methods of heat transfer, and discusses microwave and conventional cooking techniques.

Chapter 10: Mealtime Customs— Discusses the proper way to set a table and other aspects of serving a family meal; also discusses basic etiquette for meals at home or in a restaurant.

182

U N I T   T W O

Workspace, Tools, and Techniques

CHAPTER 7   **Kitchen Principles**
CHAPTER 8   **Recipe Skills**
CHAPTER 9   **Cooking Methods**
CHAPTER 10   **Mealtime Customs**

183

Motivators

- Divide the class into three groups representing the 19th, 20th, and 21st centuries. Ask each group to describe the workspace, tools, and food preparation techniques of the assigned era. What are the major food safety and sanitation considerations of the era? How is food stored? What concerns do people have about conserving natural resources during food preparation? What types of recipes are used? How are ingredients measured? What kitchen equipment is used? How are foods prepared and cooked? Have each group report to the class.

- Invite a panel of individuals who have lived in other parts of the world to discuss differences in food preparation, cooking, and service. Ask the guests to discuss food safety, sanitation, and storage. What concerns do people have for conserving natural resources during food preparation? How are foods prepared and cooked? What mealtime customs are observed?

Completing the Unit

Review

- Conduct a class discussion on the various impacts that workspace, tools, and techniques have on the way we work in the kitchen.

Evaluation

- Have students take the test for Unit Two. (Refer to the *Chapter and Unit Tests* booklet or construct your own test using the *Testmaker Software*.)

Planning the Chapter

Chapter Overview

Section 7.1: Introduction to the Kitchen

Section 7.2: Safety in the Kitchen

Section 7.3: Sanitation

Section 7.4: Storing Food

Section 7.5: Conserving Natural Resources

Introducing the Chapter

Motivators

- Ask students to identify safety, sanitation, food storage, and resource conservation concerns of pioneer families. Discuss how those concerns are the same and yet different today.

- Have students work in groups to develop kitchen principles for space station living. Ask them to include the areas of safety, sanitation, food storage, and resource conservation. Have each group share their kitchen principles with the class.

Teacher's Classroom Resources—Chapter 7

Refer to these resources in the TCR package:

Enrichment Activities

Chapter and Unit Tests

Testmaker Software

CHAPTER 7
Kitchen Principles

184

Cooperative Learning Suggestions

Conduct a Four-Pair-Share activity. Divide the class into pairs and ask one member of each pair to share a tip for conserving resources in the kitchen. Then ask the other member of each pair to share a different tip. Have each pair join another pair of students. Have the members of each original pair tell the other person's tip to all four students. Next, have each foursome move together with another foursome. No one may retell a tip he or she has already told or retold. Each member of the group of eight relates a third tip. Following sharing of the eight tips, ask group members to try to write down all eight tips for conserving resources in the kitchen.

Introduction to the Kitchen

OBJECTIVES

After studying this section, you should be able to:

- Define and give examples of major appliances, small appliances, and utensils.
- Explain what a work center is and identify the three basic kitchen work centers.

LOOK FOR THESE TERMS

major appliance
small appliance
utensil
work center

Food preparation involves many tasks and many tools. This section introduces you to the equipment and work centers you will find in a kitchen, whether at home or in the school foods lab.

Types of Kitchen Equipment

Kitchens contain three basic kinds of equipment: major appliances, small appliances, and utensils.

A **major appliance** is a large device that gets its energy from electricity or gas. Most kitchens have at least two major appliances: a refrigerator-freezer for cold storage and a range for cooking. Some kitchens have a separate cooktop and oven instead of a single range unit. Many kitchens also have a microwave oven and a dishwasher.

A **small appliance** is a small electrical device used to perform tasks such as mixing, chopping, and cooking. The blender, toaster, and mixer are examples of small appliances.

The major appliances, small appliances, and utensils in a kitchen help make efficient food preparation possible. The amount and type of equipment depend on lifestyle and budget.

Section 7.1
Introduction to the Kitchen

Introducing the Section

Motivators

- Have students prepare a bulletin board illustrating the various activities that take place in the kitchen.
- Ask students to work in groups to identify the major and small appliances and utensils they would need for a first apartment. Compare the lists developed by different groups.

Objectives

- Have students read the section objectives. Discuss the purpose of studying this section.

Vocabulary

- Pronounce the terms listed under "Look for These Terms." Have students find the terms and their definitions in the section.

Guided Reading

- Have students look at the headings within Section 7.1 to preview the concepts that will be discussed.
- Have students read the section and complete the appropriate part of the Chapter 7 Study Guide in the *Student Workbook*.

Teacher's Classroom Resources—Section 7.1

Refer to these resources in the TCR package:

Reproducible Lesson Plans
Student Workbook
Extending the Text

Reteaching Activities
Section Quizzes
Testmaker Software
Color Transparencies

186

Teaching . . .

- **Types of Kitchen Equipment**
- **Kitchen Work Centers**

(text pages 185-187)

Comprehension Check

1. Discuss the distinction between major and small appliances. *(Major appliances cost more and can do a greater variety of tasks.)*

2. Discuss why it is important to read the owner's manual before using or cleaning an appliance or utensil. *(To avoid injuring yourself or the new appliance or utensil.)*

3. Ask students to describe the concept of work centers as it relates to the kitchen. Ask them to give an example of a well-designed center.

Student Experiences

1. **Stocking a Kitchen:** Have students write a brief essay describing the appliances and utensils that would be included in their "perfect kitchen." Students may use drawings to illustrate points made in the essay but should concentrate on describing the kitchen vividly enough so that the reader can envision it. *(Key skill: writing)*

2. **Class Discussion:** Ask students to discuss the placement of small appliances in the kitchen. In which work center should each be placed? Discuss any differences of opinion. Might some items be needed in more than one location? *(Key skill: critical thinking)*

See Also . . .

- Section 14.2: "Choosing Kitchen Equipment," page 376.

Technology Tidbit

Technological advances are making kitchen designs more convenient. One example is an adjustable oven cooktop that can be raised or lowered to a convenient height.

Utensils include kitchen tools such as measuring cups, knives, and peelers. They also include cookware, such as pots and pans.

Appliances and utensils require careful use and regular care. Before using or cleaning any appliance, read the owner's manual. Following the use and care instructions carefully can prevent injuries and save costly repair bills.

As you study basic kitchen skills, you will learn how to use and care for specific pieces of equipment. In Chapter 14, you can learn about buying equipment for the kitchen.

Kitchen Work Centers

Most home kitchens and school foods labs are organized around work centers. **Work centers** are areas designed for specific kitchen tasks. A well-designed work center includes the equipment needed for the task, enough storage space, and a safe, convenient work space.

A basic principle of kitchen organization is to store items near the place they will be used most often. As you read about the kitchen work centers, notice the types of food and equipment that would logically be kept there.

Basic Work Centers

The refrigerator-freezer, sink, and range—and the counters and cabinets around them—form the three basic kitchen centers.

- ❖ **Cold storage center.** The refrigerator-freezer is the focus of this center. Items that might be stored nearby include storage bags, food wraps, and containers for leftover foods.

- ❖ **Sink center.** This center is the main source of water. It is used for a variety of tasks—washing fresh fruits and vegetables, draining foods, washing dishes, and others. Equipment such as dishpans and other cleanup supplies should be handy.

- ❖ **Cooking center.** This center includes the range and related items such as cooking tools, pots and pans, and potholders. Small cooking appliances may be kept near the range. Some canned and packaged foods may also be stored here.

This kitchen has a mixing center. Note the lowered countertop and convenient placement of appliances, utensils, and supplies.

Special Needs Strategies

Learning Disabled: Create a poster of the three basic kitchen work centers. Provide students with picture cards of items that might be stored in each center. Have students place the pictures of items in the correct work center.

Sometimes there is more than one logical place for equipment. For instance, a microwave oven could be part of the cooking center. It could also be placed near the refrigerator-freezer for quick heating of leftovers and frozen food. José's family keeps the microwave on a sturdy rolling cart so it can be moved wherever needed.

Other Work Centers

Some kitchens include additional, separate work centers.

❖ **Mixing center.** This area is used for preparing and mixing foods. Equipment such as measuring cups, bowls, mixing spoons, and an electric mixer can be stored here, along with foods such as flour and spices. In a small kitchen, this center may be combined with one of the others.

❖ **Planning center.** Some home kitchens include a planning center with space to store cookbooks, recipes, and coupons. A desk is convenient for writing out meal plans and shopping lists. Other useful features might include a calendar, a bulletin board, a telephone, and perhaps even a computer.

A well-organized and well-equipped kitchen is a place where good food can be prepared quickly, easily, and safely.

In what ways might having a planning center in the kitchen be an advantage? Would there be any disadvantages?

Section 7.1 Review

RECALL THE FACTS

1. What is a major appliance? A small appliance? A utensil?

2. What is a kitchen work center?

3. Name the three major work centers of the kitchen.

DISCUSS YOUR IDEAS

4. Which of the three kinds of kitchen equipment do you think you could most easily get along without—major appliances, small appliances, or utensils? Why?

5. Why is it important to organize a kitchen around work centers?

APPLY YOUR LEARNING

6. Draw a rough floor plan of your school foods lab kitchen. Show the location of the sink, the major appliances, cabinets, and counters. Circle and label each work center. Identify the location of at least two small appliances and three different kinds of utensils.

Section 7.1: Introduction to the Kitchen **187**

Completing the Section

Review

- Ask students to summarize the main ideas in this section.

- Have students complete the Section Review. (Answers appear below.)

Evaluation

- Give students a floor plan of a kitchen. Have students identify the three basic work centers and list the items that might be included in each work center.

- Have students take the quiz for Section 7.1. (Refer to the *Section Quizzes* booklet or construct your own quiz using the *Testmaker Software*.)

Reteaching

- Give students a picture of each basic work center and ask them to describe the appropriate work activity, appliances, and utensils for that work center.

- Refer to the *Reteaching Activities* booklet for the Section 7.1 activity sheet.

Enrichment

- Have students develop a plan for a kitchen work center other than the three basic ones (planning center, mixing center, etc.).

Closure

- Remind students of the motivating activity in which they made lists of equipment for an apartment. Ask students to categorize the equipment according to work center.

Answers to Section Review

1. A large device that gets its energy from electricity or gas; a small electrical device used to perform tasks such as mixing, chopping, or cooking; kitchen tools.

2. An area designed for specific kitchen tasks.

3. Cold storage center, sink center, cooking center.

4. Answers will vary. Possible answer: small appliances, since most of their functions can also be performed by major appliances or utensils.

5. Answers will vary.

6. Answers will vary according to your school foods lab layout.

Introducing the Section

Motivators

- Ask students to describe accidents which have occurred in their home kitchens. Ask students to identify the causes of these accidents.

- Display containers of hazardous chemicals such as oven cleaners, drain cleaners, pesticides, and polishes. Ask students to identify those that are poisonous. When they are finished, announce that all are actually poisonous.

Objectives

- Have students read the section objectives. Discuss the purpose of studying this section.

Vocabulary

- Pronounce the terms listed under "Look for These Terms." Have students find the terms and their definitions in the section.

Guided Reading

- Have students look at the headings within Section 7.2 to preview the concepts that will be discussed.

- Have students read the section and complete the appropriate part of the Chapter 7 Study Guide in the *Student Workbook*.

SECTION 7.2

Safety in the Kitchen

OBJECTIVES

After studying this section, you should be able to:

- Identify ways to prevent common kitchen accidents.
- Discuss special safety needs.
- Describe what to do if a kitchen accident results in injury.

LOOK FOR THESE TERMS

polarized plugs
Heimlich Maneuver
CPR

Cal was in a hurry and needed to fix a meal fast. As he cracked some eggs for an omelet into a bowl, some egg white fell on the floor. "I'll clean that up later," he thought. He rushed to the refrigerator to get several other omelet ingredients. He balanced them in one hand as he reached for the cutting board that hung on the wall. Just then the telephone rang. As Cal turned to answer the call, he felt something slick underfoot. "The egg white!" he thought, as his foot slid out from under him.

Safety Throughout the Kitchen

Most people think of a kitchen as a pleasant place to prepare enjoyable food. While this is true, just a few seconds of carelessness can turn the kitchen into an accident zone. Falls, electrical shocks, cuts, burns, and poisoning are all kitchen hazards. The keys to preventing kitchen accidents are careful kitchen management and safe work habits.

Safety in the kitchen begins with dressing appropriately.

Teacher's Classroom Resources—Section 7.2

Refer to these resources in the TCR package: *Reteaching Activities*
Reproducible Lesson Plans   *Section Quizzes*
Student Workbook   *Testmaker Software*
Extending the Text   *Color Transparencies*

General Safety Guidelines

Your work habits are vital to your safety in the kitchen. Here are some general guidelines:

❖ Do not let hair, jewelry, sleeves, or apron strings dangle. They could catch fire or get tangled in appliances.

❖ Keep your mind on what you're doing.

❖ Prevent clutter. Put items back where they belong as you finish with them or after you have washed them.

❖ Close drawers and doors completely after you open them. You can be seriously hurt if you bump into an open door or drawer.

❖ Use the right tool for the job. Don't use a knife to pry off a jar cover, for instance. Take the time to find the tool you need.

❖ Store heavy or bulky items, like cookware, on low shelves. That way you can reach them safely.

Safety Afoot

Many accidents occur because of what's on the floor. To prevent falls, keep the floor clean and free of clutter. Wipe up spills, spatters, and peelings so no one slips on them. Eliminate other hazards, such as slippery throw rugs and damaged or worn flooring. Don't wear untied shoes, floppy slippers, or long clothing that could cause you to trip.

To reach higher shelves, use a firm stepstool. If you use a chair or a box, you could fall and be injured.

Sharp Objects

Cuts are an everyday hazard for the cook. Here are some safety guidelines for handling knives, sharp tools, and broken glass:

❖ Keep knives sharp and use them properly. You'll learn how in Section 8.4.

❖ Use a drawer divider or knife rack for sharp cutting tools.

❖ Don't try to catch a falling knife—you might grab the blade instead of the handle.

❖ Don't soak knives or other sharp-edged utensils in a sink or dishpan of water.

Storing knives in a knife block, rack, or special drawer divider helps prevent cuts. It also keeps the knives in better condition.

When you reach into the water, you could cut yourself.

❖ Sweep up broken glass from the floor immediately using a broom and dustpan. If you need to pick up pieces by hand, use a wet paper towel instead of bare fingers.

Electrical Safety

Electrical appliances save both time and work in the kitchen. However, they can also be a source of shocks, burns, and other injuries.

Carefully read the owner's manual that comes with each kitchen appliance. Follow the directions it gives for using the appliance safely. In addition, remember these basic guidelines:

❖ *Water and electricity don't mix.* Combined, they can give you a serious shock or even kill you. Never use an electric appliance when your hands are wet or when you are standing on a wet floor.

Comprehension Check

1. Ask students to describe several types of injuries that can happen in the kitchen without careful kitchen management and safe work habits. *(slipping, falling, cutting oneself, etc.)*

2. Discuss the proper way to store and use knives and other sharp kitchen tools.

3. Discuss precautions people should take to prevent serious shocks from electrical appliances. *(See listed items on pages 189-190.)*

Student Experiences

1. **Posters:** Have students identify common types of kitchen accidents. Divide students into groups to create posters giving safety tips for preventing one type of kitchen accident. Have groups share their posters with the class, then post them in the foods laboratory. *(Key skill: cooperative learning)*

2. **Home Survey:** Have students develop a checklist for identifying kitchen hazards. Have students use the checklist to check their own homes for kitchen hazards. *(Key skill: analysis)*

3. **Electrical Emergencies:** Have students find out the correct way to turn off the electricity in their home. Discuss when it is appropriate to take this action. *(Key skill: life management)*

More About Cuts

The Consumer Product Safety Commission estimates that over 137,000 people receive hospital treatment for injuries from kitchen knives each year. Most of these are for cuts on fingers, hands, and arms.

To prevent injury, follow these tips:
- Always choose the right kind of knife for the job.
- When using scissors to snip food, hold the food so that your fingers are well away from the blades.

Teaching . . .

- **Hazardous Chemicals**
- **Range and Microwave Safety**

(text pages 190-192)

Comprehension Check

1. Ask students to list hazardous chemicals that are commonly found in the kitchen and discuss the problems they can cause. *(oven cleaners, lighter fluid, drain cleaners, pesticides, and polishes; burns, breathing difficulties, and poisoning)*

2. Ask students to list guidelines to use when buying and using products that contain hazardous chemicals. *(Read and follow the directions on the label carefully; never transfer the contents to another container; point the spray nozzle correctly; store them away from food.)*

3. Discuss safety guidelines for using ranges and microwave ovens. *(See list on page 191.)*

4. Ask students to describe two different places where fires may start in the kitchen. What should people do if a fire starts? *(Answers will vary; see page 192.)*

When you unplug an appliance, grasp the plug, not the cord. Damaged cords can cause electrical shocks and fires.

Keep small electric appliances away from water when you use them. Don't run cords around a sink. If an electric appliance falls into the water, unplug it immediately. Don't put small appliances in water for cleaning unless the owner's manual says it is safe.

❖ **Avoid damage to electrical cords.** Even a single exposed wire could start a fire or give you a shock. To keep from damaging cords, don't run them over a hot surface or try to staple or nail them in place. Never try to disconnect an appliance by tugging on the cord. Instead, grasp the plug at the electrical outlet and remove it.

❖ **Use outlets properly.** Plugging too many cords into an electrical outlet can cause a fire. Some plugs are made with one blade wider than the other. Called **polarized plugs,** they are designed to fit in the outlet in only one way. If the outlets are older, you may not be able to fit polarized plugs into them. If this happens, don't try to force the plug in or change the shape of the plug. Instead, have the outlet replaced.

190   Chapter 7: Kitchen Principles

❖ **Use care with any plugged-in appliance.** Never put your fingers or a kitchen tool inside an appliance that is plugged in. You might touch parts that could shock you, or you might accidentally turn the appliance on and injure yourself. Don't let cords dangle off the counter—an appliance could accidentally be pulled off while in use. Turn off and disconnect small appliances as soon as you are through with them.

❖ **Watch for problems.** Don't try to use a damaged appliance or one that gives you a shock. Have it repaired before you use it again. If an appliance starts to burn, unplug it immediately.

Hazardous Chemicals

Hazardous household chemicals include oven cleaners, lighter fluid, drain cleaners, pesticides, and polishes. Some can cause burns, breathing difficulties, and poisoning.

Look for less hazardous alternatives to household cleaners and chemicals. For example, orange peels and spices such as cinnamon can replace chemical air fresheners.

Thinking Skills

Reasoning: Ask students why the instructions on lye drain cleaners tell them to flush the drain with cold water after use. *(Heat increases volatility in chemicals. Hot water causes lye to "boil" up and give off harmful fumes.)*

Before you buy any household chemicals, read the label carefully to be sure you are willing to follow the directions. You will find important information about adequate ventilation, protecting yourself, and disposing of any unused product. You will also learn what to do if the product is accidentally consumed. Never transfer a hazardous product to another container. You'll need the directions that appear on the original container each time you use it.

Never mix different chemical products. They could combine to give off poisonous fumes.

With spray products, make sure you're pointing the spray nozzle where the product is supposed to go. Never point it at yourself or anyone else.

Store hazardous chemical products away from food. Be sure children can't reach them. Flammable products, such as kerosene, lighter fluid, and aerosol sprays, must be stored away from any source of heat.

Avoid using hazardous chemicals unnecessarily. Whenever you can, substitute simple, safe cleaners, such as lemon juice, vinegar, soap, baking soda, washing soda, or borax.

Range and Microwave Safety

The range is the most likely place for fires and burns. The microwave oven, too, presents some hazards. Here are some rules for using these appliances safely.

❖ Use potholders or oven mitts when picking up or uncovering hot pots and pans.
❖ When uncovering a pan, lift up the far edge of the cover first. That way, the steam will flow away from you. Otherwise it could burn your face and hands.
❖ Use only pots and pans in good condition. A loose handle or warped bottom could cause an accident.
❖ Keep pan handles turned toward the back or middle of the range top to prevent accidental spills.

Oven mitts provide more protection than potholders. They are a good choice for removing large or heavy items from the oven.

❖ Keep flammable items, such as paper towels, away from the range. A draft could blow them onto the range and start a fire. For the same reason, do not put curtains on a window that is close to the range.
❖ Do not use plastic items near the range, except for ovenproof plastic. Some plastics are highly flammable and give off poisonous fumes when they burn.
❖ Arrange oven racks properly before you start the oven. You risk a burn if you have to reposition them once the oven is hot.
❖ Stand to the side when you open the oven door. Otherwise the heat rushing from the oven can burn your face.
❖ Don't reach into a hot oven. Pull out the rack first, using a potholder.
❖ Make sure cooktop and oven/broiler controls are turned off when not in use.
❖ Keep a fire extinguisher handy and make sure everyone knows how to use it.

Student Experiences

1. **Lab Demonstration:** Conduct "burn tests" on a variety of 2" x 2" fabric swatches. Include samples from dish towels, curtains, potholders, and common clothing fabrics. Have students record how quickly each sample ignites and burns. Point out that synthetics such as polyester will melt. Discuss what effect that may have on a burn. Follow appropriate safety measures during the demonstration. Be sure to have adequate ventilation and a fire extinguisher at hand. *(Key skills: observation, analysis)*

2. **Poster Project:** Have students design and create posters to promote safety around ranges and microwaves. Display the posters in the foods laboratory or in the school cafeteria. *(Key skill: creativity)*

3. **Research:** Have students find out how people cook in areas where electricity and gas are in short supply. Have students give a short report to the class about their findings. *(Key skill: social studies)*

4. **Label Survey:** Assign students to visit a supermarket to find at least 25 different poisons that might be found in kitchens. For each, ask them to create a table to show any warnings or special directions. *(Key skill: reading)*

More About Burns from Microwave Ovens

Microwave ovens are associated with an increase in burn injuries. The most common kinds of burns related to microwave ovens result from heating whole eggs and baby bottles. The interiors develop high pressures when heated and can explode when handled.

Another common burn occurs when plastic wrap or a cover is removed from a container of hot food. People may be deceived if the container doesn't feel hot. The wrap or lid cover should always be tilted so the steam is directed away from the face.

Comprehension Check

1. Discuss extra precautions people should take when small children are likely to be in the kitchen. *(See points listed on page 192.)*

2. Discuss general safety precautions needed for elderly or handicapped people. Why do these precautions vary? *(Individual needs vary.)*

Student Experiences

1. **Create a Booklet:** Have students identify ways to childproof a kitchen as you write them on the chalkboard. Students can compile these in a booklet or brochure to be printed and given to parents of young children. *(Key skill: writing)*

2. **Library Research:** Have students locate and summarize articles on making the kitchen safe for elderly or handicapped people. *(Key skill: reading)*

If a Fire Starts

Kitchen fires can start suddenly. What to do depends on where the fire occurs.

❖ ***Range top or electric skillet:*** Turn off the heat. Put the cover on the pan or pour salt or baking soda on the flames. Never use water—the grease will spatter and burn you. Don't use baking powder—it could make the fire worse.

❖ ***Oven, broiler, microwave, toaster oven:*** Turn off or disconnect the appliance. Keep the oven door closed until the fire goes out.

Never attempt to carry a pan with burning contents. You could cause an injury or a bigger fire. If you can't immediately put out a fire, call the fire department and go outdoors.

Every kitchen should have a fire extinguisher. Do you know how to use one correctly?

✓ **SAFETY CHECK**

Gas Range Safety

❖ If you smell gas, turn off all range controls and open the windows for ventilation. Alert others and leave the building immediately. Call your local gas company from another location.

❖ To relight the pilot light on an older gas range, light the match first, then turn on the burner and light it. If you turn on the burner first, gas will accumulate and could cause an explosion when you strike the match.

Special Safety Needs

As a rule, any safety precautions you take will benefit the entire family. The very young and old, however, may need special attention.

Kitchen Safety and Children

Children like to be where adults are—especially the kitchen. They want to watch you and do what you're doing. If there are children in your kitchen, follow these guidelines for their safety and yours.

❖ Never leave young children alone in the kitchen, even for a few seconds.

❖ Protect toddlers by using safety latches on drawers and cabinet doors.

❖ If children want to help you work, set up a child-size table or a safe stepstool. Provide small utensils they can use easily for simple tasks such as mixing and mashing. Don't let young children use knives or work near the range. Supervise them at all times.

❖ Model safe work habits for children. If you have safe work habits in the kitchen, they will too.

Thinking Skills

Problem Solving: Divide the class into small groups. Ask each group what they would do in the following situations.

• Someone is choking. You think you know what to do, but you aren't sure. Everyone else around you just stares and does nothing.

• You have had first aid training. While you are in a restaurant, someone starts choking. They pass out. You are too scared to do anything because there are many adults who are trying to help. It is clear to you that none of them know the Heimlich maneuver.

Teaching children basic food preparation skills boosts self-confidence and increases independence. Teach safety first and be sure to supervise their efforts.

Kitchen Safety for the Elderly or Handicapped

Kitchen safety is an important issue for those with physical challenges, such as poor eyesight or arthritis. Changes in the workspace or equipment may be needed so that they can use the kitchen safely. Ask for their suggestions. What kitchen tasks are hard for them? How could kitchen organization be changed to make jobs easier and safer? Here are some ideas.

❖ Keep a magnifying glass in the kitchen to aid with reading small print.
❖ Relabel items in larger letters, if needed, using stick-on labels and a marking pen.
❖ Add more or better lighting.
❖ Store frequently used equipment and foods in easy-to-reach places.

❖ Add a cart with wheels to the kitchen to make it easier to move food and equipment from place to place.
❖ Use non-breakable dishes and glassware.
❖ Replace hard-to-open cabinet hardware with U-shaped or pull handles.
❖ Provide tongs or grippers to grab items that would otherwise be out of reach.
❖ Put mixing bowls on a damp dishcloth or rubber disk jar opener to keep them from sliding on a slippery countertop during mixing.
❖ Use rubber disk jar openers for gripping appliance knobs.
❖ Provide a stool or tall chair so that the person can sit while working at the counter.

Section 14.3, "Designing a Kitchen," discusses other ways to adapt a kitchen to suit special needs.

Section 7.2: Safety in the Kitchen   193

Teaching . . .

• **In Case of Accident**

(text page 194)

Comprehension Check

1. Discuss the importance of remaining calm when an accident occurs. *(Panic can make things worse, both physically and psychologically.)*

2. Ask students to explain what people can do to prepare for the possibility that an accident will occur. *(Keep emergency numbers by the telephone; keep a first aid book and kit handy.)*

Student Experiences

1. **Guest Speaker:** Invite a local paramedic, first aid instructor, or the school nurse to demonstrate proper first aid for falls, cuts, burns, choking, poisoning, and electrical shock. *(Key skill: health)*

2. **Learning CPR:** Have students find out which organizations in your community offers classes in CPR, how often the classes are offered, and what fees, if any, apply. *(Key skill: community involvement)*

More About Accidents

A major cause of accidents is distraction—not keeping your mind on your work. Much kitchen work is routine, such as washing dishes and stirring hot food. It's tempting to let the mind wander to something more interesting. You may be talking to someone as you work. However, even a slight lapse in attention can result in a burn or a cut. When working in the kitchen, keep your mind on the work at hand.

First aid training can help prepare you to handle emergencies that occur in the kitchen and elsewhere.

In Case of Accident

In spite of all your precautions, an accident may happen when you are working in the kitchen. To prepare for that possibility, keep a list of emergency numbers next to the phone. Also keep a first aid kit and book of instructions handy.

If you don't know first aid techniques, ask the local Red Cross about first aid training. Everyone should learn how to use the **Heimlich Maneuver,** a technique used in case of choking. Another vital technique is **CPR,** or cardiopulmonary resuscitation (KARD-ee-oh-PULL-muh-nair-ee rih-suhs-uh-TAY-shun). It is used if a person's breathing and heartbeat have stopped. Knowing these techniques can save a life.

If an accident does occur, stay calm. Panic will only keep you from thinking clearly. If necessary, take a few deep breaths to get yourself under control.

Never hesitate to call for help, whether for yourself or someone else. It's better to ask for help, even though you may not need it, than to try to handle an accident by yourself.

194   Chapter 7: Kitchen Principles

Section 7.2 Review

RECALL THE FACTS

1. Name three ways to prevent falls.
2. Why should you keep small appliances away from water when in use?
3. Name two safety rules for using the kitchen range.
4. Give three suggestions that might improve kitchen safety for an elderly person.
5. Name two things you should do in case of an accident in the kitchen.

DISCUSS YOUR IDEAS

6. What is the most serious kitchen accident you've ever had? Why did it happen? What safety rule did you neglect?

APPLY YOUR LEARNING

7. Make a mini-poster for the school foods lab to remind class members of one of the safety pointers discussed in this section.

Answers to Section Review

1. *Any three:* Pick up spills immediately, remove area rugs that might slip, remove damaged or worn flooring; don't wear untied shoes, floppy slippers, or long clothing.
2. To avoid electrical shock; water conducts electricity.
3. Refer to the list on page 191.
4. Refer to the list on page 193.
5. Stay calm, and never hesitate to call for help.
6. Answers will vary.
7. Posters will vary.

SECTION 7.3

Sanitation

OBJECTIVES

After studying this section, you should be able to:

- Discuss the causes of food-borne illness.
- Explain how proper food handling practices can prevent food-borne illness.

LOOK FOR THESE TERMS

sanitation
microorganism
toxins
parasites
cross-contamination
spores

James checked the chicken sizzling on the grill. "It's done!" he called to his aunt. "I'll bring it in." Looking around, he spotted the platter he had used to carry the raw chicken outside. As he started to pick up the platter, his aunt stopped him. "Don't use that! It hasn't been washed. I'll get you a clean plate."

James almost forgot an important rule of sanitation. **Sanitation** means following practices that help prevent disease. It is one of your biggest responsibilities when working with food.

Why Is Sanitation Important?

It's estimated that up to 80 million Americans suffer from food-borne illness, also known as food poisoning, every year. The illness may be mild, lasting just a day or two, or severe enough to require hospitalization. In some cases it can even result in death. Children, pregnant women, the elderly, and people with chronic illness are most at risk.

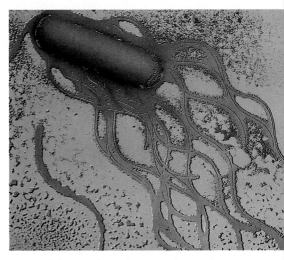

Harmful microorganisms that cause food poisoning are too small to see, but powerful enough to cause severe illness or even death. Salmonella, shown here, is one of the most common.

Teacher's Classroom Resources—Section 7.3

Refer to these resources in the TCR package:

Reproducible Lesson Plans

Student Workbook

Extending the Text

Reteaching Activities

Section Quizzes

Testmaker Software

Color Transparencies

Section 7.3 Sanitation

Introducing the Section

Motivators

- Tell the story of the old-time doctor who, upon making a house call, inevitably went first to the kitchen to thank the cook for providing him with a new patient. A grain of truth can be gleaned from this story: Anyone who chooses, prepares, and serves food influences the health of those who eat it.

- Have ready microscopes with prepared microscope slides of the four most common food poisoning bacteria. Tell students that one of the bacteria can cause death in a healthy individual. Another can cause death in infants and in elderly or ill individuals. Ask students if they can identify these two bacteria.

Objectives

- Have students read the section objectives. Discuss the purpose of studying this section.

- Pronounce the terms listed under "Look for These Terms." Have students find the terms and their definitions in the section.

Guided Reading

- Have students look at the headings with Section 7.1 to preview the concepts that will be discussed.

- Have students read the section and complete the appropriate part of the Chapter 7 Study Guide in the *Student Workbook*.

Comprehension Check

1. Ask students to explain what is involved in sanitation. Why is sanitation important in the kitchen? *(Following practices that help prevent disease; it helps prevent food-borne illness.)*

2. Ask students to list the people who are most at risk from food-borne illnesses. *(children, pregnant women, elderly people, and people with chronic illness)*

3. Ask students to list four ways in which microorganisms can cause food-borne illnesses. *(bacteria, toxins produced by bacteria, parasites, and viruses)*

Student Experiences

1. **Library Research:** Have students research major outbreaks of food-borne illnesses in the United States. In each case, ask them to identify the food that was contaminated and the food handling practices that cause the bacteria to develop. *(Key skill: research)*

2. **Creating Cartoons:** Have students draw cartoons featuring one type of food-borne illness. The cartoon should contain information on the type of food and the mode of transportation. *(Key skill: creativity)*

Most cases of food-borne illness can be traced to harmful **microorganisms**—tiny living creatures visible only through a microscope. In another sense, however, people are to blame. Poor food handling practices allow harmful microorganisms to grow and spread. It's up to you to handle food properly to prevent illness.

Types of Harmful Microorganisms

Most of the harmful microorganisms are bacteria. Bacteria are everywhere. They are carried by people, animals, insects, and objects. Many bacteria are harmless, but others can cause illness. Sometimes the illness is not caused by the bacteria themselves, but by the **toxins,** or poisons, that they produce.

Most harmful bacteria can be tolerated by the human body in small amounts. When the amounts multiply to dangerous levels, however, they create a health hazard. Bacteria reproduce quickly in the presence of food, moisture, and warmth. In just a few hours, one can multiply into thousands. You can't tell whether food contains harmful bacteria—the food generally looks, smells, and tastes normal.

Food-borne illness can also be caused by parasites or viruses. **Parasites** (PAIR-uh-sights) are organisms that get their nutrients from other living organisms. Parasites found in food can infect people and cause illness. Viruses are the simplest form of life known. A virus from an infected person can be transferred to food that the person handles. Then the food can make someone else ill.

The chart on pages 198-199 describes common food-borne illnesses.

Cleanliness in the Kitchen

Cleanliness is one of the keys to sanitation. Whenever you work with food, be sure to keep yourself and the kitchen clean.

Personal Hygiene

Personal hygiene means keeping yourself clean so you do not introduce harmful microorganisms into food as you handle it. Here are some suggestions:

- ❖ Wear clean clothes and cover them with a clean apron. Spots and stains can harbor bacteria.
- ❖ Remove dangling jewelry, roll up long sleeves, and tie back long hair to keep them out of food.
- ❖ Scrub your hands for 20 seconds before you begin to handle food. Use soap and warm water. Use a brush to clean under and around your fingernails.
- ❖ Use rubber or plastic gloves if you have an open wound on your hands. Gloves can pick up bacteria, too. Wash gloved hands as often as you wash bare hands.
- ❖ Wash your hands immediately after using the toilet or blowing your nose.
- ❖ Do not sneeze or cough into food.
- ❖ Do not touch your face, hair, or any other part of your body while working with food. If you do, stop working and scrub your hands.

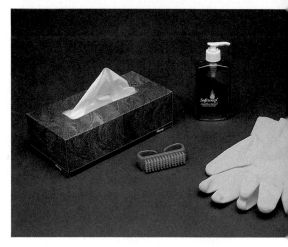

Good personal hygiene is essential for anyone preparing food. If you consistently practice the guidelines listed above, they will soon become good habits.

Food and Nutrition Science

Microorganisms Lab: Before class, prepare a sugar-sweetened gelatin mix, pour into small clear, plastic cups, and chill until set. Have students contaminate the gelatin with common items (hair, scrapings from under fingernails, saliva, mucous, scrapings of makeup, unwashed hands). Cover each plastic cup with plastic wrap and label with the name of the contaminant. Place on a tray and leave in a warm place for several days. (NOTE: Place warning signs that say "CONTAMINATED; DO NOT EAT" on each tray.) Check the cups each day for growth of microorganisms. Ask students to draw conclusions based on the results.

 **World of Variety**

As in many other African countries, people in Morocco traditionally eat food with their hands directly from a large communal bowl. It is also customary for the host to bring a pitcher of water and a basin and pour the water as the guests wash their hands. This is done both before and after the meal. Besides being a good sanitation practice, what other meaning might this custom convey?

Sanitary Work Methods

In addition to keeping yourself clean, remember to follow these important guidelines:

❖ Make sure that work areas and equipment are clean before you start preparing food.

❖ Avoid **cross-contamination**—letting microorganisms from one food get into another. For example, the juices from raw meat, poultry, or fish contain microorganisms. A knife used to cut raw meat could contaminate raw vegetables. After you have handled raw meat, poultry, or fish, wash everything that came in contact with it. This includes tools, work surfaces, and your hands.

❖ Wash the top of a can before opening it to keep dirt from getting into the food.

❖ Use a clean spoon each time you taste food during preparation. That way, you won't transfer harmful bacteria from your mouth to the food you're preparing.

❖ Keep pets out of the kitchen.

❖ Keep two towels handy in your kitchen— one for wiping hands and a separate one for drying dishes.

❖ Use a clean dishcloth each day. Dishcloths and sponges can harbor harmful bacteria. Wash sponges at the end of the day and allow them to air-dry before reusing.

Be sure you know how to use a food waste disposal correctly and safely.

Cleanup Time

After food has been prepared and eaten, it's time to clean up. A clean kitchen has no food particles and spills to encourage bacterial growth, insects, and rodents.

Using Cleanup Appliances

Many kitchens are equipped with a food waste disposal and a dishwasher to help speed cleanup.

A food waste disposal grinds food waste and flushes it down the drain. Always run plenty of cold water when grinding food. Do not overfill the disposal, but grind small batches at a time. To avoid clogging, do not put fibrous food in the disposal, such as onion skins or corn husks.

When using an automatic dishwasher, follow the instructions in the owner's manual. Make sure the dishwasher is full before running it. Small loads waste water and energy.

Section 7.3: Sanitation **197**

Teaching . . .

• **Cleanliness in the Kitchen**

(text pages 196-197)

Comprehension Check

1. Discuss elements of personal hygiene that are important to overall kitchen cleanliness. *(See list on page 196.)*

2. Ask students to list other guidelines for keeping the kitchen clean and avoiding food contamination. *(See list on page 197.)*

3. Ask students to explain what "cross-contamination" is and to give examples of how it can happen in the kitchen. *(Migration of microorganisms from one food to another; examples will vary.)*

Student Experiences

1. **Interview:** Have students interview a person who works in the food service industry. Ask the person what hygiene rules he or she must follow. Ask students present a written report on their findings. *(Key skills: interviewing, writing)*

 **World of Variety**

Have students research other cultures to find customs dealing with personal hygiene and kitchen cleanliness. Emphasize that, although the methods may be different, most cultures have developed customs that ensure cleanliness in the kitchen and at meals. Discuss how and why such customs might be established.

More About Food-Borne Illnesses

If you suspect that someone is suffering from food poisoning, you can help health professionals diagnose the problem by following these guidelines:

• Wrap a portion of the food you suspect caused the problem in a heavy plastic bag. Place it in a closed container clearly marked "DANGER" and chill it on ice.

• Write the name of the food, when it was consumed, and the date of the illness on the outside of the container.

• Save the original container in which the food was purchased.

Teaching . . .

- **Food-Borne Illnesses
(chart)**

(text pages 198-199)

Comprehension Check

1. Ask students to describe the symptoms of Toxoplasmosis. How can people avoid this disease? *(by washing hands after cleaning a cat's litter box; avoid eating undercooked meat or poultry)*

2. Ask students to name and describe the illness caused by *clostridium perfringens.*

3. Ask students which food-borne illnesses can be caught from drinking raw milk or eating cheese made from unpasteurized milk. *(Salmonellosis, Listeriosis, E. coli poisoning)*

Food-Borne Illnesses

Illness and Symptoms	Type of Microorganism	Prevention
Salmonellosis (sal-muh-nell-OH-sis) Stomach pain, diarrhea, nausea, chills, fever, and headache. Begins 6 to 48 hours after eating contaminated food. May last 3 to 5 days. Infants and young children, the ill, and the elderly may be seriously affected.	Bacteria (*salmonella*). Often found in raw or undercooked foods, such as poultry, eggs, and meat. May also be found in unpasteurized milk. May spread to other foods through cross-contamination.	❖ Follow the sanitation procedures described in the text. ❖ Don't drink unpasteurized milk.
Staph Nausea, vomiting, diarrhea. Begins 30 minutes to 8 hours after eating contaminated food. May last a day or two.	Toxin from bacteria (*staphylococcus aureus*). Staph bacteria are found on human skin, in nose, and in throat. Spread by improper food handling.	❖ Follow the sanitation procedures described in the text.
E. coli poisoning Severe abdominal cramps followed by diarrhea (often bloody), nausea, vomiting, and occasionally a low-grade fever. Begins 3 to 4 days after contaminated food is eaten. Can last up to 10 days. Often requires hospitalization. Sometimes leads to urinary tract infection and kidney failure.	Toxin from a specific type of *E. coli* bacteria. Sources include contaminated water, raw or rare ground beef, and unpasteurized milk.	❖ Follow the sanitation procedures described in the text.
Listeriosis (lih-STEER-ee-OH-sis) Rare but potentially fatal. In adults: fever, chills, headache, backache, and sometimes abdominal pain and diarrhea.	Bacteria (*listeria monocytogenes*). Found frequently in the environment. Can grow slowly at refrigerator temperatures.	❖ Follow the sanitation procedures described in the text. ❖ Avoid raw milk and cheese made from unpasteurized milk.

More About *E. Coli* poisoning

Because *E. coli* is present in the intestine of every healthy human, scientists originally dismissed it as a possible cause for disease. In fact, researchers did not discover until the early 1960s that *E. coli* was responsible for gastroenteritis in infants. Since then, this bacteria has been linked to many cases of travelers' diarrhea, in addition to other gastrointestinal problems. In some cases, *E. coli* poisoning can lead to death.

Listeriosis (continued)	Perfringens poisoning	Botulism	Toxoplasmosis
❖ Store food properly. Observe "sell by" and "use by" dates on processed products.	❖ Follow the sanitation procedures described in the text.	❖ Follow the sanitation procedures described in the text. ❖ Follow established guidelines for home canning. (See Section 24.5) ❖ See Section 7.4, pages 205–206, for signs of spoiled food and what to do with suspect foods.	❖ Follow the sanitation procedures described in the text. ❖ Wash hands after cleaning a cat's litter box. Pregnant women should not clean litter boxes.
Listeriosis (continued) In newborns: respiratory distress, refusal to drink, and vomiting. Possible complications include meningitis and blood poisoning. Can cause miscarriages and stillbirths.	**Perfringens poisoning** (purr-FRIN-jens) Diarrhea and gas pains. Begins 9 to 15 hours after eating contaminated food. Usually lasts about one day. Elderly people and ulcer patients can be affected more seriously. Toxin from bacteria (*clostridium perfringens*). The bacteria grow only where there is little or no oxygen. Spores can survive cooking. Called the "cafeteria germ" because it often strikes food served in quantity and left for long periods on a steam table or at room temperature.	**Botulism** (botch-uh-liz-um) Affects the nervous system and can be fatal if not treated. Symptoms appear 12 to 48 hours after eating contaminated food. They include double vision, droopy eyelids, trouble speaking and swallowing, and difficulty breathing. Patients who do recover may suffer nerve damage. Toxin from bacteria (*clostridium botulinum*). The bacteria grow only where there is little or no oxygen. Spores may survive cooking. Associated with improperly processed canned foods; also with cooked foods held at room or warm temperatures for an extended time with limited oxygen (such as potatoes wrapped tightly in foil).	**Toxoplasmosis** (tocks-oh-plaz-MOH-sis) Can cause nerve damage. If a pregnant woman is infected, the illness can affect the central nervous system of the unborn child. A parasite (*toxoplasmosa gondii*) common in mammals, reptiles, and birds. People are infected through eating undercooked meat or poultry that contains the parasite or by cleaning the litter box of a cat with the parasite.

Adapted from Food Safety and Inspection Service, USDA

Student Experiences

1. **Poster Project:** Have students choose one food-borne illness and make a poster explaining ways to prevent it. Donate the posters to a local clinic or school. *(Key skill: creativity)*

2. **Research:** Ask students to look up one of the food-borne illnesses listed in the text and use science books and other resources to find out more about it. Have students write a short report of their findings. *(Key skill: writing)*

3. **Bacterial Population Estimate:** Some bacteria can multiply as fast as once every 10 minutes. In other words, the number of bacteria doubles every 10 minutes. If a single *Staphylococcus aureus* bacterium were to land on food at a picnic, and the food were left at open-air temperature while people snacked on it, how many Staphylococcus aureus bacteria would be present in the food after three hours? *(262,144) (Key skill: math)*

More About Staphylococcus aureus

The food poisoning caused by *Staphylococcus aureus* (often called simply *Staph aureus* by researchers) is actually caused by a toxic substance called an *exotoxin*. This toxin is produced rapidly by *Staph aureus* growing at room temperature, which makes it a problem at picnics and other affairs where food is likely to be left at room temperature for extended periods.

Many people think that if they reheat food, they will kill any bacteria that may have grown in the food, making it safe to eat. However, the exotoxin produced by *Staph aureus* is resistant to heat. Heating food may kill the *Staph aureus*, but will not destroy the dangerous endotoxin.

Teaching . . .

• Cleanup Time

(text pages 197, 200)

Comprehension Check

1. Ask students to list the steps in washing dishes properly. *(See steps on page 200.)*

2. Emphasize that kitchen cleanup is not through when the last dish is dried. Ask students to list the other surfaces that need to be cleaned. Discuss the importance of cleaning the can opener blade and the cutting board. *(To prevent cross-contamination and to keep any bacteria present from multiplying)*

3. Ask students to explain the importance of placing garbage in a tightly closed plastic bag and putting it in the garbage can outside. What further precautions should you take regarding the outside can? *(To keep insects and small animals out; wash regularly.)*

Earth Watch

Caution students to use these or other proven methods of insect control, as opposed to relying on myths or traditions to rid the house of these pests. Ask students how they can tell the difference. *(by contacting local officials; by researching the methods at the local or school library, etc.)* What are some advantages of using these natural insecticides?

Careful dishwashing is one key to sanitation in the kitchen. Any food left on dishes or utensils allows microorganisms to multiply.

Washing Dishes by Hand

Washing dishes is faster and easier if you are well organized. Here are some suggestions.

Rinse soiled dishes and place them to one side of the sink. Group like items together and arrange in this order: glasses, flatware, dishes, kitchen tools, and cookware. Keep sharp knives separate. If food is stuck to cookware, pre-soak it. Pour a little dish detergent in, add hot water, and let the pan stand for a while.

Fill a dishpan or sink with soapy water hot enough to remove grease, but not hot enough to burn your hands. Using a sponge or dishcloth, wash the dishes in the order you grouped them. Glasses are washed first and greasy cookware last. When necessary, refill the sink or dishpan with clean, hot, soapy water.

Rinse dishes thoroughly in hot water. A safe and easy way is to put the dish rack in the sink and let hot water run over it. Be sure the insides of containers are well rinsed. Let the dishes air dry in the rack or dry them with a clean, dry towel.

What if a glass or dish breaks in a sinkful of water? Using a paper towel to protect your fingers, carefully reach into the sink and open the drain. After the water has drained, use the wet paper towel to pick up the broken pieces.

Cleaning the Work and Eating Areas

When you are through washing dishes, wipe off the dining table. Clean all the work areas and appliances that were used. Don't forget to wash the can opener blade and the cutting board. Rinse the dishcloth often as you work, using hot, soapy water.

Wipe up spills on the floor. Wash the sink to remove grease and food particles, then run the disposal.

Finally, put any garbage in a plastic bag, close it tightly, and put it in the garbage can outside. Wash garbage cans regularly to avoid attracting insects and rodents.

Earth Watch

Here are some ways to control household insects without using chemical insecticides:

- Repair holes in walls and screens. Caulk cracks and crevices.
- Keep the kitchen and other areas clean.
- Sprinkle chili powder, paprika, or dried peppermint across ant trails.
- To control roaches, dust borax lightly around the refrigerator and range.

Special Needs Strategies

Behaviorally Disabled: Motivate students by giving them recognition. Allow students to earn chef's hats by demonstrating knowledge of basic kitchen safety and sanitation practices.

Be sure to wrap garbage tightly and store it outside the home.

Proper Food Temperatures

Besides cleanliness, another important aspect of sanitation is keeping food at safe temperatures.

How Temperatures Affect Microorganisms

Bacteria multiply rapidly at temperatures between 60°F and 125°F (16°C to 52°C). Note that this range includes room temperatures. Most food-borne illnesses are caused by bacteria that thrive in these temperatures.

High food temperatures from 165°F to 212°F (74°C to 100°C) kill most of the harmful bacteria. These temperatures are normally reached during cooking. However, some bacteria produce **spores,** cells that will develop into bacteria if conditions are right. Spores can survive cooking heat.

Cold refrigerator temperatures below 40°F (4°C) slow down the growth of some of the bacteria, but do not kill them.

If food is frozen at 0°F (-18°C), bacteria stop growing. Bacteria or spores already present in the food, however, will not be killed. When the food is thawed, bacteria will start to grow again.

The diagram on page 202 shows you the proper temperatures for storing and cooking food. Red is the danger zone where bacteria grow rapidly. Bacteria also grow in the orange zone, but more slowly.

As you have learned, food-borne illness can also be caused by toxins or parasites. Some types of toxins are destroyed by heat. Others remain unchanged even after food is cooked. Thorough cooking destroys parasites.

Food Handling Guidelines

Many foods require special care to keep them out of the danger zone. These include meat, poultry, fish, eggs, and dairy products, for example.

When cooking and serving food, follow these guidelines:

❖ Cook food to the proper internal temperature or until thoroughly cooked. Avoid partial cooking—cook the food completely at one time.

❖ Taste foods containing ingredients from animal sources only after they are fully cooked. Do not taste them when they are raw or during cooking.

❖ When microwaving, take steps to ensure even, thorough cooking, as explained in Section 9.3.

❖ Do not leave food out more than two hours at room temperature, or more than one hour if the temperature is above 90°F (32°C).

❖ Keep extra quantities of food either hot—using the range or another cooking appliance—or cold, in the refrigerator.

❖ Do not add more food to a serving dish of food that has been out for a while. Instead, use a clean dish.

Section 7.3: Sanitation   201

Student Experiences

1. **Poster Project:** Have students create posters illustrating food sanitation and cleanup practices to be observed in the foods laboratory. *(Key skill: creativity)*

2. **Demonstrations:** Have students plan and present demonstrations on use of the food waste disposal, use of the automatic dishwasher, procedures for washing dishes by hand, and procedures for cleaning the work and eating areas of the foods lab. *(Key skill: health)*

3. **Field Research:** Have students visit supermarkets to find cleaning solutions such as dishwashing liquid that make cleanup chores easier but are not harmful to the environment. Have them make a list of their findings. *(Key skills: environmental studies, writing)*

Thinking Skills

Reasoning: Ask students to discuss the advantage of following the prescribed order when washing dishes. Why should glassware be washed first and cookware last? *(Keeping such items separate helps prevent breakage; the glassware will not be as greasy as the cookware. If you wash the greasy pieces last, you can avoid getting grease in the water that might adhere to other dishes—such as glassware—as you're washing them.)*

Teaching . . .

• Proper Food Temperatures

(text pages 201-202)

Comprehension Check

1. Ask students to describe the effects of heat, refrigeration, and freezing on bacteria. *(See page 201.)*

2. Ask students to list guidelines to follow when cooking and serving food. *(See list on pages 201-202.)*

3. Ask students to describe three ways to thaw food safely. Why is it important not to thaw foods at room temperature? *(Thaw in refrigerator or submerged in cold water or in a microwave oven; because bacteria grow rapidly on the food at room temperature)*

Student Experiences

1. **Rhymes:** Have students create rhymes or raps to help them remember the proper temperatures for storing, cooking, and serving food. *(Key skills: writing, creativity)*

2. **Application:** Have students work in groups to apply principles of food sanitation to holiday meals, picnics, brown bag lunches, and parties. Ask groups to develop sanitation guidelines for each of these situations. Use the guidelines to prepare a series of articles on sanitation for the local newspaper. *(Key skills: critical thinking, writing)*

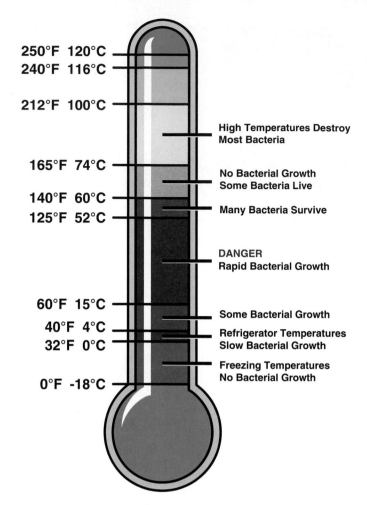

Temperature is one of the most important factors in food safety. Bacteria multiply very rapidly in the danger zone—60°F to 125°F (15°C to 52°C). What kinds of foods are most at risk?

❖ Discard foods that have been held at room temperature for more than two hours.

❖ Refrigerate food in shallow containers. Large, deep containers keep the food from cooling rapidly and evenly.

❖ When reheating food that has been refrigerated, bring it to an internal temperature of 165°F (74°C) or higher to kill any bacteria. Keep in mind that if the food has not been properly stored, it cannot be made safe just by reheating. You will learn more about storing food in the next section.

202   **Chapter 7: Kitchen Principles**

More About Spores

The word spore is a derivative of the Greek word *sporo,* which means "seed." A spore is the reproductive body produced by molds, fungi, and ferns, as well as bacteria. In turn, this spore produces a parent body. Spores are very tough. They can be frozen and heated and still live. They will not form new bacteria until specific conditions, such as a specific temperature and moisture level, are reached. Have students look at the table on pages 198-199 and note which bacteria produce spores.

How would you thaw this frozen turkey safely?

Thawing Food Safely

Do not thaw food at room temperature. If you do, the outside may contain millions of harmful bacteria by the time the inside is thawed. To thaw food safely, use one of these methods:

❖ Place food in the refrigerator, where it will thaw slowly.

❖ For faster thawing, put the package in a water-tight plastic bag and submerge it in cold water. Change the water every 30 minutes. The cold slows down the growth of bacteria as the food thaws.

❖ Use a microwave for quick, safe defrosting. Follow the manufacturer's directions. Foods thawed this way should be cooked immediately.

By handling foods carefully and practicing cleanliness, you'll avoid food-borne illnesses.

■ Section 7.3 Review ■

RECALL THE FACTS

1. Describe two kinds of microorganisms that can cause food-borne illness.

2. Name five instances when you should wash your hands while working with food.

3. What temperature range is considered the "danger zone"? Why?

4. What is the time limit for leaving most foods at room temperature?

DISCUSS YOUR IDEAS

5. Why do you think so many Americans get food poisoning each year?

APPLY YOUR LEARNING

6. Write at least six slogans or rhymes that could help you and your classmates remember important rules of sanitation.

Section 7.3: Sanitation   **203**

Completing the Section

Review

• Ask students to summarize the main ideas in this section.

• Have students complete the Section Review. (Answers appear below.)

Evaluation

• Have students prepare a picnic. Hot foods must be kept hot and cold foods, cold. Preparation techniques must include safe use of equipment and good sanitation procedures.

• Have the students take the quiz for Section 7.3. (Refer to the *Section Quizzes* booklet or construct your own quiz using the *Testmaker Software*.

Reteaching

• Have students design a bulletin board display depicting bacteria and their mode of transportation to foods.

• Refer to the *Reteaching Activities* booklet for the Section 7.3 activity sheet.

Enrichment

• Have students research current concerns about contamination of one of the following foods: eggs, poultry, ground meat. How can contamination be prevented?

Closure

• Lead a discussion about the importance of sanitation to prevent food-borne illnesses.

■ Answers to Section Review ■

1. *Any two:* bacteria, viruses, or parasites (organisms that get their nutrients from other living organisms).

2. Before you begin to handle food; after using the toilet or blowing your nose; after touching face, hair, or any other part of your body; after handling raw meat, poultry, or fish.

3. 60°F to 125°F (16°C to 52°C); because most food-borne illnesses are caused by bacteria that thrive in these temperatures.

4. Two hours (one hour if room temperature is above 90°F).

5. Answers will vary.

6. Answers will vary.

Storing Food

Introducing the Section

Motivator

- Show students pictures of kitchens in 1900 and of kitchens today. Point out differences in food storage. Compare the advantages and disadvantages of food storage today and in the past. Discuss the time spent on food storage and preservation in 1900 and today. How would today's lifestyles be affected if everyone needed to preserve their own food?

Objectives

- Have students read the section objectives. Discuss the purpose of studying this section.

Vocabulary

- Pronounce the terms listed under "Look for These Terms." Have students find the terms and their definitions in the section.

Guided Reading

- Have students look at the headings within Section 7.4 to preview the concepts that will be discussed.

- Have students read the section and complete the appropriate part of the Chapter 7 Study Guide in the *Student Workbook*.

OBJECTIVES

After studying this section, you should be able to:

- Identify causes and signs of food spoilage.
- Give examples of foods that are stored at room temperature and in cold storage.
- Give guidelines for each type of storage.

LOOK FOR THESE TERMS

shelf life
shelf-stable
perishable
freezer burn
inventory

Proper storage of food helps you in many ways. You can keep a variety of foods on hand, plan ahead, and work more efficiently. Most important, proper storage helps retain nutrients and keeps food from spoiling.

Spoilage and Nutrient Loss

Food that is not stored properly starts to lose quality and nutrients. Eventually it will spoil. Spoiled food often develops bad tastes and odors and must be thrown out. Some types of spoilage can cause food-borne illness.

What causes spoilage? Under the right conditions, harmful bacteria, yeasts, and molds can spoil food. Spoilage can also be caused by natural chemical changes within the cells of the food.

To retain the freshness and nutrition of the foods you buy, learn how to store them correctly.

Science Connection

Chemistry:

Enzymes and Spoilage

The cells of living things contain *enzymes,* protein substances that cause chemical changes to occur. When a plant or animal is processed into a food, some of the enzymes remain active. Unless foods are heated to destroy the enzymes, chemical changes continue—destroying the cells and causing the food to spoil.

■ ■ ■

Conditions in the environment can also cause or speed up nutrient loss and spoilage. Controlling these conditions is a key to proper storage.

❖ *Heat* speeds up chemical reactions that cause spoilage.
❖ *Air* contains oxygen. Exposure to oxygen can destroy some nutrients, such as vitamins C and E. It can also cause oils to become rancid—they develop an unpleasant flavor.
❖ *Too little moisture* can cause fresh foods to dry out, wilt, and lose nutrients.
❖ *Too much moisture* can lead to spoilage. Bacteria thrive in moist areas.
❖ *Light* can destroy nutrients, especially vitamin C and riboflavin.
❖ *Dirt* contains harmful microorganisms.
❖ *Damage* to food or packaging makes spoilage by microorganisms more likely.

When Food Is Spoiled

How do you know when food is starting to spoil? Some fresh foods, such as apples and celery, dry out. They may wilt, get wrinkled, or turn brown. Some foods become slimy, a sign that decay has started. Spots of fuzzy

Not all mold is bad. Blue cheese gets its flavor from a special type of mold. However, most foods with mold must be thown away.

Food and Nutrition Science

Microorganisms and Spoilage: Microorganisms such as bacteria, yeasts, and molds need food as a source of energy and nutrients. They produce waste products including acids and gases. These waste products create the bad tastes and odors typical of spoiled food.

Teaching . . .

• Spoilage and Nutrient Loss
(text pages 204-206)

Comprehension Check

1. Ask students to explain what causes food spoilage. *(harmful bacteria, yeasts, molds, and natural chemical changes within foods)*
2. Discuss conditions that you can control to eliminate or slow down nutrient loss and spoilage. *(See list on page 205.)*
3. Ask students to describe symptoms that may indicate that food is spoiling. *(bad smell, wilting, color change.)*
4. Ask students what types of moldy food should be discarded and what can be salvaged. How can these foods be salvaged? *(Hard salami, hard cheeses, and dry cured country ham; the moldy spots can be cut off.)*
5. Ask students to describe the steps you should take to keep a mold from spreading. *(Wrap it gently or place in bag before discarding.)*

Student Experiences

1. **Guest Speaker:** Invite a science teacher to discuss how enzymes and microorganisms make food spoil. Ask the speaker to explain how heat, air, moisture, light, dirt, and damage speed up or delay nutrient loss and spoilage. *(Key skill: science)*
2. **Display:** Display foods that show signs of spoilage. Ask students to point out signs of spoilage. Discuss which parts of these foods can be saved and which should be discarded. *(Key skill: health)*

Comprehension Check

1. Ask students to define the term "shelf life." What factors affect the shelf life of a product? *(The length of time a product can be stored and still retain its quality; type of food, packaging, storage temperature, and how it is handled.)*

2. Discuss guidelines people can follow to avoid loss of quality in food products. *(See list on page 206.)*

3. Ask students to give examples of shelf-stable foods. *(most unopened canned foods, dry beans and peas, oils and shortening, many grain products)*

4. Ask students to describe the ideal conditions for room temperature storage. *(Shelves should be clean and dry with doors to keep out light and dirt; temperatures no higher than 85°F and no lower than freezing; do not store near sources of heat or where they may get wet.)*

mold, damage such as holes, tears and bruises, bad flavors, and bad odors are all signs of spoilage.

Most spoiled foods should be discarded. However, spots of mold can be cut off hard cheese, hard salami, and dry cured country ham. Pare away about an inch (2.5 cm) of the food around the area where the mold spot was. Discard all other visibly moldy foods.

Mold gives off spores. To keep mold from spreading, very gently wrap the moldy food or place it in a bag before discarding. Examine other foods that may have been in contact with the moldy food. Clean the container that held the moldy food, and if necessary, wash out the refrigerator.

Basic Storage Principles

No food can be stored indefinitely. Each food has a **shelf life,** the length of time it can be stored and still retain its quality. Shelf life depends on the type of food, packaging, storage temperature, and how the food is handled.

To avoid loss of quality, follow these guidelines:

❖ Buy only what you need.

> ✔ **SAFETY CHECK**
>
> In some cases, spoiled food can make you ill. If you aren't sure whether food is spoiled, play it safe—discard it.
>
> Be alert for these signs of spoilage in canned and bottled foods: bulging cans, liquids that spurt when you open the container, or liquids that are cloudy when they should be clear. If you see these signs, *do not taste the food.* Wrap it and discard it where no people or animals can get to it.

❖ Follow the principle of "first in, first out." Store new food behind the same kind of older food. Use up the older food first.

❖ Look for "sell by" or "use by" dates on food containers. If there is none, you may want to write the purchase date on the container before storing. Use canned food within a year.

❖ Clean storage areas regularly. Throw out any food that has started to spoil or containers that have been damaged. Wash and dry surfaces thoroughly.

There are two basic kinds of food storage methods: room temperature storage and cold storage.

Room Temperature Storage

Many canned, bottled, and packaged foods will last for weeks or even months at room temperatures below 85°F (29°C). Such foods are called **shelf-stable.** Examples include most unopened canned foods, dry beans and peas, oils and shortening, and many grain products (except whole grains). In general, foods that you find on grocery shelves when shopping can be stored at room temperature when you bring them home.

Kitchen cabinets are used for most room temperature storage. They should be clean and dry with doors to keep out light and dirt. Temperatures should be no higher than 85°F (29°C) and no lower than freezing, 32°F (0°C). Do not store food on shelves near or above heat sources such as the range, refrigerator, or a radiator. Also avoid areas that may get wet, like under-sink cabinets.

Once packages or containers have been opened, storage requirements differ. Some shelf-stable foods, including most canned goods, must be refrigerated after opening. Others, such as a bag of dry beans or a box of cereal, can remain at room temperature. Reseal the package if possible. Otherwise, transfer the contents to a storage container with a tight-fitting cover. Do the same with foods you buy in bulk.

Food and Nutrition Science

Moisture Absorption Experiment: See the *Food Science Resources* booklet for the "Moisture Absorption by Cookies" teaching guide and student experiment worksheet. The experiment observes the effect of two different sweeteners and two different storage methods on moisture absorption by cookies.

Cold Storage

Shelf-stable foods may be stored at normal room temperature. To prevent food waste, buy only the amount of food you can use and store it properly.

✓ **SAFETY CHECK**

If you have to stack items to store them, put the lightest on the top. Boxes of dried soup mix, for example, can be stored on top of canned soups. That way you'll be less likely to accidentally knock over heavy items that could cause injury.

Perishable foods spoil quickly at room temperature. They require cold storage in the refrigerator or freezer, depending on the kind of food and how long you want to store it. The chart on pages 208-209 gives you a general timetable for foods in cold storage.

Refrigerator Storage

Foods normally refrigerated include:
* Foods that were refrigerated in the store, including dairy products, eggs, delicatessen foods, and fresh meat, poultry, and fish.
* Most fresh fruits and vegetables. Exceptions are onions, potatoes, and sweet potatoes, which should be stored in a cool, dry area.
* Whole grain products, seeds and nuts. They contain oils which can spoil and give foods an off-flavor.
* Leftover cooked foods.
* Baked goods with fruit or cream fillings.
* Any foods that, according to label directions, must be refrigerated. Some shelf-stable foods must be refrigerated after opening.

Some foods are very delicate and have a short shelf life. Foods with cream fillings must be refrigerated and eaten promptly.

Section 7.4: Storing Food **207**

• Cold Storage: Refrigeration

(text pages 207-209)

Comprehension Check

1. Ask students to list foods that are normally refrigerated. *(See list on page 207.)*

2. As shown on the chart on pages 208-209, some foods can be stored in the refrigerator or in the freezer. Ask students to discuss guidelines for choosing the method of storing these foods.

3. Discuss tips for storing foods in the refrigerator. *(Keep the refrigerator at 40°F; avoid overloading the refrigerator; store foods tightly covered; store meat, poultry, and fish in the store wrap unless it is damaged or leaking; wash vegetables only to remove dirt; use shallow containers for leftovers; keep all leftovers on the same shelf, so they don't get overlooked.)*

COLD STORAGE CHART

NOTE: — — — — means food should not be stored in that area.

TYPE OF FOOD	REFRIGERATOR STORAGE 40° F (4°C)	FREEZER STORAGE 0° F (-18° C)
Meats, Poultry, Fish		
Beef roasts, steaks	3-5 days	6-12 months
Pork roasts, chops	3-5 days	4-6 months
Lamb roasts, chops	3-5 days	6-9 months
Veal roasts	3-5 days	4-8 months
Chicken or turkey, whole	1-2 days	1 year
Chicken or turkey, pieces	1-2 days	9 months
Ground meats or poultry	1-2 days	3-4 months
Lean fish (cod)	1-2 days	6 months
Fatty fish (salmon)	1-2 days	2-3 months
Shellfish (shrimp)	1-2 days	3-6 months
Dairy Products		
Fresh milk, cream	5 days	— — — —
Butter, margarine	1-2 weeks	2 months
Buttermilk	2 weeks	— — — —
Sour cream	4 weeks	— — — —
Yogurt, plain or flavored	2 weeks	— — — —
Cottage cheese	1 week	— — — —
Hard cheese (cheddar), opened	3-4 weeks	— — — —
Hard cheese, unopened	3-6 months	— — — —
Ice cream, sherbet	— — — —	1 month
Miscellaneous Foods		
Bread	— — — —	3 months
Cakes, cookies, pies (not cream-filled)	1-3 days	2-3 months
Cream pies	1-2 days	— — — —
Commercially frozen foods	— — — —	3-4 months
Fresh eggs, in shell	3 weeks	— — — —
Raw yolks, whites	2-4 days	1 year
Hard-cooked eggs	1 week	— — — —
Egg substitutes, opened	3 days	— — — —
Egg substitutes, unopened	10 days	1 year
Mayonnaise, salad dressing (Refrigerate after opening)	2 months	— — — —

More About Refrigerating Food

- Many accessories are available to help you organize the refrigerator storage area. They include turntables, racks, and stackable containers.
- The vegetable drawer helps fruits and vegetables retain moister longer. Don't line the bottom with paper towels, which will get soggy. The extra moisture can encourage mold and rot.
- Avoid using large containers to store small amounts of food. You waste space and cooling energy. As you use food from

COLD STORAGE CHART (Continued)

NOTE: — — — — means food should not be stored in that area.

TYPE OF FOOD	REFRIGERATOR STORAGE 40° F (4°C)	FREEZER STORAGE 0° F (-18° C)
Cooked Foods, Leftovers		
Cooked meats, meat dishes	3-4 days	2-3 months
Fried chicken	3-4 days	4 months
Poultry covered in broth	1-2 days	6 months
Soups and stews (not creamed)	3-4 days	2 months
Fish stews, soups (not creamed)	1 day	1 month
Cured Meats		
Hot dogs, opened	1 week	1-2 months
Lunch meats, opened	3-5 days	1-2 months
Hot dogs, lunch meats, unopened	2 weeks	1-2 months
Bacon	7 days	1 month
Sausage (beef, pork, turkey)	1-2 days	1-2 months
Hard sausage (pepperoni)	2-3 weeks	1-2 months
Ham, canned (refrigerated, unopened)	6-9 months	— — — —
Ham, fully cooked, whole	7 days	1-2 months
Ham, fully cooked, half	3-5 days	1-2 months
Ham, fully cooked, slices	3-4 days	1-2 months

The refrigerator should be kept at 40°F (4°C). Do not let the refrigerator temperature fall below freezing (32°F or 0°C). Foods with a high water content, such as lettuce, may freeze and be damaged.

Avoid overloading the refrigerator. The cold air will not circulate well and some areas may become too warm to store perishables safely.

Store foods tightly covered. This will keep them from drying out and will also prevent odors from being picked up by other foods. Opened canned goods may pick up an off-flavor from the can, so transfer them to another storage container.

Store meat, poultry, and fish in the store wrap unless it is damaged or leaking. If it is, put the package in a plastic bag or on a plate. Leaking foods can contaminate other stored foods.

When storing fruits and vegetables, wash them only if necessary to remove dirt. Wipe hard-skinned ones dry and drain others well.

Leftovers require special care. To ensure thorough chilling, use shallow containers. Large, deep containers keep food from cooling rapidly and evenly. Cut large pieces of meat into smaller ones so they cool quickly. Close the containers tightly and label with the current date. Be sure to use the food within a few days. (Remember that some foods can be frozen for longer storage.) You may want to keep all leftovers on the same shelf so they don't get overlooked.

Section 7.4: Storing Food   209

1. **Demonstration:** Demonstrate how to use and read a refrigerator thermometer. Check temperatures in various parts of the refrigerator, including the top shelf, bottom shelf, door storage area, and crispers. Review which foods should be stored in warmer and colder parts of the refrigerator. Show how to control the interior temperature. *(Key skill: food management)*

2. **Demonstrations:** Have students prepare brief demonstrations on problems with overloading the refrigerator; selecting refrigerator storage containers; storing meat, poultry, and fish; storing fruits and vegetables; storing leftovers. *(Key skill: public speaking)*

3. **Poster Project:** Have students use the chart on pages 208-209 to make illustrated posters that could be mounted on a refrigerator door. Have them explain how they decided which foods to include. *(Key skill: creativity)*

a large container, transfer the remainder to a smaller one.
- Heavy cardboard containers absorb cooling energy. Transfer food (except eggs) from such containers into lightweight ones.

Teaching . . .

• Freezer Storage

(text pages 210-211)

Comprehension Check

1. Ask students to list foods that do not freeze well. Discuss what is meant "freeze well." Why might these foods not be good candidates for freezing? *(Foods that do not maintain their quality when thawed do not freeze well.)*

2. Discuss why freezers work best whey they are fairly full. *(The frozen foods help maintain the cold temperature between refrigeration cycles.)*

3. Ask students to explain what freezer burn is and how it can be avoided. *(A condition in which food dries out and loses flavor and texture; it can be avoided by packaging food properly before freezing and by using the food within the proper time period.)*

4. Ask students to list proper packaging materials for foods that will be frozen. *(vapor- and moisture-resistant plastic containers with tight-fitting covers, heavy-duty plastic freezer bags; wraps such as heavy-duty foil and freezer wrap)*

Student Experiences

1. **Demonstration:** Display containers and packaging materials appropriate for use in the freezer. Demonstrate how to package foods frozen at home to avoid freezer burn. Allow students to practice packaging "foods" for the freezer. *(Key skill: food management)*

2. **Freezer Inventory:** Demonstrate how to make a freezer inventory. Suggest students create an inventory of the foods in their home freezers. *(Key skill: writing)*

Earth Watch

Studies of residential garbage cans show that 10 to 25 percent of all the food an American family buys (not including bones and other inedible parts) gets thrown away. Reducing food waste saves both money and resources. How can proper storage help?

Freezer Storage

Freezing allows long-term storage of many foods. At temperatures of 0°F (-18°C) or below, foods keep from one month to a year, depending on the type of food and proper packaging.

These packaging materials can help prevent freezer burn. What types of wraps and containers would not provide adequate protection?

Foods purchased frozen should be stored promptly in the home freezer. Many other foods can also be frozen to increase shelf life. These include fresh meat, poultry, and fish; baked goods such as breads and rolls; and many leftovers.

Some foods do not freeze well. These include fresh vegetables that are to be eaten raw; cooked or whole raw eggs; products made with mayonnaise; meat and poultry stuffing; cream- or egg-based sauces; custards; baked goods with cream filling; and many cheeses.

To freeze foods at home, a two-door refrigerator-freezer or a separate freezer unit is needed. Separate freezer units generally maintain food quality longer than refrigerator-freezers.

Some refrigerators have only one outside door and a small freezer compartment inside. The freezer compartment maintains a temperature of 10°F to 15°F (-12°C to -9°C). It can be used for storing already frozen food for several weeks. However, it is not cold enough to freeze fresh or leftover food satisfactorily.

A freezer functions best when fairly full. Some freezers need regular defrosting.

How to Package and Freeze Foods

Foods that are purchased already frozen can be stored in their original packaging. However, foods frozen at home must be specially packaged to avoid freezer burn. **Freezer burn** results when food is improperly packaged or stored in the freezer too long. The food dries out and loses flavor and texture.

Packaging materials for freezing must be vapor- and moisture-resistant. These include plastic containers with tight-fitting covers, heavy-duty plastic freezer bags, and wraps such as heavy-duty foil and freezer wrap. Do not use regular refrigerator storage bags or plastic tubs from foods such as margarine and yogurt. They do not provide enough protection. Fresh meat, poultry, and fish need additional wrap for freezing—the store wrapping is too lightweight.

Food and Nutrition Science

Freezing and Food Quality: Have students freeze small samples of foods that generally do not freeze well, such as potatoes (become watery and fall apart), lettuce (change in texture and flavor), mayonnaise (separates), and cooked egg white (gets tough). They should package the food as for ordinary freezing. After several days, thaw the food and let students observe the results and draw conclusions.

Labeling frozen foods clearly and keeping an inventory of food in the freezer can minimize food waste. Foods freeze more quickly when air circulates between packages during the freezing process.

When wrapping solid foods, such as meat, squeeze out as much air as possible to prevent freezer burn. Seal packages with freezer tape.

When filling storage containers, leave enough space for food to expand as it freezes. This is about one inch (2.5 cm) in a quart (or liter) container. Then seal the container tightly.

Label all packages and containers with the contents, amount (or number of servings), date frozen, and any special instructions.

For best quality, freeze food quickly. Spread the packages out so they all touch the coils or sides of the freezer. Leave enough air between packages for air to circulate. When the food is frozen (at least 24 hours later), you can stack it according to the kind of food.

Keep an **inventory,** or up-to-date record, of the food in the freezer. Include the food, date frozen, and quantity. This page shows a typical freezer inventory. As you remove food, change the quantity on the inventory so you know how much is left.

When the Power Goes Off

When the power goes off or the refrigerator-freezer breaks down, the food inside is in danger of spoiling. In general, avoid opening the door of the freezer or refrigerator. This will help maintain cold temperatures longer.

Keeping Frozen Foods Safe

A full freezer will keep food frozen for about two days after losing power. A half-full freezer will keep food frozen for about one day. If the freezer is not full, stack packages closely together so they will stay cold.

Separate frozen meat, poultry, and fish from other foods. That way, if they begin to thaw, juices will not get into other foods.

FREEZER INVENTORY

Date Frozen	Food (amount in package)	Number of packages
2/8	Chicken fryers (halves)	6̸ 5
2/11	Beef stew (1 serving)	3
2/12	Mixed vegetables (2 lb.)	6̸ 5
2/13	Corn on the cob (4 ears)	4̸ 3
2/20	Eggplant Parmesan (1 serving)	4

A freezer inventory gives up-to-date information on the kind and amount of food stored in the freezer.

Section 7.4: Storing Food **211**

Food and Nutrition Science

Freezer Burn: Have students freeze two samples of cooked food, one wrapped properly and one unwrapped. Several days later, have them examine and compare the samples before thawing, after thawing, and after reheating. Discuss the results.

Comprehension Check

1. Discuss precautions people can take to prevent frozen food spoilage in case of a power outage. *(Keep freezer full or stack packages closely together; separate meat, poultry, and fish from other foods; put dry ice in the freezer.)*

2. Discuss guidelines for deciding whether to keep and use food that was in the freezer and food that was in the refrigerator during a power outage. *(See list on page 212.)*

3. Describe the procedure you should use after a power outage to clean the refrigerator and freezer. *(Wash up spills and wipe surfaces dry; clean odors with baking soda solution.)*

Student Experiences

1. **Class Discussion:** Have students why it is important to clean the refrigerator-freezer thoroughly after a power outage. *(Key skill: critical thinking)*

2. **Safety Booklet:** Have students work in groups to prepare safety booklets that explain how to determine whether to keep food after a power outage. *(Key skill: writing)*

Completing the Section

Review

- Ask students to summarize the main ideas in this section.
- Have students complete the Section Review. (Answers appear below.)

Evaluation

- Give students a list of 10 food items. Ask them to write down how they would store each item, why, and how long each item could be kept.
- Have students take the quiz for section 7.4. (Refer to the *Section Quizzes* booklet or construct your own quiz using the *Testmaker Software*.

Reteaching

- Stress that, in spite of refrigeration, most foods must be used quickly. Ask which refrigerated foods have the shortest and longest storage life. What should you do if food has been in the refrigerator a long time?
- Refer to the *Reteaching Activities* booklet for the Section 7.4 activity sheet.

Enrichment

- Have students report on how early home refrigerators compare with today's in size, appearance, cost, convenience, and other features.

Closure

- Lead a discussion to tie in with the section motivator. Discuss food storage yesterday (circa 1900), today, and tomorrow (circa 2100).

If the power will be off longer than two days, you can put dry ice (frozen carbon dioxide) in the freezer. BE CAREFUL! Never touch dry ice with bare hands or breathe its vapors in an enclosed area. Carbon dioxide gas in high concentration is poisonous.

When the freezer is working again, here's how to decide what to do with the food:

- ❖ If ice crystals are still visible, or the food feels as cold as if it were refrigerated, it is safe to refreeze. Some foods may lose quality, but they can still be eaten.
- ❖ Discard any food that thawed or was held above 40°F (4°C) for more than two hours. Also discard food that has a strange odor.

Once the freezer is working again, wash up any food spills and wipe surfaces dry. If odors remain, wash again with a solution of 2 tablespoons (30 mL) baking soda dissolved in 1 quart (1 L) warm water. Leave an open box of baking soda inside the freezer to absorb odors.

If power goes out for any period of time, discard any refrigerated or frozen food that may be unsafe to eat. Then clean the unit thoroughly to remove odors and bacteria.

Keeping Refrigerated Foods Safe

During a power outage, food will usually keep in the refrigerator for four to six hours, depending on the temperature of the room. If the power will be out for a long time, you can place a block of ice in the refrigerator.

When the refrigerator is working again, follow these guidelines to decide what to do with the food:

- ❖ Discard fresh meats, poultry, fish, lunch meats, hot dogs, eggs, milk, soft cheeses, and cooked foods if they have been held above 40°F (4°C) for more than two hours.
- ❖ Keep butter and margarine if they have not melted and do not have a rancid odor.
- ❖ Other foods, including fresh fruits and vegetables, are safe if they show no signs of mold, sliminess, or bad odor.

Once the refrigerator is working again, clean it the same way as described for the freezer.

■ Section 7.4 Review ■

RECALL THE FACTS

1. Name three signs that food has spoiled.
2. What is the difference between shelf-stable foods and perishable foods?
3. What is the ideal temperature range for room temperature storage? Refrigerator storage? Freezer storage?
4. Describe how you would wrap a package of fresh ground meat for freezing.

DISCUSS YOUR IDEAS

5. Most people have to throw away spoiled food now and then. What do you think is the major reason?

APPLY YOUR LEARNING

6. Use a refrigerator-freezer thermometer to check cold storage temperatures at home or in the foods lab. Are they at safe levels?

■ Answers to Section Review ■

1. *Any three:* It has wilted, wrinkled, or turned brown; become slimy; has mold on it; has damage such as holes, tears, and bruises; has bad odors or flavors.

2. Shelf-stable foods can be stored for much longer periods of time than perishable foods.

3. Room temperature: between 85°F and 32°F; refrigerator: 40°; freezer: 0° or below.

4. See guidelines on pages 210-211.
5. Answers will vary.
6. Answers will vary.

Conserving Natural Resources

OBJECTIVES

After studying this section, you should be able to:
- Explain the importance of conservation.
- Identify ways to conserve resources when working in the kitchen.

LOOK FOR THIS TERM

disposable

Neil was studying in the kitchen. He could hear the kitchen radio vaguely in the background, some news about environmental problems. He had heard most of it before. Conserve natural resources...use them wisely...don't waste or pollute them. He went back to his studies and ignored the radio. "I'm just one person," he thought. "Not much I can do."

Neil, like many others, never thought about the kitchen as one of the biggest polluters and household energy-guzzlers. Gas, electricity, and water are pumped into homes and used liberally in the kitchen. The kitchen is also a major source of household trash.

Some people believe they can't do much to help solve environmental problems. Yet conservation begins with the individual. If each person does his or her share, waste and pollution can be cut down. Here are some ways to conserve natural resources in the kitchen at home or at school.

Pollution is a global problem. The decisions you make daily can increase or decrease its severity.

Section 7.5: Conserving Natural Resources **213**

Teacher's Classroom Resources—Section 7.5

Refer to these resources in the TCR package:

Reproducible Lesson Plans
Student Workbook
Extending the Text

Reteaching Activities
Section Quizzes
Testmaker Software
Color Transparencies

Section 7.5 Conserving Natural Resources

Introducing the Section

Motivators
- Bring to class articles describing the need for conserving natural resources. Ask students to relate the information in the articles to energy conservation in the kitchen.
- Begin a story describing family life in a story describing family life in a time when natural resources have become very scarce. Ask each student to add something different to the story until each student has had the opportunity. What effects might scarcity have on our lifestyles?

Objectives
- Have students read the section objectives. Discuss the purpose of studying this section.

Vocabulary
- Pronounce the terms listed under "Look for These Terms." Have students find the terms and their definitions in the section.

Guided Reading
- Have students look at the headings within Section 7.5 to preview the concepts that will be discussed.
- Have students read the section and complete the appropriate part of the Chapter 7 Study Guide in the *Student Workbook*.

Teaching . . .

- Conserve Energy
- Conserve Water

(text pages 214-215)

Comprehension Check

1. Discuss the need to conserve natural resources such as energy and water.

2. Ask students to list guidelines that people can follow to conserve energy in the kitchen. *(See list on page 214.)*

Student Experiences

1. Demonstration: Have students observe a demonstration of the proper way to cook vegetables in order to conserve nutrients. Discuss other advantages of cooking vegetables properly. *(Uses less water and energy; flavor and color are preserved; foods are more appetizing.) (Key skill: observation)*

2. Efficient Meal Planning: Have students plan a meal with foods that can all be cooked together in the oven to save energy. Ask them to write out a menu for the meal. *(Key skill: writing)*

Conserve Energy

Neil wasn't listening to the radio. As a result, he wasted electricity by not turning it off. Every watt of electricity used in the home sends about two pounds (1 kg) of carbon dioxide, an air pollutant, into the atmosphere.

To save energy, follow these suggestions:

- ❖ Turn off lights and appliances when they are not in use.
- ❖ Cook as many foods as possible when using the oven. Freeze the extra for future meals.
- ❖ Use small appliances or a microwave oven when cooking small amounts of food. They use less energy than the range.
- ❖ Match the pan size to the size of the burner or heating unit for top-of-range cooking. Less energy will be lost.
- ❖ Decide what you want to eat before opening the refrigerator door. The air in the refrigerator warms up if you leave the door open. It takes more energy to cool it down.
- ❖ Keep the refrigerator and freezer well organized so you can find food easily.
- ❖ Don't run the dishwasher unless it's full.

✓ SAFETY CHECK

Never try to save energy by letting hot food cool to room temperature before refrigerating it. Remember, harmful bacteria grow quickly at room temperature.

Conserve Water

Clean, safe water is scarce in some areas. Water use may be restricted because of a shortage. Learn more about the water situation in your area. By conserving water in your home, you can help preserve this resource for all.

Look for ways to use less water during food preparation. For example, don't let tap water run unnecessarily as you pare vegetables.

Putting aerators on faucets is an easy, inexpensive way to cut water usage.

Food and Nutrition Science

Heat Conduction: Have students conduct an energy efficiency experiment to see how long it takes to boil water in glass, glass-ceramic, aluminum, and stainless steel utensils.

Cleanup takes lots of water, but you can conserve. When handwashing dishes, don't keep the water running. Wash all the dishes first and then rinse them off at the same time as quickly as possible.

Be sure to repair dripping faucets immediately. Water dripping at the rate of a drop a second can waste about 700 gallons (2700 L) a year.

Reduce Trash

Picture a four-lane highway running from Boston to Los Angeles, filled with trash about 6 feet (3 m) deep. That's about the amount of trash Americans create in a year. The trash usually ends up in landfills, which pollute soil and water. Communities are running out of landfill space.

You can help minimize the trash problem. Start by remembering three key words: reduce, reuse, and recycle.

Reduce

One way to cut down on trash is to reduce the use of **disposable,** or throwaway, products. For example, use dishcloths instead of paper towels to wipe up spills. Use cloth napkins instead of paper ones. Buy or make cloth bags to carry groceries. Choose items in reusable or recyclable containers rather than disposable ones.

Reuse

Reusing gives second life to materials. Find creative ways to reuse items that might otherwise be thrown away. In the kitchen, you might:
❖ Wash plastic tubs from margarine, yogurt, and cottage cheese and use them to refrigerate leftovers. Do not use them for freezing—they are not heavy enough and food will dry out.

Most trash ends up in landfills. Reducing use of disposable items, reusing materials, and recycling whenever possible are the keys to cutting waste.

Teaching . . .

• **Reduce Trash**
• **Show Your Concern**

(text pages 215-216)

Comprehension Check

1. Ask students to give examples of things they could do to reduce the amount of trash they generate. *(reduce, reuse, and recycle)*

2. Discuss how reusing certain kitchen items can help reduce trash. What types of things should people reuse? *(plastic margarine tubs, glass jars, plastic or paper grocery bags)*

3. Ask students to describe some ways they can influence business, industry, and government to conserve natural resources. *(by choosing products that are environment-friendly or can be recycled)*

Student Experiences

1. **Creative Solutions:** Give students five minutes to think of as many uses as possible for plastic tubs, glass jars and bottles, or plastic or paper grocery bags. Give an award to the student who thinks of the most uses in each category. *(Key skills: conservation, creativity)*

2. **Poster Project:** Have students prepare posters to illustrate the advantages of recycling. *(Key skill: creativity)*

3. **Recycling Campaign:** Have students identify recycling centers in the community and conduct a campaign to encourage the recycling of newspapers, glass, and aluminum cans. *(Key skill: citizenship)*

Special Needs Strategies

Learning Disabled: Provide students with pairs of items: one that wastes natural resources and one that conserves natural resources. Have students select the best choice for conserving natural resources from each pair.

Completing the Section

Review

- Ask students to summarize the main ideas in this section.

- Have students complete the Section Review. (Answers appear below.)

Evaluation

- Ask students to write an essay explaining the need to conserve natural resources and suggesting specific ways to do so.

- Have students take the quiz for section 7.5. (Refer to the *Section Quizzes* booklet or construct your own quiz using the *Testmaker Software*.)

Reteaching

- Bring to class magazine or newspaper pictures of natural resources being wasted. Ask students to describe what's wrong and suggest ways to correct it.

- Refer to the *Reteaching Activities* booklet for the Section 7.5 activity sheet.

Enrichment

- Have students research recent conservation legislation and report their findings to the class.

Closure

- Repeat the section motivator in which you began a story and students contributed; this time, encourage students to relate ways the family can reduce, reuse, and recycle.

❖ Turn glass jars and bottles with tight-fitting covers into storage containers. Use them for foods such as rice, pasta, and dry beans. Wash the jars and covers carefully, then let them air dry for at least 24 hours to remove odors.

❖ Reuse plastic or paper grocery bags as trash bags.

Recycle

Cooperate with recycling programs in your community. The kinds of materials recycled vary, depending on the community. Generally, newspapers, aluminum cans and foil, glass bottles, and some plastic containers are recycled.

Some communities have curb-side pickup for recycled materials. In others, the items must be brought to collection centers. Many supermarkets collect plastic shopping bags for recycling.

Many materials can be recycled and used again. What steps has your community taken to recycle waste?

Show Your Concern

Some people blame business, industry, and government for environmental problems. Even there, individual consumers have a voice. Every time you buy a product or use a service, you "vote" for it and for the policies of the organization. If you don't buy items or services that waste energy or pollute, the producers will improve them or develop new ones. Consumer power is an effective way to conserve natural resources.

By making the right choices and cooperating with community programs, you can do your share to help conserve natural resources.

Section 7.5 Review

RECALL THE FACTS

1. Why is it important for individuals to conserve resources?

2. Name five ways to conserve energy in the home.

3. What are three ways to conserve water?

4. Name three keys to reducing trash and give an example of each.

DISCUSS YOUR IDEAS

5. How might you convince someone who doesn't recycle to start recycling?

APPLY YOUR LEARNING

6. Develop a plan to reduce, reuse, and recycle at home. Where can you start? How can you proceed? How might you convince family members to take part in your plan?

Answers to Section Review

1. Environmental problems are becoming steadily worse; everyone needs to help solve them.

2. *Any five:* See list page 214.

3. Don't let tap water run unnecessarily as you pare vegetables; when handwashing, wash all dishes and then rinse all at one time; repair dripping faucets immediately.

4. Reduce, reuse, and recycle; examples will vary.

5. Answers will vary.

6. Answers will vary.

Career PROFILE

Jan Bradshaw
Family and Consumer Sciences Teacher

CURRENT POSITION

"I teach family and consumer sciences to high school students in a medium-sized urban school district."

RESPONSIBILITIES

"I help my students develop skills that they will use throughout their life—everything from preparing nutritious meals to managing a family budget to preparing for a career."

SKILLS

"Of course a teacher must be knowledgeable in his or her subject area. You also must be able to communicate with and motivate students. It helps to have a genuine enthusiasm for working with young people."

EDUCATION

"I have a bachelor's degree in education with an emphasis on home economics, and I'm certified to teach by the State Department of Education."

WORK ENVIRONMENT

"I work long hours both in and out of the classroom. Besides actually teaching, my job involves planning lessons, grading papers, preparing report cards, meeting with parents and school staff, and attending workshops and conferences."

FAVORITE PART OF THE JOB

"I love working with young people. It's very rewarding to help them learn. Often, I learn from them, too!"

- What are some of the advantages and disadvantages of a teacher's varied work schedule?
- What aspects of Jan's job do you think you might enjoy? Why?

217

CAREER PROFILE: FAMILY AND CONSUMER SCIENCES TEACHER

Thinking About . . . Teaching Careers

Have students think of additional questions they would like to ask Jan Bradshaw about the work she does. (Example: How does working in a medium-sized urban school district differ from other school settings, such as rural settings or large school districts?)

Ask students to brainstorm characteristics and personal preferences, other than liking to work with young people, a family and consumer sciences teacher should have.

Student Opportunities

Students planning a career in family and consumer sciences education should enroll in family and consumer sciences classes and get involved with their local Cooperative Extension Service. They may also wish to join clubs such as Future Teachers of America and their local 4-H club.

Occupational Outlook

Family and consumer sciences teachers who have been teaching for several years gain tenure with the school system, which can lead to higher salary and prestige. Interested teachers may also specialize or become administrators.

For More Information

For more information about educational careers in family and consumer sciences, have students contact:
- American Federation of Teachers, 555 New Jersey Avenue NW, Washington, D.C. 20001

- American Vocational Association, 1410 King Street, Alexandria, VA 22314
- American Association of Family and Consumer Sciences, 1555 King Street, Alexandria, VA 22314

Review

- Have students complete the Chapter Review. (Answers appear below.)

Evaluation

- Divide the class into two teams. Each team should brainstorm questions about Chapter 7. Then allow the teams to take turns asking each other the questions they listed. At the end of the questioning period, the team with the most correct answers wins.

- Have students take the test for Chapter 7. (Refer to the *Chapter and Unit Tests* booklet or construct your own test using the *Testmaker Software*.)

■ ANSWERS ■

REVIEWING FACTS

1. Answers will vary. Examples: Cold storage center—storage bags, food wraps, containers for leftover foods; sink center—dishpans, cleanup supplies, dish towels and cloths; cooking center—cooking tools, pots and pans, pot holders, small cooking appliances.

2. *Any two:* Keep knives sharp and use them properly; don't try to catch a falling knife; don't soak knives in sink or dishpan of water; sweep up broken glass.

3. *Any three:* Never mix chemical products; make sure you point the spray nozzle properly when using spray products; store hazardous chemicals away from food; avoid using hazardous chemicals unnecessarily.

CHAPTER 7 REVIEW

SUMMARY

SECTION 7.1

Introduction to the Kitchen: Kitchens are equipped with major appliances, small appliances, and utensils. They are organized around work centers, which include the sink, cold storage, and cooking centers.

SECTION 7.2

Safety in the Kitchen: Good management and safe work habits are the keys to kitchen safety. Common kitchen hazards include falls, sharp objects, electrical appliances, hazardous chemicals, and the range. Children, the elderly, and people with handicaps require special safety measures. Consider first aid training, including the Heimlich Maneuver and CPR.

SECTION 7.3

Sanitation: If food is handled improperly, microorganisms can multiply and cause food-borne illness. Prevent illness by practicing good personal hygiene, using sanitary work methods, keeping the kitchen clean, and keeping food at proper temperatures.

SECTION 7.4

Storing Food: Proper storage prevents spoilage and nutrient loss. Shelf-stable foods may be stored at room temperature. Store perishable foods in the freezer or in the refrigerator. Frozen and refrigerated foods require special handling after a power outage.

SECTION 7.5

Conserving Natural Resources: Conservation begins with the individual. Consider simple measures for saving energy and conserving water. To reduce trash, identify ways to reduce, reuse, and recycle.

REVIEWING FACTS

1. Name three items that might be found at each of the three basic kitchen work centers. (7.1)

2. List two knife safety rules. (7.2)

3. Give three guidelines for storing hazardous household chemicals. (7.2)

4. How can you help children learn safe kitchen work habits? (7.2)

5. List two personal hygiene habits that can help prevent food-borne illness. (7.3)

6. What is cross-contamination? How can you prevent it? (7.3)

7. Describe two procedures for thawing food safely. (7.3)

8. What is "shelf life"? (7.4)

9. Name two ways to keep frozen foods safe when the power goes off. (7.4)

10. Give three examples of alternatives to disposable items. (7.5)

LEARNING BY DOING

1. ***Foods lab:*** Prepare a food using a recipe that requires the use of three kitchen centers. Analyze how organizing a kitchen by work centers helped ease and speed this food preparation task. (7.1)

2. ***Safety demonstration:*** Perform a skit for your class showing how three different kinds of kitchen accidents can happen. Take suggestions from the class about how they could have been avoided. (7.2)

3. ***Food science lab:*** Observe spoilage in fresh fruits with this experiment. Label small samples of fresh fruits with the type of fruit and the date. Leave the samples out at room temperature (along with a sign warning "Do Not Eat"). Each day, record changes in appearance and smell. (7.4)

4. Answers will vary. Examples: Model safe work habits; allow them to watch you; assign them simple tasks.

5. *Any two:* Wear clean clothes covered with clean apron; remove dangling jewelry, roll up long sleeves and tie back long hair; scrub hands for 20 seconds before handling food; use gloves if you have open wound on hands; scrub hands immediately after using toilet or blowing nose; do not touch face, hair, etc., while working with food.

6. Letting microorganisms from one food get into another. Use clean dishcloths and sponges; wash top of can before opening; use clean spoon each time you taste food; keep pets out of the kitchen; use separate towels for wiping hands and drying dishes.

4. **Demonstration:** Collect items from home or school that could be recycled or reused (such as aluminum cans, newpapers, and glass jars). Give a demonstration showing how to prepare and sort items for recycling. Have your classmates offer suggestions for how to reuse some of the items. (7.5)

THINKING CRITICALLY

1. **Recognizing assumptions:** Elaine's mother uses a toaster with a damaged wire. She says that the toaster still works and refuses to have it fixed or buy a new one. What assumption is she making? Is it a correct one? (7.2)

2. **Predicting consequences:** What result might you expect if foods cooked for a picnic are left out on the table and eaten over the course of four or five hours? (7.3)

3. **Distinguishing between fact and opinion:** "I use up leftovers, even if they smell a little spoiled. After all, if I boil food long enough, it can't make people sick." Which of these sentences is a fact? Which is an opinion? Defend your answer. (7.4)

4. **Recognizing alternatives:** What alternatives can you suggest to reduce, reuse, and recycle the products your family uses? (7.5)

MAKING DECISIONS AND SOLVING PROBLEMS

What Would You Do?

1. Your family has a hard time functioning in the kitchen on weekday mornings. Some of you make bag lunches while others are preparing a quick breakfast. As family members get in each other's way, there are frequent accidents. (7.1, 7.2)

2. Your grandmother lives alone. Her vision and hearing are poor, but she insists on preparing her own meals. You are worried about her safety. (7.2)

3. You and your mother eat two heat-and-serve frozen meat pies out of the four purchased at the supermarket. Early the next morning, you are both nauseated and have severe diarrhea. Two of the meat pies remain in the freezer. You had planned to have them for supper the next night. (7.3)

4. You are preparing a tossed salad, hamburgers, and baked beans for your family when the power goes out. You are concerned about keeping the food safe to eat. (7.4)

LINKING YOUR STUDIES

1. **Health:** Using a first aid book as a reference, make a list of first aid supplies for the major kinds of kitchen accidents. Assemble a first aid kit for your kitchen at home, using a shoebox or other container. (7.2)

2. **Math:** Some species of bacteria can double their numbers every 20 minutes. At this rate, if you started with one bacterium, how many would there be after five hours? (7.3)

3. **Health:** Working with a partner, use library resources to find information about treatment for each of the foodborne illnesses in the chart on pages 198-199. (7.3)

4. **Science:** Investigate and report on the effects of water pollution on drinking water supplies. (7.5)

LEARNING BY DOING

Answers to "Learning by Doing" activities will vary. Evaluate students according to the effort they put into the activities as well as their results.

THINKING CRITICALLY

1. That since the toaster always has worked without a problem, there is no danger; not a correct assumption. The damaged wire is a potential fire hazard.

2. Microorganisms will multiply in the food, causing it to spoil.

3. Facts: the person uses leftovers even when they're spoiled; she boils the leftovers. Opinions: the food might be spoiled, "It can't make people sick."

4. Answers will vary.

MAKING DECISIONS AND SOLVING PROBLEMS

Answers to "Making Decisions and Solving Problems" questions will vary. Encourage students to give reasons for their answers.

LINKING YOUR STUDIES

1. You may wish to ask students to form groups to brainstorm the items to be included in the first aid kit.

2. 32,768

3. Answers will vary.

4. Answers will vary.

219

7. *Any two:* Place food in refrigerator; put package in water-tight plastic bag and submerge in cold water (change water every 30 minutes); use microwave oven.

8. The length of time a food can be stored and still retain its quality.

9. *Any two:* Stack packages closely together so they will stay cold; separate frozen meat, poultry, and fish from other foods; put dry ice into freezer.

10. Answers will vary. Examples: use dishcloths instead of paper towels to wipe up spills; use cloth napkins instead of paper ones; buy or make cloth bags to carry groceries; choose items in reusable or recyclable containers rather than disposable ones.

Planning the Chapter

Chapter Overview

Section 8.1: Recipe Basics

Section 8.2: Measuring Ingredients

Section 8.3: Changing a Recipe

Section 8.4: Preparation Tasks

Section 8.5: Time Management

Introducing the Chapter

Motivators

- Have students work in groups to prepare a simple recipe. Give groups no instruction regarding recipe use, measuring, yield adjustments, preparation techniques, time management, or teamwork. Evaluate the results. What problems did students encounter? What additional information did they need? Ask students to identify skills needed to prepare a recipe.

- Show a video of someone preparing a recipe. Ask the class to identify the knowledge and skills needed.

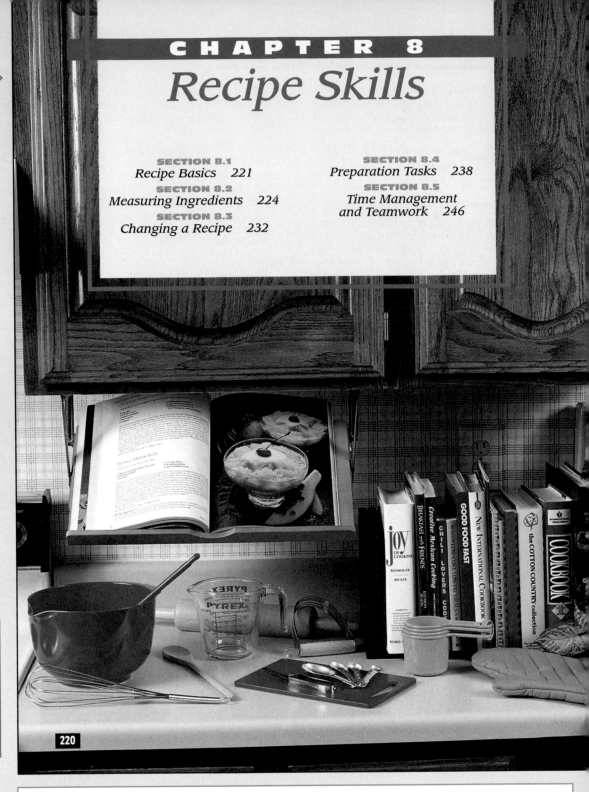

CHAPTER 8

Recipe Skills

220

Cooperative Learning Suggestions

As a review exercise, use a Simultaneous Roundtable activity. Prepare a list of food preparation tasks the class has studied with a blank line opposite each task. Have students move about the room to find someone who can describe the correct procedure for performing each task. Have students get the signature of the person who successfully describes the procedure for performing each task. Ask students to continue to move around the room to newly forming clusters of two, three, or four students until a signature has been collected for each task listed.

OBJECTIVES

After studying this section, you should be able to:
- List the kinds of information a good recipe provides.
- Give guidelines for evaluating and collecting recipes.

LOOK FOR THIS TERM

yield

A recipe is a set of directions for making a food or beverage. Your success in using it depends on how well the recipe is written, as well as your ability to understand and follow the directions.

Recipe Information

A well-written, complete recipe includes the following:

❖ **List of ingredients and amounts.** The ingredients are generally listed in the order they are used, which makes it easier for you to follow the recipe and not omit an ingredient. Amounts of ingredients are also given.

❖ **Number of servings or amount the recipe makes.** This is known as the **yield.**

❖ **Essential information about temperature, time, and equipment.** This may include pan size and type, oven temperature or power, and cooking time. The recipe will also indicate whether a conventional oven should be preheated.

❖ **Step-by-step directions.** The directions should be clear and easy to follow. Steps may be numbered so you won't skip any or lose your place. Some recipes include more than one set of directions, such as a conventional method and a microwave method.

❖ **Nutrition information.** This information is not essential, but it can be useful in helping you choose nutritious recipes. Typical nutrition information tells you the amount of calories, fat, and sodium for each serving of the food. Some recipes also include information about carbohydrates, protein, cholesterol, saturated and unsaturated fats, fiber, vitamins, and minerals.

Section 8.1: Recipe Basics **221**

Introducing the Section

Motivators

- Obtain one or more recipes dating from the 1800s or earlier. (Check your public library for reprints of old cookbooks.) Distribute copies and/or show on the overhead projector. Ask students how the recipe differs from those used today. What might account for the differences? What information should a recipe provide?

- Distribute a variety of cookbooks to the class. Ask students to choose a cookbook they like and to explain why they chose it.

Objectives

- Have students read the section objectives. Discuss the purpose of studying this section.

Vocabulary

- Pronounce the terms listed under "Look for These Terms." Have students find the terms and their definitions in the section.

Guided Reading

- Have students look at the headings within Section 8.1 to preview the concepts that will be discussed.

- Have students read the section and complete the appropriate part of the Chapter 8 Study Guide in the *Student Workbook.*

Teacher's Classroom Resources—Section 8.1

Refer to these resources in the TCR package:

Reproducible Lesson Plans
Student Workbook
Extending the Text

Reteaching Activities
Section Quizzes
Testmaker Software
Color Transparencies

8.1

Teaching . . .

- **Recipe Information**
- **Collecting Recipes**

(text pages 221-223)

Comprehension Check

1. Ask students to list and describe he elements of a well-written, complete recipe. *(list of ingredients and amounts; yield; temperature, time, equipment information; step-by-step directions; nutrition information)*

2. Discuss the advantage of compiling your own collection of recipes.

3. Ask students to explain why it's important to analyze a new recipe before you use it. What questions should you ask?

Student Experiences

1. **Display:** Display a variety of methods for organizing recipes. Discuss potential advantages and disadvantages of each method. *(Key skill: evaluating)*

2. **Recipe Comparison:** Have students study recipes written in different formats. Ask which recipe format seems easiest to follow. Identify the factors that affect the ease of using recipes written in each format. *(Key skills: reading, comparing)*

3. **Recipe Rewrites:** Have students choose a recipe and identify the parts of the recipe. Then have them rewrite the recipe a different format. *(Key skills: writing, analysis)*

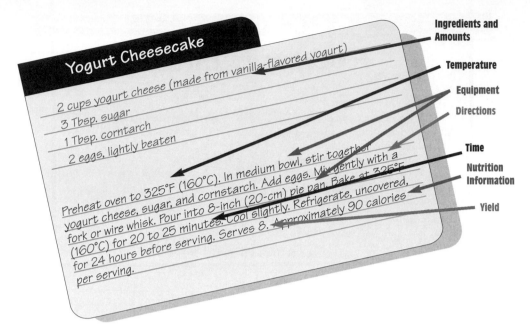

A well-written recipe should include all of the above information in an easy-to-follow format.

The standard, or most common, format for a recipe lists the ingredients first, in the order they are to be used. Then the assembly directions, which tell how to put the ingredients together, are given. This format, the clearest and easiest to follow, is used for the recipes in this book.

Less common recipe formats combine the ingredients and assembly directions. You may see a recipe written this way on a food package, for example. It takes less space than the standard format.

Collecting Recipes

The most reliable recipe source is a basic cookbook that gives standard recipes for common foods. You probably have several in

your classroom. If you don't find one you like, your teacher can make recommendations.

Once you have a basic cookbook, you can expand your recipe collection in whatever direction you choose, depending on the kinds of food you enjoy. For example, Janice collects vegetarian recipes. Recipe sources include your friends, magazines, newspapers, and the labels on many basic foods.

Recipes aren't always accurate or complete. When you first read a recipe, analyze it. Are basic ingredients missing? Are descriptions of ingredients clear? Is a direction included for each ingredient? Do you have all the information needed to prepare the recipe? If the answer to any of these questions is "no," look for another recipe.

Special Needs Strategies

Vision Impaired: Provide students with recipes printed in large type on 6" x 8" cards.
Learning Disabled: For learning disabled students or students with limited reading ability, create picture recipes.

What are the advantages of starting your own recipe collection?

Once you've tried a new recipe, you can decide whether to add it to your list of favorites. If you plan to use a new recipe on a special occasion, try it ahead of time first and evaluate the results.

Organizing your recipes can help you find them when you need them. You might want to paste your recipes on index cards and use a card file box or a shoe box for storage.

Healthy Attitudes

If you choose recipes wisely, you can prepare homemade meals that are lower in fat, sodium, and sugar than packaged convenience foods. Why not start a collection of recipes that are good-tasting, healthy, and easy to prepare?

Section 8.1 Review

RECALL THE FACTS

1. What basic information should be found in a well-written recipe?

2. What information does the yield of a recipe give?

3. Identify three things to look for when evaluating a new recipe.

DISCUSS YOUR IDEAS

4. Discuss the characteristics that make it difficult or easy to follow a recipe.

APPLY YOUR LEARNING

5. Find a recipe on a food package or in a magazine or newspaper. Analyze it to determine whether you would want to try it, using the guidelines given in this section. Write down any questions you have about the recipe. What are some ways that this recipe could be improved?

Section 8.1: Recipe Basics   223

Completing the Section

Review

- Ask students to summarize the main ideas in this section.
- Have students complete the Section Review. (Answers appear below.)

Evaluation

- Give students a recipe. Ask them to identify its parts and explain how each part helps aids in meal planning and food preparation.
- Have students take the quiz for section 8.1. (Refer to the *Section Quizzes* booklet or construct your own quiz using the *Testmaker Software.*)

Reteaching

- Have students choose a favorite recipe and identify its parts. Are any missing?
- Refer to the *Reteaching Activities* booklet for the Section 8.1 activity sheet.

Enrichment

- Have interested students trace the history of a recipe (or recipes) for a favorite food.

Closure

- Lead a class discussion on the importance of clarity and specific instructions in recipes.

Answers to Section Review

1. A list of ingredients and amounts; yield; information about temperature, time, and equipment; step-by-step instructions; nutrition information.

2. Number of servings or amount the recipe makes.

3. *Any three:* Missing ingredients, clear descriptions of ingredients, directions for use of each ingredient, all the necessary information.

4. Answers will vary.

5. Answers will vary.

SECTION 8.2
Measuring Ingredients

Introducing the Section

Motivators

- Demonstrate how pioneer women used their hands, bowls, teacups, and other containers to measure ingredients. Did these techniques work? Why? Why was it difficult for these cooks to share their recipes with others?

- Demonstrate that a cup is not always a cup. Pack flour into a cup and level, then sift the flour onto waxed paper, spoon lightly into the cup, and level with a spatula. How much was left over? Fill a cup with brown sugar (without packing) and level. Pack the sugar down. How much did the cup lack being full?

Objectives

- Have students read the section objectives. Discuss the purpose of studying this section.

Vocabulary

- Pronounce the terms listed under "Look for These Terms." Have students find the terms and their definitions in the section.

Guided Reading

- Have students look at the headings within Section 8.1 to preview the concepts that will be discussed.

- Have students read the section and complete the appropriate part of the Chapter 8 Study Guide in the *Student Workbook*.

OBJECTIVES

After studying this section, you should be able to:

- Identify customary and metric units of measure.
- Identify measuring tools.
- Describe the proper procedures for measuring various types of ingredients.

LOOK FOR THESE TERMS

volume
equivalent

Dominic bought a glass of lemonade at his little brother Carl's lemonade stand. It was so sweet he couldn't finish it. "How much sugar did you put in this?" Dominic asked. "The directions said 1 cup," Carl replied, "so I just used Mom's big coffee mug. Why?" As Dominic and his brother found out, measuring properly can be very important.

Units of Measurement

In a recipe, amounts of ingredients can be given in several ways. Most ingredients are measured by **volume,** or the amount of space they take up. For example, a salad recipe might list "1 cup cooked pasta." Some ingredients are measured by weight, or heaviness, such as a pound of fish filets. A few ingredients may be measured by the number of items, such as one medium banana or two eggs.

Accurate measurements are the key to successful food preparation.

Teacher's Classroom Resources—Section 8.2

Refer to these resources in the TCR package:

Reproducible Lesson Plans

Student Workbook

Extending the Text

Reteaching Activities

Foods Lab Resources

Section Quizzes

Testmaker Software

Color Transparencies

In addition, there are two different systems of measurement. The customary system is the system of weights and measures used in the United States. In every other country, the metric system is used. The United States is gradually moving toward adopting the metric system, especially with increasing world trade. Most recipes use either one measuring system or the other. Some, like the recipes in this book, include both customary and metric units.

Customary Units

Following are the most common customary units found in recipes. Often they are abbreviated, as shown in parentheses.

❖ *Volume:* teaspoon (tsp.), tablespoon (Tbsp.), cup (c.), fluid ounce (fl. oz.), pint (pt.), quart (qt.), gallon (gal.)
❖ *Weight:* ounce (oz.), pound (lb.)
❖ *Temperature:* degrees Fahrenheit (°F)
❖ *Length:* inches (in.)

Notice that weight may be measured in ounces. This kind of ounce is not the same as a fluid ounce, which is a measure of volume, not weight. Think of the difference between a cup of popcorn and a cup of water. Both take up the same amount of space—8 fluid ounces. However, they do not weigh the same. The water is heavier. To find out how much each weighs, you would use a scale, not a measuring cup.

Metric Units

The metric system is based on multiples of ten. For instance, just as there are 100 pennies in one dollar, there are 100 centimeters in one meter. Once you become familiar with it, the metric system is easier to use than the customary system.

Here are the metric units and symbols most often found in recipes:

❖ *Volume:* milliter (mL), liter (L)
❖ *Weight:* milligram (mg), gram (g), kilogram (kg)
❖ *Temperature:* degree Celsius (°C)
❖ *Length:* centimeter (cm)

Equivalents

You can express the same amount in different ways by using different units of measure. This is called an **equivalent**. For instance, 4 tablespoons of flour is the same amount as 1/4 cup of flour, or about 50 milliliters. The chart on page 226 shows equivalents for food preparation.

Equipment for Measuring

A well-equipped kitchen includes the following measuring tools. Each has specific uses, as you will learn.

❖ *Dry measures* usually come in a set of several sizes. A typical customary set includes 1/4 cup, 1/3 cup, 1/2 cup, and 1 cup measures. A metric set includes 50 mL, 125 mL, and 250 mL measures.

Dry measuring cups are used for accurate measuring of dry ingredients by volume.

Teaching . . .

• Units of Measurement

(text pages 224-225)

Comprehension Check

1. Ask students to list the most common units for volume, weight, temperature, and length in the customary and metric systems.
2. Discuss the difference between an ounce and a fluid ounce. *(An ounce is a unit for measuring weight; a fluid ounce is a unit for measuring volume.)* In what way does the metric system make this distinction clearer?

Student Experiences

1. **Measurement Review:** Review the two different systems of measurement, customary and metric. Which system is currently used in recipes in the United States? Why is the United States moving toward adopting the metric system? *(Key skill: math)*
2. **Chart Making:** Have students create a chart showing how volume, weight, temperature, and length are measured using customary units and metric units. *(Key skill: reading charts and tables)*
3. **Equivalent Measures Cards:** Have students work in groups to make cards listing equivalent measurements. Have students use the cards to play rummy. Give points for correctly matching equivalent measurements. *(Key skill: math)*

Special Needs Strategies

Physically Disabled: For students with physical disabilities that limit the use of their hands, provide long-handled dry measuring cups and easy-to-grasp liquid measuring cups.

Teaching . . .

• Equipment for Measuring

(text pages 225-227)

Comprehension Check

1. Ask students to describe measuring tools commonly found in a well-equipped kitchen *(liquid measuring cups, dry measures, and measuring spoons)*

2. Discuss the importance of using standard measuring cups and spoons when measuring amounts for recipes. What might happen if you used nonstandard measures? *(The dish may not turn out right, since nonstandard measures may cause you to use too much or too little of an ingredient.)*

3. Ask students to describe the intended purpose of a straight-edge spatula and a rubber scraper. What other utensils might be useful? *(To level dry measures and to make sure all of an ingredient has been scraped out of a measuring cup.)*

4. Ask students to explain why it is important to understand equivalencies when they use combinations of measures. *(Equivalencies allow people to use combinations of measures accurately.)*

Equivalents

Customary Measure	Customary Equivalent	Approximate Metric Equivalent
Volume		
1 tsp.		5 mL
1 Tbsp.	3 tsp.	15 mL
1 fl. oz.	2 Tbsp.	30 mL
1/4 cup		50 mL
1/3 cup		75 mL
1/2 cup		125 mL
2/3 cup		150 mL
3/4 cup		175 mL
1 cup	8 fl. oz. or 16 Tbsp.	250 mL
1 pt.	2 cups or 16 fl. oz.	500 mL
1 qt.	2 pt. or 4 cups or 32 fl. oz.	1000 mL or 1 L
1 gal.	4 qt.	4 L
Weight		
1 oz.		28 g
1 lb.	16 oz.	500 g
2 lb.	32 oz.	1000 g or 1 kg
Temperatures		
0°F		-18°C
32°F		0°C
350°F		180°C
400°F		200°C

More About Equivalents

When raw foods are cooked or prepared in some manner, their volume changes. Here are equivalents of some basic foods, before and after preparation:

1 cup dried beans = about 2 c. cooked
1 cup pasta = about 2 c. cooked

1 slice bread = 3/4 c. soft or 1/4 c. fine dry crumbs
14 graham crackers = 1 c. crushed
1/4 lb. American, Swiss, or cheddar cheese = 1 c. grated
1 medium apple = 1 c. sliced
1 medium banana = 1/3 c. mashed

- ❖ *Liquid measuring cups* are transparent and have measurement markings on the side. They are typically marked in fractions of a cup, fluid ounces, and milliliters. There is a headspace of about 1/4 inch above the top marking, which makes it easier to move a filled cup without spilling. A spout makes pouring easier. Common sizes are 1 cup (250 mL) and 2 cup (500 mL).
- ❖ *Measuring spoons* generally come in a set of four or five. Most customary sets include these sizes: 1/4 teaspoon, 1/2 teaspoon, 1 teaspoon, and 1 tablespoon. Metric sets include 1 mL, 2 mL, 5 mL, 15 mL and 25 mL measures.

Always use standard measuring cups and spoons. A standard 1-cup measuring cup, no matter how it is shaped or designed, always holds the same amount. Nonstandard items, such as cups and spoons used for serving food, vary in size.

Other helpful measuring tools include a straight-edge spatula for leveling off dry ingredients, a rubber scraper for removing ingredients from measuring cups, and a food scale for measuring ingredients by weight.

Measuring spoons come in a set of four or five spoons. You may need to use more than one spoon to measure an ingredient. How would you measure 3/4 teaspoon?

Using Combinations of Measures

When using measuring cups and spoons, you will sometimes need to use a combination of cup or spoon sizes to get the amount you need. For instance, if you need 3/4 cup flour, use the 1/2 cup and 1/4 cup measures. For 2/3 cup, measure 1/3 cup twice.

Sometimes you may need to measure unusual amounts of an ingredient, such as 5/8 cup. How would you measure such an amount?

First, measure out the closest amount you can with a standard size measure. For example, the closest measure to 5/8 cup is 1/2 cup (since 1/2 = 4/8). This leaves you with 1/8 cup left to measure. Since 1/8 cup is a small amount, you will need to use measuring spoons. This is where equivalents come in handy. Remember, there are 16 tablespoons in one cup. Therefore, 1/8 cup equals 2 tablespoons (1/8 x 16 = 16/8 = 2). You would add 2 tablespoons to 1/2 cup to get 5/8 cup.

You can also remove small amounts from a measuring cup to get the exact amount called for in a recipe. To get 7/8 cup milk, you would first measure one cup, then remove 2 tablespoons (1/8 cup). How would you measure 3/8 cup?

Techniques for Measuring

In addition to the correct tools, the proper procedures are essential to accurate measuring. The guidelines that follow will help you.

Measuring Liquids

Liquid measuring cups are used to measure all liquids, including oils and syrups. To measure liquids, follow these steps:
1. Set the cup on a level surface. If you try to hold it in your hand, you may tip it and get an inaccurate reading.

Student Experiences

1. **Display:** Prepare a display of tools used for measuring. Differentiate between dry and liquid measuring cups. Point out that measuring spoons can be used for measuring small amounts of both liquid and dry ingredients. Stress the importance of using standard measuring cups and spoons. *(Key skill: observation)*

2. **Demonstration:** Allow students to experiment with liquid measuring cups and dry measures to demonstrate for themselves the importance of using the correct type of measure. Ask students to write a brief report describing their experiments and results. *(Key skills: experimentation, writing)*

3. **Measuring Math:** Provide students with a list of ingredients in amounts that require the use of combinations of measures. Ask students to identify the types and sizes of cups or spoons needed. *(Key skill: math)*

1 medium orange = 1/3 c. juice and 4 tsp. grated peel
6-7 large eggs = 1 c. egg whites
1 medium potato = 1 c. sliced or 1/2 c. mashed
1 lb. cabbage = 5 c. shredded
1 lb. mushrooms = 2 c. sliced, cooked

1 medium onion = 1/2 c. chopped
1 lb. boneless raw meat = 2 c. cooked and chopped
1 lb cooked meat = 3 c. chopped

Teaching . . .

- **Measuring Liquids**
- **Measuring Dry Ingredients**

(text pages 227-229)

Comprehension Check

1. Ask students to list the steps for measuring liquids. How should you measure 1/8 teaspoon of a liquid if you do not have a 1/8 tsp. measure? *(See steps on page 227.)*

2. Ask students to explain the proper procedure for using dry measures. *(See steps on page 228.)*

3. Ask students to explain why some ingredients need to be sifted. What ingredients should not be sifted? *(Sifting loosens packed flour and sugar before measuring for more accurate measurement. Whole-grain flour and brown sugar should not be sifted.)*

Student Experiences

1. **Measuring Liquids:** Have students work in groups of three. Each one person in each group should fill a glass measuring cup with 3/8 cup, 1/4 cup, 1/2 cup 5/8 cup, or 7/8 cup water, making sure the measurement is accurate. He or she should not tell the other students how much water is in the measuring cup. Have another student read the measurement from eye level. Have the third student read the measurement by looking down into the cup. Ask students to write a paragraph explaining their results. *(Key skills: experimentation, writing)*

2. **Demonstrations:** Have students work in small groups to demonstrate procedures for measuring dry and liquid ingredients. *(Key skill: laboratory techniques)*

Check the measurement of liquids at eye level. What might happen if you looked down at the cup?

2. Carefully pour the liquid into the measuring cup.

3. Bend down to check the measurement at eye level for an accurate reading.

4. Add more liquid or pour off excess, if needed, until the top of the liquid is at the desired measurement mark.

5. Pour the ingredient into the mixing container. If needed, use a rubber scraper to empty the cup completely.

For small amounts of liquids, use measuring spoons. To measure 1/8 teaspoon of a liquid ingredient, dribble it into the 1/4 teaspoon measure until it looks half full.

Measuring Dry Ingredients

Dry measures are used to measure dry ingredients such as flour, sugar, and dry beans. They can also be used for foods such as diced meat, chopped vegetables, and yogurt. Here are the steps to take when measuring dry ingredients:

228 Chapter 8: Recipe Skills

1. Put a piece of waxed paper under the measuring cup to catch any extra ingredient. Don't measure an ingredient while holding the cup over the bowl in which you are mixing.

2. Fill the cup with the ingredient. Some ingredients must be spooned into the cup lightly. Others can be packed down if specified in the recipe.

3. Level off the top of the cup using the straight edge of a spatula. Let the excess fall on the waxed paper. Put the excess back into the original container.

4. Pour the ingredient into the mixture. With semisolid foods, such as yogurt, use a rubber scraper to make sure all of the ingredient has been emptied out of the cup.

As a general rule, spoon flour and sugar into the measuring cup lightly. If you shake the cup or pack it down, you will measure too much of the ingredient.

When measuring dry ingredients, use waxed paper to catch spills. Carefully level off the ingredient with the straight edge of a spatula, table knife, or rubber scraper.

Food and Nutrition Science

Meniscus: Have students pour water into a clear measuring cup. Tell them to look carefully at the surface of the water and note the *meniscus*, the curve formed by the surface of the liquid. Explain that when you measure clear liquids, you should make sure that the bottom of the meniscus is at the marking for the amount you want. Have students practice measuring water and other clear liquids. Walk around and make sure they are measuring properly.

Some recipes call for sifted flour. Put the flour through the sifter, then measure it. Never sift whole-grain flours—they are too coarse to go through the sifter. Instead, stir whole-grain flour with a spoon before measuring.

Sift powdered sugar before you measure it. Granulated sugar can be sifted to remove lumps, if needed.

Brown sugar contains moisture and tends to be fluffy, so pack it down with a spoon. When you empty the cup, the sugar should hold its shape.

For amounts smaller than 1/4 cup or 50 mL, use measuring spoons. Dry ingredients are usually measured by leveling them off evenly at the rim of the spoon. Sometimes, however, a recipe calls for a "heaping" measure. In this case, the ingredient is not leveled off. A heaping measure will give almost twice the amount you would get in a leveled-off measure.

If you need 1/8 teaspoon of a dry ingredient, fill the 1/4 teaspoon measure and level it off. Then, using the tip of a straight-edge spatula or table knife, remove half the ingredient.

Still smaller amounts of dry ingredients are measured as a dash or a pinch, the amount that can be held between the thumb and finger. These amounts are generally used for herbs and spices.

Measuring Fats

Fats, such as margarine or shortening, can be measured in several ways.

❖ **Stick method.** Use this for fat that comes in 1/4 lb. sticks, such as butter or margarine. The wrapper is marked in tablespoons and in fractions of a cup. Simply cut off the amount you need.

❖ **Dry measuring cup method.** Pack the fat down into the cup, pressing firmly to fill in all spaces. Level off the top. Using a rubber scraper, empty as much of the fat as possible. Use the same technique when using measuring spoons to measure fat.

❖ **Water displacement method.** This method involves combining fat with water in a liquid measuring cup. It requires some math. First, subtract the amount of fat to be measured from one cup. The difference is the amount of water to pour into the measuring cup. (For example, to measure 2/3 cup of shortening, use 1/3 cup of water.) Next, spoon the fat into the cup, making sure it is completely below the level of the water. When the water reaches the 1-cup level, you have the right amount of fat. Pour off the water and remove the fat with a rubber scraper.

Unless a recipe specifies a heaping spoonful, level off the measuring spoon.

The water displacement method is one way to measure solid fats accurately.

Section 8.2: Measuring Ingredients   **229**

8.2

Teaching . . .

- **Measuring Fats**
- **Measuring by Weight**

(text pages 229-230)

Comprehension Check

1. Ask students to list and describe the three methods for measuring fats. *(See list on page 229.)*

2. Ask students to explain why someone might want to use the water displacement method. *(Some types of fat are difficult to measure using either of the other two techniques. These fats must be measured by water displacement.)*

3. Discuss the proper way to use a food scale. Why is it important to adjust the scale to 0 after you place an empty container on the scale? *(See steps on page 230; because you do not want to include the weight of the container.)*

Student Experiences

1. **Demonstration:** Demonstrate how to measure fats using the stick method, the dry measuring cup method, and the water displacement method. Discuss when to use each method. *(Key skill: measurement)*

2. **Practice Weighing:** Have students practice weighing various ingredients in different types of containers. *(Key skill: measurement)*

More About Measuring

Some foods present special measuring challenges. For example, the amount of spaghetti needed for a recipe is usually given in terms of unit size (1 package) or weight (1 oz.). You can also use a spaghetti measure, a round plastic disk with four different sizes of holes. It can be used to measure 1 to 4 portions of uncooked spaghetti (2 oz. per portion).

Completing the Section

Review

* Ask students to summarize the main ideas in this section.
* Have students complete the Section Review. (Answers appear below.)

Evaluation

* Give students a recipe and ask them to identify the measuring tools needed to measure the ingredients properly.
* Have students take the quiz for section 8.2. (Refer to the *Section Quizzes* booklet or construct your own quiz using the *Testmaker Software*.)

Reteaching

* Have students quiz each other on equivalents by giving a customary measure and asking for an equivalent.
* Have students correctly measure 1 c. flour, 1/3 c. oats, 1/8 c. chopped celery, 1/4 c. brown sugar, 2/3 c. water, 1/2 c. shortening, and 2 Tbsp. margarine.
* Refer to the *Reteaching Activities* booklet for the Section 8.2 activity sheet.

Enrichment

* Have groups work with water, flour, and ordinary tableware to discover how close they can come to standard measurements.

Closure

* Lead a discussion on the importance of accuracy in measuring ingredients.

Measuring by Weight

As you have read, the amounts of some recipe ingredients may be given by weight. Sometimes you can buy the exact weight of food you need, such as an 8-oz. package of spaghetti. If that's not practical, a food scale comes in handy.

To use a food scale:

1. Decide what container you will put the food in. Place the empty container on the scale.

2. Adjust the scale until it reads zero. Usually this is done by turning a knob.

3. Add the food to the container until the scale shows the desired amount.

Remember, ounces of weight is not the same as fluid ounces. Do not use a dry or liquid measuring cup to measure an ingredient when the amount is given by weight. The measurement will not be accurate.

Some ingredients are normally measured by weight. Both customary and metric scales are available.

230   Chapter 8: Recipe Skills

Section 8.2 Review

RECALL THE FACTS

1. One cup is equivalent to how many fluid ounces? How many tablespoons? About how many milliliters?

2. How does a liquid measuring cup differ from a dry measuring cup?

3. Describe the basic steps you would follow to measure 2/3 cup of sifted flour.

4. Name three ways to measure fats.

DISCUSS YOUR IDEAS

5. Why is accuracy so important when measuring ingredients?

APPLY YOUR LEARNING

6. Find a recipe with at least 10 ingredients. List all the measuring tools you would need to measure the ingredients. Describe any special techniques needed.

■ Answers to Section Review ■

1. 8 fl. oz.; 16 tbsp.; about 250 mL.
2. It has clear sides and a pouring spout; it contains gradient markings on the side in fractions of a cup, fluid ounces, and milliliters; it has room above the 1-cup mark-ing to allow you to carry a liquid without spilling it.
3. Sift the flour and spoon it carefully into a 1-cup dry measure. Level the top with a straight-edge spatula.
4. Stick method, dry measuring cup method, and water displacement method.
5. A slight variation in one ingredient may be enough to spoil a recipe.
6. Answers will vary.

Thinking About the Recipe

Read the recipe for "Chocolate Citrus Shake" and answer the following questions.

1. For which ingredient(s) would you use a liquid measuring cup? Dry measuring cups? Measuring spoons?
2. What should be done to the powdered sugar before measuring it?

Chocolate Citrus Shake

Key Skill: Measuring Ingredients

Using the Recipe

- Have students read the recipe and discuss each step. Review safety and sanitation procedures that apply to this recipe. Remind students to be careful with the sharp blade on the blender, and caution them never to run the blender without first placing the cover on it.

- Have each lab team fill out a work plan. (See the *Foods Lab Resources* booklet.)

- Have students check off the ingredients and equipment listed on the recipe worksheet and prepare the recipe.

- Have students complete the evaluation and questions on the recipe worksheet.

See Also . . .

The *Foods Lab Resources* booklet for the "Chocolate Citrus Shake" recipe worksheet and other recipe alternatives.

Chocolate Citrus Shake

Customary	Ingredients	Metric
1 cup	Orange juice	250 mL
1/3 cup	Plain nonfat yogurt	75 mL
1/2 cup	Crushed ice	125 mL
1/2 medium	Banana	1/2 medium
1/2 cup	Nonfat dry milk	125 mL
1/4 cup	Powdered sugar	50 mL
2 Tbsp.	Unsweetened cocoa	30 mL
1 tsp.	Strawberry extract	5 mL

Yield: Three 8-oz. (250-mL) servings

Directions

1. Place all ingredients in blender container.
2. Cover and blend until smooth.
3. Pour into glasses and serve immediately.

Nutrition Information

Per serving (approximate): 160 calories, 7 g protein, 31 g carbohydrate, 1 g fat, 0 mg cholesterol, 85 mg sodium

---

Answers to Thinking About the Recipe

1. Liquid measuring cup: orange juice, yogurt; dry measuring cups: crushed ice, nonfat dry milk, powdered sugar; measuring spoons: cocoa, strawberry extract.

2. It should be sifted to add air and remove any lumps.

SECTION 8.3

Changing a Recipe

Introducing the Section

Motivators

- Provide students with a vanilla pudding recipe. Ask students what changes would be needed to increase or decrease the number of servings (yield). What changes would be needed to vary the flavor of the pudding? What changes could be made in the recipe to decrease the amount of fat?

- Ask students how they think new recipes are created. What would a cook need to know to create a new recipe? Why might a cook want to change a recipe? What would a cook need to know to change a recipe?

Objectives

- Have students read the section objectives. Discuss the purpose of studying this section.

Vocabulary

- Pronounce the terms listed under "Look for These Terms." Have students find the terms and their definitions in the section.

Guided Reading

- Have students look at the headings within Section 8.3 to preview the concepts that will be discussed.

- Have students read the section and complete the appropriate part of the Chapter 8 Study Guide in the *Student Workbook*.

OBJECTIVES
After studying this section, you should be able to:
- Explain how to increase or decrease recipe yield.
- Give basic strategies for changing a recipe to decrease fats and sodium.
- Describe how high altitudes affect the cooking process.

LOOK FOR THIS TERM
desired yield

Heather was in the middle of making drop biscuits when she found she didn't have any buttermilk. It didn't stop her. She substituted a mixture of skim milk and vinegar for the buttermilk and continued with the recipe.

Why Change a Recipe?

From time to time, you may find that, like Heather, you have to change a recipe. Perhaps you don't have one of the ingredients and can't take the time to go out and buy it. You might want to substitute a more healthful or less expensive ingredient for the one in the recipe. You might want to increase or decrease the recipe yield.

The success of recipe substitutions depends on choosing appropriate substitutes and measuring accurately. Chopped dates worked well as a substitute for raisins in this recipe.

Teacher's Classroom Resources—Section 8.3

Refer to these resources in the TCR package:
Reproducible Lesson Plans
Student Workbook
Extending the Text

Reteaching Activities
Section Quizzes
Testmaker Software
Color Transparencies

Changes are more likely to be successful in some recipes than others. Mixtures such as salads, stir-fried foods, soups, and stews can usually be changed easily. On the other hand, recipes for baked products such as muffins and custards are like chemical formulas. Each ingredient does a job in the recipe. They must be used in specific amounts in relation to each other. If one amount is changed or one ingredient is omitted, you risk failure.

If you change the ingredients in mixtures, you may notice a difference in flavor and texture. For instance, Olga loves to make tacos. She sometimes substitutes cooked turkey or chicken for beef, or omits the meat and doubles the refried beans. How might each change affect the flavor and texture of tacos?

Changing the Yield

Recipes may need to be changed if the yield—the number of servings the recipe makes—is not what you need. With basic math skills you can increase or decrease many recipes.

Changing the recipe is part of the tradition of preparing a *paélla* (pie-EL-uh). This Spanish main dish is based on rice, olive oil, and a spice called saffron. The rest of the ingredients are determined by the resourcefulness and creativity of the chef. Almost any meat or seafood can be used. Paellas also can include a great variety of legumes and vegetables, including broad beans, peas, onions, tomatoes, artichokes, and green peppers. What combination of ingredients do you think would make a good paella?

When increasing the yield of a recipe, you may also need to increase the size of the cooking container.

Most recipes, even those for baked goods, can be successfully doubled. Larger equipment may be needed for mixing and cooking, and cooking times often need adjustment. For most baked goods, it is best to use two baking pans of the original size rather than one larger one.

Many recipes for mixtures such as casseroles and soups can be not only doubled, but halved, tripled, and so on. The same basic process is used for both increasing and decreasing.

1. *Decide how many servings you need.* This amount is called the **desired yield.**

2. *Use the formula.* To adjust the yield of a recipe, the amount of each ingredient is multiplied by the same number. That number is determined by a simple formula:

desired yield ÷ original yield =

number to multiply by

Example: Your chili recipe serves eight and you need to serve four: 4 ÷ 8 = 0.5

Section 8.3: Changing a Recipe **233**

• Making Ingredient Substitutions

(text pages 234-236)

Comprehension Check

1. Ask students to name three general ways to reduce the amount of fat in a recipe. *(Substitute a different ingredient, change the amounts of ingredients, or change the cooking method.)*

2. Ask students to list several specific tips for cutting down the amount of fat in recipes. *(See the list on page 236.)*

3. Ask students to describe ways to cut down on the amount of sodium in recipes.

See Also . . .

- Section 9.3: "Microwave Cooking Techniques," text page 271.

- Section 9.4: "Conventional Cooking Techniques," text page 279.

---

3. **Multiply each ingredient amount by that number.** This keeps all the ingredients in the same proportion as in the original recipe.

4. **As needed, convert answers to logical, measurable amounts.** Sometimes the multiplication process gives you answers like 6/4 cups of flour or 12 tablespoons of brown sugar. Look again at the equivalents chart on page 226. Most amounts can be expressed in more than one unit of measurement. Think, too, about the equipment you will use for measuring. Then make any conversions needed.

   Examples: 6/4 cups flour = 1 ½ cups

   12 Tbsp. brown sugar = 3/4 cup

   1/6 cup oil = 2 Tbsp. + 2 tsp.

5. **Make any necessary adjustments to equipment, temperature, and time.** The depth of food in a pan affects how fast it cooks. Use pans that are the right size for the amount of food, not too large or small.

Making Ingredient Substitutions

If you don't have an ingredient you need for a recipe, you may be able to substitute another one. The chart on page 235 gives some common substitutions.

People who are concerned about healthy eating may have another reason to make substitutions. They want to reduce the fat and sodium in their diet.

Substitutions That Reduce Fat

Most recipes can be modified to reduce their fat content. Changes in the ingredients used or the amounts of ingredients can make a significant difference. A change in the cooking method can sometimes also reduce the amount of fat.

Tony decided to try to reduce the fat in his favorite spaghetti sauce. He tried two new versions. First, he reduced the amount of beef from 1 ½ pounds to 1 pound. He also

It may take some experimentation, but you can develop lower-fat versions of many of your favorite recipes.

Emergency Substitutions

For	Substitute
Baking chocolate, 1 oz.	3 Tbsp. cocoa + 1 Tbsp. butter or margarine
Buttermilk, 1 cup	1 Tbsp. lemon juice or vinegar + enough skim milk to measure 1 cup
Cake flour, 1 cup	7/8 cup sifted all-purpose flour
Garlic, 1 clove	1/8 tsp. garlic powder
Herbs, 1 tsp. dried, crushed	1 Tbsp. fresh chopped
Lemon juice	Equal amount vinegar
Milk, skim, 1 cup	1/4 cup nonfat dry milk powder + 7/8 cup water
Mustard, dry, 1 tsp.	1 Tbsp. prepared mustard
Onion, 1 small	1 Tbsp. minced dried onion or 1 tsp. onion powder
Rice, 1 cup cooked	1 cup cooked bulgur or millet
Spaghetti, uncooked, 6 oz. (3 cups cooked)	4 oz. (3 cups) uncooked egg noodles or 4 oz. (1 ¼ cup) uncooked macaroni
Sugar, granulated, 1 cup	2 cups sifted powdered sugar or 1cup packed brown sugar
Thickening, 1 ½ Tbsp. flour	1 Tbsp. quick-cooking tapioca or 1 Tbsp. cornstarch
Worcestershire sauce, 1 Tbsp.	1 Tbsp. soy sauce + dash red pepper sauce

Student Experiences

1. **Class Discussion:** Ask students to identify reasons for making ingredient substitutions. Discuss ways to reduce fat and sodium in recipes. How do some cookbooks make it easier to compare the amounts of fat and sodium in recipes? *(Key skill: health)*

2. **Adjusting Recipes:** Provide simple recipes for foods that are high in fat and/or sodium. Have students work in groups to adjust the recipes to reduce the amount of fat and sodium. *(Key skill: math)*

Lab Experience

Have students prepare a recipe twice, once as printed and once making several substitutions. Compare the results. Discuss the reasons for any differences.

chose ground round instead of ground beef because the round has less fat. Instead of cooking the onion and garlic in 2 tablespoons of oil, he used a nonstick pan and cooking spray. In the second version, he substituted 1 ¼ pounds of ground chicken meat for the ground beef. He increased the amount of seasoning because chicken has a less distinct flavor than beef. He again reduced the oil. His analysis: version one had more flavor than version two, but also more fat. He is still experimenting.

Section 8.3: Changing a Recipe   **235**

Thinking Skills

Reasoning: Discuss why it is important to check the availability of ingredients before you begin preparation. What problems might be encountered when ingredient substitutions are made? Give examples of situations where substitutions may not work.

Teaching . . .

• **High-Altitude Cooking**

(text pages 236-237)

Comprehension Check

1. Ask students to explain why pasta takes longer to cook at high altitudes. *(Water boils at a lower temperature.)*

2. Discuss the effects of low air pressure on baked goods. *(More gas bubbles tend to rise and escape, so the baked goods rise less and are heavy.)*

Student Experiences

1. Display: On a United States map, identify areas that are above 915 m (3000 ft.). Describe the effects of high altitude. What adjustments are needed when cooking at high altitudes? In what areas might people need to consider these adjustments? *(Key skill: geography)*

2. Reading Directions: Have students read directions for preparing baking mixes and note adjustments for high-altitude cooking. *(Key skill: reading)*

See Also . . .

• Section 21.1: "Ingredients and Techniques for Baking," text page 551.

• Section 21.3: "Yeast Breads and Rolls," text page 565.

Ground turkey breast meat was substituted for ground beef in this recipe. With a spicy sauce, there is little change in flavor but significantly less fat.

Here are some suggestions for reducing fat in recipes:

❖ Compare similar recipes and choose those with the least fat. Many recipes (like those in this book) show the fat content as grams of fat per serving.

❖ Use skim or low-fat dairy products in place of all or part of high-fat dairy products. For example, a mixture of half mayonnaise and half nonfat yogurt can be used instead of mayonnaise.

❖ Choose very lean cuts of meat for any recipe that requires meat.

❖ Substitute chicken or turkey for high-fat cuts of meat. Use fresh, ground, skinless turkey breast in place of ground beef for meatloaf, for instance. For more flavor, you may want to increase the seasonings.

❖ Use lemon juice, flavored vinegar, or fat-free dressings instead of salad dressings that contain oil.

❖ Substitute two egg whites for a whole egg.

❖ Use less oil for cooking food. Many foods will cook well using just a nonstick pan and vegetable oil cooking spray.

Substitutions That Reduce Sodium

Most people take in far more sodium than the body needs. This excess can have harmful effects. Here are some ideas for reducing sodium in recipes:

❖ Replace high-sodium ingredients such as broths, soy sauce, and tamari sauce with low-sodium versions.

❖ Use herbs, spices, lemon juice, or vinegar to enhance food flavors.

High-Altitude Cooking

Unless otherwise indicated, recipes are intended to be used at altitudes of 3,000 feet (about 1000 m) or below. If used at higher altitudes, they may not turn out as desired. Why? As the altitude gets higher, the air pressure gets lower. This affects food preparation in two main ways:

If you are cooking in a high-altitude area, you may need to make adjustments in recipes and package directions.

❖ First, water boils at a lower temperature. Therefore foods such as pasta are cooking at a temperature lower than 212°F (100°C), even though they are boiling. Because the temperature is lower, they take longer to cook.

❖ Second, when the air pressure is low, bubbles of gas may form more readily in liquids and escape. As a result, baked goods are likely to rise less and be heavy. Sometimes reducing the amount of baking powder or soda and sugar and increasing the liquid can help.

People who live in high-altitude areas often can get helpful information about adapting recipes from their local utility company, newspapers, or nearest Cooperative Extension office. Many packaged foods include special directions for preparation at high altitudes.

Section 8.3 Review

RECALL THE FACTS

1. Name three reasons to change a recipe.

2. List the basic steps in changing recipe yield.

3. Give three suggestions for lowering the fat in a recipe.

4. Why do some foods take longer to cook at high altitudes?

DISCUSS YOUR IDEAS

5. What are some other ways Tony might modify the spaghetti sauce to make it healthful while maintaining good flavor?

APPLY YOUR LEARNING

6. Find a simple recipe that makes four servings. Show how you would change the ingredient amounts to make twelve servings or two servings.

Section 8.3: Changing a Recipe   **237**

Completing the Section

Review

- Ask students to summarize the main ideas in this section.
- Have students complete the Section Review. (Answers appear below.)

Evaluation

- Ask students to double the yield of a recipe and to reduce the amount of fat and sodium it contains.
- Have students take the quiz for section 8.3. (Refer to the *Section Quizzes* booklet or construct your own quiz using the *Testmaker Software*.)

Reteaching

- Give students a standard biscuit recipe and help them make the adjustments needed to bake the biscuits at high altitudes.
- Refer to the *Reteaching Activities* booklet for the Section 8.3 activity sheet.

Enrichment

- Have students develop a game for improving math skills needed for cooking. Use the finished game for reteaching.

Closure

- Ask students again how they think new recipes are created. Note that many new recipes are made by altering existing recipes. Emphasize that different locations, food preferences, altitudes, and diet needs could all be reasons.

■ Answers to Section Review ■

1. To substitute for an ingredient you don't have, to change the yield, or to cut down on fat or sodium.

2. Decide how many servings you need; use the formula to find a factor for adjusting the recipe; multiply each ingredient amount by that number; convert answers to logical, measurable amounts; make any necessary adjustments.

3. Substitute a different ingredient, change ingredient amounts, or change the cooking method.

4. Because they are cooking at a lower temperature since water boils at a lower temperature at high altitudes.

5. Answers will vary.

6. Students should describe a procedure that follows the steps on pages 233-234.

Introducing the Section

Motivators

- Show students an assortment of knives. From the shape and size of each knife, can they guess the purpose of the knife?

- Without instructions, have small groups of students cut up half an apple as if for muffins. When finished, have each group show the chopped apple and explain how it was chopped. Which method produced the most finely chopped apple? What differences were there in the results? What else did the groups need to know?

Objectives

- Have students read the section objectives. Discuss the purpose of studying this section.

Vocabulary

- Pronounce the terms listed under "Look for These Terms." Have students find the terms and their definitions in the section.

Guided Reading

- Have students look at the headings within Section 8.4 to preview the concepts that will be discussed.

- Have students read the section and complete the appropriate part of the Chapter 8 Study Guide in the *Student Workbook*.

SECTION 8.4

Preparation Tasks

OBJECTIVES
After studying this section, you should be able to:
- Describe the techniques that correspond with common recipe terms.
- Identify the kitchen equipment used for each technique.

LOOK FOR THIS TERM
serrated

Success when preparing food depends a great deal on being able to follow recipe directions accurately. To do this, you first need to understand what recipe terms mean. You must also know what equipment to use for each task and the proper way to use it. In this section, you will learn about tools and techniques for some common recipe preparation tasks.

Cutting Foods

Food preparation often involves a variety of cutting tasks. You may need to trim unwanted parts from food or cut food to the desired size. With practice and attention to safety, you can become a cutting expert.

Equipment for Cutting

Cutting tools vary from graters and knives to small appliances such as the food chopper. Some basic cutting equipment is illustrated and described on page 239.

Note the proper hand position for holding a chef's knife (top). Whenever you cut, the hand holding the food should be kept away from the knife (bottom).

Teacher's Classroom Resources—Section 8.4

Refer to these resources in the TCR package:

Reproducible Lesson Plans
Student Workbook
Extending the Text
Reteaching Activities

Foods Lab Resources
Section Quizzes
Testmaker Software
Color Transparencies

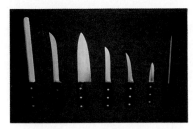

Bread knife. Has a **serrated,** or sawtooth, edge for cutting bread.

Slicing knife. Used for cutting large foods, including meat and poultry.

Chef's knife. Also called a French knife. Has a large triangular blade, wide at the handle and narrow at the tip. Used for slicing, cutting, chopping, and dicing.

Utility knife. Used for cutting small foods.

Boning knife. Has a thin blade. Used to trim fat from meat and remove meat from bones before cooking or serving.

Paring knife. Used to clean, pare, and slice small fruits and vegetables.

Sharpening steel. A long steel rod on a handle, used to sharpen knives.

Food grinder. A hand-operated tool or small electric appliance for grinding foods.

Kitchen shears. Useful for tasks such as snipping fresh herbs, trimming pastry, and cutting dried fruit.

Cutting board. Protects the kitchen counter when cutting. For proper sanitation, use a cutting board made of plastic instead of wood.

Food processor. A small electric appliance, similar to a blender but shaped differently. It comes with an assortment of blades and can do cutting jobs that a blender cannot do.

Peeler. Has a blade that swivels to cut peel thinly from fruits and vegetables.

Grater. Food is rubbed against the rough surface of the grater for grating or shredding.

Food chopper. Ranges in size from a small hand-operated nut chopper to a large chopper with several blades.

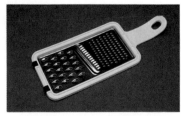

Blender. A small electric appliance used for a variety of cutting and mixing tasks. Has a tall, covered container with blades at the bottom. The container fits on a motor base that drives the blades. Most models have different speeds for specific tasks.

Section 8.4: Preparation Tasks **239**

8.4

Teaching . . .

• **Equipment for Cutting**

(text pages 238-239)

Comprehension Check

1. Ask students to list and describe tools used for cutting. *(See photos on page 239.)*
2. Discuss the proper way to sharpen a knife. *(See boxed information on page 240.)*

Student Experiences

1. **Display:** Prepare a display of basic cutting equipment. Ask students to identify cutting equipment with which they are familiar. Identify other items displayed. *(Key skill: observation)*
2. **Demonstration:** Demonstrate how to use a sharpening steel to sharpen knives. Point out that sharp knives are safer than dull ones. *(Key skill: health)*

Special Needs Strategies

Physically Disabled: For students who have physical disabilities that limit the use of their arms, follow these tips:

• Provide a cutting board with a nail for holding the food being cut in place while the student cuts it.

• Build a stand with a cutout hole the size of a mixing bowl to keep the bowl from slipping while the student mixes ingredients.

239

Teaching . . .

• Techniques for Cutting

(text pages 240-241)

Comprehension Check

1. Ask students to describe the proper way to use most knives. *(Hold the food on the cutting board with one hand and hold the knife by its handle with the other; use a back-and-forth sawing motion while pressing down gently at the same time.)*

2. Ask students to explain how to score meat. What does scoring accomplish? *(It helps tenderize meat.)*

3. Ask students to explain the difference between cubing and dicing. *(Cubed foods are cut in larger pieces than diced foods. Cubed foods should measure about 1/2 inch on each side; diced foods should measure about 1/8 to 1/4 inch.)*

Safety Check

Remind students that *all* cutting tools—not just knives—are sharp. Ask students to brainstorm guidelines for using tools such as peelers, graters, and kitchen shears safely.

Techniques for Cutting

Using knives is a basic kitchen skill. To use most knives, hold the food on the cutting board with one hand and hold the knife by its handle with the other. Use a back-and-forth sawing motion while pressing down gently at the same time.

Keep knives sharp. A dull knife is much more likely to slip and cut you because you will have to exert more pressure. A sharpening steel can be used to keep knives sharp, as shown below.

✓ SAFETY CHECK

When using a knife, keep your fingers away from the sharp edge of the blade. Never hold the food in your hand while cutting, and never cut with the blade facing your body.

Using a Sharpening Steel

Sharp knives cut more easily and safely. Regular use of a sharpening steel can keep knives in top shape. Here's how:

1. Hold the handle of the steel in your left hand. Place the point straight down, very firmly, on a cutting board. In your right hand, hold the knife by the handle, blade down. (Reverse if you are left-handed.)

2. Place the knife blade against the right side of the steel. The knife blade and steel should touch near the handles. Tip the knife away from the steel at a 20° angle.

3. Draw the blade down the steel and toward you, keeping it at a 20° angle to the steel. Use gentle pressure.

4. When the tip of the knife reaches the tip of the steel, repeat the process holding the knife against the steel on the left. Draw the blade down along the steel four or five times, alternating right and left sides.

Thinking Skills

Creativity: Have students brainstorm to identify food preparation tasks that can be done effectively with kitchen shears.

More About Chopping Garlic

The garlic press is a device that minces, or chops into fine pieces, garlic by pressing the cloves of garlic through small holes. Electric models are also available.

Recipes often use terms such as cube, grate, or score to indicate how foods are to be cut. To prepare food successfully, you need to know what each term means and how to perform the technique correctly. Here is a guide to some common cutting tasks:

❖ **Slice.** To cut a food in large, thin pieces.

❖ **Pare.** To cut off a very thin layer of peel. A peeler or paring knife works best.

❖ **Score.** To make shallow, straight cuts in the surface of a food such as a flank steak. This helps to tenderize meat. A slicing knife is most often used to score meats.

❖ **Chop and mince.** To cut food into small, irregular pieces. Minced pieces are smaller than chopped pieces. To use a chef's knife to chop or mince, hold the knife handle with one hand, pressing the tip against the cutting board. The other hand should rest lightly on the back of the blade, near the tip. Pump the knife handle up and down, keeping the tip of the blade on the board, so the blade chops through the food.

❖ **Cube and dice.** To cube or dice food means to cut it into small, square pieces. Make the pieces about 1/2 inch (1.3 cm) on each side when cubing and 1/8 to 1/4 inch (3 to 6 cm) when dicing.

❖ **Grate.** To cut food into small pieces by pressing and rubbing the food against the rough surface of the grater.

Section 8.4: Preparation Tasks **241**

Student Experiences

1. **Demonstration:** Demonstrate how to use each type of knife for cutting. Show how to hold fingers to keep them away from the sharp edges of the blade. Emphasize that you should never hold the food in your hand while cutting, and never cut with the blade facing your body. Demonstrate how to slice, pare, chop, mince, cube, dice, and grate. *(Key skill: observation)*

2. **Recipe Reading:** Have students work in groups to find recipes that call for various cutting techniques. Ask groups to share the terms they found and the foods involved. *(Key skill: reading)*

Lab Experience

Have students practice using knives by preparing meats, fruits, and vegetables for a salad bar.

Food and Nutrition Science

Retaining Nutrients: Many fruits and vegetables have a store of nutrients just beneath their skins. When paring these foods, as little of the skin as possible should be removed so nutrients can be retained. Discuss with students the best way to accomplish this. Have students practice with and compare the use of a paring knife and a peeler. Ask students to write a formal report of their findings.

Comprehension Check

1. Ask students to list and describe tools used for mixing. *(See illustration on page 243.)*

2. The electric mixer does many of the same tasks done by the wire whisk, the wooden spoon, and the rotary beater. Ask students to explain tasks for which a cook might want prefer one of these tools over another. *(Small tasks can be accomplished using manual tools in the time it takes to set up an electric mixer. Some cooks prefer different tools for specific jobs.)*

3. Discuss mixing terms often found in recipes. Have students describe each technique. *(See list on page 244.)*

Student Experiences

1. **Demonstration:** Demonstrate how to mix, combine, blend, stir, beat, cream, whip, fold, and sift ingredients. *(Key skill: observation)*

2. **Recipe Reading:** Have students work in groups to find recipes that call for each mixing technique described in the text. Ask groups to share the terms they found and the foods involved. *(Key skill: reading)*

Mixing Foods

Another common recipe task is combining ingredients. Different mixing tools and techniques are used, depending on the food and the desired results.

Equipment for Mixing

Many kinds of mixing tools, from small hand-held utensils to electric appliances, are used for mixing tasks. Some common ones are shown on page 243. The blender and food processor (shown on page 239) can also be used for some mixing tasks.

Techniques for Mixing

Mixing tools are used for a variety of tasks in the kitchen. Here are some mixing terms often found in recipes:

❖ **Mix, combine, blend.** To mix ingredients thoroughly, using a spoon, wire whisk, rotary beater, electric mixer, or electric blender.

❖ **Stir.** To mix by hand, using a spoon or wire whisk and a circular motion. Stirring can also be done while cooking to keep food from sticking to the pan and to distribute heat through foods.

242   Chapter 8: Recipe Skills

❖ **Beat.** To thoroughly mix foods using a vigorous over-and-over motion. A rotary beater, electric mixer, spoon, or wire whisk can be used. Egg whites may be beaten to add air to them.

❖ **Cream.** To beat together ingredients, such as shortening and sugar, until soft and creamy.

❖ **Whip.** To incorporate air into a mixture by beating it until light and fluffy.

❖ **Fold.** A gentle mixing method used for delicate or whipped ingredients. Usually a rubber scraper or wooden spoon is used. Cut down through the mixture, move the utensil across the bottom of the bowl, and bring it back up to the surface along with some of the mixture from the bottom of the bowl. The utensil itself is never lifted out of the mixture.

❖ **Sift.** To put dry ingredients, such as flour, through a sifter or strainer. This is done to add air, remove small lumps, or mix two ingredients.

Food and Nutrition Science

Equipment Comparison: Have students beat an egg using a wire whisk and another egg using a rotary beater, beating both eggs the same length of time. Ask students what the differences are in the two eggs after beating. In what types of recipes would each method be used?

Mixing bowls. Come in many different sizes. May be of stainless steel, glass, pottery, or plastic.

Wooden spoon. Used for many mixing tasks.

Sifter. A container with a fine wire screen at the bottom and a blade that forces dry ingredients through the screen.

Wire whisk. Made of wire loops held together by a handle. Used for mixing, stirring, beating, and whipping.

Rotary beater. Used to mix and whip foods more quickly and easily than can be done with a spoon or whisk. Often used to beat egg whites.

Electric mixer. Used to blend, beat, and whip ingredients. Lightweight, hand-held models are convenient. There are also heavy-duty models that are attached permanently to a stand.

Rubber scraper. Used to scrape food from bowls, pans, and other containers. Helpful in moving thick ingredients from the sides of the bowl to the middle while mixing. Also used for folding.

Section 8.4: Preparation Tasks **243**

Teaching . . .

• Other Tasks

(text page 244)

Comprehension Check

1. Ask students to explain the purpose of basting. *(to keep food from drying out; to help flavor food)*

2. Ask students to list occasions when a food may need to be pureed. *(For desserts or soups; sometimes people with dental problems puree food, so it is easier to eat.)*

Student Experiences

1. **Class Discussion:** Discuss the importance of understanding the terms used to describe food preparation techniques. Discuss possible results of misunderstanding a food preparation term. *(Key skill: language arts)*

2. **Flash Cards:** Have students develop and use flash cards of common food preparation terms and descriptions. *(Key skill: creativity)*

3. **Word Games:** Have students develop word games such as word searches and crossword puzzles using food preparation terms. *(Key skill: language arts)*

4. **Research:** Have students research and report on food preparation techniques used in other cultures of the world that are different from our own. *(Key skill: multicultural awareness)*

Thinking Skills

Reasoning: People in other cultures often use equipment and techniques for preparing food that differ from those we use. Ask students to discuss the problems someone from the United States might encounter while trying to cook in India, and vice versa.

Review

- Ask students to summarize the main ideas in this section.
- Have students complete the Section Review. (Answers appear below.)

Evaluation

- Have students write a short essay describing the food preparation tasks discussed in this section.
- Have students take the quiz for section 8.4. (Refer to the *Section Quizzes* booklet or construct your own quiz using the *Testmaker Software*.)

Reteaching

- Create flashcards that show different cutting and mixing tools. Have students use the cards to practice identifying each tool and describing its purpose.
- Refer to the *Reteaching Activities* booklet for the Section 8.4 activity sheet.

Enrichment

- Have students research and report on food preparation tools used by colonial or pioneer families.

Closure

- Refer students to the motivator for this section in which they cut the apple. Which tool would they choose now? Ask students to give reasons for their choices.

Other Tasks

A variety of other tools and techniques are used in food preparation. Here are some additional terms you may find in recipes:

❖ **Strain.** To separate solid particles from a liquid, such as broth or juice. The liquid is poured through a bowl-shaped fine screen called a strainer or sieve.

❖ **Drain.** To allow liquids to drain from a solid food, such as fruits, vegetables, or cooked pasta. This is done by putting the food in a colander—a bowl with small holes in the bottom—or a large strainer.

❖ **Puree** (pure-RAY or pure-REE). To make food smooth and thick by putting it through a strainer, blender, or food processer.

❖ **Baste.** To brush or pour liquid over food as it cooks.

❖ **Dredge.** To coat a food with a dry ingredient, such as flour or crumbs.

Of course, many heating and cooking tasks are also involved in food preparation. You will learn about cooking terms, equipment, and techniques in Chapter 9, "Cooking Methods."

A colander (left) and strainer (right) are useful for straining and draining foods.

■ Section 8.4 Review ■

RECALL THE FACTS

1. Describe the differences between a paring knife, boning knife, and chef's knife.

2. How is chopping different from mincing? From cubing or dicing?

3. What is meant by "beating" ingredients? Name three tools that could be used to beat a mixture.

4. Name two small electric appliances that are useful for both cutting and mixing tasks.

DISCUSS YOUR IDEAS

5. What might happen if you tried to follow a recipe without understanding the meaning of food preparation terms?

APPLY YOUR LEARNING

6. Find a salad recipe that requires the use of at least two cutting techniques and one mixing technique. Describe the tools and techniques needed.

■ Answers to Section Review ■

1. A paring knife is a small knife used to clean, pare, and slice small fruits and vegetables; a boning knife has a thin blade and is used to trim fat from meat and remove meat from bones; a chef's knife has a large triangular blade and is used for cutting, slicing, chopping, and dicing.

2. Minced pieces are smaller than chopped pieces; cubed or diced pieces are cut into more regular, cube-shaped pieces.

3. Thoroughly mixing foods using a vigorous over-and-over motion; *any three:* rotary beater, electric mixer, spoon, wire whisk.

4. Blender and food processor.

5. Answers will vary. The recipe may not turn out as expected.

6. Answers will vary.

Thinking About the Recipe

Read the recipe for "Pineapple-Pistachio Delight" and answer the following questions.

1. If you didn't have an electric mixer, what equipment could you use to beat the pineapple and pudding?
2. Why does this recipe tell you to "fold in" the whipped topping?

Pineapple-Pistachio Delight

Key Skill: Cutting and Mixing Techniques

Pineapple-Pistachio Delight

Customary	Ingredients	Metric
20 oz. can	Crushed pineapple in juice	567-gram can
3-oz. package	Instant pistachio pudding and pie filling mix	95-gram package
4-oz. carton	Light, non-dairy whipped topping, thawed	112-gram carton
1/3 cup	Pistachios or walnuts, chopped	75 mL

Yield: 8 servings

Directions

Equipment: 2 qt. (2 L) mixing bowl

1. Pour pineapple and juice into mixing bowl. Add pudding mix.
2. Beat at lowest speed with an electric mixer until well blended, about 1 to 2 minutes.
3. Fold in whipped topping and nuts.
4. Spoon into dessert dishes. Pudding will set and be ready to eat in 5 minutes.

Nutrition Information

Per serving (approximate): 151 calories, 1 g protein, 27 g carbohydrate, 7 g fat, trace of cholesterol, 181 mg sodium

Note: To reduce fat, omit nuts.

Using the Recipe

- Have students read the recipe and discuss each step. Review safety and sanitation procedures that apply to this recipe. Remind students never to run the blender without first placing the cover on it.
- Have each lab team fill out a work plan. (See the *Foods Lab Resources* booklet.)
- Have students check off the ingredients and equipment listed on the recipe worksheet and prepare the recipe.
- Have students complete the evaluation and questions on the recipe worksheet.

See Also . . .

The *Foods Lab Resources* booklet for the "Pineapple-Pistachio Delight" recipe worksheet and other recipe alternatives.

Answers to Thinking About the Recipe

1. A rotary beater, a wooden spoon, or a wire whisk.
2. So that the texture of the whipped topping, which is due to air in the mixture, does not change.

Introducing the Section

Motivator

- Display the following items: work flow chart (such as those used to study factory efficiency), employee work schedule, duty roster, memo of instructions to an employee. Ask students what these items have to do with food preparation. Explain that these are tools that help ensure efficiency in the work place.

Objectives

- Have students read the section objectives. Discuss the purpose of studying this section.

Vocabulary

- Pronounce the terms listed under "Look for These Terms." Have students find the terms and their definitions in the section.

Guided Reading

- Have students look at the headings within Section 8.5 to preview the concepts that will be discussed.
- Have students read the section and complete the appropriate part of the Chapter 8 Study Guide in the *Student Workbook*.

OBJECTIVES

After studying this section, you should be able to:

- Describe a work plan and schedule, and explain the usefulness of each.
- Give examples of efficient work techniques.
- Give guidelines for working cooperatively in the food lab or at home.

LOOK FOR THESE TERMS

work plan
pre-preparation
dovetail

Whenever you are preparing food, time is likely to be a concern. Whether it's a recipe you are preparing for a foods lab or your family's dinner, there are deadlines to meet. Good planning can help you meet your deadlines. So can learning the tricks of efficient food preparation and effective teamwork.

Time Management in the Kitchen

Winning a race takes strategy, speed, and skill. Those are also the keys to time management in the kitchen. The examples here are based on preparing a recipe, but the same process is used for preparing an entire meal. You will read more about meal management in Section 11.1.

Strategy: Making a Work Plan

Food preparation involves more than choosing a recipe and starting to work. Think it through first. Do you have the ingredients and equipment you need? Do you have the skills? Can you complete the food preparation and cleanup in the time available?

A smart strategy is to start with a **work plan.** Basically, this is a list of all the tasks required to complete the recipe and an estimate of how long each task will take.

Recipes and package directions often provide help in estimating time. A spaghetti package, for example, may say to cook the spaghetti for 9 minutes. However, you will have to draw on your experience to estimate the time for other tasks, such as chopping vegetables or cleaning salad greens. As you improve your skills, you will be able to work faster (and make more accurate time estimates). It's wise to allow a bit more time than you think you will need.

Teacher's Classroom Resources—Section 8.4

Refer to these resources in the TCR package:

Reproducible Lesson Plans

Student Workbook

Extending the Text

Reteaching Activities

Section Quizzes

Testmaker Software

Color Transparencies

Look at the recipe for "Pizza Snacks" below and the work plan on page 248 Naomi made for it. Note that some of the first steps on the work plan come from the list of ingredients, not the recipe directions. Naomi saw that the ingredients included:

- *Halved* English muffins.
- *Shredded* cheese.
- *Chopped* and *sliced* toppings.

Before beginning Step 1 of the recipe directions, Naomi would need to complete tasks such as washing and chopping the green pepper. Such tasks are called **pre-preparation** because they are done before actual recipe preparation. Measuring the ingredients is also part of pre-preparation.

A work plan often includes important tasks like washing your hands and setting the oven temperature. Including such steps insures they won't be forgotten.

Speed: Making a Schedule

Once you have a work plan, you can use it to make a schedule that shows when each task must be started. First, refer to your work plan to find the time you estimated it will take to complete each task. Add up these times to find the total preparation time. Next, subtract the total preparation time from the time you want the food to be ready. That

---

Pizza Snacks

2 English muffins, split in halves

1/2 cup prepared pizza sauce

1 Tbsp. chopped green pepper

1 Tbsp. sliced mushrooms

1 Tbsp. chopped onions

1/2 cup shredded low-fat mozzarella cheese

1. Place English muffin halves, crust-side down, on broiler pan.

2. Spread each muffin half with 2 Tbsp. pizza sauce.

3. Top with green pepper, mushrooms, and onion.

4. Sprinkle each muffin half with 2 Tbsp. cheese.

5. Position broiler pan so the tops of the muffins are about 4 inches from the heat. Turn on broiler.

6. Broil until cheese is bubbly, about 2 to 4 minutes. Remove immediately and serve hot.

NOTE: Broiling time may vary.

Yield: 4 small pizzas

Teaching . . .

- **Strategy: Making a Work Plan**

(text pages 246-247)

Comprehension Check

1. Ask students to name the three keys to time management in the kitchen. *(strategy, speed, and skill)*

2. Discuss the purpose of a work plan. What does a work plan include? *(a list of tasks and an estimate of how long each task will take)*

3. Discuss the concept of "pre preparation tasks." Ask students to list tasks that are frequently required included in pre-preparation tasks. *(Those that must be done before you can start following the recipe directions; cleaning, chopping, and measuring are common examples.)*

Student Experiences

1. **Developing a Work Plan:** Give students a recipe. Have them read it and develop a work plan for preparing that recipe. *(Key skills: reading, analysis)*

2. **Developing Skits:** Have students work in small groups to develop a short skit based on one of the keys to efficiency described in the text. Have groups present their skits to the class. Discuss how these techniques save time and energy. *(Key skills: management, creativity)*

See Also . . .

- Section 1.5: "Managing Resources and Making Decisions," text page 45.

..

Teaching . . .

- **Speed: Making a Schedule**
- **Skill: Working Efficiently**

(text pages 247-249)

Comprehension Check

1. Ask students to explain the difference between a work plan and a schedule. *(The work plan lists the tasks and how long each will take; the schedule organizes the procedure by showing when each task should be started.)*

2. Ask students the keys to working efficiently in the kitchen.

Student Experiences

1. **Recipe Analysis:** Have students analyze a recipe to see if any of the tasks listed could be simplified by using a different piece of equipment or a different cooking method. *(Key skills: reading, analysis)*

2. **Making a Schedule:** Give students a recipe for a main dish and tell them that dinner is to be served at 6:00 P.M. Have students develop a schedule that will allow them to serve the meal on time. Remind students that they should first complete a work plan. *(Key skill: math)*

Safety Check

To be sure students understand the difference between efficiency and carelessness, propose several examples of short-cuts in the kitchen (some that increase efficiency and some that are just carelessness). Have students decide which are true efficiency measures and which are carelessness.

Work Plan—Pizza Snacks

Task	Approx. Time
Gather ingredients and equipment. Scrub hands.	8 min.
Split English muffins in half.	2 min.
Chop green pepper and onion. Slice mushrooms.	7 min.
Shred cheese.	3 min.
Put muffins on broiler pan and put on toppings.	3 min.
Broil until cheese is bubbly.	6 min.
Prepare to serve.	1 min.
	Total: 30 min.

tells you what time to start. Naomi's estimated total preparation time is 30 minutes. She plans to serve the pizzas at 6:30, so she needs to start at 6:00.

To make her schedule, Naomi decides to chop and slice the vegetables first, shred the cheese next, and then split the English muffins. For this recipe, the remaining tasks match the order of the recipe directions.

When you are learning to prepare food, it's a good idea to make a work plan and schedule every time. Eventually, you may need to do so only when you prepare a new dish or plan a special meal.

Schedule—Pizza Snacks

6:00	Get ready.
6:08	Split English muffins.
6:10	Chop and slice vegetables.
6:17	Shred cheese.
6:20	Assemble pizzas.
6:23	Broil pizzas.
6:29	Prepare to serve.
6:30	Serve pizzas.

Skill: Working Efficiently

As you gain food preparation experience, you will notice an obvious improvement in your skills. You'll be able to complete many tasks more quickly than before.

However, there's more to efficiency than experience. Even a beginner can be efficient by identifying ways to save time and energy. Here are some keys to efficiency:

- ❖ *Organize the kitchen.* Always store items in the same place so you won't waste time looking for them.

- ❖ *Learn to use equipment properly.* Take the time to read the owner's manuals for the small and large appliances in the kitchen. Besides learning to use them safely, you may find they can be helpful in ways you didn't realize. Practice using your tools until you are comfortable with them.

- ❖ *Look for ways to simplify.* Could a different piece of equipment complete a task more quickly? Would a different cooking method be more efficient? Thinking through your options can help you save time and energy.

- ❖ *Gather all equipment and ingredients first.* Assembling everything you will need before you start has several advantages. You won't discover, halfway through a recipe, that you are out of an

---

More About Work Plans and Schedules

Some cooks make a combination work plan and schedule. To do this, you must be certain your work plan lists tasks in the exact order they should be started. Then add a column giving the starting time for each task.

ingredient you need. It will be easier to check whether you used every ingredient. Most important, you will be able to work efficiently because everything is at your fingertips.

❖ **Dovetail tasks.** To **dovetail** means to fit different tasks together smoothly. Not every preparation step needs your undivided attention. You could, for example, make a tossed salad while chicken pieces are baking. Checking the chicken from time to time is all that's needed. Dovetailing is especially important when you are preparing a whole meal. If you plan to dovetail tasks, be sure to adjust your time schedule.

❖ **Clean up as you work.** It's discouraging to finish the preparation and face dirty dishes and a messy kitchen. There is a more efficient way. Before you start work, fill the sink or a dishpan with hot, sudsy water. Whenever you have a few free moments, wash the equipment you have finished using. Also keep a clean, wet dishcloth handy to wipe up spills as they happen. Put away ingredients as you finish with them. Your final cleanup will take much less time.

Dovetailing tasks can help you prepare a meal quickly. For example, you could prepare a tossed salad while cooking spaghetti.

✔ **SAFETY CHECK**

Remember, there's a difference between efficiency and carelessness. Don't be in such a hurry that you ignore safety guidelines. Keep your mind on what you're doing at all times.

Teamwork in the Kitchen

In the foods lab at school, you will be working as part of a team. You will also be working against the clock. Every lab activity will need to be completed—including cleanup and evaluation—within a limited period of time. Success depends on organization and cooperation.

❖ **Organizing the job.** Start with a basic work plan. When you plan your schedule, decide not only when each task should start, but also who will do it. With every team member working, several tasks can be accomplished at the same time. You may want to use a schedule that has five-minute blocks of time down the left and columns with each person's name across the top. That way you can show what each person should be doing throughout the lab period. Be sure to consider work space and equipment as you plan your schedule.

❖ **Working together.** Foods labs, like many school and work situations, depend on everyone working together well. Be responsible for the tasks you have agreed to do. Work quickly and efficiently. Remember that accuracy is essential. If you have a question or a problem, ask another team member for help. You, too, need to be willing to help out when someone else falls behind or makes a mistake. Keeping a sense of humor will help the work go more smoothly.

More About Teamwork

There are real advantages to working with others in the foods lab at school or your kitchen at home. You can share both the work and the fun of food preparation. It's a good way to speed up preparation time.

There are also potential pitfalls, however. When two or more people share a small space,

they sometimes get in each other's way.

When you work with others in the kitchen, success depends on working well as a team. Teamwork requires good organization and communication. Each person's responsibilities must be clear.

(text pages 249-250)

Teaching . . .

● **Teamwork in the Kitchen**

Comprehension Check

1. Ask students to explain why it is important to be organized and to cooperate with other team members in the foods lab.

2. Ask students to explain the significance of teamwork in the foods lab. How can this concept be applied in students' homes? *(Teamwork allows groups to complete their assignment on time; at home, students can use the principle of teamwork to help another family member prepare a meal or to allow a younger brother or sister to help and learn at the same time.)*

3. Discuss the process of evaluating the results of a foods lab experiment or meal preparation process. What questions should students ask themselves?

Student Experiences

1. **Class Discussion:** Discuss ways food preparation in the foods lab is similar to and different from food preparation at home. Discuss the importance of organization and cooperation. Why is it important to clean up as you go? What can you learn by evaluating the results of each lab? *(Key skill: cooperation)*

2. **Developing Skits:** Have small groups develop a short, two-part skit. The first part should show how "teamwork" can create a problem if everyone doesn't help; the second part should show how teamwork can be a big advantage if everyone works together properly. *(Key skills: creativity, critical thinking)*

8.5

Completing the Section

Review

- Ask students to summarize the main ideas in this section.
- Have students complete the Section Review. (Answers appear below.)

Evaluation

- Give students a recipe and have them make a work plan and time schedule for preparing the recipe.
- Have students take the quiz for section 8.5. (Refer to the *Section Quizzes* booklet or construct your own quiz using the *Testmaker Software*.)

Reteaching

- Have students observe family members at home to identify pre-preparation tasks and work simplification practices.
- Refer to the *Reteaching Activities* booklet for the Section 8.5 activity sheet.

Enrichment

- Give students a menu for an evening meal to be served at 7:00 P.M. Include recipes for all the foods on the menu. Have students prepare a work plan and schedule, dovetailing the tasks associated with each recipe.

Closure

- Refer students to the section motivator. Ask students to review how having a work plan can help structure and organize meal preparation tasks.

❖ **Cleaning up.** Cleaning as you go will make end-of-class cleanup easier and faster. Be sure all equipment is clean and dry. Most important, return everything to its proper place. Otherwise, you will slow down the next team using the kitchen. Be sure all work surfaces and appliances are also clean. Dispose of garbage properly.

❖ **Evaluating the results.** Labs usually involve evaluating both the finished product and the preparation process. Thoughtfulness and honesty are important for both. This is especially true if the food did not turn out as expected, you experienced preparation problems, or your team did not work together well. Think about what you learned from the experience and what you might do differently the next time.

In many ways, teamwork in your kitchen at home is similar to working in the foods lab. Organization, cooperation, and cleanup are just as important. However, the atmosphere is usually much more informal. "Evaluation" may be a compliment on what you have made or simply the satisfaction of knowing you have done a good job.

Whether you are responsible for helping prepare family meals on a regular basis or just occasionally, remember that these times can be fun. You might help a younger brother or sister learn a new cooking skill or just take time to talk to a family member. When you have more time, try out a new recipe together. Daily food preparation can be a chore or an opportunity for togetherness. It all depends on your attitude.

Evaluation is one of the most important parts of the foods lab experience. You can learn from your mistakes as well as your successes.

■ Section 8.5 Review ■

RECALL THE FACTS

1. What is a work plan? How can it help you manage time when preparing food?
2. Give three examples of ways to work efficiently in the kitchen or foods lab.
3. What should you think about when evaluating a completed foods lab?

DISCUSS YOUR IDEAS

4. What other ideas for working efficiently can you think of?

APPLY YOUR LEARNING

5. Design a work plan and schedule form that could be used when planning school foods labs.

250   Chapter 8: Recipe Skills

■ Answers to Section Review ■

1. A list of all the tasks required to complete a recipe, along with the time each task requires; by organizing the tasks so that you can create a schedule.
2. *Any three:* Organize the kitchen; learn to use equipment properly; look for ways to simplify; gather all equipment and ingredients first; dovetail tasks; clean up as you work.
3. About the finished product and the preparation process; about what you learned from this experience and what you might do differently next time.
4. Answers will vary.
5. Answers will vary.

250

Career PROFILE

Beth Lane
Food Researcher

CURRENT POSITION

"I'm a researcher in a food processing lab for a large food manufacturer."

RESPONSIBILITIES

"I work as part of a team that develops prototypes for new products. It's our job to find the right formulation of ingredients to make the product as good as it can be."

SKILLS

"A background in nutrition and food science is important, as well as the ability to work well with a team. It's also important to be able to communicate well, both orally and in writing."

EDUCATION

"I have a bachelor's degree in nutrition and a master's degree in chemistry."

WORK ENVIRONMENT

"Even though I work as part of a team, I spend a lot of time alone in the lab. After doing my part of the research, I get together with others to compile our findings and work out a finished product."

FAVORITE PART OF THE JOB

"It's exciting to me to try to come up with the best-tasting and most attractive product I can. I enjoy seeing the product on the supermarket shelf and being able to say that I had a major part in putting it there."

- Why is teamwork essential to a job like Beth's?
- Do you think you might enjoy Beth's job? Why or why not?

Thinking About . . . Food Research

- Have students think of other questions they would like to ask Beth Lane about being a food researcher. Examples: How much time per week do you spend in the lab? How much contact do you have with other people? How does teamwork fit in with what you do? How do you divide the tasks? What is the salary range for a food researcher?

- Ask students to explain why food manufacturers need to hire food researchers. (To stay competitive, to introduce appealing products that sell well, etc.)

Student Opportunities

Students thinking about a career in food research should check with local food laboratories for volunteer and employment opportunities.

Occupational Outlook

Food researchers may progress from junior food chemists in research and development lab of a food company to quality assurance chemists or become section heads. Interested researchers may also go into food research administration.

251

For More Information

For more information about food research careers, contact:
- American Chemical Society, Education Division, Career Services, 1155 16th St. NW, Washington, D.C. 20036

- American Institute of Biological Sciences, 730 11th St. NW, Washington, D.C. 20001
- U.S. Department of Agriculture, 14th St. and Independence Ave. SW, Washington, D.C. 20250

Completing the Chapter

Review

- Have students complete the Chapter Review. (Answers appear below.)

Evaluation

- Give students a simple recipe written in paragraph form. Have students organize it into a standard recipe style and then alter it to double the yield.

- Have students take the test for Chapter 8. (Refer to the *Chapter and Unit Tests* booklet or construct your own test using the *Testmaker Software*.)

■ ANSWERS ■

REVIEWING FACTS

1. *Any four:* List of ingredients and amounts; number of servings or yield; essential information about temperature, time, and equipment; step-by-step directions; nutrition information.

2. Expressing the same amount using different measures. Examples will vary.

3. Set measuring cup on level surface, carefully pour liquid into cup, bend down to check the measurement at eye level, add more or pour off excess, if needed.

4. Recipes for baked products; if one amount is changed or an ingredient is omitted, the recipe may not work.

5. Divide the desired yield by the original yield.

6. *Score:* make shallow, straight cuts in the surface of a food; *pare:* cut off a very thin layer of peel; *mince:* cut food in small, irregular pieces (pieces are smaller than chopped foods); *grate:* rub food against the rough surface of a grater.

SUMMARY

SECTION 8.1

Recipe Basics: Before using a recipe, check to be sure it includes certain basic information and is clearly written. Recipes are available from many sources. A well-organized recipe collection is easier to use.

SECTION 8.2

Measuring Ingredients: Recipes include weight and volume measurements in customary or metric units. For accurate measurements, be sure to select the right measuring tools and follow the correct procedures.

SECTION 8.3

Changing a Recipe: You can alter the yield of a recipe by changing the amounts of ingredients. You might substitute different ingredients to reduce the amount of fat or sodium. High-altitude cooking may require changes in cooking time or ingredients.

SECTION 8.4

Preparation Tasks: Food preparation may involve a number of different tasks. To follow a recipe, you need to understand the meaning of the terms used. You also need to know which utensil or appliance to use and the correct technique.

SECTION 8.5

Time Management and Teamwork: A work plan can help you identify the tasks that must be done when preparing food. A schedule tells you when to do them. Look for ways to make the job easier and more efficient. Teamwork is essential when several people are working in the kitchen at once.

252

REVIEWING FACTS

1. List four kinds of information included in a well-written recipe. (8.1)

2. In measuring, what is an "equivalent"? Give an example. (8.2)

3. Describe how to measure liquids accurately. (8.2)

4. What type of recipe is more difficult to alter? Why? (8.3)

5. When changing the yield of a recipe, how do you determine the number to multiply each ingredient amount by? (8.3)

6. Define: score, pare, mince, grate. (8.4)

7. Name two small electric appliances that can be used for cutting or mixing tasks. (8.4)

8. Describe the technique for folding one ingredient into another. (8.4)

9. Give four suggestions for working efficiently in the kitchen or foods lab. (8.5)

10. Describe how a work plan for a team differs from a work plan for an individual. (8.5)

LEARNING BY DOING

1. ***Measurement lab:*** Working in groups, make a list of five amounts to be measured. Exchange lists with another group. Measure the amounts once using a dry ingredient (such as flour) and again using water. Check each other's measurements for accuracy. (8.2)

2. ***Foods lab:*** Choose a recipe from a cookbook or use one provided by your teacher. Make at least one ingredient substitution to lower the fat. Evaluate the results. (8.3)

7. Answers may vary. Examples: blender, food processor.

8. Use a rubber scraper or wooden spoon to cut down through the mixture, move the utensil across the bottom of the bowl, and bring it back up to the surface. Never lift the utensil out of the mixture.

9. *Any four:* Organize the kitchen; learn to use equipment properly; look for ways to simplify; gather all equipment and ingredients first; dovetail tasks; clean up as you work.

10. For a team, the schedule should specify not only when each task should start, but who should do it.

3. **Foods lab:** Pare a raw potato. Cut it into slices 1/2 inch (1.3 cm) thick. Set two slices aside, then cube the rest. Set some of the cubed pieces aside and dice the rest. Have your teacher check your work. (8.4)

4. **Computer lab:** Design and print out a form that could be used for a foods lab work plan and schedule. (8.5)

THINKING CRITICALLY

1. **Analyzing decisions:** Peggy looked through several cookbooks trying to find a recipe for a special meal. Finally, she decided to make a dish she had prepared many times before. What are some possible reasons for Peggy's decision? (8.1)

2. **Predicting consequences:** Dana didn't want to bother to calculate how to reduce a muffin recipe by half. He decided instead to measure out the whole amount of each ingredient and use a large spoon to put about half back. What is likely to happen when he bakes the muffins? (8.3)

3. **Recognizing alternatives:** Suppose a recipe called for sifted flour, but you didn't have a sifter. What might you use instead? (8.4)

4. **Recognizing points of view:** Some people may believe that it's not worth spending the time to make a work plan and schedule. Why might they feel this way? What could you say to change their opinion? (8.5)

MAKING DECISIONS AND SOLVING PROBLEMS

What Would You Do?

1. You've found a recipe for a casserole that you want to try. The ingredients list includes shredded cheese, but the directions do not tell you what to do with it. (8.1)

2. You and your sister are both working in the kitchen, each preparing a different recipe. You have the measuring spoons, but your sister is using the 1/4 cup dry measuring cup that you need. (8.2)

3. In the last two foods labs, your group has been unable to finish on time. You think the work would get done faster if you did it all yourself. However, part of your grade is based on how well you work as a team. (8.5)

LINKING YOUR STUDIES

1. **Writing:** Choose a recipe to put into story form. From the first person point of view ("I"), tell how you collected the ingredients and followed the directions to prepare the food. Tell how the recipe turned out. (8.1)

2. **Science:** Using references from the library, prepare a report telling how the metric system of measurement originated. (8.2)

3. **Math:** Find a recipe that makes twelve or more servings. Change the recipe so that it yields four servings. (8.3)

4. **History:** Using the library or other resources, find information about food preparation in colonial America or another historical period. Describe at least three tools that were used for common food preparation tasks. How did the tools differ from what is used today? (8.4)

5. **Math:** Make a work plan for a recipe you might use in the foods lab or at home. Estimate the time needed for each of the following: getting ready to cook, assembling the recipe, cooking or baking time, and cleanup. Express each of these as a percentage of the total time needed for the work plan. Show your findings in a chart. (8.5)

253

LEARNING BY DOING

Answers to "Learning by Doing" activities will vary. Evaluate students according to the effort they put into the activities as well as their results.

THINKING CRITICALLY

1. Answers will vary. Peggy may have decided not to try something new for the first time on a special occasion. She may have felt more comfortable with a recipe she knew would work.

2. They may not turn out right, since the exact measurements are critical in baked products.

3. Answers will vary.

4. Answers will vary.

MAKING DECISIONS AND SOLVING PROBLEMS

Answers to "Making Decisions and Solving Problems" questions will vary. Encourage students to give reasons for their answers.

LINKING YOUR STUDIES

Answers to "Linking Your Studies" will vary.

CHAPTER 9
Cooking Methods

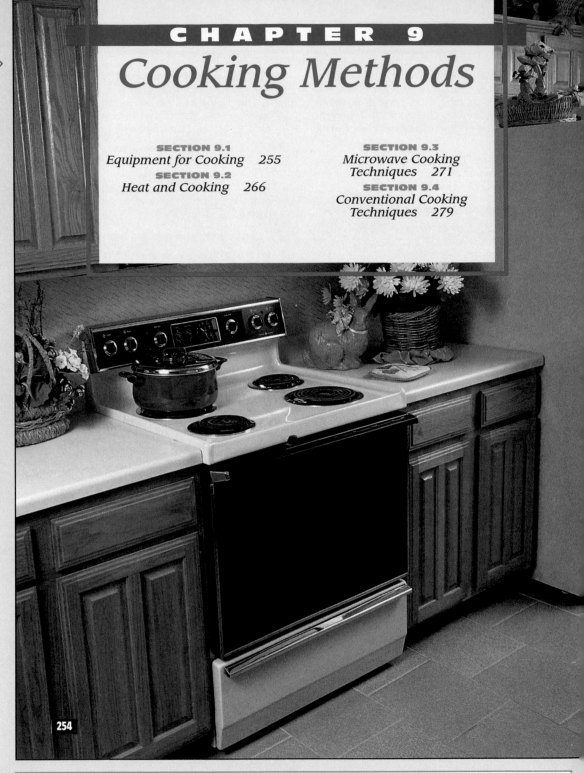

254

Planning the Chapter

Chapter Overview

Section 9.1: Equipment for Cooking

Section 9.2: Heat and Cooking

Section 9.3: Microwave Cooking Techniques

Section 9.4: Conventional Cooking Techniques

Introducing the Chapter

Motivators

- Ask students to make a list of all the major and small cooking appliances available in their kitchens at home. Which equipment is used most often? Which is used least often?

- Name several foods. Ask students to write down a method for cooking each food. Compare the methods named for each food. Suggest additional methods students many not have named.

Teacher's Classroom Resources—Chapter 9

Refer to these resources in the TCR package:

Enrichment Activities

Chapter and Unit Tests

Testmaker Software

Cooperative Learning Suggestions

After you describe a cooking technique, used the Forced Response strategy to have students name foods that could be cooked using the technique or advantages and disadvantages of the cooking technique. Continue around the classroom until each student has responded. Note: Provide students with the option at any time to say "I pass."

OBJECTIVES

After studying this section, you should be able to:

- Describe how cooktops and conventional, convection, and microwave ovens work.
- Identify small cooking appliances and describe their uses.
- Identify cookware, bakeware, and cooking tools.

LOOK FOR THESE TERMS

cookware

bakeware

Introducing the Section

Motivators

- Have students compare equipment used by backpackers and campers with that used in a home kitchen.
- Have students make predictions regarding cooking equipment in the twenty-first century. What changes do they predict? Will families continue to prepare food at home as they do today? If not, how will food preparation be done?

Objectives

- Have students read the section objectives. Discuss the purpose of studying this section.

Vocabulary

- Pronounce the terms listed under "Look for These Terms." Have students find the terms and their definitions in the section.

Guided Reading

- Have students look at the headings within Section 9.1 to preview the concepts that will be discussed.
- Have students read the section and complete the appropriate part of the Chapter 9 Study Guide in the *Student Workbook*.

Look around any kitchen and you'll find many kinds of equipment designed for cooking. These include major appliances, small appliances, and a variety of utensils.

Major Cooking Appliances

The major appliances used for cooking are the conventional range, the convection oven, and the microwave oven.

The Range

A range usually consists of a cooktop with four burners, elements, or surface units, an oven, and a broiler. The cooktop has either dials or push buttons to control the heat. Ovens have thermostatic controls so that you can set the exact temperature you need. Oven temperature settings vary from "warm," or below 200°F (93°C), to "broil," or about 500°F (260°C). The broiler cooks food by direct heat from a burner or electrical element located in the top of the compartment.

Instead of a freestanding range, some kitchens have separate cooktop and oven units built into cabinets. Another alternative is a portable oven that can be placed on a countertop or cart.

Ranges use either gas or electricity for fuel. The two types of ranges have slightly different features.

Teacher's Classroom Resources—Section 9.1

Refer to these resources in the TCR package:

Reproducible Lesson Plans

Student Workbook

Extending the Text

Reteaching Activities

Section Quizzes

Testmaker Software

Color Transparencies

Teaching . . .

Teaching . . .

> • **Major Cooking Appliances: The Range**
>
> **(text pages 255-257)**

Comprehension Check

1. Ask students to explain the differences in the features of a gas range and those of an electric range. *(In a gas range, the broiler is usually in a separate compartment below the oven; a gas range has burners that heat with a flame. In an electric range, the burners heat by passing electricity through the element or unit, causing it to heat up.)*

2. Ask students to list and describe the types of cooktops available for electric ranges. *(See list on pages 256-257.)*

Science Connection

Point out that many small electric appliances—such as toasters, toaster ovens, and small area heaters—also use high resistance and current flow to produce heat. Ask students why these appliances need to be watched more carefully than appliances that do not produce heat using this method.

■ ■ ■

Ranges use either gas or electricity for fuel. Both freestanding and built-in models are available.

Gas Range

In a gas range, the oven and broiler are usually in separate compartments. The broiler is generally located below the oven.

The heating units in gas ranges are called burners. The burners in gas cooktops heat with a flame that is easily regulated. The change in heat level is immediate. (Some gas ranges have sealed burners without a visible flame.)

In most newer ranges, when a burner is turned on, gas flows through and is ignited by an electronic spark (pilotless ignition). Older ranges contain pilot lights—small gas flames that burn continuously. When the burner is turned on, the pilot lights ignite the gas. Sometimes, however, the pilot lights go out and must be relighted. (See page 192 for information about relighting a pilot light.)

Air flow is needed for burning gas, so take care not to block the vents in a gas range. The burner bowls should not be lined with

foil for this reason. If air flow is blocked, the gas will not burn properly and will give off carbon monoxide, a deadly gas.

Electric Range

An electric range heats with heating units or elements. Electricity passes through the element or unit, causing it to heat up.

The oven and broiler in an electric range are in the same compartment. The compartment has two heating elements, one at the top and one at the bottom. The bottom element heats the oven for all cooking purposes except broiling. When broiling in the oven, only the top element comes on. When broiling in an electric range, leave the door open slightly.

Several types of cooktops are available in electric ranges. Each has its own unique characteristics.

❖ ***Coil elements.*** Elements heat up and cool down relatively quickly (although

---

More About Ranges

• *Down-draft ranges* have a built-in ventilating system that eliminates the need for a ventilating hood or fan. A duct connects the range ventilating system to the outside of the home. During cooking, blowers inside the range pull smoke, heat, and odors out through the appliance and exhaust them outdoors through the ductwork.

• *Commercial ranges,* commonly used in restaurants, are also available for home use. They usually have cast iron cooking

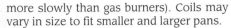

Science Connection

Physics

Electrical Resistance and Heat

As electricity passes through a material, its flow is impeded by a characteristic of the material called *resistance.* The result is that the material heats up. The greater the current flow and the higher the resistance of the material, the greater the heat produced. Cooktop elements have high resistance to produce the heat needed for cooking.

◾ ◾ ◾

more slowly than gas burners). Coils may vary in size to fit smaller and larger pans.

❖ **Solid disk elements.** New technology has made it possible to eliminate cleanup problems with this enclosed element. However, solid disks take much longer to heat up and cool down. They require special cookware with extra-flat bottoms for even cooking.

❖ **Induction cooktops.** A glass-ceramic top covers the heating elements, making this cooktop very easy to keep clean. With induction cooktops, heat is produced when a ferrous metal pan (such as stainless steel or cast iron) is placed on the element. The magnetic attraction between the pan and the heating element produces heat. This cooktop stays cool, except for any heat transferred from the pan.

New technology has simplified cleanup problems on cooktops. Both induction cooktops (left) and solid disk cooktops (below) are totally enclosed.

1. **Reading Appliance Ads:** Have students study appliance ads to identify features available on ranges, conventional ovens, convection ovens, and microwave ovens. Which features are basic? Which are extras? How do the extra features affect the price of the appliance? *(Key skill: reading)*

2. **Guest Speaker:** Invite a repair technician to answer student questions about how to select a reliable, high-quality product. Have each student develop a list of ten questions to ask the speaker. Guide students toward asking probing questions, not simply for brand name information. (For example: What happens to the durability of an oven and to the cost of repair when you add the self-cleaning feature?) *(Key skill: critical thinking)*

3. **Chart Making:** Have students make a chart comparing the features of gas and electric ranges. Discuss the advantages and disadvantages of each. *(Key skill: comparing)*

4. **Field Trip:** Take a field trip to a local appliance store. Ask the salesperson to point out features of gas and electric ranges and ovens. Ask the salesperson to explain the characteristics of coil elements, solid disk elements, and induction cooktops available on electric ranges. *(Key skill: analysis)*

surfaces, and a minimum of six burners. They are slightly deeper than standard home ranges, with well-insulated ovens. Because of their durable construction, they can last a life-time. They do, however, lack popular features such as self-

cleaning ovens, clocks, timers, and glass doors. The outside is usually finished in stainless steel, copper, black, or gray.

• When buying any range, make certain the burners are spaced far enough apart so that large pots can be used.

9.1

Teaching . . .

- **The Convection Oven**
- **The Microwave Oven**
  - **Small Cooking Appliances**

(text page 258)

Comprehension Check

1. Ask students to explain the difference between a convection oven and a conventional oven. *(A convection oven has a fan that circulates the heated air, which speeds up cooking time and keeps temperatures even throughout the oven.)*

2. Ask students to describe how a microwave oven works. *(A magnetron tube turns electricity into microwaves, which are distributed throughout the oven by a stirrer blade; the microwaves make food molecules vibrate, producing friction, which produces the heat that cooks the food.)*

3. Ask students to name several small cooking appliances that make certain cooking tasks faster and easier. *(toaster, toaster oven, electric skillet, portable electric burner, slow cooker, broiler/grill, rice cooker/steamer, etc.)*

The Convection Oven

A convection oven is like a conventional oven except that a fan circulates the heated air. This speeds up cooking time and keeps temperatures even throughout the oven. As a result, foods brown more evenly than in a conventional oven. A convection oven cooks more quickly than a conventional oven, but not as quickly as a microwave oven.

A convection oven can be combined with either a conventional or a microwave oven. The combination oven has more advantages than any single type.

The Microwave Oven

Microwaves are a form of energy that travels like radio waves. In a microwave oven, a magnetron (MAG-nuh-trawn) tube turns electricity into microwaves. The microwaves are distributed through the oven by a "stirrer blade," a fan-like device. The microwaves bounce off the oven's walls and floor until they are absorbed by food. Microwave energy is reflected from metal but passes through glass, paper, and plastic to get to food.

Microwaves make food molecules vibrate against each other, producing friction. This friction produces heat which cooks the food. Microwave ovens cook many foods in one-fourth the time that it takes to cook them conventionally, making this an energy-efficient way to cook.

Small Cooking Appliances

Many different small appliances are available for making cooking tasks faster and easier. Here are some basic ones.

- ❖ *Toaster.* Browns bread products on both sides at the same time. You set the controls for the degree of browning. Two- and four-slice models are available.
- ❖ *Toaster oven.* Toasts bread, heats up foods, and bakes small amounts of many foods. Some toaster ovens can broil food.
- ❖ *Electric skillet.* A thermostat controls the temperature on the skillet. Useful for frying, roasting, steaming, and baking.
- ❖ *Portable electric burner.* A small appliance that works like the cooktop on a range.
- ❖ *Slow cooker.* A deep pot with a heating element in the base that allows food to cook slowly over many hours. It's a convenient way to cook one-dish meals like stews.
- ❖ *Broiler/grill.* A small, portable electric grill used to broil or grill food indoors.
- ❖ *Rice cooker/steamer.* Used to cook large quantities of rice or steam vegetables. The controlled heat cooks all types of rice perfectly.

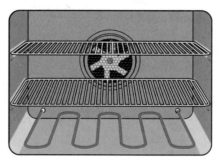

Convection ovens use a built-in fan to circulate hot air in the oven compartment. This speeds cooking and browns foods more evenly.

More About Small Appliances

- *Cordless appliances.* These operate on rechargeable batteries built into a special storage-charger base. The appliance recharges during storage.
- *Compact or mini-appliances.* Their popularity is linked to the increase in one- and two-person households. Even in larger households, family members often prepare their own meals and eat on staggered schedules. Smaller appliances are easier to store; some are designed to fit under wall cabinets.

Toaster

Toaster oven

Electric skillet

Slow cooker

Rice cooker/steamer

Broiler/grill

Cookware and Bakeware

Cookware is used for cooking food on top of the range. **Bakeware** is used to cook food in an oven. Both cookware and bakeware are made from many different materials, as shown in the chart on pages 260-261. Microwave ovens have special requirements for cooking containers.

✓ SAFETY CHECK

Don't use copper cookware if it's unlined or the lining wears out. Acidic foods can release copper into food. Too much copper in food can cause nausea, vomiting, and diarrhea.

Section 9.1: Equipment for Cooking **259**

Teaching . . .

• **Materials for Cookware (chart)**

(text pages 260-261)

Comprehension Check

1. Ask students to explain the difference between cookware and bakeware. *(Cookware is used to cook foods on top of a range; bakeware is used to cook food in an oven. Note that some items may fit both categories.)*

2. Have students use the chart to compare cookware made of different kinds of metal (aluminum, stainless steel, copper, and cast iron).

3. Discuss the advantages and disadvantages of using glass or glass-ceramic cookware.

4. Ask students to describe the use and care of cookware that has a nonstick finish. *(Use nonmetal tools to avoid scratching; follow manufacturer's directions for cleaning, since some cannot be washed in a dishwasher.)*

Materials for Cookware

Material	Advantages	Disadvantages	Use and Care
Aluminum	❖ Conducts heat quickly, evenly. ❖ Lightweight. ❖ Durable. ❖ Comes in a variety of finishes.	❖ Warps, dents, and scratches easily. ❖ Darkens and stains, especially in dishwasher. ❖ Pits if used to store salty or acid foods.	❖ Cool before washing to prevent warping. ❖ Avoid sharp tools like knives and beaters. ❖ Do not use to store salty or acid foods.
Stainless Steel	❖ Durable, tough, hard. ❖ Will not dent easily. ❖ Attractive.	❖ Conducts heat unevenly. ❖ Stains when overheated or from starchy foods. ❖ Can develop hot spots. ❖ Pits if used to store salty or acid foods.	❖ Use nonabrasive cleaners and nylon scrubbers. ❖ Use stainless steel cleaner to remove stains. ❖ Do not use to store salty or acid foods.
Copper	❖ Excellent heat conductor. ❖ Attractive.	❖ Discolors easily. ❖ Discolors food and may create toxic compounds. Inside must be lined with tin or stainless steel.	❖ Dry after washing. ❖ Do not scour inside—the thin lining may be worn away. ❖ Polish with copper cleaner or mixture of flour and vinegar.
Cast Iron	❖ Distributes heat evenly. ❖ Retains heat well.	❖ Heavy. ❖ Rusts if not wiped dry after washing.	❖ Store in a dry place. ❖ Store cover separately—pan may rust if stored covered.
Glass	❖ Attractive. Can be used for cooking and serving. ❖ Easy to clean.	❖ Breaks easily, especially if extreme temperature change. ❖ Some can be used only on the cooktop; others just in the oven. ❖ Holds heat, but does not conduct heat well.	❖ May need a wire grid if used on an electric cooktop. ❖ Use nonabrasive cleaners and nylon scrubbers. ❖ Do not plunge hot pan into cold water or put into the refrigerator.

Food and Nutrition Science

Materials Experiment: Bring to class samples of four or more types of saucepans of equal size. Ask students to hypothesize which pan will cook fastest based on the chart information. They can test their hypotheses by heating 2 cups (500 mL) of refrigerated water in each pan using the same burner preheated to the same temperature. With a candy thermometer and a stop watch, students can test how fast the water reaches a given temperature. Which pan cools most quickly? What conclusions can be drawn?

Material	Characteristics/Uses	Disadvantages	Care
Glass-Ceramic	❖ Goes from freezer to oven or cooktop. ❖ Durable, heat-resistant, attractive. ❖ Used for roasting, broiling, and baking in conventional or microwave ovens.	❖ May break if dropped. ❖ Holds heat well—reduce oven temperatures by 25°F (14°C) for baked goods.	❖ Use nonabrasive cleaners and nylon scrubbers. ❖ Dishwasher safe. ❖ Use manufacturer's care instructions.
Stoneware	❖ Attractive. ❖ Use for cooking and serving. ❖ Retains heat.	❖ Breaks easily.	❖ Dishwasher safe. ❖ Use nonabrasive cleaners and nylon scrubbers.
Enamel (glass baked on metal)	❖ Attractive. Can be used to cook and serve.	❖ Chips easily.	❖ Dishwasher safe. ❖ Use nonabrasive cleaners and nylon scrubbers.
Microwave-safe plastic	❖ Durable. ❖ Stain-resistant. ❖ Easy to clean.	❖ Some cannot be used in conventional ovens. ❖ Can be scratched by sharp kitchen tools.	❖ Dishwasher safe. ❖ Use nonabrasive cleaners and nylon scrubbers.
Nonstick Finishes	❖ Keeps foods from sticking to pans—fat may not be necessary for browning, sautéing, or frying.	❖ Easily scratched by metal kitchen tools or abrasive cleaners. ❖ High heat may stain finish or warp pan.	❖ Follow manufacturer's directions for use and care. Some cannot be washed in dishwasher. ❖ Use non-metal tools to prevent scratching.

- As a general rule, all types of cookware should be washed in hot water with detergent.
- To remove baked-on food, soak pans in hot water with a little detergent prior to washing.

Student Experiences

1. **Decision Making:** Have students study the chart on pages 260-261. Based on the information provided, ask them to choose the cookware materials they would prefer. Ask students to share their selections and the factors that influenced their decisions. Have students identify the most and least desirable cookware materials. Be sure students give reasons for their answers. *(Key skill: consumer skills)*

2. **Evaluating Cookware:** Have students work in groups to evaluate the quality of several types of cookware. Ask students to compare the quality of construction, balance, handles, covers, weight, and potential uses. Ask groups to report their findings to the class. Add additional points as needed after each presentation. *(Key skill: analysis)*

Special Needs Strategies

Learning Disabled: Make flash cards of appliances, cookware, and cooking tools. Have students practice identifying each item and its uses.

Comprehension Check

1. Ask students to list and describe several basic types of cookware. Are some more necessary than others? Why? *(See list on page 262; the cookware you use most often depends on your lifestyle, the foods you ordinarily cook, and the methods you use to cook them.)*

2. Ask students to explain why it is necessary to reduce the heat if you bake in glass. *(Glass absorbs more heat than metal, so foods get hotter faster.)*

3. Ask students to list and describe several common kinds of bakeware. Ask students if any of these items have more than one use. Why might it be best to consider buying cookware and bakeware that has multiple uses? *(Buying items that have multiple uses can save money as well as space in the kitchen.)*

Safety Check

(Page 259) Tell students that copper is not the only metal that releases metal ions into food. When acidic foods such as tomato sauce are cooked in iron cookware, the iron content of the food increases. Why is this not considered to be dangerous?

Cookware

Many kinds of cookware are available for cooktop use.

❖ **Saucepans.** The most common type of cookware. They have one long handle and often come with a cover. Sizes range from 1/2 qt. to 4 qt. (500 mL to 4 L). Usually made of metal or heatproof glass.

❖ **Pots.** Larger and heavier than saucepans, ranging in size from 3 to 20 qt. (3 to 20 L). Pots have two small handles, one on either side, making it easier to lift a heavy pot. Most pots come with covers.

❖ **Skillets** (sometimes called frypans). Used for browning and frying foods. They vary in size and often have matching covers.

❖ **Double boiler.** Consists of two saucepans—a smaller one fitting into a larger one—and a cover. Boiling water in the bottom pan gently heats the food in the upper pan. Used for cooking foods that scorch easily, such as milk, chocolate, sauces, and cereal.

❖ **Dutch oven.** A pot with a close-fitting cover. Some come with a rack to keep meat and poultry from sticking to the bottom. The Dutch oven is used on top of the range or in the oven.

❖ **Steamer.** A basketlike container that holds food. It is placed inside a saucepan containing a small amount of boiling water. Small holes in the steamer allow steam to pass through to cook food.

❖ **Pressure cooker.** A heavy pan with a locked-on cover and a steam gauge. Steam builds up inside the pan, causing very high cooking temperatures that cook food more quickly.

Dutch oven

Skillet

Saucepans

Steamer

Stockpot

Double boiler   Pressure cooker

262 Chapter 9: Cooking Methods

Food and Nutrition Science

Minimizing Nutrient Loss: Emphasize that students should check cookware thoroughly before making a purchase. Point out that the purpose of a tight-fitting cover is to prevent nutrient loss. Ask students how the nutrients would be lost if the cover was loose-fitting or not used. *(The food would take longer to cook. There would be more exposure to air. Additional water would have to be added to replace evaporation losses. All these factors would increase nutrient loss.)*

Bakeware

Most bakeware consists of pans of different sizes and shapes. Light-colored pans transfer oven heat to food quickly and give baked products a light, delicate crust. Darker pans absorb more heat from the oven and can produce thick brown crusts in baked products, though not in other foods.

Glass pans absorb more heat than metal bakeware. If you use a glass pan for baking, reduce the oven temperature by 25°F (14°C).

Here are some basic types of bakeware:

- ❖ *Loaf pan.* A deep, narrow, rectangular pan used for baking breads and meatloaf.
- ❖ *Cookie sheet.* A flat, rectangular pan designed for baking cookies and biscuits. A cookie sheet has two or three open sides.

- ❖ *Baking sheet.* Similar to a cookie sheet, except it has four shallow sides about 1 inch (2.5 cm) deep. Used for baking sheet cakes, pizza, chicken pieces, and fish.
- ❖ *Cake pans.* Come in assorted sizes and shapes.
- ❖ *Tube pan.* A cake pan with a tube in the center. Used for baking angel food cakes.
- ❖ *Pie pans.* Shallow round pans with slanted sides. Used for pies, tarts, and quiches.
- ❖ *Muffin pans.* Used for baking muffins, rolls, and cupcakes. Available with six or twelve cups.
- ❖ *Roasting pans.* Large, heavy pans, oval or rectangular in shape. They may be covered or uncovered. Used for roasting meat and poultry.
- ❖ *Casserole.* A covered or uncovered pan used for baking and serving main dishes and desserts. Various sizes are available.

A variety of bakeware is available. Shiny metal pans give a light, delicate crust. Darker metal pans give a darker, thicker crust.

Student Experiences

1. **Display:** Display different types of cookware available for cooktop use. Discuss uses for each item. *(Key skill: consumer awareness)*
2. **Materials Analysis:** Discuss the advantages and disadvantages of the materials used to make bakeware. *(Key skill: consumer awareness)*

Using the Photo

Have students identify the bakeware items shown in the photo on page 263 and discuss uses for each item. Which would they consider most versatile?

Lab Experience

Test the effects of different bakeware materials on the finished product. Pour batter into loaf pans or muffin pans made from various materials or with different finishes. Place the pans in the same preheated oven and bake for the same amount of time. Have students compare the results and draw conclusions.

Thinking Skills

Creativity: Ask students to work in groups to discuss the following questions: When making a purchase, do you ever have trouble deciding which brand, color, model, or size you should buy? Is it easier to make a selection when you know more or less about the item you are buying? Tell students to brainstorm on ways to help the indecisive buyer. Ask groups to record their best ideas and share them with the class.

Teaching . . .

• Cooking Tools

(text pages 264-265)

Comprehension Check

1. Ask students to describe cooking tools that a cook might need. *(See list on page 264.)*

2. Discuss the reasons a person might need two different kinds of thermometers: one for meat and one for candy. *(They are made differently and are used for different purposes.)*

Student Experiences

1. **Identifying Cooking Tools:** Hand students a cooking tool as they come into class. As you call on each student, ask him or her to identify the tool and tell what it is used for. *(Key skill: analysis)*

2. **Foods Lab Survey:** Have students locate the cooking tools in the foods lab. Point out that these items are stored near the range. Have students make a list of the tools they find. *(Key skill: writing)*

Ask students what familiar American cooking method the tandoor resembles. Point out the resemblance to a meat smoker. Have interested students research both methods to find further similarities and differences and report their findings to the class.

One traditional method of cooking food in India is with a *tandoor*. This is a clay oven shaped like a bucket or a beehive. Food is placed in the tandoor and cooked over a charcoal fire.

Cooking Tools

A variety of tools are available for the many different cooking tasks. Here are some you might find helpful:

❖ **Turner.** Used to lift and turn flat foods such as hamburgers and pancakes.
❖ **Tongs.** Used to grip and lift hot, bulky foods, such as broccoli spears.
❖ **Basting spoon.** Used to stir and baste foods during cooking.
❖ **Baster.** A long tube with a bulb on the end used for suctioning up juices for basting.
❖ **Ladle.** Has a small bowl and a long handle for dipping hot liquids from a pan.
❖ **Pastry brush.** Used to brush hot foods with sauce or pastry with a glaze.
❖ **Skewers.** Long rods made of metal or bamboo, with one pointed end. Pieces of food are threaded onto them for cooking or serving.
❖ **Meat thermometer.** Used to measure the internal temperature of meat and poultry. Different types are used for conventional and microwave cooking.
❖ **Wire cooling racks.** Used for holding baked goods during cooling or hot pans when they are removed from the heat.
❖ **Potholders, oven mitts.** Thick cloth pads used to protect hands while handling hot containers.
❖ **Wooden spoon.** Used to stir hot food. Does not retain heat.
❖ **Candy thermometer.** Measures the temperature of sugar syrup. or candy cooked to high temperatures.

264   Chapter 9: Cooking Methods

Turner

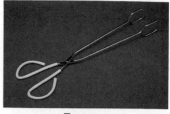

Tongs

Basting spoon

Baster

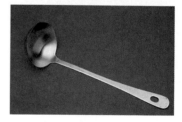

Ladle

Thinking Skills

Critical Thinking: Have students visit a discount store and a department store to record the prices of several different types of cooking tools. Were the same types and brands available in both places? Were items in general more expensive at the department store or the discount store? Were there any exceptions? Ask students to draw conclusions.

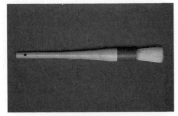
Pastry brush

Skewers

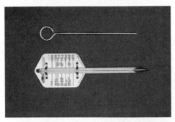
Meat thermometer

Wire cooling rack

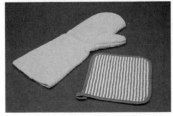
Potholders, oven mitts

Wooden spoon

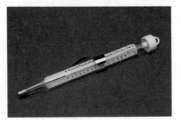
Candy thermometer

Section 9.1 Review

RECALL THE FACTS

1. How are the conventional, convection, and microwave ovens alike? How are they different?

2. Name four small appliances for cooking foods.

3. What are the key differences between a saucepan and a pot? Between a cookie sheet and a baking sheet?

DISCUSS YOUR IDEAS

4. What small cooking appliances might you find most useful in a kitchen? Why?

APPLY YOUR LEARNING

5. Working in groups, identify the cooking equipment found in the foods lab kitchen and where it is located. Be prepared to report orally to your teacher.

Section 9.1: Equipment for Cooking   265

Completing the Section

Review

• Ask students to summarize the main ideas in this section.

• Have students complete the Section Review. (Answers appear below.)

Evaluation

• Ask students to write a short essay describing the appliances, cookware, bakeware, and cooking tools that should be found in a well-equipped kitchen.

• Have students take the quiz for section 9.1. (Refer to the *Section Quizzes* booklet or construct your own quiz using the *Testmaker Software*.)

Reteaching

• Create flash cards that show different cookware and bakeware items. Have students use the cards to practice identifying each item and describing its purpose.

• Refer to the *Reteaching Activities* booklet for the Section 9.1 activity sheet.

Enrichment

• Have students research nonstick cooking materials. How and when was the coating material first discovered? What other uses does it have?

Closure

• Lead a class discussion on the importance of having the proper tools and equipment in the kitchen.

Answers to Section Review

1. Conventional and convection ovens have a bottom heating element; convection ovens also have a fan that circulates the heated air. Microwave ovens use microwaves to cause food molecules to vibrate, which produces friction, which heats the food.

2. *Any four:* Toaster, toaster oven, electric skillet, portable electric burner, slow cooker, broiler/grill, rice cooker/steamer.

3. A saucepan has one long handle and is not as heavy as a pot; a pot has two short handles, one on each side. A baking sheet has slightly higher sides so that sheet cakes and various other foods can be cooked on it.

4. Answers will vary.

5. Answers will vary.

SECTION 9.2

Heat and Cooking

OBJECTIVES

After studying this section, you should be able to:

- Explain how heat is transferred by conduction, convection, and radiation.
- Describe some changes in food brought about by cooking.
- Explain basic differences between moist heat cooking, dry heat cooking, and frying.

LOOK FOR THESE TERMS

conduction
convection
convection current
radiation
moist heat
dry heat
frying

Wonderful things happen in the kitchen. A mixture of vegetables, meat, and water becomes a savory stew. A turkey browning in the oven or soup simmering on top of the range creates delectable aromas. All these delightful changes—and many, many more—are the result of applying heat to food. Learning more about heat and its effects can help you better understand basic cooking procedures.

Methods of Heat Transfer

When any material—metal, glass, or a food—is heated, its molecules vibrate. The greater the heat, the higher the vibration.

As you learned in Section 9.1, there are many different cooking appliances. They use a variety of methods to create heat for cooking. For example, the heat may come from:

- ❖ Combustion, or burning, as in the flame on a gas burner.
- ❖ Electrical resistance, as in an electric range or a toaster oven.
- ❖ A magnetic field in an induction cooktop.
- ❖ Vibrations caused by microwave energy.

Heat affects the appearance, flavor, and texture of foods.

No matter how the heat is generated, it must travel to the food or within the food. Heat always flows from warmer areas to cooler areas. This can happen in three ways.

❖ *Conduction.* In **conduction,** heat travels by direct contact. As molecules are heated, they pass the heat on to neighboring molecules. In this way, heat can travel within an object and to other objects in direct contact. Think of a pancake cooking in a skillet. Heat from the cooktop element is conducted to the skillet. The heat from the skillet is conducted to the bottom of the pancake, and from there to the inside. To cook the top of the pancake, you flip it over. Can you see why?

❖ *Convection.* Heat can also be transferred by the movement of air or liquid. This process is called **convection.** As air or liquid is heated, the hotter portions rise above the cold. This creates a **convection current**—a circular flow of air or liquid resulting from uneven heating. Imagine a saucepan of water heating on the cooktop. The water nearest the bottom of the saucepan gets warm and rises through the colder water to the surface. The colder

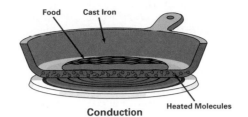

Conduction

In conduction, heat is transferred to food through direct contact with a heated surface.

water on the surface is forced down to the saucepan bottom. As the cold water on the bottom of the saucepan warms up, it again rises to the surface. This process continually repeats, creating a convection current. This same process also occurs with heated air in an oven.

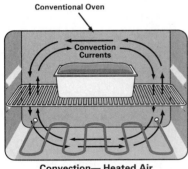

Convection— Heated Air

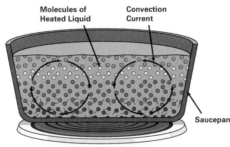

Convection— Liquids

Convection currents result from the flow of warm and cool air or liquid.

Food and Nutrition Science

Convection Currents: Convection currents create a continuous movement of air or liquid. In a convection oven, for example, as air near the heating element becomes warmer, it begins to rise, displacing the relatively cool air toward the top of the oven. Because the warmer air is now away from the heating element, it begins to cool slightly. In the meantime, the cooler air cannot escape the oven, so it is forced down toward the burner. As it gets near the burner, it begins to warm and rise back to the top of the oven, again displacing the cooler air.

Comprehension Check

1. Ask students to list three ways in which heat travels to or through foods. *(conduction, convection, and radiation)*

2. Ask students to explain what a convection current is. How is this related to cooking food? *(A convection current is the current of air or liquid that results when hotter portions rise above cooler portions. This is the principle behind the convection oven.)*

Student Experiences

1. **Menu Planning:** Have students plan a menu that includes all three methods of heat transfer. *(Key skill: science)*

2. **Making Comparisons:** Have students write a report comparing energy usage of convection, microwave, and conventional gas and electric ovens. *(Key skill: writing)*

Comprehension Check

1. Ask students to describe the various ways in which heat affects food. *(It changes the color, releases flavor and aroma, changes texture, and has an effect on nutrients.)*

2. Discuss the results of cooking in dry heat. *(Food browns and develops a crisp or tender crust yet stays moist and tender inside.)*

Student Experiences

1. **Recipe Search:** Have students bring to class recipes that specify various ways of heating or cooking foods. Have students make a chart classifying the recipes according to cooking method (moist heat, dry heat, or frying). *(Key skill: writing)*

2. **Research:** Have students find use library references to find magazine or journal articles that refer to different heating methods. Ask students to write a brief written summary of the articles. *(Key skills: reading, writing)*

Lab Experience

Have students cook a vegetable such as potatoes or carrots. Compare the taste, aroma, texture, and color of the vegetables before and after cooking. Ask students to list changes that occur when food is cooked.

❖ ***Radiation.*** Heat can travel through space in the form of waves of energy called *infrared rays.* When these rays strike an object, the object is warmed. This heat transfer method is called **radiation.** The sun radiates heat to warm the Earth. In a similar way, radiant heat from a broiler strikes the food in the pan below.

Most cooking techniques use a combination of some or all of these heat transfer processes. For example, a broiler heats the surface of a food by radiation. The heat travels through the food by conduction.

How Heat Affects Food

Heat affects food in many ways. For instance, it changes the color of foods. Some foods become darker and some lighter when cooked.

Heat also releases flavor and aroma from food. Cooking different foods together allows flavors to mingle, creating a pleasing combination.

Heat changes the texture of foods, too. Some foods become harder, some softer, some crispy, and some tender. Too much heat can dry food out, scorch or burn it, and boil away liquids. Heat also has an effect on nutrients, as you will see.

The exact effect of heat on food depends on the food and the cooking method.

Differences in Cooking Methods

Most cooking methods fall into three basic categories: moist heat, dry heat, and frying. Each has different characteristics.

Moist heat cooking involves either liquid or steam. Examples range from rice cooked in a saucepan of water to stew made in a slow cooker.

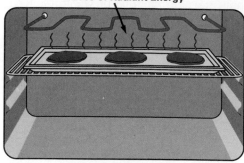

Waves of Radiant Energy

Thermal Radiation

Heat can also be transferred through infrared rays, as in a broiler or charcoal grill.

Moist heat cooking can produce tender, flavorful one-dish meals. What other types of foods are best cooked with moist heat?

Food and Nutrition Science

Frying Temperatures: Have students research and/or test the effect of cooking temperature on deep-fat fried foods. What happens when you fry foods at the proper temperature? *(The breaded or batter-coated surface quickly forms a protective shield that prevents the oil from penetrating the food.)*

What if the oil temperature is too low? *(Oil reaches the food before a protective shield can form, and the food becomes grease-soaked rather than light and crispy.)* What if the oil temperature is too high? *(The breading or batter will burn before the food cooks.)*

Moist heat may be used for a number of reasons. Long, slow moist heat cooking can help tenderize meat. Some foods, like rice or dry beans, must absorb liquid as they cook. Sometimes cooking foods together in broth or a sauce helps to blend their flavors.

Foods cooked in moist heat (or in the microwave) do not brown. They also do not develop a crisp or tender crust.

Cooking in **dry heat** means cooking food uncovered without added moisture. It requires a conventional range or similar appliance, such as a toaster oven. A microwave oven will not give the same results.

Dry heat cooking is used for tender meat, poultry, and fish and for baked products. The food develops a brown crust.

Food cooked in dry heat browns and develops a crisp or tender crust, yet stays moist and tender inside. A rack may be used under foods to help drain away fats and liquids.

Frying—cooking in fat—is a third basic method. Fat can be heated to a higher temperature than water. This high cooking temperature gives the food a brown, crisp surface and distinct flavor. A disadvantage of frying is that it adds fat to food.

As you continue your studies, you will learn more about different cooking methods and their effects on specific foods.

Science Connection

Chemistry
The Maillard Reaction

Food cooked in dry heat or in fat goes through a browning process. As food browns, the color, flavor, and texture change due to complex chemical changes. One of these changes is called the *Maillard reaction*. It occurs when carbohydrates (either sugar or starch) and amino acids combine on the surface of a food such as roasting meat. The reaction occurs only at temperatures over 300°F (150°C). The surface of food cooked in dry heat or in fat reaches that temperature. With moist heat, the cooking temperature is limited to the boiling point of water, 212°F (100°C). That is why foods cooked in moist heat do not brown.

Teaching . . .

• How Cooking Affects Nutrients

(text page 270)

Comprehension Check

1. Ask students to explain the effect of heating on beta carotene, vitamin C, thiamin, and folate. Ask students to suggest explanations for the different ways heat affects nutrients.

2. Discuss the effect of cooking in liquid. Which vitamins can be lost by cooking foods in liquid? *(The water-soluble vitamins: C and the B vitamins)*

3. Ask students if it is possible to lose fat-soluble vitamins by cooking. *(Yes, they may be lost as fat or juices drip from meat, poultry, and fish.)*

Student Experiences

1. **Guest Speaker:** Ask a nutritionist to speak to the class cooking methods that preserve nutrients in foods. *(Key skill: listening)*

2. **Chart Making:** Have students make a chart showing the effects of cooking on nutrients. How may nutrients be lost during cooking? *(Key skill: writing)*

Food and Nutrition Science

The Effects of Cooking: Ask students: Why do people cook food? Have one or more students research each of the most common cooking methods and report on what cooking does to the chemical, physical, and nutritional character of food. *(Cooking may increase palatability, kill unwanted microorganisms, soften the texture, improve digestibility, and affect nutrient content of food.)*

Completing the Section

Review

- Ask students to summarize the main ideas in this section.
- Have students complete the Section Review. (Answers appear below.)

Evaluation

- Ask students to prepare an outline of the topics covered in this chapter, using "Methods of Heat Transfer" and "How Heat Affects Food" as main topics.
- Have students take the quiz for section 9.2. (Refer to the *Section Quizzes* booklet or construct your own quiz using the *Testmaker Software*.)

Reteaching

- Name a method of cooking, then call on a student to describe the method and foods for which it is commonly used.
- Refer to the *Reteaching Activities* booklet for the Section 9.2 activity worksheet.

Enrichment

- Have students research and report to the class the number of calories added to foods by different methods of cooking in fat. Which methods add the least fat?

Closure

- Refer to the motivator at the beginning of this section. What method of heat transfer did early people use when they cooked over fires?

How Cooking Affects Nutrients

One of the goals of food preparation is to retain nutrients such as vitamins and minerals. You have already learned that proper storage helps retain nutrients. Another key is to choose cooking methods that minimize nutrient loss and use them properly.

Some nutrients can be destroyed by cooking heat. These include vitamin C, thiamin, and folate.

When foods are cooked in liquid, water-soluble vitamins and some minerals dissolve into the liquid. Unless the cooking liquid is eaten, the nutrients are lost. Some minerals and fat-soluble vitamins may be lost as fats and juices drip from meat, poultry, and fish.

Very little protein is lost during cooking. However, animal proteins are sensitive to high temperatures. Overcooking in dry heat toughens them, making them hard to eat.

As you study different foods and cooking methods, you will learn more about specific ways to retain vitamins and minerals and reduce fat.

Learning more about cooking methods will help you minimize nutrient loss in the foods you prepare.

Section 9.2 Review

RECALL THE FACTS

1. Briefly describe the three ways heat can be transferred to food during cooking.

2. Name three general ways cooking can change food.

3. What are three basic categories of cooking methods? Which could you use to make meat more tender? Which could you use to brown meat?

DISCUSS YOUR IDEAS

4. How might understanding heat transfer processes help you in using appliances to cook food?

APPLY YOUR LEARNING

5. Find a simple recipe for a cooked vegetable. Compare the taste, aroma, texture, and color of the vegetable before and after cooking. Describe your findings to the class.

Answers to Section Review

1. *Conduction:* heat travels by direct contact; *convection:* heat is transferred by the movement of air or liquid; *radiation:* heat travels in the form of energy called infrared rays.

2. It changes the color, flavor, and texture of foods.

3. Moist heat, dry heat, and frying; moist heat; frying.

4. Answers will vary; example: By understanding how the appliance heats food, you can make adjustments when necessary for the amount of food, type of food, or cooking time.

5. Answers will vary.

SECTION 9.3

Microwave Cooking Techniques

OBJECTIVES

After studying this section, you should be able to:

- Explain why the choice of power setting, foods for cooking, and cookware are important in microwave cooking.
- Describe the techniques necessary for successful microwaving.
- Identify safety precautions for microwave oven use.

LOOK FOR THESE TERMS

watts
hot spots
arcing
vent
standing time

Microwaving is a fast, healthful way to cook. Food cooks quickly with less fat and liquid than most conventional methods. That means more of the water-soluble vitamins are retained and fewer vitamins are destroyed by heat.

Microwave Oven Basics

Microwave cooking is not complicated, but it is different from conventional methods. For success, start by reading the owner's manual. It will give specific directions for using your microwave oven. It will also help you understand how the microwave power settings work, the kinds of foods that can be microwaved, and the proper equipment to use.

Power Settings

To cook in a microwave oven, you choose a power setting. The higher the power setting, the more microwaves produced and the faster the cooking. The power setting may be identified as a percentage, such as 50 or 100 percent power, or a description, such as low, medium, or high. The chart below gives typical equivalents for these two kinds of power settings. Microwave ovens do differ, so be sure to check the owner's manual.

Microwave Power Levels

Description	Percentage of Power
High	100%
Medium-High	70%
Medium	50%
Medium-Low	30%
Low	10%

Microwave ovens vary in the amount of microwaves they produce at each setting because they have different power ratings. Electrical power is measured in units called **watts.** The higher the oven wattage, the more microwaves are produced at various settings. Ovens range in wattage from about 400 to 700 watts. You'll usually find the watt rating on the back of the oven, along with the serial and model numbers.

Section 9.3
Microwave Cooking Techniques

Introducing the Section

Motivators

- Ask students how many have used microwave ovens. Where have they used them? What foods have students cooked in them? What do students perceive as their advantages and disadvantages?
- Show two examples of banana bread or another quick bread—one baked in a conventional oven and the other baked in a microwave oven. Can students identify which was baked in which oven? Have students taste the two samples and compare. Which sample do they prefer?

Objectives

- Have students read the section objectives. Discuss the purpose of studying this section.

Vocabulary

- Pronounce the terms listed under "Look for These Terms." Have students find the terms and their definitions in the section.

Guided Reading

- Have students look at the headings within Section 9.3 to preview the concepts that will be discussed.
- Have students read the section and complete the appropriate part of the Chapter 9 Study Guide in the *Student Workbook.*

Teacher's Classroom Resources—Section 9.3

Refer to these resources in the TCR package:

Reproducible Lesson Plans
Student Workbook
Extending the Text
Reteaching Activities
Section Quizzes
Testmaker Software
Color Transparencies

Teaching . . .

• **Microwave Oven Basics: Power Settings**

(text page 271)

Comprehension Check

1. Ask students to explain how the power setting affects cooking in a microwave oven. *(The higher the power setting, the more microwaves produced and the faster the food cooks.)*

2. Ask students to explain why some microwaves produce more microwaves than others at the same power setting. What is the relationship between wattage and microwaves? *(Microwave ovens have different power ratings. Higher wattages produce more microwaves at the same setting.)*

Student Experiences

1. **Reading Ads:** Have students read ads for microwave ovens to determine the range of wattage available. Discuss how the wattage of the microwave oven affects cooking times. *(Key skill: reading)*

2. **Finding Recipes:** Have students find a recipe that gives directions for conventional cooking and microwave cooking. Have students write a brief report on the differences between the two methods. *(Key skill: writing)*

> **See Also . . .**
>
> • *Food Science Resources* booklet, "Cooking Vegetables by Conventional and Microwave Cooking Methods" experiment.

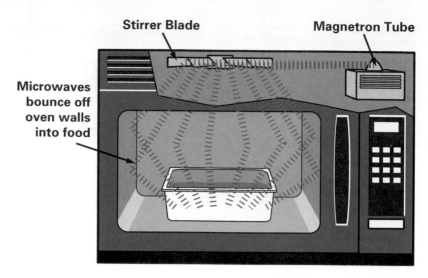

Microwaves produced by the magnetron tube are distributed throughout the oven by the stirrer blade. Those that hit the walls bounce off and back to the food.

> ✓ **SAFETY CHECK**
>
> Standards for microwave ovens require at least two independent interlock systems. Each of these systems stops the production of microwaves the moment the latch is released or the door is opened. If an interlock system fails, a monitoring system stops the oven. Don't operate the oven if the door is bent, the latches or hinges are broken or loosened, or the door seals are damaged.

Foods to Microwave

Microwaves cook by making food molecules vibrate. The microwaves penetrate food to a depth of about 1½ inches (3.8 cm). There they agitate food molecules and produce heat. If the food is thicker, conduction moves the heat deeper into the food and eventually cooks it throughout.

Microwave cooking is a better choice for some foods than others. Generally, the best choices are foods that are moist to begin with or can be cooked in moist heat.

Food Composition

What a food is made up of—its composition—affects the way it cooks in the microwave. Understanding a few basic principles will help you microwave successfully.

Food and Nutrition Science

Nutrient Retention and Microwaving: In general, there is less nutrient loss in foods cooked in a microwave oven than in those cooked conventionally. Fewer heat-sensitive nutrients are destroyed due to shorter microwave cooking times. Because less liquid is needed in many microwave recipes, there is less chance for water-soluble nutrients to dissolve in liquid.

Water, fat, and sugar are heated most quickly by microwaves. Foods high in water, such as vegetables, will cook faster than foods with a lower water content, such as meat.

Foods like pasta or rice need time to absorb liquids as they cook. As a result, there is no real time savings from cooking such foods in the microwave.

Concentrations of fat and sugar become much hotter than the rest of the food, creating **hot spots**—areas of intense heat. These hot spots can burn your skin and mouth. With a jelly doughnut, for example, the jelly may be superheated when the doughnut is only warm.

Before microwaving, use a fork to pierce foods that have a protective skin. This will keep the food from bursting as steam develops during cooking.

Salt also attracts microwaves. The food under the salt will cook faster. Wait until after cooking to sprinkle salt on food.

Foods like potatoes and winter squash have a skin that keeps moisture from evaporating. Steam can build up inside the skin and cause the food to burst. Pierce foods like these with a fork to allow steam to escape. For the same reason, do not cook eggs in the shell in the microwave—they will burst.

Other Factors

Here are some additional principles to guide you in microwave cooking.

❖ **Food density.** The more dense the food, the longer the cooking time. The heavier a food feels for its size, the more dense it is. For example, a slice of bread is less dense than a slice of meat of the same size.

❖ **Shape and size of food.** Foods of a uniform thickness cook most evenly. If foods are unevenly shaped, the thinner parts will cook through before the thicker parts. Smaller pieces cook faster than large ones.

❖ **Starting temperature of food.** The colder the food is to start with, the longer it will take to cook. Thaw most frozen foods, except vegetables, before microwaving. For commercially frozen foods, follow package directions.

❖ **Amount of food.** The more food you're cooking, the longer it will take. The same number of microwaves are produced no matter how much food you put in. One potato cooks quickly, but four potatoes take longer because they must share the microwaves.

Microwave Cookware

Microwaves are reflected by metal but pass through glass, plastic, and paper materials. These characteristics are important to remember when choosing and using containers for cooking.

Metal and foil are not generally used in microwave ovens. They can cause **arcing,** electrical sparks that can damage the oven

Teaching . . .

• **Foods to Microwave**

(text pages 272-273)

Comprehension Check

1. Ask students to list the food ingredients that are heated most quickly by microwaves *(water, fat, and sugar).*

2. Ask students to explain what "hot spots" are. *(They are areas of intense heat; created by concentrations of sugar or fat in a food.)*

3. Discuss the effects of food density on microwave cooking time.

4. Ask students to describe several factors that have an effect on microwave cooking times. *(food density; shape and size of food; starting temperature; amount of food)*

Student Experiences

1. **Class Discussion:** Discuss the advantages and disadvantages of cooking various foods in the microwave oven. Which foods cook faster? Which require as much time as by conventional methods? Which foods produce high quality results? Which are less satisfactory when cooked in the microwave? *(Key skill: analysis)*

2. **Chart Making:** Have students make a chart showing the effects of food's composition on the way it cooks in the microwave. *(Key skill: writing)*

Lab Experience

Have students cut potatoes into various sizes and shapes, then microwave the pieces of potato on High, checking frequently to see whether the pieces are done. (Rotate frequently.) Which piece was done first? Last? What conclusions can students draw?

More About the Microwave Oven

Microwaves had been used for many years before the invention of the oven. Dr. Percy L. Spencer, of Waltham, Massachusetts, was experimenting with radar in 1945.

Noticing that a chocolate bar in his pocket melted, he wondered if microwave energy could be used for cooking. He popped corn with microwaves and filed a patent for a microwave oven in 1945. At first, microwave ovens were large and expensive. By 1967, they had been modified enough to be practical for consumers. Since then, microwave ovens have become a major appliance.

Teaching . . .

• Microwave Cookware

(text pages 273-274)

Comprehension Check

1. Discuss why it is important to read the owner's manual before using metals in the microwave and to avoid the use of metal cookware. *(Metal may cause electrical sparks that can damage the oven or start a fire.)*

3. Ask students to explain why recycled paper should not be used in a microwave. *(It may contain metal fibers that could start a fire.)*

Student Experiences

1. **Display:** Prepare a display of cooking containers. Ask students to sort the containers into two groups: those that can be used safely in the microwave oven and those that cannot. Summarize characteristics of microwave-safe containers. Explain why metal causes arcing in a microwave oven. *(Key skill: classifying)*

2. **Analyzing Information:** Discuss whether type of food and cooking time may affect the choice of container for microwaving. Refer students back to the "Materials for Cookware" chart on pages 260-261. *(Key skill: analysis)*

TIPS for Success

Have students follow the instructions given to test containers to determine whether they can be used safely in a microwave oven. Discuss what conclusions can be drawn from their findings.

---

or start a fire. Use metal and foil only *if* and *how* your owner's manual specifies. Never leave metal tools, such as a spoon, in food being microwaved.

Some general guidelines are given here for choosing containers for microwave cooking. Some containers that cannot withstand the high temperatures of cooking are safe for heating foods to low temperatures.

❖ **Glass and glass-ceramic.** Use ovenproof glass and glass-ceramic for cooking. Regular glass may be suitable for heating.

❖ **Stoneware, china, and pottery.** Most items are suitable for cooking unless they have metal trim. Avoid pottery with metallic glazes.

❖ **Plastic.** For cooking, use only plastic items that are marked "microwave-safe." Some special plastic can be used both in the microwave and at low to moderate temperatures in conventional ovens.

❖ **Paper.** Use paper plates only if they are firm enough to hold food. Choose paper towels labeled "microwave-safe." Avoid products containing recycled paper. They may contain metal fragments or chemicals that could catch fire.

Be sure to choose cookware that can be used safely in a microwave oven. What are some types that would not be suitable?

When you use the microwave oven, consider the shape of the container. Round containers cook food more evenly than square or rectangular ones.

The size and shape of microwave cookware also affects the way food cooks and the cooking time. Pans should be shallow with straight sides. Ring-shaped and round pans allow for even cooking. Square and rectangular pans should have rounded corners.

TIPS for Success

Testing Containers

If a glass or pottery container is not marked microwave-safe, here's a test to tell whether or not you can use it for microwave cooking. Fill a glass measuring cup with water and place it in the oven next to the empty container you are testing. Heat for two minutes on High. If the empty container is too hot to touch, do not use it in the microwave oven.

More About Containers

The shape of the container is important in microwave cooking:

• A ring shape is most efficient because it allows microwaves to enter the food from any angle. The result is faster, more even cooking. This shape is especially recommended for foods that cannot be stirred during cooking, such as cake batter.

• A round or oval shape ranks next.

• A square or rectangular pan can be used if the corners are rounded, not sharp.

• Containers should have vertical rather than slanted sides. If the sides slope, some of the food is more shallow than the rest. Therefore it receives more microwaves and may overcook.

Microwaving Successfully

A few special techniques are needed in microwave cooking. They involve food placement in the oven and in the pan, covering, stirring, rotating, turning, and timing.

Food Placement

The best arrangement of food for microwaving is a ring shape. This allows the microwaves to enter food from as many sides as possible. A meatloaf, for example, can be shaped into a ring in a pan or cooked in a ring mold.

When possible, leave space between pieces of food. This, too, allows better microwave penetration.

When cooking foods of uneven thickness, use the characteristics of microwave patterns to your advantage. Food in the center of the oven cooks more slowly. Arrange food like the spokes of a wheel, with the thickest or toughest parts toward the outside and the thinnest or most tender parts toward the center. With broccoli spears, for example, place the tops toward the center and the stalks toward the outside.

For even cooking, arrange foods for microwaving with the thickest or toughest parts toward the outside.

Covering Food

A cover holds in steam, keeps food moist, and shortens cooking time. It also keeps food from spattering in the oven.

Foods you would cover for conventional cooking are usually covered for microwave cooking. If you want foods to steam, cover them tightly. For drier foods, cover loosely.

Foods may be covered with microwave-safe glass or plastic covers. Plastic wrap, waxed paper, and paper toweling are also useful.

❖ **Plastic wrap.** Microwave-safe plastic wrap holds in steam and heat. Too much steam may build up during cooking and split the plastic. To prevent splitting, **vent** the plastic: after covering the dish, roll back one edge slightly to allow steam to escape.

❖ **Waxed paper.** Waxed paper prevents spatters and allows some steam and moisture to escape. Use it on foods such as casseroles.

❖ **Paper towels.** Paper towels absorb excess moisture and prevent spatters. Wrap rolls, breads, and sandwiches in paper towels before microwaving to keep them from becoming soggy.

When you remove covers or plastic wrap, use a potholder and tilt the cover away from you. Escaping steam can burn.

Choose the method of covering food that will give the results you want.

- Wide, shallow containers expose more of the food to the microwaves, resulting in faster, more even cooking. However, when cooking liquids that may boil, use a container twice the size of what would be used in conventional cooking. This will allow room for the boiling liquid to expand.

Thinking Skills

Reasoning: Ask students why it is sometimes necessary to make adjustments to the cooking time recommended in a microwave cookbook *(The food or dish may not be the specified size, the oven may vary in cooking power, etc.)*

Teaching . . .

- ## Microwaving Successfully

(text pages 275-276)

Comprehension Check

1. Ask students to describe proper food placement in the microwave oven. *(Use a ring shape; leave space between pieces of food; arrange thickest portions of food toward the outside.)*

2. Ask students to list coverings that are appropriate in a microwave oven. *(microwave-safe glass or plastic lids, plastic wrap, wax paper, and paper towels)*

3. Discuss the importance of venting food that has been covered with plastic wrap. *(Venting is necessary to prevent steam from building up and splitting the plastic.)*

Student Experiences

1. **Demonstration:** Microwave two portions of a food, covering one with microwavable plastic wrap and the other with plastic wrap not suitable for use in the microwave. What happens to each type of plastic wrap? Have students write a paragraph explaining their conclusions. *(Key skills: observation, writing)*

2. **Demonstration:** Microwave two small glass bowls of green vegetables for the time suggested in the instruction book. At the end of microwave time, have students observe one bowl and evaluate for color, degree of doneness, and texture. At the end of standing time, have students observe and evaluate the other bowl. What effect did standing time have upon the vegetables? *(Key skill: analysis)*

Comprehension Check

1. Ask students to list features that a microwave recipe has in addition to the information given in conventional recipes. *(Size and shape of container; how to arrange food for even cooking; whether to cover the dish; a range of cooking and standing times.)*

2. Ask students to describe safety rules for microwave cooking. *(See page 277.)*

3. Discuss the importance of cleaning spills and spots in the microwave after each use. *(Spilled food absorbs energy, reducing cooking power, and it allows bacteria to grow.)*

Student Experiences

1. **Poster Project:** Have students make posters illustrating precautions to take when using a microwave oven. *(Key skill: creativity)*

2. **Recipe Conversion:** Provide students with a copy of a conventional recipe to be adapted for microwave cooking. Have students discuss the various changes that would need to be made for successful microwave cooking. Then have students rewrite the recipe for use in a microwave oven. If possible, test the recipes. *(Key skill: writing)*

Stirring, Rotating, and Turning

Microwaves may not be distributed evenly throughout the oven, especially in older models. To make sure that food cooks as evenly as possible, it must be stirred, rotated, or turned. Unless directed otherwise, stir or turn foods after half the cooking time.

Stirring helps foods cook evenly. If the food cannot be stirred, rotate the pan. To rotate, use a potholder to grasp the pan and give it a quarter or half turn. Dense foods such as meat and poultry also have to be turned over. Use a pair of tongs and turn the food over in the pan.

Determining Cooking Time

Microwave cooking has two parts. Cooking occurs when microwaves are being produced while the food is in the oven and the oven is on. When the oven turns off, the heat inside the food continues cooking the food as it stands. This is called **standing time.**

Recipes give directions for cooking and for standing time. If the food was cooked uncovered, cover it during standing time to retain heat.

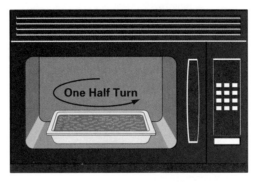

Some foods should be rotated during the cooking time so they cook more evenly. When you give a dish a half turn, the end that was at the left side of the oven is switched to the right side.

Foods continue to cook after they are removed from the microwave oven. Recipes should indicate the standing time.

Check the progress the food makes as it cooks, just as you do with conventional methods. Test food for doneness after the standing time, not before. Avoid overcooking. Foods overcooked in the microwave oven become hard and tough.

Microwave Recipes

Most microwave recipes are written for 650-watt ovens—the most common kind sold. Foods will cook slightly faster in higher wattage ovens and a bit slower in lower wattage ovens.

To adapt a standard recipe for the microwave oven, it's best to find a similar microwave recipe. A basic microwave cookbook can help you ease into microwave cooking successfully. With experience, you can begin experimenting.

A well-written microwave recipe has the same features as conventional recipes. In addition, it specifies:

- ❖ The size and shape of the cooking container.
- ❖ How to arrange food for even cooking.
- ❖ Whether or not to cover the dish.
- ❖ A range of cooking and standing times.

Thinking Skills

Reasoning: Have students explain why seasoning should be reduced in adapting a recipe to microwave cooking. *(Seasonings lose less flavor during cooking because of the microwave oven's shorter cooking time. Therefore, less seasoning is needed.)*

Food and Nutrition Science

Vegetable Cooking Experiment: See the *Food Science Resources* booklet for the "Cooking Vegetables by Conventional and Microwave Methods" teaching guide and student experiment worksheet. The experiment compares the effect of conventional and microwave cooking on fresh broccoli.

Microwave Safety and Care

Safety rules for conventional cooking also apply to microwave cooking. Review Section 7.2. Here are some additional microwave safety rules:

❖ Never turn on the oven unless there's food in it. You could damage the oven.
❖ Follow the manufacturer's directions for preparing commercially frozen foods in the microwave oven. Don't eat the food if the package turns brown. Don't reuse containers.
❖ Loosen tight-fitting covers or caps before microwaving. Otherwise, a buildup of steam pressure could cause the container to explode.
❖ Never attach kitchen magnets to the microwave oven. They can affect the electronic controls.
❖ Have your microwave oven tested by an authorized repairperson if you are concerned about microwaves leaking from the oven. Microwave leakage meters available for home use are often not reliable.

Always use potholders when removing hot foods from the microwave oven. Heat from the food can make the container too hot to handle.

Cleaning the Microwave Oven

Clean spots and spills after every use. If allowed to build up, they will absorb microwaves and cut down on the cooking power. Keep the door seal clean. Spilled food also allows bacteria to grow.

To clean the interior of the oven, wipe it with a clean, wet dishcloth. Dry it thoroughly. Do not use abrasive cleaners.

Section 9.3 Review

RECALL THE FACTS

1. What does the power setting on a microwave oven do?
2. Why are metal pans not suitable for microwave cooking?
3. What is the purpose of stirring, rotating, and turning food during cooking?
4. Give three guidelines for safe use of the microwave.

DISCUSS YOUR IDEAS

5. Many American families use their microwave ovens mainly for thawing frozen foods and for heating leftovers, commercially frozen convenience foods, and water. Why do you think more people do not use the microwave oven for other types of cooking?

APPLY YOUR LEARNING

6. Check plastic containers, tools, and cookware in the foods lab. Which items are marked microwave-safe?

9.3

Completing the Section

Review
• Ask students to summarize the main ideas in this section.
• Have students complete the Section Review. (Answers appear below.)

Evaluation
• Ask students to prepare a written summary of rules to follow when cooking in a microwave oven.
• Have students take the quiz for section 9.3. (Refer to the *Section Quizzes* booklet or construct your own quiz using the *Testmaker Software*.)

Reteaching
• Divide students into groups and assign one or more specific foods to each group. Have the groups read a microwave cookbook and report to the class how much microwave time and standing time is needed to cook each assigned food.
• Refer to the *Reteaching Activities* booklet for the Section 9.3 activity worksheet.

Enrichment
• Have students prepare a brochure explaining and illustrating techniques for successful microwave cooking. Which methods add the least fat?

Closure
• Lead a class discussion on the proper use of a microwave oven.

Answers to Section Review

1. It controls the number of microwaves produced in a given amount of time.
2. They can cause arcing and possibly start fires.
3. To make sure it cooks evenly.
4. *Any three:* Never turn on the oven unless there's food in it; follow the manufacturer's directions for preparing commercially frozen foods; loosen tight-fitting covers or caps before microwaving; never attach kitchen magnets to the microwave oven; have your microwave oven tested if you suspect microwave leakage.
5. Answers will vary. Example: They're used to cooking conventionally.
6. Answers will vary according to your lab.

9.3 Recipe

Microwave Baked Potatoes

Key Skill: Microwave Techniques

Using the Recipe

- Have students read the recipe and discuss each step. Review safety and sanitation procedures that apply to this recipe. Remind students that it is very important to pierce the potatoes before cooking them to prevent an explosion.

- Have each lab team fill out a work plan. (See the *Foods Lab Resources* booklet.)

- Have students check off the ingredient and equipment listed on the recipe worksheet and prepare the recipe.

- Have students complete the evaluation and questions on the back of the recipe worksheet.

See Also . . .

The *Foods Lab Resources* booklet for the "Microwave Baked Potatoes" recipe worksheet and other recipe alternatives.

Thinking About the Recipe

Read the recipe for "Microwave Baked Potatoes" and answer the following questions.

1. What would be the best arrangement of the potatoes for microwave cooking?
2. Why are the potatoes turned and rearranged after half the cooking time?

Microwave Baked Potatoes

Customary	Ingredients	Metric
4	Potatoes for baking	4

Yield: 4 servings

Directions

Pan: Microwave-safe dish
Power level: 100%

1. Pierce potatoes with a cooking fork.
2. Place one inch apart in microwave-safe dish. Place dish in oven.
3. Cook for 6 to 8 minutes, using 100% power.
4. Turn the potatoes over and rearrange.
5. Cook for an additional 6 to 8 minutes until done. Potatoes may still feel firm.
6. Wrap each potato in foil or paper towel. Let stand about 5 minutes to finish cooking.

Serving Suggestion: Slice potatoes in half and fluff with fork. Sprinkle with chives.

Nutrition Information

Per serving (approximate): 145 calories, 3 g protein, 34 g carbohydrate, trace of fat, 0 mg cholesterol, 8 mg sodium

---

Answers to Thinking About the Recipe

1. Answers will vary; examples: in a ring; like the spokes of a wheel (for potatoes that are thicker on one end).

2. So that the potatoes will cook evenly and get done at the same time.

Conventional Cooking Techniques

OBJECTIVES

After studying this section, you should be able to:

- Identify specific types of moist heat cooking, dry heat cooking, frying, and combination methods.
- Give guidelines for conventional cooking.

LOOK FOR THESE TERMS

stew
poach
preheating
sauté
wok

Kristie wanted to try something new, so she bought and cooked a chuck roast for her family. She cooked it the way her mother always cooked roasts—in an open pan in the oven. The roast was so tough and dry that it was hard to eat. Kristie didn't know that it was a different kind of roast than her mother usually bought and required a different cooking method.

Cooking methods vary depending on the kind of food being cooked and the results desired. In this section, you will learn about several basic methods of conventional cooking.

Moist Heat Methods

As you learned earlier, moist heat cooking methods are those in which food is cooked in a hot liquid, steam, or a combination of both. Many cooking appliances, including the microwave and slow cooker, use moist heat. When using the conventional range, you can choose between several moist heat methods. These include boiling, simmering, steaming, and pressure cooking.

Liquids bubble vigorously at boiling temperatures. The large bubbles rise quickly to the surface and break.

Section 9.4: Conventional Cooking Techniques **279**

Section 9.4
Conventional Cooking Techniques

Introducing the Section

Motivators

- Have students make a list of conventional cooking techniques. Compare the list made by students with the cooking techniques listed in the text. With which techniques are students most familiar?
- Name and briefly describe a cooking technique, then ask students to name foods that may be prepared using the technique. Point out other familiar foods that may be prepared by each technique.

Objectives

- Have students read the section objectives. Discuss the purpose of studying this section.

Vocabulary

- Pronounce the terms listed under "Look for These Terms." Have students find the terms and their definitions in the section.

Guided Reading

- Have students look at the headings within Section 9.4 to preview the concepts that will be discussed.
- Have students read the section and complete the appropriate part of the Chapter 9 Study Guide in the *Student Workbook*.

Teacher's Classroom Resources—Section 9.4

Refer to these resources in the TCR package:

Reproducible Lesson Plans
Student Workbook
Extending the Text
Reteaching Activities

Food Science Resources
Section Quizzes
Testmaker Software
Color Transparencies

Teaching . . .

• Moist Heat Methods

(text pages 279-281)

Comprehension Check

1. Ask students to explain why boiling is suitable for only a few foods. Ask students to name two foods that can be boiled. *(Because boiling may break foods apart or overcook them; it also causes more nutrient loss than other methods. Pasta and corn-on-the-cob can both be boiled.)*

2. Ask students to explain the difference between simmering and boiling. *(In simmering, the bubbles rise gently and just begin to break.)*

3. Ask students to explain the advantages of using a pressure cooker. What foods are suitable for cooking in this manner? *(It's much faster than other cooking methods; less tender cuts of meat and poultry, dry beans, soups, one-dish meals, and vegetables.)*

Using the Photo

Ask students to look again at the photo at the bottom right of page 280. Is this person lifting the cover in a safe manner? *(Yes.)* Have students identify two specific safety techniques being used in the photo. *(Potholder, opening cover to direct steam away from body.)*

Boiling

When a liquid reaches boiling temperature, it forms large bubbles that rise to the surface and break. Water boils at 212°F (100°C).

Boiling is suitable for only a few foods. Corn-on-the-cob and pasta are cooked in boiling water. Boiling is also useful when you want liquid to evaporate quickly. For instance, you might boil a sauce to thicken it or boil a soup to concentrate the flavor.

Many foods may overcook easily or break apart if boiled. Nutrient loss is higher than with other methods. Boiling also toughens foods high in protein, such as eggs.

When boiling foods, be sure to use a saucepan or pot large enough to hold the food and the boiling liquid. Bring the liquid to the boiling point, then add the food. Be sure the liquid continues boiling as the food cooks.

Simmering

Simmering differs from boiling in that bubbles in the liquid rise gently and just begin to break the surface. Water simmers at about 186°F to 210°F (86°C to 99°C).

Stewing uses simmering liquid to cook food.

Foods that would break apart or toughen if boiled can be simmered instead. Simmering is used to cook many types of food, including fruits, vegetables, and less tender cuts of meat and poultry.

To **stew** food means to cover small pieces of food with liquid, then simmer until done. To **poach** food means to simmer whole foods in a small amount of liquid until done. Eggs, fish, and whole fruits can be poached.

To simmer food, bring the liquid to a boil and then add the food. After the liquid returns to a boil, reduce the heat so the food simmers. A slow cooker can also be used to simmer some foods, such as meats and dry beans.

As with boiling, some nutrients are lost, especially water-soluble vitamins. Whenever possible, use the cooking liquid from foods such as vegetables and dry beans.

Steaming

Steaming is a method of cooking food over, but not in, boiling water. The food is usually placed in a steamer basket that fits inside a saucepan. Steam is created by a

Steaming foods helps them retain nutrients. Can you explain why?

Food and Nutrition Science

Conventional vs. Microwave Cooking Experiment: See the *Food Science Resources* booklet for the "Cooking Vegetables by Conventional and Microwave Cooking Methods" teaching guidelines and student experiment worksheet. This experiment compares the effects of both cooking method and time on the color, texture, and flavor of broccoli.

small amount of boiling water in the bottom of the pan. The boiling water does not come in contact with the food. The pan is covered during cooking to trap the steam. You can also use an electric steamer to cook food.

Many foods can be cooked in steam, including vegetables and fish. Foods retain their color, shape, and flavor well when steamed. Few nutrients are lost. Cooking time is longer with steaming than with boiling or simmering.

Pressure Cooking

A pressure cooker cooks food in steam under pressure. Because the pressure makes temperatures above 212°F (100°C) possible, the food cooks three to ten times faster than with other methods.

Use the pressure cooker for foods that take a long time to cook, such as less tender cuts of meat and poultry, dry beans, soups, one-dish meals, and vegetables. This method

has all the advantages of steaming plus faster cooking times. Follow the manufacturer's directions and safety guidelines carefully. The food in a pressure cooker is superheated and under high pressure.

Dry Heat Methods

As you have learned, cooking in dry heat means cooking food uncovered without adding any liquid or fat. Dry heat methods include roasting and baking, broiling, and pan-broiling.

Roasting and Baking

Roasting and baking both mean cooking food uncovered in a conventional or convection oven. "Roasting" generally refers to cooking large, tender cuts of meat or poultry.

Roasting and baking both refer to a dry heat cooking method used for tender foods.

Student Experiences

1. **Demonstration:** Demonstrate procedures for steaming vegetables and for using a pressure cooker. Emphasize safety practices to observe when steaming and pressure cooking. *(Key skill: safety)*

2. **Class Discussion:** What are the basic differences among the moist heat methods of cooking? How would you decide which method to use? What are the advantages of simmering foods rather than boiling them? Why is steaming a good method of preparing vegetables? What are the advantages of pressure cooking? *(Key skill: management skills)*

3. **Brainstorming:** Have students identify foods associated with each method of cooking in liquid. List the foods on the chalkboard under the appropriate methods. *(Key skill: brainstorming)*

4. **Reading Instructions:** Have students read the directions for using a pressure cooker. Ask them to make a list of safety precautions for working with pressure cookers. *(Key skills: reading, writing)*

Lab Experience

Have students use moist heat methods to prepare vegetables by boiling, simmering, steaming, and pressure cooking. Compare the results in terms of color, texture, and flavor.

More About Pressure Cookers

Atmospheric pressure affects the boiling point of water. The higher the pressure, the hotter water will get before it starts to boil. The lid of a pressure cooker is tightly sealed to trap steam, creating high pressure. The rise in pressure causes the boiling point of water to rise. The temperature of the water goes up, and food cooks faster.

• Dry Heat Methods

(text pages 281-283)

Comprehension Check

1. Ask students to describe the proper method for roasting meat and poultry. *(Use a shallow, uncovered roasting pan with a rack to drain the fat away from the food; baste it periodically with the cooking juices.)*

2. Ask students to define "preheating" and to explain why preheating is important for cooking baked goods such as breads and cakes. *(Preheating means warming up the oven for about 10 minutes before using it, so it will be at the desired temperature when the food is put in; it is important to maintain an even temperature while breads and cakes are cooking.)*

3. Ask students to list tips for broiling foods successfully. *(See "Tips for Success" on page 283.)*

4. Ask students to explain the difference between broiling and pan broiling. *(Broiling occurs in the oven, whereas pan broiling occurs in a skillet on the rangetop.)*

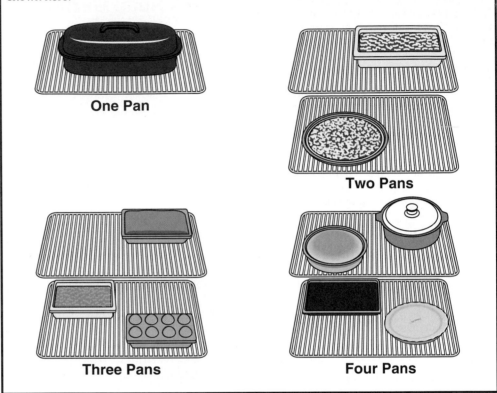

Pan Placement in the Oven

When baking, placement and spacing of pans are important. The pans must be placed so the hot air in the oven can circulate freely. If pans touch each other or the oven walls, they create a hot spot—an area of concentrated heat. The food overcooks in these areas. When baking several pans of food at one time, place them diagonally opposite one another, as shown here.

One Pan

Two Pans

Three Pans

Four Pans

"Baking" is the term used with foods such as breads, cookies, vegetables, and casseroles. However, meat, poultry, and fish may be "baked," too. (Examples include baked ham and baked chicken.)

Roasting gives tender meat and poultry a flavorful, crispy, brown crust. Use a shallow, uncovered roasting pan with a rack. The roasting rack allows fat to drain away from the food—a real benefit to those trying to reduce their fat intake.

For baked goods such as breads and cakes, preheating is important. **Preheating** means to turn the oven on about 10 minutes before using it so it will be at the desired temperature when the food is put in.

More About Cooking in a Plastic Bag

Plastic cooking bags are made specifically for cooking. It is not necessary to brown meat or poultry before placing it in a cooking bag.

Place the food in a plastic cooking bag, along with a small amount of liquid. Vegetables may be added, depending on the recipe. Close the bag and place it in a baking pan large enough to hold it. Cut slits in the bag to allow steam to escape.

Follow manufacturer's directions carefully when using a plastic cooking bag. Otherwise, the bag may burst while cooking due to a buildup of steam pressure. Hot food and grease may then spatter and catch fire.

Broiling

Broiling refers to cooking food under direct heat. The broiler pan is placed below a burner or heating element. The heat radiates down onto the food, cooking it.

Broiling is suitable for cooking tender foods such as fish, fruits, some vegetables, and tender cuts of meat and poultry. The foods cook quickly and brown well. Foods that are already cooked may be broiled for a short time to brown them or to melt cheese toppings.

A broiler pan has two parts. A slotted grid holds the food. The grid fits on the top of a shallow pan that catches drippings. This allows fat to drain away during cooking.

For broiling in most ranges, set the oven control on "broil." You cannot control the exact broiling temperature. To control the cooking, you can vary the distance of the pan from the heat and the cooking time. For thicker foods, the pan is positioned farther from the heat and the cooking time is

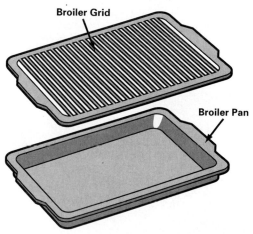

Broiler Grid

Broiler Pan

A broiler pan consists of two parts that fit together. The slots in the grid allow melted fat from the food to drain into the pan below. That makes broiling a low-fat cooking method.

SAFETY CHECK

Never cover the broiler grid with foil. The foil would keep drippings from falling through and could cause a grease fire.

Never put your hands into the broiler compartment to turn or remove food. The intense heat can burn you severely. Instead, take the broiler pan from the compartment first. Remember to use potholders. Put the pan on a heatproof surface or wire rack and turn or remove the food.

increased. This allows the food to cook all the way through without burning on the outside. Check a cookbook for guidelines about positioning specific foods for broiling.

Cooking on an outdoor or indoor grill is similar to broiling except the heat source is below the food. The food is placed on a wire grid.

TIPS for Success

Broiling Food

❖ To prevent foods from sticking, always start with a cold broiler pan.
❖ Before broiling, pat meat and poultry dry. Moisture can keep food from becoming brown and crisp.
❖ Do not salt foods before broiling. Salt draws moisture from foods, causing them to dry out.
❖ Brush fish, fruit, and vegetables lightly with oil or melted butter or margarine to keep them from charring.
❖ To turn food during broiling, use tongs instead of a fork. The fork pierces holes which allow juices to escape.

Student Experiences

1. **Demonstration:** Demonstrate how to set the oven correctly. Discuss the importance of preheating the oven for baked goods. Show correct placement of pans in the oven. Emphasize the importance of air circulation for proper baking. *(Key skill: observation)*

2. **Class Discussion:** Talk about how broiling and pan broiling differ from roasting and baking. (Only one side of the food at a time is exposed to the heat source when broiling.) Point out safety precautions when broiling and pan broiling to prevent grease fires. *(Key skill: safety awareness)*

3. **Developing Instructions:** Have students develop an instruction sheet for broiling meat. *(Key skills: critical thinking, writing)*

Safety Check

Ask students to suggest other safety tips for broiling foods. Remind students that foods that contain a large amount of fat may spatter grease as you are removing the food from the oven and even after you place it on the wire rack or heatproof surface.

Comprehension Check

1. Ask students to list and describe the three basic methods of frying *(sautéing, pan-frying, and deep-fat frying).*

2. Ask students to explain the process of braising. Why might someone choose to braise a cut of meat? *(to tenderize the meat and enhance flavor)*

3. Ask students to explain the process of stir-frying.

4. Ask students for specific examples of foods appropriate for sautéing, pan-frying, deep-fat frying, braising, and stir-frying.

Pan-Broiling

Pan-broiling is a top-of-the-range method of dry heat cooking. Foods such as hamburgers, tender cuts of steak, and some cuts of pork may be pan-broiled. The food cooks quickly and retains a minimum amount of fat.

To pan-broil, cook the food in a heavy skillet over medium heat. Do not add fat. As fat accumulates in the pan during cooking, pour it off or remove it with a baster.

Frying

Frying involves cooking food in oil or melted fat. There are several different methods:

❖ **Sautéing.** To **sauté** (saw-TAY) means to brown or cook foods in a skillet with a small amount of fat. Low to medium heat is used. This method is often used for chopped vegetables, such as onions and peppers, and small pieces of meat and fish.

❖ **Pan-frying.** Pan-frying is similar to sautéing but usually involves larger pieces of meat, poultry, or fish. The food may need to be turned several times during the cooking process for complete, even cooking. Pan-frying is often used to brown meat before cooking it in moist heat.

Sautéing is a form of frying. Small pieces of food, such as chopped onions, are cooked in a small amount of fat.

In pan-broiling, fat is removed from the skillet as it accumulates.

Special Needs Strategies

Gifted: Have students demonstrate for the class how to perform various cooking techniques.

❖ **Deep-fat frying.** This method is also called french frying. Food is immersed in hot fat and fried until done. It is used for tender foods, such as vegetables, and some breads, such as doughnuts. For best deep-fat frying results, use a deep-fat or candy thermometer to keep the fat at the correct temperature.

Combination Methods

Sometimes the best way to cook a food is by using a combination of methods. Braising and stir-frying are two popular cooking methods that combine dry heat and moist heat cooking.

Braising

Braising combines browning food (frying) with a long period of simmering to tenderize the food and enhance the flavor. It is often used for large, less tender cuts of meat and poultry.

Use a Dutch oven or other heavy pot with a tight-fitting cover. The food is pan-fried or browned on all sides. Then seasonings and a small amount of liquid are added to the food and the pot is covered. The cooking may be completed in the oven (usually at 350°F or 180°C) or on top of the range. Vegetables are sometimes added to braised meat or poultry near the end of the cooking time.

Braising combines frying and moist heat cooking. A pot roast with vegetables is prepared by braising.

Completing the Section

Review

- Ask students to summarize the main ideas in this section.
- Have students complete the Section Review. (Answers appear below.)

Evaluation

- Ask students to make a chart showing different methods of cooking using moist heat, dry heat, and frying.
- Have students take the quiz for section 9.4. (Refer to the *Section Quizzes* booklet or construct your own quiz using the *Testmaker Software*.)

Reteaching

- Show students several pictures of foods that were obviously cooked using one of the methods mentioned in this chapter. Have students identify the method used to prepare each food.
- Refer to the *Reteaching Activities* booklet for the Section 9.4 activity worksheet.

Enrichment

- Have students prepare vegetables by boiling, simmering, steaming, and pressure cooking. Compare the results in terms of color, texture, and flavor.

Closure

- Lead a discussion about the various methods of conventional cooking. Ask students to give examples.

Stir-frying is a quick way to cook foods.

Stir-Frying

Stir-frying also combines frying and moist heat cooking. Small pieces of food are fried quickly in a small amount of oil at high heat. The food is stirred constantly to keep it from sticking to the pan. During the last few minutes of cooking, a small amount of liquid is usually added to the food and the pan is covered, allowing the food to steam.

Stir-frying, which began in Asia, is most often used for cooking mixtures of vegetables and other foods. A special pan called a **wok** is traditionally used, but a skillet also works well.

Science Connection

Chemistry
Smoking Points of Fats

All fats have a *smoking point*—a temperature at which they begin to give off irritating smoke and break down chemically. Oil that has reached its smoking point is no longer good for cooking. Animal fats, such as butter and lard, have low smoking points. Safflower, soybean, corn, and peanut oils have relatively high smoking points. They make the best choices for frying.

■ □ ■

■ Section 9.4 Review ■

RECALL THE FACTS

1. Explain the difference between simmering and boiling.
2. What equipment is needed for steaming?
3. List the methods of dry heat cooking.
4. Name and describe three methods of frying.

DISCUSS YOUR IDEAS

5. Discuss some possible reasons why more people are using steamers and woks in cooking meals.

APPLY YOUR LEARNING

6. Find several recipes for each of the following: eggs for breakfast; a vegetable side dish; a ground beef dish; soup; and chicken. Which basic cooking method does each recipe use?

■ Answers to Section Review ■

1. Boiling occurs at 212°F and is characterized by bubbles rising and breaking on the surface of the liquid. Simmering is similar, but occurs at 186-210°F; the bubbles just begin to break in simmering.
2. A saucepan with a lid and a steamer basket.
3. Roasting, baking, broiling, and pan broiling.
4. Sautéing (brown or cook foods in a skillet with a small amount of fat); pan-frying (similar to sautéing but involves larger pieces of meat, poultry, or fish); deep-fat frying (food is immersed in hot fat and fried until done).
5. Answers will vary. Some people use them because more nutrients are preserved in the food.
6. Answers will vary.

Career PROFILE

Carrie Thompson
Chef

CURRENT POSITION

"I'm an executive chef for a large upscale hotel."

RESPONSIBILITIES

"I'm responsible for preparing traditional meals that are both tasty and attractively presented, as well as creating new and interesting offerings."

SKILLS

"A keen sense of taste and smell is very helpful in this career. You also need creativity and an understanding of design."

EDUCATION

"I've taken vocational courses in commercial food preparation and have completed an extensive training program sponsored by the hotel chain that employs me."

WHY I CHOSE THIS CAREER

"Even as a child I could always be found hanging around my mom in the kitchen, watching her cook. I've always enjoyed working with food."

FAVORITE PART OF THE JOB

"What's most satisfying for me is when customers take the time to send their 'compliments to the chef.'"

- Why would a sense of design be helpful in Carrie's career?
- What aspects of Carrie's job do you think you might find interesting? Why?

CAREER PROFILE: EXECUTIVE CHEF

Thinking About . . . Culinary Arts Careers

Have students think of other questions they would like to ask Carrie Thompson about being a chef. (Examples: What other options are available to chefs for employment? Do you work mostly evening hours? How many hours a week? Do you specialize in a certain kind of food?)

Ask students what other skills might be helpful for an executive chef. Why? (Administrative skills and the ability to work with other people, etc.)

Student Opportunities

Students interested in careers in culinary arts should learn to cook at home or through classes and may seek employment in a restaurant, cafeteria, or bakery.

Occupational Outlook

From cooking in small, local restaurants, cooks with experience may advance to more responsible positions or positions as chef in large establishments such as hotels and first-class restaurants.

287

For More Information

For more information about culinary arts careers, encourage students to contact:
- American Culinary Federation, P.O. Box 3466, St. Augustine, FL 32084
- The Educational Foundation of the National Restaurant Association, Suite 2620, 20 North Wacker Dr., Chicago, IL 60606
- Council on Hotel, Restaurant, and Institutional Education, 311 First St. NW, Washington, D.C. 20001

Completing the Chapter

Review

- Have students complete the Chapter Review. (Answers appear below.)

Evaluation

- Give students a simple recipe and ask them to describe how they would prepare it, naming the equipment they would use and specific method of cooking.

- Have students take the test for Chapter 9. (Refer to the *Chapter and Unit Tests* booklet or construct your own test using the *Testmaker Software*.)

■ ANSWERS ■

REVIEWING FACTS

1. Below the oven; at the top of the oven compartment.

2. To heat foods that scorch easily, such as milk, chocolate, sauces, and cereal.

3. *Any four:* Turner, tongs, basting spoon, baster, ladle, pastry brush, skewers, meat thermometer, wire cooling racks, potholders, oven mitts.

4. A method by which heat is transferred by the movement of air or liquid. It differs from conduction in that conduction requires direct contact between the heat source and the item being heated.

5. To help tenderize meat, to allow foods to absorb liquid, to blend flavors.

SUMMARY

SECTION 9.1

Equipment for Cooking: Major cooking appliances include gas and electric ranges, convection ovens, and microwave ovens. Each has different characteristics. Small cooking appliances are useful for specialized tasks. Cookware and bakeware pieces have specific uses and are available in a wide range of materials. Several small tools are also used in cooking.

SECTION 9.2

Heat and Cooking: Heat travels by conduction, convection, or radiation. When food is heated, the color, flavor, aroma, and texture are affected. The three basic types of cooking methods—moist heat, dry heat, and frying—affect food differently. Take steps to minimize nutrient losses during cooking.

SECTION 9.3

Microwave Cooking Techniques: Microwave cooking requires a basic understanding of the oven's power settings and the way microwaves affect different foods and materials. Be sure to follow instructions for arranging, covering, stirring, rotating, turning, and timing foods. Use the oven safely and care for it properly.

SECTION 9.4

Conventional Cooking Techniques: Moist heat cooking methods include boiling, simmering, steaming, and pressure cooking. Roasting or baking, broiling, and pan-broiling are methods of cooking in dry heat. Frying methods include sautéing, pan-frying, and deep-fat frying. Braising and stir-frying are cooking techniques that combine two basic methods.

288

REVIEWING FACTS

1. Where is the broiler in a gas range? In an electric range? (9.1)

2. What is a double boiler used for? (9.1)

3. List four cooking tools and tell what they are used for. (9.1)

4. What is convection? How is it different from conduction? (9.2)

5. Name three possible reasons for using moist heat cooking in certain situations. (9.2)

6. What happens when you change the power setting of a microwave oven from high to medium? How does this affect the cooking time? (9.3)

7. Name four specific materials suitable for microwave cooking. (9.3)

8. What is the difference between stewing and poaching? (9.4)

9. What kinds of foods can you roast successfully? (9.4)

10. How is pan-broiling different from broiling? (9.4)

LEARNING BY DOING

1. ***Cookware demonstration:*** Collect several cookware and bakeware items. Give a presentation explaining how the differences in size, shape, materials, and handle placement make each item helpful for particular kinds of cooking tasks. (9.1)

2. ***Foods lab:*** Cook potato slices by baking, simmering, boiling, and frying. Compare the flavors and textures. (9.2, 9.4)

6. The percentage of cooking power is reduced by 50%; cooking time increases.

7. *Any four:* Glass, glass-ceramic, stoneware, china, pottery, plastic, paper.

8. *Stewing:* covering small pieces of food with liquid, then simmer until done. *Poaching:* simmering whole foods in a small among of liquid until done.

9. Large, tender cuts of meat or poultry.

10. Pan broiling is done on top of the range.

CHAPTER 9 REVIEW

3. **Foods lab:** Work in groups to compare conventional and microwave methods of sautéing. To sauté chopped green pepper in the microwave, use a 2-qt. (2-L) casserole. Add 1 Tbsp. (15 mL) margarine and 1 cup (250 mL) chopped green pepper. Cover. Microwave at 100% power for 3 to 4 minutes until softened. Meanwhile, sauté an equal amount of green pepper on the conventional range. Compare the results, time required, and cleanup for the two methods. (9.3, 9.4)

THINKING CRITICALLY

1. **Identifying cause and effect:** Many more kinds of cookware, bakeware, and kitchen tools are available now than 50 or even 20 years ago. What are possible reasons? (9.1)

2. **Recognizing values:** The popularity of the microwave oven is the result of what trends in American values? (9.1, 9.3)

3. **Recognizing competency:** Cookbooks usually have a page describing the author or panel of authors who wrote the book. What would you expect to find in a description of the author of a microwave cookbook? (9.3)

4. **Drawing conclusions:** Joyce used a recipe to braise a mixture of meat and vegetables. When the cooking time ended, she was dismayed to find the food dried out and charred on the bottom. What might have caused this? What recommendations do you have for Joyce in the future? (9.4)

MAKING DECISIONS AND SOLVING PROBLEMS

What Would You Do?

1. Your family is packing for a week's vacation at a lakeside cabin that has a small gas range. Your parents have asked you to choose what cookware, bakeware, and kitchen tools to pack. You can only take as much as you can fit in a small cardboard box. (9.1)

2. You sometimes help an elderly neighbor prepare meals. He has purchased an inexpensive cut of meat and asks you to broil it. He tells you to be sure and broil it a long time to make it tender. (9.2, 9.4)

3. You have a favorite recipe for chicken with a sauce, but it takes so long to prepare that you seldom use it. You've been looking for a microwave version of the recipe without success. (9.3)

LINKING YOUR STUDIES

1. **Science:** Place a long all-metal kitchen tool, such as a ladle, in a saucepan of boiling water. Using a watch with a second hand, time how long it takes for the handle to become hot to the touch at the midpoint and at the end. What kind of heat transfer is involved in the movement of heat through the metal handle? (9.2)

2. **Art:** Develop a diagram that shows how to arrange fresh broccoli in a casserole for microwaving. Indicate how the microwaves will be absorbed by the food. (9.3)

3. **Reading and study skills:** Summarize Section 9.4 in outline form. Include what you feel are the most important points to remember about each cooking method discussed. (9.4)

LEARNING BY DOING

Answers to "Learning by Doing" activities will vary. Evaluate students according to the effort they put into the activities as well as their results.

THINKING CRITICALLY

1. Answers will vary, but students should realize that as methods of cooking become more varied and more types of cooking appliances appear, inevitably mean that utensils will be developed especially for each.

2. Answers will vary. Students may mention that today's fast-paced lifestyle has not diminished the desire for good-tasting, well-cooked meals. The microwave oven allows such meals to be prepared quickly.

3. Answers will vary, but the author should have had extensive experience in cooking and using microwave ovens.

4. Food may have been over-browned or not enough liquid may have been added. In future, add more liquid to simmering stage.

MAKING DECISIONS AND SOLVING PROBLEMS

Answers to "Making Decisions and Solving Problems" questions will vary. Encourage students to give reasons for their answers.

LINKING YOUR STUDIES

1. Both conduction and convection are involved. Heat is conducted up the handle from the part of the tool that is in the boiling water. The steam rising off the water will help heat the handle also.

2. The tops of the broccoli spears should be pointed toward the center of the cooking dish.

Planning the Chapter

Chapter Overview

Section 10.1: Serving Family Meals

Section 10.2: Mealtime Etiquette

Introducing the Chapter

Motivator

- Create a bulletin board entitled "Serving Food with a Flair" that illustrates ways to serve formal and informal meals attractively. Discuss how different tableware and table settings can be used to vary the atmosphere.

CHAPTER 10

Mealtime Customs

290

Cooperative Learning Suggestions

To introduce a discussion of mealtime etiquette, organize a Think-Pair-Share activity. Have students think about a time they felt uncertain or uncomfortable in a mealtime situation. Then have each student share his or her thoughts with a partner. After students have finished their work, invite students to share their thoughts with the rest of the class. Discuss how knowledge of mealtime etiquette can increase one's self-confidence in social situations.

Serving Family Meals

OBJECTIVES

After studying this section, you should be able to:

- Explain why meals together can be important to a family.
- Demonstrate how to arrange tableware for a simple family meal.
- Describe family service and plate service.

LOOK FOR THESE TERMS

place setting
serving pieces
cover

Family meals, a time when the whole family eats together, are an important part of family life. They are a time when family members can relax, enjoy food, talk with each other, and have fun. In today's fast-paced society, it may not be easy to find time to sit down and enjoy a family meal. Many families, however, make time because they know these meals strengthen the family bond.

Both of Lynette's parents work. In addition, one goes to school in the evenings. The other is a volunteer reading teacher two nights a week. Lynette and her sisters have their own after-school activities. Morning is the only time the family can get together, so breakfast is the family meal. Everyone gets up a little early and pitches in to help with the meal. Sharing news about their activities and plans for the day is part of the family routine. They know that they can depend on each other, even with their busy schedules.

Busy families may not have as much time to spend together as they'd like. When they do share a meal, it's worth a little extra effort to make the experience pleasant and enjoyable.

Teacher's Classroom Resources—Section 10.1

Refer to these resources in the TCR package:

Reproducible Lesson Plans

Student Workbook

Extending the Text

Reteaching Activities

Section Quizzes

Testmaker Software

Color Transparencies

**Section 10.1
Serving
Family Meals**

Introducing the Section

Motivators

- Before students arrive for class, prepare two tables. Set one simply but attractively using coordinated dinnerware, tablecloth, napkins, and a centerpiece. Set the other haphazardly, perhaps using mismatched plates, no tablecloth or centerpiece, silverware tossed on plates, etc. Ask students at which table they would rather sit. Why? Discuss how presentation contributes to a pleasant mealtime environment.

- Have students collect and display pictures of attractive table settings using tablecloths, placemats, runners, napkins, and centerpieces.

Objectives

- Have students read the section objectives. Discuss the purpose of studying this section.

Vocabulary

- Pronounce the terms listed under "Look for These Terms." Have students find the terms and their definitions in the section.

Guided Reading

- Have students look at the headings within Section 10.1 to preview the concepts that will be discussed.

- Have students read the section and complete the appropriate part of the Chapter 10 Study Guide in the *Student Workbook*.

- **Mealtime Atmosphere**
- **Setting the Table for Family Meals**

(text pages 292-293)

Comprehension Check

1. Ask students to explain why a pleasant mealtime atmosphere is as important as nutritious food. *(You enjoy your meal more; it helps your digestion.)*

2. Discuss ways to create a pleasant mealtime atmosphere. *(Make the eating area attractive; avoid complaining, criticizing, or discussing problems.)*

3. Ask students to explain what a "cover" is. In general, how is a cover arranged? *(A cover is the arrangement of a place setting for one person. In general, it is arranged for the convenience of the diner and is a mixture of tradition and practicality.)*

Student Experiences

1. **Table Setting Practice:** Provide students with a variety of menus. Have students work in small groups to create a place setting appropriate for each menu. *(Key skill: applying practical knowledge)*

2. **Creating a Pleasant Atmosphere:** Ask students to write a vivid description of a pleasant mealtime atmosphere, using adjectives to help the reader visualize the situation. Select several of the descriptions to read anonymously to the class. Discuss how a pleasant mealtime atmosphere makes you feel. *(Key skill: writing)*

Mealtime Atmosphere

A pleasant mealtime atmosphere is just as essential to your health as nutritious food. It helps you enjoy your meal more. Studies also show that relaxation while eating helps digestion.

The place to start is with making the eating area attractive. Take time to put a simple decoration on the table. Try a vase with a single garden flower or a few interesting seashells.

Keep family meals fun. Mealtime is not the time to complain, criticize, or air the day's problems. Focus on the pleasure of eating and each other's company. What interesting topics can you think of to discuss?

If you're eating alone, sit down and take time to eat, relax, and enjoy yourself. People who read or watch television as they eat pay little attention to what and how much they eat. They often eat more than they would if they relaxed, concentrated on the food, and enjoyed the meal.

Setting the Table for Family Meals

Tableware includes dinnerware, flatware, glassware, and linens. "Linens" can mean anything from a cloth tablecloth and napkins to wipe-clean placemats.

The pieces of tableware used by one person to eat a meal are called a **place setting**. Platters, large bowls, and other tableware used for serving food are called **serving pieces.**

The arrangement of a place setting for one person is called a **cover.** The rules of an arrangement are based on both tradition and practicality. Knowing how to set a cover will help you serve family meals, entertain guests, and feel comfortable when you eat out.

Most families choose simple table settings for everyday meals. For most meals, you need at least a dinner plate, fork, knife, teaspoon, and beverage glass. At home, the fork

For a simple meal, the cover for each person needs to include only the basic items.

For a more elaborate or formal meal, more dinnerware, flatware, and glassware are used. Note the placement of the salad plate and cup and saucer.

can be used to eat a salad as well as the main dish. It may also be used for dessert, if one is served. (When eating a formal meal, separate salad and dessert forks would be used.) Add a cup and saucer or a mug if a hot beverage is being served. If salad is on the menu, add a salad plate or bowl. For soup, you will need a bowl and soup spoon.

More About Serving Family Meals

Slow, soothing music can help create a relaxed mealtime atmosphere. Studies show that fast music makes people chew faster and eat more. Relaxing music has the opposite effect. People eat more slowly, chew the food longer, and generally eat less. What are the implications for teens' music preferences? Discuss students' reactions.

The cover is arranged for the convenience of the diner and is usually on the table before people sit down to eat. The plate is placed in the center of the cover, about one inch (2.5 cm) from the edge of the table.

Flatware is arranged in the order in which it is used, starting at the outside and working in toward the center. All forks are to the left of the plate and knives to the right. Spoons are placed to the right of the knives. If you have a soup spoon and a teaspoon, the soup spoon would probably be used first. Place it to the right of the teaspoon.

A beverage glass is placed just above the tip of the dinner knife. The cup and saucer or mug are to the right of the spoon, about one inch (2.5 cm) from the edge of the table. The napkin is usually placed to the left of the fork.

Serving Family Meals

Meals can be served in several ways. The most common styles for family meals are plate service and family service.

Plate Service

Plate service is generally used only for family meals or in restaurants. The table is set without dinner plates, but space is left on each cover for the plate. Food is placed on the plates directly from the pans in which it was cooked, and the plates are placed on the table.

The advantage of plate service is that food remaining in the pans can be kept warm in the kitchen. If people want more food, they can ask for second helpings. It also saves time because serving dishes are not used and therefore do not have to be washed.

Many families use plate service at home. When setting the table, space is left for the plates. The food is put on the plates in the kitchen and the filled plates are brought to the table.

Thinking Skills

Reasoning: Ask students: In what situations might you use cloth, plastic, or paper table linens? Why?

Comprehension Check

1. Ask students to describe family service. What are its advantages and disadvantages? *(Food is available within easy reach of all family members; food tends to cool off quickly.)*

2. Discuss plate service. How is it different from family service? What advantage does it have over family service? *(Food is brought to the table on plates; remaining food stays hot until used.)*

3. Ask students to describe how bread or rolls, salads, and desserts are handled. *(See guidelines on page 294.)*

Student Experience

1. **Class Survey:** Ask students to read the descriptions of family service and plate service. Survey the class to determine which style is most popular in their families. What other styles of service are used? *(Key skill: reading)*

Lab Experience

Have students prepare a simple meal in the foods lab and serve it using either family service or plate service. Have students observe the general guidelines for serving breads and rolls, salads, and desserts.

See Also . . .

• Section 24.3: "Entertaining," page 655.

• Section 24.4: "Outdoor Meals," page 661.

Completing the Section

Review

- Ask students to summarize the main ideas in this section.
- Have students complete the Section Review. (Answers appear below.)

Evaluation

- Have students plan and describe a pleasant eating area, complete with table settings, and explain the purpose of each item.
- Have students take the quiz for Section 10.1. (Refer to the *Section Quizzes* booklet or construct your own quiz using the *Testmaker Software*.)

Reteaching

- Have students work in pairs to create a cover for a specific menu.
- Refer to the *Reteaching Activities* booklet for the Section 10.1 activity sheet.

Enrichment

- Have students plan and create inexpensive table decorations for various occasions.

Closure

- Refer to the bulletin board you created in the first chapter motivator. Have students identify the type of service and guess what foods will be served for each picture.

Family Service

In family service, the cover is set with the necessary tableware. The food is placed in serving dishes and passed around the table, with people helping themselves. It's less confusing if all the foods are passed in the same direction, generally to the right.

Sometimes, if a serving plate is too hot or a roast or ham is sliced at the table, that food is served at the table by a family member. In that case, the dinner plates are stacked in front of the server. The food is placed on a plate and passed along to the diners, who then help themselves to other foods in the meal.

The main advantage of family service is that people can serve themselves the amount they want. The main disadvantage, however, is that hot food left on the table in serving bowls may cool quickly.

In a restaurant, dessert is brought to the table on individual plates after the other dishes have been cleared away. The same method is used when dessert is served at home.

General Guidelines

Breads and rolls are placed on a plate or in a basket and passed around the table. If a basket is used, line it with a napkin. Diners can place bread or rolls on the edge of their dinner plates. In more formal meals, a small bread-and-butter plate may be provided above the forks.

Salads may be served in individual bowls at each place setting or passed around the table in a serving bowl. If possible, serve salad dressing separately, so people can use the amount they want.

Dessert is served after the dinner plates, salad bowls, and serving dishes have been cleared from the table. If forks or spoons are needed, they are brought to the table with the dessert.

■ Section 10.1 Review ■

RECALL THE FACTS

1. Identify two benefits of a pleasant mealtime atmosphere.
2. Name the items included in a simple, everyday table setting.
3. How does family service differ from plate service?

DISCUSS YOUR IDEAS

4. What obstacles do many families face in planning meals together? How might they be overcome?

APPLY YOUR LEARNING

5. Set a cover incorrectly. Have a classmate identify the error in the setting and correct it.

☐ Answers to Section Review ☐

1. It helps you enjoy your meal and digest your food.
2. Dinner plate, fork, knife, teaspoon, beverage glass; a cup and saucer or mug, salad plate or bowl, or soup bowl and spoon may be added if necessary.
3. In family service, the food is brought to the table in serving dishes; in plate service, the food is dished onto the plate directly from the cookware and brought to the table already filled.
4. Answers will vary. Schedule clashes may be the most common obstacle.
5. Answers depend on the item that is incorrect.

Mealtime Etiquette

OBJECTIVES

After studying this section, you should be able to:

- Explain the importance of knowing simple table etiquette.
- Describe basic etiquette guidelines.

LOOK FOR THESE TERMS

table etiquette
reservations
tip

While you may enjoy a casual approach to dining, it's also important to know basic table etiquette. **Table etiquette** is simply the courtesy shown by good manners at meals. Table manners have one purpose—to make eating a pleasant experience for everyone at the table. Most rules of etiquette involve common sense and consideration of other people.

Good manners help you be more comfortable in social situations. Showing you have good table etiquette can be an asset in the working world as well. Many business transactions take place at mealtime. Often, when companies consider an applicant for a job, the interview may include a meal. This gives the interviewer a chance to find out how the applicant would act under similar business situations.

Knowing proper table etiquette is an advantage in both social and business situations.

Section 10.2 Mealtime Etiquette

Introducing the Section

Motivators

- Ask students to describe examples of poor mealtime etiquette. Discuss the impression poor mealtime etiquette makes on others.

- Ask students to make a list of mealtime etiquette guidelines they observe. Have students add additional guidelines as they study mealtime etiquette.

Objectives

- Have students read the section objectives. Discuss the purpose of studying this section.

Vocabulary

- Pronounce the terms listed under "Look for These Terms." Have students find the terms and their definitions in the section.

Guided Reading

- Have students look at the headings within Section 10.2 to preview the concepts that will be discussed.

- Have students read the section and complete the appropriate part of the Chapter 10 Study Guide in the *Student Workbook*.

Teacher's Classroom Resources—Section 10.2

Refer to these resources in the TCR package:

Reproducible Lesson Plans

Student Workbook

Extending the Text

Reteaching Activities

Section Quizzes

Testmaker Software

Color Transparencies

Teaching . . .

• Basic Etiquette

(text page 296)

Comprehension Check

1. Ask students to list reasons for using table etiquette. *(Helps you be more comfortable in social situations; can be an asset in the working world.)*

2. Ask students to list general table etiquette guidelines. Discuss any guidelines that students do not understand. *(See list on page 296.)*

Student Experiences

1. **Class Discussion:** Discuss why good table manners are important. *(Key skill: analysis)*

2. **Demonstration:** Invite an international student to demonstrate the Continental style of eating or eating with chopsticks. Let students practice these eating styles. *(Key skill: multicultural awareness)*

3. **Table Manners Drama:** Have students act out situations that illustrate good table manners. *(Key skill: building self-esteem)*

4. **Problem Solving:** Give students slips of paper detailing specific situations relating to table manners. Have them explain how to handle each situation. (Example: If you are uncertain which fork to use, what should you do?) *(Key skill: problem solving)*

5. **Research:** Have students study etiquette customs of the past or of another culture and report to the class. *(Key skill: social studies)*

Basic Etiquette

Here are some general etiquette guidelines:

❖ Place the napkin on your lap before you start eating. Don't tuck it into a belt or under your chin.

❖ If there are six or fewer people at the table, wait until everyone is served before you begin to eat. If there are more, wait until two or three have been served.

❖ You may reach for serving dishes as long as you don't have to lean across your neighbor. If you can't reach the food easily, ask the person nearest the food to please pass it to you.

❖ If you're having problems getting foods (such as peas) on your fork, push them on with a piece of bread. If you have none, use the tip of the dinner knife to push the food onto the fork.

❖ Break bread into smaller pieces before buttering or eating it.

❖ If you're dining at someone's home and aren't sure what to do, follow the actions of the host or hostess as a guide.

❖ Don't talk with your mouth full. Finish chewing, swallow the food, and then talk.

❖ Cut food into small pieces for eating. If you try to eat large pieces, you may have difficulty chewing and might choke.

❖ Sit up straight when you eat and don't lean on your elbows.

❖ If you must cough or sneeze, cover your mouth and nose with a handkerchief or a napkin. If your coughing continues, excuse yourself and leave the table.

❖ Don't leave a spoon in your cup. You might knock the cup over if your hand accidentally hits the spoon.

❖ At home and in fast food restaurants, you can eat fried chicken with your fingers. When dining in someone else's home, use the actions of the host or hostess as a guide. In fine restaurants, eat all meat except crisp bacon with a knife and fork.

❖ Some foods are normally eaten with the fingers, regardless of where you are eating. These include breads, celery, olives, carrot sticks, pickles, crisp bacon, and most sandwiches.

The acts of offering and accepting food make up interesting etiquette rituals that vary among cultures. In the Fiji Islands, for example, it is considered polite to accept all food offered and eat as much as desired. In Colombia, on the other hand, it may be considered impolite to accept a second helping. Meanwhile, a polite guest in Syria will refuse the first two offers of food, accepting only when it is offered a third time.

❖ When you have finished eating, place your fork and knife on your plate, pointing toward the center.

❖ Never comb your hair or apply makeup while at the table.

❖ Remember, people from different countries and cultures have table manners that may be different from yours. Respect and accept people with other customs.

At the end of the meal, place your knife and fork pointing toward the center of your plate and loosely fold your napkin on the table.

Thinking Skills

Problem Solving: Present this scenario to students: You have applied for a job with a large company. A representative contacts you and invites you to dinner at a fine restaurant. The representative orders chicken and proceeds to eat it with his fingers, although other people in the restaurant are eating it with a knife and fork. In general, he displays poor table manners. What should you do? *(The representative's manners should have no effect on your personal behavior. However, you will need to ignore the poor manners of the representative. Avoiding comment and not looking disgusted can be part of good table manners, too.)*

Restaurant Etiquette

Restaurant etiquette involves the same good manners that you use anywhere else. Still, there are a few basic guidelines that deal with situations found only in restaurants.

When You Enter a Restaurant

A few restaurants may require **reservations.** That means you call ahead of time to reserve a table. Give your name, the number of people in your group, and the time you plan to arrive. If you will be late or decide not to go, call and cancel the reservation.

When you arrive, you may see a coat check room, where you leave coats, umbrellas, packages, and briefcases. You are expected to tip the attendant.

Unless a sign states otherwise, never seat yourself. A restaurant employee will direct you and your group to a table.

The Meal

If you have any questions regarding the menu, ask the server. Be sure you understand the prices so you will know exactly what you must pay. Sometimes the price of the entree (or main dish) includes side dishes such as vegetables and salad. Other restaurants price each food individually.

Often, each person in a group wants to pay for his or her own meal. The bill for the food you order is called a check. If the group is small, ask the server for separate checks before you order the food. In some restaurants, however, only one check is made out for each table. Then you might ask the server to figure out the cost for each person, or have each person keep track of the cost of his or her meal.

If you want to call your server, try to catch his or her attention by raising your hand. If necessary, ask one of the other servers to get your server. Never call out or disturb other diners.

Be polite to servers, whether in a fast food or elegant restaurant. Remember, they are

If each person in a group is paying separately, be sure to tell the server before you order.

working hard to serve you and a number of other people at the same time. Be considerate and patient, especially during rush hours.

Restaurants may serve more food than some people can eat. If you have leftover food, such as part of a steak or chicken, ask to have it wrapped so you can take it home. Most restaurants have special containers and supply them to diners. However, this does not apply to all-you-can-eat buffets or salad bars.

In fast food restaurants, delicatessens, and some cafeterias, customers are expected to clear their table after they have eaten. Trays and disposables are deposited in containers provided for the purpose.

Paying the Check and Tipping

The check for the meal will be brought to you by the server. Look over the check carefully and add up the items. If there is a mistake, quietly point it out to the server. The server should correct any mistake or explain why the amount shown is right.

Section 10.2: Mealtime Etiquette   **297**

Thinking Skills

Reasoning: Many people feel awkward asking to have leftover food wrapped. Discuss why it is perfectly okay to do so. *(Not taking leftover food with you can result in food waste; there is no point in overeating to avoid food waste. Most restaurants are happy to supply containers for leftovers.)*

Teaching . . .

• **Restaurant Etiquette**

(text pages 297-298)

Comprehension Check

1. Discuss why it is important to call a restaurant at which you have a reservation if you will be late or decide not to go. *(The restaurant holds a table for you when you make a reservation at a certain time. They lose business if you decide not to go.)*

2. Ask students to describe the correct procedure for paying separately when they are with a group of people. *(For small groups, ask the server for separate checks before ordering; for larger groups, ask the server to figure the cost for each person or ask each person to keep track of his or her own costs.)*

Student Experiences

1. **Reading Menus:** Provide students with menus from different types of restaurants. Ask students to look at the menus to determine how foods are priced. Are foods priced by the meal or individually? Ask students to make a list of unfamiliar terms on the menus. *(Key skill: reading)*

2. **Skits:** Have students create and present skits to demonstrate procedures for entering a restaurant. Discuss variations in procedures in different types of restaurants. *(Key skill: creativity)*

3. **Restaurant Math:** Have students practice checking a restaurant bill and adding an appropriate tip for different situations. *(Key skill: math)*

10.2

Completing the Section

Review

- Ask students to summarize the main ideas in this section.
- Have students complete the Section Review. (Answers appear below.)

Evaluation

- Have individual students demonstrate appropriate table manners for specific situations.
- Have students take the quiz for Section 10.2. (Refer to the *Section Quizzes* booklet or construct your own quiz using the *Testmaker Software.*)

Reteaching

- Have students work in pairs to practice demonstrating good table manners in a variety of situations.
- Refer to the *Reteaching Activities* booklet for the Section 10.2 activity sheet.

Enrichment

- Take students on a field trip to a local full-service restaurant. Have students order meals and demonstrate appropriate restaurant etiquette.

Closure

- Create a class list of etiquette guidelines for use at home and in a restaurant.

Sometimes the check is brought to you inside a small folder. If so, place your money or credit card inside the folder after you have looked over the check. Your server will take the payment and return your change or credit slip.

In some restaurants you pay your server. In others you take the check to the cashier for payment. If you're not sure, ask the server.

A **tip** is extra money given to the server in appreciation for good service. Servers rely on tips as an important part of their pay. If you are paying for your meal in cash, leave the tip on the table or on the tray on which the check was presented.

If you use a credit card, the server or cashier will process the card and hand you the credit card slip. Again, go over the math and make sure the totals are correct. The slip has a space for the tip. Fill in the amount, add the final total, sign the slip, and hand it back to the server or cashier. Be sure to get your copy of the credit card slip for your records, and don't forget the credit card.

People often wonder how much to tip. The average amount for a tip is 15 percent of the total check. However, in more elegant restaurants, a tip of up to 20 percent may be expected. Also, people often tip more than 15 percent if the service has been exceptionally good. Tips may be higher in some areas of the country than in others.

In a buffet-type restaurant, servers usually fill water glasses, bring beverages, and clear the table. For this service, tip 10 percent of the bill.

In a coffee shop, the smallest tip for just a beverage should be no less than 25 cents. If food is ordered, the tip should be 15 percent of the bill or at least 50 cents, whichever is greater.

In fast food restaurants, delicatessens, and cafeterias, you usually pay for the food when you order it. Tipping is not necessary unless an employee brings the food to you.

Complaints and Compliments

If you have any complaints about the food, tell the server. If nothing is done, complain to the manager. You can also complain to the manager if the service was poor.

While people do not hesitate to voice their complaints, few remember to express their appreciation for exceptional food and service. This is just as important to the management as complaints.

Section 10.2 Review

RECALL THE FACTS

1. What is the importance of using good table manners?
2. Explain two ways of solving the problem of getting food on your fork.
3. Describe two polite ways of calling your waiter or waitress to the table.
4. What is the average percentage of tip?

DISCUSS YOUR IDEAS

5. Describe some ways that knowing dining etiquette benefits you now and in the future.

APPLY YOUR LEARNING

6. With one or two classmates, write and perform a skit demonstrating at least three dining etiquette errors. Have the rest of the class identify the errors and offer suggestions to correct them.

Answers to Section Review

1. Good manners help you feel more comfortable in social situations; they can also help you in work situations.
2. Use a piece of bread if you have any; if not, use the tip of your knife.
3. Raise your hand or ask another server to get him or her.
4. 15%
5. Answers will vary.
6. Answers will vary.

areer PROFILE

Joanne Hanson
Etiquette Consultant

CURRENT POSITION

"I'm a self-employed etiquette consultant who specializes in working with business people."

RESPONSIBILITIES

"Businesses hire me to conduct classes and workshops for their employees on etiquette and proper table manners. I also teach foreign table customs for those who travel."

SKILLS

"You must be able to communicate with people in a tactful way, so that you can teach proper manners without offending anyone. It also helps to be friendly and self-motivated, and of course you must know proper etiquette!"

EDUCATION

"I have a college degree in communications. I also received training from a school that specializes in basic and international etiquette."

HOW I GOT STARTED

"I worked for six years in the personnel department of a large firm. When the company was sold, I was laid off. My former supervisor suggested I start my own business."

FAVORITE PART OF THE JOB

"I put a lot of enthusiasm into my job. It's fun for me to know that I am helping others get ahead in their careers."

- In what ways might Joanne's former job have helped prepare her for this one?
- What do you think would be the most interesting part of Joanne's job? Why?

299

CAREER PROFILE: ETIQUETTE CONSULTANT

Thinking About . . . Etiquette Consultants

Have students think of other questions they would like to ask Joanne Hanson about being an etiquette consultant. (Examples: Do you maintain an office, or do you travel to each client location, or both? What are the business implications of being self-employed?)

Ask students why courses in communication are valuable to an etiquette consultant.

Student Opportunities

Students interested in self-employment in etiquette or food careers should organize their own part-time enterprises, such as babysitting businesses, to become familiar with the special needs of self-employed people. Students may also want to take business courses, as well as home economics courses, to prepare themselves for becoming self-employed.

Occupational Outlook

The biggest advantage of being self-employed is the freedom to set your own pace. You decide how much to charge your clients to be fair to the clients and yet make a living for yourself. As you become more experienced, you may earn more money; you may also decide to expand your business. Your business can be as large or as small as you make it.

For More Information

For more information about self-employment, encourage students to contact:
- American Association of Professional Consultants, 9140 Ward Parkway, Kansas City, MO 64114
- American Consultants League, 640 S. Washington Blvd., Sarasota, FL 34236-6951
- Professional and Technical Consultants Association, 1330 Bascom Ave., Suite D, San Jose, CA 95128

Completing the Chapter

Review

- Have students complete the Chapter Review. (Answers appear below.)

Evaluation

- Give students several scenarios that require the proper use of etiquette. Have students take turns demonstrating how they would act.
- Have students take the test for Chapter 10. (Refer to the *Chapter and Unit Tests* booklet or construct your own test using the *Testmaker Software*.)

■ ANSWERS ■

REVIEWING FACTS

1. Make the eating area attractive; keep meals fun; take time to sit down and eat, relax, and enjoy yourself.

2. Arrange it in the order in which it is used, starting at the outside and working in toward the center: all forks to the left of the plate, all knives to the right, spoons to the right of the knives.

3. Answers will vary. Examples: Advantage—people can serve themselves the amount they want; disadvantage—hot food cools quickly on the table.

4. If there are six or fewer people at the table, wait until everyone is served; if there are more than six, wait until two or three others have been served.

5. *Any five:* breads, celery, olives, carrot sticks, pickles, crisp bacon, and most sandwiches.

CHAPTER 10 REVIEW

SUMMARY

SECTION 10.1

Serving Family Meals: Family meals are important for strengthening family bonds. Creating a pleasant mealtime atmosphere, including the table setting, helps make meals more enjoyable. A basic cover includes a dinner plate, fork, knife, teaspoon, and a beverage glass. The items are arranged in a specific way based on tradition and convenience. Meals may be served using either family service or plate service.

SECTION 10.2

Mealtime Etiquette: The purpose of table manners is to make eating a pleasant experience for everyone at the table. Rules of etiquette involve common sense and consideration for others. When dining in a restaurant, follow the accepted etiquette for making reservations, ordering and paying for the meal, and leaving a tip. Be courteous to food servers and offer your compliments for good food and service.

REVIEWING FACTS

1. Give three general guidelines for creating a pleasant mealtime atmosphere. (10.1)

2. Describe how to arrange the flatware in a cover. (10.1)

3. Name one advantage and one disadvantage of family service. (10.1)

4. When dining with others, when may you begin to eat? (10.2)

5. Give five examples of acceptable finger foods. (10.2)

6. Explain the procedure for paying the bill and leaving a tip when paying with cash and by credit card. (10.2)

7. How much should you tip food servers in an elegant restaurant? A buffet-style restaurant? A coffee shop? (10.2)

8. If your food or service was poor, how should you register your complaint? (10.2)

LEARNING BY DOING

1. **Demonstration:** Design and carry out a table setting, using items available in the foods lab or brought from home. Choose a specific meal and theme. Include table linens and decorations as well as all necessary tableware items in their proper places. (10.1)

2. **Simulation:** Simulate a family meal using either family service or plate service. Include the proper arrangement of tableware, the rules of mealtime etiquette, and conversation that would contribute to a pleasant dining atmosphere. (10.1, 10.2)

6. *Cash:* look check over carefully; pay server or go to cashier to pay, leave a tip on the table or on the check tray (15% is average). *Credit card:* look check over carefully, submit credit card to server or cashier, check amount on credit card slip, add tip, and sign. Remember to get your copy of the credit slip.

7. 20%; 10%; no less than 25 cents for beverage only or 50 cents for food, and should average 15%.

8. Tell the server, or the manager if necessary.

3. **Demonstration:** Demonstrate rules of restaurant etiquette for one of the following situations: arriving at the restaurant and being seated; ordering and eating the meal; paying the bill and leaving the tip; registering a complaint or compliment with the manager. (10.2)

THINKING CRITICALLY

1. **Identifying cause and effect:** How might eating family meals together affect family members' attitudes toward food and nutrition? (10.1)

2. **Analyzing behavior:** Why do you think a meal is part of many job interviews? What might an employer learn about a job applicant by his or her dining etiquette? (10.2)

3. **Forming hypotheses:** How do you think some rules of mealtime etiquette developed? What might be the practical basis for some of these rules? (10.2)

4. **Recognizing stereotypes:** Suppose you and a friend are at a restaurant and see someone eating food in a manner that seems strange to you. Your friend thinks the person is either stupid or deliberately rude. Is this a fair judgment? What are some possible explanations for the person's behavior? (10.2)

MAKING DECISIONS AND SOLVING PROBLEMS

What Would You Do?

1. Your family would like to eat more meals together. However, conflicting schedules make it difficult to find a time that is convenient for everyone. (10.1)

2. Although your family often eats meals together, there is little conversation. You would like to encourage family members to be more open and sharing at mealtime. (10.1)

3. You are being considered for a job that you want very much. Your potential employer has asked you to lunch at an elegant restaurant. You are worried about making a good impression. (10.2)

4. A friend is eating dinner with your family. She has been making some etiquette mistakes that are embarrassing her and your family. You try to think of a way to put everyone at ease. (10.2)

LINKING YOUR STUDIES

1. **Social studies:** Visit a restaurant that serves ethnic cuisine to find information about table settings in other cultures. Share your findings with the class. If possible, bring the tableware to class and demonstrate its proper arrangement.(10.1)

2. **Reading and study skills:** Using library resources, gather information about tableware from different time periods and cultures. What materials were used for tableware and why? What serving and flatware pieces were used in previous ages? How and why have they changed? Prepare your information in outline form. (10.1)

3. **Social studies:** Use library resources to find information about mealtime etiquette in another culture. How are meals served? What is the proper way to eat the meal? Prepare a brief presentation for the class in which you act out a typical meal in that culture. (10.1, 10.2)

4. **Literature:** Many short stories and novels contain memorable scenes involving meals. Choose one and read the description of the meal. (Ask a librarian for suggestions if needed.) Be prepared to discuss the following in class: What details of the meal does the author give? What impression or mood is conveyed to the reader? Would you find this meal enjoyable? Why or why not? (10.1, 10.2)

301

LEARNING BY DOING

Answers to "Learning by Doing" activities will vary. Evaluate students according to the effort they put into the activities as well as their results.

THINKING CRITICALLY

1. The meal habits and attitudes toward nutrition of the mature family members may be picked up by younger members of the family.

2. Answers will vary. Students should realize that dining etiquette usually tells a lot about people. The potential employer may want to see how you act in company and how you might look to your clients during a meal.

3. Answers will vary. Many rules are based on common sense. Others are based on sanitation needs.

4. Answers will vary, but students should realize that mealtime etiquette differs in different cultures. Perhaps the person was using the etiquette accepted in his or her own country or culture.

MAKING DECISIONS AND SOLVING PROBLEMS

Answers to "Making Decisions and Solving Problems" questions will vary. Encourage students to give reasons for their answers.

LINKING YOUR STUDIES

Answers to "Linking Your Studies" will vary.

COMPLETING THE UNIT

Refer to page 183 for suggestions for completing the unit.

Planning the Unit

Unit Overview

Chapter 11: Planning Meals— Gives a basic overview of meal planning; gives tips to overcome challenges in meal planning, and discusses food costs and budgeting.

Chapter 12: Shopping for Food— Discusses how to prepare for shopping trips, how to read the information on food labels, and how to compare food products.

Chapter 13: The Food Supply— Traces the path of food from farmers through processing and distribution to the stores; addresses consumer safety issues and food shortages.

Chapter 14: Buying for the Kitchen— Discusses consumer skills, how to choose kitchen equipment, and designing an efficient kitchen.

UNIT THREE

Consumer Decisions

CHAPTER 11   **Planning Meals**
CHAPTER 12   **Shopping for Food**
CHAPTER 13   **The Food Supply**
CHAPTER 14   **Buying for the Kitchen**

303

Motivator

- Ask the class: "Are you smart consumers?" Follow up with questions from Unit 3 designed to show that a lot of brainwork goes into smart shopping. (For example: What are the benefits to planning a week's worth of meals at a time? What is the benefit of keeping a food budget? How can you reduce food spending through wise meal planning? How can a shopping list save you money? How can you get the most for your money when food shopping?)

Completing the Unit

Review

- Refer students to the unit motivator. Ask them what they have learned in this unit that will help them become better consumers.

Evaluation

- Have students take the test for Unit Three. (Refer to the *Chapter and Unit Tests* booklet or construct your own test using the *Testmaker Software.*)

Planning the Chapter

Chapter Overview

Section 11.1: Basic Meal Planning

Section 11.2: Challenges in Meal Planning

Section 11.3: Food Costs and Budgeting

Introducing the Chapter

Motivator

- Ask students to write a description of how they would go about planning dinner if they went home and found a note directing them to prepare the meal. Ask volunteers to share their descriptions with the class. Ask students to save their descriptions. They will need them at the end of this section.

Teacher's Classroom Resources—Chapter 11

Refer to these resources in the TCR package:

Enrichment Activities

Chapter and Unit Tests

Testmaker Software

CHAPTER 11

Planning Meals

304

Cooperative Learning Suggestions

Have students work in groups to develop a work plan and schedule for a case situation using the Co-op Co-op technique. Provide students with a menu and recipes. Identify equipment limitations. Have individual students list the steps in preparing one food and estimate the time needed for each step. Have students work together to combine the separate tasks into a work plan and schedule for the meal. As a class, compare the schedules, discuss differences, identify any potential problems, then develop a class schedule that combines the best ideas of the groups.

Basic Meal Planning

OBJECTIVES

After studying this section, you should be able to:

- Identify factors that affect meal planning.
- Describe the characteristics that make meals appealing.
- Explain how to coordinate a work plan and schedule in preparing a meal.
- Discuss the benefits of weekly meal planning.

LOOK FOR THESE TERMS

meal appeal
texture

In earlier chapters, you have learned how to make nutritious food choices and plan a schedule for a simple recipe. Planning an entire meal draws on the same skills, plus a few others. With creativity and good management, you can plan nutritious meals that are a pleasure to prepare and a pleasure to eat.

Factors to Consider

Planning a meal involves decisions about what foods to include and how to prepare them. As you begin to plan, there are a number of points to keep in mind.

Nutrition is an important goal in meal planning. Use what you have learned about the Dietary Guidelines and Food Guide Pyramid to create healthful menus. (If you need to review these guidelines, see Chapter 3.)

Think about how the meal fits in with the day's eating pattern. You might choose different foods for the main meal of the day than you would for a light lunch or supper.

Also consider those who will be eating the meal. What are their individual nutrition needs? What foods do they like and dislike? Are there certain foods that must be avoided for medical or other reasons?

Finally, consider your resources. It's an essential step in making any decision.

With a little experience, you can plan simple, delicious, attractive meals.

Teaching . . .

• **Factors to Consider**

(text pages 305–306)

Comprehension Check

1. Ask students to list and describe the resources used for meal preparations. *(time and energy, food choices and availability, money, preparation skills, and equipment.)*

2. Ask students to explain why an individual's preparation skills can be considered a resource in meal preparation.

Student Experiences

1. **Out-of-Class Project:** Have students analyze recipes to determine the resources needed to prepare them. *(Key skills: reading, analysis)*

2. **Comparing Alternatives:** Define *tradeoff* and read the examples on text page 306. Ask students to think of another example of a situation in which a tradeoff must be made when planning and preparing meals. *(Key skill: management skills)*

Earth Watch

Ask students to brainstorm other ways they could conserve natural resources in the kitchen by planning ahead. What resources are most likely to be wasted in the kitchen?

See Also . . .

• Section 1.5: "Managing Resources and Making Decisions," text page 45.

• Chapter 4: "Planning Daily Food Choices," text page 112.

Resources for Meals

Everyone works within limited resources, but you can use your creativity to make the most of what you have. Some of the resources related to meal preparation include:

❖ **Time and energy.** If there won't be much time or energy for meal preparation, plan a meal that's simple to fix. You might look for a quick and easy recipe or think about using convenience foods along with fresh ones.

❖ **Food choices and availability.** Local supermarkets offer an amazing variety of food. Still, your choices may be limited. Some foods are seasonal, especially fresh fruits. Your supermarket may not carry the items needed to prepare an unusual recipe. You might have to substitute a different ingredient or choose another recipe.

❖ **Money.** Most people have a limited amount of money to spend on food. With careful planning, however, you can stretch your food dollars. You'll find useful suggestions in Sections 11.3 and 12.3.

❖ **Your preparation skills.** If you are just learning to cook, choose simple recipes that you can prepare with confidence. As you develop your skills, you can choose more complex recipes.

❖ **Equipment.** When you find a recipe you like, consider whether you have the necessary appliances, tools, and cookware. If not, what other items might be substituted? For example, a chicken and rice one-dish meal could be cooked in a casserole dish in the oven instead of an electric skillet.

Using resources wisely often means making tradeoffs. For instance, a microwave oven lets you use one resource (equipment) to save another (time). Convenience foods also save time, but generally cost more than preparing a meal from scratch. You must decide which is more important to you, time or money.

How do you use your resources when meal planning? What tradeoffs are you willing to make?

Earth Watch

Meal planning can help you make wise use of not only personal resources, but also natural resources. For example:

• By planning meals at least a day ahead, you can remember to put frozen meat in the refrigerator to thaw. Otherwise, you might need to defrost the meat in the microwave or cook it while still frozen. Both use extra energy.

• Planning lets you make the best use of cooking appliances. Cooking several foods in the oven at one time conserves energy, as does using small appliances.

Special Needs Strategies

Learning Disabled: Have students use cognitive graphing to describe the process of planning meals. The graph should include factors to consider, resources, making meals appealing, scheduling, weekly meal planning, challenges in meal planning, reasons food costs vary, food budgeting, and food assistance programs.

Making Meals Appealing

Usually, meal planning begins with choosing a main course. Then you add side dishes that will complement it. As you do, consider **meal appeal**—the characteristics that make a meal appetizing and enjoyable. Nutritious foods that look, smell, and taste good have the most appeal. In addition, the different foods in the meal should work together to create a pleasing whole. To enhance meal appeal, pay attention to:

❖ **Color.** Plan meals that include a variety of colors. Colorful fruits and vegetables can help brighten any meal.

❖ **Shape and size.** Food is most appealing when the shapes and sizes vary. For example, carrots could be cut into strips and tomatoes into quarters. To vary the shape, food can also be chopped, diced, cubed, served whole, or shaped with molds and decorative cutters.

❖ **Texture.** The way food feels when you chew it, such as soft, hard, crisp, or chewy, is called **texture.** A meal should include a variety of textures. For example, with a soft main dish, such as pasta, you might serve toasted garlic bread and a crispy tossed salad.

❖ **Flavor.** Avoid using foods with similar flavors in one meal. If all the foods have a strong flavor, the combination can be unpleasant. Instead, serve both strong-flavored and mild foods for a meal. For example, which would you choose to eat with a spicy chili—corn bread or garlic bread? Why?

❖ **Temperature.** If you were planning lunch for a cold winter day, steaming hot soup would be more appealing than a chilled salad. Keep meal appeal in mind when you serve the food, too. Hot foods should be piping hot and cold foods crisply chilled. To make sure they stay that way, serve hot and cold foods on separate plates.

Here's an example of a well-planned menu. Notice the pleasing variety of nutritious, appetizing foods:

Barbecued chicken
Baked potatoes   Broccoli spears
Tossed salad
Whole-wheat rolls
Lemon sherbet
Milk   Coffee

Which of these meals looks more inviting to you? Why?

Teaching . . .

• Making Meals Appealing

(text page 307)

Comprehension Check

1. Ask students to describe factors that enhance the appeal of a meal. *(color, shape and size, texture, flavor, temperature)*

2. Ask students to explain how to use the flavors of strong and mild foods to make an appealing meal. *(Don't use too many strongly flavored foods in one meal—use a combination of strong and mild foods for the best effect.)*

3. Discuss reasons the sample menu on page 307 makes an appealing meal.

Student Experiences

1. **Poster Project:** Have students collect and display pictures that illustrate various ways to make meals appealing. *(Key skill: creativity)*

2. **Menu Analysis:** Provide students with a well-planned menu to analyze. Ask students to identify ways variety is provided in color, shape and size, texture, flavor, and temperature. *(Key skills: reading, analysis)*

Thinking Skills

Problem Solving: Give students a menu that is nutritious but not appealing. Ask each student to identify a way to make the meal more appealing. Ask students to share their solutions with a partner. Have each pair join another pair to form a foursome. Ask the members of each original pair to describe their partner's solution to the problem. Then ask each foursome to agree on a solution to the menu problem. Have groups report their solutions to the class.

- **Making a Schedule for the Meal**

(text pages 308-310)

Comprehension Check

1. Ask students to describe the steps required to make a work plan for an entire meal. *(List steps in preparing each dish; estimate preparation and cooking times for each step; estimate time needed for general tasks; dovetail tasks; figure out total time needed.)*

2. Discuss ways to cut down on last-minute tasks in meal preparation. *(Consider preparing some foods ahead or doing some steps in advance.)*

TIPS for Success

Remind students that dovetailing the preparation of two or more dishes should be considered at the meal planning stage. Experienced cooks do so almost automatically.

See Also . . .

- Section 8.5: "Time Management and Teamwork," text page 246.

Making a Schedule for the Meal

As stated earlier, time is an important resource to consider when planning a meal. You need to think about not only how long each food will take to prepare, but how all the preparation tasks will fit together. You want to be sure you can comfortably prepare the meal in the time available and have all the foods ready to eat at the same time.

The best way to ensure successful meal preparation is to use a work plan and schedule. Section 8.5 explained the basics of putting together a work plan and schedule for a recipe. As you recall, a work plan lists all the tasks needed to prepare the food in the order they need to be done. A schedule shows what time you need to start each task.

As soon as you have a tentative menu in mind, think about the work plan and schedule. That way, if you find the menu presents a schedule problem, you can change it.

To make a work plan for an entire meal, start by listing the basic steps in preparing each dish that will be served. Estimate the preparation time or cooking time needed for each step. Also estimate the time needed for general tasks, such as getting ready to cook and setting the table.

✓ SAFETY CHECK

As you make your work plan, remember to allow time for:

- ❖ Washing utensils and work surfaces to prevent cross-contamination.
- ❖ Returning perishable foods to the refrigerator or freezer.
- ❖ Cooking or chilling food thoroughly.

Next, look for the best way to combine the separate tasks for each food into one work plan for the meal. To do this, you will need to think about which tasks take the most time and how you might dovetail tasks.

A basic principle is start with the food that takes the longest to prepare. Suppose you plan to bake chicken pieces in the oven for an hour. If the other foods will take less time, plan to get the chicken ready to bake first. Then you can work on other parts of the meal while the chicken is in the oven.

To cut down on last-minute tasks, consider whether any foods can safely be prepared early. For instance, a tossed salad could be assembled (except for the dressing) and then put in the refrigerator. Setting the table can also be done ahead of time, or you might plan on asking a helper to do it for you.

TIPS for Success

Using Dovetailing in Your Work Plan

Dovetailing—fitting different tasks together smoothly—is a key to successfully preparing several foods at once. Here are some tips:

- ❖ Plan on no more than one complicated recipe per meal.
- ❖ Look for the "free time" in each recipe—the time it takes for water to boil, vegetables to drain, or foods to cook unattended, for instance. Think of ways to use this time for other tasks.
- ❖ Consider how to use equipment efficiently. If two different foods can be baked at the same temperature, they might share the oven. If the main dish will be prepared in the microwave, perhaps a side dish could be simmering on the range at the same time.

More About Dovetailing

The term *dovetail* is used in the furniture construction industry to describe the process of fitting two pieces of wood tightly together in an interlocking joint that resembles a dove's tail. In meal preparation, dovetailing means organizing various tasks so they fit together for efficient use of time.

A tossed salad can be made ahead and refrigerated until you're ready to serve the meal. What other types of foods might you be able to prepare ahead of time?

After you've decided on the sequence of steps in your work plan, figure out the total time needed. If the meal will take too long to prepare, think about changes that would help. For example, would chicken pieces cook faster than a whole chicken? What about changing to a different cooking method?

When you're satisfied with the work plan, you can use it to make a schedule for meal preparation. Decide what time you want to serve the meal. Count backwards from that time to determine when you need to start preparation.

The examples that follow show how the planning process works for a simple breakfast. Notice how the list of tasks for each food in the meal (below) were combined into a work plan and schedule (page 310).

Task	Preparation Time	Cooking Time
General tasks:		
Get ready to cook	10 min.	
Set table	10 min.	
Oven French Toast:		
Preheat oven		15 min.
Grease baking dish	5 min.	
Mix egg batter; dip bread slices in batter; put in baking pan	10 min.	
Bake on first side		8 min.
Turn and bake on other side		8 min.
Glazed Cherry Topping:		
Open canned cherries; put in saucepan; mix cornstarch and water and add to cherries	5 min.	
Cook cherry mixture as directed in recipe		4-6 min.
Orange juice:		
Mix frozen concentrate in pitcher; refrigerate	5 min.	
Coffee:		
Prepare in coffee maker	5 min.	15 min.
Serving tasks:		
Put food in serving dishes	2 min.	
Pour beverages	2 min.	

Section 11.1 : Basic Meal Planning **309**

Student Experiences

1. **Review:** Review the steps for preparing a recipe. Refer students to the list of tasks and the work schedule in the text. Discuss the steps in making the work plan and schedule. *(Key skill: reading)*

2. **Class Discussion:** Define *dovetailing.* Provide students with a menu for a family meal. Ask students to identify the tasks necessary for preparing the meal. Make a class list. *(Key skill: brainstorming)*

3. **Out-of-Class Assignment:** Have students plan and prepare a family meal. Before preparing the meal, they should read the recipe and prepare a work plan and schedule. When preparing the meal, the student should assemble equipment and ingredients first, do pre-preparation tasks, simplify work techniques, and clean up as they go. After the meal, family members should evaluate the results. *(Key skill: life management skills)*

Lab Experience

Have students work in lab groups to study the recipes and plan the time and sequence for preparing a simple family meal. Have students prepare and serve the meal. Assign one member of each group the role of observer. The observer should evaluate how well the group did each of the following: assemble equipment and ingredients, do pre-preparation, follow a logical work plan/schedule, simplify work techniques, and clean up. After the lab, discuss the strengths and opportunities for improvement observed in each group.

Teaching . . .

• Weekly Meal Planning

(text pages 310-312)

Comprehension Check

1. Ask students to list the advantages of planning meals a week or more in advance. *(greater meal variety, save money, avoid extra trips to the store, greater efficiency, and better organization)*

2. Discuss tips for planning meals in advance. *(Set aside time and place for meal planning; check to see what you already have on hand, check food ads for sales, aim for balanced nutrition; plan snacks as well as meals.)*

Work Plan and Schedule

7:00	Get ready to cook
7:10	Set table
7:20	Mix juice and refrigerate
7:25	Turn on oven to preheat Grease baking dish
7:30	Mix batter; dip bread slices; put in baking dish
7:40	Put French toast in oven; set timer for 8 min. Start coffee
7:45	Start preparing cherry mixture
7:48	Turn French toast; set timer for 8 min. Continue preparing cherry mixture
7:56	Remove French toast from oven; put on platter; put cherry topping in serving dish
7:58	Pour juice and milk
8:00	Serve coffee; breakfast is ready!

Weekly Meal Planning

Most people find it helpful to plan meals for a week or more at a time. Long-range planning has several advantages. It cuts down on the time and anxiety spent in deciding what to serve every day. It means a greater variety in meals. It helps you get the most for your food dollar and avoid extra trips to the supermarket for forgotten items. It also makes food preparation more organized and efficient.

When planning a week's worth of meals, use what you have already learned about planning menus. Here are some additional suggestions:

❖ Set aside a regular time and place for meal planning.
❖ Ask family members about their plans for the week. Knowing when family members need to eat early, late, or away from home can affect the menus and recipes you choose.
❖ Check the refrigerator, freezer, and kitchen cabinets to see what you already have on hand. Think of ways to use these foods (especially perishables such as leftovers and fresh fruits and vegetables).
❖ Check newspaper ads to see what foods are on sale.
❖ Aim for balanced nutrition. Include a wide variety of nutritious foods. Check to see that the meals for each day provide enough servings from the five food groups.
❖ Plan nutritious snacks as well as meals.

A sample weekly meal plan is shown on page 311. Once you have the menus for the week, you can use them to make your shopping list. As you will learn in Chapter 12, a shopping list can help you manage money as well as time.

When you first try it, planning a week's worth of meals may seem time-consuming. However, it becomes easier with practice. Once you have planned menus for several months, you can use them over and over again. In the long run, weekly planning is well worth the initial investment of time.

More About Meal Management

When it comes to the final steps of planning meals, there are many management styles you can use, such as:

• One person is primarily responsible for planning and preparing meals.
• Two or more people in the household share responsibility for the meals. For example, a husband plans and prepares breakfasts and packed lunches while his wife takes care of dinners. They shop together on weekends.
• The whole family is involved in meal planning and shopping. When family members are involved, they are more likely to make an effort to be home for mealtime.

SAMPLE WEEKLY MENU PLAN

	Breakfast	Lunch	Dinner	Snacks	Memos

MONDAY	Bran Cereal
	Sliced Bananas
	Rye Toast
	Milk/Coffee
		(Packed)
		Turkey Sandwich
		Carrot/Celery
		  Sticks
		Apple
		Milk (buy)
			Spaghetti and
			  Meatballs
			Tossed Salad
			Garlic Bread
			Milk/Coffee
				Fresh Fruits or
				  Vegetables
				Trail Mix
				Cranberry Juice
					Steve late for
					dinner.

TUESDAY	French Toast
	Sliced Kiwi
	Milk/Coffee
		(Packed)
		Peanut Butter-
		  Whole Wheat
		  Sandwich
		Broccoli/Carrots
		Pear
		Milk (buy)
			Beans and Rice
			Corn Tortillas
			Spinach Salad
			Milk/Coffee
			Sliced Fruit
				Fresh Fruits or
				  Vegetables
				Popcorn
				Vegetable Juice
					Everyone home
					for dinner.

WEDNESDAY	Bagels with Nonfat
	  Cream Cheese
	Orange Slices
	Milk/Coffee
		Parents-lunch out
		Kids-school lunch
			Baked Chicken
			Brown Rice
			Broccoli Spears
			Whole Wheat Rolls
			Coleslaw
			Milk/Coffee
				Fresh Fruits or
				  Vegetables
				Pretzels
					Mom late for
					dinner—picking
					up dry cleaning.

THURSDAY	Oatmeal with
	  Raisins
	Whole Wheat
	  Toast
	Orange Juice
	Milk/Coffee
		(Packed)
		Leftover Chicken
		  Sandwiches
		Carrot/Celery
		  Sticks
		Banana
		Milk (buy)
			Spicy Chili with
			  Beans
			Cornbread
			Tossed Salad
			Milk
				Popcorn
				Strawberry Frozen
				  Yogurt
					Mike's basketball
					game—eat
					early.

FRIDAY	Assorted Cereals
	Banana
	Whole Wheat Toast
	Milk/Coffee
		(Packed)
		Leftover Chili
		Red and Green
		  Pepper Sticks
		Mixed Fruit Cup
		Milk (buy)
			**Pick up take-out
			Pizza
			Tossed Salad
			Mixed Fruit Juice
				Fresh Fruit with
				  Plain Yogurt
				Bran Muffin
					Everyone's home
					—rent a movie.

SATURDAY	Scrambled Eggs
	Bacon
	Whole Wheat Toast
	Orange Juice
	Milk/Coffee
		Hearty Vegetable
		  Soup
		Corn Muffin
		Fruit
		Milk
			Grilled Burgers
			  with Buns
			Potato Salad
			Sliced Tomatoes
			Milk/Coffee
				Popcorn
				Flavored Yogurt
				Mixed Fruit Juice	

SUNDAY	Bran Muffins
	Grapefruit
	Milk/Coffee
		Baked Ham
		Sweet Potatoes
		Broccoli
		Fruit Salad
		Milk
		Angel Food Cake
			Sandwiches or
			  Leftover Pizza
			Cole Slaw
			Milk/Coffee
				Fresh Fruits or
				  Vegetables
				Rice Cakes
					Relax.
					Check homework.

Section 11.1 : Basic Meal Planning   311

Student Experiences

1. **Guest Speaker:** Invite the school food service director to describe how school menus are planned. What are cycle menus? Why are they used? How do they save time? Are they always reused exactly? If not, what changes are likely to be made and why? *(Key skill: management skills)*

2. **Class Discussion:** Ask students to describe how their families plan meals for the coming week. Discuss the suggestions in the text as well. *(Key skill: public speaking)*

3. **Out-of-Class Assignment:** Have students plan a week's menus for their own families using the suggestions in the text. *(Key skills: writing, critical thinking)*

Thinking Skills

Critical Thinking: Initiate a Round Robin activity by saying, "Long-range meal planning has several advantages." Point to a student to begin by giving an advantage of long-range meal planning. That student then points to another student who gives another advantage. Continue around the classroom until each student has had an opportunity to respond. Note: Always permit students the option of saying "I pass" if they cannot think of something to add.

11.1

Completing the Section

Review

- Ask students to summarize the main ideas in this section.
- Have students complete the Section Review. (Answers appear below.)

Evaluation

- Ask students to write a short essay describing the topics they studied in this section.
- Have students take the quiz for Section 11.1. (Refer to the *Section Quizzes* booklet or use the *Testmaker Software*.)

Reteaching

- Have students plan a meal that is appealing yet nutritious.
- Refer to the *Reteaching Activities* booklet for the Section 11.1 activity sheet.

Enrichment

- Ask interested students to plan meals that can be prepared on a very limited budget yet are both nutritious and appealing.

Closure

- Refer to the motivator at the beginning of this section. Ask students if they would make any changes now to the written statements they made for that motivator.

Taking a few minutes to plan meal preparation is good management. Planning makes it possible to serve nutritious, appealing homemade meals.

What might you serve along with this seafood stir-fry?

Section 11.1 Review

RECALL THE FACTS

1. Identify six factors that affect your decisions when planning meals.
2. What is meal appeal?
3. What is the first step in making a work plan for a meal?
4. Name three benefits of planning a week's worth of meals at a time.

DISCUSS YOUR IDEAS

5. Do you think that it is necessary to make a work plan and schedule for every meal? What are the pros and cons?
6. How are energy, time, and money management related in meal planning?

APPLY YOUR LEARNING

7. Plan a basic meal for you and your family. Develop a work plan and schedule for preparing this meal.

Answers to Section Review

1. Nutrition, how the meal fits in with the day's eating pattern, who will eat the meal, nutritional needs of those people, available resources.
2. The characteristics that make a meal appetizing and enjoyable.
3. List the basic steps in preparing each dish in the menu.
4. *Any three:* Cuts down on time spent deciding what to serve; greater variety in meals; helps you get the most for your money; avoids extra trips to the store; makes food preparation more organized and efficient.
5. Answers will vary.
6. All three are resources that you must manage carefully. Sometimes you can make tradeoffs among them.
7. Answers will vary.

Challenges in Meal Planning

OBJECTIVES

After studying this section, you should be able to:

- Identify meal-planning strategies for families with busy schedules.
- Give suggestions for planning meals for one.
- Discuss ways to handle unexpected changes in mealtime plans.

LOOK FOR THIS TERM

cooking style

Trends in lifestyles have made meal planning a challenge for many people today. Busy personal and family schedules may leave little time to shop, cook, or even eat. People living on their own sometimes find that cooking for one has its drawbacks.

People in these situations do face real challenges to meal planning. However, they don't have to give up nutrition, taste, or pleasurable meals. There are many possible solutions.

Each individual or family must choose the strategies that are right for them. It all depends on individual needs and wants, including cooking style. Your **cooking style** reflects how you feel about food preparation and how much time you're willing to spend on it. Some people want to spend as little time as possible in the kitchen. Others love to cook, though they may not have the opportunity as often as they'd like. No matter what your cooking style, you may find ideas in this section to help you meet the challenges of meal planning.

Your busy lifestyle may influence your cooking style. How do you and your family work together in preparing meals?

Section 11.2
Challenges in Meal Planning

Introducing the Section

Motivators

- Ask students to think about how many meals a week their families eat together. How do family schedules affect meal planning?
- Ask students to give a "thumbs up" or "thumbs down" to indicate whether they believe it would be easier or harder to plan meals for one. Ask several students to explain their reasoning.

Objectives

- Have students read the section objectives. Discuss the purpose of studying the section.

Vocabulary

- Pronounce the terms listed under "Look for These Terms." Have students find the terms and their definitions in the section.

Guided Reading

- Have students look at the headings within Section 11.2 to preview the concepts that will be discussed.
- Have students read the section and complete the appropriate part of the Chapter 11 Study Guide in the *Student Workbook*.

Teacher's Classroom Resources—Section 11.2

Refer to these resources in the TCR package:

Reproducible Lesson Plans	*Reteaching Activities*
Student Workbook	*Section Quizzes*
Extending the Text	*Testmaker Software*
	Color Transparencies

Teaching . . .

• Busy Schedules

(text page 314)

Comprehension Check

1. Discuss how planning meals at least a week in advance can help you save time and eat quick meals at home.

2. Ask students to list time-saving suggestions for planning meals in advance. *(See list on page 314.)*

3. Discuss ideas for flexible meals for families that have varied schedules.

Student Experiences

1. **Future Forecast:** Have students write a short paper on what their lifestyles might be like in five years and how their lifestyles might affect meal planning. *(Key skill: writing)*

2. **Group Research:** Divide the class into six groups. Assign each group one of the suggestions for time-saving meals on page 314. Have each group find recipes and plan menus that fit their assigned category. Use the recipes and menus to prepare a "Busy Life Cookbook" to share with parents and teachers. *(Key skills: reading, writing)*

Busy Schedules

"There's no time to cook—but I'm tired of frozen dinners and take-out food!" Does this sound like your family? When everyone is busy with work, school, and other activities, finding time for home-prepared meals may seem difficult. With planning and ingenuity, however, you can find ways around this dilemma.

Start by holding a family conference to decide who will be responsible for different food tasks such as planning, shopping, cooking, and cleaning up. You may want to rotate these responsibilities from week to week.

Planning at least a week's worth of meals at a time, as explained in Section 11.1, can help. Keep your meal plans and shopping lists to use again. After you've planned menus for two or three months, rotate them. Here are some additional suggestions for time-saving meals:

❖ Start a collection of nutritious recipes that fit your busy lifestyle. File them where they are easy to find quickly.

❖ Get acquainted with your microwave oven. It can be used for much more than heating leftovers and convenience foods.

❖ Make use of one-dish meals. They're often easier to prepare than a main dish with separate side dishes.

❖ Look for ways to combine convenience foods with fresh foods in recipes and meals.

❖ Cook for the freezer. When preparing a recipe, double it and freeze the extra.

❖ Look for recipes with versatility. For instance, Janice has a recipe for a basic seasoned meat-and-bean mixture. Once the mixture is prepared, it can be used in a number of different recipes such as chili, burritos, and taco salad. She prepares a large amount and freezes it in recipe-size quantities to use in different ways.

When family members have varied schedules, it's not always possible for everyone to sit down to a meal together. Here are some ideas for flexible meals.

TIPS for Success

Cooking for the Freezer

When you freeze a casserole, divide it into several small containers. The food will freeze faster, and thaw or cook faster, than a large frozen casserole. You'll also have the flexibility to pull out just the amount needed.

❖ Plan meals that can be cooked early and refrigerated or frozen with instructions on how to assemble or reheat.

❖ Prepare one-dish meals in a slow cooker. Family members can help themselves any time.

❖ Set up a breakfast bar near the refrigerator with assorted cereals, bowls, spoons, and glasses for a quick, nutritious breakfast. Keep milk, juice, and fresh fruit on one refrigerator shelf within easy reach.

You can often save time by choosing a simple one-dish meal recipe.

More About Cooking Styles

Your cooking style determines the kind of food you eat and how you prepare it. Here are some cooking styles with suggestions:

• *"I don't like to cook."* Visit the supermarket salad bar on the way home. Keep whole grain rolls, crackers, and fresh fruits and vegetables on hand for snacks.

• *"I cook only quick, easy recipes."* Use one-dish meals that call for convenience foods. Serve with a fresh salad and whole grain bread.

• *"I just love to cook."* Make decisions about which appliances to use and how much to cook in advance so that your experience in the kitchen goes smoothly.

Meals for One

Shopping and preparing food for one person requires thought, planning, and creativity. One common problem faced by singles is simply a matter of quantity. Most recipes provide four, six, or even eight servings, and not all can be decreased easily. Small sizes of packaged foods may be hard to find or more expensive. Yet buying and preparing large quantities of food can mean the monotony of eating the same food day after day. Here are some suggestions for getting around this problem:

❖ Buy bulk foods in just the quantity needed.
❖ Share large food packages with a friend.
❖ Ask meat and produce managers for smaller packages of fresh foods, such as two pork chops instead of six.
❖ Store as many foods as possible in single-serving packages. For example, divide a pound of ground meat into four patties, wrap them separately, and freeze.

❖ Consider buying small portions of salad ingredients at the supermarket salad bar if one is available. It may be more costly, but you'll have less waste.

Some singles slip into poor eating habits because they neglect to plan for and prepare nutritious meals. Cooking and cleaning up a meal may not seem worth the effort for just one person. Here again, management skills can help. The suggestions already given for busy lifestyles can help make meal preparation easier for singles.

Another possibility is to share mealtimes with other singles. For instance, Jorge started a weekly meal club with three friends. Once a week, the group gets together at the home of one of the members. Each person brings a dish to share. They take turns preparing different parts of the meal.

Even when dining alone, make mealtime special. Setting the table attractively and having a relaxing meal can be an enjoyable end to a busy day.

Larger packages of meat may be more economical. Singles can avoid waste by dividing the meat into single-serving portions to store in the freezer.

Food and Nutrition Science

Effects of Distractors on Eating: Weight-loss programs often suggest that a person not watch television or read while eating—that all the person's concentration be focused on eating. Some experts suggest playing music or watching television while eating alone.

To gain further insight, have interested students develop experiments to test the effects of reading, television, music, and other distractions on eating. Have students try their experiments if possible.

Teaching . . .

- **Meals for One**
- **When Plans Must Change**

(text pages 315-316)

Comprehension Check

1. Ask students to describe problems faced by people who eat alone that other people do not experience. *(Small food packages are harder to find and more expensive; buying and preparing larger quantities often results in monotony.)*
2. Discuss ways people can get around the problems associated with fixing meals for one. *(See list on page 315.)*
3. Discuss preparations you can make for sudden changes. *(Keep a small supply of "emergency" foods on hand; stock up on nutritious but quick foods.)*

Student Experiences

1. **Guest Panel:** Invite several single adults to present a panel discussion on planning, shopping for, and preparing meals for one. *(Key skill: life management)*
2. **Adopt a Grandparent:** Have students prepare a collection of "Meals for One" recipes to share with an older adult they know. Suggest that the students prepare one of the recipes and present it to their adopted "grandparent" along with the recipe collection. *(Key skill: community involvement)*
3. **Emergency Planning:** Divide students into groups. Ask each group to develop a recipe for a casserole using only the food items listed on page 316 or similar foods on hand. Have each group share their recipe and plans with the rest of the class. *(Key skills: creativity, problem solving)*

Completing the Section

Review

- Ask students to summarize the main ideas in this section.
- Have students complete the Section Review. (Answers appear below.)

Evaluation

- Have students write a short essay about special challenges in meal planning and how to overcome them.
- Have students take the quiz for Section 11.2. (Refer to the *Section Quizzes* booklet or use the *Testmaker Software*.)

Reteaching

- Give students several menus for complete meals, some that can be prepared quickly and some that cannot. Have students practice identifying those that would be good choices for people with busy schedules or for emergencies when a quick meal is necessary.
- Refer to the *Reteaching Activities* booklet for the Section 11.2 activity sheet.

Enrichment

- Have students design a menu for a full week for a family of four. Assume that every family member has a different, busy schedule.

Closure

- Lead a class discussion on the options for eating nutritious meals at home when you need to plan for a busy household.

When Plans Must Change

Even with the best plans, unexpected emergencies may arise. You may not get home in time to prepare the meal you had planned. Illness or last-minute schedule changes can also disrupt meals.

To prepare for these times, keep a small supply of "emergency" foods on hand. Stock up on nutritious, quick-to-prepare foods that can be kept on a shelf or in the freezer. Some basic items to consider are nonfat dry milk; canned chicken, tuna, and salmon; canned beans; and frozen portions of cooked dry beans, rice, and pasta. Set aside a few recipes or menus planned around your "emergency" foods. When the unexpected happens, you'll be prepared.

RECALL THE FACTS

1. What is meant by "cooking style"? How does it affect meal planning?
2. Identify five ways to make home-prepared meals fit a busy schedule.
3. Give three suggestions for helping singles plan and prepare meals.

DISCUSS YOUR IDEAS

4. Suppose you are living on your own. Which of the suggestions in this section might be most helpful to you? Why?

APPLY YOUR LEARNING

5. Plan an "emergency" meal for you and your family using foods that can be kept on hand. Evaluate it for nutrition and appeal.

When your schedule changes unexpectedly, you may not have as much time for meal preparation as you planned. If you have ingredients for quick meals on hand, you can easily adjust to these situations.

Answers to Section Review

1. How a person feels about food preparation and how much time you're willing to spend on it.
2. *Any five:* Reuse meal plans and shopping lists; collect nutritious recipes that fit busy lifestyles; use microwave oven; fix one-dish meals; combine convenience foods with fresh foods; cook for the freezer; use versatile recipes.
3. *Any three:* Buy bulk foods in just the quantity needed; share large food packages with friends; ask for smaller packages of fresh foods; store foods in single-serving packages; buy small portions of salad at supermarket salad bar.
4. Answers will vary.
5. Answers will vary.

Food Costs and Budgeting

OBJECTIVES

After studying this section, you should be able to:

- Identify reasons why food spending varies from family to family.
- Describe how using a food budget can help control spending on food.
- Identify programs that offer food assistance to persons and families in need.

LOOK FOR THIS TERM

budget

One day at the supermarket, Myra overheard a couple talking about the price of food. "Food has gotten so expensive. Many of the foods our family likes just don't fit in the budget anymore." Myra started to wonder about the food budget for her own family. "I wonder what Mom thinks about the cost of food?"

Why Budget?

A **budget** is a valuable management tool for handling money. It's a way of planning your spending so you can pay for the necessities of life, save for the future, and still have some money for other activities. Budgeting involves looking at your income and deciding how much money to set aside for different uses, such as housing, food, clothing, transportation, health care, and savings.

Food expenses make up a significant portion of most family and personal budgets. For example, an average middle-income family spends about 15 percent of the family income on food. A lower-income family will spend a greater percentage of the family income on food simply because there is less income to work with. The challenge is in meeting nutrient needs without spending more than the budget allows. (The chart below shows how a typical family spends its income.)

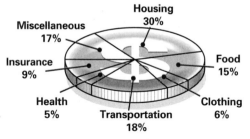

According to surveys, about 15 percent of consumer spending goes to buy food.

Housing 30%
Miscellaneous 17%
Insurance 9%
Health 5%
Transportation 18%
Food 15%
Clothing 6%

Section 11.3
Food Costs and Budgeting

Introducing the Section

Motivators

- Ask students if they think food spending varies from family to family and why. List responses on the chalkboard. Later, compare student's responses with those listed in the text.
- Ask students how they would decide how much to spend each week for food if they were living on their own.

Objectives

- Have students read the section objectives. Discuss the purpose of studying the section.

Vocabulary

- Pronounce the terms listed under "Look for These Terms." Have students find the terms and their definitions in the section.

Guided Reading

- Have students look at the headings within Section 11.3 to preview the concepts that will be discussed.
- Have students read the section and complete the appropriate part of the Chapter 11 Study Guide in the *Student Workbook*.

Teacher's Classroom Resources—Section 11.3

Refer to these resources in the TCR package:

Reproducible Lesson Plans
Student Workbook
Extending the Text

Reteaching Activities
Section Quizzes
Testmaker Software
Color Transparencies

Teaching . . .

• Why Budget?

(text pages 317-318)

Comprehension Check

1. Discuss reasons for using a budget. How can it benefit students directly? How can it benefit someone who must plan for a family? *(It can save money that might otherwise be wasted.)*

2. Ask students to list factors that affect food expenditures. *(size of family income; number of family members; age of family members; food prices; how much food is eaten away from home; time and skill available for food preparation)*

Student Experiences

1. **Class Discussion:** Ask students to define the word budget. What words do they associate with this word? Why do people make budgets? What are the major categories of a family budget? Why does the amount of money spent on food vary from family to family? *(Key skill: language arts)*

2. **Analysis of Food Expenditures:** Have students write a paper describing how each of the factors identified on page 318 affects their family's food expenditures. *(Key skills: writing, analysis)*

3. **Interview:** Ask students to interview a grandparent or other older adult about how food expenditures have changed since he or she was a young adult. Students should report their findings and relate them to modern food budgets. *(Key skill: history)*

Factors Affecting Food Expenditures

The amount of money spent on food varies depending on your personal or family resources, goals, and priorities. Here are some factors you might consider when thinking about the amount of money you spend on food:

❖ Size of family income.
❖ Number of family members.
❖ Age of family members. (It costs the most to feed teens.)
❖ Food prices in your area at different times of year.
❖ How much food is eaten away from home.
❖ Time and skills available for food preparation.

If someone in your family enjoys cooking, you might spend less money by eating more home-prepared meals. However, if busy schedules make convenience a family priority, you may spend more money on convenience foods. Every family has different priorities, so food budgets will vary.

Using a Food Budget

Whether you spend a little or a lot, you can benefit from keeping a food budget. It can show you where you may be wasting money. It can also help you think about your food choices and decide if they are wise ones.

Keeping a Spending Record

Setting up a food budget is not difficult. To begin, analyze how much you spend on food now. Keep a record of all the food you buy for two typical weeks. Divide your record into food bought at the supermarket and food eaten out. Eating out includes takeout

Keeping track of your food spending for a period of time helps you decide on a realistic amount for your food budget.

food, snacks, and foods bought from vending machines. Do not include non-food supplies in your list, such as paper products, even if you buy them at the supermarket.

Add up the expenses for groceries and eating out for the two weeks. Divide the total by two to get the average you spend per week.

TIPS for Success

Figuring Percentages

To find the percentage of monthly income that is spent on food:

❖ Total the amount spent on food per month.
❖ Divide by the monthly income.
❖ Multiply by 100 to convert the decimal to a percentage.

Thinking Skills

Creativity: To emphasize the benefits of planning food purchases, have students write and present a skit showing two approaches to food shopping. One person has come to the store with a list of everything that will be needed for the week. Another person has already made four trips to the store in the last three days and does not have a plan for what to buy this time. After the skit has been presented, have students brainstorm a list of the advantages and disadvantages of each approach.

Setting a Budget Amount

Use the information from your spending record when you plan your budget. What percentage of your income are you spending on food? Are you comfortable with the amount you are currently spending? If so, plan to spend a similar amount in future weeks. If you want to plan on spending less, set an amount that's slightly lower. Don't set an amount that's unrealistically low—you'll find it hard to stick with your budget.

Sticking With Your Budget

Once you've set an amount for your food budget, make up your mind to stick with it. Continue keeping regular records of how much you spend on groceries and eating out. You will likely spend more some weeks than others, such as when you buy staples or special items. If you have any money left over, keep it as a reserve in your food budget for emergencies.

Evaluating the Food Budget

After you have used your budget for several weeks, take a look at what you've spent. On the average, were you able to stay within your budget?

If you regularly spend more than the budget allows, don't give up. Basically, you have two choices: increase the amount budgeted or reduce your spending.

Use your spending record to evaluate your food purchases. If you made only basic purchases (with no frills) and you haven't eaten out, you may not be allowing enough money for food to begin with. Take a look at your budget again. Perhaps you can cut back in some other spending category to allow more money for food.

On the other hand, you may decide that you are spending more than you would like on food. If so, planning and money management can help you reduce your spending.

Through careful planning, many people are able to cut down on food spending. The money they save can be used to meet other goals.

More About Comparing Prices

Before the development of modern packaging methods, food arrived at a grocery store in large barrels and boxes. The grocer scooped out the quantity the customer wanted.

Today, consumers can go to the bulk foods section of a supermarket. There they can scoop out any quantity they want of certain foods from large containers. Such bulk food sales are usually limited to dry foods. However, liquid foods such as honey and oils can also be purchased in bulk.

Bulk foods are supposed to be lower in price than their packaged counterparts, but this may not always be true. Compare prices before assuming that bulk food is cheaper.

Teaching . . .

- **Using a Food Budget**

(text pages 318-320)

Comprehension Check

1. Ask students to describe the steps needed to keep an accurate spending record. *(Keep a record of all food you buy for two weeks; divide into food bought at supermarket and at restaurants; add up expenses for eating out and for groceries; divide by two.)*

2. Discuss ways to reduce spending by planning with your budget in mind. *(Look for supermarket ads; choose economical main dishes; reduce waste; prepare simple meals at home; allow some flexibility in meal planning; choose less expensive forms of food.)*

Student Experiences

1. **Guest Panel Discussion:** Invite several people who are responsible for family meals to share ways they save money on food. *(Key skill: consumer awareness)*

2. **Out-of-Class Project:** Suggest students work with their families to keep a record of food bought at the supermarket and food eaten out for two weeks. Remind students not to include non-food supplies in their records. *(Key skill: writing)*

3. **Food Budget Percentage Calculations:** Provide students with typical monthly income amounts and amounts spent on food per month. Have students determine the percentage of income spent on food for each example. *(Key skill: math)*

Comprehension Check

1. Discuss the various sources of assistance available to people who cannot afford to buy food for themselves or their families. Ask students why so many different organizations exist. *(food stamps, National School Lunch Program, Child and Adult Care Food Program, WIC Program, Nutrition Program for the Elderly, soup kitchens, food banks; they fill different needs)*

2. Ask students to explain how to find out more about food programs available in your area. *(Call local government agencies such as social services or public health services.)*

Reducing Your Spending

You can save money even before you begin spending it by planning your meals with your budget in mind. Here are some helpful tips to guide you:

❖ *Look for supermarket advertisements.* Newspaper ads can tell you about special prices on nutritious foods that your family can enjoy. Compare prices among different stores.

❖ *Choose economical main dishes.* Meat is generally the most expensive part of a meal. You can save money by serving more protein foods from plant sources, such as beans and grains. If you want to include meat, fish, or poultry in meals, use a smaller amount in combination with other nutritious foods.

❖ *Trim your food budget by reducing waste.* As you plan meals, think about how much your family eats. Prepare amounts that can be safely stored and served.

❖ *Prepare simple meals at home more often.* In general, homemade meals cost less than convenience meals or food eaten out. Your family may find it worthwhile to take the extra time needed to prepare meals at home. Sharing meal preparation tasks can cut down on preparation time and bring family members closer together.

❖ *Allow some flexibility in meal planning.* Be ready to take advantage of good prices on certain items such as seasonal fresh fruits and vegetables. Fresh produce in season is often less expensive.

❖ *Choose less expensive forms of food.* Compare prices between different forms (fresh, frozen, canned, dried) to find the best buy.

There are many other ways to save money when you go shopping for food. Careful shoppers find ways of getting more for less. You will learn more about shopping practices and techniques in Chapter 12.

Many fresh fruits and vegetables cost less at certain times of the year. You can save by learning to recognize bargains.

Food Assistance Programs

Some people may not have enough money to pay for the necessities of life, including food. They may be retired, living on a low or limited income. They may be too ill to work or unable to find a job.

Help is available from a variety of sources. Federal, state, and local governments, along with many private organizations, have food assistance programs for those who cannot afford to buy food.

❖ *Food stamps.* Low-income households that qualify receive a certain number of food stamps, depending on income and family size. The stamps are used in place of money when buying food. They cannot be used for nonfood items, such as tobacco and alcohol. They also can't be used for restaurant meals, takeout foods, and pet foods.

Thinking Skills

Problem Solving: Give students this scenario: A senior citizen on your block lives alone. You're pretty sure he cannot afford the food to create well-balanced, nutritious meals. Community organizations have offered him assistance, but he refuses out of pride. Have students brainstorm ways to help the man—tactfully—get enough food and have nutritious meals.

A variety of food assistance programs exist. They help provide nutritious meals for people of all ages who might otherwise go hungry.

Student Experiences

1. **Class Discussion:** Ask students to identify situations in which people may not have enough money for food. What food assistance programs are available at such times? *(Key skill: community involvement)*

2. **Group Research:** Divide the class into groups. Assign each group to research one of the food assistance programs listed in the text. Ask groups to report to the class on the history of the program, persons eligible for assistance, and where to get information about the program locally. *(Key skill: research)*

3. **Guest Speaker:** Invite a spokesperson from a local food assistance program to speak to the class. Ask the speaker to include information on funding and/or sources of food, eligibility for assistance, need within the community, and volunteer opportunities. Follow up with a class discussion. *(Key skill: community involvement)*

Section 11.3: Food Costs and Budgeting   321

More About Budgets and Food Types

People regularly spend more for meat than for any other part of the meal. Remember that grain products and legumes combine to make a complete protein. Popular examples are bean-and-rice dishes and pea soup with noodles. Many ethnic cooking styles are based on protein foods other than meat. Look in ethnic cookbooks for more recipe ideas.

Completing the Section

Review

- Ask students to summarize the main ideas in this section.
- Have students complete the Section Review. (Answers appear below.)

Evaluation

- Give students a spending record for a hypothetical family. Ask them to create a realistic food budget for that family and to explain how they would evaluate it.
- Have students take the quiz for Section 11.3. (Refer to the *Section Quizzes* booklet or use the *Testmaker Software*.)

Reteaching

- Provide students with index cards on which various nutritious foods are shown. Have students make up menus and shopping lists based on those foods.
- Refer to the *Reteaching Activities* booklet for the Section 11.3 activity sheet.

Enrichment

- Have students create a pamphlet listing programs and agencies in your area that are available to aid people who cannot afford to feed themselves or their families.

Closure

- Lead a discussion about the importance of budgeting. How does income affect the need for a budget?

❖ *National School Lunch Program*. Low-income students may qualify to receive free or reduced-price meals. Some schools also offer school breakfast programs. Nonprofit food services in elementary schools, secondary schools, and residential child care centers receive government surplus foods and some cash to provide for children in need. In some areas, the Summer Food Service Program provides breakfast and lunch during summer vacation.

❖ *Child and Adult Care Food Program.* Cash and food assistance are provided to child and adult care centers and family day care homes. The program operates similarly to the National School Lunch Program.

❖ *WIC (Women, Infants, and Children) Program.* This program works to improve the health of low-income pregnant and breast-feeding women, infants, and chil-

dren up to five years of age. Supplemental foods, nutrition education, and access to health services are provided. Participants receive vouchers that can be used at retail food stores for specified nutritious foods.

❖ *Nutrition Program for the Elderly.* This program provides cash and food for meals served in senior citizen centers or delivered by meals-on-wheels programs.

❖ *Soup kitchens and food banks.* These provide food for people in need of meals or food assistance. Many are run by churches, synagogues, mosques, and temples as well as by private nonprofit organizations.

If you know of anyone in need of food assistance, let him or her know of the food programs available in your area. You can get details by calling local government agencies such as social services and public health nursing services.

What organizations in your community provide assistance for people in need?

Section 11.3 Review

RECALL THE FACTS

1. Identify four factors that affect how much families spend on food.
2. What is the benefit of keeping a food budget?
3. Give five suggestions for reducing food spending through wise meal planning.
4. Give two examples of food assistance programs for those in need.

DISCUSS YOUR IDEAS

5. Why do you think many people often spend more for food than they would like?

APPLY YOUR LEARNING

6. Imagine that you have only $4.00 to spend on a meal for a family of four. Plan the meal and figure the cost by choosing foods from newspaper ads and store flyers, or by taking a trip to the store.

Answers to Section Review

1. *Any four:* Size of income; size of family; age of family members; food prices; how much food is eaten away from home.
2. It can help keep you from wasting money; it can help you make wise food choices.

3. *Any five:* Look for supermarket ads; reduce waste; prepare simple meals at home; allow flexibility in meal planning; choose less expensive forms of food.
4. *Any two:* Food stamps, National School Lunch Program, Child and

Adult Care Food Program, WIC Program, Nutrition Program for the Elderly, soup kitchens, food banks.
5. Answers will vary.
6. Answers will vary.

Anita Jaggard
WIC Manager

CURRENT POSITION

"I manage the Women, Infants, and Children (WIC) program for an urban county health department. The program provides food assistance and education to pregnant women, nursing mothers, infants, and children."

RESPONSIBILITIES

"I am responsible for seeing that the program is run properly and meets state and federal funding guidelines."

SKILLS

"For this job you must have a strong desire to help people. A background in nutrition also is required, and patience and compassion definitely help."

EDUCATION

"I have a four-year college degree in nutrition and human services. I also have a background in working for government agencies."

WORK ENVIRONMENT

"I spend much of my time in my office, where I supervise staff and meet with clients. I also teach classes on proper nutrition for women and children."

FAVORITE PART OF THE JOB

"I genuinely like helping people. It's particularly satisfying to me to know I can help a baby get a better start in life by teaching the mother about proper nutrition."

- In what ways has Anita's education and work experience prepared her for this job?
- What aspects of Anita's job do you think you might enjoy? Why?

CAREER PROFILE: WIC MANAGER

Thinking About . . . WIC Managers

- Have students think of other questions they would like to ask Anita Jaggard about being a WIC Manager. (Examples: How many hours a week do you work? In what specific ways does WIC help people?)
- Ask student volunteers to tell what they think would be the most exciting part of being a manager of a WIC program.
- Have students brainstorm other ways a county health department can help women, infants, and children.

Student Opportunities

Students interested in this type of career may volunteer to work in the WIC program at their local county health department or volunteer to work in the kitchen of a local hospital.

Occupational Outlook

WIC managers with experience may move to more responsible positions in larger counties or may become administrators of entire public health programs.

For More Information

For additional information about health/nutrition careers, have students contact:
- The National Health Council, 622 Third Ave., New York, NY 10017-6765
- American Institute of Nutrition, 9650 Rockville Pike, Bethesda, MD 20814
- National Organization for Human Service Education, National College of Education, 2840 Sheridan Road, Evanston, IL 60201

- Have students complete the Chapter Review. (Answers appear below.)

Evaluation

- Ask students to create a practical menu for one week for a family of four. Assume that every member of the family has a busy schedule, and that none of the schedules are the same. Further assume that the family is on a limited income.

- Have students take the test for Chapter 11. (Refer to the *Chapter and Unit Tests* booklet or use the *Testmaker Software*.)

■ ANSWERS ■

REVIEWING THE FACTS

1. Some fruits and vegetables are seasonal and may not be available all year; a supermarket may not carry the items you need for an unusual recipe.

2. Color, shape and size, texture, flavor, temperature.

3. Answers will vary. Examples: work around the recipe that takes the longest to prepare; prepare some foods ahead if you can do so safely.

4. Answers will vary. Examples: plans of family members, foods already on hand, what foods are on sale.

5. *Any three:* Start a collection of nutritious recipes that fit your lifestyle; use the microwave oven; make one-dish meals; look for ways to combine convenience foods with fresh foods in recipes and meals; cook for the freezer; look for versatile recipes.

CHAPTER 11 REVIEW

SUMMARY

SECTION 11.1

Basic Meal Planning: When you plan meals, consider nutrition, eating patterns, individual needs and preferences, and your resources. Meals should appeal to all the senses. Timing a meal so that all the foods are done at once requires good management skills. Weekly meal planning can help you use your resources wisely.

SECTION 11.2

Challenges in Meal Planning: Today, many individuals and families face challenges to meal planning. Whether the challenge is busy schedules or preparing meals for one, there are many possible solutions. Which you choose depends on your own cooking style. On days when plans change at the last minute, a supply of "emergency foods" can help.

SECTION 11.3

Food Costs and Budgeting: Food expenses make up a significant portion of most family and personal budgets. The amount of money spent on food depends on the family's own situation. A spending record and food budget can help you decide if you are making wise food-buying choices. If you want to reduce your food spending, planning and money management can help. A number of food assistance programs are available to help those in need.

REVIEWING FACTS

1. How do food choices and availability affect meal planning? (11.1)

2. Name five elements of meal appeal. (11.1)

3. Give two suggestions for deciding the sequence in which to prepare the foods in a meal. (11.1)

4. Name three things you should find out before writing a weekly meal plan. (11.1)

5. Give three suggestions to help families with busy schedules plan meals. (11.2)

6. List two suggestions to help single people avoid buying larger quantities than they need. (11.2)

7. Give three examples of foods to keep on hand for meal emergencies. (11.2)

8. What is the first step in setting up a food budget? (11.3)

9. How can flexibility in meal planning help you save money? (11.3)

10. What services are provided by the WIC Program? To whom are they provided? (11.3)

LEARNING BY DOING

1. *Foods lab:* Write out a work plan and schedule for a simple meal. Use them when preparing the meal in the foods lab. Evaluate how well your schedule worked. What would you change before preparing the same meal again? (11.1)

2. *Computer lab:* If menu planning software is available, use it to help you make a weekly meal plan. Or use other software, such as a word processing program. Be sure to take into consideration the factors you read about in this chapter. (11.2)

6. *Any two:* Buy bulk foods in just the quantity needed; share large food packages with friends; ask meat and produce managers for smaller packages of fresh foods; store foods in single-serving packages; buy small portions of salad ingredients at a supermarket salad bar.

7. Answers will vary. Examples: nonfat dry milk; canned chicken, tuna, salmon; frozen portions of cooked dry beans, rice, and pasta.

8. Keeping a spending record.

9. It allows you to take advantage of seasonal or sale prices on some food items.

3. **Foods lab:** Write out the menu for a meal that you might purchase from a restaurant or supermarket deli. Find or create recipes to prepare these foods yourself. Estimate the price difference between the purchased meal and the homemade meal. If possible, prepare the meal and compare it to the purchased version. (11.3)

THINKING CRITICALLY

1. **Predicting consequences:** What might be the consequences of not allowing yourself plenty of time to complete each meal preparation task? (11.1)

2. **Recognizing values:** How does a family's use of its different resources in meal planning reveal its values? (11.2)

3. **Recognizing stereotypes:** You hear a friend say that people who use food assistance programs are simply too lazy or unintelligent to get decent jobs to support themselves. How do you respond? (11.3)

MAKING DECISIONS AND SOLVING PROBLEMS

What Would You Do?

1. The main ingredients of your family's favorite chicken-rice casserole are cooked rice, diced chicken, cream soup, and shredded Swiss cheese. Usually it is served with dinner rolls and pie for dessert. You want to increase the meal's nutrition and appeal. (11.1)

2. You and your parents do most of your family's meal planning. You would like to get your seven-year-old brother and ten-year-old sister interested and involved as well. (11.2)

3. You know that one family in your neighborhood is on a very strict budget and has been skimping on food to make ends meet. You would like to help, but you don't want to offend them. (11.3)

LINKING YOUR STUDIES

1. **Writing:** Make a list of words and phrases that could be used to describe an appealing meal. Include words that describe the color, shape and size, texture, flavor, and temperature of food. Choose from your list to write a descriptive essay or poem that paints a mental picture of an appealing meal. (11.1)

2. **Social studies:** Using library resources, prepare a report on meal planning in other cultures, such as Asian and Middle Eastern. How do cultural differences (family structure, tradition, foods that are available, etc.) affect how and when meals are prepared and served? (11.2)

3. **Math:** Keep a record of your own spending for one week. Figure what percentage of your weekly spending goes toward food. Combine your findings with those of your classmates to find the average percentage for the class. (11.3)

325

LEARNING BY DOING

Answers to "Learning by Doing" activities will vary. Evaluate students according to the effort they put into the activities as well a their results.

THINKING CRITICALLY

1. Answers will vary. Examples: The meal not be done on time; some foods may be ready before others; you may become flustered and make further mistakes.

2. Answers will vary. Be sure students give reasons for their answers.

3. Answers will vary. Students should understand that, especially in times of economic hardship, some people have no choice. They may lose their jobs and be unable to find new ones, for example.

MAKING DECISIONS AND SOLVING PROBLEMS

Answers to "Making Decisions and Solving Problems" questions will vary. Encourage students to give reasons for their answers.

LINKING YOUR STUDIES

Answers to "Linking Your Studies" will vary.

10. Provides supplemental foods, nutrition education, and access to health services; available to low-income pregnant and breastfeeding women, infants, and children up to five years.

Planning the Chapter

Chapter Overview

Section 12.1: Before You Shop

Section 12.2: Food Labels

Section 12.3: In the Supermarket

Introducing the Chapter

Motivators

- Ask students to bring an item related to food shopping, such as a label from a packaged food, a coupon, a newspaper advertisement, or a shopping list. Make a bulletin board display of the items.

- Ask students to compare procedures for shopping for food in the early 1900s with food shopping today. In what ways would shopping at different shops (the greengrocer's, the bakery, and other small food shops) be more difficult than shopping at a supermarket? *(Several trips to different places would be needed; there might not be as much variety.)* In what ways would shopping in the early 1900s be better than shopping in a supermarket? *(More personal service; the greater number of choices available today makes shopping more complex.)*

Teacher's Classroom Resources—Chapter 12

Refer to these resources in the TCR package:

Enrichment Activities

Chapter and Unit Tests

Testmaker Software

326

Cooperative Learning Suggestions

Divide students into groups of four. Have each group use the Roundtable approach to plan a week's grocery list for 21 meals. Students may use newspaper ads, coupons, rebates, and sales. (Prices of some items may need to be provided.) The group planning 21 meals on the least amount of money, while maintaining quality and nutrition, wins.

OBJECTIVES

After studying this section, you should be able to:

- Give guidelines for planning where and when to shop.
- Explain the benefits of a shopping list.
- Discuss ways to make the best use of coupons.

LOOK FOR THESE TERMS

impulse buying
staples
rebate

Food shopping is one of the most important activities related to food preparation. The food you buy is the foundation for the meals you prepare. Wise food shopping can save time and money and insure nutritious meals.

Planning Where and When to Shop

Like many other activities, food shopping begins with planning.

Where to Shop

You can buy food at any one of several kinds of food stores. Each has its pluses and minuses. Your choice will depend on your own needs and wants.

❖ **Supermarkets** are large stores that sell not only food, but also many other items and services. Some have as many as 20,000 different food items. Most supermarkets offer a variety of customer services. In a large, busy supermarket, you may find it difficult to buy just a few items in a hurry.

❖ **Warehouse stores** offer basic items with few customer services. As a result, prices are lower than in most supermarkets. Most warehouse stores are large, but have a limited variety of items. Items are usually displayed in cartons rather than on shelves. Shoppers must bag their own groceries and carry them out.

❖ **Food cooperatives** are associations owned by a group of people. Members buy food in quantity and do some work, such as sorting and unloading, themselves. This reduces the cost of the food. Some cooperatives sell to the public as well as to their members.

❖ **Specialty stores** are limited to specific items, such as fish, meat, baked goods, or delicatessen foods. Prices are usually higher than in supermarkets. In return, customers may get personal attention and fast service.

❖ **Convenience stores** give fast service and are usually open early and late. Their small size makes it easy to shop quickly, but they do not carry a full line of groceries. Prices are generally higher than in supermarkets.

Section 12.1
Before You Shop

Introducing the Section

Motivators

- Have students identify services offered in stores that sell food (pharmacy, photo developing, etc.). Write their answers on the chalkboard. Discuss the pros and cons of such arrangements.
- Ask students to give a "thumbs up" or "thumbs down" in response to these questions: "Does the food shopper in your family use a shopping list?" "Does your family use coupons when purchasing food?"

Objectives

- Have students read the section objectives. Discuss the purpose of studying this section.

Vocabulary

- Pronounce the terms listed under "Look for These Terms." Have students find the terms and their definitions in the section.

Guided Reading

- Have students look at the headings within Section 12.1 to preview the concepts that will be discussed.
- Have students read the section and complete the appropriate part of the Chapter 12 Study Guide in the *Student Workbook*.

Teacher's Classroom Resources—Section 12.1

Refer to these resources in the TCR package:

Reproducible Lesson Plans
Student Workbook
Extending the Text

Reteaching Activities
Section Quizzes
Testmaker Software
Color Transparencies

Teaching . . .

- **Planning Where and When to Shop**

(text pages 327-329)

Comprehension Check

1. Ask students to list the benefits of wise food shopping. *(Can save time, money, insure nutritious meals.)*

2. Discuss the differences among supermarkets and warehouse stores. *(Warehouse stores have few customer services and less variety; they are designed to save shoppers money.)*

3. Ask students to describe what to look for when you are choosing a place to shop. *(Make sure the store is clean, and that the food is in good condition and stored at safe temperatures; then consult your own priorities.)*

4. Ask students to list considerations for deciding when to shop. *(Don't shop when you are hungry; choose a day when weekly sales are in effect; avoid shopping when stores are crowded.)*

Health Food Store

Food Cooperative

Farmer's Market

Convenience Store

Supermarket

Specialty Store

Food can be purchased at a number of different types of stores. Choose a store that meets your needs.

328 Chapter 12: Shopping for Food

Special Needs Strategies

Physically Disabled: Encourage students to identify challenges they may face when shopping for food. Discuss possible solutions to their problems.

Multicultural and/or Bilingual: Discuss cultural or language barriers which food shoppers may encounter. Discuss possible solutions.

- ❖ **Health food stores** may offer a wide range of food, including items seldom found elsewhere. However, the foods may be more expensive than those in other stores.
- ❖ **Farmer's markets** sell fresh fruits and vegetables. The selection depends on the area and the season. You may find locally grown foods that are fresher and less expensive than what you find in the supermarket. Some markets are closed during cold-weather months.

What should you consider when choosing a place to shop? First of all, make sure the store is clean. Check whether the food appears to be in good condition and is stored at safe temperatures. Beyond that, consider your own priorities. What kinds of food do you shop for most often? How far will you travel to shop? Are you willing to give up some services in exchange for lower prices?

If time is a priority, you may want to do most of your shopping at one store. That way you can become familiar with the location of the items and spend less time shopping.

Technology Tidbit

Some food stores offer a shop-at-home service. Customers place their orders over the telephone, and the store delivers the items for an extra charge. In some cases, orders can be placed using a fax machine. Another option is ordering groceries by computer. Using a modem (a device that allows computers to "talk" to one another over telephone lines), shoppers can connect to a computer information service. They can then enter their grocery order and make an appointment for delivery.

Some stores use special promotions to attract customers. These can range from prize giveaways to discount clubs for frequent shoppers. When choosing a place to shop, consider whether these promotions will actually save you money. You may find you can save as much or more by shopping at a store with low everyday prices.

When to Shop

Over half of American families do their shopping once a week. How often you shop depends on the storage space you have, including the size of your refrigerator-freezer.

Try not to shop when you are hungry. Studies show that people may spend 15 percent more if they do.

Stores often advertise in newspapers on Wednesdays. Special prices may start on Thursdays and be valid through the weekend. The days may vary, depending on the area. Choose a day when sale prices will be in effect.

If possible, avoid shopping when stores are crowded. The busiest times are usually early evenings and weekends. If you avoid the crowds, you can save time and make better choices.

When a supermarket is less crowded, employees may have more time to answer questions and fulfill special requests.

Student Experiences

1. **Class Discussion:** Ask students to identify places to shop for food in the local community. Categorize the places listed by type of store. *(Key skill: consumer awareness)*

2. **Group Activity:** Divide the class into groups to research characteristics, advantages, and disadvantages of different places to shop for food. Ask each group to summarize their discussion on a sheet of butcher paper and share it with the class. *(Key skill: research)*

3. Have students write, in order, the five factors they would consider most important in choosing where a family should shop for food. *(Key skill: analysis)*

4. **Sharing Tips:** Ask students to think of a precaution they would observe when making the decision regarding when to shop. Then ask students to turn to a partner and share their responses. Ask several pairs to share their responses with the class. *(Key skill: consumer awareness)*

Technology Tidbit

Ask students to consider these new ways of shopping for food. What are the advantages and disadvantages of shopping by telephone, fax, or modem? *(Advantages: saves the shopper time, saves gasoline; disadvantages: it's more difficult to do comparison shopping, you can't pick out the precise cut of meat, etc., that you want; you can't see what you're buying until it is delivered.)*

Thinking Skills

Critical Thinking: In 1992, the average annual grocery bill for a typical two-person family without children was $2460.30. Families with children under six years old spent an average of $2928.57. Families that included children between the ages of 6 and 17 spent an average of $3609.63. When the household included dependents age 18 and over, the annual average climbed to $3689.89. Ask students to give reasons why the annual average continues to climb as children grow older. How might such averages have been determined? What factors influence an individual family's expenditures?

Teaching . . .

• **Making a Shopping List**

(text pages 330-331)

Comprehension Check

1. Ask students to define the term *impulse buying*. How can it be avoided? *(Buying items you did not plan on and don't really need; by making a shopping list and sticking to it.)*

2. Ask students to list items a shopping list should include, in addition to those needed for the planned meals. *(Staples, emergency foods, cleaning supplies, and paper products; these should be added to the shopping list when supplies are low.)*

3. Discuss various ways to organize a shopping list. Emphasize that the "best" way is the way that works for each individual shopper.

Student Experiences

1. **Brainstorming:** Ask students to brainstorm items that are likely to be bought on impulse in the supermarket. Write responses on the chalkboard. Then have students decide which ten items teens most often buy on impulse. *(Key skill: brainstorming)*

2. **Interviews:** Ask students to interview the food shopper(s) in their families to find out whether that person makes a food shopping list. If so, how is it prepared? In class, have students share their findings and make a class list describing the steps in making a food shopping list. *(Key skill: sequencing)*

3. **List Making:** Hand out a week's menu to each student and ask the students to make out an organized shopping list. *(Key skill: life management skills)*

Making a Shopping List

A shopping list that is well thought out can save you time and money. It speeds your shopping and saves you from making special trips for forgotten items. A list also helps prevent **impulse buying**—buying items you did not plan on and don't really need. Impulse buying can ruin any food budget.

Once you get in the habit of making a shopping list, you'll find it can be done quickly and easily. The first step is to plan the meals you will serve for that shopping period. Follow the suggestions in Chapter 11. Be sure to check newspaper ads to see what's on sale—perhaps you can include those items in your meals.

After you've planned the meals, check your menus and recipes to see what foods and ingredients are needed. If you don't have them on hand, write them on your shopping list. Be sure to include the amount you'll need to buy. Increase the amount if you plan to prepare and freeze extra portions of a recipe.

Also check your supply of basic items, including:

❖ **Staples,** or items that you use on a regular basis, such as flour, honey, and nonfat dry milk.

❖ Foods you keep on hand for emergencies, such as frozen dinners.

❖ Cleaning supplies and paper products.

If you're running low on any of these items, add them to the shopping list. Many people keep a reminder list handy in the kitchen. Whenever they notice that items are running low, they jot down a reminder. Then it's easy to remember to add the items to the shopping list.

A well-organized shopping list will make it easier to find needed items when you get to the store.

Produce
Onions
Potatoes
2 butternut squash
Carrots
Kiwi
Bananas
Lettuce
Green peppers

Dairy
1 gal. skim milk
Nonfat yogurt—flavored
Margarine (stick)

Grocery aisles
3 cans tomatoes
1 can crushed pineapple
2 cans vegetable juice
1 package navy beans
1 package brown rice
Whole wheat bread
Ginger snaps
Paper towels
Dish soap

Meat
2 lb. lean ground chuck
6 lb. broiler chickens
1 lb. stew meat
4 lb. fish fillets

Frozen
3 small cans orange juice
Large bags:
   french cut green beans
   stew vegetables
   broccoli
   corn

More About Supermarkets

Large supermarkets carry many items besides food, including flowers, household items, automotive supplies, sports equipment, and stationery. There may also be a pharmacy, optical center, or banking center at the store.

Many stores run their own advertising inserts in the newspaper on Wednesday or Thursday. In addition to current sales, you may find store coupons (coupons that are good at certain stores only).

On the day newspapers feature food ads, they often have a special food section. It often includes manufacturers' advertisements with coupons good at almost all stores. You might also find menu ideas and recipes.

Organizing your shopping list will help you shop more efficiently. When writing out your list, group together items that are found in the same area of the store, such as dairy foods, meats, and frozen foods. This will help you avoid making several trips to the same area.

If you shop at one store regularly, you can make out your shopping list according to the way the store is arranged. Some stores provide a map or directory sheet showing what items are found in each aisle.

Some people keep copies of a basic shopping list that has the items they usually buy arranged in order. Each week, they just circle or check off the basic items they need and add any others. Alicia has her mother's basic shopping list in her computer. When her mother finishes the week's menus, Alicia adds the needed foods to the basic list and prints out the final one.

Using Coupons

Another consideration before you go shopping is whether you will use coupons. Coupons offer you a certain amount of savings when you buy a specific product. There are two basic ways to save with coupons.

❖ **Cents-off coupons.** These offer a reduced price on a specific item. You present the coupon to the cashier when you make the purchase. The coupon amount is subtracted from the total price of your purchases. Some stores will double or triple the amount of some coupons.

❖ **Rebate coupons.** A rebate is a partial refund given after you have purchased an item. You pay the regular price at the store. Later, you fill out the rebate coupon and mail it, along with the required proof of purchase, to a specified address. The proof of purchase might be a part of the package or a cash register receipt. A refund of part of the purchase price is sent to you by mail.

You can get coupons from many places, including newspapers, magazines, product packages, and mailed advertisements. In some stores, a checkout computer automatically prints out coupons for future use based on the purchases you have made.

32-oz. size   Limit 1 Coupon

PINEAPPLE JUICE .... 50¢OFF

Subject to Applicable Taxes. Valid for limited time only.

Cents-off coupons and rebate coupons can save you money if used wisely.

Whole Wheat Cereal $1.00 Rebate Offer

Just send us three proof-of-purchase panels from 32-oz. size boxes of Whole Wheat brand cereal.

Name_____

Street_____

City_____ State_____ Zip_____

Mail To: Whole Wheat Products, Inc.
5222 Grainery Avenue, Great Plains, Nebraska 32343

Void where prohibited. Valid for a limited time only.

Teaching . . .

- **Using Coupons**
- **Ready to Shop**

(text pages 331-332)

Comprehension Check

1. Ask students to describe the two basic types of coupons. *(cents-off, rebate)* What are the advantages and disadvantages of each?

2. Discuss the advantages and disadvantages of using coupons. *(They can save you a considerable amount of money; clipping and sorting coupons takes time.)*

3. Ask students to list suggestions for using coupons. *(See list on page 332.)*

Student Experiences

1. **Checkout Observations:** Ask students to observe two or more people at the supermarket checkout counter. How many used coupons? Combine the observations of all students and calculate the percentage of coupon use. Discuss why some people do not use them. *(Key skill: math)*

2. **Making Comparisons:** Set up a grocery display with eight food items priced and paired with a discount coupon. Ask students to compute the amount they would save by using coupons. How much would they save on "double coupon" days? Assuming that they could save that amount on grocery purchases every week, what would their yearly savings be? *(Key skill: math)*

3. **Coupon File:** Have students set up a coupon file, organizing it by categories. Encourage them to use this during the remainder of the course. *(Key skill: life management skills)*

Thinking Skills

Reasoning: Have students debate the issue: Grocery Bags—Paper, Plastic, or Cloth. What are the advantages and disadvantages of each choice?

Completing the Section

Review

- Ask students to summarize the main ideas in this section.
- Have students complete the Section Review. (Answers appear below.)

Evaluation

- Give students a meal plan for a seven-day week. Ask students to prepare a shopping list based on the meal plan.
- Have students take the quiz for Section 12.1. (Refer to the *Section Quizzes* booklet or use the *Testmaker Software*.)

Reteaching

- Give students a well-planned shopping list. Ask students to identify characteristics that make it "well-planned."
- Refer to the *Reteaching Activities* booklet for the Section 12.1 activity sheet.

Enrichment

- Have students visit several different food stores and list the services each store offers, such as photo developing, carry-out, etc. In the classroom, have students analyze these services, identifying their advantages or disadvantages for the customer.

Closure

- Lead a class discussion on the advantages of planning ahead and making a shopping list before you make the trip to the store.

Coupons can give you real savings, but it depends on what foods you usually buy. Clipping and sorting coupons takes time. For some people, the savings are well worth the effort. Others may find they can save just as much by buying less expensive products without coupons.

Here are some suggestions for using coupons:

- ❖ Be choosy. Collect coupons only for items you usually buy or want to try. Otherwise, you'll be tempted to buy an unnecessary item just because you have a coupon.
- ❖ Read coupons carefully. Some are good only on a certain size of product or only in a specific store. Most coupons have a time limit. Stores cannot accept coupons after the expiration date printed on them.
- ❖ Organize coupons so they are easy to find and use. For example, you might sort them alphabetically or by store aisle.

- ❖ Go through your coupon collection regularly. Pull out ones that expire soon so you'll remember to use them. Throw away outdated ones.

Ready to Shop

Now that you've planned your shopping, you're ready to go. Remember to take along your shopping list and your coupons. If you use cloth shopping bags, or have paper or plastic bags to return to the store, bring those too.

Consider any errands you might want to do during your shopping trip. Do them before you shop for food. That way, you can bring food home immediately so it can be properly stored.

Cloth shopping bags conserve resources because they are reusable. What items should you take to the store with you?

Section 12.1 Review

RECALL THE FACTS

1. What is an advantage of shopping in a warehouse store? Name two drawbacks.
2. Give two guidelines for choosing a time of day to shop.
3. How can a shopping list help you save money?
4. List three guidelines for using coupons.

DISCUSS YOUR IDEAS

5. Is it always wrong to buy on impulse? When is it most likely to be a problem?

APPLY YOUR LEARNING

6. List three to five places to buy food in or near your community. Identify the type of store for each. Include examples of as many different types of stores as possible.

Answers to Section Review

1. Lower prices; drawbacks will vary (examples: food stacked high in crates may be hard to reach, no carry-out service).
2. *Any two:* Consider the size of your freezer, don't shop when you're hungry; shop on days when store specials are in effect; avoid shopping when stores are crowded.
3. By discouraging impulse buying.
4. *Any three:* Collect coupons only for items you usually buy or want to try; read coupons carefully; organize coupons so they are easy to find and use; keep coupons updated.
5. Answers will vary. It may not always be wrong; it is most likely to be a problem when you make unhealthy choices or don't have much money to spend.
6. Answers will vary.

Food Labels

OBJECTIVES

After studying this section, you should be able to:
- Identify types of information found on food labels.
- Explain how to interpret nutrition information and product dates found on food labels.

LOOK FOR THESE TERMS

net weight
daily values
open dating
code dating
UPC symbol

Imagine going to the supermarket and discovering that none of the packaged foods had labels. What kinds of important information would you be missing?

Food labels are valuable tools for making wise food choices. This section will help you learn what to look for on labels.

Basic Information

Certain basic information is found on all food labels. The label tells you:
- ❖ The type of food in the package, such as "baked beans" or "chicken pot pie."
- ❖ The amount of food. This may be given as a volume measurement, such as 2 liters, or a net weight. **Net weight** means the weight of the food itself, not including the package. It includes the liquid in canned food.
- ❖ The name and place of business of the manufacturer, packer, or distributor.
- ❖ A list of ingredients (unless the food has only one ingredient). They are listed in order from largest amount to smallest by weight. If you want to avoid certain ingredients, such as a food substance you are allergic to, read the ingredients list carefully.

Food labels provide a variety of helpful information, such as the net weight of a package.

Section 12.2: Food Labels   **333**

Section 12.2
Food Labels

Introducing the Section

Motivators
- Ask students to recall and list the types of information found on food labels. Help students stretch their thinking by suggesting that they think of different types of food products such as packaged foods, canned goods, dairy products, and meats. Ask students to save their lists and add to them as you study food labels.
- Ask students to bring six food labels to class—one representing each category of the food pyramid. Encourage them to include labels from fresh foods, frozen foods, refrigerated foods, canned foods, and dehydrated foods. Use the food labels as a source of information throughout this section.

Objectives
- Have students read the section objectives. Discuss the purpose of studying the section.

Vocabulary
- Pronounce the terms listed under "Look for These Terms." Have students find the terms and their definitions in the section.

Guided Reading
- Have students look at the headings within Section 12.2 to preview the concepts that will be discussed.
- Have students read the section and complete the appropriate part of the Chapter 12 Study Guide in the *Student Workbook.*

- **Basic Information**
- **Nutrition Information: Nutrition Panel**

(text pages 333-336)

Comprehension Check

1. Ask students to list and describe basic information that is found on all food labels. *(type of food in package, amount of food, name and place of business of the manufacturer, packer, or distributor; list of ingredients)*

2. Ask students to describe the "Nutrition Facts" panel required for most processed foods under the 1993 food label laws. What information is available from this panel? *(serving size information, calorie information, nutrient amounts and daily values)*

3. Ask students to explain the meaning of "daily values." What is the purpose of daily values? *(Daily values are reference amounts based on the recommendations of health experts; they are designed to help you understand information about a product's nutrient values.)*

4. Ask students to explain why two sets of daily values are included on the new food labels for total fat, saturated fat, cholesterol, sodium, total carbohydrate, and fiber. *(The amount of these nutrients you need depends on how many calories you need.)*

Nutrition Information

Grocery stores are turning into sources of greater nutrition information, thanks to food labels. In 1993, the Food and Drug Administration (FDA) issued new food label rules. As a result, food labels offer more complete, useful, and accurate nutrition information than ever before. The format makes it easy to find the information you need. That means you can use food labels to make more healthful food choices.

Nutrition Panel

Under the 1993 rules, almost all processed foods must include a "Nutrition Facts" panel similar to the one shown on this page. Here are some guidelines for understanding and using the nutrition panel.

Serving Size Information

Near the top of the panel, you will see "Serving Size" and "Servings per Container." The serving size is the amount of food customarily eaten at one time. The FDA has established standard amounts for different types of food.

The rest of the label information, including amounts of calories and nutrients, is based on the listed serving size. When reading food labels, make sure the serving size is realistic for you. If you eat a smaller or larger serving, you will need to take this into account when reading the rest of the nutrition panel. For example, if you normally eat twice as much as the serving size shown on the container, you would need to double the amounts shown for calories and nutrients.

Calorie Information

The label lists total calories per serving. It also shows the number of calories per serving from fat. You can use this information to keep track of the number of total calories and calories from fat you eat throughout the day.

Nutrition Facts	
Serving Size 1/2 cup (114g)	
Servings Per Container 4	

Amount Per Serving	
Calories 90	Calories from Fat 27

	% Daily Value*
Total Fat 3g	**5%**
Saturated Fat 0g	**0%**
Cholesterol 0mg	**0%**
Sodium 300mg	**13%**
Total Carbohydrate 13g	**4%**
Dietary Fiber 3g	**12%**
Sugars 3g	
Protein 3g	

Vitamin A	80%	•	Vitamin C	60%
Calcium	4%	•	Iron	4%

* Percent Daily Values are based on a 2,000 calorie diet. Your daily values may be higher or lower depending on your calorie needs:

		Calories	2,000	2,500
Total Fat	Less than		65g	80g
Sat Fat	Less than		20g	25g
Cholesterol	Less than		300mg	300mg
Sodium	Less than		2,400mg	2,400mg
Total Carbohydrate			300g	375g
Fiber			25g	30g

Calories per gram:
Fat 9 • Carbohydrates 4 • Protein 4

The nutrition panel provides information to help you choose nutritious foods and follow a healthful eating plan.

More About Food Labels

The new food label rules set up by the Food and Drug Administration (FDA) meet the provisions of the Nutrition Labeling Education Act of 1990 (NLEA). The Act requires nutrition labeling for most foods, defines health- and nutrient-related terms, and limits the use of health claims. The Act called for new labels on all affected products by 1994.

According to the new guidelines, all chemicals added to preserve or enhance foods must be listed, so that people who are allergic to them can avoid the product.

Meat and poultry products regulated by USDA are not covered by NLEA. However, USDA's rules are similar to FDA's.

Nutrient Amounts and Daily Values

The nutrition panel gives information about some of the nutrients that are most important to the health of today's consumers. Amounts (in grams or milligrams) are given for total fat, saturated fat, cholesterol, sodium, total carbohydrate, dietary fiber, sugars, and protein.

For most of these nutrients, the label also gives a percent of daily value. **Daily values** are reference amounts based on the recommendations of health experts. They are designed to help you put information about nutrient content into perspective.

Here's how daily values work. Look again at the sample nutrition panel on page 334. It lists 300 milligrams of sodium per serving. Unless you know health guidelines about sodium, that information may not mean anything to you. However, the "% Daily Value" column tells you that one serving of the food provides 13 percent of the daily value for sodium. In this case, the daily value is the maximum amount of sodium recommended per day—2,400 milligrams.

The daily values for cholesterol and sodium are the same for everyone. However, recommended daily amounts for fat, saturated fat, total carbohydrate, and fiber depend on how many calories you need. (Remember, calorie needs differ depending on body size, level of activity, and so on.) A chart near the bottom of the nutrition panel shows two sets of typical daily values—one for a person who needs 2,000 calories a day, the other for a person who needs 2,500 calories a day. The daily values that are right for you may be higher or lower, depending on how many calories you need.

Look again at the numbers in the "% Daily Value" column. They are based on daily values for a 2,000 calorie diet. For instance, 3 grams of fat is 5 percent of the daily value for fat—*if* you need 2,000 calories a day. If you need more than 2,000 calories, then 3 grams of fat is *less* than 5 percent of your daily value. If you need fewer than 2,000 calories a day, then 3 grams of fat is *more* than 5 percent of your daily value.

The nutrition panel also gives information about vitamins A and C, calcium, and iron. These, too, are given in percents of daily values.

Reading labels is part of being an informed consumer.

Student Experiences

1. **Locating Nutrition Information:** Provide students with the nutrition panels from several food products. On each panel, have students locate serving size information, calorie information, nutrient amounts, and daily values. Discuss the measurements used for nutrients and the reasons percentages are also given. Discuss the basis for percentage values. Discuss how an individual can use the nutrition information to ensure healthy eating. *(Key skill: critical thinking)*

2. **Reading Labels:** Have students locate and identify the various types of information included on two food labels. Ask why it is useful to know that ingredients are listed by weight. *(Key skill: reading)*

Using the Photo

Ask students to look at the photo at the bottom of page 335. The woman is reading the food label on a carton of juice. Ask students to tell what they would look for on the food label of a carton of juice. Ask students to explain their responses.

Healthy Attitudes

Divide the class into small groups. Give each group food labels from at least two similar products (but ones which show nutritional differences, such as low-fat and regular cookies). Have students compare the products, as suggested in the feature on page 336, and draw conclusions.

Thinking Skills

Critical Thinking: The new FDA regulations define standard serving sizes. Ask students why this was necessary. *(Nutritional values based on varying serving sizes can be misleading.)* How is it helpful?

Teaching . . .

- **Label Language**
- **Health Claims**

(text pages 336-337)

Comprehension Check

1. Ask students to explain the legal meaning of terms such as "reduced," "less," and "fewer" in food labels. *(The product must have at least 25 percent less of a nutrient or calories than the regular product.)*

2. Ask students whether "high in" and "good source of" on food labels mean the same thing. *(No.)* Ask students to explain the legal difference between the terms. *("Good source of" foods must have from 10 to 19 percent of the daily value for a particular nutrient. "High in" foods must contain at least 20 percent of the nutrient.)*

3. Ask students to describe the limitations placed on health claims that food manufacturers can make. *(See page 337.)*

Student Experiences

1. **Reading:** Provide students with articles describing the most recent requirements for food label language. What changes have been made in label language? Why were these changes made? *(Key skill: reading)*

2. **Research:** Ask students to visit supermarkets to compare the health claims on various "health food" products. Ask students to write a report of their findings. *(Key consumer awareness)*

Healthy Attitudes

The nutrition panel information can be very useful to you. For instance, you can use it to keep track of how many grams of fat you eat. When shopping, you can compare nutrients in different foods. If you're looking for foods that are especially low in fat, cholesterol, sugars, or sodium, the label can help you find them easily.

For fat, saturated fat, cholesterol, and sodium, the daily value is an upper limit. In other words, the goal is to take in no more than that amount each day. For total carbohydrate, fiber, vitamin A, vitamin C, calcium, and iron, the daily value is a minimum. The goal is to take in at least that amount each day.

Label Language

You may see food packages with phrases such as "reduced calorie" or "good source of carbohydrates." These terms, and many others used to describe the level of nutrients in products, have specific meanings defined by law. Here are a few examples:

❖ **"Low in..."** The label can say "low in ..." (fat, saturated fat, cholesterol, sodium, or calories) if the food could be eaten frequently without exceeding recommended amounts. For instance, "Low in fat" means that one serving has no more than 3 grams of fat.

❖ **"Reduced..." "Less ..." or "Fewer ..."** The product must have at least 25 percent less of something (such as fat or calories) than a comparison food. The term "reduced" is used when the product has been nutritionally altered. For instance, "reduced fat cheddar cheese" has at least 25 percent less fat than regular cheddar cheese. Look for a specific comparison on the label.

Many label claims, such as "High in Fiber," cannot be used unless the product meets specific guidelines. What other types of information are found on this can of beans?

336   Chapter 12: Shopping for Food

Special Needs Strategies

Gifted: Have students write a report on the FDA's role in labeling laws. Why was there controversy about the 1993 labeling regulations?

Learning Disabled: Have students create a food label that includes all of the required label information.

- **"High in..."** This term means that one serving of the food provides at least 20 percent of the daily value for the specified nutrient. For instance, an orange juice label could say "high in vitamin C."
- **"Good source of..."** This means one serving of the food contains 10 to 19 percent of the daily value for a particular nutrient.

With these and other definitions, the law ensures that food labels do not use terms in ways that are misleading to consumers. Remember, if you're not sure what is meant by a term such as "low in sodium" or "reduced fat," read the nutrition panel. It will give you the specific amounts of nutrients and calories.

Two terms that have not yet been defined by the federal government are "organic" and "natural." Some states, and some associations of organic food growers, have set standards for organic foods. Foods labeled "certified organic" are guaranteed by that particular group to have been produced and handled without the use of synthetic chemicals. In addition, the food is produced on land to which prohibited chemicals have not been applied for at least three years immediately before the harvest. The term "natural," however, can mean whatever the food processor wants it to mean.

Health Claims

If foods meet certain specific requirements, they may make health claims. The claims are limited to relationships between the food or nutrient and the risk of osteoporosis, cancer, coronary heart disease, and high blood pressure.

The claims must use "may" or "might" in discussing the nutrient or food-disease relationship. They must state that other factors also play a role in that disease. For instance, the label may claim, "While many factors affect heart disease, diets low in saturated fat and cholesterol may reduce the risk of this disease."

Product Dating

Some food packages are stamped with a date. **Open dating** means the date can be understood by consumers. The exact meaning of the date varies, depending on the product and the wording.

- **Sell date.** This type of date indicates the last day the product should remain on the store shelf. It allows a reasonable amount of time for home storage and use after that date. Dairy products and cold cuts are among the foods that often carry a sell date. The package may say "Sell by (date)" or "Best if purchased by (date)."
- **"Use by" date.** Some packages say "Best if used by (date)." The product may still be safe to eat after the date has passed. However, the quality will start to go down. If a date alone appears on baked goods, such as breads and rolls, it is usually a "use by" date.

Open dating gives consumers an idea of how long a product can remain wholesome and safe. However, a package date does not guarantee quality. That depends on how the product was handled.

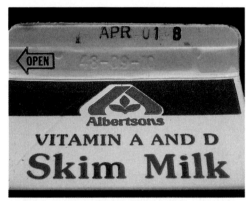

On dairy foods, package dates usually indicate the last date the product can be sold. If stored properly, the product will be safe to use for a reasonable amount of time after that date.

Teaching . . .

- **Product Dating**
- **Other Information**

(text pages 337-338)

Comprehension Check

1. Ask students to explain the significance of a "use by" date on a product. *("Use by" dates suggest the last dates for which the food should maintain its best quality.)*
2. Ask students to explain the purpose of code dating. *(Code dating is used by manufacturers to indicate where and when the product was packaged; used mostly for products that have a long shelf life.)*
3. Ask students to discuss other information that is available on food labels. *(See page 338.)*

Student Experiences

1. **Class Discussion:** Ask students to identify ways the universal product code (UPC) benefits the store and the customer. Are there any drawbacks? *(Scanned prices may not match shelf prices.) (Key skill: critical thinking)*
2. **Label Reading:** Provide students with empty food packages that have open dating. Have students group the food packages according to the type of dating. *(Key skill: reading)*
3. **Label Detectives:** Ask students to study a variety of food labels to identify other information that may be included. Make a class list of the information identified. *(Key skill: research)*
4. **Examining Labels:** Have students examine a display of package labels. Then have students explain how the pictures can be misleading. *(Key skill: consumer awareness)*

Completing the Section

Review

- Ask students to summarize the main ideas in this section.
- Have students complete the Section Review. (Answers appear below.)

Evaluation

- Provide students with a food label and ask them to explain the information it contains.
- Have students take the quiz for Section 12.2. (Refer to the *Section Quizzes* booklet or use the *Testmaker Software*.)

Reteaching

- Provide several food labels containing the information mandated by the FDA's 1993 guidelines. Help students interpret the information they contain.
- Refer to the *Reteaching Activities* booklet for the Section 12.2 activity sheet.

Enrichment

- Have interested students research the controversies between the federal government, nutritionists, and consumer alert groups. Ask them to debate the question of whether food manufacturers should be permitted to print health claims on food labels.

Closure

- Lead a discussion about the information required by 1993 FDA regulations and its impact on product labeling.

Code dating is used by manufacturers on products that have a long shelf life. The code is a series of numbers and letters that indicate where and when the product was packaged. If a recall is necessary, the products can be tracked down quickly and removed from the marketplace. Federal law requires code dating on most canned foods.

Other Information

You will find many other types of helpful information on food labels. For example, some products carry grades on their packaging, such as "U.S. Grade A." Grading is a system for identifying the quality of foods. You will learn more about food grades as you study specific foods in Unit Four.

Some label information is required only for certain products. For example, beverages that contain juice must list the percentages of juices.

The label often includes a picture of the product. If the product is not shown exactly as it appears in the package, the photo must be labeled "serving suggestion."

The label may give directions for using the product. If the product requires special handling, the label will give instructions, such as "Refrigerate after opening" or "Keep frozen."

Most products carry a **UPC symbol,** which stands for Universal Product Code. This is a bar code that can be read by a scanner. It gives the computer at the store's checkout counter the correct price for the product. It is also used to keep an automatic inventory of the product.

You may also find recipes, coupons and other special offers, or proof-of-purchase symbols on labels. There may be a toll-free number to call for consumer information.

Read the small print on the label or any information that has an asterisk (*). Such information may give exceptions to what is stated in larger type.

Whenever you shop, remember to read food labels carefully. They are the key to knowing what you are buying.

UPC symbols on packages help both the consumer and the food store. They speed checkout and make it easier to keep a record of the store's stock.

Section 12.2 Review

RECALL THE FACTS

1. List four types of information found on all food labels.

2. Why is it important to consider serving size when reading a nutrition panel?

3. What is the purpose of the "daily values" information on a nutrition panel?

4. What is the difference between a sell date and a "use by" date?

DISCUSS YOUR IDEAS

5. Why do you think it is difficult to define "natural" as a label term?

APPLY YOUR LEARNING

6. Bring to class a food label that includes nutrition information. Use the label information to identify the food's nutritional pluses and minuses. Do you think the label gives enough information to determine the food's healthfulness? Why or why not?

Answers to Section Review

1. Type of food; amount; name and address of manufacturer, packer, or distributor; ingredients.
2. The rest of the nutrition information is based on the serving size.
3. To help consumers understand the information about a product's nutrients; provides a basis of comparison.
4. Sell date: last day product should remain on store shelf. "Use by" date: last day product can be used with best quality.
5. Answers will vary.
6. Answers will vary.

In the Supermarket

OBJECTIVES

After studying this section, you should be able to:

- Describe ways of getting the most for your money when food shopping.
- Explain how to choose and handle food to preserve nutrition, quality, and safety.
- Give guidelines for courteous shopping.

LOOK FOR THESE TERMS

bulk foods
comparison shopping
unit price
store brands
generic

When you walk into a supermarket, you are faced with thousands of items attractively displayed to catch your eye. Consumer skills can help you find good nutrition and quality at the best price. You have already learned how to plan your shopping trip and how to read food labels. This section will show you some additional shopping skills that can help you make wise food-buying decisions.

How Stores are Organized

Supermarkets are generally organized into specific departments. Here are the basic areas of the store and what you will find in them:

- ❖ Produce (PROH-doos)—fresh fruits and vegetables.
- ❖ Fresh meat, poultry, and fish.

- ❖ Dairy—milk, yogurt, cheeses. Other refrigerated items, such as eggs, cured luncheon meats, and fresh pasta, may be found with the dairy foods or in sections of their own.
- ❖ Grocery section—shelf-stable foods in cans, jars, bottles, boxes, and packages.
- ❖ Frozen foods.

Many stores have other departments. For instance, there may be a delicatessen, salad bar, or bakery where you can buy freshly prepared foods.

Some stores have a bulk foods department. **Bulk foods** are shelf-stable foods that are sold loose and displayed in covered bins or barrels. Consumers place as much food as they want into a plastic bag, tie it, and stick a name tag on the bag so the checkout clerk can identify the contents. Foods that may be sold this way include grain products, nuts, dried fruits, dry beans and peas, snack foods, flour, sugar, herbs, and spices.

Section 12.3 In the Supermarket

Introducing the Section

Motivators

- Ask someone who as lived in or traveled to another country to explain how food shopping is done there.
- Ask students to think of a way to get the most for your money when food shopping. Ask each student to share his or her idea with a partner. Then ask each pair of students to join another pair. Each partner should describe the other person's suggestion for saving money. Finally, have each group of four join another group of four. Ask each person to give a suggestion they have not told before.

Objectives

- Have students read the section objectives. Discuss the purpose of studying the section.

Vocabulary

- Pronounce the terms listed under "Look for These Terms."
- Have students read the section find the terms and their definitions in the section.

Guided Reading

- Have students look at the headings within Section 12.3 to preview the concepts that will be discussed.
- Have students read the section and complete the appropriate part of the Chapter 12 Study Guide in the *Student Workbook*.

Teacher's Classroom Resources—Section 12.3

Refer to these resources in the TCR package:

Reproducible Lesson Plans

Student Workbook

Extending the Text

Reteaching Activities

Section Quizzes

Testmaker Software

Color Transparencies

Teaching . . .

- **How Stores Are Organized**
- **Saving Money with Comparison Shopping**

(text pages 339-342)

Comprehension Check

1. Ask students to name basic departments into which supermarkets are often divided. *(produce; fresh meat, poultry, and fish; dairy; grocery section; frozen foods)*

2. Ask students to explain what bulk foods are. What foods are often sold in this way? *(Shelf-stable foods sold loose and displayed in covered bins or barrels, so that people can get what they want; grain products, nuts, dried fruits, dry beans and peas, snack foods, flour, sugar, herbs, and spices.)*

3. Ask students to define *comparison shopping. (Comparing the prices of similar items to see which offers the best value.)*

4. Discuss the differences between unit price and cost per serving. *(Unit price is the price per ounce, quart, pound, or other unit; cost per serving takes into consideration unusable parts, such as bones, skin, and fat.)*

5. Ask students to explain the difference between store brands and generic items. *(Store brands are brands produced especially for a store; generic items are items produced by an independent company but packaged very plainly. Both are usually less expensive than name brands.)*

6. Ask students to list other money-saving ideas for food shopping. *(See list on page 342.)*

Each department of the supermarket carries specific types of foods.

Saving Money with Comparison Shopping

No matter what the size of your food budget, getting the most for your money is one of your main goals when shopping. Yet when faced with so many choices—different types of products, different brands and sizes—how can you spot the best bargain? Learning how to comparison shop can help. **Comparison shopping** means comparing the prices of similar items to see which offers the best value. Here are some guidelines to make comparison shopping easier.

Unit Prices

Which is a better buy, a 12-ounce package for $1.32 or a 16-ounce package for $1.52? To find out, you need to know the unit price of each item. The **unit price** is the price per ounce, quart, pound, or other unit.

In many stores, the unit price is shown on the shelf tab just below the item, next to the total price. This gives you a quick and easy way to compare prices. If the unit price is not shown, you can calculate it for yourself:

total price ÷ number of units = unit price

In the example given above, the smaller package costs 11 cents per ounce ($1.32 ÷ 12). The larger package costs 9.5 cents per ounce ($1.52 ÷ 16), so it is a better value.

Some stores provide the unit price on a shelf tab for the convenience of customers.

340 Chapter 12: Shopping for Food

More About Supermarket Organization

Foods in the grocery section of a supermarket are arranged according to basic categories, aisle by aisle. They include canned fruits; canned vegetables; canned meats, poultry, and fish; salad dressings; mustard and catsup; grain products; dried beans and peas; shelf-stable microwavable foods; and

baking ingredients and mixes. This department may also have special sections for ethnic foods, such as Mexican and Asian.

The produce department is usually located near the front of the store in a corner. That's because there is generally more space in corners than in aisles. Store clerks

Cost Per Serving

Sometimes the unit price is not the best basis for comparison. You may have to consider the cost per serving as well. This is especially true when shopping for fresh meat, poultry, or fish.

Stan was trying to decide between fish fillets on sale at $1.80 per pound (500 g) and whole broiling chickens at 94 cents per pound. At first, the chickens seemed like a better bargain. Then Stan realized that with the chickens, he would be getting less usable meat because the package included bones, skin, and fat. Even though the unit price of the chicken was lower, he would have to buy more to feed the same number of people. He needed to know the cost per serving to make a fair comparison.

To find the cost per serving, you must first decide how many servings a given amount will provide. (The chart on this page gives general guidelines for meat, poultry, and fish.) Then divide the price for that amount by the number of servings it will provide. The result is the price for one serving.

When Stan figured the cost per serving, he made a surprising discovery. A pound of fillets gives four servings, so the cost per serving would be 45 cents ($1.80 ÷ 4). A pound of chicken with bones makes only two serv-

Figuring the cost per serving can help you recognize good buys.

Servings per Pound of Meat, Poultry, and Fish	
Meat	
Lean, boneless	3 to 4 servings per pound
Some bone or fat	2 to 3 servings per pound
Large amount of bone or fat	1 to 2 servings per pound
Poultry	
Boneless	4 servings per pound
With bones	2 servings per pound
Fish	
Fillets or steaks	4 servings per pound
Dressed	2 servings per pound
Whole or drawn	1 serving per pound

ings. The cost per serving would be 47 cents ($0.94 ÷ 2). Stan chose the fish.

You can use cost per serving to help you in meal planning and budgeting. For instance, you could find the cost per serving of a homemade recipe by adding the cost of the ingredients and dividing by the recipe yield. You could find the cost per serving of a packaged food by dividing the total price by the number of servings indicated on the label.

Store Brands and Generics

You can often save money by buying store brand or generic products instead of name-brand items. **Store brands** (also called "private labels") are specially produced for the store. They are generally equal in quality to name brands, but less expensive. This is

Student Experiences

1. **Guest panel:** Invite a guest panel of consumer specialists to discuss ways to save money at the supermarket. *(Key skill: consumer awareness)*

2. **Product Comparison:** Provide three cans of a fruit or vegetable: a generic, a store brand, and a name brand. Have students compare the three products for color, size, shape, flavor, texture, and amount of liquid. Ask students to consider the price, nutrition information, and intended use, then tell which they would choose and why. *(Key skill: evaluation)*

3. **Math Game:** Have students play "The Price Is Right" by determining the unit price or cost per serving of several displayed products to find the best buy. Have students work in teams or individually. *(Key skill: math)*

4. **Calculations:** Have students calculate the cost per serving a given amount of fresh meat, poultry, or fish will provide. Discuss how this information is useful in meal planning and budgeting. *(Key skill: math)*

work constantly in this section, refilling produce and keeping the displays neat. They also clean up spills. Space is needed so clerks can do their work without getting in the way of customers.

The dairy department is usually located against a wall, as are other refrigerated sections. That way, they are closer to the refrigerated storage space behind the wall, and

the shelves can be refilled easily.

The meat, poultry, and fish departments are usually next to each other, in the back of the store. The space on the other side of the wall is usually the butcher shop where the foods are cut and packaged, and a reserve supply is stored.

- **Nutrition, Quality, and Safety**
- **Courtesy When Shopping**
- **Finishing Your Shopping**

(text page 342-344)

Comprehension Check

1. Ask students to list things they can do to ensure that the foods they buy are safe and of high quality. *(Check the date on the package; avoid packages that are dirty, bulging, dented, rusty, leaking, or damaged in any way; put meat, poultry, and fish packages in a plastic bag, so they won't drip on other foods; avoid frozen packages that are frosted with ice; keep fragile items in one part of your cart and keep moving them up so they are always on top of heavier items.)*

2. Ask students to describe courteous behavior in a supermarket. How should they treat other shoppers? How should they handle merchandise? *(Keep your cart on right side of aisle; use common courtesies such as excusing yourself if you bump into someone or have to pass them; do not block aisles; do not open containers; return products to their proper places if you decide not to buy them; handle produce gently; use scoop or tongs for bulk foods.)*

3. Ask students why it is important to check the prices as they are rung up at the cashier, even in stores that have computerized checkouts. *(The wrong price might be entered in the computer.)*

In many stores, you have a choice between name brands and store brands or generics. What factors do you consider when deciding which to buy?

because stores do not spend as much in advertising as food manufacturers do. **Generic** items are less expensive still. Their labels are very plain and not as eye-catching as name brands, but their quality may be similar. Finding out which store brands and generics are good quality may take some experimenting, but the savings will make it worthwhile.

Other Money-Saving Ideas

Here are some additional suggestions for saving money at the supermarket.

❖ Use your shopping list, but be flexible. Look for sale items that you could substitute for the ones on your list.
❖ When using coupons, make sure you are really getting the best buy. Another brand may be less expensive, even without a coupon.
❖ Continue to check the unit price of products you buy regularly. Manufacturers sometimes keep the same price but reduce the amount in the package.
❖ Consider bulk foods. They cost less because they are not prepackaged. In addition, you can buy just the amount you want.

❖ Don't buy more food than you can store properly, or more than can be used before spoiling.
❖ Beware of strategies designed to encourage impulse buying. For instance, the most popular or profitable items are often put on shelves at eye level to catch your attention. Some foods, such as high-sugar cereals, are put on lower shelves where children can see and reach them easily. Small, high-profit items such as candy and magazines are placed next to checkout lines.
❖ Take advantage of the many customer services provided by the store. You may find a coupon rack, for example, or brochures with tips on meal planning, food budgets, and shopping.

Nutrition, Quality, and Safety

There's more to shopping than looking for low prices. To get the most value for your money, you must also pay attention to nutrition, quality, and food safety.

Remember to read labels carefully. Make sure you're getting the product and amount you want. Check the date on the package. Use the nutrition information as explained in Section 12.2. Also look for nutrition information on shelf tabs or signs.

Avoid packages that are dirty, bulging, dented, rusty, leaking, or damaged in any way. Harmful bacteria may have gotten into the food. If packages of meat, poultry, and fish leak, the juices can contaminate other foods with harmful bacteria. To be safe, put meat, poultry, and fish packages in a plastic bag so they won't drip on other foods in your cart.

When buying frozen foods, avoid packages that are frosted with ice. The frost means the package may have thawed a little and was then refrozen. This can affect food safety and quality. Choose another package.

Keep fragile items in one part of your cart. As you add heavier items, move the fragile ones up so they are always on top and won't be crushed.

More About Checkout Options

Some stores now have computerized systems that can actually fill out your check for you. A printer at the checkout counter fills in the name of the store and the amount due. All you have to do is sign your name. This system helps stores avoid costly customer errors such as transposed digits.

When you use this type of system, be sure to look at the check carefully after the printer has printed the information. *Never* sign a blank check for any reason. Wait until the name of the store and the amount have been filled in.

Some stores also have systems that allow you to purchase groceries using the debit cards of local banks. There are two types of

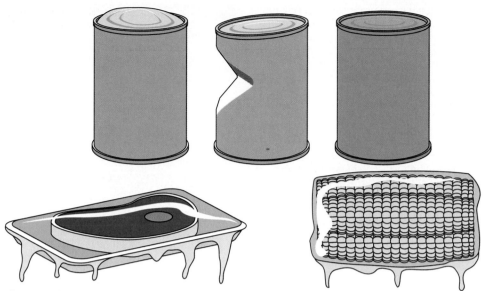

What warning signs do each of these packages show? Why should you avoid buying them?

Plan your route through the store. The frozen food department should be your last stop so the food does not begin to thaw.

Courtesy When Shopping

Be considerate of other shoppers. Keep your cart on the right side of the aisle, just like driving a car on the right side of the street. Excuse yourself if you bump into someone or have to pass them. Avoid blocking the aisle or other busy areas.

Any food that is damaged by shoppers is wasted. Consumers pay for the damage in the long run—the cost is added to the price of food. Remember:

❖ Do not open containers to look at or sample the contents.

❖ Return a product to its proper place if you decide not to buy it.

❖ Handle produce gently. Do not squeeze it or throw it back into a bin.

❖ When you buy bulk foods, use the scoop or tongs provided. Do not taste the food

or touch it with your hands. Close the bin or barrel when you are through.

Finishing Your Shopping

When you've selected all your items, it's time to head for the checkout line. If you choose an express line, be sure you have the right number of items. Don't choose a cash-only line if you intend to pay by check.

Many stores have computerized checkouts. The checkout clerk passes items over a scanner, which is the "eye" of the computer. The computer reads the UPC symbol on the package and searches its memory for the price. For fresh produce, the clerk usually enters a code into the computer.

Watch the display as the prices are rung up. The clerk could make a mistake or the incorrect price might be stored in the computer. If you think you are being charged incorrectly, politely ask the clerk to check it for you.

Section 12.3: In the Supermarket **343**

these systems. In one type, the cashier enters your card number into the computerized cash register; in the other type, the store provides a scanner that you run your debit card through. The computer sends out a request, usually over phone lines, to your bank to see that you have given a valid card number and that you have enough money in the bank to cover the cost of the groceries.

Then the system automatically charges your bank account for the amount of the groceries. Before using this system, check with the supermarket and your bank. One or both of them may charge a small fee for using the debit card in this manner.

Completing the Section

Review

- Ask students to summarize the main ideas in this section.
- Have students complete the Section Review. (Answers appear below.)

Evaluation

- Ask students to write a short summary of the various sections in a supermarket and the order in which they would visit the departments to keep foods at their best quality.
- Have students take the quiz for Section 12.3. (Refer to the *Section Quizzes* booklet or use the *Testmaker Software*.)

Reteaching

- Provide students with simple cost-per-serving and unit cost problems to build their confidence in calculating these costs.
- Refer to the *Reteaching Activities* booklet for the Section 12.3 activity sheet.

Enrichment

- Have interested students write a script for a video illustrating common mistakes made in grocery shopping. Take students to a grocery store and videotape the script (with manager's permission).

Closure

- Lead a discussion on techniques to use at the supermarket to ensure efficiency, nutrition, and safety.

Food stores vary in what forms of payment they will accept. To pay by check, you may need a store check cashing card. Some supermarkets also accept credit cards or automated banking cards. Don't let the ease of using a card tempt you to go over your food budget.

Take your purchases home right away and store them properly. (You may want to review the storage guidelines in Section 7.4). Put frozen foods away immediately so they don't thaw. Store refrigerated foods next, and finally shelf-stable ones. Remember to repackage bulk foods into airtight, durable containers.

If you come home and find a food you selected is spoiled or of poor quality, return it to the store as soon as possible. Do the same if you have any other problems with your purchase. Take the store receipt with you. Stores arc interested in keeping their customers and will do their best to satisfy you.

Have your money, checkbook, or card ready when it's time to pay for your purchases.

344   Chapter 12: Shopping for Food

Section 12.3 Review

RECALL THE FACTS

1. What is the formula for calculating unit price?
2. Give three examples of ways to save money when shopping.
3. Why is it important to avoid buying food in damaged containers?
4. In what way does handling food carelessly when shopping hurt other consumers?

DISCUSS YOUR IDEAS

5. Do you think some people are biased against buying store brands or generic items? If so, why? Is this bias justified?

APPLY YOUR LEARNING

6. Working in pairs, write and perform a skit demonstrating at least three poor shopping strategies. Have the rest of the class identify them.

Earth Watch

"Green shopping" means shopping with the environment in mind. You can make choices that help reduce waste and pollution and preserve natural resources. Here are some suggestions:

- Bring your own shopping bags. Consider using cloth ones, or reuse paper or plastic bags you received earlier. Some stores collect used bags for recycling.
- Choose products with the least amount of packaging.
- Buy products in containers that are recyclable in your area.

Answers to Section Review

1. Total price ÷ number of units = unit price.
2. See the list on page 342.
3. The food in damaged containers may have been contaminated by microorganisms and be unsafe to eat.
4. Answers will vary: damaging food items decreases the stock on hand and increases prices for all consumers.
5. Answers will vary.
6. Answers will vary.

Career PROFILE

Todd Lang
Stock Clerk

CURRENT POSITION

"I work part-time after school as a stock clerk for a large supermarket."

RESPONSIBILITIES

"My main responsibility is to keep the shelves stocked. I also unpack and check merchandise when it is delivered, help keep a record of items in the storeroom, and make sure shelf prices are up to date."

WHY I CHOSE THIS JOB

"I'm interested in food retailing and took this job to learn more about how a store operates."

SKILLS

"It helps to have a basic knowledge of business math in this job because it involves keeping track of inventory. Physically, you need a certain amount of strength for heavy lifting."

FAVORITE PART OF THE JOB

"I like being given some responsibility. It's not the most glamorous job in the world, but it's an important one. I know the store manager and the customers are all depending on me, so I try to be efficient and accurate."

FUTURE PLANS

"After I graduate from high school this spring, I'm planning to take business classes at a local community college. I'll probably also continue to work at the store. I think I'd like to become a supermarket manager or advertising director someday."

- How does Todd's positive attitude about his job affect his chances of promotion?
- What aspects of Todd's job do you think you might enjoy? Why?

345

CAREER PROFILE: STOCK CLERK

Thinking About . . . Stock Clerks

Have students think of other questions they would like to ask Todd Lang about being a stock clerk. (Examples: How many hours a week do you work? How does working as a stock clerk affect the amount of time you spend doing schoolwork? Did you receive any training for the work you do?)

Ask student volunteers to explain why they would or would not like to work part-time as a stock clerk.

Student Opportunities

Students who would like to work part-time as stock clerks should investigate employment opportunities at local stores. Many supermarkets hire students part-time.

Occupational Outlook

Few people become stock clerks for life. In many cases, however, stock clerks that show initiative and skill may be promoted to other jobs within the store and may become interested in merchandising or eventually manage or own their own stores.

For More Information

For additional information about stock clerks and merchandising careers, encourage students to contact:
- Personnel offices of local stores
- National Retail Merchants Association, 100 W. 31st St., New York, NY 10001

Completing the Chapter

Review

- Have students complete the Chapter Review. (Answers appear below.)

Evaluation

- Ask students to write a short essay describing the steps a person should take before, during, and after a trip to the supermarket.

- Have students take the test for Chapter 12. (Refer to the *Chapter and Unit Tests* booklet or construct your own test using the *Testmaker Software.*)

■ ANSWERS ■

REVIEWING FACTS

1. Supermarkets are generally less expensive and carry a greater variety of products. However, specialty stores may carry a greater variety of the product in which they specialize.

2. Plan the meals you will serve; check your menus and recipes to see what foods and ingredients are needed; write those you don't have on your shopping list along with the amounts needed; check your supply of basic items and add any you need to the list.

3. A cents-off coupon is redeemed at the checkout counter of the store; you must pay full price with a rebate coupon, then send in the proof of purchase with the coupon for a partial rebate of the purchase price.

4. The weight of the food itself, not including the package.

5. The daily value for sodium varies depending on whether you need more or less than 2000 calories per day; vitamin C is not affected by your caloric needs.

SUMMARY

SECTION 12.1

Before You Shop: A well-planned shopping trip begins with deciding where and when to shop. You can buy food from a number of different types of stores, which differ in items offered, services, and price. Which you choose depends on your priorities. You can save money and time by carefully choosing when to shop. Preparing a shopping list helps prevent impulse buying. Collecting coupons is another money-saving strategy.

SECTION 12.2

Food Labels: Food labels are valuable tools in making wise food choices. All labels must include certain basic information. Most food labels also include a nutrition panel to help you decide how well the product meets your nutritional needs. The use of certain terms and health claims on food labels is regulated by law. Open dating can help consumers judge how long products will remain safe.

SECTION 12.3

In the Supermarket: Shopping skills can help you find good nutrition and quality at the best price. Comparison shopping is easier if you know how to find the unit price and the price per serving. Store brand and generic items can save you money. Choose quality foods and handle them carefully to preserve their nutritional value and safety. Foods damaged or spoiled by careless handling result in higher prices for all consumers.

REVIEWING FACTS

1. How do supermarkets and specialty stores compare in terms of foods sold, services, and price? (12.1)

2. List four basic steps in making a shopping list. (12.1)

3. What is the difference between a cents-off coupon and a rebate coupon? (12.1)

4. What does "net weight" mean? (12.2)

5. On a nutrition panel, in what way is the daily value for sodium different from that for vitamin C? (12.2)

6. What does the phrase "low in fat" on a food label tell you about the specific fat content of the food? (12.2)

7. Does a package date that has not expired guarantee product quality? Explain. (12.2)

8. Describe the procedure for buying bulk foods. (12.3)

9. Why is it helpful to calculate the cost per serving when buying fresh meat, poultry, or fish? (12.3)

10. Name five signs that tell you a package of food may be unsafe. (12.3)

LEARNING BY DOING

1. ***Computer lab:*** Make up a basic shopping list that could be stored on the computer. Explain how you would use the list. (12.1)

2. ***Foods lab:*** Prepare two variations of a recipe. For the first, use the regular ingredients as called for. For the second, replace some of the ingredients with similar products labeled "light," "low-sodium," "low-fat," or "reduced cholesterol." Use the nutrition panels on the food labels to compare the nutritional value of the two versions. Also compare them for taste, texture, and appearance. (12.2)

6. The food has no more than 3 grams of fat; it can be eaten frequently without exceeding the recommended amount.

7. No; the way the package has been handled can affect the quality of the product also.

8. Using the scoop or tongs provided, place the desired amount of the food in a plastic bag, tie it, and stick an identifying tag on the bag; do not taste the food or touch it with your hands.

3. **Taste test:** Compare the taste, texture, and appearance of store brand or generic items to their identical name-brand equivalents. Compare a variety of types of foods, such as canned vegetables, breakfast cereals, and frozen juices. What conclusions can you draw? (12.3)

THINKING CRITICALLY

1. **Analyzing behavior:** Why do you think people buy items on impulse? (12.1)

2. **Comparing and contrasting:** Make a chart listing at least three food stores in your community, each from a different category (convenience store, warehouse store, etc.). Describe the advantages and disadvantages of each. (12.1)

3. **Identifying ambiguous statements:** A children's breakfast cereal claims to have "less sugar per serving than one apple." What conclusion does the manufacturer want you to reach? Is it a valid one? Explain your answer. (12.2)

4. **Predicting consequences:** What might be the consequences of buying frozen food that shows signs of having been thawed and then refrozen? (12.3)

MAKING DECISIONS AND SOLVING PROBLEMS

What Would You Do?

1. You are looking over your coupons as you wait in the checkout line. You discover that two of your coupons are not good for the size of the items you are buying. It is almost your turn to check out. If you go back to exchange the items, you will have to give up your place in line. (12.1, 12.3)

2. While buying milk, you notice some cartons marked "Reduced for quick sale." You see the "sell by" date is the day after tomorrow. You wonder whether you should buy one of the reduced-price cartons. (12.2)

3. You have bought a type of cheese that you've never tried before. When you open the package, you notice it has a powerful smell. You aren't sure if this is normal or if the cheese is spoiled. (12.3)

LINKING YOUR STUDIES

1. **Social studies:** Using library resources, find information about how people in other cultures do their food shopping. How are their shopping practices similar to, and different from, those in your own culture? (12.1, 12.3)

2. **Consumer economics:** Select four regular food items and their nutritionally altered equivalents (those labeled "low-fat," "low-sodium," etc.). Compare the prices of the two different types of items. Give a short report to the class telling your findings and giving possible reasons for the price differences. (12.2, 12.3)

3. **Math:** Suppose you need chicken for a dinner party of eight people. Check the prices and selections of different forms of chicken at a supermarket. Use the "Servings Per Pound of Meat, Poultry, and Fish" chart on page 341 to determine which offers the most value. What other factors would affect your decision? (12.3)

LEARNING BY DOING

Answers to "Learning by Doing" activities will vary.

THINKING CRITICALLY

1. Answers will vary.

2. Answers will vary. If students' answers vary from the general advantages and disadvantages of these types of stores, ask them to explain their answers.

3. Answers will vary. The sugar in an apple is not processed sugar and has some nutritional value. The manufacturer wants you to think that the sugar in the cereal compares favorably with the apple, even though it actually has no nutritional value.

4. The quality of the food may have been affected; the food may appear soggy or tough when cooked, or the taste may change.

MAKING DECISIONS AND SOLVING PROBLEMS

Answers to "Making Decisions and Solving Problems" questions will vary. Encourage students to give reasons for their answers.

LINKING YOUR STUDIES

Answers to "Linking Your Studies" questions will vary.

9. These foods contain bones and other parts that are not edible; the unit cost includes these parts, but cost per serving does not.

10. *Any five:* Dirty, bulging, dented, rusty, leaking, damaged.

Planning the Chapter

Chapter Overview

Section 13.1: Where Does Food Come From?

Section 13.2: A Safe Food Supply

Section 13.3: The Global Food Supply

Introducing the Chapter

Motivator

* Divide the class into groups to research the main sources of calories and protein in people's diets in different parts of the world: United States and Canada, Europe, Australia and New Zealand, Latin America, Africa, and Asia. Ask each group to report its findings to the class. Compare the percentages of protein supplied by animal protein and plant protein in different areas of the world. Why do staple foods differ in different parts of the world?

Teacher's Classroom Resources—Chapter 13

Refer to these resources in the TCR package:

Enrichment Activities

Chapter and Unit Tests

Testmaker Software

CHAPTER 13

The Food Supply

348

Cooperative Learning Suggestions

Organize a Co-op Co-op activity. Have students work in groups to research one of the following methods to increase the global food supply: making existing farmland more productive, reducing the demand for feed grain, developing new sources of food, developing solar energy as a fuel. Have each group research the topic and write a report of its findings. Then have each group present its topic to the class as a panel discussion.

Where Does Food Come From?

OBJECTIVES

After studying this section, you should be able to:

- Trace the route food takes from farm to marketplace.
- Describe innovative farming, processing, and packaging techniques.
- Identify influences on food prices.

LOOK FOR THESE TERMS

sustainable farming
hydroponic farming
aquaculture

Andre leaned back from his homework. Looking out the window, he could see huge snowflakes falling. He reached across the kitchen table for a favorite snack—an orange and corn chips. As Andre peeled the orange, he read on the chip bag that the chips were processed in Arkansas. He knew the orange had come from California. He chuckled to himself as he realized his food had traveled farther than he had in his entire life.

From Farm to Marketplace

North America has the advantage of an abundant food supply. A complicated network, involving the farmer, processor, distributor, and retailer, keeps shelves stocked with a wide variety of foods.

The Farmer

Most food begins its journey on farms where it is grown. Farmers in the United States and Canada produce enough food for their own countries and to sell elsewhere.

Farmers continually look for ways to produce more and better-quality food.

Section 13.1
Where Does Food Come From?

Introducing the Section

Motivator

- Divide the class into small groups and have each group select five processed foods. Ask groups to list the steps each basic food underwent between field, orchard, or farm and purchase.

Objectives

- Have students read the section objectives. Discuss the purpose of studying the section.

Vocabulary

- Pronounce the terms listed under "Look for These Terms." Have students read the section find the terms and their definitions in the section.

Guided Reading

- Have students look at the headings within Section 13.1 to preview the concepts that will be discussed.
- Have students read the section and complete the appropriate part of the Chapter 13 Study Guide in the *Student Workbook*.

Teacher's Classroom Resources—Section 13.1

Refer to these resources in the TCR package:

Reproducible Lesson Plans

Student Workbook

Extending the Text

Reteaching Activities

Section Quizzes

Testmaker Software

Color Transparencies

Comprehension Check

1. Ask students to explain what sustainable farming is and how it is related to integrated pest management. *(A method of farming in which farmers cut down on chemical use or do not use chemicals at all; integrated pest management allows farmers to get rid of "bad" bugs by using "good" bugs, decreasing the need for chemical pesticides.)*

2. Ask students to list methods that are used to preserve perishable foods. *(canning, freezing, during, drying, freeze-drying, controlled atmosphere storage)*

3. Discuss various developments in packaging technology that allow food manufacturers to expand their product lines. *(Discuss aseptic packages, microwavable plastic cans and trays, and modified atmosphere packaging.)*

Using the Photo

Direct students to look again at the photo on page 350. In addition to being able to grow foods indoors, what other advantages might hydroponic farming have? *(Crop rotation becomes unnecessary, since nutrients are provided by solutions—there is no soil to wear out; pests may be easier to control without the use of pesticides; weather is no longer a problem, etc.)*

Farmers are continually looking for ways to produce quality food less expensively. Environmental issues have also had an impact on farming methods. Traditional methods rely on the use of chemical fertilizers and pesticides. However, there is growing concern about these chemicals contaminating the water supply and food.

One alternative is **sustainable farming.** It means cutting back on chemicals or not using them at all. Animal manure replaces chemicals as a fertilizer. Various means are used to get rid of pests and weeds without chemicals. Some farmers are turning to *integrated pest management,* which uses "good" bugs to destroy "bad" bugs. A California strawberry grower uses a huge vacuum mounted on a tractor to suck bugs from the tops of plants.

Hydroponic farming (high-druh-PAH-nik) is a method of growing plants without soil. Various materials, such as water, gravel, or sand, can be used to hold the plants. Nutrient-enriched water provides food for the plants. Look for hydroponic lettuce, cucumbers, and tomatoes in supermarkets.

Aquaculture is a method of growing fish or seafood in enclosed areas of water. Fish farms may be located near the shore and closed off with special nets, or they may be special ponds. Aquaculture is one of the fastest growing industries in the world. For example, shrimp farmers supply about 25 percent of the world shrimp market.

Because North America has so many different climate areas, different crops are grown in various places. For example, more than 60 percent of fresh vegetables used in the U.S. are grown in California, Florida, and Texas.

At harvest, the food is shipped to processors. Depending on the kind of food, it may travel by truck, train, barge, ship, or plane.

The Processor

Processing ranges from very simple to complex, depending on the food and its final use. Fresh produce, for instance, needs minimum processing. It may just be cleaned, packaged, and shipped to the marketplace.

With hydroponic farming, plants can be grown indoors. Why would that be an advantage?

Thinking Skills

Reasoning: Most farmers still practice traditional farming methods using chemical fertilizers and pesticides. However, many are beginning to change to sustainable farming. Ask students: Aside from the pressure of consumer demand for foods grown without chemicals, what reasons might the farmers have for reducing their use of chemicals? *(Some water supplies show pollution from agricultural chemicals; the chemicals cost a great deal of money, which reduces the farmers' profit; some farmers are also worried about long-term effects of exposure to the chemicals on their own health.)*

Foods go through various amounts and types of processing, depending on what finished product is desired.

1. **Poster Project:** Have students create a poster that traces the steps in the processing of a food product from harvest to store. Remind them of the variety of processing methods and packaging procedures used. *(Key skill: creativity)*

2. **Research:** Have students research different methods of freezing foods. Which methods are the most successful in terms of maintaining product quality? Ask students to write a short report of their findings. *(Key skill: writing)*

3. **Alternative Farming Methods:** Collect current newspaper and magazine articles about alternative farming methods. Provide students with copies and ask them to discuss the advantages and disadvantages of each method. *(Key skill: reading)*

4. **Discussion:** The amount of processing food undergoes varies greatly. Have students give food examples they would classify as representing minimal, moderate, and maximum processing. Would the amount or type of processing affect their food choices? *(Key skill: critical thinking)*

As a part of processing, many perishable foods are preserved to prevent spoilage and lengthen their shelf life. Some commercial preservation methods include:

❖ **Canning.** Foods are sealed in airtight metal or glass containers and heated to destroy harmful microorganisms.

❖ **Freezing.** Foods are quickly frozen to slow down the growth of harmful bacteria.

❖ **Curing.** Ingredients such as salt, spices, sugar, sodium nitrate, and sodium nitrite are added to the food. This method is widely used in processing meats such as ham, bacon, and corned beef. It is also used to preserve fish, pickles, and some vegetables.

❖ **Drying.** Moisture, needed by harmful microorganisms, is removed from food. Drying is used for foods such as grains, dry beans, milk, and fruit.

❖ **Freeze-drying.** Food is first frozen and then dried. More flavor, texture, and nutrients are retained than with drying. Freeze-drying is used for foods such as instant coffee, dried soup mixes, strawberries, and mushrooms.

❖ **Controlled atmosphere storage.** Food is held in a cold area where the amounts of nitrogen, oxygen, and carbon dioxide in the atmosphere are controlled. This helps extend the shelf life of some foods, especially fruits.

Section 13.1: Where Does Food Come From?   351

Special Needs Strategies

Learning Disabled: Give students actual food examples of the major preservation methods described. Provide index cards labeled with the methods and ask students to place the food by the correct cards. Then discuss each method to reinforce learning. You may wish to record main points on the cards and give students photocopies for review.

Comprehension Check

1. Ask students to discuss the roles of distributors and retailers in bringing foods to the marketplace where they are accessible to many people.

2. Ask students to explain the effect of supply and demand on food prices. *(If demand is greater than supply, the price goes up; if supply is greater than demand, the price goes down.)*

3. Discuss the effects of natural disasters on food prices. *(When a natural disaster destroys crops, a shortage occurs, driving food prices up.)*

Student Experiences

1. **Creating a Game:** Have groups of students write the steps in processing and distributing a food on large index cards. Have groups exchange cards and attempt to arrange the steps in order. *(Key skill: sequencing)*

Earth Watch

Ask students to brainstorm ideas to cut down on packaging. For example, one possible idea is edible packaging. Why might this not be a good idea? Could the problems be overcome?

Packaging Technology

Several recent developments in packaging have enabled food manufacturers and processors to expand the kinds of products they offer. Here are some examples.

❖ *Aseptic packages,* commonly called "juice boxes," are made of layers of plastics, paperboard, and aluminum foil. Food and the package are sterilized separately and the package is filled under sterile conditions.

❖ *Plastic cans and trays* are used for shelf-stable foods that can be heated in a microwave oven. Some trays also can be used in a conventional oven.

❖ *Modified atmosphere packaging* inserts a mixture of carbon dioxide, oxygen, and nitrogen into the package before sealing. The gas mixture slows down bacterial growth. With this method, foods such as fresh pasta, prepared salads, and cooked meats can be kept, refrigerated, up to four weeks.

Packaging methods are continually changing to keep up with new technology and the needs and wants of consumers.

Earth Watch

Concerns for the environment are creating challenges for food processors. To cut down on trash, consumers are demanding less packaging. Food processors are looking for new ways to meet the need and still provide safe, nutritious food for the marketplace.

The Distributor

Once food is processed and packaged, it is shipped to the distributor.

Distributors are the link between food processors and retailers (the places where you buy food). There are many different kinds of distributors, depending on the food involved. Generally, the food is shipped to large warehouses. There it is stored before being sent to the retailer.

The Retailer

From the distributor, food is shipped to the many different kinds of retailers. In Section 12.1, you read of the different kinds of stores available for shopping. Supermarkets, which offer a wide selection of products, are the most popular.

A primary job of the retailer is to present food to the consumer. In an effort to satisfy consumers, food processors and manufacturers constantly develop new products. Some stores review as many as 100 new products a week. Because shelf space is limited, they cannot accept every new product. If new products are accepted but do not sell well, they are removed.

More About Food Distribution

Many supermarket chains are so large that they have their own distribution systems, either nationwide or regional. They can afford to buy huge quantities of food direct from food processors or distributors and keep it in their own warehouses until needed. This saves money for the large chains and allows them to offer lower prices than smaller chains or independent stores.

The Ups and Downs of Food Prices

For every dollar a consumer spends on food, between 3 and 25 cents goes to the farmer. The rest of the money covers processing, packaging, advertising, and distribution. The more a food is processed, the more it will generally cost the consumer. Food prices tend to go up and down for other reasons as well.

❖ **Supply and demand.** If consumer demand for a food is greater than the supply, the price will go up. Many crops reach a peak at certain times of the year. Quantities are so large that prices are lower. Other foods, offered in limited supply, are high-priced.

❖ **Natural disasters.** Storms, earthquakes, floods, and droughts affect the price of food. A severe freeze in California or Florida can damage orange trees, reducing the supply for a whole season. In 1992, Hurricane Andrew wiped out many vegetable farms in southern Florida. Vegetable prices around the country were affected.

❖ **Consumer damage.** Careless consumers sometimes damage food when they shop. The damaged items may have to be thrown out by the store. Such losses are added to the prices consumers pay.

Natural disasters, such as floods, can destroy crops and cause food prices to go up.

■ Section 13.1 Review ■

RECALL THE FACTS

1. Name the four parts of the food supply network.

2. Identify three alternatives to traditional farming methods.

3. How and why is food cured?

4. List three factors that affect food prices.

DISCUSS YOUR IDEAS

5. What trends or concerns in society are affecting how food is produced, processed, and packaged?

APPLY YOUR LEARNING

6. Find a recipe with at least three ingredients that are processed using different commercial preservation methods. Identify the methods used.

Completing the Section

Review

- Ask students to summarize the main ideas in this section.

- Have students complete the Section Review. (Answers appear below.)

Evaluation

- Ask students to draw a simple diagram describing the processes by which food goes from the farmer to the retailer.

- Have students take the quiz for Section 13.1. (Refer to the *Section Quizzes* booklet or use the *Testmaker Software*.)

Reteaching

- Using canned or packaged foods, have students practice telling the processing methods that were used to process the foods.

- Refer to the *Reteaching Activities* booklet for the Section 13.1 activity sheet.

Enrichment

- Have students report orally on the steps a locally grown food (if applicable) would pass through before packaging.

Closure

- Remind students of the motivator activity they performed for this section. Would they change anything now that they have studied this section?

■ Answers to Section Review ■

1. Farmer, processor, distributor, retailer.
2. Sustainable farming, hydroponic farming, and aquaculture.

3. Ingredients such as salt, spices, sugar, sodium nitrate, and sodium nitrite are added to the food to preserve it.
4. Supply and demand; natural disasters; consumer damage.

5. Answers will vary. Students should mention concerns about pollution and the ability to reuse or recycle products.
6. Answers will vary.

Section 13.2
A Safe Food Supply

Introducing the Section

Motivator

- Ask students to write a paragraph describing what they think makes a food safe to eat. Ask several student volunteers to read their paragraphs aloud.

Objectives

- Have students read the section objectives. Discuss the purpose of studying the section.

Vocabulary

- Pronounce the terms listed under "Look for These Terms." Have students read the section find the terms and their definitions in the section.

Guided Reading

- Have students look at the headings within Section 13.2 to preview the concepts that will be discussed.
- Have students read the section and complete the appropriate part of the Chapter 13 Study Guide in the *Student Workbook*.

A Safe Food Supply

OBJECTIVES

After studying this section, you should be able to:

- Explain how the government helps insure the safety of the food supply.
- Identify and discuss food safety issues.

LOOK FOR THESE TERMS

additives
irradiation
genetic engineering
tolerance levels
contaminants

When Ramona was choosing cucumbers at the store, she noticed they all were shiny but felt a bit sticky. She asked the produce clerk why. He explained that they were coated with a wax to prevent loss of moisture and improve their appearance. He assured her that this process met government regulations for food safety.

Safeguarding the Food Supply

Government and industry make every effort to provide a safe food supply. In doing so, they face a number of challenges. Foods must be handled properly on their way to the marketplace in order to prevent harmful microorganisms from reaching dangerous levels. **Additives**—chemicals added to food for specific reasons—must be tested and approved to be sure they will cause no harm. Questions about the safety of new food technology must be addressed. Steps must be taken to insure that harmful chemicals do not get into food accidentally.

Inspectors from various government agencies work to protect the food supply.

Teacher's Classroom Resources—Section 13.2

Refer to these resources in the TCR package:

Reproducible Lesson Plans

Student Workbook

Extending the Text

Reteaching Activities

Section Quizzes

Testmaker Software

Color Transparencies

The government usually plays a major role in monitoring the safety of a country's food supply. In the U.S., several federal agencies are responsible for food safety:

- **Food and Drug Administration** (FDA). The FDA is responsible for the general safety of food, except for meat, poultry, and eggs. It enforces laws that regulate additives, food purity, packaging, labeling, and new foods and processing methods.
- **Food Safety and Inspection Service (FSIS).** This part of the Department of Agriculture is responsible for the inspection and safety of meat, poultry, and eggs.
- **National Marine Fisheries Services.** This part of the Department of Commerce offers a voluntary inspection program to fish processors.
- **Environmental Protection Agency (EPA).** The EPA registers pesticides and sets legal limits for pesticides in food. It also regulates disposal of hazardous wastes.

What happens if tests or consumer complaints show that a food is unsafe? The FDA may first ask the manufacturer to withdraw the product voluntarily. If the manufacturer refuses, or if the situation is a life-threatening one, the FDA issues a recall. The product is removed from store shelves immediately and the public is alerted through the media. The brand name and package code numbers are announced. Consumers who have purchased any of this food are asked to return it to the store.

Food Safety Issues

Many issues related to food safety are controversial. It's important to understand the facts as well as the opinions on both sides of the issue.

Food Additives

Originally, additives were ingredients used to help preserve food or flavor it. They included basic foods such as salt and spices. As the food processing industry grew, chemicals were developed to keep foods safer or make them more appealing. By 1991, about 2,800 additives were being used. The chart on page 356 lists some common types of additives.

Hundreds of additives with a long history of use and safety are classified by the FDA as "Generally Recognized As Safe" (GRAS).

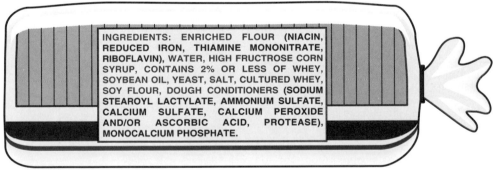

INGREDIENTS: ENRICHED FLOUR (NIACIN, REDUCED IRON, THIAMINE MONONITRATE, RIBOFLAVIN), WATER, HIGH FRUCTOSE CORN SYRUP, CONTAINS 2% OR LESS OF WHEY, SOYBEAN OIL, YEAST, SALT, CULTURED WHEY, SOY FLOUR, DOUGH CONDITIONERS (SODIUM STEAROYL LACTYLATE, AMMONIUM SULFATE, CALCIUM SULFATE, CALCIUM PEROXIDE AND/OR ASCORBIC ACID, PROTEASE), MONOCALCIUM PHOSPHATE.

Additives are used in many foods to improve the quality of the product or to lengthen shelf life.

Teaching . . .

- **Safeguarding the Food Supply**

(text pages 354-355)

Comprehension Check

1. Ask students to define *additives* and explain their implications in food safety. *(Additives are chemicals added to food for specific reasons; the chemicals must be tested to make sure that they are safe for human consumption.)*

2. Ask students to list federal agencies that are responsible for food safety in the United States. *(Food and Drug Administration, Food Safety and Inspection Service, National Marine Fisheries Services, Environmental Protection Agency.)*

Student Experiences

1. **Reading:** Provide students with copies of recent articles about the safety of our food supply. What questions about food safety were being addressed? *(Key skill: reading)*

2. **Research:** Have students research the histories of the federal agencies responsible for food safety. Why was the agency established? What is its role in ensuring food safety? What major contributions has the agency made to food safety? What are the agency's shortcomings? *(Key skill: research)*

More About Additives

Antioxidants are preservatives that keep fats and oils from spoiling and keep other foods from losing color, flavor, or texture. They include BHA and BHT, as well as vitamin E.

Monosodium glutamate (mah-noh-SOH-dee-yum GLUE-tuh-mate), also known as MSG, is an additive that used to be common in prepared foods. It is still used as a flavor enhancer in many foods, such as soups, gravy mixes, salad dressings, snack foods, frozen dinners, and processed meats. Hydrolyzed (HIGH-droh-lized) vegetable protein, another flavor enhancer, also contains some MSG. Many people now try to avoid MSG, because it causes unpleasant reactions in some people.

Teaching . . .

• **Food Safety Issues: Food Additives, Irradiation**

(text pages 355-358)

Comprehension Check

1. Ask students to explain the purpose of sugar substitutes. *(They sweeten food but add few or no calories.)*

2. Discuss the use of saccharin in the United States. Why was it banned? Why was the rule changed? *(Saccharin is an artificial sweetener first used in the 1900s; it was banned in 1977 after being linked with cancer in laboratory animals. The rule was changed by popular demand.)*

3. Ask students to explain the process of irradiation. What are the arguments for and against using irradiation? *(Irradiation is the process of exposing foods to gamma rays in controlled amounts. For: increases shelf life and destroys harmful microorganisms; it could eliminate the need for dangerous pesticides. Against: long-term effects on people who eat irradiated food have not been established. Some people claim that eating irradiated foods can cause cancer and birth defects.)*

Common Food Additives

Type of Additive	Examples
Nutritional supplements: Replace nutrients lost in processing or make food more nutritious.	• Vitamin C (often added to fruit drinks) • Vitamin D (added to milk)
Preservatives: Help extend shelf life of foods.	• BHT
Acids and alkalies: Help maintain the chemical balance in some foods. Some also help preserve food or add flavor.	• Sodium nitrite • Citric acid • Calcium propionate
Emulsifiers, stabilizers, thickeners, and texturizers: Improve the texture and "body" of foods such as baked goods.	• Vegetable gums • Modified food starch • Carrageenan
Flavoring agents: Help make foods taste more appealing.	• Natural fruit flavors • Artificial flavors • Natural and artificial sweeteners • Monosodium glutamate (MSG)
Coloring agents: Help give food a more attractive appearance.	• Caramel coloring • Artificial colors

Additives on the GRAS list can be used by food processors without further approval from the FDA. However, even these substances are undergoing additional testing to make certain they meet today's standards.

FDA approval for other additives can be a lengthy process. An additive is first tested extensively. If it proves to be safe, the FDA approves it and sets regulations for its use.

Even though additives are approved by the FDA, consumers sometimes raise questions about their safety. In some cases, the FDA undertakes a process of study and review. Consumers who are concerned about particular additives can avoid foods that contain them by reading ingredients lists carefully.

Sugar Substitutes

Sugar substitutes sweeten food, but add few or no calories. They can benefit people who must restrict the amount of sugar they eat, such as diabetics. Critics are not certain how helpful they may be for weight loss.

Artificial sweeteners currently in use include aspartame (AS-puhr-tame), acesulfame-K (ay-see-SULL-fame kay), and saccharin.

Sugar substitutes can be found in many different types of products. How many have you seen?

356   Chapter 13: The Food Supply

Sugar substitutes have sometimes proved controversial. For example, saccharin is a no-calorie artificial sweetener that was first used in the early 1900s. It was banned in 1977 after studies linked it with cancer in laboratory animals. By public demand, the rule was later changed. The new rule allowed products containing saccharin to be sold if a warning appeared on the label and in the store.

Fat Substitutes

Fat substitutes are natural or artificial substances that replace fat in processed foods such as baked goods and ice cream. They are also used in reduced-fat foods, such as low-fat cheeses.

Some natural fat substitutes are based on proteins from ingredients such as skim milk or egg whites. Others are based on carbohydrates from sources such as cornstarch and oat bran. Natural substitutes are considered safe.

Artificial fat substitutes have also been developed. Since they do not break down during digestion, they add no fat or calories to the diet. Specific FDA approval is required for artificial substitutes. One such substitute, olestra, was approved in 1996. However, it removes some fat-soluble nutrients from the body. Products containing olestra must carry a warning label about possible side effects.

Some experts are concerned that fat substitutes will not help people learn healthy eating habits. Fat-free treats such as baked goods and frozen desserts are no substitute for more nutritious low-fat foods, such as fruits and vegetables.

Irradiation

Irradiation is the process of exposing food to gamma rays to increase its shelf life and kill harmful microorganisms. Irradiation does not make foods radioactive. It can, however, cause minor changes in flavor and texture and slight vitamin loss.

The irradiation symbol (right) identifies foods that have gone through the irradiation process (below).

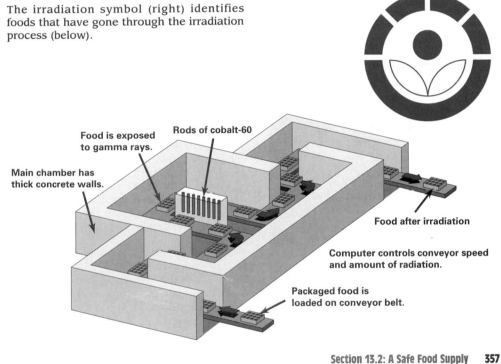

Food is exposed to gamma rays.

Rods of cobalt-60

Main chamber has thick concrete walls.

Food after irradiation

Computer controls conveyor speed and amount of radiation.

Packaged food is loaded on conveyor belt.

Student Experiences

1. **Class Discussion:** Discuss the reasons additives are added to various products. Ask students what would happen to our food supply if all additives were banned. Ask students how the GRAS list helps to ensure the safety of food additives. *(Key skill: critical thinking)*

2. **Taste Test:** Have students sample and evaluate foods that contain artificial sweeteners or fat substitutes. *(Key skill: evaluation)*

3. **Product Comparison:** Give each student a food product. Tell students to read the label, identify the additives present, and determine their function. Refer students to the chart on page 356. *(Key skill: reading)*

4. **Debate:** Have students debate the benefits and risks posed by irradiating foods. *(Key skill: critical thinking)*

5. **Research:** Have students investigate and report on the process of obtaining FDA approval to use an additive not on the GRAS list. *(Key skill: research)*

More About Irradiated Foods

In 1992, the first irradiation plant opened in Mulberry, Florida. More than 1,000 pounds (500 kg) of strawberries were irradiated and shipped to a retailer. They sold quickly and consumers were pleased with the flavor and appearance of the strawberries.

Even with modern laboratory techniques, it is almost impossible to determine whether foods have been irradiated or how much exposure they have had to the gamma rays. Thus, it would be difficult to enforce laws meant to limit the amount of irradiation foods receive.

Teaching . . .

**• Food Safety Issues:
Biotechnology, Illegal
Chemical Residues,
Contaminants**

(text pages 358-359)

Comprehension Check

1. Ask students to identify several improvements that have been achieved or are being investigated in the field of plant biotechnology. *(Tomatoes that ripen but do not soften during shipping; more nutritious varieties of plant foods; more insect-resistant plants, and plants better able to survive harsh weather.)*

2. Ask students to define biodiversity. In what way might biotechnology pose a threat? *(Biotechnology could eventually lead to dependence on a few genetically engineered plants for food; in the event of a sudden change in conditions, the whole food supply could be threatened.)*

3. Discuss sources of chemical residues in food. *(Chemicals injected into animals to improve health; pesticides in animal feed and in plant foods.)*

Student Experiences

1. **Guest Speaker:** Invite an agriculture teacher or extension agent to speak to the class on the use of biotechnology to improve food products. Discuss the potential advantages and disadvantages of genetically engineered foods. *(Key skill: science)*

2. **Reading:** Provide students with copies of articles voicing concerns about chemical residues in food. What are some sources of chemical residues in food? How do government agencies try to control the amount? *(Key skill: reading)*

Those in favor of irradiation cite its potential to improve food safety. It could reduce food-borne illness and eliminate the need for dangerous pesticides.

Critics of irradiation point to other concerns. They claim that irradiation produces harmful by-products that can cause cancer and birth defects. They also fear that the radioactive chemicals used in irradiation plants pose a danger to workers and the community.

The FDA approved the use of irradiation for spices years ago. It has also approved the process for fruits, vegetables, poultry, and seafood. Irradiated foods must be identified with the symbol that appears on page 357.

Genetic Engineering

Genetic engineering is based on a knowledge of genetics. Genes carry specific, hereditary traits from one generation to the next. By modifying the genes for specific traits, scientists can produce new varieties of plants with improved characteristics.

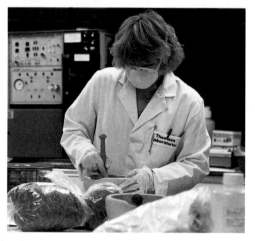

Through genetic engineering, scientists work to improve the food supply.

Scientists have already used genetic engineering to produce new varieties of tomatoes, squash, and potatoes. They are working to develop other plants that are easier to grow and process, stay fresh longer, and have more nutrients.

Some critics have questioned the safety of foods that have been genetically altered. The FDA has developed guidelines for assessing the safety of such foods as they become available to consumers. It has also considered the question of product labeling. As with all foods, labeling is required if the product contains a food allergen or if the nutritional content has been altered.

Some people are concerned that genetic engineering could result in a food supply that is dependent on a few specifically designed plants. If so, unforeseen problems, such as a sudden change in climate, could endanger the entire food supply. However, others see genetic engineering as a way to increase the diversity of the world's crops.

One thing is certain—genetic engineering raises issues that have never had to be dealt with before. They will probably be debated for years to come.

Illegal Chemical Residues

In recent years, concern about chemical residues in food have increased. These residues are substances left behind in food after processing. Chemical residues have the potential to cause health problems, some serious.

Chemical residues can come from a variety of sources. In meat and poultry, they are usually from drugs used to improve animal health or from pesticides in animal feed. Residues gather in animal tissues. In plant foods, including grains, fruits, and vegetables, pesticides are usually the main residues.

Government agencies establish **tolerance levels**—maximum safe levels for certain chemicals in the human body. It is illegal for foods to contain more of a chemical than the tolerance level set for it. Government agencies test food samples regularly for illegal residue levels.

Thinking Skills

Reasoning: People tend to become very upset over the risks of additives, contaminants, and chemical residues, when they actually face a much higher risk of food-borne illness from poor sanitation in the home. Why? *(Possible answers: People may be more alarmed by things they feel they have little control over; poor sanitation is a less "glamorous" topic, so it doesn't cause as much controversy and isn't written up in popular magazines as much as the more controversial topics of additives, contaminants, and chemical residues in foods.)*

Pesticides serve a purpose, but they may also contribute to the problem of chemical residues and contaminants. Government agencies monitor the levels of chemicals in food and take action if problems are suspected.

Contaminants

Contaminants are substances that accidentally get into food as it moves from the farm to the table. One type of contaminant is chemical pollutants. Hazardous chemicals from industries, farms, or careless consumers can easily get into water supplies. Plants drawing on polluted water can become contaminated. Fish and animals are also affected.

Microorganisms are another source of contamination. Salmonella bacteria, for example, can contaminate eggs and chickens, causing food-borne illness. Aflatoxins (af-luh-TOCK-suns) are poisonous substances produced by certain types of mold. They can sometimes be found in grains, milk, cheese, and peanuts.

As with illegal residues, various government agencies test food for contaminants to insure the safety of the food supply.

Earth Watch

Never dump household chemicals down the drain or on the ground. The chemicals could contaminate the water and food supply. Follow package directions for proper disposal or call your local waste disposal department.

What Consumers Can Do

Contradictory reports regarding the safety of the food supply can be confusing to consumers. For reliable information, turn to a reputable consumer group concerned with food safety. Many such groups serve as watchdogs of both government and industry. Before you accept facts presented by a consumer group, however, be sure you know how it is funded. Some are merely agents for food and chemical industries.

Section 13.2: A Safe Food Supply **359**

Comprehension Check

1. Ask students to identify sources of reliable information about the safety of the food supply. *(reputable consumer groups)*

2. Ask students to identify suggestions for promoting a safe food supply. *(Support consumer groups that reflect your views; avoid buying products from companies whose policies you do not support; keep track of laws introduced relating to food and write to your representatives to let them know your views.)*

Student Experiences

1. Letter Writing: Ask students to select a food safety issue about which they are concerned. Have them write letters to the appropriate government agency outlining their concern and asking for information on the government's role in this issue. *(Key skills: writing, citizenship)*

Healthy Attitudes

Ask students whether organically grown produce is readily available in your area. Point out that many people grow some of their own food in gardens and can control the pesticides used. However, they cannot control contaminants in the soil or water.

Food and Nutrition Science

Interpreting Data: When you read about the results of scientific experiments that relate to food safety, be sure you understand the real impact of the conclusions presented.

For example, if a report states that a certain chemical doubles the risk of cancer, find out what the *original* risk was. It may have been so small that doubling it may be insignificant.

Completing the Section

Review

- Ask students to summarize the main ideas in this section.
- Have students complete the Section Review. (Answers appear below.)

Evaluation

- Ask students to present a brief report on the effects of technology on food supplies and safety.
- Have students take the quiz for Section 13.2. (Refer to the *Section Quizzes* booklet or use the *Testmaker Software*.)

Reteaching

- List federal and state agencies that regulate food safety. Present several situations regarding food safety and ask students to choose the agency to contact in each case.
- Refer to the *Reteaching Activities* booklet for the Section 13.2 activity sheet.

Enrichment

- Ask students to write a consumer guide listing common problems with food safety and the agencies that can help with each problem.

Closure

- Remind students of the motivator for this section. Would they change their answers now? What makes foods safe or unsafe?

Healthy Attitudes

If you are concerned about residues and contaminants, here are some suggestions.

- Wash produce with water before eating it.
- Consider buying organic fruits and vegetables—those grown without chemicals.
- Choose lean cuts of meat and remove visible fat from meat and poultry. If harmful residues are present, they are concentrated in fat and organs.

Here are some additional suggestions for promoting a safe food supply:

- ❖ Support consumer groups that reflect your views.
- ❖ Avoid buying products from companies whose policies you do not support.
- ❖ Keep track of any laws that are being introduced relating to food. Write to your representatives. Tell them how you feel about any aspect of food safety.

Consumers have the right to be informed about issues affecting food safety, such as laws about disposing of hazardous chemicals. What can consumers do to make their voices heard?

Section 13.2 Review

RECALL THE FACTS

1. Name four government agencies responsible for food safety.
2. What is a food additive? Give two examples.
3. How might irradiation improve food safety?
4. Name one benefit and one concern associated with biotechnology.

DISCUSS YOUR IDEAS

5. How large a role do you think government should play in maintaining a safe food supply?
6. What role should consumers play in food safety?

APPLY YOUR LEARNING

7. Select a food safety issue you are concerned about. Write a letter to the appropriate government agency. Identify your concern and ask for information on the government's role in this issue.

Answers to Section Review

1. Food and Drug Administration; Food Safety and Inspection Service; National Marine Fisheries Services; Environmental Protection Agency.
2. A chemical added to food for specific reasons; examples will vary (see chart on page 356).
3. By retarding the growth of harmful microorganisms.
4. Answers will vary; examples: it can increase the food supply or create a safer food supply; it may decrease biodiversity.
5. Answers will vary.
6. Answers will vary. Students should realize that consumers play a very important role in food safety by letting government agencies know their preferences and concerns.
7. Answers will vary.

The Global Food Supply

OBJECTIVES

After studying this section, you should be able to:

- Explain why staple foods differ around the world.
- Identify the causes of food shortages.
- Discuss the possible ways to remedy global food problems.

LOOK FOR THESE TERMS

industrialized nations
developing nations
staple foods
famine
subsistence farming

Imagine 100 people eating at an unusual banquet. Fifteen of the guests sit at tables set with fine china. They eat an elegant meal prepared by world-famous chefs. Twenty-five others have a simple meal of cooked grain, flavorful sauce, and water. Meanwhile, sixty of the banquet guests sit on the floor with a meal of plain cooked grain and water.

A similar scene occurs at the annual Hunger Banquet served by an international nonprofit organization. The different groups at the banquet represent the percentage of the world's people who live in high, middle, and low income countries. The banquet dramatizes the differences in food supplies that exist around the world. How would you feel if you were one of the 60 percent who had little to eat?

The Global View

Differing economic conditions are one reason for differences in the food supply around the world. Countries are often categorized according to their economic progress. The **industrialized nations,** also called "developed" countries, are the richest. People in these countries rely on a sophisticated, organized food industry to supply them with food.

Developing nations are not yet industrialized or are just beginning to become so. People often cannot afford to buy food and must grow their own.

Many countries rank between industrial and developing countries. As they progress economically, they are able to provide more food for their people.

Section 13.3
The Global Food Supply

Introducing the Section

Motivator

- Ask students to identify reasons the world's food supply varies from year to year. (Examples: droughts, floods, or other natural disasters, amount of land in cultivation.) Why does the food supply vary from country to country? (Examples: soil, climate, agricultural research, farming methods, industrialization, transportation, distribution, fuel shortages, overpopulation, economics, wars and politics, natural disasters, waste.)

Objectives

- Have students read the section objectives. Discuss the purpose of studying the section.

Vocabulary

- Pronounce the terms listed under "Look for These Terms." Have students read the section find the terms and their definitions in the section.

Guided Reading

- Have students look at the headings within Section 13.3 to preview the concepts that will be discussed.

- Have students read the section and complete the appropriate part of the Chapter 13 Study Guide in the *Student Workbook*.

Teacher's Classroom Resources—Section 13.3

Refer to these resources in the TCR package:

Reproducible Lesson Plans

Student Workbook

Extending the Text

Reteaching Activities

Section Quizzes

Testmaker Software

Color Transparencies

Teaching . . .

• The Global View

(text pages 361-363)

Comprehension Check

1. Ask students to explain what determines the staple foods in an area. *(the types of foods that can be grown in the area)*

2. Discuss the factors that limit the types of food that can be grown in an area. *(Geography and climate are the two largest factors.)*

3. Ask students to explain why feeding grain to animals used for food could be considered an inefficient use of the grain. *(Animals are inefficient in converting grain to meat.)*

Earth Watch

Remind students that one problem that has led to the destruction of vital rainforests in developing countries is the people's need to grow food. People burn the rainforest land to clear it so that they can raise crops. However, most rainforest soil is unsuited to growing crops. The poor soil, combined with the people's lack of knowledge and technology, mean that each portion of land they clear only supports crops for a year or two. Then the people move on and clear more land for farming.

In industrialized nations, most people buy their food from supermarkets and other stores. In developing nations, most people grow their own food. The specific foods that can be grown depend on geography and climate.

Staple Foods

The food supply in any region also depends on what foods can be grown there. Only certain foods can be grown in each region. They make up the basic food supply, or **staple foods.**

Geography is one factor that determines the staple foods in an area. Food is most easily grown in areas where the soil is rich, such as in valleys or on plains. In mountainous areas, farming is more difficult. Animals that can live on rocky slopes, such as goats, may be raised.

Climate is another factor. Moderate temperatures make it possible to grow a wide variety of food. In some climates, temperatures vary and food can be grown only during the warm months. Extreme temperatures, either high or low, limit the kinds of food that can be grown. Staple foods also vary depending on the amount of rainfall an area typically receives. Some crops thrive in wet areas, while others require moderate rainfall. Little, if any, food can be grown in dry areas such as deserts.

More About Staple Foods

Crops grown for food provide the main source of nourishment for the world's population. Wheat grows best in the temperate climates and rye in northern regions. Grains such as rice and corn need warmer temperatures.

Special Needs Strategies

Multicultural and/or Bilingual: Have students develop posters showing the staple foods in different areas of the world. Label each food.

Earth Watch

Did you know?...

- Only about 11 percent of the Earth's land masses can be used for growing food.
- Fresh water, needed for drinking and for growing crops, makes up only about 1 percent of the Earth's water.

In many parts of the world, grains are the main staple foods. This is especially true in developing countries. Each type of grain, such as wheat, rice, corn, and rye, is best suited to a particular climate. For example, rice grows in warm, wet climates.

Grain is also fed to animals used for food. However, animals are inefficient in converting grain to meat. With cattle, for example, it takes about 8 to 10 pounds (3.6 to 4.5 kg) of grain to produce 1 pound (500 g) of meat.

WORLD of Variety

Around the world, people include a variety of protein foods in their diet. Their choices depend on availability and resources. Members of the Libinza tribe in Zaire cook and eat grubs (immature insects). Some people in South America, Africa, Australia, and Japan enjoy fried grasshoppers—a convenient, inexpensive source of protein.

What Causes Food Shortages?

It's estimated that about 700 million of the world's people don't have enough to eat. For some, it means going hungry for several days at a time. The severest form of hunger is **famine**—food shortages that continue for months or years. Many die of starvation.

The problem of world hunger is a complex one. Some of the basic causes include economics, inefficient farming methods, fuel shortages, overpopulation, wars and politics, and natural disasters. These factors may affect food production, or they may cause problems in distributing and using the food.

Economics

In many developing countries, most people have small plots of land where they must grow their own food. This is known as **subsistence farming.** They are too poor to buy food and they live on very meager meals.

Some farmers have enough land to grow crops they can sell, known as cash crops. However, when cash crops are exported, local food shortages often occur. Also, world food prices change so frequently that cash crop farmers cannot depend on a steady income.

In developing countries, good roads are rare. Villages are separated, with no modern transportation to connect them. As a result, it's difficult to distribute food. One area may have a surplus of food while a few miles away people have nothing to eat. During famine, poor distribution keeps food aid from reaching starving people.

Student Experiences

1. **Class Discussion:** Have students write a list of characteristics of industrialized nations and developing nations. Discuss the effects of economic conditions on food supply. *(Key skill: writing)*

2. **Display:** Display the major staple foods of the world. Using colored flags to represent each staple food, have students identify the parts of the world in which the food is a staple. Discuss factors that influence the basic food supply of different parts of the world. *(Key skills: geography, critical thinking)*

WORLD of Variety

Encourage students to research other protein sources used in other parts of the world. Do some seem strange to them? Why do the people choose these sources? How are the foods prepared?

Food and Nutrition Science

Soil Fertility Experiment: Prepare soil mixtures that represent the dominant soil types in various developing countries. You may need to ask a science teacher to help you with the percentages of components. Provide seeds for three or four staple foods that grow in the United States. Have students try to grow each food in each soil type and report on their results. Remind students that the climate in your area will have an effect on the results of the experiment. Have interested students repeat the experiment, adjusting the "climate" to simulate conditions in various areas of the world.

13.3

• What Causes Food Shortages?

(text pages 363-365)

Comprehension Check

1. Ask students to define *subsistence farming. (Farming a small plot of land to raise the food you need.)*

2. Ask students to explain what a cash crop is and to list problems that developing countries have with cash crops. *(Raising food to sell; when food is exported, the town in which the food was grown may experience a shortage; food prices vary so much that the income from cash crops is unstable; poor distribution system keeps cash crops from being an efficient internal source of food.)*

3. Discuss the various factors that contribute to food shortages. *(economics, inefficient farming methods, fuel shortages, overpopulation, wars and politics, and natural disasters)*

Student Experiences

1. Reading About Food Crises: Have students bring to class newspaper or magazine clippings about food crises around the world. Discuss the circumstances that create such crises. What relief efforts are being undertaken? *(Key skill: reading)*

Using the Photo

Ask students to identify, if possible, the methods and equipment used in the photos on page 364. Then have students suggest modern replacements for the methods and equipment. Why might the modern replacements not work in these countries?

364

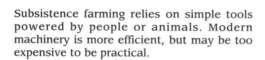

Subsistence farming relies on simple tools powered by people or animals. Modern machinery is more efficient, but may be too expensive to be practical.

364   Chapter 13: The Food Supply

More About Alternative Fuel Sources

Solar energy is an inexpensive alternative in many countries in which wood is in short supply. Various models of solar appliances can meet the needs of most regions. One model of a solar oven is as large as a car and can bake 72 loaves of bread at one time.

Camels are the main means of transportation in hot desert areas. A small refrigerator can be strapped to the camel's back and a solar panel mounted on top. The solar panel converts the sun's rays into energy that runs the refrigerator. The refrigerator is currently being used to carry perishable medicines, but the technology opens possibilities for food storage.

Inefficient Farming Methods

Subsistence farming makes use of ancient methods. Animals supply the power instead of gas-powered machinery. Farm tools are simple; the designs date back hundreds of years. With such tools and methods, food production is low. However, modern farming equipment and methods are costly and not always suited to the crops and conditions in developing countries.

Fuel Shortages

Most food must be cooked before eating. That means fuel for cooking is essential. In developing countries, wood is the most common cooking fuel. However, many areas are experiencing serious shortages of wood. Without fuel for cooking, people may go hungry.

Overpopulation

The world population, which now stands at more than 5.5 billion people, could increase to 6.2 billion by the year 2000. The population is increasing most quickly in developing countries. As population increases, there is a demand for more food. At the same time, more land is taken for housing, leaving less land for farming. When people clear forests to get more farmland, they destroy their source of fuel.

Will the food supply keep up with the increase in population? Some experts think not.

Wars and Politics

Wars can have a devastating effect on food supplies. Animals are killed and crops destroyed. People are forced to abandon their farms. Fighting disrupts food distribution systems.

Food is also used as a political weapon. Opposing parties may interfere with food distribution or manipulate supplies. Food aid may never reach the needy because it is stolen and sold on the black market.

Wars can result in famine. Political problems sometimes keep food aid from reaching those who need it.

Natural Disasters

Natural disasters such as floods and earthquakes can destroy a region's food supply. Crops may be damaged and animals killed. If soil erosion occurs or roads are destroyed, food supplies can be affected for years. Prolonged drought, especially in developing countries, can result in famine and starvation.

Section 13.3: The Global Food Supply   365

Teaching . . .

• **What Can Be Done?**

(text page 366)

Comprehension Check

1. Ask students to explain the most common focus of food aid to developing countries. *(Educating people to help themselves using the means available to them.)*

2. Ask students to describe the role technology plays in decreasing food shortages. *(Through biotechnology, scientists may be able to produce varieties of grains and other plant foods that are resistant to drought and other environmental problems or that are more nutritious. The development of solar energy may also help decrease food shortages.)*

Student Experiences

1. **Guest Speaker:** Invite an agriculture specialist, food researcher, or nutritionist to speak to the class on the development of new food sources. How can these help solve global food shortages? *(Key skill: science)*

2. **Class Discussion:** Discuss problems that could result from trying to introduce modern farming machinery and methods in developing nations. *(Key skill: critical thinking)*

3. **Research:** Have students research local or worldwide agencies that work to solve food crises and report to the class. *(Examples: CARE, World Vision International, Bread for the World, Food Banks) (Key skill: research)*

Thinking Skills

Reasoning: Ask students: Why do you think there is so much food wasted in this country? What could be done to prevent food waste? *(Teaching people about food shortages in other parts of the world might make them aware of the need to avoid waste.)*

Special Needs Strategies

Gifted: Have students research the history and mission of an organization concerned with the world food supply, such as the Agency for International Development, Food and Agriculture Organization, or Food for Peace. Have students report their findings to the class.

Review

- Ask students to summarize the main ideas in this section.
- Have students complete the Section Review. (Answers appear below.)

Evaluation

- Have students write a short essay explaining the reasons for food shortages and what can be done about them.
- Have students take the quiz for Section 13.3. (Refer to the *Section Quizzes* booklet or use the *Testmaker Software*.)

Reteaching

- Using a world map, help students identify areas of the world in which food shortages are likely to occur (developing countries).
- Refer to the *Reteaching Activities* booklet for the Section 13.3 activity sheet.

Enrichment

- Have students conduct an energy efficiency experiment to see how long it takes water to boil in glass, earthenware, aluminum, and stainless steel utensils. Ask students to relate their results to fuel shortages in underdeveloped and developing countries.

Closure

- Lead a discussion on world food shortages and what people in the United States can do about them.

What Can Be Done?

Many efforts are being made to increase the global food supply. The most common goal is to educate people in developing countries to help themselves. They are too poor to use modern farming machinery and methods. Therefore, programs help people work within the means available to them.

The United Nations, government agencies such as the Peace Corps, and private non-profit organizations such as the American Friends Service Committee and Oxfam International are involved in the education process. They show farmers how to improve farming methods and equipment and how to increase water supplies. In Ethiopia, for instance, food production increased just by broadening the tiny steel blade on the crude wooden plows used by farmers.

Food technology also has an important role in increasing the world's food supply. Through genetic engineering (see Section 13.2), scientists hope to produce varieties of grains and other plant foods that are resistant to drought and other environmental problems.

Nutritious products are also being developed. For instance, people in some developing countries cannot easily digest milk or milk products. A nutritious product is being obtained from leaf curd made by grinding leaves into a paste. It is made into a highly nutritious crumbly cake, which is being introduced in developing countries around the world.

Solar energy offers much hope as a solution to the problem of fuel shortages. It has great potential in the tropics because the sun shines almost constantly. Several solar ovens are already being used successfully in developing countries. One type can be made inexpensively from cardboard and aluminum foil.

Solar-powered ovens like this one provide a means of cooking food in areas where fuel is scarce.

Section 13.3 Review

RECALL THE FACTS

1. What is meant by "staple foods"? Name two reasons why different regions may have different staple foods.

2. Identify five causes of food shortages.

3. What are two ways of helping to increase the global food supply?

DISCUSS YOUR IDEAS

4. Is hunger a problem in industrialized nations? Explain.

5. What problems could result from trying to introduce modern farming machinery and methods in developing nations?

APPLY YOUR LEARNING

6. In magazines and newspapers, find articles about regions that are experiencing famine. Identify the causes of the food shortage and any relief efforts being undertaken.

Answers to Section Review

1. Foods that can be grown in an area and are the major food supply; geography and climate.
2. *Any five:* Economics, inefficient farming methods, fuel shortages, overpopulation, wars and politics, natural disasters.
3. Using genetic engineering to create new varieties of plant foods; developing new fuel sources.
4. Yes, usually due to economic and political factors.
5. Students should realize that most modern machinery is expensive.

Also, introducing the equipment and methods without adequate training and support (such as repair facilities) becomes a waste of materials.
6. Answers will vary.

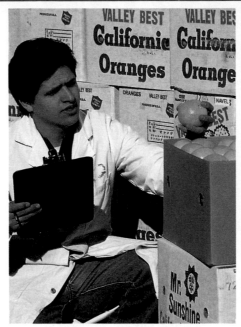

Juan Gloria
Food Safety Inspector

CURRENT POSITION

"I'm a consumer safety inspector specializing in food for the U.S. Food and Drug Administration."

RESPONSIBILITIES

"I inspect firms that deal with food, checking for violations such as inaccurate product labeling or possible contamination. I also meet with plant managers and write reports on my findings."

SKILLS

"To be successful in this line of work, it helps to be detail-minded. It's also necessary to be able to communicate well with people, both orally and in writing."

EDUCATION

"I have a college degree in agriculture and previous experience in the food industry. I also passed a required government examination to qualify for my current job."

WORK ENVIRONMENT

"I'm on the road quite a bit, traveling from one inspection site to another. Sometimes my hours can be long and irregular. However, I enjoy traveling and meeting a lot of different people."

FAVORITE PART OF THE JOB

"It's satisfying to me to know that I take part in helping to make sure our country's food supply is safe to eat."

- What are the advantages and disadvantages of working irregular hours?
- What aspects of Juan's job do you think you might find interesting? Why?

367

CAREER PROFILE: FOOD SAFETY INSPECTOR

Thinking About . . . Food Safety Inspection

Have students think of other questions they would like to ask Juan Gloria about being a food safety inspector. (Examples: How do you go about getting a job with the FDA? How do you check for violations? Do you have a laboratory to which you can send samples of foods from food companies? What's the salary range for food safety inspectors?)

Ask student volunteers to tell what they think would be the most exciting part of being a food safety inspector.

Have students discuss the responsibilities inherent in the food safety inspection business.

Student Opportunities

Students planning a career in consumer and food safety should check with local food laboratories for volunteer and employment opportunities.

Occupational Outlook

To become an inspector with the FDA, you have to pass a civil service exam. After you have passed the exam and been hired by the government, advancement is based on the civil service "career ladder" and usually occurs at one-year intervals.

For More Information

For additional information about careers in consumer and food safety, encourage students to contact:

- Office of Higher Education Programs, U.S. Dept. of Agriculture, Administration Bldg., 14th St. and Independence Ave. SW, Washington, D.C. 20250.
- U.S. Food and Drug Administration, 5600 Fishers Lane, Rockville, MD 20850

Completing the Chapter

Review
- Have students complete the Chapter Review. (Answers appear below.)

Evaluation
- Divide the class into two teams (A and B). Each team should brainstorm questions about Chapter 13. Then allow the teams to take turns asking each other questions. At the end of the questioning period, the team with the most correct answers wins.
- Have students take the test for Chapter 13. (Refer to the *Chapter and Unit Tests* booklet or construct your own test using the *Testmaker Software*.)

■ ANSWERS ■

REVIEWING FACTS

1. *Any two:* Using manure as fertilizer, using integrated pest management to manage pests, using huge vacuums to suck the bugs off plants.

2. *Any four:* Canning, freezing, curing, drying, freeze-drying, controlled atmosphere storage.

3. As supply goes up, prices go down; as demand goes up, prices go up.

4. Food and Drug Administration (general safety of food, except for meat, poultry, and eggs); Food Safety and Inspection Service (meat, poultry, and eggs)

5. Those with a long history of use and safety.

6. Chemical substances left behind in food after processing; by drugs given to animals or by pesticides in the food animals eat or in other plant foods.

SUMMARY

SECTION 13.1

Where Does Food Come From?: Most food eaten in North America begins its journey to the consumer as a farm product. It is then sent to a processor, where it is prepared for its final use. Processing may include one of several preservation methods used to prevent spoilage and lengthen shelf life. The processor sends the food to the distributor, who stores it until it is purchased by the retailer. The retailer then sells the food to the consumer. The price consumers pay for the food depends on many factors, such as the amount of processing, supply and demand, natural disasters, and consumer damage.

SECTION 13.2

A Safe Food Supply: In the U.S., the federal government plays a major role in monitoring the safety of the nation's food supply. Various government agencies inspect food for contamination and regulate food processing, packaging, and labeling. However, some food safety issues remain controversial. As a consumer, you can affect food-related policies through your buying decisions and by staying informed, supporting consumer groups, and contacting lawmakers about your concerns.

SECTION 13.3

The Global Food Supply: The basic food supply, or staple foods, in a region depends on geography and climate. Food shortages are caused by a number of factors that affect food production and distribution. International agencies and scientists are working to increase the food supply in developing countries.

REVIEWING FACTS

1. Give two examples of sustainable farming practices. (13.1)

2. List four commercial preservation methods. (13.1)

3. How does supply and demand affect food prices? (13.1)

4. Identify what FDA and FSIS stand for. What types of food is each agency responsible for keeping safe? (13.2)

5. What types of food additives are found on the GRAS list? (13.2)

6. What are chemical residues? How do they get into food? (13.2)

7. How does food production differ in industrialized nations and developing nations? (13.3)

8. Explain two problems associated with growing cash crops in developing countries. (13.3)

9. Explain the relationship between the growing population, food supplies, and fuel supplies. (13.3)

10. How does genetic engineering play a role in increasing the world's food supply? (13.3)

LEARNING BY DOING

1. **Foods lab:** Cook or heat equal amounts of the same kind of vegetable, one fresh, the other canned or frozen. Compare the two for taste, texture, appearance, price per serving, and convenience. (13.1)

2. **Food science lab:** Conduct an experiment using two different loaves of bread—one homemade and one a commercial brand containing preservatives. Place one slice of each loaf on a plate,

7. In industrial countries, people have the technology and other resources to create and use modern equipment. In developing countries, the people cannot afford the equipment, and they do not yet understand the technologies.

8. *Any two:* Local food shortages occur, world food prices are unstable, distribution systems are poor.

9. As the population increases, there is a demand for more housing, leaving less land for farming; as people clear more land for farming, they destroy their source of fuel.

uncovered. Wrap another slice from each loaf in plastic wrap. Leave the slices out at room temperature. After two, five, and seven days, compare the slices for mold and other signs of spoilage. Record your findings. What conclusions can you draw? (13.2)

3. **Foods lab:** Prepare and serve a "World Hunger Banquet," similar to the one described in this chapter, for the class. Base the menus and the percentage of students in each group on the information given in the chapter. (13.3)

THINKING CRITICALLY

1. **Recognizing alternatives:** What are some ways of obtaining food besides the network of food production and distribution described in this chapter? What are the advantages and disadvantages of each? (13.1)

2. **Determining credibility:** A respected scientist testifies before the FDA that a certain pesticide is safe and effective. Later it is discovered that the university where the scientist teaches receives large donations from the company that makes the pesticide. How does this affect your opinion of the scientist's findings? (13.2)

3. **Predicting consequences:** What might be some long-term effects of several consecutive poor growing seasons in a region? (13.3)

MAKING DECISIONS AND SOLVING PROBLEMS

What Would You Do?

1. When you go grocery shopping, you are disturbed by the amount of bruised, wilted, and otherwise damaged fruits and vegetables in the produce section. You know this drives prices up, and wonder how to solve the problem. (13.1)

2. Your friend wants to lose weight. She tells you that her weight-loss plan is based mainly on low-calorie foods and beverages made with artificial sweeteners and fat substitutes. She asks for your opinion. (13.2)

3. A friend tells you that, unless you are a scientist or politician, there is nothing you can do to increase the world's food supply. You want to prove him wrong by reducing food waste and helping the hungry in your own community. (13.3)

LINKING YOUR STUDIES

1. **Science:** Using library resources, write a brief report about one of the commercial methods used to preserve food. Describe the process and tell what foods it is usually used for. Also identify the advantages and disadvantages of this preservation method. (13.1)

2. **Social studies:** Using library sources, investigate the history of a food additive that has been in use for at least 100 years. What was the original purpose of the additive? What foods was it used in? Is it still in use today? What are its advantages and disadvantages? (13.2)

3. **Social studies:** Using library sources, locate five farming regions on at least three different continents. For each region, identify the main crops, describe the geography and climate conditions that make the crops successful, and tell what products they are used in. (13.3)

LEARNING BY DOING

Answers to "Learning by Doing" activities will vary.

THINKING CRITICALLY

1. Answers will vary.

2. The scientist might have been biased, in spite of his excellent reputation.

3. Hunger, famine, starvation.

MAKING DECISIONS AND SOLVING PROBLEMS

Answers to "Making Decisions and Solving Problems" questions will vary. Encourage students to give reasons for their answers.

LINKING YOUR STUDIES

Answers to "Linking Your Studies" will vary.

10. Scientists are trying to create more stable varieties of grains that can withstand drought and other problems; they are also looking for ways to make foods more nutritious.

Planning the Chapter

Chapter Overview

Section 14.1: Consumer Skills

Section 14.2: Choosing Kitchen Equipment

Section 14.3: Designing a Kitchen

Introducing the Chapter

Motivator

- Number and arrange mounted photos of cookware, utensils, and small appliances on the bulletin board. Then ask students to write each item number and name under one of three columns: "Necessities," "Clutter," and "Luxuries." Discuss the difference between needs and wants and talk about how to distinguish between the two.

Teacher's Classroom Resources—Chapter 14

Refer to these resources in the TCR package:

Enrichment Activities

Chapter and Unit Tests

Testmaker Software

CHAPTER 14
Buying for the Kitchen

SECTION 14.1
Consumer Skills 371

SECTION 14.3
Designing a Kitchen 382

SECTION 14.2
Choosing Kitchen Equipment 376

370

Cooperative Learning Suggestions

Organize a Co-op Co-op activity. Have students work in groups of three to five to design a kitchen. Provide each group with a different case situation to use. Examples: kitchen for a single adult who doesn't like to cook; kitchen for a couple who enjoy entertaining, kitchen for a large family; kitchen for an elderly woman with arthritis; kitchen for a family with a blind homemaker. Have students identify the needs to be met, research appropriate kitchen equipment, and decide on kitchen design features. Have groups draw a floor plan and sketches of the kitchen. Have each group present its kitchen design to the class as a panel discussion.

Consumer Skills

OBJECTIVES

After studying this section, you should be able to:

- Describe the decisions that must be made before shopping for kitchen equipment.
- List four important steps of shopping that can help you make wise kitchen purchases.

LOOK FOR THESE TERMS

principal
interest
annual percentage rate
finance charge
warranty
EnergyGuide label
service contract

Introducing the Section

Motivator

- Ask students to identify the least used kitchen equipment in their home kitchens. Was the item purchased or a gift? What is its intended purpose? Why is it seldom used? What can be done to prevent purchase of such items?

Objectives

- Have students read the section objectives. Discuss the purpose of studying the section.

Vocabulary

- Pronounce the terms listed under "Look for These Terms." Have students read the section find the terms and their definitions in the section.

Guided Reading

- Have students look at the headings within Section 14.1 to preview the concepts that will be discussed.

- Have students read the section and complete the appropriate part of the Chapter 14 Study Guide in the *Student Workbook*.

Shopping for a new refrigerator took Shasta's family to several different appliance stores. While her parents talked to salespeople, Shasta compared the features of the various models. The family finally chose one that fit their budget and had most of the features they wanted.

Buying equipment for a kitchen can vary from shopping for a mixing spoon to spending thousands of dollars for major appliances. No matter what you plan to buy, be a smart consumer.

Before You Shop

Before you begin, think about your reasons for buying. Decide how much you can pay and how you will pay.

Kitchen equipment can be purchased at appliance stores, department stores, discount stores, and other places. Planning your purchase makes it easier to sort out the many choices you have.

Section 14.1: Consumer Skills **371**

Teacher's Classroom Resources—Section 14.1

Refer to these resources in the TCR package:

Reproducible Lesson Plans
Student Workbook
Extending the Text

Reteaching Activities
Section Quizzes
Testmaker Software
Color Transparencies

Comprehension Check

1. Ask students to explain the terms principal and interest. *(Principal is the amount you borrow when you buy an item on credit; interest is the fee the lender charges for the loan; the fee is a percentage of the amount you borrow.)*

2. In addition to interest, what other fees may be included in finance charges? *(service charges, insurance premiums, etc.)*

3. Discuss the problems with using credit. How can they be avoided? *(The biggest problem is the temptation to buy more than you can really afford; you can avoid it by choosing a price range you can afford and sticking with it.)*

Student Experiences

1. **Class Discussion:** Ask students to identify appropriate uses of credit when purchasing kitchen equipment. Why should you shop for credit as carefully as for your purchase? *(Key skill: consumer awareness)*

2. **Total Price Calculation:** Ask students to assume they have purchased a range that cost $695. With a down payment of $100 and a 14% annual percentage rate on the remainder, how much interest would you have to pay in one year? *($83.30)* Suppose you pay the remainder at the end of one year. How much did you actually pay for the range? *($778.30) (Key skill: math)*

Why Buy?

Start by asking yourself why you want the item. If you are updating something you already have, will the replacement be enough of an improvement to justify its cost? If you are buying a new item, will you use it? John's mother bought an electric skillet to save energy. She uses it instead of the range for many main dishes. She also bought an electric chopper, but soon decided that she prefers using a knife. Make sure that what you plan to buy is an item you need and will use.

Paying for Your Purchase

Most people pay cash for small items. Some save so they can pay cash for larger purchases, too. However, many people use credit for at least part of the cost of major purchases.

Buying on Credit

Buying on credit means paying for a product with money you borrow from a lender. This method is more expensive than paying cash, but it allows you to use the item while you pay for it.

Before you sign a credit agreement, read it carefully. Ask questions about any points you don't understand.

Credit has a vocabulary of its own. The money you borrow is the **principal.** The lender charges you a fee for the loan, called **interest.** Interest is a percentage of the amount you borrow, such as 15 or 20 percent.

Interest rates vary. By law, they must be stated in terms of **annual percentage rate** (APR), which gives you the yearly cost of the loan.

When considering credit, look carefully at the **finance charge**—the total amount you will pay for borrowing. It includes interest and other costs, such as service charges and credit-related insurance premiums. Monthly payments are usually calculated by dividing the total cost (principal + finance charge) by the number of months of the loan.

For major purchases, you may have several financing options. Many stores offer financing. Loans are available from institutions such as banks and finance companies. Credit cards can also be used.

Shop for credit as carefully as for your purchase. Ask each lender for the APR and finance charges, so you can compare the cost of borrowing. The differences in total cost may surprise you.

One problem with using credit is that you may be tempted to spend more than you can afford. Failure to make monthly payments on time can cause significant problems. The item you purchased may be taken away from you, and you may find it difficult to get credit in the future. You can avoid these problems by deciding on a price range you are comfortable with and sticking to it.

Buying Guidelines

Following a few simple shopping guidelines can help you make wise choices in buying for the kitchen. Any item you plan to keep a long time should be chosen with special care.

More About Credit

Failure to make monthly payments on time can have serious consequences. These can include:
• Late payment fees.
• Loss of good credit rating. This may prevent being able to borrow money the next time it is needed.

• Repossession. With large purchases such as major appliances, the item may be taken back if payments are not made regularly. This means losing all the money already paid on the item, as well as the item itself.

Anyone having a problem making payments should tell the lender immediately. Often a new payment can be worked out until finances improve.

Consider Your Needs and Wants

Begin by identifying the characteristics and features most important in the item you plan to buy. For instance, if you're buying a new appliance, write down the measurements of the space it must fit. If your new dishes must be microwave-safe, note that.

Also write down the features you would like the item to have. Rank your "wants" from most to least important. You may not be able to find an item with all these features within your price range, so it is helpful to set priorities.

Gather Information

Well-informed shoppers usually are happier with the items they purchase and often get a better price. Many sources of information are available. Look at advertisements and articles in magazines and newspapers. Some consumer magazines conduct unbiased tests to compare similar items from different manufacturers. You can also contact manufacturers directly for up-to-date information.

The reliability of the store is also important, especially for major purchases. Check with the closest Better Business Bureau to see if the business has satisfactorily settled any complaints.

Look for Consumer Safeguards

As you shop, look for consumer safeguards. Government agencies, manufacturers, and dealers have provided means for ensuring the quality of products.

Seals of Approval

Seals of approval are given by nonprofit testing agencies to show that a product meets certain standards for safety and performance.

❖ On gas appliances, look for the *American Gas Association* seal. It indicates that a gas appliance's design, performance, and reliability have been tested and certified.
❖ On electrical appliances, look for the *Underwriters Laboratories* seal. It indicates that an electrical appliance's design is reasonably free from the risk of fire, electric shock, and other hazards.

Testing agencies work to make sure that products meet standards of safety and performance. The American Gas Association has different seals for appliances (above left) and accessories (above right). The UL seal (right) is found on electrical appliances tested by Underwriters Laboratories.

Section 14.1: Consumer Skills   **373**

Teaching . . .

• Buying Guidelines

(text pages 372-375)

Comprehension Check

1. Ask students what type of information consumers should gather before making a purchase. *(Compare similar items from different manufacturers; check the reliability of the store with the Better Business Bureau; check warranties and/or service contracts offered by companies.)*

2. Ask students to list and describe seals of approval. What is their purpose? *(See description on page 373.)*

3. Ask students to list suggestions for becoming an active shopper. *(See list on page 375.)*

Student Experiences

1. **Comparing Features:** Have students work in small groups to compare the features available for one type of kitchen equipment. Ask students to identify situations when certain features might be considered needs and others when the same features might be wants. Have each group report their findings to the class. *(Key skill: evaluation)*

2. **Class Discussion:** Bring to class warranties from appliances. Have students work in groups to rate the warranties in terms of coverage and limitations. Discuss how useful to the consumer each warranty might be. How do the warranties protect the manufacturer? *(Key skills: reading, critical thinking)*

• When You Get Your Purchase Home

(text page 375)

Comprehension Check

1. Ask students to describe the documents that usually accompany an appliance when you buy it. *(receipt, warranty, and owner's manual)*

2. Ask students why people should fill out and return the registration card that comes with most warrantied items. *(The manufacturer may need to notify you about a safety or other problem.)*

Student Experiences

1. **Class Discussion:** Ask the class to identify things you should do when you get your kitchen equipment purchase home. Why is it important to keep appliance documents? Why is it important to read the owner's manual? *(Key skill: critical thinking)*

Other seals of approval may be found on a product or package. Find out more about who issued the seal and what it means. Don't assume that every seal comes from a reliable product-testing agency.

Warranties

A **warranty** is a manufacturer's guarantee that a product will perform as advertised. If you have problems with the product, the manufacturer promises to replace or repair it. A warranty often has limits on the length of time it is in effect and what is covered.

EnergyGuide Labels

An **EnergyGuide label** gives information to help you estimate the energy costs of an appliance. Such labels are required for most major appliances. A dollar figure tells the average yearly energy costs for that model. You can compare the costs for different models. You can also project your own energy expenses based on the cost of gas or electricity in your area.

Service Contracts

A **service contract** is repair and maintenance insurance purchased to cover a product for a specific length of time. It is usually sold by the store that sells you the product. Service contracts often don't cover the total costs of repairs and parts. They may duplicate the protection received free with the warranty. Service contracts are often expensive and are only as good as the company that issues them.

The EnergyGuide label gives the appliance's estimated energy cost. Why is this information important?

Earth Watch

Ten percent of the electricity used in the average home is used for refrigeration. Here are some energy-saving tips:

• Vacuum the condenser coils on the back or bottom of the refrigerator frequently.

• Keep the seals (gaskets) around the doors clean. Dirt and spills can keep them from sealing tightly.

Look for other energy-saving suggestions in the owner's manuals for your appliances.

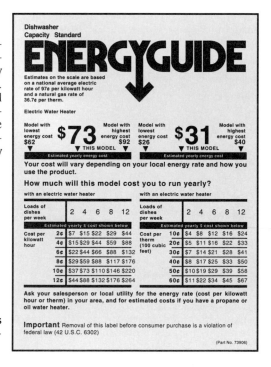

More About Solving Appliance Problems

If problems show up in the appliance, call the dealer or service agency. Keep a written record of all the calls you make. If the dealer fails to help, call the manufacturer. Look for an 800 number in the owner's manual or on the product's packaging, or call 1-800-555-1212 to find out if the manufacturer has an 800 number. If you are not satisfied by the response to your phone call, write a letter to the manufacturer's consumer office. Include a copy of your receipt. Keep a copy of your letter for your files. If you can't get help from the manufacturer, call the Better Business Bureau and your local office of consumer affairs.

Be an Active Shopper

While shopping, don't just look. Think about how the product will perform and last.

* Keep written notes. Making a list of your likes and dislikes as you shop can help you make a final decision.
* Consider safety. Look for a seal of approval. Check carefully for safety features and potential hazards.
* Handle tools, cookware, and appliances. Do they seem comfortable to use and durable?
* Look at the warranty and owner's manual. What exactly does the warranty cover? Will the item be easy to use and care for?
* Compare prices. More features and better quality usually mean a higher price. Some brands are generally more expensive than others.
* Ask the dealer about additional costs. Are there separate charges for delivery and installation?

When You Get Your Purchase Home

You will probably bring home some important documents with your purchase, especially if it's an appliance. You may have your receipt, a warranty, and an owner's manual. Keep these documents together in a safe place. If the warranty has a registration card, fill it out and send it in. Even if you don't have problems with the product, the manufacturer may need to notify you about a safety problem.

Read the owner's manual before you use the product. Then test the product to make certain it works. If it doesn't, return it to the store or call the dealer.

The owner's manual will tell you how to use the product safely and care for it properly. It may also provide tips to help you get the most out of your purchase.

■ Section 14.1 Review ■

RECALL THE FACTS

1. What decisions should you make before shopping for kitchen equipment?

2. What costs should you consider when buying on credit?

3. List the four steps to follow while shopping for the kitchen.

4. What should you do when you get your purchase home?

DISCUSS YOUR IDEAS

5. What are some ways the choice of kitchen equipment affects the way a family plans and prepares meals?

APPLY YOUR LEARNING

6. Collect magazine and newspaper advertisements for different brands of a major kitchen appliance. Make a chart showing the different features.

Section 14.1: Consumer Skills **375**

■ Answers to Section Review ■

1. Exactly what you are shopping for, whether you really want or need the item, and whether you will use it after you purchase it.
2. All of the finance charges (interest, service charges, built-in insurance costs, etc.)

3. Consider your needs and wants; gather information; look for consumer safeguards; be an active shopper.

4. Store important documents in a safe place; read the owner's manual; try the appliance to make sure it works properly.
5. Answers will vary.
6. Answers will vary.

Section 14.2
Choosing Kitchen Equipment

SECTION 14.2

Choosing Kitchen Equipment

OBJECTIVES

After studying this section, you should be able to:

• Give examples of choices available in appliances, small equipment, and tableware.
• Discuss features to look for when buying items for the kitchen.

LOOK FOR THESE TERMS

self-cleaning oven
continuous cleaning oven
patterns
open stock

Just what equipment is included in a kitchen depends on budget, space, and personal preference. Equipping any kitchen is an expensive process. Most people start with the basics and add equipment over the years.

Section 14.1 gave basic strategies for making good buying decisions. In this section, you will learn more about what to look for when choosing major and small appliances, cookware, tools, and tableware.

Buying Appliances

Appliances can take up a major portion of your equipment budget. To save money, some people choose used, rather than new, appliances. Whatever the choice, it pays to shop carefully.

Both large and small appliances come in a wide range of models. Careful shopping can help you find one that meets your needs and fits your budget.

Underwriters Laboratories, Inc.

Refrigerator-Freezers

Today, there are more options than ever in refrigerator-freezers. The freezer may be placed at the top, side, or bottom. Some models defrost the freezer automatically. Manual defrost models must be emptied, thawed, and cleaned regularly.

Special features add to convenience, but also to cost. Decide which are most important and within your budget. In the refrigerator, choices include adjustable shelves, temperature- and humidity-controlled compartments for vegetables and meat, and special areas for tall or large items such as milk and soda. You will also find automatic ice makers and doors with ice and chilled water dispensers on the outside.

Consumer Checklist: Refrigerator-Freezers

✓ Fits available kitchen space. Door opens in correct direction.
✓ Size and features meet needs.
✓ Energy efficiency compares well with other models.
✓ Has separate temperature controls for refrigerator and freezer.
✓ Has good warranty and UL seal of approval.
✓ Dealer is reputable and service is available.

Teaching . . .

- **Buying Appliances: Refrigerator-Freezers**

(text pages 376-377)

Comprehension Check

1. Ask students to list options available for refrigerator-freezers. *(Placement of the freezer portion of the appliance; automatic or manual defrost; adjustable shelves, temperature/humidity-controlled compartments for vegetables and meat; special areas for tall or large items; automatic ice makers; doors with ice and chilled water dispensers on the outside.)*

2. Ask students what features and characteristics they should check before buying a refrigerator-freezer. *(See the chart at the top of page 377.)*

Student Experiences

1. **Magazine Comparison:** Bring to class different consumer magazines that compare the same appliance. Ask pairs or small groups to analyze the same appliance in more than one magazine. How do the test procedures and criteria differ? Have students decide which brand of the appliance they would select on the basis of each report. They should then list their reasons. *(Key skill: evaluation)*

Using the Photo

Ask students to look again at the refrigerators pictured at the bottom of page 377. What extras are shown on these models? Ask students to decide whether these features are necessary for them. Might some features be necessary for some people, yet unnecessary for others?

Some refrigerator-freezers have adjustable shelves for more efficient use of space. What are the advantages and disadvantages of other special features?

Section 14.2: Choosing Kitchen Equipment   **377**

More About Refrigerator-Freezer Features

Some refrigerator-freezers offer advanced features, such as:
- Pull-down counter for serving snacks.
- Electronic monitors alert you to any problems.
- Adjustable humidity levels that can be set for different foods.

- Tempered glass shelves that wipe up easily and prevent foods from dripping to lower shelves.
- Adjustable storage and wider door shelves that offer more efficient use of space.

Comprehension Check

1. Ask students to describe various types of cooktops that are now available. *(See list on page 378.)*

2. Ask students to explain how an induction cooktop works. *(See illustration on page 378.)*

3. Ask students to explain the difference between a self-cleaning oven and a continuous cleaning oven. *(Self-cleaning oven: has a special cleaning cycle. Continuous cleaning oven: soil residue can be wiped off easily.)*

Student Experiences

1. **Group Decision-Making:** Have students work in small groups to make a list of essential appliances for a 20-year-old single adult who lives alone. Have groups share their lists and justify each selection. *(Key skill: critical thinking)*

2. **Research:** Have students work in groups to compare features and prices of a range, cooktop, or oven. Ask students to report their findings to the class. *(Key skill: research)*

3. **Brochure Writing:** Have students write a sales brochure for a small appliance. They should include information about features, safety, care, and use. *(Key skill: writing)*

See Also . . .
- Section 9.1: "Equipment for cooking," page 255.

Ranges, Cooktops, and Ovens

When buying a major cooking appliance, some basic decisions must be made first. Are you looking for an all-in-one range, a countertop oven, or separate built-in cooktop and oven units? Do you want a gas or electric model? If you are replacing appliances in an existing kitchen, these decisions may already be determined. If you are remodeling or planning a new kitchen, your options are probably more open.

Cooktops

While the traditional gas burners or electric coils are still most typical, there are many new choices in cooktops. For example:

- **Sealed gas burners** have no visible flame and no pilot light. This adds safety and aids cleanup.
- **Solid cast-iron disks** are very energy efficient, though slow to heat.
- **Smooth cooktops** are easy to clean. They include induction cooktops, which use electromagnetic energy. Heat is generated when a pan made of a magnetic metal is placed on the induction cooktop.
- **Modules** are units that allow greater flexibility. A grill, griddle, or other accessory can be substituted for standard surface units.

Ovens

Shopping for an oven—as a separate unit or part of a range—begins with the choice of conventional, convection, or microwave models. You may prefer a range with two ovens—one below the cooktop and a smaller one at eye level. Another option is an oven that combines two or more cooking methods in a single unit, such as a microwave-convection oven. (As you have learned, convection ovens use a fan to circulate the heated air and reduce cooking time.)

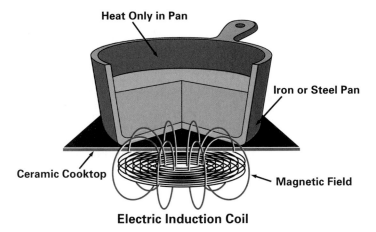

An induction cooktop uses electromagnetic energy. A magnetic field forms when cookware made of iron or steel comes in contact with the cooktop. The magnetic field causes the cookware to heat up. The heat is transferred to the food inside.

Food and Nutrition Science

Pilotless Ignition: Science and technology have greatly improved the characteristics of gas ranges. Lighting a gas burner or oven requires igniting the gas released when the unit is turned on. Early ranges required use of a match. Then small, continuously burning flames called "pilot lights" were developed. This increased convenience but wasted energy. Today, technology offers an alternative. *Pilotless ignition* electrically generates a spark when the burner is turned on. This method is both safe and energy efficient.

Conventional and convection ovens are available with easy-clean options. A **self-cleaning oven** has a special cleaning cycle using high heat to burn off food stains. A **continuous cleaning oven** has special rough interior walls that absorb spills and spatters. Soil residue can be easily wiped off.

Microwave ovens have many feature options. Some come equipped with a turntable. Others have a rack which increases the capacity of the oven. Electronic programming can cook food automatically. Browning units improve the appearance of microwaved foods. Temperature probes allow heating to a specific temperature.

Small Appliances

The list of small appliances available seems endless, from sandwich makers to automatic bread machines. Small electric appliances can save time, money, and energy. However, having too many can cause storage problems. Before you buy, consider whether the appliance will be helpful enough to justify the cost and space required.

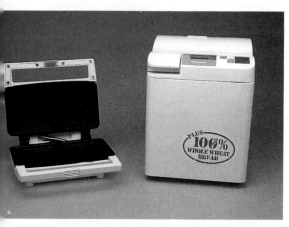

Many small appliances serve just one specific purpose, such as making toasted sandwiches or baking bread automatically. Consider how often you would use the appliance before you decide to purchase one.

As with any kitchen equipment, look for safety, comfort, ease of use and care, and the features you want and need. Doing research ahead of time will help you learn what to look for. For example, important safety features on a food processor include a safety lock, food pusher, and overload switch.

Buying Other Equipment

Equipment needs don't end with major and small appliances. Kitchens also need cookware and tools.

Cookware

Cookware includes the utensils used for cooking and baking. They can be made from a variety of materials, ranging from metal and glass to special plastics, depending on their intended use. Each material has advantages and disadvantages. (See Section 9.1 for more information on cookware items and materials.)

Both rangetop and oven cookware are available as sets or by the individual piece. Keep in mind that cookware is a major investment that should last for years. Consider these purchasing guidelines:

❖ Look for materials and finishes that are strong and durable enough to withstand daily use. Edges should be smooth. Handles should be heat-resistant.

❖ Choose quality. Look for seamless construction. Metal should be heavy enough to resist warping.

❖ Check the balance of each piece. Look for flat bottoms and secure lids.

Tools

As you learned in Chapters 8 and 9, dozens of different hand tools are available to make the process of preparing food faster and more convenient. Many of these tools

Teaching . . .

- **Buying Other Equipment**

(text pages 379-380)

Comprehension Check

1. Ask students to list guidelines to follow when purchasing cookware. *(See the list on page 379.)*

2. Ask students to list guidelines to follow when you purchasing kitchen tools. *(See the list on page 380.)*

Student Experiences

1. **Display:** Have students create displays of cookware with signs pointing out purchasing guidelines. How many kinds of materials can students accurately identify? *(Key skill: consumer awareness)*

2. **Cost Comparisons:** Ask students to visit a store or consult a catalog. Have them compare and report on the cost of four 10-inch skillets, each made of a different material. *(Key skill: math)*

WORLD of variety

Ask students to compare the various uses of chopsticks to the various uses of certain kitchen tools commonly used in this country. For example, spoons used to stir food on the stove are usually larger than their tableware counterparts. What other examples can students think of?

See Also . . .

- Section 9.1: "Equipment for cooking," page 255.

Thinking Skills

Creativity: Have students work in groups to dream up a small appliance of the future. Tell them to explain the need for this appliance, then sketch it and describe how it works. You may also want to ask students to develop a magazine advertisement promoting their creation.

Comprehension Check

1. Ask students to list the items included in the term *tableware*. *(dinnerware, flatware, glassware, and table linens)*

2. Ask students to define the term open stock. *(tableware that can by bought by the piece)*

Student Experiences

1. **Displays:** Have students make a display of photos showing place settings for various formal and informal occasions. The place settings should use a variety of the types of tableware available. Point out the advantages and disadvantages of each. *(Key skill: life management skills)*

2. **Small Group Discussion:** Have students work in small groups to examine catalogs, brochures, and other promotional materials and compare the characteristics and cost of stainless steel, silver plate, and sterling silver flatware. *(Key skills: reading, consumer awareness)*

3. **Poster Project:** Have students collect and display pictures of attractive table settings using tablecloths, placemats, runners, and napkins. *(Key skill: creativity)*

Cookware and kitchen tools range from everyday necessities to unusual items. What are some signs of quality to look for?

are designed for specific tasks. Others can be used for several different jobs. Follow these guidelines when selecting kitchen tools:

❖ Choose tools that fill a real need. Avoid buying ones you will seldom use.
❖ Well-designed, quality tools are easier to use and last longer. Knives, for example, should have a sturdy handle that is firmly attached to the blade. Look for at least two rivets (fasteners) through the handle and blade. Higher quality knives have three.
❖ Tools used for hot foods should be heat-resistant.
❖ Keep storage in mind. Unless you can store the tool in a convenient place, you won't use it often.

Many people in Asian cultures use chopsticks not only to eat their food, but also for food preparation. They might use a single chopstick for stirring. A person skilled in handling chopsticks can use a pair to add, remove, or turn pieces of food. Chopsticks used in preparing food are longer than those used as eating utensils.

The tools used for eating and food preparation may vary in different cultures.

380   **Chapter 14: Buying for the Kitchen**

More About Tableware

Because expensive, fine-quality tableware needs special care and handling, many people use it only for special occasions. Before buying expensive tableware, it is important to consider whether it will be used enough to justify the cost.

Buying Tableware

Tableware refers to the items used for serving and eating food—dinnerware, flatware, and glassware. The amount, type, and formality of tableware people choose varies. Some people have one set, others two or more.

Dinnerware, flatware, and glassware are available with many different designs on them. These designs are called **patterns.** Remember, however, that patterns in tableware do not have to match. You can mix and match pieces that complement one another.

Most tableware is priced and sold by the place setting—the pieces used by one person to eat a meal. Sometimes you can buy sets for a certain number of people. Serving pieces may be sold individually or grouped as a set. Some tableware is also sold **open stock**—you can buy each piece separately.

Prices for tableware vary widely, depending on quality and brand name. Fine china, crystal glassware, and silver flatware are the most formal and most expensive choices. Most people who have them use them only for special occasions. For everyday use, there are many less costly, easy-care, yet attractive options. These include stainless steel flatware, informal glassware, and dishes made of stoneware, glass-ceramic, or plastic. Microwave-safe dinnerware and dishwasher-safe tableware are practical choices.

Expensive, fine-quality tableware usually needs special care and handling. For everyday use, choose tableware that is durable as well as attractive.

✓ SAFETY CHECK

Lead is a toxic metal that can travel from a container into food. It may be in tableware and cookware made from pottery. Lead crystal glassware also contains lead. Do not use lead crystal regularly or store beverages in lead crystal for more than a few hours.

Section 14.2 Review

RECALL THE FACTS

1. Give four examples of options available in ranges.

2. List three things to look for when buying cookware.

3. What does buying tableware "open stock" mean? What are two other ways tableware may be sold?

DISCUSS YOUR IDEAS

4. Suppose you and a friend decided to share an apartment while in college. How might you go about equipping a kitchen effectively on a limited budget?

APPLY YOUR LEARNING

5. Choose a large or small kitchen appliance. Using magazines or other resources, make a list of the special features that are available.

Section 14.2: Choosing Kitchen Equipment   381

Answers to Section Review

1. Sealed gas burners, solid cast-iron disks, smooth cooktops, modules; type of oven.

2. Materials and finishes that are strong and durable; quality; balance of pieces.

3. The tableware is sold by the individual piece; by place setting or as a package of several place settings.

4. Answers will vary.

5. Answers will vary.

Section 14.3
Designing a Kitchen

Designing a Kitchen

OBJECTIVES

After studying this section, you should be able to:

- Discuss considerations in kitchen design.
- Explain how the floor plan and other elements of a kitchen can affect safety and convenience.
- Give examples of barrier-free kitchen design.

LOOK FOR THESE TERMS

work flow
peninsula
island
grounding
task lighting
life-span design

Understanding the basics of kitchen design and planning has several advantages. When choosing housing, you can evaluate how convenient and safe a kitchen might be. You may someday have an opportunity to plan a totally new kitchen or remodel an existing one. Even without remodeling, you

can find low-cost ways to improve your kitchen. Kitchen design also offers excellent career opportunities.

Thoughtful planning can make any kitchen convenient, safe, and easy to clean. The key is a good design, not necessarily an unlimited budget or large space.

Planning a successful kitchen depends on understanding the lifestyle of those who will use it. Following well-researched principles of kitchen design helps ensure efficiency.

A well-designed kitchen begins with careful planning, including an analysis of needs and wants.

Considering Lifestyle

A single person who rarely cooks has different kitchen needs than a family that uses cooking as a form of entertainment. Kitchen design must take into account how the kitchen will be used. Think about:

- ❖ What activities, besides cooking, will take place in the kitchen?
- ❖ How much kitchen equipment and food must be stored?
- ❖ Will more than one person generally work in the kitchen at one time?
- ❖ What are the needs and preferences of those who will use the space?

A kitchen design that would work well for one family might not be right for another. It all depends on how the kitchen will be used.

Teaching . . .

- **Considering Lifestyle**
- **Designing for Efficiency**

(text pages 382-383)

Comprehension Check

1. Ask students to list lifestyle factors to be considered when you plan a kitchen. *(See the list on page 382.)*

2. Ask students to define work flow and give an example of a work flow in a kitchen. *(Any kind of work routine; examples will vary.)*

3. Ask students to give a situation in which the traditional work triangle would not be the most efficient layout for a kitchen. *(When more than one person will be working in the kitchen simultaneously.)*

Student Experiences

1. **Class Survey:** Have students write answers to the lifestyle questions on page 382 based on their own family. Ask several student volunteers to read their responses. Discuss how the variations in lifestyle might affect kitchen design. *(Key skills: writing, critical thinking)*

2. **Observation:** Ask students to observe someone preparing a meal and record the person's movements about the kitchen. Ask students to draw conclusions about the efficiency of work flow. *(Key skill: drawing conclusions)*

Designing for Efficiency

An efficient kitchen starts with a well-designed floor plan. It should provide enough space for working but also keep walking to a minimum.

Any kind of work routine is known as the **work flow.** In food preparation, food is removed from storage, washed if necessary, prepared, and served. This involves moving from one area of the kitchen to another. The design of the room affects the work flow.

As you learned in Section 7.1, the sink, cooking, and cold storage centers are the three major kitchen work centers. They make up the primary path of work called the work triangle. Each work center is located at a point in the triangle. For an efficient work flow, the legs of the triangle should total between 12 and 22 feet (about 3 and 7 m).

When only one person works in the kitchen, the work triangle is an efficient arrangement. However, today's kitchens are often used by several people at one time. Additional work space and duplicate work centers help avoid traffic jams. For example, a second sink or a separate microwave oven can give space for two cooks. The kitchen may have adjacent or overlapping work triangles.

The kitchen should be arranged so that people going from one room to another do not pass through the work triangle. Such traffic can cut efficiency and may cause accidents.

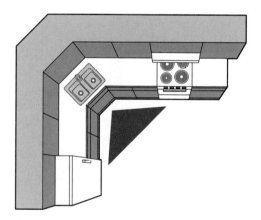

The sink, cooking, and cold storage centers form the three points of the work triangle.

Section 14.3: Designing a Kitchen **383**

See Also . . .

- "Kitchen Work Centers," text pages 186-187.

Thinking Skills

Reasoning: Give students descriptions of families or individuals who have different lifestyles (examples: single parents, college roommates, dual-worker couple), and have them describe the type of kitchen that would suit the lifestyle. Then ask them what generalizations they made about each type of family or individual. How are generalizations helpful? How can they be limiting?

14.3

Teaching . . .

• **Basic Kitchen Plans**
• **Storage and Work Space**

(text pages 384-386)

Comprehension Check

1. Ask students to describe the four basic types of kitchen plans. *(one-wall, corridor, L-shaped, and U-shaped)*

2. Ask students to explain the difference between a peninsula and an island. *(A peninsula is an extension of a kitchen counter, whereas an island is a freestanding unit, usually in the center of the kitchen.)*

3. Ask students to list storage aids that can be ordered as part of new cabinets or added to existing cabinets. *(Possibilities include roll-out shelves; cabinets with vertical dividers for cookie sheets and trays; pull-out, ventilated baskets for produce, pop-up shelves in base cabinets for appliances such as mixers.)*

4. Ask students to explain the advantages and disadvantages of different types of countertops. *(Plastic laminates are inexpensive but sometimes difficult to clean; seamless solid surfacing is easier to clean but expensive; ceramic tile is attractive but requires more care.)*

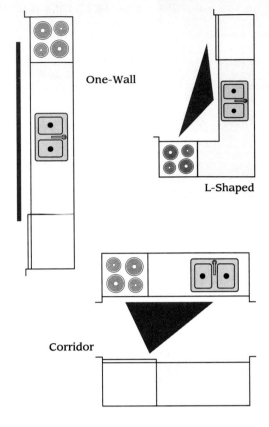

One-Wall

L-Shaped

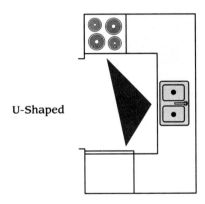

Corridor

U-Shaped

Kitchen plans can be identified by their basic shape.

384   **Chapter 14: Buying for the Kitchen**

Basic Kitchen Plans

Kitchens are often categorized by the shape or pattern formed by the cabinets and major appliances. These common shapes have certain characteristics.

❖ **One-wall.** All three work centers are on one wall. One-wall kitchens tend to be small with limited storage and counter space.

❖ **Corridor.** The work centers are located on two parallel walls. This is efficient for one cook. However, efficiency is lessened if the corridor is a traffic lane through the kitchen.

❖ **L-shaped.** The work centers are on two connecting walls. There is no through traffic to interrupt work.

❖ **U-shaped.** This efficient plan has work centers on three connecting walls, forming a U.

These basic kitchen plans may be modified by the addition of a peninsula or an island. A **peninsula** is an extension of a kitchen counter. An **island** is a freestanding unit, often in the center of the kitchen. Both can include storage space below the countertop. They can be equipped with a sink or cooktop or may serve as an eating area.

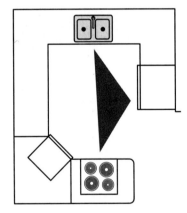

This U-shaped kitchen has been modified by the addition of a peninsula, where the cooktop is located.

Thinking Skills

Reasoning: Discuss how time spent organizing a kitchen can result in time savings when the kitchen is in use. Ask students to explain why this is an example of good time management.

Storage and Work Space

The amount of storage and counter space in a kitchen also affects how pleasant and efficient it is to work in.

Storage

Many kitchens lack adequate storage. As you learned in Section 7.1, items should be stored near the area where they are used. For new or remodeled kitchens, the key is to identify storage needs and develop a plan to meet them. In existing kitchens, storage can often be improved inexpensively.

Kitchen cabinets include base cabinets, which rest on the floor, and wall cabinets. Base cabinets are generally 36 inches high (about 3 m) and about 24 inches (61 cm) deep. Wall cabinets, placed on the wall above the countertop, vary in size. Kitchens may also include some floor-to-ceiling cabinets for additional storage.

Many storage aids can be ordered as part of new cabinets. Some of these can also be added to existing cabinets. They include:

❖ Roll-out shelves.
❖ Cabinets with vertical dividers for cookie sheets and trays.
❖ Pull-out, ventilated baskets for produce such as potatoes and dry onions.
❖ Pop-up shelves in base cabinets for appliances such as mixers.

Cabinets can be made of a variety of materials, including wood and plastic laminate. Look for well-made units with durable hardware. Cabinets receive more use than most other furniture in a home.

Special storage aids, such as turntables and vertical tray compartments, make kitchens more efficient. The cabinet shown at left includes an area for storing small appliances behind a sliding door.

Student Experiences

1. **Poster Project:** Have students work in four small groups to collect and display pictures of the four basic kitchen plans. Let each group present the poster to the class and describe the major features and the advantages and disadvantages. *(Key skill: creativity)*

2. **Field Trip:** Visit a kitchen planning center to see examples of various types of kitchens. Ask the sales consultant to discuss trends, new products and technology, and costs. *(Key skill: consumer awareness)*

3. **Display:** Create a display of kitchen storage devices, including low-cost ideas. Discuss other ways to stretch storage space in the kitchen. *(Key skill: critical thinking)*

4. **Bulletin Board:** Have students collect pictures of ideas for providing additional storage and work space in the kitchen. Use the pictures to create a bulletin board titled "Space Stretchers." *(Key skill: creativity)*

More About Designing a Kitchen

• Standard counter height is 36 inches (about 1 m). For tasks such as kneading dough and mixing, 30 inches (76 cm) is more comfortable for most people. If you're short, buy or build a wooden skid on which to stand while you work. If you're tall, stack cutting boards for a higher, more comfortable work surface.

• An island should not interrupt the work triangle, and its placement should not cause overly narrow traffic lanes within the kitchen.

• Reaching deep inside base cabinets can result in strained muscles. To reduce the risk of injury, equip deep base cabinets with pull-out racks that glide easily.

• The Kitchen Environment

(text pages 386-387)

Comprehension Check

1. Ask students to explain why grounding is so important. *(It provides a safe path for electricity to travel to the ground.)*

2. Ask students to describe the correct way provide grounding for a three-prong plug when an outlet only has two holes. *(See illustration on page 386.)*

3. Ask students to explain why task lighting is important in some areas of a kitchen. *(To keep you from working in your own shadow.)*

4. Ask students to describe factors to consider when buying flooring for a kitchen. *(It should be durable, easy to care for, and comfortable.)*

Student Experiences

1. **Panel of Experts:** Invite a panel of experts to discuss how to plan an efficient, comfortable, and attractive kitchen. Have students develop a list of questions to ask and write a summary of what they learn. *(Key skill: writing)*

2. **Design Study:** Have students collect and analyze pictures of well-designed kitchens. *(Key skill: evaluation)*

Safety Check

Remind students that other rooms have the potential for inadequate wiring: rooms in which electronic equipment is used, bathrooms, garages, and workshops.

Counter Space

Each work center needs its own counter space. Additional counter areas are needed for preparing and mixing food.

Work space often can be improved in an existing kitchen without remodeling. Adding a cart, table, or island can give more work space. So can a flip-down shelf, pull-out breadboard, or an adjustable cutting board that fits over the sink.

Countertops should be durable and easy to clean. Plastic laminates are the most common. Solid surfacing is seamless and easier to clean than laminates. It is also more expensive. Ceramic tile is attractive but requires more care.

The Kitchen Environment

Cabinets and major appliances are the obvious elements of a kitchen. There are other components, however, that make up the kitchen environment. Some of these are essential but work behind the scenes. Others make the kitchen comfortable and attractive.

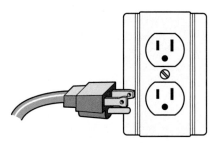

On plugs with three prongs, the rounded prong provides grounding for the appliance. If outlets have three holes, the home's wiring is probably grounded. However, the outlets should be tested to be certain.

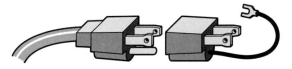

Adapters are available that allow plugs with three prongs to be inserted in outlets that have only two holes.

The Electrical System

Much of the electric usage in a home comes from the kitchen. Small appliances, many large appliances, and lighting all depend on electric power.

In planning a new kitchen or remodeling an old one, providing adequate electricity should be a priority. This means having enough electric power coming into the kitchen, sufficient outlets, and a grounded electrical system.

Electricity follows the path of least resistance to the ground. If there is a problem in the wiring, **grounding** provides a path for the electrical current to travel back through the electrical system to the ground, rather than through your body.

The National Electrical Code requires that new homes have a grounding wire as part of their wiring system. Outlets with three holes usually indicate the wiring is grounded. (Check with an electrician to be certain.) These outlets accept plugs from grounded appliances, which have three prongs. For a grounded system with two-hole outlets, special adapters can be used to plug in grounded appliances.

To provide grounding, the wire or metal clip on the adapter plug must be fastened to the outlet screw. However, you should check with an electrician to be sure this will properly ground appliances. It depends on how the house wiring was installed.

✔ SAFETY CHECK

Many kitchens have inadequate wiring that can cause fires. Have a qualified electrician check out the electrical system if:

❖ Lights dim when an appliance goes on.
❖ Appliances take a long time to heat.
❖ Mixers and motors slow down.
❖ The power frequently goes out due to a blown fuse or tripped circuit breaker.
❖ Extension cords are used regularly with appliances.

Lighting

Good lighting is essential in a kitchen for both comfort and safety. General lighting, usually from lighted ceiling panels or a ceiling light fixture, provides overall light. During the day, natural light from windows may also help light the room. However, **task lighting** is also needed to provide brighter, shadow-free light over specific work areas.

Task lighting is usually used over the counters, sink, and range. Spotlights or fluorescent fixtures are often mounted beneath overhead cabinets to light countertop areas. Recessed spotlights or track lights on the ceiling can also be positioned to light specific locations. Dimmer switches allow adjustment of the light to any brightness.

Ventilation

Cooking produces moisture, heat, grease, and odors. Good ventilation is needed to clear these from the kitchen. Windows, exhaust fans, and range hoods can all provide ventilation. Some cooktops and grills are available with built-in ventilation systems called downdraft systems.

No-wax vinyl flooring is a popular choice for kitchens. It is durable, comfortable, and easy to care for.

Plumbing

The plumbing system brings water to the kitchen and takes away waste water. With the addition of a garbage disposal, most food waste can also be carried away.

Sinks are the most visible parts of the system. Today, there are alternatives to traditional sinks, including ones mounted without rims and others that are part of the countertop itself. In addition, there are many bowl shapes, sizes, and combinations.

Walls and Floors

Wall coverings and flooring must look good and be durable and easy to clean. There are options available at different price levels.

❖ **Wall covering** may be paint or wallpaper. Look for "scrubbable" types. Kitchen walls have to be cleaned frequently, especially areas near the sink and range.
❖ **Flooring** should be durable and easy to clean, but also comfortable to stand on. Ceramic tile has excellent durability but can be uncomfortable during long periods of standing. Vinyl or hardwood floors are resilient and easier on the feet. Choose flooring that does not have to be waxed or polished.

Section 14.3: Designing a Kitchen   387

Teaching . . .

• **Designing Barrier-Free Kitchens**

(text page 388)

Comprehension Check

1. What is the purpose of the movement among kitchen designers known as "life-span design"? *(To make kitchens adaptable to people of various ages and degrees of physical ability.)*

2. Ask students to describe characteristics of life-span designs. *(Wide doorways, work surfaces at various heights, open shelving and drawers rather than closed cabinets, easy-to-grasp handles on drawers and cabinets.)*

Student Experiences

1. **Guest Speakers:** Invite several individuals who have physical challenges to explain how they have adapted their kitchens to meet their needs. *(Key skill: life management skills)*

2. **Letter Writing:** Have students write to the Association of Home Appliance Manufacturers or to the American Foundation for the Blind, to obtain information about adaptations for the handicapped. Some appliances manufacturers also have information. Have students report their findings to the class. *(Key skill: writing)*

Special Needs Strategies

Physically Disabled: Have physically disabled students research kitchen equipment and kitchen design features that would enable them to function more easily when preparing meals.

Visually Disabled: Have visually disabled students research kitchen equipment that is adapted to meet their needs.

Hearing Impaired: Have students investigate kitchen timers that provide visual rather than auditory warnings.

Completing the Section

Review

- Ask students to summarize the main ideas in this section.
- Have students complete the Section Review. (Answers appear below.)

Evaluation

- Have students write a list of guidelines for designing a kitchen.
- Have students take the quiz for Section 14.3. (Refer to the *Section Quizzes* booklet or use the *Testmaker Software*.)

Reteaching

- Provide floor plans of kitchens of several different designs. Have students practice identifying each type of kitchen plan.
- Refer to the *Reteaching Activities* booklet for the Section 14.3 activity sheet.

Enrichment

- Have students visit a professional kitchen remodeler or a kitchen specialty shop to identify low-cost ways to update kitchens.

Closure

- Lead a discussion on ways to update a kitchen inexpensively to make it safer and more efficient.

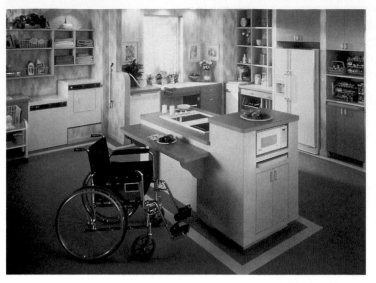

Barrier-free kitchen design makes it easier for everyone to use the kitchen. What specific features make this kitchen convenient for someone in a wheelchair to use?

Designing Barrier-Free Kitchens

Food preparation is a basic activity. Kitchen designers are working to make it easier for everyone. This movement, called **life-span design,** emphasizes kitchens adaptable to people of various ages and degrees of physical ability. Life-span designs incorporate wider doorways and aisles in the kitchen to accommodate wheelchairs or walkers. Work surfaces are placed at various heights so preparation can be done sitting or standing. Open shelving and drawers, rather than closed cabinets, provide easier access.

Kitchens can also be designed, remodeled, or adapted to meet specific physical challenges. For example, cabinet knobs can be replaced with easy-to-grasp handles. Braille controls can be added to appliances. Kitchen designers, appliance manufacturers, and support organizations are good sources of information.

Section 14.3 Review

RECALL THE FACTS

1. List three questions to consider when planning the design of a kitchen.
2. Give two guidelines for evaluating the efficiency of a kitchen floor plan.
3. Name a material suitable for each of the following: countertops, kitchen wall coverings, kitchen flooring.
4. What is meant by "life-span design"? Give an example.

DISCUSS YOUR IDEAS

5. Imagine the kitchen in which you'll be preparing food 20 years from now. How will it be different from the kitchen of today?

APPLY YOUR LEARNING

6. Describe how you could reorganize one work center in your kitchen at home. List tasks done at the center and food and tools located there. Tell what should be added and what should be moved elsewhere.

■ Answers to Section Review ■

1. See the list on page 382.
2. Traffic flow should not cut through the work triangle; it should have enough space for working but should keep walking to a minimum.

3. Countertops: plastic laminate, seamless solid surfacing, ceramic tile; wall coverings: scrubbable paint or wallpaper; flooring: vinyl or hardwood floors, possibly ceramic tile.

4. Making kitchens adaptable to people of various ages and degrees of physical ability. Examples will vary (see page 388).
5. Answers will vary.
6. Answers will vary.

Career PROFILE

Denise Chambers
Appliance Salesperson

CURRENT POSITION

"I sell appliances for a department store chain."

RESPONSIBILITIES

"I talk with customers to get a sense of what their needs and wants are. Then I show them the features of different appliances and answer any questions they may have."

SKILLS

"To be good at this job, you must be able to put people at ease and communicate clearly. It helps to have a good memory for details so you can keep track of the features of many different appliances. Basic math skills are essential for writing out sales slips, figuring tax and discounts, and discussing payment plans."

EDUCATION

"I have a high school diploma and previous retail experience."

WORK ENVIRONMENT

"I work a lot of nights and weekends, and I have to be on my feet for long periods."

FAVORITE PART OF THE JOB

"I've always liked working with people. It's fun to be able to help them find exactly what they're looking for."

BIGGEST CHALLENGE

"When a customer is rude or difficult, it can be frustrating. I just tell myself there must be some reason why this person is having a bad day. I can't take it personally or let it affect my attitude."

- Does Denise seem well suited to her job? Why or why not?
- Do you think you might enjoy working with the public as Denise does? Why or why not?

389

Thinking About . . . Appliance Sales

Have students think of other questions they would like to ask Denise Chambers about being an appliance salesperson. (Examples: How much do you have to know about each appliance you sell? Does the store have a training program to help you learn about the appliances? How many hours a week do you usually work?)

Ask students what other skills might be helpful for an appliance salesperson. Why? (general business skills, possibly administrative skills, the ability to work with other people, etc.)

Student Opportunities

Students interested in careers in sales should check with local retail stores about employment opportunities.

Occupational Outlook

Salespeople with experience and skill may advance to sales managers for individual stores or even district or regional sales managers. Some people may prefer to open their own store.

For More Information

For more information about careers in sales, encourage students to contact:
- National Retail Merchants Association, 100 W. 31st St., New York, NY 10001

- Personnel offices of local retail stores and state merchants' associations
- National Association of Professional Salespersons, P.O. Box 76461, Atlanta, GA 30358

Review

Have students complete the Chapter Review. (Answers appear below.)

Evaluation

- Describe various lifestyles for students and have them design a kitchen plan to suit each lifestyle.

- Have students take the test for Chapter 14. (Refer to the *Chapter and Unit Tests* booklet or construct your own test using the *Testmaker Software*.)

■ ANSWERS ■

REVIEWING FACTS

1. *Advantage:* you can use the item while you are paying for it. *Disadvantage:* you might be tempted to spend more than you can afford, the item costs more when you include the cost of interest.

2. A label that gives information that helps you estimate the energy costs of an appliance. It helps you compare energy costs for different models and project your own energy expenses based on the cost of gas or electricity in your area.

3. See the list on page 375.

4. *Any three:* adjustable shelves, temperature/humidity-controlled compartments for vegetables and meat, special areas for tall or large items, automatic ice makers, doors with chilled water and ice dispensers on the outside.

5. *Any three:* Whether the appliance will be helpful enough to justify the cost and space required; safety, comfort, ease of use and care, features you want and need.

CHAPTER 14 REVIEW

SUMMARY

SECTION 14.1

Consumer Skills: Before you buy any kitchen equipment, make sure you need and will use it. If you decide to buy on credit, investigate the costs of borrowing. When you shop for equipment, consider your needs and wants. Gather information about several different products. Look for consumer safeguards and consider your purchase carefully.

SECTION 14.2

Choosing Kitchen Equipment: It's easier to shop for appliances, cookware, tools, and tableware when you are familiar with some of the basic options you will find. A wide range of choices is available. Some features are essential for safety and quality, while others depend on personal needs and preferences.

SECTION 14.3

Designing a Kitchen: An efficient kitchen is planned according to how it will be used and by whom. The floor plan should allow an uninterrupted work flow. Storage units and counter space should be adequate, accessible, and durable. Other elements, such as electricity, lighting, and plumbing, should provide safety and convenience. Lifespan design helps make the kitchen easier to use for people of various ages and degrees of physical ability.

REVIEWING FACTS

1. Name one advantage and one disadvantage of buying on credit. (14.1)

2. What is an EnergyGuide label? How is it helpful when buying appliances? (14.1)

3. List four ways of being an active shopper. (14.1)

4. Identify three special features that may be found in refrigerator-freezers. (14.2)

5. List three things to consider when buying small appliances. (14.2)

6. Describe two signs of quality construction in knives. (14.2)

7. List four basic kitchen floor plans. (14.3)

8. In kitchen design, how does a peninsula differ from an island? What is the purpose of both? (14.3)

9. Why is good lighting important in a kitchen? (14.3)

10. Identify three features of good flooring. (14.3)

LEARNING BY DOING

1. **Simulation:** With one or two classmates, simulate an appliance-shopping trip. Pretend you are interested in buying one of the appliances in the foods lab. Through dialogue, identify the important points to consider when buying. Use the suggestions and checklists found in this chapter. (14.1, 14.2)

2. **Computer lab:** Using software that includes drawing tools, design an efficient kitchen floor plan. Include the location of large appliances and the dimensions of the work triangle. (14.3)

6. Sturdy handle, handle that is firmly attached to the blade by at least two rivets.

7. One-wall, corridor, L-shaped, U-shaped.

8. A peninsula is attached at one end to a countertop; an island is freestanding. Both provide additional working space in the kitchen.

9. Good lighting is important to prevent mistakes and accidents.

10. *Any three:* Durable, easy to keep clean, resilient, does not have to be waxed or polished.

THINKING CRITICALLY

1. **Determining credibility:** Sources of information about a product could include advertisements, reports in consumer magazines, and salespersons. Which do you think is most accurate and reliable? Explain your answer. (14.1)

2. **Analyzing decisions:** Which do you think is a greater problem when buying appliances: paying more for features that are seldom used, or not having needed features? Explain your answer. (14.2)

3. **Predicting consequences:** What might be the disadvantages of having work centers too close together? Too far apart? (14.3)

MAKING DECISIONS AND SOLVING PROBLEMS

What Would You Do?

1. One evening, you and your family go shopping for a microwave oven. At the first store you visit, you find a model that has most of the features you want and is on sale. You would like to compare it to other stores' selections, but the sale ends that day. (14.1)

2. You and your family are planning to buy a new refrigerator. The list of special features that family members would like is long and beyond your budget. You are having trouble reaching an agreement about which features are most important. (14.1, 14.2)

3. A new student in your foods lab group uses a wheelchair. The appliances, storage areas, and work space are sometimes difficult for him to use. Your teacher has asked you to suggest long-range and short-range solutions to the problem. (14.3)

LINKING YOUR STUDIES

1. **Math:** Compare the EnergyGuide labels on three different models of an appliance. Calculate the cost of using each one for one week, one month, and one year. Determine the difference in energy costs and rank the appliances from least to most expensive to use. (14.1)

2. **Social studies:** Choose one major appliance and research its development over time. How have the available options changed? What technological advances and social trends have made these changes in features possible and desirable? (14.2)

3. **Fine arts:** Plan and sketch an attractive, efficient kitchen design for a small apartment. Point out the features that make the kitchen efficient (either on the drawing or in a separate written description). Use colored pencils, paint chips, or wallpaper samples to show the color scheme. (14.3)

4. **Math:** Measure the distances between work centers in three different kitchens. Compare the results. Which kitchen would be most efficient for preparing food by one person? Two or more people at once? (14.3)

LEARNING BY DOING

Answers to "Learning by Doing" activities will vary.

THINKING CRITICALLY

1. Answers will vary. Independent consumer magazines are usually the most reliable. Ask students to explain their reasoning.

2. Answers will vary.

3. Answers will vary. Work centers that are too close together may cause accidents when more than one person works in the kitchen; there may not be enough space even for one person to work efficiently. When they are too far apart, extra steps are necessary, which reduces efficiency in the kitchen.

MAKING DECISIONS AND SOLVING PROBLEMS

Answers to "Making Decisions and Solving Problems" questions will vary. Encourage students to give reasons for their answers.

LINKING YOUR STUDIES

Answers to "Linking Your Studies" will vary.

COMPLETING THE UNIT

Refer to page 303 for suggestions for completing the unit.

391

UNIT FOUR
Foods for Meals and Snacks

Planning the Unit

Unit Overview

Chapter 15: Convenience Foods—Discusses guidelines for choosing, preparing, and using convenience foods, as well as making your own convenience foods.

Chapter 16: Fruits and Vegetables—Describes the characteristics of fruits and vegetables and discusses preparation techniques for raw and cooked fruits and vegetables.

Chapter 17: Grains, Legumes, Nuts, and Seeds—Describes the characteristics of grains and grain products, legumes, nuts, and seeds and discusses cooking methods.

Chapter 18: Dairy Foods and Eggs—Gives a general discussion on dairy products and eggs, as well as guidelines for preparing dairy products and eggs and using eggs in recipes.

Chapter 19: Meat, Poultry, and Fish—Describes the characteristics of meat, poultry, and fish and discusses preparation techniques for each.

Chapter 20: Food Combinations—Discusses sandwiches, snacks, salads, dressings, soups, sauces, casseroles, and other foods and dishes that are actually a combination of foods.

Chapter 21: Baking—Discusses methods and techniques for baking various foods.

Teacher's Classroom Resources—Unit Four

Refer to these resources in the TCR package:

Chapter and Unit Tests

Testmaker Software

UNIT FOUR

Foods for Meals and Snacks

393

Introducing the Unit

Motivator

- Prepare two stacks of index cards. On each card in one stack, write the name of a basic ingredient, such as apples, cheese, or chicken. On each card in the other stack, describe a simple procedure for preparing one of these foods. However, leave the name of the food out. (For example: "Wash four large _____ and remove their cores. Fill the cores with sugar, cinnamon, and butter or margarine . . .") Shuffle each stack separately and have students randomly choose a card from each stack. Have them read their "recipes" aloud, inserting the name of the food they drew. Afterwards, discuss the mixed-up recipes. Why were they often humorous? Point out that it is not enough to understand basic preparation and cooking methods. Success in the kitchen also depends on using the right method in the right way for a particular type of food. Then ask students to swap cards until all the foods are matched up with the correct preparation method.

Completing the Unit

Review

- Refer students to the unit motivator. Ask them to expand on the "mixed-up recipes" problem using what they have learned in this unit.

Evaluation

- Have students take the test for Unit Four. (Refer to the *Chapter and Unit Tests* booklet or construct your own test using the *Testmaker Software.*)

Planning the Chapter

Chapter Overview

Section 15.1: Choosing Convenience Foods

Section 15.2: Cooking with Convenience

Introducing the Chapter

Motivator

- Ask students to define the term *convenience food*. What foods do they consider convenience foods? Make a list. Do all students agree that all of these are convenience foods?

Teacher's Classroom Resources—Chapter 15

Refer to these resources in the TCR package.

Enrichment Activities

Chapter and Unit Tests

Testmaker Software

CHAPTER 15

Convenience Foods

394

Cooperative Learning Suggestion

Have students work in small groups to become experts on one type of convenience food. Then initiate a Simultaneous Roundtable activity. Give students a list of questions to answer. Ask students to move about the room and talk with each other while gathering answers to the questions. Statements should begin, "Find someone who...." Examples: ". . . can explain which nutrients are likely to be lost during canning," ". . . can compare the cost of fresh and frozen foods," ". . . can identify additives frequently used in convenience foods." Have students continue their quest until all of their questions are answered.

Choosing Convenience Foods

OBJECTIVES

After studying this section, you should be able to:

• Identify different types of convenience foods and their uses.

• Discuss the pros and cons of convenience foods.

LOOK FOR THESE TERMS

analogues
formed product

What does the word "convenience" mean to you when it comes to food? Joanne thinks of convenience foods as those that are "easy to cook—no mess—no clean up." Ricco thinks of packaged mixes that save time. Chantel uses the term to describe any ready-to-eat foods, whether she buys them in a supermarket or from a vending machine.

Convenience Food Choices

In general, a convenience food is one that has been commercially processed to make it more convenient to store or use. Some convenience foods have been around for such a long time that they have become staples in the American food supply. Today you might not think of baked, sliced breads or bottled salad dressings as convenience foods. Yet when they first appeared, these products were time-saving innovations.

What are the advantages and disadvantages of frozen fruit compared to fresh?

**Section 15.1
Choosing Convenience Foods**

Introducing the Section

Motivator

• Have students read the first two paragraphs on page 395 and look at the photo. Then have each student list two convenience foods their families use. Tally students' answers. Which types of convenience food were mentioned most often?

Objectives

• Have students read the section objectives. Discuss the purpose of studying the section.

Vocabulary

• Pronounce the terms listed under "Look for These Terms." Have students find the terms and their definitions in the section.

Guided Reading

• Have students look at the headings within Section 15.1 to preview the concepts that will be discussed.

• Have students read the section and complete the appropriate part of the Chapter 15 Study Guide in the *Student Workbook*.

Teacher's Classroom Resources—Section 15.1

Refer to these resources in the TCR package:

Reproducible Lesson Plans

Student Workbook

Extending the Text

Reteaching Activities

Section Quizzes

Testmaker Software

Color Transparencies

• Convenience Food Choices

(text pages 395-396)

Comprehension Check

1. Ask students to define the term convenience food. *(One that has been commercially processed to make it more convenient to store or use.)*

2. Discuss the purpose of convenience foods. *(They make certain foods more convenient to use, they reduce meal preparation time.)*

3. Ask students to describe analogues and give two examples. *(They are foods made from a vegetable protein but processed to resemble animal foods; TVP and egg substitutes.)*

4. Ask students to explain what a formed product is. *(A product made from a less expensive food and substituted for a more expensive one.)*

Student Experiences

1. **Class Discussion:** Discuss reasons people use convenience foods. Ask students to name some convenience foods that have a longer shelf life than fresh foods. Ask students to name some convenience foods that reduce meal preparation time. Ask students to identify some convenience foods that are already prepared. *(Key skill: brainstorming)*

2. **Research:** Have students research manufactured foods, including egg substitutes and other analogues, imitation crab and other substitutes for more expensive foods. *(Key skill: research)*

Convenience foods include items that have been processed for a longer shelf life. For example, nonfat dry milk can be stored without refrigeration and kept for a longer time than fluid milk.

Another purpose of convenience foods is to reduce meal preparation time. Food that is partially prepared when purchased can save time in the kitchen. For example, you can buy cheese that is already shredded and vegetables that are already cleaned and cut up. Some foods are combined and packaged for specific uses, such as a mixture of frozen stew vegetables. Dry mixes are available for everything from macaroni and cheese to salad dressing to baked goods. Often you need only add one or two ingredients and complete a few simple steps to prepare the food.

Of course, convenience can go even further. You can buy snacks, main dishes, side dishes, desserts, and even complete meals that are already prepared. Some need only be thawed or heated, while others are ready to eat.

Manufactured Foods

As you have seen, processing can result in products that are more convenient. In addition, processing can result in manufactured foods—products developed to serve as substitutes for other foods. Many manufactured foods have been developed to meet special nutritional needs or to provide low-cost alternatives. There are several types of manufactured foods.

Analogues (AN-uh-logs) are foods made from a vegetable protein and processed to resemble animal foods. Textured vegetable protein, also known as TVP, is one of the most widely used analogues. When flavored and processed, it can be substituted for meat and poultry in foods such as meatless burgers, pot pies, and hot dogs. These products are generally low in fat and cholesterol, although they may be high in sodium. TVP can also be purchased as granules so you can make your own meatless main dishes.

Egg substitutes are another example of a manufactured food. They are usually made

You can use granules of textured vegetable protein as a meat extender. Just mix the granules with ground meat or poultry for good nutrition at a lower cost. Egg substitutes can be scrambled or used in many recipes.

from egg whites with other ingredients added. Because they have no yolks, they have little or no saturated fat and cholesterol. They are usually sold in the freezer or refrigerator sections of the supermarkets. You can also buy ready-to-cook and ready-to-eat foods made with egg substitutes, such as baked goods.

A **formed product** is made from a less expensive food and substituted for a more expensive one. For example, surimi (soo-REE-mee) is made from white fish that is processed, flavored, and shaped to resemble expensive shellfish such as crab or lobster. The prices of imitation foods are lower than the prices of foods they replace. Such foods must be labeled "imitation" and can't be called by the name of the food they replace.

Sometimes manufactured foods are substituted for more expensive ones in convenience products. For example, "blueberry waffles" may not contain real blueberries. Instead, blueberry "buds" may be used which are made of sugar, oil, artificial flavor, salt, plus dyes and other additives.

Food and Nutrition Science

Processing Technology: One of the results of food science research in recent years has been new technology for food processing. For example, aseptic containers are replacing traditional cans and jars of food. Have students research and report on these new methods. Ask them to focus on the difference in procedure between traditional canning and newer methods, and what implications the differences have for convenience foods. For example, what temperatures are used for aseptic and traditional processing? How does processing time differ? What makes these differences possible, and what is the effect on the finished product?

Formed foods, such as products made with surimi, can be a good value. They are less expensive than the foods they replace.

The Pros and Cons of Convenience Foods

Every day, about 30 new convenience foods appear in the marketplace. The demand for new and more convenience foods emphasizes the important role they play in consumer food choices.

Most consumers are aware of the advantages of convenience foods. They cut down on the amount of preparation needed, saving time and energy. Because they need less preparation, less work space and equipment may be required. Many substitutes help people who are on special diets.

Although there are many advantages, there are also some disadvantages of convenience foods. They include cost, nutrition, and meal appeal.

Cost

Convenience is costly. Every additional step in processing adds to the price of the food. For example, at one supermarket, ready-to-cook meat loaf costs over twice as much as regular ground beef. Check the cost per serving of whole chicken versus cut-up chicken pieces. Will you save money if you cut up the chicken yourself?

Not all convenience forms have great price contrasts. To be certain, compare prices of different forms before buying.

Nutrition

Every step in processing usually destroys some nutrients. Heat, for example, destroys vitamin C. When grains are processed, much of the fiber and some of the nutrients are lost.

Frozen plain vegetables tend to lose the fewest nutrients during processing. In addition, no sodium, sugar, or fat is added to them.

Many convenience foods tend to be high in sodium, sugar, and fat. Even simple canned foods like vegetables usually have some salt added. Many fruits are canned in sugar syrups. Ready-to-cook and ready-to-eat foods often contain high amounts of sodium and fat.

Because the emphasis is now on good nutrition, low-sodium and low-fat convenience foods are becoming more common. Even so, the amounts of sodium and fat may still be above those recommended for good health. With careful shopping, you can buy nutritious convenience foods.

Food processing companies are making more nutritious convenience foods available, such as premixed salad ingredients.

More About Convenience Foods

- Frozen vegetables may actually have more nutrients than fresh vegetables because they are frozen immediately after harvest.
- Convenience products commonly labeled as "sandwich steaks" may contain beef that has been chopped, shaped, and thin-ly sliced. Most of these products do not really contain steak.
- If commercial convenience foods cost less than homemade ones, it's probably because they contain less of an expensive food, such as meat, poultry, or fish.

Teaching . . .

- **The Pros and Cons of Convenience Foods**

(text pages 397-398)

Comprehension Check

1. Ask students to compare the cost of convenience foods with the same foods prepared at home. *(Convenience foods are generally more expensive.)*
2. Discuss the impact of convenience foods on nutrition. *(Processing usually destroys at least some nutrients; convenience foods also tend to be high in sodium and sometimes fat, although many low-sodium and low-fat products are now available.)*

Student Experiences

1. **Taste Tests:** Have students conduct taste tests to compare convenience and homemade foods. They should develop score sheets to rank the flavor, color, and texture of each. *(Key skill: evaluation)*
2. **Nutrient Comparisons:** Have students use the Appendix chart and product labels to compare the nutrients in fresh, homemade, and convenience products. *(Key skill: reading)*
3. **Price Comparisons:** Have students compare the prices of different forms of the same food, such as fresh, canned, frozen, and dried peaches. Have students make charts to show the price comparisons. *(Key skill: math)*
4. **Degrees of Convenience:** Convenience foods vary significantly in the amount of preparation that remain for the consumer. Ask students for examples of convenience foods requiring slight, moderate, and significant additional preparation.

Completing the Section

Review

- Ask students to summarize the main ideas in this section.
- Have students complete the Section Review. (Answers appear below.)

Evaluation

- Have students write a short essay describing convenience foods, their purpose, and the things consumers should watch for when purchasing them.
- Have students take the quiz for Section 15.1. (Refer to the *Section Quizzes* booklet or use the *Testmaker Software*.)

Reteaching

- Bring empty packages from several convenience foods to class. Have students practice reading the labels to discover additives in the products and identify sodium and fat content.
- Refer to the *Reteaching Activities* booklet for the Section 15.1 activity sheet.

Enrichment

- Have students choose a common convenience food and describe the steps that would be necessary to prepare that food "from scratch" at home.

Closure

- Lead a discussion on the role convenience foods play in today's society. In what ways does society contribute to the prevalence of convenience foods?

Often, nutrients are added to convenience foods to increase the nutritional quality. Keep in mind that, even though many nutrients have been identified by scientists, there are probably others that are still unknown. When nutrients are added to food, only those that are known can be added. If you rely on convenience foods with nutrients added for good nutrition, you may be missing out on important nutrients that are present only in fresh foods.

Meal Appeal

Processing affects the flavor, color, and texture of food. Often, additives are used to make the final product resemble fresh ones. When it comes to convenience foods, the flavor and appearance may not compare with similar foods that are homemade.

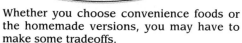

Whether you choose convenience foods or the homemade versions, you may have to make some tradeoffs.

TIPS for Success

Buying Convenience Foods

- ❖ Read labels carefully. Choose products that are low in sodium, sugar, fat, and additives.
- ❖ Compare the cost of the convenience product with making it from scratch at home.
- ❖ Find out if any ingredients have to be added to the convenience food. How much will this add to the cost and preparation time?
- ❖ Ask yourself whether the product will help you have and enjoy a pleasant meal.

■ Section 15.1 Review ■

RECALL THE FACTS

1. What are the two main purposes of convenience foods? Give an example of a convenience food for each.

2. What is an analogue?

3. Name two ways in which convenience foods are often less nutritious or healthful than fresh foods.

DISCUSS YOUR IDEAS

4. With today's busy schedules, many people consider convenience foods essential and use them regularly in meals. What might be some effects of this trend?

APPLY YOUR LEARNING

5. Compare the cost and nutrition of at least three different convenience forms of a food. For example, you might want to compare different forms of macaroni and cheese (canned prepared, boxed mix, frozen). Which form might be the best choice? Why?

■ Answers to Section Review ■

1. To give foods a longer shelf life (example: nonfat dry milk); to reduce meal preparation time (example: shredded cheese). Examples will vary.

2. A food made from a vegetable protein and processed to resemble animal foods.

3. Some nutrients are destroyed in processing; convenience foods tend to be high in sodium, sugar, and fat.

4. Answers will vary. Students should realize that convenience foods are more widely used because of this outlook; also, people may consume more sodium, sugar, and fat than they realize.

5. Answers will vary. Students should give reasons for their answers.

Cooking with Convenience

OBJECTIVES

After studying this section, you should be able to:

- Give suggestions for planning healthful meals around convenience foods.
- Describe general methods for preparing basic convenience foods.
- Discuss the benefits of making your own convenience foods.

LOOK FOR THIS TERM

reconstitute

As you read this section, think of convenience foods in terms of your own food choices. Which convenience foods are you more likely to use? Why? How do you and your family use convenience foods in meals?

Planning Meals with Convenience Foods

Meals that use convenience foods can be nutritious and help you meet your daily food needs. Here are some guidelines for making daily food choices when you use convenience foods:

❖ If you use convenience products for one part of the meal, plan the rest of your choices carefully. Make other parts of the meal from fresh foods that can be prepared quickly. These include fresh fruits and vegetables, whole grain breads and cereals, and low-fat dairy products.

❖ When using dry mixes to make main dishes, side dishes, and sauces, reduce the amount of fat called for in the directions. Use skim milk or water instead of whole milk.

❖ Use quick-cooking grains as a side dish to add variety to meals. These include rice, bulgur, millet, kasha, and couscous. (For more information, see Chapter 17.)

❖ Keep shelf-stable or frozen main dishes and meals on hand for emergencies, but try to avoid using them regularly for meals.

What fresh foods would you serve with this main dish?

Section 15.2
Cooking with Convenience

Introducing the Section

Motivator

- Ask students to describe their family's favorite convenience food meal. When is this meal most likely to be prepared?

Objectives

- Have students read the section objectives. Discuss the purpose of studying the section.

Vocabulary

- Pronounce the terms listed under "Look for These Terms." Have students find the terms and their definitions in the section.

Guided Reading

- Have students look at the headings within Section 15.2 to preview the concepts that will be discussed.

- Have students read the section and complete the appropriate part of the Chapter 15 Study Guide in the *Student Workbook*.

Teacher's Classroom Resources—Section 15.2

Refer to these resources in the TCR package:

Reproducible Lesson Plans

Student Workbook

Extending the Text

Reteaching Activities

Foods Lab Resources

Section Quizzes

Testmaker Software

Color Transparencies

- **Planning Meals with Convenience Foods**
- **Preparing and Using Convenience Foods**

(text pages 399-401)

Comprehension Check

1. Ask students to list guidelines for making daily food choices when you use convenience foods. *(See the list on page 399 for examples.)* Reinforce that the nutritional content of the specific foods must be considered in planning (frozen peas vs. a high-fat, high-sodium entree).

2. Ask students to explain what precautions should be taken with chilled convenience foods. *(They should be treated the same as fresh foods; keep them refrigerated until you are ready to use them; use by date shown on package.)*

3. Ask students to explain how to reconstitute a dried food. *(Reconstitution usually consists of adding back the liquid that was removed when the food was dried.)*

When planning a meal around convenience main dishes, be sure to include nutritious fresh foods as well. Many require little preparation time.

Preparing and Using Convenience Foods

Most convenience foods have directions for use on the package. Always read the directions carefully, even if you have used the product before. Manufacturers often change the ingredients or the preparation methods. Follow the directions exactly for best results.

If you want microwavable convenience foods, check the package directions before buying. Not all convenience foods can be successfully microwaved.

Here are some general guidelines for using common convenience foods. You'll also find information about specific convenience foods in later chapters.

❖ **Canned foods.** Many canned foods are ready to eat or need little preparation other than heating. Some canned soups must be mixed with water or milk. Once canned food is opened, any leftovers must usually be refrigerated.

HEATING INSTRUCTIONS

MICROWAVE OVEN:
Microwave ovens vary. Heating time may require adjustment.
• Remove dinner from carton.
• Cut and remove film cover from fruit compartment only.
• Cut a slit in center of film cover over main entree.
• Heat on HIGH 6 to 7 minutes or until hot, rotating dinner once.
• Let stand in microwave oven 1 to 2 minutes.
• Stir main entree before serving.
When heating TWO dinners, follow instructions above, heating approximately 12 to 14 minutes or until hot, rotating once.

CONVENTIONAL OVEN:
Preheating oven is not necessary.
• Remove dinner from carton.
• Cut and remove film cover from fruit compartment only.
• Cut a slit in center of film cover over main entree.
• Heat at 350°F on COOKIE SHEET in center of oven 30 to 35 minutes or until hot.
• Remove dinner from oven on COOKIE SHEET.
• Let stand 1 to 2 minutes before serving.
Temperatures above 350°F AND/OR failure to use a COOKIE SHEET may cause damage to the plastic tray, food and/or oven.

NOTE: When removing cover, be careful to avoid steam burns.
Do not prepare in toaster oven.

Many convenience food packages include specific directions for preparing the food. Follow them exactly for best results. What cautions are given on the package directions shown here?

❖ **Frozen foods.** Some frozen foods may need to be thawed. Others must be cooked without thawing. Check the package for special instructions, such as "Do not heat in toaster oven."

Special Needs Strategies

Learning Disabled: Help students learn to use the picture directions often used on dry mixes.

Gifted and Talented: Have students compare the additives to convenience and nonconvenience versions of the same food. What is the purpose of each additive?

Food and Nutrition Science

Dried Foods: Have students research the methods used to dry convenience foods and devise a an experiment to determine the best way for the average person to dry foods. If possible, allow students to carry out their experiments.

SAFETY CHECK

Before opening canned goods, wipe the top of the can with a clean, wet dishcloth. That will keep dirt and germs from getting into the food.

* **Chilled foods.** Use the same care in handling chilled convenience foods, such as fresh pasta and sauces, that you do when preparing foods from scratch. Keep them refrigerated until you are ready to use them. Use a chilled food product by the date shown on the package or check to see if it can be frozen. As an alternative, consider using it in a recipe which can be frozen.
* **Dried foods.** Many dried foods, such as nonfat dry milk, need to be reconstituted. To **reconstitute** means to add back the liquid that was removed in processing.
* **Dry mixes.** Most mixes contain the dry ingredients needed to prepare the food. You add other ingredients, such as liquids. Along with the basic directions, the package may have suggestions for variations.

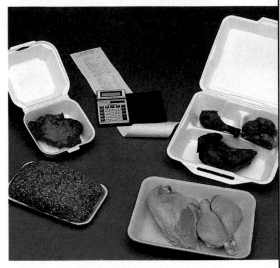

The cost of buying already-prepared foods is usually more than preparing similar recipes at home. Making your own convenience foods is an alternative that can save both time and money.

Making Your Own Convenience Foods

Even though people are busy, they may be concerned about the cost or nutritional qualities of convenience foods. Some solve the problem by making their own convenience foods. Homemade convenience foods have several advantages:

* You decide on the kind and quality of ingredients to put into the product.
* You can control the amount of sodium, sugar, and fat used.
* Homemade convenience foods often cost less to prepare than the commercial ones.
* They have few or no additives.
* You enjoy meals with a homemade appearance and flavor.

Here are some ideas for making your own convenience foods.

Pre-prepared Ingredients

Perhaps there are some basic ingredients that you often use in recipes. You can save time by preparing a quantity of these foods ahead of time and refrigerating or freezing them.

* **Sautéed chopped vegetables.** Recipes often call for sautéed chopped garlic, onions, celery, or green pepper. Chop and sauté the combinations you use often. Freeze them in recipe-size quantities, such as 1/2 cup (125 mL). You can also freeze chopped vegetables without sautéing them, as long as you plan to cook them. Freezing softens crisp vegetables.

Section 15.2: Cooking with Convenience   401

Student Experiences

1. **Group Activity:** Have students work in groups to study typical preparation techniques for canned foods, frozen foods, chilled foods, dried foods, and dry mixes. Provide students with convenience food packages to study. Have each group report its findings to the class. *(Key skill: reading)*
2. **Menu Planning:** Have students work in small groups to plan a meal around convenience foods. Have students observe the guidelines on page 399. Have each group share its menu with the class. *(Key skill: life management skills)*

Lab Experience

Have students prepare a meal featuring one or more convenience foods. Emphasize the importance of reading and following package directions carefully. Students should develop a rating scale for convenience products including time savings, clear directions, ease of preparation, cost, nutrition, and taste. Would they purchase these foods again? Why or why not?

Safety Check

Remind students that keeping the can opener clean is another important safety step that is often forgotten. If you wipe a can before opening it, but the can opener blade has a buildup of food and microorganisms, the microorganisms can still get in the food.

Thinking Skills

Reasoning: Ask students to explain the reasons for the addition of "mini-marts" at gasoline service stations. *(People can quickly buy a single food item, such as milk, as they get gas. People are willing to pay a higher price for this convenience. Also, people eat while traveling.)* Ask students if this is a new idea. *(Actually, many small grocery stores in the 1940s and 1950s added gas stations for similar reasons.)*

Teaching . . .

• Making Your Own Convenience Foods

(text pages 401-403)

Comprehension Check

1. Ask students to list advantages of preparing your own convenience foods. *(See the list on page 401.)*

2. Ask students to name recipe ingredients that can be pre-prepared and stored in the freezer. *(Examples include sautéed vegetables, dry beans and grain products, cubed or shredded cheese, bread crumbs or cubes.)*

3. Discuss the advantages of creating your own frozen main meals and homemade mixes.

Student Experiences

1. **Class Discussion:** Discuss reasons people might choose to make their own convenience foods. *(Key skill: critical thinking)*

2. **Group Activity:** Have students work in groups to research homemade convenience foods. Include pre-prepared ingredients, frozen main dishes, and homemade mixes. *(Key skill: research)*

Lab Experience

As a demonstration, prepare a homemade mix. Then have students work in groups to prepare a variety of foods using the mix as a base. What conclusions can they draw?

See Also . . .

• "Freezer Storage," pages 210-211.

❖ **Dry beans and grain products.** Cook dry beans and grain products, such as rice and pasta, in quantity. Freeze them in 1-cup (125 mL) portions. Use them for salads, casseroles, soups, and side dishes.

❖ **Cubed or shredded cheese.** Cube or grate the kind of cheese you use frequently, such as cheddar or mozzarella. Store in a container with a tight-fitting cover and keep refrigerated or frozen until used.

❖ **Bread crumbs or cubes.** Cut bread into cubes and dry them. For crumbs, grind dried bread slices in a blender or food processor. You can also crush them with a rolling pin between two pieces of waxed paper or in a large, sealed plastic bag. Store the crumbs or cubes in an airtight container in the refrigerator or freezer. For added flavor and fiber, use whole wheat bread.

Frozen Main Dishes

At first, it may sound time-consuming to cook your own meals and freeze them. By preparing and freezing your own main dishes, however, you can save time and money in the long run. Considering the advantages, it may be worth the little extra time it takes.

Some busy people set aside one or two weekend days to "cook for the freezer." They prepare as many of their favorite recipes as they can and freeze them. Karen's mother gets the family involved in their "cooking weekend." They have a large freezer and can prepare enough main dishes to last about two months. Because everyone is involved, it has become a fun activity the family enjoys.

Others cook for the freezer regularly by preparing more than they need whenever they cook. The leftover food is frozen for future meals.

When packing the food, consider how it will be used. If family members eat at different times, freeze the food in single-serving packages.

When labeling the packages, include any instructions needed to serve the food. For example, if the recipe is to be served over rice, write that on the package so the rice can be thawed at the same time. (See pages 210-211 for information on packing and labeling foods to be frozen.)

Consider stocking your freezer with recipe ingredients that you have prepared ahead of time. They can cut down on the time needed to prepare recipes in the future.

More About Making Your Own Convenience Foods

In addition to freezing main meals, ingredients for recipes, and mixes, you can prepare meats in advance for sandwiches. Slice cooked, leftover meat or poultry and freeze it in serving-size portions.

"Cooking for the freezer" is a way to use time efficiently. Several recipes can be prepared and frozen in one cooking session, especially when family members work together.

Homemade Mixes

You can make your own mixes for foods that you prepare regularly, such as quick breads or beverages. Seasoning mixes are great time-savers because you handle just one container instead of many different jars of herbs and spices.

The secret to making a successful mix is to be sure the ingredients are thoroughly combined and evenly distributed. Then, when you measure out the quantity you need, you will be sure to get the right amount of all the ingredients. Some ingredients may be heavier than others and may settle down in the container. Before measuring the amount you need, mix well to be sure the ingredients are evenly distributed.

Commercial mixes usually have preservatives added to extend the shelf life. You may not be able to store homemade mixes as long as commercial ones. Make only the quantity you think you will use before the mix spoils.

On page 404, you'll find an example of a basic baking mix and a recipe that can be prepared with it.

Section 15.2 Review

RECALL THE FACTS

1. List three tips for using convenience foods in meals.

2. Why is it important to read the directions on convenience foods even if you have used the product before?

3. Name two guidelines for using chilled convenience foods.

4. What are three benefits of making your own convenience foods?

DISCUSS YOUR IDEAS

5. How might you and your family use homemade convenience foods? What types of foods would be most helpful?

APPLY YOUR LEARNING

6. Plan a menu that combines a main-dish convenience food with easy-to-prepare fresh foods as side dishes. Evaluate the menu for nutrition, cost, and appeal.

Section 15.2: Cooking with Convenience **403**

15.2

Completing the Section

Review

- Ask students to summarize the main ideas in this section.

- Have students complete the Section Review. (Answers appear below.)

Evaluation

- Have students create an outline of the topics covered in this section. Students may use section headings for main topics, but subtopics should be in their own words.

- Have students take the quiz for Section 15.2. (Refer to the *Section Quizzes* booklet or use the *Testmaker Software*.)

Reteaching

- Bring to class packages from several commercially packaged convenience foods. Have students analyze the contents and discuss how a similar convenience food could be prepared at home.

- Refer to the *Reteaching Activities* booklet for the Section 15.2 activity sheet.

Enrichment

- Have students make a plan for a "cooking day" to prepare foods ahead for their family. Students should create a work plan and schedule for accomplishing the cooking.

Closure

- Hold a class debate on the relative advantages of buying convenience foods and making your own.

Answers to Section Review

1. See the list on page 399.
2. Manufacturers often change the ingredients or the preparation methods.
3. Keep them refrigerated until you're ready to use them; use them by the date on the package or check to see if it can be frozen.
4. See the list on page 401.
5. Answers will vary.
6. Answers will vary.

15.2 Recipes

Favorite Wheat Pancakes

Whole Wheat Quick Bread Mix

Key Skill: Preparing and using homemade mixes.

Using the Recipe

- Have students read both recipes and discuss the steps for each. Review safety and sanitation procedures that apply to each recipe. For the Whole Wheat Quick Bread Mix, check to be sure the storage container is airtight.
- Have each lab team fill out a work plan. (See the *Foods Lab Resources* booklet.)
- Have students check off the ingredients and equipment listed on the recipe worksheet and prepare the recipe.
- Have students complete the evaluation and questions on the recipe worksheet.

See Also . . .

The *Foods Lab Resources* booklet for the "Favorite Wheat Pancakes" and "Whole Wheat Quick Bread Mix" recipe worksheets and other recipe alternatives.

Thinking About the Recipe

Read the recipes for "Favorite Wheat Pancakes" and "Whole Wheat Quick Bread Mix" and answer the following questions.

1. In what way does using a homemade mix like this one save time?
2. Why is it important to stir the quick bread mix before using it in the pancakes?

Favorite Wheat Pancakes

Customary	Ingredients	Metric
1	Egg, slightly beaten	1
1 ½ cups	Water	375 mL
2 Tbsp.	Oil	30 mL
2 ¼ cups	Whole Wheat Quick Bread Mix	550 mL

Yield: About 15 4-inch (10-cm) pancakes

Directions

Pan: Skillet
Temperature: Medium-high

1. Spray skillet with vegetable oil cooking spray. Preheat skillet.
2. Combine egg, water, and oil in a medium bowl.
3. Stir in Quick Bread Mix until just moistened.
4. Cook pancakes in hot skillet until browned on both sides, about 3 or 4 minutes.

Nutrition Information

Per 3-pancake serving : 257 calories, 8 g protein, 41 g carbohydrate, 7 g fat, 43 mg cholesterol, 425 mg sodium

Whole Wheat Quick Bread Mix

Customary	Ingredients	Metric
6 cups	Whole wheat flour	1500 mL
3 cups	All-purpose flour	750 mL
1 ½ cups	Instant nonfat dry milk	375 mL
1 Tbsp.	Salt	15 mL
1 cup	Sugar	250 mL
1/2 cup	Wheat germ	125 mL
1/4 cup	Baking powder	50 mL

Yield: About 12 cups baking mix

Directions

1. Combine all ingredients in a large bowl.
2. Put baking mix in a large container with a tight-fitting cover. Label with the name of the mix and the date.
3. Store baking mix in the refrigerator. Use within 12 to 14 weeks.

Note: Mix well again before measuring to use in recipes.

Answers to Thinking About the Recipe

1. You only have to do the mixing one time. From then on, whenever you use the mix, you just take out the amount you need.

2. Because some of the ingredients may be heavier than others, so they may tend to settle to the bottom of the mixture.

Career PROFILE

Marilyn Lakota
Processing Plant Worker

CURRENT POSITION

"I work in a large food processing plant. My current job involves inspecting and sorting ears of corn prior to freezing and packaging."

SKILLS

"To be successful in this job, you must be able to handle repetitive tasks quickly and accurately. You also must be able to pay attention to details and work well as part of a team."

EDUCATION

"In addition to my high school diploma, I have completed on-the-job training at the plant."

WORK ENVIRONMENT

"My hours are steady—40 hours a week—and I work third shift. I work in a clean environment, though it can be noisy. Safety is always a factor with the various machines in the plant, so I have to be careful to follow all safety rules and pay attention to what I'm doing."

FUTURE PLANS

"I'm in line for a promotion to machine operator. My long-term goal is to become a supervisor or manager. As a first step, I volunteered for the quality-control team in my work unit."

- What are the advantages and disadvantages of Marilyn's work environment?
- What aspects of Marilyn's job do you find interesting? Why?

405

Thinking About . . . Production Careers

- Have students think of other questions they would like to ask Marilyn Lakota about being a processing plant worker. (Examples: What hours do third-shift workers work? What machines do you currently work with? What other foods are processed at your facility? What does it take to become a supervisor or manager?)

- Ask students to brainstorm types of products that are processed at processing plants.

Student Opportunities

Students who are interested in production careers should check employment opportunities at local food production plants.

Occupational Outlook

Processing plant workers with motivation and on-the-job training can advance to machine operators, senior inspectors, or supervisors or managers of processing areas.

For More Information

For additional information about production careers, encourage students to contact:
- Personnel offices of local food production plants
- Local chapters of the United Food and Commercial Workers International Union (AFL-CIO)
- American Frozen Food Institute, 1764 Old Meadow Lane, Suite 350, McLean, VA 22102

Review

- Have students complete the Chapter Review. (Answers appear below.)

Evaluation

- Provide a list of well-known convenience foods or make a display of packages. Have students write menus for nutritious, home-cooked meals using the foods.

- Have students take the test for Chapter 15. (Refer to the *Chapter and Unit Tests* booklet or construct your own using the *Testmaker Software*.)

■ ANSWERS ■

REVIEWING THE FACTS

1. It can be stored for much longer periods than fluid milk.

2. To meet special nutritional needs; to provide low-cost alternatives for expensive foods.

3. Textured vegetable protein; it is substituted for meat or poultry in various foods.

4. Nutrients are lost in processing; they may contain high amounts of sodium, sugar, and fat.

5. Replace the liquid that was removed during the drying process.

6. *Any three:* Sautéed chopped vegetables; dry beans and grain products; cubed or shredded cheese; bread crumbs or cubes, or other examples.

CHAPTER 15 REVIEW

SUMMARY

SECTION 15.1

Choosing Convenience Foods: Convenience foods include a wide variety of food items. They have been processed for longer shelf life, ease of preparation, or both. Manufactured foods are developed to serve as substitutes for other foods. Using convenience foods can save time and energy. However, convenience foods may be more costly, less nutritious, and less appealing than home-prepared or fresh foods.

SECTION 15.2

Cooking with Convenience: With careful planning, convenience foods can be part of a nutritious meal. Prepare convenience foods according to package directions. You can make your own convenience foods by pre-preparing ingredients, freezing main dishes, and making homemade dry mixes. Homemade convenience foods usually have advantages over store-bought versions, such as lower cost, better nutrition, and more meal appeal.

REVIEWING FACTS

1. In what way is nonfat dry milk more convenient than fluid milk? (15.1)

2. Name two reasons for the development of manufactured foods. (15.1)

3. What is TVP? How is it used? (15.1)

4. Identify two nutritional disadvantages of some convenience foods. (15.1)

5. What does "reconstitute" mean? (15.2)

6. Identify three types of recipe ingredients that you can pre-prepare. (15.2)

7. Describe two practices many people use to make and freeze main dishes. (15.2)

8. Do homemade dry mixes last as long as commercial varieties? Explain. (15.2)

LEARNING BY DOING

1. ***Taste test:*** Prepare a ready-to-cook entree or side dish and a similar recipe from scratch in the foods lab. Compare them for meal appeal and nutritional value. (15.1)

2. ***Foods lab:*** Pre-prepare different types of recipe ingredients. Divide them into convenient quantities, label them, and store them properly. Use these in a later foods lab. (15.2)

3. ***Food science lab:*** Using a recipe from this book or another source, prepare a dry mix. Store it and a similar commercial variety under identical conditions. Check both mixes regularly for texture and appearance. Prepare recipes using the mixes at regular intervals. How does time affect the quality of each mix? (15.2)

4. ***Foods lab:*** Prepare a commercial dry mix according to the basic package directions. Prepare another batch using a variation suggested on the package or one of your own creation. Compare the two recipes for taste, texture, appearance, and nutritional value. (15.2)

7. Set aside one or two weekend days to "cook for the freezer"; regularly cook more than you need and freeze the rest.

8. No, because the commercial varieties have added preservatives that homemade mixtures don't have.

THINKING CRITICALLY

1. **Identifying cause and effect:** Identify one positive effect and one negative effect of convenience foods on family life. (15.1)

2. **Identifying solutions:** How might convenience foods be used to help improve the global food supply? (15.1)

3. **Drawing conclusions:** You notice that your homemade convenience foods cost much less per serving than similar store-bought varieties. What do you think accounts for this price difference? (15.2)

MAKING DECISIONS AND SOLVING PROBLEMS

What Would You Do?

1. Your family uses convenience foods every day. You are worried about the effect on your family's health and budget. However, with everyone's busy, conflicting schedules, there doesn't seem to be much choice. (15.1)

2. You have promised to prepare a homemade pizza for your family's dinner tonight. However, you are late getting home from school and don't have time to prepare yeast dough crust or to simmer the tomato sauce. (15.2)

3. You are preparing your family's dinner when some old friends drop by. You would like to invite them to stay for the meal, but aren't sure you have enough food. You wonder how you can stretch the recipes using convenience foods. (15.2)

LINKING YOUR STUDIES

1. **Social studies:** Trace the history of convenience foods. What were some of the first commercially sold convenience foods? What technologies made them possible? How has their use affected family life? (15.1)

2. **Science:** Find information on the use of convenience foods by the armed forces and the space program. How has the technology used in preparing foods for these groups been applied to supermarket convenience foods, and vice versa? (15.1)

3. **Math:** Prepare a homemade convenience food. Calculate the cost per serving. Compare this to the per-serving cost of a similar commercial variety. Express the price difference in dollars and cents and as a percentage. (15.2)

4. **Writing:** Imagine that you can invent any kind of convenience food. Write a description of the product you would invent. Describe its appearance, texture, flavor, nutritional value, and how to store and prepare it. Then write an advertisement for your product. (15.1, 15.2)

LEARNING BY DOING

Answers to "Learning by Doing" activities will vary. Evaluate students on the effort they put into the activity as well as their results.

THINKING CRITICALLY

1. Answers will vary.

2. Answers will vary. Students may say that foods that can be stored for longer periods could withstand the poor or slow distribution systems in developing countries.

3. Answers will vary. The packaged convenience foods include the price of processing, packaging, and additives, in addition to the basic foods.

MAKING DECISIONS AND SOLVING PROBLEMS

Answers to "Making Decisions and Solving Problems" activities will vary. Encourage students give reasons for their answers.

LINKING YOUR STUDIES

Answers to "Linking Your Studies" activities will vary. Encourage students to give reasons for their answers.

407

Planning the Chapter

Introducing the Chapter

Motivator

- Provide a variety of unusual fruits and vegetables for students to taste test. Provide students with a check sheet for recording the ones they like and dislike. Tally students' responses and discuss reasons some fruits and vegetables may be more popular than others. Encourage students to try fruits and vegetables prepared in a variety of ways before deciding that they don't like them.

Teacher's Classroom Resources—Chapter 16

Refer to these resources in the TCR package:

Enrichment Activities

Chapter and Unit Tests

Testmaker Software

CHAPTER 16

Fruits and Vegetables

408

Cooperative Learning Suggestion

Organize a Total Group Response (Human Graph) activity. Have students indicate how much they like or dislike various fruits and vegetables by taking a position on an imaginary graph. Ask students to draw conclusions about their fruit and vegetable preferences. Do students like a variety of fruits and vegetables? Discuss possible ways to increase the variety of fruits and vegetables in students' diets, if needed.

OBJECTIVES

After studying this section, you should be able to:

- Describe types of fruits and vegetables.
- Identify nutrients found in fruits and vegetables.
- Discuss guidelines for buying and storing fresh produce.
- Give suggestions for using convenience forms of fruits and vegetables.

LOOK FOR THESE TERMS

drupes
tuber
cruciferous vegetables
unitized
mature fruits
ripe fruits

When she stopped at the supermarket one day, Marla was surprised to find that the produce section was being remodeled. "With all the emphasis on eating more fresh fruits and vegetables," said the manager, "we just didn't have enough space to handle the different kinds people want. So we're expanding."

Until that day, Marla was in the habit of eating only apples, bananas, potatoes, and carrots. She didn't even realize how many other kinds of fruits and vegetables are available. Now Marla likes to try a new one at least once or twice a month.

Types of Fruits and Vegetables

Think of the many varieties of fruits that are available. For example, there are:

- ❖ Melons, such as cantaloupe, honeydew, and casaba.
- ❖ Berries, including raspberries, strawberries, blackberries, and blueberries, as well as grapes.
- ❖ Citrus fruits, such as grapefruit, oranges, and tangerines.

- ❖ Many varieties of apples and pears.
- ❖ Cherries, plums, peaches, nectarines, and apricots. These fruits, called **drupes,** all have a central pit enclosing a single seed.
- ❖ Tropical fruits, including bananas, pineapple, and papayas.

In most supermarkets, you can find many other fruits from around the world. How many of the fruits and vegetables shown on page 410-411 have you tried?

Choose many different fruits for variety and good nutrition.

Introducing the Section

Motivators

- Show students the week's newspaper advertisements. If they were shopping, which fruits and vegetables would they buy? Why? Are all advertised fruits "good buys"? Why or why not?
- Compare the changes in fresh produce which have occurred during the history of the United States. What caused these changes? How have consumers benefited?

Objectives

- Have students read the section objectives. Discuss the purpose of studying the section.

Vocabulary

- Pronounce the terms listed under "Look for These Terms." Have students find the terms and their definitions in the section.

Guided Reading

- Have students look at the headings within Section 16.1 to preview the concepts that will be discussed.
- Have students read the section and complete the appropriate part of the Chapter 16 Study Guide in the *Student Workbook*.

Teacher's Classroom Resources—Section 16.1

Refer to these resources in the TCR package:

Reproducible Lesson Plans
Student Workbook
Extending the Text
Reteaching Activities

Food Science Resources
Section Quizzes
Testmaker Software
Color Transparencies

Teaching . . .

• **Types of Fruits and Vegetables**

(text pages 409-412)

Comprehension Check

1. Ask students to describe the different types of fruits available. *(melons, berries, citrus fruits, apples and pears, drupes, tropical fruits.)*

2. Ask students to list the various parts of plants that are eaten as vegetables. *(roots, stems, tubers, leaves, bulbs, flowers, seeds, and fruits.)*

3. Ask students to list and describe fruits from around the world that are considered unusual in this country. *(See the photos and captions on pages 410-411 for some examples.)*

4. Ask students to give examples of vegetables that are roots. *(carrots, beets, turnips.)*

Carambola is also called star fruit because of its shape when cut. In taste and texture, it is similar to a blend of apples, grapes, and citrus fruit. Carambola is a good source of vitamin C and also supplies some vitamin A.

Atemoya has a sweet flavor and creamy, custard-like texture. It is a good source of vitamin C and potassium.

Lychees (LEE-chees) are small, round, sweet fruits about the size of cherries. The skin is bumpy and red to red-brown in color. Lychees are a good source of vitamin C and also supply potassium.

Pummelo (PAHM-uh-low) originated in the Far East. It resembles a large grapefruit, but is sweeter. It's a good source of vitamin C and potassium.

Special Needs Strategies

Learning Disabled: Have students place pictures of fruits and vegetables in the correct categories.

Physically Disabled: Have physically disabled students investigate adaptive aids for paring produce. (Example: a cutting board with a nail to hold the fruit or vegetable in place so it can be pared by someone who has the use of only one hand.)

Gifted and Talented: Have students analyze recipes featuring fruits and vegetables, comparing their calorie and fat content. What are the main sources of calories and fat. What conclusions can they draw about preparing fruits and vegetables to avoid extra calories and fat?

Calabaza is also called West Indian pumpkin. It may be green, tan, or orange and has bright orange flesh. Calabaza is a good source of vitamin A, vitamin C, and potassium.

Chayote (chy-OH-tay) is a tropical summer squash with a flavor similar to zucchini. It's a good source of vitamin C and also supplies potassium.

Malanga is a starchy vegetable popular in Cuba and in Puerto Rico, where it is called *yautia*. When boiled, the texture and flavor resemble a blend of dry beans and potatoes. Malanga is a good source of vitamin C.

Boniato is a tropical sweet potato. It's a good source of vitamin C and potassium.

Section 16.1: Choosing Fruits and Vegetables **411**

Student Experiences

1. **Categorizing:** On the chalkboard, list all of the fruits students can think of. Identify the categories into which fruits can be divided based on page 409 or as temperate, subtropical, or tropical. Have students categorize the fruits listed on the chalkboard. Have students look up any fruit they cannot categorize. *(Key skill: categorizing)*

2. **Vegetable Identification:** Identify the parts of plants eaten as vegetables. Have students think of an example of each, then turn to a partner and share their examples. Have each pair of students join another pair and have each partner share the other person's examples. Then have the foursome join another foursome and ask each person to give an example they have not repeated before. *(Key skill: cooperative learning)*

Food and Nutrition Science

Horticulture Science: Horticulturists—scientists who study the growth of plants—define vegetables as "the edible products of herbaceous plants." *Herbaceous (her-BAY-shuss) plants* have stems that are softer than those of shrubs and trees.

Horticulturalists classify fruits based on the temperatures they require for growth:
- *Temperate fruits* include common fruits such as apples and peaches.
- *Subtropical fruits* include citrus fruits, such as oranges, grapefruit, and tangerines, as well as dates and figs.
- *Tropical fruits* include bananas, pineapples, and mangoes.

Teaching . . .

• **Nutrients in Fruits and Vegetables**

(text pages 412-413)

Comprehension Check

1. Ask students to list cruciferous vegetables and explain their importance in the diet. *(Broccoli, brussels sprouts, cabbage, collards, kale, mustard greens, cauliflower, rutabagas, and turnips; they may lower the risk of certain kinds of cancer.)*

2. Ask students to list fruits and vegetables that are high in vitamin C. *(Citrus fruits, kiwi, strawberries, cantaloupe, cabbage, potatoes.)*

Student Experiences

1. **Review:** Review the nutritional value of fruits and vegetables. Emphasize that, in general, vegetables are high in nutrition and low in calories. Refer students to Chapters 2 and 3 for further review. *(Key skill: reading)*

2. **Research:** Have students research the possible role of cruciferous vegetables in lowering the risk of certain kinds of cancer. Have students report their findings to the class. *(Key skills: reading, research)*

Did you know that some "vegetables" are really fruits? Various parts of plants are eaten as vegetables.

❖ **Roots.** Carrots, beets, and turnips are examples of root vegetables. Roots store a plant's food supplies and send nutrients and moisture to the rest of the plant.

❖ **Stems.** Celery is a common stem vegetable.

❖ **Tubers.** A **tuber** (TOO-burr) is a large underground stem that stores nutrients. Potatoes are tubers.

❖ **Leaves.** Spinach, lettuce, and cooking greens such as kale and collards are leafy vegetables. Leaves are thc plant's manufacturing areas. Through a process called photosynthesis (foe-toe-SIN-thuh-siss), they turn sunlight, carbon dioxide, and water into high-energy carbohydrates.

❖ **Bulbs.** Onions and garlic are examples of bulbs. A bulb is made up of layers of fleshy leaves surrounding a portion of a stem.

❖ **Flowers.** Broccoli is an example of a vegetable that includes the flowers of a plant, along with the attached stems.

❖ **Seeds.** Corn, beans, and peas are vegetables which come from the edible seeds of plants. Seeds are high in carbohydrates and other nutrients because they are the part of the plant from which new plants grow.

❖ **Fruits.** Some foods commonly called vegetables, including cucumbers, eggplants, and tomatoes, are really the fruit of the plant. The fruit is the part of the plant that holds the seeds.

Nutrients in Fruits and Vegetables

In general, fresh fruits and vegetables are excellent sources of vitamins, minerals, and fiber. Some have higher amounts than others. They are also low in fat and sodium and have no cholesterol.

As you may recall, only plant foods contain beta carotene, which the body uses to make vitamin A. Carotene gives food an orange color, so yellow or orange fruits and vegetables are excellent sources.

Dark green leafy vegetables, such as cooking greens and broccoli, are also excellent sources of beta carotene. Eat dark-green leafy vegetables several times a week—they are a good source of vitamins and minerals.

Research shows that a group of vegetables, called **cruciferous** (crew-SIH-furruss) **vegetables,** may also lower the risk of certain kinds of cancer. Cruciferous vegetables include broccoli, brussels sprouts, cabbage, collards, kale, mustard greens, cauliflower, rutabagas, and turnips.

Most people think of citrus fruits as the main source of vitamin C. However, many other fruits and vegetables are rich in this vitamin, including kiwi, strawberries, cantaloupe, cabbage, and potatoes.

Cruciferous vegetables are members of the cabbage family. They not only provide vitamins, minerals, and fiber, but may help protect against cancer. Make them a regular part of your food choices.

Food and Nutrition Science

Nutrition Comparison: Have students compare the nutrition information on the labels of fruits packed in water or fruit juice with those packed in syrup. Which has the most calories? Are there other differences in nutritional value among the fruits?

The Food Guide Pyramid recommends two to four servings of fruits each day and three to five servings of vegetables. Typical servings of fruit include 1 medium apple, banana, or orange; 1/2 cup (125 mL) of chopped, cooked, or canned fruit; or 3/4 cup (175 mL) of pure fruit juice. Vegetable servings might include 1 cup (250 mL) of raw, leafy vegetables; 1/2 cup (125 mL) of other vegetables (cooked or chopped raw); or 3/4 cup (175 mL) of vegetable juice.

Buying Fresh Produce

Some fruits and vegetables, such as bananas, apples, pears, grapes, spinach, and broccoli, are available all year. Others, such as asparagus, peaches, plums, and mangoes, have a specific growing season. During this season, the fruit or vegetable is plentiful,

Produce is often priced by the pound. In many stores, you can check the weight of loose produce using the scale provided in the department.

prices usually are lower, and the quality is better. Seasonal items are often imported during the off-season months, but prices are higher. When shopping, look for items that are in season as well as year-round favorites.

Produce can be purchased loose, in a bag or plastic-covered tray, or unitized. **Unitized** means that large produce, such as broccoli, is held together with a rubber band or a plastic tie. If you want a smaller amount of produce than is in a package, ask a clerk to open it and repackage the amount you want.

Here are some additional general guidelines for buying produce.

❖ Buy top-quality fruits and vegetables. They will give you the most nutrients for the money and will last longer. Poor-quality produce is a waste of money.

❖ Buy only what you can store and use. Most high-quality fresh fruits and vegetables last about a week in the refrigerator.

❖ Inspect packaged produce carefully. If the package has stains or an unpleasant odor, it may be a sign of damaged or spoiled produce.

❖ Avoid any produce that looks wilted, shriveled, bruised, or decayed. Some produce may have natural blemishes, which do not affect quality. Grapefruit and oranges, for instance, may have a brownish scale.

❖ Buy by weight, when possible. Except for leafy vegetables, fruits and vegetables should feel heavy for their size.

Buying Fresh Fruits

Fruits are usually picked when they are mature. **Mature fruits** have reached their full size and color but may not have ripened. That means they are hard and have not yet reached full flavor.

Ripe fruits are tender with a pleasant aroma and fully developed flavors. To test for ripeness on most fruit, press very gently. The fruit should give a little under the pressure. Don't press so hard that you damage the fruit.

Teaching . . .

• **Buying Fresh Produce**

(text pages 413-415)

Comprehension Check

1. Ask students to identify three ways in which produce can be purchased. *(loose, in a bag or plastic-covered tray, and unitized.)*

2. Ask students to list general guidelines for buying produce. *(See the list on page 413.)*

3. Ask students to explain the difference between mature and ripened fruits. *(Mature fruits have reached their full size but are still hard and have not yet reached full flavor. Ripened fruits are tender and have fully developed flavors.)*

Student Experiences

1. **Display:** Using a display of fresh fruits and vegetables, discuss guidelines for buying them. *(Key skill: evaluation)*

2. **Supermarket Survey:** Have students visit one supermarket and record the convenience forms of fruits and vegetables available (such as ready-to-eat carrot and celery sticks). Discuss their findings. *(Key skill: consumer awareness)*

3. **Field Trip:** Take a field trip to the produce department of a supermarket or to a farmer's market. Ask the produce manager to point out signs of quality and to give buying tips for fresh produce. Ask the manager to explain how fruits and vegetables are priced and how price is affected by season. Have students look for examples of loose, packaged, and unitized produce. Which fruits and vegetables are priced per pound, each, or per package or unit? *(Key skill: consumer awareness)*

Teaching . . .

• Storing Fresh Produce

(text pages 415-416)

Comprehension Check

1. Ask students to explain why it is better not to wash produce until just before you use it. *(The added moisture speeds up spoiling caused by bacteria and can cause mold to grow.)*

2. Ask students to explain why potatoes, onions, and sweet potatoes should not be refrigerated. Where should these foods be stored? *(The flavor of potatoes changes because the starch turns to sugar; onions and sweet potatoes decay; they should be kept in a cool, dark, dry place.)*

3. Discuss guidelines for buying and using convenience fruits and vegetables. *(See the list on page 416.)*

Ask students if they have ever eaten plantains. Ask students who have to describe the taste and the method of preparation. You may want to prepare plantains for students to taste test. Ask how they might determine how to store plantains.

Bananas grow in the tropics. The large bunches are harvested while the fruit is still green. They will ripen naturally on the way to the marketplace or after purchase.

Fruits are easy to ripen. Place them in a brown paper bag at room temperature until they reach the stage of ripeness you want. If you use a plastic bag, punch holes in it to allow excess moisture to evaporate. Otherwise, the fruit may mold and decay before it ripens.

To avoid having fresh fruits ripen too quickly or all at once, buy fruits at different stages of ripeness. You can also refrigerate unripe fruits, which slows down the ripening process. As you need ripe fruit, take it out and let it ripen at room temperature.

When buying fresh fruits, look for fruit that is mature and at the stage of ripeness you want. Choose fruits that are typical in shape and size. Fruits that are much smaller than usual, or misshapen, are usually of lower quality.

Choose fruits that have reached their natural color, with no green showing anywhere. Green fruits, in most cases, will not ripen well. There are some exceptions:

❖ Some fruits are naturally green in color, such as certain varieties of pears, apples, and grapes.

❖ A few fruits, such as bananas, are picked green and will turn their natural color when they ripen.

❖ The skins of oranges sometimes turn green when exposed to light, but flavor and quality are not affected. Oranges, like all citrus fruits, must be ripe when picked.

In Puerto Rican cuisine, *plantains* are a staple. A plantain resembles a green banana, but because it is starchy, like a potato, it is cooked before eating. Plantain can be roasted, fried, boiled, baked, stuffed, or used in casseroles.

414 **Chapter 16: Fruits and Vegetables**

More About Produce

Some produce that you buy in the store has been waxed. The wax replaces the natural protective coating that is removed when the produce is washed after harvest. It also helps make the foods look better and helps prevent moisture loss, which would make the produce wither. Produce such as apples, bananas, cucumbers, oranges, peppers, and squash is often waxed.

All waxes used have been approved by the FDA as safe. However, some people have questioned whether consumers are being given enough information about the types of wax found on the produce they buy.

Buying Fresh Vegetables

Fresh vegetables are already ripe when you buy them. Select those typical in shape and medium in size. Misshapen vegetables may not be of the best quality. Large vegetables might be overripe. Avoid vegetables that look like they have discoloring which indicates decay.

Storing Fresh Produce

Unless the produce is dirty, it should not be washed until you are ready to use it. The added moisture will speed up spoiling caused by bacteria. Moisture remaining on produce can also cause mold to grow. If it's necessary to wash produce before storing, be sure it is thoroughly dry before you refrigerate it.

Most fresh fruits and vegetables, except potatoes, sweet potatoes, and onions, should be stored in the refrigerator. Refrigerate produce in the crisper section or in brown paper bags. If you use plastic bags, punch holes in them so some of the moisture can escape. Don't line the bottom of the crisper with paper towels. They get soggy and might cause produce to decay or get moldy.

When potatoes are refrigerated, the starch turns to sugar, changing their flavor. Onions and sweet potatoes will mold and decay when refrigerated. Therefore, store potatoes, sweet potatoes, and onions in a cool, dark, dry place. Sometimes it's difficult to find such a spot in today's homes. If stored at room temperature, these foods will keep for a relatively short time. Therefore, buy only what you can use during that time.

✔ SAFETY CHECK

Potatoes that are exposed to light may develop a greenish color. The green color itself is harmless. However, it indicates that the potato may contain a harmful, bitter-tasting compound called solanine. Potato sprouts also contain solanine. Cut away sprouts and green portions before using potatoes. Discard potatoes that have a bitter taste.

Storing potatoes and onions separately will lengthen their shelf life. What type of storage area is best?

1. **Demonstrations:** Have students demonstrate showing the correct way to store various fresh fruits and vegetables. Discuss storage guidelines. (Key skill: management skills)

2. **Posters:** Have students prepare posters that illustrate the guidelines for buying fresh fruits and vegetables. (Key skill: creativity)

3. **Checklists:** Have students develop a checklist of guidelines for storing fresh fruits and vegetables. Have students use the checklist when storing fruits and vegetables at home or in the foods lab. (Key skill: writing)

Safety Check

Have interested students research solanine to find out in what ways it is harmful and why it appears when potatoes are exposed to light. Ask students to report their findings to the class. Point out that refrigerator storage is not recommended because this causes sugar to build up and the potatoes to discolor during cooking due to the Maillard reaction. (See page 269.)

Food and Nutrition Science

Ethylene and Ripening: As fruit ripens, it gives off ethylene (EH-thuh-lean) gas which acts as a ripening agent. Scientists are still working to understand exactly how ethylene works to ripen fruit. However, they do know that ethylene produced by a ripe fruit can stimulate the ethylene production in under-ripe fruit, speeding the ripening process.

Completing the Section

Review

- Ask students to summarize the main ideas in this section.
- Have students complete the Section Review. (Answers appear below.)

Evaluation

- Display a variety of fruits and vegetables in various stages of maturity, ripeness, and quality. Number each fruit or vegetable. Have students examine each piece and write a short summary of whether the fruit is mature, ripe, damaged in any way, etc.
- Have students take the quiz for Section 16.1. (Refer to the *Section Quizzes* booklet or use the *Testmaker Software*.)

Reteaching

- Provide students with a list of plant parts that can be eaten as vegetables. Have students write an example of each, along with storage methods for that vegetable.
- Refer to the *Reteaching Activities* booklet for the Section 16.1 activity sheet.

Enrichment

- Have students research and write short reports about the countries in which the fruits shown on page 410-411 are grown.

Closure

- Lead a discussion about the proper storage and handling of fruits and vegetables.

Convenience Fruits and Vegetables

Here are some tips for buying and using convenience forms of fruits and vegetables:

❖ Canned fruits usually have less fiber than fresh fruits, but are still a good source of vitamins and minerals. Choose whole fruit, slices, or pieces, depending on how you will use them. To cut down on sugar, avoid fruits canned or frozen in heavy syrups.

❖ For a quick, low-fat dessert, try pureeing canned fruit in a blender and serving it over angel food cake.

❖ To serve frozen fruits, thaw them only partially. A few ice crystals should remain so the fruit is firm and cold, not mushy.

❖ Dried fruits are sweet and chewy—a concentrated form of energy. They can be eaten as snacks, cooked, or used in recipes.

❖ Most canned vegetables contain added sodium. To reduce the amount of sodium, drain the liquid from vegetables and rinse them before cooking. However, you will lose some nutrients that are found in the liquid, too.

❖ If you have freezer space, buy frozen vegetables in large bags so you can use just the amount you need. Cook frozen vegetables as directed before serving.

❖ Dried vegetables may be found in boxed casserole mixes and soup mixes. They must be rehydrated during the cooking process before you can eat them.

❖ Many fruit and vegetable juices are available. They do not contain fiber, but are good sources of many nutrients. If the label says "juice," the product must be 100 percent juice. Products that are not pure juice must be called by another name, such as fruit drink.

Convenience forms of fruits and vegetables give consumers more options.

■ Section 16.1 Review ■

RECALL THE FACTS

1. What is a tuber? Give an example of a tuber vegetable.

2. What is the difference between mature and ripe fruit?

3. Name three qualities to look for when choosing fresh vegetables.

4. Why should most produce be stored unwashed?

5. Give two suggestions for using convenience forms of fruits and vegetables.

DISCUSS YOUR IDEAS

6. Twenty years ago, supermarkets did not display as great a variety of fruits and vegetables as most do today. Discuss the reasons for this change. How does this benefit consumers?

APPLY YOUR LEARNING

7. Use the "Nutritive Value in Foods" chart in the Appendix to identify five fruits and five vegetables that are high in vitamins A and C.

■ Answers to Section Review ■

1. A large underground stem that stores nutrients; potatoes.
2. Mature fruits are fully grown but are still hard and have not yet reached full flavor. Ripened fruits are tender and have fully developed flavors.

3. Typical in shape, medium in size, no discoloration.
4. Because the added moisture speeds up bacterial decay and promotes mold.

5. See the list on page 416.
6. Answers will vary. Example: Distribution systems have become more advanced.
7. Answers will vary.

Preparing Raw Fruits and Vegetables

OBJECTIVES

After studying this section, you should be able to:

- Describe how to wash produce.
- Give suggestions for preparing and serving raw fruits and vegetables.

LOOK FOR THIS TERM

enzymatic browning

Fresh fruits and vegetables, eaten raw, are nature's nutritious convenience foods. They need little preparation. In minutes, you can have a raw carrot for a snack, strawberry slices to top your cereal, or a pear for a quick dessert.

Unlike fruits, not all vegetables can be eaten raw. Those which can be include broccoli, carrots, cauliflower, celery, cucumbers, jicama, mushrooms, radishes, sweet peppers, and tomatoes.

Vegetables such as these, which are easy to chew and digest, can be eaten raw for snacks. How might raw vegetables be used in meals?

Section 16.2 Preparing Raw Fruits and Vegetables

Introducing the Section

Motivators

- Ask students to name a food that is tasty, eaten raw, and easily prepared in minutes. How many students named fresh fruits and vegetables? Which ones were named?
- Demonstrate a variety of ways to cut fresh produce to create interesting shapes.

Objectives

- Have students read the section objectives. Discuss the purpose of studying the section.

Vocabulary

- Pronounce the terms listed under "Look for These Terms." Have students find the terms and their definitions in the section.

Guided Reading

- Have students look at the headings within Section 16.2 to preview the concepts that will be discussed.
- Have students read the section and complete the appropriate part of the Chapter 16 Study Guide in the *Student Workbook.*

Teacher's Classroom Resources—Section 16.2

Refer to these resources in the TCR package:

Reproducible Lesson Plans

Student Workbook

Extending the Text

Reteaching Activities

Foods Lab Resources

Food Science Resources

Section Quizzes

Testmaker Software

Color Transparencies

Teaching . . .

- **Washing Fresh Produce**
- **Cutting Fresh Produce**
- **Serving and Storing Cut Produce**

(text pages 418-420)

Comprehension Check

1. Ask students to explain why it is important to wash fresh fruits and vegetables before eating or cooking them. *(It helps remove dirt, microorganisms, and residues.)*

2. Ask students to describe various ways to cut fruits and vegetables. *(Wedges, slices, cubes; vegetables may also be shredded.)*

3. Ask students to explain how to prevent fruits from darkening. *(Coat them with some form of ascorbic acid—vitamin C—as soon as they are cut.)*

4. Ask students to explain how cut vegetables should be stored. *(in the refrigerator, tightly sealed)*

TIPS for Success

For some recipes, students may need to section citrus fruits. To do so easily, follow these steps: 1) Slice off both ends with a sharp knife; 2) score and peel of the skin; 3) With a sharp knife, loosen the sections from the membranes. Steaming the fruit for two to four minutes before step 1 makes peeling easier.

See Also . . .

- "Illegal Chemical Residues," text page 358.
- "Contaminants," text page 359.

Washing Fresh Produce

Fresh fruits and vegetables should be washed before they are eaten or cooked. Washing helps remove pesticide residues, dirt, and germs. Even if you're going to peel or pare produce, washing helps keep chemicals and dirt from being transferred to the edible parts.

For tender fruits and vegetables, wash carefully in cool, clear water. Be sure all visible dirt is removed and that cracks and crevices are clean. Use a stiff brush to scrub thick-skinned produce, such as squash. Also scrub vegetables that might have a lot of dirt, such as potatoes. To minimize nutrient loss, do not let produce soak in water.

Cutting Fresh Produce

After it is washed, produce may need to be peeled, pared, or cut into pieces.

Cut or peel away the thick, inedible skins of some fruits, such as oranges and pineapples. A few vegetables may have to be pared, such as jicama. Also remove other inedible parts, such as the seeds of sweet peppers, the stems of fruits, and any soft spots or damaged areas.

✔ SAFETY CHECK

Never use detergent to wash produce. The produce may absorb the detergent, which can make people ill if swallowed. In addition, it's possible that the detergent could react with any pesticides and waxes found on the produce. The reaction might produce other chemicals, possibly harmful ones.

TIPS for Success

Peeling Citrus Fruit

Here's an easy way to peel an orange or grapefruit. First, divide the peel into quarters by scoring it with a sharp knife. Begin the cuts at the stem end and continue around to the opposite end. Then pull each section of the peel away with your fingers.

To retain the most nutrients, don't pare produce with edible skins, such as apples. However, if you're concerned about removing wax and residues, pare the produce. Even though some nutrients will be lost in the skin, most will remain in the produce.

Fruits and vegetables can be cut into pieces to make them easier to eat or more attractive. To keep nutrient losses to a minimum, cut fruits and vegetables into the largest possible pieces. Also, serve them as soon after cutting as possible.

Fruits can be cut into many different shapes. For example, fruits such as bananas, oranges, and kiwis can be sliced crosswise. You might cut apples, pears, or peaches into wedges and remove the core or pit. Some fruits can be cut into cubes and served with wooden picks.

Vegetables may be cut in the same shapes as fruits or shredded on a grater. Most can also be cut into strips.

More About Serving Fruits

Some fresh fruits are treated with chemicals to maintain quality and increase storage time. These include apples, lemons, some melons, bananas, grapefruit, and watermelons. In some cases, the chemicals are mixed with the wax that is used to prevent moisture loss. Fungicides, batericides, ripening inhibitors, and coloring agents may also be added.

Preventing Cut Fruits from Darkening

Some fruits retain an attractive appearance after they are cut. These include citrus fruits, melons, pineapples, and kiwis. However, many other fruits will turn dark when the flesh inside is exposed to the air. The discoloration is due to a process called **enzymatic browning.**

The easiest way to keep fresh fruits from discoloring is to coat them with some form of ascorbic acid (vitamin C) as soon as they are cut. One solution is to dip the pieces of cut fruit in lemon juice. You can also buy an ascorbic acid powder to mix with water and sprinkle on cut fruit.

Unlike fruits, vegetables do not turn brown when they are cut. If they are allowed to stand for several days, however, they may begin to darken.

Lemon juice can keep banana slices from turning dark. Would you need to use lemon juice on any other fruits in this salad? Why or why not?

Science Connection

Chemistry:
Enzymatic Browning

Oxygen in the air will eventually cause any cut fruit to turn brown. However, the reaction occurs more quickly in fruits that contain a specific enzyme (called *polyphenoloxidase*.) The fruit, the enzyme, and oxygen in the air react to cause the discoloration. Enzymatic browning can be prevented with an acid, which slows down the action of the enzyme.

■ ■ ■

Serving and Storing Cut Produce

An assortment of cut-up raw fruits and vegetables is a welcome addition to any gathering. When arranging the fruits and vegetables on a platter, use your imagination. Don't just heap the food in any way. Instead, try to arrange it in an artistic pattern. That way, you have more fun preparing the food and your guests will enjoy the beauty of the arrangement. For instance, you could arrange the different kinds of produce into wedge-shaped sections, like pieces of pie. Keep in mind that color contrasts make a pleasing display.

If you've arranged the platter ahead of time, cover it tightly with plastic wrap, squeezing out as much air as possible. Refrigerate until serving time. You might want to serve the produce with a tasty low-fat dip, such as one made with yogurt.

Student Experiences

1. **Demonstration:** Demonstrate how to wash fresh fruits and vegetables to remove pesticide residues, dirt, and germs. Show how to use a vegetable brush. Point out that soaking produce in water causes nutrient loss. Note that produce should never be washed in detergent. *(Key skill: health)*

2. **Student Demonstrations:** Have students work in pairs to demonstrate how to cut fresh fruits and vegetables. Discuss reasons to avoid paring produce with edible skins. Have students demonstrate different ways to cut fruits and vegetables. *(Key skill: kitchen management skills)*

Lab Experience

Have students arrange attractive trays of cut-up raw fruits and vegetables to serve for a special occasion. Have students make yogurt-based dips to serve with the fruit and vegetable trays.

Food and Nutrition Science

Enzymatic Browning Experiment: See the *Food Science Resources* booklet for the "Enzymatic Browning of Fruit" teaching guidelines and student experiment worksheet. The experiment allows students to compare the effects of various liquids on the browning of fresh fruit.

Completing the Section

Review

- Ask students to summarize the main ideas in this section.
- Have students complete the Section Review. (Answers appear below.)

Evaluation

- Give students fresh fruit and vegetables and have them wash and prepare the produce for use on a snack tray.
- Have students take the quiz for Section 16.2. (Refer to the *Section Quizzes* booklet or use the *Testmaker Software*.)

Reteaching

- Show pictures of various fruits. Have students identify the fruits and describe at least one way each could be prepared.
- Refer to the *Reteaching Activities* booklet for the Section 16.2 activity sheet.

Enrichment

- Have students research interesting ways to prepare and serve raw fruits and vegetables. Ask students to write a short report of their findings.

Closure

- Lead a brainstorming session to list a variety of occasions for which fresh fruits and vegetables might be appropriate.

A display of raw produce can be a work of art, as this example from Thailand shows. Simple arrangements using basic shapes can also be attractive and take little time to create.

Try keeping cut-up vegetables in the refrigerator as handy snacks. Store them in a tightly sealed plastic bag or on a plate covered with plastic. Squeeze out as much air as possible to keep nutrients from being destroyed by oxygen.

Section 16.2 Review

RECALL THE FACTS

1. How should thick-skinned produce be washed?

2. Name two ways to keep cut fruit from turning brown.

3. Why might you want to arrange raw fruits and vegetables in a pleasing pattern before serving?

DISCUSS YOUR IDEAS

4. How might people be encouraged to think of raw fruits and vegetables as convenience foods?

APPLY YOUR LEARNING

5. Plan an attractive platter of raw fruits or vegetables that you might serve at a party. What fruits or vegetables would you include? What shape would you use for each? Describe or sketch how the foods would be arranged on the platter. Evaluate your plan for nutrition as well as variety of shape and color.

Answers to Section Review

1. With a vegetable brush.

2. Dip it in lemon juice or sprinkle a mixture of powdered ascorbic acid and water on the fruit.

3. It makes the food more aesthetically pleasing.

4. Answers will vary. Example: Educate the people about the ease with which fresh fruits and vegetables can be prepared.

5. Answers will vary.

Thinking About the Recipe

Read the recipe for "Strawberry Fruit Dip" and answer the following questions.

1. How would you prepare this recipe if you didn't have a blender or electric mixer?
2. What are some creative ways you could arrange and serve the fresh fruit and dip?

Strawberry Fruit Dip

Key Skills: Preparing fresh fruit and dip.

Strawberry Fruit Dip

Customary	Ingredients	Metric
8-oz. package	Nonfat or low-fat cream cheese	224-gram package
16-oz. package	Frozen sweetened strawberries, thawed	384-gram package
2 Tbsp.	Plain, nonfat yogurt	30 mL
	Assorted fresh fruit (strawberries, pineapple, banana, kiwi), cut into bite-size pieces	

Yield: 2 ¾ cups (675 mL)

Directions

Equipment: Blender or electric mixer
1. Place the cheese, strawberries, and yogurt in the blender or mixer bowl.
2. Whip until smooth.
3. Refrigerate for at least 2 hours before serving.
4. Serve dip with fresh fruit.

Nutrition Information

Per 1/4 cup (50 mL) serving (approximate): 78 calories, 2 g protein, 11 g carbohydrate, 3 g fat, 7 mg cholesterol, 109 mg sodium

Using the Recipe

- Have students read the recipe and discuss each step. Review safety and sanitation procedures that apply to this recipe. Caution students never to run the blender without first putting the lid on securely. Remind students that the blades of the blender are extremely sharp.
- Have each lab team fill out a work plan. (See the *Foods Lab Resources* booklet.)
- Have the students check off the ingredients and equipment listed on the recipe worksheet and prepare the recipe.
- Have students complete the evaluation and questions on the recipe worksheet.

See Also . . .

The *Foods Lab Resources* booklet for the "Strawberry Fruit Dip" recipe worksheet and other recipe alternatives.

Answers to Thinking About the Recipe

1. Allow fruit to soften somewhat and use a pastry blender, masher, or fork.
2. Answers will vary. Suggest attractive arrangement of fruit and creative containers for dip.

Section 16.3
Cooking Fruits and Vegetables

Cooking Fruits and Vegetables

OBJECTIVES

After studying this section, you should be able to:

- Identify the effects of cooking on fruits and vegetables.
- Describe methods for cooking fruits.
- Describe methods for cooking vegetables.

LOOK FOR THIS TERM

chlorophyll

"I've never tasted vegetables this flavorful," thought Jolene as she enjoyed a meal with her friend's family. "The colors are so bright, too. I wonder what makes the difference?"

The difference Jolene noticed may have been due to the way the vegetables were prepared. Paying close attention to cooking methods can make a big difference in how cooked vegetables and fruits look and taste.

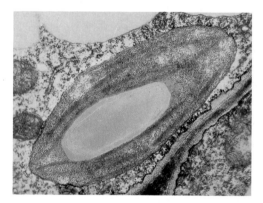

This image shows part of the leaf cell of a garden pea, greatly magnified by an electron microscope. Colors have been added to highlight the different areas. The green strands contain the chlorophyll pigments that give green plants their color. With proper cooking, green vegetables keep their natural color.

Effects of Cooking on Fruits and Vegetables

Cooking results in noticeable changes in fruits and vegetables, especially in texture, color, and flavor.

- ❖ **Texture.** Heat softens the cell walls, making fruits and vegetables more tender. Many vegetables, such as green beans and winter squash, must be cooked to be edible. Starchy vegetables are easier to digest when cooked. If overcooked, fruits and vegetables become mushy.
- ❖ **Color.** When properly cooked, fruits and vegetables retain pleasing colors. Green vegetables get their color from **chlorophyll** (KLORE-uh-fill), the chemical compound that plants use to turn the sun's energy into food. If overcooked, green vegetables can turn an unpleasant olive green.
- ❖ **Flavor.** The heat of cooking releases flavors, making them more noticeable. Fruit flavors mellow somewhat and taste less acid. Herbs, spices, or other foods can be added during cooking, allowing their flavors to mingle with the natural flavor of the fruit or vegetable. When overcooked, fruits and vegetables lose their flavor and may even develop an unpleasant flavor.

Cooking can also result in nutrient losses. To minimize loss of vitamin C when cooking fruits and vegetables, keep them whole or in large pieces. Cook them quickly using methods that require only a small amount of water, such as simmering in a tightly covered pan or microwaving. Serve cooked vegetables and fruits with the cooking liquid whenever possible.

Cooking Fresh Fruits

Cooking fruits is a way of adding variety to your food choices. Cooked fruits can be served hot or chilled. They may be part of the main course, a snack, or a dessert.

Before cooking, remember to wash fresh fruits as described in Section 16.2. Fruits can be cooked by several different methods.

Poaching Fruits

Poaching, or stewing, is a method of cooking fruit in simmering liquid. The goal is to retain the shape of the fruit as it cooks.

Fruits that can be poached include plums, berries, apples, and pears. Small fruits, such as berries, are left whole. Apples and pears may be cut in large pieces.

When poaching, use enough water to cover the fruit. Add sugar at the beginning of cooking. The sugar is not just for sweetness, but to help retain the shape of the fruit. Sugar added at the beginning of cooking strengthens the cell walls so that the heat won't break down the texture.

For flavoring, you may also want to add lemon or orange rind, a cinnamon stick, or vanilla. Simmer, uncovered, until the fruit is tender but still holds its shape.

Poaching is a way to add flavor to fruit while retaining the shape for an attractive presentation.

Food and Nutrition Science

Effects of Acids and Bases Experiment: See the *Food Science Resources* booklet for the "Effects of Acids and Bases on Vegetables" teaching guidelines and student experiment worksheet. The experiment tests the effects of acids and bases on the color, aroma, texture, and flavor of cooked vegetables.

Teaching . . .

- **Effects of Cooking on Fruits and Vegetables**
- **Cooking Fresh Fruits**

(text pages 422-424)

Comprehension Check

1. Ask students to describe three ways in which cooking affects fresh fruits and vegetables. *(Makes them more tender; enhances or retains color; enhances flavors.)*

2. Ask students to explain why it is important to serve cooked vegetables and fruits with their cooking liquids whenever possible. *(Cooking results in nutrient loss; the nutrients are retained in the cooking liquids.)*

3. Discuss various ways to prepare cooked fruits. *(Poaching, making fruit sauces, baking, and microwaving.)*

Student Experiences

1. **Class Discussion:** Ask students to describe ways in which cooking affects fruits and vegetables. What happens when fruits and vegetables are overcooked? How can nutrient loss be reduced? *(Key skill: kitchen management skills)*

2. **Finding Recipes:** Have students find recipes for poaching, baking, and microwaving fruits. *(Key skill: reading)*

Lab Experience

Have students prepare homemade applesauce, with some students adding sugar before cooking the apples, and others adding sugar after the apples are cooked. What conclusions can students draw about when the sugar should be added?

Teaching . . .

- **Simmering Vegetables**
- **Steaming Vegetables**
- **Microwaving Vegetables**

(text pages 424-425)

Comprehension Check

1. Ask students to describe the procedure for simmering vegetables. *(Pour a small amount of water into a medium saucepan. Cover and bring to a boil. Add vegetables, cover, and bring to a boil again. Lower the heat until the water just simmers then cook, covered, until vegetables are tender.)*

2. Ask students to explain how steaming vegetables differs from simmering them. *(In steaming, the vegetables do not touch the water, so more nutrients are retained. They are cooked by the steam produced by the boiling water.)*

3. Ask students why it is important to remember to pierce the skins of vegetables such as potatoes and squash before cooking them in the microwave. *(The vegetables will burst or explode if they are not pierced.)*

TIPS for Success

Tell students that the reason tomatoes keep their color when cooked, even though they are red, is because that are naturally acid. Ask students if they can think of other red vegetables that retain their color when cooked. See the "Food and Nutrition Science" box on page 423 for a related experiment.

Fruit Sauces

Fruit sauces, such as applesauce, are also made by cooking the fruit in liquid. In this case, however, the goal is to break down the texture. Therefore, sugar is not added until after cooking.

Besides apples, many fruits—such as peaches, plums, apricots, and pears—can be made into a sauce. Try combining two kinds of fruit for a different flavor.

To make a fruit sauce, pare the fruit and cut it into small pieces for faster cooking. Add water to a saucepan to a depth of about 1/4 inch (0.6 cm). Put the fruit in the saucepan. Bring to a boil, lower the heat to simmer, and cover the pan. Cook, stirring occasionally, until the fruit has broken down. The time will vary, depending on the kind of fruit and the size of the pieces. Sweeten as desired with sugar, honey, or syrup. Spices or other flavorings may also be added.

Baking Fruits

Care must be taken when you bake fruits to avoid overcooking. Best results are obtained with firm fruits, such as apples, pears, and bananas, that are whole or in large pieces.

Apples are probably the most popular baked fruit. They are easy to prepare and make a delicious ending to any meal. Use a variety of apple suited to cooking, such as Rome Beauty. Before cooking, core the apples and cut a thin strip of skin from around the middle. This will enable the apples to expand as they cook so they will not burst. You can fill the core cavity with raisins and seasonings such as cinnamon or nutmeg. Place the apples in a baking dish and pour hot water around them to a depth of 1/4 inch (6 mm). Bake at 350°F (180°C) until tender, about 45 to 60 minutes.

Microwaving Fruits

Fruits are easy to prepare in the microwave oven. They cook quickly and keep their fresh flavor and their shape.

For variety, try baking sliced apples instead of the whole fruit. Seasonings such as cinnamon and nutmeg can give the flavor of apple pie with less fat and fewer calories.

Because they are so tender, however, they can easily overcook. Watch the timing carefully.

Cover fruits when microwaving them, but leave a small opening for excess steam to escape. If you're cooking whole fruits, such as plums, puncture them with a fork in several places to keep them from bursting.

The basic steps in poaching, making a fruit sauce, and baking fruit are similar for microwave and conventional cooking. Power level and cooking time will vary, so check the owner's manual or a microwave cookbook.

Cooking Fresh Vegetables

Before cooking vegetables, wash them carefully and trim away inedible parts. If necessary, pare and cut the vegetables into pieces. Small pieces will cook faster than larger ones, but will also lose more nutrients.

Food and Nutrition Science

Size and Cooking Time Experiment: See the *Food Science Resources* booklet for the "Effect of Vegetable Piece Size on Cooking Time" teaching guidelines and student experiment worksheet. This experiment clearly illustrates the effects of cooking and overcooking vegetables, as well as the link between piece size and cooking time.

Fresh vegetables can be cooked by several different methods. The timing and method depends on the tenderness of the vegetable and the size of the pieces.

Simmering Vegetables

Vegetables can be simmered in a covered pan in a small amount of water. Allow about 1/2 cup (125 mL) water for four servings of vegetables. Pour the water into a medium-size saucepan, cover, and bring to a boil. Add the vegetables, cover, and bring to a boil again. Then lower the heat until the water just simmers. Cook, covered, until vegetables are tender.

Steaming Vegetables

Steaming is a nutritious way to cook vegetables. Fewer nutrients are lost because the vegetables are not cooked in water. However, steaming sometimes takes a little longer than simmering.

Place the steamer basket in a saucepan with a tight-fitting cover. Add water to a depth just below the bottom of the steamer. Cover the pan and bring the water to a boil. Add the vegetables to the steamer basket and cover. Reduce the heat slightly, but not so much that the water stops boiling and producing steam. Steam the vegetables until tender.

Microwaving Vegetables

Microwaving cooks vegetables quickly using only a small amount of water. Therefore, the vegetables lose few nutrients and keep their color, texture, and flavor.

Remember, larger pieces will take longer to cook than smaller ones. Pieces that are the same size and shape will cook more evenly.

When cooking whole vegetables that have a skin, such as potatoes or squash, pierce the skin with a fork to keep them from bursting.

If parts of a vegetable are more tender than others, arrange the tender parts toward the center and the less tender ones toward the edge of the baking dish. For instance, the stems of broccoli and asparagus are less tender and would be placed toward the edge.

Always cover the container to retain moisture. Follow directions in the owner's manual or cooking guide for cooking times and special instructions.

TIPS for Success

Retaining Color in Vegetables

❖ Some red vegetables, such as red cabbage and beets, can turn blue if simmered in water that contains certain minerals. To avoid discoloration, add a small amount of an acid food, such as lemon juice or vinegar, to the water during cooking.

❖ Don't add baking soda when simmering vegetables. Although it helps retain color in green vegetables, baking soda destroys vitamins and creates a mushy texture. For a bright green color, avoid overcooking the vegetable.

Recipes for cooking red cabbage or beets often include lemon juice or vinegar. Why?

Student Experiences

1. **Demonstration:** Have students view a demonstration of cooking vegetables in the microwave oven. Review guidelines for using the microwave oven (Section 9.3, page 271) and discuss the advantages of microwave cooking. *(Key skill: kitchen management skills)*

2. **Demonstration:** Demonstrate the proper way to cook vegetables in liquid and steam. Sample for flavor and discuss the advantages of each method. *(Key skill: evaluation)*

3. **Recipe Comparisons:** Have students locate recipes for preparing a specific vegetable. By what methods may the vegetable be prepared? Which recipes retain the vegetables' natural nutritional advantages? Which recipes add fat to the vegetables? Which cooking methods require the longest cooking times? *(Key skill: reading)*

4. **Small Group:** Have students work in small groups and use brainstorming and problem-solving techniques to think up ways to encourage a young child to eat vegetables. You may want to ask the class to put together a booklet of ideas to distribute to parents of a preschool or kindergarten class. *(Key skill: problem solving)*

Conventional vs. Microwave Cooking Experiment: See the *Food Science Resources* booklet for the "Cooking Vegetables by Conventional and Microwave Cooking Methods" teaching guidelines and student experiment worksheet. This experiment compares the effects of both cooking method and time on the color, texture, and flavor of broccoli.

Teaching . . .

- **Baking Vegetables**
- **Frying Vegetables**

(text pages 426-427)

Comprehension Check

1. Ask students to list vegetables that are suitable for baking. *(Potatoes, winter squash, sweet potatoes.)*

2. Ask students to explain the advantage of the wide temperature range at which potatoes can be baked. *(They can be baked at the same time as other foods.)*

3. Ask students to name three different methods of frying vegetables. *(Sautéing, stir frying, and deep-fat frying.)*

Student Experiences

1. **Class Discussion:** Discuss the nutritional advantages of vegetables. What can cause normally low-fat vegetables to become high-fat items? How can vegetables be flavored without adding fat during cooking or at the table? *(Key skill: health)*

2. **Finding Recipes:** Have students look for recipes for baking or frying vegetables. Ask students to compare the recipes on the basis of added fats, cooking time, and nutritional value of the food after cooking. *(Key skill: reading)*

Lab Experience

Have each lab group prepare fresh and convenience forms of the same vegetable in a different way. Each group should label their food with cooking time, cost, and nutrition information, if available. Have students taste-test each food, then lead a class discussion about the results.

Healthy Attitudes

Vegetables are naturally low in fat. To keep them that way, go easy on the high-fat foods sometimes added to vegetables at the table or during cooking. These include butter, margarine, salad dressings, mayonnaise, cheese, and the rich sauces that come with some frozen vegetables. Instead, use low-fat seasonings to add "zip" to fresh vegetables or plain frozen ones. Try lemon juice, flavored vinegar, herbs, spices, or low-fat salad dressings.

Baking Vegetables

Vegetables with a high moisture content, such as winter squash, potatoes, and sweet potatoes, can bake in the dry heat of an oven.

Winter squash is usually cut in half, the seeds removed, and the halves placed on a baking sheet. Squash usually bakes at 350°F (180°C) for 30 minutes or longer, until it is tender. The time depends on the variety and size of the squash.

Potatoes baked in the skins are usually placed right on the oven rack. They can bake at any temperature between 300°F (150°C) and 450°F (230°C). The baking time will depend on the temperature. Such flexibility in temperatures makes it possible to bake potatoes with other foods that need more exact temperatures. For example, you can bake muffins at 375°F (190°C) and still bake potatoes at the same time.

Sweet potatoes can also be baked with the skins on. Put them in a shallow pan in case juices begin to run out. They bake best at 400°F (200°C).

Pared whole vegetables such as carrots, onions, and potatoes can be baked in the same pan with a roast. This method adds fat to the vegetables, but it also browns them and gives them a flavorful crust.

There are many varieties of potatoes. Russet potatoes are best for baking. They are oval and have thick skins.

Thinking Skills

Creativity: Have students invent stir-fry recipes using creative combinations of foods. As a class, choose one or more recipes to prepare and taste-test. Have students evaluate the finished product for taste, texture, appearance, nutrition, cost, and ease of preparation.

Frying Vegetables

Vegetables such as chopped onions, garlic, celery, and sweet peppers are sometimes sautéed before they are used in recipes. Sautéing brings out the flavor of the vegetables. Stir-frying is also a popular method of cooking.

Many people enjoy the flavor of deep-fried vegetables, such as potatoes, zucchini slices, cauliflower, mushrooms, and onions. Except for potatoes, deep-fried vegetables are usually covered with a batter first.

Keep in mind that frying in even a small amount of oil adds fat and calories to any vegetables. If a large amount of fat is used, as in deep-fat frying, much more fat is absorbed by the vegetables.

Vegetables are often stir-fried with other foods. Use just a small amount of oil.

Cooking Convenience Fruits and Vegetables

❖ Canned vegetables may be simmered in liquid on the range top or heated in the microwave oven.

❖ Frozen vegetables may be steamed, simmered in liquid, or cooked in the microwave oven. Follow package directions for best results.

❖ Dried fruits may be poached in water or fruit juice and served as a tasty side dish or dessert.

■ Section 16.3 Review ■

RECALL THE FACTS

1. Name three undesirable changes that can occur if fruits or vegetables are overcooked.

2. Identify two ways poaching fruit differs from making a fruit sauce. What is the reason for the differences?

3. Describe two differences between simmering and steaming a vegetable.

DISCUSS YOUR IDEAS

4. Which do you think might be the best way to cook vegetables? Why?

APPLY YOUR LEARNING

5. Write an article for the local newspaper's food page, giving ideas for cooking vegetables to retain nutrients, appearance, texture, and flavor.

Completing the Section

Review

- Ask students to summarize the main ideas in this section.
- Have students complete the Section Review. (Answers appear below.)

Evaluation

- Have students write a short essay describing ways to cook fruits and vegetables.
- Have students take the quiz for Section 16.3. (Refer to the *Section Quizzes* booklet or use the *Testmaker Software*.)

Reteaching

- Have students gather recipes for fruits and vegetables. Ask students to classify the recipes according to cooking method.
- Refer to the *Reteaching Activities* booklet for the Section 16.3 activity sheet.

Enrichment

- Have students work in groups to stir-fry a variety of vegetables. Sample and evaluate for flavor and appearance.

Closure

- Remind students of the second motivator for this section. Have them think about foods they did not like and suggest alternate methods of preparation that they might like better.

■ Answers to Section Review ■

1. *Any three:* The texture becomes mushy, the color can become unpleasant, the nutrients can be lost, they may lose their flavor or develop an unpleasant flavor.

2. Sugar is added before cooking, and pieces are larger; they help fruits retain their shape. Fruit sauces are supposed to break down.

3. In steaming, the vegetable does not touch the water; foods may take longer to cook.

4. Answers will vary.

5. Answers will vary.

16.3 Recipe

Herbed Vegetable Combo

Key Skill: Simmering vegetables in a small amount of water.

Using the Recipe

- Have students read the recipe and discuss each step. Review safety and sanitation procedures that apply to this recipe.
- Have each lab team fill out a work plan. (See the *Foods Lab Resources* booklet.)
- Have the students check off the ingredients and equipment listed on the recipe worksheet and prepare the recipe.
- Have students complete the evaluation and questions on the back of the recipe worksheet.

See Also . . .

The *Foods Lab Resources* booklet for the "Herbed Vegetable Combo" recipe worksheet and other recipe alternatives.

Thinking About the Recipe

Read the recipe for "Herbed Vegetable Combo" and answer the following questions.

1. If you planned to make this recipe, how much time would you allow for pre-preparation tasks?
2. Do you consider this to be a healthful method for cooking vegetables? Why or why not?

Herbed Vegetable Combo

Customary	Ingredients	Metric
2 Tbsp.	Water	30 mL
1 cup	Zucchini squash, thinly sliced	250 mL
1 1/4 cups	Yellow summer squash thinly sliced	300 mL
1/2 cup	Green pepper, cut into 2-inch (50 mm) strips	125 mL
1/4 cup	Celery, cut into 2-inch (50 mm) strips	50 mL
1/4 cup	Onion, chopped	50 mL
1/2 tsp.	Caraway seed	3 mL
1/8 tsp.	Garlic powder	0.5 mL
1 medium	Tomato, cut into wedges	1 medium

Yield: 4 servings

Directions

Pan: Large skillet
Temperature: Medium

1. Heat water in skillet.
2. Add zucchini, yellow squash, green pepper, celery, and onion.
3. Cook, covered, over medium heat for about 4 minutes, or until vegetables are tender-crisp.
4. Sprinkle seasonings over vegetables. Top with tomato wedges.
5. Cook, covered, over low heat for about 2 minutes, or just until tomato wedges are heated.
6. Serve hot.

Nutrition Information

Per serving (approximate): 32 calories, 2 g protein, 7 g carbohydrate, trace of fat, 0 mg cholesterol, 12 mg sodium

---

Answers to Thinking About the Recipe

1. Pre-preparation time would vary, depending on the cutting, slicing, and chopping skills of the cook. A professional chef could prepare the raw vegetables for cooking in about 5 minutes, and a skilled cook in less than 10. A less experienced cook should allow longer.
2. Yes, it uses no fat, a small amount of water, and cooks the vegetable only to tender-crisp. Nutrient loss is minimized.

Career PROFILE

Ed Quintero
Wholesale Buyer

CURRENT POSITION

"I'm a produce buyer for a grocery whole-saler."

RESPONSIBILITIES

"I purchase produce from farmers and other wholesale firms for resale to clients such as grocery stores, school cafeterias, and restaurants."

SKILLS

"My job requires some knowledge of accounting and marketing to stay informed about prices and availability. And, of course, you must be familiar with produce!"

EDUCATION

"I have a four-year college degree in purchasing, and a background in produce sales."

WORK ENVIRONMENT

"This can be a highly competitive job with long hours and a certain amount of travel. During a typical day, I might get together with some of our vendors, meet with store executives, and discuss sales promotions with the advertising department."

FAVORITE PART OF THE JOB

"I enjoy the variety of working with many different people."

- Does Ed seem well qualified for his job? Why or why not?
- What aspects of Ed's job do you think you might find challenging? Why?

429

CAREER PROFILE: WHOLESALE BUYER

Thinking About . . . Buying Produce

- Have students think of other questions they would like to ask Ed Quintero about buying produce for a grocery whole-saler. (Examples: How many hours a week do you usually work? In what way is your job competitive? How much math do you need to know?)

- Ask student volunteers to tell what they think would be the most exciting part of being a wholesale buyer.

- Have students brainstorm decisions that a wholesale buyer might have to make in the course of a day. What might the effects of a wrong decision be?

Student Opportunities

Students thinking about a career as a wholesale buyer may want to seek an entry-level job, such as in the stockroom or shipping department of a wholesale produce company, to learn about the business. Foods and nutrition classes can provide important knowledge and skills.

Occupational Outlook

Wholesale buyers with experience may be promoted to general or regional managers in charge of buying produce for wholesale companies. Some people may start their own wholesale business.

For More Information

For additional information about careers in wholesale buying and selling, encourage students to contact:
- National Retail Merchants Association, 100 W. 31st St., New York, NY 10001
- Local wholesale houses or associations of wholesalers in many of the larger cities
- National Food Brokers Association, 1010 Massachusetts Ave. NW, Washington, D.C. 20001

Review

- Have students complete the Chapter Review. (Answers appear below.)

Evaluation

- Divide the class into two teams (A and B). Each team should brainstorm questions about Chapter 16. Then allow the teams to take turns asking each other questions. At the end of the questioning period, the team with the most correct answers wins.

- Have students take the test for Chapter 16. (Refer to the *Chapter and Unit Tests* booklet or construct your own test using the *Testmaker Software*.)

■ ANSWERS ■

REVIEWING FACTS

1. Because they store nutrients to be sent to the rest of the plant.

2. *Any three:* Broccoli, brussels sprouts, cabbage, collards, kale, mustard greens, cauliflower, rutabagas, and turnips.

3. *Any three:* Buy top-quality produce; buy only what you can store and use; inspect packaged produce carefully for stains and odors; avoid any produce that looks wilted, shriveled, bruised, or decayed; buy by weight when possible.

4. To keep pesticide residues, dirt, and germs from contaminating the food.

5. Enzymatic browning; by coating the fruit with ascorbic acid.

6. In the refrigerator covered tightly with plastic wrap or in a tightly sealed plastic bag with all the excess air squeezed out.

CHAPTER 16 REVIEW

SUMMARY

SECTION 16.1

Choosing Fruits and Vegetables: You can choose from a wide variety of produce. Fruits and vegetables are excellent sources of vitamins, minerals, and fiber. Shop carefully for the best quality and value on in-season and year-round produce. Some fruits can be ripened after purchase. Store fresh produce properly to preserve its quality. Convenience forms of fruits and vegetables give you still more options.

SECTION 16.2

Preparing Raw Fruits and Vegetables: Fresh produce should be washed before it is used. To retain the most nutrients, keep paring and cutting to a minimum. Take steps to prevent cut fruits from turning dark. Raw produce can be served on a platter for a party or kept on hand in the refrigerator for snacks.

SECTION 16.3

Cooking Fruits and Vegetables: Cooking affects the texture, color, and flavor of fruits and vegetables. Overcooking can result in discoloration and loss of texture, flavor, and nutrients. Fresh fruits may be poached, baked, made into sauces, or prepared in a microwave oven. Fresh vegetables may be simmered, steamed, baked, or prepared in a microwave oven. They may also be fried in oil, which adds flavor but also fat.

REVIEWING FACTS

1. Why are roots high in nutrients? (16.1)

2. Give three examples of cruciferous vegetables. What is a possible benefit of eating them? (16.1)

3. Give three tips for buying fresh produce. (16.1)

4. Why should you wash produce, even if you're going to peel it before eating? (16.2)

5. What is the process that causes cut fruit to darken? How can it be prevented? (16.2)

6. How should cut produce be stored? (16.2)

7. Give three tips for minimizing vitamin C loss when cooking fruits and vegetables. (16.3)

8. What characteristics make some fruits better for baking than others? (16.3)

9. Explain how to simmer vegetables. (16.3)

10. Give three tips for microwaving vegetables. (16.3)

LEARNING BY DOING

1. ***Food science lab:*** Select two similar potatoes. Store one in a cool, dry, dark place. Store the other in the refrigerator. After at least one week, bake the potatoes. Compare their taste and texture. What caused the difference? (16.1)

2. ***Demonstration:*** Using your knowledge of handling fresh produce and of meal appeal, demonstrate how to create an attractive fresh fruit or vegetable platter. (16.2)

7. *Any three:* Keep them whole or in large pieces; cook them quickly; use methods that require only a small amount of water; serve with cooking liquid.

8. Firm fruits bake better.

9. Pour a small amount of water (1/2 cup for each four servings) into a medium saucepan; cover and bring to a boil; add vegetables, cover, and bring to a boil again; lower the heat until the water just simmers; cook, covered, until vegetables are tender.

3. **Food science lab:** Cut an apple into wedges. Sprinkle half of the wedges with lemon juice. Let all the wedges stand at room temperature. Record any changes in appearance after 5, 10, and 15 minutes. Explain what happened and why. (16.2)

4. **Foods lab:** Select one fruit or vegetable and prepare it using three of the methods described in this chapter. Compare the results on appearance, taste, texture, and convenience. Identify when you might want to use each method. (16.3)

THINKING CRITICALLY

1. **Predicting consequences:** What are some possible consequences of not getting enough fruits and vegetables in your diet? (16.1)

2. **Forming hypotheses:** A hypothesis is sometimes called an "educated guess." Based on what you know about the effect of lemon juice on cut fruit, do you predict that any other juices would have the same effect? Which ones? How could you test your hypothesis? (16.2)

3. **Comparing and contrasting:** Compare and contrast the advantages and disadvantages of the cooking methods described in this chapter. (16.3)

MAKING DECISIONS AND SOLVING PROBLEMS

What Would You Do?

1. The supermarket is having a sale on fruits and vegetables. However, they are packaged in quantities that are too large for your family's use. You want to take advantage of the low price, but are afraid some of the produce will spoil before you can eat it. (16.1)

2. You are watching your neighbor's children, ages seven and nine, and are responsible for making sure they eat their dinner. Your neighbor has warned you that they do not like to eat vegetables. You wonder how you can make vegetables more appealing to the children. (16.2, 16.3)

LINKING YOUR STUDIES

1. **Science:** Research and report on the ways fruits and vegetables are classified by scientists. (16.1)

2. **Math:** Use newspaper ads or visit a supermarket to conduct a price survey. Compare the per-serving price of several similar fruits or vegetables (for example, different types of berries or cruciferous vegetables). Compare the prices of different forms such as fresh, frozen, and canned. Make a bar graph showing your findings. What are some possible reasons for the price differences? (16.1)

3. **Fine arts:** Many artists have included arrangements of fruits or vegetables in their works. Using art books, find such artworks by at least five different artists. Be prepared to discuss the works and your reactions to them in class. Suggested works: Henri Rousseau, *Still Life with Tropical Fruit;* Paul Cezanne, *Fruit Bowl, Glass, and Apples;* Gabriel Metsu, *Vegetable Market at Amsterdam.* (16.1, 16.2)

4. **Social studies:** In cookbooks, magazines, and other sources, find recipes for cooked fruits and vegetables that are popular in other cultures. Identify the cooking methods used. (16.3)

LEARNING BY DOING

1. The potato stored in the refrigerator underwent a chemical change: some of the starch changed to sugar.

2. Answers will vary.

3. Students' results should show that the half not treated with the lemon juice browned much more quickly than the half treated with lemon juice.

4. Answers will vary.

THINKING CRITICALLY

1. Answers will vary. You will not get a balanced diet, you probably won't get all of the nutrients you need.

2. Answers will vary.

3. Answers will vary.

MAKING DECISIONS AND SOLVING PROBLEMS

Answers to "Making Decisions and Solving Problems" will vary. Encourage students to give reasons for their answers.

LINKING YOUR STUDIES

Answers to "Linking Your Studies" will vary. Evaluate students on the amount of effort they put into the activities as well as their results.

431

10. *Any three:* Pierce vegetables that have a skin to keep them from bursting; arrange tender parts toward the center and less tender parts toward the outside; cover the container to retain moisture; follow directions in the owner's manual or cooking guide for cooking times and special instructions.

Planning the Chapter

Chapter Overview

Section 17.1: Choosing Grains and Grain Products

Section 17.2: Preparing Grains and Grain Products

Section 17.3: Legumes, Nuts, and Seeds

Introducing the Chapter

Motivators

- Have students make a list of ways they eat grains, legumes, nuts, and seeds. Beginning with grains, wrap around the class to hear responses from the entire class. Follow with examples of legumes, nuts, and seeds.

- Have students prepare snack foods using grains, legumes, nuts, and seeds. Possibilities include bean dip and trail mix. Have students identify other ways grains, legumes, nuts, and seeds may be included in the diet.

Teacher's Classroom Resources—Chapter 17

Refer to these resources in the TCR package:

Enrichment Activities

Chapter and Unit Tests

Testmaker Software

CHAPTER 17

Grains, Legumes, Nuts, and Seeds

432

Cooperative Learning Suggestions

Initiate a Group Investigation (Jigsaw) activity. Have students work in groups to research one of the following topics: grains, legumes, nuts, and seeds grown in a particular country, imports of these foods, sources of protein in people's diets in the country, or popular dishes made with grains, legumes, nuts, and seeds in the country. Have students draw conclusions about the use of grains, legumes, nuts, and seeds in people's diets. Discuss the benefits of using these sources of protein in the diet. Have students choose and prepare a recipe featuring grains, legumes, nuts, or seeds for the class to taste.

Choosing Grains and Grain Products

OBJECTIVES

After studying this section, you should be able to:

- Describe the nutrients in grains and grain products.
- Identify different grain products and their uses.
- Give guidelines for buying and storing grain products.

LOOK FOR THESE TERMS

germ
endosperm
bran
enrichment
fortified

Grains have been the most important staple in the world's food supply for thousands of years. How many grains and grain products can you name? After reading this section, you may be familiar with a few more than before.

What Are Grains?

Grains are the seeds of plants in the grass family. Common grains in North America include wheat, rice, corn, buckwheat, oats, rye, triticale (trih-tih-KAY-lee), barley, and millet.

Besides grains, a number of other foods also come from the seeds of plants: dry beans and peas, nuts, and sunflower seeds, for example. All of these edible seeds are alike in some ways. The seed is usually encased in a container of some kind—a soft pod (beans and peas), a hard shell (nuts and seeds), or a husk of dried plant material (grains). The seed itself has several parts:

❖ A tiny embryo that will grow into a new plant. In grains, this is called the **germ.**

❖ A food supply for the embryo, made up of proteins, starches, and other nutrients. In grains, this part of the seed is called the **endosperm.**

❖ An outer protective coat or skin. In grains, it is called the **bran.**

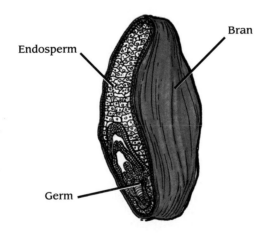

The three parts of the grain kernel are each nutritious.

Section 17.1
Choosing Grains and Grain Products

Introducing the Section

Motivators

- Create a display of stalks of wheat, oats, and/or other grain products. Ask students to identify the stalks and name products made from the displayed grains. Discuss ways grains were prepared by early peoples. Identify modern methods of preparing grains. Point out the use of grain as a continuous link among people since the beginning of time.

- Have students taste-test a variety of grain products. Which have students eaten before? Which do they think are most and least nutritious? Why?

Objectives

- Have students read the section objectives. Discuss the purpose of studying the section.

Vocabulary

- Pronounce the terms listed under "Look for These Terms." Have students find the terms and their definitions in the section.

Guided Reading

- Have students look at the headings within Section 17.1 to preview the concepts that will be discussed.

- Have students read the section and complete the appropriate part of the Chapter 17 Study Guide in the *Student Workbook.*

Teacher's Classroom Resources—Section 17.1

Refer to these resources in the TCR package:

Reproducible Lesson Plans
Student Workbook
Extending the Text

Reteaching Activities
Section Quizzes
Testmaker Software
Color Transparencies

- **What Are Grains?**
- **Nutrients in Grains**

(text pages 433-434)

Comprehension Check

1. Ask students to define *grains* and list several grains that grow in North America. *(The seeds of plants in the grass family; wheat, rice, corn, buckwheat, oats, rye, triticale, barley, and millet.)*

2. Ask students to identify the parts of a seed. *(embryo [germ], endosperm, and bran.)*

3. Ask students to explain the purpose of the endosperm in a seed. *(It contains a food supply for the embryo, made up of proteins, starches, and other nutrients.)*

4. Ask students to identify the nutrients in each part of a grain seed. *(Germ: B vitamins, vitamin E, iron, zinc, and other trace minerals; endosperm: complex carbohydrates and proteins; bran: fiber, B vitamins, and some minerals.)*

5. Ask students to explain the difference between enrichment and fortification in grain products. *(Enrichment replaces some of the nutrients lost in processing, so that the nutritional value of the product is similar to the original wheat; fortifying a product means that 10 percent or more of the daily value for a nutrient has been added, regardless of the original nutrient content of the grain.)*

After they are harvested, all grains are processed. However, some undergo more processing than others. Products made with the whole grain retain most of the nutrients found in the kernel.

Nutrients in Grains

Like all plant seeds, grains are packed with nutrients. The endosperm is high in complex carbohydrates and proteins. The bran is rich in fiber, B vitamins, and some minerals. The germ provides B vitamins, vitamin E, iron, zinc, and other trace minerals, along with unsaturated fat.

All grains must be processed before consumers can use them. The outer husk is removed, leaving the actual grain seed, called a kernel. The nutrients in the grains and grain products you eat depend on the way they are processed from that point on.

Sometimes the entire kernel is used to make whole grain products. Examples include whole wheat flour, brown rice, and whole grain breakfast cereals. These products contain most of the kernel's original nutrients.

In another method, the bran and germ are removed, along with the fiber and nutrients they contain. The remaining endosperm is made into products such as white flour or breakfast cereals. Usually, some of the nutrients lost in the processing are added to the product so the total is close to the original levels. This is known as **enrichment.** Some products are **fortified,** which means that the manufacturer has added 10 percent or more of the daily value for that nutrient.

The Food Guide Pyramid recommends eating 6 to 11 daily servings of enriched or whole grains and grain products. Typical servings include one slice of bread, 1/2 cup (125 mL) cooked cereal, rice, or pasta, or one ounce (28 g) ready-to-eat cereal.

Buying Grains and Grain Products

When you buy grains and grain products, keep nutrition in mind. Choose whole grain products as much as possible. Otherwise, be sure the product is enriched. Look for products low in fat, sugar, and sodium. Try different grains for variety.

When buying, read the labels to make certain you get the product you want. If the grain is visible in the package, inspect it carefully to be sure you are getting good quality. For example, be sure pasta is not cracked or broken.

434 Chapter 17: Grains, Legumes, Nuts, and Seeds

Thinking Skills

Reasoning: Ask students: Since by law processed grains are enriched to replace lost nutrients, what is the nutritional advantage of choosing whole grain products? *(They provide fiber and may contain undiscovered nutrients.)*

The following information will help you select specific types of grains and grain products.

Rice

Several different varieties of rice are grown. You can choose from rice with short, medium, or long grains.

* **Short grain.** The grains are almost round. When cooked, the rice is moist and the grains stick together. Short-grain rice is a good choice for creamy dishes, molded rice rings, or eating with chopsticks.
* **Medium grain.** The grains are plump, tender, and moist. They stick together, but not as much as short-grain rice.
* **Long grain.** When cooked, the grains are fluffy and dry and stay separated.

Rice can also vary in the way it is processed. *Brown rice* is the whole grain form of rice. Only the outer hull has been removed; the bran and germ remain. *White rice* has had the bran and germ removed. *Converted rice* has been parboiled (briefly boiled) to save nutrients before the hull is removed. It takes longer to cook than regular white rice. *Instant rice* has been precooked and dehydrated. It takes only a few minutes to prepare.

Other Cooked Grains

Besides rice, many other types of grain can be cooked and served as a side dish. Cooked grains are also popular as a hot breakfast cereal. Some can be used in baking or other recipes. Here are some types of grains you might want to try:

* **Oats.** Usually eaten as a breakfast cereal or used in cooking. Quick-cooking types are available.
* **Cornmeal.** Coarsely ground dried corn. Available in yellow or white types. Used as a breakfast cereal and in baked goods.

Many of the grain products you may find in the supermarket originally came from different places around the world. For example:

* Basmati (bahz-MAH-tee) rice is a variety from India, now also grown in America. It is fragrant with a rich, nutty flavor.
* Ramen (RAH-men) are Japanese noodles made of wheat and deep-fried. (Low-fat ramen are available.)
* Couscous (described on page 436) is very popular in the Middle East.
* Chapati (chah-PAH-tee) is a flat bread from India.
* Tortillas originated in Mexico.

The type of rice you choose may depend on how you plan to use it. What else would you consider when buying rice?

1. **Classifying Grain Products:** Bring a variety of packaged grain products to class. Have students classify them into two groups: whole-grain and enriched. Discuss reasons for choosing one type of product over another. *(Key skill: classification)*

2. **Drawing:** Have students draw diagrams of different types of grains and identify the parts of each. Why is it beneficial to eat whole grain products? *(Key skill: creativity)*

3. **Student Reports:** Have each student select a particular grain and prepare a report on where it is grown, its nutrient content, and how it is processed and used. *(Key skill: writing)*

Special Needs Strategies

Gifted and Talented: Some people are allergic to wheat (celiac sprue disease). Have students identify specific products that those who are allergic to wheat should avoid. Ask students to suggest possible substitutions using other grains.

17.1

Teaching . . .

- Buying Grains and
  Grain Products
- Storing Grains and
  Grain Products

(text pages 434-438)

Comprehension Check

1. Ask students to describe the different varieties of rice grains. *(short grain, medium grain, and long grain)*

2. Ask students to list grains that are usually cooked and describe their general use. *(See the list on pages 435-436.)*

3. Ask students to name two ways in which pasta may be purchased. *(dried [in the grocery section of the supermarket] and fresh [in the refrigerated section])*

4. Ask students to explain the difference between the terms "wheat" and "whole wheat" on bread labels. *(Those that say "whole wheat" mean that the product is made from the whole grain; those that merely say "wheat" may have had some part of the grain removed or white flour was used.)*

5. Ask students to list guidelines for storing grains and grain products. *(See the list on page 438.)*

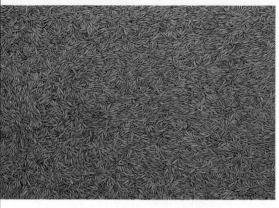

Oats, shown here in kernel form, are just one of many grains that can be used as a breakfast cereal, as a side dish, or in recipes. How many different kinds have you tried?

❖ **Grits.** Coarsely ground endosperm of corn. Used as a breakfast cereal or side dish.

❖ **Bulgur.** Wheat kernels that have been steamed, dried, and crushed. Tender with a chewy texture. Used in main dishes, salads, and as a side dish.

❖ **Wheat berries.** Whole, unprocessed wheat kernels. Can be cooked as a cereal or added to other foods.

❖ **Couscous** (KOOS-koos). Steamed, cracked endosperm of wheat kernel. Has a nutty flavor. Used as a cereal, in salads and main dishes, or sweetened for dessert.

❖ **Cracked wheat.** Very hard with tough and chewy texture. Often added to bread.

❖ **Barley.** Mild-flavored grain. Usually used in soups and stews.

❖ **Kasha** (KAH-shah). Roasted buckwheat that is hulled and crushed. Has a pleasant, nutty flavor. Used as a breakfast cereal or side dish.

❖ **Millet.** Small, yellow grains with a mild flavor. Used as a breakfast cereal or side dish.

❖ **Triticale** (trih-tih-KAY-lee). A cross between wheat and rye, with more protein than wheat. Can be used in cereals and main dishes and combined with other cooked grains.

❖ **Brans.** The ground bran of oat, rice, or wheat can be purchased to use as a hot cereal or in cooking. All are high in fiber.

Instant and Ready-to-Eat Cereals

Some of the hot cereals already described, such as oats and grits, are also available in instant forms. Cooking time is shorter. Often sugar and other flavorings have been added.

Dry, ready-to-eat cereals come in many different varieties. Use the nutrition information on the label to help you make wise choices. Look for cereals that are high in complex carbohydrates and fiber, low in sugar and sodium. It's not necessary for a cereal to provide 100 percent of the nutrients you need in a day. You can get a nutritious product at a lower cost by buying cereals that are not so highly fortified.

Another ready-to-eat grain product is wheat germ. It has a pleasant, nutty flavor and is an excellent source of proteins, vitamins, and minerals. Wheat germ can be added to other foods for more nutrition. For example, you might sprinkle it on cereal or use it in recipes. Use wheat germ in small amounts—it contains fat, which could add up to more than you need.

Pasta

Pasta (PAH-stah) is an Italian word that means "paste." To make pasta, dough made from flour and water is rolled thin, then formed into hundreds of different shapes. Examples include spaghetti and macaroni.

Both enriched and whole-wheat pasta is available. Sometimes pasta is flavored and colored with other foods, such as spinach. Noodles are pasta made with eggs.

436 Chapter 17: Grains, Legumes, Nuts, and Seeds

Food and Nutrition Science

Converted Rice: Converted rice retains more nutrients than other types of rice, although it takes longer to cook. When a food is parboiled, it is cooked partially by boiling for a brief period of time. When rice is parboiled, the intense heat drives the nutrients from the hull and the bran into the endosperm, so that they remain in the rice when the hull and bran are removed.

Pasta comes in many different shapes and colors for use in a variety of recipes.

Packages of dried pasta are found in the grocery section with other shelf-stable foods. You may find fresh pasta in the refrigerated section.

Breads

Breads range from enriched white bread to whole wheat and mixed whole grains. They come in assorted flavors, shapes, and sizes, including individual rolls.

Leavened (LEV-uhnd) breads are made with leavenings, ingredients such as yeast or baking powder that cause them to rise. Unleavened, or flat, breads—such as tortillas—are made without leavenings. Pita (PEE-tuh), also called pocket bread, is a flat bread that can be split horizontally to make a pocket which can be filled with food.

When buying bread, read the label carefully. "Whole wheat" means the product is made from the whole grain. If only the word

Leavened breads have a very different texture from unleavened breads. What makes the difference?

Section 17.1: Choosing Grains and Grain Products   **437**

Student Experiences

1. **Taste Tests:** Show students raw and cooked examples of long-grain, medium-grain, and short-grain rice, both white and brown. What visual differences can students identify? Have students compare the taste and texture of the cooked rice. *(Key skill: evaluation)*

2. **Comparing Directions:** Provide students with directions for preparing brown rice, white rice, converted rice, and instant rice. Have students compare directions for preparing each. What are the main differences? *(Key skill: reading)*

3. **Store Survey:** Have students survey the cereal section of a grocery store to compare regular, quick-cooking, and instant hot cereals and ready-to-eat cereals. Which are most and least expensive per serving? Which are most and least nutritious? Which contain the most fiber? Which are high in fat, sugar, and sodium? Ask students to note the location of presweetened cereals on the grocery shelves. What conclusions can they draw? *(Key skills: reading, evaluation)*

4. **Product Comparison:** Have students compare a vegetable-flavored pasta with a regular pasta in appearance, ease of preparation, taste, nutritional value, and cost. *(Key skill: analysis)*

5. **Student Demonstrations:** Have students demonstrate procedures for storing grains and grain products. *(Key skill: kitchen management skills)*

Thinking Skills

Problem Solving: Have students choose ten different ready-to-eat cereals sold at a nearby grocery store. Have students calculate the unit cost per 1 oz. (28 g) of each cereal. Which has the highest unit cost? Lowest? Do students see a relationship between unit cost and nutritional value? If so, what is that relationship?

Completing the Section

Review

- Ask students to summarize the main ideas in this section.
- Have students complete the Section Review. (Answers appear below.)

Evaluation

- Have students write a short essay describing the various types of grains and at least one food in which each is used.
- Have students take the quiz for Section 17.1. (Refer to the *Section Quizzes* booklet or use the *Testmaker Software*.)

Reteaching

- Tape samples of various types of grains to the front of a stack of index cards. On the back of each card, write the name of the grain. Have students work in pairs to drill each other on the names of the grains.
- Refer to the *Reteaching Activities* booklet for the Section 17.1 activity sheet.

Enrichment

- Have students research the spread of pasta from its beginnings in the Far East to Italy to America and create a classroom display of their findings.

Closure

- Refer to the second motivator activity for this section. Have students reevaluate their answers. Now which grains do they think are most and least nutritious?

"wheat" is used, it usually means some part of the grain has been removed or white flour is used. Some dark breads are made with white flour with caramel or molasses added for color.

Storing Grains and Grain Products

To maintain the quality of grains and grain products, follow these storage guidelines:

❖ Store whole grains and whole grain products in the refrigerator. Because they contain oil, they can spoil at room temperature if not used quickly.
❖ Refrigerate fresh pasta.
❖ Store other uncooked grains and grain products, such as white rice and dried pasta, in a cool, dry place in tightly covered containers.
❖ Store breads at room temperature for short-term storage. Otherwise, freeze. If bread is refrigerated, it gets stale faster. However, in humid weather, refrigerate bread to prevent mold from growing.
❖ Store cooked grains in the refrigerator if they will be used within a few days. For longer storage, freeze.

A label that says "wheat bread" doesn't necessarily mean the bread is made from the whole grain. Remember, wheat is used to make both whole wheat flour and enriched white flour.

■ **Section 17.1 Review** ■

RECALL THE FACTS

1. Identify the three parts of the grain kernel and the nutrients found in each.
2. Name four grains that can be cooked and eaten as a side dish.
3. What should you look for when choosing a nutritious ready-to-eat cereal?
4. How should bread be stored?

DISCUSS YOUR IDEAS

5. What qualities have made grain products so popular around the world?

APPLY YOUR LEARNING

6. Find three recipes that each use a different grain or grain product. Identify the type of grain or grain product and describe its nutritional value.

■ Answers to Section Review ■

1. Germ: B vitamins, vitamin E, iron, zinc, and other trace minerals; endosperm: complex carbohydrates and proteins; bran: fiber, B vitamins, and some minerals.

2. See the list on pages 435-436.
3. Cereals that are high in complex carbohydrates and fiber.
4. Store at room temperature or freeze.

5. Answers will vary.
6. Answers will vary.

Preparing Grains and Grain Products

OBJECTIVES

After studying this section, you should be able to:

- Explain the general principles of cooking grains.
- Describe how to successfully prepare rice and other grains, pasta, and breakfast cereals.

LOOK FOR THIS TERM

al dente

Section 17.2
Preparing Grains and Grain Products

Introducing the Section

Motivators

- Have students prepare and taste-test various unusual grains, such as grits, hominy, barley, kasha, millet, quinoa, and amaranth. How does the unit cost of these grains compare with more common varieties?
- Have students compare the package directions for preparing several different grain products. Ask students to develop a set of general guidelines that would apply to most grain products.

Objectives

- Have students read the section objectives. Discuss the purpose of studying the section.

Vocabulary

- Pronounce the terms listed under "Look for These Terms." Have students read the section find the terms and their definitions in the section.

Guided Reading

- Have students look at the headings within Section 17.2 to preview the concepts that will be discussed.
- Have students read the section and complete the appropriate part of the Chapter 17 Study Guide in the *Student Workbook*.

Properly prepared, grains can be a nutritious, flavorful part of any meal, from breakfast to a meal for company. You can serve them plain or use recipes that might add vegetables, seasonings, and sauces. Some can even be served as desserts if sweeteners and fruit are added.

Principles of Cooking Grains

Because they are dry, grains must be cooked in water. They need enough time to absorb the amount of water needed to make them edible.

Even though most grains are cooked in a similar way, cooking methods and times do vary. Always follow package or recipe directions.

Unless package directions state otherwise, do not rinse enriched grains before cooking. Rinsing causes loss of the added B vitamins.

Microwaving grains is not always practical. Because grains need time to absorb the liquid and soften, microwaving does not usually save time. Pasta, for instance, takes just as long to microwave as it does to cook conventionally. However, check the package for microwave directions.

Grains are a delicious part of many dishes, such as this mulligan stew served with rice.

Teacher's Classroom Resources—Section 17.2

Refer to these resources in the TCR package:

Reproducible Lesson Plans
Student Workbook
Extending the Text
Reteaching Activities

Foods Lab Resources
Section Quizzes
Testmaker Software
Color Transparencies

- **Principles of Cooking Grains**
- **Preparing Rice and Other Grains**
- **Preparing Pasta**
- **Preparing Breakfast Cereals**

(text pages 439-442)

Comprehension Check

1. Ask students to explain why microwaving grains is not a timesaving technique. *(Grains need time to absorb the liquid, so they take just about as long to microwave as to cook conventionally.)*

2. Ask students to explain why long-grain rice should be stirred only if necessary while cooking. *(The stirring scrapes starch off the rice, making the grains stick together.)*

3. Ask students to explain what the term "al dente" means. *(It is a stage of doneness for pasta at which the pasta is firm to the bite.)*

4. Ask students to describe methods of sweetening breakfast cereals without adding processed sugar. *(Add fresh or dried fruit, honey, molasses, or syrup.)*

Preparing Rice and Other Grains

Rice is usually simmered, using just the amount of water that the grain can absorb. Bring the water to a boil, add the rice, cover, and bring to a boil again. Then reduce the heat so the rice simmers gently.

Package directions may tell you to stir the rice at intervals as it cooks. Do not stir long-grain rice unless necessary. Stirring scrapes off starch, making the grains stick together.

Near the end of cooking time, check the rice for doneness. It should be tender but firm. There should be no water left. If any water remains, continue cooking without the cover until the excess water evaporates.

Many other grains, such as barley, grits, and kasha, are cooked in much the same way. The chart below gives information about cooking different grains.

Instant rice requires a slightly different method. Follow package directions.

Preparing Pasta

Unlike rice and other grains, pasta is cooked, uncovered, in a large amount of boiling water. Pasta is one of very few foods that must be boiled. The boiling helps circulate the pasta so it cooks evenly.

TIPS for Success

Cooking Pasta

Pasta sometimes tends to stick together during or after cooking. Here are some suggestions to prevent sticking:

- ❖ Use plenty of water.
- ❖ Bring the water to a rapid boil. Then add the spaghetti slowly so the boiling does not stop.
- ❖ Stir frequently during cooking.

Cooking Grains

To cook 1 cup (250 mL) dry grain, use the amount of water shown and cook for the time indicated.

Grain	Amount of Water	Cooking Time	Cooked Yield (approx.)
Barley (pearl)	2 ½ cups (625 mL)	40-45 min.	3 cups (750 mL)
Bulgur	2 cups (500 mL)	30 min.*	2 ½ cups (625 mL)
Cornmeal	4 cups (1 L)	25 min.	3 cups (750 mL)
Grits (regular)	4 cups (1 L)	25 min.	3 cups (750 mL)
Kasha	2 cups (500 mL)	15 min.	2 ½ cups (625 mL)
Millet	2 ½ to 3 cups (625 to 750 mL)	35 to 40 min.	3 ½ cups (875 mL)
Rice (long or medium grain)	2 cups (500 mL)	45 min. (brown) 15 min. (white)	3 cups (750 mL)

*Do not cook bulgur; pour boiling water over it and let stand 30 minutes.

Food and Nutrition Science

Rice Preparation Comparison: Have students prepare 1/2 cup (125 mL) long-grain rice according to the directions on the package. Direct half of the students to stir the rice as little as possible and the other half to stir every five minutes. Have students compare the appearance, texture, and taste of the samples. What conclusions can students draw?

After the water has come to a rapid boil, add the pasta slowly. That way it will be less likely to stick together.

Check the package for the amount of water to use. With spaghetti, for example, use about 1 quart (1 L) of water for every 4 ounces (112 g) of spaghetti. Be sure the pot is large enough for the amount of water used and the boiling action of the water.

Pasta is generally cooked to a doneness stage known as **al dente** (ahl DEHN-tay), which means it is firm to the bite. Cooking time varies from 5 to 20 minutes, depending on the thickness of the pasta. If the pasta is to be further cooked in a recipe (such as lasagne), cook it for a shorter time so it is slightly more firm.

Unless directions state otherwise, fresh pasta will cook in a fraction of the time needed by dried pasta. Otherwise, the methods are the same.

After cooking, drain the pasta in a colander or strainer. Never rinse pasta after cooking—it loses valuable nutrients. To keep cooked pasta hot, set the colander or strainer over a pan of hot water and cover.

The chart at the bottom of the page gives the yield of cooked pasta from a given amount of dry.

If you have leftover cooked pasta, freeze it. First, stir 1 tsp. (5 mL) cooking oil into the hot drained pasta to keep it from sticking. Freeze in serving-size portions.

Healthy Attitudes

Pasta, in itself, is a low-fat, low-calorie, high-protein and high-carbohydrate food. However, sauces and other foods added to pasta can greatly increase fat and calories. Look for low-fat sauces for pasta, or adapt recipes to lower the fat.

Dry Pasta Quantities

Type of Pasta	Dry Weight	Dry Volume	Cooked Yield (approx.)
Small pasta, such as macaroni, shells, spirals, twists	4 oz. (112 g)	1 cup (250 mL)	2 ½ cups (675 mL)
Long, slender pasta, such as spaghetti, linguini	4 oz. (112 g)	1-inch diameter bunch	2 cups (500 mL)

Section 17.2: Preparing Grains and Grain Products   **441**

1. **Poster Project:** Have students prepare posters outlining the basic steps in cooking grains. *(Key skill: creativity)*

2. **Finding Recipes:** Have students find recipes that use rice and other grains. Classify the dishes as main dishes, side dishes, and desserts. Discuss with students how different grains or grain products are associated with ethnic foods or specific cultures or countries. *(Key skills: reading, multicultural awareness)*

3. **Demonstration:** Demonstrate how to cook pasta, having students taste the pasta at the "al dente" stage and when the pasta is overcooked. Emphasize the points listed in Tips for Success. *(Key skill: evaluation)*

4. **Product Comparison:** Have students prepare and taste-test regular, quick-cooking, and instant oatmeal. How do these products compare in ease of preparation, time required for preparation, appearance, texture, taste, and cost? *(Key skill: evaluation)*

Healthy Attitudes

Have students brainstorm ways to fix pasta that do not add fat and calories. Provide cookbooks and have students find additional low-calorie pasta recipes.

More About Cooking Pasta

Point out to students that draining pasta requires special care because of the heavy pot and boiling water. Remind students of the following safety points:

- Have the strainer or colander ready in an empty sink with the drain open.

- Lift the pot or kettle carefully with both hands, using potholders.
- Be sure the path to the sink is clear before carrying the pot there.
- Pour out the pasta and water slowly to avoid splashing. Be sure the water drains out of the sink.

17.2

Completing the Section

Review

- Ask students to summarize the main ideas in this section.
- Have students complete the Section Review. (Answers appear below.)

Evaluation

- Have students prepare 1/2 cup (125 mL) pasta to the "al dente" stage. Observe the procedure and safety techniques they use and evaluate the final product.
- Have students take the quiz for Section 17.2. (Refer to the *Section Quizzes* booklet or use the *Testmaker Software*.)

Reteaching

- Have students prepare posters outlining the steps in cooking top-quality pasta.
- Refer to the *Reteaching Activities* booklet for the Section 17.2 activity sheet.

Enrichment

- Assign a grain type to students and ask them to plan an entire, well-balanced meal around it.

Closure

- Lead a class discussion on the various ways grains can be prepared and used to create nutritious meals.

Preparing Breakfast Cereals

Follow the package directions for cooking hot breakfast cereals. Some can be cooked in either water or milk. Instant hot cereals usually require only that you add boiling water. Some ready-to-eat cereals can be microwaved to serve hot.

Cereals, cold or hot, are usually eaten with milk. For natural sweetness and added nutrients, try adding fresh or dried fruit, such as strawberries, raisins, dried apricots, or sliced bananas. If more sweetness is desired, you can add a small amount of sugar, honey, molasses, or syrup.

Try adding your own toppings to breakfast cereals for added flavor and nutrients. It's usually more economical than buying cereal with fruit already in it.

There are many ways to use grains in meals. How many can you think of?

442   Chapter 17: Grains, Legumes, Nuts, and Seeds

■ Section 17.2 Review ■

RECALL THE FACTS

1. Why shouldn't you rinse grains before cooking them?
2. Does microwaving grains save time? Explain.
3. How can you tell when rice is properly cooked?
4. How does the preparation of pasta differ from that of most other foods? What is the reason for using this preparation method?

DISCUSS YOUR IDEAS

5. What are some creative ways to use grains in meals?

APPLY YOUR LEARNING

6. Find recipes for a variety of pasta sauces. Which appear to be low in fat? How might you reduce the fat in the other recipes?

■ Answers to Section Review ■

1. Rinsing washes off the added B vitamins.
2. No, because the grains need a certain amount of time to absorb water.
3. It should be tender but firm, and there should be no water left.
4. Answers will vary.
5. Answers will vary.

Thinking About the Recipe

Read the recipe for "Western Beans with Rice" and answer the following questions.

1. What foods provide most of the protein in this recipe?
2. If you wanted to reduce the sodium in this recipe, what changes would you make?

Western Beans and Rice

Key Skill: Cooking Grains

Western Beans and Rice

Customary	Ingredients	Metric
(See package directions)	Instant brown rice	(See package directions)
(See rice package directions)	Water	(See rice package directions)
1 Tbsp.	Vegetable oil	15 mL
1 cup	Chopped onion	250 mL
1 cup	Diced celery	250 mL
3 cups	Canned pinto beans, drained	750 mL
8-oz. can	Tomato sauce	224-g can
1/2 cup	Water	125 mL
1/4 tsp.	Hot pepper sauce	1 mL

Yield: 6 servings

Conventional Directions

Pan: Saucepan; large skillet
Temperature: High, then low

1. Prepare instant brown rice in saucepan, according to package directions, using amount of rice and water to make 3 cups cooked rice.
2. While rice is cooking, heat oil in skillet. Cook onions and celery in oil until tender.
3. Stir in beans, tomato sauce, 1/2 cup water, and hot pepper sauce.
4. Heat mixture thoroughly..
5. Serve over hot rice.

Microwave Directions

Pan: Saucepan; 1-qt. (1-L) microwave-safe dish with cover
Power level: 100 percent power

1. Prepare rice as in Step 1 of conventional directions.
2. Combine onions and celery in microwave-safe dish. Cover.
3. Cook onions and celery at 100 percent power for 2 minutes, stirring after 1 minute.
4. Stir in beans, tomato sauce, 1/2 cup water, and hot pepper sauce. Cover.
5. Cook mixture at 100 percent power for 5 to 8 minutes, stirring after 4 minutes.
6. Serve over hot rice.

Nutrition Information

Per serving—conventional directions (approximate): 246 calories, 9 g protein, 46 g carbohydrate, 4 g fat, 0 mg cholesterol, 752 mg sodium

Section 17.2: Preparing Grains and Grain Products   **443**

Using the Recipe

- Have students read the recipe and discuss each step. Point out that students will have to determine when to start preparing the beans so that the rice will be done at the same time as the beans. Review safety and sanitation procedures that apply to this recipe. Caution students always to lift the lids of saucepans so that the steam is directed away from them.

- Have each lab team fill out a work plan. (See the *Foods Lab Resources* booklet.)

- Have students check off the ingredients and equipment listed on the recipe worksheet and prepare the recipe.

- Have students complete the evaluation and questions on the back of the recipe worksheet.

See Also . . .

The *Foods Lab Resources* booklet for the "Western Beans and Rice" recipe worksheet and other recipe alternatives.

Answers to Thinking About the Recipe

1. The brown rice and pinto beans provide the most protein.

2. You could use low-sodium tomato sauce, rinse the canned beans before using, or substitute cooked dry beans for canned.

Section 17.3
Legumes, Nuts, and Seeds

Introducing the Section

Motivators

- Have students work in small groups to review recipes from different cultures to identify ways legumes, nuts, and seeds are used. Have groups identify the types of legumes, nuts, and seeds used in the recipes they found. Also have them describe the types of dishes. Point out that legumes are considered to be the second most important food in the world, after grains.

- Have students identify favorite foods that combine grains with legumes, nuts, or seeds. Review the benefits of combining essential amino acids in grains with those in legumes, nuts, or seeds to create a complete protein.

Objectives

- Have students read the section objectives. Discuss the purpose of studying the section.

Vocabulary

- Pronounce the terms listed under "Look for These Terms." Have students find the terms and their definitions in the section.

Guided Reading

- Have students look at the headings within Section 17.3 to preview the concepts that will be discussed.

- Have students read the section and complete the appropriate part of the Chapter 17 Study Guide in the *Student Workbook*.

SECTION 17.3

Legumes, Nuts, and Seeds

OBJECTIVES

After studying this section, you should be able to:

- Identify the nutrients in legumes, nuts, and seeds.
- Give guidelines for buying, storing, and preparing legumes, nuts, and seeds.

LOOK FOR THIS TERM

legumes

Legumes are plants whose seeds grow in pods. They include beans, peas, and lentils.

Legumes come in different shapes, sizes, and colors. In one form or another, they are available in most parts of the world. They are considered to be the second most important food in the world, after grains.

Nutrients in Legumes

As explained in Section 17.1, all edible seeds have several parts. The inside of a legume contains the embryo, the tiny seedling that will grow into a plant under the right conditions. Surrounding the seedling is its food supply, rich in proteins, carbohydrates, vitamins, and minerals.

When beans and peas are green, they are eaten as vegetables. At that stage in their growth, however, they have not yet developed the proteins and some of the other nutrients found in legumes. As legumes mature, they store up nutrients for the embryo's food supply.

Legumes are excellent sources of complex carbohydrates, proteins, fiber, B vitamins, iron, calcium, potassium, and some trace minerals. Except for soybeans, they are low in fat.

Lima beans may be harvested while still green, as shown here, or left in the field until fully mature and dry.

Teacher's Classroom Resources—Section 17.3

Refer to these resources in the TCR package:

Reproducible Lesson Plans
Student Workbook
Extending the Text

Reteaching Activities
Section Quizzes
Testmaker Software
Color Transparencies

The combination of grains and legumes, as in this lasagne made with dry beans, provides complete protein. What are the advantages of using legumes and grains as protein sources?

Teaching . . .

- **Nutrients in Legumes**
- **Buying and Storing Legumes**

(text pages 444-445)

Comprehension Check

1. Ask students to define the word "legumes." *(plants whose seeds grow in pods)*

2. Ask students to list the nutrients commonly found in legumes. *(complex carbohydrates, proteins, fiber, B vitamins, iron, calcium, potassium, and some trace minerals)*

3. Ask students to describe what to look for when you buy legumes. *(bright color, no visible damage, and uniform size)*

Student Experiences

1. **Making Comparisons:** Have students compare the parts of a kernel of grain with the parts of legumes. *(Key skill: comparing)*

2. **Sharing Knowledge:** Provide each student with the answer to a question related to buying and storing legumes. Provide each student with a list of all the questions used. Ask students to move about the room and search for people who have the answers to the questions on their sheet. Have students record answers and get signatures of the student giving the answer. *(Key skill: cooperative learning)*

3. **Calculations:** Have students compare the nutrients in legumes with those in grains. How can eating both improve their nutrient quality? What are the advantages of eating dry beans, peas, or lentils at least twice a week instead of meat? *(Key skills: math, health)*

Legumes are included in the Meat, Poultry, Fish, Dry Beans, Eggs, and Nuts Group in the Food Guide Pyramid. Health experts urge people to eat dry beans, peas, or lentils at least twice a week instead of meat. When counting your servings, 1/2 cup (125 mL) of cooked dry beans counts as 1 ounce (28 g) of lean meat.

Legumes and grains work perfectly as a team. Each has the amino acids the other one lacks. By eating both sometime during the day, you can get the essential amino acids needed for good health. Grains and legumes make up about two-thirds of the protein eaten by people around the world.

Buying and Storing Legumes

Many types of legumes are available. The box on page 446 describes some examples.

When buying legumes, purchase only as much as you will use within six months. Legumes continue to dry out when stored. The drier they are, the longer they will take to cook.

If legumes are visible in the package, inspect them carefully to be sure you are getting good quality. Look for bright color, no visible damage, and uniform size. Mixed sizes result in uneven cooking, since smaller ones cook faster than larger ones.

Store dry legumes in a cool, dry place. Once the package has been opened, transfer the remainder to a tightly covered container.

Cooked legumes should be stored in the refrigerator if they will be used within a few days. For longer storage, freeze. When putting the beans in freezer containers, add enough cooking liquid to cover them so they will not dry out. Frozen cooked beans can be thawed in a microwave oven or in the refrigerator.

Preparing Legumes

Like grains, legumes are prepared by cooking in water. They need time to absorb water until they become soft enough to eat. Always follow package or recipe directions.

Cooked beans can be served as a side dish or used in recipes such as casseroles, soups, and salads. Preparing dry beans takes time, but is relatively easy. Lentils and dry peas cook in less than an hour. Dry peas are usually used in soup. Lentils are used in soup or as a side dish.

More About Legumes

Legume pods usually grow above ground on vines or small bushes. The legume has a seed coat, or skin, to protect the interior. The inside of a legume is called the *cotyledon* (cat-uhl-LEAD-uhn). The *hilum* (HIGH-lehm) is a tiny spot where the seed was attached to the pod. It absorbs water through this area.

Teaching . . .

• Preparing Legumes: Sorting and Rinsing, Soaking Beans

(text pages 445-447)

Comprehension Check

1. Ask students in what ways legumes are similar to grains. *(Both require time to absorb water; both contain incomplete proteins, although their proteins complement each other.)*

2. Ask students to list several types of legumes and describe their typical uses. *(See the chart on page 446.)*

3. Ask students to explain why it is important to sort and rinse dry legumes carefully. *(There may be pebbles and stems, as well as damaged or unsuitable legumes in the bag.)*

4. Ask students to describe the procedure for rinsing legumes. *(Rinse carefully in cool water and drain; rinse again and again until the rinsing water runs clear.)*

5. Ask students to explain the advantage of soaking beans before cooking them. *(Soaking reduces the amount of time the beans have to cook.)*

Type of Legume	Typical Uses
Black beans (turtle beans) Black skin, cream-colored inside, sweet flavor.	Soups, other dishes. Popular in Latin American and Asian cooking.
Black-eyed peas Actually beans, not peas. Small, oval, with black "eye" on one side.	Main dishes; "Hoppin' John" (popular Southern recipe).
Dry peas Available whole or split, green or yellow.	Soups.
Garbanzo beans (chickpeas) Round, roughly shaped, nut-like flavor, firm texture. Hold their shape when cooked.	Appetizers, salads, main dishes.
Lentils Thin, tiny, disc-shaped. Come in colors ranging from grayish brown to green to reddish orange.	Soups, stews, salads, side dish. Main ingredient in East Indian dish *dal*.
Lima beans White, flat beans in assorted sizes. Baby limas are smallest with mild flavor. Butter beans are largest with a rich, buttery flavor.	Soups, casseroles, side dish.
Pink and red beans Vary in size, flavor, and intensity of color. Kidney beans are largest with a hearty flavor.	Chili and other Latin American main dishes.
Pinto beans Pink and white, speckled. Similar in flavor and texture to pink and red beans.	Mexican foods, such as chili and refried beans.
Soybeans Distinct flavor. High in fat and protein. Difficult to digest.	Usually eaten in form of soy products, such as tofu and soy milk.
White beans Vary in size and flavor, but all have a firm texture. Great Northern are largest.	Navy beans are medium size. Soups, baked beans.

More About Lentils

Lentils have a mild, distinctive flavor. They can be served plain as a vegetable or pureed and used as a meat extender. Cooked lentils can be frozen for future use.

Lentils were one of the first crops to be cultivated. Legend has it that lentils were introduced into the United States in the early 1900s by a German minister. Traveling in the state of Washington, he gave a farmer a small amount of lentil seeds. That was the beginning of the lentil industry in the United States. Currently, most of the lentils in the United States are grown in Idaho and Washington.

Sorting, rinsing, and soaking are the first steps in preparing beans.

Sorting and Rinsing

Before cooking, sort legumes carefully. Pick out foreign material such as pebbles and stems. Also discard any legumes that are damaged, are smaller than the others, or have a greenish tint.

Rinse the legumes carefully by placing them in cool water. Drain them and rinse again. Repeat, if necessary, until the water is clear.

Soaking Beans

Beans normally take from one and a half to three hours to cook. Soaking before cooking can cut down on the cooking time by 15 to 30 minutes. Dry peas and lentils do not have to be soaked.

To soak beans, use a large pot. For every pound (500 g) of any kind of beans, sorted and washed, add 10 cups (2500 mL) hot water. Simmer for two to three minutes, then turn off the heat and cover the beans. Let them soak for at least an hour. The longer beans soak, the less cooking time they need.

Healthy Attitudes

People sometimes avoid beans because they may produce gas in the digestive system. The effect is caused by certain complex sugars in the beans that cannot be digested. Here are some suggestions that may help minimize the problem.

- Add beans to your food choices gradually. Start with a small amount once a week and gradually work up to larger amounts. This helps your body adapt.
- Soak beans before cooking. Change the soaking water several times. Use fresh water for cooking.
- Try different varieties of beans. Some cause more gas than others.

Most people find that if they add beans to their food choices gradually, they are better able to digest them.

Student Experiences

1. **Small Group Discussion:** Have students work in small groups to review cooking instructions on the labels of dried legumes. Why should legumes be sorted before cooking? Why should beans be soaked? Why should the soaking water be changed several times? Why should fresh water be used for cooking? Why should salt and acid foods, such as vinegar and tomatoes, be added near the end of the cooking time? *(Key skill: critical thinking)*

2. **Label Reading:** Have students read the ingredients and nutrition labels on convenience forms of beans. For what reason would you rinse plain canned beans before using them in recipes? What types of canned beans are available? *(Key skill: reading)*

Healthy Attitudes

Tell students that there are several products now on the market that, when sprinkled on beans, have the effect of reducing gas in the digestive system. Have interested students find out more about these products and how they work.

Food and Nutrition Science

Using Legumes as Thickeners: Have students choose a recipe that calls for a thickener such as flour or cornstarch. Have some students prepare the recipe as it is written. Have other students prepare the recipe but substitute mashed legumes for the thickener. Compare the two dishes. Ask students to evaluate the substitution in terms of taste, texture, and appearance.

Teaching . . .

• Simmering Beans

(text pages 448-449)

Comprehension Check

1. Ask students why it is important to choose a large pot when cooking beans. *(The beans double in volume as they cook.)*

2. Ask students to describe two ways to cook beans, other than simmering on a stovetop. *(In a slow cooker; in a pressure cooker; in a microwave oven.)*

Student Experiences

1. **Finding Recipes:** Have students find recipes for cooking beans. What cooking methods do the recipes use? *(Key skill: reading)*

2. **Making a Chart:** Have students make a chart showing the proper steps to cook a pot of beans. Have them take turns explaining their charts to each other. In what ways do they differ, if any? *(Key skill: creativity)*

Lab Experience

Have students cook beans by simmering on the range top, in a slow cooker, in a pressure cooker, and in a microwave oven. Compare the results. What might influence a person's choice of method?

Simmering Beans

The next step is to cook the legumes. If beans have been soaked, drain and rinse them first.

Place the beans in a large pot—they double in volume as they cook. Add water, using the amount specified in the package directions as a guide. More water may be needed if the legumes are older and drier. If desired, you can add chopped onions, garlic, and dried herbs for a flavorful broth.

Cover the pot and bring the water to a boil. Then lower the heat to a simmer.

Use the package directions as a guide for cooking time. For best results, start checking at the minimum cooking time given. If the beans are not tender enough, continue cooking. If the beans will be used in a salad or further cooked in a recipe, cook them a shorter time so they are a little more firm. If you plan to mash them, cook longer so they are a little more soft.

TIPS for Success

Cooking Beans

❖ Simmer beans gently. If boiled, they get mushy and the skins break.

❖ Leave the cover slightly ajar during cooking. If the pot is tightly covered, the cooking liquid foams up and can boil over.

❖ Check several times during cooking to make sure the beans are always covered with water. If more water is needed, add hot water, not cold.

❖ Salt and acid foods, such as vinegar and tomatoes, toughen beans. Add them near the end of the cooking time, if desired.

If you were cooking beans to use in a salad such as this one, would you shorten or lengthen the cooking time? Why?

More About Beans

Beans, like other legumes, are complex carbohydrates. They digest more slowly than many other carbohydrate foods, such as fruit. Therefore, they give a feeling of fullness longer.

When done, the beans should have only a little cooking liquid left. Serve the liquid with the beans—it contains B vitamins. If you plan to use only the beans, save the liquid for soups, sauces, or broth.

Other Methods

An easy way to cook beans is with a slow cooker. Do not presoak them. Check the owner's manual of the slow cooker for exact directions. In general, the beans are combined with boiling water in the cooker. Mix well, cover, and cook on the high setting. This method generally takes three to eight hours, depending on the kind of beans.

Beans can also be cooked in a pressure cooker. Follow directions in the owner's manual.

Convenience Forms of Beans

If you don't have time to cook dry beans, don't let that stop you from using them in meals. Canned beans are a time-saver because they are already cooked. Use plain canned beans in recipes as you would cooked dry beans. Rinse them first to cut down on sodium. They can be mashed by hand or in a blender to make dips, sandwich spreads, and fillings for tacos. You can also buy canned beans with sauces and seasonings added.

Legumes can be cooked in the microwave, too. It takes about the same amount of time as conventional cooking. If you want to prepare a bean recipe in the microwave oven, use canned beans to save time.

Nuts and Seeds

Like legumes, nuts and seeds are included in the Meat Group in the Food Guide Pyramid. Nuts and seeds are high in protein and B vitamins. Because they are also very high in fat, however, they should be used sparingly.

A wide assortment of nuts are available, including almonds, filberts, cashews, Brazil nuts, and walnuts. Even though peanuts are legumes, most people use them as they do other nuts. The most popular edible seeds include pumpkin, squash, sunflower, and sesame.

Sunflower seeds are a popular type of edible seed. What nutrients do they provide?

More About Nuts and Seeds

Unlike peanuts, nuts grow on trees. Because trees mature slowly, the supply of nuts is limited.

Nuts have a hard outer shell and a tender, chewy inside. Seeds have a hard outer shell that can be easily removed before eating.

Many seeds, such as safflower, are used mainly for the oils they contain.

Teaching . . .

• Nuts and Seeds

(text pages 449-450)

Comprehension Check

1. Ask students to describe the nutritional advantages and disadvantages of including nuts and seeds in daily meals. *(Advantages: high in protein and B vitamins, tasty; disadvantages: high in fat.)*

2. Ask students to list popular edible seeds. Which ones have students eaten? *(Edible seeds include pumpkin, squash, sunflower, sesame.)*

Student Experiences

1. **Class Discussion:** Discuss guidelines for buying nuts and seeds. How should nuts and seeds be stored? What are some ways to use nuts and seeds? *(Key skill: kitchen management skills)*

2. **Comparing Nutrients:** Have students compare the nutrients in nuts and seeds with those in grains and legumes. In which nutrients are nuts and seeds high? Why should they be used sparingly? *(Key skill: health)*

3. **Supermarket Survey:** Have students survey a local supermarket to make a list of the nuts and edible seeds available. In what forms are nuts and seeds available? *(Key skill: analysis)*

Lab Experience

Have students make homemade peanut butter. Try using other nuts or seeds if desired. Evaluate the results. Discuss possible uses of homemade nut or seed spreads.

Review

- Ask students to summarize the main ideas in this section.
- Have students complete the Section Review. (Answers appear below.)

Evaluation

- Have students write a short essay explaining how to choose, prepare, and store legumes, nuts, and seeds.
- Have students take the quiz for Section 17.3. (Refer to the *Section Quizzes* booklet or use the *Testmaker Software*.)

Reteaching

- Provide a display of various types of legumes. Help students identify each type and explain how he or she might use the legume in a meal or recipe.
- Refer to the *Reteaching Activities* booklet for the Section 17.3 activity sheet.

Enrichment

- Have students calculate the nutritional value of recipes that combine legumes with grain and animal products.

Closure

- Discuss various ways to include legumes, nuts, and seeds in a weekly meal plan.

Nuts and seeds can add flavor, texture, and nutrients to many recipes.

Buying and Storing Nuts and Seeds

Nuts and seeds are sold with or without the shell. Some are roasted with oil, which adds more fat. Dry roasting is a special process that roasts nuts and seeds without adding oil.

Nuts and seeds can be ground into a thick, spreadable paste. Peanut butter is a common example. Tahini (tuh-HEE-nee) is a spread made from ground sesame seeds. It is popular in Middle Eastern cooking as a spread and flavoring.

When buying nuts and seeds, avoid those in shells that are cracked or broken. Harmful germs may be present in the edible parts.

Store nuts and seeds in the refrigerator. Because they contain oil, they can spoil at room temperature if not used quickly.

Using Nuts and Seeds

You can enjoy nuts and seeds in a variety of ways. Chopped or ground nuts and seeds add flavor and texture to baked goods, salads, cereal, and yogurt. They can also be used in meatless main dishes for added protein. Nut butters and spreads can be used in sandwiches or recipes.

450   Chapter 17: Grains, Legumes, Nuts, and Seeds

Section 17.3 Review

RECALL THE FACTS

1. Name five nutrients supplied by legumes.
2. Within how many months should dry legumes be used? Why?
3. What are the three basic steps in preparing dry beans?
4. Why should nuts and seeds be used sparingly?

DISCUSS YOUR IDEAS

5. What characteristics of legumes might account for their importance in the world food supply?

APPLY YOUR LEARNING

6. Look through cookbooks to find recipes that use legumes in each of the following: a vegetarian main dish, a main dish with meat or poultry, a soup, a salad, and a side dish. Be prepared to discuss how the recipe directions relate to the preparation principles you have learned in this section.

■ Answers to Section Review ■

1. *Any five:* Complex carbohydrates, proteins, fiber, B vitamins, iron, calcium, potassium, and some trace minerals.

2. Six, because the legumes continue to dry out while they are being stored.

3. Sorting and rinsing, soaking, and simmering (cooking).

4. They contain a high amount of fat.

5. Answers will vary. They are easy to grow, abundant, easy to cook, etc.

6. Answers will vary.

Steve Helman

Farmer

JOB DESCRIPTION

"I own a Midwestern crop farm that's been in my family for five generations."

RESPONSIBILITIES

"When most people think of farming, they picture you out in the field on a tractor, planting and harvesting. That's part of the job, of course, but there's a lot more to it. Our farm is a family business. We have to plan how to use our land, what type of seed to buy, what yield to expect, when to buy new equipment—everything involved in getting a crop to market."

WHY I CHOSE THIS JOB

"I grew up on this farm, and I couldn't imagine ever leaving it. To me, farming is not just a job, but a way of life."

EDUCATION

"I took time off from farming to earn a four-year college degree in agriculture. When I was in high school I participated in the Future Farmers of America and 4-H."

SKILLS

"Besides the physical stamina you need to be a farmer, you must be organized and able to plan ahead. You also have to be aware of outside influences, such as the weather and fluctuations in prices, and you must be able to keep financial and inventory books."

FAVORITE PART OF THE JOB

"It's very rewarding to be my own boss. My goal is to produce the highest yield of top-quality corn and soybeans possible."

- In what ways could a personal computer be useful in managing the business aspects of a farm?
- What aspects of Steve's job do you think you might enjoy? Why?

451

CAREER PROFILE: FARMER

Thinking About . . . Farming

- Have students think of other questions they would like to ask Steve Helman about farming. (Examples: What do you do when prices fluctuate wildly? How do you decide what to plant? In what ways do you use your degree in agriculture on the farm?)
- Ask student volunteers to tell what they think would be the most exciting part of farming.
- Have students brainstorm additional decisions that might have to be made by farmers.

Student Opportunities

Students planning a career in farming should join their local 4-H club, get involved with their local Cooperative Extension Service, and/or seek a job as a farmhand at a local farm.

Occupational Outlook

Advancement in farming can be had only by buying more land (getting a bigger farm) or by using techniques that make the existing land more profitable.

For More Information

For additional information about farming and agricultural careers, encourage students to contact:
- National FFA Organization, Box 15160, 5632 Mt. Vernon Memorial Highway, Alexandria, VA 22309
- American Farm Bureau Federation, 225 Touhy Ave., Park Ridge, IL 60068
- National Association of State Universities and Land Grant Colleges, Division of Agriculture, One DuPont Circle, Suite 710, Washington, D.C. 20036

Review

- Have students complete the Chapter Review. (Answers appear below.)

Evaluation

- Have students choose a recipe that contains both a grain and a legume and prepare the recipe. Watch students' technique and procedure, and evaluate the final product.

- Have students take the test for Chapter 17. (Refer to the *Chapter and Unit Tests* booklet or construct your own test using the *Testmaker Software*.)

■ ANSWERS ■

REVIEWING FACTS

1. Whole grain products use the whole wheat grain (germ, endosperm, and bran). Enriched products have usually had some parts of the grain removed by processing, and are enriched with nutrients to make their nutritional value similar to what it was before processing.

2. *Couscous:* steamed, cracked endosperm of wheat kernel; used as cereal, in salads and main dishes, or sweetened for dessert. *Kasha:* roasted buckwheat that is hulled and crushed; used as breakfast cereal or side dish. *Triticale:* cross between wheat and rye; used in cereals and main dishes and combined with other cooked grains.

3. Whole grains or grain products, fresh pasta, refrigerate bread only for short time if humidity is high.

4. Because they are dry.

CHAPTER 17 REVIEW

SUMMARY

SECTION 17.1

Choosing Grains and Grain Products: Grain kernels are made up of the germ, endosperm, and bran. Grains are generally high in complex carbohydrates, proteins, fiber, vitamins, and minerals. However, the nutrition of grains depends on how they are processed. Cooked grains are popular as side dishes and breakfast cereals. Grain products include instant and ready-to-eat cereals, pasta, and breads. Look for nutrition and quality when buying. Store grains and grain products properly to maintain their quality.

SECTION 17.2

Preparing Grains and Grain Products: Grains must be cooked before eating. Although cooking methods for many grains are similar, always check the package directions. Rice and many other grains are simmered in only as much water as they can absorb. Pasta is boiled in a large amount of water, then drained. Breakfast cereals are served hot or cold, often with milk and fruit.

SECTION 17.3

Legumes, Nuts, and Seeds: Legumes are high in protein, fiber, and other nutrients. Most are low in fat. The many types of legumes can be used in main dishes, side dishes, and salads. Dry beans require long cooking in water. Soaking dry beans first decreases the cooking time. Nuts and seeds are high in protein, but also fat. They may be eaten plain or added to baked goods and other dishes.

REVIEWING FACTS

1. What is the difference between whole grain and enriched products? (17.1)

2. Describe the following grain products and tell how they are used: couscous, kasha, triticale. (17.1)

3. Name three specific instances when grains or grain products should be refrigerated. (17.1)

4. Why must grains be cooked before they are eaten? (17.2)

5. What type of rice should not be stirred during cooking? Why? (17.2)

6. What term is used to describe properly cooked pasta? What does it mean? (17.2)

7. Describe the following legumes and tell how they are used: garbanzo beans; lentils; soybeans. (17.3)

8. Give three guidelines for buying legumes. (17.3)

9. Briefly describe how to cook beans. (17.3)

10. What is dry roasting? (17.3)

5. Long-grain rice, because stirring scrapes off the starch and makes the rice grains stick together.

6. "Al dente"; firm when you bite into it.

7. *Garbanzo beans:* round, roughly shaped "chickpeas" with a nut-like flavor; used in appetizers, salads, main dishes. *Lentils:* thin, disc-shaped, come in several colors; used in soups, stews, salads, side dishes. *Soybeans:* have a distinct flavor and are high in fat and protein, but difficult to digest; used soy products such as tofu and soy milk.

8. Bright color, no visible damage, uniform size.

CHAPTER 17 REVIEW

LEARNING BY DOING

1. **Taste test:** Prepare a variety of different grains, such as couscous, bulgur, and millet. Compare them for taste, texture, and appearance. Decide what types of dishes or recipes each grain might be used in. Give reasons for your answers. (17.1, 17.2)

2. **Foods lab:** Prepare a dessert dish using rice or pasta. What nutritional value does rice or pasta add to the dessert? (17.2)

3. **Foods lab:** Make your own spread from nuts or seeds. (Look in a cookbook for a basic peanut butter recipe and adapt it to use different nuts or seeds if desired.) Evaluate the results on taste, texture, and appearance. Explain how you might use the product. (17.3)

THINKING CRITICALLY

1. **Drawing conclusions:** Why do you think the bran and germ are sometimes removed when processing grains, even though it results in a less nutritious product? (17.1)

2. **Recognizing fallacies:** A friend of yours who wants to lose weight avoids pasta because he thinks it is fattening. Do you agree? Explain your answer. (17.1, 17.2)

3. **Identifying cause and effect:** Your friend tells you that the last time she cooked beans, they were tough and chewy. What are some possible explanations for this? (17.3)

MAKING DECISIONS AND SOLVING PROBLEMS

What Would You Do?

1. Your family relies mostly on processed grain products and eats very few whole grains. You would like to start introducing more whole grains to make your family's meals more nutritious. (17.1)

2. You have cooked too much rice for your family's dinner. You wonder what to do with the leftovers. (17.2)

3. You would like to cook beans for your family's dinner tonight, but you will be out of the house all day. (17.3)

LINKING YOUR STUDIES

1. **Social studies:** Using library sources, write a report on a grain that is popular in a specific foreign country. How was the grain introduced in that country? Why is it popular? How is it used? What percentage of the population is employed in growing and processing the grain? (17.1)

2. **Math:** Draw a graph comparing the cooking times of various grains and legumes. (17.2, 17.3)

3. **Science:** Write a short report on scientist George Washington Carver. What contributions did he make to the use of peanuts? What were some of his creations or discoveries? How do you benefit today from his work? (17.3)

LEARNING BY DOING

1. Answers will vary.

2. Using rice or pasta in a dessert adds the nutrients present in the rice or pasta.

3. Answers will vary.

THINKING CRITICALLY

1. Answers will vary.

2. No, the pasta itself is a low-calorie, low-fat food; the sauces that are usually put on the pasta add the calories.

3. Answers will vary. She may have added salt, vinegar, or some other type of acid early in the cooking process.

MAKING DECISIONS AND SOLVING PROBLEMS

Answers to "Making Decisions and Solving Problems" will vary. Encourage students to give reasons for their answers.

LINKING YOUR STUDIES

Answers to "Linking Your Studies" will vary. Encourage students to give reasons for their answers.

453

9. Sort and rinse them; add hot water and simmer for two or three minutes, then turn off heat and soak for at least an hour; drain and rinse beans; simmer beans in fresh water until done.

10. A special process that roasts nuts and seeds without adding oil.

Planning the Chapter

Chapter Overview

Section 18.1: Choosing Dairy Foods

Section 18.2: Preparing Dairy Foods

Section 18.3: Egg Basics

Section 18.4: Using Eggs in Recipes

Introducing the Chapter

Motivators

- Provide students with a list of dairy foods and egg dishes. Ask students to identify those they have eaten in the past three days. Point out that dairy foods and eggs are also used as ingredients in foods. Have students add foods that may have contained dairy foods or eggs to their lists. Discuss the importance of dairy foods and eggs in the diet.

- Provide students with cookbooks. Give them five minutes to list as many recipes as they can find that include dairy foods and eggs as ingredients. Discuss the variety of dishes made with dairy foods or eggs.

Teacher's Classroom Resources—Chapter 18

Refer to these resources in the TCR package:

Enrichment Activities

Chapter and Unit Tests

Testmaker Software

CHAPTER 18

Dairy Foods and Eggs

454

Cooperative Learning Suggestions

Initiate a Co-op Co-op activity. Have students work in groups to research uses of dairy foods and eggs in other parts of the world. Assign each group a different area of the world: Latin America, Europe, Asia, Africa, and Australia. What dairy foods and egg dishes originated in each part of the world? In what countries did the various cheeses originate? What different names are given to common dishes such as omelets? Have each group report its findings to the class in an interesting way.

Choosing Dairy Foods

Section 18.1
Choosing Dairy Foods

OBJECTIVES

After studying this section, you should be able to:

- Identify nutrients in dairy foods.
- Describe the types of dairy foods available.
- Give guidelines for buying and storing dairy foods.

LOOK FOR THESE TERMS

nonfat milk solids
pasteurized
ultra-pasteurization
homogenized
cultured
ripened cheese
unripened cheese

Dairy foods include milk and the many products made from milk, such as yogurt and different kinds of cheeses.

Nutrients in Dairy Foods

Milk has been called an "almost-perfect" food. It is especially high in proteins, vitamin A, riboflavin, vitamin B_{12}, calcium, phosphorus, magnesium, and zinc. When fortified, it is an excellent source of vitamin D.

Milk also contains saturated fat and cholesterol. Some or most of the fat can be removed to produce skim and low-fat milk. These products also have less cholesterol.

The fat in other dairy products depends on the kind of milk from which they are made. Those made with skim or low-fat milk have less fat.

Wisconsin produces more dairy products than any other state. Other leading dairy states include California, Minnesota, New York, and Pennsylvania.

Introducing the Section

Motivators

- Create a bulletin board entitled "Milk Power." Show a personified glass of milk with large muscles. List the nutrient content of milk and equivalent servings of other dairy products.
- Provide a variety of cheeses for students to taste. Discuss the consistency, shape, color, texture, and flavor of the cheeses.

Objectives

- Have students read the section objectives. Discuss the purpose of studying the section.

Vocabulary

- Pronounce the terms listed under "Look for These Terms." Have students find the terms and their definitions in the section.

Guided Reading

- Have students look at the headings within Section 18.1 to preview the concepts that will be discussed.
- Have students read the section and complete the appropriate part of the Chapter 18 Study Guide in the *Student Workbook*.

Teacher's Classroom Resources—Section 18.1

Refer to these resources in the TCR package:

Reproducible Lesson Plans	*Section Quizzes*
Student Workbook	*Testmaker Software*
Extending the Text	*Food Science Resources*
Reteaching Activities	*Color Transparencies*

Teaching . . .

- **Nutrients in Dairy Foods**
- **Milk**
- **Yogurt**

(text pages 455-457)

Comprehension Check

1. Ask students to identify the percentage of fat that comes from whole milk, lowfat milk, and skim milk. *(Whole milk: 48 percent; lowfat milk: 38 percent; skim milk: only a trace)*

2. Ask students to explain what UHT milk is. What might be some uses for UHT milk? *(Ultra-high temperature milk, which goes through a high-temperature pasteurization process and is packaged in aseptic containers so that it is shelf stable. It might be used in developing countries where refrigeration may not be available; small families without children may use it to keep the milk from going bad before they use it all.)*

3. Ask students to identify other types of milk and describe their characteristics. *(See list on page 457.)*

4. Ask students to explain how yogurt is made. *(By adding a harmless bacteria culture to milk.)*

Special Needs Strategies

Learning Disabled: Ask students to develop a word game on: types of dairy foods, varieties of cheeses, nutrients in dairy foods and eggs, or guidelines for preparing dairy foods and eggs. Have students exchange and play the word games.

The Food Guide Pyramid recommends two to three servings a day from the Milk Group. A typical serving includes 1 cup (250 mL) of milk or yogurt, 1½ ounces (42 g) of natural cheese, or 2 ounces (56 g) of process cheese.

Types of Dairy Foods

An array of dairy foods are available in the marketplace. They include fresh and convenience forms of milk, cheeses, cream, butter, and frozen dairy desserts.

Milk

As stated earlier, milk is available with varying fat content. The dairy industry measures fat in milk by weight. From a nutrition standpoint, however, it is more useful to know the percentage of calories that come from fat.

- ❖ **Whole milk** is 3.3 percent fat by weight with 48 percent of the calories from fat.
- ❖ **Low-fat milk** is 1 to 2 percent fat by weight with 16 to 38 percent of calories from fat.
- ❖ **Skim milk** contains only a trace of fat.

Fresh whole milk contains about 87 percent water and 13 percent solids. Some of the solids are milkfat. The **nonfat milk solids** contain most of the protein, vitamins, minerals, and lactose (milk sugar) found in milk.

Processing of Fluid Milk

Before milk reaches the marketplace as a beverage, it must be processed. Government regulations state that milk must be **pasteurized,** or heat-treated to kill harmful bacteria and stop enzyme activity. Enzymes in milk can make it spoil quickly. **Ultra-pasteurization** heats milk to a higher temperature, which means it can be kept refrigerated longer than pasteurized milk.

UHT (ultra-high temperature) milk is processed the same as ultra-pasteurized milk. It is packaged in aseptic containers (sometimes called "juice boxes"), which makes it a shelf-stable product.

Milkfat is lighter than other milk fluids and easily separates, rising to the top of the milk. When milk is **homogenized,** the fat is broken down and evenly distributed in the milk so it does not separate.

Inspectors test milk during and after processing to ensure quality and safety.

Food and Nutrition Science

Lactobacillus acidophilus: Some people develop an intolerance to lactose and cannot digest milk properly. One way to make milk easier to digest is to add a bacteria, *lactobacillus acidophilus*. It consumes the lactose, producing lactic acid. However, it may make the milk taste slightly sour.

Low-fat milk is the most common form of acidophilus milk, although whole and skim forms are also available. The label must state that the milk contains the acidophilus bacteria.

When milk is skimmed, most of the vitamin A is removed. By law, any vitamin A removed when making low-fat and skim milk must be replaced. In addition, some manufacturers voluntarily fortify milk with vitamin D.

Other Types of Milk

Besides plain fluid milk, various flavored milks and convenience products are available.

Some milk products are **cultured**. This means a harmless bacteria culture is added to them after pasteurization. The bacteria cause fermentation to take place. This gives cultured dairy products, such as yogurt and buttermilk, a characteristic tangy, acidic flavor.

- ❖ **Buttermilk** has a tart, buttery flavor and smooth, thick texture. It was originally a fluid left after cream was churned into butter. Now it is made from cultured low-fat or skim milk. Often nonfat dry milk solids are added.
- ❖ **Chocolate milk** has chocolate or cocoa and sweetener added.
- ❖ **Kefir** (keh-FUR) is a beverage similar in flavor to yogurt. The authentic Middle Eastern beverage is made of fermented camel's milk. In the United States, kefir is made from cultured cow's milk.

A variety of milk products are available for use as beverages or in cooking.

- ❖ **Nonfat dry milk** is a powdered form of skim milk. When reconstituted, use and refrigerate as you do liquid skim milk. The instant variety mixes with water more easily. Add the powder directly to recipes to increase nutrients, especially protein and calcium, without adding fat.
- ❖ **Evaporated milk** is canned whole or skim milk that contains only half the amount of water as regular milk. Use evaporated skim milk as a nonfat cream substitute in beverages.
- ❖ **Sweetened condensed milk** is concentrated, sweetened canned milk. It is used to make candy and desserts.

Yogurt

Yogurt is made by adding a harmless bacteria culture to milk, resulting in a thick, creamy, custard-like product with a tangy flavor. Yogurt may be purchased plain or with added flavorings such as vanilla and fruits.

Science Connection

Chemistry:

Coagulating Milk Protein

Milk contains many different proteins, but two major ones are involved in making milk products such as yogurt and cheese. The two proteins are casein (kay-SEEN) and whey (way). When an acid food or milk-clotting enzymes such as rennin (REH-nihn) are added to milk, the two proteins separate. Casein clumps together into solid groups called curds, as in cottage cheese. The whey is a thin, bluish liquid that remains after the curds clump. By turning proteins into curds, many different dairy products are made.

■ ■ ■

Student Experiences

1. **Class Survey:** Survey the class to find out how many students get the recommended two to three servings a day of dairy products. Discuss typical servings of various dairy foods. *(Key skill: health)*

2. **Display:** Display containers from a variety of dairy foods. Have students identify the fresh and convenience forms of milk, cheeses, cream, butter, and frozen dairy desserts. Have students compare the nutrients in different forms of dairy foods. *(Key skill: evaluation)*

3. **Demonstration:** Demonstrate how to reconstitute nonfat milk solids to fluid milk. Have students sample it. Refrigerate and have students sample again the next day. Compare the taste of the reconstituted milk with the taste of other milks. Discuss cost, nutritive value, taste, and use. *(Key skill: kitchen management skills)*

4. **Supermarket Survey:** Have students visit a supermarket and make a list of the types of milk available. Which products are cultured? Which are flavored? How do nonfat dry milk and evaporated milk compare with whole or skimmed milk? *(Key skill: consumer awareness)*

5. **Demonstration:** Demonstrate how to make homemade yogurt using nonfat dry milk. Have students experiment with different ways to flavor it. *(Key skill: science)*

Food and Nutrition Science

Effects of Acids Experiment: See the *Food Science Resources* booklet for the "Effect of Acid on Protein" teaching guides and student experiment worksheet.

The experiment tests the effects of acid (vinegar) on the physical appearance of proteins in milk.

Using the Photo

Refer students to the photo on page 457. Ask students how many of the products they have used in the past. What might be a practical use for each form of milk? What are some other forms of milk?

18.1

Teaching . . .

- • Cheeses
- • Cream
- • Butter

(text pages 457-460)

Comprehension Check

1. Ask students to name the two basic categories of cheeses and to explain the difference between them. *(Ripened and unripened; ripened cheeses are aged for a period of time, so that they can be stored for a relatively long time. Unripened cheeses last only a few days in the refrigerator.)*

2. Ask students to name three types of ripened cheeses and three types of unripened cheeses and to describe the characteristics of each. *(See the chart on page 459.)*

3. Ask students to list various types of cream. Which has the highest fat content? Which have lower fat content? *(heavy cream [highest fat content], light cream, half and half, sour cream)*

4. Ask students to explain how butter is graded. *(Grade AA is superior in quality, with a delicate, sweet flavor and a smooth, creamy texture. Grade A is very good in quality and has a pleasing flavor with a smooth texture. Grade B butter is made from sour cream and has a pleasing flavor.)*

Science Connection

Have students find out more about how milk products are separated. Is there more than one way to separate milk proteins? What products are made from curds and whey after separation?

■ ■ ■

Yogurt is a concentrated form of milk and is therefore higher in nutrients. For example, 1 cup (250 mL) of nonfat yogurt has 452 milligrams of calcium, while a cup (250 mL) of skim milk has 302 milligrams.

Cheeses

Cheese is made from curds with the whey drained off. There are two basic categories of cheeses—ripened (also called aged) and unripened.

Ripened cheese is made from curds to which ripening agents, such as bacteria, mold, yeast, or a combination of these, have been added. The cheese is then aged under carefully controlled conditions. Aging time depends on the kind of cheese. The result is a cheese that can be stored for a relatively long time.

The texture of ripened cheeses can be categorized as soft, semi-soft, semi-hard, hard, and very hard cheeses.

Specialty cheeses are created by combining several ripened cheeses by either cold or hot processing methods. *Cold pack* cheese is a blend of ripened cheeses processed without heat. Flavorings and seasoning are often added. *Pasteurized process cheese* is a blend of ripened cheeses processed with heat. Examples include process American cheese, cheese spread, and cheese food.

Unripened cheese is made of curds that have not been aged. Most unripened cheeses will keep only a few days in the refrigerator.

The chart on page 459 describes some different varieties of cheeses.

Cream

Cream is a liquid separated from milk. Several types are available that vary in fat content. Heavy cream, the highest in fat, whips easily. Light cream, which is not as high in fat, is used in coffee. Half and half is a mixture of milk and cream. Sour cream, made by adding lactic acid bacteria to cream, is thick and rich with a tangy flavor.

Cheese is made by adding enzymes or other ingredients to milk, causing it to thicken and form curds. The curds are then separated from the whey and further processed into cheese.

Thinking Skills

Critical Thinking: Discuss whether adding chocolate to milk is a good way to entice children to drink milk.

Food and Nutrition Science

Separation of Fat Experiment: See the *Food Science Resources* booklet for the "Separating Fat From Cream" teaching guides and student experiment worksheet. The experiment demonstrates turning invisible fat into visible fat using agitation.

Types of Cheese

RIPENED CHEESES	Appearance	Texture and Flavor
Blue Cheese	White cheese with a blue vein.	*Semi-soft.* Tangy flavor.
Brick	Light yellow in color.	*Semi-soft.* Sweet, mild but pungent flavor.
Brie (bree)	White, edible crust with a creamy yellow interior.	*Soft.* Mild to pungent flavor.
Camembert (KAM-ehm-behr)	White, edible crust with a creamy yellow interior. Similar to Brie.	*Soft.* Mild to pungent flavor.
Cheddar	White to orange in color.	*Hard.* Mild to sharp in flavor.
Colby	Similar to Cheddar, but more moist.	*Hard.* Mild to sharp in flavor.
Edam (EE-duhm)	Creamy yellow Dutch cheese with red wax coating.	*Semi-hard.* Mild, nut-like flavor.
Feta (FAY-tuh)	White, crumbly cheese.	*Semi-hard.* Salty "pickled" flavor.
Gouda	Creamy yellow cheese with red wax coating. Similar to Edam, but higher in fat.	*Semi-hard.* Mild, nut-like flavor.
Monterey Jack	Creamy white cheese with tiny cracks.	*Semi-soft.* Mild flavor.
Muenster (MUHN-stir)	Orange exterior and white interior.	*Semi-soft.* Mild flavor.
Parmesan (PAHR-muh-zahn)	Creamy white, granular cheese.	*Very hard.* Tangy, robust flavor.
Provolone (proh-vo-LOW-nee)	Creamy golden yellow, plastic-like cheese.	Hard. Bland to sharp, smoked. flavor.
Romano (roh-MAH-noh)	Creamy white, similar to Parmesan.	Very hard. Rich, tangy flavor.
Swiss	Creamy white cheese with holes in it.	Hard. Firm with a nut-like flavor.
UNRIPENED CHEESES	Appearance	Texture and Flavor
Cottage Cheese	Moist, soft cheese with large or small curd.	Bland flavor, but flavorings such as chives may be added. May be creamed.
Cream Cheese	Smooth, spreadable white cheese.	Mild, slightly acid flavor. Flavorings such as strawberry may be added.
Farmer's Cheese	Firm and dry. Similar to cottage cheese.	Bland flavor.
Mozzarella	Creamy white, plastic-like cheese.	Semi-soft. Mild flavor.
Ricotta	Moist, white cheese.	Mild, sweet flavor.

Student Experiences

1. **Class Discussion:** How is fresh cheese used? *(finger food, in salads or sandwiches, baking, cooking) (Key skill: critical thinking)*

2. **Poster Project:** Have each student research the history, production, characteristics, and uses of one type of cheese. Ask students to make posters to present their findings to the class. *(Key skills: research, creativity)*

3. **Demonstration:** Demonstrate how to churn butter. *(Key skill: analysis)*

Lab Experience

Have students prepare dips using sour cream, plain yogurt, and blended cottage cheese. Serve with raw vegetable dippers. Have students compare the calories and milk fat in the dips, as well as the tastes. What conclusions can students draw? In what other recipes could you substitute yogurt or cottage cheese for sour cream? *(potato toppings, dressings)*

Food and Nutrition Science

Lactose Intolerance: Have students find out more about lactose intolerance and what causes it. Why can lactose-intolerant people consume some dairy products but not others?

Teaching . . .

- **Frozen Dairy Desserts**
- **Buying and Storing Dairy Foods**

(text pages 460-461)

Comprehension Check

1. Ask students to list types of frozen desserts made from dairy products. *(ice cream, sherbet, frozen yogurt)*

2. Ask students how long milk products can be used safely. *(up to five days after the "sell by" date, if they have been stored properly)*

3. Ask students to list guidelines for storing dairy foods. *(See list on pages 460-461.)*

Student Experiences

1. **Taste Testing:** Have students conduct taste tests of three brands of ice cream and one low-fat ice cream of the same flavor. Cover the containers and color-code. Dip small samples into mini paper baking cups in the same colors as the container labels. Have students compare taste, quality, and price. *(Key skill: evaluation)*

2. **Product Comparison:** Have students compare labels from frozen dairy desserts, including regular ice cream, low-fat ice cream, frozen custard, frozen yogurt, fruit sherbet, and water ice. Which provides the most nutrients? Which are highest and lowest in milkfat and calories? *(Key skill: reading)*

Healthy Attitudes

Ask students why the calories and fat in the chart are given for vanilla flavor. Does the flavoring add calories? If so, how? *(It depends on the product and the type of flavoring.)*

Butter

Butter is made from milk, cream, or a combination of both. Because it is high in saturated fat and also contains cholesterol, it should be used in moderation.

Butter is graded for quality by the USDA. *Grade AA* is superior in quality. It has a delicate sweet flavor, a smooth creamy texture, and spreads well. It may be purchased salted or unsalted. *Grade A* butter is very good in quality and has a pleasing flavor with a smooth texture. *Grade B* butter is made from sour cream and has a pleasing flavor.

Frozen Dairy Desserts

Several different types of frozen desserts are available. They differ in fat content and ingredients. All come in a variety of flavors. Here are some examples:

❖ **Ice cream** is a whipped frozen mixture of milk, cream, sweeteners, flavorings, and other additives. In addition to regular ice cream, you can buy reduced-fat, low-fat, nonfat, and no-sugar-added versions.

❖ **Frozen yogurt** is similar to ice cream but with yogurt cultures added. Low-fat and nonfat varieties are the most popular.

Healthy Attitudes

What's the scoop on frozen dairy desserts? Below are typical amounts of calories and fat in a 1/2 cup (125 mL) serving of various products (vanilla flavor). Values do vary by brand and flavor, however, so check the nutrition label when you buy.

	Calories	Fat (g)
Premium ice cream	175	12
Regular ice cream	135	7
Low-fat ice cream	92	3
Sherbet	135	2
Low-fat frozen yogurt	125	3

❖ **Sherbet** is made from milkfat, sugar, water, flavorings, and other additives. It generally has less fat and more sugar than regular ice cream.

Buying and Storing Dairy Foods

When buying dairy products, look for the date on the package. Most milk products can be safely used up to five days beyond the "sell by" date if they have been stored properly. Yogurt and some ripened cheeses may be stored for longer periods of time. Make sure containers are sealed tightly and have not been opened before you buy them.

The different types of frozen dairy desserts differ in ingredients, fat, and calories. Check the label to be sure you know which kind you are buying.

Effects of Gelatin Experiment: See the *Food Science Resources* booklet for the "Effect of Gelatin on a Frozen Dessert" teaching guides and student experiment worksheet. The experiment tests the appearance, texture, flavor, and melting characteristics of adding gelatin to a frozen dessert.

Cheese can be frozen for later use in cooked dishes, such as this turkey and rice casserole.

Dairy foods are highly perishable. Store them immediately when you get home from shopping. Refrigerate all dairy foods in their original containers, if possible.

Here are some additional tips for storing dairy foods:

❖ Tightly close milk and cream containers. These products can pick up aromas from other foods and develop off-flavors.

❖ Store milk away from light. Light destroys the riboflavin (a B vitamin) in milk.

❖ Keep cheeses tightly wrapped.

❖ Hard cheeses can be frozen, but the texture will change. Freeze in 1/2 pound (250 g) portions. Use crumbled, shredded, or in cooked dishes.

❖ Refrigerate butter up to several weeks. For longer storage, freeze up to nine months.

❖ Store ice cream tightly covered in the freezer.

SAFETY CHECK

After pouring milk, return the container to the refrigerator immediately. Do not pour milk that has been sitting in a serving pitcher back into the original container. Instead, if the milk has been at room temperature less than two hours, refrigerate it in a separate container and use soon. Discard milk that has been left at room temperature more than two hours.

■ Section 18.1 Review ■

RECALL THE FACTS

1. Identify four nutrients in milk products.

2. Why is milk pasteurized?

3. What is the difference between ripened and unripened cheese?

4. Give three tips for storing milk.

DISCUSS YOUR IDEAS

5. Discuss the benefits of using nonfat yogurt instead of other dairy foods in cooking.

APPLY YOUR LEARNING

6. Use the chart "Nutritive Value in Foods," in the Appendix, to compare the nutrients in various dairy products. Which are highest in calcium? Which are lowest in fat?

Section 18.1: Choosing Dairy Foods   461

Completing the Section

Review

• Ask students to summarize the main ideas in this section.

• Have students complete the Section Review. (Answers appear below.)

Evaluation

• Have students write a short essay describing the various types of dairy products available.

• Have students take the quiz for Section 18.1. (Refer to the *Section Quizzes* booklet or use the *Testmaker Software*.)

Reteaching

• Ask students to write a newspaper article on choosing low-fat dairy foods.

• Refer to the *Reteaching Activities* booklet for the Section 18.1 activity worksheet.

Enrichment

• Have students research trends in America's tastes in frozen dairy desserts.

Closure

• Lead a discussion on the various types of dairy products available, the nutrients in each, and how to include these products in a weekly menu.

■ Answers to Section Review ■

1. *Any four:* proteins, vitamin A, riboflavin, vitamin B$_{12}$, calcium, phosphorus, magnesium, and zinc.

2. To kill enzymes and harmful bacteria that make milk spoil quickly.

3. Ripened cheese has been aged to make it more stable (so it can be stored for a longer time).

4. See list on pages 460-461.

5. Answers will vary. Students should realize that nonfat yogurt can give a very similar taste without adding the fat and calories in other foods.

6. Answers will vary according to the dairy products students choose. See the "Nutritive Value in Foods" chart in the Appendix.

Motivators

- Ask students if they know what causes a skin to form on the surface of milk as it cooks, what causes milk to scorch, what makes milk curdle when mixed with an acid food, what you should do if yogurt separates when it is stored, what happens if cheese is overcooked. Point out that the answers to these questions and more will be answered in this section.

- Ask students if they have ever encountered any problems when cooking with milk, yogurt, or cheese. What problems did they encounter?

Objectives

- Have students read the section objectives. Discuss the purpose of studying the section.

Vocabulary

- Pronounce the terms listed under "Look for These Terms." Have students find the terms and their definitions in the section.

Guided Reading

- Have students look at the headings within Section 18.2 to preview the concepts that will be discussed.

- Have students read the section and complete the appropriate part of the Chapter 18 Study Guide in the *Student Workbook*.

SECTION 18.2
Preparing Dairy Foods

OBJECTIVES

After studying this section, you should be able to:

- Identify ways to prevent problems when cooking with milk.
- Discuss ways to use yogurt in recipes.
- Identify guidelines for preparing cheese.

LOOK FOR THIS TERM
scalded milk

Dairy foods are delicate proteins. They must be cooked carefully at moderate temperatures and for a limited amount of time.

Cooking with Milk

Milk can be the base for preparing delicious cooked foods, including cocoa and soups. However, when cooking milk, several problems can arise.

- ❖ **Skin.** As milk cooks, protein solids clump together, forming a skin on the surface. The skin can make the milk bubble up and boil over. To keep a skin from forming, cover the pan or stir the mixture regularly. If a skin forms, use a wire whisk to beat it back into the mixture. Removing it would remove nutrients.
- ❖ **Scorching.** Milk can scorch, or burn, easily. The milk solids fall to the bottom of the pan, stick, and burn. To prevent scorching, use low heat. Also, stir the mixture to keep the solids circulating.
- ❖ **Curdling.** When milk curdles, it has separated into curds and whey. Curdling may occur when milk is heated with acid

foods, such as vegetables and fruits. It can also be caused by salt or high heat. To prevent curdling, use low temperatures, stir the mixture, and combine milk with acid foods gradually.

When milk-based recipes are cooked carefully, the result is smooth and flavorful.

Teacher's Classroom Resources—Section 18.2

Refer to these resources in the TCR package:

Reproducible Lesson Plans

Student Workbook

Extending the Text

Reteaching Activities

Section Quizzes

Testmaker Software

Color Transparencies

TIPS for Success

Making Hot Cocoa

❖ Cocoa powder by itself is difficult to mix with liquids. To prevent lumping, mix the cocoa powder and sugar thoroughly. Gradually add a little liquid, stirring well to make a smooth paste. Then continue adding the rest of the liquid, stirring constantly.

❖ To cut down on fat, use skim milk. For greater richness and more nutrients, add nonfat dry milk when combining the cocoa and sugar.

❖ Use low heat to prevent scorching.

❖ For a flavor variation, add vanilla or peppermint extract, cinnamon, or nutmeg.

Cocoa is one of the favorite hot beverages prepared with milk. It can be prepared on the range or in the microwave.

Some recipes call for **scalded milk.** This means the milk is heated to just below the boiling point. Use low heat and cook only until bubbles appear around the sides of the pan.

Milk and milk-based recipes can be prepared easily in the microwave oven. Be sure to use a large enough container in case the milk foams up.

Using Yogurt in Recipes

Yogurt can be a nutritious substitute for ingredients such as sour cream, cream cheese, milk, and mayonnaise. It can be used in many recipes, from soups to main dishes to salads.

Here are some basic guidelines to remember when cooking with yogurt.

❖ Yogurt can be cooked, baked, or frozen. The active bacterial cultures may not survive, but the nutrients will still be the same.

❖ Whey may separate from the curd in yogurt when it is stored. Stir it back into the yogurt before you use it.

❖ Cook yogurt at moderate temperatures for only the time needed. Yogurt is just as delicate as other dairy foods. If overcooked, it will curdle.

❖ To keep yogurt from separating during cooking, blend 1 Tbsp. (15 mL) cornstarch with a small amount of yogurt. Combine with the remaining yogurt and use according to recipe directions.

A yogurt maker is an appliance that can be used to make yogurt at home. Packaged yogurt starter can supply the bacterial culture.

Section 18.2: Preparing Dairy Foods   **463**

Food and Nutrition Science

Serving Temperature of Cheese: Have students prepare cheese trays of ripened cheeses. Have students refrigerate one tray and allow the other to reach room temperature. Have students taste cheese from both trays. What conclusions can students draw?

Teaching . . .

* **Cooking with Milk**
* **Using Yogurt in Recipes**
* **Preparing Cheese**

(text pages 462-464)

Comprehension Check

1. Ask students what problems can arise when you cook with milk. *(See list on page 462.)*

2. Ask students to list guidelines to follow when you cook with yogurt. *(See list on pages 463-464.)*

3. Ask students to explain how to thicken yogurt. *(Let the whey drain off.)*

4. Ask students to explain which cheeses should be served chilled, and which should be served at room temperature. *(Unripened cheeses should be chilled; ripened cheeses should be served at room temperature.)*

Student Experiences

1. **Demonstration:** Demonstrate how to heat milk to scalding temperature on top of the range and in a microwave oven. *(Key skill: kitchen management skills)*

2. **Demonstration:** Demonstrate how to make a cheese sauce in different ways (using evaporated milk, a white sauce base, natural shredded cheese, processed cheese). Discuss the advantages and disadvantages of each method. *(Key skill: evaluation)*

Lab Experience

Have students make homemade hot cocoa. Students should take precautions to avoid skin formation, curdling, and scorching.

❖ You can thicken yogurt by letting the whey drain off. Line a strainer with a double thickness of cheesecloth. Empty the yogurt into the strainer and set the strainer over a bowl. (The bowl should be a size and shape that prevents the strainer from touching the bottom.) Refrigerate up to 12 hours or until enough whey has drained off to give the desired thickness. If thick enough, you can use the yogurt as a cheese. Use the nutrient-rich whey in soups and casseroles, or substitute it for water, buttermilk, or milk in baking.

Yogurt can also be used as a salad dressing, dip, sauce, or dessert topping. For example, top cooked vegetables such as asparagus with plain yogurt and sprinkle with chopped nuts and minced chives.

Preparing Cheese

Unripened cheeses, such as cottage cheese and cream cheese, should be served chilled. They can be used to make dips by adding seasonings and chopped vegetables.

Ripened cheese tastes best when served at room temperature. Remove it from the refrigerator at least 30 minutes before serving to allow it to reach room temperature. You can also bring it to room temperature by microwaving it at 30 percent power for about 20 seconds, then letting it stand five minutes. Times will vary, depending on size and texture of the cheese. Repeat if necessary.

Follow these guidelines when cooking cheese:

❖ Heat cheese just long enough to melt it. If overcooked, cheese gets stringy and tough.
❖ To speed up cooking time, shred, grate, or cut cheese into small pieces.
❖ Be careful when microwaving cheese—the fat in it attracts microwaves. The cheese may be hotter than the rest of the microwaved food.
❖ To lower the fat in recipes with cheese, choose sharp-flavored varieties. Since they have more flavor, you can use less cheese.

When cheese is used as a topping, it is often shredded or grated and added near the end of cooking time. Then only brief heating is needed to melt it, reducing the chance of overcooking.

■ Section 18.2 Review ■

RECALL THE FACTS

1. List two ways to prevent milk from curdling.
2. How can yogurt be used as a substitute for cheese?
3. What happens to cheese if it is overcooked?

DISCUSS YOUR IDEAS

4. What are some ways to use milk and dairy products in cooking to meet the nutritional needs of someone who doesn't like plain milk?

APPLY YOUR LEARNING

5. Locate a recipe for homemade cream of tomato soup. Read through the directions carefully. What does the recipe recommend to prevent curdling? How might you improve upon the directions?

Thinking About the Recipe

Read the recipe for "Easy Macaroni and Cheese" and answer the following questions.

1. Why is the cheese cut into cubes before it is cooked?
2. What are some low-fat foods you could serve with this dish to make a nutritionally balanced menu?

Easy Macaroni and Cheese

Customary	Ingredients	Metric
8 oz.	Elbow macaroni	224 g
4 oz.	Process cheese spread (sold in loaves)	112 g
1/2 cup	Green pepper, chopped	125 mL
1/4 cup	Onion, finely chopped	50 mL
1 tsp.	Margarine	5 mL
1 cup	Evaporated skim milk	250 mL
1/4 tsp.	White pepper, ground	1 mL
1/2 cup	Bread crumbs	125 mL
1 tsp.	Margarine, melted	5 mL

Yield: 4 servings

Directions

Pans: Saucepan; 1½ quart (1.5 L) casserole dish
Oven Temperature: 350°F (180°C)

1. Cook and drain macaroni according to package directions. Set aside.
2. Cut cheese into cubes and set aside.
3. Sauté green pepper and onion over medium-low heat in 1 teaspoon (5 mL) margarine, about 1 to 2 minutes, stirring constantly.
4. Stir in evaporated skim milk and cheese cubes.
5. Cook over medium-low heat, stirring constantly, until cheese is melted and mixture is well blended. Stir in pepper.
6. Combine milk and cheese mixture with macaroni in casserole dish. Mix gently.
7. Combine bread crumbs and 1 teaspoon (5 mL) melted margarine.
8. Sprinkle bread crumb mixture over macaroni and cheese mixture.
9. Bake at 350°F (180°C) 20 to 30 minutes until hot and bubbly.
10. Serve hot.

Nutrition Information

Per serving (approximate): 274 calories, 15 g protein, 28 g carbohydrate, 11 g fat, 30 mg cholesterol, 531 mg sodium

Using the Recipe

- Have students read the recipe and discuss each step. Review safety and sanitation procedures that apply to this recipe.
- Have each lab team fill out a work plan. (See the *Foods Lab Resources* booklet.)
- Have students check off the ingredients and equipment listed on the recipe worksheet and prepare the recipe.
- Have students complete the evaluation and questions on the recipe worksheet.

See Also . . .

The *Foods Lab Resources* booklet for the "Easy Macaroni and Cheese" recipe worksheet and other recipe alternatives.

Answers to Thinking About the Recipe

1. To help it melt more evenly and more quickly.
2. Answers will vary. Make sure students' choices are nutritionally balanced.

SECTION 18.3

Egg Basics

Introducing the Section

Motivators

- Ask students to name their favorite methods of preparing eggs. List the methods on the board in order of popularity from the most popular to least popular.

- Ask students why you should never microwave an egg in the shell. Discuss precautions to take when microwaving eggs.

Objectives

- Have students read the section objectives. Discuss the purpose of studying the section.

Vocabulary

- Pronounce the terms listed under "Look for These Terms." Have students find the terms and their definitions in the section.

Guided Reading

- Have students look at the headings within Section 18.3 to preview the concepts that will be discussed.

- Have students read the section and complete the appropriate part of the Chapter 18 Study Guide in the *Student Workbook*.

OBJECTIVES

After studying this section, you should be able to:

- Describe the structure of an egg.
- Identify the nutrients provided by eggs.
- Give guidelines for buying and storing eggs.
- Explain how to cook eggs by conventional and microwave methods.

LOOK FOR THESE TERMS

albumen
chalazae
coagulate
shirred eggs

Eggs are an economical food source and can be prepared in a variety of ways. Many people enjoy them for breakfast. However, they can be featured in other meals as well.

The Structure of an Egg

The egg is shaped like an oval, with one end more narrow than the other. It has a hard outer shell lined with several membranes. The shell color may be brown or white, depending on the breed of hen. The color does not affect the nutrients in the egg. A pocket of air occupies the space between the shell and membrane at the wide end. As the egg ages, the air pocket grows.

Inside the egg is a thick, clear fluid called the **albumen** (al-BYOU-men). It is commonly called the egg white. The yolk is the round, yellow portion of the egg, floating in the albumen. **Chalazae** (kuh-LAH-zuh) are twisted, cordlike strands of albumen that anchor the yolk in the center of the egg.

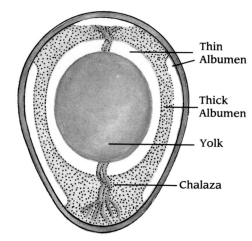

Thin Albumen

Thick Albumen

Yolk

Chalaza

Whether the shells are brown or white, eggs have the same nutrients and the same structure.

Teacher's Classroom Resources—Section 18.3

Refer to these resources in the TCR package:

Reproducible Lesson Plans

Student Workbook

Extending the Text

Reteaching Activities

Section Quizzes

Testmaker Software

Color Transparencies

Nutrients in Eggs

Eggs are an excellent source of protein, riboflavin, and iodine. In addition, they are good sources of vitamin A, some other B vitamins, vitamin D, iron, and trace minerals. However, egg yolks also contain saturated fats and cholesterol.

Eggs are part of the Meat, Poultry, Fish, Dry Beans, Eggs, and Nuts Group. When counting servings from that group, one egg counts as 1 ounce (28 g) of meat. However, because whole eggs are so high in cholesterol, health experts recommend that people eat no more than four a week. There is no limit on eating egg whites because they are cholesterol-free.

Buying and Storing Eggs

Eggs are sold according to size and grade standards set by the USDA. Both size and grade are clearly marked on the package.

The USDA grade shield on the package means that the eggs have been federally inspected for wholesomeness. The grade is determined by the inner and outer quality of the egg at the time it was packaged. It has nothing to do with the freshness of the egg or the size.

The three egg grades are AA, A, and B. There is no difference in nutritive value among them. However, there is a difference in appearance when cooked. Grade AA and

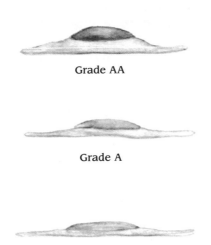

Grade AA

Grade A

Grade B

Egg grades indicate thickness and appearance.

A eggs have a thicker white and are used when appearance is important, such as with fried or poached eggs. Grade B eggs are used when appearance is not important, such as in baked products or scrambled eggs. As a rule, grades AA and A are most common in supermarkets. The illustration above shows the differences in the grades.

The size is determined by the minimum weight for a dozen eggs, as shown in the chart below. The sizes most commonly sold are "large" and "extra large." As a general rule, recipes assume that large eggs will be used.

Jumbo	X-Large	Large	Medium	Small	Peewee
30 OZ.	27 OZ.	24 OZ.	21 OZ.	18 OZ.	15 OZ.

Egg sizes indicate the minimum weight of a dozen eggs. About how much would a single large egg weigh?

Teaching . . .

- **The Structure of an Egg**
  - **Nutrients in Eggs**
  - **Buying and Storing Eggs**

(text pages 466-468)

Comprehension Check

1. Ask students to explain the purpose of chalazae in an egg. *(They anchor the yolk in the center of the egg.)*

2. Ask students to list the nutrients present in eggs. *(protein, riboflavin, iodine, vitamin A, some other B vitamins, vitamin D, iron, and trace minerals)*

3. Ask students to describe proper storage for eggs. *(Refrigerate eggs in the original carton immediately when you arrive at home; do not store in refrigerator door shelf.)*

Student Experiences

1. **Observation:** Have students hold an egg up to a strong light and observe the contents. Have students locate the air pocket at the wide end, then break the egg onto a saucer and locate its parts: shell, membranes, albumen, yolk, and chalazae. *(Key skill: science)*

2. **Observation:** Have students break Grade AA, Grade A, and Grade B on separate plates. Note differences in size, shape, and consistency. *(Key skill: science)*

3. **Demonstration:** Demonstrate how to freeze whole eggs and egg whites. *(Key skill: kitchen management skills)*

Thinking Skills

Reasoning: Discuss why raw eggs should not be frozen in their shells. *(Freezing expands the contents of the egg more than the shell's capacity. Result: cracked egg.)*

Using the Photo

Answer to caption question: One large egg weighs about 2 oz. on the average (24 oz. ÷ 12).

- **Preparing Eggs**
- **Eggs Cooked in the Shell**

(text pages 468-469)

Comprehension Check

1. Ask students to explain what happens to eggs when they are overcooked. *(The yolks toughen and turn gray-green on the surface.)*

2. Ask students to explain the difference in the way eggs cook in the microwave and in conventional cooking. *(When eggs are cooked conventionally, the egg whites cook faster than the yolks; when they are microwaved, the yolks cook faster.)*

3. Ask students to describe the procedure for cooking eggs in the shell. *(See page 469, right column.)*

Safety Check

Emphasize that even eggs that are not cracked may be contaminated with salmonella bacteria. Recent cases have lead researchers to believe that salmonella may be transferred from an infected hen to the egg.

Although the risk of getting sick from eating soft-cooked or underdone eggs is small, cooking eggs thoroughly is a wise precaution. This is especially true if the eggs will be served to children, the elderly, or the infirm. Foods normally made with raw or under-cooked eggs can be safely made with pasteurized eggs.

✓ SAFETY CHECK

Harmful bacteria in raw or undercooked eggs have caused food-borne illness. To make sure that eggs are safe to eat, follow these guidelines:

- ❖ Do not use eggs that are cracked or broken. They may contain harmful bacteria.
- ❖ Always cook eggs thoroughly until the whites and yolks are firm.
- ❖ Use the proper sanitation procedures when preparing eggs. (See Section 7.3, pages 195-197 and 201-202).
- ❖ Serve cooked eggs and egg-rich foods right after cooking.
- ❖ Never eat raw eggs or any foods containing raw eggs, such as homemade eggnog, homemade ice cream, and raw cookie dough. (Raw eggs in commercial products are usually pasteurized, which destroys harmful bacteria.)

Eggs are usually priced according to size and supply. Check the unit price to determine which size is the best buy. Be sure to open the carton and inspect the eggs. They should be clean and whole, without any cracks.

Eggs are highly perishable. Store them immediately when you get home from shopping. Refrigerate eggs in the original carton. Do not put them in the egg tray commonly found on the refrigerator door—the drop in temperature each time the door is opened may cause eggs to lose quality more quickly. In addition, egg shells are porous and pick up aromas from other foods if stored uncovered. Do not wash eggs before storing—washing destroys the egg's natural protective covering.

Leftover raw yolks or whites should be refrigerated in a covered container if they will be used within two to four days. For longer storage, freeze them. Refrigerate cooked egg dishes immediately and use them within three days.

To reduce the risk of illness, egg-rich dishes should be cooked thoroughly and served right away.

TIPS for Success

Freezing Eggs

- ❖ To freeze whole raw eggs, beat the eggs until well-blended and pour them into freezer containers. Three tablespoons (45 mL) of beaten whole egg equals one large egg.
- ❖ To freeze raw whites, place the white of one egg in each compartment of an ice cube tray. After freezing, put frozen cubes in a tightly sealed freezer container and use as needed. Two tablespoons (30 mL) of egg white equals one large white.
- ❖ Use frozen eggs only in dishes that will be thoroughly cooked.

Food and Nutrition Science

Protein Coagulation: Ask students if they can explain why adding vinegar to the cooking water will help keep a cracked egg from running. *(Vinegar is an acid. Acids cause the egg protein to coagulate faster.)*

Coagulation Experiment: See the *Food Science Resources* booklet for the "Heat and Protein Coagulation" teaching guides and student experiment worksheet. The experiment tests the effects of different cooking time on the coagulation of protein.

Preparing Eggs

Like dairy foods, eggs are delicate proteins. They must be cooked at moderate temperatures for a limited amount of time. When overcooked, egg whites shrink and become tough and rubbery. When egg yolks are overcooked, they toughen and turn gray-green on the surface.

Eggs can be prepared easily, either on top of the range or in a microwave oven. There are a few differences in basic cooking principles, depending on which method you use.

In conventional cooking, use medium to low heat. Time the eggs carefully to make sure they are thoroughly cooked. The whites will **coagulate,** or become firm, before the yolks.

When eggs are cooked in a microwave oven, the yolks cook faster than the whites. That is because the fat in the yolks attracts

Before microwaving, pierce egg yolks. If you don't, trapped steam could cause the yolk to burst.

✓ **SAFETY CHECK**

Never microwave an egg in the shell. Steam builds up in the egg and is held in by the shell. The egg can burst and seriously injure you.

more microwaves than the whites. Eggs are usually removed from the microwave oven while still moist and soft. Standing time completes the cooking.

Eggs can be prepared in several basic ways: cooked in the shell, fried, baked, poached, or scrambled.

Eggs Cooked in the Shell

When cooking eggs in the shell, place a single layer of eggs in a saucepan. Add water to a level at least 1 inch (2.5 cm) above the eggs. Cover the saucepan and bring the water just to boiling. Turn off the heat (and remove the pan from the heating unit, if using an electric range). Let the eggs stand in the hot water, covered. If you want soft-cooked eggs, let them stand about four to five minutes for a safe doneness. For hard-cooked eggs, let stand about 15 minutes if using large eggs (about 18 minutes if using extra large eggs).

After cooking, immediately run cold water over the eggs to stop the cooking process. To serve soft-cooked eggs, break the shell with a knife and scoop the egg out of the shell into a serving dish. To remove the shell from a hard-cooked egg, gently tap the egg all over to crackle the shell. Roll the egg between your hands to loosen the shell. Peel the shell away starting at the large end.

Student Experiences

1. **Demonstration:** Show how to peel a hard-cooked egg. (Or have a student give the demonstration after practicing ahead of time.) *(Key skill: kitchen management skills)*

2. **Poster Project:** Have students prepare a poster that shows what happens to the protein and water molecules in an egg as it heats. *(Key skill: science)*

Lab Experience

Hard-boiled Eggs: Have lab groups each prepare three hard-cooked eggs. Simmer two eggs for 15 minutes; boil one for 20 minutes. Let one of the first two eggs cool at room temperature. Cool the others in cold water. Compare the results. Have students draw conclusions.

More About Egg Protein

Ovomucin is the protein that makes albumen thick. It does not coagulate as quickly as the other proteins in the egg white. When you begin to fry an egg, the thin albumen flows away from the egg. Because it is thin and low in ovomucin, it coagulates first. The thicker the albumen, the longer it takes to coagulate. Chalazae is the thickest part of the albumen. It may only partially coagulate.

As the egg heats (using conventional methods), the albumen coagulates first. The yolk proteins begin to set at a slightly higher temperature than the albumen.

Teaching . . .

- **Fried Eggs**
- **Baked Eggs**
- **Poached Eggs**
- **Scrambled Eggs**
- **Basic Omelet**

(text pages 470-471)

Comprehension Check

1. Ask students to describe the procedure for frying an egg. *(Use a small amount of fat or vegetable oil cooking spray on the skillet. Heat skillet until it is hot enough to sizzle a drop of water; break egg into small bowl; if yolk doesn't break, slip the egg from the bowl into the heated pan. Reduce heat immediately. Cover pan and cook eggs slowly until done. Turn eggs over to cook both sides.)*

2. Ask students to explain why it is necessary to pierce the yolks before baking an egg in a microwave oven. *(If it is not pierced, the yolk will burst as it heats.)*

3. Ask students to explain the difference between boiling and poaching eggs. *(Boiled eggs are cooked in the shell; poached eggs are cooked in simmering water, but out of the shell.)*

4. Ask students to explain why it is important not to stir scrambled eggs constantly while they cook. *(They will get mushy.)*

Fried Eggs

Eggs can be fried in a small amount of fat or using a vegetable oil cooking spray. Heat a skillet over medium-high heat until it is hot enough to sizzle a drop of water. Gently break one egg at a time into a small bowl or custard cup. If the yolk breaks, save the egg for another use. Otherwise, gently slip the egg from the bowl into the heated pan. Reduce the heat to low immediately. Cover the pan and cook the eggs slowly until done. Turn the eggs over to cook both sides.

Baked Eggs

Baked eggs are sometimes called **shirred eggs.** Break the eggs into a small bowl, then slip them into a greased, shallow baking dish or custard cup. You can use individual dishes or place several eggs in one dish. Top the eggs with a small amount of milk, if desired.

To bake conventionally, place in an oven preheated to 325°F (160°C). Bake until done—about 12 minutes for two eggs.

To microwave, first pierce the yolks with the tip of a knife or a wooden pick so that steam can escape. Otherwise, the eggs may burst. Cover the baking dish with plastic wrap and vent it to allow steam to cscape. Follow the power level and timing instructions in the owner's manual or recipe book.

Baked eggs are easy to prepare. If you like, you can sprinkle on toppings such as chopped parsley, ham, or mushrooms.

Thinking Skills

Problem Solving: Ask students to brainstorm ways to prepare eggs with fewer calories. (Examples: For fried eggs, use a spray coating or a nonstick skillet instead of oil, margarine, or butter. Choose poached eggs rather than fried or scrambled.)

Scrambled Eggs

When making scrambled eggs, beat the eggs together with water or milk. Use one tablespoon (15 mL) liquid for each egg.

To cook conventionally, melt a small amount of butter or margarine in a skillet, or use a vegetable oil cooking spray. Pour the egg mixture into the hot skillet. As the mixture starts to thicken, gently draw a spatula across the bottom and sides of the pan. This forms large curds and allows the uncooked egg to flow to the bottom of the skillet. Continue this procedure until the eggs are thickened and no visible liquid remains. Do not stir the eggs constantly. They will get mushy.

To make scrambled eggs in the microwave oven, cook the egg mixture in a custard cup or other microwave-safe container. Follow the power level and timing instructions in the owner's manual or recipe book. Stir once or twice during cooking and again at the end of the cooking time. Let stand to complete cooking.

Basic Omelet

A basic omelet, also called a French omelet, is made with beaten eggs, just as scrambled eggs are. However, an omelet is cooked in a skillet without stirring. The result is shaped somewhat like a large pancake. During cooking, occasionally lift the edge of the omelet to allow uncooked egg to flow to the bottom. When the omelet is almost done, you may add a filling, such as sautéed vegetables. Fold the omelet in half to serve.

There are many variations of omelets. The recipe on page 473 is for an Italian-style omelet, called a *frittata* (frih-TAH-tuh). In the next section, you will learn how to make a puffy omelet using beaten egg whites.

When poaching, start with fresh, cold eggs– they will hold their shape better. Drain poached eggs well before serving.

Poached Eggs

Poaching is a method of cooking eggs, out of the shell, in simmering water. To poach eggs conventionally, bring the water to a boil in a saucepan or deep skillet, then reduce the heat to a gentle simmer. Break one egg at a time into a small dish. Hold the dish close to surface of the water and slip the egg in. Simmer about five minutes or until done.

Eggs can also be poached in the microwave oven. Follow the directions in the owner's manual or recipe book. Be sure to pierce the yolks first to let steam escape.

After cooking, use a slotted spoon to lift the eggs out of the water and drain them. Serve the eggs in a dish or over toast.

Student Experiences
1. **Guest Speaker:** Have the chef of an area restaurant speak to the class about interesting ways to prepare eggs for different types of meals (breakfast, brunch, lunch, dinner). *(Key skill: kitchen management skills)*
2. **Recipe Collection:** Have students compile a collection of recipes for preparing eggs. Which ones are students' favorites? Have students check the nutritional value of each recipe. *(Key skill: reading)*
3. **Recipe Creation:** Have students develop their own creative recipes for scrambled eggs. *(Key skill: creativity)*

Lab Experience
- Have students fry several eggs, experimenting with various cooking times and temperatures. Have them compare the results for texture and appearance.
- Have students prepare eggs using different preparation methods.

Food and Nutrition Science

Coagulation Temperature of Egg Yolks: Ask students if they know why it is technically impossible to fry eggs until the yolks are done. Explain that the egg white sets at about 149°F (65°C), but the yolk must be cooked to about 156°F (69°C) before it coagulates. This means that the white will become rubbery if the yolk is cooked beyond the point of being firm but tender.

18.3

Completing the Section

Review

- Ask students to summarize the main ideas in this section.
- Have students complete the Section Review. (Answers appear below.)

Evaluation

- Assign a method for cooking eggs and have students prepare the eggs correctly.
- Have students take the quiz for Section 18.3. (Refer to the *Section Quizzes* booklet or use the *Testmaker Software*.)

Reteaching

- Have students write a booklet giving step-by-step instructions for preparing eggs in different ways.
- Refer to the *Reteaching Activities* booklet for the Section 18.3 activity worksheet.

Enrichment

- Have students compile a collection of recipes using hard-cooked eggs.

Closure

- Lead a discussion on the various methods of cooking eggs. Emphasize the necessity of cooking eggs completely.

WORLD of variety

"Thousand-year eggs" are a Chinese delicacy. However, they are not really that old. The eggs are cooked, preserved in a mixture of fine ash, clay, and salt, and then wrapped in straw. After about 45 days, they are considered ready to eat.

"Thousand-year eggs" are usually made from duck eggs. The unique preservation method gives the eggs a distinctive flavor and appearance.

472   **Chapter 18: Dairy Foods and Eggs**

Section 18.3 Review

RECALL THE FACTS

1. What is another name for the white of an egg?
2. Name four nutrients found in eggs.
3. What does the grade shield on an egg carton tell you?
4. Why shouldn't whole eggs in the shell be cooked in the microwave oven?

DISCUSS YOUR IDEAS

5. What are the advantages and disadvantages of the various cooking methods for eggs?

APPLY YOUR LEARNING

6. Design an advertisement to promote the use of eggs. You may want to focus on their versatility or nutritional value.

Answers to Section Review

1. Albumin.
2. *Any four:* protein, riboflavin, iodine, vitamin A, some other B vitamins, vitamin D, iron, and trace minerals.
3. Eggs have been federally inspected for wholesomeness (based on inner and outer quality at the time the eggs were packaged).
4. They expand when they are heated; the egg will burst.
5. Answers will vary.
6. Answers will vary.

Thinking About the Recipe

Read the recipe for "Italian Frittata" and answer the following questions.

1. How does the preparation method for this recipe differ from that for scrambled eggs?
2. Name two ways you might reduce the amount of fat in the frittata.

Italian Frittata

Key Skill: Cooking Eggs

Italian Frittata

Customary	Ingredients	Metric
1/4 lb.	Fresh mushrooms, thinly sliced	112 g
2	Green onions, minced	2
1 ½ Tbsp.	Margarine	20 mL
6	Eggs	6
3 Tbsp.	Fresh parsley, chopped	45 mL
1/2 tsp.	Basil, dried and crumbled	2 mL
1/4 cup	Grated Parmesan cheese	50 mL
	Salt and pepper to taste	

Yield: 4 servings

Conventional Directions

Pan: Large skillet with oven-safe handle
Oven Temperature: Broil

1. Sauté mushrooms and onions in margarine over medium heat until tender-crisp.
2. Preheat broiler.
3. Beat eggs in medium bowl.
4. Add parsley, basil, salt and pepper, and half the cheese to the eggs. Mix well.
5. Pour egg mixture over vegetables in skillet. Cook over medium heat, without stirring, until edges are lightly browned.
6. Sprinkle with remaining cheese.
7. Broil until top is golden brown.
8. Cut into wedges and serve hot.

Microwave Directions

Pan: 9-inch glass pie pan, microwave-safe
Power level: 100% power

1. Combine mushrooms, onions, and margarine in glass pie pan. Cover with plastic wrap and vent.
2. Cook 2 to 3 minutes at 100% power, rotating the pan after 1 minute.
3. Beat eggs, parsley, basil, salt, pepper, and half the cheese in a small bowl.
4. Pour egg mixture over vegetables.
5. Cook at 70% power 4 to 5 minutes.
6. Move cooked portions to center of dish and uncooked parts to outside. Lightly level the top. Rotate pan.
7. Cook 4 to 5 minutes more at 70% power until eggs are set but glossy.
8. Sprinkle remaining cheese on eggs.
9. Cook 2 to 3 minutes at 70% power.
10. Let stand 2 to 3 minutes. Cut into wedges and serve hot.

Nutrition Information

Per serving (approximate): 188 calories, 13 g protein, 3 g carbohydrate, 14 g fat, 324 mg cholesterol, 263 mg sodium

Section 18.3: Egg Basics   473

Using the Recipe

- Have students read the recipe and discuss each step. Caution students not to get the burner too hot while sautéing the mushrooms and onions to avoid being splattered with hot margarine. Review other safety and sanitation procedures that apply to this recipe.

- Have each lab team fill out a work plan. (See the *Foods Lab Resources* booklet.)

- Have students check off the ingredients and equipment listed on the recipe worksheet and prepare the recipe.

- Have students complete the evaluation and questions on the recipe worksheet.

See Also . . .

The *Foods Lab Resources* booklet for the "Italian Frittata" recipe worksheet and other recipe alternatives.

Answers to Thinking About the Recipe

1. The eggs are not stirred in this recipe as they are in scrambled eggs.

2. Use a vegetable oil spray instead of margarine; use a low-calorie substitute for the cheese.

Section 18.4
Using Eggs in Recipes

Introducing the Section

Motivators

- Challenge students to see who can think of the most uses of eggs in cooking. Give a prize to the person who thinks of the most different uses.

- Create a bulletin board entitled "Egg-citing Eggs." Include illustrations of dishes that feature eggs, such as soufflé, meringue pie, omelet, and eggs Benedict. Point out that eggs can be prepared in more ways than fried, scrambled, hard or soft cooked, and poached.

Objectives

- Have students read the section objectives. Discuss the purpose of studying the section.

Vocabulary

- Pronounce the terms listed under "Look for These Terms." Have students find the terms and their definitions in the section.

Guided Reading

- Have students look at the headings within Section 18.4 to preview the concepts that will be discussed.

- Have students read the section and complete the appropriate part of the Chapter 18 Study Guide in the *Student Workbook*.

SECTION 18.4
Using Eggs in Recipes

OBJECTIVES

After studying this section, you should be able to:

- Describe the difference between stirred custard and baked custard.
- Explain how to separate and beat egg whites.
- Identify uses for beaten egg whites.

LOOK FOR THESE TERMS

quiche
soufflé
meringue

Eggs perform different functions in recipes. They add richness and nutrients. They bind ingredients together, as in a meat loaf. They are also used for thickening foods such as sauces. When beaten, they incorporate air and can be used to help baked products rise.

Custards

One example of a recipe made with eggs is custard. Custard is a tender blend of milk thickened with eggs. It serves as the base for main dishes, such as **quiche** (keesh). Quiche

is a pie with a custard filling that contains foods such as chopped vegetables, cheese, and chopped cooked meat. Sweetened, flavored custard is a popular dessert.

There are two types of custard, stirred and baked.

- ❖ **Stirred custard** is also known as soft custard. It is cooked on top of the range, stirred constantly, until it thickens enough to coat a spoon. It is pourable, creamy, and can be served as a pudding or as a sauce over cake or fruit.

- ❖ **Baked custard** is baked in the oven. It has a firm, delicate consistency, similar to yogurt. If prepared in individual custard cups, the cups are set in a pan of hot water to keep the mixture from overcooking. The custard is baked until a knife inserted in or near the center comes out clean. Baking time varies, depending on the size of the pans. If overbaked, the custard will curdle. If not baked long enough, it will not set.

Custards are versatile combinations of milk and eggs. What is the difference between stirred and baked custard?

474   Chapter 18: Dairy Foods and Eggs

Teacher's Classroom Resources—Section 18.4

Refer to these resources in the TCR package:
Reproducible Lesson Plans
Student Workbook
Reteaching Activities

Extending the Text
Section Quizzes
Testmaker Software
Color Transparencies

TIPS for Success

Making Stirred Custard

If stirred custard curdles and looks lumpy, you can still rescue it. Pour it gradually into a blender or food processor and beat. The sauce will be frothy instead of velvety. However, it will be usable, unless it is very badly curdled.

Separating Eggs

Sometimes recipe directions call for only the yolk or white of the egg. In that case, you need to separate the egg. Eggs separate more easily when they are cold.

An easy, sanitary way to separate whites from yolks is to use an inexpensive egg separator. Simply break the egg into the separator. The white will flow through, leaving the yolk in the separator.

Beating Egg Whites

When egg whites are beaten, air is incorporated into them. Beaten egg whites can be used to add volume and lightness to baked products. For example, they can be used to prepare soufflés. A **soufflé** (soo-FLAY) is

✓ SAFETY CHECK

The traditional method for separating whites calls for passing the yolk back and forth from shell half to shell half. This method is no longer recommended. Bacteria may be present in the pores of the shell and could be picked up by the yolks and whites.

Professional chefs and bakers use beaten egg whites in many creative dishes. You can, too, if you know the "secrets" to successfully beating egg whites.

made by folding stiffly beaten whites into a sauce or batter, then baking the mixture in a deep casserole until it puffs up.

Here are some guidelines for beating egg whites:

❖ When separating the yolks from the whites, be careful that no yolk mixes with the whites. Yolks contain fat, and even a drop of fat can keep whites from reaching full volume.

❖ Before beating, let egg whites stand at room temperature for 30 minutes. This will allow them to reach the fullest volume when beaten.

❖ Use beaters and bowls that are clean and completely free of fat. Plastic bowls tend to absorb fat, so use only glass or metal bowls.

Comprehension Check

1. Ask students to explain the difference between stirred custard and baked custard. *(See page 474.)*
2. Ask students to explain the easiest ways to separate eggs. *(Do it while they're cold; use an egg separator.)*
3. Ask students to explain the purpose of beating egg whites. *(To add air; to add volume and lightness to baked products.)*
4. Ask students to list guidelines for beating egg whites. *(See list on page 475.)*

Student Experiences

1. **Demonstration:** Demonstrate the procedure used to prevent eggs from curdling when they are used as a thickener in a hot mixture such as custard. *(Key skill: kitchen management skills)*
2. **Demonstration:** Demonstrate how to fold egg whites into other ingredients. *(Key skill: kitchen management skills)*
3. **Class Discussion:** Discuss safety concerns related to separating eggs. How can you avoid contaminating the yolk and white with bacteria present in the pores of the shell? *(Key skills: science, critical thinking)*

Food and Nutrition Science

Variables in Beating Eggs: Have students experiment with beating egg whites in bowls made of various materials. Compare results obtained using each type of bowl with and without cream of tartar. Discuss the results. Point out that because plastic or wooden bowls tend to absorb grease from other foods, they should not be used for beating egg whites. An aluminum bowl causes dark egg whites; copper reacts with the whites and helps stabilize the foam. However, if cream of tartar is used with a copper bowl, the egg whites will turn green. Have students work in groups to research and report on what causes these reactions.

Effects of Added Ingredients Experiment: See the *Food Science Resources* booklet for the "Effects of Added Ingredients on Egg White Foams" teaching guides and student experiment worksheet. The experiment tests the effects of adding different ingredients to egg white foams on the stability, beating time, and volume of the foam.

Comprehension Check

1. Ask students to describe the procedure for making a puffy omelet. *(Separate eggs; beat whites and yolks separately. Fold stiffly beaten whites into yolks; pour mixture into ovenproof skillet; cook on top of range until puffed and lightly browned on bottom (about 5 min.); bake at 350°F (180°C) for 10-12 min. or until knife inserted in center comes out clean.)*

2. Ask students to explain what a meringue is. *(A foam made of beaten egg white and sugar used for desserts.)*

3. Ask students to explain why it is better to put a meringue on a pie while the filling is still hot. *(The meringue weeps less if put on while filling is hot.)*

Student Experiences

1. **Discussion:** Discuss the various uses for soft meringue. What fillings could you use in a meringue shell? *(Key skill: critical thinking)*

2. **Finding Recipes:** Ask students to find recipes that require beaten egg whites. What types of recipes use beaten eggs most? *(Key skill: reading)*

3. **Research:** Have students find out how eggs are used in recipes in other parts of the world. Have students write a short report on their findings. *(Key skills: research, reading)*

As egg whites are beaten, they turn white and foamy and begin to form peaks. The peaks reach two different stages.

❖ **Soft peak stage.** The peaks bend over slightly when the beaters are lifted out of the whites.

❖ **Stiff peak stage.** The peaks are glossy and hold their shape when the beaters are lifted out of the mixture.

Stop beating egg whites as soon as they reach the stage called for in the recipe. Do not try to beat past the stiff peak stage. If the whites are overbeaten, they will turn dry and dull and begin to fall apart. They cannot be used since they have lost air and moisture.

When used in mixtures, beaten egg whites must be folded in. If they are stirred or beaten, the whites lose air and volume. To fold beaten whites into a mixture, add them to the bowl containing the mixture. Use a flat tool, such as a rubber scraper, for folding. (See Section 8.4 for directions on folding.)

Puffy Omelet

Beaten egg whites can be used to make a puffy omelet. A puffy omelet is made by separating the eggs and beating the whites and yolks separately. The stiffly beaten whites are folded into the yolks. The mixture is poured into a skillet with an ovenproof handle. It is first cooked on top of the range until puffed and lightly browned on the bottom, about five minutes. Then it is baked at 350°F (180°C) for 10 to 12 minutes or until a knife inserted in the center comes out clean.

The omelet can be served open-faced or folded. To serve the omelet folded, cut partially through the center of the omelet for ease in folding. The omelet can be filled with foods such as cheese, vegetables, and meats.

Meringues

A **meringue** (mehr-ANG), a foam made of beaten egg white and sugar, is used for desserts. There are two types of meringue, soft and hard. Soft meringue is used to top precooked pies and puddings. Hard meringue is used to make baked meringue shells that can be filled like a pie.

To make a meringue, beat the whites until they are foamy. Sometimes cream of tartar is added to the whites before beating to make the meringue more stable. When the whites are foamy, gradually beat in the sugar, one tablespoon at a time. Most soft meringue recipes call for 1 to 2 Tbsp. (15 to 30 ml) sugar per egg white. A hard meringue may use 4 Tbsp. (50 mL) sugar per egg white. Continue beating until the sugar is dissolved.

A puffy omelet is light in texture and lends itself to a variety of nutritious fillings.

More About Omelets

A French or puffy omelet has a puffy texture. It is made by folding stiffly beaten egg whites into well-beaten egg yolks. The omelet is baked in the oven.

Ideas for omelet fillings:
• Chili, sloppy joe mixture, or taco filling.
• Drained, canned bean sprouts or water chestnuts.
• Yogurt, plain or mixed with fresh fruit.
• Macaroni and cheese or any heated leftover casserole.

To find out if the sugar is dissolved, rub a little meringue between the thumb and forefinger. If it feels gritty, all the sugar is not dissolved.

Spread soft meringue over hot, pre-cooked pie filling or pudding. On a pie, the meringue should touch the crust all around the edge or it may shrink during baking. Bake it in a pre-heated oven according to recipe directions until the peaks are lightly browned.

Sometimes a liquid accumulates between the meringue and pie filling, a condition known as "weeping." This happens when the sugar is not completely dissolved or the meringue is not beaten to the soft-peak stage. Meringue weeps less when put on a hot filling.

Hard meringue can be baked on a baking sheet. Line the sheet with parchment paper (a special paper used for baking in the oven), waxed paper, or foil. Shape the meringue into individual or large shells using a spoon, spatula, or pastry tube.

A baked hard meringue is crispy. It must bake at a low enough temperature to dry out thoroughly, but not overcook. Unless it dries well, the meringue may be sticky and chewy. Bake according to the time and temperature in the recipe directions. Turn off the oven and leave the meringue in it for at least another hour to dry out.

Lemon meringue pie is a popular dessert. Which type of meringue is used to make the fluffy, delicate topping?

RECALL THE FACTS

1. What is the difference between a baked custard and a stirred custard?

2. What is the safest way to separate egg whites from the yolks?

3. Give three guidelines for beating egg whites.

4. Name two dishes that use beaten egg whites.

DISCUSS YOUR IDEAS

5. What might baked meringue shells be filled with?

APPLY YOUR LEARNING

6. Beat one egg white using 1/8 teaspoon (0.5 mL) cream of tartar. Beat another egg white without cream of tartar. Compare the results.

Section 18.4: Using Eggs in Recipes   **477**

Completing the Section

Review

- Ask students to summarize the main ideas in this section.
- Have students complete the Section Review. (Answers appear below.)

Evaluation

- Have students prepare a puffy omelet. Observe their procedure and evaluate the finished product.
- Have students take the quiz for Section 18.4. (Refer to the *Section Quizzes* booklet or use the *Testmaker Software*.)

Reteaching

- Have students draw pictures of beaten eggs at the three most commonly used stages.
- Refer to the *Reteaching Activities* booklet for the Section 18.4 activity worksheet.

Enrichment

- Have students make and fill meringue shells.

Closure

- Refer students to the bulletin-board motivator for this section. Ask students to think of other creative ways to prepare and serve eggs.

■ Answers to Section Review ■

1. Baked custard is firmer than stirred custard.
2. Using an egg separator.

3. See list on pages 475-476.
4. Answers will vary. Soufflés, puffy omelets, and meringues are three possible answers.

5. Answers will vary.
6. Ask students to give reasons for their answers.

18.4 Recipe

Meringue-Swirled Fruit

Key Skill: Beating Egg Whites

Using the Recipe

- Have students read the recipe and discuss each step. Review safety and sanitation procedures that apply to this recipe. Have each lab team fill out a work plan. (See the *Foods Lab Resources* booklet.)

- Have students check off the ingredients and equipment listed on the recipe worksheet and prepare the recipe.

- Have students complete the evaluation and questions on the recipe worksheet.

See Also . . .

The *Foods Lab Resources* booklet for the "Meringue-Swirled Fruit" recipe worksheet and other recipe alternatives.

Thinking About the Recipe

Read the recipe for "Meringue-Swirled Fruit" and answer the following questions.

1. What combination of fruits would you use in this recipe?
2. What should you check for when beating the egg whites?

Meringue-Swirled Fruit

Customary	Ingredients	Metric
4 cups	Fresh or frozen fruit (any combination, such as blueberries, strawberries, orange sections, banana slices)	1 L
2 Tbsp.	Cherry or almond extract	30 mL
5	Egg whites	5
2/3 cup	Sugar	150 mL

Yield: 6 servings

Directions

Pans: Six large custard cups; cookie sheet
Temperature: 500°F (260°C)

1. Preheat oven.
2. Mix fruit and extract together. Chill.
3. Beat egg whites in large bowl until foamy.
4. Add sugar gradually, about 2 Tbsp. (30 mL) at a time, beating after each addition. Stop beating when stiff peaks form.
5. Divide fruit mixture evenly among custard cups.
6. Top and seal each dish of fruit with meringue. Use spoon to swirl meringue to a decorative peak.
7. Place custard cups on cookie sheet. Bake at 500°F (260°C) for 3 minutes or until meringue is golden. Serve immediately.

Nutrition Information

Per serving (approximate): 147 calories, 4 g protein, 35 g carbohydrate, trace of fat, 0 mg cholesterol, 48 mg sodium

---

Answers to Thinking About the Recipe

1. Answers will vary. Encourage students to use combinations that are pleasing to the eye as well as to the taste.

2. Make sure there is no yolk in the egg whites; that the egg whites are at room temperature; that the beaters and bowls are clean and free of fat.

Kristen Todd
Dairy Writer

CURRENT POSITION

"I'm a public relations writer for a dairy industry organization."

RESPONSIBILITIES

"I research and write articles for company newsletters as well as for public distribution. My articles are intended to keep the public and other interest groups aware of our organization's activities and accomplishments."

SKILLS

"Organization is a key skill, since I usually have several projects going at once. Creativity and strong communication skills are also necessary."

EDUCATION

"I have a four-year college degree with a double major in communications and home economics."

WORK ENVIRONMENT

"The majority of my time is spent at my desk doing research or writing on a computer. I also meet weekly with other staff members in my department. I usually work 40 hours a week, but must sometimes work extra hours to meet deadlines."

FAVORITE PART OF THE JOB

"Writing has always been my first love. I enjoy being able to gather facts and put them all together in an article that people will find informative and interesting to read."

- Does Kristen seem well suited to her job? Why or why not?
- What aspects of Kristen's job do you think you might enjoy? Why?

479

CAREER PROFILE: DAIRY WRITER

Thinking About . . . Dairy Writers

- Have students think of other questions they would like to ask Kristen Todd about being a public relations writer for a dairy industry organization. (Examples: How much work do you do on your computer? What types of programs do you use? What types of activities and accomplishments do you write about?)

- Ask student volunteers to tell what they think would be the most exciting part of being a writer for a dairy industry organization.

Student Opportunities

Students interested in public relations writing should join the yearbook staff in their schools, as well as any literature or writing clubs the school may have. Students may also want to join their local 4-H club.

Occupational Outlook

Public relations writers for the food industry can be promoted within their organizations or can freelance, writing articles for several different companies or magazines.

For More Information

For additional information about careers in dairy writing, encourage students to contact:
- National Dairy Council, 6300 N. River Rd., Rosemont, IL 60018
- The Association for Business Communications, University of North Texas, Denton, TX 76203
- Women in Communications Inc., P.O. Box 9561, Austin, TX 78766

Review

- Have students complete the Chapter Review. (Answers appear below.)

Evaluation

- Divide the class into two teams. Have each team think of questions about the chapter. Allow teams to ask each other their questions. At the end of the question period, the team with the most correct answers wins.

- Have students take the test for Chapter 18. (Refer to the *Chapter and Unit Tests* booklet or construct your own test using the *Testmaker Software*.

■ ANSWERS ■

REVIEWING FACTS

1. Whole: 48 percent; lowfat: 16 to 38 percent; skim: trace of fat.

2. Answers will vary. Yogurt, buttermilk, and cheeses are all cultured products.

3. Ripened cheeses are processed with heat.

4. Protein solids clump together on the surface as liquid evaporates; prevent it by covering the pan or stirring regularly.

5. It contains many nutrients; use it in soups and casseroles or substitute for water, buttermilk, or milk in baking.

6. The changes in temperature whenever the door is opened may cause the eggs to lose quality faster; eggs may pick up aromas from other foods.

7. Freeze in an egg tray or similar container.

SUMMARY

SECTION 18.1

Choosing Dairy Foods: Milk is high in protein, vitamin A, and B vitamins. You can choose from whole, low-fat, or skim milk as well as a variety of flavored and convenience milk products. Yogurt is made by adding live bacterial culture to milk. The many kinds of cheese fall into two basic categories, ripened and unripened. Other dairy products include cream, butter, and frozen dairy desserts. Dairy foods are highly perishable and must be refrigerated or frozen.

SECTION 18.2

Preparing Dairy Foods: When heating milk, use care to avoid scorching, curdling, and skin formation. Yogurt can be a nutritious substitute for higher-fat dairy products. Unripened cheese should be served chilled, while ripened cheese tastes best at room temperature. Avoid overcooking cheese.

SECTION 18.3

Egg Basics: Eggs are good sources of protein, several vitamins, and iron. The yolks are high in fat and cholesterol. Eggs are sold by size and grade. They should be refrigerated in their original cartons. When cooking with eggs, take steps to prevent food-borne illness. Eggs may be cooked in the shell, fried, baked, poached, scrambled, or made into a basic omelet.

SECTION 18.4

Using Eggs in Recipes: Eggs perform different functions in recipes. They thicken and add richness to custards and quiches. Egg whites can be beaten to add volume and lightness to soufflés, puffy omelets, and meringues.

REVIEWING FACTS

1. Identify the percent of calories from fat in whole, low-fat, and skim milk. (18.1)

2. Give two examples of cultured milk products. (18.1)

3. How is pasteurized process cheese made? (18.1)

4. What causes skin formation in milk? How can you prevent it? (18.2)

5. Why should you save the whey from thickened yogurt? How can it be used? (18.2)

6. Give two reasons why you should not store eggs in the egg tray on the refrigerator door. (18.3)

7. Describe how to freeze leftover raw egg whites. (18.3)

8. Briefly describe the procedure for making hard-cooked eggs. (18.3)

9. Describe the characteristics of egg whites beaten to the soft-peak stage and the stiff-peak stage. (18.4)

10. Identify two ways of keeping meringue from "weeping." (18.4)

LEARNING BY DOING

1. ***Food science lab:*** Add 1 Tbsp. (15 mL) lemon juice to 1 cup (250 mL) room-temperature milk. Let the milk stand for ten minutes. Describe the results. What do you think is happening to the milk? What is this process called? (18.1)

2. ***Foods lab:*** Select a recipe calling for sour cream. Prepare it first as directed. Prepare again using yogurt instead of sour cream. Compare the results on taste, texture, appearance, and nutritional value. (18.2)

8. Use a small amount of fat or vegetable oil cooking spray on the skillet. Heat skillet until it is hot enough to sizzle a drop of water; break, egg into small bowl; if yolk doesn't break, slip the egg from the bowl into the heated pan. Reduce heat immediately. Cover pan and cook eggs slowly until done. Turn eggs over to cook both sides.

9. Soft peak stage: peaks bend over slightly when beaters are lifted out of whites; stiff peak stage: peaks are glossy and hold their shape when the beaters are lifted out of the mixture.

10. Dissolve the sugar completely; put it on while filling is still hot.

3. **Foods lab:** Develop your own recipes for scrambled eggs. Experiment by adding seasonings and other ingredients. Evaluate the results for taste, appearance, nutritional value, and cost per serving. (18.3)

4. **Demonstration:** Demonstrate the proper method for making baked meringue shells, including beating the egg whites, forming the shells, and baking the meringue. (18.4)

THINKING CRITICALLY

1. **Forming hypotheses:** Why do you think food manufacturers developed UHT milk and canned milk? In what situations would these products be valuable? (18.1)

2. **Making generalizations:** Would you try to dovetail other food preparation tasks with cooking dairy products? Why or why not? (18.2)

3. **Recognizing alternatives:** How can you reduce the amount of cholesterol in recipes that use eggs? (18.3)

4. **Comparing and contrasting:** Compare the texture and composition of quiches and soufflés. Explain when you might want to serve each dish. (18.4)

MAKING DECISIONS AND SOLVING PROBLEMS

What Would You Do?

1. You have found a recipe for a cheese sauce that you would like to try. However, it calls for Edam and Gouda cheese, which you have not been able to find in your local food stores. You wonder if you can substitute other types of cheese. (18.1)

2. You offer to make a dip for a friend's party. You want to make it attractive and tasty, but low in fat and cholesterol as well. (18.2)

3. You want to reduce a recipe that calls for three eggs by one-half. (18.3)

4. You want to make meringue shells for your family's dessert tonight. However, it will take half an hour for the egg whites to come to room temperature, and you don't have that much time. (18.4)

LINKING YOUR STUDIES

1. **Social studies:** Using library resources, find information on milk products that are popular in other cultures. Present your findings to the class. (18.1)

2. **Math:** Compare the per-serving price and nutritional value of sour cream and its lower-fat substitutes, including yogurt and reduced-fat sour cream products. Record your findings on a chart or bar graph. Also tell how each product's nutritional value affects your decision about which is the best buy. (18.2)

3. **Writing:** Select your favorite cheese and trace its history. Write an article for a popular food magazine, including historical information, how the cheese is produced, and some ways to use it. (18.2)

4. **Science:** Using library resources, find more information on the reproductive purposes of the egg. How does the yolk develop? What is the purpose of the albumen? What is the shell's composition? Share your findings with the class in a short report. (18.3)

5. **Social studies:** Write a report on the international origins of dishes mentioned in this section. Where and when did soufflés and meringues originate? What other international dishes use beaten egg whites? (18.4)

LEARNING BY DOING

Answers to "Learning by Doing" activities will vary. Evaluate students on the effort they put into the activities as well as their results.

THINKING CRITICALLY

1. Answers will vary. For people who do not have access to refrigerators; for people who do not drink much milk.

2. Answers will vary. Students should realize that dairy products are very delicate and easily overcooked. It may not be a good idea to try to do something else while watching them.

3. Use two egg whites in place of one whole egg; use an egg substitute.

4. Answers will vary.

MAKING DECISIONS AND SOLVING PROBLEMS

Answers to "Making Decisions and Solving Problems" activities will vary. Encourage students to give reasons for their answers.

LINKING YOUR STUDIES

Answers to "Linking Your Studies" activities will vary. Encourage students to give reasons for their answers.

Planning the Chapter

Chapter Overview

Introducing the Chapter

Motivator

- If you had lived in the 15th century, you might have eaten seven meat dishes in a single meal; you might also have eaten none. The wealthy ate a great deal of meat; the poor ate very little. Discuss why meat holds such intrinsic value in many cultures. *(Throughout history, meat has been prized both for its nutritional value—its ability to "stick to your ribs—and because of its relative scarcity. Plant foods have always been easier to come by than animal foods. Because meat has typically been eaten by the wealthy, it has come to symbolize wealth and prestige in many cultures.)*

Teacher's Classroom Resources—Chapter 19

Refer to these resources in the TCR package:

Enrichment Activities

Chapter and Unit Tests

Testmaker Software

CHAPTER 19

Meat, Poultry, Fish, and Shellfish

SECTION 19.1
Looking at Meat, Poultry, Fish, and Shellfish 483

SECTION 19.2
Meat Selection and Storage 489

SECTION 19.3
Poultry Selection and Storage 496

SECTION 19.4
Fish and Shellfish Selection and Storage 500

SECTION 19.5
Preparing Meat, Poultry, Fish, and Shellfish 506

482

Cooperative Learning Suggestions

Initiate a Co-op Co-op activity. Have students work in groups to research and report on the latest studies on the relationship between the amounts and types of meat, poultry, fish, and shellfish eaten and the occurrence of health risks. Have the groups report their findings to the class as a panel discussion.

Looking at Meat, Poultry, Fish, and Shellfish

OBJECTIVES

After studying this section, you should be able to:

- Identify nutrients in meat, poultry, fish, and shellfish.
- Discuss factors affecting tenderness.
- Give guidelines for comparing costs of meat, poultry, fish, and shellfish.

LOOK FOR THESE TERMS

cut
marbling

Cerise looked at the long meat display case in the supermarket. It seemed like hundreds of different packages of meat were on display to her left and poultry to her right. Beyond the poultry, she could see dozens of different kinds of fresh fish and shellfish.

Cerise wondered how all these different foods compared to one another. Were some more nutritious than others? How else did they differ? How could she find the best buys?

Your Choices

Like Cerise, you face many choices when shopping for meat, poultry, fish, and shellfish. Each of these categories includes foods from several different sources.

- ❖ Meat includes beef (from mature cattle), lamb (from young sheep), pork (from hogs), and veal (from young cattle).
- ❖ Poultry refers to birds raised for food, such as chicken, turkey, duck, and goose.
- ❖ Dozens of different fish and shellfish are available, from cod and salmon to lobsters and clams.

When you shop for meat, poultry, fish, and shellfish, consider nutrition, tenderness, and cost.

Section 19.1: Looking at Meat, Poultry, Fish, and Shellfish   **483**

Section 19.1
Looking at Meat, Poultry, Fish, and Shellfish

Introducing the Section

Motivators

- Have students make a list of sources of meat, poultry, fish, and shellfish. Give a small prize to the student who identifies the most sources.
- Ask students to identify recent nutritional concerns related to meat, poultry, fish, and shellfish. How have these concerns affected their families' eating habits?

Objectives

- Have students read the section objectives. Discuss the purpose of studying this section.

Vocabulary

- Pronounce the terms listed under "Look for These Terms." Have students find the terms and their definitions in the section.

Guided Reading

- Have students look at the headings within Section 19.1 to preview the concepts that will be discussed.
- Have students read the section and complete the appropriate part of the Chapter 19 Study Guide in the *Student Workbook*.

Teacher's Classroom Resources—Section 19.1

Refer to these resources in the TCR package:

Reproducible Lesson Plans
Student Workbook
Extending the Text
Reteaching Activities

Section Quizzes
Testmaker Software
Food Science Resources
Color Transparencies

Teaching . . .

- **Your Choices**
- **Nutrition of Meat, Poultry, Fish, and Shellfish**

(text pages 483-484, 486)

Comprehension Check

1. Ask students to name four sources of meat and four sources of poultry. *(Beef, lamb, pork, and veal; chicken, turkey, duck, goose.)*

2. Ask students to explain what a "cut" of meat, poultry, or fish is. *(A particular edible part of the meat, poultry, or fish.)*

3. Ask students to list the nutrients available in meat, poultry, fish, and shellfish. *(complete protein, B vitamins, phosphorus, trace minerals)*

4. Ask students to name two types of animal foods that are generally lower in fat content than other animal foods. *(most fish, turkey breast meat)*

Student Experiences

1. **Display:** Display recommended serving sizes of cooked lean meat, poultry, or fish. Ask students to compare these serving sizes with the amounts they typically eat at a meal. Discuss the nutrition implications. *(Key skill: health)*

2. **Supermarket Survey:** Have students survey a local supermarket to identify the choices of meat, poultry, fish, and shellfish available. *(Key skill: analysis)*

Healthy Attitudes

Have students practice creating menus that would allow a family of four to enjoy meat, poultry, and fish while limiting fat and cholesterol.

Within each category, you can choose from many different fresh or frozen cuts. A **cut** refers to a particular edible part of meat, poultry, or fish as it is sold in the marketplace. For instance, cuts of beef include steaks, chops, roasts, and organ meats (such as liver).

You can also buy cured meat and poultry products, such as ham, bacon, cold cuts, and sausages. Many other convenience forms are available as well. (For more information on choosing convenience foods, see Chapter 15.)

How can you make wise decisions when shopping for meat, poultry, fish, and shellfish? Start by taking a look at how the different choices vary in nutrition, tenderness, and cost.

Nutrition of Meat, Poultry, Fish, and Shellfish

Meat, poultry, fish, and shellfish are all nutritious foods. They are excellent sources of complete protein. All three provide B vitamins, phosphorus, and certain trace minerals.

The Food Guide Pyramid recommends two to three servings daily from the Meat, Poultry, Fish, Dry Beans, Eggs, and Nuts Group. A typical serving can be 2 to 3 ounces (56 to 84 g) of cooked lean meat, poultry, or fish.

Many Americans eat larger servings of meat, poultry, and fish than the recommended portions. That means they eat more protein than needed. The larger servings may also add more fat and cholesterol to daily food choices.

Fat and Cholesterol Content

Because they are animal foods, meat, poultry, fish, and shellfish all contain cholesterol. All animal muscle contains about the same amount of cholesterol per ounce. Organ meats have more cholesterol.

Fat content varies. Most fish is very low in fat. So is turkey breast meat. Other poultry and meat cuts generally have more fat, but the amount varies depending on the cut and the preparation method. Meat, poultry, fish, or shellfish that has less than 10 grams of fat in a 3 ½ ounce (100 gram) serving is considered lean.

Besides the amount of fat, another consideration is the type of fat that is present. In general, beef has the largest amount of saturated fat. Pork has more polyunsaturated fats than beef or lamb. Chicken and turkey generally have less saturated fat than red meat. Fish has the least amount of saturated fat and the most polyunsaturated.

Meat and poultry include both invisible fat—which is part of the chemical composition of the food—and visible fat. In poultry, most of the visible fat is located in the skin

Healthy Attitudes

Here are some suggestions for enjoying meat, poultry, and fish while limiting fat and cholesterol.

- Follow the Food Guide Pyramid recommendations for serving sizes.
- Combine moderate amounts of meat, poultry, or fish with grains and vegetables.
- Substitute legumes for meats at least several times a week.
- Choose cuts with less fat. (You'll learn more about choosing cuts in later sections.)
- Trim fat layers from meat. Remove poultry skin before eating.
- Use low-fat cooking methods, such as broiling or roasting. Avoid cooking methods that add fat, such as frying.

Special Needs Strategies

Learning Disabled: Have students make flash cards of types, forms, and cuts of meat, poultry, fish, and shellfish. Have students use the flash cards to practice identifying each of these.

More About Meat

- *Bloom.* The main pigment of animal muscle is myoglobin. It stores oxygen and is normally a bright red color. After the animal is slaughtered, myoglobin gets no oxygen and turns a purplish-red. However, when the meat is cut, the surface is exposed to air and turns a pink-

Comparing Fat and Cholesterol Content

The following chart lists just a few examples of meat, poultry, fish, and shellfish. It shows the approximate amount of fat, saturated fat, and cholesterol in each. Notice that within each category, some choices are higher and some are lower in fat. How does the cholesterol content compare?

Type of food (3 oz. [84 g] serving)	Total Fat (g)	Saturated Fat (g)	Cholesterol (mg)
Fish and shellfish:			
Cod, cooked	1	0	47
Tuna, canned in water	1	0	48
Mackerel, cooked	15	4	64
Shrimp, cooked	1	0	166
Poultry:			
Chicken, light meat, without skin, roasted	3	0	73
Chicken, dark meat, without skin, roasted	4	1	80
Turkey, breast meat, without skin, roasted	1	0	71
Meat:			
Beef, top round, trimmed, broiled	5	2	71
Beef, ground, regular, broiled	18	7	76
Beef liver, pan-fried	7	2	410
Pork loin, trimmed, roasted	11	4	77

Teaching . . .

- **Comparing Fat and Cholesterol Content (Chart)**

(text page 485)

Comprehension Check

1. Ask students to name the type of fish listed in the chart on page 486 that has the most fat. *(cooked mackerel)*

2. Ask students which of the foods on the chart on page 486 people with high cholesterol levels should avoid. *(cooked shrimp, pan-fried beef liver)*

Student Experiences

1. **Chart Reading:** Have students compare the amounts of fat and cholesterol in meats, poultry, fish, and shellfish. *(Key skill: math)*

2. **Research:** Have students find out why dark chicken meat has more fat, saturated fat, and cholesterol than white chicken meat. Ask students to report their findings to the class. *(Key skill: research)*

3. **Research:** Have students find out why beef liver has a much higher cholesterol content than other items in the chart on page 486. Have students write a brief report of their findings. *(Key skills: writing, research)*

ish-red, known as "bloom." Consumers associate the pinkish-red with freshness. Therefore retailers usually sell meat in packaging that allows oxygen to flow through, maintaining the bloom.
- *Aging.* Letting meat age improves the flavor and makes it more tender. In aging, meat is stored at low temperatures that limit the growth of microorganisms. Beef can benefit from being aged up to three weeks. Aging adds to the cost, so most meat is shipped almost immediately. Still, some aging takes place during shipping in refrigerated transport.

Teaching . . .

• Factors Affecting Tenderness

(text pages 486-488)

Comprehension Check

1. Ask students to list the four types of tissue that may be present in meat, poultry, or fish. *(muscle tissue, connective tissue, fat, bone)*

2. Ask students to explain the relationship between thickness of muscle fibers and tenderness. *(The thicker the muscle fiber, the tougher and coarser the meat or poultry becomes.)*

3. Ask students to explain the difference between collagen and elastin. What methods can be used to tenderize each? *(Both are connective tissues, but collagen can be broken down by heat methods; elastin cannot be softened by heat, so it must be pounded, cut, or ground to break down the elastin.)*

4. Discuss the relationship between marbling and tenderness. *(The more marbling a cut has, the more tender it seems to be.)*

Student Experiences

1. **Class Discussion:** Discuss ways to enjoy meat, poultry, and fish while limiting fat and cholesterol. *(Key skill: critical thinking)*

2. **Research:** Have students find out the percentage of fat to muscle in various types of meat. Have students write a report of their findings. *(Key skills: writing, research)*

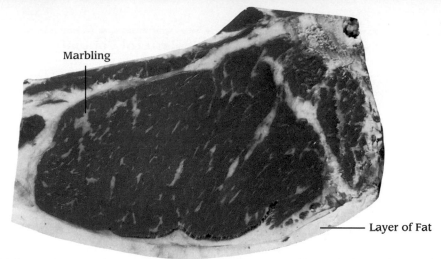

Marbling

Layer of Fat

Visible fat in meat occurs in two ways—as fat layers surrounding muscle sections and as marbling within muscle sections.

and in layers under the skin. In meat, there may be a layer of visible fat surrounding the lean muscle portion of the cut. In addition, small white flecks, called **marbling,** may appear within the muscle tissue of meat.

Factors Affecting Tenderness

Tenderness is another consideration when shopping for meat, poultry, and fish. As you will see later on, tenderness can affect your choice of cooking method.

Different cuts of meat, poultry, and fish may vary in tenderness. Why? To answer that question, it helps to know a little about the composition of meat, poultry, and fish.

A cut may contain four basic types of tissue: muscle tissue, connective tissue, fat, and bone. When it comes to tenderness, the most important factors are muscle tissue and connective tissue.

Composition of Meat and Poultry

Meat and poultry have very long, thin muscle cells (sometimes called "muscle fibers").

486   Chapter 19: Meat, Poultry, Fish, and Shellfish

Some are as long as 12 inches (30 cm). They are thinnest in young animals and in parts of the animal that get little exercise (such as the back). As animals get older, the fibers thicken. They are thickest in those parts that get the most exercise (such as the legs). Thicker muscle fibers give the meat or poultry a tougher, coarser texture.

Tenderness also depends on the amount and type of connective tissue that is present. Connective tissue is a protein material that surrounds cells. The more connective tissue, the tougher the cut of meat or poultry.

There are several kinds of connective tissue in meat and poultry, but two are important when it comes to tenderness and cooking.

❖ *Collagen* (KAHL-eh-jen) is a thin, white or transparent connective tissue. When meat or poultry is cooked using moist-heat methods, such as simmering in liquid, the collagen softens and turns into a gelatin.

❖ *Elastin* (ee-LASS-tin) is a yellowish, very tough connective tissue. It cannot be softened by heat. Other tenderizing methods, such as pounding, cutting, or grinding, must be used to break down elastin.

Food and Nutrition Science

Identifying and Comparing Animal Tissues: Have students use a hand lens to examine samples of tender meat cuts and tougher cuts. Have them identify muscle tissue, connective tissue, fat, and bone. Define marbling, collagen, and elastin. Discuss the factors that affect tenderness. Compare the muscles observed in meat with the muscles in fish. What differences were observed? Ask students to write a brief report of their findings.

Tenderizing Experiment: See the *Food Science Resources* booklet for the "Tenderizing Meat" teaching guides and student experiment worksheet. The experiment tests the effects of tenderizing methods on the appearance, texture, flavor, and color of meat.

Beef and Poultry Muscle

Single Muscle Cell

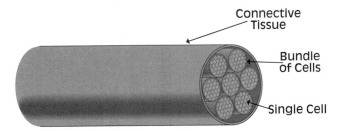

Connective
Tissue

Bundle
of Cells

Single Cell

**Many bundles of cells
form muscle tissue**

Fat content can also have an effect on tenderness. Meat that has more marbling seems more tender. In addition, fat gives meat and poultry flavor and helps keep it juicy as it cooks.

In meat and poultry, the muscle tissue is made up of long fibers held together in bundles by connective tissue. The thicker the fibers, the less tender the meat.

TIPS for Success

Cutting Across the Grain

The lengthwise direction of the muscle cells is known as the "grain." One solution for less tender cuts of meat is to cut across the grain. The long fibers are cut into pieces and the meat can be easier to chew. Most meats are generally cut this way for retail sale. It's also a good way to cut cooked meat and poultry for serving.

 SAFETY CHECK

When shopping for meat, poultry, or fish, be sure the department smells fresh. Foul odors could indicate leaking packages or temperatures that may be too high for safety. The fish department may have a characteristic fish aroma, but should have no foul odors. (See Section 12.3 for more shopping tips.)

Thinking Skills

Reasoning: Have students check the forms of turkey available in a local supermarket. Ask them to note prices and figure the cost per serving. Why do some forms of turkey cost more than others?

Teaching . . .

• Comparing Costs

(text page 488)

Comprehension Check

1. Ask students to explain why cooking less tender cuts can save money. *(Less tender cuts are less expensive than tender cuts.)*

2. Ask students to explain why it is important to consider cost per serving when you compare boneless meat and poultry with cuts that are sold with the bone. *(The boneless cuts yield more servings per pound.)*

Student Experiences

1. **Comparing Cost per Serving:** Collect labels from a variety of meat, poultry, and fish. Have students compare the cost per serving of different cuts. Discuss factors that influence prices. *(Key skills: math, consumer awareness)*

2. **Price Comparisons:** Have students price several types of meats: boneless lean, boneless with fat, small bone, and bony meats. (Use ads or visit a supermarket.) Determine price per serving. Make a comparison chart beginning with the lowest price per serving. *(Key skills: writing, consumer awareness)*

Lab Experience

Have students cook identical amounts of several types of ground beef and thoroughly drain (use microwave, if possible). They should weight the portions before and after to determine the percentage of fat loss and recalculate price per pound. Then have them conduct a taste test and determine the best buy.

Completing the Section

Review

- Ask students to summarize the main ideas in this section.
- Have students complete the Section Review. (Answers appear below.)

Evaluation

- Ask students to write a short essay describing the fat and cholesterol content of different types of meat, poultry, fish, and shellfish.
- Have students take the quiz for Section 19.1. (Refer to the *Section Quizzes* booklet or construct your own quiz using the *Testmaker Software.*)

Reteaching

- Have students prepare a poster that shows the differences in nutritional value and fat and cholesterol content of meats, poultry, fish, and shellfish.
- Refer to the *Reteaching Activities* booklet for the Section 19.1 activity worksheet.

Enrichment

- Ask students to research what the beef industry is doing to produce and promote the use of leaner meat.

Closure

- Lead a discussion about the importance of choosing meats, poultry, fish, and shellfish wisely.

Fish Muscles Are Different

The muscles in fish are arranged differently. Instead of the long fibers found in meat and poultry, fish have very short fibers that are arranged in layers. The layers are separated by sheets of very thin, fragile connective tissue. When heated, this connective tissue turns into gelatin. As a result, all fish and shellfish is very tender. When cooked, the flesh "flakes" or breaks up into small pieces because the muscle fibers are short.

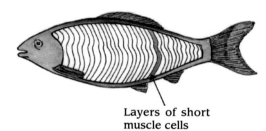

Layers of short muscle cells

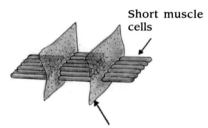

Short muscle cells

Very thin sheets of connective tissue divide muscle cells

Fish is naturally tender because it has short muscle fibers and fragile connective tissue.

Comparing Costs

When shopping, cost is an important point of comparison. Meats, poultry, fish, and shellfish are generally the most expensive part of the food budget. However, cuts can vary widely in cost.

Remember to compare the cost per serving of different cuts of meat, poultry, and fish. (Refer to Section 12.3, page 341.) If you find a bargain that's not on your shopping list, consider changing your plans. You may save a considerable amount.

Here are some general guidelines:

- ❖ Tender cuts are often more expensive than less tender cuts. Knowing how to cook less tender cuts can help you save money.
- ❖ Boneless meat and poultry is generally more expensive than cuts sold with the bone. You may be able to save money by removing the bones yourself. Remember, however, that boneless cuts yield more servings per pound. Be sure to check the cost per serving.

■ Section 19.1 Review ■

RECALL THE FACTS

1. List three nutrients found in meat, poultry, and fish.

2. Identify two factors that affect the tenderness of meat and poultry.

3. What is the most accurate way to compare the cost of different cuts of meat, poultry, or fish?

DISCUSS YOUR IDEAS

4. What factors might affect the price of meat, poultry, and fish?

APPLY YOUR LEARNING

5. In magazines and cookbooks, find at least six recipes for meat, poultry, or fish. Identify the cut and preparation method for each recipe. Why do you think some preparation methods are preferred for certain cuts?

■ Answers to Section Review ■

1. *Any three:* Complete protein, B vitamins, phosphorus, certain trace minerals.
2. *Any two:* The age of the animal, the amount of exercise the animal has had, the amount and type of connective tissue that is present.
3. By cost per serving.
4. Answers will vary. Tenderness and length of aging, if any, affect the price.
5. Answers will vary. Students should realize that some of the tougher cuts must be prepared in certain ways to keep them from being too tough when they are served.

Meat Selection and Storage

OBJECTIVES

After studying this section, you should be able to:

- Describe the four basic types of meat.
- Identify tender and less tender cuts of meat.
- Identify processed meat products.
- Give guidelines for storing meat.

LOOK FOR THESE TERMS

wholesale cuts
retail cuts
variety meats
curing

The more you know about meat, the easier it will be to find the best buys. Even though there are many different cuts of meat, with an understanding of just a few basic guidelines you can become a smart meat shopper.

Types of Meat

Each of the four basic types of meat has a distinct flavor and appearance. When shopping, look for color typical of the meat.

- ❖ **Beef** is meat from cattle over one year old. It has a hearty flavor. The cuts have bright red flesh. The fat is firm with a white, creamy white, or yellowish color.
- ❖ **Veal** is meat from very young calves, one to three months old. It has a mild flavor and light pink color with very little fat. "Special fed veal" has been fed a special milk-base diet; the flesh is more tender with a grayish-pink color and white fat.

- ❖ **Lamb** has a mild but unique flavor. Cuts are a bright pink-red color with white, brittle fat. The fat is sometimes covered with a "fell," a colorless connective tissue.
- ❖ **Pork** has a mild flavor. Fresh meat is a grayish-pink color with white, soft fat.

Because of changes in breeding and feeding practices, the pork produced today is leaner than in the past.

Section 19.2
Meat Selection and Storage

Introducing the Section

Motivators

- Organize a visit to a meat processing plant where students can observe meat cutting, storage, packaging, and sanitation procedures.
- Display the bone shapes that can be used to identify cuts of meat. Ask students if they can identify the cut of meat from which each bone comes.

Objectives

- Have students read the section objectives. Discuss the purpose of studying this section.

Vocabulary

- Pronounce the terms listed under "Look for These Terms." Have students find the terms and their definitions in the section.

Guided Reading

- Have students look at the headings within Section 19.2 to preview the concepts that will be discussed.
- Have students read the section and complete the appropriate part of the Chapter 19 Study Guide in the *Student Workbook*.

Teacher's Classroom Resources—Section 19.2

Refer to these resources in the TCR package:

Reproducible Lesson Plans

Student Workbook

Extending the Text

Reteaching Activities

Section Quizzes

Testmaker Software

Color Transparencies

Comprehension Check

1. Ask students to identify the four basic types of meat and the typical color of each. *(Beef—bright red flesh and white to yellowish fat; veal—light pink color with very little fat; lamb—bright pink-red with white, brittle fat; pork—grayish-pink with white, soft fat.)*

2. Ask students to explain how knowing wholesale cuts and bone shapes can help you make wise choices among the hundreds of retail cuts of meat. *(Knowing wholesale cuts and bone shapes can help you decide how tender the meat is and how it can be cooked.)*

3. Ask students to identify lean cuts of beef, pork, veal, and lamb. *(Beef—roasts and steaks: round, loin, sirloin, chuck arm; pork—roasts and chop: tenderloin, center loin, ham; veal—all cuts except ground veal; lamb—roasts and chops: leg, loin, fore shanks.)*

4. Ask students to identify the amount of fat that should be present around the cut. *(no more than 1/4 inch [0.6 cm])*

Using the Diagram

Discuss the similarities and differences in the diagrams of beef, veal, pork, and lamb wholesale cuts. For example, which has the most wholesale cuts? *(Beef, because it is largest.)* Where is the loin located in all four animals? *(The back.)*

Cuts of Meat

For marketing, meat is first divided into large **wholesale cuts** (also called primal cuts). Wholesale cuts for beef, veal, pork, and lamb are identified in the illustrations on this page.

These wholesale cuts are divided into the smaller **retail cuts** which you find in the supermarket. For example, one of the wholesale cuts of beef is the chuck, from the shoulder area. Retail cuts from the chuck include blade roast and chuck short ribs.

The price label on the meat package identifies the cut. The type of meat is listed first (beef, veal, pork, or lamb). The wholesale cut is listed second. This tells you the part of the animal the meat comes from, such as chuck, rib, or round. The retail cut, such as spareribs, chops, or steak, is listed third.

Compare the wholesale cuts for the four types of meat animals. In what ways are they similar? How are they different?

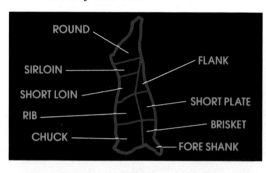

Beef

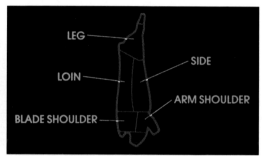

Pork

Veal

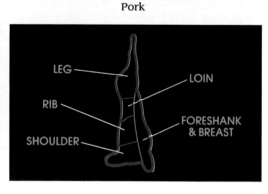

Lamb

Thinking Skills

Critical Thinking: Ask students to collaborate to compare the price per pound of hamburger and rib-eye steak at a meat market and two supermarkets. Ask them to compute the cost of making chili for four using 1/2 lb. (227 g) of hamburger. How does that compare to the cost of four rib-eye steaks? What about the comparative nutritional value and caloric content? Instruct students to make a chart using the information collected and draw conclusions.

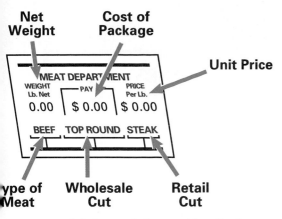

Net Weight

Cost of Package

Unit Price

Type of Meat

Wholesale Cut

Retail Cut

Meat labels can help you identify the cut. They also provide information about the size of the package and the price.

Which Cuts Are Lean?

When shopping for meat, lean choices (less than 10 grams of fat in a 3½ ounce [100 gram] serving) include:

❖ **Beef** roasts and steaks: round, loin, sirloin, chuck arm.
❖ **Pork** roasts and chops: tenderloin, center loin, ham.
❖ **Veal** cuts: all except ground veal.
❖ **Lamb** roasts and chops: leg, loin, fore shanks.

When shopping, you can also use appearance as a clue to leanness. Inspect the package carefully. How much fat can you see? The fat that surrounds the cut should be trimmed to less than 1/4 inch (0.6 cm). If there is more, you pay for the excess and waste money.

Using Bone Shape to Identify Cuts

Each wholesale cut has a distinctive bone shape. Therefore, you can use bone shape as a method to identify meat cuts. The bone shape for a particular area of the animal is almost identical in beef, pork, lamb, and veal, although the bones differ in size.

The bones are also your clue to the tenderness of the cut. For example, the rib or T-shaped bones, which are part of the backbone, indicate the meat is tender. Knowing whether a cut is tender will help you decide what cooking method to use.

The diagram on page 492 shows typical bone shapes for the wholesale cuts of meat. It also identifies which wholesale cuts are tender.

Lean cuts of meat can be a part of an overall low-fat eating plan.

Student Experiences

1. **Taste Testing:** Cook samples of beef, veal, lamb, and pork. Have students observe the appearance of each meat, then taste it. Discuss the differences in taste and appearance. *(Key skill: evaluation)*

2. **Display:** Refer students to the illustration on page 492. Point out that bones are the clue to what part of the animal the retail cut comes from. With that information you can judge tenderness by determining whether the muscle fiber in that area would get heavy or light use. (In general, the cuts from the areas that get heavy muscle use are tougher.) *(Key skill: consumer awareness)*

3. **Class Discussion:** Refer students to the list of lean cuts on page 491. What are some other clues to leanness? *(Key skills: reading, critical thinking)*

4. **Reading Charts and Labels:** Display charts of wholesale and retail cuts of beef, veal, lamb, and pork. Provide students with labels from different cuts of beef, veal, lamb, and pork. Point out that the type of meat is listed first, the wholesale cut is listed second, and the retail cut is listed third. Example: pork loin chop. *(Key skill: reading charts and graphs)*

Thinking Skills

Problem Solving: Discuss why it is important to keep fat in mind when choosing cuts and quality of meat and making up serving portions. Point out that research indicates that too much fat in the diet is unhealthy. Fat is a suspected contributor to heart disease and certain cancers. It is also highest of all nutrients in calories. Ask students to work in groups to plan a one-day menu for a family of four concerned about lowering fat intake. Ask students to write out the menu, including an estimate of the fat intake per person for the day. Then have students find out the actual fat content, if possible.

Teaching . . .

- **Ground Meat**
- **Organ Meats**

(text page 493)

Comprehension Check

1. Ask students to explain what ground meat is made from. *(Ground meat is made from beef trimmings, the meat attached to the bone.)*

2. Ask students to identify the maximum percent fat by weight allowed by law in ground beef. *(30 percent)*

3. Ask students to define variety meats. *(The edible organs of animals.)*

4. Ask students to give examples of variety meats. *(liver, kidneys, chitterlings, brains, heart, tongue, tripe, and sweetbreads)*

Student Experiences

1. **Class Discussion:** Have students identify organ meats available. Which organ meats are associated with regional or ethnic foods? *(Key skill: multicultural awareness)*

2. **Survey:** Have students survey the types of ground beef sold locally (hamburger, ground chuck, ground round, hamburger plus extended, lean ground beef, etc.). Have students find the cost per pound and ask the meat cutter what the differences are, especially fat content. *(Key skills: reading, consumer awareness)*

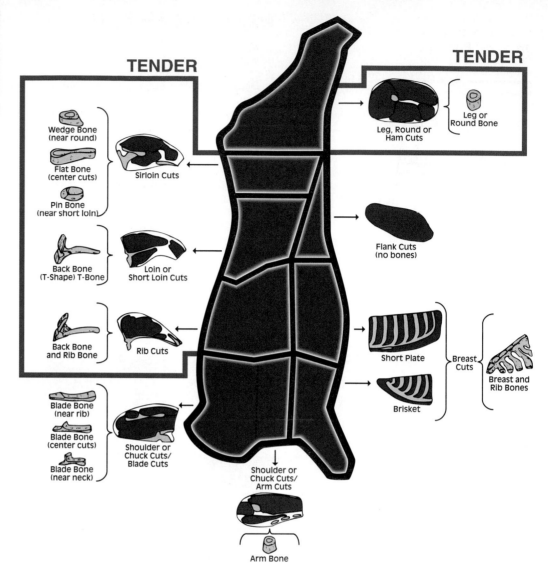

Bone shapes can help you decide how tender meat is and what cooking method to use. Notice the typical bone shapes for each part of the animal. An example of a retail cut is also shown for each wholesale cut. Tender cuts include those from the rib, loin or short loin, sirloin, and leg or round.

More About Beef

The amount of fat in a beef cut varies, depending on the part of the animal. While the "Select" grade is generally lowest in fat, some cuts are proportionately higher in fat than others.

Some cuts in Select grade can be heavily marbled. In fact, a lean cut of Choice beef can have less fat than a marbled cut of Select. For example, a rib steak is more heavily marbled than a sirloin. A rib steak in the Select grade may have more fat than a sirloin steak, Choice grade.

When buying meat, look carefully at the amount of visible fat, and, even more

These stuffed peppers are just one example of the many uses for ground meat. When buying, look for an indication of fat content on the label. For example, "85 percent lean" would mean that the ground meat is 15 percent fat by weight.

Comprehension Check

1. Ask students why people may not often see the USDA inspection stamp on retail cuts of meat. *(The stamp is placed in only a few places on the animal.)*

2. Ask students to list and explain the most common grades for beef. *(see the list on page 493)*

Student Experiences

1. **Observation:** After describing prime, choice, and select grades, have students examine and try to identify the grades of beef cuts that are unlabeled. Have then fry a thin piece of each and rank the samples by taste and tenderness. Do the results of the visual examination agree with taste test results? *(Key skill: evaluation)*

2. **Research:** Have students research and write about state meat inspection laws and procedures. *(Key skills: reading, writing)*

Ground Meat

Ground beef is made from beef trimmings, the meat attached to the bone. By law, ground beef cannot have more than 30 percent fat by weight. Lean ground beef is available, although it may cost more.

You may also find packages of ground lamb, pork, and veal. If not, you can ask to have meat ground for you.

Organ Meats

Edible animal organs are usually called **variety meats.** Here are some examples.

❖ Liver is highly nutritious and tender, with a pronounced flavor.

❖ Lamb and veal kidneys are tender with a mild flavor. Beef and pork kidneys are strong flavored and less tender.

❖ Chitterlings usually refers to the intestines of pigs, but they may also come from calves. They are thoroughly cleaned and sold whole in containers.

Other organ meats include brains, heart, tongue, tripe (stomach lining of cattle), and sweetbreads (thymus gland).

Inspection and Grading

Meat is inspected before it can be sold. The USDA inspects meat for wholesomeness. A round inspection mark is stamped on the meat with a harmless vegetable dye. The inspection mark is stamped in only a few places on the animal, so you will probably not see it on retail cuts.

Meat may also be graded. Grading is a voluntary program available to the meat industry, which pays for the service. Meat is graded according to standards which include amount of marbling, age of the animal, and texture and appearance of the meat. Following are the most common grades for beef.

❖ **Prime** is the highest and most expensive grade. The meat is well marbled with fat. It is very tender and flavorful.

❖ **Choice** is the most common grade sold in supermarkets. It has less marbling than prime but is still tender and flavorful.

❖ **Select** contains the least amount of marbling and is least expensive. It is sometimes sold as a store brand.

important, the marbling. Fat around the edges can and should be trimmed. But marbling cannot be trimmed. As the meat cooks, some of the marbling melts, but not all of it.

• **Processed Meats**

• **Storing Meat**

(text pages 494-495)

Comprehension Check

1. Have students name at least four processed meats sold in the United States. *(ham, bacon, sausage, cold cuts)*

2. Discuss the advantages and reasons why some meats are processed. *(To extend shelf life and create a distinctive flavor.)*

3. Ask students to list and describe common processing methods. *(curing, drying, salting, and smoking, or a combination of these methods)*

4. Ask students to explain how to store meat. *(Meat requires cold storage.)*

Student Experiences

1. **Taste Testing:** Purchase and cook a variety of processed meats. Ask blindfolded students to try to identify the meat by taste and texture. Can students identify some of the spices added to the meats? *(Key skill: evaluation)*

2. **Class Discussion:** Discuss reasons processed meats should be eaten in moderation. *(Key skill: critical thinking)*

3. **Group Research:** Have students work in small groups to research methods of processing meats. Which methods were used more in the past than today? *(Key skills: reading, research)*

See Also . . .
• "Room Temperature Storage," text pages 206-207
• "Cold Storage," text pages 207-212

Meat that has been graded is identified by a grade shield. Which of these grades is least expensive?

Lamb and veal are also graded. The same grades are used, except that "Good" replaces "Select." Pork is not graded because the meat is more uniform in quality.

Processed Meats

Meats can be processed into products such as ham, bacon, sausage, and cold cuts. Processed meats give consumers a wider variety of products from which to choose. About 35 percent of the meat produced in the United States is processed.

Processing involves treating the meat to extend its shelf life and to create a distinctive flavor. One common processing method is **curing.** This method uses a mixture of salt, sugar, nitrite, ascorbic acid, and water. The meat may be soaked in the solution or the solution may be pumped into the meat.

Other processing methods include drying, salting, and smoking. Drying and salting help preserve the meat. Smoking originally meant exposing meat to wood smoke to preserve and flavor it. Today, liquid smoke is used for flavoring only.

Often, more than one of these processing methods is used. For example, bacon is cured and smoked. Chipped beef has been dried, salted, and smoked.

Ham is pork that has been cured and either smoked or canned. Check the label carefully for instructions. Some hams are precooked, but others must be cooked before eating. If the label does not specify, cook the ham.

Healthy Attitudes

Processed meats should be eaten in moderation. Many of them are high in sodium, fat, or both. In addition, nitrites and nitrates found in cured meats may be linked to certain types of cancer. The National Cancer Institute and the American Cancer Society recommend that people eat fewer smoked, salt-cured, and nitrate-cured foods.

Many people enjoy the flavor of hot dogs and other cured meats. Health experts recommend such meats be eaten only occasionally, since most are high in fat and sodium.

Food and Nutrition Science

Sodium Nitrite: Cured meats such as ham and bacon are treated with sodium nitrite to inhibit the growth of the bacterium that causes botulism, a sometimes deadly disease. Some studies have shown that nitrite consumption can cause cancer. Have interested students research the nitrite controversy and report their findings. Use the report to stimulate a class discussion on the merits of using nitrites in meats. Or you may want to have students form teams (for and against nitrite use), and allow each side five minutes to present its point of view, with a two-minute rebuttal after each presentation. Give the class 10 minutes to question the teams, then take a vote.

Sausages are made from ground meat, often mixed with fat, salt, sugar, preservatives, seasonings, and other additives. Many different types of sausages are available. Some, such as fresh pork sausage, must be cooked before eating. Others are ready to eat, although they may be heated. Again, check the label carefully.

Cold cuts are processed meats that have been sliced and packaged. They are ready to eat.

Kielbasa, or Polish sausage, is an example of a sausage associated with a particular country or region. Others include chorizo from Spain, pepperoni from Italy, and braunschweiger from Germany.

Storing Meat

Meat requires cold storage. Ground meat and variety meats, if stored in the refrigerator, should be used within one to two days. Other fresh meat will keep in the refrigerator for three to five days. For longer storage, freeze the meat. See the chart in Section 7.4, pages 208-209, for more specific storage times, including leftovers.

■ Section 19.2 Review ■

RECALL THE FACTS

1. How does pork differ from beef in flavor and color?

2. Name three wholesale cuts of beef that are considered tender.

3. Give four examples of processed meat products.

4. How long can fresh meat be stored safely in the refrigerator?

DISCUSS YOUR IDEAS

5. How do you think the cut and grade of meat affect its price?

APPLY YOUR LEARNING

6. Bring to class several price labels from packages of meat. (Clean them thoroughly first.) Using the information found on the labels, identify the type of animal, the wholesale cut, the retail cut, the unit price, and the total price for the package.

Completing the Section

Review

- Ask students to summarize the main ideas in this section.

- Have students complete the Section Review. (Answers appear below.)

Evaluation

- Use a chart similar to those on page 491, but without the labels. Have students identify the wholesale cuts.

- Have students take the quiz for Section 19.2. (Refer to the *Section Quizzes* booklet or use the *Testmaker Software*.)

Reteaching

- Show pictures of different bone types. Have students identify the cut of meat that has each bone type.

- Refer to the *Reteaching Activities* booklet for the Section 19.2 activity worksheet.

Enrichment

- Have students research and write about state meat inspection laws and procedures.

Closure

- Refer to the second motivator for this section. Ask students if they feel more comfortable identifying cuts of meat by looking at the bones.

■ Answers to Section Review ■

1. Pork is a grayish-pink color and mild flavor; beef is bright red and has a hearty flavor.
2. Sirloin, loin, rib cuts.
3. Ham, bacon, sausage, cold cuts.
4. Ground and variety meats should be stored only one to two days. Other meats: 3 to 5 days.
5. Answers will vary. Students should understand that the more tender the cut and the better the grade, the higher the price will be.
6. Answers will vary.

Section 19.3
Poultry Selection and Storage

Introducing the Section

Motivators

- Ask students to identify the types of poultry they have eaten. Which types do they like best? Least?

- Discuss reasons people are eating poultry more often now than in the past. Have students identify their families' favorite poultry dishes. Discuss the type of poultry used in each and the method of preparation.

Objectives

- Have students read the section objectives. Discuss the purpose of studying the section.

Vocabulary

- Pronounce the terms listed under "Look for These Terms." Have students find the terms and their definitions in the section.

Guided Reading

- Have students look at the headings within Section 19.3 to preview the concepts that will be discussed.

- Have students read the section and complete the appropriate part of the Chapter 19 Study Guide in the *Student Workbook*.

Using the Photo

Answer to caption question (page 496): Possible reasons include: chicken is widely available, relatively economical, available in a variety of market forms, and versatile. The smaller size of chickens makes them more convenient to cook for most families than a whole turkey.

Poultry Selection and Storage

OBJECTIVES

After studying this section, you should be able to:

- Describe types and market forms of poultry.
- Give guidelines for buying and storing poultry.

LOOK FOR THIS TERM

giblets

Poultry is an increasingly popular food. Some poultry is relatively low in fat, which makes it a good choice for health-conscious consumers. Its mild flavor lends itself to many different recipes.

Types and Market Forms of Poultry

The different types of poultry—chicken, turkey, duck, and goose—are sold in a wide variety of market forms.

Chicken

Chicken has light and dark meat. The light meat is leaner and has a milder flavor.

Tenderness and cooking method are determined by the age of the bird. The terms used on the label give an indication.

Chicken is the most popular type of poultry in the United States. Why do you think this is so?

Teacher's Classroom Resources—Section 19.3

Refer to these resources in the TCR package:

Reproducible Lesson Plans

Student Workbook

Extending the Text

Reteaching Activities

Section Quizzes

Testmaker Software

Color Transparencies

- **Broiler-fryer** chickens are the most tender and most common. They can be cooked using almost any method.
- **Roaster** chickens are raised to be roasted whole. They are slightly larger and older than broiler-fryers and yield more meat per pound.
- **Stewing chickens** are older, mature birds. Since they are less tender than others, they must be cooked in moist heat.
- **Rock Cornish game hens** are young, small chickens of a special breed. They have less meat in relation to size than other chickens. One hen usually makes one serving. They can be broiled or roasted.
- **Capons** are desexed roosters under 10 months old. Tender and flavorful, they are best roasted.

Chicken can be purchased in various market forms—whole, cut up, or in packages of specific parts. Poultry labeled "fresh" has never been chilled below 26°F (-4°C). If it has been chilled between 0°F and 26°F (-18°C to -4°C), it is labeled "hard chilled." "Frozen" or "previously frozen" means that the poultry has been chilled to below 0°F (-18°C).

Turkey

Turkeys are larger than chickens and have a stronger flavor. The light meat is leaner and more tender with a more mild flavor than the dark meat.

When buying a whole turkey, you can choose from several types. They differ mainly in size. All are suitable for roasting, the most common cooking method for turkey.

To cut up a whole chicken, follow these steps...

1. Slice the skin between one leg and the body.

2. Bend the leg to crack the joint. Then cut through the joint and remove the leg. Repeat for the other leg and the wings.

3. If desired, separate the drumstick from the thigh by cracking the joint and cutting through it.

4. Use kitchen shears to cut along the backbone on both sides, separating the breast from the back.

5. Hold the breast skin side down and snap it in two.

6. Cut the breast in half, leaving the breastbone on one of the halves.

Section 19.3: Poultry Selection and Storage **497**

Teaching . . .

- **Types and Market Forms of Poultry**

(text pages 496-499)

Comprehension Check

1. Ask students to name the different types of chicken commonly available in supermarkets. *(broiler-fryer, roaster, stewing chickens, Rock Cornish game hens, capons)*

2. Ask students to list the various market forms in which broiler-fryers can be purchased. *(whole, cut up, specific parts)*

3. Ask students to list the three most common types of whole turkeys available and the approximate size or weight of each. *(Beltsville or fryer-roaster—5 to 9 pounds; hen turkeys—8 to 16 pounds; tom turkeys—up to 24 pounds.)*

4. Ask students how to tell whether poultry was ground with or without the skin. *(If the package description contains the word "meat," the skin was not used.)*

Student Experiences

1. **Class Discussion:** Discuss the classes of poultry available. How are tenderness of the bird and cooking method related? *(Key skill: critical thinking)*

2. **Demonstration:** Demonstrate how to cut up a whole chicken. Compare the cost of buying a whole chicken with the cost of buying chicken parts or boned chicken. *(Key skills: consumer awareness, kitchen management skills)*

3. **Display:** Show students packages of ground poultry, giblets, and processed poultry. Discuss the terms used on the labels. Discuss possible uses of each in cooking. *(Key skill: reading)*

Food and Nutrition Science

Substituting Ground Meat: Have students choose a recipe calling for ground beef. Have half the students prepare the recipe using ground beef, and the other half prepare the recipe using ground poultry instead. Have students compare the results in terms of taste, texture, and appearance. Ask students to write a brief report of their results.

Teaching . . .

- **Inspection and Grading**
- **Buying and Storing Poultry**

(text page 499)

Comprehension Check

1. Ask students to describe the characteristics of poultry that is labeled "Grade A." *(The poultry is practically free of defects, has a good shape and appearance, and is meaty.)*

2. Ask students to explain what to look for when buying poultry. *(plump, meaty bird with smooth, soft skin, no tiny feathers or bruised or torn skin)*

3. Discuss how long poultry can be stored in the refrigerator. *(one to two days only)*

Student Experiences

1. **Grade Comparisons:** Have students observe and compare Grade A and Grade B poultry. Ask students to record the differences and compare their observations with the information in the text. *(Key skills: writing, evaluation)*

2. **Research:** Have students research poultry production, inspection, or marketing and report to the class. How have they changed over time? What changes are expected in the future? *(Key skills: reading, research)*

3. **Practice:** Have students practice preparing fresh or frozen poultry for storage. Why is storage important for maintaining quality and preventing contamination? How can proper storage save money? *(Key skill: kitchen management skills)*

Turkeys are categorized by size.

- ❖ **Beltsville or fryer-roaster** turkeys are smallest, with an average weight of 5 to 9 lbs. (2.5 to 4.5 kg). They are not always available.
- ❖ **Hen** turkeys (female) weigh about 8 to 16 lbs. (4 to 8 kg).
- ❖ **Tom** turkeys (male) can weigh up to 24 lbs. (12 kg).

Whole turkeys are sold fresh or frozen. You can also buy turkey parts, such as drumsticks, thighs, and wings. Turkey breast is sold bone-in, boneless, or cut into tenderloins and cutlets.

Ducks and Geese

Ducks and geese have all dark meat, which is very flavorful but relatively high in fat. Usually, only whole, frozen ducks and geese are sold.

Ground Poultry

Ground chicken or turkey can be purchased. Read the label carefully. If it states "ground turkey breast" or "ground chicken," both the flesh and skin were used. As you may recall, most of the fat is in the skin. If

the word "meat" is part of the description, such as "ground turkey breast meat" or "ground chicken meat," the poultry was ground without the skin. Poultry ground without skin is leaner.

Ground poultry can be used instead of ground beef, but it gives a drier, more bland product. Usually, a little more liquid and seasonings must be used in the recipe.

Giblets

Edible poultry organs are called **giblets** (JIB-lets). Giblets are usually included in a package stuffed inside of whole cleaned poultry. They include the liver, gizzard (stomach), and heart. Chicken livers and gizzards are also sold separately.

Processed Poultry

Turkey is processed the same as meat into products such as ham and bacon. Turkey and chicken are also processed into sausages, such as frankfurters.

Strings of ducks hang in Hong Kong, in preparation for use in popular dishes of the region.

Food and Nutrition Science

Drugs in Poultry Feed: Have students research the pros and cons of using antibiotics and hormones in poultry and livestock feed. Ask them to report their findings to the class.

Science Connection

Biochemistry:
Light and Dark Meat

Why does poultry have light and dark meat? The difference in color is due partly to the amount of exercise that different parts of the bird get. Muscles that get frequent, strenuous exercise need more oxygen than others. The oxygen is stored in a red-colored protein pigment called *myoglobin* (MY-uh-GLOW-bin). The amount of myoglobin in the muscle tissue determines the color. Dark meat is found in those parts of chickens and turkeys that get the most exercise, such as the legs. Because chickens and turkeys do not fly, their breast and wing muscles do not need as much oxygen to function. The tissue does not contain as much myglobin, which makes breast meat a lighter color.

■ ■ ■

Inspection and Grading

Poultry is inspected and graded by the USDA. Grading is a voluntary program, just as it is with meat. The inspection and grade

Processed chicken or turkey products may be lower in fat and sodium than processed meats. Check the nutrition facts on the label.

marks can appear on the label or on a wing-tag attached to the bird.

Grade A is the grade of poultry most commonly found in supermarkets. It indicates the poultry is practically free of defects, has a good shape and appearance, and is meaty.

Buying and Storing Poultry

When buying poultry, look for plump, meaty birds. The skin should be smooth and soft. Color of the skin may vary from a creamy white to yellow, depending on the food eaten by the bird. Avoid poultry with tiny feathers or bruised or torn skin.

When stored in the refrigerator, poultry should be used within one to two days. For longer storage, freeze. See the chart in Section 7.4, pages 208-209, for more specific storage times, including leftovers.

■ Section 19.3 Review ■

RECALL THE FACTS

1. Tell which cooking method is best for each of the following types of chicken: broiler-fryer, stewing chicken, capon.

2. What is the main difference among types of turkeys?

3. How are ducks and geese usually sold?

4. List three characteristics of good quality poultry.

DISCUSS YOUR IDEAS

5. Review the different market forms of poultry. When might you prefer to buy each one?

APPLY YOUR LEARNING

6. Make a list of as many different ways of using poultry in recipes as you can. Identify the type or form of poultry that might be used in each.

Section 19.3: Poultry Selection and Storage   **499**

Completing the Section

Review

- Ask students to summarize the main ideas in this section.
- Have students complete the Section Review. (Answers appear below.)

Evaluation

- Have students write a short essay describing the different types of poultry available and the characteristics to look for in each.
- Have students take the quiz for Section 19.3. (Refer to the *Section Quizzes* booklet or use the *Testmaker Software*.)

Reteaching

- Have students write a consumer information article on buying and storing poultry.
- Refer to the *Reteaching Activities* booklet for the Section 19.3 activity worksheet.

Enrichment

- Have students survey adults they know to find out whether they handle poultry safely. Compile the results and discuss.

Closure

- Lead a discussion on the importance of choosing poultry carefully and storing it correctly.

■ Answers to Section Review ■

1. Broiler-fryer: almost any cooking method; stewing chicken: moist heat only; capon: roasted.
2. Their size.
3. Whole and frozen.
4. *Any three:* Plump, meaty, smooth and soft skin, no tiny feathers, no bruised or torn skin.
5. Whole, cut up, or by the piece; answers will vary.
6. Answers will vary.

Introducing the Section

Motivators

- Survey students to discover how many have eaten fish and/or shellfish in the last 24 hours, week, and month. On the chalkboard, list the fish and shellfish students have eaten.

- Ask students how many have eaten fish they caught themselves. What benefits and drawbacks are there in catching fish to eat?

Objectives

- Have students read the section objectives. Discuss the purpose of studying the section.

Vocabulary

- Pronounce the terms listed under "Look for These Terms." Have students find the terms and their definitions in the section.

Guided Reading

- Have students look at the headings within Section 19.4 to preview the concepts that will be discussed.

- Have students read the section and complete the appropriate part of the Chapter 19 Study Guide in the *Student Workbook*.

SECTION 19.4

Fish and Shellfish Selection and Storage

OBJECTIVES

After studying this section, you should be able to:

- Describe different types and market forms of fish.
- Identify different types and market forms of shellfish.
- Give guidelines for buying and storing fish and shellfish.

LOOK FOR THESE TERMS

crustaceans
mollusks

Fish and shellfish have long been favorite foods of people living in coastal regions. Today, people almost everywhere can enjoy the nutrition and flavor of the many varieties of fish and shellfish that are available.

Types and Market Forms of Fish and Shellfish

What is the difference between fish and shellfish? Fish have fins and a bony skeleton with a backbone. Shellfish have no fins or bones but have a shell instead.

Some fish and shellfish come from inland waters such as lakes, rivers, and ponds. They are known as freshwater varieties. Saltwater varieties, also known as seafood, come from oceans and seas. Today, both freshwater and saltwater fish and some shellfish are being raised on fish farms.

Fish farms provide much of the fish sold in the U.S. today, as well as some shellfish.

Teacher's Classroom Resources—Section 19.4

Refer to these resources in the TCR package:

Reproducible Lesson Plans

Student Workbook

Extending the Text

Reteaching Activities

Section Quizzes

Testmaker Software

Color Transparencies

Types of Fish

There are dozens of varieties of fish. However, when it comes to cooking, many of them are similar to one another. If a specific fish recommended in a recipe isn't available, a fish similar in color and texture can be substituted. The box at the bottom of the page gives some examples.

As you have learned, most fish are very low in fat. A few of the darker fish have a higher fat content.

Market Forms of Fish

Fish can be purchased in several market forms. The most common are:
- ❖ **Drawn:** Whole fish with scales, gills, and internal organs removed.
- ❖ **Dressed or pandressed:** Drawn fish with head, tail, and fins removed.
- ❖ **Fillets:** Sides of fish cut lengthwise away from bones and backbone. Usually boneless. Large fillets may be cut into smaller ones.
- ❖ **Steaks:** Cross sections cut from large, dressed fish. May contain bones from ribs and backbone.

Drawn

Dressed

Fillet

Steaks

You can purchase drawn or dressed fish, fillets, or steaks. Which would you choose if you wanted boneless fish?

Fish Choices

Fish with a light color, mild flavor, and tender texture:

Catfish	Perch	Sole
Cod	Pike	Trout
Flounder	Pollock	Turbot
Haddock	Pompano	Whitefish
Halibut	Red Snapper	

Fish with a dark color, more pronounced flavor, and firm texture:

Bluefish	Salmon	Tuna
Mackerel	Swordfish	

Thinking Skills

Drawing Conclusions: Have students compare the protein and calorie content of three kinds of fish, three cuts of beef, and three cuts of chicken. What conclusions can students draw?

Teaching . . .

- • **Types of Fish**
- • **Market Forms of Fish**

(text pages 500-501)

Comprehension Check

1. Ask students to explain the difference between fish and shellfish. *(Fish have fins and a bony skeleton; shellfish have a shell instead.)*

2. Ask students to explain the difference between a fish that has been drawn and one that has been dressed. *(Dressed fish have had the head, tail, and fins removed.)*

3. Ask students to list five fish that have a light color and five that have a dark color. Nutritionally, what is the difference? *(See box on page 501. The dark fish may have a higher fat content.)*

Student Experiences

1. **Identifying Choices:** Have students identify as many fish choices as they can. Categorize the choices as light or dark in color. *(Key skill: consumer awareness)*

2. **Demonstration:** Show students a whole fish. Dress the fish and explain how it could be prepared. Cut steaks or fillets or have samples available. *(Key skill: kitchen management skills)*

3. **Research:** Have students find articles that warn about high levels of heavy metals, such as mercury and lead, in fish. Ask students to report on any current problems in this area. How can these problems be prevented? *(Key skills: reading, research)*

Using the Diagram

Answer to caption question: Fish fillets are usually boneless.

Comprehension Check

1. Ask students to explain the difference between crustaceans and mollusks. *(Crustaceans have long bodies with jointed limbs, covered with shells; mollusks have soft bodies that are covered by at least one shell.)*

2. Ask students to list various names for crayfish. How are crayfish sold? *(crawfish, crawdads; whole, live or cooked.)*

3. Discuss the various types of mollusks and ask students to give the characteristics of each. *(See list on page 503.)*

Shellfish

Shellfish generally have a mild, sweet flavor. Almost all shellfish come from oceans and seas, but a few come from fresh water. There are two types of shellfish: crustaceans and mollusks.

Crustaceans

Crustaceans (kruss-TAY-shuhns) have long bodies with jointed limbs, covered with shells. They include crabs, crayfish, lobsters, and shrimp.

❖ **Crabs** have a round shell with eight legs and two claws. Different varieties and sizes are available. Whole crabs are sold live, cooked, or frozen. Crab legs and claws are sold cooked and frozen. Cooked crabmeat is available refrigerated, frozen, and canned.

❖ **Crayfish** are freshwater crustaceans. They are also called "crawfish" or "crawdads." They look like small lobsters. Crayfish are sold whole, live, or cooked.

❖ **Lobsters** have a long, jointed body with four pair of legs and two large claws, all covered with a hard shell. Average weight is from 1 ¼ lb. (625 g) to 2 ¼ lb. (1125 g). Maine lobster is the most popular. Fresh lobster is sold live.

❖ **Shrimp** vary in size and color. They are usually sold frozen or previously frozen and thawed. You can buy raw shrimp, with or without the shell, as well as shelled, cooked shrimp.

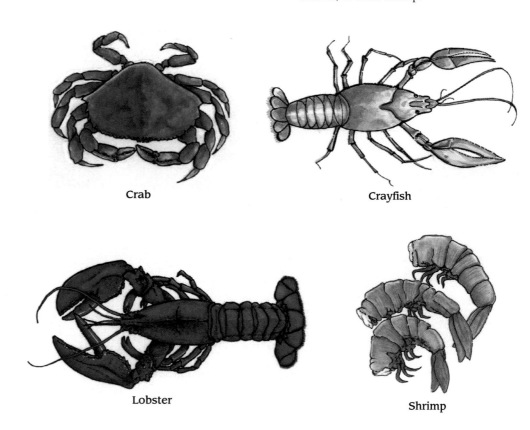

Crab

Crayfish

Lobster

Shrimp

Thinking Skills

Critical Thinking: Ask students to brainstorm to think of reasons why some types of mollusks vary so greatly in size. *(The size is usually linked to the location in which they grow. The available nutrients and other environmental factors play a role in size. Genetic factors also help determine size.)*

Mollusks

Mollusks have soft bodies that are covered by at least one shell. They include clams, mussels, oysters, scallops, and squid.

- ❖ **Clams** have two shells hinged at the back with edible flesh inside. Many varieties are available, from small to large. They are sold live (still in the shell) or shucked (removed from the shell).
- ❖ **Mussels** have a thin, oblong shell. Depending on type, the length varies from 1½ inches (3.8 cm) to 6 inches (15 cm). Shell colors also vary. The flesh is creamy tan and not as tender as oysters or clams. Mussels are sold live in the shell.

- ❖ **Oysters** have a rough, hard, gray shell. They come in different sizes. The flesh varies in color, flavor, and texture. Oysters are sold live or shucked.
- ❖ **Scallops** grow in beautiful fan-shaped shells. Only the muscle that hinges the two shells is sold. Bay scallops are very tiny, about 1/2 inch (1.3 cm) in diameter, sweet and tender. Sea scallops are larger (about 1½ inches (3.8 cm) in diameter) and not as tender as bay scallops.
- ❖ **Squid** is also known as calamari (cah-lah-MAH-ree). It is sold fresh. Squid is popular in Asia and the Mediterranean area and is becoming popular in the United States.

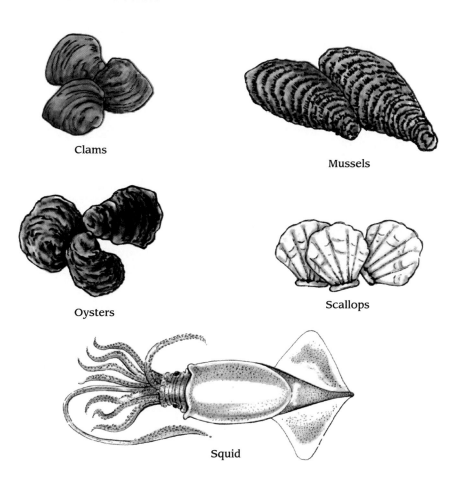

Clams

Mussels

Oysters

Scallops

Squid

19.4

Student Experiences

1. **Taste Test:** Provide samples of cured, dried, smoked, or pickled fish for students to taste-test. *(Key skill: evaluation)*
2. **Store Survey:** Have students survey a supermarket to discover what shellfish are available for purchase, what forms they are available in, and how much they cost per pound. *(Key skills: reading, consumer awareness)*
3. **Product Comparison:** Have students taste-test cooked shellfish in different forms, such as clams that were live in the shell, shucked, frozen, and canned. How do the products compare in taste, appearance, and cost per serving? For what purposes would each product be most useful? Ask students to write a summary of their responses. *(Key skills: writing, evaluation)*

Food and Nutrition Science

Effect of Canning Liquid: Remind students that most of the darker fish are available in canned form. Point out that fish canned in water contains fewer calories than fish canned in oil. Provide samples of tuna canned in water and tuna canned in oil. Have students sample each one and evaluate for taste, and odor, appearance. Provide the labels from the cans so students can compare the calories present in each one. Ask students to write a short report of their findings.

Comprehension Check

1. Ask students to describe the inspection and grading process used for fish. Who does the inspection and grading? *(FDA and National Marine Fisheries Service)*

2. Ask students to describe the characteristics of fresh, high-quality fish. *(Shiny, glistening skin; mild, fresh aroma; skin springs back when pressed; eyes clear and full; gills bright red or pink.)*

3. Ask students to explain the proper way to store fresh fish. *(Refrigerate for use in a few days, or freeze.)*

Student Experiences

1. **Display:** Show two samples of fresh fish to students—one of good quality and one of poor quality. Point out the differences. *(Key skill: evaluation)*

2. **Letter Writing:** Have students write letters to the FDA and the National Marine Fisheries Service to obtain information about the voluntary inspection and grading program for fish. Discuss the information students receive. *(Key skill: writing)*

3. **Cost Comparison:** Have students compare the cost per serving of fresh, frozen, and canned shrimp. *(Key skill: math)*

Processed Fish

Fish may be dried, pickled, smoked, or cured. Sometimes more than one method is used. For example, lox is a type of cured, smoked salmon. Cod is often salted and dried. Herring may be cut into chunks, pickled in vinegar and spices, and then packed in jars.

Canned fish is ready to eat as is, heat, or use in recipes. To cut down on fat, look for fish packed in water instead of oil. If fish is packed in oil, drain well and rinse off the oil before using. Many other convenience forms of fish are available, such as frozen, breaded, fish sticks.

Inspection and Grading

A voluntary inspection and grading program is carried on jointly by the Food and Drug Administration (FDA) and the National Marine Fisheries Service of the U.S. Department of Commerce. The program attempts to focus on those parts of fish processing that may be risks to consumer safety. Some state and local fish inspection services are also available.

Fish that has been inspected carries this seal. Look for it on the package.

> ✓ **SAFETY CHECK**
>
> People with certain types of health problems—including liver disease, diabetes, and immune disorders—should be careful never to eat raw or undercooked fish or shellfish. If they do, they risk serious illness or even death. The cause is a bacteria that may be present in the fish or shellfish. Thorough cooking kills the bacteria.

Buying and Storing Fish and Shellfish

Buy fish from a reliable source. When buying fresh fish, notice the way it is displayed. If layers are piled on ice, the top layer may be too warm for safe keeping. Don't buy ready-to-eat fish that is piled next to fresh fish. Harmful bacteria from the fresh fish may have transferred to the ready-to-eat products.

Judge the quality of fresh fish by its appearance and aroma. Fresh fish should have shiny skin and a glistening color. It should have a mild, fresh aroma, similar to cucumbers or seaweed. The skin should spring back when pressed. Whole fish should have clear, full eyes and bright red or pink gills.

Using the Photo

Answer to caption question (p. 505): The live shellfish should be refrigerated in a container covered with a clean, damp cloth. The rest should be refrigerated or frozen in a tightly sealed package.

Thinking Skills

Reasoning: Have students look in the frozen food section of the supermarket for imitation crab meat. What are its ingredients? Ask students what nutritional problems may arise when people use imitation shellfish such as crab. *(The imitation crab still has nutrients, but those nutrients are different from those in real crab. You need to take these differences into account when you substitute imitation products for real shellfish.)*

Remember to look for signs of quality when buying fish and shellfish. How would you store the varieties shown here?

Review

- Ask students to summarize the main ideas in this section.
- Have students complete the Section Review. (Answers appear below.)

Evaluation

- Ask students to write a short essay on the characteristics of edible fish and shellfish.
- Have students take the quiz for Section 19.4. (Refer to the *Section Quizzes* booklet or use the *Testmaker Software*.)

Reteaching

- Show students pictures of various types of shellfish. Ask students to identify the shellfish and its type (crustacean or mollusk).
- Refer to the *Reteaching Activities* booklet for the Section 19.4 activity worksheet.

Enrichment

- Have students research the effects of water pollution on fish and shellfish. How has this affected the fishing industry?

Closure

- Lead a discussion on the characteristics of high-quality fish and shellfish.

Some shellfish must be live if bought fresh. Look for signs that they are live, such as movement in lobsters. Mollusk shells should be closed when they are tapped.

Fresh fish and shellfish that have gone bad will smell "fishy" or have an unpleasant ammonia odor.

After you bring fish home, store it in the refrigerator or freezer immediately. Refrigerate live shellfish in containers covered with a clean, damp cloth. They need breathing space to stay alive. Do not put live saltwater shellfish in fresh water—they will not live.

Fish stored in the refrigerator should be used within one to two days. For longer storage, freeze. See the chart in Section 7.4, pages 208-209, for more specific storage times, including leftovers.

■ Section 19.4 Review ■

RECALL THE FACTS

1. How are drawn fish and dressed fish alike? How are they different?

2. Define "crustacean" and "mollusk." Give three examples of each.

3. List four signs to look for when buying fresh fish and shellfish.

4. How should live shellfish be stored?

DISCUSS YOUR IDEAS

5. Do you think it would be safe to eat fish that you and your friends had caught on a fishing trip? Why or why not?

APPLY YOUR LEARNING

6. Find recipes for fish and shellfish in magazines or cookbooks. Identify whether each recipe calls for a light-colored fish, dark-colored fish, crustacean, or mollusk.

■ Answers to Section Review ■

1. Both have scales, gills, and internal organs removed. Dressed fish have head, tail, and fins removed.

2. Crustaceans have long bodies with jointed limbs, covered with shells; examples are lobsters, crabs, crayfish, shrimp. Mollusks have soft bodies that are covered by at least one shell; examples are clams, mussels, oysters, scallops, squid.

3. Shiny skin; glistening color; mild, fresh aroma; skin springs back when pressed; clear, full eyes; bright red or pink gills.

4. In containers covered with a clean, damp cloth.

5. Answers will vary, depending on the area in which the fish was caught and the pollutants, if any, in the water.

6. Answers will vary.

Introducing the Section

Motivators

- Ask students if their families have changed the amounts of meat, poultry, fish, and shellfish they eat or the methods for preparing these foods in recent years. If so, what were their reasons? Discuss changes in recommendations from experts regarding meat, poultry, fish, and shellfish. Discuss changes in preparation methods that have resulted from health concerns.

- Survey students to identify the most popular preparation methods for meat, poultry, fish, and shellfish. Point out nutritional advantages and disadvantages of various methods.

Objectives

- Have students read the section objectives. Discuss the purpose of studying the section.

Vocabulary

- Pronounce the terms listed under "Look for These Terms." Have students find the terms and their definitions in the section.

Guided Reading

- Have students look at the headings within Section 19.5 to preview the concepts that will be discussed.

- Have students read the section and complete the appropriate part of the Chapter 19 Study Guide in the *Student Workbook*.

506

SECTION 19.5

Preparing Meat, Poultry, Fish, and Shellfish

OBJECTIVES

After studying this section, you should be able to:

- Explain how to select a cooking method for different cuts of meat, poultry, fish, and shellfish.
- Identify ways of preparing cuts for cooking.
- Tell how to test cuts for doneness.
- Give guidelines for cooking cuts by different methods.

LOOK FOR THIS TERM

doneness

Meat, poultry, fish, and shellfish are different in some ways. However, when it comes to cooking, there are also many similarities. Many of the same basic cooking methods can be used for each.

Principles of Cooking Meat, Poultry, and Fish

When cuts from animal foods cook, several changes occur in color, flavor, and texture.

❖ **Color.** The red color changes to brown. For instance, beef, which is dark red, turns a dark brown. Pork and the white meat of poultry, which are a light pink, turn beige.

❖ **Flavors.** Heat develops the flavors by creating chemical reactions within the cut.

❖ **Texture.** When heated, a cut loses fat and moisture. As a result, it shrinks. In addition, muscle fibers get firmer and connecting tissue becomes more tender.

When cooked in dry heat, animal foods lose some juices, carrying off some B vitamins. Some thiamin is destroyed by high temperatures. In general, however, few nutrients are lost unless the food is overcooked.

When properly cooked, meat is tender and flavorful and retains most of its nutrients.

Teacher's Classroom Resources—Section 19.5

Refer to these resources in the TCR package:

Reproducible Lesson Plans

Student Workbook

Extending the Text

Reteaching Activities

Section Quizzes

Testmaker Software

Foods Lab Resources

Color Transparencies

Moist heat methods are a good choice for less tender cuts. Why?

When a cut is overcooked in dry heat, it dries out and gets tough, stringy, and chewy. In moist heat, an overcooked cut gets mushy and loses its flavor. When overcooked in a microwave oven, the cut can get so hard that it cannot be chewed.

Choosing a Cooking Method

The cooking method depends on the tenderness of the cut. Tender cuts can be cooked using dry heat methods, such as broiling and roasting. Broiling, the fastest of the two methods, cooks tender cuts in a matter of minutes. Examples of tender cuts include steaks, rib and loin roasts, certain kinds of chops, ground meat and poultry, broiler-fryers, fish, and some shellfish. Less tender cuts include blade roasts, arm steaks, stewing hens, and some shellfish.

These cuts can be tenderized using cooking methods that involve moist heat, such as simmering, stewing, and braising. These methods involve long, slow cooking which breaks down the collagen in the meat and makes it tender.

Moist heat methods also give you an opportunity to add seasonings, sauces, and other foods to the dish. You can create many different flavor combinations in this way. You may sometimes choose to cook tender cuts in moist heat for this reason. When tender cuts are cooked in moist heat, the cooking time is generally shortened. Otherwise, the cut can easily be overcooked and fall apart.

Preparing to Cook

For best results, thaw frozen raw meat, poultry, and fish before cooking. Follow the guidelines for safe thawing in Section 7.3, page 203. If the cut is not thawed, the cooking time will have to be increased. In general, increase the cooking time by about 50 percent. For example, if the normal cooking time is 40 minutes, the cooking time for frozen cuts would be about 60 minutes. However, the extra time needed depends on size of the food and whether or not it was partially thawed.

Before cooking meat, poultry, or fish, be sure the cut is clean. Rinse it under cold water and pat dry with a paper towel. If you are cooking whole poultry, first remove the giblets and neck from the body and neck cavities. Rinse the cavities of whole poultry and whole fish several times. Remove any foreign matter that may be present in the cavities.

Trimming Fat

Before cooking meat and poultry, remove as much fat as possible. Trim visible fat from meat as shown in the illustration on page 508.

Thinking Skills

Problem Solving: Have the class discuss what they would do if they came home and discovered that the meat for the evening meal was still in the freezer. Explore with them the options depending on the type of meat and cooking facilities available. Introduce microwave thawing techniques.

See Also . . .

- "Thawing Food Safely," text page 203
- "How Heat Affects Food," text pages 268-270
- "Moist Heat Methods," text pages 279-281
- "Dry Heat Methods," text pages 281-284

Teaching . . .

- **Principles: Choosing a Cooking Method**
- **Preparing to Cook**

(text pages 506-508)

Comprehension Check

1. Ask students to list characteristics that change when animal foods are cooked. *(Color changes to brown; flavors develop; texture gets firmer and connecting tissue becomes more tender; cut shrinks as fat melts.)*

2. Ask students to list cuts that can be cooked using dry heat methods. *(Steaks, rib and loin roasts, certain kinds of chops, ground meat and poultry, broiler-fryers, fish, and some shellfish.)*

3. Ask students to explain how less tender cuts should be prepared in order to tenderize them. *(In moist heat: braising, simmering, stewing.)*

4. Ask students to explain how much cooking time must be increased if the meat is cooked frozen and why. *(By about 50 percent; to allow the food to thaw.)*

Student Experiences

1. **Categorizing:** Have students categorize cooking methods as dry heat or moist heat methods. Relate appropriate cooking methods to the tenderness of the cut. *(Key skill: categorization)*

2. **Student Demonstrations:** Have students work in groups to demonstrate ways of tenderizing less tender cuts of meat before cooking. Include mechanical methods such as grinding, pounding, and scoring, use of acids, and use of meat tenderizer. *(Key skill: kitchen management skills)*

• Judging Doneness

(text pages 508-510)

Comprehension Check

1. Ask students to describe two general measures of doneness. *(The cut should be cooked long enough to be a pleasure to eat and long enough so that it is safe to eat.)*

2. Ask students to identify the minimum temperature to which meat and poultry should be heated. Why should cuts reach at least this temperature? *(160°F [71°C]; because this is the lowest temperature at which you can be sure that harmful bacteria have been destroyed.)*

3. Ask students to explain why the meat may turn dark around the bones of some poultry when it is cooked. *(In some young broiler-fryers, the bones have not hardened completely, and a color pigment seeps out from inside the bones.)*

4. Ask students to identify the internal temperatures for rare, medium, and well-done beef. *(Rare: 140°F [60°C]; medium: 160°F [71°C]; well-done: 170°F [77°C].)*

Safety Check

Ask students to brainstorm ideas for salvaging a meal that is half-cooked if something happens and you absolutely have to leave the kitchen. Evaluate the safety of students' ideas.

A boning knife is useful for trimming fat from meat. Cut the muscle sections apart and trim away the fat found around and between them.

As you have learned, much of the fat in poultry is in or just under the skin. When cooking poultry in moist heat, remove the skin. However, when using dry heat methods, leave the skin on to keep the poultry from drying out. Most of the fat will melt and drip away during cooking. Remove the skin before eating.

Judging Doneness

Doneness means that the cut has cooked long enough for the necessary changes to take place so it is a pleasure to eat. All cuts must be cooked long enough so they are safe to eat. If any part is not cooked, there is a risk of food-borne illness.

✓ SAFETY CHECK

Once you start to cook a cut, regardless of the method, finish cooking it. Don't cook food partially and then complete the cooking later. Partial or interrupted cooking often produces conditions that encourage the growth of harmful bacteria.

Testing Meat and Poultry for Doneness

To be safe to eat, all meat and poultry should reach an internal temperature of at least 160°F (71°C). This insures that harmful bacteria have been destroyed.

When roasting or microwaving cuts more than two inches (5 cm) thick, use a meat thermometer to check for doneness. The thermometer, when inserted into the thickest part of the cut, will tell you the internal temperature. The chart on page 509 gives internal temperatures for meat and poultry cooked in dry heat.

With other cooking methods, with thinner cuts, or if you do not have a meat thermometer, test for doneness by checking the inside color. With a sharp knife, pierce the cut about halfway through. The juices running out should be clear, with no pink color. The center of the meat should not show any pink color.

When testing chicken, you may find the meat has turned dark around the bones. This is common in young broiler-fryers. Their bones have not hardened completely. During cooking, color pigment from the inside of the bone seeps out. The meat is safe to eat.

More About Cooking Meat

- Do not salt a roast before cooking. The salt will draw out juices and nutrients.
- When roasting, keep the meat out of the drippings, or the portion in the drippings will fry in its own fat. If you do not have a roasting rack, improvise with several metal jar lids. Wash them in warm, soapy water and rinse. Punch holes in the tops so heat and steam can flow. Place lids top side up on the bottom of the roasting pan and rest the meat on them.

✓ SAFETY CHECK

Trichinosis is an illness caused by a parasitic worm sometimes found in pork or wild game. It can cause diarrhea, nausea, vomiting, and other symptoms. Thorough cooking to an internal temperature of 160°F (71°C) destroys the parasite.

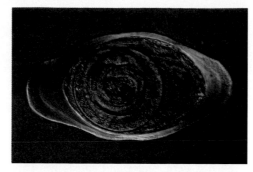

The parasite that causes trichinosis is shown here greatly magnified. Trichinosis is much less common now than in the past. Still, cook pork to the recommended temperature to reduce the risk of any food-borne illness.

Internal Temperatures for Meat and Poultry

Cooking food to an internal temperature of 160°F (71°C) usually protects against food-borne illness. However, some foods are considered more tasty when they are cooked to a higher internal temperature. The higher temperatures in this chart reflect a greater degree of doneness.

Food	Internal Temperature	
	°F	°C
Beef		
Rare (some bacterial risk)	140	60
Medium	160	71
Well Done	170	77
Pork, Lamb, Veal		
Medium	160	71
Well Done	170	77
Poultry		
Whole poultry	180	82
Turkey breasts or roasts	170	77
Stuffing (cooked alone or in bird)	165	74
Ham		
Fresh (raw) or shoulder	160	71
Precooked (to reheat)	140	60
Ground meat and poultry		
Turkey, chicken	170	77
Beef, veal, lamb, pork	160	71

Section 19.5: Preparing Meat, Poultry, Fish, and Shellfish   **509**

Student Experiences

1. **Demonstration:** Demonstrate methods for checking meat and poultry for doneness. Show how to use a meat thermometer to ensure accuracy. Refer students to the "Internal Temperatures for Meat and Poultry" chart on page 509. Demonstrate how to test fish for doneness. Explain how to use the "ten-minute rule." *(Key skill: evaluation)*

2. **Class Discussion:** Discuss reasons to avoid eating undercooked meat, poultry, and fish. Refer students to the "Internal Temperatures for Meat and Poultry" chart on page 509. *(Key skill: critical thinking)*

Safety Check

Refer students to the "Food-Borne Illnesses" chart on pages 198-199 for more information about Trichinosis and other food-borne illnesses. How many of the microorganisms in the chart are caused by underdone cuts of meat, poultry, fish, or shellfish?

Lab Experience

Have students cook samples of the same inexpensive cut of meat in four different ways: slow cooker, dry heat, moist heat at low temperature, and moist heat at high temperature. Ask students to compare and rank the taste and tenderness of the cooked meats. Also have students compare the time it takes to cook the cut using each method. What can students conclude?

Food and Nutrition Science

Broiling Temperatures: Broiling is just a modern name for the oldest cooking technique of all: roasting over an open fire or glowing coals. All heat sources used in broiling—coals, electric metal rod, gas flame, etc.—emit visible light, which means they also emit intense infrared radiation. It is this infrared heat, not hot air, that does the cooking when meat is broiled. The temperatures reached by broiler elements are much higher than those of an oven wall. Since the energy radiated by an element is proportional to the fourth power of the temperature, a broiler can radiate about 80 times as much energy as the wall of an oven set at 500°F.

Comprehension Check

1. Ask students to identify the lowest oven temperature that should be used for roasting or baking and why. *(325°F [160°C]; to keep harmful bacteria from growing.)*

2. Ask students to describe the proper placement of a meat thermometer in a large meat roast. *(It should be inserted so that the tip of the thermometer is in the center of the roast, not touching bone, fat, or thick connective tissue.)*

3. Ask students to explain why it is better to tie the legs together and tuck tips of wings under back of a chicken before roasting or baking. *(The chicken will cook more evenly; the legs and wings will not overcook before the rest of the chicken is cooked thoroughly.)*

4. Ask students to explain why whole turkey pieces should not be broiled. *(They are too thick.)*

5. Ask students to list guidelines for broiling. *(See list on page 512.)*

Safety Check

Discuss with students the reasons for each safety precaution listed in the Safety Check on page 511. Point out that if the stuffing does not reach a high enough temperature during cooking, harmful bacteria that may be present will not be killed.

When testing small pieces or cubes of meat or poultry, pierce with a fork. If it slides easily to the bottom, the cut is done.

Meat and poultry cooking times vary, depending on the method and cut used. The cooking time given in the recipe is just a guide. Begin testing meat and poultry for doneness about ten minutes before the end of the cooking time.

Testing Fish for Doneness

Fish is very tender and cooks in a short time. When using conventional cooking methods, remember the "ten-minute rule." Cook fish ten minutes for every inch (2.5 cm) of thickness, as measured at the thickest part. However, there are a few exceptions. If fish is being baked in a sauce, add about five minutes to total cooking time. Some moist heat recipes may call for longer cooking times to allow flavors to blend. Remember to increase the cooking time if the fish is frozen.

Begin to check fish for doneness about two or three minutes before the cooking time is up. Fish is done when its flesh turns opaque. When gently lifted with a fork, the flesh flakes easily.

Basic Cooking Methods

A number of different cooking methods can be used for meat, poultry, fish, and shellfish. They include roasting, broiling, poaching, and microwaving. You may want to review basic information on these cooking methods in Sections 9.3 and 9.4.

Roasting or Baking

When roasting or baking meat, poultry, or fish, it is usually not necessary to preheat the oven. However, follow recipe directions. The roasting temperatures in a conventional oven should be at least 325°F (160°C) to keep harmful bacteria from growing. Fish can bake at high temperatures, such as 450°F (230°C).

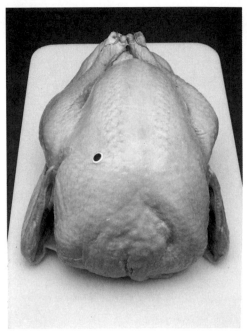

When roasting whole poultry, make the bird as compact as possible. Some turkeys, like this one, have a small plastic cylinder that pops up to indicate doneness. However, check the internal temperature with a thermometer to be sure.

Thinking Skills

Reasoning: Discuss the advantages and disadvantages of buying a self-basting bird.

Reasoning: Ask students: Why is "roasting" poultry in aluminum foil or in a special cooking bag more like steaming than roasting?

The way you prepare meat, poultry, and fish for roasting or baking varies:

❖ **Large meat roasts.** Put the roast, fat side up, on a rack in the pan to hold the cut out of the drippings. Some rib cuts of meat form a natural rack. Insert the meat thermometer so the tip is in the center of the roast. The thermometer should not touch bone, fat, or thick connective tissue.

❖ **Whole poultry.** Make the bird as compact as possible so it cooks evenly. Tie the legs together. Tuck tips of wings under the back. Insert the thermometer deep into the thickest part of the thigh next to the body. Be sure it is not touching bone or fat.

❖ **Poultry pieces.** Place in a shallow pan, skin side up.

❖ **Fish.** Place the fish in a lightly oiled, shallow baking dish. If baking fillets, place skin side down so you can test for doneness. To keep the fish moist, brush with seasoned melted fat or a sauce. It can also be breaded. If so, dot the fish with a teaspoon (5 mL) of butter or margarine after breading.

Follow recipe directions for turning the food. Generally, large roasts and fish do not have to be turned. Poultry pieces may need to be turned after half the cooking time.

For low-fat cooking, use broth or juice for basting instead of drippings.

Roast or bake for the time specified in the recipe. Remove from the oven when done.

Broiling

Many tender cuts are suitable for broiling. These include many steaks and chops; hamburgers; chicken halves, quarters, or pieces; fish steaks, fillets, or whole fish; and some shellfish, such as shrimp. Do not broil whole turkey pieces—they are too thick. However, thinner cuts may be broiled, such as cutlets or ground turkey patties.

By broiling tender cuts, you can prepare delicious main dishes, such as this broiled mullet, in a short time.

✓ **SAFETY CHECK**

Roasting whole poultry with stuffing requires a few special precautions.

❖ Do not stuff the poultry ahead of time. The inside of a refrigerated stuffed bird does not chill fast enough for safe storage. Harmful bacteria will multiply. Instead, stuff the poultry just before roasting.

❖ Allow extra cooking time for poultry with stuffing. If you want to shorten the cooking time, bake the stuffing separately.

❖ After cooking, use a meat thermometer to make sure the stuffing has reached an internal temperature of 165°F (74°C).

❖ Remove stuffing from poultry immediately after cooking.

❖ Store leftover poultry and stuffing separately, divided into small portions.

19.5

Student Experiences

1. **Demonstration:** Demonstrate procedures for preparing whole poultry for roasting with and without stuffing. Demonstrate how to truss poultry using metal skewers. Show how to insert a meat thermometer to check for doneness. Show how to baste the bird using a baster. Point out safety precautions for roasting whole poultry with stuffing. *(Key skill: kitchen management skills)*

2. **Chart Making:** Distribute beef and pork cut charts to students and have them color code the cuts according to basic cooking methods appropriate for each cut. *(Key skill: evaluation)*

3. **Poster Project:** Have students work in groups to prepare posters listing the basic steps for roasting meat, poultry, and fish. *(Key skills: creativity, kitchen management skills)*

4. **Writing:** Have students develop a brochure on "Holiday Hazards Involving Poultry." Have them include information on thawing, cooking, and storing cooked poultry. *(Key skill: writing)*

Lab Experience

Have students practice broiling using cubes of meat, poultry, or firm fish. Alternate meats with pieces of vegetables such as tomato quarters, mushrooms, and green pepper chunks. Brush with melted butter or margarine, or a sauce, to keep vegetables from drying out. Broil, turning so all sides are done.

Food and Nutrition Science

Barbecue Sauces for Chicken: Ask students if they have ever had home-barbecued chicken that was black-crusted and bitter. Explain that the primary cause is adding barbecue sauce too early. High heat burns sugar, a major ingredient of barbecue sauces. In addition, spices become bitter when scorched. To avoid this, do not brush on the sauce until 15 minutes before the chicken will have finished cooking. Also, keep the food four to six inches above the coals.

Comprehension Check

1. Ask students to describe how to poach fish fillets. *(Pour seasoned cooking liquid into large, deep skillet. Bring to boil, then reduce to simmer. Place fillets in single layer in the pan; add enough liquid to cover by at least 1 inch [2.5 cm]. Cover pan and simmer gently until fish is just opaque throughout. Do not turn fish while cooking.)*

2. Ask students to explain why it is important to buy cuts of meat, poultry, fish, and shellfish that are uniform in shape and size if you intend to cook them in the microwave oven. *(They will cook more evenly.)*

3. Ask students to list guidelines for microwaving meat, poultry, fish, and shellfish. *(See the discussion on page 514.)*

Follow the guidelines for broiling in Section 9.4. Here are some additional tips:

❖ Slash the fat around the edges of meat before broiling. This will keep the cut from curling.

❖ When broiling chicken, begin with the skin side down. Halfway through the broiling time, turn skin side up.

❖ Because fish is lean, brush it lightly with melted butter or margarine to keep it from charring.

❖ To add flavor to broiled foods, brush them with a sauce, such as barbecue or salsa.

For variety, make kabobs (kuh-BOBS). Cut meat, poultry, or firm fish into cubes. Put them on a skewer, alternating with pieces of vegetables such as tomato quarters, mushrooms, and green pepper chunks. Brush with melted butter or margarine, or a sauce, to keep vegetables from drying out. Broil, turning so that all sides are done.

Poaching

As you may recall, poaching involves simmering whole foods in a small amount of liquid. Fish is one of the foods most commonly poached. Many people consider poached fish a delicacy, and it is often served in fine restaurants.

Whole drawn fish, fillets, or steaks may be poached. The cooking liquid may be plain water, water with lemon or grapefruit juice, fish or vegetable stock, or milk. Usually, it is seasoned to add more flavor to the fish. Try using herbs or spices, such as dill or grated fresh ginger, and sautéed vegetables, such as onions and green peppers.

To poach fish fillets:

1. Pour the cooking liquid (seasoned as desired) into a large, deep skillet. Bring to a boil, then immediately reduce the heat to a simmer.

2. Place the fillets in a single layer in the pan. Add enough liquid, if necessary, to cover the fish by at least 1 inch (2.5 cm).

3. Cover the pan and simmer gently until the fish is just opaque throughout. Do not turn the fish while poaching.

Fish fillets can be poached in seasoned liquid. Add the fillets to the simmering liquid, cover, and cook gently until done.

To poach whole fish or fish steaks, first wrap the fish in cheesecloth. Allow enough length at the ends so the cheesecloth can be twisted, knotted, and used as handles to lower and raise the fish. Otherwise, follow the same procedure as for fillets.

If you like, you can serve hot poached fish with a sauce made from the cooking liquid. After removing the fish from the pan, boil the cooking liquid to reduce the amount of liquid and reach the desired flavor.

Poached fish may also be eaten chilled. You might serve cold poached fish with dill or cucumber sauce or use it in a salad.

Microwave Cooking

All types of meat, poultry, fish, and shellfish can be microwaved. When buying for microwaving, choose cuts that are uniform in shape and size. Frozen raw meat, poultry, fish, and shellfish should be completely thawed before cooking in the microwave.

For best results, follow the directions in microwave recipes exactly. Here are some general guidelines.

Food and Nutrition Science

Microwave vs. Conventional Preparation: Have students prepare meat, poultry, or fish dishes in the microwave oven and by conventional methods. Have them compare cooking times and taste. Which methods do students most prefer? Least prefer?

A cooking bag can be used when microwaving roasts and whole poultry. What are the advantages of this method?

✓ SAFETY CHECK

Do not use a conventional meat thermometer inside the microwave oven. Use a thermometer made for the microwave, or wait until after cooking to use a conventional thermometer.

Microwaving Meat and Poultry

Remember that microwave ovens do not always cook evenly. This is especially important when microwaving large cuts, such as meat roasts or a whole turkey. Follow recipe directions exactly to be sure the meat or poultry cooks completely throughout.

When microwaving pork roasts, special care must be taken to cook the meat thoroughly. Place the meat in a covered dish or in a loosely sealed microwave-safe cooking bag. This will hold in moist heat to help ensure even cooking and tender, juicy meat. If you like, add a small amount of liquid such as water, broth, fruit juice, or a sauce. A cooking bag can also be used for whole poultry, if desired.

When microwaved, roasts and whole poultry are cooked to a lower internal temperature than with conventional cooking. That is because the internal temperature continues to rise during standing time. If the microwave oven has a temperature probe, you can program the oven to shut off when the food reaches the desired temperature.

Follow microwave directions carefully for meat that is evenly cooked, tender, and juicy. Use a sauce, a browning grill, or a broiler to add color to the surface of the meat.

Section 19.5: Preparing Meat, Poultry, Fish, and Shellfish   **513**

Student Experiences

1. **Taste Testing:** Provide samples of fish poached in various liquids. Have students taste test each variety and write a short summary of their conclusions. (Key skills: writing, evaluation)

2. **Finding Recipes:** Have students find recipes for broiled or poached fish. Ask students to compare the nutritional value and calories for each recipe. (Key skill: reading)

3. **Menu Planning:** Have students select a recipe and plan a menu featuring poached fish fillets. Have students prepare and serve the meal. Evaluate the results. (Key skill: kitchen management skills)

4. **Demonstration:** Demonstrate methods of making light-colored meats cooked in a microwave look more appetizing. Show how a browning effect can be created using a dark-colored sauce, a browning dish or grill, or by broiling for a few minutes after cooking in the microwave oven. (Key skill: kitchen management skills)

Using the Photo

Answer to caption question (upper photo on p. 513): Advantages include more even cooking; tender, juicy meat; easier cleanup.

Thinking Skills

Creativity: Have students brainstorm ways to add color and flavor to broiled chicken. Have students choose two or three of the best ideas and try them in the laboratory.

Teaching . . .

• Other Cooking Methods

(text pages 514-515)

Comprehension Check

1. Ask students to list guidelines for frying. *(Use as little fat as possible; pan-broil meat that is marbled.)*

2. Ask students to explain why frying leaves foods higher in fat content than other cooking methods. *(Food absorbs fat as it fries.)*

Student Experiences

1. **Research:** Have students research other methods for cooking meat, poultry, fish, and shellfish. Have students work in groups to prepare demonstrations of these cooking methods. *(Key skill: research)*

2. **Finding Recipes:** Ask students to find recipes that use as many different cooking methods as possible. Discuss the merits of each cooking method. *(Key skill: reading)*

Healthy Attitudes

Ask students to think about the advantages and disadvantages of cooking ground beef in a microwave oven. When might students use this method? When might they prefer to use the conventional browning method?

Using the Photo

Answer to caption question (upper photo on p. 515): Answers will vary but may include broiling and oven-frying.

During standing time, cover roasts loosely with foil to hold heat in. After standing time, check the meat or poultry in several spots with a meat thermometer to be sure it has reached the proper internal temperature throughout.

Light-colored cuts cooked in a microwave oven may look unappetizing because they have not browned. You may want to use one of the following methods to create a "browned" effect:

❖ Before cooking, brush or rub with a dark-colored sauce such as barbecue, tamari, or Worcestershire.

❖ Use a browning dish or grill. It is specially made so it becomes extremely hot. Small cuts can be pressed down against the bottom to brown them.

❖ After microwaving, put the cut in the broiler for a few minutes to brown it.

Healthy Attitudes

The microwave oven gives you an easy, healthy way to cook ground meat for use in recipes. Crumble the meat in a microwave-safe colander. Set the colander in a large microwave-safe bowl or casserole dish. Cook on high power for the time specified in the oven's instruction book. As the meat cooks, the fat drains into the bowl or dish. Discard the fat and use the meat as desired.

Microwaving Fish

When microwaving fish, allow about three to six minutes per pound (500 g) at 100 percent power. Thick fillets and whole fish take a little more time than thin ones.

Take care to avoid overcooking—fish is tender and the microwave cooks quickly. Remove the fish from the microwave when it is still slightly underdone in the center. Let it stand five minutes to complete the cooking, then test for doneness.

Shellfish cooks quickly, so be careful not to overcook. If you do, it will get tough and rubbery.

Other Cooking Methods

Meat, poultry, fish, and shellfish may be pan-fried. Often the food is breaded or dipped in batter first. Remember, however, that food absorbs fat as it fries. Other cooking methods are lower in fat.

Since most meat has fat of its own, you do not need to fry it in added fat. Pan-broil it instead.

More About Pan-frying Fish

• Before you begin to fry fish, have paper towels ready for draining the fried fish. Keep the towels away from the burner so they do not catch fire. Soaked with fat, they would burn fiercely.

• Use several layers of paper towels to drain fried fish. Have enough so that, as fat accumulates on the towels, you can replace them quickly. Don't use newspapers under a single layer of paper towel. Newspaper is loaded with chemicals, as well as ink, that can transfer to the fish through the oil-soaked paper towel.

Batter-dipped fried chicken is a traditional favorite, but adds more fat than you may want or need. What are some alternative cooking methods that give a similar texture and flavor?

If you do fry, use as little fat as possible. For example, when sautéing small pieces of meat, poultry, fish, or shellfish, use no more than 1 tsp. (5 mL) of oil or a vegetable oil spray.

Most meat (except veal) is marbled with fat. Therefore, it can be pan-broiled—cooked in a skillet without added fat—instead of fried. For instance, you can pan-broil hamburgers, bacon, or tender steaks and chops. Be sure to remove the fat that accumulates during cooking.

Some cooking methods—such as stewing, braising, and stir-frying—usually involve cooking several different foods together, such as meat and vegetables. These methods are discussed in Chapter 20, "Food Combinations."

Section 19.5 Review

RECALL THE FACTS

1. Name two specific cooking methods you might use for tender cuts and two you might use for less tender cuts.

2. Name three steps that might be involved in preparing raw meat or poultry for cooking.

3. Name two signs that fish is done cooking.

4. Briefly explain how to prepare whole poultry for roasting.

DISCUSS YOUR IDEAS

5. What is the advantage of knowing basic guidelines for a number of different methods of cooking meat, poultry, and fish?

APPLY YOUR LEARNING

6. Choose one of the cooking methods discussed in this chapter. Write the name of the method vertically down the left-hand side of a piece of paper. Next to each letter, write a sentence that begins with that letter and gives a fact about the cooking method.

Section 19.5: Preparing Meat, Poultry, Fish, and Shellfish   515

Completing the Section

Review

- Ask students to summarize the main ideas in this section.
- Have students complete the Section Review. (Answers appear below.)

Evaluation

- Have students write a short essay about the cooking concepts covered in this section.
- Have students take the quiz for Section 19.5. (Refer to the *Section Quizzes* booklet or use the *Testmaker Software*.)

Reteaching

- Demonstrate how to determine when fish or shellfish cooked in the microwave oven is done, taking into account that further cooking will occur during standing time.
- Refer to the *Reteaching Activities* booklet for the Section 19.5 activity worksheet.

Enrichment

- Have students investigate current medical research on Omega-3 fatty acids and their relationship to cardiac health and disease.

Closure

- Discuss preparation methods for meat, poultry, fish, and shellfish. Ask students to list new methods and/or foods they have discovered while studying this chapter.

Answers to Section Review

1. Tender cuts: broiling, roasting; less tender cuts: simmering, stewing, braising, etc.
2. Thaw, clean by rinsing under cold water and patting dry with paper towel; rinse cavities; trim fat.
3. Flesh turns opaque; flesh flakes easily when lifted gently with a fork.
4. Make the bird as compact as possible; tie legs together; tuck tips of wings under back. Insert meat thermometer deep into thickest part of thigh next to body. Be sure it is not touching bone or fat.
5. Answers will vary.
6. Answers will vary.

Breaded Perch with Parmesan

Key Skill: Baking Fish

Using the Recipe

- Have students read the recipe and discuss each step. Caution students to be sure to grease the baking pan so that the fish doesn't stick to the pan. Review other safety and sanitation procedures that apply to this recipe.
- Have each lab team fill out a work plan. (See the *Foods Lab Resources* booklet.)
- Have students check off the ingredients and equipment listed on the recipe worksheet and prepare the recipe.
- Have students complete the evaluation and questions on the recipe worksheet.

See Also . . .

The *Foods Lab Resources* booklet for the "Breaded Perch with Parmesan" recipe worksheet and other recipe alternatives.

Thinking About the Recipe

Read the recipe for "Breaded Perch with Parmesan" and answer the following questions.

1. If the fish fillets are 1½ inches thick at the thickest part, about how long will they take to cook?
2. What other types of fish could you substitute for perch? (See Section 19.4.)

Breaded Perch with Parmesan

Customary	Ingredients	Metric
1/2 cup	Dry bread crumbs	125 mL
2 Tbsp.	Grated Parmesan cheese	30 mL
1/2 tsp.	Oregano, thyme, or basil	3 mL
1 lb.	Perch fillets	0.45 kg
1/4 cup	Skim milk	50 mL
1 Tbsp.	Margarine, melted	15 mL

Yield: 4 servings

Directions

Pan: Shallow baking pan
Temperature: 425°F (220°C)

1. Preheat oven. Grease baking pan.
2. Combine bread crumbs, Parmesan cheese, and choice of herbs.
3. Dip fillets in milk, then coat with bread crumb mixture. Lay in single layer on baking pan.
4. Drizzle fillets with melted margarine.
5. Bake at 425°F (220°C) until fish flakes easily with a fork (approximately 10 minutes per inch of thickness).

Nutrition Information

Per serving (approximate): 197 calories, 26 g protein, 10 g carbohydrate, 5 g fat, 104 mg cholesterol, 260 mg sodium

---

Answers to Thinking About the Recipe

1. 15 minutes.

2. Possible answers: catfish, cod, flounder, haddock, halibut, pike, pollock, pompano, red snapper, sole, trout, turbot, whitefish.

Thinking About the Recipe

Read the recipe for "Simply Deluxe Microwave Chicken" and answer the following questions.

1. Why is it important to arrange and turn the chicken pieces as specified in the recipe?
2. What is the purpose of the soy sauce?

Simply Deluxe Microwave Chicken

Key Skill: Microwaving Poultry

Simply Deluxe Microwave Chicken

Customary	Ingredients	Metric
4	Boneless, skinless chicken breast halves	4
2 Tbsp.	Soy sauce	30 mL
1/2 cup	Plain nonfat yogurt	125 mL
1/2 tsp.	Grated onion	3 mL
1/2 tsp.	Prepared mustard	3 mL
1/4 tsp.	Seasoned salt	1 mL
Dash	Pepper	Dash

Yield: 4 servings

Directions

Pan: Round microwave-safe dish with removable rack
Power level: 100% power

1. Brush chicken pieces with soy sauce.
2. Arrange chicken on rack close to edges of dish. Cover loosely with waxed paper.
3. Microwave at 100% power for 6 minutes.
4. Mix together yogurt, onion, and mustard in small bowl. Set aside.
5. Remove chicken pieces from rack. Turn pieces over and place in bottom of dish, arranging them in a circle around the edge.
6. Sprinkle chicken with seasoned salt and pepper. Spoon yogurt mixture over each piece.
7. Cover loosely with waxed paper. Microwave at 100% power for about 6 minutes, or until fork can be inserted in chicken with ease.
8. Sprinkle with additional salt and pepper, if desired. Let stand, covered, 2 minutes before serving.

Nutrition Information

Per serving (approximate): 148 calories, 29 g protein, 3 g carbohydrate, 3 g fat, 73 mg cholesterol, 739 mg sodium

Section 19.5: Preparing Meat, Poultry, Fish, and Shellfish   517

Using the Recipe

- Have students read the recipe and discuss each step. Remind students that waxed paper should cover the chicken only loosely, so that steam can be vented from the cooking chicken. Review safety and sanitation procedures that apply to this recipe.
- Have each lab team fill out a work plan. (See the *Foods Lab Resources* booklet.)
- Have students check off the ingredients and equipment listed on the recipe worksheet and prepare the recipe.
- Have students complete the evaluation and questions on the recipe worksheet.

See Also . . .

The *Foods Lab Resources* booklet for the "Simply Deluxe Microwave Chicken" recipe worksheet and other recipe alternatives.

Answers to Thinking About the Recipe

1. So that it cooks evenly.

2. Answers will vary. The actual purpose is to give the effect of "browning" the chicken.

19.5 Recipe

Beef Patties with Herbs

Key Skill: Pan-broiling Meat

Using the Recipe

- Have students read the recipe and discuss each step. Remind students not to get the burner too hot; the fat and grease will spatter and could cause severe burns. In addition, the spattered grease can be difficult to clean up from the kitchen surfaces. Review safety and sanitation procedures that apply to this recipe.

- Have each lab team fill out a work plan. (See the *Foods Lab Resources* booklet.)

- Have students check off the ingredients and equipment listed on the recipe worksheet and prepare the recipe.

- Have students complete the evaluation and questions on the recipe worksheet.

See Also . . .

The *Foods Lab Resources* booklet for the "Beef Patties with Herbs" recipe worksheet and other recipe alternatives.

Thinking About the Recipe

Read the recipe for "Beef Patties with Herbs" and answer the following questions.

1. What other cooking methods could you use for ground beef patties?
2. If you substituted ground turkey meat for ground beef, what other changes might you need to make in the recipe? Why?

Beef Patties with Herbs

Customary	Ingredients	Metric
1 lb.	Extra-lean ground beef	0.45 kg
1/2 tsp.	Black pepper, ground	3 mL
1/2 tsp.	Rosemary, dried	3 mL
1/2 tsp.	Thyme, dried	3 mL
4 slices	Tomato	4 slices
4 thin slices	Onion	4 thin slices
4	Crusty rolls, split	4

Yield: 4 servings

Conventional Directions

Pan: Nonstick skillet
Temperature: Medium

1. Combine ground beef, pepper, and herbs until well blended.
2. Shape the ground beef mixture into four patties about 1/2 inch (1 cm) thick.
3. Panbroil ground beef patties about 8 minutes, turning once.
4. Serve patties with tomato and onion slices on crusty rolls.

Microwave Directions

Pan: Microwave-safe dish
Power level: 100% power

1. Follow Steps 1 and 2 of conventional directions.
2. Place ground beef patties in microwave-safe dish. Cover with waxed paper.
3. Cook patties for about 6 minutes at 100% power, turning once after 2 minutes.
4. Let stand 1 minute.
5. Serve patties with tomato and onion slices on crusty rolls.

Nutrition Information

Per serving (approximate): 382 calories, 27 g protein, 33 g carbohydrate, 16 g fat, 70 mg cholesterol, 374 mg sodium

---

Answers to Thinking About the Recipe

1. Answers will vary; broiling and grilling are possible answers.

2. More seasonings may need to be used because turkey has a milder flavor than beef.

Career PROFILE

Bill Mayokok
Fisherman

CURRENT POSITION

"I'm a boatswain (a highly experienced deckhand) on a large fishing vessel."

RESPONSIBILITIES

"Basically, I help carry out the ship's sailing and fishing operations. After removing the catch from the nets, we have to see that it's washed, salted, iced, and properly stored. Once we're back on land, we help unload the catch."

SKILLS

"This work can be physically demanding, so you must be in good health. You also must have a certain amount of mechanical aptitude to work the equipment. And you must be patient and able to work as a team with others."

EDUCATION

"This line of work is learned on the job. I sometimes attend workshops on the newest improvements in fishing gear."

WORK ENVIRONMENT

"I prefer to work outdoors, so this job suits me. The days can be long and hot, but at the same time satisfying and relaxing. Sometimes the job can be hazardous, though, when an unexpected storm or fog blows up."

CAREER GOALS

"I'm hoping to obtain my license from the U.S. Coast Guard to captain my own fishing vessel someday."

- Why do you think teamwork is so important in Bill's job?
- What aspects of Bill's job do you think you might enjoy? Why?

519

CAREER PROFILE: FISHERMAN

Thinking About . . . Fishing

Have students think of other questions they would like to ask Bill Mayokok about the fishing profession. (Examples: How many hours a week do you work? Do your duties change when a storm blows up? How is fish packed at sea so that it does not spoil before you get back to the dock?)

Have students brainstorm decisions that Bill Mayokok might have to make on a daily basis. What techniques might he use to make the decisions?

Student Opportunities

Students interested in fishing as a career may consider volunteering to help on small commercial fishing vessels.

Occupational Outlook

As fishermen become more experienced they may advance to positions of higher authority on the fishing boats. Those with a business aptitude may own their own fishing fleet some day.

For More Information

For additional information about careers in the fishing industry, encourage students to contact:
- American Fisheries Society, 5410 Grosvenor Lane, Suite 110, Bethesda, MD 20814-2199
- National Fisheries Institute, 2000 M St., Washington, D.C. 20036
- International Game Fish Association, 1301 E. Atlantic Blvd., Pompano Beach, FL 33060

Review

- Have students complete the Chapter Review. (Answers appear below.)

Evaluation

- Have students prepare guidelines for buying, storing, preparing, and cooking meat, poultry, fish, and shellfish.
- Have students take the test for Chapter 19. (Refer to the *Chapter and Unit Tests* booklet or construct your own test using the *Testmaker Software*.)

■ ANSWERS ■

REVIEWING FACTS

1. Beef; fish.

2. A yellowish, very tough connective tissue in meat and poultry that cannot be softened by heat. It must be tenderized by other methods.

3. Beef—roasts and steaks: round, loin, sirloin, chuck arm; pork—roasts and chops: tenderloin, center loin, ham; lamb—roasts and chops: leg, loin, fore shanks.

4. Prime (highest and most expensive grade, meat well marbled with fat, tender and flavorful); choice (less marbling than prime, but still tender and flavorful); select (least expensive, least amount of marbling; sometimes sold as store brand.)

5. Roasters, Rock Cornish game hens, capons.

6. "Ground turkey" was ground with the skin, so it contains more fat. "Ground turkey meat" was ground without the skin.

CHAPTER 19 REVIEW

SUMMARY

SECTION 19.1

Looking at Meat, Poultry, Fish, and Shellfish: Meat, poultry, fish, and shellfish are sources of complete protein, B vitamins, and several minerals. They also contain cholesterol and varying amounts of fat. Cuts of meat and poultry that include thicker muscle fibers or more connective tissue are less tender. Meat, poultry, fish, and shellfish are usually the most expensive part of the food budget.

SECTION 19.2

Meat Selection and Storage: Beef, veal, lamb, and pork each have a characteristic flavor and color. You can identify cuts of meat by the package label or by bone shape. The USDA inspects meat for wholesomeness. Grading for quality is a voluntary program. Some meats are processed by curing and other methods. Store meat properly to retain its quality.

SECTION 19.3

Poultry Selection and Storage: Chicken and turkey may be purchased fresh or frozen, whole or in parts. Ducks and geese are usually available whole and frozen. Poultry is inspected, and may be graded, by the USDA. Poultry requires cold storage.

SECTION 19.4

Fish and Shellfish Selection and Storage: Fish that are similar in color and texture can be substituted for one another. Fish may be bought fresh or frozen in several market forms. Shellfish include crustaceans and mollusks. Many are sold live. Fish may also be dried, pickled, smoked, or cured. Judge the quality of fish and shellfish by appearance and aroma. Fish should be refrigerated or frozen.

SECTION 19.5

Preparing Meat, Poultry, Fish, and Shellfish: Tender cuts can be cooked with dry heat methods. Less tender cuts need moist heat methods. Cuts should be thawed, cleaned, and trimmed of fat before cooking. You can test for doneness by using a meat thermometer or checking the color and texture of the cut. Basic cooking methods include roasting or baking, broiling, poaching, and microwaving.

REVIEWING FACTS

1. Of beef, pork, chicken, and fish, which generally has the most saturated fat? The least? (19.1)
2. What is elastin? Why is it a factor in meat and poultry preparation? (19.1)
3. Give two examples of lean cuts of each of the following: beef; pork; lamb. (19.2)
4. List and describe three grades of meat. (19.2)
5. Name three types of chicken suitable for roasting. (19.3)
6. What is the difference between "ground turkey" and "ground turkey meat"? (19.3)
7. What does "seafood" refer to? (19.4)
8. What is the difference between fish fillets and fish steaks? (19.4)
9. Describe how cuts from animal foods change in color, flavor, and texture when they are cooked. (19.5)
10. Give three tips for broiling meat, poultry, or fish. (19.5)

LEARNING BY DOING

1. ***Demonstration:*** Choose a less tender cut of meat. Demonstrate ways of tenderizing it before cooking. (19.1, 19.2)

520

7. Saltwater fish and shellfish; those that come from the sea or ocean (as opposed to freshwater fish and shellfish).

8. Fillets are skimmed from along the side of the fish and rarely contain bones. Steaks are cut across the fish and usually contain back and rib bones.

9. The red color changes to brown and pink colors turn to beige; flavors are developed; cut shrinks, muscle fibers get firmer, and connective tissue becomes more tender.

2. **Taste test:** Compare the taste of different types of processed meat, poultry, or fish. Identify the processing method used and tell what characteristics it gives the food. (19.2, 19.3, 19.4)

3. **Foods lab:** Choose a recipe calling for ground meat. Prepare it once using meat, then using ground poultry instead. Compare the results. (19.3)

4. **Demonstration:** Demonstrate how to judge the quality of fresh fish. (19.4)

5. **Foods lab:** Cook a thicker cut of meat or poultry. Test for doneness by using a meat thermometer and by piercing with a knife. Which method do you think is more reliable? (19.5)

THINKING CRITICALLY

1. **Analyzing decisions:** Besides cost and tenderness, what other factors might affect your choice when buying meat, poultry, and fish? (19.1)

2. **Recognizing bias:** A friend refuses to try organ meats, giblets, or shellfish. She is sure she won't like them. Why might she feel this way? What might be some benefits of trying these foods? (19.2, 19.3, 19.4)

3. **Predicting consequences:** How do you think overcooking affects the appearance, flavor, and texture of fish? (19.5)

MAKING DECISIONS AND SOLVING PROBLEMS

What Would You Do?

1. You would like to reduce the amount of money you spend on meat, poultry, and fish, while still providing your family with good-tasting, quality protein foods. (19.1)

2. You have just moved to a new town and would like to prepare dinner for some new friends. You choose a favorite recipe that calls for loin of lamb, but discover that none of the stores in your area carry it. (19.2)

3. A supermarket is having a sale on fresh, whole catfish. You enjoy catfish, but you don't know how to dress them. (19.4)

4. You are cooking a blade roast in the oven and figure it will be done in about 15 minutes. You get a phone call from the school that your ten-year-old sister attends. The school explains that your sister is not feeling well. You know that it will take at least half an hour to pick her up and bring her home. (19.5)

LINKING YOUR STUDIES

1. **Social studies:** Find information about which foods from animal sources are most popular in another culture. (19.1)

2. **Science:** Find information about meat processing methods. How were meats treated for preservation and flavoring in the past? How is this done today? What chemicals and chemical processes are involved? If possible, conduct an experiment or demonstration showing these principles at work. (19.2)

3. **Math:** Compare the prices of similar forms of chicken and turkey in your area. Figure the cost per serving for each. Show your findings on a bar graph. Also list the possible reasons for any price differences. (19.3)

4. **Science:** Write a report about the latest studies on the relationship between the amount of fish eaten and the occurrence of heart disease. (19.4)

LEARNING BY DOING

Answers to "Learning by Doing" will vary. Encourage students to give reasons for their answers.

THINKING CRITICALLY

1. Answers will vary. Nutritional value and fat or calorie content are possible answers.

2. Answers will vary. Students should understand that people who have never been served certain foods in their homes may inherit biases or think they don't like foods based on family preferences.

3. The fish will become tough and rubbery.

MAKING DECISIONS AND SOLVING PROBLEMS

Answers to "Making Decisions and Solving Problems" activities will vary. Encourage students to give reasons for their answers.

LINKING YOUR STUDIES

Answers to "Linking Your Studies" activities will vary. Evaluate students on the amount of effort they put into the activities as well as their results.

521

10. *Any three:* Slash the fat around the edges before broiling; when broiling chicken, begin with skin side down and turn when halfway through broiling time; brush fish lightly with melted butter or margarine to keep it from charring; brush broiled foods with sauce to add flavor.

Planning the Chapter

Chapter Overview

Section 20.1: Sandwiches, Snacks, and Packed Lunches

Section 20.2: Salads and Dressings

Section 20.3: Soups and Sauces

Section 20.4: Casseroles and Other Combinations

Introducing the Chapter

Motivator

- Ask students to find pictures of food combinations. Divide the pictures into the following categories: sandwiches, snacks, salads, soups, sauces, casseroles, and other combinations. Use the pictures to create a bulletin board titled "Putting It All Together."

CHAPTER 20

Food Combinations

522

Cooperative Learning Suggestions

Initiate a Co-op Co-op activity. Have students work in groups to research sandwiches, salads, soups, casseroles, and other food combinations popular in other countries. Have each group choose a country to research. Have each group member select one type of food to research. Have group members share their findings with their group, then have the group develop a one-page summary of the food combinations popular in the country. Combine the work of all groups into a study guide for the entire class.

Sandwiches, Snacks, and Packed Lunches

OBJECTIVES

After studying this section, you should be able to:

- Describe how to make sandwiches using a variety of breads and fillings.
- Give suggestions for nutritious snacks.
- Explain how to pack an interesting, nutritious lunch and keep it safe to eat.

LOOK FOR THESE TERMS

club sandwich
vacuum bottle

In the last three chapters, you have learned about specific types of foods, ranging from fruits to fish. Different kinds of foods can be put together to make pleasing combination dishes. For example, a variety of nutritious foods can be used in making sandwiches, snacks, and packed lunches. All three are an important part of daily food choices.

Making Sandwiches

When making a sandwich, focus on healthful ingredients. Start with whole grain breads. As a change from sliced bread, make sandwiches with rolls, pita bread, taco shells, bagels, or tortillas. Try toasting the bread.

The variety of fillings is limited only by your imagination. Try leftover cooked lean meat, poultry, or fish; mashed, cooked dry beans; egg or fish salad; or low-fat cottage cheese mixed with chopped fruit. Choose luncheon meats that are low in fat.

Top the fillings with other foods. Use fruits and vegetables such as tomatoes, lettuce, pickles, onions, shredded carrot, sliced apples, and cucumbers. Mustard and salsa are often added for extra flavor.

Sandwiches can be heated easily in a microwave oven. Prepare the sandwich, omitting fresh vegetables and fruit which would wilt during heating. Add those later. Wrap the sandwich in a paper towel and microwave it on 100 percent power for 30 to 60 seconds.

**Section 20.1
Sandwiches, Snacks, and Packed Lunches**

Introducing the Section

Motivator

- Ask students to describe their favorite snacks. Differentiate between healthful snacks and those that are less nutritious.

Objectives

- Have students read the section objectives. Discuss the purpose of studying the section.

Vocabulary

- Pronounce the terms listed under "Look for These Terms." Have students find the terms and their definitions in the section.

Guided Reading

- Have students look at the headings within Section 20.1 to preview the concepts that will be discussed.
- Have students read the section and complete the appropriate part of the Chapter 20 Study Guide in the *Student Workbook.*

Teacher's Classroom Resources—Section 20.1

Refer to these resources in the TCR package:

Reproducible Lesson Plans
Student Workbook
Extending the Text
Reteaching Activities

Section Quizzes
Testmaker Software
Foods Lab Resources
Color Transparencies

Teaching . . .

• Making Sandwiches

(text pages 523-524)

Comprehension Check

1. Ask students to list possible substitutions for sliced bread when making a sandwich. *(rolls, pita bread, taco shells, bagels, tortillas)*

2. Discuss the procedure for heating sandwiches in a microwave oven. *(Prepare the sandwich, except for fresh fruit and vegetables; wrap sandwich in a paper towel; microwave on 100 percent power for 30 to 60 seconds.)*

3. Ask students to describe four ways to make sandwiches. *(traditional sandwiches, sandwiches with fancy shapes, club sandwiches, filled pocket sandwiches)*

Student Experiences

1. **Taste-Testing:** Have students work in groups to prepare small amounts of sandwich fillings and toppings. Use a variety of breads to make small sandwiches for the class to taste. *(Key skill: evaluation)*

2. **Sandwich Filling Listing:** Make a class list of possible fillings for sandwiches. *(Key skill: creativity)*

3. **Recipe Reading:** Have students find recipes for sandwiches. Discuss the variety of sandwiches possible. *(Key skill: reading)*

Using the Photo

Answer to caption question: The photo shows (left to right) a filled pocket sandwich, a traditional sandwich, and an open-face sandwich.

Here are several basic ways to make sandwiches:

❖ **Traditional sandwich.** Use two slices of bread and your choice of fillings. To keep moist fillings from soaking the bread, spread one side of each slice with a very thin coat of butter or margarine. Place the filling between the two buttered slices of bread. For easier eating, cut the sandwich into halves or quarters.

❖ **Fancy sandwiches.** Cut the bread into fancy shapes with cookie cutters before or after you add the filling. Serve these sandwiches at formal events or on special occasions.

❖ **Club sandwich.** A **club sandwich** uses three slices of bread and two different kinds of fillings, such as turkey and ham. Prepare a traditional sandwich. Then but- ter the top slice, add a second filling, and top it with third slice of bread, buttered side down. Cut the sandwich into quarters. Secure quarters with decorative toothpicks, if necessary.

❖ **Filled pocket sandwiches.** Make pocket sandwiches with pita bread or hard rolls. Taco shells can also be used to hold a filling. To make a pocket from a pita, first warm the pita briefly in the microwave oven to make it easier to handle. Then cut the pita in half with a sharp knife. Gently slit or pull the two sides apart. To make a pocket from a hard roll, slice off the top and scoop out the bread to form a hollow for the filling. (Dry the leftover bread and crust for bread crumbs.) To keep pockets from absorbing the filling, line them first with shredded lettuce or alfalfa sprouts.

By using different breads, fillings, and flavorings, you can create an endless variety of sandwiches. Can you identify the basic types of sandwiches shown here?

Special Needs Strategies

Learning Disabled: Have students develop picture cards of different types of sandwiches, salad ingredients, types of salads, types of salad dressings, types of soups, and types of main dish combinations. Have students use the pictures to practice identifying each type of food.

Physically Disabled: Have students with physical impairments develop a system for making sandwiches that works for them.

Healthful Snacks

As you have learned, snacks are as much a part of your daily eating plan as meals are. (If you need to review information about snacks and eating patterns, see Section 4.1.)

There are many simple, nutritious ways to satisfy between-meal hunger. For instance, fresh fruits and vegetables are easy to prepare. You could also have a glass of skim milk, a small sandwich, or a cup of soup with whole grain crackers as a snack.

Here are more ideas for healthful, tasty snacks to make in a jiffy:

❖ **Fruit shake:** Put 1 cup (250 mL) of frozen fruit, such as strawberries or peaches, in a blender. Add 1 cup (250 mL) of skim milk, 2 teaspoons (10 mL) of honey, and 1/2 teaspoon (2.5 mL) of vanilla extract. Cover and blend until smooth. Serve immediately.

❖ **Yogurt pops:** Pour flavored yogurt into a paper cup. Put a wooden popsicle stick or a plastic spoon in the center. Freeze the yogurt pop for at least an hour. The stick or spoon serves as a handle.

❖ **Frozen fruit bites:** Freeze whole grapes or strawberries. They make candy-like snacks.

❖ **Low-fat tortilla or pita chips:** Cut tortillas or pita bread into six or eight wedge-shaped pieces. Spread a single layer in a baking pan. Bake them in a preheated oven at 450°F (230°C) for about five minutes or until the wedges are crispy.

Packing a Lunch

It's estimated that about 30 percent of American workers carry a packed lunch. Their reasons vary from saving money to having a better choice of foods. Packed lunches can be taken to school, too.

With a little organization, packed lunches can be easy to assemble. Here are a few simple guidelines:

Fruit shakes make nutritious beverages or snacks. Try blending orange juice, nonfat yogurt, and honey for a refreshing treat.

❖ Keep hot foods hot and cold foods cold. Since the lunch may have to stand at room temperature four to five hours before eating, use an insulated lunch bag or containers such as vacuum bottles. You can also buy a freezer gel pack, freeze it, and pack it with the lunch.

❖ To pack foods such as hot soup, chili, or stew, use a wide-mouth vacuum bottle. A **vacuum bottle** has a vacuum space between the outer container and the inner liner, which is made of glass or metal. Vacuum bottles do a better job of keeping foods hot than less expensive foam-insulated bottles. Before packing the vacuum bottle, preheat it—fill it with hot tap water and let it stand a minute or two. Empty the water, fill the bottle with piping hot food, and close tightly.

❖ Pack foods that are easy to handle. Avoid foods that are drippy or oily. If foods must be cut up, cut them before packing the lunch.

More About Sandwich Alternatives

For an interesting sandwich, make a wraparound. Use a soft, flat bread, such as a tortilla or chapati. Place it on a napkin or piece of foil. Spoon the filling down the center of the bread, leaving an even border on either side. Fold the bottom and side portions of the bread over the filling to create a cone which is open at one end. Wrap a napkin or foil around the outside to prevent dripping.

Teaching . . .

- **Healthful Snacks**
- **Packing a Lunch**

(text pages 525-526)

Comprehension Check

1. Ask students to describe the procedure for making a fruit shake. *(Put 1 cup (250 mL) frozen fruit in a blender; add 1 cup (250 mL) skim milk, 2 tsp. (10 mL) honey, and 1/2 tsp. (2.5 mL) of vanilla extract. Cover and blend until smooth. Serve immediately.)*

2. Ask students to describe other healthful snacks that don't take long to prepare. *(yogurt pops, frozen fruit bites, low-fat tortilla or pita chips)*

3. Discuss guidelines for packing and assembling packed lunches. *(See list on pages 525-526.)*

Student Experiences

1. **Snack Ideas:** Have students identify foods to keep on hand for healthful snacks. *(Key skill: brainstorming)*

2. **Finding Recipes:** Have students work in small groups to find recipes for healthful snacks. *(Key skill: reading)*

3. **Handout:** Ask students to make a list of Do's and Don'ts for packing lunches. Have them combine their suggestions and prepare a handout on packed lunches for school lunches, work lunches, and picnics. *(Key skills: writing, critical thinking)*

Lab Experience

Have students plan, prepare, and serve healthful snacks. Discuss the nutritional benefits of the snack foods prepared.

Teaching . . .

• Assembling the Lunch

(text pages 526-527)

Comprehension Check

1. Ask students to identify foods appropriate for packed lunches. *(cold chicken, meat loaf, or pizza; warmed-up chili, stew, or soup (in a vacuum bottle); salads; bean dips and spreads.)*

2. Ask students to explain why it is important to pack salad dressings and crunchy items separately when you pack a salad for lunch. *(The dressing will make the salad limp by lunchtime; the crunchy items will become soggy.)*

Student Experiences

1. Class Discussion: Discuss considerations for packing different types of foods, including sandwiches, salads, and beverages. *(Key skill: critical thinking)*

2. Demonstration: Demonstrate how to preheat a vacuum bottle. Point out the use of refreezable "ice". *(Key skill: health)*

3. Menu Planning: Have students work in small groups to plan interesting and nutritious packed lunches. Have students plan and write out menus for lunches featuring sandwiches, lunches without sandwiches, and lunches using leftovers. Provide articles on packed lunches to provide sources of ideas. *(Key skills: writing, reading)*

Earth Watch

Have students brainstorm other ways to reduce, reuse, and recycle items commonly used in packed lunches.

When packing a lunch, keeping the food safe and fresh is an important consideration. So is avoiding waste. How can these items help?

❖ To speed up lunch packing, set aside an area in the freezer, refrigerator, and a nearby cabinet for lunch foods and equipment.

❖ Make packing lunches a family affair. Take turns as the "designated lunch packer" for everyone.

Assembling the Lunch

To prepare an interesting and nutritious lunch, use a variety of foods, following the guidelines in the Food Guide Pyramid. Use your imagination. Think of leftover foods you enjoy eating cold—barbecued chicken, meat loaf, roast turkey, or pizza. You can also heat up leftover chili, stew, or soup to pack in a vacuum bottle.

If you take salads with greens, mix the fruits and vegetables but pack the dressing and any crunchy additions separately. Add them just before you eat.

Bean dips and spreads make tasty sandwich fillings. Try using them as dips for fresh fruits and vegetables, too.

Earth Watch

When you pack a lunch, remember to reduce, reuse, and recycle. For example, plastic containers from yogurt, sour cream, and cottage cheese can be washed out and used to pack foods. Reuse plastic bags from the grocery store as lunch sacks. Save used aluminum foil if it can be recycled in your area. Avoid one-use containers and wraps. Use a cloth napkin instead of paper ones. These tips will help you save money and cut down on waste.

More About Packed Lunches

Here are some ideas for packed lunches, featuring complex carbohydrates:

• Pita bread sandwich made with refried beans and lettuce. (Carry taco sauce in a separate container.)

• Hummus (pureed garbanzo beans and ground sesame seeds) with crackers.

• Pita bread sandwich filled with herb-seasoned cooked vegetables such as zucchini, mushrooms, peas, beans, and onions.

• Avocado and tomato slices with lettuce or alfalfa sprouts; use in a sandwich with either whole-wheat or pita bread.

Where necessary, add a salad or vegetable. Round out the packed lunch with dessert and milk.

Be sure your food choices include whole grain breads or rolls as well as fresh fruits and vegetables.

What will you choose for a beverage? Remember that a regular soft drink has about 10 teaspoons (50 mL) of sugar and very few nutrients. Milk and fruit juice, on the other hand, are both flavorful and nutritious.

Don't forget to include such nonfood items as forks, spoons, and napkins. Tuck in a wet wipe or a wet washcloth in a plastic bag when you pack foods that are especially messy.

Nutritious packed lunches are based on the Food Guide Pyramid. How would you rate this lunch?

■ Section 20.1 Review ■

RECALL THE FACTS

1. Name four kinds of bread that might be used to make a sandwich.

2. Identify two healthful snacks made with fruit.

3. Describe how to preheat a vacuum bottle.

DISCUSS YOUR IDEAS

4. How do the snack suggestions in the text compare to the snacks you choose at home in terms of nutrition, expense, and ease of preparation?

APPLY YOUR LEARNING

5. Draw a diagram showing how you would set up an ideal lunch-packing area in your kitchen at home. Explain the advantages of your plan.

Completing the Section

Review

- Ask students to summarize the main ideas in this section.
- Have students complete the Section Review. (Answers appear below.)

Evaluation

- Have students prepare a menu for a packed lunch that is nutritious and appealing.
- Have students take the quiz for Section 20.1. (Refer to the *Section Quizzes* booklet or use the *Testmaker Software*.)

Reteaching

- Show pictures of foods that are commonly used for lunch. Have students practice choosing nutritious, healthful lunches.
- Refer to the *Reteaching Activities* booklet for the Section 20.1 activity worksheet.

Enrichment

- Have students plan, prepare, and serve healthful snacks or lunches and explain the nutritional benefits of the foods they prepared.

Closure

- Lead a discussion on the benefits of packing and eating a nutritious lunch every day.

Section 20.1: Sandwiches, Snacks, and Packed Lunches   **527**

■ Answers to Section Review ■

1. *Any four:* Whole grain sliced bread, rolls, pita bread, taco shells, bagels, or tortillas.

2. Fruit shake and frozen fruit bites.
3. Fill it with hot tap water and let it stand a minute or two.

4. Answers will vary.
5. Answers will vary.

20.1 Recipe

Apple-Tuna Sandwiches

Key Skill: Making a sandwich

Using the Recipe

- Have students read the recipe and discuss each step. Encourage students to be creative in making an attractive presentation of the sandwich. Review safety and sanitation procedures that apply to this recipe.
- Have each lab team fill out a work plan. (See the *Foods Lab Resources* booklet.)
- Have students check off the ingredients and equipment listed on the recipe worksheet and prepare the recipe.
- Have students complete the evaluation and questions on the recipe worksheet.

See Also . . .

The *Foods Lab Resources* booklet for the "Apple-Tuna Sandwiches recipe worksheet and other recipe alternatives.

Thinking About the Recipe

Read the recipe for "Apple-Tuna Sandwiches" and answer the following questions.

1. Which food groups are represented in this sandwich?
2. What ingredients might you add or substitute for a flavor variation?

Apple-Tuna Sandwiches

Customary	Ingredients	Metric
7-oz can	Water-pack tuna, drained and flaked	198-g can
1/2 cup	Celery, finely chopped	125 mL
2 Tbsp.	Onion, finely chopped	30 mL
1/2 cup	Mayonnaise, nonfat variety	125 mL
4	Lettuce leaves	4
4 slices	American cheese (optional)	4 slices
1	Apple, cored and thinly sliced—about 12 slices	1
4	Whole wheat buns, split	4

Yield: 4 servings

Directions

1. Combine tuna, celery, onion, and mayonnaise.
2. Cover the bottom of each bun with a lettuce leaf. (Be sure leaves are dry.)
3. Place a cheese slice on top of the lettuce leaf, if desired. (For a decorative effect, try cutting each cheese slice in half diagonally to form two triangles.)
4. Spread tuna mixture on top of lettuce or cheese slices on each bun. Place apple slices on top of tuna. Cover with top half of bun.

Nutrition Information

Per serving (approximate): 119 calories, 6 g protein, 11 g carbohydrate, 7 g fat, 16 mg cholesterol, 302 mg sodium

---

Answers to Thinking About the Recipe

1. The Milk, Yogurt, and Cheese Group; Meat, Poultry, Fish, Dry Beans, Eggs, and Nuts Group; Vegetable Group; Fruit Group; Bread, Cereal, Rice, and Pasta Group.

2. Answers will vary.

Salads and Dressings

OBJECTIVES

After studying this section, you should be able to:

- Describe how to select, wash, store, and serve several kinds of salad greens.
- Plan and assemble a salad using a variety of methods and ingredients.
- Identify ways to serve salads.

LOOK FOR THESE TERMS

emulsion
base
body

A salad is a versatile combination of foods. It can be simply an assortment of greens served as a side dish, or it can be a hearty main dish. Fresh fruit salads can serve as desserts or refreshing snacks any time of day. Depending on the ingredients, a salad can provide servings from each of the five food groups.

Ingredients for Salads

Almost any solid, ready-to-eat food from the five food groups can be used in a salad. Some of the basic foods include:

❖ **Salad greens.** Lettuce is the most common salad green. It comes in many varieties, such as iceberg, romaine, bibb (also known as Boston or butterhead), and red or green leaf lettuce. Other greens include spinach, escarole, chicory, and radicchio (rah-DEE-kee-oh). Remember, the darker the color, the more nutrients the greens contain. Flavors vary from mild to slightly bitter.

❖ **Other vegetables and fruits.** Any fresh fruits and fresh or cooked vegetables may be used in salads. They can be sliced, diced, shredded, quartered, or cubed.

Salad greens include (clockwise from lower left): iceberg lettuce, spinach, leaf lettuce, curly endive, escarole, romaine lettuce, and (center) bibb lettuce.

Section 20.2 Salads and Dressings

Introducing the Section

Motivators

- Create a bulletin board entitled "Be a Salad Star." Cut out pictures of various salad ingredients from magazines, or make your own illustrations from construction paper. Discuss how the ingredients could be combined to make salads.

- Purchase some potted herbs and seeds to sprout. Herbs thrive on a sunny window sill, and sprouts will grow anywhere. Discuss the nutrients and the flavor each will add to a salad.

Objectives

- Have students read the section objectives. Discuss the purpose of studying the section.

Vocabulary

- Pronounce the terms listed under "Look for These Terms." Have students find the terms and their definitions in the section.

Guided Reading

- Have students look at the headings within Section 20.2 to preview the concepts that will be discussed.

- Have students read the section and complete the appropriate part of the Chapter 20 Study Guide in the *Student Workbook*.

Teacher's Classroom Resources—Section 20.2

Refer to these resources in the TCR package:

Reproducible Lesson Plans
Student Workbook
Extending the Text
Reteaching Activities

Section Quizzes
Testmaker Software
Foods Lab Resources
Color Transparencies

Teaching . . .

- **Ingredients for Salads**
- **Salad Dressings**

(text pages 529-531)

Comprehension Check

1. Ask students to identify greens that are commonly used in salads. What different types of lettuce are available? *(lettuce, spinach, escarole, chicory, radicchio; types of lettuce: iceberg, romaine, bibb, red or green leaf lettuce.)*

2. Ask students to name ingredients that can turn a salad into a hearty main-dish food. *(cooked grains, legumes, meat, poultry, fish, or eggs; cheese.)*

3. Ask students to explain why salad dressings have traditionally been high in fat and calories. How has this changed? *(The oil used in making them contained many calories; today, many low-fat and fat-free dressings are available.)*

Science Connection

Encourage students to think of other foods that might benefit from an emulsifier. (Example: Casseroles that contain meat.) Ask students if an egg yolk would be an appropriate ingredient in these foods. Have interested students find out about other emulsifiers that are commonly used in food.

■ ■ ■

❖ **Cooked grains, legumes, meat, poultry, fish, eggs, or cheese.** Make hearty main dish salads by mixing these foods with fruits and vegetables. For example, combine leftover rice with cooked dry beans, chopped onions, chopped tomatoes, seasonings, and greens. Any cooked, chilled pasta can be used in salads, too.

Salad Dressings

Salad dressings are sauces poured on salads to give them richness and flavor. They also act as binding agents to hold salads together. There are several basic types of dressings.

❖ **Oil-based dressings** are also called "French," "Italian," or "vinaigrette" (vihn-uh-GREHT) dressings. They are a mixture of oil, vinegar, and seasonings. Oil-based dressings separate easily and must be mixed again each time you use them.

❖ **Mayonnaise** is made with oil, vinegar or lemon juice, seasonings, and eggs. Eggs create an emulsion, which keeps the oil and vinegar from separating. An **emulsion** is an evenly blended mixture of two liquids that do not normally stay mixed.

❖ **Cooked dressings** are similar to mayonnaise, but use white sauce to replace some of the eggs and oil.

❖ **Dairy dressings** include "ranch-type" dressings. They have buttermilk, yogurt, sour cream, or cottage cheese as a main ingredient. Seasonings are added.

Salad dressings have traditionally been high in fat and calories because of the oil used in making them. Today, however, there are many low-fat and fat-free dressings available. Check the fat content on the label when you are selecting salad dressings. Remember, the nutrients listed on the label are for one serving of 2 tablespoons (30 mL). Many people use far more than that.

Try using nonfat yogurt to make a flavorful, low-calorie salad dressing. Add your favorite seasonings or a dry prepared mix to vary the flavor. For example, stir a little prepared mustard into the yogurt for a main dish salad dressing.

As a change from purchased salad dressings, try using nonfat yogurt to make your own dressings.

Food and Nutrition Science

Water Content in Lettuce: With just 8 calories per cup, lettuce is a staple to many calorie counters. The reason lettuce provides so few calories is that the leaves contain about 95 percent water by weight. Ask students to research and write about how this high water content gives crunch to a properly prepared salad but makes lettuce leaves prone to drooping if mishandled. Students should explain how they as consumers can use this information to prevent lettuce from wilting.

Science Connection

Chemistry:
Emulsifying Agents in Mayonnaise

Oil and water do not ordinarily stay mixed. If they are shaken together, the oil is broken down into tiny droplets. As soon as you stop shaking the mixture, however, the oil droplets begin to combine with one another. Soon the oil and water are separate again.

The egg yolks in mayonnaise contain a natural substance that acts as an *emulsifying agent*. This agent coats the oil droplets and causes them to repel one another. It also reduces the ability of the vinegar (which is mainly water) to repel the oil. Therefore, the oil stays in small droplets that remain evenly mixed throughout the dressing.

■ ■ ■

Before washing iceberg lettuce, remove the core. Striking the head against a flat surface loosens the core so that it can be removed easily with the fingers.

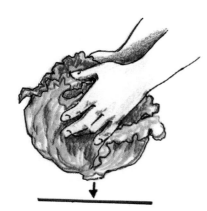 

Making a Salad

What kind of a salad should you make? First, decide how you plan to serve it. *Appetizer salads* are small, tasty salads served at the beginning of a meal to stimulate your appetite. For example, a shrimp cocktail or small tossed salad might be served. An *accompaniment salad* is a small salad served with a meal. Coleslaw, fruit salads, and tossed salads are examples. *Main dish salads* make up the main course of a meal. They generally contain a protein food along with grains, fruits, and vegetables. For instance, a chef's salad is made with cooked meat, poultry, and eggs, as well as cheese, on a thick bed of lettuce. A main dish salad is a great way to use leftovers. *Dessert salads* are usually made with fruit.

Preparing Salad Greens

Refrigerate salad greens as soon as you get home from the supermarket. You can wait to clean them until you use them, or you may clean them first so they will be ready to use.

❖ *Iceberg lettuce.* Hold the head in your hands, core side down. Hit the core on the counter once or twice to loosen it. Remove the core from the head. Let cold water run into the cavity for a minute or two until it pours out between the leaves.

Student Experiences

1. **Class Discussion:** Discuss the basic types of salad dressings—oil-based, mayonnaise, cooked, and dairy. What is the basic difference between an oil-based dressing and a mayonnaise dressing? What can you do to reduce the calories in cooked and mayonnaise dressings? How can you reduce the calories from salad dressings when you eat out? *(Key skill: critical thinking)*

2. **Display:** Display an assortment of salad greens. Number each type. Have students practice identifying the greens. What does the color of salad greens indicate? *(Key skill: kitchen management skills)*

3. **Taste-Testing:** Have students compare the taste of traditional commercial salad dressings that are high in fat and calories with low-fat and fat-free dressings. Which products are most and least acceptable? Ask students to write a summary of their findings. *(Key skills: writing, evaluation)*

4. **Group Activity:** Have students work in small groups to identify types of salads and salad ingredients that tend to be high in nutrients and low in fat and those that tend to be high in calories and fat. Following group discussions, develop a class list of nutritious salads and those that add calories and fat. *(Key skill: health)*

5. **Product Comparison:** Have students compare the cost and taste of a generic brand, a name brand, and a homemade salad dressing. Which one would they recommend? Why? *(Key skills: math, reasoning)*

More About Salads

Early salads consisted of greens and many fresh herbs, such as fennel, garlic, leeks, mint, onions, parsley, rosemary, and sage. These were washed, torn apart, and mixed with oil, salt, and vinegar. A 14th century English recipe said that even a plain salad should have at least 35 ingredients, including whole or candied flowers. A 19th century recipe book had only a summer and a winter salad. The winter salad had sliced hard-boiled eggs and beets but fewer greens.

Comprehension Check

1. Ask students to describe four ways in which salads can be used in a meal. *(appetizer, accompaniment served with a meal, main dish, dessert)*

2. Ask students to explain how to prepare iceberg lettuce. *(Hold the head, core side down. Hit the core on the counter to loosen it. Remove the core and let cold water run into the cavity. Drain the lettuce and place it in a covered plastic container or bag in the refrigerator.)*

3. Ask students to describe ways of combining salad ingredients. *(See list on page 532.)*

Student Experiences

1. **Demonstration:** Demonstrate how to core iceberg lettuce and separate the leaves. Demonstrate how to wash and prepare leafy greens. *(Key skill: kitchen management skills)*

2. **Group Discussions:** Have students work in groups to identify appetizer, accompaniment, and main dish salads. Develop a written list of characteristics for each type of salad. *(Key skill: writing)*

3. **Finding Recipes:** Have students find and analyze salad recipes. Ask students to identify the base, body, and dressing. Have students categorize the recipes as tossed or mixed salads, arranged salads, or molded salads. *(Key skills: reading, analysis)*

Lab Experience

Have students prepare a variety of salads and salad ingredients for a salad bar.

Place the head, core-side down, in a colander and let it drain. Store the drained lettuce in a covered plastic container or bag in the refrigerator.

❖ **Leafy greens.** Pull the leaves away from the core and wash them under cold running water. Place each leaf, stem side down, in a colander so the water can drain off easily. You may also need to pat the greens dry before storage. Put the washed greens in a plastic container with a cover or in a large plastic bag and store them in the refrigerator.

Assembling the Salad

Salads are fun and easy to assemble. Be creative! Choose colorful combinations of greens, fruits, vegetables, and other foods for an attractive, healthful dish.

A salad can be served in a small or large bowl or on a plate, depending on the foods used. For an attractive touch, line the bowl or plate with greens first—creating a **base** for the salad. Other salad ingredients make up the **body**, or main part of the salad.

Salad ingredients can be combined in many different ways. Here some common methods:

❖ **Tossed or mixed salads.** Greens and vegetables can be gently tossed together. Ingredients may be stirred together with a dressing, as in potato salad. They may also be put together in layers instead. For example, you might layer shredded greens, cooked mashed beans, chopped tomatoes, and yogurt in a dish.

❖ **Arranged salads.** Salad ingredients may be arranged in an attractive pattern, usually on a base of greens. For example, you might arrange fresh fruit slices around a mound of cottage cheese.

❖ **Molded salads.** Any salad mixture that holds its shape can be molded in a decorative container. Many molded salads are made with gelatin.

Making an arranged salad is an opportunity to develop your artistic skills.

Tossed or mixed salads lend themselves to a wide variety of ingredients. What are some of your favorite combinations?

Thinking Skills

Creativity: Give students a description of leftover fruits, vegetables, or grain products and have them suggest ways to use the foods in salads.

A fruit-and-gelatin mixture is not the only possibility for a molded salad. This shrimp mousse could be served as an appetizer or snack.

Serving Salads

Salads may be dressed up with decorative vegetables, such as green or red pepper rings or carrot sticks, and sprinkled with seeds, chopped nuts, or raisins.

Add the dressing to a tossed salad just before serving it. If dressing is added too soon, the greens will wilt. Better still, serve the salad without dressing. Pass the dressings separately at the table, so people can add their own.

Section 20.2 Review

RECALL THE FACTS

1. Name three kinds of salad greens.

2. How should salad greens be stored?

3. List three ways to prepare salads and give an example of each.

4. When should salad dressing be added to a tossed salad? Why?

DISCUSS YOUR IDEAS

5. Discuss some suggestions for cutting down on the fat and calories commonly found in salad dressings.

6. Brainstorm ways to use leftover cooked foods in salads. What combinations can you think of?

APPLY YOUR LEARNING

7. Describe two ways that you could change a small tossed salad into a main dish salad.

Section 20.2: Salads and Dressings   **533**

20.2

Completing the Section

Review

- Ask students to summarize the main ideas in this section.
- Have students complete the Section Review. (Answers appear below.)

Evaluation

- Have students prepare a salad of their choice. The salad must be both nutritious and appealing.
- Have students take the quiz for Section 20.2. (Refer to the *Section Quizzes* booklet or use the *Testmaker Software*.)

Reteaching

- Prepare a salad or buy one from the school cafeteria. Have students determine the nutritional value of the salad.
- Refer to the *Reteaching Activities* booklet for the Section 20.2 activity worksheet.

Enrichment

- Have students research and write about the kinds of greens used in salads in other parts of the world.

Closure

- Refer to the first motivator for this section. Ask students if they can add any other suggestions.

Answers to Section Review

1. *Any three:* Lettuce, spinach, escarole, chicory, and radicchio.
2. In a covered plastic bowl or in a sealed plastic bag.
3. See list on page 532. Examples will vary.
4. Just before it is served; otherwise it will wilt the greens.
5. Answers will vary.
6. Answers will vary.
7. Answers will vary. Adding legumes and grain; adding meat or poultry and cheese. etc.

533

Garbanzo Salad
Honey Mustard Dressing

Key Skill: Preparing a salad

Using the Recipe

- Have students read the recipe and discuss each step. Remind students to allow excess water to drain from the lettuce leaves before using them in the salad. Students may need to pat the lettuce dry. Review safety and sanitation procedures that apply to this recipe.

- Have each lab team fill out a work plan. (See the *Foods Lab Resources* booklet.)

- Have students check off the ingredients and equipment listed on the recipe worksheet and prepare the recipe.

- Have students complete the evaluation and questions on the recipe worksheet.

See Also . . .

The *Foods Lab Resources* booklet for the "Garbanzo Salad" and "Honey Mustard Dressing" recipe worksheets and other recipe alternatives.

Thinking About the Recipe

Read the recipes for "Garbanzo Salad" and "Honey-Mustard Dressing" and answer the following questions.

1. Name one substitution you might make for each ingredient in the recipe.
2. What could you do to keep the chopped apple from turning brown while you make the dressing?

Garbanzo Salad

Customary	Ingredients	Metric
8 leaves	Romaine lettuce	8 leaves
16-oz. can	Garbanzo beans	454-g can
1 large	Apple	1 large
1 medium	Red or green pepper	1 medium
1/2 cup	Raisins	125 mL

Yield: 4 servings

Conventional Directions

1. Tear lettuce into bite-size pieces.
2. Rinse and drain garbanzo beans.
3. Core apple. Chop apple and pepper into bite-size pieces.
4. Toss all ingredients in salad bowl.
5. Serve with Honey-Mustard Dressing.

Honey-Mustard Dressing

Customary	Ingredients	Metric
2 tsp.	Prepared mustard	10 mL
2 Tbsp.	Vinegar	30 mL
.2 tsp.	Oil	10 mL
2 tsp.	Honey	10 mL
1/4 tsp.	Celery seed	1 mL

Yield: 4 servings

Directions

1. Mix together mustard and vinegar in small bowl.
2. Add oil, honey, and celery seed. Mix well.

Nutrition Information

Per serving (approximate—salad plus dressing): 227 calories, 7 g protein, 42 g carbohydrate, 4 g fat, 0 mg cholesterol, 487 mg sodium

534   Chapter 20: Food Combinations

Answers to Thinking About the Recipe

1. Answers will vary. Examples: Bibb lettuce, kidney beans, orange sections, jalapeño peppers, cashews.

2. Sprinkle it with lemon juice; use an ascorbic acid mixture.

Soups and Sauces

OBJECTIVES

After studying this section, you should be able to:

- Describe how to prepare clear, vegetable, and cream soups.
- Explain how to make and use white sauce and gravy.

LOOK FOR THESE TERMS

bouillon
white sauce
aromatic vegetables
au jus

People often think of homemade soups as delicious foods that take a long time to prepare. While that may have been true in the past, today's quick and easy methods can result in soups as flavorful as the ones great-grandma used to make. As you will see, there are also ways to make soups and sauces with less fat than traditional versions.

Kinds of Soups

There are basically three kinds of soups:

❖ **Clear broth** is also called stock, consommé (kahn-soh-MAY), or **bouillon** (BOOL-yon). It is the seasoned liquid made from cooking meat, poultry, fish, or vegetables. The liquid is strained to remove any solids. Serve broth as part of a meal or as a snack. It is also used as a base for sauces and other soups.

A hearty soup is almost a meal in itself. Broth or cream soup might be served as an appetizer or a meal accompaniment.

Section 20.3
Soups and Sauces

Introducing the Section

Motivators

- Prepare samples of the three basic kinds of soups: clear broth, hearty vegetable, and cream soups. Include a hot soup, a cold soup, and a sweet soup. Have students taste the soups. Ask students in what ways this motivator has broadened their definition of a soup.

- Put out samples of flour, cornstarch, tapioca, an egg, a potato, and a legume. Ask students to guess what common cooking purpose all of these foods serve. *(They are all thickeners.)*

Objectives

- Have students read the section objectives. Discuss the purpose of studying the section.

Vocabulary

- Pronounce the terms listed under "Look for These Terms." Have students find the terms and their definitions in the section.

Guided Reading

- Have students look at the headings within Section 20.3 to preview the concepts that will be discussed.

- Have students read the section and complete the appropriate part of the Chapter 20 Study Guide in the *Student Workbook*.

Teacher's Classroom Resources—Section 20.3

Refer to these resources in the TCR package:

Reproducible Lesson Plans

Student Workbook

Extending the Text

Reteaching Activities

Section Quizzes

Testmaker Software

Foods Lab Resources

Food Science Resources

Color Transparencies

Teaching . . .

- **Kinds of Soups**
- **Making Soups**

(text pages 535-537)

Comprehension Check

1. Ask students to describe the three basic kinds of soup. *(clear broth, hearty vegetable soups, cream soups)*

2. Ask students to identify aromatic vegetables. Why are they usually sautéed first when used in soups? *(chopped onions, garlic, celery, and green peppers; to help develop the flavor)*

3. Ask students to explain how you can make a cream soup lower in fat than traditional cream soups. *(Use nonfat dry milk instead of whole milk.)*

4. Ask students to explain why care must be used when cooking milk-based soups in a microwave oven. *(The milk tends to foam up during cooking.)*

❖ **Hearty vegetable soups** are thick soups, made with assorted vegetables, legumes, and grain products. Chunks of cooked meat, poultry, or fish can be added.

❖ **Cream soups** are traditionally made with a **white sauce**—a milk-based sauce thickened with starch—plus cooked vegetables, poultry, or shellfish. Cream soups made this way can be high in fat.

Soups are usually highly nutritious. Some B vitamins and vitamin C may be destroyed by heat, especially if the soup is cooked for a long time. Other water-soluble vitamins and minerals, however, remain in the liquid.

Making Soups

Many people today use canned convenience broths or bouillon cubes as a base for making soup. You can also combine broth with a seasoned vegetable juice for additional flavor. Here are some easy, basic ways to make vegetable and cream soups.

The first step in making most soups is to sauté **aromatic vegetables,** such as chopped onions, garlic, celery, and green peppers, in a small amount of fat. These vegetables are used in small amounts to flavor most soups. Sautéing them first helps develop the flavors. Use a stockpot and about 1 teaspoon (5 mL) of oil.

Vegetable Soup

To make vegetable soup, combine the sautéed aromatic vegetables with broth. Add other vegetables according to the recipe or make up your own combinations. Use at least three or four different vegetables for a rich flavor.

When adding the vegetables, begin with those that take the longest to cook. Then add the remaining vegetables according to the time needed for cooking. Season the soup with herbs and spices. Cover and simmer the soup only until the vegetables are tender.

For variety, flavor, and nutrients, add other foods such as cooked legumes or grain products (pasta, rice, or barley). These foods contain starch and will thicken the soup. You can also add cooked leftover meat and poultry sliced in thin strips or cut into small cubes.

Homemade soup doesn't have to take all day. Try starting with ready-made broth or vegetable juice. Add vegetables, grains, and leftover meat or poultry. A stockpot is useful for making large amounts of soup.

536   **Chapter 20: Food Combinations**

Thinking Skills

Reasoning: Since fat adds flavor to clear broths, ask students why directions for making a broth, or stock, often say to trim excess fat off the meat before making the broth. *(The fat may add flavor, but too much fat adds needless calories and can be harmful. The fat is removed during degreasing anyway, so removing it before cooking saves time later.)*

Problem Solving: Ask students what they could do if they wanted a darker, more flavorful beef broth. *(Brown the meat before putting it into the stock pot.)*

Cream Soup

A traditional cream soup is thickened with a white sauce (see page 538).

You can also make a cream soup using pureed cooked vegetables and nonfat dry milk. This method is quick, easy, and low in fat. The recipe on page 540 is an example of this type of soup. You can vary the recipe by substituting other vegetables, such as chopped broccoli or cauliflower. Just be sure to include either potatoes or 1/4 cup (60 mL) cooked rice to thicken the soup. If you prefer a smooth soup rather than a chunky one, puree all the cooked vegetables (and the rice, if used).

Cooking Soup in the Microwave Oven

Try making your own broth in the microwave oven. It takes much less time than by conventional cooking. Check a microwave cookbook for directions.

Vegetable soups can be easily prepared in the microwave oven. Chop the vegetables into uniform pieces and add hot water or broth. The hot liquid will help speed up the cooking process. Cook larger quantities of soup in a covered container to speed up cooking time. Still, you may find that larger quantities of soup take longer than on a conventional range.

Milk-based soups may foam up during microwave cooking. Follow the directions in the owner's manual for the best results. Be sure to use a large enough container. You may prefer to cook milk-based soups on the conventional range.

Convenience soups can be heated quickly in the microwave oven. When using a temperature probe, heat cream soups to about 140°F (60°C) and other soups to about 160°F (71°C).

Section 20.3: Soups and Sauces **537**

Student Experiences

1. **Display:** Display convenience products to use as a base for making soup. Have students identify other liquids that can be combined with the broth for added nutrition and flavor. *(Key skill: critical thinking)*

2. **Demonstration:** Demonstrate how to sauté aromatic vegetables to flavor soups. *(Key skill: kitchen management skills)*

3. **Class Discussion:** Ask students to identify their favorite types of soups. Discuss how soup can help meet your nutritional needs. How might serving soup as the main dish help stretch the family's food budget? *(Key skill: critical thinking)*

Lab Experience

• Have students create their own combinations of vegetables and prepare a vegetable soup. Have students add other foods such as cooked legumes or grain products for variety, flavor, and nutrients. Students can also add cooked leftover meat and poultry sliced in thin strips or cut into small cubes.

• Have groups of students prepare cream soup using the traditional method and the easier, faster, low-fat method. Have students taste both versions. Compare the taste, fat content, preparation difficulty, and preparation time for the two versions.

Special Needs Strategies

Gifted and Talented: Have students research soups and sauces popular in other parts of the world. Ask students to collect several recipes representing soups and sauces that appeal to them. Have students select one recipe and prepare it.

Teaching . . .

• Sauces and Gravies

(text pages 538-539)

Comprehension Check

1. Ask students what a basic white sauce is and its use. *(A sauce made by thickening milk with flour; as a base for cream soups.)*

2. Ask students to describe the procedure for making a white sauce. *(See page 538.)*

3. Ask the difference between white sauce and pan gravy. *(Pan gravy is made with meat juices instead of milk.)*

Student Experience

1. **Class Discussion:** Discuss ingredients that can be used to thicken liquid to make white sauce or pan gravy. *(Key skill: critical thinking)*

Lab Experience

In groups have students make a thin white sauce, medium, and thick white sauce. Have students compare the three sauces. How would they use each sauce?

TIPS for Success

One reason for lumps in a white sauce is cooking the sauce over too high a heat setting. Slow cooking and patience are the keys to making sauces and gravies without lumps.

Using the Photo

Answer to caption (lower photo): To reduce fat, skim fat off pan juices and use only a small amount, see p. 539 for making lower-fat gravy.

Sauces and Gravies

Sauces and gravies are thickened liquids used to add flavor to cooked food. There are many different kinds of sauces and gravies. Most, however, are variations on a few basic types. Added ingredients and seasonings give each variation a distinct flavor.

Basic White Sauce

The most common sauce is white sauce. It is made by thickening milk with flour.

Flour contains starch granules which lump together as they cook. If flour alone were added to the milk, the mixture would be lumpy. For a smooth sauce, the flour is cooked in fat. The fat coats the starch granules and helps keep them from lumping.

For a medium-thick sauce, use 2 tablespoons (30 mL) each of butter and flour for every 1 cup (250 mL) of milk. For a thinner sauce, use 1 tablespoon (15 mL) each of butter and flour.

Melt the fat and add the flour. Cook the mixture over low heat, stirring constantly, for about two minutes or until the mixture is smooth and bubbly. Gradually add the milk while continuing to stir. Cook the mixture, stirring constantly, until it thickens. The sauce should be thick enough to coat the back of a wooden spoon.

Pan Gravy

Pan gravy is made like white sauce, but with meat juices instead of milk. Remove the meat from the pan and pour the juices into a measuring cup. Skim off and reserve the fat.

TIPS for Success

Rescuing Lumpy Sauce or Gravy

If a few lumps occur, put the sauce or gravy through a strainer or blender. Reheat the mixture, stirring constantly, and serve.

538 Chapter 20: Food Combinations

When making white sauce, stir constantly until the mixture is thick enough to coat a spoon.

Gravy made with pan juices adds flavor to meat. How can you reduce the fat in the gravy?

Food and Nutrition Science

Have students heat 1 cup (250 mL) water in each of three saucepans until boiling. Have them stir one of the following into each saucepan: 1 Tbsp. (15 mL) cornstarch; 1 Tbsp. (15 mL) cornstarch mixed with 1 Tbsp. (15 mL) sugar; 1 Tbsp. (15 mL) cornstarch mixed with 2 Tbsp. (30 mL) cold water. What conclusions do students draw? Ask them to write a summary of their findings.

Creating Sauce Experiment: See the *Food Science Resources* booklet for the "Creating a Smooth Sauce" teaching guide and student experiment worksheet. The experiment determines which preparation method is best for producing a smooth sauce when flour is used as a thickener.

Measure the remaining liquid. For each 1 cup (250 mL) of liquid, use 2 tablespoons (30mL) each of fat and flour. Heat the fat, then blend in the flour and cook the mixture until it is smooth and bubbly. Gradually add the remaining liquid and stir constantly until smooth and thickened. Scrape the bottom of the pan to loosen browned meat particles that add flavor to the gravy.

Lower-Fat Alternatives

White sauce and gravy are high in fat. Consider using seasoned nonfat yogurt in place of white sauce. Instead of serving roasts with gravy, try serving them **au jus,** or "in the juice." Use the pan drippings after the fat has been skimmed off.

To make lower-fat gravy, remove the meat from the pan and skim the fat from the meat broth. Measure the broth. You may need to add some water or boullion to obtain enough broth for gravy. Measure out 2 tablespoons (30 mL) of flour or cornstarch and 1/4 cup (50 mL) of cold water for every 1 cup (250 mL) of broth. (Note: Mixing starch with cold water before adding it to a hot mixture prevents lumping.) Shake the starch and water mixture together in a covered container. Add the starch mixture to the broth and heat the mixture to boiling, stirring constantly. Cook the mixture until it thickens, about one minute.

Traditional French cooking—famous throughout the world—relies on rich sauces for its delicious flavors. *Nouvelle cuisine* ("new cooking") is a more recent style of French cooking. The emphasis has shifted to smaller portions, attractive presentations, more vegetables, and sauces that are lower in fat.

Thickened, defatted pan drippings can add flavor to meat.

■ Section 20.3 Review ■

RECALL THE FACTS

1. Describe how to make a clear broth.

2. Name three aromatic vegetables. Why are they sautéed?

3. Why must flour be coated with fat when making a white sauce?

4. What is a lower-fat alternative to gravy served with roasted meat?

DISCUSS YOUR IDEAS

5. How might a family's food budget be stretched by serving soup as the main dish?

APPLY YOUR LEARNING

6. Create a recipe for a hearty vegetable soup that you can prepare in one hour. What pre-preparation tasks could you do beforehand to cut down even further on the cooking time?

Section 20.3: Soups and Sauces **539**

■ Answers to Section Review ■

1. Cook meat, poultry, fish, or vegetables in a seasoned liquid until done. Strain the resulting broth to remove any solids.
2. *Any three:* Onions, garlic, celery, green peppers; to develop the flavor.
3. To keep the sauce from being lumpy.
4. Serve the roast au jus.
5. Answers will vary. Soups are filling and can stretch meat, poultry, and fish to cover more meals; they can also be made without meat, poultry, or fish.
6. Answers will vary.

20.3 Recipe

Creamy Vegetable Soup

Key Skill: Preparing a vegetable soup

Using the Recipe

- Have students read the recipe and discuss each step. Remind students to use only the amount of oil recommended in the recipe to sauté the vegetables. Adding more than that can make the finished soup seem greasy. Review safety and sanitation procedures that apply to this recipe.
- Have each lab team fill out a work plan. (See the *Foods Lab Resources* booklet.)
- Have students check off the ingredients and equipment listed on the recipe worksheet and prepare the recipe.
- Have students complete the evaluation and questions on the recipe worksheet.

See Also . . .

The *Foods Lab Resources* booklet for the "Creamy Vegetable Soup" recipe worksheet and other recipe alternatives.

Thinking About the Recipe

Read the recipe for "Creamy Vegetable Soup" and answer the following questions.

1. What is used to thicken this soup?
2. How could you prepare a low-sodium version of this recipe?

Creamy Vegetable Soup

Customary	Ingredients	Metric
1	Green pepper, chopped	1
1	Onion, small, chopped	1
3	Celery stalks, chopped	3
1	Garlic clove, chopped or pressed	1
1 tsp.	Oil	5 mL
32-oz. can	Stewed tomatoes	896-g can
3	Potatoes, pared and cubed	3
1 cup	Carrots, sliced	250 mL
1 cup	Corn, frozen or canned	250 mL
1 cup	Green beans, frozen or canned	250 mL
1 cup	Water	250 mL
2	Beef boullion cubes	2
1/2 cup	Instant nonfat dry milk	125 mL

Yield: About 4 servings

Directions

Pan: Dutch oven

1. Sauté green pepper, onion, celery, and garlic in oil.
2. Add stewed tomatoes (with liquid), potatoes, carrots, corn, green beans, water, and beef boullion cubes to sautéed vegetables.
3. Simmer mixture over medium heat until vegetables are tender.
4. Drain the cooking liquid from the vegetables, reserving the liquid.
5. Puree half of the cooked vegetables in a blender or food processor.
6. Return pureed vegetables to the Dutch oven. Thin the mixture with reserved cooking liquid.
7. Add the instant nonfat milk and remaining vegetables. Mix well.
8. Simmer until thoroughly heated.
9. Season to taste and serve hot.

Nutrition Information

Per serving (approximate): 268 calories, 10 g protein, 58 g carbohydrate, 2 g fat, 1.5 mg cholesterol, 1315 mg sodium

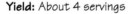

Answers to Thinking About the Recipe

1. Potatoes are the main thickening agent.

2. Use salt-free canned green beans; use low-sodium bouillon.

Casseroles and Other Combinations

OBJECTIVES

After studying this section, you should be able to:

- Plan and prepare hearty one-dish meals using a variety of ingredients, including those low in fat.
- Explain several methods used to prepare one-dish meals.

LOOK FOR THESE TERMS

extender
binder

Depending on the foods used, combination dishes can often provide servings from the five food groups. To complete the meal, add a salad and whole grain bread. Some main dishes can be served over a grain. A stir-fry or stew, for example, tastes great over cooked rice or noodles.

Some common main dish combinations are stews, braised meats with vegetables, stir-fries, pizza, and casseroles.

Stews

Stewing is an efficient way to cook less tender cuts of meat or poultry. Cut meat into cubes, but leave poultry in pieces. Remove poultry skin to reduce fat. Browning meat before stewing it adds flavor and color to the gravy.

Fish and shellfish stews are delicious, too. Oyster stew, for instance, is traditional for some people during holiday seasons.

Many different kinds of vegetables can be used in stews. Starchy ones, such as potatoes, add thickness. If you're not following a recipe, make up your own combination. Also consider using fruits, such as dried apricots.

An oyster stew is one example of a hearty main dish combination. What would you serve with it to make an appealing, nutritionally balanced meal?

Section 20.4: Casseroles and Other Combinations   **541**

Introducing the Section

Motivators

- Ask students to identify as many examples of one-dish meals as they can.
- Display cookware and appliances that lend themselves to one-dish meals. Ask students to tell what these items have in common. Discuss how specialized cookware and appliances can aid in simplifying food preparation for busy people.

Objectives

- Have students read the section objectives. Discuss the purpose of studying the section.

Vocabulary

- Pronounce the terms listed under "Look for These Terms." Have students find the terms and their definitions in the section.

Guided Reading

- Have students look at the headings within Section 20.4 to preview the concepts that will be discussed.
- Have students read the section and complete the appropriate part of the Chapter 20 Study Guide in the *Student Workbook*.

Teacher's Classroom Resources—Section 20.4

Refer to these resources in the TCR package:
Reproducible Lesson Plans
Student Workbook
Extending the Text
Reteaching Activities

Section Quizzes
Testmaker Software
Foods Lab Resources
Color Transparencies

- **Stews**
- **Braised Foods**
- **Stir-Frying**

(text pages 541-544)

Comprehension Check

1. Ask students to identify liquids that can be substituted for some of the water in stews. What is the advantage of doing this? (broth, vegetable juice; adds flavor and variety)

2. Ask students to identify typical cooking times for beef stew in different appliances. *(Pressure cooker: 30 minutes; microwave oven: 1 hour; range top or conventional oven: 2 1/2 hours; slow cooker: 9 hours.)*

3. Discuss the basic method for braising a cut of beef. *(Brown the beef and place in Dutch oven or heavy pot; add enough liquid to cover the bottom; add seasonings; cover and bake at 350°F (180°C) or simmer on top of the range.)*

4. Ask students to explain why it is important to be organized and to know exactly what you are going to do and in what order when you stir-fry foods. *(The foods cook so quickly that there is no time to do preparation tasks such as chopping vegetables.)*

Although water is the basic liquid in stew, try substituting other liquids, such as broth or vegetable juice, for part of it. Tomato juice, for example, contains acid which helps tenderize meat and adds flavor.

Cooking time depends on the tenderness of the meat. Beef may need two or three hours to cook, while poultry may cook in an hour. Because fish is already tender, fish stews take little time to cook. As a rule, cook them just until the fish flakes and the flavors are blended.

Cooking times also vary with the appliance used. A beef stew can cook in thirty minutes in a pressure cooker, an hour in a microwave oven, two and one-half hours on the range top or in a conventional oven, or about nine hours in a slow cooker.

Vegetables and fruits may need different amounts of cooking time, depending on tenderness and the size of the pieces. Add them to the stew according to the amount of cooking time needed. Those that will take longest to cook, such as fresh carrot pieces, should be added early in the process. Those that

Fresh or dried fruits can be included in stews. They add nutrients and complement the flavor of the other ingredients.

take less time to cook, such as frozen corn, can be added later. Add canned vegetables or leftover cooked vegetables near the end of cooking time.

To stew meat on the range top, brown cubes of meat without added fat in a large pan. Remove the meat to a clean plate. Sauté aromatic vegetables in a small amount of fat, then return the browned meat to the pan. Add seasonings and enough liquid to cover the meat. Cover the pan and simmer until tender, adding the other ingredients during the cooking time as explained above.

Braised Foods

Braising is used to cook large, less tender cuts of meat and poultry. It can also be used to give flavor to tender cuts. For example, fish is sometimes braised in a flavorful sauce.

Meat is often browned before braising; usually poultry is not. Place the meat or poultry in a Dutch oven or heavy pot. Add enough liquid to cover the bottom and create steam. Add seasonings such as onions, garlic, herbs, and spices. Cover the pan and bake at 350°F (180°C) or simmer on top of the range.

Add other vegetables as the meat braises. The timing depends on how long they will take to cook. Use large pieces of vegetables, such as halved or quartered potatoes and carrot halves. Add quick-cooking vegetables, such as peas and corn, near the end of the cooking time.

Check the food regularly to make sure there is enough liquid covering the bottom of the pan. Add hot water when needed. Cold water will increase the cooking time. To thicken the gravy, add a diced potato an hour before serving.

The cooking time depends on the size and cut of the meat. Cook until the ingredients are tender and the flavors are well blended.

More About Stir-Fry Combinations

An unlimited number of stir-fry combinations are possible. The following suggestions will get you started:
- Sliced raw beef, garlic, beef bouillon, soy sauce, ginger, onion, fresh tomato, broccoli, green pepper, water chestnuts.
- Raw chicken breast, chicken bouillon, ginger, garlic, green onion, zucchini, snow peas.

The French term *fricassee* (FRIK-uh-SEE) means to cut up meat, stew it or fry it, and serve it in a sauce or its own gravy. In America the term has come to refer to stewed dishes of chicken or veal.

Consider using fresh or canned fruit to flavor the sauce. Some tasty combinations are pork with apples (applesauce or peeled and quartered fresh apples), poultry with pineapple or orange juice, fish with lemon or grapefruit juice, beef with prunes or dried apricots, and lamb with canned plums.

Stir-Frying

Stir-frying is a quick and easy way to make a flavorful, nutritious dish. It can be a low-fat dish if you choose the ingredients carefully.

The secret of a successful stir-fry is to cut up all the ingredients and assemble them in the order in which they are to be cooked. Because stir-frying is fast, there's no time to stop and cut up foods while you're cooking.

Cut raw meat or poultry across the grain into thin, narrow strips. Meat that has been chilled in the freezer will be easier to slice. Cubes or strips of tofu or cooked meat, poultry, or fish can also be used.

Select a variety of vegetables. Cut each into pieces of the same size for even cooking.

The wok is ideal for stir-frying. It has a rounded bottom and sits on a metal ring which is placed on the range. Electric woks are also available. If you don't have a wok, you can use a large skillet.

Heat just a small amount of oil in the skillet or wok. High heat is necessary to cook food quickly and give vegetables a crispy texture. The wok or skillet is hot enough for cooking when a few drops of water sizzle and evaporate immediately. Add seasonings and cook for a few seconds to flavor the oil. Stir foods constantly as they cook, or they will burn.

Begin stir-frying raw meat, poultry, or fish first. When cooked, remove it to a clean platter. Next, cook dense, fibrous vegetables

You can use almost any combination of protein foods, fruits, vegetables, seasonings, and sauces in a stir-fry. Be sure to slice each type of food uniformly for even cooking.

Section 20.4: Casseroles and Other Combinations   **543**

Comprehension Check

1. Ask students to list the basic types of ingredients used to make a pizza. *(base or crust, seasonings, sauce, toppings, and grated cheese)*

2. Ask students to explain the purpose of the extender and the binder in a casserole. *(The extender helps thicken the casserole; the binder helps hold it together.)*

3. Ask students to give examples of extenders and binders for casseroles. *(Extenders: dry bread crumbs, cooked diced potatoes, pasta, rice, grits, barley, beans that have been cooked and mashed; binders: skim milk, broth, fruit juice, soup, thickened sauces.)*

Student Experiences

1. **Group Discussion:** Have students work in groups to develop a list bases, binders, and extenders in addition to those mentioned in the text. *(Key skills: writing, creative thinking)*

2. **Recipe Analysis:** Have students find recipes for casseroles and list the food groups contained in each. Have students compile a written list of well-balanced main-dish casseroles that sound appealing to them. *(Key skills: writing, analysis)*

Lab Experience

• Have students work in groups to prepare low-fat versions of pizza using their own choice of ingredients.

544

> ### Stir-Fry Suggestions
>
> ❖ **Seasonings:** 1/4 to 1/2 teaspoon (1 to 3 mL) grated raw ginger, pressed garlic, crushed dried thyme or marjoram.
> ❖ **Protein:** 1 cup (250 mL) tofu, meat, poultry, or fish.
> ❖ **Vegetables or fruits:** 3 cups (750 mL) of at least three vegetables and fruits.
> ❖ **Sauce:** Mix 1 tablespoon (15 mL) cornstarch with 1 tablespoon (15 mL) tamari sauce, soy sauce, or prepared mustard to make a paste. Add 1 cup (250 mL) canned broth, fruit juice, or vegetable juice and mix well.

such as broccoli, carrots, and cauliflower. (You can also precook them in the microwave oven.) Then cook the other vegetables. Add the cooked meat, poultry, or fish when the vegetables are done.

As you cook, avoid overloading the pan. Putting too much food in the pan at one time will result in vegetables that are steamed, not stir-fried.

After all the foods in the stir-fry have been cooked, add a sauce for flavor. The sauce is usually mixed ahead of time and allowed to stand until needed. Stir it just before adding it to the wok or skillet.

The box on this page will give you ideas for making stir-fries. The recipe on page 545 shows one possible combination of ingredients.

Pizza

Pizza is a hearty main dish served on a crust. Traditional pizza calls for a yeast bread crust topped with a tomato-based sauce, cheese (generally mozzarella), and other toppings. However, many variations are possible. Pizza can be baked in any large shallow pan.

Here are some suggestions for making pizza. For a low-fat pizza, use smaller amounts of low-fat or fat-free cheese.

❖ **Base.** One ready-made or homemade crust.
❖ **Seasonings.** Small amounts of garlic, oregano, basil, marjoram, pepper, cayenne, cinnamon, nutmeg, or chili powder.
❖ **Sauce.** Canned pizza, pasta, taco, or chili sauce; salsa; pureed fresh or canned fruit.
❖ **Toppings.** Chopped broccoli, cauliflower, green or red peppers; grated carrots; sliced mushrooms, onions, or pineapple slices; cooked or canned meat, poultry, or fish; browned, drained ground beef or sausage.
❖ **Grated cheese.** Mozzarella, feta, Gouda, Cheddar, Swiss, or Parmesan.

Pizza is generally baked in an oven preheated to 425°F (220°C). The cooking time may vary depending on the size pizza you are making and the ingredients used. Check a cookbook for cooking times.

It's easy to make pizza at home. Try new combinations, such as a rice crust with vegetable toppings.

> ### More About Pizza
>
> Pizzas are usually round, but you can bake them in any large, shallow pan. Try various shapes for variety.
>
> You may also want to try these combinations of pizza ingredients:
> • Tex-Mex: salsa, chili powder, ground beef and Mexican sausage, green pepper, onion; cheddar cheese.
> • Polynesian: drained, crushed pineapple and applesauce; ground ginger; tamari sauce; thinly-sliced cooked ham or chicken; mozzarella or Swiss cheese.
> • All-vegetable: spaghetti sauce, basil, oregano, broccoli, zucchini, onions, red or green pepper, mozzarella and Parmesan cheese.

Thinking About the Recipe

Read the recipe for "Whitefish Stir-Fry" and answer the following questions.

1. What would you do if you did not have already-cooked fish on hand to use in the recipe?
2. How can you tell when the oil is hot enough for cooking?

Whitefish Stir Fry

Customary	Ingredients	Metric
1 Tbsp.	Cornstarch	15 mL
1 Tbsp.	Tamari sauce	15 mL
1 cup	Pineapple juice	250 mL
1 Tbsp.	Oil	15 mL
1/2 tsp.	Fresh ginger, grated	2 mL
1	Garlic clove, pressed	1
1 cup	Snow peas	250 mL
1/2 cup	Green bell pepper, chopped	125 mL
1/2 cup	Red bell pepper, chopped	125 mL
1/2 cup	Water chestnuts, sliced	125 mL
1 cup	Pineapple chunks	250 mL
1 cup	Whitefish fillets, cooked and cubed	250 mL
	Hot cooked rice	

Yield: 4 servings

Directions

Pan: Wok or large skillet
Temperature: Medium-high

1. Combine cornstarch with tamari sauce. Add pineapple juice and set aside.
2. Heat oil in wok. Add ginger and garlic and cook for a few seconds to flavor the oil.
3. Add snow peas, green and red pepper, water chestnuts, and pineapple chunks to wok. Cook, stirring constantly, until snow peas and pepper are tender but still slightly crisp.
4. Add cooked whitefish to vegetables in wok.
5. Mix the sauce from Step 1 and pour it over the food. Cook, stirring constantly, until mixture is thickened and fish is hot.
6. Serve over hot cooked rice.

Nutrition Information

Per serving (approximate—without rice): 226 calories, 13 g protein, 28 g carbohydrate, 7 g fat, 34 mg cholesterol, 286 mg sodium

Section 20.4: Casseroles and Other Combinations   **545**

20.4 Recipe

Whitefish Stir Fry

Key Skill: Stir-frying

Using the Recipe

- Have students read the recipe and discuss each step. Caution students not to allow too much food to cook in the wok or skillet at one time to avoid steaming the food. Review safety and sanitation procedures that apply to this recipe.
- Have each lab team fill out a work plan. (See the *Foods Lab Resources* booklet.)
- Have students check off the ingredients and equipment listed on the recipe worksheet and prepare the recipe.
- Have students complete the evaluation and questions on the recipe worksheet.

See Also . . .

The *Foods Lab Resources* booklet for the "Whitefish Stir Fry" recipe worksheet and other recipe alternatives.

Answers to Thinking About the Recipe

1. Answers will vary but may include: adapt recipe to include stir-frying raw fish before cooking vegetables; cook raw fish in microwave oven and proceed with recipe; substitute canned fish.

2. A few drops of water should sizzle and evaporate immediately.

Completing the Section

Review

- Ask students to summarize the main ideas in this section.
- Have students complete the Section Review. (Answers appear below.)

Evaluation

- Have students prepare a menu for a meal featuring stewed, braised, or stir-fried foods. The menu should be nutritional and appealing.
- Have students take the quiz for Section 20.4. (Refer to the *Section Quizzes* booklet or use the *Testmaker Software*.)

Reteaching

- Ask students to create a poster that lists guidelines for stir-frying foods.
- Refer to the *Reteaching Activities* booklet for the Section 20.4 activity worksheet.

Enrichment

- Ask students to research casseroles common in the 18th century in the United States. In what ways does environment affect the types of foods we cook and eat?

Closure

- Ask students to debate the question: "Are specialized small cooking appliances are essential for busy people?"

Casseroles

A casserole is a tasty blend of cooked ingredients which are heated together to develop flavor. The base of a casserole provides its main texture and flavor. A casserole also needs an **extender,** such as pasta or rice, to help thicken it, and a liquid **binder** to hold it together. Seasonings and aromatic vegetables give more flavor and texture.

Here are some suggestions for casserole combinations:

- ❖ *Base.* Cubed, cooked meat, poultry, or fish; browned, drained ground beef or turkey; grated or cubed cheese.
- ❖ *Vegetables.* Any cooked or canned vegetables.
- ❖ *Extenders.* Dry bread crumbs; cooked diced potatoes, pasta, rice, grits, or barley; cooked, mashed dry beans.
- ❖ *Aromatic vegetables.* Chopped celery or parsley; sautéed mushrooms, onions, or chives.
- ❖ *Seasonings.* Dried, crushed oregano, basil, thyme, or marjoram; ground ginger, mace, cinnamon, chili powder, cayenne or black pepper. Start out using 1/4 teaspoon (1 mL). You can always add more to taste.
- ❖ *Binder.* Skim milk, broth, fruit juice, soup, or a thickened sauce.

To make a casserole for four people, try combining 1 cup (250 mL) of each ingredient choice (except seasonings) in a greased 1½ quart (1.5 L) baking dish with a cover. Bake the casserole about 30 minutes in an oven preheated to 350° F (180° C). Remove the cover after 20 minutes if the liquid needs to thicken.

To microwave a casserole, combine the ingredients in a ungreased baking dish with a cover. Cook the casserole at 100 percent power for six to 18 minutes, depending on the ingredients. Stir once or twice during cooking and rotate the casserole after half the cooking time.

In what ways do casseroles save time and energy when planning and preparing meals?

■ Section 20.4 Review ■

RECALL THE FACTS

1. What kind of meat works well for stewing and braising? Give two examples.

2. Why must stir-fry ingredients be cut up and assembled before you start cooking?

3. Name the main parts of any casserole. Give an example of each.

DISCUSS YOUR IDEAS

4. Discuss reasons why food combinations are good, economical choices for many families.

APPLY YOUR LEARNING

5. Develop a list of at least six ingredients that you could use in making three of the one-dish meals discussed in this section. What foods might you need to have on hand for "emergency" one-dish meals?

■ Answers to Section Review ■

1. Tougher cuts. Examples will vary.
2. Because the foods cook so quickly that there is no time to cut up or assemble them after you start cooking.
3. Base (meat, poultry, or fish; browned, drained ground beef or turkey; grated or cubed cheese); extender (dry bread crumbs, cooked diced potatoes, pasta, rice, grits, barley, cooked mashed dry beans); binder (skim milk, broth, fruit juice, soup, thickened sauce).
4. Answers will vary.
5. Answers will vary.

Career PROFILE

Rick Joseph
Pizza Maker

Thinking About . . . Making Pizza

Have students think about other questions they would like to ask Rich Joseph about his job. (Examples: Do you plan to go into the restaurant business when you finish college? What rules does the restaurant have about personal hygiene and kitchen sanitation? What's the secret to hand-tossing pizza dough?)

Student Opportunities

Students planning on a career in food preparation may want to volunteer in the kitchen of a local hospital, soup kitchen, or senior citizen's center. Part-time work may also be available at local restaurants.

Occupational Outlook

People who make pizza and do other food preparation jobs advance on the basis of their skill and knowledge. An expert in food preparation may become a chef at an expensive restaurant or may even own a restaurant some day.

CURRENT POSITION

"I'm a college student working part-time at a pizza restaurant."

RESPONSIBILITIES

"I make the dough, prepare the other ingredients, and then put them all together to make the pizzas. When I'm not cooking, I make sure my area of the kitchen is clean. I also help train new workers."

SKILLS

"Employers are looking for people who can handle responsibility and get along well with other workers. The food preparation skills can be learned through on-the-job training. My previous experience as a short-order cook helped me get this job. Oh, and you have to be willing to follow rules about personal hygiene and kitchen sanitation. They're very important for any food service worker."

WORK ENVIRONMENT

"I work mostly nights and weekends, and spend a lot of time on my feet in a hot kitchen!"

FAVORITE PART OF THE JOB

"I've always enjoyed cooking, and pizza is especially fun to make. I like using my creativity to come up with new flavor combinations for our weekly specials. And I love to hand-toss the dough the traditional way—it gives my work a special flair, and it entertains the customers."

- Does Rick seem to enjoy his work? Explain.
- What aspects of Rick's job do you think you would enjoy? Why?

547

For More Information

For additional information about food preparation careers, encourage students to contact:
- The Educational Foundation of the National Restaurant Association, 20 N. Wacker Dr., Suite 2620, Chicago, IL 60606
- American Culinary Federation, P.O. Box 3466, St. Augustine, FL 32084

Review

• Have students complete the Chapter Review. (Answers appear below.)

Evaluation

• Have students write a short essay describing the topics covered in this chapter.

• Have students take the test for Chapter 20. (Refer to the *Chapter and Unit Tests* booklet or construct your own test using the *Testmaker Software*.

▮ ANSWERS ▮

REVIEWING FACTS

1. A traditional sandwich uses two slices of bread; a fancy sandwich has bread cut into fancy shapes, and a club sandwich has three slices of bread.

2. *Any two:* Rolls, pita bread, taco shells, bagels, or tortillas.

3. *Any two:* Use a freezer gel pack, insulated lunch bags, vacuum bottles; to keep bacteria from growing and spoiling the food.

4. They contain eggs, so the oil doesn't separate from other ingredients.

5. Yes.

6. Both are thick and can contain vegetables; cream soups are traditionally made with white sauce.

7. Add a small amount of fat to the mixture.

8. To create a darker, more flavorful stew.

9. Just enough to cover the bottom.

10. It cooks the vegetables while keeping them crisp.

CHAPTER 20 REVIEW

SUMMARY

SECTION 20.1
Sandwiches, Snacks, and Packed Lunches: Sandwiches can be as varied, nutritious, and hearty as the ingredients from which they are made. Choose breads, fillings, and toppings creatively. Nutritious, easy-to-prepare snacks are part of a healthful eating plan. When packing lunches, keep hot foods hot and cold foods cold.

SECTION 20.2
Salads and Dressings: Salads tend to be nutritious and low in calories. They may include greens, fresh fruits or vegetables, cheese, and cooked grains, legumes, meat, poultry, fish, or eggs. Basic dressings include oil-based, mayonnaise, cooked, and dairy varieties. Salads are assembled and served in a number of ways.

SECTION 20.3
Soups and Sauces: There are three basic kinds of soup: clear broth, hearty vegetable, and cream soup. Soups, which are usually very nutritious, often rely on aromatic vegetables for flavoring. You can use quick and easy methods to make low-fat soup. Sauces and gravies can add flavor to cooked foods. You can make a basic white sauce from a mixture of fat, flour, and seasonings added to milk. Pan gravy is made with meat juice.

SECTION 20.4
Casseroles and Other Combinations: One-dish meals can be healthful choices, depending on the ingredients. Types of one-dish meals include stews, braised dishes, stir-fries, pizza, and casseroles. Combination dishes lend themselves to variety and creativity in the kind and amounts of ingredients used.

548

REVIEWING FACTS

1. What are the differences between a traditional sandwich, a fancy sandwich, and a club sandwich? (20.1)

2. Name two kinds of bread, other than sliced bread, which can be used to make sandwiches. (20.1)

3. What are two ways to keep packed lunches cold? Why is the temperature of the food important? (20.1)

4. What is the basic difference between an oil-based dressing and a mayonnaise dressing? (20.2)

5. How should leafy greens be washed? (20.2)

6. Name one way cream soups and hearty vegetable soups are the same and one way they are different. (20.3)

7. When making a sauce, how can you keep the flour from becoming lumpy? (20.3)

8. Why is meat often browned before stewing? (20.4)

9. When braising, how much liquid should you add to the pan? (20.4)

10. Why is high heat essential for stir-frying? (20.4)

LEARNING BY DOING

1. ***Taste test:*** Plan and prepare one or two sandwich fillings and toppings. Use a variety of breads to make up enough sandwiches so that members of the class can sample a piece of each sandwich. (20.1)

2. ***Foods lab:*** Plan and prepare a salad luncheon and invite some teachers to share it. (20.2)

3. **Foods lab:** In groups, choose and prepare several foods to stir-fry. Chop vegetables and slice meats uniformly and arrange them in cooking order. One group should prepare a mixture to make sauce. Another could cook rice to serve with the stir-fry. Choose a designated "stir-fryer" or take turns stirring the mixture. (20.4)

THINKING CRITICALLY

1. **Identifying cause and effect:** You decide to take packed lunches to school. Will your lunches the first week or so of school be different from those later on during the year? Why or why not? If your lunches tend to be the same, what effect will that have on you? (20.1)

2. **Determining accuracy:** Compare the labels of several popular salad dressings including some varieties lower in fat. Rate them in terms of fat content and primary ingredients. How do their ratings compare with the claims or descriptions on the label? (20.2)

3. **Comparing and contrasting:** Examine a can of ready-made gravy, a package of gravy mix, and a can of cream soup, such as mushroom, that may be used for gravy. Using the same serving size for each, calculate the calories and fat. Which rates the best? The worst? How do your findings compare with the commonly-held assumption that gravies are a calorie-laden addition to a meal? How do they compare to other sauces? (20.3)

4. **Recognizing alternatives:** You have all the ingredients to make stew for dinner—all except the stew meat. Could you alter the recipe using another meat or no meat at all? Why or why not? How? (20.4)

MAKING DECISIONS AND SOLVING PROBLEMS

What Would You Do?

1. Your sports team is leaving for an all-day tournament in the morning. The coach told each of you to pack one meal to eat at noon and another to eat in the evening because there will be no stops along the way. (20.1)

2. Your family needs to cut down on cholesterol. Tossed salad is on your menu often—as well as oil-based and mayonnaise salad dressings. (20.2)

3. It's your turn to cook soup and you're short of fresh ingredients. You do, however, have loads of leftovers. (20.3)

LINKING YOUR STUDIES

1. **Social studies:** Use library references or cookbooks to find out what sandwiches and salads are popular in other cultures. Report to the class. (20.1, 20.2)

2. **Math:** Alter the yield of a soup recipe to make one or two servings. Using a microwave cookbook (or experimenting on your own), figure out how long it would take to cook the soup in a microwave oven as compared to a conventional range. What can you conclude about cooking a single serving of soup in the microwave? (20.3)

3. **Writing:** Write a short essay on one of the following topics:

   A. The sandwiches I ate as a child were memorable. (20.1)

   B. If I were a salad, I would be a (name a type of salad) because... (20.2)

   C. Soup is more than a meal: it is a way of showing you care. (20.3)

   D. Pizza is an almost perfect food. (20.4)

LEARNING BY DOING

Answers to "Learning by Doing" activities will vary. Evaluate students on the effort they put into the activities as well as their results.

THINKING CRITICALLY

1. Answers will vary. Packed lunches should be varied from day to day. Too much repetition can be boring. Hot foods may sound better in cold weather, and salads and sandwiches may sound better in hot weather.

2. Answers will vary.

3. Answers will vary.

4. Answers will vary. In most cases, you could substitute another meat or even omit the meat if you made appropriate nutritional substitutions.

MAKING DECISIONS AND SOLVING PROBLEMS

Answers to "Making Decisions and Solving Problems" activities will vary. Encourage students to give reasons for their answers.

LINKING YOUR STUDIES

Answers to "Linking Your Studies" activities will vary.

549

Planning the Chapter

Chapter Overview

Section 21.1: Ingredients and Techniques for Baking

Section 21.2: Quick Breads

Section 21.3: Yeast Breads and Rolls

Section 21.4: Cakes, Cookies, and Pies

Introducing the Chapter

Motivators

- When students arrive in class, have cookies or quick bread baking in the oven. Let the aroma introduce the lesson topic.

- Invite students to share their baking experiences, whether success stories or tales of bread that wouldn't rise and pie crust that stuck to the counter. Point out that a familiarity with baking ingredients, tools, and techniques can put "baker's magic" in anyone's hands.

Teacher's Classroom Resources—Chapter 21

Refer to these resources in the TCR package:

Enrichment Activities

Chapter and Unit Tests

Testmaker Software

CHAPTER 21

Baking

550

Cooperative Learning Suggestions

Initiate a Co-op Co-op activity. Have students bring their family's favorite recipes for baked goods from home. Have students work in groups to sort the recipes by type of baked product. Have each group alphabetize one category of baked goods. Arrange to have the recipes typed and edited to create a Family Bakery Recipe Collection. Have students design a cover and section dividers for the booklet. Use the recipe collection as gifts to parents, teachers, guest speakers, etc.

Ingredients and Techniques for Baking

OBJECTIVES

After studying this section, you should be able to:

- Identify the basic ingredients in baking and the function of each.
- Name methods for combining ingredients.
- Explain how to select and prepare pans for baking.
- Compare conventional and microwave baking.

LOOK FOR THESE TERMS

gluten
leavening agent
knead

How can just a few basic ingredients make such taste-tempting treats as a cinnamon yeast roll, a rich buttery cake, or an apple pie with a crust that melts in your mouth? The secret lies in the amounts of the ingredients used and how they are combined and baked. With a little understanding of baking ingredients and techniques, you can prepare a wide array of delicious baked products.

Ingredient Basics

All baked products are made by using a combination of the following basic ingredients: flour, liquid, leavening agents, fat, sweeteners, eggs, and flavoring. Some of these ingredients affect the nutrient density. Baked goods are generally nutritious, but many are high in fat, sugar, and calories.

Ingredients such as these are common to many different baked goods. Each ingredient has a specific role to play in the mixture.

Section 21.1: Ingredients and Techniques for Baking   551

Section 21.1
Ingredients and Techniques for Baking

Introducing the Section

Motivators

- Ask students to identify ingredients they have used in baking. Point out that all baked products are made from just a few basic ingredients. The different products result from differences in amounts of ingredients, the order in which the ingredients are combined, how they are mixed, and how they are baked.
- Display several baked products. Have students point out the differences in the appearance and textures of the products.

Objectives

- Have students read the section objectives. Discuss the purpose of studying the section.

Vocabulary

- Pronounce the terms listed under "Look for These Terms." Have students find the terms and their definitions in the section.

Guided Reading

- Have students look at the headings within Section 21.1 to preview the concepts that will be discussed.
- Have students read the section and complete the appropriate part of the Chapter 21 Study Guide in the *Student Workbook*.

Comprehension Check

1. Ask students to list three liquids commonly used in baking. *(water, milk, and buttermilk)*

2. Ask students to list and describe leavening agents used in baked products. *(See list on page 553.)*

3. Discuss the various sweeteners available. Why is it important to read the manufacturer's directions when using artificial sweeteners? *(Sugar, honey, corn syrup, molasses, powdered sugar, artificial sweeteners; because some are not suitable for baking.)*

4. Ask students to discuss flavorings that are commonly used in baked goods. *(fruits, nuts, herbs, spices, extracts)*

While all-purpose flour is the most commonly used type, there are others. Top row, left to right: pastry, durum, oat, soy, and triticale flours. Middle row, left to right: barley, millet, rice, and buckwheat flours. Bottom row, left to right: unbleached flour, whole wheat flour, cornmeal, and rye flour.

Flour

Flour is usually one of the main ingredients in baked products. The protein and starch in flour make up most of the structure. One of the proteins is called **gluten** (GLOO-ten). Gluten affects the texture of the product and helps determine how a product will rise. As you will see later on, other ingredients also affect the texture.

When liquid and flour are mixed, the starch absorbs some of the liquid. More is absorbed as the product bakes.

There are many types of flours, which vary in gluten content. *All-purpose flour*—a wheat flour—gives good results for most products. *Bread flour* has the highest gluten content and gives bread a strong structure. *Cake flour* contains less gluten and gives cakes a tender structure.

Whole wheat flour has weaker gluten than all-purpose flour. Products made with only whole wheat flour rise less and have a heavy texture. Other whole grain flours, such as rye or cornmeal, have either weak gluten or no gluten. They are generally combined with all-purpose flour in equal proportions. Stir whole grain flours rather than sift them—the particles are too large to go though a sifter.

Whole grain flours should be stored in the refrigerator to keep them fresh. Store other flours in an airtight container in a cool, dry place.

Liquid

Liquid is needed to help form the structure of the product. It takes part in the many physical and chemical changes that occur during baking. Water and milk are the most common liquids used in baking. Milk adds flavor and nutrients and helps baked goods brown better. To reduce fat in a recipe, use skim milk instead of whole milk.

Some recipes call for buttermilk, which gives a slightly tangy flavor. Buttermilk also makes the mixture more acid and affects the kind of leavening needed.

Leavening

Most baked products include a leavening agent. **Leavening agents** provide air, steam, or gas to help baked products rise. This makes the baked product less compact and gives it a softer texture.

More About Leavening

• Baking powder includes an ingredient to absorb moisture, such as cornstarch, so it does not lose its leavening power. Because baking powder is highly perishable, it should be stored in a cool, dry place and used before the expiration date on the container.

Special Needs Strategies

Gifted and Talented: Have students find out more about how leavening agents work. Have students design a demonstration based on their findings to share with the class.

Here is a description of how each leavening agent works:

❖ **Air** is trapped in mixtures as they are beaten. Creaming fat and sugar, sifting flour, and adding beaten egg whites are some of the ways to add air. When the mixture is heated, the air expands and the product rises. Angel food cake is leavened mainly by air in beaten egg whites.

❖ **Steam** leavens products that contain high amounts of water. As the product bakes, the water heats and produces steam. Steam expands, causing the product to rise. Popovers and cream puffs use steam for leavening.

❖ **Yeast** is a microorganism that produces carbon dioxide gas as it grows. It needs food (such as flour or sugar), liquid, and a warm temperature to grow. Several forms of yeast are available. *Active dry yeast* and *quick-rising dry yeast* come as dry granules in a packet. The quick-rising type leavens the dough about twice as quickly. Both can be stored at room temperature. *Compressed yeast* comes in individually wrapped cakes and must be refrigerated. Use yeast before the expiration date on the package.

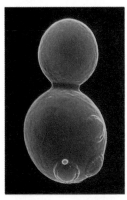

Under the right conditions, yeast cells multiply (shown here greatly magnified). They also produce carbon dioxide, which causes the dough to rise.

❖ **Baking soda** is used whenever the recipe calls for an acid liquid such as buttermilk, yogurt, or sour milk. It produces carbon dioxide gas when combined with liquids.

❖ **Baking powder** is leavening made of baking soda and a powdered acid such as cream of tartar. The most common type, double-acting baking powder, releases some carbon dioxide gas when it is first mixed with a liquid. The remainder is released when it is heated.

Fat

Fat adds richness, flavor, and tenderness to baked products. Fats can be solid or liquid. Shortening, lard, butter, and margarine are solid fats. Oils are liquid fats.

Solid and liquid fats cannot be substituted for one another. In place of butter or shortening, you can use regular margarine, but do not use soft, whipped, or liquid margarine or spreads. They may contain water or oil which can affect the results. You can also substitute solid shortening for butter or margarine. Any cooking oil may be used in baking, as long as it has a mild flavor.

Refrigerate lard, butter, and margarine. Store shortening and oils at room temperature unless the label directs otherwise.

Section 21.1: Ingredients and Techniques for Baking   **553**

Student Experiences

1. **Taste Test:** Have students taste baked products made with water, milk, and buttermilk. What differences can students observe? Discuss differences in nutritive value of the products. Point out that buttermilk also affects the kind of leavening needed. *(Key skill: evaluation)*

2. **Observation:** Display different types of flour used in baking. Ask students to observe and taste the flour and list differences in color, taste, and texture. Point out that the flour most commonly used for baking is wheat flour. *(Key skill: evaluation)*

3. **Recipe Analysis:** Photocopy and distribute to students recipes for baked products that use a variety of leavening agents. Ask students to identify the leavening agent, the gas produced during baking, and other ingredients that make the leavening action possible. *(Key skill: reading)*

Food and Nutrition Science

Reaction Speed Experiment: See the *Food Science Resources* booklet for the "Reaction Speed of Chemical Leavening Agents" teaching guide and student experiment worksheet. The experiment tests the effects and reaction times of leavening agents mixed with liquids.

Effects of Sugar and Salt Experiment: See the *Food Science Resources* booklet for the "Effects of Sugar and Salt on Yeast Growth" teaching guide and student experiment worksheet. The experiment tests the effects of sugar and salt on the leavening action of yeast.

Teaching . . .

• **Combining the Ingredients**

(text pages 554-556)

Comprehension Check

1. Ask students to explain why it is important to mix or stir flour and liquid ingredients only as long as directed by the recipe. *(The texture is affected by how much the gluten develops; gluten is developed by mixing.)*

2. Ask students to list and describe four types of batters and doughs. *(Pour batters are thin enough to pour; drop batters are thick and are usually spooned into pans; soft doughs are soft and sticky but can be touched and handled; stiff doughs are firm to the touch and are easy to work with and cut.)*

3. Ask students to tell what kneading is and explain its purpose. *(Working dough with the hands; to further mix the ingredients and develop the gluten.)*

Eggs

Eggs add flavor, nutrients, richness, and color to baked products. They also help to form the structure. When beaten, eggs add air to the mixture. To reduce fat and cholesterol, two egg whites can usually be substituted for one whole egg.

Sweeteners

Sugar is the most commonly used sweetener. It helps make baked products tender, adds sweetness and flavor, and helps the crust to brown. Granulated white sugar and brown sugar are used in many recipes. Other sweeteners include honey, corn syrup, molasses, and powdered sugar. Some artificial sweeteners are suitable for baking, but others are not. Follow the manufacturers' recommendations.

Store most sweeteners in tightly covered containers in a cool place. Some sweeteners should be refrigerated after opening. Follow label directions.

Flavorings

Fruits and nuts add both flavor and texture to baked goods. Herbs, spices, and extracts are used in small amounts to add flavor. Extracts are flavorings in a liquid form. Vanilla and almond are two common varieties. Store herbs, spices, and extracts in tightly closed containers.

Hawaii

Combining the Ingredients

The characteristics of a baked product depend on not only what ingredients are used, but how they are combined. During the mixing process, changes take place that affect the texture of the finished product.

The Role of Gluten

When flour and liquid are mixed together, the gluten in flour "develops," or becomes strong and elastic. It forms a network of tiny air cells. Air, steam, or gas produced by the leavening agent is trapped by these cells. When heated, the trapped gasses expand and the product rises.

The longer the mixing time, the greater the extent to which gluten is developed. For example, ingredients for cakes and quick breads are mixed only long enough to combine them. As a result, the gluten is not strong. The cells remain small and the network stretches very little. This results in a fine, tender texture.

Yeast breads, on the other hand, are mixed much longer than cakes. The dough for yeast bread is worked with the hands to develop the gluten. As a result, the gluten is very elastic and expands easily. Larger air cells are produced, giving yeast breads a coarser texture.

Sugar cane is one of the sources of granulated sugar, a common sweetener in baked goods.

Special Needs Strategies

Physically Disabled: Assist students as needed in finding the best way to do the steps required for each baked product. Students may need assistance in solving problems in mixing, preparing pans, kneading dough, shaping products, using the oven, and handling hot pans. Stress safety rules and precautions in using the food mixer and the oven.

Batters and doughs have different consistencies—thick or thin, soft or firm. Waffle batter and cookie dough are two examples.

Batters and Doughs

The amount of liquid in relation to the flour determines whether a mixture is a batter or dough and affects how you handle the mixture. Batters have more liquid than doughs. There are four kinds of batters and doughs:

- ***Pour batters*** are thin enough to pour in a steady stream. They are used to make cakes, pancakes, and waffles.
- ***Drop batters,*** which are thick, are usually spooned into pans. They are used to make some quick breads and cookies.
- ***Soft doughs*** are soft and sticky but can be touched and handled. Rolled biscuits, yeast breads and rolls, and some cookies start with soft doughs.
- ***Stiff doughs*** are firm to the touch. Easy to work with and cut, they form the basis for pie crust and some cookies.

TIPS for Success

Kneading Dough

1. Turn the dough out on a very lightly floured surface.
2. With the heel of your hands, push down on the edge of the dough nearest to you.
3. Fold the dough in half toward you and give it a quarter turn.
4. Continue pushing, folding, and turning for the time directed in the recipe.

Methods of Mixing

There are several basic methods for combining ingredients. Other methods are usually variations. Use the method described in the recipe you have chosen. The chart on page 556 summarizes common mixing methods used in baking. You will read more about these later in the chapter.

Unless the recipe directs otherwise, have all ingredients at room temperature before mixing. Thirty minutes is long enough to warm refrigerated items.

Some doughs must be kneaded after they are mixed. To **knead** dough means to work it with the hands in order to further mix the ingredients and develop gluten. For directions, see "Tips for Success" on this page.

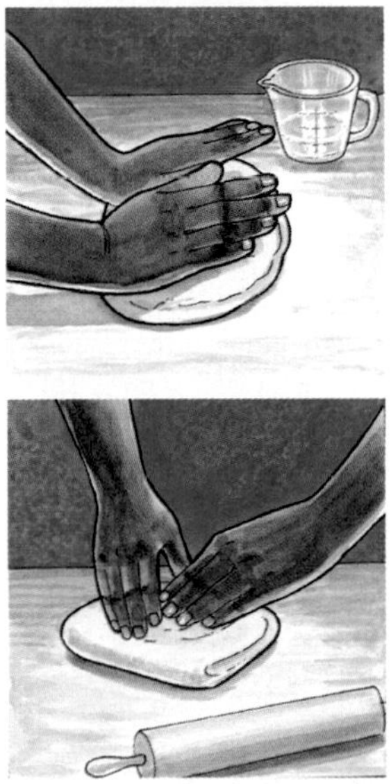

When making biscuits and yeast breads, knead the dough by pushing, folding, and turning it.

Student Experiences

1. **Class Discussion:** Explain the differences between batters and doughs. Ask students to suggest uses for each. *(Key skill: critical thinking)*
2. **Student Demonstrations:** Have students work in small groups to demonstrate procedures for creaming, beating, cutting in, folding, and kneading. Have each group define the technique they demonstrate. Discuss differences between the techniques. *(Key skill: kitchen management skills)*
3. **Analyzing recipes:** Provide students with recipes for a variety of breads. Have students study the mixing methods in each recipe and group those that use the same method. Have students list the general steps for mixing each group of similar recipes. Identify the methods as the standard mixing method, muffin method, one-bowl method, and pastry and biscuit method. *(Key skills: reading, analysis)*

More About the Role of Gluten

When a product is heated, the air, steam, or gas expands further and stretches the gluten. As the product bakes, the proteins and starch in the flour set, giving the baked product its final shape.

• Preparing to Bake

(text pages 556-557)

Comprehension Check

1. Ask students to explain why it is important to use a baking pan of the correct shape and size for a recipe. *(The product will not bake properly if the pan is not the correct shape and size.)*

2. Ask students to identify the correct temperature to use when using a glass pan to bake a product that normally bakes at 375°F (190°C). *(350°F [180°C])*

3. Ask students to describe three ways to prepare a pan for baking a product. *(grease and flour, vegetable oil cooking spray, lining a pan with paper)*

Student Experiences

1. **Display:** Create a display of baking pans. Discuss the effects of different types of baking materials on baked products. *(Key skill: kitchen management skills)*

2. **Recipe Use:** Give students several recipes. Have them select appropriate pans and describe how the product should be prepared and placed in the oven. *(Key skill: critical thinking)*

3. **Creating a Baking Demonstration:** Ask students to develop a baking demonstration for an elementary classroom. In the presentation, they should instruct children in how to prepare a cake mix, grease and flour the pan, and place the pan safely and correctly in the oven. *(Key skills: critical thinking, creativity)*

Summary of Common Mixing Methods

Method	Uses	Highlights	Where Described
Standard mixing method	• Cakes • Quick breads • Cookies	• Cream solid fat and sugar • Add dry ingredients alternately with liquids	• Section 21.4, page 572
Muffin method	• Muffins and other quick breads • Some cakes and cookies	• Use liquid fats • Pour liquids all at once into dry ingredients	• Section 21.2, page 560
One-bowl method	• Cakes • Cookies • Quick breads	• Use solid fat • Only one bowl needed	• Section 21.4, page 572
Pastry and biscuit method	• Pastry • Rolled biscuits	• Use pastry blender to mix solid fat and flour	• Section 21.2, page 562

Preparing to Bake

The baking pans you choose can affect the results of baking. Use the size and type of pan specified in the recipe. If the pan is too large or small, the product will not bake properly.

Pan materials are important, too. Most recipes are developed for light-colored metal pans. If you use glass pans, lower the temperature by 25°F (14°C). Glass retains more heat than metal, and at the higher temperature, a dark, thick crust may result.

Dark pans also retain more heat than light ones and can create a thick crust. If you use dark metal pans, you may have to lower the oven temperature by about 10°F (6°C).

Glass bakeware or special microwave bakeware must always be used when baking in the microwave oven.

Pan Preparation

Baking pans must be properly prepared so products can easily be removed from the pans. Follow recipe directions carefully. The pans should be prepared before the ingredients are mixed.

Here are several different methods for preparing pans:

❖ **Grease and flour** means to lightly grease a pan and dust it with flour. Use waxed paper to spread the fat. Sprinkle a little all-purpose flour into the pan. Tilt the pan to different angles until the flour is spread evenly. Turn the pan upside down over the sink and tap it gently to remove any excess flour. The flour allows the product to come out of the pan easily. Never grease and flour pans for microwave baking—they become sticky.

Thinking Skills

Reasoning: Some cake recipes recommend that you grease and flour the bottom of the pan but not the sides. Ask students to determine why. *(The bottom is greased and floured for ease in removing the cake from the pan. The sides are left ungreased so the cake will rise properly.)*

In order to make the finished product easy to remove, you may need to prepare the pans. If so, the recipe will tell you which method to use. Some recipes require ungreased pans—otherwise the product will not rise properly.

❖ *Vegetable oil cooking spray* is the easiest method, but may not work with all products. Follow the directions on the label.

❖ *Lining a pan with paper* requires parchment paper. Do not use brown paper or waxed paper. Brown paper contains chemicals that may be transferred to the food when it is heated. The wax in waxed paper may melt. Parchment paper is made for cooking and baking. Cut a piece of parchment the same shape and size as the pan bottom. Grease the pan and line the bottom with the parchment paper. When the product is removed, peel the paper off the bottom. This method is used for rich cakes, such as fruitcake.

Conventional and Microwave Baking

Most batters and doughs are baked. In a conventional oven, the dry heat creates desirable changes. The product browns and, depending on the ingredients, a crispy crust may develop. Because a microwave oven cooks with moist heat, baking results differ from a conventional oven. Microwave baked products do not brown or develop a crispy

crust. They have more of a steamed texture than a baked one and are very tender and moist.

Unless the recipe states otherwise, preheat the conventional oven. Before you turn on the oven, make sure the oven racks are in the proper position. See page 282 to review proper pan placement.

Brownies are an example of a cookie that can be baked in the microwave oven with good results. Use a recipe written for the microwave.

Section 21.1: Ingredients and Techniques for Baking   **557**

Comprehension Check

1. Ask students to explain why microwave ovens produce different baking results than a conventional oven. *(Conventional ovens use dry heat; microwave ovens don't.)*

2. Ask students to explain why it is necessary to preheat a conventional oven before baking. *(Oven temperature must be relatively constant for the product to bake evenly; a cool oven may alter baking time.)*

3. Discuss the use of cooling racks.

4. Ask students to explain why most baked products should not be refrigerated. *(They would get stale quickly.)*

Student Experiences

1. **Class Discussion:** Discuss why you should avoid opening the oven door while baking is in progress. *(It lowers oven temperature, can affect the product, and wastes energy.) (Key skill: critical thinking)*

2. **Product Comparison:** Have students compare a product baked in a conventional oven with one baked in a microwave oven. Discuss the advantages and disadvantages of microwave baking vs. conventional baking. *(Key skill: analysis)*

3. **Adapting a Recipe:** Have students adapt a conventional recipe for the microwave oven. Ask them to prepare and evaluate the product. *(Key skills: writing, kitchen management skills)*

More About Removing Baked Products from Pans

• To remove a cake from a pan, run a spatula around the inside of the pan to loosen the sides. Place a cooling rack over the pan and turn both upside down. The cake should come out easily, but it will be upside down. To turn the cake over, place another cooling rack over the bottom immediately and turn both so the cake is now right-side up.

• To remove bread from a loaf pan, turn the pan on its side. Using clean potholders, pull the hot loaf out of the pan and place it on a cooling rack.

Completing the Section

Review

- Ask students to summarize the main ideas in this section.
- Have students complete the Section Review. (Answers appear below.)

Evaluation

- Have students write a short essay explaining the various ingredients used in baked products and the purpose of each.
- Have students take the quiz for Section 21.1. (Refer to the *Section Quizzes* booklet or use the *Testmaker Software*.)

Reteaching

- Create flash cards with various ingredient names on one side and the purpose of the ingredients on the other. Have students practice explaining the purpose of each.
- Refer to the *Reteaching Activities* booklet for the Section 21.1 activity sheet.

Enrichment

- Ask students to research, sketch, and describe some of the special baking pans used in other countries to bake cookies and cakes.

Closure

- Lead a discussion on the importance of using exactly the right amount of each ingredient listed in a recipe for baked goods.

After you put the pans in the oven, set a timer for the baking time. Begin to check the product for doneness about five minutes before the time is up.

Only certain kinds of cakes, quick breads, and cookies can be baked successfully in a microwave oven. Follow the directions in the owner's guide or in a microwave recipe.

Removing Baked Products from Pans

Some baked products must be removed from the pans immediately when they come out of the oven. Others must cool for a few minutes. Still others need to stay in the pan until they are completely cool. Follow the recipe directions.

Use cooling racks so baked goods will cool faster and stay crisp. When baked goods are allowed to cool on a solid surface, such as a cutting board, moisture collects and baked goods become soggy.

Storing Baked Products

Fruit pies and products with cream filling must be refrigerated to prevent spoilage. Studies show that other baked products get stale quickly when stored at refrigerator temperatures. Store them at room temperature if they will be used within three days. To store them longer, freeze them in airtight freezer containers.

How should this chiffon pie be stored?

RECALL THE FACTS

1. List the basic ingredients in baked products. Identify one function of each.
2. Identify three methods for combining ingredients.
3. What type of paper is used for lining baking pans? Why?
4. In general, how do microwaved baked products differ from conventionally baked products?

DISCUSS YOUR IDEAS

5. Discuss the pros and cons of microwave baking versus conventional baking. When might you choose each?

APPLY YOUR LEARNING

6. Locate a basic muffin recipe. Identify the function of each ingredient.

■ Answers to Section Review ■

1. Flour (gives structure, provides gluten); liquid (helps form structure, helps leavener work); leavening (helps product rise); fat (adds richness, flavor, tenderness); eggs (add flavor, nutrients, richness, and color and help form the structure); sweetener (tenderness, sweetness, flavor, browning); flavorings (add flavor and sometimes nutrients).
2. See the chart on page 556.
3. Parchment paper; it is made for the purpose and contains no harmful chemicals or wax to get in the food.
4. They have a more steamed texture and are very tender and moist.
5. Answers will vary.
6. Answers will vary.

Quick Breads

OBJECTIVES

After studying this section, you should be able to:

- Suggest several additions to quick breads which increase the nutritional value.
- Discuss the differences and similarities between the muffin method and the pastry method of mixing.
- Describe the quality characteristics of properly mixed and baked muffins and biscuits.

LOOK FOR THESE TERMS

cut in
rolled biscuits
drop biscuits

As their name implies, quick breads are quick and easy to make. Most use baking powder as a leavening agent. Muffins, biscuits, pancakes, corn bread, and fruit breads are common examples.

Quick breads are good sources of carbohydrates, protein, B vitamins, and iron. Using whole grains adds fiber and trace minerals. If fruits and nuts are included, they provide more vitamins and minerals.

Some quick breads are high in fat. By choosing wisely, though, you can use quick breads to add variety, flavor, and nutrition to your meals and snacks.

Muffins

Muffins are prepared using the muffin method of mixing. The most important part of this procedure is properly mixing the dry and liquid ingredients.

Quick breads can add nutrients and variety to meals. What are some of your favorite types of quick breads?

Section 21.2
Quick Breads

Introducing the Section

Motivators

- Display several pictures or samples of quick breads such as muffins, biscuits, pancakes, waffles, corn bread, and fruit bread. Ask students if they can identify each of the breads and tell what they have in common.

- Display several variations of a quick bread, such as plain muffins, bran muffins, pumpkin muffins, and banana muffins. Ask students to taste each and guess what changes were made to the recipe to make each variation.

Objectives

- Have students read the section objectives. Discuss the purpose of studying the section.

Vocabulary

- Pronounce the terms listed under "Look for These Terms." Have students find the terms and their definitions in the section.

Guided Reading

- Have students look at the headings within Section 21.2 to preview the concepts that will be discussed.

- Have students read the section and complete the appropriate part of the Chapter 21 Study Guide in the *Student Workbook*.

Teacher's Classroom Resources—Section 21.2

Refer to these resources in the TCR package:

Reproducible Lesson Plans

Student Workbook

Extending the Text

Reteaching Activities

Section Quizzes

Testmaker Software

Foods Lab Resources

Food Science Resources

Color Transparencies

559

Teaching . . .

• **Muffins**

• **Loaf Breads**

(text pages 559-561)

Comprehension Check

1. Ask students to list the steps in mixing muffins properly. *(Sift or mix all dry ingredients into large bowl; beat all liquid ingredients; pour liquid into center well of dry ingredients; fold ingredients such as chopped nuts and raisins in gently.)*

2. Ask students to explain why it is important not to overmix the batter for muffins. *(Overmixing results in tough, heavy muffins and creates large gas bubbles or tunnels in the finished product.)*

3. Ask students to describe two characteristics to look for when you check to see if they're done. *(They are nicely browned; a wooden pick inserted in the center comes out clean.)*

4. Ask students to explain why quick breads that contain dried fruits and nuts should be cooked in loaf pans lined with parchment paper. *(The paper keeps the fruit and nuts from sticking to the bottom of the pan.)*

Muffin method:

1. Sift together or mix all dry ingredients (flour, sugar, baking powder, spices) in a large bowl. Make a well in the center of the dry ingredients using the back of a spoon.
2. Beat all liquid ingredients (eggs, milk or water, oil or melted fat, liquid flavorings) together in a small bowl until they are well blended.
3. Pour the liquid into the center well of the dry ingredients. Mix just enough to moisten the dry ingredients. A few floury spots can remain and the batter should be lumpy.
4. Fold ingredients such as chopped nuts and raisins in gently.

It is important not to overmix the batter. Muffins that are properly mixed have a rounded, pebbly top with a coarse but tender texture inside. Overmixed muffins will have peaks on the tops and be tough and heavy. The inside will have long, narrow tunnels.

The flavor of muffins can easily be varied with different ingredients. Fresh and dried fruits are often included. Try cranberries, blueberries, chopped dates, or dried apricots. Muffin recipes may also include yogurt or sour cream, tofu, raw vegetables (zucchini and carrots, for example), or cooked vegetables (such as sweet potatoes and winter squash). These ingredients add flavor and important nutrients, too. Adding extra ingredients to just any recipe may not work. Instead, start with recipes that already include them.

To add fiber to muffins, substitute 1/2 cup (125 mL) bran for an equal amount of flour. More than that will affect the texture.

Instead of greasing muffin pans, you can line them with paper baking cups. Fill the cups only two-thirds full. If you add more than that, the batter will overflow and the muffins will have odd shapes.

When baking muffins, test them for doneness about five minutes before the end of the baking time. They are done when they are nicely browned. A wooden pick inserted in the center should come out clean. Serve warm.

560   Chapter 21: Baking

Mix the dry ingredients and make a well in the center.

Beat the liquid ingredients together.

Add the liquids to the dry ingredients all at once. Stir briefly—do not overmix.

More About the Muffin Method

Sifting the dry ingredients together (step 1) insures they are evenly distributed. Some people prefer to simply mix them together by hand to save time.

Thinking Skills

Creativity: Ask students to think of nutritious toppings or spreads that could be used on quick breads instead of high-sugar or high-fat toppings.

With what other foods might quick loaf breads such as these be served?

Student Experiences

1. **Muffin Variations:** Have students identify ways to vary the flavor of muffins with different ingredients. *(Key skill: brainstorming)*

2. **Recipe Comparison:** Have students compare recipes for quick breads with recipes for yeast breads. Do they have the same ingredients? What additional ingredients are added for flavor? *(Key skill: reading)*

Using the Photo

Upper photo, p. 561: Encourage students to suggest a variety of menus for meals that might include quick breads, such as breakfast, brunch, a soup-and-salad lunch, or dinner. Point out that quick breads can also be a dessert or snack.

Lab Experience

- Have a group of students demonstrate how to make muffins. Have students place half of the muffins in greased muffin pans and half in paper baking cups. Discuss the advantages of each. Have students demonstrate procedures for testing muffins for doneness.

- Have a group of students demonstrate how to make loaf breads. Have students grease one loaf pan and line another with parchment paper. Have students demonstrate how to check loaf breads for doneness. How did the different pan preparations affect the finished product?

Loaf Breads

Many quick loaf breads are mixed in the same manner as muffins. They often have the same basic ingredients. Cranberry-orange-nut bread, for instance, is a holiday favorite. Other breads, such as corn bread, are less sweet. Some loaf breads are flavored with herbs.

Quick breads are generally baked in greased loaf pans. If the bread contains dried fruit and nuts, line the bottom of the pan with parchment paper so the loaf can be removed easily.

Check for doneness as you would with muffins. Don't be surprised if the top of the loaf cracks. That is typical for quick breads.

Biscuits

Biscuits are delicate, small breads. Properly made, they have a tender but crisp crust and are an even, light-brown color. The inside is slightly moist, creamy white, and peels apart in tender layers.

There are two kinds of biscuits—rolled and dropped. Both are made using the pastry and biscuit method of mixing.

Mixing Biscuit Dough

In the pastry and biscuit method, the fat is cut into the flour. To **cut in** means to mix solid fat and flour using a pastry blender or two knives and a cutting motion. This technique leaves the fat in fine particles in the dough. During baking, the fat melts between layers of flour, giving a flaky texture.

A pastry blender is a tool designed for cutting fat into flour.

Food and Nutrition Science

Cause of Tunnels in Muffins: Ask students if they can explain why overmixing muffins causes tunnels. *(The more the batter is mixed, the more gluten is formed. This results in a tough, rubber texture. The gluten prevents the escape of CO_2. As the muffins bake, the tunnels form.)*

Effects of Gluten Development Experiment: See the *Food Science Resources* booklet for the "Effect of Gluten Development on Muffins" teaching guidelines and student experiment worksheet. The experiment tests the effects of mixing methods on muffins.

Teaching . . .

• Biscuits

(text pages 561-563)

Comprehension Check

1. Ask students to explain what is meant by "cutting" fat into flour. *(Mix the two using a pastry blender or two knives and a cutting motion.)*

2. Ask students to list the steps to mix biscuit dough. *(See steps on page 562.)*

3. Discuss reasons why you might choose to make drop biscuits instead of rolled biscuits, and vice versa. *(Drop biscuits take less time to make, since they do not have to be rolled; rolled biscuits have a nicer, more uniform appearance.)*

Student Experience

1. **Class Discussion:** Discuss uses of dropped and rolled biscuits. How can the flavor be varied? What are the advantages of making biscuits ahead of time, freezing them, and reheating them in the microwave oven? *(Key skill: critical thinking)*

Lab Experience

Have students prepare biscuit dough to serve as a base for strawberry shortcake. What other fruits could be used with the shortcake?

Handle the dough as little as possible. If the shortening and flour are overmixed, the texture will be mealy, not flaky.

Pastry and biscuit method:

1. Sift together or mix the dry ingredients in a large bowl. Sifting ensures the ingredients are distributed evenly.

2. Cut the shortening into the flour until the particles are the size of peas or coarse bread crumbs.

3. Make a well in the center of the dry ingredients and add the liquids. Stir just until the ingredients are blended and form a soft dough.

Making Rolled Biscuits

Rolled biscuits are rolled out to an even thickness and cut out with a biscuit cutter. If you don't have a biscuit cutter, you can use the rim of a water glass.

To make rolled biscuits, mix the dough as explained above. If necessary, use your hands to form a ball of dough.

Turn the dough out on a lightly floured board and knead about ten strokes. (See page 555 for specific kneading instructions.) The goal is to blend the ingredients but not develop too much gluten. Overkneading results in tough, compact biscuits.

Next, roll the dough out until it is about ½-inch (1.3 cm) thick. Cut the biscuits out with a biscuit cutter that is slightly dusted with flour. Press the cutter straight down, so the biscuits have straight sides and even shapes. Don't twist the cutter.

Place the biscuits on an ungreased baking sheet, about 1 inch (2.5 cm) apart. Bake according to recipe directions.

Making Drop Biscuits

Drop biscuits contain more liquid than rolled biscuits. This creates a batter that is too sticky to handle but which can be dropped from a spoon. Although these biscuits have irregular shapes, they are just as flavorful and flaky as the rolled variety.

After kneading biscuit dough, roll it out to an even thickness so the biscuits will be uniform in size.

Cut the biscuits out, being careful not to pull or tear the dough. You can reroll the leftover dough to make more biscuits.

Mix drop biscuits using the same method as rolled biscuits. Drop the batter in mounds on a greased cookie sheet about 1 inch (2.5 cm) apart. Bake according to recipe directions. You can also spoon drop biscuits onto a casserole as a topping.

Food and Nutrition Science

Types of Leavening for Biscuits: Have students experiment with different types of leavening using a basic rolled biscuit recipe. Variations might include using baking powder, using baking soda and buttermilk or sour milk, and using baking soda and cream of tartar. Ask students to evaluate the results. How did the biscuits compare in flavor, texture, and color?

Drop biscuits save time because you do not have to knead or roll dough.

Serving Biscuits

Biscuits are best when they are eaten warm, right out of the oven. Serve them with meals or use them for sandwiches. Biscuits can be made ahead of time, frozen, and then reheated in the microwave oven.

Traditionally, biscuits provide the base for one of America's favorite desserts—strawberry shortcake. See the recipe on page 564.

Biscuits and muffins are usually served fresh from the oven or reheated.

Section 21.2 Review

RECALL THE FACTS

1. List five ingredients you can add to quick breads to vary the nutritional value.

2. Name two ways that the muffin method and biscuit method are similar and two ways they are different.

3. Describe the characteristics of a well-made muffin after baking.

4. What are the differences between a drop biscuit and a rolled biscuit?

DISCUSS YOUR IDEAS

5. Brainstorm ways that you can use quick breads to add variety to meals.

APPLY YOUR LEARNING

6. Find three recipes for quick breads. Identify the mixing method used in each.

Section 21.2: Quick Breads   **563**

Completing the Section

Review

- Ask students to summarize the main ideas in this section.
- Have students complete the Section Review. (Answers appear below.)

Evaluation

- Have students prepare a quick bread according to a recipe you provide. Evaluate student procedures and results.
- Have students take the quiz for Section 21.2. (Refer to the *Section Quizzes* booklet or use the *Testmaker Software*.)

Reteaching

- Ask students to prepare posters showing the steps used to make rolled biscuits.
- Refer to the *Reteaching Activities* booklet for the Section 21.2 activity worksheet.

Enrichment

- Have students vary the amount of leavening used in quick bread and report their results to the class.

Closure

- Lead a class discussion about quick breads and how they can be used to help create a well-rounded meal.

Answers to Section Review

1. *Any five:* Fruits, nuts, yogurt, sour cream, tofu, raw vegetables, cooked vegetables, bran.
2. Answers will vary.
3. It should be nicely browned and a wooden pick inserted in the center comes out clean.
4. Drop biscuits contain more liquid than rolled biscuits. Drop biscuits have irregular shapes; rolled biscuits are uniform.
5. Answers will vary.
6. Answers will vary.

21.2 Recipe

Strawberry Shortcake

Key Skill: Making Quick Breads

Using the Recipe

- Have students read the recipe and discuss each step. Review safety and sanitation procedures that apply to this recipe.
- Have each lab team fill out a work plan. (See the *Foods Lab Resources* booklet.)
- Have students check off the ingredients and equipment listed on the recipe worksheet and prepare the recipe.
- Have students complete the evaluation and questions on the recipe worksheet.

See Also . . .

The *Foods Lab Resources* booklet for the "Strawberry Shortcake" recipe worksheet and other recipe alternatives.

Thinking About the Recipe

Read the recipe for "Strawberry Shortcake" and answer the following questions.

1. What other fruits or combinations of fruits could you use to make shortcake?
2. What tools can be used to cut the margarine into the dry ingredients?

Strawberry Shortcake

Customary	Ingredients	Metric
2 cups	Fresh or frozen strawberries, sliced	500 mL
1/4 cup	Sugar (optional—omit if using frozen strawberries)	50 mL
1 cup	All-purpose flour	250 mL
1 Tbsp.	Sugar	15 mL
1 ½ tsp.	Baking powder	7 mL
1/2 tsp.	Salt	2 mL
2 Tbsp.	Margarine	30 mL
1/2 cup	Skim milk	125 mL
1/2 cup	Whipped topping or low-fat vanilla yogurt	125 mL

Yield: 4 servings

Directions

Pan: Baking sheet
Temperature: 450°F (232°C)

1. Thaw strawberries if frozen. If using fresh strawberries, clean and slice. Add 1/4 cup (50 mL) sugar to the fresh strawberries and refrigerate for about an hour to draw out the juices.
2. Preheat the oven. Lightly grease the baking sheet.
3. Sift flour, 1 Tbsp. (15 mL) sugar, baking powder, and salt together into a bowl.
4. Cut the margarine into the flour mixture until it resembles coarse bread crumbs. Make a well in the center of the mixture.
5. Add the milk and stir with a fork until ingredients are moistened and form a drop batter.
6. Drop biscuits onto baking sheet about 1 inch (2.5 cm) apart.
7. Bake at 450°F (232°C) about 15 minutes or until golden brown.
8. For each serving, tear a warm biscuit in half and place the bottom half in a small bowl.
9. Spoon 1/2 cup (125 mL) strawberries and juice over each biscuit half.
10. Cover the berries with the top half of the biscuit. Add 2 tablespoons (30 mL) whipped topping or yogurt to each shortcake. Serve.

Nutrition Information

Per serving (approximate): 102 calories, 1 g protein, 11 g carbohydrate, 6 g fat, trace of cholesterol, 168 mg sodium

---

Answers to Thinking About the Recipe

1. Answers will vary. Peaches, cherries, and blackberries are some examples.

2. A pastry blender or two knives.

Yeast Breads and Rolls

OBJECTIVES

After studying this section, you should be able to:

- Identify ways to simplify bread making.
- Describe the procedure for making yeast breads.
- Explain how to tell when yeast breads are done baking.

LOOK FOR THIS TERM

quick-mix method

As their name indicates, yeast breads use yeast for leavening. The yeast also gives the bread a characteristic flavor and contributes to the wonderful aroma of baking.

Time Savers

Many people think that baking yeast bread is too time-consuming for today's fast-paced lifestyles. With a little organization, however, bread baking can be a part of regular food preparation. Making yeast dough is a flexible process. The tasks can be timed to fit into the cook's schedule.

Several appliances can help speed up the bread-making process. Use a microwave oven to heat the liquid before adding it to yeast, to bring refrigerated ingredients to room temperature, and to let the dough rise. Check the owner's manual for specific directions. These vary, depending on the power and controls.

A heavy-duty mixer with dough hook or a powerful food processor will mix yeast dough quickly. They will knead it in about six minutes compared to eight or ten minutes by hand.

As different as these breads appear, all use yeast for leavening.

Section 21.3
Yeast Breads and Rolls

Introducing the Section

Motivators

- Display several pictures or samples of yeast breads such as white bread, sweet white bread, whole grain bread, batter bread, sourdough bread, rolls, and croissants. Ask students if they can identify each of the breads and tell what they have in common.

- Have students create a bulletin board showing some of the ways yeast dough can be shaped.

Objectives

- Have students read the section objectives. Discuss the purpose of studying the section.

Vocabulary

- Pronounce the terms listed under "Look for These Terms." Have students find the terms and their definitions in the section.

Guided Reading

- Have students look at the headings within Section 21.3 to preview the concepts that will be discussed.

- Have students read the section and complete the appropriate part of the Chapter 21 Study Guide in the *Student Workbook*.

Teacher's Classroom Resources—Section 21.3

Refer to these resources in the TCR package:
Reproducible Lesson Plans
Student Workbook
Extending the Text
Reteaching Activities

Section Quizzes
Testmaker Software
Foods Lab Resources
Food Science Resources
Color Transparencies

Teaching . . .

- **Time Savers**
- **Steps in Making Yeast Bread and Rolls**

(text pages 565-567, 570)

Comprehension Check

1. Ask students to name three ways to use a microwave oven to speed tasks associated with making yeast bread. *(Heat the liquid before adding it to yeast, bring refrigerated ingredients to room temperature, let the dough rise.)*

2. Ask students to explain how to add fiber and nutrients to recipes that use only all-purpose flour. *(Substitute whole wheat or rye flour for as much as two thirds of the all-purpose flour.)*

3. Ask students to describe the steps of the quick-mix method. *(See the steps on pages 566-567.)*

4. Ask students to explain how long yeast bread should be kneaded. *(About 8 to 10 minutes; long enough that the dough becomes a smooth, shiny ball.)*

Technology Tidbit

You may want to ask interested students read manufacturer's materials or instruction booklets to find out how automatic bread makers and similar appliances work. Have students report their findings to the class.

Technology Tidbit

Do you think that you don't have time to make bread? Automatic bread makers allow you to make bread with almost no effort. All you do is accurately measure the ingredients into the machine. This handy appliance mixes, kneads, allows the dough to rise, and then bakes it. Depending on the type of bread you make, you have a loaf of bread in about four hours.

Use a thermometer to check the temperature of the liquids.

Steps in Making Yeast Bread and Rolls

There are just a few easy steps to follow in making yeast bread and rolls. These include mixing the dough, kneading it, letting it rise, shaping it, and finally baking it.

Mixing the Dough

Yeast bread is simply a mixture of flour, salt, sugar, liquid, fat, and yeast. Sugar provides food for the yeast so that it will grow. Salt controls the action of the yeast. Consult a recipe for the exact ingredients and amounts.

Bread flour is ideal for yeast breads. However, most recipes for homemade bread call for all-purpose flour. It is more readily available than bread flour and makes a loaf with good texture.

If a recipe uses only all-purpose flour, you can mix whole grain flour with it for added fiber and nutrients. For yeast doughs, a general rule is to use at least one-third all-purpose flour. The other two-thirds can be whole grain flours such as whole wheat or rye. Other amounts of ingredients remain the same.

Before you begin, be sure the ingredients are at room temperature and the liquid is

After mixing the liquid and dry ingredients, use a spoon to beat in the additional flour. The amount needed will vary. It depends on the moisture content of the flour and even the humidity in the air that day.

heated to the right temperature. Yeast will not grow if the liquid is too cold. If the liquid is too hot, it will kill the yeast.

The **quick-mix method** combines active dry yeast with the dry ingredients. A standard mixer will work for the first part of the mixing until the dough thickens and becomes too heavy for it. Beat the rest of the flour in with a wooden spoon.

Quick-mix method for yeast bread:

1. Combine part of the flour with the undissolved active dry yeast, sugar, and salt in a large bowl.
2. Heat the liquid and fat to 120°F to 130°F (49°C to 54°C).

Food and Nutrition Science

Yeast Experiment: Have each group of students prepare a small-necked bottle with varying amounts and kinds of yeast, water of varying amounts and temperature, and added ingredients such as sugar and salt. Put a balloon over the mouth of the bottle and tie it with string. Note results at varying time intervals. Have students suggest reasons for variations in results.

Gluten Development Experiment: See the *Food Science Resources* booklet for the "Gluten Development in Yeast Bread" teaching guidelines and student experiment worksheet. The experiment determines the effect of kneading on the development of gluten in yeast dough.

Yeast goes to work during the rising time. Cover the dough to keep it from drying out.

Gently "punching" the dough after the first rising eliminates excess gas bubbles.

3. Add the liquid to the dry ingredients, beating them with a mixer until they are well blended. At this point, the gluten is beginning to develop.
4. Beat in enough of the remaining flour to make the kind of dough specified in the recipe. You may need more or less flour than the recipe calls for. Some kinds absorb more liquid than others.

Kneading the Dough

Turn the dough out on a lightly floured surface. Knead the dough until it becomes a smooth, shiny ball, about 8 to 10 minutes. Use just enough flour to keep the dough from sticking to the work surface or to your hands. Too much flour will give a tough texture.

Don't be concerned if bubbles develop in the dough. That's a clue that gluten is developing. The cell walls are becoming elastic and expanding with carbon dioxide given off by the yeast.

Letting Dough Rise

Shape the dough into a ball and place it in a well-oiled bowl to rise. Turn the dough over so all sides are coated with oil. Put a piece of plastic wrap over the top of the

dough to keep it from drying out. Cover the bowl with a clean dish towel. Set the bowl in a warm (not hot), draft-free place for about an hour to rise.

After the first rising, "punch" the dough down by gently pressing your fist down in the center. Gently pull the dough from the sides of the bowl to the center and press down to eliminate the large air bubbles. If you're not ready to shape the dough, let it rise again. You can also cover the dough and refrigerate it overnight. It will rise in the refrigerator and be ready to shape the next day.

TIPS for Success

Identifying Readiness for Shaping

In general, the dough is ready to shape when it has doubled in size. However, "doubled in size" is a little difficult to measure. Try this method:
❖ Push two fingers gently into the surface of the dough. If the finger indentations remain, the dough is ready to shape.

1. **Demonstration:** Demonstrate how to use the microwave oven and heavy-duty mixer with a dough hook to speed up breadmaking. *(Key skill: kitchen management skills)*
2. **Taste Test:** Have students compare the taste of homemade yeast bread with commercially prepared yeast breads. Consider cost, nutrition, flavor, and texture. *(Key skill: evaluation)*
3. **Recipe Comparison:** Have students compare the steps for making yeast bread and rolls. Based on these recipes, have students make a list of tips for success and a list of basic steps. *(Key skills: reading, writing)*
4. **Analysis:** Have students write an essay discussing the advantages and disadvantages of making yeast breads by hand versus using a breadmaker. *(Key skill: writing)*

Lab Experience

- Have students make and bake a whole-wheat yeast bread. Students should evaluate the bread in terms of flavor, texture, nutrition, and cost.
- Have students use store-bought refrigerated dough (such as crescent roll dough) to practice shaping breads and rolls.

More About Kneading Dough

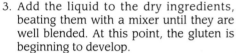

Kneading affects the molecular structure of yeast dough, changing its texture and appearance. When the dough is first mixed, the protein molecules are long and coiled, forming a mass. As the dough is kneaded, the molecules begin to line up in a more orderly fashion. Coiled gluten molecules

unwind and form layers in the dough. This firms the dough, giving it a satinlike surface.

Overkneading can break down the protein structure. Usually, it's difficult to overknead dough by hand. But it can be overworked with a food processor. Overkneaded dough will not rise properly.

21.3 Recipe

Honey Whole Wheat Bread

Key Skill: Making Yeast Breads

Using the Recipe

- Have students read the recipe and discuss each step. Review safety and sanitation procedures that apply to this recipe. Caution students to follow the directions carefully so that they don't accidentally miss a step. It is very important that the steps be done in the correct order when you make bread.
- Have each lab team fill out a work plan. (See the *Foods Lab Resources* booklet.)
- Have students check off the ingredients and equipment listed on the recipe worksheet and prepare the recipe.
- Have students complete the evaluation and questions on the recipe worksheet.

See Also . . .

The *Foods Lab Resources* booklet for the "Honey Whole Wheat Bread" recipe worksheet and other recipe alternatives.

Thinking About the Recipe

Read the recipe for "Honey Whole Wheat Bread" and answer the following questions.

1. What is the name of the mixing method used in this recipe?
2. Why isn't an exact amount of all-purpose flour specified?

Honey Whole Wheat Bread

Customary	Ingredients	Metric
2 ½ to 3 cups	All-purpose flour	625 to 750 mL
3 cups	Whole wheat flour	750 mL
2 tsp.	Salt	10 mL
1 pkg.	Active dry yeast	1 pkg.
1 cup	Skim milk	250 mL
1 cup	Water	250 mL
1/4 cup	Honey	50 mL
3 Tbsp.	Shortening	45 mL

Yield: Two loaves

Two-day Directions

Pan: Small saucepan; two 9 x 5 x 3 inch (23 x 13 x 8 cm) loaf pans
Temperature: 400°F (200°C)
Day One

1. Mix 1 cup (250 mL) all-purpose flour, 1 cup (250 mL) whole wheat flour, salt, and undissolved active dry yeast in a large bowl. Set aside.
2. Combine milk, water, honey, and shortening in a small saucepan.
3. Heat liquids over low heat until warm, about 120°F(49°C). Shortening does not have to melt.
4. Add the heated liquid to the dry ingredients.
5. Blend at low speed with a mixer about 2 minutes. Occasionally scrape the bowl.
6. Add another 1/2 cup (125 mL) all-purpose flour and 1/2 cup (125 mL) whole wheat flour to the mixture.
7. Beat about 2 minutes at medium speed, scraping the bowl occasionally.
8. Stir in 3/4 cup (175 mL) all-purpose flour and 1 ½ cups (375 mL) whole wheat flour with a wooden spoon until the mixture forms a soft dough. If necessary, add more all-purpose flour.

Answers to Thinking About the Recipe

1. The quick-mix method.

2. Some types of flour absorb more liquid than others, so the amount of flour may vary.

Honey Whole Wheat Bread (cont.)

9. Put the dough on a lightly floured surface.
10. Knead the dough about 8 to 10 minutes until it is smooth and elastic.
11. Place the dough in a large, well-oiled bowl. Turn the dough in the bowl to be sure all sides are oiled.
12. Cover the dough with a piece of plastic wrap. Place a clean dish towel over the bowl.
13. Refrigerate the dough overnight.

Day Two

1. Remove dough from the refrigerator.
2. Gently push your fist into the center of the dough. Pull the sides of the dough toward the center.
3. Turn the dough out of the bowl onto a lightly floured surface. Allow the dough to rest 10 to 15 minutes.
4. Divide the dough into two equal portions.
5. Shape the dough into two loaves.
6. Put each loaf into a well-greased loaf pan.
7. Cover the loaves with a clean dish towel and let them rise in a warm place until doubled in size, about one hour, or until finger indentations remain.
8. Preheat the oven to 400°F (200°C).
9. Bake the loaves about 25 to 30 minutes or until done.
10. Remove loaves from pans and cool on a cooling rack away from drafts.

Nutrition Information

Per serving (1 slice or 1/20 of loaf—approximate): 80 calories, 2 g protein, 15 g carbohydrate, 1 g fat, trace of cholesterol, 110 mg sodium

More About Yeast Dough

- As dough rises, yeast grows, multiplies, and gives off gases. The dough ripens, becoming softer and more pliable. If ripened too long or too quickly, dough sours. If the rising temperature is too warm, the dough becomes stickier and may be difficult to shape.
- Punching the dough down relaxes it. It also redistributes its ingredients, feeding the yeast.
- When dough is being shaped, by hand or with a rolling pin, it may "squeak." That is the sound of gas escaping from the dough.

Completing the Section

Review

- Ask students to summarize the main ideas in this section.
- Have students complete the Section Review. (Answers appear below.)

Evaluation

- Provide a recipe for yeast bread and have students make the bread. Evaluate procedure and result.
- Have students take the quiz for Section 21.3. (Refer to the *Section Quizzes* booklet or use the *Testmaker Software*.)

Reteaching

- Demonstrate steps in making yeast bread. Have students observe the size, shape, and texture of the dough at each step.
- Refer to the *Reteaching Activities* booklet for the Section 21.3 activity worksheet.

Enrichment

- Have students prepare two batches of bread according to a recipe, but for one batch, eliminate the kneading step. Have students evaluate and explain the results.

Closure

- Lead a discussion about the various ways yeast breads can be made even if you have a busy lifestyle.

Shaping the Dough

Shape the dough into loaves or rolls, according to recipe directions. Place the bread in greased pans or on baking sheets. Cover the pans and let the shaped dough rise until double or until finger indentations remain when you lightly press the dough.

Baking

Bake as directed in the recipe. Bread and rolls are nicely browned when done baking. Check loaves for doneness by tapping them with your finger. If they sound hollow, they are done.

Remove the bread or rolls from the pans and place them on a wire cooling rack. The rack prevents moisture from forming on the bottom crust and making it soggy. Let loaves stand about 20 minutes for easier cutting.

After shaping, bread dough is allowed to rise a final time in the pan.

Yeast dough can be shaped in many creative ways, such as this braided ring. Notice the evenly browned crust.

Section 21.3 Review

RECALL THE FACTS

1. What appliances can help speed up the bread-making process? Why?
2. What happens if the liquids in yeast breads are too hot or too cool?
3. How can you tell if dough is ready to shape and bake?
4. How can you tell if a loaf of bread is done baking?

DISCUSS YOUR IDEAS

5. Discuss the pros and cons of making yeast breads yourself by hand versus using an automatic bread maker or commercially frozen bread dough.

APPLY YOUR LEARNING

6. Using cookbooks or other references, describe at least five different ways of shaping yeast breads or rolls other than a loaf.

Answers to Section Review

1. Microwave oven, automatic breadmaker, heavy-duty mixer with dough hook.
2. The yeast will not grow if the temperature is too cold; if the liquid is too hot, it will kill the yeast.
3. By pushing two fingers gently into the surface of the dough. If the finger indentations remain, the dough is ready to shape.
4. The bread is nicely browned and sounds hollow when you tap the loaf with your finger.
5. Answers will vary.
6. Answers will vary.

Cakes, Cookies, and Pies

OBJECTIVES

After studying this section, you should be able to:
- Describe types of cakes, cookies, and pies.
- Give guidelines for preparing cakes, cookies, and pies.

LOOK FOR THESE TERMS

shortened cakes
foam cakes

Who doesn't enjoy a freshly-baked cookie or a warm slice of homemade pie? Cakes, cookies, and pies are among the most popular baked goods. While many are nutritious, most are high in fat, sugar, and calories, so eat them sparingly. When you do prepare sweet treats for your family and friends, there are some choices you can consider.

Cakes

Although cakes are easy to make, accurately measuring ingredients is essential for good results.

Cake recipes sometimes call for cake flour, which is low in gluten. If you do not have cake flour, substitute all-purpose flour. For each 1 cup (250 mL) of cake flour, use 1 cup (250 mL) minus 2 tablespoons (30 mL) of all-purpose flour.

There are two basic kinds of cakes, shortened and foam cakes.

Besides being beautifully decorated, these desserts have something else in common— they are all shortened cakes.

Section 21.4: Cakes, Cookies, and Pies **571**

Section 21.4
Cakes, Cookies, and Pies

Introducing the Section

Motivators

- Write the word "cookie" on the chalkboard. Have students quickly name the kinds that first come to mind when they hear the word "cookie." Do the same with the words "cake" and "pie." Do students think of the same kinds of cookies, cakes, and pies, or do the lists contain a wide variety of kinds?

- Describe a favorite holiday cookie, cake, or pie. Discuss with students the cookies, cakes, and pies they associate with holidays and special occasions.

Objectives

- Have students read the section objectives. Discuss the purpose of studying the section.

Vocabulary

- Pronounce the terms listed under "Look for These Terms." Have students find the terms and their definitions in the section.

Guided Reading

- Have students look at the headings within Section 21.4 to preview the concepts that will be discussed.

- Have students read the section and complete the appropriate part of the Chapter 21 Study Guide in the *Student Workbook*.

Teacher's Classroom Resources—Section 21.4

Refer to these resources in the TCR package:

Reproducible Lesson Plans	*Section Quizzes*
Student Workbook	*Testmaker Software*
Extending the Text	*Foods Lab Resources*
Reteaching Activities	*Food Science Resources*
	Color Transparencies

• Cakes

(text pages 571-574)

Comprehension Check

1. Ask students to name the two basic types of cakes and list the characteristics of each. *(Shortened cakes are rich and tender and contain a solid fat such as shortening, butter, or margarine or sometimes oil; foam cakes are leavened with beaten egg whites.)*

2. Ask students to describe the standard method for mixing cakes. *(See the steps listed on page 572.)*

3. Ask students to explain how to test a shortened cake and a foam cake for doneness. *(Shortened cake: insert a wooden pick in the center; if it comes out free of wet batter, the cake is done. Foam cake: touch the top lightly; if it springs back the cake is done.)*

4. Ask students to explain why it is important not to grease the pans when baking foam cakes. *(The batter clings to the sides of the pan as it rises during baking; if the pan were greased, the cake would not be able to rise.)*

5. Ask students to list low-calorie alternatives to traditional high-calorie frostings for cakes. *(Make a glaze with confectioners' sugar and lemon, orange, or pineapple juice; sift a little confectioners' sugar over the top of the cake.)*

Using the Photo

Answer to caption question (p. 572): If dishes are washed by hand, the one-bowl method saves time and personal energy because there is only one bowl to wash.

Shortened Cakes

Shortened cakes are rich and tender. They most often contain a solid fat such as shortening, butter, or margarine, but may contain oil. Shortened cakes appear in a variety of flavors including chocolate, lemon, and spice. Some contain chopped nuts and dried fruits.

As you learned in Section 21.1, several methods can be used for mixing cakes. The standard method is most common for shortened cakes. An electric mixer is helpful for creaming and beating the ingredients.

Standard method for mixing cakes:

1. Cream the solid fat and sugar until the mixture is light and fluffy, as in whipped cream.
2. Beat the eggs into the mixture thoroughly, usually one at a time.
3. Sift the dry ingredients together.
4. Mix the liquids together.
5. Add the dry ingredients to the creamed mixture alternately with the liquid. Begin and end with the dry ingredients. This helps keep the fat from separating, which could affect the texture. Add the dry ingredients in fourths and the liquids in thirds. After each addition, beat the batter just enough to mix the ingredients.

You can also use the *one-bowl method* to mix shortened cakes. The dry ingredients are combined by sifting or mixing. Solid fat, liquids, and flavorings are added and beaten with the dry ingredients until well blended. The eggs are beaten in last.

You can bake shortened cakes in pans of many shapes and sizes, from individual cupcakes in muffin pans to large sheet cakes. Fancy molds can turn an ordinary cake into a centerpiece for a special event.

To check a shortened cake for doneness, insert a wooden pick in the center. If it comes out free of wet batter, the cake is done.

A shortened cake should have a slightly rounded top with a tender, shiny crust. When the cake is cut, it should have a fine, even grain and be moist and tender.

The one-bowl method saves time because there are fewer steps in mixing. How else might this method save time and personal energy?

Foam Cakes

Foam cakes are leavened with beaten egg whites, which give them a light, airy texture. Angel food, sponge, and chiffon cakes are examples.

Angel food cakes use only beaten egg whites for leavening. They have neither egg yolks nor fat. This makes them good choices for low-fat, low-calorie desserts. In sponge cakes, beaten egg yolks are added to the batter before the batter is folded into the egg whites. Some foam cake recipes call for baking powder as well. Chiffon cakes include yolks, oil, and baking powder, which are blended and then folded into beaten egg whites.

Foam cakes must be baked in ungreased pans. As the batter rises during baking, it clings to the sides of the pan. If the pan were greased, the cake would not be able to rise. A tube pan is often used for foam cakes.

Food and Nutrition Science

Mixing Methods Experiment: See the *Food Science Resources* booklet for the "How Mixing Methods Affect a Shortened Cake" teaching guidelines and student experiment worksheet. The experiment observes how different mixing times and methods can affect a shortened cake.

Leavening Experiment: See the *Food Science Resources* booklet for the "How Shortened Cakes Rise" teaching guidelines and student experiment worksheet. The experiment tests the effects of leavening agents on the appearance, texture, and flavor of shortened cakes.

Foam cakes have a light texture because they include beaten egg whites.

To test a foam cake for doneness, touch the top lightly. It should spring back.

Foam cakes are generally cooled upside down in the pan to keep them from losing volume or falling. If the tube pan does not have legs to support it upside down, use an empty glass bottle with a slender neck or a large metal funnel turned upside down. Invert the tube pan over the neck of the bottle or funnel.

When the cake is cool, gently loosen the cake from the sides with a spatula. Turn the pan upside down to remove the cake. If the pan has a removable bottom, use a spatula to loosen the cake from the bottom.

TIPS for Success

Using a Tube Pan

Most tube pans are made in two parts. The bottom (which contains the center tube) detaches from the sides, making it easy to remove the cake. If the pan is in one piece, line the bottom with parchment paper so the cake can be removed more easily.

Section 21.4: Cakes, Cookies, and Pies 573

Student Experiences

1. **Taste Test:** Have students taste the two basic kinds of cakes: shortened and foam. Ask students to identify similarities and differences. *(Key skill: evaluation)*

2. **Recipe Comparison:** Provide students with a variety of recipes for shortened and foam cakes. Have students work in groups to separate recipes according to the mixing technique used. Read the descriptions for the standard and foam methods for mixing cakes. Have students check their recipes to see if they correctly categorized each recipe. *(Key skill: reading)*

TIPS for Success

Some one-piece tube pans have fluted bottoms. Ask students to brainstorm ways to make it easier to remove the cake from this type of pan.

Lab Experience

Have students prepare shortened and foam cakes. Remind students that pan shape, size, and material will affect baking time. Have students check the cakes for doneness using the appropriate technique. Have students cool the cakes using an appropriate technique. Have students evaluate the results according to shape, crust, grain, moistness, and tenderness.

Food and Nutrition Science

Cooked Frosting: The success of cooked frosting depends on achieving the right concentration of sugar and water. Concentration is related to the temperature at which a sugar-water solution will boil: the higher the concentration, the higher the boiling point. Emphasize to students that the accurate use of a candy thermometer when making cooked frosting will help ensure success.

Comprehension Check

1. Ask students to list and describe the six basic types of cookies. *(bar cookies, drop cookies, cut-out or rolled cookies, molded cookies, pressed cookies, sliced or refrigerator cookies)*

2. Ask students to explain how to tell when cookies are done baking. *(Bar cookies are done when they pull away slightly from the sides of the pan and a slight impression remains when they are tapped gently; other cookies are done when the bottoms are lightly browned and the edges are firm.)*

3. Ask students to explain how to store cookies. *(Store in covered containers with waxed paper between layers.)*

Decorating Cakes

Cakes are often frosted. Since frostings are usually high in fat, sugar, and calories, you may want to try one of these alternatives.

❖ Make a glaze with confectioners' sugar and lemon, orange, or pineapple juice. Drizzle it over the cake and let it flow down the sides.

❖ Sift a little confectioners' sugar over the top of the cake. Try putting a cutout paper design, such as a snowflake, on top before sifting the sugar.

You may also serve the cake with fresh or frozen fruit instead of icing.

These simple cake toppings are attractive, easy to make, and lower in calories than frosting.

Cookies

Cookies are easy to prepare. Many people consider homemade cookies well worth the little time and effort they require. The main difference between cakes and cookies is that cookies have little, if any, liquid. This gives cookies a heavier texture than cakes.

Cookies vary in texture from soft to crisp. They can be made in assorted shapes and decorated in many ways. The thousands of cookie varieties can be divided into six basic kinds.

❖ **Bar cookies** are baked in square or rectangular pans and then cut into bars, squares, or diamonds. They can be made from a batter or a soft dough that is pressed into a pan. Textures vary from cake-like to chewy. Brownies are one example of bar cookies. Usually, bars are cooled in the pan and then cut.

❖ **Drop cookies** are made from a soft dough that is dropped from a teaspoon onto cookie sheets. During baking, the dough spreads out to make a thick cookie. Remember to allow enough space between cookies so they can spread without touching. Most chocolate chip cookies are drop cookies.

❖ **Cut-out cookies** (also called rolled cookies) are made from stiff dough that is rolled out and cut with cookie cutters.

❖ **Molded cookies** are formed by shaping the dough by hand into balls. These balls can be rolled in chopped nuts or other toppings before baking, or they can be flattened with a fork or the bottom of a glass.

❖ **Pressed cookies** are made by pushing dough through a cookie press, which can create a variety of shapes. Spritz cookies are an example of pressed cookies.

❖ **Sliced cookies** (sometimes called refrigerator cookies) are made by forming a soft dough into a long roll and refrigerating it. When the roll is chilled and firm, the cookies are sliced and baked.

Thinking Skills

Problem Solving: Have students imagine they are making a batch of oatmeal drop cookies. When they take the first pan from the oven, they discover that the cookies have flattened and run together. What should they do before baking the rest of the cookies? *(Add more flour or oatmeal and make a test cookie to see if enough flour or oatmeal has been added.)*

Student Experiences

1. **Class Discussion:** Discuss differences between cakes and cookies. List the six basic kinds of cookies across the top of the chalkboard. Have students name examples of cookies that fit each category. Have students identify keys to successful cookie baking. *(Key skill: classification)*

2. **Product Evaluation:** Have students evaluate four types of chocolate chip cookies: ready-made, refrigerated dough, packaged mix, and homemade. Ask students to compare cost, preparation time, taste, texture, and appearance. Ask students to write their conclusions. *(Key skills: writing, analysis)*

3. **Finding Recipes:** Have students find and compare two recipes for each of the six basic kinds of cookies. *(Key skill: reading)*

Cookies range from simple to decorative. Try baking and freezing batches of different kinds until you have an assortment. Then you can put together a sampler for a homemade gift.

Most cookies are baked on cookie sheets —flat pans with only one edge. Let cookie sheets cool before baking more cookies. Otherwise, the warm pan will soften the dough and the cookies will lose their shape.

Bar cookies are done baking when they pull away slightly from the sides of the pan. A slight impression remains when they are tapped gently. Other cookies are done when the bottoms are lightly browned and the edges are firm.

Store cookies in covered containers. Waxed paper between layers will keep them from sticking together.

Dutch immigrants introduced cookies to America in the early 1600s. The Dutch word *koekjes,* which means "little cakes," soon was Americanized to "cookies."

Pies

A pie is a flaky crust filled with either a sweet or a savory mixture. A sweet pie may contain a fruit, custard, or cream filling and is generally served as dessert. A savory pie, filled with a meat or a custard and vegetable mixture, is served as a main dish. Two examples are quiche and potpie.

Pies can have one or two crusts made with flour, fat, salt, and water.

A lattice crust is made with strips of dough.

Section 21.4: Cakes, Cookies, and Pies   **575**

More About Storing Cookies

When preparing cookies, make an extra batch to freeze. Most cookie batters and doughs freeze well, except those made by the foam method. When freezing a batter, pour it into a freezer container and seal well. Doughs may be shaped into rolls and frozen. Thaw in the refrigerator.

Food and Nutrition Science

Moisture Absorption Experiment: See the *Food Science Resources* booklet for the "Moisture Absorption by Cookies" teaching guidelines and student experiment worksheet. The experiment observes the effect of different sweeteners and storage methods on moisture absorption by cookies.

Lab Experience

Have students make various kinds of cookies. Serve the cookies at a school function.

Teaching . . .

• Pies

(text pages 575-577)

Comprehension Check

1. Ask students to describe the two main types of pies and give two examples of each. *(Sweet pies and savory pies; examples will vary.)*

2. Ask students to explain how to patch dough if it cracks or tears while you're rolling it. *(Moisten the area to be patched, press a piece of dough over it, sprinkle flour over patched area, and continue to roll.)*

Student Experiences

1. **Display:** Display pie crust mixes and ready-to-use crusts. What are the advantages and disadvantages of these alternatives? *(Key skill: critical thinking)*

2. **Recipe Analysis:** Have students work in small groups to locate several pie recipes. Have students identify short-cut ingredients or preparation methods suggested in the recipes. Have students suggest ways to modify the recipes to make them lower in fat. *(Key skill: reading)*

See Also . . .

• Mixing Biscuit Dough, text pages 561-562

Using the Photo

Answers to caption questions:

• *p. 576, lower right:* A two-crust pie, since the pastry is being trimmed even with the edge of the pan.

• *p. 577, upper right:* Examples may include pumpkin pie, custard pie, etc.

To mix pastry, use the pastry and biscuit method. Follow the same steps as you would to mix biscuit dough (see page 562). For a flaky pastry, handle the dough as little as possible.

Use a lightly floured surface to roll out pastry dough. Roll the dough in a large, round circle about 1/8 inch (0.3 cm) thick and 2 inches (5 cm) larger than an inverted (upside-down) pie pan. If the dough cracks or tears, patch it with another piece of dough. Moisten the area to be patched with a little water and press a piece of dough over it. Sprinkle some flour over the patched area and continue to roll it with rolling pin.

For a two-crust pie, fold a rolled pastry circle in half and gently place it in a pie pan. Unfold the circle and fit it into the pan without stretching the pastry. Trim the pastry even with the edge of the pan. Fill it with a sweet or savory mixture. Place another circle of pastry over the filling to form the top crust. Trim it so that 1/2 inch (1.3 cm) extends over the edge of the pan. Moisten the bottom pastry around the edge with water. Tuck the top pastry under the bottom edge of the pastry and gently pinch the layers together. Make a decorative edge that also seals the top and bottom crusts. (See "Tips for Success," p. 577, for directions.)

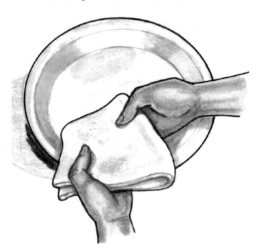

Fold the pastry so that you can transfer it to the pan without stretching or tearing it.

Roll pastry dough from the center outward to form a circle of even thickness.

Make several small slits in the top crust to allow steam to escape.

When making a one-crust pie, roll out one pastry circle for the bottom crust. Put the pastry into the pie pan. Trim it, leaving a 1/2-inch (1.3 cm) overhang. Turn the overhang under to form a double thickness along the pan rim. Flute the edge or make a forked edge.

Trim the pastry with kitchen shears. Will this be a one-crust or two-crust pie? How can you tell?

Thinking Skills

Reasoning: Ask students why pie dough should not be stretched as it is placed in the pan. *(The dough will shrink during baking and will split or crack where it was stretched.)*

Creativity: Have students brainstorm to develop a list of fillings for a one-crust pie.

Food and Nutrition Science

Effects of Fats Experiment: See the *Food Science Resources* booklet for the "Effects on Fats on Pastry" teaching guidelines and student experiment worksheet. The experiment tests the effects of four different fats on pastry.

Some recipes call for a baked pie shell. The filling is added later. If you bake the pie shell before filling it, pierce the bottom with a fork about every 1 inch (2.5 cm) to prevent the crust from bubbling up while baking.

One-crust pies can also be made with crumb crusts. Mix fine crumbs from graham crackers or gingersnaps with melted butter or margarine and press them into the pan. These crusts are usually used with unbaked fillings.

Pecan pie is an example of a pie that is traditionally made without a top crust. What others can you name?

TIPS for Success

Making a Decorative Edge

The edge of a pie crust can be finished in several ways. Here are two you can try:

❖ **Forked edge.** To make a forked edge, dip the tines of a fork in flour. Use the fork to press the pastry crust against the edge of the pan around the entire crust.

❖ **Fluted edge.** To make a fluted edge, place the index finger of one hand on the inside edge of the crust and the thumb and index finger of the other hand on the outside edge. Gently push the crust to form a curved shape. Repeat this process around the entire crust edge.

Section 21.4 Review

RECALL THE FACTS

1. What are the two basic kinds of cakes? Name two ways they are different and two ways they are alike.

2. What are six basic kinds of cookies?

3. Give two examples of dessert pies and one example of a savory pie.

4. What should you do if pastry dough tears as you are rolling it?

DISCUSS YOUR IDEAS

5. Why do you think homemade cakes and pies were more common (and perhaps more popular) 60 or 70 years ago?

APPLY YOUR LEARNING

6. In small groups, locate several pie recipes in magazines and food advertisements. Write down any shortcut ingredients or preparation methods suggested in the recipes. Make suggestions for modifying the recipes to make them lower in fat.

Section 21.4: Cakes, Cookies, and Pies   **577**

Completing the Section

Review

• Ask students to summarize the main ideas in this section.

• Have students complete the Section Review. (Answers appear below.)

Evaluation

• Provide a recipe for cookies and have students prepare them. Evaluate procedure and results.

• Have students take the quiz for Section 21.4. (Refer to the *Section Quizzes* booklet or use the *Testmaker Software*.)

Reteaching

• Have students deliberately make a tear when rolling out pie crust to practice patching the dough.

• Refer to the *Reteaching Activities* booklet for the Section 21.4 activity worksheet.

Enrichment

• Have students prepare brochures or posters entitled "Tips for a Top-Notch Pie Crust."

Closure

• Lead a discussion on the traditional role of cakes, pies, and cookies as dessert items and ways to reduce the calories and increase nutrition in various desserts.

Answers to Section Review

1. Shortened and foam; differences and likenesses will vary.
2. Bar cookies, drop cookies, cut-out or rolled cookies, molded cookies, pressed cookies, and sliced or refrigerator cookies.
3. Examples will vary.
4. Patch it with another piece of dough.
5. Answers will vary. Remind students that many people did much more physical labor than people do today, so they could afford the extra calories.
6. Answers will vary.

21.4 Recipe

Apple Bran Bars

Key Skill: Baking cookies

Using the Recipe

- Have students read the recipe and discuss each step. Review safety and sanitation procedures that apply to this recipe.
- Have each lab team fill out a work plan. (See the *Foods Lab Resources* booklet.)
- Have students check off the ingredients and equipment listed on the recipe worksheet and prepare the recipe.
- Have students complete the evaluation and questions on the recipe worksheet.

See Also . . .

The *Foods Lab Resources* booklet for the "Apple Bran Bars" recipe worksheet and other recipe alternatives.

Thinking About the Recipe

Read the recipe for "Apple Bran Bars" and answer the following questions.

1. What are two other methods you could use to test the bars for doneness?
2. How might you adapt this recipe for microwave preparation?

Apple Bran Bars

Customary	Ingredients	Metric
1 cup	100 percent bran cereal	250 mL
1/2 cup	Skim milk	125 mL
1 cup	All-purpose flour	250 mL
1 tsp.	Baking powder	5 mL
1/2 tsp.	Cinnamon, ground	2 mL
1/4 tsp.	Nutmeg, ground	1 mL
1/3 cup	Margarine	75 mL
1/2 cup	Brown sugar, packed	125 mL
2	Egg whites	2
1 cup	Pared, chopped apple	250 mL

Yield: 16 servings

Directions

Pan: 9 x 9 inch (23 x 23 cm) baking pan
Temperature: 350°F (180°C)

1. Preheat oven. Grease baking pan.
2. Soak bran in milk until milk is absorbed.
3. Mix flour, baking powder, cinnamon, and nutmeg thoroughly in a bowl. Set aside.
4. Beat margarine and sugar until creamy in a separate bowl. Add the egg whites and beat again.
5. Add the dry ingredients to the creamed mixture.
6. Stir in apples and the bran mixture; mix well.
7. Put mixture into greased baking pan.
8. Bake at 350°F (180°C) about 30 minutes or until a toothpick inserted in the center comes out clean.
9. Cool. Cut into bars and serve.

Nutrition Information

Per serving (approximate): 107 calories, 2 g protein, 17 g carbohydrate, 4 g fat, trace of cholesterol, 106 mg sodium

---

Answers to Thinking About the Recipe

1. Watch for the sides to pull away from the edges or press gently to see if it springs back.

2. Use a microwave-safe pan; cut down some on the liquid ingredients; oven does not have to be preheated; check a microwave cookbook for cooking time; test for doneness by pressing gently instead of using a wooden pick.

Career PROFILE

Cal Chandler
Retail Bakery Manager

CURRENT POSITION

"I manage the bakery department of a large supermarket."

RESPONSIBILITIES

"It's my job to see that the bakery runs efficiently and profitably. Among my specific duties are ordering supplies, hiring and supervising employees, and managing the payroll."

SKILLS

"Leadership abilities are important. In managing my staff, I've had to learn how to build a strong team out of individuals with very different personalities. Good communication skills and the ability to handle many details at one time also are necessary to succeed in this job."

EDUCATION

"I have a bachelor's degree in food service management. While I was in college, I worked part-time as a baker for a doughnut chain."

TYPICAL DAY ON THE JOB

"During a typical day, I might interview potential employees, prepare the next week's schedule, arrange for the repair of faulty equipment, and meet with a dissatisfied customer to try to make things right."

FAVORITE PART OF THE JOB

"I enjoy working with people, and this job certainly gives me ample opportunity to do that. I also like to see that operations run smoothly and that customers are happy with our services."

- What are some examples of leadership skills that a manager might need?
- What part of Cal's job appeal to you? Why?

579

CAREER PROFILE: RETAIL BAKERY MANAGER

Thinking About . . . Managing a Retail Bakery

Have students think of other questions they would like to ask Cal Chandler about managing a retail bakery. (Examples: What is the salary range for managing a retail bakery? How does the bakery department interact with other departments in the store? What do you look for in the people you hire?)

Ask student volunteers to tell what they think would be the most exciting part of managing a retail bakery.

Student Opportunities

Students planning a career as a food service manager should first gain experiences as a food service worker. They may also want to volunteer in the kitchen of a local hospital or other nonprofit organization.

Occupational Outlook

Managers of bakeries in supermarkets can be transferred to bigger stores for better salaries, or they may open their own independent bakery or chain of bakeries.

For More Information

For additional information about careers in food service management, encourage students to contact:
- The Educational Foundation of the National Restaurant Association, 20 N. Wacker Dr., Suite 2620, Chicago, IL 60606
- Council on Hotel, Restaurant, and Institutional Education, 311 First St. NW, Washington, D.C. 20001
- American Culinary Federation, P.O. Box 3466, St. Augustine, FL 32084

Review

- Have students complete the Chapter Review. (Answers appear below.)

Evaluation

- Evaluate cookies, cakes, and pies prepared by students in the foods lab.

- Have students take the test for Chapter 21. (Refer to the *Chapter and Unit Tests* booklet or construct your own test using the *Testmaker Software*.)

■ ANSWERS ■

REVIEWING FACTS

1. Pour batters, drop batters, soft doughs, stiff doughs.

2. They add lightness and volume to baked products; by expanding as the baking progresses.

3. Dark pans retain more heat than light pans and can create a thick crust.

4. Fruit and custard pies and baked items that have fillings should be refrigerated. All others should not be.

5. Muffins, quick loaf breads, biscuits.

6. To avoid overdeveloping the gluten, which would make them tough.

7. At least one third of the total amount of flour.

8. After the first rise; by pushing gently with your fist into the center of the dough.

CHAPTER 21 REVIEW

SUMMARY

SECTION 21.1

Ingredients and Techniques for Baking: Basic ingredients for baked products include flour, liquid, leavening agents, fat, sweeteners, eggs, and flavoring. Each plays a specific role in the mixture. When flour and liquid are mixed, gluten develops. The mixture forms a batter or dough. Recipes use different mixing methods depending on the desired results. Follow recipe directions for the size and type of pans to use and how to prepare them for baking. Conventional and microwave baking produce different results. After baking, remove products from pans and store them properly.

SECTION 21.2

Quick Breads: Breads, biscuits, and muffins made without yeast are called quick breads. They are mixed using the muffin method or the pastry and biscuit method. Quick breads can be nutritious, but some are high in fat and calories.

SECTION 21.3

Yeast Breads and Rolls: You can use time-saving techniques to speed up yeast bread preparation. Yeast bread dough consists of flour, salt, sugar, liquid, fat, and yeast. After kneading and rising, the dough can be shaped and baked a number of ways.

SECTION 21.4

Cakes, Cookies, and Pies: There are two basic kinds of cakes, shortened cakes and foam cakes. Foam cakes generally rely on beaten eggs instead of a chemical leavening agent. Cookies can be shaped in a variety of ways. Pies can have sweet or savory fillings, and can be made with one or two crusts. These baked goods are often high in fat and calories.

REVIEWING FACTS

1. Name two kinds of batters and two kinds of doughs. (21.1)

2. What can air, steam, and carbon dioxide do for baked goods? How do they work? (21.1)

3. What is the difference between using a dark pan or a light pan for baking? (21.1)

4. Which baked goods should be refrigerated? Which should not? Why? (21.1)

5. What are three kinds of quick breads? (21.2)

6. Why are quick breads mixed only briefly? (21.2)

7. When making whole grain yeast dough, how much all-purpose flour should be used in the dough? (21.3)

8. When and how is dough "punched" down? (21.3)

9. What are two examples of low-fat ways to decorate a cake? (21.4)

10. What are the six basic kinds of cookies? (21.4)

LEARNING BY DOING

1. ***Food science lab:*** Demonstrate the action of leavening agents. Dissolve one package of yeast in water. Add both sugar and water to another package of yeast. Combine baking powder with water and baking soda with water. Compare the results of all the samples. (21.1)

2. ***Foods lab:*** Prepare yeast dough and freeze it. At a later time, allow it to thaw and rise in the refrigerator overnight. Bake it the next day. Evaluate the results. (21.3)

9. Combine confectioners' sugar and lemon, orange, or pineapple juice; sprinkle a small amount of confectioners' sugar over a cake.

10. Bar cookies, drop cookies, cut-out or rolled cookies, molded cookies, pressed cookies, and sliced or refrigerator cookies.

3. **Foods lab:** Prepare enough pastry for a two-crust pie. Roll out all the dough in a large square. Sprinkle one-fourth of it with cinnamon and sugar, cut it into strips, and put the strips on a baking sheet. Re-roll the rest of the dough, sprinkle cinnamon and sugar on one-third of it, cut it into strips, and place the strips on another sheet. Repeat this process two more times. You should have four baking sheets of dough strips. Keep track of which sheet is which. Bake them and compare the results. Which pastry is more flaky and tender? Why? (21.4)

THINKING CRITICALLY

1. **Recognizing alternatives:** To cut down on fat and calories, Mick has decided to streamline his bread recipe to include only flour, water, and yeast. Will his "no-frills" bread be a satisfactory product? Why or why not? What are some alternative plans? (21.1)

2. **Predicting consequences:** Jan is baking bread for 45 minutes in a disposable aluminum pan. Because she plans to throw the pan out after using it, she doesn't grease it. What are two problems using this pan might cause? (21.1)

3. **Determining accuracy:** Paula's friend heard that you could substitute applesauce for oil in a muffin recipe to cut down on fat. How can Paula find out whether this is true? (21.2)

4. **Forming hypotheses:** Bread has been called the staff of life. Those selling homes are sometimes encouraged to bake bread before showing their house so it smells appealing. Why do you think bread has such importance? (21.3)

MAKING DECISIONS AND SOLVING PROBLEMS

What Would You Do?

1. A friend invites you over to make cookies for a party. She says that she likes to bake by just throwing a bunch of ingredients together. Directions are not for her. (21.1, 21.4)

2. Your life is hectic, with school sports, music lessons, and other activities. Your grandmother, who lives with you, is turning eighty later this week. You know she would love to have fresh yeast rolls for her birthday breakfast. (21.3)

3. Some family friends drop by just before dinner time. Your dad asks you to prepare a special dessert within an hour. (21.4)

LINKING YOUR STUDIES

1. **Science:** Research and report on one of the following topics: What is yeast and how does it grow? What is in baking powder and baking soda that brings about a chemical reaction to form carbon dioxide? Why does baking soda need to be mixed with an acid? (21.1)

2. **Social studies:** Use your school or public library to find out how the American colonists (or other groups) baked bread before the invention of the kitchen range. (21.3)

3. **Social studies:** Read about ancient Egypt and find out how bread baking developed. Report to the class. (21.3)

4. **Math:** Make a chart comparing one kind of pie made in several ways: totally from scratch; using a purchased crust and canned filling; or purchased from a bakery. Rate each kind in terms of preparation time, cost, and fat and calorie content. (21.4)

LEARNING BY DOING

Answers to "Learning by Doing" activities will vary. Evaluate students on the procedures they use as well as their results.

THINKING CRITICALLY

1. No, because there is no food for the yeast in the mix. Alternatives will vary.

2. The bread might stick to the pan; the bread might not rise correctly.

3. By talking with her home economics teacher or another expert; by performing an experiment.

4. Answers will vary.

MAKING DECISIONS AND SOLVING PROBLEMS

Answers to "Making Decisions and Solving Problems" activities will vary. Encourage students to give reasons for their answers.

LINKING YOUR STUDIES

Answers to "Linking Your Studies" activities will vary. Encourage students to give reasons for their answers.

COMPLETING THE UNIT
Refer to page 393 for suggestions for completing the unit.

UNIT FIVE

Expanding Your Horizons

Teacher's Classroom Resources—Unit Five

Refer to these resources in the TCR package:

Chapter and Unit Tests

Testmaker Software

582

UNIT FIVE

Expanding Your Horizons

583

Introducing the Unit

Motivators

- As students enter the class-room, greet them with exotic music and the aroma of foods you have purchased or pre-pared. Include a variety of the foods and artistic touches (gar-nishes, etc.) discussed in Chapters 22-24. Invite students to sample the foods. Discuss how food choices and prepara-tion methods reflect both cul tural traditions and creativity.

- Create a bulletin board illus-trating food and nutrition careers in the areas of food technology, food service, and home economics. Discuss the jobs involved in each area.

Completing the Unit

Review

- Refer students to the first unit motivator. Ask them what they have learned in this unit that will help them prepare and present food more effectively.

- Lead a discussion about the various careers open to stu-dents interested in food and nutrition.

Evaluation

- Have students take the test for Unit Five. (Refer to the *Chapter and Unit Tests* booklet or con-struct your own test using the *Testmaker Software*.)

Planning the Chapter

Chapter Overview

Section 22.1: Latin America

Section 22.2: Africa and the Middle East

Section 22.3: Europe

Section 22.4: Asia and the Pacific

Introducing the Chapter

Motivators

• Show students photos or samples of five or more foods from other countries. Ask them to guess the countries from which the foods originated. Why did they make the guesses they did?

• Obtain menus from restaurants that serve foreign foods. Have students choose from the menus three unfamiliar foods. Ask them to find out what the foods are, the ingredients, and how they are prepared.

CHAPTER 22

Foods of the World

584

Cooperative Learning Suggestions

Initiate a Co-op Co-op activity. Have students work in groups to research foods from different parts of the world. Assign a region to each group. Each student can research a different country within that region. Research should include climate, foods grown, cultural influences, and common foods. Have members of each group share their information with their own group. Have students work together to collect pictures and items depicting the culture of each country. Assign each group a day to put up a display about the culture of the area, to present information on the region, and to share typical foods for the class to taste.

Latin America

OBJECTIVES

After studying this section, you should be able to:

- Describe food choices available in the various regions of Latin America.
- Identify the cultural influences on foods in Latin America.

LOOK FOR THIS TERM

maize

Over twenty countries in Central and South America make up what is called Latin America—the land where people speak languages based on Latin (Spanish, French, Portuguese). This region of over 300 million people stretches from Mexico and the Caribbean Islands to the tip of South America. It contains the fastest growing city in the world, Mexico City.

The early history of this area is dominated by three native cultures: Aztec, Inca, and Maya. The Aztecs flourished in Mexico, the Incas in South America, and the Mayans in Central America.

Because the area is so vast, it includes climates and geographical features of all kinds—tropical rain forests, snow-capped mountains, arid deserts, and temperate zones. Foods vary according to the growing conditions, but there are many similarities from country to country.

Corn, or **maize,** is the staple grain in much of Latin America. Wheat and rice are grown in some areas.

Dry beans, corn products, chili peppers, and avocados are common ingredients in Latin American cooking.

Section 22.1: Latin America   **585**

**Section 22.1
Latin America**

Introducing the Section

Motivators

- Ask students to name foods they associate with Latin America. How many of these foods are fast-food varieties of Mexican food?
- Display fruits and vegetables that are popular in Latin America. Have students identify the ones with which they are familiar. Identify and provide information about the uses of those that are unfamiliar to students.

Objectives

- Have students read the section objectives. Discuss the purpose of studying this section.

Vocabulary

- Pronounce the terms listed under "Look for These Terms." Have students find the terms and their definitions in the section.

Guided Reading

- Have students look at the headings within Section 22.1 to preview the concepts that will be discussed.
- Have students read the section and complete the appropriate part of the Chapter 22 Study Guide in the *Student Workbook*.

Teacher's Classroom Resources—Section 22.1

Refer to these resources in the TCR package:

Reproducible Lesson Plans

Student Workbook

Extending the Text

Reteaching Activities

Section Quizzes

Testmaker Software

Foods Lab Resources

Multicultural Resources

Color Transparencies

Comprehension Check

1. Ask students to list and describe foods common in Mexican meals. *(tortillas, tacos, tostadas, enchiladas, frijoles, tamales, moles)*

2. Ask students to describe the use of flan in Mexico. What is flan made of? *(Flan is a dessert made of sweet custard topped with a sauce of caramelized sugar.)*

3. Ask students to list the countries that make up Central America. *(Belize, Costa Rica, El Salvador, Guatemala, Honduras, Nicaragua, Panama.)*

4. Ask students to explain what chayote is. How do the people in Costa Rica prepare it? *(A crisp vegetable with a delicate flavor; mixed with cheese and eggs.)*

5. Ask students to name the staple foods in the Caribbean islands. *(fish and shellfish)*

This street vendor in Mexico holds a basket of churros, fried pastries sprinkled with sugar and cinnamon.

Mexico

Mexico's wide variety of foods have developed both from the native foods which abound and the influence of the Spanish conquerors.

Cornmeal, rice, cooked dry beans, and chili peppers are basic to Mexican food. The bland taste of corn and beans provides a mild contrast to the variety of spicy peppers.

Here are some foods that are common in Mexican meals:

❖ *Tortillas* are thin discs of bread. They are generally made from *masa,* dried corn that is soaked in limewater and ground while wet.

❖ *Tacos* are folded tortillas filled with foods such as meat, chicken, refried beans, avocadoes, onion, lettuce, cheese, tomatoes, and salsa, a spicy sauce.

❖ *Tostadas* begin with a crispy fried tortilla spread with the same kinds of foods used to make tacos.

❖ *Enchiladas* are made from a soft tortilla rolled around a meat, bean, or cheese filling and topped with salsa and grated cheese.

❖ *Frijoles* are cooked dry beans. *Frijoles refritos* are cooked dry beans that are mashed and fried in lard.

❖ *Tamales* are made of finely chopped fillings encased in masa dough, wrapped in corn husks or banana leaves, and steamed.

❖ *Moles* are Mexican sauces. Mole poblano is made from tomatoes, chili, fruit, seasonings, and chocolate, which gives it richness.

Mexicans like to finish off a meal with a popular dessert called *flan,* a sweet custard topped with a sauce of caramelized sugar.

With years of experience and centuries of tradition behind her, this Mexican woman makes a batch of tortillas. She uses the traditional tools: a metate to hold the dough and a metlalpil to roll it.

Special Needs Strategies

Learning Disabled: Have students make signs to put on a world map summarizing the dietary staples in different regions of the world. Each day, call on a different student to present the list for his or her area.

Gifted and Talented: Provide students with menus from foreign restaurants. Have students find definitions of commonly used terms and create a Foreign Menu Dictionary to share with the class.

Gifted and Talented: Have students research ways meals are served in different parts of the world. Have students create display of table settings and demonstrate serving styles as closely as possible.

Central America

A bridge of seven countries connects Mexico to South America: Belize, Costa Rica, El Salvador, Guatemala, Honduras, Nicaragua, and Panama. This is where the Mayan empire flourished. People who live in these countries today are of Mayan, European, African, and mixed descent. The cooking has Mayan and Aztec roots with Spanish and Caribbean influences.

Corn and beans are the staple crops. Bananas, coffee, coconuts, and cacao are exported to other countries.

Chicken is widely eaten in Central America. It might be prepared with pineapple, or in a mixture of ingredients such as pumpkin seeds, tomatoes, and raisins.

A favorite food is the chayote, a crisp vegetable with a delicate flavor. (See the illustration in Section 16.1, page 411). Chayote is often sliced and simmered. Costa Ricans mix it with cheese and eggs, while cooks in the Dominican Republic may fry it with eggs, tomatoes, and hot peppers.

The Caribbean

The tropical islands of the Caribbean Sea are to the south and east of Mexico, between Florida and South America. Caribbean nations include Cuba, Jamaica, Haiti, the Dominican Republic, and Puerto Rico.

Columbus landed on the islands on his trek to find spices and a shorter route to India. The Spanish came later as did the Dutch, Portuguese, British, and French. All of these cultures left their mark on the people who live there today, in the languages they speak, their customs, and their food.

Fish and shellfish are staple foods on the islands. Flying fish, conchs, shrimp, codfish, clams, grouper, and red snapper are just a few of the choices available.

Tropical fruits and vegetables grow in abundance. Mangoes, bananas, coconuts, papayas, pineapples, sweet potatoes, yams, pumpkins, and chili peppers are basic in island cooking. Islanders use coconut milk and fruit juice to prepare many kinds of foods.

The staple food is the *plantain*, a starchy food that looks like a green banana and is cooked as a vegetable. It can be roasted, fried, boiled, or baked, as well as combined in dishes with meat and cheese.

Cooking techniques and sauces vary, giving each island unique dishes even though many of the ingredients are the same. Here are some examples of foods found among the Caribbean Islands:

❖ ***Moros y Cristianos*** is a Cuban national dish made with black beans and rice.
❖ ***Djon-djon*** are black mushrooms found only on Haiti. Haitian food generally reflects French and African influences.
❖ ***Jamaican Saturday Soup*** includes hot peppers (originally from Africa), carrots, turnips, and pumpkin added to beef stock.

This buffet from the island of Barbados includes beans, rice, plaintain, fish, pineapple, and other locally available foods.

Student Experiences

1. **Guest Demonstration:** Invite a person who prepares homemade tortillas to demonstrate the procedure to the class. Discuss ways tortillas are used in Mexican meals. *(Key skill: kitchen management skills)*

2. **Taste Test:** Prepare plantain by roasting, frying, boiling, or baking. Have students taste the dish. Show students that the raw plantain looks like a banana, but point out that it is cooked like a vegetable. *(Key skill: evaluation)*

3. **Display:** Create a display of the staple foods of Central America: corn, beans, bananas, coffee, coconuts, cacao, chicken, and chayote. Ask each student to choose a food and research to find out how the food is used in Central American cooking. Have students write a short report of their findings. *(Key skills: writing, research)*

4. **Store Survey:** Have students survey a grocery store to see what types of Mexican foods are available locally. What do they cost? *(Key skill: multicultural awareness)*

Lab Experience

Have students prepare a typical Mexican meal including dishes based on tortillas; a typical Mexican sauce such as salsa, picante, or guacamole sauce; and flan, the popular Mexican dessert.

More About Mexican Foods

- Guacamole is a rich and delicious Mexican sauce that is now popular in the United States. It is made from avocados, onion, and tomatoes.
- *Sopa secas*, or dry soups, are widely eaten in Mexico. Spanish rice is the American version of sopa seca.
- The combination of cinnamon and chocolate is popular in Mexico; they are sometimes mixed with coffee to make a tasty beverage.

Teaching . . .

• South America

(text pages 588-589)

Comprehension Check

1. Ask students to name and describe three foods native to Brazil. *(See list on page 588.)*

2. Ask students to name the staple food of Peru. *(potatoes)*

3. Ask students to explain why the people in Argentina eat a lot of beef. *(Raising beef is one of Argentina's major industries.)*

Student Experiences

1. **Mapping:** Have students draw a map of South America, listing foods typical of each country and identifying European influences, where appropriate. *(Key skill: mapping)*

2. **Geography:** Have students look up the geography of Argentina. Ask students to speculate about why beef is a major industry in that country. *(Key skill: geography)*

Healthy Attitudes

In many Latin American countries, staple foods include grains, beans, and fresh fruits and vegetables. These food choices are relatively low in fat, sugar, and sodium. How might the food customs that originated in the past benefit people now and in the future?

❖ **Conchs** are shellfish that come from beautiful shells. The meat must be beaten before it is tender enough to eat.

❖ **Crapaud**, a huge bullfrog which lives in the mountaintops of the island of Dominica, is considered a delicacy.

For dessert, a pudding or ice cream made with an exotic fruit would be a popular choice.

South America

Twelve nations make up South America, the southern half of the Western Hemisphere: Argentina, Bolivia, Brazil, Chili, Colombia, Ecuador, Guyana, Paraguay, Peru, Suriname, Uruguay, and Venezuela. It also includes French Guiana, a European possession.

As in the rest of Latin America, the population is of native Indian, European, and African ancestry. The climate, culture, people, and growing conditions vary greatly from country to country and from rural area to city.

Brazil

Brazil, the largest country in South America, is located on the eastern part of the continent. It produces great amounts of beef,

coffee, and cocoa. The people of Brazil are mainly a mixture of native Indians, Portuguese, and Africans.

Brazilian food reflects this mixture. From West Africa comes *dende* or palm oil (which gives a bright yellow-orange color to foods), *malagueta* peppers, and coconut milk. All are widely used to prepare food in Brazil. From the Portuguese comes the love for sausages and kale in soups.

Here are some examples of foods you might find in Brazil:

❖ **Feijoada** is the national dish of Brazil. It's made of stewed black beans, smoked sausages, dried beef, pork, onions in hot sauce, rice, collard greens, and sliced oranges.

❖ **Churrasco** is beef that is marinated and barbecued.

❖ **Mariscada** is a fish stew made with an assortment of fish: clams, mussels, codfish, shrimp, and crabmeat. They are all cooked together with tomatoes and spices.

Black beans are a staple in Brazil. What popular Brazillian dish is made with black beans?

Thinking Skills

Critical Thinking: Have students discuss how the geography, farm products, and food supply of a particular area affect cuisine. *(The foods commonly eaten in a country tend to reflect what is grown or available locally,* *which is in turn affected by the geography of the country. This was more true before food processing and storage techniques became as advanced as they are today.)*

Peru

Peru is located on the Pacific coast of South America. When Pizarro, the Spanish conqueror, came to Peru in the 16th century, the local people were eating corn, potatoes, squash, beans, cassava, sweet potatoes, peanuts, tomatoes, avocados, and chili peppers. While these foods are still popular, today Peru is also noted for its fishing industry. The potato remains its staple food. Popular meats include seafood, beef, and guinea pig.

Peru was a Spanish colony for almost 300 years. The Spanish influence can be seen in foods such as *gazpacho*, a cold tomato-based soup of Spanish origin. (See the recipe on page 590).

Ceviche is a native Peruvian dish in which raw fish is marinated in lime. Other foods often eaten in more affluent (wealthy) areas include meat, poultry, vegetables, and grains that are highly seasoned with onions, garlic, and hot peppers. Rice, potatoes, and bread accompany the main meals.

In poorer areas, meals include potatoes, corn, squash, and soups made of wheat and barley. The foods of those living in jungle areas consist of a variety of fish, small game, fruits, and nuts.

Argentina

South of Brazil, along the eastern coast of South America, lies Argentina. Today most of its inhabitants are of European descent.

Raising beef is one of Argentina's major industries, and as a result most people eat beef. It is often grilled outdoors and served with spicy sauces. *Puchero* is a meat and vegetable stew.

Another widely-eaten dish is the *empanada*, a turnover of dough filled with vegetables, meat, fruit, or a combination of the three. Meats are also combined with fruits in local stews such as *Carbonada Criolla*—beef mixed with peaches.

This gaucho, or South American cowboy, is engaged in producing one of Argentina's largest exports—beef.

Section 22.1 Review

RECALL THE FACTS

1. What is the staple grain in most of Latin America?

2. What is the most popular type of bread in Mexican cooking?

3. What cultures have influenced Caribbean food?

DISCUSS YOUR IDEAS

4. What factors influence the food customs of a particular area?

APPLY YOUR LEARNING

5. In groups, make a list of the foods described in this section with which you are familiar. What other Latin American foods have you tasted that were not listed in the text? What ingredients appear regularly in the dishes you listed?

Section 22.1: Latin America   **589**

Answers to Section Review

1. Corn.
2. Tortillas.
3. Italy, Spain, Holland, Portugal, Great Britain, and France.

4. Answers may include the geography of the area, weather conditions, what products are grown there, dominant religious beliefs, etc.

5. Answers will vary.

22.1 Recipe

Gazpacho
(Cold Vegetable Soup)

Key Skill: Preparing soups

Using the Recipe

- Have students read the recipe and discuss each step. Review safety and sanitation procedures that apply to this recipe. Remind students never to run the blender without first putting the lid in its proper place.
- Have each lab team fill out a work plan. (See the *Foods Lab Resources* booklet.)
- Have students check off the ingredients and equipment listed on the recipe worksheet and prepare the recipe.
- Have students complete the evaluation and questions on the recipe worksheet.

See Also . . .

The *Foods Lab Resources* booklet for the "Gazpacho (Cold Vegetable Soup)" recipe worksheet and other recipe alternatives.

Thinking About the Recipe

Read the recipe for "Gazpacho" and answer the following questions.

1. How does this recipe illustrate European influence on Latin American food customs?
2. How might you puree the ingredients if you didn't have a blender?

Gazpacho (Cold Vegetable Soup)

Customary	Ingredients	Metric
16-oz. can	Whole tomatoes, with liquid	454-g can
1/2 cup	Finely chopped green peppers, divided	125 mL
1/2 cup	Finely chopped cucumber, divided	125 mL
1/4 cup	Chopped onion, divided	50 mL
1 Tbsp.	Vegetable oil	15 mL
1½ tsp.	Ground cumin	7 mL
1½ tsp.	Cider vinegar	7 mL
1/4 tsp.	Salt	1 mL
1/4 tsp.	Pepper	1 mL
1/2 cup	Croutons, unseasoned	125 mL

Yield: 4 servings

Directions

1. Put in a blender: tomatoes (with liquid), 1/4 cup (50 mL) of green pepper, 1/4 cup (50 mL) of cucumber, 1/4 cup (50 mL) of onion, the vegetable oil, cumin, cider vinegar, salt, and pepper. (Save remaining ingredients to serve as accompaniments to the soup.)
2. Cover and blend ingredients on medium speed until smooth.
3. Place blended mixture in a covered container. Refrigerate for 1 hour or longer.
4. Serve soup cold with the croutons and remaining chopped ingredients as accompaniments.

Nutrition Information

Per serving (approximate): 71 calories, 2 g protein, 9 g carbohydrate, 4 g fat, 0 mg cholesterol, 330 mg sodium

---

Answers to Thinking About the Recipe

1. Answers will vary.

2. You could use a food processor; you could use a strainer or food mill to puree the tomatoes, then dice other ingredients for a chunky soup.

SECTION 22.2

Africa and the Middle East

OBJECTIVES

After studying this section, you should be able to:
- Describe food choices available in Africa and the Middle East.
- Identify the cultural and geographical influences on the foods of Africa and the Middle East.

LOOK FOR THESE TERMS

berbere
kibbutz

Although Africa is an ocean away from Latin America, the two continents share some of the same foods. This is the result of journeys by explorers and settlers, the transportation of Africans to the New World as slaves, and the similarities in climate.

The mixing of cultures and food traditions often makes it difficult to determine the origins of particular foods. Unleavened breads, for example, are common in many cultures. Variations of pita bread can be found throughout the Middle East and much of Africa. For example, a staple bread of Ethiopia, a country in eastern Africa, is *injera*, a giant pancake baked on a griddle. It is used to wrap and scoop other foods.

The Sahara Desert forms a natural east-west dividing line through Africa. It separates the five nations in the north, along the Mediterranean Sea, from the rest of the continent.

The people living south of the Sahara are mainly Africans. Those living north of the Sahara are mostly Arabs, with a culture similar to the Middle East. For purposes of discussion, the five countries north of the Sahara will be included later in this section, in "North Africa and the Middle East."

Members of a Middle Eastern family gather for the evening meal. By tradition, the diners sit on the floor.

Section 22.2
Africa and the Middle East

Introducing the Section

Motivators

- Ask students to recall information about the geography and history of Africa and the Middle East. Ask students to identify possible influences on foods in that part of the world. What forces contributed to the mixing of cultures? What effect do you think mixing the cultures would have on food traditions of the region?
- Ask students to identify foods that have been brought to this country from Africa and the Middle East.

Objectives

- Have students read the section objectives. Discuss the purpose of studying this section.

Vocabulary

- Pronounce the terms listed under "Look for These Terms." Have students find the terms and their definitions in the section.

Guided Reading

- Have students look at the headings within Section 22.2 to preview the concepts that will be discussed.
- Have students read the section and complete the appropriate part of the Chapter 22 Study Guide in the *Student Workbook*.

Teacher's Classroom Resources—Section 22.2

Refer to these resources in the TCR package:

Reproducible Lesson Plans	*Section Quizzes*
Student Workbook	*Testmaker Software*
Extending the Text	*Foods Lab Resources*
Reteaching Activities	*Multicultural Resources*
	Color Transparencies

Teaching . . .

• **Africa Below the Sahara**

(text pages 592-594)

Comprehension Check

1. Ask students to explain why food customs in sub-Saharan African countries are more likely to be based on kinship ties than to political boundaries of the countries. *(The society has always been very kinship-oriented; people usually jointly owned the surrounding farmlands and made joint decisions about which food crops to grow.)*

2. Ask students to identify the chief crops of the sub-Sahara region. *(Plantains, rice, bananas, yams, cassava in the tropical areas; corn, millet, and sorghum in the grasslands; onions, garlic, plantains, pumpkins, watermelons, cucumbers, chili, dates, and figs in other areas.)*

3. Ask students to identify the typical eating African pattern. *(They eat one large meal a day, usually in the evening, and snack during the rest of the day.)*

4. Ask students to explain what berbere is and how it is used. *(A blend of spices, including garlic, red and black peppers, salt, coriander, fenugreek, and cardamom; it's used in Ethiopia in soups and stews.)*

Africa Below the Sahara

The area south of the Sahara Desert is sometimes known as the sub-Sahara region. Most of this area has a tropical or subtropical climate. However, there is a wide range in geographical features, including mountains, coastlines, river valleys, tropical rain forests, and the Sahara Desert. Consequently, different foods are raised in various regions.

Historically, African society has been based on kinship groups of related people. These kinship groups linked together into clans, and clans formed into tribes that might have thousands of members. Clans often lived together in villages and jointly owned the surrounding farmland. Food traditions are often linked to these associations rather than the political borders of specific countries.

Large cities are scattered throughout Africa, centers of business, trade, and government. International settlers in these cities brought their customs with them. Thus the lifestyles and foods in cities differ from those in rural areas. People in less developed areas eat foods traditional to that particular region.

At this market in the West African nation of Mali, peanuts and yams are among the foods sold.

Shoppers in this Nairobi, Kenya, market have a wide variety of beans from which to choose.

More About European Settlements

The first Europeans to come to Africa were the Portuguese explorers. They were followed by the Dutch, who decided to stay and establish farms. The French Huguenots (Protestants) came next, looking for religious freedom. Germans and other Europeans also came, but did not remain in large numbers as the Dutch and French did.

This peanut snack shows an African influence. According to some historians, peanuts were brought to Africa from South America over two hundred years ago.

1. **Group Discussion:** Discuss why hunger is one of Africa's most urgent problems and the causes of this hunger. How do geography and politics contribute to the problem? What part does religion play in people's food choices in Africa? *(Key skill: critical thinking)*

2. **Cultural Influences:** Have students research foods that are native to Africa and those that were brought by the explorers, traders, and settlers. What effect has this had on food customs? *(Key skill: social studies)*

3. **Recipe Search:** Have students find recipes for preparing yams in a traditional African manner. Are any similar recipes popular in the United States? *(Key skill: reading)*

4. **Nutritional Analysis:** Have students consider the nutritional benefits of using meat as a flavoring ingredient rather than as the main focus of the meal. What foods provide protein in the African diet? *(Key skill: health)*

Climate varies, which influences the kinds of crops that can be grown. Western and central Africa are wet, tropical areas. Their chief crops include plantains, rice, bananas, yams, and cassava. In the grasslands in the east and south, corn, millet, and sorghum are among the crops grown. Wheat is grown in many areas, along with foods such as onions, garlic, plantains, pumpkins, watermelons, cucumbers, chili, dates, and figs.

Chickens, cattle, sheep, and goats may be raised wherever possible. Small herds of animals have traditionally provided income, as well as food, for small farmers and herders. Meat, however, is usually eaten just for special occasions. People living along waterways, such as rivers, lakes, and seacoasts, have an abundant supply of fish.

Over the centuries, food crops introduced from other continents were incorporated into African food traditions. Coconuts were introduced from Asia in the 1500s. Sweet potatoes and corn came from America at roughly the same time. In the 1600s, cassava became an important food source. It thrived in much of Africa, even in difficult growing conditions. In the 1700s, peanuts were introduced, possibly from South America.

Yams continue to be important in Africa. The traditional way to prepare them is to boil, peel, and slice or pound them until they form a paste called *fufu*. In West Africa, cooks mash and deep fry them, make them into croquettes, or slice and bake them. In some areas, cooks make fufu by mashing cassava and plantains.

Most Africans eat one large meal a day, and this is generally in the evening. A typical meal may include a grain such as millet cooked into a porridge or a vegetable such as yams. This is served with a seasoned stew made with vegetables and flavored with meat, poultry, or fish, if available. During the rest of the day, Africans eat light snacks.

Section 22.2: Africa and the Middle East   593

Thinking Skills

Critical Thinking: Point out that Africa is a frequent site of wars and natural disasters. Ask students to think about the effect these problems have on sanitary conditions. How does this affect the health of many African people? *(The problems usually bring unsafe and unsanitary conditions, which frequently cause illness and death. For example, food distributed in a war-torn country may be spoiled or infected with pests because of the time it takes to get it to those in need. This increases the problems of malnutrition and hunger in these countries. War-devastated cities often have no running water or sewage disposal, creating conditions for the rampant spread of disease.)*

- **North Africa and the Middle East**

(text pages 594-596)

Comprehension Check

1. Ask students to explain why traditional foods in the countries of North Africa and the Middle East include foods typical of Asia, Europe, and southern Africa. *(This region is bordered by Asia, Europe, and southern Africa, and has therefore been well traveled by the inhabitants of those areas.)*

2. Ask students to identify the staple grains in North Africa and the Middle East. What other foods are common? *(Wheat and barley; olive oil, rice, yogurt, chickpeas, fava beans, lentils, lamb, and goat; various fruits.)*

3. Ask students to list and describe foods popular in the Arab countries. *(tabbouleh, felafel, kubaybah, stuffed vine leaves, herrira, pastilla, couscous, kebabs, chelo, koresh)*

The meal is always a social occasion. The food may be served in one large bowl, set on the ground. People sit around the bowl, using either pieces of bread or their fingers to scoop up the food.

In many areas of Africa, spicy hot foods are preferred. Cooks make up their own seasoning mixes, based on the many kinds of hot chili and spices available. One blend, called **berbere,** is commonly used in Ethiopia in soups and stews. It is a spicy hot combination of garlic, red and black peppers, salt, coriander, fenugreek, and cardamom. Other spices are added, depending on the cook's preference.

South Africa was visited and also settled by many waves of Europeans looking for trade routes or escaping persecution. These French, Dutch, British, and German Europeans brought their own food preferences and preparation methods. African cooks modified them with local produce and techniques. *Bredie*, for example, is a stew made with meat or fish, vegetables, onions, and chili peppers.

The fruit-filled triangles on the left are made with phyllo, very thin sheets of pastry. Phyllo dough is common in Middle Eastern cuisine and can hold either sweet or savory fillings. Stuffed vegetables are also popular, such as these onions stuffed with ground meat and spicy stuffed artichokes.

North Africa and the Middle East

The five main countries in North Africa include Libya, Egypt, Algeria, Morocco, and Tunisia. The population is clustered along the Mediterranean, in desert oases, or in irrigated parts of Egypt along the Nile.

The Middle East is located just east of North Africa, between Southeast Europe and Southwest Asia. The countries of the Middle East include Lebanon, Syria, Iran, Iraq, Israel, Jordan, Kuwait, Turkey, and Saudi Arabia, along with many others.

Because of its location between Asia, Europe, and southern Africa, this area has been well-traveled. Its cuisine reflects the influence of those early travelers. The use of rice as a staple and the variety of produce are some of the results of foreign visitors.

Most of the inhabitants of this area share many food traditions. Because all of these nations were occupied by European countries some time in the past, there is also French and British influence in the food customs.

More About North Africa

North Africans also enjoy porridge, grilled lamb, meatballs, roasted locusts, and mint tea. Poorer people must be content with a diet of cereal, legumes, seasonal vegetables, and bread. In Egypt, peasants have even less. They exist on a porridge of brown beans, lentils, or rice.

In the desert live nomads, who trade goods or do short-term work. They eat camel meat and drink camel milk, among other things. In an oasis, the date palm is common. Dates have become a symbol of hospitality, and they are always offered to visitors.

Tabbouleh is a popular, refreshing salad from the Middle East. It is made with bulgur (steamed, dried, crushed wheat kernels).

Staples in this area are wheat and barley. Other commonly used foods include olive oil, rice, yogurt, chickpeas (or garbanzo beans), fava beans, lentils, lamb, and goat. Fruits include apricots, pomegranates, dates, figs, grapes, and oranges. Vegetables include eggplant, peppers, olives, cucumbers, and tomatoes. Seasonings include parsley, dill, mint, cinnamon, lemon juice, pine nuts, onion, and garlic. *Tahini*, a sesame seed paste, is popular.

Most people in this area are Arabs. Israel, which is a Jewish nation, is the exception.

Arab Countries

There are many similarities in the foods of these countries. The names and some seasonings may vary, but the ingredients and cooking methods are similar.

While lamb is commonly eaten, chicken and fish are also used when they are available. Chicken is sometimes an ingredient in stews made with lentils, beans, rice, and vegetables.

Tabbouleh is a popular salad made with bulgur, olive oil, tomatoes, mint, parsley, and onions.

Healthy Attitudes

Throughout much of Africa, meat is used as a flavoring ingredient rather than as the main focus of the meal. The people get more of their protein from combinations of plant foods, such as rice and beans. Plant proteins are a staple in Latin America and the Middle East, also. As you have learned, health experts encourage Americans to use plant foods as a source of protein more often. What might Americans learn about healthful eating from their global neighbors?

22.2

Student Experiences

1. **Taste Test:** Have students taste stuffed vine leaves and couscous. Discuss other dishes commonly found in the countries of North Africa. *(Key skill: multicultural awareness)*

2. **Map Reading:** On a map of Africa, have students locate the areas in North Africa where the population is clustered. Discuss reasons other areas are virtually unpopulated. *(Key skill: geography)*

3. **Map Reading:** Have students locate the countries of the Middle East on a world map. Discuss how the food traditions of these countries have been affected by their location. *(Key skill: geography)*

Healthy Attitudes

Ask students to brainstorm American dishes that use meat only for flavoring or that could be altered and prepared so that meat is used only for flavoring.

Teaching . . .

• Israel

(text page 597)

Comprehension Check

1. Ask students to name condiments typically used in Israeli foods. *(zhoug, shatta, and tahini)*

2. Ask students to explain what a kibbutz is and describe the foods normally eaten on a kibbutz. *(A communal organization that raises its own food; fresh produce, cold meats, cheese, fish, eggs, condiments, vegetable salads, hot coffee, chicken, and lamb.)*

3. In what way does the Jewish religious law affect cooking methods among many families in Israel? *(Traditional religious laws forbid cooking on the Sabbath, a day of rest and worship. Food is often slow cooked, which allows the foods to be started the day before.)*

Student Experiences

1. **Guest Speaker:** Invite a guest speaker to discuss ways Jewish food traditions and laws affect food customs in Israel. *(Key skill: multicultural awareness)*

2. **Research:** Have students research the history of Israel and the land that makes up what is now the nation of Israel. How has history influenced Israeli culture and food customs? *(Key skill: history)*

A major food in this area is yogurt. Depending on where you are, you might find yogurt made from the milk of cows, goats, camels, or buffalo. In several countries, yogurt is called *leban*. Leban is often mixed with vegetables, especially cucumbers and dates, for a side dish or part of a main dish.

Here are some other dishes commonly found in this area.

❖ **Felafel** are patties made from ground chickpeas, well-seasoned and fried. They are served in pita bread with tahini and vegetables.

❖ **Kubaybah or kibbi** is a mixture of ground lamb, bulgur, cinnamon, and allspice.

❖ **Stuffed vine leaves** are filled with a rice and meat mixture and served with a sauce made of yogurt, garlic, and mint.

❖ **Herrira,** a mutton and vegetable soup, is eaten often during Ramadan, the month when Muslims fast during daylight hours.

❖ **Pastilla,** a dish from Morocco and Algeria, is a pigeon pie made with phyllo dough, eggs, vegetables, spices, and nuts.

❖ **Couscous** has a double meaning. It refers to a type of pasta popular in this region, which looks like tiny beads of dough. It also refers to the main dish that is made with a variety of stews served over steamed couscous.

❖ **Kebabs** are made of marinated cubes of lamb on a metal skewer and grilled with herbs. Ground meat is also formed into long patties and cooked on skewers.

In Iran, Iraq, and Lebanon, some of the following dishes might be served:

❖ **Chelo** is steamed rice accompanied by a meat or vegetable dish.

❖ **Koresh** is a stew of meat or poultry with vegetables, fruit, nuts, seasoning, and perhaps cereal. Most Iranians will eat a *chelo koresh* for one meal a day.

Desserts in this area are often fresh, seasonal fruits. In the winter, a compote of dried fruits may be served. Sweeter treats include *baklava* (phyllo dough layered with nuts and syrup), *halva* (a sweetened candy), and rice pudding.

For a feast, such as a wedding, it is common to roast a whole sheep and serve it with couscous. A salad of tomatoes, peppers, cucumbers, mint, oranges, melon, grapes, dates, and figs might be included.

Soon these ingredients will become a tasty North African stew, or tagine, of lamb, chickpeas, vegetables, raisins, and spices, served over couscous. The mild flavor of the couscous is a fitting background for stronger-flavored foods.

More About Jewish Foods and Customs

Gefilte fish is a traditional meal of the Jewish people. It is a combination of different fishes, bread crumbs, eggs, and seasonings, mixed and stuffed into a whole fish, then baked. Because it can be made ahead of time and served cold, it is popular on the Sabbath—the holy day of the week—when work is forbidden by Jewish law.

Israel

Israel includes people native to the Middle East along with others from around the world. Consequently, its food customs combine Middle Eastern traditions with those of many other countries. Customs also reflect Jewish food traditions and laws.

Traditional condiments which find their way into most recipes include *zhoug, shatta,* and *tahini. Shatta* is a red chili pepper mixture. *Zhoug* is a combination of green chili peppers, parsley, coriander, cumin, garlic, olive oil, and salt and pepper.

Some Israelis live in a **kibbutz,** a communal organization which raises its own food. Breakfasts at a kibbutz are known to be substantial. They may consist of fresh produce, cold meats, cheese, fish, eggs, condiments, vegetable salads, and hot coffee.

Chicken and lamb are widely used. Many main dishes are prepared using slow cooking procedures. Traditional Jewish religious laws forbid cooking on the Sabbath, a day of rest and worship. Slow cooking allowed foods to be started the day before.

Traditional Jewish dishes are familiar in America and elsewhere, as well as in Israel. They include (above) challah bread, gefilte fish, blintzes, and knishes, among others. Another Jewish tradition is the seder plate (left), part of the Passover holiday. Each of the foods on the plate has a symbolic meaning.

Section 22.2 Review

RECALL THE FACTS

1. What are two important food plants which found their way from the Americas to Africa?
2. What is couscous?
3. How has location influenced the food customs of the Middle East?
4. Give an example of how religion influences eating habits in Middle Eastern countries.

DISCUSS YOUR IDEAS

5. How does global travel influence the exchange of food customs today? How does this compare with the influence of travel in the past?

APPLY YOUR LEARNING

6. Find a recipe for making yogurt (using milk and a small amount of cultured yogurt). Come up with a work plan for making some at home or in a foods lab.

Section 22.2: Africa and the Middle East   597

Completing the Section

Review
- Ask students to summarize the main ideas in this section.
- Have students complete the Section Review. (Answers appear below.)

Evaluation
- Have students write a short essay describing foods available and commonly eaten in Africa and the Middle East.
- Have students take the quiz for Section 22.2. (Refer to the *Section Quizzes* booklet or construct your own quiz using the *Testmaker Software.*)

Reteaching
- Use maps to identify the various areas in discussed in this section and attach tags listing the various foods in each area.
- Refer to the *Reteaching Activities* booklet for the Section 22.2 activity worksheet.

Enrichment
- Have students locate a recipe for, prepare, and taste-test felafel or couscous.

Closure
- Lead a discussion on the foods and food preparation methods used in Africa and the Middle East. Emphasize the relationship between geography, foods, and food preparation.

Answers to Section Review

1. *Any two:* Sweet potatoes, corn, cassava, peanuts.
2. A pasta that looks like tiny beads of dough; also a main dish made with a variety of stews served over steamed couscous.
3. It is centrally located among Europe, Asia, and Africa, so it is greatly traveled; travelers leave their influences.
4. Answers will vary; students may say that in Israel, slow cooking is used to avoid cooking during the Sabbath.
5. Answers will vary. Students should realize that travel is more common and much faster than it used to be, so the effects of travelers on food customs is likely to be greater, or at least more immediate.
6. Answers will vary.

22.2 Recipe

Senegalese Couscous

Key Skill: Preparing Pasta Dishes

Using the Recipe

- Have students read the recipe and discuss each step. Review safety and sanitation procedures that apply to this recipe.
- Have each lab team fill out a work plan. (See the *Foods Lab Resources* booklet.)
- Have students check off the ingredients and equipment listed on the recipe worksheet and prepare the recipe.
- Have students complete the evaluation and questions on the recipe worksheet.

See Also . . .

The *Foods Lab Resources* booklet for the "Senegalese Couscous" recipe worksheet and other recipe alternatives.

Thinking About the Recipe

Read the recipe for "Senegalese Couscous" and answer the following questions.

1. What other grains might you substitute for couscous if it is unavailable?
2. What suggestions do you have for lowering the fat in this recipe?

Senegalese Couscous

Customary	Ingredients	Metric
8-oz. package	Couscous mix	226-g package
1/4 cup	Pistachio nuts, shelled	50 mL
1/4 cup	Almonds, blanched	50 mL
1/2 cup	Golden raisins	125 mL
1 Tbsp.	Orange peel, grated	15 mL
1 oz.	Semisweet chocolate, grated (optional)	28 g
1/2 tsp.	Cinnamon, ground	3 mL
1 tsp.	Margarine, lowfat	5 mL
Dash	Salt	Dash
2 Tbsp.	Powdered sugar	30 mL
1/4 cup	Dates, pitted and chopped	50 mL

Yield: 4 servings

Directions

Pan: Medium saucepan

1. Prepare couscous according to package directions, but omit any seasoning packet enclosed.
2. Grind remaining ingredients, except dates, in a food processor until well mixed.
3. Stir the dates, nut mixture, and couscous together in a large bowl.
4. Mound the couscous mixture on a platter and form it into a pyramid shape.
5. Serve.

Nutrition Information

Per serving (approximate): 373 calories, 11 g protein, 63 g carbohydrate, 11 g fat, 0 mg cholesterol, 60 mg sodium

---

Answers to Thinking About the Recipe

1. Answers will vary; rice or bulgur could probably be used.

2. Answers will vary; you could eliminate the nuts or chocolate.

Europe

OBJECTIVES

After studying this section, you should be able to:

- Identify foods commonly found in Western and Eastern Europe.
- Identify ways that culture, history, geography, and climate influence European foods.

LOOK FOR THESE TERMS

scones
high tea
haute cuisine
nouvelle cuisine
antipasto

The European countries tend to be small and there is considerable travel among them. They share many food customs and seasoning choices, especially neighboring countries with similar climates. On the other hand, most European countries have had distinctive histories and traditions which give their foods national identities.

Western Europe

Western Europe includes the British Isles, France, Spain, Portugal, Germany, Austria, Italy, Greece, and Scandinavia.

The European nations have much in common, yet each has its own identity. This scene shows a French fishing village on the Mediterranean coast.

Introducing the Section

Motivators

- On the chalkboard, list foods commonly found in Western and Eastern Europe. Ask students to identify those with which they are familiar. Ask if they know the national origin of the dishes with which they are familiar.

- Identify the Western and Eastern European countries from which ancestors of the local population migrated to the United States. Ask students to identify any foods associated with these groups that are still popular in the area.

Objectives

- Have students read the section objectives. Discuss the purpose of studying this section.

Vocabulary

- Pronounce the terms listed under "Look for These Terms." Have students find the terms and their definitions in the section.

Guided Reading

- Have students look at the headings within Section 22.3 to preview the concepts that will be discussed.

- Have students read the section and complete the appropriate part of the Chapter 22 Study Guide in the *Student Workbook*.

Teacher's Classroom Resources—Section 22.3

Refer to these resources in the TCR package:

Reproducible Lesson Plans
Student Workbook
Extending the Text
Reteaching Activities

Section Quizzes
Testmaker Software
Foods Lab Resources
Multicultural Resources
Color Transparencies

Teaching . . .

- **The British Isles**
- **France**

(text pages 600-602)

Comprehension Check

1. Ask students to list and describe dishes commonly served at lunch or dinner in the British Isles. *(Roast beef and Yorkshire pudding, shepherd's pie, Cornish pasties, bubble and squeak, and Finnan haddie.)*

2. Ask students to explain the British meal known as "tea" and list some items that might be served at that meal. *(A meal served at about 4:00 that features hot tea and some type of bread or dessert; typical items are crumpets, scones, and savories such as Welsh rarebit.)*

3. Ask students to define the term "haute cuisine." *(The term means "high cooking" and refers to the classic dishes of France, which have been elaborately and skillfully prepared.)*

4. Ask students to explain how haute cuisine differs from nouvelle cuisine. *(Nouvelle cuisine uses less flour and sugar, and is lower in fat content.)*

5. Ask students to list and describe examples of popular French foods. *(See list on pages 601-602.)*

Plum pudding is a Christmas tradition in England. It is a heavy food made with raisins, currants, nuts, and flavorings, steamed for many hours.

The British Isles

The British Isles are an island group just off the European continent. The two largest islands are Great Britain—which includes England, Scotland, and Wales—and Ireland.

British food tends to be hearty and cooked by plain, simple methods. Beef, mutton (meat from older sheep), pork, and fish are favorite foods. Many Britons eat four meals a day: breakfast, lunch, tea, and dinner (or supper).

Breakfast has historically been a meal of great variety and quantity. Today it tends to be smaller. Even so, it usually includes cereal, toast and marmalade, tea, and either eggs, bacon, sausage, tomatoes, or fried bread. In Scotland, oatmeal porridge is standard breakfast fare.

Here are some dishes often served at lunch or dinner:

- ❖ **Roast beef and Yorkshire pudding** consists of beef baked in the oven, with a popover-like mixture cooked in the pan drippings. Roast beef is usually served with a horseradish sauce or mustard.

- ❖ **Shepherd's pie** is a meat pie that is covered with mashed potatoes and baked. It is often made with leftover ground lamb or beef cooked with onions, garlic, tomatoes, and seasonings.
- ❖ **Cornish pasties**, popular in the south of England, are a combination of steak, onions, chopped potatoes and carrots, baked in a pastry crust. In former times, these baked turnovers were carried to work by miners and eaten cold.
- ❖ **Bubble and squeak** uses chopped leftover meat and vegetables. They are mixed with mashed potatoes and fried until brown and crisp.
- ❖ **Finnan haddie** is smoked haddock prepared with milk, onion, lemon juice, pepper, and parsley.

The British also enjoy a variety of game—pigeon, quail, pheasant, and deer. Fish such as sole, salmon, turbot, monkfish, and shellfish are also common to British menus.

A light afternoon meal, called tea, is an English tradition. This tea features scones topped with thick clotted cream.

More About England

- Ancient Britons had three staple grains: barley, wheat, and oats, which they used for bread and porridge. These grains are still popular today.
- Puddings are common, made with any food from meat and vegetables to fruit. Some are served plain; others are served with a sauce. Most are steamed or boiled, but some are baked.
- A dark, rich fruitcake is served for afternoon tea on Christmas day. It is often decorated with a white, fluffy frosting and Christmas designs.

A meal which is uniquely British is "four o'clock tea." Tea itself, the national beverage, was brought from China to England by Dutch traders at the beginning of the 1600s. Most Britons add milk to their tea. Tea, the meal, is generally served with a bread of some kind or dessert. The bread may be sandwiches made with cucumbers, watercress, or meat or fish fillings. Crumpets, which are similar to what Americans call English muffins, may also be served. **Scones,** a tasty variation of baking-powder biscuits, are served with butter and jam in parts of Britain. In Scotland, tea may be served with oatcakes or oatmeal biscuits.

Another British favorite is the *savory*, a dish somewhere between an appetizer and a main dish. *Welsh rarebit*, for example, is seasoned melted Cheddar cheese on toast. Adding a savory to tea and serving it a bit later turns a regular tea into **high tea,** which then may replace the supper meal.

Often, dessert is fresh fruit and cheese or a pastry. Cookies are called *biscuits*. *Shortbread*, a rich mixture of butter, flour and sugar, is usually associated with Scotland.

Popular British condiments include marmalade, lemon curd, and mincemeat. Another is chutney, one of the dishes brought back from India when it was a British territory.

France

France has long been known for the quality and complicated preparation of its food. The goal of French cooking is to blend foods and seasonings to either enhance one another or to create a new flavor altogether. One flavor does not dominate the dish.

The classic dishes of France have been called **haute cuisine,** or "high cooking"— food that is elaborately and skillfully prepared. Originally, great chefs prepared huge numbers of these time-consuming dishes for the aristocrats of France. Preparing food was considered a fine art, just as painting was. Rich sauces, elegantly decorated dishes, exotic ingredients, and puff pastries characterized haute cuisine. Today this type of food is found mainly in expensive restaurants.

Modern French cooking is called **nouvelle cuisine,** or "new cooking." The trend is to lower flour, sugar, and fat content.

French people rarely eat between meals. A typical breakfast might be tea or coffee and some kind of bread—toast, a croissant, or *brioche*, a round roll made from a rich yeast dough. Lunch or dinner might include an *hors d'oeuvre* (appetizer), a light fish course, a main dish of meat and vegetables, a salad, bread and cheese, and fresh fruit or a sweet dessert. This menu sounds hearty, but remember that there are no between-meal snacks. Portion sizes are moderate. Food is eaten slowly and enjoyed.

Many French dishes vary from region to region and from city to rural area. Local food customs make up a style called provincial cooking, a much simpler type of cooking than haute cuisine. Hearty one-dish meals are characteristic of provincial cooking.

Here are some examples of popular French foods:

❖ *Ragout* is a flavorful stew made with vegetables and meat, poultry, or fish. It is often named after the region where it originated.

In France, one often sees shoppers carrying fresh, unwrapped bread home from the bakery. The long loaves are called baguettes.

Student Experiences

1. **Guest Speaker:** Invite a person who comes from Great Britain to speak to students about the English custom of afternoon tea, describing how the tea itself is prepared and describing foods that are customarily served at high tea. *(Key skill: multicultural awareness)*

2. **Finding Recipes:** Have students look for recipes typical of Great Britain. Do these recipes give some idea of the variety of foods eaten by the British? In what way? *(Key skill: reading)*

3. **Finding Recipes:** Have students look through cookbooks to find at least two French recipes—one crepe recipe and one soup or stew recipe. Ask students whether the recipes they found are examples of haute cuisine, nouvelle cuisine, or provincial French cooking. *(Key skill: critical thinking)*

Lab Experience

- Have students locate a recipe for chutney, prepare the chutney, and taste-test it.

- Have students prepare several crepe recipes, including meat-filled crepes, vegetable-filled crepes, and dessert crepes.

Thinking Skills

Problem Solving: A restaurant offers a table d'hote of soup du jour (soup of the day), beef Bourguignon, salad, and chocolate mousse for $13.99. A la carte, the items are soup du jour—$2.25, chicken crepes—$6.95, salad—$1.99, and chocolate mousse—$3.95. Ask students how they would order and why.

- **Spain and Portugal**
- **Germany and Austria**

(text pages 602-603)

Comprehension Check

1. Ask students to describe a typical breakfast and lunch in Spain. *(Breakfast may be hot coffee or hot chocolate and a bread such as churros; lunch is a large meal, such as a salad, fish, a meat course, and a fruit or light dessert.)*

2. Ask students to describe paella. *(Paella is a Spanish dish that has a base of rice, olive oil, and saffron. Other ingredients vary from cook to cook, but may include meats, vegetables, legumes, fish, and seafood.)*

3. Ask students to identify the major difference between Spanish and Portuguese foods. *(Portuguese foods are spicier.)*

4. Ask students to identify breads for which the Germans are famous. What are some other traditional German baked goods? *(Pumpernickel, rye, stollen, and streuselkuchen; Bavarian cream, marzipan, and gingerbread.)*

This pot of **bouillabaisse** includes many different kinds of seafood, shells and all.

- ❖ **Pot-au-feu** is a popular soup of beef and veal cooked with vegetables such as carrots, celery, onions, and turnips.
- ❖ **Beef Bourguignon** is a famous French stew of cubed beef, onions, mushrooms, carrots, and seasonings served over boiled potatoes.
- ❖ **Bouillabaisse** is a hearty soup that combines several types of fish and shellfish, tomatoes, and herbs.

French people enjoy salads after the main course. They are made with salad greens topped with seasoned oil and vinegar. Vegetables are usually enhanced with a sauce.

Spain and Portugal

Spain and Portugal have access to the sea, so many of their dishes contain at least one kind of fish. The cooking of Spain varies greatly from region to region.

Breakfast in Spain is similar to breakfast in France. It generally consists of coffee or hot chocolate and a bread. The bread might be *churros*, fried strips of dough.

Lunch often consists of a salad, fish, a meat course, and fruit or a light dessert. Supper at home may be a light meal, but at a restaurant, it may be another large meal.

There are a few dishes which are enjoyed throughout the country. These include chicken and garlic, garlic shrimp, potato omelets, *gazpacho* (cold vegetable soup), and *paella*. Paella has a base of rice, olive oil, and saffron. From there cooks add a mixture of ingredients such as meats, vegetables, legumes, and especially fish and seafood.

Portuguese cooking is similar to Spanish cooking, except the Portuguese prefer spicier food. The cuisine was greatly influenced by travelers to India, South Africa, and South America. Portuguese foods tend to be rich because they contain more cream and butter.

Appetizers, or tapas, are favorites in Spain. This assortment features peppers, ground meat, eggs, and olives.

A paella of shrimp, clams, chicken, vegetables, and rice makes a colorful meal.

More About Spain

Because it is generally mountainous, Spain is more able to support olive trees (brought to Spain by the Romans) and vineyards than dairy farms and grazing cattle. Therefore, menus are more likely to include small animals, such as suckling pigs, rather than beef. Olive oil is used almost exclusively in recipes; butter is rarely called for. Fruit grows well in Spain and is usually available. Vegetables—except for tomatoes and peppers—are not often served alone, but they do appear in many dishes.

Germany and Austria

Generally speaking, German food tends to be rich and heavy. Sausages abound, with different combinations and seasonings in each region. Familiar favorites include liverwurst, bratwurst, knockwurst, and frankfurters.

Pork is probably the most popular meat, although beef and veal are common, too. Poultry is important, but fish is not popular.

Two characteristics of German cooking are the use of one-dish meals and the blending of fruit, meat, and vegetables to get sweet-sour flavors. Pork, for example, may be served with applesauce or cooked prunes.

People in Austria, a nation south of Germany, share a common language with the Germans and have many similar food customs. Austrian cooking has also been influenced by that of its Eastern European neighbors.

Here are some examples of German and Austrian foods:

❖ **Sauerbraten** is a beef roast marinated for several days in a sweet/sour sauce, then simmered in the same sauce. It is served with noodles, dumplings, or boiled potatoes.

❖ **Schnitzel** means "cutlet" in German. The meat cutlet is usually dipped in egg, breaded, and fried.

❖ **Kartoffelsalat** is a potato salad made with red potatoes, oil, vinegar, herbs, mustard, and other seasonings. It is served lukewarm. Bacon is sometimes added to potato salads.

Germans are famous for their rye and pumpernickel breads as well as *stollen*, a yeast bread with raisins and candied fruit. Another favorite is *streusel-kuchen*, a coffee cake topped with a mixture of flour, sugar, butter, nuts, and cinnamon.

Cabbage is important in German cooking. This meal includes both red cabbage slaw and sauerkraut, or fermented cabbage, along with potato pancakes, apples, sausages, and pumpernickel bread.

German desserts include rich cakes and cookies. *Bavarian cream* is a delicious mold of custard and cream. *Marzipan*, a rich mixture of ground almonds and sugar formed into exotic shapes, has its origins in Germany. So does *nürnberger lebkuchen*, better known as gingerbread.

Austrians are famous for rich desserts, most notably their cakes or tortes. For example, *linzertorte* is cake made with ground walnuts which is spread with jam.

1. **Finding Recipes:** Have students locate recipes that contain saffron. For what types of dishes did they find recipes? *(Key skill: reading)*

2. **Analyzing Recipes:** Have students study recipes from Spain and Portugal. Have students write a short report of their findings. *(Key skills: writing, analysis)*

3. **Social Influences:** Have students study the historical relationships between Germany and Austria. Why are the food customs in some parts of Austria so similar to customs in Germany? *(Key skill: social studies)*

Lab Experience

Have students prepare and taste-test several varieties of German wurst. Do students like the sausages? Why or why not?

Food and Nutrition Science

Lactic acid and sauerkraut: Sauerkraut is made when cabbage is fermented by bacteria that produce lactic acid. The lactic acid produced gives the sauerkraut its characteristic tart flavor. Locate a recipe for sauerkraut and have students prepare a batch of this typical German food.

Comprehension Check

1. Ask students to list and describe popular Italian dishes. *(Cannelloni are large pasta tubes that are cooked, stuffed with meat or cheese, then baked in a sauce; ravioli are "pillows" of pasta filled with various mixtures; polenta is cornmeal cooked in milk or water, cooled, and sliced; risotto is rice that is sautéed and then cooked in stock and flavorings.)*

2. Ask students to describe ways vegetables are usually cooked in Italy. *(Preparation varies according to region: simmered, fried, grilled, stuffed, sautéed, or eaten raw.)*

3. Ask students explain why many Greek dishes resemble Turkish dishes. *(Greece was ruled by Turkey for nearly 400 years.)*

4. Ask students to list the Scandinavian countries and describe the general cuisine. *(Denmark, Norway, Sweden, and Finland; it relies heavily on fish.)*

5. Ask students to explain why root vegetables such as potatoes, carrots, onions, and rutabagas often used in Scandinavian cooking. *(Vegetables and fruits do not grow well because of the short growing season.)*

Italy

Where did pasta come from? The most popular explanation is that Marco Polo brought it to Italy from China. Today pasta is still the national dish of Italy. It is made from durum wheat, the staple grain of Italy, which is not suitable for baking but perfect for pasta. Pasta is prepared in many ways, depending on the region.

In Northern Italy, the cooking is similar to that of France. It is characterized by herbs and rich sauces as well as the use of butter and lard.

In the south of Italy, foods are heartier. Tomato sauces and garlic are commonly used.

Here are some popular Italian dishes:

- ❖ **Cannelloni** are large pasta tubes that are cooked, stuffed with a meat or cheese filling, then baked in a sauce.
- ❖ **Ravioli** are pasta "pillows" filled with a savory mixture which varies by region.
- ❖ **Polenta** is cornmeal cooked in milk or water, cooled, and sliced. It's a staple food in Northern Italy.

- ❖ **Risotto** is a grain dish made from rice which is sautéed and then cooked in stock and flavorings.

Pasta sauces often, but not always, depend on tomatoes for a base. Some have a cream sauce base. *Pesto* is a sauce of fresh basil leaves, garlic, olive oil, grated cheese, and pine nuts.

Italians eat a variety of meat, poultry, fish, and game foods, such as rabbit.

Vegetables vary in kind and preparation according to region. They may be simmered, fried, grilled, stuffed, sautéed, or eaten raw. An Italian meal might include cauliflower, eggplant, cabbage, artichokes, peas, squash, or potatoes.

Salads may begin or end the meal. They are usually served with an oil and vinegar dressing. Salads, pickled vegetables, cheeses, and other appetizers are called **antipasto,** which means "before the meal."

Italy is famous for its cheeses, from the hard Parmesan and Romano, which must be grated, to ricotta, similar to cottage cheese.

At a production plant in Trentino, Italy, wheels of cheese are being carefully aged to just the right point.

A colorful assortment of pasta awaits an equally colorful array of sauces. Parmesan cheese and bread are typical accompaniments.

Thinking Skills

Critical Thinking: Have students point out the similarities and differences between a cafeteria and a smorgasbord. *(Both have a variety of foods displayed so people can choose the foods they want to eat. A smorgasbord usually includes "all you can eat" for one price, while in a cafeteria, foods are priced by the serving.)*

Greece

Lamb is the most popular meat in Greece. Fish and shellfish are also important, since Greece is located on the Mediterranean Sea.

Greek cooking often makes use of tomatoes, green peppers, garlic, lemon juice, and olive oil. Rice appears in many dishes. *Feta cheese*, made from sheep's or goat's milk, is widely eaten as an appetizer and in salads.

The history of Greece includes nearly four hundred years when it was ruled by Turkey. As a result, many Greek dishes, such as vine leaves stuffed with seasoned meat and rice, are similar to the foods of the Middle East.

Here are some other dishes popular in Greece:

❖ *Avgolemono* is a well-known Greek soup of chicken broth and rice flavored with eggs and lemon juice.

❖ *Moussaka* is a layered casserole made with seasoned ground lamb and sliced eggplant. A rich white sauce is poured over the mixture before baking.

Scandinavia and Northern Europe

Denmark, Norway, Sweden, and Finland make up the Scandinavian countries. Although these countries do not have a lavish cuisine, they have used the foods available to them creatively and tastefully.

The Swedish *smorgasbord* is perhaps the finest example of a bountiful buffet. Originally, smorgasbord meant a "sandwich board." Now it is a collection of assorted meats and fish dishes, raw vegetables, salads, and hot dishes.

Scandinavians rely heavily on fish for food. Dried and salted cod is a staple. Fish may also be fried, poached, or grilled, as well as used in soups and fishballs.

Smorrebrod are open-faced sandwiches which the Danes eat daily. They top thin slices of buttered bread with foods such as pickled herring, cooked pork, raw cucumbers, onion rings, apple slices, mustard, and horseradish.

Dairy products are also important to Scandinavian cooks. Each country seems to have a version of thick or sour milk which may be eaten with sugar. Milk, butter, and cream are essential ingredients in many dishes. For instance, the Danes are well-known for their rich, flaky, buttery pastries with touches of sugar, almonds, or jam. Scandinavians also bake an array of rye and white breads.

Because the local growing season is so short, Scandinavian meals are somewhat low in fresh fruits and vegetables. However, root vegetables such as potatoes, carrots, onions, and rutabagas are used regularly. Fresh berries (lingonberries, raspberries, and strawberries) are often used to accent desserts. *Fruksoppa*, or fruit soup, is a mixture of dried fruit and tapioca cooked in a sweetened liquid and served cold.

Christmas is special in Scandinavia. Weeks in advance, cooks prepare traditional sweet treats using butter, cream, almonds, eggs, and sugar. Swedes celebrate *Lucia Day* on December 13, when the eldest daughter, wearing a crown of seven white candles, serves coffee and Lucia buns, or *lussekake*, to her family.

Fish is a prominent part of this Swedish smorgasbord. Why is fish so common in Scandinavian cooking?

Student Experiences

1. **Class Discussion:** Discuss ways in which the cooking of northern Italy differs from that of southern Italy. What might account for these differences? *(Key skill: critical thinking)*

2. **Taste Test:** Have students sample several varieties of Scandinavian breads. How are they similar to and different from breads students regularly eat? Discuss other foods popular in Scandinavia. *(Key skill: evaluation)*

3. **Interview:** Have students interview someone of Italian, Greek, or Scandinavian descent. What foods does he or she eat that are typical of the culture? Does the person still follow the culinary traditions of the country? *(Key skill: multicultural awareness)*

Lab Experience

Have students prepare and taste-test antipasto. Discuss the meaning of the term "antipasto." What other foods are popular in Italy? Which are typically found in Italian restaurants?

More About Italy

• As in most other European countries, fresh fruit is the preferred dessert. "Biscotti" are cookies which are also popular.

• Italy is also the place where ice cream making was perfected. The Italians learned about ice cream from the Arabs, who had learned about it from the Chinese. Several familiar kinds of ice cream are named for their Italian background. "Spumoni," for example, contains fruits, nuts, or candies, and "Neapolitan" is layers of chocolate, vanilla, and strawberry ice cream.

Teaching . . .

• **Eastern Europe**

(text pages 606-607)

Comprehension Check

1. Ask students to list and describe dishes common to Russian cuisine. *(Piroshky are little pies stuffed with meat, vegetables, or cheese; blini are small yeast pancakes served with caviar or smoked salmon and sour cream; kasha is crushed buckwheat.)*

2. Ask students to list and describe foods preferred by other nations of eastern Europe. *(See the discussion on page 607.)*

Student Experiences

1. **Taste Test:** Have students taste test cabbage soup, borscht, and black bread. How do the Russian bread and soups differ from those students are most familiar with? *(Key skill: evaluation)*

2. **Reasoning:** Have students compare the foods eaten in other Eastern European nations with those eaten in Russia and in the Middle East. What factors may have contributed to these similarities? *(Key skills: history, evaluation)*

Eastern Europe

The countries of Eastern Europe have undergone changing borders and names in the late twentieth century. For ease in describing culinary history and tradition, general areas will be referred to by their traditional names. The following discussion will include the foods and culture of Russia, Poland, Czechoslovakia, Hungary, Bulgaria, Yugoslavia, and Rumania.

Russia

Russia is one of the many countries that once made up the Soviet Union. It covers a vast area, from Eastern Europe to the Pacific Coast in Asia.

Food in Russia differs from region to region, as it does in most countries. Over the years, Russian people have experienced many times of meager food supplies. Still, national dishes have evolved, based mainly on available staple foods. One example is Russian black bread, a dark, heavy, moist bread of rye and wheat flavored with chocolate, caraway, coffee, and molasses.

Hearty soups are also common. *Schchi* is a soup made from sauerkraut. Other popular soups are made with fresh cabbage and potatoes. *Borscht*, or beet soup, is one of the best known Russian soups. If available, meat

Borscht is a well-known Russian dish. The colorful beet-based soup is served with a dollop of sour cream.

or sausage is added. Most soups either contain sour cream or are served with it.

Russians have a fondness for sour cream and include it in many dishes. A popular combination is sliced cucumbers and onions with sour cream, seasoned with dill weed.

Fish is common in Russia. Sardines, salted herring, and salmon are especially popular.

Russia is noted for its caviar, the roe of eggs from certain fish. The roe is sieved, lightly salted, and served as an appetizer. Sturgeon roe is most expensive but considered the best.

Here are some other dishes common to Russian cuisine:

❖ *Piroshky* are little pies stuffed with meat, vegetables, or cheese.

❖ *Blini* are small yeast pancakes served with caviar or smoked salmon and sour cream.

❖ *Kasha* is crushed buckwheat, cooked and served as a side dish or used as an ingredient.

Tea is the most popular beverage. On cold evenings, you might find a gathering of Russians drinking tea and enjoying good conversation.

Easter has been one of the most important holidays. For Easter, Russians color eggs in beautiful, complex designs. *Kulich* is a sweet, fruit-filled yeast bread, drizzled with a thin white frosting.

Other Eastern European Nations

The food in other nations of eastern Europe has many similarities to that of Russia and, sometimes, the Middle East. The use of wheat, kasha, and cabbage, for example, is widespread.

In Poland, the national dish, *bigos*, is a stew of game meat with mushrooms, onions, sauerkraut, sausage, apples, and tomatoes. Barley is commonly used, especially in soup. *Krupnik* is a barley and vegetable soup to which sour cream and dill are added.

The Hungarian people enjoy grilled skewered lamb or beef in addition to the stew for which they are most famous, *goulash*.

Thinking Skills

Reasoning: Ask students why many Russians traditionally eat cabbage soup in the summer and sauerkraut soup in the winter. *(Cabbage is grown in the summer and is used in soup when it is fresh. To preserve the cabbage, the people ferment it to make sauerkraut, which is used in soup in the winter.)*

Holidays and family gatherings are an important part of life in Poland. Roast mutton cooked over a wood fire will be the main dish at this feast.

Goulash consists of simmered cubed beef, onions, paprika, potatoes, and perhaps garlic, caraway seeds, tomatoes, green peppers, and honey.

Hungarians also enjoy sauerkraut, pork-stuffed cabbage rolls, strudels, and *dobos torta*, a chocolate-filled sponge cake of many layers, glazed with caramel.

The Slovakian, Moravian, and Bohemian people of the Czechoslovakia area rely on dumplings as the cornerstone of their meals. Dumplings may be made from a variety of foods and come in many shapes and forms. A national favorite is liver dumplings in beef bouillon. Pork, beef, and game are common, as are cabbage and sauerkraut with caraway. One of the most famous Czech dishes is *kolacky*, yeast buns filled with fruit, cottage cheese, poppy seeds or jam.

In the region of former Yugoslavia, pilafs (seasoned rice dishes) are a favorite, as are cornmeal dishes, vegetables, and pasta. *Sarma*, the national dish, is rolled cabbage or sauerkraut leaves stuffed with a mixture of rice and ground pork. Also popular are thick, dark coffee, baklava, and desserts made with sweet noodles, dumplings, and fried yeast dough.

Corn is the mainstay of cooking in the area of Rumania. Cornmeal mush, the national dish, is served with melted butter, sour cream, or yogurt. Rumanian cooks also use peppers in their dishes and are known for their richly-flavored stews.

Meals in the Bulgarian region are some of the most healthy in this part of the world. Grains, vegetables, fruit, nuts, and yogurt are mainstays. Fresh vegetables are eaten widely in salads. Fruits, nuts, and herbs grow well in this region. The people prefer fish and lamb to other meats. A favorite dish is *potato musaka*, a casserole of vegetables, meat, potatoes, onions, garlic, tomato, eggs, cream, and grated cheese.

Section 22.3 Review

RECALL THE FACTS

1. Name five foods commonly found in the countries of Western Europe.

2. What is the difference between haute cuisine and nouvelle cuisine?

3. Name two characteristics of German cooking.

4. Identify five foods commonly found in Eastern European countries.

DISCUSS YOUR IDEAS

5. Discuss the similarities and differences among the foods of Western and Eastern Europe. What factors appear to have influenced food choices and how foods are prepared?

APPLY YOUR LEARNING

6. Choose a European country. Assume you are inviting two teens from this country to dinner with your family. Write a menu showing what you would serve to make these teens feel at home. Give reasons to support your selections.

Section 22.3: Europe   **607**

22.3

Completing the Section

Review

- Ask students to summarize the main ideas in this section.
- Have students complete the Section Review. (Answers appear below.)

Evaluation

- Ask students to write a short essay on the variety of foods and food customs in Europe.
- Have students take the quiz for Section 22.3. (Refer to the *Section Quizzes* booklet or construct your own quiz using the *Testmaker Software*.)

Reteaching

- Have students prepare and use flash cards to help them remember the names of foods from different countries.
- Refer to the *Reteaching Activities* booklet for the Section 22.3 activity worksheet.

Enrichment

- Have students research to discover how Italian pizza is similar to and different from American pizza.

Closure

- Lead a discussion about European food; analyze the differences between eastern European food and western European food.

Answers to Section Review

1. Answers will vary. Be sure the foods students mention are commonly found in Western Europe.
2. Nouvelle cuisine is lower in flour, sugar, and fat content.
3. *Any two:* Rich, heavy, use of one-dish meals, blending of fruit, meat, and vegetables to get sweet-sour flavors.
4. *Any five:* Piroshky, blini, kasha, tea, Russian black bread, borscht, fish, caviar, bigos, krupnik, goulash, dobos torta, kolacky pilafs, sarmadark coffee, baklava, potato musaka.
5. Answers will vary.
6. Answers will vary.

22.3 Recipe

Scandinavian Marinated Cod

Key Skill: Preparing fish fillets

Using the Recipe

- Have students read the recipe and discuss each step. Review safety and sanitation procedures that apply to this recipe. Caution students to use the proper safety devices, such as pot holders, when turning the fish.
- Have each lab team fill out a work plan. (See the *Foods Lab Resources* booklet.)
- Have students check off the ingredients and equipment listed on the recipe worksheet and prepare the recipe.
- Have students complete the evaluation and questions on the recipe worksheet.

See Also . . .

The *Foods Lab Resources* booklet for the "Scandinavian Marinated Cod" recipe worksheet and other recipe alternatives.

Thinking About the Recipe

Read the recipe for "Scandinavian Marinated Cod" and answer the following questions.

1. What other varieties of fish might you substitute for the cod that would commonly be eaten by Scandinavian people?
2. Give two suggestions for reducing the fat in this recipe.

Scandinavian Marinated Cod

Customary	Ingredients	Metric
1 lb.	Cod fillets	454 g
1/4 cup	Olive oil	50 mL
2 Tbsp.	Lemon juice	30 mL
1/4 cup	Onion, finely chopped	50 mL
1 tsp.	Salt	5 mL
	Black pepper, freshly ground	
2 Tbsp.	Butter or margarine, melted	30 mL
2 Tbsp.	Vegetable oil	30 mL

Yield: 4 servings

Directions

Pans: Shallow baking dish, broiler pan

1. Wash cod fillets in cold water and pat dry. Place in shallow baking dish.
2. Combine olive oil, lemon juice, onion, salt, and a small amount of freshly ground black pepper in a small bowl.
3. Pour marinade over cod fillets. Allow fish to marinate 30 minutes (15 minutes on each side). Drain marinade from fillets and discard.
4. Blend melted butter or margarine with vegetable oil in a small bowl.
5. Brush cold broiler pan with 1 tablespoon of the butter and vegetable oil mixture.
6. Place cod fillets on cold broiler pan.
7. Broil fillets 10 minutes for each inch of thickness, turning halfway through cooking time. Occasionally brush fillets with butter and vegetable oil mixture to keep fish from drying out. Fish should flake easily with a fork when done.
8. Serve immediately.

Nutrition Information

Per serving (approximate): 146 calories, 20 g protein, 2 g carbohydrate, 6 g fat, 54 mg cholesterol, 348 mg sodium

608   Chapter 22: Foods of the World

Answers to Thinking About the Recipe

1. Answers will vary. See the list on page 501 for fish that can be substituted for cod.

2. Answers will vary. Reduce the amount of oil; substitute a cooking spray for butter when possible.

Asia and the Pacific

OBJECTIVES
After studying this section, you should be able to:
- Identify foods common to the countries of Asia and the Pacific.
- Point out how culture and climate influence the foods of Asia and the Pacific.

LOOK FOR THIS TERM
masala

Rice is the staple grain in most of Asia, the largest continent in area and in population. In Northern China and parts of India and Japan, wheat is the staple grain.

Wood is the main cooking fuel in most of Asia. Because fuel is often scarce and expensive, food is cut into small pieces that cook quickly. The basic cooking methods include boiling, steaming, and frying.

Main dishes are usually a mixture of fried or steamed vegetables, mixed with a small amount of meat, poultry, or fish. Flavorful sauces add variety and spice to meals in Asia.

Another staple is soybeans, which are used to make many products, such as soy sauce, tamari sauce, and tofu. Soybean sprouts are used fresh and in cooked dishes.

Coastal areas enjoy an abundant variety of seafood. Seaweed is an important part of Asian cooking. It is used in soups, sauces, and main dishes and also served as a side dish.

Traditional Asian cooking emphasizes grains and legumes and uses an abundance of fresh ingredients. As a result, most traditional Asian meals are generally healthy and nutritious.

A Japanese woman cleans vegetables at her family farm. Fresh ingredients are essential in Asian cooking.

Section 22.4
Asia and the Pacific

Introducing the Section

Motivators

- Locate and identify countries in Asia and the Pacific on a world map. Ask students to identify foods they associate with Asia and the Pacific.
- Have students taste-test samples of tofu prepared in different ways. Point out that tofu is made from soybeans. Discuss the nutritive value of tofu and describe other ways it can be prepared. Discuss reasons soybeans are a staple in the Far East.

Objectives

- Have students read the section objectives. Discuss the purpose of studying this section.

Vocabulary

- Pronounce the terms listed under "Look for These Terms." Have students find the terms and their definitions in the section.

Guided Reading

- Have students look at the headings within Section 22.4 to preview the concepts that will be discussed.
- Have students read the section and complete the appropriate part of the Chapter 22 Study Guide in the *Student Workbook.*

Teacher's Classroom Resources—Section 22.4

Refer to these resources in the TCR package:
Reproducible Lesson Plans
Student Workbook
Reteaching Activities
Extending the Text

Section Quizzes
Testmaker Software
Foods Lab Resources
Multicultural Resources
Color Transparencies

Teaching . . .

- **Japan**
- **China**

(text pages 610-611)

Comprehension Check

1. Ask students to explain what tempura is. *(Crispy, deep-fried vegetables and seafood that are batter-dipped before frying.)*

2. Ask students to list characteristics common to Japanese foods. *(They are economical, nutritious, and attractive in appearance.)*

3. Ask students to explain how Chinese food ingredients are selected and why. *(They are selected and cut into pieces to retain the sense of harmony and symmetry that reflects Chinese philosophy about the universe.)*

4. Ask students to list and describe the four major styles of Chinese cooking. *(See list on page 611.)*

5. Ask students to describe a typical Chinese serving arrangement for a meal. *(A variety of hot dishes are arranged in the center of the table. Each person is served a bowl of rice. Diners help themselves to a small amount of each food.)*

The tea ceremony is a centuries-old Japanese custom. The tea is prepared and served in a ritual of grace and precision.

Sushi is popular in Japan. Cooked rice is flavored with vinegar, then combined with ingredients such as fresh raw fish, cucumber, and seaweed. The sushi is presented in artistically arranged, bite-size portions.

Japan

Japanese cuisine features foods that are economical, nutritious, and attractive in appearance. Traditionally, Japanese people have eaten mainly vegetables, seaweed, and fish, as well as some fruit. Popular seafood includes squid and eel.

Meals usually consist of small amounts of a variety of foods, since this is considered a healthy way to eat. The Japanese dietary guidelines recommend that a person eat 30 different foods a day. Here are a few of the dishes commonly found in Japan:

- ❖ **Sukiyaki** is a mixture of vegetables and meat cooked quickly in a wok.
- ❖ **Tempura** is the Japanese version of crispy, deep-fried vegetables and seafood which are batter-dipped before frying.
- ❖ **Soba** are buckwheat noodles, widely eaten for lunches and snacks.
- ❖ **Miso**, a paste made from soybeans, is often used as a flavoring.

In addition to having a pleasing flavor, Japanese food must also appeal to the eye. Foods and table settings are attractively arranged to provide beauty for the meal.

China

Chinese cuisine ranks among the best in the world. It dates back thousands of years.

Preparing and serving food reflects the philosophy of the people. Food preparation balances opposites, just as, according to Chinese philosophy, the universe is balanced. Ingredients are carefully selected and cut into pieces to retain the sense of harmony and symmetry. Whether for a banquet or a simple family meal, the food is a blend of simplicity and elegance.

China has always had a wide variety of foods. Instead of depending on expensive ingredients, the Chinese rely on their skill and cooking methods.

610 Chapter 22: Foods of the World

More About Japan

Japan has been known as one of the healthiest nations, with low rates of heart disease and cancer. One possible explanation is that the Japanese have traditionally eaten a large amount of fish. On the average, individuals consumed about 3 ½ ounces of fish a day.

As Japan became industrialized and the people became wealthier, they began to eat more meat and chicken. American fast foods, such as fried chicken and hamburgers, are popular in large cities. Since the advent of these foods in Japan, both cancer and heart disease have started to increase among the Japanese.

A Chinese meal does not have a main dish or a specific pattern. Instead, a variety of hot dishes are arranged in the center of the table. Each person is served a bowl of rice. The diners then help themselves to a small amount of each food. Soup is eaten during the meal or at the end of it, but never at the beginning. Hot tea is always served.

The variety of dishes in a meal depends on the number of people being served. If large amounts are needed, cooks prepare an additional number of recipes instead of making larger quantities of a few foods.

China is a such a large country that each region developed its own style of cooking. Generally, there are four different styles:

❖ *Northern or Peking* food is named after the capital, Peking, now called Beijing. The climate is dry and cold and the winters bitter. Wheat, the staple grain, is used to make dumplings, noodles, and steamed bread. The dumplings, known as *won ton*, are made from small sheets of dough filled with stuffings and folded into packets. The seasonings are usually mild, although spicy sweet and sour flavors are popular.

❖ *Coastal or Shanghai/Fukien* food comes from a region with a temperate climate. Fish and shellfish are the main foods in this area. Pork, chicken, and duck are also popular. They are mixed sparingly with large amounts of well-seasoned vegetables. *Red cooking* describes food simmered in a sauce that colors the food red.

❖ *Inland or Szechwan* food is prepared in central China, which also has a temperate climate. This area is noted for its hot peppers, which, along with garlic and ginger, create a zesty, spicy cuisine. Szechwan cooking also mingles sweet, sour, salty, and bitter flavors.

A chef in Hong Kong (top photo) displays the noodles he has made by swinging the dough in his hands, a traditional Chinese method. At right, diners enjoy a buffet in Guangzhou City.

❖ *Southern or Canton* food is prepared in an area with a subtropical climate. Foods are generally steamed or stir-fried. Although meals are based on seafood, pork, or poultry, other ingredients include mushrooms, nuts, and chicken broth. Steamed dumplings stuffed with meat, seafood, or fruit pastes are popular. *Egg rolls* are small sheets of dough rolled around a flavorful filling, sealed with a water/flour mixture, and deep-fried.

Section 22.4: Asia and the Pacific   **611**

Student Experiences

1. **Class Discussion:** Discuss reasons Japanese cuisine features foods that are economical, nutritious, and attractive in appearance. How do the geography and culture of Japan help to explain the Japanese cuisine? *(Key skill: critical thinking)*

2. **Taste Test:** Have students taste tempura, the Japanese version of deep-fried vegetables and seafood. *(Key skill: evaluation)*

3. **Class Discussion:** Discuss the influence of Chinese philosophy on food preparation. *(Key skill: social studies)*

4. **Field Trip:** Take students to a Chinese restaurant for a meal. Have students write a paper describing the Chinese meal pattern and the dishes served. *(Key skill: writing)*

5. **Guest Speaker:** Invite someone who is skilled in preparing Chinese food to discuss the different styles of cooking in China. Ask the guest to demonstrate the use of a wok to make typical Chinese dishes. *(Key skill: kitchen management skills)*

More About Chinese Foods

• To make *thousand year eggs*, a Chinese delicacy, raw duck eggs are wrapped in a special clay for weeks. The eggs thicken, becoming vivid blue and green inside. Because they are so rich, half an egg or less is enough for one portion.

• The Mongolian Hot Pot is a Northern specialty. The pot, similar to a fondue pot, is heated with charcoal and contains broth. Individuals dip small pieces of food into the broth and then into a sauce. The broth is eaten at the end of a meal.

Teaching . . .

- **Korea**
- **Southeast Asia**

(text pages 612-613)

Comprehension Check

1. Ask students to describe a typical meal in Korea. *(A soup or stew plus a grilled or stir-fried fish.)*

2. Ask students to list the countries of Southeast Asia and to describe the general types of food that are grown there. *(Burma, Laos, Thailand, Vietnam, Cambodia, and Indonesia; tropical fruits and vegetables, such as bananas, coconuts, rice, and spices.)*

3. Ask students to name the staple foods of Vietnam. *(rice and fish)*

4. Ask students to describe nasi goreng. *(A mound of fried rice surrounded by assorted meats and vegetables, mixed by the individual diners in Indonesia.)*

Ask students to compare this Chinese tradition with various American food traditions associated with New Year's meals.

Dim Sum can be roughly translated as "hits the spot," or "heart's delight." They are an assortment of bite-sized snacks that include dumplings which are steamed, boiled, or fried. Dim sum is traditional for Chinese New Year's meals. Cooks often hide a coin inside one filled dumpling. The finder is assured prosperity for the coming year.

Korea

As in much of Asia, rice is essential in Korea. It is sometimes cooked with barley or millet, which adds nutrients, texture, and flavor to the rice.

Meals usually consist of a soup or stew plus a grilled or stir-fried dish. Fish and fish pastes appear regularly in Korean foods. Garlic, in many forms, is used in meals. In fact, some of the hottest foods in the world can be found in South Korea.

Pickles add interest and flavor to Korean dishes. They might be made from almost any foods, such as pumpkins, cabbage, or ginseng. They can be rich in minerals and vitamin C.

Southeast Asia

Southeast Asia includes Burma, Laos, Thailand, Vietnam, Cambodia, and Indonesia. These countries are in the tropics and have a variety of tropical fruits and vegetables, as well as a huge assortment of spices. The cooking reflects the influence of Chinese and European settlers.

Thailand

Coconut milk, the juice from coconuts, is frequently used as a liquid in Thai cooking, from main dishes to desserts. Noodles are a favorite and appear in casseroles and in soups. They are also mixed with sauces made of oysters, black beans, or fish. Then they are topped with chopped peanuts, coconut, and green onions.

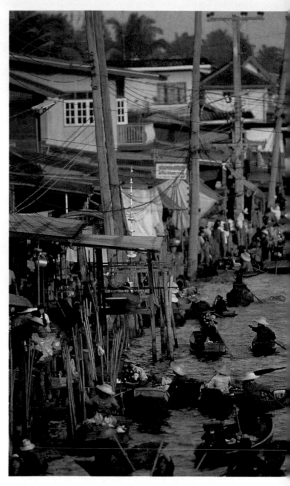

Like many nations in Southeast Asia, Thailand is a blend of old and new, as this scene at a floating market shows.

Food and Nutrition Science

Heat Transfer and Food Size: The small size of the food pieces in Asian cooking allows rapid transfer of heat to the center of the pieces of food, causing them to cook much faster than larger pieces of food. Have students stir-fry grated, diced, sliced, and stalks of celery and compare the time needed to cook each.

Pad Thai is made with the flat noodles characteristic of Thai cooking.

Most food combinations in Thailand have four basic flavors—sweet, sour, salty, and spicy. They also meet four texture requirements—soft, chewy, crunchy, and crispy. The most popular dish is *pad Thai*, a well-seasoned mixture of noodles, shrimp, peanuts, egg, and bean sprouts.

Vietnam

Rice and fish are the staple foods in Vietnam. The Vietnamese eat rice every day, by itself and combined with other foods. Rice starch is used to make noodles and dumpling wrappers. Foods are usually seasoned with *nuoc-mam*, a spicy fish sauce.

Fish has always been the main source of protein for the Vietnamese. Fish and other foods are commonly seasoned with fresh ginger, coriander, lemon grass, and sweet basil. Many foods are rolled in lettuce or rice paper wrappers which are easily dipped into spicy sauces.

Indonesia

Indonesian foods are highly spiced. One of the most popular dishes is *nasi goreng*, which is a mound of fried rice surrounded by assorted meats, such as beef and shrimp, and vegetables. The diner mixes them to obtain a wide variety of flavor combinations.

The Philippines

The inhabitants of the Philippines are a blend of Chinese, Arab, and Indian people living on 7000 islands. The culture and food reflect the influences of those who have settled there, including the Spanish and Americans of the last few centuries.

The staple foods are fish, pork, and rice, which is made into cakes, noodles, and pancakes. Fish sauces are also widely used.

The national dish is *adobo*, which is pork marinated and browned in soy sauce, vinegar, garlic, bay leaves, and peppercorns.

It takes a lot of rice to feed the great number of people in the world who depend on it as their staple grain. These terraced rice fields in Bali, Indonesia, are beautiful as well as productive.

Section 22.4: Asia and the Pacific   613

Comprehension Check

1. Ask students to describe masala. To what American food is it similar? (*It's an Indian seasoning that is similar to curry powder.*)

2. Ask students to list and describe interesting foods used in India. (*See list on page 614.*)

3. Ask students to name the European nationalities whose influence is still seen in cooking in Australia and New Zealand. (*English, Scottish, and French.*)

Student Experiences

1. **Class Discussion:** Discuss factors that influence the diets of people in India. What effects do the Hindu and Muslim religions have? How does population influence cost of food and its availability? (*Key skill: multicultural awareness*)

2. **Taste Test:** Have students taste pilaf. Have students tasted pilaf before? Ask them to write a paragraph summarizing the taste. (*Key skill: writing*)

3. **Reasoning:** Have students read about the geography and history of Australia and New Zealand. What foods are plentiful in these countries? What European countries contributed settlers to Australia and New Zealand? (*Key skills: geography, history*)

India

Cooking in India varies from region to region, according to climate and culture. In the northern and central areas, wheat is the staple grain and lamb is the most common meat. In the south, rice is the staple grain and the food is much spicier.

The most common Indian seasoning is similar to American curry powder and is called **masala.** Most cooks grind and mix their own blend of spices and keep a jar on hand at all times. Yogurt is used widely.

Many people eat little or no meat. As a result, India has a wide variety of delicious, spicy, meatless main dishes. However, poultry and fish are popular wherever they are available. In northern India, for example, chicken stuffed with rice, almonds, and raisins is a favorite. Here are some other interesting foods found in meals in India.

❖ **Kebabs** are made of meat—often lamb—and herbs on a skewer.
❖ **Pilaf** is cooked, seasoned rice often mixed with chopped almonds, raisins, or yogurt.
❖ **Raita** is a salad which combines yogurt with several vegetables and spices.
❖ **Dal** is a dish of dry beans or lentils cooked in a seasoned broth.
❖ **Puri** is an Indian bread. (See the recipe on page 616.)

The food for an Indian meal is a pleasant blend of flavors and textures. It is served all at once. Indian people also enjoy candy made from sugar and almonds, rice flour, or coconut.

This spicy lamb dish is seasoned with masala. Rice and chapati, a flat Indian bread, complement its distinctive flavor.

614   Chapter 22: Foods of the World

More About India

Meals are usually eaten from plates or bowls, but in some areas large flat leaves are used. People sit on the floor. In cities, tableware is used, but in other areas people usually eat with their fingers. The meal begins with grace to give thanks for the food. Rice is ladled onto a plate, and then other foods are added. All foods, except desserts, are served at the same time. Hot tea is the common beverage in the north and hot coffee with milk in the south.

Pavlova is a popular dessert in Australia and New Zealand. The meringue-like mixture is topped with whipped cream and berries or sliced kiwis.

Australia and New Zealand

The food in Australia and New Zealand is very similar to that of the European countries that contributed settlers to it. These include English in particular, but also Scottish and French people in some regions.

Menus vary according to location, from the outback of Australia to the large cities along its coasts to the smaller cities and rural areas of New Zealand. Meals usually feature foods which are locally available. Meat and seafood are plentiful. Many people eat steaks and chops (beef or mutton) for breakfast. New Zealanders enjoy toheroas, which resemble clams.

One uniquely Australian dish is *Pavlova*, a rich mixture of meringue, fruit, and cream. Pies and sweet rice dishes are also common desserts.

Shrimp and other seafood are widely eaten in Australia and New Zealand.

Section 22.4 Review

RECALL THE FACTS

1. What is the staple grain in Asia and the Pacific?

2. Give four examples of protein foods commonly used throughout Asia and the Pacific.

3. How does food preparation relate to Chinese philosophy?

4. What four food flavors are common to the foods of Thailand?

5. Name three foods eaten by the people of India.

DISCUSS YOUR IDEAS

6. Why do you think Asian cooking methods are popular in the United States today?

APPLY YOUR LEARNING

7. Plan a meal using foods from an Asian or Pacific country. Look up the calories, grams of protein and fat, and the amounts of vitamins A and C found in these foods. Are the foods in this meal a good source of these nutrients?

Section 22.4: Asia and the Pacific **615**

Answers to Section Review

1. Rice.
2. Fish, shellfish, rice, and beans.
3. The Chinese prepare their foods to balance, the way they believe the universe is balanced.

4. Sweet, sour, salty, and spicy.
5. *Any three:* Kebabs, pilaf, raita, and puri.
6. Answers will vary. Students should realize that a large number

of Asians now live in the United States.
7. Answers will vary.

22.4 Recipe

Puri (Bread of India)

Key Skills: Making quick breads; deep-frying

Using the Recipe

- Have students read the recipe and discuss each step. Review safety and sanitation procedures that apply to this recipe. Remind students to use care when deep-frying to avoid serious burns.
- Have each lab team fill out a work plan. (See the *Foods Lab Resources* booklet.)
- Have students check off the ingredients and equipment listed on the recipe worksheet and prepare the recipe.
- Have students complete the evaluation and questions on the recipe worksheet.

See Also . . .

The *Foods Lab Resources* booklet for the "Puri (Bread of India)" recipe worksheet and other recipe alternatives.

Thinking About the Recipe

Read the recipe for "Puri" and answer the following questions.

1. What other whole-grain flours might you substitute for whole wheat flour?
2. What foods of India might you eat with Puri for a meal?

Puri (Bread of India)

Customary	Ingredients	Metric
1¼ cup	Whole wheat flour	300 mL
1/2 tsp.	Salt	3 mL
1/4 cup	Margarine, softened	50 mL
3/4 cup	Low-fat yogurt, plain	175 mL
	Vegetable oil for frying	
	Honey	

Yield: About 2 dozen small biscuits

Directions

Pan: Deep saucepan
Temperature: Medium to medium-low heat

1. Mix flour and salt together in a bowl.
2. Cut in margarine until mixture resembles pea-size pieces.
3. Stir in yogurt and mix until well blended.
4. Roll dough out on a lightly-floured surface to 1/8 inch (3 mm) thickness and cut with a biscuit cutter.
5. Pour oil into deep saucepan, about 1 inch (2.5 cm) deep.
6. Heat oil until a small piece of dough sizzles quickly when dropped into the oil.
7. Lower biscuits into oil using a slotted spoon. Hold biscuits under the oil. (Otherwise they rise as soon as they begin to puff.)
8. Fry biscuits a few seconds until they turn golden brown.
9. Remove from oil and drain on paper towels.
10. Serve warm, plain or with honey.

Nutrition Information

Per serving (approximate): 62 calories, 1 g protein, 5 g carbohydrate, 4 g fat, trace of cholesterol, 75 mg sodium

---

Answers to Thinking About the Recipe

1. Answers will vary. Barley or rye flour might be used.

2. Answers will vary but may include kebabs, pilaf, and raita.

Tab Sagi
Specialty Store Owner

CURRENT POSITION

"I'm the owner of a Middle Eastern grocery store located in a major city."

RESPONSIBILITIES

"I have family members and employees who help me, but I am ultimately responsible for maintaining the store's inventory and finances."

SKILLS

"You need a variety of skills to successfully run your own business. You definitely need to be self-motivated and have leadership abilities, and you need to be skilled in management and accounting."

EDUCATION

"My education has primarily been on-the-job, but my son, who will take over the business one day, has a bachelor's degree in food service management."

WORK ENVIRONMENT

"You might think that by owning your own store you can take many days off! In reality I work very long hours, and my life often seems to revolve around the store."

FAVORITE PART OF THE JOB

"It's very satisfying for me to get to know my regular customers on a personal level. I enjoy being able to help them find particular items they are looking for, and to offer menu suggestions from time to time."

- What do you think Tab means when he says a business owner must be "self-motivated"?
- What aspects of Tab's job appeal to you? Why?

617

CAREER PROFILE: SPECIALTY STORE OWNER

Thinking About . . . Owning a Specialty Store

Have students think of other questions they would like to ask Tab Sagi about owning a specialty grocery store. (Examples: What courses could students take to help them if they wanted to own their own specialty store? What are the advantages to having a degree in food service management?)

Ask student volunteers to tell what they think would be the most exciting part of owning their own specialty store.

Student Opportunities

Students planning a career in working for or owning a grocery may gain experience through an entry-level job at a supermarket or grocery store. They may also want to volunteer in the kitchen of a local hospital or other non-profit organization.

Occupational Outlook

Owners of specialty stores can continue to expand their stores to make them as big as they want, as long as they have the skills and the business to make the store profitable.

For More Information

For additional information about grocery careers, encourage students to contact:
- National Association of Grocers, 1825 Samuel Morse Dr., Reston, VA 22090
- Grocery Manufacturers of America, 1010 Wisconsin Ave., Suite 800, Washington, D.C. 20007
- Small Business Administration (SBA), 1441 L St. NW, Washington, D.C. 20416

- Have students complete the Chapter Review. (Answers appear below.)

Evaluation

- Ask each student to choose a country mentioned in this chapter, research its traditional celebrations, and plan a menu for one of these events.

- Have students take the test for Chapter 22. (Refer to the *Chapter and Unit Tests* booklet or construct your own test using the *Testmaker Software*.)

■ ANSWERS ■

REVIEWING FACTS

1. A starchy food that looks like a green banana and must be cooked before it is eaten. It can be roasted, fried, boiled, or baked, or combined in dishes with meat and cheese.

2. The people are a mixture of native Indians, Portuguese, and Africans; foods: dende, malagueta peppers, and coconut milk.

3. Coconuts, sweet potatoes, corn, cassava, peanuts.

4. See list on page 596.

5. Zhoug, shatta, and tahini.

6. Tea, sandwiches made with cucumbers, watercress, or meat or fish fillings, crumpets, scones, savories.

7. In the north of Italy, cooking is more similar to that of France and is not as hearty as cooking in southern Italy.

CHAPTER 22 REVIEW

SUMMARY

SECTION 22.1

Latin America: Latin American cooking is a combination of native foods and European influences. Corn is the staple grain in most areas. Mexican meals include masa, rice, beans, and chili peppers. Staples in the Caribbean include fish, tropical fruits, and vegetables. Beef is popular in Brazil, Peru, and Argentina.

SECTION 22.2

Africa and the Middle East: In Africa, staples include yams, cassava, and peanuts. Geography, climate, native traditions, religion, and foreign influence have shaped food customs. The same is true of countries in the Middle East. This region's location on trade routes from Europe to Asia brought many travelers who influenced food.

SECTION 22.3

Europe: The cooking of the British Isles tends to be plain but hearty. The goal of French cooking is to blend flavors to enhance one another. Spanish foods are fairly simple and light. German cooking tends to be rich and heavy. Pasta is the national dish of Italy. Many Greek foods are similar to those in the Middle East. In Scandinavia, fish and dairy products are basic foods. Eastern European cooking emphasizes root vegetables, grains, and sour cream.

SECTION 22.4

Asia and the Pacific: Rice, seafood, soybeans, and vegetables are the staples of Japanese and Chinese cooking. Foods in Korea and Southeast Asia are spicy and include tropical fruits and vegetables. Indian cuisine is known for its spicy, often meatless recipes. Australian and New Zealand cuisine has European roots.

REVIEWING FACTS

1. What is a plantain? How can it be prepared? (22.1)

2. Identify the two major influences on Brazilian cooking. Name two foods that reflect these influences. (22.1)

3. Name five foods that were introduced to Africa between the fourteenth and eighteenth centuries. (22.2)

4. Name and describe three dishes often eaten in Arab countries. (22.2)

5. Name three traditional condiments used in Israel. (22.2)

6. Name four foods commonly served at British tea. (22.3)

7. Identify two ways in which the cooking of northern Italy differs from that of southern Italy. (22.3)

8. Identify five mainstays of Bulgarian cooking. (22.3)

9. Name the four basic styles of Chinese cooking and give one characteristic of each. (22.4)

10. What is *nasi goreng*? How is it eaten? (22.4)

LEARNING BY DOING

1. *Foods lab:* Choose one popular food of Latin America. Find two recipes for preparing it: one traditional, the other as it is usually prepared in the United States. Prepare and sample both recipes. Tell how they differ in ingredients and flavor. Offer reasons for these differences. (22.1)

2. *Computer lab:* Design a table or database showing the dietary staples, their origins, and dishes made from these staples, for the different regions of Africa and the Middle East. Print out this information for the class. (22.2)

8. Grains, vegetables, fruit, nuts, and yogurt.

9. See list on page 611.

10. A popular dish in Indonesia in which a mound of fried rice is surrounded by assorted meats, shrimp and vegetables; the diners mix them individually to obtain a wide variety of flavor combinations.

CHAPTER 22 REVIEW

3. **Foods lab:** Find a French recipe that is traditionally considered haute cuisine. Modify the recipe to make it nouvelle cuisine. Prepare your new version. Be ready to explain how your modifications made this recipe nouvelle cuisine. (22.3)

4. **Demonstration:** Investigate the traditional ways of serving Japanese and Chinese meals. Then demonstrate these serving methods. Duplicate the foods, serving pieces, and serving styles as closely as possible. (22.4)

THINKING CRITICALLY

1. **Predicting consequences:** Review the dietary staples of the different regions of Latin America. For each region, identify one possible health advantage and one disadvantage of the typical way of eating. (22.1)

2. **Comparing and contrasting:** Find examples of bean-and-grain dishes served in several countries from different continents. How are they similar and different? (22.1,, 22.2, 22.3, 22.4)

3. **Recognizing bias:** Do people sometimes make assumptions about a national or ethnic group based on the foods they eat? What do you think about this practice? (22.3)

4. **Recognizing values:** You have read how Chinese meals reflect the Chinese people's traditional philosophy of life. What philosophies might meals in the United States reflect? (22.4)

MAKING DECISIONS AND SOLVING PROBLEMS

What Would You Do?

1. Your new neighbors are a Jewish family. You would like to invite them to dinner. However, you are not familiar with Jewish food customs and are unsure about what foods they may and may not eat. (22.2)

2. Your new acquaintance, an exchange student from Czechoslovakia, tells you that she is having trouble adapting to American foods. You wonder what common American foods might be similar to the foods she is accustomed to. (22.3)

3. One of your teammates on the basketball team is a practicing Hindu. When you play games in other cities and eat in restaurants, he has trouble finding foods that are acceptable. (22.4)

LINKING YOUR STUDIES

1. **Social studies:** Locate information on the controversy surrounding cattle raising in the rain forest regions of South America. What are the arguments of the opposing sides? What are the strengths and weaknesses of these arguments? Which side do you feel has the stronger case, and why? Share your findings with the class in a brief report. (22.1)

2. **Social studies:** Find out more about Jewish and Islamic dietary laws and customs. What foods are forbidden, and why? How else do these rules affect the cooking of Israel and Arab countries? (22.2)

3. **Literature:** Read the passages in Charles Dickens' *A Christmas Carol* regarding the Cratchits' Christmas pudding. Why is the family so concerned with its preparation and outcome? (22.3)

4. **Fine arts:** Learn more about how Japanese cuisine fits into the wider Japanese philosophy on the arts. How are the Japanese people's ideas about color, balance, and symmetry reflected in their art, music, and dance, as well as their meals? Make a presentation to the class using examples to support your conclusions. (22.4)

LEARNING BY DOING

Answers to "Learning by Doing" will vary. Evaluate students on the procedures they use as well as their results.

THINKING CRITICALLY

1. Answers will vary. Be sure the advantages and disadvantages agree with the health principles students have learned.

2. Answers will vary.

3. Answers will vary. Students should realize that people often do make assumptions and generalizations about people from other countries based on the foods they eat, but that this practice is very unfair.

4. Answers will vary.

MAKING DECISIONS AND SOLVING PROBLEMS

Answers to "Making Decisions and Solving Problems" activities will vary. Encourage students to give reasons for their answers.

LINKING YOUR STUDIES

Answers to "Linking Your Studies" may vary. Encourage students to give reasons for their answers.

Planning the Chapter

Chapter Overview

Section 23.1: Regional Foods of the East, Midwest, and South

Section 23.2: Regional Foods of the Wcst and Canada

Introducing the Chapter

Motivators

- Ask students to imagine that they are moving to another country. Ask: "What food(s) or food habits would you take with you? Why?"

- Have students refer to an American history text to make a time line of the arrival of various ethnic groups to the United States from 1600 to the present. Display the time line in class and discuss how each group influenced American cuisine. Refer to the time line as you study each region of the country.

Teacher's Classroom Resources—Chapter 23

Refer to these resources in the TCR package:

Enrichment Activities

Chapter and Unit Tests

Testmaker Software

CHAPTER 23
Foods of the U.S. and Canada

620

Cooperative Learning Suggestions

Initiate a Co-op Co-op activity. Divide the class into groups of four. Assign each group a region of the country. Assign each member one of these tasks: geography and climate of the region, food production in the region, food traditions of immigrants, and cooking techniques commonly used in the region. Have individual members share their findings with the group. Have students work together to find recipes of popular regional dishes. Have students select the five most representative recipes based on the group's findings. Have the group present a report of its findings to the class and prepare one of the recipes for the class to taste.

Regional Foods of the East, Midwest, and South

OBJECTIVES

After studying this section, you should be able to:

• List foods common to the East, Midwest, and the South.
• Identify cultural and climate influences on the foods of the East, Midwest, and the South.

LOOK FOR THIS TERM
roux

Cornbread, clam chowder, barbecued meat, key lime pie, grits, sourdough bread—do you think of these foods as typically American? Today, any of them can be enjoyed throughout the country. However, at one time each was known only in the region where it originated.

The Foundation of American Cooking

How did regional differences come about? As you learned in Section 13.3, the foods common to an area depend in part on the geography and climate of the region. The pattern of North American settlement also affected the development of food customs.

The first known inhabitants, the Native Americans, developed their own food customs based on locally available foods. Those foods are the foundation for American cooking. Later, immigrants from other parts of the world made additional contributions to the foods of America.

Corn, or maize, played an important role in the life of many Native American tribes. It is still a staple crop in the United States today. How many different uses for corn can you name?

Section 23.1: Regional Foods of the East, Midwest, and South   **621**

Teacher's Classroom Resources—Section 23.1

Refer to these resources in the TCR package:

Reproducible Lesson Plans
Student Workbook
Extending the Text
Reteaching Activities

Section Quizzes
Testmaker Software
Foods Lab Resources
Multicultural Resources
Color Transparencies

Section 23.1
Regional Foods of the East, Midwest, and South

Introducing the Section

Motivators

• Ask students who have visited or lived in the East, Midwest, or South to describe the geography, climate, and culture of the area. Discuss how these characteristics have influenced food traditions of the area.

• Ask students to name foods they associate with the East, Midwest, or South. Write these regions on the chalkboard and under each, list the foods students name. With which region's foods were students most familiar? Have students copy the lists for future use.

Objectives

• Have students read the section objectives. Discuss the purpose of studying the section.

Vocabulary

• Pronounce the terms listed under "Look for These Terms." Have students find the terms and their definitions in the section.

Guided Reading

• Have students look at the headings within Section 23.1 to preview the concepts that will be discussed.

• Have students read the section and complete the appropriate part of the Chapter 23 Study Guide in the *Student Workbook*.

Teaching . . .

• **The Foundation of American Cooking**

(text pages 621-623)

Comprehension Check

1. Ask students to name the first known inhabitants of North America. On what basis did they develop food customs? *(The Native Americans; they based their food customs on locally available foods.)*

2. Ask students to describe the types of food eaten by the Native Americans. *(Animals they could hunt, fish, berries, fruit, corn.)*

3. Ask students to describe the cultural exchange between the early immigrants and the Native Americans in North America. *(The Native Americans helped the immigrants survive by introducing them to native foods.)*

Student Experiences

1. **Brainstorming:** Have students name foods made from corn. *(Key skill: brainstorming)*

2. **Bulletin Board:** Have students draw or find pictures of foods eaten by Native Americans. What preservation methods were used? *(Key skill: history)*

3. **Writing:** Have students pretend they are immigrants to North America in the year 1700. Ask them to write an entry in their diary describing the foods and cooking methods of the Native Americans. *(Key skills: writing, creativity)*

Lab Experience

Have students prepare a meal based on food preparation techniques of Native Americans.

Foods of the Native Americans

The philosophy of the Native Americans was to live in harmony with nature. They relied on hunting, fishing, and gathering local berries for meals. Some cultivated wild maize (corn) so that it would yield greater amounts of food and seed. They also stored the seed in dry places to protect it from moisture. The seed could be used as food in the lean months of winter. In a sense, Native Americans were early pioneers in food technology.

Corn was prepared in a variety of ways, some of which are still used today. Native Americans roasted and boiled the corn in the husk. Some removed the kernels and made them into a powder which was then made into flatbreads, drinks, and mush. Sometimes the Native Americans softened the kernels in homemade lye and made hominy, which was cooked with bits of meat.

Regional differences in climate and soil meant that different foods were available in different places. In the cold climates, food was dried, smoked, and frozen to use in the winter. *Pemmican,* for example, was dried meat, pounded into a paste with fat and preserved in cakes which were easy to carry when traveling.

In coastal areas, seafood was a staple. Fish were usually steamed or cooked over an open fire. Native Americans in the South concocted soups and stews from fish and small game.

In the Southwest, tribes grew peppers and beans to use in soups and chili-type dishes. They also made barbecue sauces to put on meat which was roasted over open fires. These foods are still part of the heritage of the region in which they originated.

Native Americans and the Immigrants

In the fifteenth century, immigration from Europe began. Immigrants coming to America brought their food customs with them. They tended to settle as groups in areas that reminded them of their homelands. These national clusters helped preserve their traditions.

Native Americans played an important role in the survival of the immigrants in the New World. They introduced the immigrants to such foods as maize, potatoes, tomatoes, peppers, pumpkin, squash, and many types of beans. Gradually, the immigrants adapted their favorite recipes to local produce and methods of cooking and preserving food.

Foods of the Native Americans varied from region to region. For example, in the Southwest, locally available foods included the edible flowers and fruits of cactus plants.

622   Chapter 23: Foods of the U.S. and Canada

More About Native Americans

Because corn was the primary food source for many Native Americans, maize took on a certain magical quality to some people. It became the center of many tribal religious beliefs. Planting and harvesting corn became times for special rituals and yearly festivals.

Cultural exchange also occurred between different colonies and different immigrant groups. Over time, this process resulted in the unique cooking styles of each region of North America.

The Northeast

Among the first settlers in the Northeast were English, Dutch, French, and Germans. Native Americans taught early immigrants to use available foods such as deer, rabbit, wild turkey, and berries. They also taught the immigrants to plant native crops such as corn, beans, squash, and pumpkins. Corn and dry beans provided carbohydrates and protein to help the immigrants survive in the New World.

Dried corn was ground and made into breads, pancakes, puddings, mush, and fish batter. Corn cakes, called *journey cakes* or *Johnnycakes*, were a simple baked mixture of water and ground corn.

Baked beans also have their origins in these early days. The immigrants learned how to soak the beans and cook them slowly for hours. Over a period of time, through trial and error, they developed a tasty dish that is now known as *Boston baked beans*.

Seafood, which was plentiful along the Atlantic coast, was another source of protein for the early settlers. They learned to cook shellfish between layers of seaweed and heated rocks. They also cooked shellfish dishes called *chowders* in huge kettles hung in the fireplace. The most famous was clam chowder, made with milk, butter, onions, and clams. In some areas, cooks used tomatoes instead of milk. Either way, clam chowder is one of the most well-known dishes of New England.

The Irish came to the Northeast somewhat later than other immigrants. They introduced Irish stew and corned beef with cabbage, known throughout the United States as traditional Irish dishes.

Boston baked beans and pumpkin pie are two traditional New England dishes. Both beans and pumpkin were introduced to the European settlers by Native Americans.

With miles of coastline, New England is rich in seafood. Here empty lobster traps await the next fishing trip.

More About the Northeast

Because the climate was harsh and the people worked hard, breakfast was an important and hearty meal. A typical winter breakfast might include codfish cakes, baked beans, steamed brown bread, and pancakes. Breakfast often ended with a large piece of apple pie.

Lab Experiences

- Have students prepare clam chowder with milk and with tomatoes. Invite other students in for a taste test.
- Have students prepare baked goods for a traditional Kaffeeklatsch.

Teaching . . .

• The Northeast

(text pages 623-624)

Comprehension Check

1. Ask students to list foods that Native Americans and early European settlers made from corn. *(bread, pancakes, puddings, mush, fish batter, corn cakes)*

2. Ask students to explain what a clam chowder is and to describe the two kinds that evolved in New England. *(A shellfish dinner made with milk, butter, onions, and clams; the second variety uses tomatoes instead of milk.)*

3. Ask students to describe the foods of the Pennsylvania Dutch settlers. From what European country did these settlers actually come? *(pork, cabbage or sauerkraut, noodles, sausage, spiced fruit, pickled fruits and vegetables, fruit butters, baked goods; from Germany)*

Student Experiences

1. **History Review:** Review the history of the Northeast. Who were the early settlers? What food resources were available to these pioneers? What native crops did Native Americans teach them to plant? *(Key skill: history)*

2. **Finding Recipes:** Have students find recipes for traditional Northeastern foods. Discuss how these recipes used the food resources of the region. *(Key skill: reading)*

3. **Recipe Analysis:** Provide students with recipes for traditional German foods. Ask students to work in groups to analyze the recipes. Ask students to identify recipes that could be used or adapted for use by the early settlers in North America. *(Key skill: critical thinking)*

Comprehension Check

1. Ask students to name crops grown by settlers in the Midwest. Why did settlers choose these crops? *(They planted wheat, corn, other grains, fruits, and vegetables; because they knew these crops would grow well in the Midwestern climate.)*

2. Ask students to list foods that people in the South made from corn. Why are these different from foods made from corn in the Northeast? *(Cornbread, spoonbread, corn pone, fritters, cornmeal batters, grits, and hush puppies; food customs were influenced by different nationalities, such as the Africans, French, and Spaniards.)*

3. Ask students to describe the effect of African-American cooks on Southern cooking. *(These cooks introduced turnip and dandelion greens, black-eyed peas, catfish, fried okra, yams, red beans, rice, and peppers into Southern cooking.)*

4. Discuss the various recipes that African-Americans developed. *(They include chitterlings, ham hocks and turnip greens, spicy hot sauces and gravies, hopping John, hush puppies, among others.)*

Hearty and filling foods were a trademark of the Irish. These foods utilized a wide range of vegetables, including cabbage, carrots, and potatoes, which provided good sources of vitamins and minerals. Vegetables were combined with eggs, bread crumbs, butter, and spices to make puddings. Irish cooks also used leeks, onions, and garlic to flavor foods.

Pennsylvania Dutch

The early German, or *Deutsch,* immigrants to Pennsylvania were given a different name by the English settlers. The closest the English could come to pronouncing "Deutsch" properly was "Dutch." As a result, the Germans in this area became known as Pennsylvania Dutch.

These Germans were known for their hearty soups, stews, and homemade breads. They were farmers, which required hard physical labor and large quantities of flavorful, filling food.

The Pennsylvania Dutch immigrants continued to eat familiar foods from their homeland: pork, cabbage or sauerkraut, noodles, and sausage. Their meals included sweet and sour flavors from foods such as spiced fruit, pickled fruits and vegetables, and fruit butters.

The Pennsylvania Dutch are also known for tasty baked goods. Pies, cakes, rolls, and crumb-topped cakes were shared with neighbors over mid-morning coffee or *kaffeeklatsch.*

624   Chapter 23: Foods of the U.S. and Canada

The Midwest

In the eighteenth century, as people in the East settled into a comfortable lifestyle, adventurous pioneers set out to explore the unknown land to the west. Settlers followed, opening up new lands in the Midwest. During the nineteenth century, newly arrived immigrants from Europe joined this westward movement.

Soon the prairies of the heartland were supporting farms and dairies. Settlers planted familiar crops that grew well in that climate—wheat, corn, other grains, fruits, and vegetables. Farms also produced beef, pork, and poultry. Fish was available from rivers and lakes.

The Midwest is home to acres of rich farmland. Corn and soybeans are just two of the crops the region is famous for.

Rye bread with apple butter and pecan sticky buns reflect the Pennsylvania Dutch fondness for baked goods and sweets. Potato salad with a vinegar dressing provides one of the "sour" flavors included in each meal.

More About the Midwest

Among settlers in the Midwest was a religious group known as the Shakers. They contributed much to agriculture, improving many of the implements commonly used. Skilled horticulturists, they established successful plant nurseries and orchards, and they placed special emphasis on herbs. Vast herb gardens flourished, and the harvest flavored many of their foods. Marjoram, thyme, and rosemary were especially popular.

This bounty provided the basis for Midwestern cooking. It was also influenced by the cooking styles of settlers from the East and the food traditions brought by the new wave of immigrants from Europe.

In general, Midwestern menus were hearty and relied on the taste of the foods themselves rather than on much seasoning for flavor. The great supply of wheat made home-baked breads, cakes, and pies a way of life. Meat, potatoes, bread, vegetables, and dessert: this was food to provide energy for hard-working pioneers. It was simple fare, simply cooked, but a part of what is now known as American cooking.

The South

In the eighteenth century, life in the South generally revolved around the plantation and other rural areas. Crops in the South were bountiful because the earth along the lakes, rivers, and deltas was rich and the temperatures were warm. These lakes and rivers, as well as the ocean, provided fish and shell-

This appetizer features shrimp freshly caught along the southern coast of the United States.

fish. Corn was the staple food and was dried and ground so it could be used in a variety of recipes: cornbread, spoonbread, corn pone, fritters, cornmeal batters, grits, and hush puppies. These foods are still served in the South today.

The English were the primary settlers in the area. Food customs, however, were also influenced by the Africans, French, and Spaniards.

African-American Influence on Southern Cooking

African-American cooks on the plantations made their mark on Southern food. They incorporated turnip and dandelion greens, black-eyed peas, catfish, fried okra, yams, red beans, rice, and peppers into their cooking.

African-Americans developed their own special recipes for foods such as pig's feet and hog jowls. Chitterlings (small pieces of hog intestine) were fried and dipped into a spicy sauce. Pig tails were cooked with lima beans in a sweet-spicy sauce. Ham hocks (legs) and turnip greens became a popular dish. The backbone of the hog was simmered to make a tasty stew topped with dumplings.

The African-Americans had come to appreciate chili peppers, which had been transported to Africa from Latin America. They enjoyed spicy hot sauces and gravies. They also depended on one-pot cooking. Dishes were cooked in an iron pot and made with a wide variety of foods, including cooking greens.

African-American cooks also combined foods to make new recipes. *Hopping John,* for instance, is a mixture of black-eyed peas and rice. *Hush puppies,* made of cornmeal batter dropped by spoonfuls into hot oil, are often served with fried catfish. According to legend, hush puppies got their name in early days when they were thrown to silence barking dogs around campfires.

Student Experiences

1. **Class Discussion:** Discuss the three influences on the types of foods people ate in the Midwest. How did these influences lead to a new type of cooking? Why was this type of cooking well-suited for rural living? *(Key skill: critical thinking)*

2. **Listing:** Have students list five foods typical of midwestern cooking. Randomly ask students to share their lists with the class. *(Key skill: writing)*

3. **Naming Examples:** Ask students to think of five foods typical of Southern cooking. Have each student pair with another student to share lists. Have each student tell his or her partner which foods seem appealing and why. *(Key skill: cooperative learning)*

4. **Finding Recipes:** Have students find recipes for dishes that reflect African-American influence on Southern cooking, including pig's feet, hog jowls, chitterlings, hopping John, and hush puppies. *(Key skills: reading, multicultural awareness)*

Lab Experience

Have students prepare and taste hush puppies.

Food and Nutrition Science

Thickening Properties of Okra: Ask students to design and carry out an experiment comparing the thickening properties of okra and other thickeners. (Refer students to page 538, "Sauces and Gravies.")

23.1

Teaching . . .

• Creole and Cajun Cooking

(text pages 626-627)

Comprehension Check

1. Ask students to explain the difference between Creole and Cajun cooking. *(Creole is more sophisticated and has rich sauces; Cajun emphasizes improvisation and has stronger, hotter flavors.)*

2. Ask students to describe the blending of cultures that resulted in Creole cooking. *(It is a blend of traditions from Europe; Africa and the West Indies; and Native Americans.)*

3. Ask students to define *roux* and explain its use in Creole and Cajun cooking. *(Mixture of browned flour and fat used to thicken sauces.)*

Student Experiences

1. **Recipe Comparison:** Have students compare the ingredients and cooking methods of recipes for French foods, Creole foods, and Cajun foods. Have them write a report on similarities and differences. *(Key skill: writing)*

2. **Group Activity:** Have students plan a menu of Southern foods. Ask each group to obtain ingredient prices and figure the cost of preparing their meal. Discuss what location has to do with the price and availability of food items. *(Key skill: math)*

WORLD of variety

Have interested students find out more about the French Acadians and the contribution they made to the Cajun style of cooking.

African cooks helped create the special blend that is Southern cooking. Peanuts, yams, and peppers were familiar foods from their homeland. Here, they appear in an African-inspired peanut soup with red pepper garnish and a traditional Southern favorite, sweet potato pie.

Desserts were sweet and rich. They included pecan pie, sweet potato pie, and peach cobbler.

Creole and Cajun Cooking

Creole and Cajun are two specialized kinds of cooking that developed in southern Louisiana. Both feature ingredients such as seafood, pork, rice, peppers, celery, onions, and a variety of herbs and spices. Both are famous for their blending of flavors. This is

Jambalaya is a Creole or Cajun mixture of rice cooked with tomatoes, onions, and other flavorings, to which foods such as shrimp, ham, sausage, and chicken are added.

only natural, since Creole and Cajun cooking each resulted from a blending of cultures.

Creole cooking developed in New Orleans. Many European immigrants had settled there, including natives of France, Spain, and Italy. In many families, the meals were prepared by servants. To the European cuisine, these cooks added some of their own food traditions from Africa and the West Indies, as well as ingredients borrowed from Native Americans.

Creole cooking is considered by many to be a more sophisticated style than Cajun. Creole meals are likely to include a variety of separate dishes, each featuring a delicate, subtle blending of flavors. Shrimp, oysters, and crabs appear often. As in classic French cooking, sauces are often based on butter or cream. Creole cooking is sometimes described as a "city-style" cuisine.

Food and Nutrition Science

Effect of Spices on Foods: Point out that spices can enhance or spoil the flavors of foods. Have students compare the effects of a variety of spices on the taste and texture of various meats and vegetables. Have students identify foods that are palatable without spices, those made worse by spices, and those that are improved by spices.

Crawfish are a Louisiana specialty.

stews. The use of okra, and the method of simmering foods for a long time in iron pots, are examples of the African influence on the region's cooking. Still another thickener was borrowed from the Native Americans. They used dried, crushed sassafras leaves to thicken stews and add a delicate flavor. This was called "filé powder" by the settlers.

A famous Louisiana dish is gumbo, a thick stew that begins with a roux. From there, many variations are possible. A Creole gumbo might include shrimp, crab, and oysters, while a Cajun gumbo is more likely to feature ham and crawfish. Vegetables and seasonings are also added. Either okra or filé powder is used as a thickener. Gumbos are simmered slowly for hours, then served over rice.

In contrast, Cajun cooking is a "country-style" cuisine. The term "Cajun" is derived from "Acadian." The Acadians were French colonists who had settled in Canada. After being expelled from Canada by the British, some eventually found their way to the bayous and farmlands of southern Louisiana. The style of cooking that resulted combines French traditions with locally available foods and the influences of other cultural groups.

One of the key features of Cajun cooking is the ability to improvise. The Cajuns had to learn to live off the land, making meals from whatever they could hunt, catch, or grow at home. Authentic Cajun cooking often includes freshwater fish, crawfish (the Southern term for crayfish), and game such as rabbit, turtle, squirrel, and even alligator. One-dish meals, made from whatever foods are on hand, are common. Compared to Creole cooking, Cajun foods tend to feature stronger, hotter flavors.

Despite these distinctions, Creole and Cajun cuisine have much in common. Many dishes owe their distinctive flavor to a **roux** (ROO), a mixture of browned flour and fat. This thickener, of French origin, gives a subtle, dark, roasted flavor to sauces. Okra is also commonly used to thicken soups and

Section 23.1 Review

RECALL THE FACTS

1. Name two foods native to North America.

2. What are hominy and pemmican? What people made and ate these dishes?

3. Name three contributions made by the Africans to the American food culture.

4. What is roux?

DISCUSS YOUR IDEAS

5. What factors do you think encouraged the immigrants to try new foods?

APPLY YOUR LEARNING

6. Plan a dinner meal combining different foods from the South. (You may need to check some recipe books.) Survey a supermarket and gather ingredient prices for the foods in this meal. Which items were most or least expensive? Which were the easiest and most difficult to find? What does location have to do with the price and availability of food items?

Completing the Section

Review

- Ask students to summarize the main ideas in this section.
- Have students complete the Section Review. (Answers appear below.)

Evaluation

- Have students write a short essay on the development of food customs in the Northeast, Midwest, and South.
- Have students take the quiz for Section 23.1. (Refer to the *Section Quizzes* booklet or use the *Testmaker Software*.)

Reteaching

- Have students list five foods typical of the Northeast, the Midwest, and the South. Have them tell which foods appeal to them and why.
- Refer to the *Reteaching Activities* booklet for the Section 23.1 activity worksheet.

Enrichment

- Have students find a recipe for a Creole or Cajun dish and prepare the dish for the class.

Closure

- Refer to the second motivator for this section. Have students add items to their lists.

Answers to Section Review

1. *Any two:* Berries, fruit, maize (corn), seafood, peppers, beans, pumpkin, squash.
2. Pemmican is dried meat, pounded into a paste with fat and preserved in cakes; hominy is corn that has been soaked in lye; the Native Americans.
3. *Any three:* Turnip and dandelion greens, black-eyed peas, catfish, fried okra, yams, red beans, rice, peppers, chitterlings, pig's feet, hog jowls, pig tails, chili peppers, hopping John, hush puppies.
4. A mixture of browned flour and fat used to flavor and thicken Creole cooking.
5. Answers will vary. Students should realize that they had to try new foods to survive.
6. Answers will vary.

23.1 Recipe

Creole Green Beans

Key skill: Cooking ethnic dishes

Using the Recipe

- Have students read the recipe and discuss each step. Remind students to use the proper temperature to sauté the ham, onion, and garlic to avoid excessive spattering and possible burns. Review other safety and sanitation procedures that apply to this recipe.
- Have each lab team fill out a work plan. (See the *Foods Lab Resources* booklet.)
- Have students check off the ingredients and equipment listed on the recipe worksheet and prepare the recipe.
- Have students complete the evaluation and questions on the recipe worksheet.

See Also . . .

The *Foods Lab Resources* booklet for the "Creole Green Beans" recipe worksheet and other recipe alternatives.

Thinking About the Recipe

Read the recipe for "Creole Green Beans" and answer the following questions.

1. How might you adapt this recipe to use fresh green beans?
2. What suggestions do you have for lowering the sodium in this recipe?

Creole Green Beans

Customary	Ingredients	Metric
3 oz.	Ham, cubed	85 g
1	Onion, medium, chopped	1
1 clove	Garlic, minced	1 clove
1 lb.	Frozen cut green beans	454 g
1/2 cup	Water	125 mL

Yield: 4 servings

Conventional Directions

Pan: 3 qt. (3 L) covered saucepan
1. Sauté ham in saucepan over medium heat until lightly browned. Remove ham from saucepan and set aside.
2. Sauté onion and garlic in saucepan with ham drippings until tender, about 2 to 3 minutes.
3. Add green beans, ham, and water to saucepan. Cover.
4. Simmer over medium heat until beans are tender, about 12 to 15 minutes.
5. Serve hot in cooking liquid.

Microwave Directions

Pan: 3 qt. (3 L) microwave-safe baking dish
Power level: 100 percent power
1. Cook ham in covered baking dish 1 to 2 minutes at 100 percent power, stirring halfway through cooking time. Remove ham from baking dish and set aside.
2. Sauté onions and garlic with ham drippings in baking dish 1 to 2 minutes at 100 percent power, stirring halfway through cooking time.
3. Add green beans, ham, and water to baking dish.
4. Cook at 100 percent power for 10 to 12 minutes, stirring after 4 minutes and 8 minutes.
5. Serve hot with the cooking liquid.

Nutrition Information

Per serving (approximate): 80 calories, 7 g protein, 10 g carbohydrate, 2 g fat, 13 mg cholesterol, 334 mg sodium

---

Answers to Thinking About the Recipe

1. Answers will vary. You might have to change the cooking time; you might have to add a little more water.

2. Answers will vary. Students should recognize that the ham is the major source of sodium in the recipe.

Regional Foods of the West and Canada

OBJECTIVES

After studying this section, you should be able to:

• Identify foods characteristic of the western United States and Canada.

• Describe the cultural influences on foods of the western United States and Canada.

LOOK FOR THESE TERMS

sourdough starter
hibachi

Early settlers in the American West brought with them the cuisine of their native homelands. In adapting their traditional recipes to the climate and foods available to them, these early settlers developed foods that are commonly found in these regions today.

The Southwest

Most people associate the Southwest with cowboys and huge cattle ranches. Spaniards introduced cattle to this area in the sixteenth century. By the 1800s, ranches dotted the Texas plains, raising large herds of Longhorn cattle tended by cowboys.

Long before the Spaniards arrived, Native Americans were raising crops such as corn, beans, pumpkins, squash, and chilies. They also had an abundant supply of fish and wild game as well as berries, nuts, and seeds.

The use of chilies in Southwestern cooking illustrates the Native American influence, as well as the use of locally available foods.

Teacher's Classroom Resources—Section 23.2

Refer to these resources in the TCR package:

Reproducible Lesson Plans
Student Workbook
Extending the Text
Reteaching Activities

Section Quizzes
Testmaker Software
Foods Lab Resources
Multicultural Resources
Color Transparencies

Section 23.2
Regional Foods of the West and Canada

Introducing the Section

Motivators

• Discuss ways the settlement of the American West differed from the settlement of the rest of the United States. From what countries did early settlers in the American West come?

• On the chalkboard, write the regions: Southwest, Pacific Coast and Northwest, Hawaii, Ontario and Western Provinces, Quebec, Atlantic Provinces. Ask students to list foods from each region and write the foods under the appropriate region. With which region's foods were students most familiar? Have students copy the lists for future use.

Objectives

• Have students read the section objectives. Discuss the purpose of studying the section.

Vocabulary

• Pronounce the terms listed under "Look for These Terms." Have students find the terms and their definitions in the section.

Guided Reading

• Have students look at the headings within Section 23.2 to preview the concepts that will be discussed.

• Have students read the section and complete the appropriate part of the Chapter 23 Study Guide in the *Student Workbook*.

1. Ask students to explain why a cook traveled with cowboys. What typical early meals were prepared over campfires? *(The cowboys could not come home for meals; they roasted, barbecued, or stewed meat in a pot and had biscuits and sweet syrup for dessert.)*

2. Ask students to explain how Tex-Mex foods came about. *(When Mexican foods began to become popular among the cowboys, they blended the Mexican foods with their own styles and preferences. The result was Tex-Mex.)*

Student Experiences

1. **Guest Speaker:** Invite a historian who has studied the settlement of the Southwest to discuss the influences of different cultures on Southwestern dishes. *(Key skill: history)*

2. **Class Discussion:** Discuss the increased popularity of Tex-Mex food. What has contributed to this increase? What evidence can students see locally of interest in Tex-Mex foods? *(Key skill: social studies)*

3. **Recipe Finding:** Have students find recipes typical of the Southwest, including barbecued beef, Son-of-a-Gun stew, biscuits, pinto beans, tamales, tacos, tortillas, and chili con carne. What foods are used in these dishes? *(Key skill: reading)*

While Native Americans and Spaniards influenced the cooking in the region, so did other cultures. These included Mexicans, French, English, and other settlers moving from the east. Settlers moving westward found rich soil for growing abundant crops.

Because cowboys couldn't come home for meals, a cook traveled with them. Food and essential equipment to cook over a campfire were carried in a chuckwagon.

At first, cowboy cooks prepared simple meals over the open campfires. Meat was cooked by roasting, barbecuing, or stewing in a pot. To save time in the morning, the cook made a biscuit mix the night before, mixing flour, salt, and baking powder in a sack. The next day he added fat and water and baked the biscuits over the campfire. For the cowboys, "dessert" consisted of biscuits topped with a sweet syrup. Very strong coffee completed the meal.

Before long, Mexican foods made their way across the Texas border and influenced Southwest cooking. Beans, corn, and chilies were added to the cowboys' meals. Soon

other Mexican foods became popular, such as tamales, tacos, and tortillas. When the foods of the two cultures blended, the result was known as Tex-Mex. The seasoning in Tex-Mex can vary from mild to fiery hot. It depends on personal preference.

Many believe that Southerners moving to the Southwest introduced the barbecue. The word *barbecue* may be derived from the Spanish *barbacoa,* which refers to the grid on which meat is roasted in Latin America. However, records show that meat was barbecued in Virginia as early as the seventeenth century. Cowboy cooks bathed the roasting meat with a spicy tomato-based sauce. Soon, the barbecue was a major cooking method, especially in Texas.

There's a difference of opinion as to where *chili con carne* originated, in Texas or Mexico. There's little debate, however, over the popularity of chili, as it is now known. Originally, chili was made with diced beef cooked in a spicy sauce laced with red chilies and marjoram. Later, chili powder replaced the chilies and the beef was ground. Pinto beans, tomatoes, onions, cilantro, and spices were also added. Today, local contests are held yearly from coast to coast to find out who can make the best chili.

As in Mexican cooking, corn continues to be the mainstay of Tex-Mex cooking. Corn products are usually served at every meal. In addition, beans, chili peppers, fresh vegetables, and fruit, sometimes cooked with meats, are included in Southwestern meals.

Nachos are popular, made by smothering tortilla chips with refried beans, cheese sauce, and chilies. *Fajitas* (fah-HEE-tuhs) are tortillas wrapped around a thin, marinated, grilled steak. They are usually served with grilled onions and sweet peppers, guacamole, refried beans, and salsa.

Chili con carne is an all-American favorite, but nowhere is it more popular than in the Southwest. Many chili chefs create their own special blend of ingredients.

More About Tex-Mex

Much of the Southwestern cooking that is considered Mexican is actually Tex-Mex. For example, flour tortillas are an American invention.

Most true Mexican dishes contain little meat. In Mexico, meat was a luxury. Tex-Mex dishes, however, rely heavily on meat. The burrito, a folded tortilla filled with meat, beans, and cheese, is an American dish with Mexican seasoning.

The Pacific Coast and the Northwest

Early settlers in the Pacific Coast and the Northwest found an abundant food supply. Natural resources such as seafood and game were plentiful. The settlers used simple food preparation methods to bring out the natural flavors of these foods. For example, elk, deer, and goat were grilled or roasted. Seafood was steamed, boiled, or grilled.

The coast also had a rich supply of tasty fresh fruits and vegetables. The temperate climate of Southern California provided the perfect growing conditions.

As with most seacoasts, great shipping ports grew on the Pacific Coast, including San Francisco, Seattle, and Los Angeles. When gold was discovered in California and Alaska, people from Asia flocked to the New World. These Japanese, Chinese, Russian, and Korean immigrants were joined by Mexicans, French, and Canadians.

The immigrants brought their food specialties with them and mingled them with local food customs. For example, *chow mein* is a dish created in California about 100 years ago. It is not an authentic Chinese dish, but an Americanized version of Chinese cooking.

Early sailing ships brought food from China, Japan, and the Polynesian islands to America. The influence of Asian cooking is still strong in the Pacific Coast and Northwest regions.

Sourdough bread today is considered one of the classic breads in America. Yet it had humble beginnings in the mid-19th century, during the days of the gold rush. Many early settlers in California and Alaska came looking for gold. Most of the prospectors were poor and relied on bread as their staple. They had no yeast, but made bread with a **sourdough starter,** a mixture of flour, water, and salt on which wild yeast cells grew. The mixture fermented and became a leavening agent.

The prospectors never put all their starter in the bread. A small amount was always left in a crock and then replenished by adding flour and water. In this way sourdough starter was always on hand and the prospector was assured of a food supply. As long as the prospector had the crock of sourdough starter, he knew he would not starve. Because they were so dependent on the starter, prospectors came to be known as "sourdoughs."

The Northwest corner of the United States was the last to be settled. Settlers in Oregon and Washington came to these Northwestern states by way of the Oregon Trail. Many brought seeds from fruit trees to begin orchards. Fruit orchards, which later became

San Francisco is the undisputed capital of sourdough bread.

Along the Pacific Coast, fish has always been a staple food. These cooks in Alaska are grilling salmon and other varieties for an outdoor festival.

Comprehension Check

1. Ask students to explain the effect the discovery of gold in California and Alaska had on the cultural background of the people who settled in these areas. *(It encouraged people from Asia to come to this area, so Japanese, Chinese, Russian, and Korean cultures were blended with those already there.)*

2. Ask students to describe the use of sourdough starter by prospectors. *(They mixed flour, water, and salt and allowed wild yeast cells to grow and ferment to become a leavening agent. Once they had the starter, they never used all of it, but saved a little to make the next batch.)*

Student Experiences

1. **Geography Review:** Review with students the geography of the Pacific coast and the Northwest. What natural food resources are readily available? How have the great shipping ports of San Francisco, Seattle, and Los Angeles influenced the foods available? *(Key skill: geography)*

2. **Finding Recipes:** Have students find recipes for foods popular on the pacific coast and in the Northwest, including those associated with Asian cultures and those for fish, seafood, fruits, and vegetables. *(Key skill: reading)*

Food and Nutrition Science

Sourdough Starter: Have students research to find out how the sourdough starter works and why it is possible to keep an endless supply by adding more flour, water, and salt to a little of the starter left over from the previous batch.

Provide students with sourdough starter and have them bake bread from it. Give each student a supply of the starter to take home with them for future use. Survey students at the end of the term to find out who is still using the starter, and how often students used it.

Teaching . . .

- **Hawaii**
- **Canada**

(text pages 632-634)

Comprehension Check

1. Ask students to explain why Hawaii contains so many different cultures. *(It has been a midway stopping point for ships traveling between Asia and North America for several hundred years.)*

2. Ask students to list the cultures that have had an effect on Hawaiian cooking. *(Polynesian, Chinese, Japanese, Korean, Filipino, French, English, Portuguese, and American.)*

3. Ask students to explain what a hibachi is and identify the culture that introduced it to Hawaiian cooking. *(A small charcoal grill; introduced by the Japanese.)*

4. Ask students to identify the most heavily populated province in Canada. *(Ontario)*

5. Ask students to explain why the dominant culture in Quebec is French. *(From 1534 until 1763, the area was under the control of France. When it was given to Great Britain, the culture was already established firmly enough that it is still dominant.)*

profitable businesses for settlers, remain a major industry in the Northwest today. Along with raising fruits, such as pears, peaches, and apples, these settlers created delicious dishes from the abundance of fish and seafood. Dungeness crab and coho salmon were often steamed or served with creamy sauces.

Earth Watch

Today in the Pacific Northwest, the salmon which was once so abundant is less available. Environmental hazards, such as over-fishing and pollution, have taken their toll on the availability of this tasty fish. What suggestions might you have for preventing problems like this with other food sources?

Many tropical fruits, such as papaya (right), are grown in Hawaii. A tempting buffet (below) illustrates the bounty of the islands.

Hawaii

Hawaiian cuisine is a very complex blend of different cultures. Hawaii is a small chain of islands located in the middle of the Pacific Ocean, west of Mexico. For centuries, it has been the midway stopping point for ships traveling the long shipping lanes between Asia and North America.

The original inhabitants were Polynesian, but many other cultures have settled in the islands, bringing their food customs with them. Today, Hawaiian cooking is a blend of Polynesian, Chinese, Japanese, Korean, Fil-

More About Hawaii

Common in Hawaiian cooking, the coconut is the seed of the coconut palm. It provides both a refreshing beverage and an edible pulp called "coconut meat." The clear liquid inside the coconut is often called "milk."

Another kind of coconut milk is made by grating coconut meat, mixing it with a small amount of water, then squeezing and straining it to produce a white, sweet juice. This milk is used in many Hawaiian main dishes and desserts.

ipino, French, English, and Portuguese, as well as mainland American.

The rich soil and warm climate offer a wide variety of tropical fruits, including mango, papaya, pineapple, and bananas. The surrounding waters and inland streams provide a bounty of flavorful fish. Other foods were introduced by settlers. The Japanese introduced seaweed, teriyaki sauce for marinating, a new kind of noodle, and many rice and bean products. They also brought the **hibachi,** a small charcoal grill. The Chinese brought rice, soybeans, pork, and Asian vegetables such as Chinese cabbage. These, along with chicken, are the mainstay of Hawaiian cooking.

The early Polynesians had no pots and pans, so they invented techniques for preparing food. One was *poi* pounding. They pounded fruits or roots into a bland, sticky paste. This was their staple. Today, poi is made from ground taro root and is often used in cooking or served as a side dish. If allowed to ferment for several days, it develops a more sour flavor. Duck may be steamed in a banana leaf with cabbage, pineapple, and poi. Taro chips, similar to potato chips, are deep-fried thin slices of taro root.

Another cooking method was the open pit, which became famous as the *luau,* or feast. The luau is a tradition observed on special occasions, such as birthdays, marriages, and other events. Tourists visiting Hawaii are usually treated to the luau, which also features native entertainment.

The highlight of the luau is a pig roasted in an open pit. Fish and other meats are wrapped in leaves and roasted with sweet potatoes and bananas on the hot coals. Besides poi, other Hawaiian dishes that might be served include *lomi lomi salmon*—salted salmon with onions and tomatoes—and *haupia*, a sweet pudding made with arrowroot and coconut milk.

Canada

As in the United States, the foods of Canada reflect the nation's natural resources and cultural diversity. The natural resources include wild rice, fish, and beef. As for the people, Canada is populated by many nationalities that have, for the most part, retained their identities.

Ontario and the Western Provinces of Canada

Ontario is centrally located in Canada, lying to the north of Minnesota, Wisconsin, and Michigan. Over one-third of Canada's population lives in Ontario, making it the most heavily-populated province in the country.

Beef and dairy foods are among the chief products of Ontario. Poultry, eggs, fruits, vegetables, and maple syrup are also plentiful.

Food customs in Ontario are as varied as the people who live there. Many are of British, French, German, Italian, Ukrainian, or Asian descent, among others. In addition, more Native Americans live in Ontario than in any other province.

To the west of Ontario are the prairie provinces of Manitoba, Saskatchewan, and Alberta. Here, the traditional foods are similar to those in the Midwest of the United States.

In British Columbia, on the North Pacific coast, salmon is a staple. Vancouver, the largest city in British Columbia, is located just north of Seattle. It has a significant Chinese population and its own Chinatown. Foods from all regions of China can be found there.

The Northwest Territories stretch across northern Canada. Native Americans and Inuit (Eskimos) are the primary inhabitants. Until the 19th century, most Inuit hunted and fished for food. Seal meat, caribou, trout, and cod were staples.

Student Experiences

1. **Demonstration:** Help students obtain references on the preparation of fresh coconut, pineapple, papaya, and mango. Ask for volunteers to demonstrate ways to prepare the tropical fruits for eating. *(Key skill: reading)*

2. **Class Discussion:** Compare the countries from which people immigrated to Canada with those who immigrated to the United States. What similarities and differences in food traditions have resulted? *(Key skill: social studies)*

3. **Letter Writing:** Have students exchange letters with students in different provinces of Canada. Have students ask questions about the geographic and cultural influences, food production, and food traditions. Have students request that the Canadian students send recipes that reflect the food traditions of the area. Have students read the letters they receive to the class. *(Key skill: writing)*

Lab Experiences

- Have students prepare a Hawaiian luau complete with decorations and entertainment.

- From the recipes received from Canadian students (see Student Experience 3), select several for students to prepare and serve in class. Are any of these dishes also popular in the United States? If so, where?

More About Quebec

Great Britain became the official owner of the Quebec area as a result of the Treaty of Paris, which ended the Seven Year War. This and previous wars between Great Britain and France determined the official country to which Quebec belonged, but had little to do with the sentiments of the inhabitants.

The tensions between Canadians with French and English backgrounds continues even today. Because of these tensions between Canadian provinces, a vote was taken in 1992 to see if Quebec should be separate from the rest of Canada. Canadians voted for a unified Canada under one national government. The people of Quebec remain loyal to their heritage, however.

• **Cultural Diversity Today**

(text page 635)

Comprehension Check

1. Ask students to explain why the United States and Canada have recently experienced so much growth in their minority populations. *(Millions of immigrants from around the world have come to North America in search of a better life and have settled in communities all across the country.)*

2. Ask students to name four factors that have affected the cultural diversity in North America in recent decades. *(Immigration, mobility, the media, and technology.)*

Student Experiences

1. **Class Discussion:** Discuss other factors that have helped people become familiar with foods from all over. *(world travel, restaurants, more interaction with people from other cultures) (Key skill: critical thinking)*

2. **Class Discussion:** Discuss other factors that have led to changes in traditions. Ask students how time and energy constraints may affect traditions. *(People may use convenience foods and shortcuts rather than traditional preparation methods.)* Ask how health consciousness affects traditions. *(Traditional dishes that are high in fat and calories may be modified or saved for special occasions.) (Key skill: multicultural awareness)*

Quebec

In 1534, Jacques Cartier landed in Gaspé, in what is now Quebec, and claimed the territory for France. The next year he traveled up the St. Lawrence River to the present site of Quebec and Montreal. By 1663, the area was under the firm control of Paris and was called New France.

One hundred years later, the Treaty of Paris gave Britain control of all of New France. By this time, though, French culture was firmly established and has continued to be dominant in the region.

Due to cultural and linguistic ties to France and Switzerland, Quebec shows the most European influence of any Canadian province. About a fourth of the population of Canada resides in Quebec. These French Canadians are proud of their language and heritage. French is spoken almost exclusively in that province.

It is not surprising, then, that food in Quebec displays a distinct French influence. Common dishes include French pastries, apple tarts, French breads, seafood soups, and special cheeses. Maple syrup, a local contribution, is a favorite in desserts. The cuisine of Quebec is considered some of the finest in North America.

Apples, pumpkins, and other produce are for sale at this orchard in Quebec. Besides fruits and vegetables, Quebec produces dairy products, pork, poultry, and beef.

634   Chapter 23: Foods of the U.S. and Canada

Atlantic Provinces

Newfoundland, New Brunswick, Nova Scotia, and Prince Edward Island make up the Atlantic provinces. The ethnic origins of the people are largely English and French, with some German, Dutch, and Irish as well. Almost half of the people speak both English and French.

Fish is one of the most important foods of the region. The coast provides an abundance of lobster and crab, which are relatively common and quite inexpensive. Seafood provides great sources of protein and iodine. Fresh fruits and vegetables are grown locally, but the growing season is short due to the cold. Potatoes are raised on Prince Edward Island, showing the influence of the Irish who settled the region.

Blueberries are one of the main fruits grown in the Atlantic provinces. They are often featured in desserts and baked goods.

More About Cultural Diversity

By 1990, one-fourth of the population of the United States was made up of non-white people from non-Western European backgrounds. In North America, more than 100 languages are spoken and all the world's major religions are practiced. In 25 of the largest cities in the United States, one-half of the students in public schools are considered "minorities."

No matter what region you live in, you can find ethnic restaurants such as this one in major cities and even small towns. This is just one sign of the cultural diversity characteristic of the U.S. and Canada today.

Review

- Ask students to summarize the main ideas in this section.
- Have students complete the Section Review. (Answers appear below.)

Evaluation

- Have students create a menu for and prepare a typical Tex-Mex meal that is attractive and nutritious.
- Have students take the quiz for Section 23.2. (Refer to the *Section Quizzes* booklet or use the *Testmaker Software*.)

Reteaching

- Ask students to prepare a chart of regional foods in the United States and Canada.
- Refer to the *Reteaching Activities* booklet for the Section 23.2 activity worksheet.

Enrichment

- Have students sponsor a chili cook-off at school. They should make arrangements for publicity, preparation areas, serving areas, and judges.

Closure

- Refer to the second motivator for this section. Have students add to their lists the foods they learned about in this section.

Cultural Diversity Today

In recent decades, the United States and Canada have experienced much growth in their minority populations. Millions of immigrants have flocked to North America in search of a better life and settled in communities all across the country.

In addition to immigration, other factors that affect the cultural diversity in North America include:

❖ **Mobility.** People move from one region to another more often now than in the past. They carry their food traditions with them.

❖ **The media.** Through television, magazines, and other sources, people are exposed to various cultures and their traditions.

❖ **Technology.** Due to modern transportation and packaging methods, foods from many regions and cultures are available all across the U. S. and Canada.

For these and other reasons, today the food in a specific region is as diverse as the people who live there. Many food habits and patterns now reflect the traditions of individual families more than the area in which they live.

■ Section 23.2 Review ■

RECALL THE FACTS

1. Describe the special touch contributed to barbecued beef by inhabitants of the Southwest.

2. Explain two ways in which the geography of the Pacific Coast and Northwest affected the food supply.

3. Describe the contribution of the Polynesians to Hawaiian cuisine.

4. Identify one Irish influence on the foods of the Atlantic provinces of Canada.

DISCUSS YOUR IDEAS

5. Do you think the type of foods people were accustomed to influenced their decision about where to settle? Explain.

APPLY YOUR LEARNING

6. List ten foods that you enjoy eating. Identify the regional or ethnic source of each food.

Section 23.2: Regional Foods of the West and Canada   **635**

■ Answers to Section Review ■

1. They added a spicy, tomato-based sauce, with which they basted the meat.
2. Seafood was abundant on the coast; the temperate climate of Southern California allowed fresh fruits and vegetables to grow well.
3. Poi is made of fruits or roots pounded into a bland, sticky paste.
4. Potatoes.
5. Answers will vary. People might have looked for land that was similar to the land they had in their former country; similar land would grow similar foods.
6. Answers will vary.

23.2 Recipe

Southwest Guacamole

Key skill: Making fruit and vegetable spreads

Using the Recipe

- Have students read the recipe and discuss each step. Review safety and sanitation procedures that apply to this recipe.
- Have each lab team fill out a work plan. (See the *Foods Lab Resources* booklet.)
- Have students check off the ingredients and equipment listed on the recipe worksheet and prepare the recipe.
- Have students complete the evaluation and questions on the recipe worksheet.

See Also . . .

The *Foods Lab Resources* booklet for the "Southwest Guacamole" recipe worksheet and other recipe alternatives.

Thinking About the Recipe

Read the recipe for "Southwest Guacamole" and answer the following questions.

1. How could this recipe be varied to suit individual tastes?
2. How might you adapt this recipe if you wanted to use a blender to make guacamole?

Southwest Guacamole

Customary	Ingredients	Metric
2	Ripe avocados	2
1 small	Tomato, diced	1 small
4-oz. can	Chopped mild green chilies, drained	112-g can
1/4 cup	Onion, minced	50 mL
2 Tbsp.	Lemon juice	30 mL
1 Tbsp.	Cilantro (fresh coriander leaves), minced	15 mL
1/8 tsp.	Garlic powder	0.5 mL

Yield: About 2 cups (500 mL)

Directions

1. Peel and seed avocados.
2. Mash avocados in a medium bowl.
3. Stir in tomato, chilies, onion, lemon juice, cilantro, and garlic powder.
4. Serve as a spread on warm tortillas, as a dip with baked tortilla chips, or as a condiment with Tex-Mex foods. To store, cover surface of guacamole with plastic wrap and refrigerate.

Nutrition Information

Per 1/4-cup (50-mL) serving (approximate): 87 calories, 1 g protein, 5 g carbohydrate, 7 g fat, 0 mg cholesterol, 174 mg sodium

Answers to Thinking About the Recipe

1. Answers will vary. Students may say that the chilies could be hotter or more garlic powder could be added. Other ingredients may also be added.

2. Cut the avocados into pieces and blend; add ingredients in step 3 and blend.

Joyce Nitobe
Foods Writer

CURRENT POSITION

"I'm a journalist assigned to the food section in a medium-sized newspaper."

RESPONSIBILITIES

"I'm responsible for producing a weekly page in the newspaper on regional food specialties. I write the articles and obtain photographs or arrange to have them taken. Of course it's necessary to be a good cook in this business. It also helps to be very well-organized and personable."

SKILLS

"First and foremost, you must be able to meet deadlines to be successful in this job. You also must have good interviewing skills, organizational skills, and writing skills. It helps to be knowledgeable about foods, although some of what you need to know can be learned on the job."

EDUCATION

"I have a bachelor's degree in journalism and a background in foods and cooking that goes back to my high school years."

TYPICAL DAY ON THE JOB

"I spend a lot of time gathering information through mail I receive, my own research, and interviews. Often I test out recipes in my own kitchen. After I have the information I need, I spend time writing at a computer."

FAVORITE PART OF THE JOB

"I'm a natural born writer and I love to cook, so this is a perfect job for me! I enjoy learning so many new things in my job and being able to pass on that information to others."

- Why are organizational skills important in Joyce's job?
- What aspects of Joyce's job do you think you might enjoy? Why?

637

Thinking About . . . Writing About Foods

Have students think of other questions they would like to ask Joyce Nitobe about being a foods writer. (Examples: What is the salary range for writing the foods section in a newspaper? How much time do you spend on your job weekly? How much of that time do you spend at the computer? What types of information do people send you through the mail? What percentage of this information can you actually use?)

Ask student volunteers to tell what they think would be the most exciting part of being a foods writer.

Student Opportunities

Students planning a career in journalism should get involved in their school publications and seek internship opportunities with local newspapers or magazines. Future foods writers should also take home economics and foods courses.

Occupational Outlook

Foods writers for newspapers can go to work for larger newspapers; those who are interested can write books on the subject of food. Others may want to go into a management position.

For More Information

For additional information about careers in foods writing and journalism, encourage students to contact:
- The American Newspaper Publishers Association Foundation, The Newspaper Center, Box 17407, Dulles International Airport, Washington, D.C. 20041
- Association for Education in Journalism and Mass Communication, University of South Carolina College of Journalism, 1621 College St., Columbia, SC 29208
- National Newspaper Association, 1627 K St. NW, Suite 400, Washington, D.C. 20006

Review

- Have students complete the Chapter Review. (Answers appear below.)

Evaluation

- Using a map of the United States and Canada, have students name the various regions and describe foods typical of the regions.

■ ANSWERS ■

REVIEWING FACTS

1. *Any three:* Roasted corn, boiled corn, flatbreads, hominy.

2. In cold climates, food was dried, smoked, and frozen for use in the winter; in coastal areas, seafood was a staple; in the Southwest, tribes grew peppers and beans to use in soups and chili-type dishes.

3. The climate, the cultural heritage of immigrants, and the cultural heritage of the Native Americans.

4. *Any four:* French, Spanish, Italian, African, West Indian, and Native American.

5. *Any six:* Fish, crawfish, rabbit, turtle, squirrel, alligator, ham, rice, okra, peppers, celery, onions.

6. Because they were simple methods and made use of the campfire that they had already built.

7. Chinese and American.

8. It is made from a mixture of flour, water, salt, and yeast; the mixture is allowed to ferment, which creates a leavening agent. Advantages: it costs little; once you have a yeast culture started, you can keep it going indefinitely by saving a little from each batch and adding flour, water, and salt to make a new batch.

CHAPTER 23 REVIEW

SUMMARY

SECTION 23.1

Regional Foods of the East, Midwest, and South: Native Americans lived on fish and game, wild berries, and corn. They shared these foods with European immigrants, who adapted them to their own lifestyles and cooking traditions. British, Dutch, and German groups in the Northeast developed recipes to supply their energy needs and get them through the harsh winters. Midwestern farmers raised cattle, grains, and vegetables that became the basis of that region's flavorful food. Southern staples such as corn, catfish, and black-eyed peas were incorporated into new dishes by African-Americans living in the South. Creole and Cajun cuisines, which originated in and around Louisiana, are famous for their distinctively spiced, seafood-based recipes.

SECTION 23.2

Regional Foods of the West and Canada: Foods and preparation methods of the American Southwest reflect the influence of Native American and Mexican cultures. On the Pacific Coast and in the Northwest, shipping ports brought the influence of Asian cooking to native food supplies. Hawaiian cuisine combines Polynesian, Chinese, Japanese, Korean, and Filipino traditions. Foods in Canada's Western provinces show the influence of Native Americans, the French, British, and other immigrant groups. The cuisine of Quebec reflects its historical ties to France. Fish and potatoes are staples in the Atlantic provinces.

REVIEWING FACTS

1. Name three ways that Native Americans prepared corn that are still used today. (23.1)

2. Describe three ways in which regional differences affected the foods and preparation methods of Native Americans. (23.1)

3. Identify the three influences on the development of Midwestern cooking styles. (23.1)

4. What four cultures are blended in Creole cooking? (23.1)

5. Name six foods that are often combined in Cajun cooking. (23.1)

6. Why was grilling and barbecuing a common food preparation method among cowboys? (23.2)

7. *Chow mein* reflects a blending of what two cultures? (23.2)

8. How is sourdough bread made? What is the advantage to this method? (23.2)

9. Identify two uses of the taro root. (23.2)

10. Name three foods that show the French influence in Quebec. (23.2)

LEARNING BY DOING

1. ***Foods lab:*** Find and prepare an authentic recipe for one of the regional favorites described in this chapter. Compare its basic flavor to those of the foods you enjoy today. Describe and give reasons for the similarities and differences you find. (23.1)

2. ***Foods lab:*** Find and prepare a recipe for sourdough starter and bread. Experiment with different flavor combinations that show the influence of the different regions and ethnic cuisines that you have read about. (23.2)

9. Poi and taro chips are made from taro root.

10. *Any three:* French pastries, French breads, apple tarts, seafood soups, special cheeses.

3. **Foods lab:** Combine the preferences and cooking traditions of your lab group to create your own "regional" cuisine. Prepare a meal of these favorite recipes, explaining how each one became part of the group's "heritage." (23.1, 23.2)

THINKING CRITICALLY

1. **Recognizing alternatives:** Identify the traditional cooking methods used to prepare the regional foods described in this chapter. Suggest some modern methods that could replace the traditional methods. (23.1, 23.2)

2. **Analyzing behavior:** What personal qualities did immigrants and settlers show by trying new foods and developing new recipes? In what other situations did those qualities help them survive? How might people today benefit from trying new foods? (23.1, 23.2)

3. **Predicting consequences:** How do you think appreciating the food traditions of other cultures affects your attitudes and feelings toward the people of these cultures? (23.1, 23.2)

MAKING DECISIONS AND SOLVING PROBLEMS

What Would You Do?

1. You are spending a few months with friends in the South. You are concerned that many of the foods they prepare— fried chicken and fish, hush puppies, meat gravy—are high in fat and calories. You would like to suggest ways of preparing foods that are more healthful, but retain the flavors and textures your friends enjoy. (23.1)

2. You want to prepare *poi* for your family's dinner. However, taro root is not available where you live. (23.2)

3. A friend of yours, who grew up in Texas, has recently moved to Vermont. In one of her letters, she says she misses the flavor of an authentic outdoor barbecue, especially in the winter. (23.2)

LINKING YOUR STUDIES

1. **Literature:** In Willa Cather's *My Antonia*, find a passage related to food, or the lack of it. What does the scene tell you about meals, food supplies, and preparation methods of people of that time and place? What might the scene tell you about the characters involved? (23.1)

2. **Social studies:** Interview people of different cultural backgrounds who live in your community. What are some traditional foods of their ethnic group? If they originally came from another country or region, how has moving affected their cooking and eating habits? How have their cooking traditions affected the way they prepare common American dishes? (23.1, 23.2)

3. **Writing:** In diary form, describe your first encounter with some of the foods, recipes, and preparation methods of another region of North America. (23.1, 23.2)

639

LEARNING BY DOING

Answers to "Learning by Doing" activities will vary. Evaluate students on their procedures as well as their results.

THINKING CRITICALLY

1. Answers will vary.

2. They showed courage, adaptability, and a willingness to try new things. They also applied these characteristics to the homes they built, the local governments they formed, and every other aspect of their lives. People today might benefit by trying new foods that are lower in fat, cholesterol, or salt content.

3. Answers will vary. Understanding the food traditions of a culture helps you understand the people a little better.

MAKING DECISIONS AND SOLVING PROBLEMS

Answers to "Making Decisions and Solving Problems" activities will vary. Encourage students to give reasons for their answers.

LINKING YOUR STUDIES

Answers to "Linking Your Studies" activities will vary. Encourage students to give reasons for their answers.

Planning the Chapter

Chapter Overview

Introducing the Chapter

Motivator

- Discuss the following creative cooking tips: 1) once you have experience in preparing a dish, you can use the recipe as a guideline rather than an instruction sheet; 2) when preparing a simple meal, try new ways to present or decorate the food; 3) don't be afraid of failure; 4) don't be caught saying "I'm just not creative"—that usually means you don't have the courage to try new things.

CHAPTER 24

Special Ways
with Food

640

Cooperative Learning Suggestions

Initiate a Co-op Co-op activity. Have students work in small groups to plan a party. Assign one group to each of the following: theme, menu, recipes, invitations, decorations, entertainment, and time schedule. Discuss and evaluate the plans according to the text guidelines. Have each group present its plans to the class in a creative manner. Have students combine their plans and carry them out.

Creative Techniques

OBJECTIVES
After studying this section, you should be able to:
- Describe how to use a variety of seasonings and marinades.
- Explain how to use your creativity in cooking.
- Describe ways to improve the appearance of foods with garnishes.

LOOK FOR THESE TERMS
seasoning blends
julienne
en papillote

Once you learn the basics of food preparation, you can begin to use creative techniques that can easily turn simple foods into special meals. For instance, different seasonings can vary the flavor of any basic recipe. Other creative techniques include cooking in parchment paper and making garnishes.

Seasoning Secrets

Seasonings are ingredients that are used in small amounts to flavor foods. They include herbs and spices, condiments, and marinades. Seasonings can be helpful to health-conscious people who are limiting their use of salt and fat.

When you begin to experiment with seasonings, start out using a small amount. You can always add a little more. If you add too much at the beginning, there's little you can do to correct the flavor.

Would you recognize these objects as spices in their natural form? The seeds, bark, stems, and roots of certain plants yield seasonings that are essential for creative cooking.

Section 24.1: Creative Techniques   **641**

Teacher's Classroom Resources—Section 24.1

Refer to these resources in the TCR package:
Reproducible Lesson Plans
Student Workbook
Extending the Text

Reteaching Activities
Section Quizzes
Testmaker Software
Color Transparencies

Section 24.1
Creative Techniques

Introducing the Section

Motivators
- Place six common spices in test tubes or small glass containers. Number the containers and keep a master list to identify the spices. Have students smell the spices. Can they identify each?
- Ask students how many ways they can cook ground beef. Have students list as many ways as they can. Compare lists. Give a small prize to the student who lists the most ways to cook ground beef.
- Display several dishes served plainly. Ask students to comment about the appeal of these foods. Add garnishes to the dishes. Discuss the difference in appeal.

Objectives
- Have students read the section objectives. Discuss the purpose of studying the section.

Vocabulary
- Pronounce the terms listed under "Look for These Terms." Have students find the terms and their definitions in the section.

Guided Reading
- Have students look at the headings within Section 24.1 to preview the concepts that will be discussed.
- Have students read the section and complete the appropriate part of the Chapter 24 Study Guide in the *Student Workbook*.

Teaching . . .

• Seasoning Secrets

(text pages 641-645)

Comprehension Check

1. Ask students to list guidelines for using herbs and spices. *(See list on pages 642-643.)*

2. Ask students to define "condiments" and name three popular condiments. *(Condiments are liquid or semi-liquid, flavorful accompaniments to food. Examples include mustard, salsa, ketchup, soy sauce, tamari sauce, hot pepper sauce, and Worcestershire sauce.)*

3. Ask students to identify the three basic ingredients in most marinades. *(oil, an acid, and seasonings)*

4. Ask students to explain the procedure for marinating food. *(Pour the marinade ingredients into a large container and shake well. Place the food in a glass or plastic covered container, pour the marinade over the food, and refrigerate. Occasionally turn and stir the food to marinate evenly.)*

TIPS for **Success**

Have interested students grow and air-dry or microwave some fresh herbs. Have students compare the taste and cost of their herbs to those sold commercially. What do students conclude?

Herbs and Spices

Herbs are the flavorful leaves and stems of soft, succulent plants that grow in the temperate zone. Some familiar examples include basil, oregano, sage, and bay leaf. They are usually sold dried, but some, such as parsley and basil, are available fresh.

Spices are usually dried, ground buds, bark, seeds, stems, or roots of aromatic plants and trees. Most grow in tropical countries. Some are sold whole or in pieces, such as whole nutmeg, peppercorns, or cinnamon sticks. A few are sold fresh, such as ginger root, which is commonly used in Asian cooking.

Seasoning blends are convenient combinations of herbs or spices. Most are used for specific purposes. For instance, Italian seasoning combines flavors typical in Italian cooking. You can buy blends or mix your own.

Because herbs and spices are used in such small amounts, consider buying them in bulk. That way, you can buy just the amount you can use in a short time.

Light, air, and heat are the main enemies of herbs and spices. Store them in tightly closed, opaque containers in a cool, dark place. Do not keep them next to the range.

Dried crushed herbs keep their flavor about six months. To test dried herbs for freshness, rub a small amount in the palm of your hand with your thumb for about five to ten seconds. If there is little or no aroma, the herb is probably too old to use. It might give food a bitter flavor.

Ground spices keep their flavor about a year. Whole spices may last as long as three years.

Here are some guidelines for using herbs and spices:

❖ Begin with a few basic herbs and spices as suggested on the chart on pages 644-645. Once you learn how to use them, you can add others.

❖ Herbs and spices vary in strength and are used in differing amounts. Dried herbs are more potent than fresh. As a rule, one tablespoon of fresh herbs can be substituted for one teaspoon of dried and crushed herbs.

You can grow your own fresh herbs in a garden or on a windowsill. Starter plants are available at many garden shops.

642 Chapter 24: Special Ways with Food

TIPS for **Success**

Drying Herbs

You can successfully dry your own fresh herbs. Here are two simple methods:

❖ *Air-dry method.* Rinse sprigs of herbs and shake off excess water. Tie herbs into bunches and label so you can identify them when they dry. Hang them in a dry, shady, well-ventilated place. They should dry in about two weeks.

❖ *Microwave method.* Place rinsed herbs between several layers of paper toweling. Microwave on 100 percent power, 15 to 30 seconds at a time, until the herbs are dry and can be crumbled.

More About Herbs and Spices

The American Heart Association has developed a salt substitute composed of herbs and spices. This "herb shaker blend" can be used instead of salt at the table and also to season foods while cooking.
Yield: 1/4 c.
1 Tbsp. garlic powder (not garlic *salt*)

1 tsp. each dried, ground, or crushed basil, thyme, parsley, savory, mace (or nutmeg), onion powder, black pepper, and sage.
1/2 tsp cayenne

Mix all ingredients together and store in a cool, dark place.

Fresh herbs can be dried in the microwave oven. After drying, store herbs in airtight containers and use as needed.

❖ When preparing hot foods, add herbs and spices at least ten minutes before tasting or serving. This allows time for the heat to release the flavor. Do not add herbs more than 45 minutes before serving—they will lose their flavor if overcooked.
❖ When preparing cold mixtures, add herbs and spices 30 minutes to several hours before serving so that flavors can be released.

Condiments

Condiments are liquid or semi-liquid accompaniments to food. They can also be used as flavorful seasonings. Condiments vary in flavors, such as sweet, salty, and spicy hot. Mustard, salsa, and ketchup are popular condiments. Here are some others.
❖ *Soy and tamari (tuh-MA-ree) sauces* are made from fermented soybeans. Soy sauce has a sharper, more pungent flavor than tamari. Low-sodium types are available.

❖ *Hot pepper sauce* is made from hot chili peppers. It's measured by drops because it is so strong.
❖ *Worcestershire (WOO-stir-sheer) sauce* is a dark, spicy sauce used in soups, stews, and meat mixtures.

Marinades

Marinades (MAIR-ih-nayds) are flavorful liquids in which food is placed before it is cooked. Marinades can tenderize less tender cuts of meat and can add flavor to food. Low-fat salad dressings can be used as marinades, or you can make your own.

Most marinades contain three basic ingredients—oil, an acid, and seasonings. Any mild oil can be used. It coats the outside of the food and keeps it from drying out as it broils or grills. The acid ingredient helps tenderize the food. Options include flavored vinegars, citrus juices, plain nonfat yogurt, and buttermilk. Seasonings add flavor. Try using herbs and spices or aromatic vegetables such as onions, peppers, garlic, and celery.

You can vary the flavor of marinades by the ingredients you choose.

Student Experiences

1. **Class Discussion:** Discuss the reasons for using marinades. What basic ingredients do most marinades contain? What determines marinating time? What happens if you over-marinate a food? Why should the marinade be discarded? Why should an extra batch be made for basting? *(Key skill: critical thinking)*

2. **Oral Reports:** Have each student prepare and present a three-minute report on the history and use of a spice or herb. *(Key skill: research)*

3. **Store Survey:** Have students survey a local supermarket to identify the variety of condiments available. Include mustard, salsa, ketchup, and other sauces. (See also "Food and Nutrition Science" at the bottom of this page.) *(Key skill: writing)*

4. **Finding Recipes:** Have students find recipes for marinades to use for meat, poultry, and fish. *(Key skill: reading)*

Food and Nutrition Science

Salt Content of Seasoning Blends: Ask students to include seasoning blends in their survey for Student Experience #3. Have students read the ingredients in the seasoning blends. How many of the seasoning blends contain salt? How many list salt as the first ingredient? What are the implications of this for people who are on low-salt diets?

Teaching . . .

• **Basic Herbs, Spices, and Blends (Chart)**

(text pages 644-645)

Comprehension Check

1. Ask students to identify herbs, spices, and blends that are specifically recommended for use with poultry. *(basil, dillweed, marjoram, oregano, rosemary, thyme, dry mustard, curry powder, poultry seasoning)*

2. Ask students to identify "all-purpose" herbs, spices, and blends—those that can be used with a variety of foods. Why might it be a good idea to buy these before you buy those that have narrower uses? *(Basil, bay leaves, mint, oregano, rosemary, cumin, dry mustard, ground ginger, nutmeg; because you will probably need them more frequently.)*

Student Experiences

1. **Class Discussion:** Discuss the use of the herbs, spices, and blends in the chart on pages 644-645. Ask students which herbs and spices they have used together in one dish. Which ones are often used together? Why? *(Key skill: critical thinking)*

2. **Research:** Have students research the history and use of herbs and spices not mentioned in the chart on pages 644-645, such as allspice, cayenne, savory, mace, parsley, and barbecue blend. *(Key skill: research)*

Basic Herbs, Spices, and Blends	
Herbs	**Uses**
Basil Mild, spicy-licorice flavor with a hint of mint.	Dishes containing tomatoes; meat and poultry; carrots; peas; rice.
Bay leaves Strong, aromatic, pungent flavor.	Braised meats, stews, soups, bean dishes. Use leaf whole. Remove before serving.
Dillweed Sharp flavor, similar to caraway seeds.	Cruciferous vegetables; carrots; green beans; cucumbers; fish; poultry; breads.
Marjoram Delicate, sweet, spicy flavor with hint of mint.	Soups; stews; poultry; stuffings; salads; tomato sauces.
Mint Strong, refreshing, aromatic flavor.	Yogurt dishes; tomato dishes; rice; bulgur; vegetables; lentils; fruits; tea.
Oregano Strong, clove-like flavor.	Italian and Mexican dishes; bean dishes; pork; poultry; salads; green beans.
Rosemary Strong, piney flavor.	Poultry; lamb; pork; potatoes; breads; bean dishes; pasta sauces; soups.
Sage Strong, slightly bitter flavor.	Poultry; pork; stuffings; potatoes; white beans; chowders.
Thyme Strong, clove-like flavor.	Poultry and stuffings; lamb; dry beans; stews; soups.
Spices	**Uses**
Cinnamon Sweet flavor.	Meat dishes; desserts; legumes; sweet potatoes; squash.
Cloves Strong, hot, pungent flavor.	Meat dishes; grains; legumes; fruit desserts.
Cumin Strong, musty flavor.	Mexican and Mideastern foods; legumes; tomato sauces and soups; rice.
Dry mustard Hot, sharp, spicy flavor.	Meat; poultry; soups; stews; egg dishes; salad dressings.
Ground ginger Hot, pungent, spicy flavor.	Stir-fries; stews; soups; squash; sweet potatoes; grains; legumes; desserts.

Thinking Skills

Reasoning: Ask students to explain why bay leaves should always be removed from food before serving. *(Bay leaves do not soften when cooked. Therefore, pieces of bay leaf can become lodged in a person's throat, causing the person to choke.)*

Basic Herbs, Spices, and Blends (continued)

Nutmeg Mild, spicy flavor; best if purchased whole and grated fresh.	Cooked spinach, zucchini, and carrots; sweet potatoes; soups; stews; ground meat; bulgur; fruits; desserts.
Blends	**Uses**
Chili powder Spicy hot, pungent flavor.	Tex-Mex cooking; chili; stews; soups; barbecue sauces; dishes made with corn.
Curry Powder Pungent, spicy flavor.	East Indian cooking; poultry; meats; fish; yogurt dishes; legumes.
Italian seasoning Blend of basil, marjoram, oregano, rosemary, sage, savory, and thyme.	Italian recipes.
Poultry seasoning Blend of lovage, marjoram, and sage.	Any recipes made with poultry, including stuffing.

Pour the marinade ingredients into a large container, such as a reusable glass jar, and shake well. Place the food into a glass or plastic covered container, pour the marinade over the food, and refrigerate. Occasionally turn and stir the food so it marinates evenly. Do not marinate food in metal pans—the acid may react with the metal and give an unpleasant flavor.

Marinating time depends on the food. Tender foods, such as fish, can marinate for an hour or less. Meat and poultry can marinate up to six or eight hours. Be careful not to over-marinate foods because they will get mushy. If you are marinating foods just for flavor, 30 minutes is long enough.

Before cooking, drain the food well. Discard marinade used for meat, poultry, and fish as it may contain harmful bacteria. If you want to baste with the marinade, make an extra batch for basting.

Using Your Creativity

What's the secret to making food look appealing? Using your creativity and your "meal appeal" skills—that's the secret! For many people, preparing food is more than just cooking. It's a form of self-expression. A creative cook may plan the appearance of a plate of food much like Michaelangelo or Picasso planned a painting. Think about the colors and shapes of food or how the flavors blend together. What would your edible "work of art" look like?

You might want to look in a variety of cookbooks for different ways to present food. Here are a few possibillities:

❖ Swirl whipped potatoes into a fluffy mound by using a pastry bag with a decorative tip similar to those used in cake decorating.
❖ Cut foods into **julienne** strips. Julienne strips are long, thin strips of food.
❖ Use a small scoop to mold fruits such as melons into balls.

Section 24.1: Creative Techniques   **645**

Teaching . . .

• **Using Your Creativity**

(text pages 645-646)

Comprehension Check

1. Ask students to list ways to present food attractively. *(Swirl whipped potatoes into a fluffy mound by using a pastry bag with a decorative tip similar to those used in cake decorating; cut foods into julienne strips; use a small scoop to mold fruits such as melons into balls.)*

2. Ask students to explain what is meant by cooking "en papillote." *(Baking in parchment paper so that the flavors of the foods blend; the sealed package retains the flavor and aroma.)*

Student Experiences

1. **Class Discussion:** Compare creative cooking with other forms of creativity, such as art or music. Discuss ways creative cooking could be an enjoyable leisure activity. *(Key skill: critical thinking)*

2. **Poster Project:** Have students clip illustrations from magazines that show examples of creative cooking and create a poster display. *(Key skill: creativity)*

More About Cooking en Papillote

Here is a simple recipe for one serving of sweet potatoes en papillote:
• Preheat oven to 425°F (220°C).
• Pare a sweet potato and cut in bite-size chunks.
• Mound in the center of a square of parchment paper.

• Chop one medium apple and spread over sweet potatoes.
• Dot with 1 tsp. (5 mL) butter.
• Sprinkle with 1/4 tsp. cinnamon and 1/4 tsp. fresh grated nutmeg.
• Close the package and place on baking sheet.
• Bake at 425°F (220°C) for 25 minutes. Serve hot.

Teaching . . .

• **Garnishes**

(text pages 646-648)

Comprehension Check

1. Ask students to define "garnish." What is the purpose of garnishes? *(Garnishes are small, colorful, edible bits of food; they are used to enhance the appearance and texture of food.)*

2. Ask students to suggest garnishes for use with sandwiches. *(Crisp, fresh vegetables, such as scored cucumber slices, carrot curls, celery fans, radish roses, and fruit slices or wedges.)*

3. Ask students to identify soups with which they might use each of the garnishes listed on page 646 for use with soups. *(Answers will vary. Yogurt, cucumber slices, and lemon slices might be better served on cold soups; the remaining garnishes might be better served on hot soups.)*

✔ **SAFETY CHECK**

Do not use brown paper bags for cooking. They are not made to withstand the high cooking temperatures and may burn. Chemicals in the paper also may be transferred to the food.

Cooking in parchment paper, or cooking **en papillote** (ehn pah-pee-YOHT), is another method used by creative cooks. Fish and tender cuts of meat and poultry are often cooked by this method. One serving is placed in the center of a square of parchment paper along with other ingredients, such as vegetables, butter, or a sauce. The paper is folded around the food to form a package. The ends are tightly closed and folded under so food does not leak out. As the food cooks, flavors blend. The sealed package retains the flavor and aroma.

The packages are placed on baking sheets and baked in the oven. To serve, each package is placed on a dinner plate. An X is cut into the top of the paper, which is peeled back. As you read on about garnishes, think about ways you might dress up foods served en papillote.

Even simple foods can be served with a creative flair.

Garnishes

Garnishes are small, colorful, bits of food that are used to enhance the appearance and texture of any dish. They can be used on appetizers, salads, main dishes, vegetables, desserts, and beverages. Presenting foods that are attractive, as well as tasty, helps make mealtime an enjoyable experience.

Keep size in mind when garnishing foods. If a garnish is too large, it may overpower the food. Choose garnish colors and flavors that complement the food it is served with. Here are some ideas for simple garnishes:

❖ **Soups.** Float a spoonful of yogurt, cucumber slices, lemon slice, croutons, or chopped parsley or chives on soups.

❖ **Salads.** Add green pepper rings, cherry tomatoes, pimiento strips, red onion rings, tomato wedges, pickle fans, radish roses, chopped nuts, or seeds to salads.

Food and Nutrition Science

Keeping Garnishes Crisp: The crispness of a fresh fruit or vegetable depends on the amount of water in the cells of the food. Water, called free water because it is not chemically bound to other molecules in the food, is lost through evaporation and can be restored by soaking the food in water. Placing the garnishes described on pages 646-647 in ice water helps swell the cells with water, making the garnishes crisp.

Carrot curls

Celery fan

1. **Class Discussion:** Have students develop a list of possible garnishes to make food more attractive. *(Key skill: writing)*

2. **Demonstration:** Demonstrate the use of a decorating tube. Have students identify various foods with which the decorating tube could be used. *(Key skill: critical thinking)*

3. **Student Practice:** Have students use mashed potatoes and large dark-colored paper plates to practice using the various tips of the decorating tube. *(Key skill: kitchen management skills)*

Radish rose

Lemon basket

Citrus cartwheels

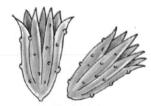
Pickle fan

Citrus twist

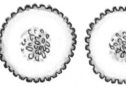
Scored cucumber

Garnishes add only a little extra time to food preparation, but a lot of appeal to the foods you serve. How might you use these garnishes?

Thinking Skills

Problem Solving: Ask students to imagine that they are trying to make the carrot curls shown on page 647. However, the carrot keeps breaking when they try to cut or roll up the paper-thin strips. Why is this happening? How could it be remedied? *(There is too much water in the carrot. It should be allowed to sit until some of the cellular free water evaporates and the carrot becomes more limp.)*

Completing the Section

Review

- Ask students to summarize the main ideas in this section.
- Have students complete the Section Review. (Answers appear below.)

Evaluation

- Ask students to prepare garnishes to accompany specific foods that you mention.
- Have students take the quiz for Section 24.1. (Refer to the *Section Quizzes* booklet or use the *Testmaker Software*.)

Reteaching

- Show students pictures of meat loaf, au gratin potatoes, baked fish, and applesauce. What garnishes could they use with these foods? What herbs and spices might they use?
- Refer to the *Reteaching Activities* booklet for the Section 24.1 activity worksheet.

Enrichment

- Have students work in groups to prepare new kinds of pizza using various herbs, spices, and seasoning blends.

Closure

- Lead a discussion about the importance of presentation when you prepare foods, especially for special occasions.

- ❖ **Meat, poultry, and fish dishes.** Use citrus fruit slices, twists, or wedges, a small bunch of grapes, cranberry sauce, spiced crabapples, currant or mint jelly in lemon baskets, sprigs of parsley or fresh herbs, pineapple slices, or olives.
- ❖ **Sandwiches.** Use crisp, fresh vegetables, such as scored cucumber slices, carrot curls, celery fans, radish roses, and fruit slices or wedges.
- ❖ **Beverages.** Try citrus twists on a skewer, lemon or lime slices slipped on the edge of a glass, marshmallows or peppermint sticks in cocoa, or fruit slices and whole fruits frozen in an ice ring for punch.

Garlic and red peppers are among the vegetables that can add flavor to food mixtures such as stews and marinades. What others can you name?

Section 24.1 Review

RECALL THE FACTS

1. When should herbs be added to hot foods and to cold foods?
2. Briefly explain how to marinate food.
3. Explain how foods are arranged and cooked en papillote.
4. Name one way to garnish each of the following dishes: tomato soup, tossed salad, roasted whole chicken, tuna sandwich, and iced tea.

DISCUSS YOUR IDEAS

5. How can seasoning with herbs and spices replace other methods of flavoring food that are higher in fat and sodium?

APPLY YOUR LEARNING

6. Make a list of herbs and spices your family uses regularly. Create a recipe using some of these herbs and spices. Explain how you would use them and describe the flavor they would give to the foods.

■ Answers to Section Review ■

1. Hot foods: at least 10 but no more than 45 minutes before the food is done; cold foods: 30 minutes to several hours before serving.
2. Combine the marinade ingredients and shake well. Place the food in a glass or plastic covered container, pour the marinade over it, and refrigerate. Occasionally turn and stir the food to marinate evenly.
3. One serving is placed in the center of a square of parchment paper along with other ingredients; the paper is folded around the food to form a package; package is placed on baking sheet and baked.
4. Answers will vary.
5. Answers will vary. The herbs and spices add flavor so salt and fat are not necessary.
6. Answers will vary.

Beverages

OBJECTIVES

After studying this section, you should be able to:

• Identify different types of beverages.

• Describe correct procedures for preparing and serving beverages.

• Explain how to store beverages.

LOOK FOR THESE TERMS

infuser

steep

Beverages are refreshing any time of day. No meal is complete without one. Offering guests a beverage is a sign of hospitality. In this section, you will learn about several types of beverages including coffee, tea, and punch.

Coffee

Coffee is brewed from ground coffee beans, which are the seeds from trees grown in South and Central America, Asia, and Africa. Ground coffee can be made from just one variety of coffee beans or a blend of several. Gourmet coffee is more expensive because it is made from costlier beans.

Coffee contains caffeine, a mild stimulant to the nervous system. Most forms of coffee are also available in a decaffeinated (dee-KAFF-in-ay-ted) version.

Instant coffee is brewed coffee that has been dried and ground. It comes either as a powder or freeze-dried crystals, regular or decaffeinated. All you do is add hot water.

Besides regular and gourmet coffee, flavored coffees are also available. Flavors include mocha, vanilla, and assorted spices.

Coffee trees produce berries that turn red when they ripen. Inside each berry are two coffee beans, which are the seeds of the plant.

Section 24.2: Beverages **649**

Teacher's Classroom Resources—Section 24.2

Refer to these resources in the TCR package:

Reproducible Lesson Plans

Student Workbook

Extending the Text

Reteaching Activities

Section Quizzes

Testmaker Software

Foods Lab Resources

Color Transparencies

Section 24.2
Beverages

Introducing the Section

Motivators

• Show a videotaped recording of a televised coffee, tea, or hot cocoa advertisement. If the ad is appealing to students, ask them why. Ask them what kind of feelings the people in the ad were portraying. Have them note the social importance of beverages in society.

• Discuss ways in which beverages are related to human needs and desires. Point out that beverages provide water and sometimes other nutrients, but they can also play a part in meeting emotional and social needs.

Objectives

• Have students read the section objectives. Discuss the purpose of studying the section.

Vocabulary

• Pronounce the terms listed under "Look for These Terms." Have students find the terms and their definitions in the section.

Guided Reading

• Have students look at the headings within Section 24.2 to preview the concepts that will be discussed.

• Have students read the section and complete the appropriate part of the Chapter 24 Study Guide in the *Student Workbook*.

Teaching . . .

- **Coffee**
- **Tea**

(text pages 649-652)

Comprehension Check

1. Ask students to explain the difference between regular coffee and decaffeinated coffee. *(Regular coffee contains caffeine, a mild stimulant to the nervous system; decaffeinated coffee contains no caffeine.)*

2. Ask students to explain why various coffee grinds are available. *(Different brewing methods require different grinds; drip coffee needs a fine grind, percolator coffee needs a coarser grind; all-purpose grinds are also available.)*

3. Ask students to explain how to determine the correct amount of coffee and water to use in an automatic drip coffeemaker. *(Follow the directions that come with the coffeemaker and those on the coffee container; then change the amounts to suit your taste preference.)*

4. Ask students to name and describe the three basic types of tea. *(Black tea is made from leaves that have been oxidized to give them a dark, rich color and hearty flavor; green tea is processed without being oxidized and has a very mild flavor; Oolong tea is partly oxidized.)*

The type of coffee to buy depends on the way you plan to brew it. Popular coffeemakers include the electric percolator (left), the automatic drip coffeemaker (center), and the nonautomatic drip model.

Buying Coffee

Ground coffee comes in different grinds to suit the brewing method. For example, drip coffee brews quickly, so a fine grind is needed. Percolator coffee takes longer, so it requires a coarser grind. Some coffee manufacturers offer an all-purpose grind that can be used for several brewing methods. Buy the grind recommended for your coffeemaker.

Most ground coffee is sold in vacuum-packed containers. Gourmet shops and many supermarkets also sell coffee beans that can be ground to order. Specialty coffees are sold in bags that are not vacuum-packed.

Storing Coffee

Unopened containers of vacuum-packed coffee can be stored at room temperature for about a year. Once opened, refrigerate fresh coffee, whether ground or whole beans, in an airtight container. It will generally keep in the refrigerator up to two weeks. For longer storage, freeze. Instant coffee can be kept at room temperature.

Making Coffee

The most popular appliance for making coffee is the automatic drip coffeemaker. Most automatic drip coffeemakers have four parts—a water reservoir, a basket that holds a filter and coffee, a carafe that catches the coffee as it brews, and a hotplate which keeps the carafe and coffee warm. Some automatic drip coffeemakers are equipped with timers which can start the brewing cycle at a preset time.

Here are a few popular coffee beverages:

- ❖ *Espresso* (ehs-SPRESS-oh) is dark, strong coffee made by steaming in a pressure coffeemaker using a specially blended Italian coffee. The surface of the coffee has a thin layer of light-colored froth.
- ❖ *Café au lait* (kaff-FAY oh-LAY) is a French beverage made with equal parts of hot milk and regular coffee.
- ❖ *Cappuccino* (kap-oo-CHEE-noh) is the Italian version of café au lait. It is made with espresso coffee and frothy steamed milk or cream. The foamy top is often dusted with cocoa or cinnamon.

An espresso machine uses pressure and steam to produce the dark, frothy beverage.

650 Chapter 24: Special Ways with Food

Food and Nutrition Science

Methods of Decaffeination: The caffeine in coffee beans is removed by one of two basic methods before the beans are roasted. In one method, the beans soak in hot water containing a solvent such as methylene chloride, which dissolves the caffeine. The solvent is removed from the water, the beans soak in the water to restore their flavor, and then they are rinsed. This method is sometimes advertised as "water processed." "Natural decaffeination" means that ethyl acetate is used as the solvent.

In the Swiss Water Process method, the beans soak in plain water with no solvent. Charcoal filters are used to remove the caffeine from the water.

Automatic drip coffeemakers are easy to use. Just put ground coffee into a filter inside the basket, pour cold water into the reservoir, and turn on the controls. The coffeemaker quickly heats the water which drips through the coffee grounds into the carafe.

How much coffee and water should you use? The final decision depends on your taste preferences. Begin by following the directions that come with the coffeemaker as well as those on the coffee container. If desired, change the amounts to get the strength of coffee you want. Coffeemakers usually have convenient markings on the carafe or sides of the reservoir so you can measure the water easily.

Clean the coffee carafe and basket in hot sudsy water after every use. Coffee contains oils that cling to the inside of the carafe and basket. They can give the next carafe of coffee an unpleasant flavor.

Serving Coffee

Serve coffee piping hot, right after it is made. If coffee is held at a high temperature for too long or reheated, it loses its flavor and aroma.

Coffee can also be served iced. Make double strength coffee and pour it over ice cubes.

Tea

Tea is a beverage made from the leaves of a shrub grown in tropical mountainous areas. Three basic types of tea are produced and used worldwide. *Black tea* is made from leaves that have been oxidized or fermented, which turns them black. Black tea has a dark, rich color and deep hearty flavor. *Green tea* is processed without being oxidized, so the leaves retain their green color. It has a delicate, light green color and a very mild flavor. *Oolong tea* is partly oxidized, so the leaves are partly brown and partly green. Its flavor and color are between black and green teas. Tea is sold loose or in teabags.

Most of the world's tea is grown in Asia. This tea estate is in Japan.

Tea contains caffeine, although not as much as coffee. It is also available decaffeinated. The same processes are used to decaffeinate tea as coffee.

In addition to plain tea, you can also buy flavored and instant teas. Flavored tea includes fruit, herb, and spice flavors. Instant tea is brewed tea which has been dried and ground to a powder. It is available plain, flavored, and presweetened.

Herb Teas

Herb teas are made from herbs and other plants. They do not contain regular tea and are caffeine-free.

Buying Tea

Because there are so many different varieties, read labels carefully. Be certain you are buying the type and form of tea you want.

Buy herb teas from reliable sources. Most supermarkets carry the major brands. Avoid teas that make health claims, such as weight-loss teas.

Section 24.2: Beverages   651

Student Experiences

1. **Store Survey:** Have students list the various brands, grinds, and forms of coffee and coffee products in the grocery stores. Have them compare costs. *(Key skill: writing)*

2. **Research:** Have students research the cultivation, picking, and processing of coffee beans. *(Key skills: reading, research)*

3. **Consumer Survey:** Have students conduct a survey of teachers or parents regarding their use of coffee (coffee, decaffeinated coffee, or no coffee). Have students compile their data and determine the percentage of people who drink each. Discuss the results. *(Key skill: math)*

4. **Research:** Have students research the cultivation and processing of tea and herb teas. *(Key skill: reading, research)*

WORLD of **variety**

Have students list other coffee specialties they have heard of or tried. With what countries are the coffees primarily associated?

Lab Experiences

- Have students make several types of coffee using different methods. Include one or more specialty coffees.

- Have students demonstrate how to brew loose and bagged tea correctly and incorrectly. Have students taste the teas and evaluate their differences.

Food and Nutrition Science

Effect of Temperature on Solute: Demonstrate to students what happens when a cube of sugar is added to hot tea and to iced tea. Which cube dissolves faster? (Sugar dissolves faster in hot tea.) Point out that in this solution, the tea is the *solvent* and the sugar is the *solute*. Explain that a solution can hold a greater amount of solute at a higher temperature. Have students test this phenomenon using tea.

Comprehension Check

1. Ask students to describe how to prepare and serve a cold punch. *(Combine all liquids except carbonated beverages and chill; chill carbonated liquids separately and add just before serving; ladle the punch from punch bowl into small glasses or cups.)*

2. Ask students to name two types of garnish commonly used in punches. *(fresh fruit, ice mold or decorative ice cubes)*

3. Ask students to list common forms of specialty waters. *(mineral water, spring water, seltzer water, and club soda)*

Student Experiences

1. **Garnishing Beverages:** Have students find ideas for garnishing and serving hot and cold beverages. *(Key skill: reading)*

2. **Taste Test:** Have students taste several varieties of bottled water. Discuss reasons bottled water has increased in popularity in recent years. What are the nutritional advantages and disadvantages of bottled waters? *(Key skill: evaluation)*

Lab Experience

Have students prepare a variety of hot and cold punches for the class to sample. Have students make a variety of ice rings and garnishes from fruits to garnish their punches. Ask the class to rate the punches on a scale of 1 to 5 for taste, attractiveness, nutrition, and economy.

The many varieties of tea and herb teas can be purchased loose or in bags. What tea-making utensils are shown here?

Storing Tea

Store tea in an airtight container at room temperature. Keep different flavored teabags in separate containers so the flavors don't intermix. Properly stored, tea will keep up to two years.

Brewing and Serving Tea

Tea can be brewed in a teapot or right in the cup. An automatic hot tea maker is also available. It works in much the same way as an automatic coffeemaker. It preheats the tea pot, brews the tea, and keeps it at serving temperature.

To brew tea yourself, begin by heating fresh, cold water in a teakettle. Using water that has been standing or is reheated gives tea a flat taste. Bring the water to a rolling boil.

Preheat the teapot or cup by rinsing it with hot water. Then put in the tea or tea bags. As a rule, use one teaspoon (5 mL) of tea, or one tea bag, for each serving. To make loose tea easier to use, put it in an **infuser**—a small container with tiny holes that let water in but don't allow the tea leaves to come out. Like tea bags, the infuser is easy to remove at the end of the brewing time.

Pour boiling water over the tea. The tea **steeps,** or brews in water just below the boiling point. Follow package directions for brewing time and set a timer. Do not judge the strength of tea by its color since different varieties brew to different colors.

Stir the tea before pouring or drinking to make sure it's uniformly strong. If the brewed tea is too strong, add a little hot water. Tea may be served with milk or lemon and sweetener.

To make iced tea, brew as for hot tea but use fifty percent more tea. That allows for melting ice when the hot tea is poured into ice-filled glasses. For six servings, use nine teabags or nine teaspoons (45 mL) of tea. Steep. Remove tea and pour into ice-filled glasses.

You can also use an automatic iced tea maker to prepare iced tea or iced coffee. Instant tea is another option. Just follow the directions on the label.

More About Ice Molds

To make an ice mold, select the size and shape of mold you want. Choose decorative ingredients to freeze in the mold, such as citrus slices, cherries, strawberries, grapes, and fresh herbs such as mint.

Some fruit floats and some sinks in liquid. To distribute the fruit evenly in the mold, pour about an inch of cold water into the mold and freeze until it is like slush. Arrange fruit and herbs in the slush, working quickly. Then very carefully add very cold water and freeze. If you want to add more fruit, freeze to a slush and repeat the procedure. Otherwise, freeze solid. Do not make a mold more than 3 inches (7.5 cm) high or it may be top heavy and tip over.

Punch

A punch is generally a mixture of fruit juices and either carbonated beverages, such as ginger ale or seltzer, or tea. It is usually served in a punch bowl. Sherbet, ice cream, or fruit may be added. To serve the punch, ladle it from the bowl into small glasses or cups.

If the punch is to be served cold, combine all liquids except the carbonated beverages ahead of time and chill well. Chill the carbonated beverages separately and add them just before serving.

Fruit is often floated in the bowl as a garnish, the kind depending on the fruit flavors in the punch. Another popular garnish is an ice ring. Besides being decorative, it helps keep the punch cold. The ice ring is usually made with punch or water. Fruit is placed in the ring mold in a decorative design. You can also freeze fruit in ice cubes.

Other Beverages

As you learned in Section 2.4, water is an essential nutrient. Beverages that can supply your body's need for water include plain water, milk, and fruit juices.

Fruit and vegetable juices are healthful choices because they supply vitamins and minerals as well as water. When shopping, remember that only products labeled "juice" are made of 100 percent juice. Others may contain large amounts of added sugar.

Many carbonated soft drinks are also high in sugar. In "diet" soft drinks, the sugar is replaced with artificial sweeteners and other additives. These beverages do not supply the natural vitamins and minerals of fruit juices.

Bottled specialty waters are popular. There are many different kinds, such as mineral water, spring water, seltzer water, and club soda. They vary in mineral content and flavor. Some are carbonated. Check the list of ingredients on the label.

Milk is not only a nutritious beverage in itself, but is the basis for many other beverages, such as cocoa. For information about milk and cocoa, see Section 18.2.

When making punch, mix and chill fruit juices ahead of time to blend flavors. Why should you wait until just before serving to add carbonated beverages?

■ Section 24.2 Review ■

RECALL THE FACTS

1. What is decaffeinated coffee?
2. How should coffee be stored?
3. What is the difference between tea and herb tea?
4. What is punch? How is it served?

DISCUSS YOUR IDEAS

5. What are the nutritional drawbacks of coffee, tea, and punch? How do these compare with other beverage choices?

APPLY YOUR LEARNING

6. Look through cookbooks and magazines to find a punch recipe. How might you change the ingredients in this recipe to make it more healthful?

Section 24.2: Beverages   **653**

Completing the Section

Review

- Ask students to summarize the main ideas in this section.
- Have students complete the Section Review. (Answers appear below.)

Evaluation

- Have students prepare charts or posters showing the correct way to prepare coffee or tea by various methods.
- Have students take the quiz for Section 24.2. (Refer to the *Section Quizzes* booklet or use the *Testmaker Software*.)

Reteaching

- Provide various brands of tea and have students categorize them according to type of tea, loose or bagged, instant, caffeine or no caffeine.
- Refer to the *Reteaching Activities* booklet for the Section 24.2 activity worksheet.

Enrichment

- Have students research the ingredients of sparkling fruit juices and fruit-juice drinks. What is the nutritional value of these beverages?

Closure

- Lead a discussion about the use of coffee and tea in our society. Emphasize the various alternatives that do not contain caffeine.

■ Answers to Section Review ■

1. Coffee from which the caffeine has been removed.
2. Store unopened vacuum-packed coffee at room temperature; once opened, refrigerate in an airtight container, or freeze. Keep instant coffee at room temperature.
3. Tea is made from tea leaves and contains caffeine (unless decaffeinated); herb tea contains no tea leaves or caffeine.
4. A mixture of fruit juices and carbonated beverages or tea; usually served in a punch bowl.
5. Coffee and tea contain caffeine, a mild stimulant; punch may contain caffeine. The nutritional value of most beverages, except milk and fruit or vegetable juices, is very low.
6. Answers will vary.

24.2 Recipe

Fruit Punch

Key Skill: Preparing a beverage

Using the Recipe

- Have students read the recipe and discuss each step. Point out the warning in the recipe that advises students not to put frozen juice concentrate directly into a punch bowl—the bowl may crack. Review safety and sanitation procedures that apply to this recipe.

- Have each lab team fill out a work plan. (See the *Foods Lab Resources* booklet.)

- Have students check off the ingredients and equipment listed on the recipe worksheet and prepare the recipe.

- Have students complete the evaluation and questions on the recipe worksheet.

See Also . . .

The *Foods Lab Resources* booklet for the "Fruit Punch" recipe worksheet and other recipe alternatives.

Thinking About the Recipe

Read the recipe for "Fruit Punch" and answer the following questions.

1. How could you serve punch if you didn't have a punch bowl?
2. What liquids and fruits could you use to make an ice ring for the punch?

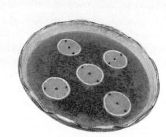

Fruit Punch

Customary	Ingredients	Metric
6 oz.	Frozen lemonade concentrate, thawed	177 mL
6 oz.	Frozen orange juice concentrate, thawed	177 mL
32 oz.	Tropical fruit punch, canned, chilled	1 L
2 qt.	Ginger ale or lemon-lime soda	2 L

Yield: 32 servings (approximate)

Directions

1. Combine thawed juice concentrates and tropical fruit punch in a half-gallon (2L) pitcher. (Note: Do not put frozen juice concentrate directly into punch bowl—you may crack the bowl.)
2. Pour juice mixture into punch bowl.
3. Add ginger ale or lemon-lime soda and stir the mixture gently.
4. Garnish with citrus fruit slices or an ice ring.
5. Serve chilled.

Nutrition Information

Per serving (approximate): 54 calories, 0 g protein, 14 g carbohydrate, 0 g fat, 0 mg cholesterol, 11 mg sodium

Answers to Thinking About the Recipe

1. You could use a large mixing bowl or serve the punch from pitchers. Other answers are possible.

2. Water, punch, or fruit juice; fruits named will vary.

Entertaining

OBJECTIVES

After studying this section, you should be able to:

- Identify ways to plan for entertaining.
- Develop menus and organize food preparation and cleanup for entertaining.
- Describe different methods of serving food depending on the occasion.

LOOK FOR THESE TERMS

modified English service
service plate
reception

Entertaining is a way of expressing hospitality to people, making them feel welcome and special. Although food is generally served, entertaining involves much more than this.

Entertaining does not have to be elaborate. You can have a successful party with a simple soup-and-salad meal if the atmosphere is right. With planning and organization, entertaining can be just as much fun for the person giving the party as it is for the guests.

Planning for Entertaining

When you think about entertaining, what do you think of? Perhaps you think of a formal dinner party, a meal with a few close friends, a brunch, or even a potluck supper. Whatever the event or occasion, careful planning goes a long way.

Holidays and other special occasions are a perfect time for entertaining. This group of family and friends has gathered to celebrate Tet, the Vietnamese New Year.

Introducing the Section

Motivators

- Ask students to make a list of occasions for entertaining guests. Have students categorize these occasions as formal or informal. What factors help determine whether an occasion will be formal or informal?
- Have students describe orally or in writing the best party they ever attended and explain what made it enjoyable.

Objectives

- Have students read the section objectives. Discuss the purpose of studying the section.

Vocabulary

- Pronounce the terms listed under "Look for These Terms." Have students find the terms and their definitions in the section.

Guided Reading

- Have students look at the headings within Section 24.3 to preview the concepts that will be discussed.
- Have students read the section and complete the appropriate part of the Chapter 24 Study Guide in the *Student Workbook*.

Teacher's Classroom Resources—Section 24.3

Refer to these resources in the TCR package:

Reproducible Lesson Plans
Student Workbook
Extending the Text

Reteaching Activities
Section Quizzes
Testmaker Software
Color Transparencies

- **Planning for Entertaining**

(text pages 655-658)

Comprehension Check

1. Ask students to explain what a theme is and how it relates to entertaining. *(A theme is a specific idea on which the occasion is based; it helps make parties or entertaining more fun.)*

2. Ask students what they should consider when making up a guest list. *(Try to put together a combination of people who are likely to get along and be interesting to one another; a good blend of listeners and talkers.)*

3. Ask students to list the items that should be included on a formal invitation. *(The date, location, and time of the event; the occasion, if there is one; your name as host or hostess; R.S.V.P. and your telephone number.)*

4. Discuss guidelines for selecting foods for a party menu. *(See list on page 657.)*

TIPS for Success

Have students brainstorm to think of other decorations that are inexpensive, yet attractive for use at formal parties and informal parties. Ask students if they would consider the same types of decorations for both formal and informal occasions. Why?

Parties are more memorable when both the food and decorations relate to a theme. Besides a Mexican fiesta, what are some other possible themes? What foods and decorations would you choose to go with each?

Informal and Formal Events

Entertaining can be as simple or elaborate as you like. When you begin making your plans, think about the type of occasion. Is it an informal event such as a simple evening party, a family-style dinner with friends, or perhaps a buffet (buh-FAY) meal for a larger number of guests? You may be planning a formal sit-down dinner for a special event such as a birthday or graduation.

Whether the occasion is to be formal or informal affects the menu and the way you will serve food. Think about your skills in entertaining. If this is the first party you are giving, it's probably best to start with a simple, informal event.

Themes and Decorations

After you've decided whether you are having an informal or formal event, decide on a theme for the occasion. Most parties or get-togethers are more fun if they have a theme. A theme is a specific idea on which the occasion is based. Holidays, birthdays, and gradu-

ations provide a ready-made theme. Be creative! You might want to choose an interest you and your guests share such as sports or old movies, or an ethnic theme such as a Mexican fiesta. After you have chosen your theme, plan the menu, activities, and decorations to go with it.

A pleasant atmosphere makes a party or meal more enjoyable for everyone. Whether you are serving snacks to your guests from a card table or eating a meal in the dining room, providing attractive decorations makes everyone feel comfortable.

TIPS for Success

Simple Decorations

Here are a few decorating ideas:
- ❖ A potted plant on a placemat.
- ❖ An arrangement of fresh or silk flowers.
- ❖ A grouping of seashells on a wicker mat.
- ❖ A basket of fresh fruit or colorful gourds.
- ❖ A fresh flower floating in water in a glass bowl beside some candle-holders.

656   Chapter 24: Special Ways with Food

More About Entertaining

People sometimes hesitate to entertain for many reasons. Some think they do not have the right kind of tableware or their cooking is too plain. People often don't have much time to prepare fancy foods for entertaining. Budgets limit the kind of food that can be served or the number of people who can be invited. Most of these objections can be overcome with a little ingenuity. Have students brainstorm to think of ways to get around the objections stated above.

Invitations

As you decide on a list of guests, try to put together a combination of people who are likely to get along and be interesting to one another. Look for a good blend of listeners and talkers. Avoid inviting people that you know don't get along.

For informal events, you will most likely ask your guests in person or by telephone about one week before the event. (Of course, impromptu gatherings are fun, too! Just be sure to check with your parents first.)

Formal occasions or larger parties require a written invitation. This will help eliminate any mixups about the time or date. Send your invitations ten days to two weeks before the event is to occur. On your invitation, be sure to include the following information:

❖ The date, location, and time of the event.
❖ The occasion, if there is one.
❖ Your name as host or hostess.
❖ R.S.V.P. and your telephone number. This informs your guests that you would like them to "Reply, please." You might also include a date by which they are to reply so that you can buy the appropriate amount of food.

If, as an invited guest, you are asked to R.S.V.P., it is your responsibility to follow through with this request. If you can't reach a person by telephone, send a brief note in the mail.

Menus for Entertaining

Planning food for parties and other special occasions follows the same guidelines as planning meals. Choose a variety of nutritious, attractive foods. If you are planning foods for a special theme, try to choose some foods that are liked by many people. Here are a few guidelines for selecting foods for your menu:

❖ Find out about special food needs or preferences that your guests might have.

❖ Keep food choices simple. Choose foods that can be prepared ahead of time with a minimum of last-minute preparation. For example, you might want to prepare lasagne as the main course and do all the preparation except baking it the day before. Add a tossed salad, bread, beverage, and perhaps some fruit for dessert.

❖ You might want to select a simple appetizer, such as a dip and crackers or fruit, that your guests can nibble on while you make a few last-minute preparations.

Making a Schedule

After you have planned your meal or refreshments, the next step is to identify the tasks to be accomplished before the event. You might start with a list organized by

Help us celebrate
Westview High Marching Band's
first place trophy!

Please come to a Pizza Party
Saturday, November 9 at 7 p.m.
417 Ridgeway Road

Hosted by Sheila Wilson and Carlos Morales
R.S.V.P. to Sheila (555-9843)
by Thursday, November 7

Does this invitation include all the information a guest would need?

Student Experiences

1. **Identifying Party Themes:** Have students take turns identifying possible party themes. Discuss how a theme helps you plan a party. *(Key skill: brainstorming)*

2. **Decorations:** Have students write a list of simple, inexpensive ideas for party decorations. *(Key skill: writing)*

3. **Poster Project:** Have students collect and display pictures that illustrate party themes. *(Key skill: creativity)*

4. **Display:** Create a display of invitations appropriate for different types of occasions. Have students categorize the invitations as formal or informal. *(Key skill: classification)*

Using the Illustration

Ask students whether the invitation shown on page 657 includes all the information mentioned in the text. *(yes)* What other optional information might an invitation include? *(suggested dress, whether guests are to bring anything)*

More About Parties

If you have received an invitation to a party, answer it immediately. When you reply, repeat the date and time, in case the invitation had an error. Arrive on time. Don't arrive too early, unless you've been asked to help.

As a guest, offer to help wherever you can. Remove empty soft drink bottles as they accumulate. If food falls on the floor, pick it up. Wipe up spills, whether on the floor or furniture, immediately.

Comprehension Check

1. Ask students to describe the use of modified English service. *(Modified English service is a technique for serving small groups in a formal atmosphere; dinner plates and the food for the main course are brought to the table in serving dishes and placed in front of the host or hostess; the host carves meat and places the meat and vegetables on the plate and passes it to the right; when all the people on the right have been served, the plates are passed down the left side of the table.)*

2. Ask students to explain the use of a service plate. *(It's a large, decorated plate used only for the first course; food is never put directly on the service plate, but in a separate dish put on top of the service plate.)*

3. Ask students to list foods that are good choices for buffet meals. *(casseroles, stir-fries, sandwiches, and salads)*

categories such as food shopping and preparation, decorations, set-up, and clean-up. List the tasks in order, beginning with the one that must be done first. Think about ways to accomplish the items on your list efficiently. Some jobs can be done far ahead of the event. Make a special list for things to be done the day before and the day of the event. Cross each item off your list as it is accomplished.

Serving Food

There are several ways to serve food, depending on the type of event, the number of people eating, the time available for serving and eating, the menu, and your personal preference.

Informal Table Service

Informal table service may include several ways to serve food. Your menu and the space you have for serving will affect the method you choose.

Most people want to do something special when they have guests for a meal. Even with informal sit-down meals, you will want to set your table properly. (See pages 292-293.) In addition, you may want to add a bread and butter plate or a salad bowl above the forks on the left side of the cover.

Many people feel most comfortable serving a meal family style. Food is brought to the table in serving dishes and people help themselves. To avoid confusion, all foods should be passed to the right.

If space and tableware are limited, you might want to consider using plate service. As you learned in Section 10.1, this means food is portioned out on individual dinner plates and served to each person at the table. This eliminates the need for serving dishes and makes cleanup easier.

An attractive table setting helps make the meal special.

Formal Service

For formal occasions, there are several ways you might handle serving food. If your guest list is limited to eight people (including yourself), you can easily handle serving the meal yourself. For larger groups, you will need help serving the meal so that all of your guest are served quickly and efficiently.

For serving small groups yourself, use **modified English service.** Dinner plates and the food for the main course are brought to the table in serving dishes and placed in front of the host or hostess. If meat is to be carved, this is done by the person hosting. He or she places the meat and vegetables on the plate and passes it to the right. The first plate is passed down to the person at the end of the table. When all people on the right have been served, those on the left are served.

The salad is often served on individual plates from the kitchen and placed on the table before the guests are seated. Accompaniments, such as rolls and butter, are usually passed at the table.

Formal service for large groups is rarely done at home because additional help is needed to serve the meal. This style of service is often used in fine restaurants, at hotels for banquets, and other formal occasions.

Thinking Skills

Reasoning: Ask students: Why is plate service the style most often used in restaurants? *(It is easier to control portion size and reduce waste.)* Ask student volunteers to explain which serving style would be most appropriate for them and why.

For most formal occasions, the table is set with silver, glassware, and a service plate for the appetizer course. A **service plate** is a large and beautifully decorated plate used only for the first course. It is removed from the table before the main course is served. Food is never put directly on the service plate—it is served in a separate dish and place on the service plate.

As a rule, formal service includes a number of courses, each served separately on clean plates. Flatware is needed for each course. It is not uncommon to have three pieces of flatware on each side of the plate.

Buffet Service

A buffet is an easy, practical way to entertain if you don't have enough seating space at a dining table. For eating space, you can set up card tables or other small snack tables. People can also hold plates of food on their laps.

The prepared food is placed in serving dishes on a large table, kitchen counter, or perhaps on several card tables. When setting up the buffet, stack the plates where you want the guests to begin. After the plates, place the main dish, followed by vegetables, salad, rolls, and butter. The flatware, rolled up in a napkin, should be the last items your guests pick up.

When planning a buffet meal, choose foods that are easy to serve and that do not have to be cut with a knife. This makes the food easier to eat. Casseroles, stir-fries, sandwiches, and salads are good choices. You may want to serve beverages to your guests after they are seated.

Receptions

Receptions are social gatherings usually held to honor a person or an event, such as a wedding anniversary or a graduation. These gatherings are usually formal. Buffet service is most often used to serve food.

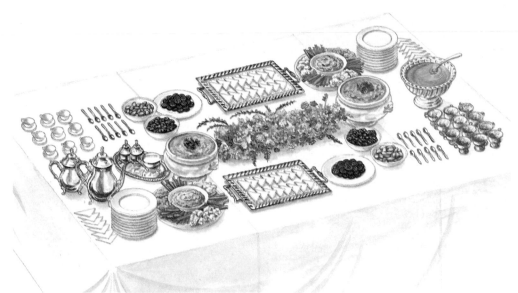

A reception table should be organized for the convenience of both servers and guests. This table is set up to handle two serving lines. What is the starting point for each line? Which direction would each line move?

1. **Class Discussion:** Discuss the methods of service that might be used for different types of entertaining. How would you serve an informal meal for guests? What styles of services might you choose for formal occasions? Why is buffet service popular? What type of service is used at a reception? *(Key skill: critical thinking)*

2. **Student Demonstrations:** Have students work in small groups to plan and give demonstrations of the types of service appropriate for entertaining. *(Key skill: cooperative learning)*

3. **Reception:** Ask interested class members to volunteer to help serve at a reception sponsored by the school. *(Key skill: community involvement)*

Lab Experience

Have students plan and prepare a simple meal in the foods lab and serve it buffet style, following the guidelines outlined in the text. Discuss the advantages of buffet service and the occasions for which it might be used.

Using the Drawing

Answer to caption question: Each line starts at the point where plates are stacked and moves from left to right (as you face each side of the table).

More About Receptions

Special occasions, such as receptions, give many people an excuse for eating foods high in fat, sugar, and calories. Some people may be restricted from such foods.

When planning the menu for a reception, consider those who may be on restricted diets. Have at least one finger food they can eat. This might be:
• Fresh fruit on skewers.
• Raw vegetables with a tofu or yogurt dip.
• Dry-roasted nuts.

Completing the Section

Review

- Ask students to summarize the main ideas in this section.
- Have students complete the Section Review. (Answers appear below.)

Evaluation

- Ask students to identify the different ways food can be served and the various occasions for which each type of service is appropriate.
- Have students take the quiz for Section 24.3. (Refer to the *Section Quizzes* booklet or use the *Testmaker Software*.)

Reteaching

- Have students plan a party for an occasion of their choice.
- Refer to the *Reteaching Activities* booklet for the Section 24.3 activity worksheet.

Enrichment

- Have students research styles of food service used in other countries and report to the class.

Closure

- Discuss the various elements that go into successful entertaining. Emphasize that the host must plan more than just which foods to serve.

A large table is generally used to serve food at a reception. It is covered with a floor-length tablecloth with an attractive centerpiece placed in the center of the table.

Indicate the starting point at the reception table by where you place the plates. For large groups, divide the table in half lengthwise and offer the same food on both sides of the table. This allows people to move in two lines instead of one.

Types of Foods to Serve

Hot beverages, such as coffee or tea, are generally served at one end of the table while a cool beverage, such as fruit punch, is served at the opposite end. Food choices often include small fancy sandwiches, nut-breads, cheese, crackers, small fruit kabobs, delicate cookies and small pastries, candies, and nuts that are attractively arranged on plates and trays.

When preparing foods for a buffet or reception table, remember to arrange and garnish them attractively. Also be sure to provide appropriate serving utensils.

■ Section 24.3 Review ■

RECALL THE FACTS

1. Identify two factors that help determine whether an occasion will be formal or informal.

2. What is one point to remember as you decide on a guest list?

3. Give three guidelines for planning a menu for a party.

4. How should you set up a buffet table for serving food?

DISCUSS YOUR IDEAS

5. Name three foods or dishes that you would include at a buffet and three that you would serve at a formal dinner. What factors influence your choice?

APPLY YOUR LEARNING

6. In small groups, brainstorm a list of themes that might be appropriate for a party for teens. Chose one theme and describe how you would carry it out with invitations, decorations, music, and menu. How would you serve the food?

■ Answers to Section Review ■

1. Answers will vary. Examples: the amount of space and resources available, the type of occasion.
2. Invite compatible people; invite a good blend of listeners and talkers.
3. Find out about special food needs or preferences of guests; keep food choices simple; select a simple appetizer.
4. Place the food in serving dishes on the serving surface; stack the plates where you want the guests to begin; after the plates, place the main dish, followed by vegetables, salad, rolls, and butter. The flatware, rolled up in a napkin, should be the last items your guests pick up.
5. Answers will vary.
6. Answers will vary.

Outdoor Methods

OBJECTIVES

After studying this section, you should be able to:

- Describe how to choose and pack picnic foods.
- Identify ways to safely cook foods outdoors.
- Identify foods for outdoor cooking.

LOOK FOR THESE TERMS

micro-grill

Outdoor cooking is a favorite way to prepare meals for many families. It's a way for family and friends to gather and enjoy the out-of-doors while preparing and eating a meal.

You can apply many of the food preparation skills that you have already learned to outdoor cooking. Keeping food at safe temperatures is especially important when cooking and eating outdoors.

Picnic Foods

The food you choose for a picnic may depend on how far you have to travel. Avoid taking hot cooked food unless you know it will be eaten within two hours. For safety, keep hot foods in an insulated container.

Cooking foods on a grill at the picnic site is often safer than transporting hot food. Cook raw foods, like hamburgers, or warm up cold cooked foods. For safety, don't partially cook food at home and then finish cooking it at the picnic.

Outdoor cooking seems to add a special flavor to foods. What are some other reasons for its popularity?

Introducing the Section

Motivators

- Ask students to identify their favorite foods for a picnic or for outdoor cooking.
- Ask students to describe problems they have encountered at picnics or when cooking outdoors. How could these problems have been avoided?

Objectives

- Have students read the section objectives. Discuss the purpose of studying the section.

Vocabulary

- Pronounce the terms listed under "Look for These Terms." Have students find the terms and their definitions in the section.

Guided Reading

- Have students look at the headings within Section 24.4 to preview the concepts that will be discussed.
- Have students read the section and complete the appropriate part of the Chapter 24 Study Guide in the *Student Workbook*.

Teacher's Classroom Resources—Section 24.4

Refer to these resources in the TCR package:

Reproducible Lesson Plans

Student Workbook

Extending the Text

Reteaching Activities

Section Quizzes

Testmaker Software

Color Transparencies

Teaching . . .

- **Picnic Foods**
- **Outdoor Cooking**

(text pages 661-664)

Comprehension Check

1. Ask students to list things they would need for a picnic. *(Food, tableware, cleanup equipment, can and bottle openers, paring knife, paper towels, trash bags, extra plastic bags to bring back dirty utensils.)*

2. Ask students to explain why it is important to pack raw meat or poultry in a separate cooler. *(To prevent cross-contamination with prepared foods.)*

3. Ask students to list considerations for buying an outdoor grill. *(See the feature box on page 662.)*

4. Discuss safety guidelines for safe grilling. *(See items on pages 663-664.)*

5. Ask students to explain why it is important never to pour water on burning charcoal. *(The charcoal might explode.)*

Using the Photo

Ask students how they would pack the foods shown in the photo on page 662. Emphasize the importance of keeping foods cold on the way to the picnic. Point out that the cake should be packed at the bottom of the cooler because it is needed last.

A picnic can have almost any kind of food, as long as it is properly packed and kept at a safe temperature. How would you pack the foods shown here?

Packing the Picnic

If you're traveling to the picnic area, make a list of everything you will need, including food, tableware, and cleanup equipment. Don't forget items such as premoistened cleaning wipes, can and bottle openers, a paring knife, paper towels, trash bags, and extra plastic bags to bring back dirty utensils. As you pack for the picnic, check off each item on your list.

Be sure to follow the same safety and sanitation precautions given for packing a lunch in Section 20.1, page 525.

Pack nonperishable items in a basket or any other container. Use an insulated cooler for chilled food. To keep the food chilled, put ice cubes in the cooler or a reusable frozen gel pack. Frozen food, such as sandwiches or boxed frozen juices, will help keep other food cold.

If you're taking raw meat or poultry to cook at the picnic, pack it in a separate cooler to prevent cross-contamination with ready-to-eat foods.

When packing the cooler and picnic basket, put the last item you will need on the bottom and the first one on top. To pack the cooler, start with the end of the meal, so put the dessert on the bottom (if it's fragile, put it

662   Chapter 24: Special Ways with Food

Earth Watch

Before you leave the picnic area, clean up the trash and dump it in on-site trash containers. If there are none, gather your trash in a plastic bag and bring it home for disposal.

If your picnic is at the beach or on a boat, remember that it is illegal to dump plastic trash in the ocean or navigable waters. Violators may be fined up to $25,000.

in a crush-resistant plastic container first). Packing food in this order eliminates the need to unpack the whole cooler every time you want something. Don't remove food from the cooler until you need it.

At the picnic site, keep the cooler in a cool, shady spot. Keep the cover on the cooler at all times. Don't leave the cooler in the sun, a hot car, or a car trunk. Even an insulated cooler won't stay cool under such conditions.

Thinking Skills

Critical Thinking: Have students discuss the factors that might affect a family's decision to buy a gas grill instead of a charcoal grill.

Reasoning: Have students discuss why special barbecue tools are essential for cooking on a grill.

Outdoor Cooking

Grilling food outdoors is also called barbecuing. Before barbecuing, be sure you have the proper tools and understand how to use an outdoor grill safely.

Safety First

The simplest grill is a round, kettle-shaped metal container that holds burning charcoal. It is topped with a wire grid for holding food above the hot coals. There are many other kinds of grills that vary in price. Some cook with bottled (propane) gas instead of charcoal.

All grills cook by the same principle. Heat radiates upward and cooks the food held on the grid above. Grilling is a dry-heat method of cooking, similar to broiling. Cooking time depends on the kind and thickness of food and the distance from the heat.

Follow the directions in the owner's manual for using the grill. Methods vary, depending on the kind of grill you have.

Here are some guidelines for safe grilling:

❖ Use fireproof gloves and heavy-duty grilling tools with long handles. The long handles keep your hands away from the intense heat.

In a basic grill, hot coals provide radiant heat that cooks the food above it.

❖ Set the grill on a level surface so it won't tip over. Keep it away from flammables such as buildings, shrubs, and trash containers.

❖ Use a clean grill. Before using it, remove baked-on grime from the inside and the grid with a hard-bristled brush. Baked-on food and grease can cause flames to flare up when you light the fire.

❖ Apply enough of the starter fluid (if you use it) before striking the match. Never add more fluid after the coals have been lighted—it might explode.

❖ Never use kerosene or gasoline as fire-starters—they can explode.

❖ Fat and meat juices dripping on coals can cause flare-ups. If that happens, raise the grid, cover the grill, or use a long-handled tool to spread the coals apart. You can also remove the food from the grid and use a pump-spray bottle filled with water to spray a mist on the flare-up. Then put the food back on the grid. Don't pour water on the burning charcoal—it might explode.

Section 24.4: Outdoor Meals   663

Student Experiences

1. **Class Discussion:** Discuss picnickers' responsibility to clean up before they leave the picnic site. What are the penalties in your area for littering and illegal dumping? (Key skill: community involvement)

2. **Writing Brochures:** Have students work in groups to create a brochure on picnic foods. Include sections on planning, safety, packing, and cleanup. Have students include a picnic checklist. (Key skill: writing)

3. **Consumer Decisions:** Have students study catalogs, advertisements, and consumer publications to obtain information on the types of outdoor grills available. Have students compare features, durability, stability, size, and cost of various grills. (Key skill: consumer awareness)

4. **Finding Recipes:** Have students find recipes for outdoor cooking. Discuss how techniques for outdoor cooking differ from the usual techniques. (Key skill: reading)

Healthy Attitudes

Point out that when fat drips onto a flame or hot coals, polycyclic aromatic hydrocarbons (pah-lee-SIGH-click air-oh-MAAH-tick HIGH-droh-kar-bins), known as PAHs, form. The smoke carries them up and deposits them on food. PAHs can also form right on the meat when it is charred. PAHs have been linked to certain kinds of cancer.

More About Using the Grill Safely

• Keep pets away from the cooking area. They could knock over the grill or work table.

• When you are through grilling, allow the briquets to cool in the fire bowl. They retain heat for a long time, so don't discard them where people or animals might walk on them. Don't dump them in a combustible box—it could ignite.

• Don't remove the grid until it is cool. Don't place a hot grid on the ground. Someone could step on it barefoot and suffer serious burns.

Completing the Section

Review

- Ask students to summarize the main ideas in this section.
- Have students complete the Section Review. (Answers appear below.)

Evaluation

- Have students write a short essay on issues that pertain to outdoor meals and their preparation.
- Have students take the quiz for Section 24.4. (Refer to the *Section Quizzes* booklet or use the *Testmaker Software*.)

Reteaching

- Have students prepare posters that illustrate safety rules for using an outdoor grill.
- Refer to the *Reteaching Activities* booklet for the Section 24.4 activity worksheet.

Enrichment

- Have students find a recipe for a tomato-based barbecue sauce, prepare it, and compare it to two commercial varieties.

Closure

- Lead a discussion on safety measures to take when you plan, prepare, and eat outdoor foods.

Healthy Attitudes

Some people are concerned about the chemicals that are deposited on food as it cooks over hot charcoal. Some studies have linked these chemicals to certain kinds of cancer. Here are some steps you can take to prevent chemicals from forming on grilled food:

- ***Stop fat from dripping on the heat source.*** Trim fat from meat before cooking. Make a drip pan from heavy-duty foil and place it in the center of the charcoal, under the food on the grid, to catch drippings.
- ***Micro-grill foods.*** To **micro-grill** means to cook food—usually meat or poultry—by a combination of microwaving and grilling. Foods cook faster and remain moist and juicy. Begin by partially cooking the meat or poultry on a rack in the microwave oven. Discard any juices that collect. Finish cooking the meat or poultry on the outdoor grill immediately.

Kabobs are a popular food for grilling.

❖ When you have finished grilling, let the coals burn out until only ashes are left. Douse the ashes with water and then put them in a metal trash can. Do not dump hot coals or ashes on the ground. They damage the grass and can even start a fire.

Food for Grilling

Grilling is used mainly for tender cuts of meat and poultry. Cook them thoroughly, turning after half the cooking time.

Fish is also easy to grill. Place fillets skin-side down on a lightly oiled grid so they do not stick. Grill until fish flakes easily. Thick pieces may have to be turned.

Most fruits and vegetables can be grilled. Thread small pieces of fruits and vegetables on metal skewers. Brush them lightly with melted butter or a basting sauce. Place them on the grid. Turn the skewers frequently until foods are hot and lightly browned.

Section 24.4 Review

RECALL THE FACTS

1. Give three safety tips for choosing and preparing picnic foods.
2. In what order should foods be packed in a cooler? Why?
3. Give four guidelines for safe grilling.
4. Briefly explain how to grill fruits and vegetables.

DISCUSS YOUR IDEAS

5. What are some advantages of outdoor cooking?
6. What effect might local government regulations have on outdoor cooking in your area?

APPLY YOUR LEARNING

7. Bring to class a favorite recipe for indoor cooking. Explain how it might be modified for preparation on a grill.

Answers to Section Review

1. Use insulated containers for hot or chilled foods; pack raw meat or poultry in a separate cooler; take hot foods only if they will be eaten within two hours.
2. So that the things you will need first are on top; to avoid having to unpack the cooler every time you need something.
3. See list on pages 663-664.
4. Thread small pieces on metal skewers; brush lightly with melted butter or basting sauce; place on grid; turn frequently.
5. Answers will vary.
6. Answers will vary according to your local government.
7. Answers will vary.

Preserving Food at Home

OBJECTIVES

After studying this section, you should be able to:

- Identify ways to safely freeze fruits and vegetables while retaining quality and nutrients.
- Explain how to safely can fruits and vegetables at home.
- List the benefits of drying foods at home.

LOOK FOR THESE TERMS

antioxidant
blanched
processing
raw pack
hot pack
headspace

Preserving food at home serves several purposes for some families. For many families, it's a way to stretch the food budget. In other families, it's a way to spend time working together and have some fun while preserving food at the same time. People who garden usually preserve some of the food they have grown.

There are several ways to preserve food at home, including freezing, canning, and drying. Whichever method you use depends on personal preference and the equipment you have available.

If you do not grow your own food, you may be able to buy seasonal foods at lower rates and save money. Farmers often have lower prices for fruits and vegetables that people pick themselves. Stores may have specials on locally grown produce.

Always use ripe, high quality food. At best, freezing and canning do not improve the quality of the food. Buy only the amount you can process in the time you have available. Wash the food carefully and prepare it according to recipe directions, keeping cleanliness and sanitation in mind.

When preserving foods at home, choose high-quality produce for the best results.

Introducing the Section

Motivators

- Create a bulletin board entitled "Preserving Summer's Harvest—A Time-Honored Tradition." Use historical and modern illustrations and photographs of different methods of food preservation (for example, salting, smoking, drying, storing in a root cellar, canning, and freezing). Discuss the history of food preservation.

- Ask students to describe their own experiences with home canning, freezing, and drying. Ask students to list the advantages of preserving foods at home.

Objectives

- Have students read the section objectives. Discuss the purpose of studying the section.

Vocabulary

- Pronounce the terms listed under "Look for These Terms." Have students find the terms and their definitions in the section.

Guided Reading

- Have students look at the headings within Section 24.5 to preview the concepts that will be discussed.

- Have students read the section and complete the appropriate part of the Chapter 24 Study Guide in the *Student Workbook.*

Teacher's Classroom Resources—Section 24.5

Refer to these resources in the TCR package:

Reproducible Lesson Plans
Student Workbook
Extending the Text
Reteaching Activities

Section Quizzes
Testmaker Software
Food Science Resources
Color Transparencies

(text page 666)

Comprehension Check

1. Ask students to explain how to stop or slow the enzymatic activity in fresh fruits before freezing. *(Use an antioxidant, such as ascorbic acid.)*

2. Ask students to describe three methods of freezing fresh fruits. *(Dry-pack plain— for fruits that do not darken; dry-pack with ascorbic acid— for fruits that would otherwise darken; sugar-packed fruits— for sweetened fruits or fruits in syrup to use as a sauce.)*

3. Ask students to describe the blanching process. *(Prepare vegetables, put them in strainer and immerse into boiling water. When water returns to rolling boil, begin timing according to a blanching chart; when time is up, remove strainer and plunge into cold water until completely cooled; drain and pat dry; pack into containers and freeze.)*

Using the Photo

Answer to caption question: Pineapple—dry-pack plain because the fruit does not darken; peaches—ascorbic acid to keep fruit from darkening; strawberries—sugarpacked because syrup is desired.

Freezing Fresh Fruits and Vegetables

In Section 7.4, you read about freezing as a method for storing food. Follow those directions for packing, labeling, and freezing.

Freezing Fruits

Most fruits can be frozen. Pears, oranges, and bananas do not freeze well. Applesauce freezes better than apples.

Before freezing fresh fruits, enzyme activity must be stopped. Since enzymes need oxygen, cutting off the oxygen supply stops enzyme activity. Ascorbic acid is an **antioxidant**—a substance which slows down enzyme activity. It is used for fresh fruits that darken. Those that do not darken have enough natural ascorbic acid. Fruits can also be packed in syrup or water to eliminate the oxygen supply, but this limits the way they can be used.

❖ **Dry-pack plain.** Put prepared fruit on a cookie sheet, leaving space in between the pieces. Use this method for fruits that do not darken, such as most berries, melons, pineapple, and cherries. Freeze. Package food pieces when solidly frozen.

What freezing method is being used for each of these kinds of fruits? Why?

❖ **Dry-pack with ascorbic acid.** Sprinkle fruit with a ready-prepared ascorbic acid mixture according to package directions. Use for fruits that darken, such as apples, figs, peaches, nectarines, and plums. Freeze as directed for "Dry-pack plain."

❖ **Sugar-packed fruits.** Toss fruits in sugar until they are well coated. Pack in containers and freeze. Use this method whenever you want sweetened fruits or fruits in syrup to use as a sauce. When fruits defrost, their juices combine with the sugar to form a sweet syrup.

Freezing Vegetables

Vegetables must be **blanched**, or precooked, to kill enzymes. Tomatoes do not need to be blanched. Work with 1 pound (500 g) of vegetables at a time.

To blanch vegetables, you will need the following items: a large pan of boiling water; about a gallon (4 L) of water to blanch 1 pound (500 g) of vegetables; a large strainer to hold the vegetables while blanching; a large pan of ice water; a supply of ice cubes; and clean, dry towels for draining vegetables.

Put the prepared vegetables into the strainer and immerse them in boiling water. Allow the water to return to a rolling boil and begin timing the vegetables. Timing depends on the type and size of vegetable pieces. The larger the pieces, the longer they must blanch. Follow the time recommended in a blanching chart.

When the time is up, remove the strainer of vegetables and plunge them into cold water until completely cooled. Be sure the water remains ice cold. Drain the vegetables on clean, dry towels and pat dry. Pack them into containers and freeze.

Vegetables may also be blanched in a microwave oven. Use the same method as for microwaving vegetables. Blanching times are generally similar to those for top-of-the-range blanching.

Food and Nutrition Science

Maximum freezer storage times: Some people think you can put food in the freezer and preserve it forever. Not so. Have students research maximum storage times for frozen fruits and vegetables. Using the information, have students create a chart for the most commonly frozen fruits and vegetables.

Antioxidant Experiment: See the *Food Science Resources* booklet for the "Enzymatic Browning of Fruit" teaching guidelines and student experiment worksheet. The experiment compares the effects of various liquids on the browning of fresh fruit.

Canning Fruits and Vegetables

Before canning, make sure you have up-to-date recipes, instructions, and equipment. Canning methods have changed in recent years to prevent serious food-borne illness. A reliable source of information is your local cooperative extension service.

Follow the recipe directions and do not take shortcuts or change recipes. Sugar and salt in recipes may act as preservatives. If you want low-sugar or low-sodium foods, look for that type of recipe.

Jars and Lids

Only use jars made for home canning. Be sure they are all perfect. Discard any that have cracks or chips that might keep the lids from sealing tightly.

Use two-piece metal covers, which combine a flat lid with a screw band. The lid is used only once. The band may be reused. Follow the manufacturers' directions for preparing the covers. Do not use one-piece covers that seal with separate rubber rings, such as glass or metal with a porcelain lining. They do not seal properly.

If filled jars are to be heated more than 10 minutes, they do not need to be sterilized before packing the food. Others should be sterilized. Follow the recipe directions.

Processing the Food

When canning, the food is heated in specific ways to stop enzyme activity and kill harmful microorganisms. This is called **processing** food. Two different heating methods are used. *Water bath canning* is used for high- acid foods such as fruits and most tomatoes. Acid protects canned food

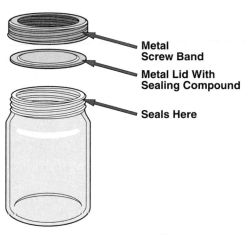

Metal Screw Band

Metal Lid With Sealing Compound

Seals Here

Two-piece metal covers provide a tight, safe seal for home-canned goods.

Home economists from the local cooperative extension service can provide information about home canning.

1. **Display:** Display appropriate containers for freezing fruits and vegetables. Point out that it is false economy to skimp on containers and wrappings. Show various types of labels and emphasize the importance of good labeling. *(Key skill: consumer awareness)*

2. **Demonstration:** Demonstrate procedures for freezing fruits. Point out that pears, oranges, and bananas do not freeze well. Show how to prepare fruits using dry-pack plain, dry-pack with ascorbic acid, and sugar-packed methods. *(Key skill: kitchen management skills)*

3. **Demonstration:** Demonstrate procedures for freezing vegetables. Point out that blanched vegetables retain their nutrients, color, flavor, and texture far longer than vegetables that have not been blanched. *(Key skill: kitchen management skills)*

More About Freezer Packaging

Here are some guidelines for choosing packaging materials and containers for freezing:

• They should withstand freezer temperatures. Some materials, such as waxed paper and cellophane, will crack at freezer temperatures. Some glass jars and brittle plastics will crack when frozen.
• Packaging should suit the food.
• Packaging should be strong. Packages are shifted frequently in the freezer. This can tear or crack weak materials.
• Empty cottage cheese and margarine tubs are not heavy enough for freezer storage. However, they can be used to hold freezer bags.

Teaching . . .

• **Canning Fruits and Vegetables**

(text pages 667-669)

Comprehension Check

1. Ask students to explain why the amount of salt and sugar in canning recipes should not be altered. *(The salt and sugar may act as preservatives.)*

2. Ask students to name foods that are processed using water bath canning. *(fruits and most tomatoes)*

3. Ask students to explain the difference between raw pack and hot pack foods. *(Raw pack foods are placed into jars raw and hot liquid is poured over them; hot pack foods are heated in liquid before they are put into the jars.)*

Student Experiences

1. **Demonstration:** Demonstrate the hot pack method and the raw pack method of packing food in jars. Point out recommended foods for each method. *(Key skill: kitchen management skills)*

2. **Guest Speaker:** Invite a Cooperative Extension Home Economist to speak to the class on canning methods. Ask the guest why recommendations for home canning change periodically. *(Key skill: health)*

Safety Check

Bring a pressure canner to class so that students can examine it and become familiar with the various parts.

---

against the growth of harmful microorganisms. Low-acid foods, such as all vegetables, require *pressure canning* to be safe. A pressure canner is like a pressure cooker, only larger. It heats foods under pressure to temperatures above the boiling point to kill harmful microorganisms.

There are several methods you can use to pack the jars for processing. To **raw pack** jars, place raw foods into the jars and then pour in hot syrup, water, or juice. To **hot pack** foods, heat the food in liquid first, then pack it into the jars.

When packing jars, leave about 1/2 to 1 inch (1.3 to 2.5 cm) **headspace**, the space between the top of the food and the rim of the jar, for the food to expand. Run a spatula between the food and the jar to remove air bubbles. Wipe the jar top clean. Apply the covers. Screw the metal band on tightly by hand. Process the jars using one of the recommended processing methods. Do not process canned food in conventional or microwave ovens.

❖ *Canning fruits.* After raw packing or hot packing fruits into jars, process the jars in a boiling water bath canner for the time directed on recipe. The canner is a large, covered pot, with a rack to hold the jars.

A pressure canner heats foods to temperatures higher than 212°F (100°C). It is used for low-acid foods, such as vegetables.

SAFETY CHECK

A pressure canner contains a rack to hold jars, a steam-tight cover, a safety release valve, and a pressure gauge which measures accurate pressure during processing. To use a pressure canner safely:

❖ Read the manufacturer's directions for using the canner *carefully*.

❖ Process foods at the pressure indicated in the instructions for each type of food.

❖ Make sure the cover of the canner is fastened securely to avoid injuries.

❖ When the processing time is over, remove the pressure canner from the heat and allow it to cool until the pressure gauge returns to zero pressure. Open the safety release. If no steam escapes, the pressure is down and the canner can be safely opened. *Do not attempt opening the canner until the pressure is down and no steam escapes from the canner. Failure to do this could result in serious injury.*

Food and Nutrition Science

Botulism: Botulinus, the bacterium responsible for botulism, produces a toxin that's the most potent biological poison known. Ask students how you can detect the presence of the botulinus bacterium. *(You can't always. It may be present even when there is no odor or color change in the food. That's why home canners must "go by the rules.")* Which foods can provide a growth medium? *(Low-acid foods.)*

Effect of Pectin Experiment: See the *Food Science Resources* booklet for the "Role of Pectin in Jelly" teaching guidelines and student experiment worksheet. The experiment determines the effects of pectin and sugar when making jelly.

Many people enjoy canning their own fruits, vegetables, and homemade jellies as a hobby. State and local fairs often give prizes for the best results.

Teaching . . .

• **Drying Food**

(text pages 669-670)

Comprehension Check

1. Ask students to list the two conditions that are necessary for drying food at home. Why do these conditions make it difficult for people in the United States to dry foods at home? *(High temperature and dry climate; that combination is difficult to find in this country.)*

2. Ask students to explain how food dehydrators work. *(They look much like a microwave oven, but have a 24-hour timer and an adjustable thermostat that allows you to dry foods between 90°F and 155°F [32°C and 68°C].)*

3. Ask students to name foods that can be dried easily at home. *(fruits, vegetables, granola, and beef jerky)*

Student Experiences

1. **Demonstration:** Demonstrate how to prepare foods for drying. Using a food dehydrator, dry several types of foods. Have students taste the results. *(Key skill: kitchen management skills)*

2. **Store Survey:** Have students visit a supermarket and make a list of the dried foods available. Which ones can be eaten as they are? Which need to be reconstituted? *(Key skill: writing)*

3. **Cost Comparison:** Have students compare the features and cost of several food dehydrators. Ask them to determine whether a food dehydrator could help a family save money on food. Under what circumstances? *(Key skill: math)*

❖ *Jams and fruit spreads:* Fill the jars with the prepared jam or fruit spread and apply the two-part covers. Process them in the boiling water bath canner for the time specified in the recipe. Do not seal jars with paraffin—it does not make a tight seal.

❖ *Canning vegetables:* After raw packing or hot packing the jars with vegetables, process the jars in a pressure canner.

After processing, let the jars cool on a rack or clean dish towel away from drafts until completely cool, usually about 12 hours.

Check the covers to make sure they have sealed. Press the center of the cover or tap it with a spoon. The cover should stay down and give a clear, ringing sound when tapped. If the jar has not sealed, reprocess or remove the food and refrigerate or freeze it.

Store home-canned foods in a clean, cool, dry place. Before tasting or using home-canned vegetables, boil them for 10 to 15 minutes to be certain that any harmful microorganisms are destroyed.

Drying Food

Drying food at home is a time-consuming process that requires special equipment. Most people find it easier to buy dried foods. Sun-dried tomatoes, for example, are popular. However, sun drying requires both a high temperature and a dry climate, which is difficult to find in the United States.

The easiest way to dry foods at home is with the use of a food dehydrator. A food dehydrator is similar in size, shape, and cost

Section 24.5: Preserving Food at Home   669

More About Drying Foods

Early American explorers often traveled alone, on foot, and needed a food supply that was easy to carry and required little if any preparation. They relied heavily on dried foods, which were lightweight and needed no special care. One of the most popular dried foods was beef jerky, devel-oped by the Native Americans.

Legend has it that jerky was originally developed by the Indians in Peru. Lean beef was sliced 1/4 inch thick and preserved with salt or brine for about 12 hours. Then it was dried in the sun and tied into convenient bundles. Its Native American name, "charqui," eventually was pronounced as "jerky."

24.5

Completing the Section

Review

- Ask students to summarize the main ideas in this section.
- Have students complete the Section Review. (Answers appear below.)

Evaluation

- Have students list the steps for freezing, canning, or drying foods.
- Have students take the quiz for Section 24.5. (Refer to the *Section Quizzes* booklet or use the *Testmaker Software*.)

Reteaching

- Ask students to explain how drying helps keep food from spoiling.
- Refer to the *Reteaching Activities* booklet for the Section 24.5 activity worksheet.

Enrichment

- Have students collect recipes for fruit spreads that could be used as gifts.

Closure

- Lead a discussion about the advantages and disadvantages of preserving your own food.

to a microwave oven. However, it functions much differently. Most food dehydrators have a 24-hour timer and an adjustable thermostat which allows you to dry foods between 90°F and 155°F (32°C and 68°C). Follow the manufacturer's directions for drying times and temperatures.

Foods such as fruits and vegetables, granola, and beef jerky can be dried easily at home. By taking advantage of lower seasonal prices on fruits and vegetables, you can save money, too.

Food dehydrators make it easy to dry fruits and vegetables at home.

Dried foods are convenient to store and make delicious snacks. They are especially popular with hikers because they are a lightweight, nutritious source of energy.

■ Section 24.5 Review ■

RECALL THE FACTS

1. Briefly explain why and how vegetables are blanched.
2. Give four guidelines for using a pressure canner safely.
3. What should you do with food in a jar that has not sealed?
4. Name two foods that can be easily dried at home.

DISCUSS YOUR IDEAS

5. Why do you think preserving food at home has remained popular even with today's busy lifestyles?

APPLY YOUR LEARNING

6. Brainstorm a list of all the frozen, canned, and dried products your family uses regularly. Identify those that you might preserve at home. Why might it be impractical or unwise to preserve the others at home?

■ Answers to Section Review ■

1. Vegetables are blanched to kill enzymes; prepare vegetables, put them in strainer, immerse into boiling water. When water returns to rolling boil, begin timing according to blanching chart; when time is up, remove strainer and plunge into cold water until completely cooled.
2. See the "Safety Check" feature on page 668.
3. Reprocess or remove the food and refrigerate or freeze it.
4. *Any two:* Fruits, vegetables, granola, and beef jerky.
5. Answers will vary.
6. Answers will vary.

Career PROFILE

Eugenia Snyder
Wedding Cake Baker

CURRENT POSITION

"I'm a baker specializing in wedding cakes."

RESPONSIBILITIES

"After helping customers pick out the right kind of cake to match their wedding, I bake the cake, decorate it, and deliver it to the reception site."

SKILLS

"To be successful in this career, it helps to have some artistic ability. You also must be able to communicate with people and manage your own finances."

EDUCATION

"I have a high school diploma and previous experience as a cook and baker. I took cake decorating classes to learn how to create the 'special effects' that are so important to wedding cakes. I've also taken a few accounting classes."

TYPICAL DAY ON THE JOB

"Most of my days are divided between preparing cakes and meeting with new customers. I also spend time ordering supplies and cleaning up the kitchen."

FAVORITE PART OF THE JOB

"I've always thought the wedding cake was an important part of any wedding reception, and I find a lot of pleasure in contributing to the bride and groom's special day."

- Does Eugenia seem to have the skills necessary for her job? Why or why not?
- What parts of Eugenia's job do you think you might find interesting? Why?

671

Thinking About . . . Baking Wedding Cakes

Have students think of other questions they would like to ask Eugenia Snyder about baking wedding cakes. (Examples: How can people receive training in the artistic side of decorating cakes? Are you planning to take any more courses? What college degree might help you in your job? Do you work for yourself or for a company? How many hours a week do you work? Do you have to work many weekends?)

Student Opportunities

Students interested in a career in baking wedding cakes may learn to bake in their own kitchens at home or seek experience as a cook in a restaurant, cafeteria, or catering business.

Occupational Outlook

Bakers that specialize in wedding cakes usually own their own businesses. They can expand their businesses to be as large as they want, as long as they have the baking and business skills necessary to run the business.

For More Information

For additional information about careers in baking, encourage students to contact:
- American Culinary Federation, P.O. Box 3466, St. Augustine, FL 32084
- The Educational Foundation of the National Restaurant Association, 20 N. Wacker Dr., Suite 2620, Chicago, IL 60606
- Small Business Institute, P.O. Box 30149, Baltimore, MD 21270

Review

Have students complete the Chapter Review. (Answers appear below.)

Evaluation

Have students write a short essay discussing the topics covered in this chapter.

Have students take the test for Chapter 24. (Refer to the *Chapter and Unit Tests* booklet or construct your own test using the *Testmaker Software*.)

■ ANSWERS ■

REVIEWING FACTS

1. Oil (keeps food from overcooking under intense heat); acid (helps tenderize the food); seasonings (flavor the food).

2. The bags are not made to withstand high cooking temperatures and may burn; the chemicals in the paper may be transferred to the food.

3. Water reservoir, basket that holds a filter and coffee, carafe that catches the coffee as it brews, and hotplate to keep the carafe and coffee warm.

4. Black tea—rich, dark brown color and hearty flavor; green tea—green leaves are unaltered, has mild flavor; oolong tea—mixture of green and brown color; flavor between black tea and green tea; amount of oxidation accounts for the differences.

5. Start with a list organized by categories; list the tasks in order; make a special list for things to be done the day before and the day of the event; cross each item off the list as it is accomplished.

CHAPTER 24 REVIEW

SUMMARY

SECTION 24.1

Creative Techniques: You can add flavor to foods with seasonings such as herbs, spices, condiments, and marinades. Cooking foods *en papillote* allows the flavor of several foods to blend in a sealed paper package. Garnishes are colorful bits of food that complement a dish's appearance and texture.

SECTION 24.2

Beverages: Coffee and tea come in several different varieties and are easy to prepare. Punch is a mixture of fruit juices and carbonated beverages or tea.

SECTION 24.3

Entertaining: Good planning helps make any occasion, whether formal or informal, a success. When you plan, consider the theme, decorations, invitations, and menu. Options for serving the food include modified English service, formal service, and buffet service. Receptions are usually formal gatherings at which buffet service is used.

SECTION 24.4

Outdoor Meals: Safety is especially important when planning and preparing outdoor meals. Pack foods with care and follow rules for safe grilling. Meats, fish, and fruits and vegetables can all be successfully grilled.

SECTION 24.5

Preserving Food at Home: When freezing fruits and vegetables, take steps to stop enzyme activity. To can safely, use up-to-date recipes and equipment and follow recipe instructions exactly. Some foods can be dried at home with a food dehydrator.

REVIEWING FACTS

1. Identify the three basic ingredients in a marinade and the purpose of each one. (24.1)

2. Give two reasons for not using brown paper bags for cooking foods *en papillote*. (24.1)

3. Identify the four basic parts of a coffeemaker. (24.2)

4. Compare the three basic types of tea for taste and appearance. What accounts for their differences? (24.2)

5. Give four suggestions for making a schedule of things to do when organizing a party. (24.3)

6. Describe modified English service. (24.3)

7. Give two guidelines for packing chilled food in a cooler. (24.4)

8. Explain how to handle grill flare-ups. (24.4)

9. Describe two differences between the dry-pack plain and sugar-pack methods of freezing fruits. (24.5)

10. Briefly describe how to prepare raw packed and hot packed jars for processing. (24.5)

LEARNING BY DOING

1. ***Foods lab:*** Create your own herb or spice blend or marinade. Experiment with different combinations and proportions of seasonings. Prepare a recipe using your blend or marinade. (24.1)

2. ***Demonstration:*** Design and demonstrate for the class the arrangement of two different table settings: one for a six-year-old's birthday party, the other for a formal dinner. Explain the differences between the two and the reasons for your selections. (24.3)

---

6. Dinner plates and the food for the main course are brought to the table in serving dishes and placed in front of the host or hostess; the host carves meat and places the meat and vegetables on the plate and passes it to the right; when all the people on the right have been served, the plates are passed down the left side of the table.

7. Put the last item you will need on the bottom and the first one on top; at the picnic site, keep the cooler in a cool, shady spot.

8. Raise the grid, cover the grill, or use a long-handled tool to spread the coals apart; remove the food from the grid and spray a mist of water on the flare-up using a pump-spray bottle.

3. **Demonstration:** Demonstrate safe grilling practices. Include such things as using utensils properly, starting the fire, preparing different foods on the grill, cleaning up after grilling, and handling flare-ups. (24.4)

4. **Food science lab:** Blanche and freeze green beans. Freeze another batch without blanching. After one week, thaw and compare the two packages' appearance and texture. Cook the beans and compare their taste. How do you explain your findings? (24.5)

THINKING CRITICALLY

1. **Forming hypotheses:** Why do you think dried herbs are more potent than fresh ones? (24.1)

2. **Drawing conclusions:** Why are carbonated beverages added to punch mixtures just before serving? (24.2)

3. **Recognizing alternatives:** Suppose you wanted to host a sit-down dinner but had limited space. How might you creatively use the space available to seat your guests? (24.3)

4. **Recognizing fallacies:** You are cleaning up after a picnic with friends. One of your friends says you can leave your dirty paper plates at the picnic site, since paper is biodegradable. Do you agree? Explain your answer. (24.4)

5. **Forming hypotheses:** Why do you think fruits such as oranges and bananas do not freeze well? (24.5)

MAKING DECISIONS AND SOLVING PROBLEMS

What Would You Do?

1. You are doing the grocery shopping for a friend. He has written "tea" on his shopping list, but he hasn't specified any particular kind. (24.2)

2. Some of the guests at your dinner party do not seem to be enjoying themselves. They don't eat or speak much and generally seem uncomfortable. (24.3)

3. You have several items to pack in your cooler for a picnic for yourself and three family members: a large container of ham salad for sandwiches; a six-pack of soda; a chunk of cheese; a chocolate cake; and ice for the drinks. As you pack, however, you realize that there is not enough room in the cooler for everything. (24.4)

LINKING YOUR STUDIES

1. **Social studies:** Choose five different herbs or spices and find out where they are commonly grown. Make a display using a world map identifying the herb or spice, the region in which it is produced, and the geographic conditions that help it grow there. (24.1)

2. **Science:** Research the latest findings on the possible effects of caffeine on health. Summarize your findings in a brief report. (25.2)

3. **Fine arts:** From a library's music collection or your own, select music that would provide an enjoyable accompaniment to the following meals: a seven-year-old's birthday party; a neighborhood potluck dinner; an elegant anniversary dinner. (24.3)

4. **Science:** Find more information about one of the chemical processes involved in preserving food at home, such as oxidation, the action of enzymes, or dehydration. If possible, set up an experiment or other demonstration to illustrate the principles involved. (24.5)

673

LEARNING BY DOING

Answers to "Learning by Doing" activities will vary. Evaluate students on their procedures as well as their results.

THINKING CRITICALLY

1. Answers will vary.
2. Because they would lose their carbonation if they were combined with other liquids ahead of time.
3. Answers will vary.
4. Answers will vary. Littering is against the law in most parks, cities, and counties.
5. Answers will vary.

MAKING DECISIONS AND SOLVING PROBLEMS

Answers to "Making Decisions and Solving Problems" activities will vary. Encourage students to give reasons for their answers.

LINKING YOUR STUDIES

Answers to "Linking Your Studies" activities will vary. Encourage students to give reasons for their answers.

9. Dry-pack plain does not contain sugar; in dry-pack plain method, the food must be frozen before it is put into its container, but sugar-packed fruits are frozen in their containers.

10. Raw pack: place raw foods into the jars and then pour in hot syrup, water, or juice; hot pack: heat the food in liquid before putting it into the jars and then pack heated food into the jars.

CHAPTER 25

Careers in Food and Nutrition

SECTION 25.1
Career Opportunities 675

SECTION 25.2
The Successful Worker 681

Planning the Chapter

Chapter Overview

Section 25.1: Career Opportunities

Section 25.2: The Successful Worker

Introducing the Chapter

Motivator

- Ask students to think of three careers in food and nutrition. Ask each student to turn to a partner and describe one of the careers. Ask the partners to try to guess the career. Have each pair join another pair. Ask each student to describe the career first described by his or her partner. If the career has already been described, the student should describe another career. Then have each foursome join another group. Ask each person to describe one career. Each career may be used only once. As a class, make a list of all the careers described.

674

Cooperative Learning Suggestions

Organize a Co-op Co-op activity. Have students work in groups of four to research one of the types of food and nutrition careers described in the text. Assign each group member one of the following tasks: research the job outlook for the career; identify qualities and skills needed for suc- cess; describe the experience, training, and education needed; describe the typical duties of a person in the career. Have students share their information with the group. Randomly select a member of each group to summarize the group's findings for the class.

Career Opportunities

OBJECTIVES

After studying this section, you should be able to:

- Identify career opportunities in food and nutrition.
- Describe the training and education needed for various careers.

LOOK FOR THESE TERMS

career
entry-level job
career ladder
entrepreneur

Carrie had always enjoyed preparing food for her family and friends. When she entered high school, she thought she might like to become a chef or a baker. After a few foods and nutrition courses, she discovered her opportunities in the foods area were even more varied. She could also choose from a career in food science, research and development, or communications, to name just a few. After thinking about her skills and interests, Carrie set herself a new goal. She decided she wanted to develop low-fat recipes for a large food corporation.

Thinking About Careers

Like Carrie, you can prepare for a career in the food and nutrition field. Now is the time to explore your opportunities, to learn about training requirements, and to develop good work habits.

A **career** is a profession or a life's work within a certain field. It usually begins with an **entry-level job,** one that requires little or no experience. These jobs often lead to better paying jobs with more responsibility.

An interest in food that starts as a hobby could someday turn into a career.

Section 25.1 Career Opportunities

Introducing the Section

Motivators

- Create a bulletin board illustrating food and nutrition careers in the areas of food technology. Discuss the jobs involved in each area.
- Discuss how high school courses might help you get an entry level job or even lead to a career.

Objectives

- Have students read the section objectives. Discuss the purpose of studying the section.

Vocabulary

- Pronounce the terms listed under "Look for These Terms." Have students find the terms and their definitions in the section.

Guided Reading

- Have students look at the headings within Section 25.1 to preview the concepts that will be discussed.
- Have students read the section and complete the appropriate part of the Chapter 25 Study Guide in the *Student Workbook.*

Teacher's Classroom Resources—Section 25.1

Refer to these resources in the TCR package:

Reproducible Lesson Plans
Student Workbook
Extending the Text

Reteaching Activities
Section Quizzes
Testmaker Software
Color Transparencies

Teaching . . .

- **Thinking About Careers**
  - **Food Service**
- **Family and Consumer Sciences**

(text pages 675-678)

Comprehension Check

1. Ask students to explain the difference between a career and a job. *(A job is work you do for a salary or wage; it may be one in a series of jobs that makes up a career. A career is a profession or life's work within a certain field.)*

2. Ask students to describe the types of jobs available within the food service industry. *(serving food, developing recipes, merchandising food products)*

3. Ask students to explain why educational requirements vary. What is the advantage of getting a higher education? *(Lower-level jobs, such as entry-level and part-time jobs, do not require much education—but they don't pay much, either. The more education you have, the better the salary you can receive.)*

4. Ask students to name the types of jobs available in family and consumer sciences. *(Teaching in schools, colleges, and universities; communication jobs in television, magazines, books, and newspapers; research and development for new products and appliances.)*

TIPS for Success

Have students use these guidelines to identify several careers in which they might be interested. Have students write their responses to the items and save the responses for their own future reference.

TIPS for Success

Choosing a Career

These guidelines can help you choose a career that you will enjoy and do well in:

- ❖ **Think about the classes and activities you enjoy.** Why do you like them?
- ❖ **List your skills and talents.** Do any point toward a specific career you might enjoy?
- ❖ **Identify your values.** They can direct you toward a career area.
- ❖ **Work in community service and part-time jobs.** Even though they may not be in the career area that interests you, they can provide you with valuable information about yourself, your abilities, and your preferences.

Many entry-level jobs are available in the food service industry. Employees who show motivation and pride in their work have a better chance of moving up to higher-paying jobs.

Employees advance in a career by mastering the skills needed for their job and showing they are qualified to take on new responsibilities. Many seek additional education or training throughout their lives to further their career.

Career Areas

A recent study on job growth for the coming years predicted great expansion in service industries, including food and nutrition. The job outlook for this field is bright. More people are eating out. Consumers are more interested in the relationship between food and health. The growing world population and other global factors make producing and utilizing quality food efficiently more important than ever. All this means a growing demand for service and information.

Here is a summary of some of the careers in food and nutrition.

Food Service

The food service industry includes all aspects of preparing and serving food for the public. It is expected to create more new jobs than any other retail industry in the next decade.

Thinking Skills

Reasoning: Ask students: Why are nutrition and good personal health essential for success in a food service career? *(People who serve food to the public must meet certain health standards; the work is hard and the hours are often long; they must have lots of energy and be able to work quickly under pressure.)*

Jobs in food service can vary from serving food, to developing recipes, to merchandising food products. They are usually available in every part of the country. If you like to travel, you might even consider food service jobs with cruise lines or airlines, or even in different countries.

Educational requirements vary, depending on the job you want. Part-time, entry-level jobs are often a good start. Food preparation classes in high school can also provide a valuable foundation. For more training, consider vocational schools, junior or community colleges, and four-year colleges and universities. Many companies offer on-the-job training to help employees advance.

As a rule, more education and training allows you to start higher on the **career ladder**—a series of jobs through which a person can advance in a career. Food service offers many different career ladders. One is shown on this page.

Brent started working in a restaurant bussing tables. Through hard work and study, he moved up the ladder to become assistant manager. His goal is to become a manager.

Food service requires certain personal traits. Employees must enjoy and be able to work successfully with people. They must be willing to do their share as part of a team. Producing quality food on schedule can mean hard work and long hours. Good health, enthusiasm, ambition, and a sense of humor are essential. So are good work habits, such as punctuality and the ability to follow directions and accept criticism.

Family and Consumer Sciences

Family and consumer sciences—called home economics, human ecology, or family studies at some universities—involves using knowledge and skills to solve problems and make decisions about the home and family. Professionals with degrees in food and nutrition have many career options in addition to food service, including:

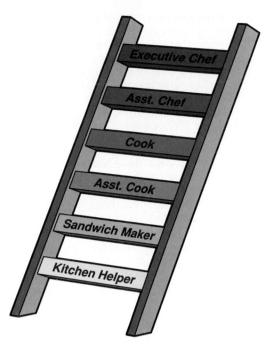

Having a long-range goal, such as becoming an executive chef, can help you plan your career. An entry-level job, such as kitchen helper, is often the first step. From there, you can work your way up the career ladder. Each promotion takes you a step closer to your long-term goal.

❖ *Teaching.* Family and consumer science specialists may teach in schools, colleges, and universities. They may teach classes ranging from nutrition to ethnic foods. Nutritionists may work for county or regional extension services, teaching consumers about food preparation and related topics. They are also needed by other government agencies and health organizations to teach consumers how to make wise food choices.

Section 25.1: Career Opportunities   **677**

1. **Class Discussion:** Have students who have worked in food service describe their experiences. What traits are needed by food service workers? What opportunities do entry-level food service workers have to move up the career ladder? What effect does education have on their chance to be promoted? *(Key skill: critical thinking)*

2. **Field Trip:** Visit a restaurant, cafeteria, hotel, or institution to observe what employees in the different areas of food service do. *(Key skill: observation)*

3. **Writing:** Have students write a paragraph on why they would or would not consider a career in food service. *(Key skill: writing)*

4. **Panel Discussion:** Invite people who work in food and nutrition careers to discuss their work, education, and training. *(Key skill: career planning)*

5. **Small Group Discussion:** Have students work in small groups to find out what family and consumer science specialists do in teaching, communications, and research and development, and what training is required in each field. *(Key skill: research)*

Special Needs Strategies

Learning Disabled: Have students collect and display pictures illustrating the food and nutrition careers described in the text.

Thinking Skills

Reasoning: Ask students: What factors have contributed to the increase in the number of meals eaten away from home and to the increased demand for processed foods?

Teaching . . .

- **Food Science**
- **Dietetics**
- **Food Production, Processing, and Marketing**
- **Entrepreneurship**

(text pages 678-680)

Comprehension Check

1. Ask students to define *food science*. What education do food scientists usually need? *(Food science is the study of the physical, chemical, and microbiological makeup of food; food scientists need at least a bachelor's degree with a major in food science, food engineering, or food technology, but higher degrees are needed for research and management jobs.)*

2. Ask students to explain what a dietitian does. *(Dietitians work in large institutions, such as hospitals, HMOs, company cafeterias, and food service companies, to help develop special diets and counsel groups or individuals in making wise food choices.)*

3. Ask students to describe the education needed by a dietitian. *(Bachelor's degree in food and nutrition and a one-year internship at an approved institution; to become a registered dietitian, they must pass an exam, also.)*

4. Ask students to explain what an entrepreneur is. *(A person who runs his or her own business.)*

❖ ***Communication.*** This involves communicating information to the public through television, magazines, books, and newspapers. People with strong communication skills are needed to help write speeches, articles, and advertisements about food products and services. Food stylists create attractive arrangements of foods for photographs. Employers include food producers, manufacturers, government agencies, and trade associations.

❖ ***Research and development.*** Food researchers help develop new products and appliances in test kitchens or research laboratories. They may work for universities, food producers, appliance manufacturers, or the government.

Jobs in family and consumer sciences require at least a bachelor's degree. Some, such as teaching, research, and management, require higher degrees. Study and experience in related fields also helps. Specialists in communications, for example, might have a background in journalism or public relations.

Food Science

Food science is the study of the physical, chemical, and microbiological makeup of food. Food scientists develop food products and new ways to process and package them. They also test foods and beverages for quality and purity to make sure they meet company standards and federal food laws.

Food scientists are generally employed by the food processing industry. They may work in laboratories, test kitchens, or on the production line. The many careers in food science include basic research, product development, quality control, and sales.

Food scientists need at least a bachelor's degree with a major in food science, food engineering, or food technology. Higher degrees are needed for research and management jobs.

A college education can lead to a rewarding career as a food scientist.

Dietetics

A dietitian (die-uh-TISH-en) is a professional who is trained in the principles of food and nutrition. Dietitians may work for large institutions such as hospitals, health maintenance organizations, company cafeterias, and food service companies. They help develop special diets and counsel groups or individuals in making wise food choices.

Dietitians must have a bachelor's degree in food and nutrition. They must then serve a one-year internship at an approved institution. A registered dietitian (RD) must pass the Registration Examination for Dietitians. Some community colleges offer two-year programs for dietetic technicians, who work as assistants to dietitians.

Thinking Skills

Creativity: Ask students to imagine themselves as the successful entrepreneurs of the year 2100. Tell them to write a short story describing their business (including the product or service it provides) and their typical day's work as head of the business.

Food Production, Processing, and Marketing

A vast network of people is involved in producing food and getting it to the marketplace. Career opportunities vary from hydroponic farming to supermarket management.

Training and education also vary, but a combination of experience and formal education is best. Farmers, for example, need to know how to do the everyday work on the farm itself, but can also benefit from studies in related topics such as soil conservation and plant and animal genetics. A bakery owner must have experience in preparing the food as well as knowledge about business management, marketing techniques, and tax laws.

Entrepreneurship

Many people dream of owning their own business. A person who runs his or her own business is called an **entrepreneur** (on-truh-pruh-NOOR). Successful entrepreneurs share certain personal qualities. They are willing to work hard and take risks. They can make sound decisions, are well organized, and understand basic business management practices. Opportunities for entrepreneurs in food and nutrition include catering; running a snack shop; home delivery from restaurants or supermarkets; nutrition consultation; and preparing and selling food, such as homemade baked goods.

Entrepreneurs sometimes invest in a franchise, which allows them to own a business with an established name and guidelines. Some fast food restaurants are franchises. Not all franchises are reliable, however, so potential owners should investigate carefully before buying one. Also, a franchise cannot guarantee success. It's up to the businessperson to provide the skills and commitment needed to succeed.

Owning a business takes hard work, but the results are worthwhile. Entrepreneurs feel the special satisfaction of building their own success. They also contribute to the strength and growth of their communities.

Section 25.1: Career Opportunities   **679**

1. **Field Trip:** Take a field trip to a food processing plant to learn about careers in food science. Where were food scientists working: in a laboratory, in a test kitchen, or on the line? Were food scientists involved in basic research, product development, quality control, or sales? *(Key skill: career planning)*

2. **Guest Speaker:** Invite a dietitian to speak to the class about career opportunities in dietetics. Where do dietitians work? What do they do? What education do they need? Have students write a summary of what they learn. *(Key skill: writing)*

3. **Research:** Have students research local career opportunities in food production, processing, and marketing. Resources may include the telephone directory, local business and industry directories, the Chamber of Commerce, interviews, etc. *(Key skill: research)*

4. **Interviews:** Have students interview local food and nutrition entrepreneurs. Were any of the businesses franchises? If so, what assistance was provided by the franchisor? Ask students to give brief presentations summarizing their interviews. *(Key skill: public speaking)*

5. **Letter writing:** Have students write to one of the sources listed on page 680 for more information about food and nutrition careers. *(Key skill: writing)*

More About Franchises

A franchise is actually a license to conduct a business enterprise in the name of an established corporation or, in some cases, the government. The franchisee usually pays an initial fee and a percentage of gross receipts to the franchisor in exchange for the privilege of marketing a well-known product or service. In corporate franchises, the franchisor usually helps the franchisee with merchandising and advertising.

Franchising can be a good way to get started in a business of your own if you have enough capital to pay the initial fees. By selling brands that are already established, you may even have a preestablished clientele.

Businesses that are often franchised in the United States include fast-food restaurants, gasoline stations, motels, and real estate offices. Encourage students to find out what local companies are actually franchises in your area.

Completing the Section

Review

- Ask students to summarize the main ideas in this section.
- Have students complete the Section Review. (Answers appear below.)

Evaluation

- Have students write a short essay describing the various careers available in food and nutrition.
- Have students take the quiz for Section 25.1. (Refer to the *Section Quizzes* booklet or use the *Testmaker Software*.)

Reteaching

- Have students make a chart of the various occupations and the educational requirements for each.
- Refer to the *Reteaching Activities* booklet for the Section 25.1 activity worksheet.

Enrichment

- Have students develop plans for a small business that could be operated on a part-time basis or in the summer.

Closure

- Lead a discussion about the importance of education in the appropriate field so that you can advance in your career.

Sources of Food and Nutrition Career Information

The Council on Hotel, Restaurant, and Institutional Education (CHRIE)
1200 17th Street NW
Washington, DC 20036

American Association of Family and Consumer Sciences
1555 King Street
Alexandria, VA 22314

The Institute of Food Technologists
221 N. LaSalle Street, Suite 300
Chicago, IL 60601

The American Dietetic Association
216 W. Jackson Blvd., Suite 800
Chicago, IL 60601

U.S. Department of Agriculture
14th Street and Independence Ave. SW
Washington, DC 20250

Small Business Administration
409 3rd Street SW
Washington, DC 20416

■ Section 25.1 Review ■

RECALL THE FACTS

1. List four types of education or training for a career in food service.
2. Name three food and nutrition career options other than food service.
3. Briefly describe the educational and training requirements for registered dietitians.
4. Name three business opportunities for entrepreneurs.

DISCUSS YOUR IDEAS

5. Discuss what social trends contribute to the increased need for workers in food and nutrition.

APPLY YOUR LEARNING

6. Choose one food that you enjoy. List as many workers as you can that are involved in producing, processing, and distributing that food.

A culinary arts school is just one example of the opportunities for education and training in the foods area.

■ Answers to Section Review ■

1. *Any four:* Food preparation classes in high school, vocational schools, junior or community colleges, four-year colleges and universities, on-the-job training.
2. *Any three:* Family and consumer sciences, food science, dietetics, food production, food processing, food marketing, entrepreneurship.
3. Bachelor's degree in food and nutrition and a one-year internship at an approved institution; to become a registered dietitian, they must pass an exam, also.
4. *Any three:* Catering, running a snack shop, home delivery from restaurants or supermarkets, nutrition consultation, preparing and selling food.
5. Answers will vary.
6. Answers will vary.

The Successful Worker

OBJECTIVES

After studying this section, you should be able to:
- Identify qualities of successful workers.
- Describe the steps in applying for a job.
- Give guidelines for job interviews.
- Explain how to handle leaving a job.

LOOK FOR THESE TERMS

networking
resumé
references

Even if you haven't decided on a career, having a part-time or summer job offers several advantages. Finding and keeping a job teaches responsibility and increases self-confidence. It sharpens your management and decision-making skills. It also lets you enjoy the benefits of earning a paycheck. In addition, working can also help you decide what type of career you might enjoy.

Qualities of Successful Workers

Recent surveys have identified some of the qualities employers look for. You can develop these skills while still in school:

❖ **Communication skills.** These include writing, reading, speaking, and listening. Employees often write reports. They must read and understand company bulletins and guidelines. They must listen carefully to instructions they receive or to customer requests.

Learning how to communicate effectively and becoming familiar with computers are two ways you can prepare for a career while you are still in school.

Section 25.2: The Successful Worker   **681**

Teacher's Classroom Resources—Section 25.2

Refer to these resources in the TCR package:

Reproducible Lesson Plans
Student Workbook
Extending the Text

Reteaching Activities
Section Quizzes
Testmaker Software
Color Transparencies

**Section 25.2
The Successful Worker**

Introducing the Section

Motivators

- Ask students who work to describe how they found their jobs. How many had to fill out an application form? How many had a job interview? What did they learn that would help them do better next time?

- Ask students to identify qualities they have that will help them be successful workers. Ask several volunteers to share their lists with the class.

Objectives

- Have students read the section objectives. Discuss the purpose of studying the section.

Vocabulary

- Pronounce the terms listed under "Look for These Terms." Have students find the terms and their definitions in the section.

Guided Reading

- Have students look at the headings within Section 25.2 to preview the concepts that will be discussed.

- Have students read the section and complete the appropriate part of the Chapter 25 Study Guide in the *Student Workbook*.

- **Qualities of Successful Workers**
- **Looking for a Job**
- **Applying for a Job**

(text pages 681-683)

Comprehension Check

1. Ask students to list qualities employers look for that they can develop while they are still in school. *(Communication skills such as reading, writing, speaking, and listening; computer skills; critical thinking and problem solving; positive attitude; math skills; teamwork and self-responsibility; ability to learn.)*

2. Ask students to identify three ways to find a job. *(Check with school counselor or employment office; read newspaper want ads and community bulletin boards; network.)*

3. Ask students to explain what a resumé is and what information needs to be included on it. *(A written summary of your past experience, skills, and achievements that are related to the job you seek.)*

4. Ask students to list documents and information they should take with them when they apply for a job. *(Social Security number; work permit; health certificate; names, addresses, and telephone numbers of references.)*

❖ **Computer skills.** Most jobs involve the use of a computer in some way. In many restaurants, for instance, servers use computers to send customer food orders to the kitchen.

❖ **Critical thinking and problem solving.** Employees who can analyze situations and suggest solutions to problems are valued by their employers.

❖ **Positive attitude.** Employees must be enthusiastic about their work and interested in what they do.

❖ **Math skills.** Even though computers and calculators are widely used, employees must understand basic math. They may have to make change, keep a time schedule, or solve math-related problems.

❖ **Teamwork and self-responsibility.** Employees must be willing to do their share, and more if necessary. They must work well with others to achieve common goals.

❖ **Ability to learn.** New technology will continue to cause rapid changes in the workplace. That means learning new skills will be a lifelong process for employees.

Develop good learning and work habits while you are still in school. Volunteer work, school projects, and social activities can provide opportunities to develop essential skills.

Looking for a Job

As a student, right now you may be looking for only a part-time job. Even so, the experience of finding and keeping a job will be valuable to you personally as well as professionally.

There are many ways to find a job. Check with your school employment or counseling office. Read the newspaper want ads and community bulletin boards. You can also contact employers directly and ask if they have any job openings.

Networking can help you find a job. Ask teachers, neighbors, and friends for advice. The more people who know you are looking for employment, the more likely you will be to find out about any openings.

Another idea helpful to job hunting is **networking.** This means making connections among people who can provide information about job openings. When Anton began exploring careers in food science, his network included his home economics teacher, a nutritionist at the county extension office, and the writer of a foods column in the local newspaper. Remember, however, that other people can only help you find a job. Getting the job and keeping it are up to you.

Thinking Skills

Critical Thinking: Ask students why it is so important to follow directions exactly when answering want ads. *(If the applicant does not follow directions in answering the want ad, the employer will assume that he or she may not follow directions well on the job.)*

Special Needs Strategies

Gifted and Talented: Have students assist students who need help filling out job application forms and developing resumés.

Applying for a Job

Your next step is to apply for a specific job. This usually involves filling out a job application form or writing a letter of application.

A job application form requires basic personal information, such as your age and home address, and information about your education and experience. Remember to print your answers in ink, answering all questions as concisely as possible.

A letter of application serves the same purpose as an application form. However, you have a choice of what information to include. Include basic personal information plus any other helpful facts about yourself. As with the application form, focus on those things that will demonstrate your suitability for the job you are seeking. For example, being editor of the school yearbook shows that you can work well with people and delegate authority. Good grades in food science courses indicate your knowledge of foods and related fields.

For some jobs, you may need to submit a **resumé** (REH-zoo-may). This is a written summary of your past experience, skills, and achievements that are related to the job you seek. A chronological resumé lists jobs and experiences from most recent to the earliest. A functional resumé describes your skills and accomplishments as they relate to the job you are seeking. A sample of a functional resumé is shown on this page.

Although a resumé is more detailed than a letter of application, it should be brief—not more than one page—and contain only relevant information. If you have no previous work experience, don't mention it. Focus instead on those activities that show your skills and abilities.

When applying for a job, you may be asked for **references.** These are people who know you well and can give information about your previous work or your character. A teacher or former work supervisor might be good references. Be sure to ask them first. You will need their names, addresses, and phone numbers.

Employers are prohibited by law from asking, in person or on application forms, for certain information such as your race, gender, religion, or marital status. They may not ask questions about some aspects of your personal or past life.

An application form, letter of application, and resumé all demonstrate your ability to communicate in writing. All three should be carefully thought out and neatly written or typed. Be sure the grammar and punctuation are correct. Remember that this will be your potential employer's first—and possibly only—impression of you as a worker. Make it a positive one.

SAMPLE RESUME

Ginny Arnold   Social Security: 000-00-000
800 Southwest Street
Anytown, US 11111
Home Phone: (000)000-000

OBJECTIVE: Kitchen helper, part-time.

QUALIFICATIONS:
- Received high grades in food preparation class.
- Have ability to organize work.
- Know how to use a computer.
- Would like to become a chef.

EXPERIENCE:
- Help with Friday night suppers at church.
- Organized successful pancake breakfast for parents, sponsored by Home Economics Club.
- Worked at the Community Center soup kitchen, helping with meals for homeless.

EDUCATION:
- Junior at Anytown High School.
- Currently taking advanced food preparation class.

A well-written resumé is brief, but provides the information that employers need in order to consider you for the job.

Student Experiences

1. **Group Discussion:** Divide the class into small groups. Assign each group one of the following topics: volunteer work, school projects, social activities, part-time jobs. Ask students to consider how each activity would help them develop qualities needed for job success. *(Key skill: critical thinking)*

2. **Guest Speaker:** Invite a school counselor to discuss the job placement assistance programs offered by the school. *(Key skill: career planning)*

3. **Want Ad Analysis:** Have students collect "Help Wanted" ads from the national and local newspapers. What jobs are available in the food and nutrition area? Ask students to look through the ads in search of jobs that look attractive and accessible for a young applicant. How many listings request a written reply? How many ask you to apply in person? By phone? *(Key skill: analysis)*

4. **Completing Forms:** Provide students with two different job application forms. Have them fill out the forms neatly and completely. *(Key skill: writing)*

5. **Developing a Resumé:** Have students develop a resume showing past experience, skills, and achievements that would help them get an entry level food service job. *(Key skills: writing, career planning)*

More About Writing a Resumé

Here are some tips for avoiding pitfalls when you create your resume:
- Do not include references, unless you are specifically asked for them.
- Do not include previous salary or wages.
- Do not include personal information that is not related to the job, such as age, height, weight, and marital status.

Teaching . . .

- **Interviewing for a Job**
- **On the Job**
- **Leaving Your Job**

(text pages 684-686)

Comprehension Check

1. Ask students what characteristics and attitudes people should show to give a good impression during an interview. How can you accomplish this? *(That you are enthusiastic, qualified, and willing to work hard; by arriving on time and being neatly groomed and polite.)*

2. Ask students to describe the proper way to end an interview. *(Thank the interviewer and repeat your interest in the job; ask when you may call to find out about the final decision; write a note of thanks to the interviewer after you get home, again expressing your interest in the job.)*

3. Ask students to list tips that can help you keep a job. *(See list on page 685.)*

4. Ask students to describe the proper way to leave a job. *(At least two weeks ahead of time, inform your employer in a brief, polite letter of resignation; do not be negative; thank the employer for the opportunity to have worked there.)*

At many high schools, you can apply for a work permit in the school counseling office.

Interviewing for a Job

If the employer thinks you might be a good prospect for employment, you will be called for an interview. This is a meeting with the employer during which you can both get more information and perhaps reach a conclusion regarding the job.

The impression you make at the interview should continue the one you began in your application. You want to show that you are enthusiastic, qualified, and willing to work hard. You convey this by arriving on time and being neatly groomed and polite.

Interviews can be stressful, but try to relax. Let the interviewer direct the conversation. Show your interest in the job and familiarity with the company. Explain how you can help the company and be prepared to answer questions such as, "What are your strengths and weaknesses?" Remember to phrase your answers in ways that will stress your abilities and qualifications. Ask questions about the nature of the job, but don't focus on money or benefits yet.

Documents You May Need for Employment

❖ *Social Security number.* This lifelong identification number allows you to receive Social Security payments when you retire or are disabled. You probably already have a number. If not, you can get one at the nearest Social Security office.

❖ *Work permit.* Some states require students to have a work permit.

❖ *Health certificates.* If you work with food, you may need one.

Your school counselor can tell you how to obtain these and other necessary documents.

It's natural to feel a little nervous when going to a job interview. Think of the interview as an opportunity to visit a workplace, learn more about an interesting job, and meet new people. Try to make a good impression, but also relax and be yourself.

More About Interviewing for a Job

- Most hiring decisions are made at the first interview. Therefore, the impression you make on your first interview is important.
- Do not chew gum or smoke during an interview.
- As part of the interview, you may be asked to take some tests, such as personality, aptitude, knowledge, or medical.
- After the interview, evaluate it. How did you perform? Did you answer the questions well? Did you get all the information you need about the job? Were you dressed appropriately? Did you close the interview effectively? What can you do to improve future interviews?

TIPS for Success

Preparing for an Interview

An interview can go more smoothly with a bit of advance preparation:

❖ Write down the time and place of the interview. Make sure you know how to get there and how long it will take. Be sure to arrive on time.
❖ Make up an interview package. Include your resumé (if needed), a good pen, and a small notebook for taking notes.
❖ Learn all you can about the company, including the job you are applying for.
❖ Go to the interview alone. Don't bring family members or friends.
❖ Dress neatly. Avoid jeans, excessive make-up, and too much jewelry.

What questions should you ask when making an appointment for an interview?

At the end of the interview, thank the interviewer and repeat your interest in the job. If you are not told whether you are being offered the job, ask when you may call to find out about the decision. When you get home, write the interviewer a note of thanks, again expressing your interest in the job.

If you didn't get the job, you may politely ask why. Whatever the reason, use the interview as a learning experience.

If you are offered the job, you have completed the first step in reaching your career goals. Now you must work to continue making progress toward those goals.

On the Job

Once you have found a job, it is up to you to keep it. These tips can help you:

❖ Get to work on time and appropriately dressed.
❖ Follow company rules, such as those about taking breaks and eating on the job.
❖ Pay attention when receiving instruction or training.

❖ Don't be afraid to ask questions about your responsibilities.
❖ Accept criticism and suggestions without resentment.
❖ If you make a mistake, admit it and learn from it.
❖ Take pride in your work. Remember that even small jobs can make a big difference.

Balancing Your Life

Balancing the demands of school, work, and family life takes good stress management skills:

❖ Recognize that your life must include a balance of activities. Set your priorities and focus on the most important ones.
❖ Keeping fit and healthy helps you do your best. Make wise food choices and allow time for exercise.
❖ You also need rest and relaxation. Find time for your family, your friends, and quiet time for yourself.

Section 25.2: The Successful Worker   **685**

Student Experiences

1. **Guest Speaker:** Invite the manager of a fast food restaurant to speak to the class. Ask the guest to explain the preparation, appearance, social skills, body language, etc., that make a job applicant successful. Encourage the guest to relate pertinent anecdotes. What are the most serious mistakes people make when they interview for a job? Have the manager interview a student volunteer in front of the class and evaluate the interview. *(Key skill: career planning)*

2. **Class Discussion:** Discuss how students can balance the demands of school, work, and family life. Identify good stress management skills. *(Key skill: critical thinking)*

3. **Practice Interviews:** Have students work in groups of three to conduct practice job interviews for an entry-level food service job. Ask students to come to class dressed as they would for a job interview. Have one student interview another. Have the third student evaluate the interviewee's performance. Have students rotate until all have been interviewed. *(Key skill: communication skills)*

4. **Class Discussion:** Ask students to identify good and poor ways to leave a job. What steps should you take to leave the job on good terms? What should you do if you are fired? *(Key skill: communication skills)*

Thinking Skills

Reasoning: Ask students why it is important to do a job right, no matter how insignificant it seems. *(Possible answers: For personal satisfaction, to improve chances of promotion, to get a good recommendation, and because each job contributes to the team effort.)*

Critical Thinking: Ask students how getting fired could be seen as a positive event. *(When it causes the person to evaluate him-or herself and improve on the next job.)*
Creativity: Have students brainstorm to develop a list of ways food service workers can help make customers happy.

Completing the Section

Review

- Ask students to summarize the main ideas in this section.
- Have students complete the Section Review. (Answers appear below.)

Evaluation

- Have students fill out a job application correctly and completely.
- Have students take the quiz for Section 25.2. (Refer to the *Section Quizzes* booklet or use the *Testmaker Software*.)

Reteaching

- Ask students to write a brief letter asking for a job interview. Discuss what they should say in the letter.
- Refer to the *Reteaching Activities* booklet for the Section 25.2 activity worksheet.

Enrichment

- Have students develop a list of opportunities for volunteer work in your community that could give students valuable job-related experience.

Closure

- Lead a discussion on the personal qualifications and skills needed to get a job and keep it.

When writing a letter of resignation, give careful consideration to what you say. In the future, a prospective employer may ask you for the name of a previous employer as a reference. If your letter of resignation was critical or angry, you'll wish you had left on a more positive note.

Leaving Your Job

There will probably come a time when you will want to leave your job. Here again you can make a good impression. At least two weeks ahead of time, inform your employer with a brief but polite letter of resignation. You may mention your reasons for leaving, but do not be negative. Thank your employer for the opportunity of having worked for the company.

Continue to do your best work until your last day. Remember, you may want to use your employer as a reference in the future.

If you are fired, find out exactly why. How can you improve your job performance so you won't have the same problem again?

When you interview for the next job, be honest about the reasons for leaving. If you were fired, explain why. Also explain how you plan to change so you won't have the same problem again. Employers are more willing to give employees a chance if they seem eager to improve and change.

Remember, success doesn't depend on just your skills and talent. It also depends on your attitude and commitment to do the best you possibly can.

■ Section 25.2 Review ■

RECALL THE FACTS

1. Name six qualifications of successful workers.
2. How are a job application form and a letter of application similar? How do they differ?
3. Give five suggestions for interviewing successfully.
4. How much notice should you give an employer before leaving a job?

DISCUSS YOUR IDEAS

5. What do you think is the most serious mistake people make when they interview for a job?

APPLY YOUR LEARNING

6. Review the qualities of successful workers described in this section. Using job listings from the newspaper want ads, give specific examples of how each skill might be needed in a particular job.

■ Answers to Section Review ■

1. *Any six:* Communication skills such as reading, writing, speaking, and listening; computer skills; critical thinking and problem solving; positive attitude; math skills; teamwork and self-responsibility; ability to learn.

2. Both list your skills and qualifications for the job; letters of application allow you to choose the information that you want to include.

3. See the "Tips for Success" box on page 685.

4. At least two weeks.
5. Answers will vary.
6. Answers will vary.

Debra Munson

Fast Food Worker

CURRENT POSITION

"I'm a high school student working part-time at a fast food restaurant."

RESPONSIBILITIES

"I take orders from customers, take their money and give them change, and serve the food at the counter. Occasionally, I fill in as a cook in the kitchen."

SKILLS

"It's important to be pleasant in this job, since you have to deal directly with customers. It also helps to be able to keep a clear head under pressure."

WORK ENVIRONMENT

"Things can get pretty hectic during the breakfast, lunch, and dinner rush. But with all of us working efficiently as a team, we get through it smoothly."

WHY I CHOSE THIS JOB

"I started looking for a job so I could save up some money for college. At first I didn't have anything particular in mind, except that I would need a job with evening and weekend hours. After checking the want ads and talking with friends about their jobs, I applied here. One of the things that appealed to me was their training program for entry-level workers."

FUTURE PLANS

"I haven't decided on a college major yet, but I plan to investigate family and consumer sciences courses. I think I may be interested in a career in the food industry."

- Do you think Debra chose wisely in seeking this job? Why or why not?
- What aspects of Debra's job do you think you might enjoy? Why?

687

CAREER PROFILE: FAST FOOD WORKER

Thinking About . . . Working in a Fast-Food Restaurant

Have students think of other questions they would like to ask Debra Munson about working in a fast-food restaurant. (Examples: Can you give any tips on how to manage work, school, and family life? What is the salary range for working in a fast-food restaurant? How many hours a week do you work? What do you do when customers become rude or angry?)

Ask student volunteers to tell what they think would be the most exciting part of working in a fast-food restaurant.

Student Opportunities

Students planning a career in food service should look for entry-level employment at local fast-food restaurants.

Occupational Outlook

Fast-food workers who want to stay in the food service business work their way from entry-level positions to the manager of their restaurant or even a regional or district manager. Some may prefer to open their own fast-food restaurant or restaurants.

For More Information

For additional information about careers in food service, encourage students to contact:
- The Educational Foundation of the National Restaurant Association, 20 N. Wacker Dr., Suite 2620, Chicago, IL 60606
- Council on Hotel, Restaurant, and Institutional Education, 311 First St. NW, Washington, D.C. 20001
- National Association of Trade and Technical Schools, P.O. Box 10429, Department BL, Rockville, MD 20850

Review

Have students complete the Chapter Review. (Answers appear below.)

Evaluation

Ask students to prepare a written plan for looking for a job for the upcoming summer. Where would they look, how would they get any required experience, and how would they apply?

Have students take the test for Chapter 25. (Refer to the *Chapter and Unit Tests* booklet or construct your own test using the *Testmaker Software*.)

■ ANSWERS ■

REVIEWING FACTS

1. More people are eating out; consumers are more interested in the relationship between food and health; the growing world population and other global factors make producing and utilizing quality food efficiently more important than ever.

2. Must be able to work successfully with people; must be willing to do his or her share as part of a team; can take the long hours and hard work; has good health, enthusiasm, ambition, and a sense of humor; good work habits.

3. Teaching—*any two:* teach classes in anything from nutrition to ethnic foods, work for county or regional extension services, work for other government agencies and health organizations. Communication—*any two:* working in television, magazines, books, newspapers; help write speeches, articles, and advertisements about food products and services; food stylist.

CHAPTER 25 REVIEW

SUMMARY

SECTION 25.1

Career Opportunities: Career opportunities in food and nutrition are growing and varied. Food service jobs include all those needed to prepare and serve food for the public. Home economists are needed to inform consumers about food, food choices, and related topics. Food scientists develop new foods and test foods for safety and quality. Dietitians help develop special diets for individuals or large groups. Many opportunities exist in food production, processing, and marketing. The food industry offers many options for entrepreneurs. The training and education needed for these careers also varies. Some require extensive formal education and advanced degrees. For others, a combination of on-the-job experience and additional training is most effective.

SECTION 25.2

The Successful Worker: Successful workers share certain qualities. They can communicate well, solve problems, and learn new things. They have a positive attitude and work well alone and with others. Applying for a job may involve filling out an application form, writing a letter of application, and submitting a resumé. These documents require you to give basic personal information and allow you to describe your strengths and qualifications. They should be brief, concise, and well-written. Interviews can be successful if you are relaxed, positive, and show an interest in the job and a willingness to learn. Even if you decide to leave a job or are fired, it can be a learning experience.

REVIEWING FACTS

1. Give three reasons for the expected job growth in food and nutrition. (25.1)

2. Name six personal traits needed to succeed in food service. (25.1)

3. Identify two career options for home economists in teaching and two in communications. (25.1)

4. What degrees and majors are needed to become a food scientist? (25.1)

5. Identify two risks of investing in a franchise. (25.1)

6. Name three benefits of having a job. (25.2)

7. Identify three instances when employees need good communication skills. (25.2)

8. What is networking? (25.2)

9. Give three tips for preparing for an interview. (25.2)

10. Give four tips for being a valuable employee. (25.2)

LEARNING BY DOING

1. ***Computer lab:*** Design and print a form that might be used by an entrepreneur in the food industry, such as an inventory or an employee schedule. (25.1)

2. ***Foods lab:*** Suppose you are a dietitian working in an institution. Think of some of the special diets that might be needed by people in an institutional setting. Create one such diet and prepare one or more of your recipes. (25.1)

3. ***Demonstration:*** Working in pairs, demonstrate how to successfully interview for a job. Have the rest of the class identify the positive points of the interview. (25.2)

---

4. At least a bachelor's degree in food science, food engineering, or food technology.

5. Some franchises are not reliable; the franchise is not a guarantee of success.

6. *Any three:* Teaches responsibility, increases self-confidence, sharpens management and decision-making skills, earns a paycheck, can help you decide what type of career you might enjoy.

7. Writing reports, reading and understanding company bulletins and guidelines, listening to instructions they receive or to customer requests.

THINKING CRITICALLY

1. *Recognizing fallacies:* A friend comments that he thinks bussing tables in a restaurant is an unimportant, dead-end job. How would you respond? (25.1)

2. *Comparing and contrasting:* How might the training and personal traits needed by a teacher in family and consumer sciencesbe similar to those needed by a family and consumer sciences professional in research and development? How might they differ? (25.1)

3. *Comparing values:* Which do you think is more important for a job—technical ability and experience, or enthusiasm and a positive attitude? Explain your answer. (25.2)

4. *Predicting consequences:* How can one employee's poor work habits affect other workers? (25.2)

MAKING DECISIONS AND SOLVING PROBLEMS

What Would You Do?

1. You have been working for almost a year as a cook in a fast-food restaurant and hoping to work your way up the career ladder. However, others who have been working at the restaurant less time than you are being promoted ahead of you. (25.1)

2. Your friend is an excellent baker. He would like to sell his baked goods for profit, but he cannot afford to start a business of his own. (25.1)

3. You and a friend work at the same restaurant. One day he asks you to tell your boss that he is sick so he can go to a concert that night. (25.2)

4. While filling out a job application form, you come to some questions that you feel are inappropriate. (25.2)

LINKING YOUR STUDIES

1. *Art:* Use your creative talents to arrange foods in an appealing manner. You may also photograph or make sketches of your arrangement. Bring your display or illustrations to class. (25.1)

2. *Economics:* Interview at least two local entrepreneurs about the economic aspect of their businesses. What economic factors encouraged them to start their business? What social and economic trends affect their business decisions? What role does their business play in the local or national economy? Do they feel the economy is a good one now for starting a business? If so, what kind? Write a transcript or a summary of your interview, including an explanation of what you learned from it. (25.1)

3. *Social studies:* Trace the history of child labor and child labor laws in this country. At what jobs and under what conditions have children worked in the past? How have attitudes toward child labor changed over time? What circumstances led to the enactment of child labor laws? How do these laws protect children in the workplace? Are there any disadvantages to these laws? Share your findings in a short report to the class. (25.2)

4. *Writing:* Choose a want ad from the newspaper. Write a letter of application for the job, using the suggestions given in this chapter. (25.2)

689

LEARNING BY DOING

1. Forms will vary.

2. Answers will vary; diets might include those for people with high blood pressure and diabetics.

3. You may want to videotape the interviews so that students can see how they appear in an interview situation.

THINKING CRITICALLY

1. Answers will vary; students should understand that the task is not as important for advancement as the attitude of the person; with the proper attitude, bussing tables might lead to a good career in food service.

2. Answers will vary.

3. Answers will vary. Students should realize that both types of attributes are extremely important.

4. Answers will vary. One employee's bad work habits may create extra work for other employees; they may have to cover for the employee, for example, if he or she consistently arrives late to work.

MAKING DECISIONS AND SOLVING PROBLEMS

Answers to "Making Decisions and Solving Problems" activities will vary. Encourage students to give reasons for their answers.

LINKING YOUR STUDIES

Answers to "Linking Your Studies" activities will vary. Encourage students to give reasons for their answers.

8. Making connections among people who can provide information about job openings.

9. See the "Tips for Success" feature on page 685.

10. See list on page 685.

COMPLETING THE UNIT

Refer to page 583 for suggestions for completing the unit.

Glossary

A

additives. Chemicals added to food for specific reasons, such as to preserve freshness or to enhance color or flavor. (Section 13.2)

aerobic exercise (uh-ROW-bick). Exercise that gives the heart and lungs a workout. (Section 5.3)

a la carte (ah-lah-CART). On a restaurant menu, describes items that are priced individually. (Section 4.3)

albumen (al-BYOU-men). The thick, clear fluid inside an egg; also call the egg white. (Section 18.3)

al dente (ahl-DEHN-tay). Used to describe pasta that is tender, but still firm in the center. (Section 17.2)

amino acids (uh-MEE-no). Chemical compounds that combine to make up protein. (Section 2.2)

anabolic steroids (AN-uh-boll-ick STEER-oyds). Drugs used illegally by some athletes to build up muscles; have dangerous side effects that create serious physical and psychological health risks. (Section 5.4)

analogues (AN-uh-logs). Foods made from a vegetable protein and processed to resemble animal foods. (Section 15.1)

annual percentage rate (APR). The percent of interest that is charged per year on a loan. (Section 14.1)

anorexia nervosa (an-uh-RECK-see-yuh ner-VOH-suh). An eating disorder characterized by an irresistible urge to lose weight through self-starvation. (Section 6.3)

antioxidant. A substance that slows down enzyme activity; used to keep cut or pared fresh fruits from darkening. (Section 24.5)

antipasto (ahn-tee-PAH-stoh). An assortment of appetizers served before the main meal in Italy. (Section 22.3)

aquaculture. Method of growing fish or seafood in enclosed areas of water. (Section 13.1)

arcing. Electrical sparks produced when metal is used in a microwave oven; can damage the oven or start a fire. (Section 9.3)

aromatic vegetables. Flavorful vegetables, such as onions, garlic, celery, and green peppers, that are frequently sautéed to provide flavoring for other foods. (Section 20.3)

au jus. Describes meat served in its own juices. (Section 20.3)

B

bakeware. Containers used to cook food in an oven. (Section 9.1)

basal metabolism (BAY-suhl muh-TAB-oh-lih-zum). The amount of energy needed by the body to carry out automatic processes, such as breathing and digesting food. (Section 2.5)

base. A lining of salad greens on which the main part of a salad is placed. (Section 20.2)

behavior modification. Gradually making permanent changes in eating and exercise habits to lose weight and keep it at a healthy level. (Section 5.2)

berbere. A spicy seasoning mixture popular in Ethiopia. (Section 22.2)

binder. A liquid, such as broth or soup, used to hold a casserole together. (Section 20.4)

blanch. To briefly cook vegetables to kill enzymes before freezing. (Section 24.5)

body. The main part of a salad. (Section 20.2)

bouillon (BOOL-yon). a clear, seasoned liquid made from cooking meat, poultry, fish, or vegetables. Also called broth or consommé. (Section 20.3)

bran. The outer protective coat or skin of a grain kernel. (Section 17.1)

budget. A plan for spending one's income. (Section 11.3)

bulimia nervosa (byou-LIM-ee-yuh ner-VOH-suh). Eating disorder characterized by episodes of binge eating (rapidly consuming large amounts of food) followed by purging (using self-induced vomiting, laxatives, and/or vigorous exercise to prevent weight gain). (Section 6.3)

bulk foods. Foods that are sold loose and displayed in covered bins or barrels; consumers buy as much or as little as they want. (Section 12.3)

C

calorie. A unit used to measure the energy that food supplies the body. (Section 2.1)

carbohydrates (kar-boh-HY-drates). Nutrients that are the body's main source of energy; commonly known as starches and sugars. (Section 2.1)

career. A profession or a life's work within a certain field. (Section 25.1)

career ladder. The steps from entry-level to top-level jobs through which a person can advance in a career area. (Section 25.1)

career ladder. The steps from entry-level to top-level jobs through which a person can advance in a career area. (Section 25.1)

chalazae (kuh-LAH-zuh). The twisted, cord-like strands of albumen that anchor the yolk in the center of an egg. (Section 18.3)

chlorophyll (KLORE-uh-fill). The chemical compound that plants use to turn the sun's energy into food; gives plants their green color. (Section 16.3)

cholesterol (kuh-LESS-tehr-all). A fat-like substance present in all body cells and needed for essential body processes. (Section 2.3)

club sandwich. A layered sandwich made using three slices of bread and two types of fillings. (Section 20.1)

coagulate (koh-AGG-yoo-LATE). To cause a liquid to become a soft, semisolid mass, such as curdled milk or the white of a baked or poached egg. (Section 18.3)

code dating. A series of numbers and letters printed on food packages to indicate in code form where and when the product was packaged. (Section 12.2)

colostrum (kuh-LAW-strum). A thick, yellowish fluid produced by the mother's breasts the first few days after a baby's birth. (Section 6.1)

comparison shopping. Comparing prices of similar items to see which offers the best value. (Section 12.3)

complete proteins. Protein foods that supply all of the essential amino acids. Foods from animal sources supply complete protein. (Section 2.2)

conduction. A method of transferring heat by direct contact from one molecule to another. (Section 9.2)

contaminants. Substances that accidentally get into food as it moves from the farm to the table. Chemical pollutants and bacteria are examples. (Section 13.2)

continuous cleaning oven. An oven with special rough interior walls that absorb spills and spatters; residue can then be easily wiped off. (Section 14.2)

convalescence. The period of recovery after a serious illness or injury. (Section 6.2)

convection. A transfer of heat by the movement of currents in air or liquid. (Section 9.2)

convection current. A circular flow of air or liquid resulting from uneven heating. (Section 9.2)

cooking style. An individual's approach to food preparation as determined by personal feelings and priorities. (Section 11.2)

cookware. Containers used for cooking food on top of the range. (Section 9.1)

cover. Arrangement of a place setting for one person. (Section 10.1)

CPR. Stands for cardiopulmonary resuscitation, a first-aid technique used if a person's breathing and heartbeat stop. (Section 7.2)

critical thinking. Judging an idea on its soundness and truthfulness. (Section 3.3)

cross-contamination. Letting microorganisms from one food get into another. (Section 7.3)

cruciferous vegetables (crew-SIH-fur-uss). Vegetables in the cabbage family, including broccoli, brussels sprouts, cabbage, collards, kale, mustard greens, cauliflower, rutabagas, and turnips. (Section 16.1)

crustaceans (kruss-TAY-shuhns). Shellfish that have segmented bodies and limbs covered with a shell. Lobsters and crabs are examples. (Section 19.4)

cultural diversity. A variety of cultures in a single geographical area. (Section 1.3)

culture. The shared customs, traditions, and beliefs of a large group of people, such as a nation, race, or religious group. (Section 1.2)

cultured. Describes milk products to which a harmless bacteria culture has been added, causing fermentation, which results in a tangy, acidic flavor. (Section 18.1)

curing. A method of processing meat using a mixture of salt, sugar, nitrate, ascorbic acid, and water; extends shelf life and adds distinctive flavor. (Section 19.2)

cut. Refers to a piece of meat, poultry, or fish as it is sold in the marketplace. (Section 19.1)

cut in. To mix solid fat, such as butter or shortening, and flour using a pastry blender or two knives and a cross-cutting motion. (Section 21.2)

D

daily values. Reference amounts shown on the nutrition panel of food labels. Consumers can compare the amount of calories and nutrients in the food with the daily values, which are based on the recommendation of health experts. (Section 12.2)

dehydration (dee-high-DRAY-shun). Lack of adequate fluids in the body; can lead to serious health problems. (Section 5.4)

desired yield. When changing the yield of a recipe, the number of servings you want the revised recipe to make. (Section 8.3)

developing nations. Countries that are not yet industrialized or are just beginning to become so. (Section 13.3)

diabetes. A condition in which the body cannot control blood sugar properly. (Section 6.2)

dietary fiber. Mixture of plant materials that are not fully broken down in the digestive system; needed for good health. (Section 2.1)

Dietary Guidelines for Americans. A set of guidelines developed by the U.S. government to help people make healthy food choices. (Section 3.1)

digestion. The process of breaking food down into usable nutrients. (Section 2.5)

disposable. Refers to products that are thrown away after use. Examples include paper towels and food packaging. (Section 7.5)

doneness. Point at which food has cooked long enough so that it is both pleasurable and safe to eat. (Section 19.5)

dovetail. To fit tasks together in order to make the best use of time. (Section 8.5)

drop biscuits. Biscuits made by dropping sticky batter from a spoon onto a baking sheet. (Section 21.2)

drupes. Fruits with a central pit enclosing a single seed. Cherries and peaches are examples. (Section 16.1)

dry heat. Cooking food uncovered without added moisture. (Section 9.2)

E

eating disorder. Extreme, unhealthy behavior relating to food, eating, and weight. (Section 6.3)

eating patterns. Patterns that individuals follow when it comes to eating meals and snacks (such as what they eat, where, when, and how much). (Section 4.1)

electrolytes. The minerals potassium, sodium, and chloride, which work together to help maintain the body's fluid balance. (Section 2.4)

emulsion. An evenly blended mixture of two liquids that do not normally stay mixed, such as oil and water. (Section 20.2)

endosperm. The part of the grain kernel that contains the food supply for the embryo or germ; made up mostly of proteins and starches. (Section 17.1)

EnergyGuide label. Label on a large appliance that gives consumers information about estimated yearly energy costs. (Section 14.1)

en papillote (ehn pah-pee-YOHT). Describes technique for cooking foods in parchment paper. (Section 24.1)

enrichment. Adding nutrients to a product to make up for those lost in processing. (Section 17.1)

entree (AHN-tray). Main course in a meal. (Section 4.3)

entrepreneur (AHN-truh-pruh-NOOR). A person who runs his or her own business. (Section 25.1)

entry-level job. A beginning-level job that requires little or no experience. (Section 25.1)

enzymatic browning (EN-zie-MATT-ik). Browning that occurs in cut fruit when it is exposed to air. (Section 16.2)

equivalent. The same amount expressed in different ways by using different units of measure. For example, 4 tablespoons is the equivalent of 1/4 cup. (Section 8.2)

ergonomics (urr-guh-NAHM-iks). The study of how to make tools and equipment easier and more comfortable to use. (Section 1.4)

esophagus (ih-SOFF-uh-gus). The long tube connecting the mouth to the stomach. (Section 2.5)

ethnic group. A cultural group based on a common heritage. (Section 1.3)

extender. A starchy food, such as a grain or vegetable, used in a casserole to thicken it. (Section 20.4)

F

fad diets. Current, popular weight-loss methods that ignore good nutrition. (Section 5.2)

famine. Food shortages that continue for months or years, frequently resulting in starvation. (Section 13.3)

fat. Nutrient that provides a concentrated source of energy, provides essential fatty acids, and carries fat-soluble vitamins. (Section 2.1)

fat-soluble vitamins. Vitamins that dissolve only in fat, not in water; include vitamins A, D, E, and K. (Section 2.4)

fetus (FEE-tus). The unborn baby in the mother's womb. (Section 6.1)

finance charge. The total amount a person is charged for borrowing money; includes interest plus any service charges or insurance premiums. (Section 14.1)

foam cakes. Light, airy cakes that are leavened (made to rise) with beaten egg whites. Angel food, sponge, and chiffon cakes are examples. (Section 21.4)

food allergy. Condition in which eating even a small amount of a certain food causes an unwanted reaction, such as itching, rash, hives, nausea, or difficulty breathing. (Section 6.2)

Food Guide Pyramid. A guide developed by the U.S. government to help people make wise food choices. It divides foods into five food groups, plus a Fats, Oils, and Sweets category, and indicates a range of the number of servings needed daily from each group. (Section 3.2)

food record. A record kept over a specific period of time that lists all the foods one eats, the amount, and when it was eaten. (Section 4.2)

food science. A scientific study of food and its preparation. (Section 1.4)

formed product. A food product that is processed, flavored, and shaped to resemble a more expensive food. (Section 15.1)

fortified. Describes a food to which the manufacturer has added 10 percent or more of the daily value for a particular nutrient to make the food more nutritious. (Section 17.1)

freezer burn. Condition that results when food is improperly packaged for freezing or stored in the freezer too long; food dries out and loses flavor and texture. (Section 7.4)

frying. Cooking food in fat. (Section 9.2)

G

generic. Describes products in plain labels with no brand name; less expensive than name brands or store brands. (Section 12.3)

genetic engineering. A method of improving the characteristics of plants and animals by modifying genes for specific traits. (Section 13.2)

germ. The embryo in a grain kernel. The germ can sprout and grow into a new plant. (Section 17.1)

giblets (JIB-lets). Edible poultry organs, such as the liver and gizzard (stomach). (Section 19.3)

glucose. Blood sugar; the body's basic fuel supply. The body breaks carbohydrates down into glucose during digestion. (Section 2.5)

gluten (GLOO-ten). A protein in flour that affects the texture of a baked product and helps determine how it will rise. (Section 21.1)

glycogen (GLIE-kuh-juhn). The stored form of glucose. (Section 2.5)

grazing. Eating five or more small meals throughout the day. (Section 4.1)

grounding. A method of providing a safeguard against electrical shock. (Section 14.3)

H

haute cuisine (HOAT kwee-ZEEN). The classic cooking of France, characterized by rich sauces, exotic ingredients, and puff pastries. (Section 22.3)

headspace. The space left between the food and the cover of the container when packing food for freezing or canning. (Section 24.5)

Heimlich Maneuver. A first-aid technique used in case of choking. (Section 7.2)

hibachi (hih-BAH-chee). A small cast iron charcoal grill. (Section 23.2)

high tea. In England, a light meal served in the late afternoon or early evening. (Section 22.3)

homogenized (huh-MAH-jen-ized). Used to describe milk that has been processed so that the fat does not separate. (Section 18.1)

hot pack. A method of filling jars for canning. The food is first heated in liquid, then packed in jars. (Section 24.5)

hot spots. Areas of intense heat, as in a microwaved food. (Section 9.3)

hydrogenation (hi-DRAH-juh-NAY-shun). A process used to turn vegetable oils into solids; makes fat more saturated. (Section 2.3)

hydroponic farming (high-druh-PAH-nik). Using nutrient-enriched water to grow plants without soil. (Section 13.1)

I

impulse buying. Buying an item you did not plan on and don't really need just because it seems appealing at the moment. (Section 12.1)

incomplete protein. Protein lacking one or more essential amino acids. Foods from plant sources provide incomplete protein. (Section 2.2)

industrialized nations. Countries that use machines and equipment to manufacture many products and process foods. Also called "developed countries." (Section 13.3)

infuser. A small container with tiny holes that holds loose tea while brewing. (Section 24.2)

insoluble fiber. Type of dietary fiber that contributes bulk to help move waste through the large intestine. (Section 2.2)

interest. The amount of money a lender charges as a fee for a loan; equals a specific percentage of the amount borrowed. (Section 14.1)

inventory. An up-to-date record, as of food stored in the freezer. (Section 7.4)

irradiation. Exposing food to gamma rays to increase its shelf life and kill harmful microorganisms. (Section 13.2)

island. A freestanding kitchen counter. (Section 14.3)

J K L

julienne. Term for long, thin strips of food. (Section 24.1)

kibbutz (kih-BOOTS). An Israeli communal organization that raises its own food. (Section 22.2)

knead. To work dough with the hands (or an appliance) to further mix the ingredients and develop the gluten. (Section 21.1)

lacto-ovo vegetarians. People who do not eat meat, poultry, or fish, but do eat dairy products and eggs in addition to foods from plant sources. (Section 4.4)

lacto-vegetarians. People who do not eat meat, poultry, fish, or eggs, but do eat dairy products in addition to foods from plant sources. (Section 4.4)

leavening agents. Substances that produce the air, steam, or gas that helps baked products rise. (Section 21.1)

legumes. Edible seeds that develop in pods of plants; include dry beans and peas, lentils, and peanuts. (Section 17.3)

life cycle. The various stages of life a person passes through from the prenatal stage through old age. (Section 6.1)

life-span design. Designing kitchens to be adaptable to people of various ages and degrees of physical ability. (Section 14.3)

lifestyle. A person's typical way of life; includes how one spends one's time and one's values and attitudes. (Section 1.2)

M

macrominerals. Minerals that are needed in relatively large amounts; include calcium, phosphorus, magnesium. (Section 2.4)

maize. Another name for corn. (Section 22.1)

major appliance. A large electrically- or gas-powered device that performs a specific task, such as cook foods, keep foods cold, or wash dishes. (Section 7.1)

malnutrition. Serious health problems caused by poor nutrition over a long period of time. (Section 2.1)

management. Specific techniques that help one use resources wisely. (Section 1.5)

marbling. Small white flecks of fat that are visible within the muscle tissue of meat. (Section 19.1)

masala. A common seasoning powder used in India; similar to American curry powder. (Section 22.4)

mature fruits. Fruits that have reached their full size and color. (Section 16.1)

meal appeal. Characteristics that make a meal appetizing and enjoyable. (Section 11.1)

media. Channels of mass communication, such as newspapers, television, and radio. (Section 1.2)

meringue (mehr-ANG). A foam made of beaten egg whites and sugar, used for desserts. (Section 18.4)

micro-grill. A combination cooking method in which food is partially cooked in a microwave oven and then immediately placed on an outdoor grill to finish cooking. (Section 24.4)

microorganisms. Tiny living creatures, such as bacteria, that are visible only through a microscope. (Section 7.3)

minerals. Nutrients that help the body work properly; many become part of the body's bones, tissues, and fluids. (Section 2.1)

moderation. Avoiding extremes, as in eating moderate (average or medium size) amounts of a wide variety of foods. (Section 3.1)

modified English service. A method of serving food in which the host or hostess serves the main course at the table. (Section 24.3)

moist heat. Method for cooking food that involves using either liquid or steam. (Section 9.2)

mollusks. Shellfish with soft, unsegmented bodies that are enclosed in a rigid outer shell. Clams and oysters are examples. (Section 19.4)

monounsaturated (MAH-no-uhn-SAT-chur-ay-ted). Term for fatty acids, found mainly in olive oil and certain other foods, that appear to lower only LDL ("bad") cholesterol levels. (Section 2.3)

multicultural. Describes a society that includes many cultures. (Section 1.3)

myths. Beliefs that are not based on fact. (Section 3.3)

N

net weight. The weight of the food itself without the weight of its container or any packaging. (Section 12.2)

networking. When job hunting, making connections among people who can provide information about job openings. (Section 25.2)

nonfat milk solids. Solids in milk that contain most of the protein, vitamins, minerals, and lactose (milk sugar). (Section 18.1)

nouvelle cuisine (new-VELL kwee-ZEEN). Modern French cooking, which uses less flour, sugar, and fat than the classic cooking. (Section 22.3)

nutrient deficiency. A severe shortage of a nutrient, which can cause illness or interfere with normal growth or development. (Section 2.1)

nutrient-dense. Describes a food that is low or moderate in calories, yet rich in nutrients such as complex carbohydrates, protein, vitamins, and minerals. (Section 3.2)

nutrients. Chemicals in food that the body uses to carry out its functions. (Section 1.1)

nutrition. The study of nutrients and how they are used by the body. (Section 1.1)

O

obstetrician. A physician who specializes in pregnancy. (Section 6.1)

open dating. A date on a food product that can be understood by consumers, such as a "sell by" date or an expiration date. (Section 12.2)

open stock. Pieces of tableware that are sold individually rather than in a set. (Section 14.2)

osteoporosis (AH-stee-oh-puh-RO-sis). Condition in which human bones gradually lose their minerals, causing them to become weak and fragile and break easily. (Section 2.4)

ovo-vegetarians. People who do not eat meat, poultry, fish or dairy products but do eat eggs in addition to foods from plant sources. (Section 4.4)

oxidation. Process in which fuel is combined with oxygen to produce energy. In the body, the fuel is glucose. (Section 2.5)

P

parasites (PAIR-uh-sights). Organisms that get their nutrients from other living organisms (their hosts). Some parasites, when found in food, can cause food-borne illness. (Section 7.3)

pasteurized. Describes milk or other substance that has been heat-treated to kill enzymes and harmful bacteria. (Section 18.1)

patterns. Designs used in dinnerware, flatware, and glassware. (Section 14.2)

pediatrician. A physician who cares for infants and children. (Section 6.1)

peninsula. An extension of a kitchen counter. (Section 14.3)

perishable. Refers to foods that spoil quickly at room temperature. (Section 7.4)

peristalsis (PAIR-uh-STALL-suhs). Muscular action that forces food through the digestive system. (Section 2.5)

place setting. The pieces of tableware (dinnerware, glassware, flatware, and napkin) needed by one person to eat a meal. (Section 10.1)

poach. To simmer whole food, such as eggs or fish, in a small amount of water until done. (Section 9.4)

polarized plug. An electrical plug designed, as a safety measure, with one wide prong and one narrower one; may not fit in some older electrical outlets. (Section 7.2)

polyunsaturated (PAH-lee-uhn-SAT-chur-ay-ted). Term for certain fatty acids that seem to help lower cholesterol levels. Many vegetable oils are high in polyunsaturated fatty acids. (Section 2.3)

preheating. Bringing an oven to the desired temperature before putting the food in. (Section 9.4)

pre-preparation. Food preparation tasks done before one begins to actually assemble a recipe. Measuring the ingredients is an example. (Section 8.5)

principal. The amount of money that is borrowed from a lender. (Section 14.1)

processing. Heating filled canning jars at boiling temperatures or above to kill enzymes and harmful microorganisms. (Section 24.5)

proteins. Nutrients that help the body to grow and to repair tissue; also provide energy and help fight disease. (Section 2.1)

provitamin. A substance that can be converted into a vitamin in the human body. (Section 2.4)

psychological. Having to do with the mind and emotions. (Section 1.1)

Q

quacks. People who promote a particular food, diet, or supplement as a health aid without some scientific evidence. (Section 3.3)

quiche (keesh). A main-dish pie with a custard filling that contains foods such as chopped vegetables, cheese, and chopped cooked meat. (Section 18.4)

quick-mix method. Method for mixing yeast bread dough in which the active dry yeast is mixed with the dry ingredients before warmed liquid and fat are added. (Section 21.2)

R

radiation. A method of transferring heat by waves of energy called infrared rays. When the rays strike an object, the object is warmed. (Section 9.2)

raw pack. A method of filling jars for canning in which raw foods are placed in jars and covered with hot liquid. (Section 24.5)

RDA. Recommended Dietary Allowances. Scientifically-developed guidelines that specify the amounts of protein and certain vitamins and minerals needed daily by people, according to their age and gender. (Section 2.1)

rebate. A partial refund paid to the buyer after an item has been purchased. (Section 12.1)

reception. A social gathering to honor a person or an event, such as an anniversary or a graduation. (Section 24.3)

reconstitute. To add back the liquid that was removed from a food or beverage during processing. (Section 15.2)

references. People a job applicant knows well who can give information about the applicant's previous work or character. (Section 25.2)

refined sugars. Sugars that have been removed from plants and processed to be used as sweeteners, such as table sugar and maple syrup. (Section 2.2)

reservations. Arrangement made by calling a restaurant ahead of time to have a table set aside for you and any of your guests for a particular time. (Section 10.2)

resources. Objects and qualities that can help one reach one's goal. Time, money, skills, knowledge, and equipment are examples. (Section 1.2)

resumé (REH-zoo-MAY). A written summary of skills and past experiences and achievements that are related to the job a person is seeking. (Section 25.2)

retail cuts. Smaller cuts of meat into which wholesale cuts are divided for sale to consumers. Steaks, roasts, and chops are examples. (Section 19.2)

ripe fruits. Tender fruits that have a pleasant aroma and fully developed flavors and are just ready to eat. (Section 16.1)

ripened cheese. Cheese made from milk curds to which ripening agents, such as bacteria, mold, yeast, or a combination of these, have been added; the cheese is then aged, or ripened, for a certain period of time. (Section 18.1)

rolled biscuits. Biscuits made by rolling dough out to an even thickness and cutting it. (Section 21.2)

roux (ROO). A mixture of browned flour and fat; thickens sauces and gives them a subtle roasted taste. (Section 23.1)

S

sanitation. Keeping disease-causing bacteria down to as small a number as possible through cleanliness and proper food handling. (Section 7.3)

saturated. Term for fatty acids that appear to raise the level of LDL ("bad") cholesterol in the bloodstream. Meat, poultry skin, whole-milk dairy products, and tropical oils (coconut, palm, and palm kernel oils) are high in saturated fatty acids. (Section 2.3)

sauté (saw-TAY). To brown or cook foods in a skillet with a small amount of fat, using low to medium heat. (Section 9.4)

scalded milk. Milk that has been heated to just below the boiling point. (Section 18.2)

science. Research to develop knowledge of a particular part of nature. (Section 1.4)

scones. A tasty variation of biscuits popular in parts of Britain. (Section 22.3)

seasoning blends. Convenient combinations of herbs or spices, such as Italian seasoning. (Section 24.1)

self-cleaning oven. An oven with a special cleaning cycle that uses high heat to burn off food stains. (Section 14.2)

self-esteem. A healthy recognition of your strengths and weaknesses and the ability to accept yourself as you are. (Section 1.1)

serrated. Refers to a knife with sawtooth notches along the edge of its blade. (Section 8.4)

service contract. Insurance purchased to cover repair and maintenance of a product for a specific length of time. (Section 14.1)

service plate. A large, decorative plate on which the dish containing the first course of a formal meal is placed; removed before the main course is served. (Section 24.3)

serving pieces. Tableware used for serving food. Platters and large bowls are examples. (Section 10.1)

shelf life. The length of time a food can be stored and still retain its quality. (Section 7.4)

shelf-stable. Describes processed foods that can be stored at room temperatures up to 85°F (29°C). (Section 7.4)

shirred eggs. Baked eggs. (Section 18.3)

shortened cake. Rich, tender cake, usually made with a solid fat and leavened with baking powder or baking soda. (Section 21.4)

small appliance. A small electrical device used to perform tasks such as mixing, chopping, and cooking. (Section 7.1)

snacks. Small amounts of food eaten between meals. (Section 4.1)

soluble fiber. Type of dietary fiber that may help lower blood cholesterol levels. (Section 2.2)

soufflé (soo-FLAY). Dish made by folding stiffly beaten egg whites into a sauce or batter, then baking the mixture in a deep casserole until it puffs up. (Section 18.4)

sourdough starter. A mixture of flour, water, and salt, which when allowed to sit for a few days, ferments and grows wild yeast cells, turning the mixture into a leavening agent; used to make sourdough bread. (Section 23.2)

spores. Cells that will develop into bacteria if conditions are right. (Section 7.3)

standing time. The amount of time a food must stand after microwave power is turned off. The heat inside the food causes the cooking process to continue during this time. (Section 9.3)

staple foods. Locally grown foods that make up the basic food supply of a particular region. (Section 13.3)

staples. Items you use on a regular basis, such as flour, honey, and margarine. (Section 12.1)

steep. To allow tea leaves to soak in hot water until the flavor is extracted from the leaves. (Section 24.2)

stew. To cover small pieces of food with liquid and simmer until done. (Section 9.4)

store brands. Packaged foods specially produced for the store; also called "private labels." (Section 12.3)

stress. Physical or mental tension triggered by an event or situation in one's life. (Section 6.2)

study. A scientific experiment conducted on a specific group of people or animals. (Section 3.3)

subsistence farming. A farming method in which people grow and raise their own food supply on small plots of land; common in many developing countries. (Section 13.3)

supplements. Nutrients people take in addition to those that are in the food they eat; usually in the form of pills, capsules, liquids, or powders. (Section 2.1)

sustainable farming. A farming method that uses few, if any, chemicals. (Section 13.1)

T

table etiquette. Rules for polite, appropriate mealtime behavior in a particular culture. (Section 10.2)

task lighting. Bright, shadow-free light over specific work areas, such as counters and sinks. (Section 14.3)

technology. The practical application of scientific knowledge to develop new or improved products and processes. (Section 1.4)

texture. The way food feels when you chew it, such as soft, hard, crispy, or chewy. (Section 11.1)

tip. Extra money given to the server in a restaurant in appreciation for good service. (Section 10.2)

tolerance levels. Maximum safe levels of certain chemicals that may be present in food. By law, foods cannot contain more of a chemical than the tolerance level set for it. (Section 13.2)

toxins. Poisons produced by bacteria. (Section 7.3)

trace minerals. Minerals that are needed in small amounts; include iron, copper, zinc, iodine, and selenium. (Section 2.4)

tuber (TOO-burr). Thickened, fleshy part of an underground stem that stores a plant's nutrients. Potatoes are an example. (Section 16.1)

U

ultra-pasteurization. Heating milk to a higher temperature than in normal pasteurization so the milk can be kept refrigerated longer than regularly pasteurized milk. (Section 18.1)

unitized. Describes produce that is held together with a rubber band or plastic tie and sold as a single unit. (Section 16.1)

unit price. Cost per ounce, quart, pound, or other unit of measurement. (Section 12.3)

unripened cheese. Cheese made of milk curds that have not been aged, or ripened; highly perishable. Cottage cheese and cream cheese are examples. (Section 18.1)

UPC symbol. Universal Product Code. A bar code on food labels and other products; it carries coded information (such as the price of the product) that can be "read" by a laser scanner. (Section 12.2)

utensils. Tools or containers used for specific tasks in food preparation. Examples include measuring cups, peelers, and cookware. (Section 7.1)

V

vacuum bottle. Container with two walls enclosing a vacuum (empty space), which provides insulation; used to keep heated foods and beverages hot for several hours. (Section 20.1)

variety meats. Edible animal organs, such as liver and kidneys. (Section 19.2)

vegans (VEE-guns *or* VEE-juns). People who eat only foods from plant sources. They do not eat meat, poultry, fish, eggs, or dairy products. (Section 4.4)

vegetarians. People who do not eat meat, poultry, or fish; some also do not eat dairy foods or eggs. (Section 4.4)

vent. To allow steam to escape from food as it cooks by slightly rolling back one edge of a plastic wrap cover on a dish to be microwaved. (Section 9.3)

vitamins. Chemicals in food that are needed in small amounts to help the body function properly and to help other nutrients do their jobs. (Section 2.1)

volume. The amount of three-dimensional space something takes up. (Section 8.2)

W

waist-to-hip ratio. Waist measurement divided by hip measurement; helps determine how weight is distributed in the body. (Section 5.1)

warranty. Manufacturer's written guarantee that for a specified period of time, it will repair or replace a product that does not perform properly. (Section 14.1)

water-soluble vitamins. Vitamins that dissolve in water, not in fat; include B vitamins and vitamin C. (Section 2.4)

watts. Units by which electrical power is measured. (Section 9.1)

wellness. Taking responsibility for one's own health by making choices and developing habits that help one become and stay physically, emotionally, and mentally healthy. (Section 1.1)

white sauce. A milk-based sauce thickened with starch. (Section 20.3)

wholesale cuts. Large pieces of meat into which an animal carcass is divided. Examples include flank, rib, and loin. (Section 19.2)

wok. A special pan used for stir-frying. It is wide at the top and has a narrower, rounded bottom. (Section 9.4)

work center. An area in the kitchen designed for specific tasks; includes equipment needed for the task and adequate storage and work space. (Section 7.1)

work flow. The sequence of movement from one area of the kitchen to the next while performing food preparation tasks. (Section 14.3)

work plan. A list of all the tasks required to complete a recipe in the order they must be done; includes an estimate of how long each task will take. (Section 8.5)

X Y Z

yield. Number of servings or amount a recipe makes. (Section 8.1)

"yo-yo" dieting. Repeated cycle of losing weight while dieting and then gaining weight when the diet stops. (Section 5.2)

Appendix: Nutritive Value of Foods

Item No.	Food Description	Approximate Measure	Weight Grams	Food energy Calories	Protein Grams	Fat Grams	Cholesterol Milligrams	Calcium Milligrams	Iron Milligrams	Sodium Milligrams	Vitamin A value* Retinol equivalents	Vitamin C Milligrams
	Beverages											
9	Club soda	12 fl oz	355	0	0	0	0	18	Tr	78	0	0
10	Regular cola	12 fl oz	369	160	0	0	0	11	0.2	18	0	0
11	Diet, artificially sweetened cola	12 fl oz	355	Tr	0	0	0	14	0.2	32	0	0
20	Fruit punch drink	6 fl oz	190	85	Tr	0	0	15	0.4	15	2	61
	Dairy Products											
	Natural Cheese											
32	Cheddar, cut pieces	1 oz	28	115	7	9	30	204	0.2	176	86	0
38	Cottage cheese, lowfat (2%)	1 cup	226	205	31	4	19	155	0.4	918	45	Tr
43	Mozzarella, part skim milk	1 oz	28	80	8	5	15	207	0.1	150	54	Tr
46	Parmesan, grated	1 tbsp	5	25	2	2	4	69	Tr	93	9	0
52	Pasteurized process American cheese	1 oz	28	105	6	9	27	174	0.1	406	82	0
	Milk, fluid:											
78	Whole (3.3% fat)	1 cup	244	150	8	8	33	291	0.1	120	76	2
79	Lowfat (2%)	1 cup	244	120	8	5	18	297	0.1	122	139	2
83	Nonfat (skim)	1 cup	245	85	8	Tr	4	302	0.1	126	149	2
85	Buttermilk	1 cup	245	100	8	2	9	285	0.1	257	20	2
88	Evaporated skim milk	1 cup	255	200	19	1	9	738	0.7	293	298	3
	Dried, nonfat, instantized:											
91	Cup	1 cup	68	245	24	Tr	12	837	0.2	373	483	4
	Milk beverages:											
94	Chocolate milk, lowfat (1%)	1 cup	250	160	8	3	7	287	0.6	152	148	2
105	Shakes, thick: Vanilla	10 oz	283	315	11	9	33	413	0.3	270	79	0
	Milk desserts, frozen:											
	Ice cream, vanilla, regular (about 11% fat):											
107	Hardened	1 cup	133	270	5	14	59	176	0.1	116	133	1
109	Soft serve (frozen custard)	1 cup	173	375	7	23	153	236	0.4	153	199	1
	Ice cream, vanilla, low-fat:											
113	Hardened (about 4% fat)	1 cup	131	185	5	6	18	176	0.2	105	52	1
116	Sherbet (about 2% fat)	1 cup	193	270	2	4	14	103	0.3	88	39	4
	Yogurt, made with lowfat milk:											
117	Fruit-flavored	8-oz	227	230	10	2	10	345	0.2	133	25	1
118	Plain	8-oz	227	145	12	4	14	415	0.2	159	36	2

Eggs

Eggs, large (24 oz. per dozen):
Cooked:

No.	Food	Measure	Grams	Food energy (cal)	Protein (g)	Fat (g)	Cholesterol (mg)	Calcium (mg)	Iron (mg)	Sodium (mg)	Vit. A	Vit. C
124	Fried in margarine	1 egg	46	90	6	7	211	25	0.7	162	114	0
125	Hard-cooked, shell removed	1 egg	50	75	6	5	213	25	0.6	62	84	0

Fats and Oils

No.	Food	Measure	Grams	Food energy (cal)	Protein (g)	Fat (g)	Cholesterol (mg)	Calcium (mg)	Iron (mg)	Sodium (mg)	Vit. A	Vit. C
129	Butter (4 sticks per lb) (1/8 stick)	1 tbsp	14	100	Tr	11	31	3	Tr	116	106	0
138	Margarine (1/8 stick)	1 tbsp	14	100	Tr	11	0	4	Tr	132	139	Tr
147	Corn oil	1 cup	218	1,925	0	218	0	0	0.0	0	0	0
	Salad dressings, commercial:											
162	French, Regular	1 tbsp	16	85	Tr	9	0	2	Tr	188	Tr	Tr
163	French, Low calorie	1 tbsp	16	25	Tr	2	0	6	Tr	306	Tr	Tr

Fish and Shellfish

No.	Food	Measure	Grams	Food energy (cal)	Protein (g)	Fat (g)	Cholesterol (mg)	Calcium (mg)	Iron (mg)	Sodium (mg)	Vit. A	Vit. C
177	Fish sticks, frozen, reheated, (stick, 4 by 1 by 1/2 in.)	1 fish stick	28	70	6	3	26	11	0.3	53	5	0
181	Haddock, breaded, fried	3 oz	85	175	17	9	75	34	1.0	123	20	0
182	Halibut, broiled, with butter and lemon juice	3 oz	85	140	20	6	62	14	0.7	103	174	1
195	Tuna, canned, oil pack, chunk light	3 oz	85	165	24	7	55	7	1.6	303	20	0
196	Tuna, canned, water pack, solid white	3 oz	85	135	30	1	48	17	0.6	468	32	0

Fruits and Fruit Juices

No.	Food	Measure	Grams	Food energy (cal)	Protein (g)	Fat (g)	Cholesterol (mg)	Calcium (mg)	Iron (mg)	Sodium (mg)	Vit. A	Vit. C
198	Apples, raw, unpeeled, 2-3/4-in. diam.	1 apple	138	80	Tr	Tr	0	10	0.2	Tr	7	8
202	Apple juice, bottled or canned	1 cup	248	115	Tr	Tr	0	17	0.9	7	Tr	2
204	Applesauce, canned, unsweetened	1 cup	244	105	Tr	Tr	0	7	0.3	5	7	3
215	Bananas, raw, without peel, whole	1 banana	114	105	1	1	0	7	0.4	1	9	10
229	Fruit cocktail, canned, juice pack	1 cup	248	115	1	Tr	0	20	0.5	10	76	7
230	Grapefruit, raw, without peel, 3-3/4-in. diam.	1/2 grapefruit	120	40	1	1	0	14	0.1	Tr	1	41
233	Grapefruit juice, canned, unsweetened	1 cup	247	95	1	Tr	0	17	0.5	2	2	72
237	Grapes, Thompson Seedless	10 grapes	50	35	Tr	Tr	0	6	0.1	1	4	5
239	Grape juice, canned or bottled	1 cup	253	155	1	Tr	0	23	0.6	8	2	Tr
242	Kiwifruit, raw, without skin	1 kiwifruit	76	45	1	1	0	20	0.3	4	13	74
250	Mangos, raw, without skin and seed	1 mango	207	135	1	1	0	21	0.2	4	806	57
251	Cantaloup, orange-fleshed, 5-in. diam.	1/2 melon	267	95	2	1	0	29	0.6	24	861	113
253	Nectarines, raw, without pits	1 nectarine	136	65	1	1	0	7	0.2	Tr	100	7
254	Oranges, raw, whole	1 orange	131	60	1	Tr	0	52	0.1	Tr	27	70
260	Orange juice, frozen concentrate, diluted	1 cup	249	110	2	Tr	0	22	0.2	2	19	97
262	Papayas, raw, 1/2-in. cubes	1 cup	140	65	1	Tr	0	35	0.3	9	40	92
263	Peaches, raw, whole, 2-1/2 in. diam.	1 peach	87	35	Tr	Tr	0	4	0.1	Tr	47	6
273	Pears, raw, with skin, cored, Bartlett, 2-1/2-in. diam.	1 pear	166	100	1	1	0	18	0.4	Tr	3	7

Item No.	Food Description	Approximate Measure	Weight (Grams)	Food energy (Calories)	Protein (Grams)	Fat (Grams)	Cholesterol (Milligrams)	Calcium (Milligrams)	Iron (Milligrams)	Sodium (Milligrams)	Vitamin A value* (Retinol equivalents)	Vitamin C (Milligrams)
283	Pineapple, chunks or tidbits, juice pack	1 cup	250	150	1	Tr	0	35	0.7	3	10	24
287	Plantains, without peel, cooked, boiled, sliced	1 cup	154	180	1	Tr	0	3	0.9	8	140	17
288	Plums, raw, 2-1/8-in. diam.	1 plum	66	35	1	Tr	0	3	0.1	Tr	21	6
297	Raisins, seedless, cup, not pressed down	1 cup	145	435	5	1	0	71	3.0	17	1	5
303	Strawberries, raw, capped, whole	1 cup	149	45	1	1	0	21	0.6	1	4	84
309	Watermelon, 4 by 8 in. wedge	1 piece	482	155	3	2	0	39	0.8	10	176	46

Grain Products

Breads:

Item No.	Food Description	Approximate Measure	Weight (Grams)	Food energy (Calories)	Protein (Grams)	Fat (Grams)	Cholesterol (Milligrams)	Calcium (Milligrams)	Iron (Milligrams)	Sodium (Milligrams)	Vitamin A value* (Retinol equivalents)	Vitamin C (Milligrams)
311	Bagels, plain or water, enriched	1 bagel	68	200	7	2	0	29	1.8	245	0	0
314	Biscuits, from mix, 2 in. diameter	1 biscuit	28	95	2	3	Tr	58	0.7	262	4	Tr
319	Cracked-wheat bread (18 per loaf)	1 slice	25	65	2	1	0	16	0.7	106	Tr	Tr
332	Pita bread, enriched, white, 6-1/2-in. diam.	1 pita	60	165	6	1	0	49	1.4	339	0	0
346	White bread, enriched (18 per loaf)	1 slice	25	65	2	1	0	32	0.7	129	Tr	Tr
353	Whole-wheat bread (16 per loaf)	1 slice	28	70	3	1	0	20	1.0	180	Tr	Tr
355	Bread stuffing, dry type, from mix	1 cup	140	500	9	31	0	92	2.2	1,254	273	0

Breakfast cereals:

Item No.	Food Description	Approximate Measure	Weight (Grams)	Food energy (Calories)	Protein (Grams)	Fat (Grams)	Cholesterol (Milligrams)	Calcium (Milligrams)	Iron (Milligrams)	Sodium (Milligrams)	Vitamin A value* (Retinol equivalents)	Vitamin C (Milligrams)
359	Cream of Wheat®, cooked	1 cup	244	140	4	Tr	0	54	10.9	5	0	0
367	Cheerios®	1 oz	28	110	4	2	0	48	4.5	307	375	15
368	Kellogg's® Corn Flakes	1 oz	28	110	2	Tr	0	1	1.8	351	375	15
383	Shredded Wheat	1 oz	28	100	3	1	0	11	1.2	3	0	0
386	Sugar Frosted Flakes, Kellogg's®	1 oz	28	110	1	Tr	0	1	1.8	230	375	15
390	Wheaties®	1 oz	28	100	3	Tr	0	43	4.5	354	375	15

Cakes prepared from cake mixes:

Item No.	Food Description	Approximate Measure	Weight (Grams)	Food energy (Calories)	Protein (Grams)	Fat (Grams)	Cholesterol (Milligrams)	Calcium (Milligrams)	Iron (Milligrams)	Sodium (Milligrams)	Vitamin A value* (Retinol equivalents)	Vitamin C (Milligrams)
394	Angelfood, 1/12 of cake	1 piece	53	125	3	Tr	0	44	0.2	269	0	0
396	Coffeecake, crumb, 1/6 of cake	1 piece	72	230	5	7	47	44	1.2	310	32	Tr
398	Devil's food with chocolate frosting, 1/16 of cake	1 piece	69	235	3	8	37	41	1.4	181	31	Tr

Cookies, commercial:

Item No.	Food Description	Approximate Measure	Weight (Grams)	Food energy (Calories)	Protein (Grams)	Fat (Grams)	Cholesterol (Milligrams)	Calcium (Milligrams)	Iron (Milligrams)	Sodium (Milligrams)	Vitamin A value* (Retinol equivalents)	Vitamin C (Milligrams)
424	Brownies with nuts and frosting	1 brownie	25	100	1	4	14	13	0.6	59	18	Tr
426	Chocolate chip, 2-1/4 in. diam.	4 cookies	42	180	2	9	5	13	0.8	140	15	Tr
429	Fig bars, square, 1-5/8 in. square	4 cookies	56	210	2	4	27	40	1.4	180	6	Tr
430	Oatmeal with raisins, 2-5/8-in. diam.	4 cookies	52	245	3	10	2	18	1.1	148	12	0
437	Corn chips	1-oz pkg.	28	155	2	9	0	35	0.5	233	11	1

Crackers:

Item No.	Food Description	Approximate Measure	Weight (Grams)	Food energy (Calories)	Protein (Grams)	Fat (Grams)	Cholesterol (Milligrams)	Calcium (Milligrams)	Iron (Milligrams)	Sodium (Milligrams)	Vitamin A value* (Retinol equivalents)	Vitamin C (Milligrams)
444	Graham, plain, 2-1/2 in. square	2 crackers	14	60	1	1	0	6	0.4	86	0	0
448	Snack-type, standard	1 cracker	3	15	Tr	1	0	3	0.1	30	Tr	0
449	Wheat, thin	4 crackers	8	35	1	1	0	3	0.3	69	Tr	0

No.	Food	Measure	Grams									
	Doughnuts, made with enriched flour:											
456	Cake type, plain, 3-1/4-in. diam.	1 doughnut	50	210	3	12	20	22	1.0	192	5	Tr
457	Yeast-leavened, glazed, 3-3/4-in. diam.	1 doughnut	60	235	4	13	21	17	1.4	222	Tr	0
458	English muffins, plain, enriched	1 muffin	57	140	5	1	0	96	1.7	378	0	0
461	Macaroni, enriched, cooked	1 cup	130	190	7	1	0	14	2.1	1	0	0
	Muffins, 2-1/2-in. diam., commercial mix:											
467	Blueberry	1 muffin	45	140	3	5	45	15	0.9	225	11	Tr
468	Bran	1 muffin	45	140	3	4	28	27	1.7	385	14	0
470	Noodles (egg noodles), enriched, cooked	1 cup	160	200	7	2	50	16	2.6	3	34	0
	Pancakes, 4-in. diam.											
474	Plain, from mix (with enriched flour), egg, milk, and oil added	1 pancake	27	60	2	2	16	36	0.7	160	7	Tr
	Pies, 9-in. diam:											
478	Apple, 1/6 of pie	1 piece	158	405	3	18	0	13	1.6	476	5	2
488	Lemon meringue, 1/6 of pie	1 piece	140	355	5	14	143	20	1.4	395	66	4
494	Pumpkin, 1/6 of pie	1 piece	152	320	6	17	109	78	1.4	325	416	0
	Popcorn, popped:											
497	Air-popped, unsalted	1 cup	8	30	1	Tr	0	1	0.2	Tr	1	0
498	Popped in vegetable oil, salted	1 cup	11	55	1	3	0	3	0.3	86	2	0
499	Sugar syrup coated	1 cup	35	135	2	1	0	2	0.5	Tr	3	0
500	Pretzels, stick, 2-1/4 in. long	10 pretzels	3	10	Tr	Tr	0	1	0.1	48	0	0
	Rice:											
503	Brown, cooked, served hot	1 cup	195	230	5	1	0	23	1.0	0	0	0
505	White, enriched, cooked, served hot	1 cup	205	225	4	Tr	0	21	1.8	0	0	0
	Rolls, enriched, commercial											
509	Dinner, 2-1/2-in. diam.	1 roll	28	85	2	2	Tr	33	0.8	155	Tr	Tr
510	Frankfurter and hamburger	1 roll	40	115	3	2	Tr	54	1.2	241	Tr	Tr
514	Spaghetti, enriched, cooked	1 cup	130	190	7	1	0	14	2.0	1	0	0

Legumes, Nuts, and Seeds

No.	Food	Measure	Grams									
526	Almonds, shelled, whole	1 oz	28	165	6	15	0	75	1.0	3	0	Tr
	Beans, dry, cooked, drained:											
527	Black	1 cup	171	225	15	1	0	47	2.9	1	Tr	0
528	Great Northern	1 cup	180	210	14	1	0	90	4.9	13	0	0
531	Pinto	1 cup	180	265	15	1	0	86	5.4	3	Tr	0
536	Black-eyed peas, dry, cooked (with cooking liquid)	1 cup	250	190	13	1	0	43	3.3	20	3	0
544	Chickpeas, cooked, drained	1 cup	163	270	15	4	0	80	4.9	11	Tr	0
550	Lentils, dry, cooked, with peanuts	1 cup	200	215	16	1	0	50	4.2	26	4	0
553	Mixed nuts, dry roasted, salted	1 oz	28	170	5	15	0	20	1.0	190	Tr	0
555	Peanuts, roasted in oil, salted	1 cup	145	840	39	71	0	125	2.8	626	0	0
557	Peanut butter	1 tbsp	16	95	5	8	0	5	0.3	75	0	0
564	Refried beans, canned	1 cup	290	295	18	3	0	141	5.1	1,228	0	17
	Soy products:											
567	Miso	1 cup	276	470	29	13	0	188	4.7	8,142	11	0
568	Tofu, piece 2-1/2 by 2-3/4 by 1 in.	1 piece	120	85	9	5	0	108	2.3	8	0	0
569	Sunflower seeds, dry, hulled	1 oz	28	160	6	14	0	33	1.9	1	1	Tr
570	Tahini	1 tbsp	15	90	3	8	0	21	0.7	5	1	1

Nutrients in Indicated Quantity

Item No.	Food Description	Approximate Measure	Weight (Grams)	Food energy (Calories)	Protein (Grams)	Fat (Grams)	Cholesterol (Milligrams)	Calcium (Milligrams)	Iron (Milligrams)	Sodium (Milligrams)	Vitamin A value* (Retinol equivalents)	Vitamin C (Milligrams)
Meat and Meat Products												
	Beef, cooked, braised, or pot roasted:											
575	Chuck blade, lean and fat, piece	3 oz	85	325	22	26	87	11	2.5	53	Tr	0
577	Round, bottom, lean and fat, piece	3 oz	85	220	25	13	81	5	2.8	43	Tr	0
578	Lean only from item 577	2.8 oz	78	175	25	8	75	4	2.7	40	Tr	0
580	Ground beef, regular, broiled, patty	3 oz	85	245	20	18	76	9	2.1	70	Tr	0
585	Round, eye of, lean and fat, roasted	3 oz	85	205	23	12	62	5	1.6	50	Tr	0
587	Sirloin, steak, broiled, lean and fat	3 oz	85	240	23	15	77	9	2.6	53	Tr	0
590	Beef, dried, chipped	2.5 oz	72	145	24	4	46	14	2.3	3,053	Tr	0
	Lamb:											
593	Chops, loin, broiled, lean and fat	2.8 oz	80	235	22	16	78	16	1.4	62	Tr	0
	Pork, cured, cooked:											
599	Bacon, regular	3 slices	19	110	6	9	16	2	0.3	303	0	6
601	Ham, light cure, roasted, lean and fat	3 oz	85	205	18	14	53	6	0.7	1,009	0	0
	Luncheon meat:											
605	Chopped ham (8 slices per 6 oz pkg)	2 slices	42	95	7	7	2	3	0.3	576	0	8
	Pork, fresh, cooked:											
610	Chop, loin, pan fried, lean and fat	3.1 oz	89	335	21	27	92	4	0.7	64	3	Tr
614	Rib, roasted, lean and fat	3 oz	85	270	21	20	69	9	0.8	37	3	Tr
	Sausages											
618	Bologna, slice (8 per 8-oz pkg)	2 slices	57	180	7	16	31	7	0.9	581	0	12
620	Brown and serve, browned	1 link	13	50	2	5	9	1	0.1	105	0	0
621	Frankfurter cooked (reheated)	1	45	145	5	13	23	5	0.5	504	0	12
Mixed Dishes and Fast Foods												
	Mixed dishes:											
629	Beef and vegetable stew, home recipe	1 cup	245	220	16	11	71	29	2.9	292	568	17
631	Chicken a la king, home recipe	1 cup	245	470	27	34	221	127	2.5	760	272	12
642	Spaghetti in tomato sauce with cheese, home recipe	1 cup	250	260	9	9	8	80	2.3	955	140	13
	Fast food entrees:											
645	Cheeseburger, regular	1 sandwich	112	300	15	15	44	135	2.3	672	65	1
648	English muffin, egg, cheese, bacon	1 sandwich	138	360	18	18	213	197	3.1	832	160	1
649	Fish sandwich, regular, with cheese	1 sandwich	140	420	16	23	56	132	1.8	667	25	2
651	Hamburger, regular	1 sandwich	98	245	12	11	32	56	2.2	463	14	1
653	Pizza, cheese, 1/8 of 15-in. diam.	1 slice	120	290	15	9	56	220	1.6	699	106	2
654	Roast beef sandwich	1 sandwich	150	345	22	13	55	60	4.0	757	32	2
655	Taco	1 taco	81	195	9	11	21	109	1.2	456	57	1

Poultry and Poultry Products

	Food	Measure											
	Chicken:												
	Fried, flesh, with skin and bones:												
656	Breast, 1/2 breast, batter dipped	4.9 oz	140	365	35	18	119	28	1.8	385	28	0
657	Drumstick, batter dipped	2.5 oz	72	195	16	11	62	12	1.0	194	19	0
	Roasted, flesh only:												
660	Breast, 1/2 breast	3.0 oz	86	140	27	3	73	13	0.9	64	5	0
662	Stewed, flesh only, light and dark meat	1 cup	140	250	38	9	116	20	1.6	98	21	0
	Turkey, roasted, flesh only:												
665	Dark meat, piece, 2-1/2 by 1-5/8 by 1/4 in.	4 pieces	85	160	24	6	72	27	2.0	67	0	0
666	Light meat, piece, 4 by 2 by 1/4 in.	2 pieces	85	135	25	3	59	16	1.1	54	0	0
667	Chopped or diced	1 cup	140	240	41	7	106	35	2.5	98	0	0

Soups, Sauces, and Gravies

	Food	Measure											
	Soups, condensed												
	Canned, prepared with milk:												
679	Cream of mushroom	1 cup	248	205	6	14	20	179	0.6	1,076	37	2
680	Tomato	1 cup	248	160	6	6	17	159	1.8	932	109	68
	Canned, prepared with water:												
681	Bean with bacon	1 cup	253	170	8	6	3	81	2.0	951	89	2
682	Beef broth, bouillon, consomme	1 cup	240	15	3	1	Tr	14	0.4	782	0	0
684	Chicken noodle	1 cup	241	75	4	2	7	17	0.8	1,106	71	Tr
693	Vegetarian	1 cup	241	70	2	2	0	22	1.1	822	301	1
	Dehydrated, prepared with water:												
697	Onion	1 pkt (6-fl-oz)	184	20	1	Tr	0	9	0.1	635	Tr	Tr
	Sauces; ready to serve:												
703	Barbecue	1 tbsp	16	10	Tr	Tr	0	3	0.1	130	14	1
704	Soy	1 tbsp	18	10	2	0	0	3	0.5	1,029	0	0
	Gravies:												
708	Brown, from dry mix	1 cup	261	80	3	2	2	66	0.2	1,147	0	0
709	Chicken, from dry mix	1 cup	260	85	3	2	3	39	0.3	1,134	0	3

Sugars and Sweets

	Food	Measure											
	Candy:												
711	Chocolate, milk, plain	1 oz	28	145	2	9	6	50	0.4	23	10	Tr
712	Chocolate, milk, with almonds	1 oz	28	150	3	10	5	65	0.5	23	8	Tr
717	Fondant, uncoated (mints, other)	1 oz	28	105	Tr	0	0	2	0.1	57	0	0
720	Hard candy	1 oz	28	110	0	0	0	Tr	0.1	7	0	0
723	Custard, baked	1 cup	265	305	14	15	278	297	1.1	209	146	1
724	Gelatin dessert	1/2 cup	120	70	2	0	0	2	Tr	55	0	0
726	Honey, strained or extracted	1 tbsp	21	65	Tr	0	0	1	0.1	1	0	Tr
727	Jams and preserves	1 tbsp	20	55	Tr	Tr	0	4	0.2	2	Tr	Tr
739	Pudding, vanilla, instant	1/2 cup	130	150	4	4	15	129	0.1	375	33	1

Nutrients in Indicated Quantity

Item No.	Food Description	Approximate Measure	Weight (Grams)	Food energy (Calories)	Protein (Grams)	Fat (Grams)	Cholesterol (Milligrams)	Calcium (Milligrams)	Iron (Milligrams)	Sodium (Milligrams)	Vitamin A value* (Retinol equivalents)	Vitamin C (Milligrams)
	Sugars:											
741	Brown, pressed down	1 cup	220	820	0	0	0	187	4.8	97	0	0
742	White, granulated	1 tbsp	12	45	0	0	0	Tr	Tr	Tr	0	0
745	White, powdered, sifted	1 cup	100	385	0	0	0	1	Tr	2	0	0
	Syrups:											
748	Molasses, cane, blackstrap	2 tbsp	40	85	0	0	0	274	10.1	38	0	0
749	Table syrup (corn and maple)	2 tbsp	42	122	0	0	0	1	Tr	19	0	0
	Vegetables and Vegetable Products											
750	Alfalfa seeds, sprouted, raw	1 cup	33	10	1	Tr	0	11	0.3	2	5	3
	Beans, snap, cooked, drained:											
761	From frozen (cut)	1 cup	135	35	2	Tr	0	61	1.1	18	71	11
	Broccoli:											
771	Raw	1 spear	151	40	4	1	0	72	1.3	41	233	141
772	Cooked	1 spear	180	50	5	1	0	82	2.1	20	254	113
	Cabbage, common varieties:											
778	Raw, coarsely shredded or sliced	1 cup	70	15	1	Tr	0	33	0.4	13	9	33
	Cabbage, Chinese:											
780	Pak-choi, cooked, drained	1 cup	170	20	3	Tr	0	158	1.8	58	437	44
	Carrots:											
784	Whole, 7-1/2 by 1-1/8 in.	1 carrot	72	30	1	Tr	0	19	0.4	25	2,025	7
786	Cooked, sliced, drained, from raw	1 cup	156	70	2	Tr	0	48	1.0	103	3,830	4
	Celery, pascal type, raw:											
792	Stalk, large outer, 8 by 1-1/2 in.	1 stalk	40	5	Tr	Tr	0	14	0.2	35	5	3
	Collards, cooked, drained:											
795	From frozen (chopped)	1 cup	170	60	5	1	0	357	1.9	85	1,017	45
	Corn, sweet:											
	Cooked, drained:											
796	From raw, ear 5 by 1-3/4 in.	1 ear	77	85	3	1	0	2	0.5	13	17	5
798	From frozen kernels	1 cup	165	135	5	Tr	0	3	0.5	8	41	4
	Canned:											
799	Cream style	1 cup	256	185	4	1	0	8	1.0	730	25	12
800	Whole kernel, vacuum pack	1 cup	210	165	5	1	0	11	0.9	571	51	17
801	Cucumber, with peel, slices 1/8 in. thick, 2-1/8-in. diam.	6 slices	28	5	Tr	Tr	0	4	0.1	1	1	1
806	Kale, cooked, drained, from raw	1 cup	130	40	2	1	0	94	1.2	30	962	53
	Lettuce, raw:											
813	Crisphead, as iceberg, chopped	1 cup	55	5	1	Tr	0	10	0.3	5	18	2
814	Looseleaf, chopped or shredded	1 cup	56	10	1	Tr	0	38	0.8	5	106	10

No.	Food	Measure										
830	Peas, green, frozen, cooked, drained	1 cup	160	125	8	Tr	0	38	2.5	139	107	16
832	Peppers, sweet, raw	1 pepper	74	20	1	Tr	0	4	0.9	2	39	95
834	Potatoes, cooked: Baked, with skin	1 potato	202	220	5	Tr	0	20	2.7	16	0	26
	French fried, strip, frozen:											
838	Oven heated	10 strips	50	110	2	4	0	5	0.7	16	0	5
839	Fried in vegetable oil	10 strips	50	160	2	8	0	10	0.4	108	0	5
849	Potato chips	10 chips	20	105	1	7	0	5	0.2	94	0	8
852	Radishes, raw	4 radishes	18	5	Tr	Tr	0	4	0.1	4	Tr	4
	Spinach:											
856	Raw, chopped	1 cup	55	10	2	Tr	0	54	1.5	43	369	15
858	Cooked, drained, from frozen (leaf)	1 cup	190	55	6	Tr	0	277	2.9	163	1,479	23
	Squash, cooked:											
861	Summer, sliced, drained	1 cup	180	35	2	1	0	49	0.6	2	52	10
862	Winter, baked, cubes	1 cup	205	80	2	1	0	29	0.7	2	729	20
863	Sweet potatoes, baked in skin, peeled	1 potato	114	115	2	Tr	0	32	0.5	11	2,488	28
	Tomatoes:											
868	Raw, 2-3/5-in. diam	1 tomato	123	25	1	Tr	0	9	0.6	10	139	22
869	Canned, solids and liquid	1 cup	240	50	2	1	0	62	1.5	391	145	36
870	Tomato juice, canned	1 cup	244	40	2	Tr	0	22	1.4	881	136	45
877	Vegetable juice cocktail, canned	1 cup	242	45	2	Tr	0	27	1.0	883	283	67

Miscellaneous Items

No.	Food	Measure										
885	Catsup	1 cup	273	290	5	1	0	60	2.2	2,845	382	41
894	Mustard, prepared, yellow	1 tsp	5	5	Tr	Tr	0	4	0.1	63	0	Tr
895	Olives, canned, green, medium	4	13	15	Tr	2	0	8	0.2	312	4	0
	Pickles, cucumber:											
901	Dill, medium, whole, 3-3/4 in.	1 pickle	65	5	Tr	Tr	0	17	0.7	928	7	4
903	Sweet, small, whole, 2-1/2 in. long	1 pickle	15	20	Tr	Tr	0	2	0.2	107	1	1

*1 RE = 3.33 IU from animal foods or 1 mcg retinol.
1 RE = 10 IU from plant foods or 6 mcg beta carotene.
Tr = Trace amount.
Source: USDA Home and Garden Bulletin No 72, "Nutritive Value of Foods"

NOTE: Nutritive values of most packaged foods may be obtained from the "Nutrition Facts" label on the container.

American Dry Bean Board (NE)/Peter Monge, 445
447, 448.
American Egg Board, 476.
American Gas Association, 373.
Angelo's/Brent Phelps, 295.
Arnold & Brown, 135, 149, 170, 177, 375, 415, 475.
Ashby, David/Morgan Cain & Associates,
418, 497, 659.

Ballard, James, 25, 81, 171.
Bean, Roger B., 33, 321, 332, 637, 681, 684, 685,
686.
Bemis Company, Inc., 397.
Berry, Keith M., 9, 328, 449, 682.
Bettmann Archive, 43, 141, 158.
Black Star
Holbrook, Andrew, 365.
Turnley, Peter, 365.
Brooks, J.R. & Son, Inc., 37, 69, 410, 411, 532.
Burns-Milwaukee, 366.

Circle Design/Carol Spengle, 74, 81, 82, 83.
Cupboard, Denton, TX

de Wys, Leo, Inc.
Lavine, Arthur, 649.
Naclivet, Jean Paul, 641.
Phillips, Van, 414.
Denton West/Ann Garvin, 184, 223, 250, 441.
Dillard's Department Store, Golden Triangle Mall,
Denton, TX/Christine Rowell, Trish Steinmetz,
and Karen Washington
Dotter, Earl, 84, 328, 475.

Florida Dept. of Agriculture and Consumer
Services/Bureau of Seafood & Aquaculture,
68, 312, 512, 533, 541.
Frazier, David R., Photolibrary, 251, 340, 344, 351,
354, 367, 405, 429, 444, 451, 456, 458,554, 586,
601, 624, 627, 632, 635, 667, 687.
Frazier, David R., Photolibrary,
Kevin Syms, 547.
Jim Patrico, 624.
Fuller, Tim, 41, 45, 59, 62, 91, 93, 94, 95, 108, 116,
127, 128, 133, 138, 150, 157, 167, 176, 182, 183,
189, 194, 197, 203, 207, 224, 225, 228, 237, 287,
299, 313, 316, 328, 332, 349, 370, 380, 382, 394,
395, 398, 399, 426, 450, 460, 471, 499, 508, 528,
530, 551, 585, 600, 674, 675, 676

Garvin, Ann, 9, 10, 11, 12, 13, 14, 15, 16, 40, 47,
57, 61, 63, 67, 71, 80, 104, 109, 112, 123, 126,
129, 146, 152, 159, 162, 166, 168, 188, 191,
200, 205, 211, 220, 231, 232, 236, 245, 249, 254,
266, 273, 277, 278, 280, 281, 284, 285, 286, 290,
291, 292, 293, 296, 304, 307, 309, 319, 345, 372,

387, 389, 402, 403, 404, 421, 423, 424, 428, 432,
437, 443, 462, 463, 465, 466, 470, 473, 474, 477,
478, 479, 482, 505, 511, 513, 515, 518, 522, 525,
527, 532, 534, 538, 540, 545, 550, 557, 561, 563,
564, 565, 568, 570, 571, 573, 574, 575, 578, 584,
588, 590, 597, 598, 603, 604, 605, 606, 613, 615,
616, 620, 623, 624, 626, 628, 631, 640, 642, 652,
654.
Greenberg, Jeff Isaac, 321, 420, 494, 634.

Hamptons/Arnold & Brown, 371, 234.
Health Connection, 131.
Hershey Foods Corporation, 31, 377.
Hopkins, John, 172, 179, 676.
Hutchings, Richard, 48, 680.

Idaho Bean Commission, 130, 134, 630.

Kraft General Foods, 13, 461, 464, 468, 524, 558,
559, 646.

Marshall, James M., 17, 294, 364, 472, 498, 604,
607, 611, 617.
Maytag, 185, 256, 257, 272.
Merillat, 10, 186, 187, 189, 385.
Mishima, 38, 151, 322, 328, 362.
Morgan Cain & Associates, 58, 68, 240.
Morse, P.C., 222, text/cover design

National Broiler Council/Newman, Saylor and
Gregory, 427, 442.
National Live Stock and Meat Board, 485, 489,
490, 492, 493, 507, 516, 517, 524, 538.
National Pork Producers Council, 11, 268, 269,
491, 506, 514, 539.
National Turkey Federation, 498, 535.

Peerless Photography, 100, 101, 437, 658, 660.
Peterson, Judith, 433, 531.
Phelps, Brent, 30, 56, 66, 68, 78, 90, 92, 107, 113,
114, 117, 124, 125, 131, 156, 165, 190, 192, 196,
201, 210, 212, 214, 227, 228, 230, 233, 239, 243,
244, 259, 262, 263, 264, 265, 274, 275, 276, 279,
293, 298, 306, 312, 315, 318, 328, 333, 337, 338,
340, 341, 342, 352, 356, 379, 381, 396, 397, 400,
401, 415, 416, 417, 425, 442, 447, 457, 463, 469,
510, 514, 524, 526, 529, 536, 537, 543, 544, 555,
557, 643, 650, 652, 663, 666, 670.
Photo Edit
Aron, Bill, 587, 594, 597, 602.
Conklin, Paul, 364.
Denny, Mary Kate, 321.
Dreyfess, Hermine, 364.
Ferguson, Myrleen, 24, 29.
Freeman, Tony, 328, 656, 669.

Index

Dairy desserts, frozen, 460
Dairy products
    butter, 458, 460
    buying, 460
    cheese, 457-458, 459. *See also* Cheese
    cholesterol in, 455
    cooking with, 462-465
    cultured, 457
    fat in, 68, 455, 456
    in Food Guide Pyramid, 99, 100
    frozen desserts, 460
    low-fat, 92, 99
    milk, 456-457
    nutrients in, 455, 457
    safety with, 460, 461
    storing, 208, 460-461
    yogurt, 457, 460, 463-464, 525
Dal, 64
Dating, on food packages, 337-338
Decision making, 46-48
Decorations
    garnishes, for foods, 646-647
    for parties, 656, 657
Deep-fat-frying, 285
Deficiency, nutrient, 54-55, 74-75
Dehydration, 156
Dehydrator, food, 669-670
Design, life-span, 388
Designing a kitchen, 382-388
Desserts
    See also Baked products
    dairy, frozen, 460
    serving, 294
Developing nations, food supply in, 361, 363, 365, 366
Diabetes, and diet, 173
Diet(s)
    for dental problems, 174
    fad, 144
    for medical conditions, 172-174
    during pregnancy, 144, 165
    weight control, 144-145, 148
Dietary fiber. *See* Fiber
Dietary Guidelines for Americans, 89-95
Dietary laws, religious, 34
Dietitian, 109, 678
Digestion, 79-81
Dinnerware, buying, 381
Discoloration, of fruits and vegetables,
    preventing, 419, 425, 666
Dishes
    buying, 381
    placement of, on table, 292-293
    washing, 197, 200, 215
Disposables, and environment, 215
Disposal, food waste, 197

Distribution, food, 352, 363
Dominican foods, 588
Doneness, determining
    of cakes, 572, 573
    of cookies, 575
    of fish, 510
    of meats, 508-509
    of muffins, 560
    of poultry, 508-509
    of yeast bread, 570
Dough
    biscuit, mixing, 561-562
    kneading, 555, 567
    pastry, 576
    rolling, 562, 576
    shaping, 567, 570
    yeast, 555, 566-567
Dovetailing, 249, 308
Dressing, salad, 530, 534 (recipe)
Dried fruit, 416, 427
Drop biscuits, 562
Drupes, 409
Dry beans, cooking, 447-449
Dry-heat, cooking with, 269, 281-284
Drying food, 669-670
Dry ingredients, measuring, 228-229

E

E. coli poisoning, 198
East Coast, foods of, 623-624
Eastern Europe, foods of, 606-607
Eating disorders, 175-178
Eating habits
    children's, promoting, 168
    identifying, 118
    improving, 119-120, 147-148
    throughout life cycle, stages of, 167-169
    and weight management, 147-148
Eating out
    etiquette when, 297-298
    and nutrition, 121-126
    vegetarian style, 133
Eating patterns, 113-117
Economy, and food supply, 361, 363
Efficiency, in food preparation tasks, 248-249
Eggs. *See also* Egg whites
    baked, 470
    in baked goods, role of, 554
    buying, 467
    cholesterol in, 467
    cooking, 468-473
    in custards, 474
    and food-borne illness, 468, 475
    in Food Guide Pyramid, 99, 100

freezing, 469
frying, 470
functions of, in recipes, 471
grades of, 467
hard-cooked, 469
in mayonnaise, 531
microwaving, 469, 470, 471
nutrients in, 467
in omelets, 471, 473, 476
poached, 471
scrambled, 471
separating, 475
sizes of, 467
soft-cooked, 469
storing, 208
structure of, 466
"thousand year," 472
Egg substitutes, 208, 396
Egg whites
    beating, 475-476
    and cholesterol, 467
    freezing, 469
    as leavener, 553, 572
    in meringues, 476-477, 478
    separating from yolk, 475
    substituting for whole eggs, 554
Elastin, 486
Elderly
    kitchens designed for, 193, 388
    nutrition for, 169, 322
    safety for, in kitchen, 193
Electricity
    conserving, 214
    grounded outlets for, 386
    outage of, and food safety, 211-212
    safety with, 189-190, 387
    wiring for, 386-387
Electric range, 256-257
Electrolytes, 74, 77
Emergency foods, stocking, 316
Emotions
    and food choices, 23, 31
    and digestive problems, 81
Endosperm, 433, 434
Energy (body)
    athletes' need for, 155
    body's use of, 84
    and calories, 56-57, 146
    and nutrients, 54, 56-57, 60, 63, 84
Energy (fuel), conserving, 214, 306, 374
EnergyGuide labels, 374
England, foods of, 600-601
En papillote, 646
Entertaining, 655-660
Entrée, 123
Entrepreneurs, 49, 671, 679
Environment
    and chemical contaminants, 350, 359

and canned goods, 206
and dairy products, 460, 461
and eggs, 468, 475
and fish, 504
and meat, 508, 509
and packing a lunch, 525
and picnicking, 622
and poultry, 197, 508, 509
and poultry stuffing, 511
and sanitation, 195-197
and shellfish, 504
and shopping for food, 342, 343, 344
and temperature of foods, 201-203, 211-212
and thawing food, 203
types of, 198-199, 509
Food choices
and eating out, 121-126, 133
and emotions, 23, 31
using Food Guide Pyramid for, 96-102
and health, 21-22, 54-55, 67, 90-95
influences on, 26-31
planning, 113-133
and wellness, 22-24
Food cooperatives, 327
Food customs. *See* Customs
Food dehydrator, 669-670
Food groups, 98-102
Food Guide Pyramid, 96-102
Food poisoning. *See* Food-borne illness
Food record, 118-119, 120
Food researcher, 251
Food safety, 354-360. *See also* Food-borne illness
Food Safety and Inspection Service, 355
Food safety inspector, 367
Food scale, using a, 230
Food science
careers in, 85, 251, 678
general discussion, 40-41
Food service, careers in, 49, 547, 579, 671, 676-677, 687
Foods lab, teamwork in, 249-250
Food stamps, 320
Food supply, global, 361-366
Formal dinner service, 658-659
Formed foods, 396
France, foods of, 601-602
Freeze-dried foods, 351
Freezer burn, avoiding, 210-211
Freezer inventory, 211
Freezer storage, 208-209, 210-211
Freezing foods
beans, cooked, 445
cheese, 461
eggs, 469
fruits, 666
meals ahead, 314, 402

vegetables, 401, 666
French cooking, 539, 601-602
Fricassee, 543
Frittata, 471, 473 (recipe)
Frosting, alternatives to, 574
Frozen dairy desserts, 460
Fruit
baking, 424
buying, 413-414
canned, 416
canning, 668
citrus, peeling, 418
convenience forms of, 416, 427
cooking, 423-424
darkening of, preventing, 419, 666
and Dietary Guidelines, 91
dried, 416, 427
in Food Guide Pyramid, 99, 101
freezing, 666
as garnish, 646, 653
grilling, 664
Meringue-Swirled (recipe), 478
microwaving, 424
nutrients in, 412
poaching, 423
ripeness of, testing, 413
ripening, 414
snacks made with, 525
storing, 207, 415
types of, 409-410, 412
washing, 418
Fruit Group, 99, 101
Fruit juice, 156, 416, 653
Fruit punch, 653, 654 (recipe)
Fruit sauces, 424
Fruit shake, 525
Frying
eggs, 470
general discussion, 269
meat, fish, and poultry, 514-515
safety when, 285
types of, 284-285
vegetables, 427

G

Garbage, reducing, 215-216, 344, 526
Garbanzo Salad (recipe), 534
Garnishes, 646-647
Gas range, 192, 256, 373, 378
Gazpacho, 589, 590 (recipe)
Generic products, 342
Genetic engineering, 41-42, 358, 366
Geography
and food customs, 36
and food supply, 362
Germ, of grains, 433, 434
Germany, foods of, 603
Giblets, 498

Global food supply, 361-366
Glucose, 80, 82, 84, 173
Gluten, 552, 554
Glycogen, 82, 155
Government, and food safety, 355-356, 358
Grades
of eggs, 467
of meat, 493-494
of poultry, 499
Grains and grain products
breads, 437-438, 559-570. *See also* Bread(s)
buying, 434-439
cereals, 436, 442
and Dietary Guidelines, 91
enriched, 434
flour, 552, 566, 571
in Food Guide Pyramid, 98, 101
fortified, 434
nutrients in, 434, 559
pasta, 436-437, 440-441
rice, 435, 440
storing, 206, 207, 208, 438
types of, 435-438
in vegetarian diet, 131
GRAS list, 355-356
Gravy, making, 538, 539
Grazing, 116-117
Grease fire, 192
Greece, foods of, 605
Green Beans, Creole (recipe), 628
Greens, salad, 529, 531-532
"Green shopping," 344
Grill, outdoor, buying a, 663
Grilling foods, 663-664
Grits, 436, 440
Grocer, Middle Eastern, 617
Grounded electrical systems, 386
Ground meat
beef, 485, 493, 509, 518 (recipe)
cholesterol in, 485
doneness of, and internal temperatures, 509
fat in, 485, 493, 498
microwaving, 514
poultry, 498, 509
Guacamole, Southwest (recipe), 636
Guidelines, Dietary, 89-95

H

Haiti, foods of, 588
Handicaps, and kitchen design, 193, 388
Hands, washing, 196
Haute cuisine, 601
Hawaiian foods, 632-633
HDL, 67, 68
Health
and cholesterol, 66-67
and dehydration, 156
and Dietary Guidelines, 89-95